International Directory of
COMPANY
HISTORIES

International Directory of
COMPANY HISTORIES

VOLUME 101

Editor

Jay P. Pederson

ST. JAMES PRESS
A part of Gale, Cengage Learning

GALE
CENGAGE Learning

Detroit • New York • San Francisco • New Haven, Conn • Waterville, Maine • London

GALE
CENGAGE Learning

International Directory of Company Histories, Volume 101

Jay P. Pederson, Editor

Project Editor: Miranda H. Ferrara

Editorial: Virgil Burton, Donna Craft, Louise Gagné, Peggy Geeseman, Julie Gough, Linda Hall, Sonya Hill, Keith Jones, Daniel King, Lynn Pearce, Holly Selden, Justine Ventimiglia

Production Technology Specialist: Mike Weaver

Imaging and Multimedia: John Watkins

Composition and Electronic Prepress: Gary Leach, Evi Seoud

Manufacturing: Rhonda Dover

Product Manager: Jenai Mynatt

For product information and technology assistance, contact us at
Gale Customer Support, 1-800-877-4253.
For permission to use material from this text or product,
submit all requests online at **www.cengage.com/permissions.**
Further permissions questions can be emailed to
permissionrequest@cengage.com

Gale
27500 Drake Rd.
Farmington Hills, MI, 48331-3535

LIBRARY OF CONGRESS CATALOG NUMBER 89-190943
ISBN-13: 978-1-55862-635-5
ISBN-10: 1-55862-635-2

This title is also available as an e-book
ISBN-13: 978-1-55862-764-2   ISBN-10: 1-55862-764-2
Contact your Gale, a part of Cengage Learning sales representative for ordering information.

BRITISH LIBRARY CATALOGUING IN PUBLICATION DATA
International directory of company histories, Vol. 101
Jay P. Pederson
33.87409

Contents

Preface

The St. James Press series *The International Directory of Company Histories* (*IDCH*) is intended for reference use by students, business people, librarians, historians, economists, investors, job candidates, and others who seek to learn more about the historical development of the world's most important companies. To date, *IDCH* has covered more than 10,050 companies in 101 volumes.

INCLUSION CRITERIA

Most companies chosen for inclusion in *IDCH* have achieved a minimum of US$25 million in annual sales and are leading influences in their industries or geographical locations. Companies may be publicly held, private, or nonprofit. State-owned companies that are important in their industries and that may operate much like public or private companies also are included. Wholly owned subsidiaries and divisions are profiled if they meet the requirements for inclusion. Entries on companies that have had major changes since they were last profiled may be selected for updating.

The *IDCH* series highlights 25% private and nonprofit companies, and features updated entries on approximately 35 companies per volume.

ENTRY FORMAT

Each entry begins with the company's legal name; the address of its headquarters; its telephone, toll-free, and fax numbers; and its web site. A statement of public, private, state, or parent ownership follows. A company with a legal name in both English and the language of its headquarters country is listed by the English name, with the native-language name in parentheses.

The company's founding or earliest incorporation date, the number of employees, and the most recent available sales figures follow. Sales figures are given in local currencies with equivalents in U.S. dollars. For some private companies, sales figures are estimates and indicated by the abbreviation *est.* The entry lists the exchanges on which the company's stock is traded and its ticker symbol, as well as the company's NAICS codes.

Entries generally contain a *Company Perspectives* box which provides a short summary of the company's mission, goals, and ideals; a *Key Dates* box highlighting milestones in the company's history; lists of *Principal Subsidiaries, Principal Divisions, Principal Operating Units, Principal Competitors*; and articles for *Further Reading.*

American spelling is used throughout *IDCH*, and the word "billion" is used in its U.S. sense of one thousand million.

SOURCES

Entries have been compiled from publicly accessible sources both in print and on the Internet such as general and academic periodicals, books, and annual reports, as well as material supplied by the companies themselves.

CUMULATIVE INDEXES

IDCH contains three indexes: the **Cumulative Index to Companies**, which provides an alphabetical index to companies profiled in the *IDCH* series, the **Index to Industries**, which allows researchers to locate companies by their principal industry, and the **Geographic Index**, which lists companies alphabetically by the country of their headquarters. The indexes are cumulative and specific instructions for using them are found immediately preceding each index.

SPECIAL TO THIS VOLUME

This volume of *IDCH* contains an entry on one of Scottish-born American Industrialist Andrew Carnegie's greatest cultural legacies, The Carnegie Hall Corporation.

SUGGESTIONS WELCOME

Comments and suggestions from users of *IDCH* on any aspect of the product as well as suggestions for companies to be included or updated are cordially invited. Please write:

The Editor
International Directory of Company Histories
St. James Press
Gale, Cengage Learning
27500 Drake Rd.
Farmington Hills, Michigan 48331-3535

St. James Press does not endorse any of the companies or products mentioned in this series. Companies appearing in the *International Directory of Company Histories* were selected without reference to their wishes and have in no way endorsed their entries.

Notes on Contributors

M. L. Cohen
Novelist, business writer, and researcher living in Paris.

Jeffrey L. Covell
Seattle-based writer.

Ed Dinger
Writer and editor based in Bronx, New York.

Paul R. Greenland
Illinois-based writer and researcher; author of two books and former senior editor of a national business magazine; contributor to *The Encyclopedia of Chicago History, The Encyclopedia of Religion,* and the *Encyclopedia of American Industries.*

Robert Halasz
Former editor in chief of *World Progress* and *Funk & Wagnalls New Encyclopedia Yearbook*; author, *The U.S. Marines* (Millbrook Press, 1993).

Kathleen Peippo
Minnesota-based writer.

Nelson Rhodes
Editor, writer, and consultant in the Chicago area.

David E. Salamie
Part-owner of InfoWorks Development Group, a reference publication development and editorial services company.

Ted Sylvester
Photographer, writer, and editor of the environmental journal *From the Ground Up.*

Mary Tradii
Colorado-based writer.

Frank Uhle
Ann Arbor-based writer; movie projectionist, disc jockey, and staff member of *Psychotronic Video* magazine.

A. Woodward
Wisconsin-based writer.

List of Abbreviations

¥ Japanese yen
£ United Kingdom pound
$ United States dollar

A

AB Aktiebolag (Finland, Sweden)
AB Oy Aktiebolag Osakeyhtiot (Finland)
A.E. Anonimos Eteria (Greece)
AED Emirati dirham
AG Aktiengesellschaft (Austria, Germany, Switzerland, Liechtenstein)
aG auf Gegenseitigkeit (Austria, Germany)
A.m.b.a. Andelsselskab med begraenset ansvar (Denmark)
A.O. Anonim Ortaklari/Ortakligi (Turkey)
ApS Amparteselskab (Denmark)
ARS Argentine peso
A.S. Anonim Sirketi (Turkey)
A/S Aksjeselskap (Norway)
A/S Aktieselskab (Denmark, Sweden)
Ay Avoinyhtio (Finland)
ATS Austrian shilling
AUD Australian dollar
ApS Amparteselskab (Denmark)
Ay Avoinyhtio (Finland)

B

B.A. Buttengewone Aansprakeiijkheid (Netherlands)
BEF Belgian franc

BHD Bahraini dinar
Bhd. Berhad (Malaysia, Brunei)
BND Brunei dollar
BRL Brazilian real
B.V. Besloten Vennootschap (Belgium, Netherlands)

C

C.A. Compania Anonima (Ecuador, Venezuela)
CAD Canadian dollar
C. de R.L. Compania de Responsabilidad Limitada (Spain)
CEO Chief Executive Officer
CFO Chief Financial Officer
CHF Swiss franc
Cia. Companhia (Brazil, Portugal)
Cia. Compania (Latin America [except Brazil], Spain)
Cia. Compagnia (Italy)
Cie. Compagnie (Belgium, France, Luxembourg, Netherlands)
CIO Chief Information Officer
CLP Chilean peso
CNY Chinese yuan
Co. Company
COO Chief Operating Officer
Coop. Cooperative
COP Colombian peso
Corp. Corporation
C. por A. Compania por Acciones (Dominican Republic)
CPT Cuideachta Phoibi Theoranta (Republic of Ireland)
CRL Companhia a Responsabilidao Limitida (Portugal, Spain)
C.V. Commanditaire Vennootschap (Netherlands, Belgium)
CZK Czech koruna

D

D&B Dunn & Bradstreet
DEM German deutsche mark
Div. Division (United States)
DKK Danish krone
DZD Algerian dinar

E

EC Exempt Company (Arab countries)
Edms. Bpk. Eiendoms Beperk (South Africa)
EEK Estonian Kroon
eG eingetragene Genossenschaft (Germany)
EGMBH Eingetragene Genossenschaft mit beschraenkter Haftung (Austria, Germany)
EGP Egyptian pound
Ek For Ekonomisk Forening (Sweden)
EP Empresa Portuguesa (Portugal)
E.P.E. Etema Pemorismenis Evthynis (Greece)
ESOP Employee Stock Options and Ownership
ESP Spanish peseta

Et(s). Etablissement(s) (Belgium, France, Luxembourg)
eV eingetragener Verein (Germany)
EUR euro

F
FIM Finnish markka
FRF French franc

G
G.I.E. Groupement d'Interet Economique (France)
gGmbH gemeinnutzige Gesellschaft mit beschraenkter Haftung (Austria, Germany, Switzerland)
G.I.E. Groupement d'Interet Economique (France)
GmbH Gesellschaft mit beschraenkter Haftung (Austria, Germany, Switzerland)
GRD Greek drachma
GWA Gewerbte Amt (Austria, Germany)

H
HB Handelsbolag (Sweden)
HF Hlutafelag (Iceland)
HKD Hong Kong dollar
HUF Hungarian forint

I
IDR Indonesian rupiah
IEP Irish pound
ILS new Israeli shekel
Inc. Incorporated (United States, Canada)
INR Indian rupee
IPO Initial Public Offering
I/S Interesentselskap (Norway)
I/S Interessentselskab (Denmark)
ISK Icelandic krona
ITL Italian lira

J
JMD Jamaican dollar
JOD Jordanian dinar

K
KB Kommanditbolag (Sweden)
KES Kenyan schilling
Kft Korlatolt Felelossegu Tarsasag (Hungary)
KG Kommanditgesellschaft (Austria, Germany, Switzerland)

KGaA Kommanditgesellschaft auf Aktien (Austria, Germany, Switzerland)
KK Kabushiki Kaisha (Japan)
KPW North Korean won
KRW South Korean won
K/S Kommanditselskab (Denmark)
K/S Kommandittselskap (Norway)
KWD Kuwaiti dinar
Ky Kommandiitiyhtio (Finland)

L
LBO Leveraged Buyout
Lda. Limitada (Spain)
L.L.C. Limited Liability Company (Arab countries, Egypt, Greece, United States)
L.L.P. Limited Liability Partnership (United States)
L.P. Limited Partnership (Canada, South Africa, United Kingdom, United States)
Ltd. Limited
Ltda. Limitada (Brazil, Portugal)
Ltee. Limitee (Canada, France)
LUF Luxembourg franc

M
mbH mit beschraenkter Haftung (Austria, Germany)
Mij. Maatschappij (Netherlands)
MUR Mauritian rupee
MXN Mexican peso
MYR Malaysian ringgit

N
N.A. National Association (United States)
NGN Nigerian naira
NLG Netherlands guilder
NOK Norwegian krone
N.V. Naamloze Vennootschap (Belgium, Netherlands)
NZD New Zealand dollar

O
OAO Otkrytoe Aktsionernoe Obshchestve (Russia)
OHG Offene Handelsgesellschaft (Austria, Germany, Switzerland)
OMR Omani rial
OOO Obschestvo s Ogranichennoi Otvetstvennostiu (Russia)
OOUR Osnova Organizacija

Udruzenog Rada (Yugoslavia)
Oy Osakeyhtî (Finland)

P
P.C. Private Corp. (United States)
PEN Peruvian Nuevo Sol
PHP Philippine peso
PKR Pakistani rupee
P/L Part Lag (Norway)
PLC Public Limited Co. (United Kingdom, Ireland)
P.L.L.C. Professional Limited Liability Corporation (United States)
PLN Polish zloty
P.T. Perusahaan/Perseroan Terbatas (Indonesia)
PTE Portuguese escudo
Pte. Private (Singapore)
Pty. Proprietary (Australia, South Africa, United Kingdom)
Pvt. Private (India, Zimbabwe)
PVBA Personen Vennootschap met Beperkte Aansprakelijkheid (Belgium)
PYG Paraguay guarani

Q
QAR Qatar riyal

R
REIT Real Estate Investment Trust
RMB Chinese renminbi
Rt Reszvenytarsasag (Hungary)
RUB Russian ruble

S
S.A. Société Anonyme (Arab countries, Belgium, France, Jordan, Luxembourg, Switzerland)
S.A. Sociedad Anónima (Latin America [except Brazil], Spain, Mexico)
S.A. Sociedades Anônimas (Brazil, Portugal)
SAA Societe Anonyme Arabienne (Arab countries)
S.A.B. de C.V. Sociedad Anónima Bursátil de Capital Variable (Mexico)
S.A.C. Sociedad Anonima Comercial (Latin America [except Brazil])
S.A.C.I. Sociedad Anonima Comercial e Industrial (Latin America [except Brazil])

S.A.C.I.y.F. Sociedad Anonima Comercial e Industrial y Financiera (Latin America [except Brazil])

S.A. de C.V. Sociedad Anonima de Capital Variable (Mexico)

SAK Societe Anonyme Kuweitienne (Arab countries)

SAL Societe Anonyme Libanaise (Arab countries)

SAO Societe Anonyme Omanienne (Arab countries)

SAQ Societe Anonyme Qatarienne (Arab countries)

SAR Saudi riyal

S.A.R.L. Sociedade Anonima de Responsabilidade Limitada (Brazil, Portugal)

S.A.R.L. Société à Responsabilité Limitée (France, Belgium, Luxembourg)

S.A.S. Societá in Accomandita Semplice (Italy)

S.A.S. Societe Anonyme Syrienne (Arab countries)

S.C. Societe en Commandite (Belgium, France, Luxembourg)

S.C.A. Societe Cooperativa Agricole (France, Italy, Luxembourg)

S.C.I. Sociedad Cooperativa Ilimitada (Spain)

S.C.L. Sociedad Cooperativa Limitada (Spain)

S.C.R.L. Societe Cooperative a Responsabilite Limitee (Belgium)

Sdn. Bhd. Sendirian Berhad (Malaysia)

SEK Swedish krona

SGD Singapore dollar

S.L. Sociedad Limitada (Latin America [except Brazil], Portugal, Spain)

S/L Salgslag (Norway)

S.N.C. Société en Nom Collectif (France)

Soc. Sociedad (Latin America [except Brazil], Spain)

Soc. Sociedade (Brazil, Portugal)

Soc. Societa (Italy)

S.p.A. Società per Azioni (Italy)

Sp. z.o.o. Spólka z ograniczona odpowiedzialnoscia (Poland)

S.R.L. Sociedad de Responsabilidad Limitada (Spain, Mexico, Latin America [except Brazil])

S.R.L. Società a Responsabilità Limitata (Italy)

S.R.O. Spolecnost s Rucenim Omezenym (Czechoslovakia

S.S.K. Sherkate Sahami Khass (Iran)

Ste. Societe (France, Belgium, Luxembourg, Switzerland)

Ste. Cve. Societe Cooperative (Belgium)

S.V. Samemwerkende Vennootschap (Belgium)

S.Z.R.L. Societe Zairoise a Responsabilite Limitee (Zaire)

T

THB Thai baht

TND Tunisian dinar

TRL Turkish lira

TWD new Taiwan dollar

U

U.A. Uitgesloten Aansporakeiijkheid (Netherlands)

u.p.a. utan personligt ansvar (Sweden)

V

VAG Verein der Arbeitgeber (Austria, Germany)

VEB Venezuelan bolivar

VERTR Vertriebs (Austria, Germany)

VND Vietnamese dong

V.O.f. Vennootschap onder firma (Netherlands)

VVAG Versicherungsverein auf Gegenseitigkeit (Austria, Germany)

W–Z

WA Wettelika Aansprakalikhaed (Netherlands)

WLL With Limited Liability (Bahrain, Kuwait, Qatar, Saudi Arabia)

YK Yugen Kaisha (Japan)

ZAO Zakrytoe Aktsionernoe Obshchestve (Russia)

ZAR South African rand

ZMK Zambian kwacha

ZWD Zimbabwean dollar

Adecoagro LLC

Catamarca 3454
Martínez, Buenos Aires B1640FWB
Argentina
Telephone: (54 11) 4836-8600
Fax: (55 11) 3079-3683 (in Brazil)
Web site: http://www.adecoagro.com

Limited Liability Company
Founded: 2002
Employees: 3,800
Sales: $105 million (2006 est.)
NAICS: 111110 Soybean Farming; 111120 Oilseed (Except Soybean) Farming; 111140 Wheat Farming; 111160 Rice Farming; 111334 Berry (Except Strawberry) Farming; 111920 Cotton Farming; 111930 Sugarcane Farming; 112111 Beef Cattle Ranching and Farming; 112120 Dairy Cattle and Milk Production; 311311 Sugarcane Mills; 311514 Dry, Condensed, and Evaporated Dairy Product Manufacturing; 325193 Ethyl Alcohol Manufacturing

∎ ∎ ∎

Adecoagro LLC is a private partnership/limited liability company active in Argentina, Uruguay, and Brazil, where it owns large farms producing a variety of crops and raising cattle. Backed by hedge fund billionaire George Soros, it sees South America as a significant source of the food supplies needed to feed the world's growing population. Adecoagro's plan calls for acquiring similar but smaller operations that are underfinanced and not sufficiently diversified in output. The company has spent over $500 million in pursuit of this goal.

SEEKING PROFIT IN ARGENTINA'S RICH FARMLAND

The fertile pampas of Argentina provided the raw materials, chiefly wheat and beef, that enabled the country to become one of the most prosperous in the world during the early 20th century. Even after decades of economic mismanagement and neglect of the nation's agricultural treasures, Argentina's farms and ranches, in the mid-1980s, were providing more than half of its exports, and agribusiness was accounting for more than 40 percent of employment.

For a variety of reasons, including inflation that reached triple digit levels in some years, and price controls and export taxes on their output, Argentina's farmers were reluctant to make the investments needed to fully exploit the natural advantages of their land and compete with farmers turning out similar food products in North America, Europe, and Australia. Writing in the *Financial Times* in 1985, Jimmy Burns declared, "agriculture remains the most highly taxed and the least subsidized sector of the economy." By the 1990s, agriculture accounted for only 6 percent of Argentina's gross domestic product.

In the early 1990s Argentina adopted free market policies and conquered inflation by pegging its currency to the U.S. dollar. Investors abroad, aware that land was a commodity that could not be increased in size, came shopping. In 1994 Soros, who had made a fortune in New York, much of it by speculating on the rise and fall

COMPANY PERSPECTIVES

Our mission is to become a world leading food and renewable energy producer, effectively becoming an attractive, solid, liquid and trustworthy investment alternative.

of currencies, purchased 47 percent of the agricultural company Cresud S.A.C.I.F. y A., which became the largest landowner in Argentina. Dedicated chiefly to livestock raising on vast tracts of land, Cresud was the first enterprise of its kind to go public and be traded on the Bolsa de Comercio de Buenos Aires. As the nation's economy fell into recession near the end of the century, Soros sold his investment in Cresud.

The severe recession resulted in national bankruptcy and the devaluation of the Argentine peso at the end of 2001, reducing its value from parity with the dollar to about 30 cents. All of debt-ridden Argentina became a shopper's paradise, with many Brazilian companies buying into, or buying out, their Argentine counterparts. The Pérez Companc family, once the nation's richest, had to sell Argentina's biggest privately owned oil company to Brazil's state-owned Petróleo Brasileiro S.A. (Petrobrás). Pecom Agropecuaria S.A., the family's large farming and ranching holding, was also on the block.

While most Europeans and Americans who had invested in Argentina, badly burned by the economic collapse, kept their distance, Soros and his 20 or so partners, Argentines and foreigners, stepped in, purchasing Pecom's more than 74,000 hectares (183,000 acres) in 2002 for $53 million. At the time Pecom Agropecuaria was the third largest agricultural company in Argentina.

The purchase was made by a Delaware-based entity, Argentine Farmland Investors. Adecoagro was not really a new company but rather a continuation of Adeco Agropecuaria S.R.L., which was formed in 1977 by Alejandro Quentin and a nephew, Octavio Carabello, to invest in Argentine agriculture. Its headquarters were in Martínez, Buenos Aires, where Adecoagro continued to occupy a main office. It had another one in the city of Buenos Aires.

MORE FARMS, MORE PRODUCTS: 2004–07

Under Adecoagro's direction, crops, employing no-till technology, replaced beef as the former Pecom Agropec-

uaria's most important product. The cattle were rerouted to land without capabilities for growing crops. Dairy production was emphasized in place of beef. In 2005 the company established Adeco Lattina as the brand for marketing its dairy products. Adecoagro had already begun exporting powdered milk to Africa and the Middle East.

The success of this model resulted in higher profits. However, to diversify its business and thus reduce exposure to risk, Adecoagro in 2004 purchased a 5,000-hectare (12,500-acre) farm in Uruguay and, in 2005, three farms in Brazil, including two totaling 20,400 hectares (50,400 acres). In early 2006 the company entered the growing field of "green" energy, or biofuels, in Brazil by purchasing Usina Monte Alegre, a plantation and mill in the state of Minas Gerais producing sugar and alcohol, the latter in the form of ethanol, from about one million metric tons a year of harvested sugarcane.

Almost immediately after this acquisition, Adecoagro initiated the Angélica Agroenergía project in Brazil by establishing sugarcane nurseries and building a sugar producing mill in the state of Mato Grosso do Sul. The project called for a yearly productive capacity of 3.6 million metric tons of sugarcane to be converted to sugar and ethanol, with bagasse as a byproduct serving as a fuel source for electricity generation. BNDES, Brazil's state-owned development bank, later approved BRL 151 million (about $75 million) in financing for the project.

Before the year was out, Adecoagro had made further investments in Brazil relating to tropical products. The company acquired Fazenda Lagos de Oeste, a coffee plantation of 1,000 hectares (2,470 acres) in the state of Bahia. In January 2007, five months later, it took a half-share in Fazenda Mimosa, a neighboring plantation of 500 hectares. Both holdings had equipment for irrigation, mechanical harvesting, and processing the beans. Alfenas Café was incorporated to market the coffee and the production of other parties to Europe and Japan. Adecoagro was also growing cotton in Brazil.

Marcelo Vieira, whose family had sold Usina Monte Alegre to Adecoagro, became a partner and the administrator of the company's Brazil holdings, whose revenues totaled BRL 95 million (about $43 million) in 2006. In addition to his more than 30 years' experience in the sugar industry, Vieira was an exponent for the development of specialized varieties of coffee, including some that had been long forgotten. He was appointed manager for Adecoagro's sugar and ethanol activities.

For the enterprise as a whole, Mariano Bosch Jr., a young Argentine agronomist, was chief executive officer.

KEY DATES

2002: Private investors purchase Argentina's third largest agricultural company.
2004: Adecoagro purchases a farm in Uruguay.
2005: Adecoagro buys three farms, with a combined 50,000 acres, in Brazil.
2006-07: The firm buys Brazilian properties producing sugar, coffee, and ethanol.
2007: Purchase of Argentina's Pilagá property makes Adecoagro a rice grower as well; joint venture is established to produce cheese and powdered milk for export.

Despite the Brazil acquisitions, Argentina remained the center of its activities. By late 2006 the former Pecom lands were producing 160,000 metric tons of grain, compared to only 60,000 on the same amount of land prior to the acquisition. The cows, which had been averaging 16 liters of milk a day in yield, were producing 26.

These results encouraged Adecoagro to make an even bigger purchase: 94,000 hectares (233,000 acres) bought from Grupo Pilagá for $90 million. The acquisition, incorporated in 2007 as Pilagá S.A., included two rice mills and the recognized brands in Argentina of Cabaña Pilagá and Molinos Ala. By late 2008 Adecoagro was the leading rice producer in Argentina, with 15,000 planted hectares (about 37,000 acres) yielding 100,000 metric tons a year and two mills. The Pilagá spread also was enabling the company to sell about 500 bulls and 8,000 metric tons of beef a year.

Adecoagro's thirst for productive rural properties could not always be appeased. By late 2006 the company was on the verge of acquiring a majority stake in SanCor Unidas Cooperativas Ltda., the second largest dairy producer in Argentina and a cooperative of thousands of affiliated dairy farmers. Adecoagro was preparing to pay $120 million, in return for 62.5 percent of the cooperative, to help retire much of the $167 million debt that had pushed SanCor to the edge of bankruptcy. The prospective purchase incited a furious reaction in Argentina from defenders of the cooperative system, and SanCor found, instead, a white knight in the form of Venezuelan President Hugo Chávez, who extended a substantial advance payment for the first of an annual shipment of powdered milk and baby formula.

After failing in this attempt Adecoagro settled in mid-2007 for a smaller dairy acquisition: Córdoba-based La Lácteo S.A., for $6 million. This company, with its plant in nearby Ferreyra, produced 150,000 liters of milk a day (compared to SanCor's four million) and also yogurt, cheese, and related products. Adecoagro at this time, on three farms in the province of Santa Fe, had seven dairy operations yielding a total of 100,000 liters of milk a day. Later in 2007 the company formed a joint venture with Agropur, the largest dairy cooperative in Canada, to build a $40 million plant with capacity to convert 1.5 million liters of fresh milk daily to powdered milk and cheese. This facility would abut the state-of-the-art dairy farm, with more than 3,000 cows (and ultimately 45,000), that Adecoagro was building in a location named Venado Tuerto (One-Eyed Deer). It also had plans to build a plant in Argentina that would produce ethanol from corn and send a byproduct, distilled mash, to feed the 45,000 cows.

ADECOAGRO IN 2008

By late 2008 Adecoagro had ten farms with a total of more than 225,000 hectares (555,000 acres) of land in four Argentine provinces, of which 105,000 hectares (260,000 acres) was being planted. There were three farms in Brazil with a total of 21,000 hectares (52,000 acres), plus the one in Uruguay. Annual crop output of 380,000 metric tons in Argentina was mainly in wheat, soybeans, corn, rice, and sunflowers. The Brazilian farms produced coffee and cotton in addition to sugar and ethanol.

Fueled by the boom that was enabling all commodities to rise rapidly in price, South American farmland had increased precipitously in price by late 2008, when a gathering world economic recession began threatening all gains. In the fertile area of Argentina nicknamed "The Nuclear Zone," a hectare of land was commanding $12,000 to $15,000 or more (or in acreage, from nearly $5,000 to $6,000 or more), an increase of threefold to sixfold in only six years. One important reason was the boom in soybean exports, particularly to a voracious China.

By this time the Argentine government had decided to put a lid on the speculative frenzy in land and to prevent the increasing concentration of farmland in a few hands. According to one agronomist, six foreign enterprises or ones with foreign partners controlled one-quarter of the nation's cultivated area. There were widespread fears, too, that intensive agriculture risked soil erosion and water contamination and that growing soybeans without the rotation of other crops would ruin the fertility of the land.

In the space of a few weeks the government announced two new measures, mandating that it be informed of all plans for soybean planting and banning the sale to foreigners of land within a zone 50 kilometers (31 miles) from the nation's borders. Argentina had only about one million hectares (about 2.5 million acres) of arable land not being cultivated.

In Brazil, where this amount—even excluding the Amazon basin and areas already eroded—was estimated at 90 million hectares (over 220 million acres), the case for development was stronger. After a 2007 *Washington Post* article expressed alarm that increased planting of sugarcane and soybeans threatened wooded savanna that included a rich variety of flora, Vieira replied in a letter, "We have an explicit policy of not clearing native vegetation, and we don't subcontract to farmers who do. Adecoagro restores land surrounding springs, streams, wetlands, steep hills, hilltops and other sensitive areas."

While Adecoagro owned land and buildings, it contracted out most of the production, except for chemical applications. The company marketed all its own crops and paid for all the inputs. Adecoagro's investors, in addition to Soros, included U.S.-based Halderman Farm Management Services, Inc., and HBK Investments, a Dallas-based hedge fund manager. An Argentine investor was Buenos Aires Capital Partners. Adecoagro was an operating company of International Farmland Holding LLC. It was planning to make an initial public offering of stock at some point, but the difficult economic climate made this prospect unlikely in 2009.

Robert Halasz

PRINCIPAL SUBSIDIARIES

Adeco Agropecuaria Brasil Ltda. (Brazil); Pilagá S.A.; Usina Monte Alegre S.A. (Brazil).

PRINCIPAL COMPETITORS

BrasilAgro-Companhia Braileira de Propriedades Agrícoles; Calyx Agro Ltd.; Cresud S.A.C.I.F. y A.; Grupo Los Grobo; El Tejar.

FURTHER READING

"Argentina: The Silver Giant," *LatinFinance,* September 1996, p. 33.

Bertello, Fernando, "Invertirán US$40 millones para contruir una planta láctea," *La Nación de Argentina,* November 9, 2007.

———, "Tras el intento por SanCor, Adecoagro quiere otro láctea," *La Nación de Argentina,* July 23, 2007.

Burns, Jimmy, "The Argentine Pampa Gets a New Lease on Life," *Financial Times,* November 20, 1985, p. 16.

Del Río, José, and Carla Quiroga, "Empresarios y CEOs '06," *Apertura,* December 2006, pp. 20–22.

Grondona, Carlos, "Los dueños del campo," *Apertura,* November 2006, pp. 24–25.

Lara Serreno, Rodrigo, "El nuevo real estate," *AméricaEconomía,* September 29, 2008, pp. 42, 44, 46.

Miller, Ben, "Flipping Crops," *LatinFinance,* September 29, 2008.

Pilling, David, "Signs of Wealth Return to the Pampa," *Financial Times,* November 5, 1996, p. 33.

Schneyer, Joshua, "The Money Flying down to Brazil," *Business Week,* June 18, 2007, p. 70.

Vieira, Marcelo, "Brazilian Ethanol's Green Methods," *Washington Post,* August 16, 2007, p. A14.

Adolor Corporation

700 Pennsylvania Drive
Exton, Pennsylvania 19341-1129
U.S.A.
Telephone: (484) 595-1500
Fax: (484) 595-1520
Web site: http://www.adolor.com

Public Company
Incorporated: 1994
Employees: 108
Sales: $9.1 million (2007)
Stock Exchanges: NASDAQ
Ticker Symbol: ADLR
NAICS: 325412 Pharmaceutical Preparation Manufacturing

■ ■ ■

Adolor Corporation is an Exton, Pennsylvania-based biopharmaceutical company devoted to the development and marketing of prescription pain-management products. The company's lone product on the market, Entereg, provides the pain relief offered by opioids such as morphine, but without adverse effects on the gastrointestinal (GI) tract. After an arduous approval process, the U.S. Food and Drug Administration (FDA) in 2008 granted permission for the use of Entereg after partial large or small bowel resection surgery, to alleviate the pain caused by postoperative ileus when the disruption of the intestines results in nausea, vomiting, and general discomfort. Adolor has worked with partner GlaxoSmithKline to win FDA approval, and the two companies are also collaborating on the development and commercialization of Entereg for other uses, including the management of adverse GI side effects related to opioid use. In addition, Adolor collaborates with Pfizer Inc. on its Delta Opioid Receptor Program, developing new pain compounds that target opioid receptors outside the brain and spine, to provide topical relief from inflammation and itching. Adolor is also pursuing other opioid and non-opioid targets. Adolor is a public company, listed on the NASDAQ since 2000.

COMPANY FOUNDED: 1994

Adolor was formed in the fall of 1994 by John J. Farrar with $1.5 million in financial backing provided by three venture-capital firms: ARCH Venture Fund II; Falcon Technology Partners; and Weiss, Peck & Greer Venture Partners. The seed round of funding was completed in November 1994. Serving as president and chief executive officer, Farrar held an undergraduate degree and a master's degree in zoology from Miami University, and a Ph.D. in microbiology/immunology from the University of Notre Dame. He had worked for Hoffmann-La Roche, serving as group director of biological research in immunology, cancer, and virology. He then became senior vice-president and director at the research division of Sterling Winthrop Pharmaceuticals, a research division of Eastman Kodak that maintained a facility in Collegeville, Pennsylvania, north of Philadelphia. "When Kodak dismantled Sterling in 1994," according to an article by Dan Stets in the *Philadelphia Inquirer* in 1996, "selling pieces to SmithKline and Sanofi and passing out pink slips to nearly 500 Collegeville researchers,

COMPANY PERSPECTIVES

Committed to innovation, focused on invention.

'it was like a piñata breaking and all these other companies tumbling out,' said Mary G. Gregg, deputy director of Greater Philadelphia First." Scores of start-up companies sprang up, as Sterling units and former Sterling researchers linked up with venture-capital firms. Like many of these new enterprises, Farrar set up shop for his new biotechnology company in Malvern, Pennsylvania.

Adolor took its name from the Latin phrase *a do lor,* meaning "without pain." The company's goal was straightforward yet ambitious. In the words of the *Inquirer,* Adolor was "on the hunt for the Holy Grail of the pharmaceutical industry: a nonaddictive painkiller that works as effectively as morphine." Farrar told the paper, "A side-effect-free morphine is a billion-dollar drug."

The search for new classes of opiate-type substances with fewer side effects than morphine was clearly a long-term vision for Adolor. To generate a more immediate source of revenue, the company initially focused on painkillers that it hoped it could get to market in a relatively short period, in particular a topical preparation that could provide the pain-killing effect of an opiate without affecting the brain, thus avoiding the controlled drug label and regulation by the federal Drug Enforcement Administration. The medical compound Adolor focused on was a formulation of loperamide, a narcotic that targeted opioid receptors outside the brain and spinal cord. It was hardly a new compound, having been tested previously for use with acute pain. Because it could not cross into the brain through the bloodstream like morphine or other opiates, however, it failed as an acute painkiller. What Adolor did was to create a cream-based formulation of loperamide to provide topical pain relief for such surface inflammations as burns, hemorrhoids, and cornea abrasions.

SECOND ROUND OF FUNDING HELD: 1996

As Adolor made preparations to begin clinical trials on its loperamide compound, code named ADL 2-1294, it raised additional funds in a second venture-capital round in March 1996, taking in $9.6 million. The initial three backers participated, as did three newcomers: Alta California Partners, OneLiberty Ventures, and

TL Ventures. Phase I clinical trials for ADL 2-1294 were then initiated in November 1996 and completed in the spring of 1997. Phase II trials were subsequently launched on a topical formulation for pain and itching associated with burns and other skin wounds and inflammation.

Given the high cost of testing new compounds, Adolor began looking for pharmaceutical partners to help share the financial burden of bringing formulations of ADL 2-1294 to market. In 1997 Adolor licensed the ADL 2-1294 topical formulation to a South Korean firm. In 1999 SmithKline Beecham licensed the formulation on a worldwide basis (except for Korea), in a licensing and development pact that could net Adolor $48 million plus future royalty payments. By that time Phase II trials were also underway for an ophthalmic formulation of ADL 2-1294 for inflammatory pain associated with corneal abrasions and eye surgery. In addition, other compounds in the Adolor pipeline entered Phase I trials.

INITIAL PUBLIC OFFERING: 2000

In three subsequent rounds with private investors, Adolor raised another $32.4 million. In 2000 Adolor made plans to go public in an initial public offering (IPO) it hoped could raise as much as $84 million, underwritten by Warburg Dillon Read LLC, Robertson Stephens, and Pacific Growth Equities Inc. The stock market, however, was experiencing a difficult stretch, due in large part to the implosion of the technology sector, the bursting of the Internet bubble, and a crash in the biotechnology sector in April 2000. Adolor postponed the offering and several times delayed pricing the shares. As the company waited for better market conditions, it signed a licensing agreement with Santen Pharmaceutical Co. of Japan for the ophthalmic formulation of ADL 2-1294, and it raised $36.6 million in a sixth round of private funding, completed in July 2000. The IPO was then conducted in November 2000, netting Adolor another $103.6 million.

A secondary stock offering in 2001 raised a further $60 million to supplement Adolor's cash position, which totaled $156.4 million by the end of 2001, including cash equivalents and short-term investments. The company was enthusiastic about another drug compound, ADL 8-2698, intended for use as a painkiller following abdominal surgery. Because it blocked the ill effects caused by other painkillers, including nausea and vomiting, it allowed patients to leave the hospital one day sooner. Adolor hoped to file for a new drug application in 2002 and begin marketing the product in 2003. Known as alvimopan, the drug would eventually be branded as Entereg.

In April 2002 Adolor signed a collaboration agreement with GlaxoSmithKline for the worldwide development and commercialization of alvimopan for certain indications, receiving a $50 million signing fee and the possibility of another $220 million in milestone and other payments. Also noteworthy in 2002 was Farrar's decision to retire. He was replaced as president and chief executive officer by Bruce A. Peacock, a biotech veteran in the Philadelphia area with more than 20 years of executive experience.

FIRST NEW DRUG APPLICATION

Hopes of getting Entereg to market in 2003 were overly optimistic. Instead, more studies were conducted. Other drug compounds in the pipeline also took part in clinical trials, and another product was added to the pipeline when the company licensed a sterile lidocaine patch for treating postsurgery pain caused by incisions. In June 2004, nearly ten years since its founding, Adolor submitted its first new drug application to the FDA for Entereg to treat postoperative ileus. During 2004 Phase II studies were also completed for the use of Entereg to treat opioid-induced bowel dysfunction and chronic idiopathic constipation.

Entereg was given a "fast track" review because it fulfilled the requirements of addressing unmet medical needs. In anticipation of soon earning FDA approval, Adolor began recruiting a sales force. Thus, it was a bitter blow when in July 2005 the company received an "approvable" letter. Although approval was not denied, it required that Adolor perform another clinical trial to provide additional proof that Entereg was effective following bowel-resection surgery. At the very least the commercial launch of the product would be delayed by 18 months. A month later, Peacock resigned, accepting an offering to run a chain of walk-in neighborhood medical clinics. Replacing him as president and CEO on an interim basis was Chairman David Madden.

Adolor submitted the results of its new Entereg study in 2006 and again waited for FDA approval on the drug. In the meantime, the company received disappointing news when final-stage clinical trials for the use of Entereg to mitigate the effects of narcotic medicines offered mixed results. Wall Street punished the stock, which lost almost half of its value in a single day, falling below $12 per share. Matters grew worse in November 2006 when the FDA replied with another approvable letter for the primary use of Entereg, asking for further information. The FDA asked the company to provide 12-month safety data and a risk-management plan.

Adolor's stock took another hit, falling 45 percent to $7.69. A month later Madden stepped down as president and CEO, turning over day-to-day control to COO Michael R. Dougherty. An experienced biotechnology executive, Dougherty had joined Adolor in November 2002 as senior vice-president of commercial operations. He then became chief financial officer in April 2003, and was named senior vice-president and chief operating officer in October 2005. In addition to the change at the helm, Adolor disbanded its 35-person sales force, which given the uncertainty of the FDA's final decision would not be needed for the foreseeable future. Another 17 people were laid off as well. The company was fortunate, however, to have plenty of cash on hand to see it through this difficult, uncertain time.

The focus of 2007 was on compiling and analyzing the long-term safety data that had been compiled by GlaxoSmithKline in opioid bowel dysfunction in order to meet the FDA request. The response was completed in August 2007 and in November of that year the FDA announced that its Gastrointesinal Drugs Advisory Committee (GIDAC) of outside experts would review the application at the start of 2008. In the meantime, Adolor made progress on its search for the "Holy Grail," its Delta Opioid Receptor Program. Conventional opioids bind to what is called the mu receptor. While they provide excellent pain relief, they come with many well-known side effects. Adolor focused on a different opioid receptor, delta, which it believed offered significant pain relief with fewer side effects. The first of these delta compounds, ADL5859, entered Phase IIa studies in 2007 and steps were taken to initiate Phase I trials on a second delta compound, ADL5747. The potential of the compounds was strong enough that in December 2007 Pfizer Inc. signed an exclusive worldwide collaboration agreement with Adolor to develop and commercialize the delta compounds, paying $30 million up front as well as $1.9 million for prior development costs.

FDA APPROVES ENTEREG: 2008

In early 2008 the GIDAC offered a favorable recommendation to the FDA for Entereg. The persistence of Adolor and GlaxoKlineSmith finally paid off in May 2008 when the FDA approved Entereg for postoperative ileus. It was a milestone moment for the company, which would soon enjoy its first sales revenues after nearly 15 years of effort. Should the other uses of Entereg also receive FDA approval and the delta compounds eventually pan out, it would be the beginning of a prosperous enterprise.

Ed Dinger

PRINCIPAL COMPETITORS

Endo Pharmaceuticals Holdings Inc.; Progenics Pharmaceuticals, Inc.; Wyeth Pharmaceuticals, Inc.

FURTHER READING

George, John, "Adolor Puts Its Initial Public Offering on Hold," *Philadelphia Business Journal,* April 14, 2000, p. 5.

Hilton, Christopher, "Adolor Names Dougherty CEO, Disbands 35-Person Sales Force," *Wall Street Journal,* December 15, 2006, p. B5.

Knox, Andrea, "High-Tech but Low-Key," *Philadelphia Inquirer,* September 28, 1997, p. L01.

Loftus, Peter, "Bowel-Surgery Drugs Are on the Way," *Wall Street Journal,* March 22, 2006, p. B3A.

Loyd, Linda, "Adolor Shares Up 20% After Pfizer Drug Deal," *Philadelphia Inquirer,* December 6, 2007.

———, "Adolor Trims 52 Jobs After Drug's Delay," *Philadelphia Inquirer,* December 15, 2006.

———, "Another Delay, Blow for Adolor," *Philadelphia Inquirer,* November 7, 2006.

———, "Experimental Drug from Exton, Pa., Firm Shows Promise for Abdominal Surgery," *Philadelphia Inquirer,* October 2, 2001.

———, "Exton, Pa., Drug Firm Seeks FDA Approval for New Medicine," *Philadelphia Inquirer,* June 29, 2004.

———, "FDA Again Delays Decision on Adolor Drug," *Philadelphia Inquirer,* May 9, 2008.

———, "Not a Ringing Endorsement," *Philadelphia Inquirer,* January 24, 2008.

Stets, Dan, "Venture Investing Rises 47% in Region," *Philadelphia Inquirer,* June 10, 1996, p. C01.

Winslow, Ron, "Glaxo, SmithKline Plan Collaborations," *Wall Street Journal,* July 28, 1999, p. B8.

Agria Corporation

Building 16, No. 26 Xihuan South Road
Beijing Economic-Technological Development Area
Beijing, 100176
China
Telephone: (+86 10) 8785-9000
Fax: (+86 10) 8785-9001
Web site: http://www.agriacorp.com

Public Company
Incorporated: 2007
Employees: 333
Sales: RMB 490 million ($91.9 million) (2007)
Stock Exchanges: New York
Ticker Symbol: GRO
NAICS: 115112 Soil Preparation, Planting, and Cultivating

■ ■ ■

Agria Corporation is a publicly listed investment vehicle focused on the agricultural sector in mainland China. The company, which calls itself an "agri-solutions provider," primarily operates through its effective control of subsidiary Primalights III Agriculture Development Co. Ltd. (P3A). That company in turn operates in three distinct product categories: corn seed, sheep breeding, and seedlings. Corn seed is the company's largest business, accounting for 50 percent of its revenues of RMB 490 million ($92 million) in 2007. The Corn Seed division targets especially the high-margin, proprietary seed market, led by the group's four Primalights III corn varieties developed for different soil

and weather conditions. The company also boasts a product pipeline of some 20 corn seed varieties in various stages of approval by the Chinese government. Agria claims 3 percent of the highly fragmented Chinese corn seed market.

The sheep breeding business includes breeder sheep from the company's own herds, as well as the production of frozen semen and frozen embryos. The company's sheep breeding program includes its Primalights III hybrid sheep, developed by crossing domestic and foreign sheep breeds, which offer enhanced reproductive capacity and adaptability. The Sheep Breeding division produced 40 percent of the group's revenues, but 50 percent of its profits, in 2007.

The third division, Seedlings, focuses on producing whitebark pine, raspberry, and date seedlings, among others. This division generated 10 percent of the company's sales. Agria Corporation itself was formed in 2007 in order to list the group's shares on the New York Stock Exchange (NYSE). The company is led by Chairman and CEO Guanglin Lai, whose wife, Juan Li, is one of the major shareholders in P3A.

"AGRI-SOLUTIONS" BUSINESS IN 2000

Agria Corporation was formed in 2007 as a holding company for a number of companies engaged in the research and development of products for China's agricultural sector. The main component of Agria's holdings, and its sole source of revenue, was Primalights III Agriculture Development Co. Ltd. (P3A).

COMPANY PERSPECTIVES

At Agria, we are dedicated to providing top quality products and service. We also put a strong focus on building on our established network of relationships to provide seamless support to our clients and partners. With that, we strive to maintain contentious efforts and awareness of our corporate responsibilities to our environment, our employees and our investors.

P3A had been founded in 2000 by Zhixin Xue, who led a team of scientists in the research and development of what the company later labeled "agri-solutions," that is, premium and high-margin products designed to improve the quality and quantity of certain agricultural sectors in China. From the start, P3A focused on three primary markets, each of which held significant potential for future growth.

The first of these was corn seed, a booming market as China emerged as the world's second largest producer of corn at the start of the 21st century. The majority of the country's corn production was used as livestock feed, and most of the remainder served as biofuel. By 2000, however, as the increasingly affluent Chinese consumers adopted Western dietary habits, the demand for food-grade corn increased dramatically. While the country experienced an oversupply of corn, primarily produced domestically, the growth in demand had begun to outpace the growth in production. However, the great variety in China's agricultural regions, where geography and climate and other growing conditions often exhibited wide differences, introduced a need for seeds developed for specific conditions.

P3A's second area of focus involved sheep breeding. China was by far the world's largest producer of sheep—and the largest consumer of both mutton and wool—nearly doubling the output of the next largest market, Australia. In terms of productivity, however, China's herds lagged far behind these other markets. The breeding of stronger and more productive livestock faced a number of obstacles. Chief among them was the peculiarity of China's sheep sector, which remained dominated by small, household farms. The vast majority of the country's sheep (and goats) were kept on these small farms, with an average of fewer than 30 head of sheep. Only a tiny percentage of China's sheep farms boasted herd numbers of 500 or more. This compared to an average of 2,700 sheep per herd in Australia.

The small size of individual herds meant that farmers were unable to afford to own breeder sheep that might improve the quality of their herds. Control over the sector by local and regional governments and farmers cooperatives also provided another obstacle to breeding initiatives. Yet this market also presented an opportunity to develop breeding products based on sales of frozen semen and frozen embryos, in addition to the creation of breeder herds. P3A's operations focused on all three of these breeding products and services.

The company's third operational area targeted the fast-growing market for seedlings in China. The country's massive pollution problem, especially in its cities, had sparked a growing environmental awareness among the people and the government. This resulted in a new tree-planting effort, driven largely by government programs. Consumer demand also played a major role in the regreening of China, prompting residential developers to incorporate trees and greenery in their developments. However the country's regulation prohibited the uprooting and transplanting of trees for these purposes.

HYBRID SUCCESS IN 2003

P3A responded to the demand by developing its own catalog of tree seedlings and other plants. The company's focus turned particularly to whitebark pine, a fast-growing tree variety. At the same time, the rising affluence of Chinese consumers encouraged the company to develop a number of higher-margin seedlings, including raspberries and dates. Into the middle of the first decade of the 2000s, P3A compiled a catalog of some 20 plant species.

P3A grew strongly and by 2002 the company had begun to post its first profits. Research and development drove much of the company's early growth, backed by the creation, in 2002, of the company's Bioresearch Institute. In that year, also, the company received certification for both its sheep breeding and forestry businesses.

In the seedling sector, the company teamed up with the Chinese Academy of Forestry to develop methods of speeding the growth of whitebark pine seedlings, successfully reducing the seed-to-sale period from three years to two years and even less. The company's main customer for its whitebark pine seedlings was Taiyuan Relord Enterprise Development Group, which also became one of the company's main shareholders. P3A founder Xue was to serve as chairman of Taiyuan Relord as well.

P3A's strongest growth came from its corn seed and sheep breeding operations. In 2003 the company achieved a breakthrough in its breeding program when

KEY DATES

■

2000: Zhixin Xue founds Primalights III Agriculture Development Co. (P3A), focusing on developing corn seed, breeder sheep, and seedlings for the Chinese market.

2003: P3A introduces the Primalights III hybrid sheep variety.

2004: P3A launches production of Primalights III corn seed; company forms a contractual arrangement with the predecessor company to Agria Corporation.

2007: Agria Corporation is founded and listed on the New York Stock Exchange.

2008: Agria acquires two corn seed varieties from NKY Company of Beijing.

it successfully developed a new hybrid sheep variety. For this, the company had crossed domestic Chinese sheep with varieties from overseas. The result was a sheep that remained highly adaptable to China's environment, while boasting the reproductive hardiness and enhanced fleshiness of foreign sheep. The new variety was named after the company itself, becoming known as the Primalights III hybrid sheep. P3A began building its herd and by 2005 was able to begin marketing its breeder sheep, as well as frozen semen and frozen embryos, to the Chinese market.

By the end of 2007, the company's Primalights III herd had grown to more than 4,700 head. This also meant that the population approached stabilization, enabling the company to apply to register the Primalights III hybrid sheep as a new sheep variety. By then, too, the company had built up additional herds of more than 5,500 other sheep varieties, including Suffolk, Texel, Merino, and Poll Dorset. The company's breeding operations had expanded to include five farms, for a total of 3,700 acres.

P3A's sales had kept pace as well: through 2007 the company's sales of breeder sheep had topped 36,500, nearly 32,000 of which were Primalights III sheep. The company had also built a strong sales base for its frozen semen and frozen embryo sales, selling 25 million containers of frozen semen and nearly 9,500 frozen embryos that year.

NEW CORN VARIETY IN 2004

P3A's corn seed development wing had in the meantime been busy with its own research and development program. In 2004 the company achieved a new milestone with the successful development of its first proprietary corn seed. By the end of the year, the company had created corn seed production centers, in cooperation with local farmer networks, in Shanxi, Inner Mongolia, Gansu, and Xinjiang.

These four regions corresponded with the four types of corn seed, also branded under the Primalights name, developed by the company. The first, Primalights III 28, produced a straight cornstalk capable of high yields. The second, called Primalights III 591, produced corn with a high starch content, with a hardier plant capable of resisting harsh weather conditions. Primalights III 891 coupled greater disease resistance with higher yields. The last of the first four Primalights varieties was Primalights III 391, developed for China's more arid regions.

The launching of Primalights corn provided a new successful product for the company. P3A quickly built up a strong farmer-based network of seed producers. By the end of 2007, the company's corn seed production spanned more than 23,000 acres. The success of the Primalights III seeds helped place the company among the top seed producers in China; the higher-margin seeds also made the company one of the fastest-growing agricultural products companies. The company was also aided by the Chinese government's refusal to allow the entry of genetically modified organisms into the country's food crops, effectively restricting the entry of foreign seed varieties, and agroindustrial giants such as Monsanto, from entering the Chinese market.

FIRST STEPS TOWARD AGRIA IN 2004

Toward the middle of the first decade of the 2000s, P3A began seeking capital for further expansion. This brought the company into contact with Guanglin Lai, a Chinese native who had a bachelor's degree in accounting from Monash University, in Melbourne, Australia. Lai had also qualified as a certified public accountant in Australia. However, the realm of new business opportunities available led Lai to soon return to China to try his hand as an entrepreneur. Lai turned toward the investment sector, joining Shenzhen Keding Venture Capital Management Co. as its managing director in 2000. By 2002 Lai had decided to establish his own investment company, called Ace Choice Management Limited, which served as a liaison between business interests in China and abroad.

Lai proved instrumental in helping guide P3A to a public offering, targeting a listing on the NYSE. Chinese companies seeking listing on foreign exchanges

KEY DATES

1994: Company is incorporated.
1999: Company signs licensing agreement with SmithKline Beecham.
2000: Adolor goes public on the NASDAQ.
2007: Adolor signs licensing agreement with Pfizer Inc.
2008: Company's first product receives Food and Drug Administration approval.

were often required to develop a complex network of holding companies, subsidiaries, and shareholders in order to navigate the legal and financial hurdles set up by the Chinese government. P3A's own route toward a public listing proved equally convoluted. In 2004 P3A nominally became an affiliated subsidiary of Lai's company, listed in the Cayman Islands, which became the predecessor to Agria Corporation.

Chinese law prohibited foreign ownership from entering the company's agricultural sector directly. As a result, Agria would in fact own no shares in P3A, but instead put into place operating agreements that transferred all of P3A's revenues and profits to Agria. Instead, 100 percent of P3A was owned by just four shareholders. These included P3A founder Xue and Juan Li, the wife of Guanglin Lai.

In 2005 Lai founded another entity, Aero-Biotech Group, registered in the British Virgin Islands. That company's primary purpose was to serve as the holding company for another corporate entity, Hong Kong–registered China Victory International Holdings Ltd. This company then provided the link to a domestic company, Aero-Biotech Science & Technology Co. Ltd., founded by Lai as an agricultural research and development company. This latter company then effectively took control of P3A, which in turn became the company's sole revenue source.

NYSE LISTING IN 2007

The complicated structure permitted Lai and Xue to turn to the international investment market to fund P3A's fast-growing operations. As a next step, Lai created a new holding company, Agria Corporation, registered in the Cayman Islands, which became the ultimate parent to the group's other corporate entities. Like many Chinese companies, Agria chose to list its shares on the NYSE, benefiting from the huge interest in Chinese stocks. Lai became Agria's chairman and

chief executive officer, while Xue became the company's chief operating officer and continued as chairman of P3A. Agria completed its listing in November 2007.

The successful offering appeared to turn sour soon after, however, when Xue suddenly resigned his chief operating officer position as a result of a pay dispute. Agria's share prices collapsed in half at the announcement. Nonetheless, investor confidence was quickly restored, after it became evident that Xue and his team of scientists planned to remain at P3A. Nonetheless, the incident highlighted Agria's vulnerability, as its revenues and profits remained entirely dependent on a company it did not own.

Its complex shareholding aside, Agria Corporation continued to enjoy strong growth prospects into the end of the decade. Agria's successful Primalights III brand placed it in a strong position to gain market share ahead of what many observers saw as a coming consolidation of the country's highly fragmented seed industry.

Agria itself intended to lead that consolidation. As a sign of this, the company announced that it had completed its first acquisition, of the proprietary rights to two corn seed varieties from Beijing-based NKY Company. The two varieties, initially developed by the Beijing Academy of Agricultural Services, enabled Agria to expand its own corn seed portfolio to include fresh corn for human consumption. Agria looked forward to its own growth as a major Chinese agri-solutions provider.

M. L. Cohen

PRINCIPAL SUBSIDIARIES

Aero-Biotech Group Ltd. (British Virgin Islands); Aero-Biotech Science & Technology Co. Ltd.; Agria Brother Biotech (Shenzhen) Co. Ltd.; China Victory International Holdings Ltd. (Hong Kong); Primalights III Agriculture Development Co. Ltd.

PRINCIPAL COMPETITORS

Tata Sons Ltd.; D1 Oils PLC; SABCO L.L.C.; Balanoor Plantations and Industries Ltd.; Koninklijke Cooperatie Cosun U.A.; Cooperative des Agriculteurs de Bretagne S.C.A.; Eastern Produce Kenya Ltd.; YTL Corporation Bhd.; Groupe Glon S.A.

FURTHER READING

"Agria Announces Management and Board Changes," *Internet Wire*, November 24, 2008.

"Agria Confirms No Disruptions to the Business," *Internet Wire,* April 8, 2008.

"Agria to Acquire Rights to Two Proprietary Corn Seeds," *Internet Wire,* June 11, 2008.

Kumar, Vivek, "Chinese Ag Solution Provider Agria: A Compelling IPO," *Seeking Alpha,* November 6, 2007.

"Our Progressive Review of GRO," *M2 Presswire,* October 27, 2008.

"The Pomerantz Firm Charges Agria Corporation with Securities Fraud—GRO," *PrimeZone Media Network,* May 13, 2008.

"Progressive Following on Agria Corporation," *M2 Presswire,* February 25, 2008.

Roe, Timothy, "Agria Corporation Slumps on IPO," *Seeking Alpha,* November 8, 2007.

"Three Chinese Companies to List on New York Stock Exchange," *AsiaPulse News,* October 26, 2007.

SECURING THE GLOBAL VILLAGE

Aladdin Knowledge Systems Ltd.

35 Efal Street
Kiryat Arye
Petach Tikva,
Israel
Telephone: (972 3) 978 1207
Fax: (972 3) 978 1010
Web site: http://www.aladdin.com

Public Company
Incorporated: 1985
Employees: 464
Sales: $105.9 million (2007)
Stock Exchanges: NASDAQ (GM)
Ticker Symbol: ALDN
NAICS: 541512 Computer Systems Design Services

∎ ∎ ∎

Based in Petach Tikva, Israel, Aladdin Knowledge Systems Ltd. is a leading player in the area of enterprise security and software digital rights management. The company provides solutions and services that Internet security professionals and software developers use to protect a wide variety of digital content. From 14 offices around the globe, Aladdin serves a customer roster that includes governments, leading corporations, as well as educational and financial institutions.

Aladdin Knowledge Systems markets software rights management products under its long-established HASP brand. In addition, the company offers integrated content security solutions under the eSafe nameplate, as well as a next-generation authentication key (technology used to verify one's identity) called eToken.

FORMATIVE YEARS: 1985–94

Aladdin Knowledge Systems' history dates back to 1985, when the company was established in Israel by Yanki Margalit. A former computer hacker, Margalit gained experience tapping into the computer system at Tel Aviv University around the age of 16. While serving in the Army, he continued to tinker with technology by building his own computer.

Instead of pursuing a college education, Margalit went into business for himself. In 1984 he developed the HASP (Hardware Against Software Piracy) anti-piracy dongle, an innovative device that thwarted even the most skilled software pirates. Essentially, HASP was a physical device that had to be plugged into the back of a computer in order for a given software program to function.

Margalit formed Aladdin Knowledge Systems at the age of 22, with his brother Dany and an initial investment of $10,000. On the strength of its sole product, the fledgling enterprise grew steadily throughout the remainder of the 1980s.

By 1989 Aladdin Knowledge Systems was marketing the next generation of its product, which it called the HASP II. From a small apartment located near Dizengoff Circle, a staff of approximately 12 workers produced some 5,000 HASP II units per month. The device's effectiveness was maximized by Margalit's experience with artificial intelligence technology, which

COMPANY PERSPECTIVES

■

Aladdin Knowledge Systems has spent over two decades providing the most innovative and secure solutions. Its reputation is built upon a comprehensive line of products satisfying the security needs of organizations operating in a world where fast and secure information accessibility is a necessity.

he had applied in other areas. One example of this was Rabi, a software development tool Margalit developed during the late 1980s.

International expansion soon began. In late 1992, Aladdin formed a wholly owned subsidiary in the United States named Aladdin Software Security Inc. The company went public in October of the following year, listing on the NASDAQ under the symbol ALDN.

On the strength of burgeoning sales in Europe and the United States, Aladdin sold about 60,000 HASP devices in the first quarter of 1993 alone. By this time, the company exported approximately 60 percent of its products and benefited from a geographically dispersed customer base that spanned some 40 different countries.

By 1993 Aladdin was marketing MacHASP, a version of its original product that protected Macintosh software. One advantage of the product was that a single system could be used to protect multiple applications on a computer network. MacHASP's popularity was affirmed when Europe's Alcatel selected the product, joining other noteworthy customers such as BBC Television and the Associated Press.

Another development in 1993 was the formation of Aladdin France SA, which enabled the company to begin marketing its products in France. Aladdin ended 1993 with annual sales of $4.2 million, up from $2.6 million in 1992.

Aladdin's sales continued to climb in 1994, reaching $4.2 million. That year, profits totaled $2.4 million, up from $1.3 million in 1993. International expansion continued as the company formed a new wholly owned subsidiary in the United Kingdom named Aladdin Knowledge Systems UK Ltd.

ACQUISITIONS AND PRODUCT DEVELOPMENT: 1995–99

The company enjoyed a steady pace of growth during the mid-1990s. In March 1995, Aladdin Knowledge Systems completed the acquisition of EliaShim Microcomputers. By May of that year, the company had sold more than one million HASP keys, and its client base had grown to include IBM, NEC, and Honeywell.

An important development unfolded in November 1995 when a new product named Aladdin Smartcard Environment (ASE) was introduced. Embedded with computer chips, smartcards were capable of storing information such as health records, security data, highway tolls, and even money. The company's new system came with programmable cards, and allowed software developers to create applications for them.

A flurry of acquisition activity unfolded in 1996. Aladdin Knowledge Systems kicked off the year by securing a 51 percent stake in distributor Aladdin Japan Co. Ltd. In March, the company revealed plans to acquire the Munich, Germany-based software protection systems provider FAST Software Security AG, along with the software security operations of FAST Software's independent North American licensee, Glenco Engineering Inc.

Other deals that year included the acquisition of full ownership in Aladdin Knowledge Systems (Deutschland) GmbH and Hafalad B.V. (Netherlands). The company rounded out the year with record sales of $28.7 million, up from $24.8 million in 1995. By this time Aladdin Knowledge Systems served more than 20,000 customers in approximately 100 countries.

New product developments continued at a rapid pace as the company headed into the late 1990s. In October 1997 Aladdin Knowledge Systems unveiled ASE-II, the second iteration of its smartcard development product. That same month the company reached an important milestone in the areas of quality and customer satisfaction when it received ISO 9002 accreditation.

By 1998 Aladdin Knowledge Systems' reach had extended to Russia, where the company operated under the name Aladdin Software Security. In the wake of faltering Russian economic conditions, and a corresponding rise in software piracy, Aladdin found a strong market for its products.

Aladdin Knowledge Systems concluded 1998 with more acquisition activity. In December, the company acquired the assets of Eliashim Ltd. Co., along with its subsidiaries eSafe Europe and Seattle, Washington-based eSafe Technologies Inc. These companies collectively served as the basis of a new Internet Security unit. By this time, Aladdin Knowledge Systems was generating net profits of approximately $10 million on annual revenues of $35 million.

International expansion continued in early 1999 when the company formed a new wholly owned

KEY DATES

1985: Aladdin Knowledge Systems is established in Israel by Yanki Margalit.

1993: The company lists on the NASDAQ under the symbol ALDN.

1998: The assets of Eliashim Ltd. Co. and subsidiaries eSafe Europe and eSafe Technologies Inc., are acquired, leading to the formation of a new Internet Security unit.

2004: Aladdin opens its first corporate office in China, with a location in Hong Kong.

2008: Secure SafeWord line of products is acquired from Secure Computing Corp. for $65 million; Attack Intelligence Research Center is established at the company's Israel headquarters.

subsidiary in the Netherlands named Aladdin Knowledge Systems BV. Around the same time, the company parted with $700,000 to acquire the assets of Micro Macro Technologies Ltd. Co. At this time, Aladdin Knowledge Systems employed a workforce of 300 people, and roughly half of the company's sales came from Germany.

Aladdin Knowledge Systems concluded the 1990s by receiving industry recognition. The company received *PC* magazine's Editor's Choice Award for its eSafe Protect Desktop antivirus software. In addition, Aladdin Knowledge Systems' eToken e-commerce security product was recognized with the European IST Award.

A NEW MILLENNIUM: 2000–07

At the dawn of the new millennium, Aladdin Knowledge Systems continued its transformation from a provider of software protection to an Internet security enterprise. By this time, the company's customer base had grown to include Microsoft, Lucent, and Hewlett-Packard, among others.

Aladdin Knowledge Systems continued along the acquisition path at this time. In February 2000, full ownership in Aladdin France was acquired, and the company bought eSafe-related assets held by Commerce Technology International. Midway through 2001, a $5.24 million deal was made for Preview Systems Inc.'s electronic software distribution operations.

Aladdin Knowledge Systems generated record revenue of $54.7 million in 2003. A noteworthy highlight that year was the establishment of a strategic partnership with the software vendor Aspelle.

Developments continued to unfold into 2004, when full ownership in Aladdin Knowledge Espana S.L. was acquired. In March, the company opened its first corporate office in China, with a location in Hong Kong. By the year's end, Aladdin made plans to double its business in that country, where it already had approximately 600 customers.

In March 2004, Aladdin Knowledge Systems' stock reached $19.79 per share, more than double from a year before. Highlights that year included the settlement of a patent dispute with Cupertino, California-based Symantec Corp., as well as the release of version 6.4 of the company's HASP SL software.

Progress continued at Aladdin Knowledge Systems during the middle of the first decade of the 2000s. In early 2006, the company was granted a U.S. patent for technology used to detect computer viruses and spyware via the process of emulation. That year, a number of product enhancements and introductions were made. In addition to rolling out the latest iteration of its eToken solution, Aladdin Knowledge Systems rounded out the year by adding HASP support for the Microsoft Windows Vista operating system.

In early 2007, Aladdin Knowledge Systems introduced eToken PKI Client 4.0 for Windows, as well as eToken PKI Client 3.65 for Linux and Mac. Around the same time, the company unveiled its Token Management System (TMS) 2.0 authentication management software.

A deal worth as much as $30 million was announced in April 2007, when the Indian Information Technology Consortium inked a deal with Aladdin Knowledge Systems for the use of its eToken software. By this time, the company was flush with about $90 million in cash. Plans were made to spend $10 million to repurchase 500,000 shares of Aladdin Knowledge Systems' common stock.

CONTINUED GROWTH: 2008

More important deals unfolded in 2008. Early in the year, the Thai government chose eToken as a solution for providing staff with secure access to its fiscal management information system.

In mid-2008, Aladdin Knowledge Systems partnered with Iden Trust as part of an effort between Asian, European, and U.S. banks to heighten e-commerce security and hamper identity theft.

In August, Aladdin Knowledge Systems received an unsolicited takeover proposal from the San Francisco,

California-based equity fund Vector Capital, which already was a major shareholder. Calling the offer too low, Aladdin rejected Vector's bid of $13 per share. Vector also made an alternative $125 million offer to acquire Aladdin's Digital Rights Management (DRM) business, which the company also rejected.

A $65 million cash deal with Secure Computing Corp. followed in September, at which time Aladdin Knowledge Systems acquired the Secure SafeWord line of products. By doing so, the company broadened the scope of its offerings in the area of security and authentication solutions. Following the deal, Aladdin announced that its annual revenues would total between $124 million and $132 million.

In October, Vector Capital came back with a new takeover proposal, offering $14.50 per share. CEO Yanki Margalit, who also considered that offer to be too low, flew to the United States in an effort to convince Aladdin Knowledge Systems' other institutional shareholders to reject the proposal.

It was also in October that the company established the Attack Intelligence Research Center at its Israel headquarters, as part of an effort to thwart Internet security cybercrime. In addition to offering around-the-clock threat research, the new center promised to deliver security threat forecasts on a monthly basis, as well as regular security updates, emergency support, and technical blogs.

The new center was headed by forensic web specialist Ian Amit, the company's director of security research. What made it unique was its predictive focus. In a company news release, Amit explained: "Our mission is to go beyond threat detection and malicious code to identify where the threat came from, who is benefiting from it, and how threats ultimately affect real organizations today and in the future. It is only through the understanding of how these threats are developed and delivered that we can protect our businesses today, and become educated and better prepared for tomorrow."

Aladdin Knowledge Systems ended 2008 on a high note. In mid-December, the company was named as a finalist in *SC* magazine's 2009 SC Awards Program, in recognition of outstanding achievement in information technology security.

Specifically, the company's eSafe product was named as a finalist in the Best Web Filtering Solution category of the Reader Trust Award competition, and its eToken product was named in the Best Multi-and Second-Factor solution category. Making the recognition significant was the fact that eSafe and eToken were chosen from a pool of approximately 600 entries.

As the 21st century's second decade loomed in the distance, Aladdin Knowledge Systems seemed well-positioned for future success. From its humble roots as a one-product company, the organization had transformed itself into a leading information security provider with multiple solutions and offices in approximately 15 countries worldwide.

Paul R. Greenland

PRINCIPAL SUBSIDIARIES

Aladdin Europe BV (Netherlands); Aladdin Europe GmbH (Germany); Aladdin Europe Ltd. (UK); Aladdin Europe S.A.R.L. (France); Aladdin Europe S-L (Spain); Aladdin Japan & Co. Inc.; Aladdin Knowledge Systems Inc. (USA); Aladdin Knowledge Systems India Pvt; Aladdin Knowledge Systems Italy SRL; Hafalad BV (Netherlands).

PRINCIPAL COMPETITORS

Macrovision Solutions Corp.; RSA Security Inc.; SafeNet Inc.

FURTHER READING

"Aladdin Launches Attack Intelligence Research Center," Petach Tikva, Israel: Aladdin Knowledge Systems Ltd., October 15, 2008.

"Aladdin to Double Business in China's Market," *China Daily,* March 25, 2004.

Blackburn, Nicky, "Back to the Future," *Jerusalem Post,* March 7, 1999.

Kushner, Leonard, "Fighting Piracy," *Jerusalem Post,* May 17, 1995.

Mallon, Jack, "Yanki Margalit of Aladdin Stakes Company's Claim in Internet Security," *Access Control & Security Systems Integration,* November 2000.

Petreanu, Dan, "Making Language a Valuable Resource," *Jerusalem Post,* May 18, 1989.

Alexandria Real Estate Equities, Inc.

385 East Colorado Boulevard, Suite 299
Pasadena, California 91101-6104
U.S.A.
Telephone: (626) 396-4828
Fax: (626) 578-0896
Web site: http://www.labspace.com

Public Company
Incorporated: 1994 as Health Science Properties Holding Corporation
Employees: 150
Sales: $405.4 million (2007)
Stock Exchanges: New York
Ticker Symbol: ARE
NAICS: 525930 Real Estate Investment Trusts

■ ■ ■

Alexandria Real Estate Equities, Inc., is a real estate investment trust (REIT) listed on the New York Stock Exchange that specializes in buildings used by life science companies, universities, and research organizations for office and laboratory space. The Pasadena, California-based company owns and manages more than 160 properties in ten states as well as a handful of properties in Canada, accounting for about 12.1 million square feet of rentable space. Alexandria focuses on certain life science markets, including Los Angeles, San Diego, and San Francisco, California; eastern Massachusetts; New York City; Philadelphia, Pennsylvania/New Jersey; suburban Washington, D.C.; and Seattle, Washington. Eastern Massachusetts, with 38 properties, is the company's largest market, followed by San Diego with 33 properties, and suburban Washington, D.C., with 31. Leasing seven properties, the U.S. government is the largest tenant, followed by GlaxoSmithKline plc with five leases. Other major tenants include Novartis AG; ZymoGenetics, Inc.; Massachusetts Institute of Technology; Theravance, Inc.; Scripps Research Institute; and Amylin Pharmaceuticals.

FOUNDER, A BIOTECH PIONEER

Alexandria Real Estate Equities was founded by Jerry M. Sudarsky, who had already enjoyed a rewarding career in the life sciences field before putting his knowledge of laboratory space to use as a landlord. Sudarsky was born in Russia in 1918, although his family came from Lithuania, where it was involved in the brush business. At the dawn of the 20th century, one of Sudarsky's uncles moved to the United States to start a brush factory in Chicago. Sudarsky's father was asked in 1916 to travel to Russia to purchase hog bristles for the factory, but once there, he and his wife were unable to leave because of World War I. As a result, Jerry Sudarsky, originally Jerahmiel Sudarsky, was born in a Russian hospital.

After the war, the Sudarsky family lived in Berlin, Germany, for several years before coming to the United States and settling in Brooklyn, New York, where some other family members lived. It was also here that his fifth-grade teacher decided that Jerahmiel was too difficult to pronounce and bestowed upon Sudarsky the more American name of Jerry. He became a U.S. citizen and was so acclimated to his new home that when he

COMPANY PERSPECTIVES

■

World Class Labspace for World Class Life Science.

was 16 years old, during the Great Depression when the rest of the family decided to return to Europe because of financial considerations, Sudarsky elected to remain in Brooklyn to finish high school and live with a classmate whose father was doing well in the toy business.

Jerry Sudarsky embraced his new culture in other ways as well. He became an excellent baseball player, a pitcher who was good enough to receive an athletic scholarship in 1936 from the University of Iowa, where he enrolled in the chemical engineering program. His catcher at Iowa for a time would be Nile Kinnick, who would become better known as a football player, winning the Heisman Trophy in 1939. Although hardly a star athlete himself, Sudarsky was good enough to be invited to a Boston Red Sox tryout camp, but he quickly realized that he would be better off focusing on his education. By the end of his junior year, however, he could no longer afford to remain at Iowa, despite the scholarship, and he returned to New York, taking a laboratory job at the Atlantic Yeast Company, testing yeast during the day while completing his chemical engineering degree at night at Brooklyn Polytechnic University.

SUDARSKY STARTS OWN POSTWAR BUSINESS

After graduation, Sudarsky quickly worked his way up through the ranks at Atlantic Yeast, becoming plant superintendent by the time he left in 1943 for a stint in the U.S. Navy during World War II. Although trained as a radar specialist, Sudarsky became a ping-pong champion and spent most of his time in the service touring military bases giving ping-pong exhibitions. Upon his discharge in California, he decided to stay in the state and start his own business producing autolyzed yeast, which he had read was being touted as a cure for ulcers. He found suitable drying equipment for sale in a creamery in Wasco, California, leased space in the plant, and established Pacific Yeast Products to produce autolyzed yeast. Soon a medical journal was reporting that the substance proved ineffective on ulcers, and Sudarsky was forced to find a new use for his equipment. He began buying used brewer's yeast, processed it, and sold it as a dried protein additive for animal feed, useful in helping animals to grow.

Through his new association with the feed industry, Sudarsky learned that pharmaceutical companies were also drying out the mold and bacteria left over from the production of antibiotics and selling that to feed companies as well. This additive was even more effective in stimulating animal growth, prompting Sudarsky to switch gears and begin producing the residue. In his laboratory Sudarsky was able to locate a microorganism that produced greater quantities of animal growth factor, providing Pacific Yeast with a competitive edge. Later he learned that what was thought to be animal growth factor was in reality vitamin B12, prompting a search for a microorganism that produced large quantities of B12. His team of researchers was successful in the effort and the company changed its name to Bioferm Corporation; around 1955 the company began selling a B12 concentrate.

SUDARSKY BECOMES INTERESTED IN REAL ESTATE: 1994

Sudarsky steadily grew Bioferm, adding a bacteria-based pesticide and monosodium glutamate as products. In 1960 he sold the company to International Minerals & Chemical Corporation, staying on for five years to run the business before retiring for the first time. Sudarsky became a volunteer for the United Nations Industrial Development Organization to aid undeveloped countries and was soon recruited by Israel to organize that country's chemical industry. He served as chairman of Israel Chemicals, Ltd., from 1967 to 1972, growing it into the country's largest company. After five years of splitting time between Israel and California, Sudarsky returned to the United States to become vice-chairman of Daylin Corporation in Los Angeles. After retiring once again, Sudarsky in 1982 became vice-chairman of Jacobs Engineering Group Inc., a Pasadena engineering and construction company, a post he held until 1994, when in his mid-70s he turned his attention to real estate.

Sudarsky decided to combine his knowledge of the space requirements of research companies with what he had learned with an engineering and construction firm, then created a real estate investment trust (REIT) to acquire properties with laboratory space and lease them to biotechnology companies. REITs had suddenly become popular vehicles for holding and growing real estate portfolios, despite being in existence since 1960 when Congress created them as a way for small investors to become involved in real estate, similar to the way a mutual fund operated. REITs could be taken public and their unit shares traded like stocks, but unlike stocks, REITs were required to pay out at least 95 percent of

KEY DATES

1993: Health Science Properties Holding Corporation is founded by Jerry Sudarsky.
1994: Company is incorporated in Maryland.
1997: Name is changed to Alexandria Real Estate Equities, Inc.; company goes public.
2000: Revenues top $100 million.
2007: Sudarsky retires.
2008: Credit crunch forces halt to development projects.

their annual taxable income to shareholders. As a result, REITs were limited in their ability to raise funds internally. Moreover, they were allowed to own only real estate, and third parties had to be employed to actually manage the properties. The tax code also made direct real estate investments more attractive because of their tax shelter ramifications, thereby absorbing funds that might have been invested in REITs. It was not until the Tax Reform Act of 1986 eliminated these shelters that the nature of real estate investments began to shift. The act also permitted REITs to operate and manage the properties they owned.

When capital dried up in the early 1990s, REITs finally became an attractive way for many private real estate companies to raise funds. New REITs quickly staked out category positions, concentrating on such areas as office buildings, apartment buildings, and shopping centers. Sudarsky was unique in focusing on biotech facilities, an area other REITs shied away from because of the high cost of tenant improvements and the difficulty encountered in retrofitting properties to meet the needs of biotech tenants.

Sudarsky and his partners, which included Jacobs Engineering, formed Health Science Properties Holding Corporation in Maryland in September 1993. It was capitalized at the start of 1994 and incorporated in Maryland in October 1994, with Sudarsky serving as both chairman and chief executive officer. Focusing initially on San Diego, the San Francisco area, New England, and the mid-Atlantic region, Health Science Properties completed its first purchases in October 1994, paying $23 million for a pair of scientific research and manufacturing facilities in San Diego's Torrey Pines Science Park. In December of that year Health Science Properties also acquired two more properties in the Torrey Pines area, a pair of adjacent two-story facilities that were fully leased.

Health Science Properties added no further properties in 1995. During the first full year managing its four San Diego properties, the company posted revenues of $9.92 million, resulting in net income of $761,000. In 1996 the company completed several acquisitions. In May it paid $31.75 million for a Seattle, Washington, property. Next, in July 1996 a Rockville, Maryland, building was acquired at a cost of nearly $12 million. Two Gaithersburg, Maryland, acquisitions followed in September and October for $14.34 million and $17.74 million, respectively. Finally, in December 1996, Health Science Properties paid $19.4 million for three buildings in Alameda, California. These additions to the portfolio helped to increase revenues to $17.7 million and net earnings to $2.2 million in 1996.

COMPANY TAKEN PUBLIC: 1997

To fuel further growth and pay off accumulated debt, Health Science Properties prepared for an initial public offering (IPO) of shares in 1997. Although he remained chairman, Sudarsky stepped down as CEO, turning over the helm to Joel S. Marcus, an accountant and attorney who had specialized in corporate finance and acquisition as a lawyer and the financing and taxation of real estate as a certified public accountant. He had also served as general counsel of one biotech company and on the board of another. Health Science Properties took the name Alexandria Real Estate Equities, Inc.; shares were listed on the New York Stock Exchange in May 1997 and the IPO was completed on June 2. Combined with a subsequent exercise of an underwriter's over-allotment option, the company netted $138.9 million. Some of the proceeds were then used the following month to close on three more Maryland properties at the cost of $13.3 million. When the year came to a close, revenues had increased to $34.84 million.

Alexandria went on an acquisition spree during the first three months of 1998, spending about $110 million to acquire 11 properties with a combined 927,000 square feet of rentable space. Another 18 properties and approximately 900,000 square feet were to follow by the end of the year, and the company's footprint was expanded to include eastern Massachusetts, San Francisco, and the Philadelphia, Pennsylvania, area. Total rentable square footage approached 3.6 million. Revenues for the year increased to $61 million and net income improved to $19.4 million.

Another 437,000 square feet of rentable space was added in 1999 through the acquisition of seven more properties, including four in the northern portion of New Jersey. Although the focus had been on acquisitions, Alexandria was also becoming a developer. In 1999 it completed a property to add another 55,000 rentable square feet to the portfolio. Hence, rental revenues grew 41 percent to $86.3 million for the year and net income increased to more than $22 million.

A pair of offerings raised $52.1 million for Alexandria in 2000, helping the company finance the acquisition of 12 properties with an aggregate of about 450,000 rentable square feet and the completion of five developed properties adding another 380,000 rentable square feet. A year later the company raised another $16.8 million in a private placement of stock, added another 345,000 rental square feet through the acquisition of five properties, as well as 108,000 square feet from two new developed properties. The enlarged portfolio led to an increase of revenues to $106.9 million in 2000 and $127.8 million in 2001, and net income that increased from $26 million in 2000 to $30.3 million a year later.

A further 427,000 square feet of rentable space was added in 2002 through the acquisition of four properties and the opening of two developed properties. Alexandria also conducted a secondary public offering of shares, netting a further $55.1 million. Net income improved to $31.45 million on total revenues of $144.67 million. The following year, Alexandria adjusted its portfolio, selling three properties containing 289,000 square feet in San Francisco, eastern Massachusetts, and Washington, D.C. The company recouped 267,000 square feet through the acquisition of four properties. Despite the loss in overall rentable space, Alexandria increased revenues to $160.6 million and net income to $59.64 million in 2003.

Alexandria accelerated its growth in 2004, almost entirely through external means. During the year, 23 properties with 1.63 million square feet of rentable space were acquired, and a single developed property contributed a further 104,000 square feet. Revenues grew to $183.3 million and net income held steady around $60.2 million.

The next three years brought rapid expansion to the REIT. In 2005, 19 properties and 1.2 million rentable square feet were acquired, followed by 25 properties totaling 2.4 million rentable square feet in 2006, and 16 properties containing another 1.3 million rentable square feet in 2007. During this period Alexandria also completed the development of three properties in 2005, four properties a year later, and another property in 2007 for a total of more than 700,000 additional rentable square feet. Moreover, 21 properties underwent redevelopment during this period. The company also tapped the equity markets again, raising $189.4 million in 2005 and $535.3 million in 2006 through four public offerings. As a result of the growing portfolio, revenues increased to $405.4 million in 2007 and net income kept pace, approaching $79 million.

SUDARSKY RETIRES: 2007

Along the way, Alexandria acquired a good deal of land in promising markets and was also successful in securing a variety of loans and credit facilities to develop these properties. A downturn in the economy and a credit crunch that ensued in the fall of 2008 put a halt to the company's rapid expansion. Some projects had to be put on hold, including a 1.1 million-square-foot laboratory complex in New York City, located on Manhattan's East Side, but there was every reason to expect that when funds became available Alexandria would resume its development efforts. The Manhattan project alone, according to *Forbes,* "could be something of a game-changer for Manhattan by setting off a miniboom in science parks, while contributing significantly to Alexandria's profits." The company would be doing so without the direct benefit of its founder, Jerry Sudarsky, who in 2007 retired as chairman and was succeeded by Marcus, who also continued to serve as CEO. Sudarsky, who turned 90 in 2008, told interviewer Gilbert Gia that it was the seventh time he had retired.

Ed Dinger

PRINCIPAL SUBSIDIARIES

ARE—QRS Corp.; Alexandria Real Estate Equities, L.P.; AREA—MA Region No. 31, LLC; ARE—Tech Square, LLC.

PRINCIPAL COMPETITORS

BioMed Realty Trust, Inc.; HRPT Properties Trust; Liberty Property Trust.

FURTHER READING

Davey, Tom, "REIT Pursues Biotech Properties Worth $72M," *San Francisco Business Times,* July 1, 1994, p. 5.

Fikes, Bradley J., "BioREITs Get Hopeful Welcome," *San Diego Business Journal,* February 28, 1994, p. 1.

———, "Biotech REIT Buys Two La Jolla Buildings," *San Diego Business Journal,* July 4, 1994, p. 1.

Gia, Gilbert, "Interview with Jerry and Milly Sudarsky," http://www3.igalaxy.net/~ggia/Articles/2008-InterviewwithJerryan.html, May 21, 2008.

Green, Frank, "Biotech REIT Enters SD Market; Pays $23 Million for Torrey Pines Sites," *San Diego Union-Times,* June 24, 1994, p. C1.

Lueck, Thomas J., and Jim Rutenberg, "Science Park Is Planned at Bellevue," *New York Times,* August 11, 2005, p. B1.

Shook, David, "Four Labs Sold to California REIT," *Record* (Bergen County, N.J.), January 15, 1999, p. B1.

Slatin, Peter, "Office Space Is Cheap," *Forbes,* November 17, 2008, p. 140.

Smith, Ray A., "Public Real Estate Firms Weather a Storm," *Wall Street Journal,* October 4, 2000, p. B10.

Allen Brothers, Inc.

3737 South Halsted Street
Chicago, Illinois 60609
U.S.A.
Telephone: (773) 890-5100
Toll Free: (800) 548-7777
Fax: (773) 890-9146
Web site: http://www.allenbrothers.com

Private Company
Incorporated: 1893
Employees: 120
Sales: $110 million (2007 est.)
NAICS: 424470 Meat and Meat Product Merchant Wholesalers; 424420 Packaged Frozen Food Merchant Wholesalers; 424440 Poultry and Poultry Product Merchant Wholesalers; 454111 Electronic Shopping

■ ■ ■

Allen Brothers, Inc., is a wholesaler and retailer of meat, seafood, and other food products. The company supplies a broad range of hand-cut steaks and other cuts of meat to some of the leading restaurants in the nation, including Del Frisco's Restaurant Group, LLC, and Morton's Restaurant Group, Inc., as well as hotels, resorts, and country clubs. Allen Brothers' retail operation sells products directly to consumers through a 60-page catalog and a web site. Customers can choose from a vast array of items such as wet-aged beef, Kobe Wagyu beef, USDA Prime steaks, veal, lamb, pork, duck, seafood, dessert, and precooked, ready-to-heat entrees.

The company utilizes two processing facilities and two holding facilities in the Chicago area to support its wholesale and retail operations. Allen Brothers serves all 50 states and Puerto Rico.

THE HATOFF ERA

Aside from founding the company, giving it their surname for a corporate title, and establishing it in Chicago's Union Stockyards, the Allen brothers did little else to affect the development of their company. The brothers sold the business soon after they formed it in 1893. The level of success enjoyed by the business more than a century later was achieved through the contributions of the Allen brothers' successors, notably the Hatoff family. The Hatoffs were responsible for giving the meat-processing venture the signature characteristics that defined Allen Brothers in the 21st century.

Allen Brothers was not the first meat-processing business that fell under the influence of the Hatoffs. Todd Hatoff, who led Allen Brothers in the 21st century, came from a family of meat processors, although he somewhat reluctantly followed in his ancestors' footsteps. His great-grandfather Jack Hatoff owned a meat-processing business named Queen's; his grandfather Lloyd ran United American Meat Processors. Todd Hatoff's father, Robert "Bobby" Hatoff, served as the link between the family and Allen Brothers, bringing his particular vision to the company operating in Union Stockyards.

Bobby Hatoff joined Allen Brothers as an employee, spending years working at the company's facility before circumstances and his skill eventually put him in charge

COMPANY PERSPECTIVES

The old-time neighborhood butcher valued his customers and was likely to be a trusted friend. He specialized in personal and knowledgeable customer-friendly service. Today, Allen Brothers offers that same devotion to old-fashioned service and customer satisfaction that's now so hard to find.

of the entire operation. He was hired by a man named Mel Solomon, whose uncle had purchased the business from the Allen brothers not long after they had founded the company.

ALLEN BROTHERS CATERS TO HIGH-END RESTAURANTS

Bobby Hatoff took control of Allen Brothers in the early 1980s. He exerted his influence on the company immediately, becoming an advocate of portion control and, most significantly, steering the company toward upscale customers in the foodservice market. "My father took the high road—only the best, in product and service," Todd Hatoff said in a March 2007 interview with the *National Provisioner*. Bobby Hatoff focused on supplying the best grades of meat to the best restaurants. He cultivated relationships with prestigious restaurateurs, gradually building a customer base that spread out geographically and included many of the most respected names in the fine dining market. He made Allen Brothers the source of meat for Morton's of Chicago, Dallas's Al Biernat's, Dominic's Steak House in Philadelphia, and Wichita, Kansas-based Del Frisco's, among others.

Bobby Hatoff succeeded in carving a niche for Allen Brothers as one of the premier suppliers of the best grades of meat to upscale restaurants. The U.S. Department of Agriculture (USDA), responsible for determining the quality of beef, rated only 2 percent of all the beef it examined as "prime" beef, the grade of beef that became Allen Brothers' hallmark. The company supplied its trademarked Great Steakhouse Steaks to the nation's leading restaurants and steakhouses, becoming the largely anonymous wholesaler who underpinned part of the success of its decidedly more high-profile clientele. Allen Brothers remained relatively unknown until Bobby Hatoff's son joined the business and ushered in an era of robust growth, developing a new facet of the company's operations that thrust it into the public eye.

RETAIL BUSINESS TAKES SHAPE IN 1991

For years, Allen Brothers had operated a small retail component of its wholesale business, but it had never amounted to much. Bobby Hatoff's talents and passion were wholly focused on catering to the foodservice industry, and he never gave his retail business anything more than a cursory look. That level of attention changed dramatically when Todd Hatoff joined the company in the early 1990s, but he never intended to make his father's business his life's work. "I wanted to be more of an academic," he recalled in the March 2007 issue of the *National Provisioner*. "I stuck around and promised to for a year or two to get the retail division going, and here I am still."

Without much conviction at first, Todd Hatoff fully committed himself to developing a substantial retail arm to Allen Brothers' operation within months of joining the company. He developed what he dubbed Allen Brothers' "Unique Selling Proposition," a marketing approach that attempted to leverage the consumer recognition of its clients for the company's own promotion. In essence, restaurants had won over customers with their steaks and Hatoff wanted the restaurants to assist in informing those customers that Allen Brothers had provided the steaks. "We went to our prime steakhouses and asked if they wanted to be part of this marketing campaign, and many did, more than I expected," Hatoff explained in the March 2007 issue of the *National Provisioner*. "We put them into our marketing campaign—logos, names, quotes—to add credibility into the marketplace."

FEDEX LENDS A HAND

With Allen Brothers' clients offering their support, Hatoff launched a direct-mailing campaign in 1991. Consumers were presented with a 16-page catalog that offered the same steaks and chops they had enjoyed at some of the nation's leading restaurants. To accomplish the vital task of shipping Allen Brothers' products, Hatoff consulted with the Memphis, Tennessee-based courier FedEx Corporation and developed a packaging and shipping plan to ensure the perishable strip steaks, porterhouse steaks, and filet mignons retained their quality during transport. Through its catalog, the company primarily offered frozen products and, to a lesser extent, never-frozen products. For frozen products, Hatoff and his FedEx representative devised a packaging system. Products were individually shrink-wrapped, frozen, and packed in a box placed within a reusable polystyrene cooler with a tight-fitting lid. Next, the cooler was placed in a heavy-duty corrugated box and shipped with enough dry ice to ensure the product's

KEY DATES

1893: Allen Brothers is established as a meat-processing business in Chicago's Union Stockyards.
1980s: Early in the decade, the Hatoff family takes control of Allen Brothers.
1991: The company's retail business begins to grow after a 16-page catalog is released.
2003: Todd Hatoff, responsible for developing the company's retail business, is named president.
2007: Annual sales eclipse $100 million.

integrity. For the never-frozen line, products were vacuum-sealed and packed with the same layered protection as the frozen line, using a special gel-pack refrigerant instead of dry ice.

Allen Brothers' relationship with FedEx was integral to the success of its retail operation. "We knew their delivery commitment and knew that was going to work for our product," Hatoff said in the June 2005 issue of *Frozen Food Age.* "Because of the life of the dry ice, we needed a guaranteed two-day delivery commitment. We wanted to go to air shipments—we had to get away from ground services—in order to meet that delivery commitment window in those two days."

Allen Brothers' retail operation took several years before becoming a profitable business. The path toward profitability was expedited by the addition of a web site that allowed customers to place their orders online. With both a catalog and an Internet presence, the retail operation compensated for its slow start by blossoming into a bustling business, recording its greatest activity between mid-November and the beginning of January. Orders poured in during the holiday season, underscoring the importance of the company's relationship with its courier. Each October, the company's FedEx representative met with Hatoff to plan for the peak season. Expected volume for the coming season was determined, a review of the previous year's shipping history was conducted, and a plan of attack was devised.

As the company's retail sales mushroomed, the volume of traffic became large enough for FedEx to "spot" trailers at Allen Brothers' warehouse, a practice that involved leaving empty trailers at a customer's facility for loading. "One day we picked up four or five trailers," a FedEx representative recalled in the June 2005 issue of *Frozen Food Age.* "While the trailer was spotted there, we had another one in another yard just waiting. So, as soon as one was full, we'd pull that out. We'd drop another empty trailer. We'd fill that up. We'd pull that out, then we would drop another one. It was just immediate for them. As soon as they boxed the product and affixed a FedEx label, we scanned it and moved it to the airport so it didn't sit in their building."

ALLEN BROTHERS' VAST SELECTION

In the company's two processing facilities all the meat was hand-cut by butchers. Every Allen Brothers' butcher was highly skilled, required to attend a formal, three-and-a-half-year training program at the company's state-of-the-art training facility in Chicago. Once the butchers had mastered the art of butchering meat, they were put to work fulfilling orders for wholesale and retail customers that arrived from all 50 states and Puerto Rico. A decade after Hatoff organized the company's retail business, it was thriving, offering a 38-page catalog that kept the company's butchers inundated with orders. The 2002 holiday catalog featured a seemingly endless assortment of products: steak, veal, lamb, pork, lobster-stuffed filet mignon, chicken, duck, sausages, turkey, ham, and braised shanks. Customers could order Asian-style stuffed dumplings, lobster tails from New Zealand, South Africa, Australia, Maine, and Canada, Scottish smoked salmon, precooked, ready-to-eat entrees, and desserts such as tiramisu and mango mousse.

TODD HATOFF BECOMES PRESIDENT IN 2003

Hatoff took control of the family business in 2003, when he was named president of the 110-year-old Allen Brothers. The company's retail business enjoyed a surge in orders in 2005, when, for the first time in four years, Japanese Kobe beef was allowed back in the United States (the meat was banned after the discovery of mad cow disease in Japan in 2001). "We cannot meet demand," Hatoff said in the December 30, 2005 edition of the *Star Ledger,* referring to Kobe beef. "I don't see it going away ever," he added. "It's not a fad."

Allen Brothers' retail business hardly needed an extra boost in sales from a single product. By 2007, the company's catalog had stretched to 60 pages. Together, the catalog and online orders accounted for roughly $50 million in yearly sales, representing half of the company's annual sales. More than 100,000 customers from all 50 states and Puerto Rico turned to Allen Brothers each year for the company's dizzying array of products, which generally were not available from supermarket butchers. "We're experiencing rapid growth right now," Hatoff said in the March 2007 issue of the

National Provisioner. To accommodate the company's growing business, he revealed Allen Brothers was in the planning stages of a major expansion project as it looked to the future. He discussed several options that were being explored, including adding a new fulfillment center to one of the company's four existing buildings or, more ambitiously, building an entirely new operation. "We're starting now," he informed the *National Provisioner* in March 2007, "and we're weighing everything and talking with our consultants, figuring out what's going to be the best for us to do."

Jeffrey L. Covell

PRINCIPAL COMPETITORS

Omaha Steaks International, Inc.; Colorado Boxed Beef Co.; Atlantic Premium Brands, Ltd.

FURTHER READING

Gazdziak, Sam, "Hand-Picked and High-End," *National Provisioner,* March 2007, p. 20.

Morganti, Carol S., "Delivering on a Promise," *Frozen Food Age,* June 2005, p. 33.

Quaid, Libby, "Kobe-Style Beef Replaces the Real Thing," *Record,* December 30, 2005, p. A15.

"U.S. Comeback for Kobe Beef? Fat Chance!" *Star-Ledger,* December 30, 2005, p. 4.

Anchor BanCorp Wisconsin, Inc.

——————■——————

25 West Main Street
Madison, Wisconsin 53703
U.S.A.
Telephone: (608) 252-8700
Toll Free: (800) 252-6246
Fax: (608) 252-8783
Web site: http://www.anchorbank.com

Public Company
Incorporated: 1992 as AnchorBank, SSB
Employees: 990
Total Assets: $5.15 billion (2008)
Stock Exchanges: NASDAQ (OTC)
Ticker Symbol: ABCW
NAICS: 551111 Offices of Bank Holding Companies;
522120 Savings Institutions

■ ■ ■

Anchor BanCorp Wisconsin, Inc., is the holding company for Wisconsin's largest thrift. AnchorBank, the company's wholly owned subsidiary, is a leading lender in residential housing and commercial real estate. The bank serves over 170,000 households and businesses through more than 74 locations, spanning 19 counties, and by way of Internet and telephone banking capabilities. The Anchor Investment Services division provides a full range of investment services.

BUILDING ASSETS: 1918–90

The Anchor Savings, Building and Loan Association held an organizational meeting in December 1918. The following year, the first office "opened at 1 E. Main St., Madison, with one desk, one chair and one part-time employee," AnchorBank's web site history recounted. By 1923, the Wisconsin association had accumulated over $500,000 in assets. The figure approached $1.5 million five years later.

A corporate name change came in 1940. Operating as Anchor Savings and Loan Association, the S&L held more than $10 million in assets by the end of the decade. Over the 1950s into the early 1960s, Anchor's assets grew tenfold.

In 1964, Anchor Savings and Loan occupied its new ten-story office building, located at 25 West Main Street. Beginning in 1967 and through the 1970s, Anchor added branch offices. The growing operation passed the $500 million mark in assets in 1979.

Anchor increased the number of its locations through a string of mergers, an acquisition, and organic growth during the early 1980s. A merger with Provident Savings, in 1984, propelled Anchor past $1 billion in assets. A new subsidiary, Anchor Insurance Services, also came into existence that year. The growth drive continued into the next decade.

SWITCH TO PUBLIC OWNERSHIP: 1992–98

Anchor BanCorp Wisconsin, Inc., incorporated into a holding company in 1992. The operating unit was renamed AnchorBank, SSB. According to the company's web site history, five million shares of common stock were issued at $10 per share to about 2,800 depositors.

COMPANY PERSPECTIVES

We are constantly evolving our products and services to meet the changing needs of our customers.

President and CEO Douglas Timmerman led the transition. Timmerman, a former economics and finance professor, had served on the board prior to joining the company in 1978. Anchor followed the trend toward demutualization occurring in the industry. The switchover created ownership opportunities for employees and provided a vehicle to raise capital for future growth, according to the *Wisconsin State Journal.*

The decision to go public, made in 1990, came at the heels of the late 1980s savings and loan industry collapse. The federal government had to step in with a $135 billion bailout. Among the hardest hit states were Arizona, Texas, and California. Wisconsin, however, weathered the collapse, leaving Anchor's reputation and financial strength intact.

Moreover, spreads between earnings on assets and payments to depositors had improved, fueling interest in financial stocks, the *Wisconsin State Journal* explained. In 1992, about one-third of the bank's business was in refinancing.

During the mid-1990s, AnchorBank expanded the number of its locations and added services, such as telephone and Internet banking.

By 1998, Anchor was trading at about ten times its adjusted initial offering, according to the *Madison Capital Times.* Not only was the nation in the midst of a prolonged bear market, low interest rates created a favorable climate for home mortgages, Anchor's core business. The thrift posted record earnings of $20.5 million in fiscal 1998.

RIDING THE WAVES: 1999–2005

Anchor initiated a $172 million stock deal for FCB Financial Corp. of Oshkosh, in early 1999. FCB held $535 million in assets and ranked second in terms of market share in the fast-growing Fox Valley region.

Anchor's stock declined upon word of the purchase, squelching a surge driven by takeover speculation. The $2.1 billion thrift holding company was itself viewed as a potential expansion vehicle for other financial institutions. Suspension of its stock program, as required by the Securities and Exchange Commission during a

pooling-of-interests acquisition, also contributed to the 19 percent drop-off in Anchor stock, according to a mid-January *American Banker* article.

In February 2000, Milwaukee-based Mutual Savings Bank, with $1.8 billion in assets, announced plans to acquire First Northern Capital Corp. of Green Bay. A blending of the two would propel Mutual Savings past Anchor into the position of Wisconsin's largest thrift.

At about mid-year, Anchor opened two new lending-only offices, one in Green Bay and the other near the Minnesota border, in Hudson, Wisconsin. In July, the bank became a federal stock savings association resulting in a name change to AnchorBank, fsb.

Anchor purchased Ledger Capital Corp. in June 2001. Through Ledger Bank, the $507 million-asset holding company owned banking offices in Glendale, Greenfield, New Berlin, and West Allis, according to the *Milwaukee Journal Sentinel.* By entering the Milwaukee metropolitan area, Anchor could claim a presence in all five of the largest population areas of the state.

The country saw record levels of mortgage lending in 2001 and into 2002, a bright spot in an economy staggering in the wake of the September 11, 2001, terrorist attacks on the United States. For fiscal 2003, ending March 31, Anchor posted record earnings of $49.6 million, up from $36.4 million the prior year. Loan sales increased 134 percent, year over year.

Interest rates on home loans were at 45-year lows in the summer of 2003, continuing to drive up revenue for lenders. An uptick in interest at the end of July, though, produced a major drop-off in refinancing activity. New home loans showed less sensitivity to the rate changes, falling marginally.

"Michael Helser, chief financial officer for Anchor BanCorp, said higher interest rates would bring his company a chance to hold onto more home loans instead of selling them to avoid a loss in their value. Out of worry that rising interest rates would cause lower-yielding loans to depreciate in value, Anchor has been selling more of its mortgages," Jason Stein reported for the *Wisconsin State Journal,* in August 2003. Anchor held $900 million in home loans.

In 2004, Anchor settled with the Wisconsin Department of Revenue over allegations of tax improprieties. A change in the state's executive office triggered auditing of roughly 200 Wisconsin banks' attribution of income to tax-exempt Nevada investment subsidiaries. Marshall & Ilsley Corp., a $37.1 billion-asset Milwaukee-based bank, and Anchor were among 26 banks agreeing to pay back taxes, accrued interest, and penalties, according to *American Banker.* The Wisconsin Bankers Association maintained banks had

KEY DATES

1918: Anchor Savings, Building and Loan Association holds organizational meeting.
1928: Assets reach $1.4 million.
1940: Name is changed to Anchor Savings and Loan Association.
1962: Anchor claims more than $104 million in assets.
1979: Decade of branch expansion takes assets above the half-billion-dollar mark.
1984: Anchor Insurance Services is created as new subsidiary.
1992: Company converts to stock ownership and changes name to AnchorBank, SSB.
1999: Company enters fast growing Fox Valley through merger.
2001: Merger brings AnchorBank into greater Milwaukee metropolitan area.
2005: AnchorBank assets top $4 billion.
2008: Acquisition helps AnchorBank exceed 70 locations.
2009: AnchorBank marks 90th year.

been given the go-ahead to use the tax-shelter device and admitted no wrongdoing.

Late in the year, Anchor agreed to pay the Office of Thrift Supervision a $100,000 fine for lax compliance of government rules intended to detect and prevent money laundering. Anchor violated regulations related to reporting large cash transactions and implementing customer-identification programs. Systems already in place under the Bank Secrecy Act had been enhanced by the 2001 Patriot Act, as had rule enforcement.

Rounding out a trio of bad news, an accounting error forced Anchor Bank to restate earnings for its three previous fiscal years, the company reported in July 2005.

On the upside, Anchor topped the $4 billion mark in assets, during fiscal 2005. Anchor followed Marshall & Ilsley and Associated BanCorp of Green Bay, as the largest Wisconsin-headquartered banks.

Since 1979, Anchor had acquired more than a dozen smaller banks, expanding geographically in the state. As for the future, Chairman Douglas J. Timmerman said the bank planned to continue expanding in the Milwaukee and Green Bay areas, *Knight-Ridder/ Tribune Business News* reported in May 2005.

NAVIGATING A CHANGING COURSE: 2006–09

In September, AnchorBank opened its 60th location, the seventh in the Milwaukee area. A third Green Bay location opened in February 2006. Also during 2006, the wholly owned investment products and services subsidiary, Anchor Investment Services, Inc., was integrated into the bank as a department.

In July 2007, Anchor announced plans to acquire S&C Banco Inc. of New Richmond, Wisconsin. The move elevated the bank to second place in deposit share in St. Croix County. Bordering Minnesota's Twin Cities metropolitan area, St. Croix had been Wisconsin's fastest-growing county since 2000 with the population up by 29 percent. S&C Bank held nearly 15 percent of the county's deposits, *American Banker* reported. The deal was Anchor's first for a commercial bank.

Nationally, the number of bank acquisitions had been holding steady over the past few years, according to the *Wisconsin State Journal.* Banks in attractive markets, though, had been demanding higher prices.

The S&C deal, completed in January 2008, was Anchor's first since 2001. The $400 million-asset, family-owned bank had operated 17 branches, although Anchor sold the three in east central Minnesota and combined the Hudson bank with its lending-only site.

The nation's economic downturn put pressure on the bank's net income, which fell to $31.1 million in fiscal 2008, down from $39.0 million the prior fiscal year. The rising number of non-performing loans reduced interest revenue and necessitated higher reserves for potential loan losses. Yet, according to Timmerman's letter to shareholders, the bank's rate of residential delinquencies and foreclosures at 0.43 percent, as of March 31, 2008, was well below state and national averages of 4.10 percent and 6.35 percent, respectively.

In October 2008, Anchor BanCorp sought permission from the Securities and Exchange Commission to raise up to $200 million via stock and securities sales. Proceeds would go toward reducing acquisition-related debt and countering bad commercial loans, Marv Balousek explained to the *Wisconsin State Journal.* Moreover, seeing problems with loans for business, investment residential property, and speculative home building, Anchor had increased the provision for loan losses.

Following suit of many other banks, Anchor had also pared down the quarterly dividend and was considering sale of stock to the U.S. Treasury under the Troubled Assets Relief Program. The nation's economic system faced continued uncertainty as the bank entered 2009 and marked its 90th year of operation.

Kathleen Peippo

PRINCIPAL SUBSIDIARIES

AnchorBank, fsb.

PRINCIPAL DIVISIONS

Anchor Investment Services.

PRINCIPAL COMPETITORS

Associated BanCorp; Marshall & Ilsley Corp.; Mound City Financial Services.

FURTHER READING

"Anchor BanCorp Wisconsin Inc. Announces Fourth Quarter and Fiscal Year End Earnings," *PR Newswire,* May 22, 2006.

Balousek, Marv, "Anchor Parent Chalks Up Loss," *Wisconsin State Journal,* November 8, 2008, p. C1.

Gores, Paul, "Anchor BanCorp in Expansive Mood," *Knight-Ridder/Tribune Business News,* May 24, 2005.

———, "Anchor Bank Files to Raise $200 Million," *Milwaukee Journal Sentinel,* October 7, 2008, p. D3.

———, "Anchor to Acquire Ledger Capital," *Milwaukee Journal Sentinel,* June 16, 2001, p. 1D.

———, "U.S. Fines AnchorBank for Lax Oversight," *Milwaukee Journal Sentinel,* December 23, 2004, p. 1.

Ivey, Mike, "Anchors Aweigh for Thrift's Stock," *Madison Capital Times,* May 5, 1998, p. 1D.

Jackson, Ben, "Anchor of Wis. Deals to Expand in Growing Market," *American Banker,* July 13, 2007, p. 5.

Kulikowski, Laurie, "FHLB Loan Errors Force Anchor to Restate Profits," *American Banker,* July 1, 2005.

Lutton, Laura Pavlenko, "Wis. Thrift Deal Thwarts Sale Speculation," *American Banker,* January 14, 1999, p. 10.

Newman, Judy, "Anchor Bancorp Expanding," *Wisconsin State Journal,* July 13, 2007, p. C8.

Riddle, Jennifer, "Going Public: Ex-Prof Leads AnchorBank's Profitable Transition," *Wisconsin State Journal,* December 3, 1992.

Stein, Jason, "Bank's Parent Acts to Stay on NASDAQ," *Wisconsin State Journal,* July 8, 2005, C10.

———, "In a Free Fall," *Wisconsin State Journal,* August 17, 2003, p. C1.

———, "Small Banks Say New Laws Are Heavy Load," *Wisconsin State Journal,* February 13, 2005, p. C1.

"Wis. Banks Beat a Retreat in Tax-Shelter Crackdown," *American Banker,* September 20, 2004.

Woker, Craig, "Deal Lifts Mutual Savings to No. 1 Wisconsin Thrift," *American Banker,* February 23, 2000, p. 4.

Andrew Peller Ltd.

697 South Service Road
Grimsby, Ontario L3M 4E8
Canada
Telephone: (905) 643-4131
Fax: (905) 643-4944
Web site: http://www.andreswines.com

Public Company
Incorporated: 1961 as Andrés Wines Ltd.
Employees: 1,236
Sales: CAD 237.1 million (2008)
Stock Exchanges: Toronto
Ticker Symbol: ADW
NAICS: 312130 Wineries; 312120 Breweries

■ ■ ■

Andrew Peller Ltd. is one of the largest winemakers in Canada. Long known for mid-grade table wines and its best-selling sparkling wine Baby Duck, the company has also established itself as a maker of premium brands. It makes Canadian bestsellers such as Schloss Laderheim, Royal Sommet, Domaine D'Or, and Hochtaler, as well as upper-end brands including Calona Vineyards, Hillebrand, Peller Estates, Red Rooster, Sandhill, Thirty Bench, and Trius. It also produces the Granville Island brand of beer, and markets three brands of wine kits, Winexpert, Wine Kitz, and Vineco, for home vintners. The company operates vineyards in Ontario, Nova Scotia, and British Columbia. It cultivates approximately 400 acres of its own land, and has another 350 acres under long-term lease. Andrew Peller also operates a chain of over 100 retail wine stores in Ontario, under the names Vineyards Estate Wines and WineCountry Vintners. Most of Andrew Peller's wines are sold in Canada. The company holds about 10 percent of the total Canadian wine market. While the company is publicly traded, members of the founder's family control the voting shares.

CANADIAN WINE

The company that became Andrew Peller Ltd. was founded in 1961, at a crucial point in the development of the Canadian wine industry. Wine had been produced in Canada since the early 1800s. European settlers brought their grape varieties to the New World, but these tender plants could not survive Canada's climate. Canadian vintners made use of the native grape varieties, which were hardy in the cold winters and hot summers. These grapes, however, could not produce the fine wines of Europe. Principally they were made into fortified wines, and sold at affordable prices. Despite some limitations in the types of wine the native soil could support, Canada's wine industry thrived in the late 19th century. Much Canadian wine was exported to England. The two centers of wine production were southern Ontario and British Columbia.

The Canadian government tightly controlled production of alcohol, and offered only a strictly limited number of licenses to wine producers. During the first 20 years of the 20th century, Canadian provinces adopted legislative measures that prohibited alcohol production and sales. This legislation was piecemeal, with Prohibition lasting only a short time in Quebec,

COMPANY PERSPECTIVES

Andrew Peller Ltd. is a leading producer and marketer of quality wines in Canada. With wineries in British Columbia, Ontario and Nova Scotia, the company markets wines produced from grapes grown in Ontario's Niagara Peninsula, British Columbia's Okanagan and Similkameen Valleys and vineyards around the world.

for example, while other provinces banned alcohol earlier and for many years. By 1927, Prohibition was effectively repealed nationwide.

Following the repeal of Prohibition, control of alcohol licenses moved from the central government to the provinces. Large producers then bought the smaller ones. The industry remained somewhat stagnant until the 1960s. At that point, changes in consumer preference and better grape growing and wine-making technology allowed new vintners such as Andrew Peller to come to the fore.

AN IMMIGRANT'S DREAM

Andrew Peller was born in Hungary in 1903. He immigrated to Canada in 1927 and became involved in several business ventures. His interest in brewing led him to Chicago, where he became certified as a brewmaster. Then he worked for Congrave's Brewery in Toronto. During World War II, Peller went into business producing equipment for the British Navy. At the war's end, he moved to Hamilton, Ontario. There, in 1945, Peller and a group of investors built a new brewery, operating as Peller Brewing Company Limited.

Peller was evidently a prominent force in Hamilton. In 1954, he founded a newspaper, the *Hamilton News*. This served as a counterpoint to the other existing daily newspaper. A front page article on Peller described him not as a brewer but as an "industrialist." Although he had tried his hand at a variety of businesses, he seemed to have a flair for alcoholic beverages. In 1961, Peller invested CAD 600,000 in a winery in British Columbia, far from Hamilton. This took the more European-sounding name Andrés Wine Ltd.

It was around this time that Canadian growers began finding ways to grow European grapes successfully. The government began granting more licenses to produce and sell wine, and the Canadian wine industry entered a new phase. Andrés Wines

expanded quickly. Only three years after its founding, it broke ground on two new wineries, one in Calgary, Alberta, and the other in Truro, Nova Scotia. Peller's son Joseph, a doctor, also joined Andrés Wines at this time.

Over the next several years, Andrés Wines established several popular wine brands in Canada. Perhaps its best known was its brand of sparkling wine, called Baby Duck. A sweet, bubbly wine, it became a market leader and one of the most widely recognized Canadian brands. By 1973, Andrés Wines Ltd. had prospered to the point of investing CAD 2 million in an expansion of its Ontario headquarters, located in the city of Winona.

In the 1970s and 1980s, Andrés Wines was one of the preeminent wineries in Canada. In addition to Baby Duck, it had other widely recognized brands. Its Hochtaler table wine was the best-selling wine in Canada in 1978. At the company's 20th anniversary celebration in 1981, the premier of Ontario honored Andrés with a scroll recognizing its leadership in the domestic wine industry. In an industry where some European wines traced their lineage back to medieval times, Andrés Wines was still a very young company. However, it had come on the scene at an opportune time, and apparently grasped the taste of Canadian consumers.

FREE TRADE CHANGES COMPETITIVE LANDSCAPE

The Canadian wine industry began to alter with the passage of landmark legislation in 1988. In the mid-1980s, Andrés Wines had annual sales of around CAD 60 million. It was known as Canada's leading winery, with about one-third of its sales coming from its local territory of Ontario. The mix of imported and domestic wines was split nearly half and half in Canada, with domestic wines having a slight edge. Canadian trade laws had protected domestic wines from competition from imports, and the government had done much to support Andrés and other native vintners.

In 1988, the governments of Canada and the United States signed a new trade agreement that dismantled the domestic wine industry's protections. The Canada/USA Free Trade Agreement coincided with a new ruling under the General Agreement on Tariffs and Trade, known as GATT, that also confirmed that Canada's wine industry would have to compete directly with imports. Price markups that had made imports more expensive for Canadians were reduced, and were set to disappear entirely by 1995. This meant that Andrés's popular Hochtaler and other leading brands would have to face lower-priced European wines. At the

KEY DATES

1961: Company is founded as Andrés Wines Ltd.
1988: New trade agreement forces changes in Peller strategy.
1991: First premium wine, Peller Estates, debuts.
1994: Company acquires Hillebrand Estates Winery.
2005: Company acquires three more premium wineries.
2006: Name is changed to Andrew Peller Ltd.

same time, wineries in Australia, Chile, and other newer wine-growing regions were gaining notice for affordable, palatable, and sometimes premium products.

Andrés Wines responded to these changing conditions by beginning to move into premium wines. With more scientifically advanced procedures in horticulture, Andrés and other Canadian wineries began replacing Canadian grape varieties with the more tender Old World varieties. Also in 1988, Andrés and other Ontario wine growers banded together and formed the Vintners Quality Alliance, or VQA. This group agreed to submit their wines to certain standards the VQA would set, in order to raise the quality of the entire Ontario wine-growing region. With better grape varieties, a standard-setting body, and the stimulation of stiffer competition from outside Canada, Andrés and other domestic wine producers entered a new era.

By 1991, Andrés was producing a new wine brand, Peller Estates, that rose to be the leading premium wine in Canada. The Peller Estates wines, both red and white, were made from grapes grown in southern Ontario's Niagara Peninsula. Andrés also bought wineries in British Columbia, Quebec, and Manitoba. It also acquired a California winery. While it strove to make its wines of such a quality that they competed well with imports, Andrés also opened its own import business and sold wines from around the world.

The company continued to be solidly profitable through this time of change, although it did not experience a lot of revenue growth. Andrés had little debt despite the improvements and acquisitions it had made. Its stock was highly regarded, so much so that investors tended to hold onto it, and very little of it changed hands. Though Andrés was publicly traded, it operated in many ways like a family company. It was under the leadership of the founder's son Joseph through the early 1990s. Andrew Peller's grandson John took over as chief executive in 1995. His father remained chairman.

Though Andrés Wines did not have an ancient pedigree, the wine industry was relatively slow moving. The company looked ahead for long-term growth rather than quick profits. In 1992, Andrés Wines still prevailed as one of Canada's foremost winemakers, with a total market share across Canada of just under 10 percent.

STRATEGIC ACQUISITIONS

Although the company led an industry where vineyards took decades to flourish and vintages years to reach their peak, increasing global competition forced Andrés to make some quick decisions. After launching Peller Estates in 1991, Andrés began bolstering its stable of premium wines through acquisitions. In 1993 it failed in its bid to purchase a competitor, T.G. Bright & Co. Andrés owned a minority stake in Bright, and it offered to acquire the whole company for CAD 19 a share. Andrés was outbid by another contender and let its offer lapse. Andrés nevertheless made money by eventually selling its minority stake, leaving it in a good cash position to make other buys.

In 1994, Andrés acquired the Hillebrand Estates Winery of Niagara-on-the-Lake, Ontario. Hillebrand was Ontario's largest producer of VQA wine. It had annual revenue of around CAD 14 million. Now Andrés had its own premium brands, Peller Estates and French Cross, plus Hillebrand's stable of fine wines. It was important for Andrés to establish a niche in the high end of the market, where the pressure from imports was greatest.

The other competitive pressure on Andrés was from illegal manufacturers. Canadians could make wine at home for their own use, and home wine kits had long been popular. Yet some vintners manufactured "home" wines out of imported grape concentrate, making bulk vintages in warehouses with unsophisticated equipment. They sold this wine at a fraction of the cost of legal wines. While the market share of imports held steady, domestic producers' market share eroded because of the impact of these illegal vintners.

Andrés Wines responded by buying one of the largest producers of home wine kits in 1996. It acquired Vineco International Products that year, and in 1997 bought a similar company, Brew King. Brew King had a large market share in the western part of the country. By owning both Brew King and Vineco, Andrés became the leading company in the home wine kit market in Canada.

Andrés bought more land in late 1997. It acquired 210 acres of cropland in Ontario's prime grape-growing Niagara Peninsula, and planted these with European (vinifera) grape varieties. The increased grape cultivation would allow the company to produce more high-end wines in coming years. In 2001 it opened Peller Estates Winery in Niagara-on-the-Lake. The winery produced ultra-premium wines, and also offered tours and fine dining. Also in the late 1990s and early 2000s, the company sold land and facilities in Quebec and Alberta, concentrating its grape-growing in Ontario and British Columbia. Sales rose gradually over this period of time, from CAD 135.4 million in 1999 to CAD 147.9 million in 2003.

In another response to the increasing pressure from imported wines, Andrés distributed a small portfolio of Californian, Chilean, and Australian wines. These were premium wines sold at prices consumers considered reasonable. At the same time, Andrés began exporting its wines both to Europe and to the Pacific Rim countries. By 2003, the company was selling its brands in more than 20 countries abroad.

MORE INROADS IN THE HIGH END

Andrés Wines Ltd. had made its reputation selling middle-of-the-road table wines such as its best-selling Hochtaler and Schloss Laderheim brands. It was also well-known for its sparkling wine, Baby Duck. However, by the middle of the first decade of the 2000s, the company had moved firmly into the high end of the market. Its vineyards in Ontario and British Columbia occupied some of the finest grape-growing land in North America. These were planted with pedigreed European grape varieties. Many of its wines had won Canadian and international awards. In 2005, the company bought three wineries that produced premium wines. It acquired Thirty Bench, a winery on the Niagara Peninsula, and two British Columbia producers, Sandhill and Red Rooster. The company announced that it would continue to look for acquisitions.

Both the Niagara Peninsula region and the Okanagan Valley area of British Columbia, where its western properties were concentrated, were still developing as wine regions. Although Andrés had begun to move into premium wines in the early 1990s, its vineyards were not expected to reach their full capability for another 20 or 30 years. Therefore, there was still plenty of room for Andrés to bring out more award-winning wines, and to buy up small wineries that flourished in these areas.

The company had been under the direction of the third generation of Pellers since 1995, when Joseph's son John became chief executive. In 2006, the company voted to change its name from Andrés Wines Ltd. to

Andrew Peller Ltd., in order to honor its founder. Changes made under the new masthead contributed to the company's growth over the next several years. Sales increased steadily, to CAD 237.1 million in 2008. Investments in vineyards, in upgrades to its wineries and restaurants, and the acquisition of premium producers, led the company to continue its long trajectory of stable growth. The Canadian wine market was expected to continue to grow, and Andrew Peller predicted no drastic change in its business strategy. Its grape capacity at its British Columbia vineyards was expected to double by 2011 as newly cultivated land and acquired wineries reached their peak. The company's export business also trended upward, with 25 percent year over year growth in 2008. Its wines continued to win prizes in Canada, where consumers widely recognized Peller's leading brands. The company anticipated keeping to proven ways, weathering short-term downturns with a long-range strategy of diverse and moderate growth.

A. Woodward

PRINCIPAL SUBSIDIARIES

4384814 Canada, Inc.; Granville Island Brewery Co. Ltd.; Canrim Packaging Ltd.; Sandhill Vineyards Ltd.

PRINCIPAL COMPETITORS

Vincor International Inc.; Magnotta Winery Corp.; E & J Gallo Winery.

FURTHER READING

"Andres to Buy Hillebrand," *Globe and Mail,* May 18, 1994, p. B2.

Bertin, Oliver, "Andres Abandons Bid to Buy Bright," *Globe and Mail,* April 17, 1993, p. B14.

———, "Discount Vintners Threaten Andres," *Globe and Mail,* August 2, 1993, p. B7.

Clifford, Edward, "Stock Scene: Andres Shares Aging in Portfolios," *Globe and Mail,* November 12, 1992, p. B11.

———, "Stock Scene: Andres Shares Sag After Dividend," *Globe and Mail,* September 24, 1993, p. B9.

McKeough, Patrick, "Profits Flowing Freely for Sleeman and Andres," *Money Digest,* August 2002, p. 3.

———, "Winemaker Andres Mixes Versatile Blend," *Money Digest,* November 1998, p. 3.

Motherwell, Catherine, "Andres' Sales Hurt by Bad Industry Publicity," *Globe and Mail,* January 9, 1986, p. B1.

Stueck, Wendy, "Andrew Peller Puts Andres Wines Behind It," *Globe and Mail,* December 9, 2006, p. B4.

Arlington Tankers Ltd.

■

**22 Bermudiana Road, 1st Floor, The Hayward
Building
Hamilton, HM 11
Bermuda
Telephone: (+441) 292 4456
Fax: (+441) 292 4258
Web site: http://www.arlingtontankers.com**

Subsidiary of General Maritime Corporation
Incorporated: 2004
Employees: 2
Sales: $69.4 million (2007)
NAICS: 483111 Deep Sea Freight Transportation

■ ■ ■

Arlington Tankers Ltd. provides tanker shipping services to the global oil industry. The Bermuda-registered company can lay claim to operating the world's youngest fleet, with an average vessel age of under three years, compared to the industry average of 12.5 years. At the end of 2008, Arlington owned eight vessels: two V-MAX tankers in the 200,000 to 320,000 deadweight ton (dwt) class; two Panamax tankers, in the 50,000 to 80,000 dwt class; and four product tankers, at the 50,000 to 80,000 dwt class. All of the company's vessels are double-hulled carriers. The larger vessels are designed for transporting crude oil, while the product tankers are capable of transporting crude oil, and both "clean" (i.e., diesel, gasoline, jet fuel) and "dirty" (i.e., fuel oil) products. All of Arlington Tankers' vessels are chartered to the company's primary shareholders, Stena Bulk and

its subsidiary, publicly listed Concordia, and/or their subsidiaries. These companies are in turn subsidiaries of Stena AB, which also operates in the bulk freight, ferry, and other shipping sectors. Arlington Tankers was created in 2004 as a vehicle to enable the investor community to invest directly in the oil tanker sector. After struggling to maintain profitability amid the economic downturn of 2008, Arlington Tankers agreed to merge its operations with those of General Maritime Corporation. Under terms of the merger, both companies became subsidiaries of a "new" General Maritime Corporation. The deal, completed in December 2008, gives General Maritime control of 73 percent of Arlington Tankers.

CREATING A TANKER INVESTMENT VEHICLE FOR THE 21ST CENTURY

Arlington Tankers Ltd. was founded as an offshoot of Swedish shipping giant Stena AB in 2004. The new company, registered in Bermuda, with offices in the United States, took its name from the street on which Stena's London offices were located. Arlington Tankers' creation came specifically in order to fill a growing demand for direct investment opportunities in the oil tanker sector.

This market was then experiencing a major expansion, driven by two important factors. The first lay in the international shipping agreements put into place in the early 1990s, which called for the phasing out of all single-hulled tanker vessels by 2010. The new regulations responded to demands for increasing environ-

COMPANY PERSPECTIVES

Our mission continues to be the generation of stable and predictable cash flow from our fleet of tankers that enables the payment of quarterly dividends to shareholders. The key elements of our strategy are to acquire tankers of high quality, to charter our tankers to experienced charterers under long-term, fixed-rate charters and to arrange for experienced ship managers to operate our fleet.

mental protection standards following a series of ecological disasters caused by tanker oil spills. As a result, more than half of the international tanker fleet quickly approached obsolescence. Demand for new-buildings (newly constructed vessels) quickly outstripped shipbuilders' capacity.

At the same time, the global oil and gas industry was undergoing a surge in demand for oil and petroleum products, as well as natural gas. Driven by the booming Chinese and Indian economies, in particular, and the strong growth exhibited in the Asian markets in general, oil prices soared into the second half of the decade. The rising demand in turn strengthened demand for shipping services. In consequence, tanker chartering fees rose strongly as well.

Exposure to spot market pricing also left the tanker industry vulnerable to the highly cyclical nature of the global shipping market. This vulnerability presented certain risks to the investment community. Arlington Tankers' business model, however, was developed specifically to mitigate these risks. Instead of adjusting its pricing according to the spot market, Arlington Tanker focused on fixed-rate, time-charter contracts. The company's vessel operating costs were similarly fixed by contracting for these services with a third-party manager. In this way, Arlington Tankers was able to present investors with minimum revenue and earnings guarantees. The downside of this strategy lay in the fact that the company could not take full advantage of subsequent spikes in spot market rates. Nonetheless, the company's charter agreements included provisions for sharing some of the profits generated by its clients.

DEVELOPING AN OIL TANKER FLEET: 2004

Arlington Tankers was formally created as a 50-50 joint venture between Stena Bulk and its publicly listed

subsidiary Concordia Maritime in September 2004. Leading the new company was Arthur Regan, who had more than ten years' experience in the oil tanker services sector, including serving as a vice-president at Stena Bulk. By November of that year, Arlington Tankers had completed its initial public offering on the New York Stock Exchange, raising more than $270 million. The company complemented this equity issue with $135 million in bank loans.

The company immediately used its capital to carry out the purchase of six vessels from Stena Bulk and Concordia. These included two V-MAX tankers from Concordia, the sister ships *Stena Victory* and the *Stena Vision,* both built in 2001 and featuring a size of 314,000 dwt. Both VLCCs (very large crude carriers) were also among the most modern in the industry, featuring an extrawide hull that not only increased carrying capacity by some 20 percent, but also provided significant fuel reduction and other operating economies. The ships were designed with several advanced safety features, including redundant rudders, propellers, and propulsion systems.

Arlington's new fleet also included the *Stena Compatriot* and *Stena Companion.* These vessels, also sister ships, were newly built in 2004, and provided Arlington with operations in the Panamax—so-called because these were the largest vessels capable of passing through the Panama Canal—class, with 72,750 dwt. Both vessels also featured fully epoxy-coated tanks, allowing them to provide transport services both for crude oil and petroleum products including fuel oil. The Panamax tankers largely served the North, Central, and South American markets.

Arlington Tankers rounded out its offering with a smaller Handymax class vessel, the *Stena Consul,* built in 2004, and its sister ship, the *Stena Concept,* which was delivered only in 2005. Both vessels offered a deadweight tonnage of 47,400, and featured ten independent cargo tanks, in contrast to the conventional six tank design. This allowed these vessels, which focused on the oil product transport market, a wider flexibility in carrying a variety of primarily clean products, such as jet fuel, diesel, and gasoline.

INHERITING A SHIPPING LINEAGE

All of Arlington Tankers' vessels operated under fixed-rate time-charter contracts with Stena, Concordia, and their subsidiaries. Both Stena and Concordia also maintained equity stakes in Arlington Tankers, holding 14 percent of the company, further enhancing the company's attractiveness as a stable investment.

KEY DATES

1982: Stena AB creates Stena Bulk as a tanker shipping subsidiary.

1984: Stena Bulk spins off part of its tanker operations into a publicly listed subsidiary, Concordia Maritime.

2001: Concordia takes delivery of two V-MAX class VLCC carriers.

2004: Stena Bulk and Concordia create Arlington Tankers, which takes over Concordia's V-MAX vessels and four vessels from Stena, then goes public on the New York Stock Exchange.

2006: Arlington Tankers buys two new product tankers from Stena.

2008: Arlington Tankers agrees to merge with General Maritime Corporation and removes its stock exchange listing.

Arlington Tankers could also lay claim to operating the industry's youngest fleet, with an average vessel age of just 1.5 years at the outset, compared to an industry average of more than 12 years.

Despite the young age of its fleet, and its own newcomer status, Arlington Tankers benefited from Stena's long involvement in the shipping industry. Stena had been founded in 1939 by Sweden's Sten A. Olsson, the son of a shipowner and ship's captain. Olsson's business initially focused on metals trading, but in 1946 the company acquired its first cargo ship. By the early 1960s, Stena, as the company became known, had branched out into ferry operations as well. Through the 1970s, Stena explored a number of diversified shipping markets, such as Ro-Ro (roll-on, roll-off) container ships and offshore vessels. In 1983, the company set up a new subsidiary, Stena Bulk, as a specialist in tanker shipping.

The first tankers had appeared as early as the late 19th century. Their importance to the shipping market really took off in the years following World War II, which saw a surge in the international demand for petroleum and chemicals. The discovery and exploitation of the major oil and gas fields in the Middle East brought about a demand for vessels capable of transporting large quantities of petroleum, chemicals, and other liquids over great distances. Safety and environmental concerns also drove the industry, leading to the creation of the first parcel tankers by the late

1950s. Over the following decades, vessel sizes grew dramatically. Ships rarely surpassed 10,000 dwt in the 1960s; by the 1970s, vessels of 30,000 dwt had become quite common. Into the 1980s, the introduction of the VLCC class introduced vessels of 200,000 dwt and even more. By the end of that decade, the largest ships neared 500,000 dwt.

Stena Bulk acquired its first vessel, the *Stena Adriatica,* in 1983. That vessel provided just 20,000 dwt. Yet the company had begun to exhibit the flexibility that became a hallmark of Arlington Tankers as well. By the end of its first year, Stena Bulk had already acquired a second vessel, the *Stena Atlantica,* this time in the VLCC class with a dryweight tonnage of 270,000.

Stena Bulk foreshadowed Arlington Tankers' creation in another way. Parent company Stena remained a privately owned company. In 1984, however, Stena Bulk formed a new subsidiary, Concordia Maritime, in order to gain access to the public market. Concordia listed its shares on the Stockholm Stock Exchange that year. Concordia grew into a major tanker player in its own right. By 1988, the company had taken delivery on what was then the fifth and sixth largest vessels in the world, the *Stena King* and *Stena Queen,* both at 458,000 dwt. This boosted Concordia's total fleet size to 3.5 million dwt. The following year, Concordia bought six VLCC vessels from Universe Tankships. In 1996, Concordia purchased that company outright, adding its remaining fleet.

Stena Bulk, including Concordia, continued to build its fleet through the 1990s. The company had also begun to phase out its older single-hull vessels, many of which were converted for use as offshore vessels. Stena Bulk's fortunes were further lifted in 1994, when it reached a Strategic Maritime Alliance with Texaco, which included agreements governing more than 50 million tons of oil shipments. The two companies formed the joint venture StenTex, which later built up its own fleet of more than 20 vessels, before becoming a wholly owned subsidiary of Stena Bulk.

EXPANDING THE FLEET IN 2006

The beginnings of Arlington Tankers' initial fleet appeared by the turn of the millennium. In 1999, Concordia placed an order with Hyundai Heavy Industries to build a revolutionary new VLCC carrier. Called the V-MAX, the new vessel design featured a wider hull than conventional VLCCs. This design not only enabled a 20 percent increase in storage capacity, it also reduced the depth at which the bottom of the vessel rested in the water. This reduced draft, as it was called, permitted the wider vessel design to navigate safely in ports with draft restrictions, while also providing for significant fuel economy underway. The double-hulled V-MAX design also boasted a number of other safety and performance features, such as dual propeller, rudder, and propulsion systems, which made navigation easier, while boosting speed and stability on the ocean. The V-MAX design also offered an expanded life cycle, rated for 40 years as opposed to just 25 years for the conventional VLCC design.

Concordia took delivery of the two vessels, the *Stena Victory* and the *Stena Vision,* in 2001. In that year, Stena Bulk placed an order for a number of new Panamax vessels, including a series of 72,000 dwt vessels to be built at China's Dalian Shipyard. These were complemented by a number of other vessel orders. By 2003, Stena Bulk's order book had topped 16 vessels, including four 47,000 dwt product tankers under construction at the Uljanik shipyard in Croatia.

Soon after its creation, Arlington Tankers too targeted an expansion of its fleet, in part in response to the rising demand for product tanker capacity. By 2006, the company had taken delivery of two more vessels, the *Stena Concord* and *Stena Contest,* both in the Handymax class and sister ships to the company's initial two product tankers. Both vessels had been owned by Stena, and operated under chartering contracts with that company.

As a result, Stena, through Stena Bulk, Concordia, and other subsidiaries, remained the primary source of Arlington Tankers' revenues, which topped $69 million into 2008. Nonetheless, as it turned toward the end of the decade, Arlington Tankers announced its intention to broaden its customer base beyond Stena once its chartering contracts were completed into the beginning of the next decade. These contracts provided somewhat of a shield for the company from the brunt of the global economic downturn in 2008. As oil prices plummeted, Arlington Tankers' revenues remained protected by its fixed-rate chartering contracts. Nonetheless, Arlington found itself struggling against losses into the middle of 2008. In August, the company launched merger discussions with General Maritime Corporation, also listed on the NYSE. Led by CEO Peter Georgiopoulos, General Maritime had been founded in 1997 and focused on providing oil transportation in the Aframax and Suezmax classes, commanding a fleet of 20 vessels by 2008. General Maritime's operations spanned most of the

major oil and gas producing markets, including the South, Central, and North American, Mediterranean, West African, Black Sea, and North Sea markets. The merger, completed in December of that year, gave General Maritime control of 73 percent of Arlington Tankers. The addition of Arlington Tankers' fleet allowed General Maritime to expand its fleet into the larger tanker classes, while providing Arlington with the financial security of a larger group.

M. L. Cohen

PRINCIPAL SUBSIDIARIES

Arlington Tankers LLC (USA).

PRINCIPAL COMPETITORS

Sumitomo Corporation; A.P. Møller-Maersk A/S; TUI AG; Marubeni Corporation; Companhia Vale do Rio Doce; Louis Dreyfus S.A.S.; Nippon Yusen KK; Mitsui OSK Lines Ltd.; Kawasaki Kisen Kaisha Ltd.

FURTHER READING

"Arlington in Chase for Chartering Opportunities," *Europe Intelligence Wire,* October 27, 2006.

"Arlington Lifts Payout After Setback," *Europe Intelligence Wire,* February 1, 2007.

"Arlington Shares Profits As Income Increases," *Europe Intelligence Wire,* April 26, 2007.

Gray, Tony, "Arlington Refinances Debt to Buy Two Tankers," *Europe Intelligence Wire,* December 14, 2005.

———, "Better Freight Rates Helps Arlington Beat Dividend Targets," *Europe Intelligence Wire,* January 30, 2006.

———, "Stena and Concordia Back Arlington Merger," *Lloyds' List,* December 10, 2008.

Lee, Richard, "Arlington Tanker Officials Like Being Part of Region's Shipping Scene," *Stamford (Conn.) Advocate,* August 2, 2005.

Reeves, Amy, "Tanker Operator Tests the Water on Wall Street," *Investor's Business Daily,* November 10, 2004, p. A09.

"Tanker Co. to Raise $335m in Equity, Debt," *Corporate Financing Week* November 1, 2004, p. 1.

Wolfe, Daniel, "Oil Firm's CEO Joins S1 Board," *American Banker,* April 19, 2007, p. 17.

Art's Way Manufacturing Co., Inc.

5556 Highway 9
Armstrong, Iowa 50514-7566
U.S.A.
Telephone: (712) 864-3131
Fax: (712) 864-3154
Web site: http://www.artsway-mfg.com

Public Company
Incorporated: 1956
Employees: 107
Sales: $25.52 million (2007)
Stock Exchanges: NASDAQ
Ticker Symbol: ARTW
NAICS: 333111 Farm Machinery and Equipment Manufacturing

■ ■ ■

Art's Way Manufacturing Co., Inc., is a NASDAQ-listed manufacturer of specialized agricultural equipment sold under its own and private labels. The Armstrong, Iowa-based company offers several lines of equipment. The grinder mixer line, the company's original business, includes equipment to grind and mix grain and protein for livestock feed; feed grain processing equipment, including stationary hammer mills and roller mills to create feed grain rations; the forage blending line, including machinery to plant seed and spread fertilizer, and shredders to destroy insect habitats and quickly restore nutrients to the soil; land management equipment, including land planes to level the ground for the even distribution of rainfall or irrigation water; and sugar beet harvesters to lift beets out of the ground for removal and defoliators to cut and remove leaves, the particles of which are reincorporated into the soil. Products are sold mostly through a network of about 1,650 independent dealers in the United States and Canada. Art's Way also exports to several countries, an increasingly important source of revenues.

In addition, the company does business through a pair of subsidiaries. Art's Way Scientific Inc. operating out of Monona, Iowa, manufactures and markets modular laboratory buildings for biocontainment, animal science, public health, and biomedical and security purposes. The units can be produced in Iowa, certified, and then transported wherever needed. Another subsidiary, Art's Way Vessels, Inc., based in Dubuque, Iowa, manufactures pressurized tanks and vessels used in such markets as agriculture, chemical, food and beverage, heavy equipment, marine, mining, pharmaceutical, and storage.

COMPANY FOUNDED: 1956

Art's Way Manufacturing was founded by Arthur Luscombe, an Iowa farmer with a penchant for invention and a knack for business. Living in Dolliver, Iowa, close to the Minnesota border, he invented a grinder-mixer to feed his own hogs. His neighbors were so impressed that Luscombe decided to start a company to manufacture the equipment for sale. Thus, in 1956 Luscombe established a downtown plant in nearby Armstrong, Iowa, to manufacture his invention. The grinder-mixer caught on, becoming a standard hog-feeding machine in the United States. In 1959 the company moved to a

COMPANY PERSPECTIVES

Mission: To deliver high quality market responsive products and services, which will exceed customer expectations, and maximize shareholder value.

new location in Armstrong, its present-day site, where there was ample room for future expansion. The new facility also allowed Art's Way to extend the product line as well as take on original equipment manufacturing work for large farm machinery companies, including Massey Ferguson, Owatonna, and International Harvester.

In the 1960s Art's Way became a public company and began diversifying, not only developing new products but also adding niche lines of farm equipment through acquisition. In 1966 the company purchased the Siamix chain feed wagon line. A complementary line of scale products was developed for both the grinders and feed wagons as well as industrial applications. This sideline led to the creation of Weigh-Tronix, incorporated in 1971. In the early 1980s the unit was split off from Art's Way, eventually merging with other companies to become Avery Weigh-Tronix Inc.

Sales of grinder-mixers peaked in the mid-1970s at 10,000 a year, after which the numbers steadily declined because of the failure of small farms and the ever growing importance of large agricultural enterprises. Sales dipped below 500 by the end of the 20th century. As a result, the need for diversification and new product development increased at a comparable pace for Art's Way. In the early 1980s the company added mowers, cutters, and shredders by acquiring the Sunmaster product line from Rotech of Olathe, Kansas. In 1982 Art's Way entered the sugar beet harvesting and defoliator market with the purchase of the product lines of Fort Collins, Colorado-based Heath Farm Equipment. Later in the decade Art's Way acquired the rights to the John Deere–designed "wheel" harvester, and emerged as the industry leader in the sugar beet harvesting niche market. Art's Way also used the expertise developed with sugar beet harvesting to introduce a potato harvester as well.

ACQUISITION OF PEERLESS PRODUCT LINE: 1991

The next major development in Art's Way business was the late 1991 acquisition of the Peerless product line from a Joplin, Missouri, company, allowing it to add a

roller mill option to the feed processing line. It was also in the early 1990s that Art's Way introduced stationary feed processing and mixing equipment. In addition, the company purchased the Eversman, Inc., line of land preparation equipment, including land planes, levelers, ditchers, scrapers, and the PreSeeder minimum tillage tool. In 1994 a vertical mixer was developed for the cattle market.

Much of the 1990s was a challenging period for Art's Way. Annual sales hovered around $20 million from fiscal 1993 to fiscal 1995, but the company lost more than $1 million in 1995 and a year later lost another $772,000 on sales that fell to $13.8 million. The company had relatively little long-term debt compared to its total assets, however, allowing it to continue to invest in product development and take advantage of tough times to buy new product lines on the cheap. In June 1996, the start of fiscal 1997, Art's Way introduced a portable roller mixer for use by hog producers. Then, in September of that year, Art's Way acquired the potato farm equipment line of Idaho-based Logan Harvesters, Inc., providing it with harvesters, windrowers, planters, and bulk beds. Later in the fall, Art's Way also acquired the DMI Grain Wagon product line from Goodfield, Illinois-based DMI, Inc. These new products helped Art's Way to rebound in fiscal 1997, when the company returned to profitability, netting $80,000 on revenues that improved to $16.44 million.

21ST CENTURY BRINGS INTERNATIONAL PUSH

Sales continued to grow in fiscal 1998, when the end of the fiscal year was moved from May 31 to November 30, totaling $23.63 million, though the company posted a net loss of $324,000. The agricultural economy was suffering another downturn, leading to a dip in demand for farm equipment. As a result, Art's Way experienced an erosion in sales to $17.22 million in fiscal 1999 and a further net loss of $630,000. All of those sales came from the United States and Canada, but in the new century, Art's Way would begin to look overseas for much needed new sources of revenues, while continuing to seek avenues for diversification. Even as the 1990s came to a close, in fact, the company remained healthy enough to acquire several product lines from Oelwein, Iowa-based United Farm Tools, including a no-till grain drill, a multicrop shredder, a high dump wagon, and the "Speedy" bean cutter. Nevertheless, some cost reductions were necessary, including a reduction in the workforce from 123 employees to 97.

Art's Way was better positioned than other farm equipment companies that fell by the wayside during

KEY DATES

1956: Arthur Luscombe establishes company in Armstrong, Iowa.
1959: Company moves to present-day site.
1966: Siamix feed wagon line is acquired.
1982: Company begins producing sugar beet harvesting and defoliator equipment.
1991: Peerless product line of roller mills is acquired.
2005: Vessel Systems Inc. is acquired.
2006: Subsidiary Art's Way Scientific, Inc., is formed.

these tough times, and it remained optimistic as the new century dawned, but the market had yet to bottom out. Declining commodity and livestock prices had an adverse impact on all of Art's Way's niche markets. The sugar beet sector was hit especially hard. Not only did the industry have to contend with overproduction, there was also increased competition from the sugarcane industry and other foreign sugar-producing sources. One positive item in the first decade of the 2000s was improved beef prices, which spurred demand for the feed processing and land maintenance equipment offered by Art's Way. Sales of this equipment could not make up for losses in other areas, however. In fiscal 2000 total sales fell to $14.23 million, resulting in a net loss of $2.17 million, and a year later sales decreased further to $10.9 million, while the net loss grew to $2.4 million.

OBECO, INC., ACQUISITION: 2003

Revenues held steady in fiscal 2002, but because of cost reductions, Art's Way was able to turn a net profit of $569,000. In 2003 the company looked to diversify beyond farm equipment, acquiring Cherokee, Iowa-based Obeco, Inc., maker of steel truck bodies. The business was renamed Cherokee Truck Bodies, Inc., and plans were made to relocate it to Armstrong. During the four months of that fiscal year that it contributed to the balance sheet, Cherokee generated sales of $471,000. Sales from the farm machinery side of the company stayed flat as the farm economy remained weak, but with the help of an $801,000 tax benefit, Art's Way was able to record a net profit of $1.64 million. The company also had enough financial resources to continue to invest in engineering, resulting in an improved grinder-mixer product and the industry's first 12-row sugar beet harvester, aimed at the large farm

operators. The prototype was unveiled in fiscal 2003 and introduced to the market, with the new grinder-mixer debuting a year later.

Cherokee did not fare well in fiscal 2004, nor did the company's potato harvesters, but making up the difference were improved sales of sugar beet equipment grinders, land planes, plows, and other farming equipment. Total revenues improved 8.9 percent to nearly $12.8 million, while net earnings dipped slightly to $1.4 million, due to the Cherokee move and the high price of steel that hindered the unit's performance.

Without the benefit of tax credits in fiscal 2005, Art's Way posted net income of $977,000 on revenues of $14.62 million, a 14.3 percent increase over the previous year. Contributing $358,000 in sales was a new subsidiary, Art's Way Vessels, Inc., which took shape in October 2005 following the acquisition of Dubuque, Iowa-based Vessel Systems Inc., a manufacturer of pressurized tanks and vessels. Again, Art's Way was able to diversify its business at a modest cost, picking up a company that was struggling. Cherokee Truck Bodies, on the other hand, proved not to be a good fit and was divested. In August 2006 Art's Way completed another acquisition to further its diversification efforts, paying about $1.14 million for Monona, Iowa-based Tech Space Inc., a manufacturer of modular laboratories. It was subsequently renamed Art's Way Scientific, Inc.

Not only did Art's Way celebrate its 50th anniversary in the summer of 2006, it recorded its first international sales, exporting grinders and sugar beet harvesters to Australia and England, resulting in sales of $843,000. The company's chairman, Ward McConnell, spearheaded the push, having begun the previous year to attend agricultural shows in Europe and Asia, setting up displays of the Art's Way equipment lines. In fiscal 2007, China, France, Russia, and Ukraine would be added as customers as export sales improved to about $2 million.

FIRE DESTROYS PLANT: 2007

With contributions from Art's Way Vessels, Art's Way Scientific, and international sales, the company was able to increase revenues 36 percent to $19.85 million in 2006. Because of start-up costs related to Art's Way Scientific, net earnings fell slightly to $934,000. The following year proved even better despite a fire in January 2007 that completely destroyed the main factory of Art's Way Scientific in Monona. Nevertheless, revenues increased 29 percent to $25.52 million, due in large part to the performance of Art's Way Scientific. Net income more than doubled to $2.23 million.

Although located in a remote corner of Iowa, the company's performance did not go unnoticed. In 2008

Art's Way was ranked 58th on the *Fortune Small Business* list of the nation's fastest-growing small public companies. Going forward, Art's Way still had to contend with the problematic farm equipment sector, ameliorated somewhat by a growing export business, but perhaps the key to the company's future lay with Art's Way Scientific. Because of the complex certification process that had to be mastered to enter the market for these portable laboratory facilities, it was a business with few competitors, one that a fund manager interviewed by *Fortune Small Business* called "the gold mine hidden behind the house."

Ed Dinger

PRINCIPAL SUBSIDIARIES

Art's Way Scientific Inc.; Art's Way Vessels, Inc.

PRINCIPAL COMPETITORS

AGCO Corporation; Alamo Group Inc.; Deere & Company.

FURTHER READING

"A Gold Anniversary for Art's Way," *Implement & Tractor,* September 1, 2006, p. 423.

"J. David Pitt: Art's Way Manufacturing," *Wall Street Transcript,* October 4, 1999.

Kittle, M. D., "Iowa Manufacturer Buys Vessel Systems," *Dubuque (Iowa) Telegraph Herald,* October 12, 2005, p. A1.

Knudson, Brooke, "Building on Tradition," *U.S. Business Review,* June 2007, p. 150.

Oechslin, Russ, "Art's Way Turns 50 with Growth," *Sioux City Journal,* October 22, 2006.

O'Reilly, Brian, "Art's Way," *Fortune Small Business,* July/August 2008, p. 84.

AtheroGenics Inc.

8995 Westside Parkway
Alpharetta, Georgia 30004
U.S.A.
Telephone: (678) 336-2500
Fax: (678) 336-2501
Web site: http://www.atherogenics.com

Public Company
Incorporated: 1993
Employees: 70
Sales: $52.3 million (2007)
Stock Exchanges: Over the Counter (OTC)
Ticker Symbol: AGIXQ
NAICS: 325412 Pharmaceutical Preparation Manufacturing

■ ■ ■

Alpharetta, Georgia-based AtheroGenics Inc. is an emerging pharmaceutical company. With a senior leadership team comprised of executives from leading academic institutions and drug companies, its efforts are concentrated on discovering, developing, and commercializing novel drugs in several areas, including atherosclerosis, chronic inflammatory diseases, and diabetes. Due to a mounting debt burden, the company filed for Chapter 11 bankrupty in October 2008.

ORIGINS: 1993–95

AtheroGenics emerged from a Georgia state program that sought to create new companies from research universities. The company was founded in 1993 by Emory University cardiologists Russell M. Medford and Wayne Alexander.

Drs. Medford and Alexander theorized that it was possible to prevent the arterial swelling and inflammation that leads to heart attacks by blocking a chemical process called oxidation. While the theory proved to be correct, the oxidation-halting chemical they initially identified turned out to be unsafe for human use.

The two physicians ultimately secured the rights to a cholesterol drug named Probucol from Marion Merrell Dow Inc., which was no longer marketed due to undesirable side effects. By 1996 AtheroGenics had reformulated Probucol and renamed it AGI-1067, which eventually become the company's lead compound.

Initial start-up funding for AtheroGenics was provided from Alliance Technology Ventures. Michael A. Henos, Alliance Technology's managing partner, served as AtheroGenics' chairman, with Medford fulfilling the role of CEO. These same two executives continued to guide the company in 2008.

During AtheroGenics' early years, the company focused on developing an operational structure and hiring scientists from academic and industry laboratories, including senior management from fields such as biochemistry, biology, cell biology, and synthetic chemistry.

INITIAL DEVELOPMENTS: 1996–99

By early 1996 AtheroGenics had finished construction of a 7,500-square-foot leased facility in Norcross,

COMPANY PERSPECTIVES

Our objective is to become a leading pharmaceutical company focused on discovering, developing and commercializing novel drugs for the treatment of chronic inflammatory diseases.

Georgia, which included a research laboratory, offices, and space for manufacturing and storage. In January AtheroGenics completed a second round of financing, bringing the company's total to approximately $5.1 million. Six months later, a third round ($9.3 million) of financing was completed, bringing AtheroGenics' total to about $14 million.

At this time, AtheroGenics was focused on AGI-H15 and AGI-H1, two oral compounds that it hoped would stop, and potentially reverse, the development of atherosclerosis, a medical condition that causes heart attacks.

A number of important developments occurred on the scientific leadership front during the mid- to late 1990s. In March 1996, AtheroGenics named Uday Saxena, Ph.D., who had worked in Parke-Davis's Department of Atherosclerosis Therapeutics, as director of preclinical research. Midway through 1997, Dr. Saxena was promoted to vice-president of preclinical research and Patricia K. Somers, who attended Harvard University as an American Cancer Society postdoctoral fellow, was named as director of chemistry. By this time AtheroGenics' lead products included the aforementioned AGI-H1, as well as a compound named AGI-3.

Progress continued at AtheroGenics in 1998. In January the company began Phase I clinical trials on AGI-1067. The oral compound was part of a new class of drugs called composite vascular protectants, or v-protectants, which were based on AtheroGenics' proprietary drug discovery platform. Unlike existing atherosclerosis drugs, which reduced risk factors for heart disease, v-protectants actually stopped the onset and progression of heart disease by lowering LDL cholesterol levels and controlling inflamed arteries.

In mid-1998, AtheroGenics signed a ten-year lease for a 50,000-square-foot, $8.5 million facility in Alpharetta, Georgia. The company's building was one of ten planned in the 26-acre North Point Research Park. Developed by Cousins Properties Inc., the park was the only one of its kind in Georgia.

In mid-1999, Phase II trials had commenced on AGI-1067, which had become AtheroGenics' lead compound, with the potential to become a multibillion-dollar heart drug. With hopes of bringing AGI-1067 to market in 2003, the second round of trials involved some 800 people.

Around this time, a major milestone was reached when AtheroGenics closed a third, $15.9 million round of venture capital funding, bringing its total to roughly $30 million. The funding was especially meaningful, given that the Georgia-based firm competed against drug developers in such high-profile markets as North Carolina (Research Triangle), California, and Boston.

During the late 1990s, AtheroGenics' workforce included nearly 40 employees. In addition to developing new drugs to treat atherosclerosis, the company also was working on compounds for treating asthma and arthritis.

In October 1999, AtheroGenics forged a global collaboration and licensing deal with Schering-Plough Corporation for the development of coronary artery disease drugs. The agreement included the development of AGI-1067, and involved up to $189 million in milestone payments, as well as royalties.

PUBLIC ENTERPRISE: 2000–02

AtheroGenics kicked off the new millennium with a bang. In February, the company filed for its initial public offering (IPO), with plans to trade on the NAS-DAQ National Market under the symbol AGIX. By this time, AtheroGenics' development pipeline had grown to include v-protectants for solid organ transplant rejection, as well as cystic fibrosis.

With shares priced at $8, AtheroGenics' August IPO generated $48 million, which was earmarked for the company's drug discovery program, including AGI-1067, which was in Phase II clinical trials. Driving the company's efforts was a staff that had grown to include 17 Ph.D.s, as well as five medical doctors and 12 employees with master's degrees.

AtheroGenics capped off 2000 with annual revenues of $8.2 million and operating expenses of $15.9 million. The company bolstered its discovery pipeline in early 2001, announcing plans to file an investigational new drug application for a compound aimed at treating rheumatoid arthritis. According to CEO Dr. Russell Medford, the development was especially important in that it demonstrated the wide range of potential applications for the company's v-protectant technology platform.

In March, an important leadership development occurred when James A. Sikorski, Ph.D., was named direc-

KEY DATES

1993: AtheroGenics is founded by Emory University cardiologists Russell M. Medford and Wayne Alexander.

1998: The company signs a ten-year lease for a new, $8.5 million facility in Alpharetta, Georgia.

2000: AtheroGenics generates $48 million from its initial public offering and begins trading on the NASDAQ National Market.

2002: The company is added to the Russell 2000 Index.

2003: AtheroGenics is included in the NASDAQ Biotechnology Index.

2007: When AGI-1067, a potential heart disease drug, fails to meet a composite benchmark score in a Phase III clinical trial, the company's stock price falls 60.5 percent.

2008: AtheroGenics announces positive results from a Phase III clinical trial that demonstrates AGI-1067 is effective as a type 2 diabetes treatment; files for Chapter 11 bankruptcy in October.

tor of medicinal chemistry and given the responsibility for developing AtheroGenics' medicinal chemistry strategies. Dr. Sikorski had invented or co-invented roughly 50 U.S. and foreign patents before joining the company, and had authored or coauthored approximately 90 research publications.

Midway through the year, AtheroGenics raised $20.6 million through the private placement of 3.59 million shares of common stock. Investors included JP-Morgan H&Q, SAFECO Growth Opportunities Fund, and Vulcan Ventures Inc. The placement provided funds needed for continued research and development efforts.

Around the same time, cofounder Dr. Russell Medford was recognized in the Emerging category of Ernst & Young's Entrepreneur of the Year award for the Southeast region. The recognition continued in January 2002 when Drs. Medford and Alexander, along with Michael Henos, received the Biomedical Community Award for 2001 from the Georgia Biomedical Partnership.

In mid-2002, an important milestone was reached when AtheroGenics was added to the Russell 2000 Index. By joining this stock market index, the company

and its shareholders stood to benefit from increased visibility.

Talented individuals continued to join AtheroGenics' executive staff during the early 2000s. New faces included Dr. Rob Scott, who had formerly served as Pfizer's vice-president and worldwide medical and therapeutic head. At AtheroGenics, Scott was chosen to serve as the company's senior vice-president of clinical development and regulatory affairs.

In November 2002 AtheroGenics announced that, in conjunction with the Montreal Heart Institute, it had received a CAD 5 million grant from the Canadian Institutes of Health Research to support a 12-month Phase IIb clinical trial of AGI-1067 that involved 500 patients at 24 clinical sites.

AGI-1067 MISSES BENCHMARK: 2003–06

In early 2003, AtheroGenics generated about $48 million from a public stock offering of 7.2 million shares, which it priced at $6.25 each. Midway through the year, the company moved forward with a Phase III clinical trial program for AGI-1067 that sought to prove if the drug was effective at reducing cardiac-related hospitalizations and deaths among heart attack patients. Developed by the Montreal Heart Institute's Jean-Claude Tardif and Harvard Medical School's Marc Pfeffer, the trial cost approximately $40 million and ultimately involved more than 6,000 patients who agreed to take AGI-1067 over a two-year period.

Positive developments continued into late 2003. On November 24, AtheroGenics was included in the NASDAQ Biotechnology Index. Early the following year, the company revealed plans to collaborate with Fujisawa Pharmaceutical Co. Ltd. for the development of AGI-1096, a new oral treatment for preventing organ transplant rejection.

Heading into the middle of the first decade of the 2000s, AtheroGenics' cash holdings totaled $67 million. In early 2005, this figure was bolstered with $200 million from the sale of convertible notes, the proceeds of which were earmarked for funding research and development efforts, including the Aggressive Reduction of Inflammation Stops Events (ARISE) Phase III clinical trial of AGI-1067.

Two years after announcing plans to develop its AGI-1096 organ transplant rejection drug, AtheroGenics reported positive results from its early studies of the compound. In early 2006 the company extended a research and development agreement with Astellas Pharma Inc. to continue studying AGI-1096.

Midway through the year, AtheroGenics promoted three key executives. Rob Scott, M.D., was named executive vice-president, research and development. Mark P. Colonnese was elevated to the position of executive vice-president, commercial operation. Finally, W. Charles Montgomery, Ph.D., became senior vice-president, business development and alliance management.

After posting no revenues for 2005, AtheroGenics saw its revenues increase to $31.7 million in 2006, most of which ($22.9 million) came from licensing fees the company received from a partnership with AstraZeneca. The tie-up, for the development and possible commercialization of AGI-1067, had been recognized as Best Partnership Alliance of the Year at the Annual Scrip Awards. Analysts estimated that, if successful, AGI-1067 held the potential to generate annual sales of $5 billion.

The company's research and development expenditures increased steadily during the middle years of the first decade of the 2000s, from $59.2 million in 2004 to $71.3 million in 2005 and $82.9 million in 2006. This largely stemmed from the ARISE Phase III clinical trial of AGI-1067.

CHANGING FOCUS: 2007–08

AGI-1067's success in the ARISE Phase III clinical trials depended on a composite benchmark score that was based on a number of different measures, including bypass surgery, death, heart attack, and stroke. When the compound failed to meet the composite benchmark at the conclusion of the trial in March 2007, the company's stock price fell 60.5 percent.

Following this setback, AtheroGenics focused on the potential of AGI-1067 as a diabetes treatment. In October 2007, Executive Vice-President of Research & Development and Chief Medical Officer Rob Scott left the company. He was succeeded by G. Alexander Fleming, M.D., a former senior physician at the U.S. Food and Drug Administration, who assumed the role of act-

ing chief medical officer. Dr. Fleming was given the responsibility of bringing AGI-1067 through a Phase III trial called Novel Anti-Diabetic Agent Evaluation Study (ANDES).

In July 2008, AtheroGenics announced positive results from the ANDES Phase III clinical trial, which demonstrated that AGI-1067, also known as succinobucol, was effective as a type 2 diabetes treatment.

In a July 31, 2008, news release, President and CEO Russell Medford said: "Based on the results of this successful trial, AtheroGenics intends to rapidly move forward with development of AGI-1067. We believe that AGI-1067, through its unique mechanism of action, could become the first diabetes treatment with demonstrated cardiovascular safety, and with the potential to reduce cardiovascular hard events including cardiovascular death, heart attack and stroke."

The fate of AGI-1067, in which the company had invested significant resources, remained in doubt. In October 2008, due to its "substantial debt burden," the company, by that time delisted from the NASDAQ, was forced to file for Chapter 11 bankruptcy protection. Atherogenics intended to sell virtually all of its assets, including the compound on which it had pinned its hopes.

Paul R. Greenland

PRINCIPAL COMPETITORS

Eli Lilly and Co.; GlaxoSmithKline plc; Merck & Co. Inc.

FURTHER READING

"AtheroGenics Shares Plunge After Heart Drug Fails in Trial," *New York Times,* March 20, 2007.

Herper, Matthew, "Inflamed Hearts," *Forbes,* June 23, 2003.

Robbins, Roni B., "$15 Million Capital Infusion," *Atlanta Business Chronicle,* July 2, 1999, p. A1.

Autostrada Torino-Milano S.p.A.

—■—

Corso Regina Margherita 165
Turin, I-10144
Italy
Telephone: (+39 011) 439211
Fax: (+39 011) 4392218
Web site: http://www.autostradatomi.it

Public Company
Incorporated: 1928 as S.A. Autostrada Torino-Milano
Employees: 1,705
Sales: EUR 823.44 million ($1.1 billion) (2007)
Stock Exchanges: Borsa Italiana
Ticker Symbol: AT.MI
NAICS: 237310 Highway, Street, and Bridge Construction

■ ■ ■

Autostrada Torino-Milano S.p.A. (ASTM) is the holding company for the second largest of the Big Three owner-operators of Italy's freeway system. ASTM, through its 63.4 percent control of publicly listed subsidiary SIAS (Società Iniziative Autostradali e Servizi), controls more than 1,100 kilometers of freeways, compared to sector leader Atlantia/Autostrade's 3,400-kilometer network, and smaller rival Autostrada del Brennero's 314 kilometers. ASTM's freeway holdings are operated through a number of separate companies. These include Società Autostrada Torino-Alessandria-Piacenza (SATAP), which operates both the 130-kilometer stretch of the A4 freeway between Turin and Milan, and the nearly 168-kilometer A21 freeway connecting Turin and

Piacenza. Other companies include SALT (Società Autostrada Ligure Toscana), nearly 155 kilometers; Autocamionale della Cisa, 182 kilometers between La Spezia and Parma; Società Autostrade Valdostane, 59.5 kilometers between Quincinetto and Aosta; Autostrada dei Fiori S.p.A., 113.2 kilometers between Savona and Ventimiglia; Società Autostrada Asti-Cuneo, 90 kilometers; and Autostrada Torino-Ivrea-Valle d'Aosta, 155.8 kilometers.

The company also has shareholdings in another 234 kilometers of freeways, including 43 kilometers of freeway in Chile operated by Costanera Norte S.A. These companies focus primarily on freeway operations and toll collection; other subsidiaries include SINA, SINECO, Ativa Engineering and Cisa Engineering, which provide planning and engineering services; and construction subsidiaries, including ABC Costruzioni and Itinera. Freeway revenues accounted for more than 86 percent of ASTM's total revenues of EUR 823 million ($1.1 billion) in 2007. ASTM is listed on the Borsa Italiana; more than 50 percent of the company is controlled by Italian construction conglomerate Gavio Group. Alberto Sacchi is ASTM's chief executive officer.

ITALIAN FREEWAY OPERATOR IN 1928

Italy's road system remained relatively rudimentary compared to its European neighbors in the early 20th century. The development of the automotive industry, and the need to provide more rapid roadways for automobiles, motorcycles, and trucks, prompted the Italian government to launch a new road-building effort

KEY DATES

1928: S.A. Autostrada Torino-Milano (later ASTM) is founded and begins construction of the Turin-Milan freeway, completed in 1932.
1969: The company goes public with a listing on the Turin stock exchange.
2002: ASTM creates SIAS, which takes over the group's freeway concessions along Italy's western corridor.
2007: ASTM transfers the remainder of its freeway operations into SIAS.

in the years following World War I. The government began building the country's first highways.

By 1922, a new term had been coined to describe a new type of highway, the *autostrada*. The autostrada featured limited access, relatively straight roads, with no stop signs, traffic lights, or other obstacles to slow the flow of traffic. The concept soon caught on, and Italy's European counterparts began developing their own freeway systems. Many countries simply adapted the name "Autostrada" to their own languages. As a result, the French developed the Autoroute, the Germans, the Autobahn, and the Spanish, the Autopistas.

The Fascist takeover of the Italian government in 1922 led to a new surge in Autostrada construction efforts. Indeed, the development of the country's freeway system played an important role in the Fascists' political, economic, and military objectives. In December 1992, the Fascist government created the country's first state-owned freeway company, Società Anonima Autostrade. That company became responsible for building and operating most of the country's original highways.

Italy's initial freeway construction efforts focused almost entirely on the northern regions, where most of the country's wealth and industrial infrastructure was located. Milan's role as the country's financial capital gave it strategic importance as a major hub for the developing motorway network. Many of the country's earliest road-building projects served to connect Milan to other major cities in the region. These included the Milan-Laghi roadway, and the Milano-Bergamo roadway, completed in 1927. While Autostrade oversaw this development, construction of new freeways often became the responsibility of dedicated state-owned enterprises created specifically for each new roadway.

This led to the formation of a new company, S.A. Autostrada Torino-Milano, in 1928. The Milan-Turin link was at the time one of the longest of the new freeway projects, with an initial length of 127 kilometers. Like the other branches of the freeway system, the Milan-Turin roadway crossed a relatively flat, easy-to-construct landscape. Construction of the freeway began in 1929, and was completed in 1932. The Turin-Milan highway ultimately reached a total length of 130 kilometers. The development of the Milan-Turin freeway helped play a role in the codification of the country's freeway system. In 1933, the Italian government established new legislation governing the specifications for subsequent extensions of the Autostrada network. Freeway construction continued through the end of the decade, including the construction of the Milan-Genova highway, the first to be built through the mountainous region. Also during the decade, the Italian government established plans to extend the Autostrada system as a fully integrated network of more than 6,850 kilometers.

REBUILDING AFTER WORLD WAR II

The Autostrada system's strategic importance made it a primary target for Allied bombing raids during World War II. By the end of the war, the country's highway and freeway systems had suffered massive damage. Hundreds of bridges had been destroyed, and nearly 15,000 kilometers of roads had been damaged.

Following the war, the new Italian government immediately set out to rebuild its roadway infrastructure. In order to facilitate the reconstruction effort, the government created a new body, ANAS, the Italian Roads Agency, as a central body to coordinate and regulate the construction and extension of the country's roadway system. With financial assistance from the Marshall Plan, ANAS succeeded in repairing the country's existing Autostrada system by 1954. At that time, the total network consisted of just 311 kilometers.

The extension of the Autostrada network began in earnest in the second half of the 1950s as ANAS. During this period, the government established the Autostrada as a toll-based system, and construction of the individual highways were turned over to a new pool of state-owned franchises.

This period saw the creation of most of the companies that were to make up the future ASTM group. The earliest of these was Autocamionale della Cisa SpA, founded in 1950. That company became responsible for the 102-kilometer freeway between La Spezia and Parma. In the later years of the first decade of the 2000s, it also began construction of an 81-kilometer extension to the Autostrada del Brennero.

Another of ASTM's holdings originated in the first half of the 1950s. The Autostrada Torino-Ivrea-Valle d'Aosta (ATIVA) was founded in 1954. ATIVA then launched construction of the Turin ring-road system, including extensions to nearby Santhia and Quincinetto, for a total length of 153 kilometers. Rounding out the 1950s was the establishment of Società Italiana Traforo del Gran San Bernardo, which held the concession for the 12.4-kilometer Gran San Bernardo tunnel.

The 1960s saw a new boom in freeway construction, with the founding of three future ASTM companies, Autostrada dei Fiori, Traforo del Frejus, and Società Autostrada Torino-Alessandria-Piacenza. The first company held the concession for the 113-kilometer Savona-Ventimiglia expressway. The second became the operator of the Frejus tunnel into France as well as the 94-kilometer freeway between Turin and Bardonecchia. The third, SATAP, was responsible for the nearly 168-kilometer motorway between Turin and Piacenza. That company later took over the original Turin-Malin freeway as well.

PUBLIC COMPANY IN 1969

Most of the remaining components of the future ASTM groups were in place by the early 1960s. One of the most important of these was Società Autostrada Ligure Toscana (SALT), founded in 1961. That company ultimately acquired the concessions for three motorways, Fornola to La Spezia; Viareggio to Lucca; and Sestri Levante to Livorno. The three combined reached a total length of nearly 155 kilometers. In 1962, the Autostrade Valdostane was created to build and operate a 59.5-kilometer highway linking Aosta and Quincinetto.

By the end of the 1960s, the Italian government's road-building program had succeeded in creating the second longest freeway network (after Germany) among Europe's major markets. The Autostrada system boasted more than 3,900 kilometers in 1970. Some two-thirds of the network remained under control of government-owned Autostrade, which had been re-formed in the 1950s. However, at the end of the 1960s, a number of the companies controlling the country's highway concession underwent a privatization.

Among these companies was Autostrada Torino-Milano (ASTM), which went public with a listing on the Turin Stock Exchange in 1969. The following year, the company moved its listing to the Borsa Italiana. ASTM quickly came under control of Marcellino Gavio and the Gavio Group, one of Italy's major engineering and construction companies.

The oil crisis of the 1970s led the Italian government to curtail its planned extensions to the freeway system. In 1975, the government placed a freeze on new highway construction, permitting only contracts already in place to proceed. As a result, Italy's highway network soon lagged behind its European counterparts. Into the new century, Italy's freeway system ranked fourth in the five largest European markets, behind Germany, Spain, and France, but ahead of the United Kingdom.

The difficult economic period saw a consolidation of much of Italy's Autostrada system. State-owned Autostrade remained by far the industry leader, continuing to control more than half of the country's total network into the next decade. Nonetheless, ASTM grew strongly as well, building up a range of companies and extending the motorways under its control to more than 1,000 kilometers. ASTM also remained unusual in its status as a publicly listed company; Autostrade's own privatization came only in 1999.

RESTRUCTURING IN THE 21ST CENTURY

The 1980s were marked by a series of measures to improve the Italian freeway system, notably through the widening of the highways to include more lanes. ASTM carried out its own upgrades program during this time. The company also began diversifying its operations, adding a number of subsidiaries specializing in planning and engineering for roadways and related networks, as well as technological services. In 1985, for example, the company founded Sinelec SpA, which specialized in developing advanced traffic management and toll payments systems. ASTM's operations also included its own roadway maintenance and other subsidiaries.

ASTM also became a vehicle for the Gavio Group's entry into a number of other sectors, especially the telecommunications sector. By 2000, ASTM held a 10.3 percent stake in Sitech, controlled by Autostrade, which in turn held 32 percent of Italy's then fourth largest mobile phone operator, Blu. ASTM's stake in Sitech also placed the company in position to become a minority partner in Autostrade's proposed entry into the fixed-line, fiber-optic based telecommunications market as well.

ASTM also eyed a number of other telecommunications initiatives at the time, particularly the entry into the regional telecommunications markets through a series of partnerships. In order to explore these opportunities, ASTM set up a joint venture with Argofin, the investment vehicle controlled by the Gavio family, which in turn controlled the majority of ASTM. In 2000, ASTM changed its bylaws in order to authorize the company's entry into the telecommunications market.

In any event, the crash of the global high-technology market, and the telecommunications market in general, cut short ASTM's telecommunications strategy. Instead, in 2002, ASTM moved to restructure parts of its freeway holdings, creating a new company, SIAS - Società Iniziative Autostradali e Servizi S.p.A. ASTM then transferred control of a number of its concessions to SIAS, focused on Italy's west coast corridor. These concessions included SALT, Autostrada dei Fiori, and Autocamionale della CISA, as well as Sinelec and the majority of ASTM Telecommunications. SIAS was then listed on the Borsa Italiana, with ASTM's stake in the company reduced to 63.4 percent.

The restructuring of the ASTM group continued in 2004. In that year, ASTM transferred the concession for the Turin-Milan freeway to its SATAP subsidiary. In this way ASTM itself moved toward more of a holding company status. The conversion of the company came in part because of the Gavio Group's increasing interest in investing in foreign highway groups. In 2005, for example, the company began talks with Autostrade toward launching a bid for one or more of the soon-to-be privatized French Autoroute operators. While the company failed in this ambition, it did acquire a 20 percent stake in Road Link (A69) Holdings Ltd., which held the management contract for the motorway between Newcastle and Carlisle in England. Another ASTM investment brought it to South America, where it acquired a stake in a 43-kilometer stretch of freeway in Chile operated by Costanera Norte S.A.

ASTM's focus remained, however, on the Italian motorway market, which continued to represent more than 86 percent of the company's revenues. ASTM launched a number of expansion and improvement efforts. Of note among these were the widening of the Turin-Milan freeway in order to accommodate traffic increases expected for the 2006 Winter Olympics; and the construction of the 81-kilometer linkup between Parma and the Autostrada del Brennero. Also in the later years of the first decade of the 2000s, the company launched construction of a new highway connecting Novara and Malpensa.

ASTM took the final step in its restructuring in 2007, when the company announced that it was transferring all of its remaining freeway operations to SIAS. The move helped increase the transparency of the company's operations and enhanced SIAS's own appeal to investors. The creation of a single, large-scale freeway company provided SIAS with the critical mass to raise the investment capital needed, while promising greater use of the company's financial resources. The ASTM-SIAS group remained Italy's second largest freeway concessionaire.

M. L. Cohen

PRINCIPAL SUBSIDIARIES

ADF: Autostrada dei Fiori S.p.A. (60.77%); Asti-Cuneo: Società Autostrada Asti-Cuneo S.p.A. (60%); ATIVA: Autostrada Torino-Ivrea-Valle d'Aosta S.p.A. (41.17%); CISA: Autocamionale della Cisa S.p.A. (84.44%); SALT: Società Ligure Toscana p.A. (87.39%); SATAP: Società Autostrada Torino-Alessandria-Piacenza S.p.A. (99.87%); SAV: Società Autostrade Valdostane S.p.A. (67.63%); SIAS - Società Iniziative Autostradali e Servizi S.p.A. (63.4%).

PRINCIPAL COMPETITORS

Autostrade per l'Italia S.p.A.; Autostrada del Brennero S.p.A.; Autostrada Brescia Verona Vicenza Padova S.p.A.; Autostrada dei Fiori S.p.A.

FURTHER READING

"Autostrada To-Mi H1 Net Down on Construction Ops, One-Off South America Cost," *AFX Europe,* August 5, 2008.

"Autostrada To-Mi, SIAS Reorganisation Delay Seen up to 3 Wks—Officials," *AFX Europe,* March 30, 2007.

"Autostrada To-Mi, SIAS See Asset Switch, Reorganisation Completed by End-June," *AFX Europe,* February 1, 2007.

"Autostrade e Gavio insieme in Francia per la Torino-Lione," *La Stampa,* August 10, 2005.

Benfratello, Luigi, Alberto Iozzi, and Paola Valbonesi, "Technology and Incentive Regulation in the Italian Motorway Industry," *Journal of Regulatory Economics,* October 25, 2008.

Greco, Andrea, "Regulation and Licensee Companies in the Italian Highways Network" (Università Degli Studi di Bergamo, 2004), http://www.unibg.it/highways.

Bank of America Corporation

———————◼———————

Bank of America Corporate Center
100 North Tryon Street
Charlotte, North Carolina 28255-0001
U.S.A.
Telephone: (704) 386-5681
Fax: (704) 386-6699
Web site: http://www.bankofamerica.com

Public Company
Incorporated: 1904 as Bank of Italy; 1960 as North Carolina National Bank
Employees: 299,000
Total Assets: $1.84 trillion (2008)
Stock Exchanges: New York London Tokyo
Ticker Symbol: BAC
NAICS: 522110 Commercial Banking; 522190 Other Depository Credit Intermediation; 522210 Credit Card Issuing; 522291 Consumer Lending; 522293 International Trade Financing; 522294 Secondary Market Financing; 523110 Investment Banking and Securities Dealing; 523120 Securities Brokerage; 523210 Securities and Commodity Exchanges; 523920 Portfolio Management; 523930 Investment Advice; 523991 Trust, Fiduciary, and Custody Activities; 525910 Open-End Investment Funds; 551111 Offices of Bank Holding Companies

◼ ◼ ◼

Bank of America Corporation is one of the largest financial institutions in the world, offering individuals, small and middle-market businesses, and large corporations a full range of banking, investing, asset management, and other financial products and services. The company serves more than 59 million consumer and small-business customers via one of the largest retail banking networks in the United States, encompassing more than 6,100 bank branches and nearly 18,700 ATMs across the nation, and through a heavily used online banking service as well. Bank of America is ranked number one or number two in terms of deposit market share in Arizona, California, Connecticut, Florida, Illinois, Kansas, Maryland, Massachusetts, Michigan, Missouri, New Jersey, New Mexico, North Carolina, Rhode Island, South Carolina, and Washington. After its acquisition of Merrill Lynch & Co., Inc., at the beginning of 2009, Bank of America ranked among the leading wealth management companies in the world and also became a global leader in corporate and investment banking and trading across a broad array of asset classes serving corporations, governments, institutions, and individuals in more than 40 countries around the world.

Bank of America is the product of the September 1998 merger of NationsBank Corporation and BankAmerica Corporation. The company bulked up further in the early 21st century through a series of major acquisitions: New England banking giant FleetBoston Financial Corporation (March 2004); credit and debit card behemoth MBNA Corporation (January 2006); leading private banking specialist U.S. Trust Corporation (July 2007); LaSalle Bank Corporation (October 2007), a major Midwest bank; mortgage giant Countrywide Financial Corporation (July 2008); and finally Merrill Lynch (January 2009), an investment banking titan with an extensive retail brokerage network. Bank of America's

COMPANY PERSPECTIVES

At Bank of America, our heritage is woven into our very name. When our earliest predecessor, the Massachusetts Bank, opened for business on July 5, 1784, the United States Constitution had yet to be adopted. The inauguration of George Washington as the nation's first president would not take place for another five years.

John Hancock signed the bank's charter in his role as Massachusetts Governor, making it the second bank to receive a state charter and one of only three commercial banks in existence in the United States at the time.

Generation after generation, the financial institutions that are part of the Bank of America legacy have played a role in the development of our nation's culture and economy. With a commitment to delivering higher standards and a drive to exceed expectations, Bank of America continues a proud tradition of service and performance.

stock has been a component of the Dow Jones Industrial Average since February 2008.

EARLY HISTORY OF BANKAMERICA CORPORATION

BankAmerica was founded in 1904 as the Bank of Italy. Its credo was radical at the time: to serve "the little fellows." From its humble beginnings in a former tavern, BankAmerica grew to become a force that revolutionized U.S. banking. With deregulation, however, its traditional emphasis on the general consumer created problems for the bank.

Amadeo Peter Giannini, founder of BankAmerica, became one of the most important figures in 20th-century American banking. Giannini, an Italian immigrant, was seven when his father died. By age 21, he had earned half ownership of his stepfather's produce business. He married into a wealthy family, and profits from the produce business, combined with shrewd real estate investments in San Francisco, enabled him to retire at age 31.

His retirement was brief. When his father-in-law died, he left a sizable estate, including a directorship of a small San Francisco savings bank. When Giannini failed to convince the board of this bank that the poor but hardworking people who had recently come to the West Coast were good loan risks, he resigned his position and set out to start his own bank, a bank for "people who had never used one."

The year, 1904, was an inauspicious one; an up-and-down economy and the financial irresponsibility of many banks during this period gave banking such a bad name that the government was eventually prompted to create the Federal Reserve system, in 1917. However, Giannini's bank was atypical. His policy of lending money to the average citizen was unheard of in the early 1900s, when most banks lent only on a wholesale basis to commercial clients or wealthy individuals.

Giannini raised capital for his new bank, called the Bank of Italy, by selling 3,000 shares of stock, mostly to small investors, none of whom were allowed to own more than 100 shares. Although Giannini never held a dominant share of stock, the extreme loyalty of these and subsequent stockholders allowed him to rule the bank as though it were closely held. His innovative policies made the Bank of Italy and its successor, the Bank of America of California, the most controversial bank in the United States. The nation watched with wary eyes as he created a system of branch banking that made it the world's largest bank in a mere 41 years.

During the famous San Francisco earthquake of 1906, Giannini rescued $80,000 in cash before the bank building burned by hiding it in a wagon full of oranges and bringing it to his house for safekeeping. With this money he reopened his bank days before any other bank and began making loans from a plank-and-barrel counter on the waterfront, urging demoralized San Franciscans to rebuild an even better city.

Giannini's original vision led naturally to branch banking. Expense made it difficult for small depositors to travel long distances to a bank, so Giannini decided his bank would go to them, with numerous well-placed branches. Accordingly, the Bank of Italy bought its first branch, a struggling San Jose bank, in 1909.

Giannini made up the rules as he went; he was not a banker, and his was the first attempt ever at branch banking. Going his own way included loudly denouncing the "big interests," and he repeatedly offended influential members of the financial community, including local bankers, major Californian bankers, and many state and federal regulators, who were already uncertain about how to handle an entirely new kind of banking. Some did support Giannini's vision though, including William Williams, an early California superintendent of banks, and the Crocker National Bank, which lent money to a subsidiary of the Bank of Italy expressly for acquiring branch banks.

KEY DATES

1865: In Virginia, the First National Bank of Richmond, forerunner of First & Merchants Corporation, is formed.

1874: Several prominent Charlotte, North Carolina, citizens form The Commercial National Bank.

1887: The Citizens Bank of Savannah, Georgia, begins operation.

1904: Amadeo Peter Giannini forms the Bank of Italy in San Francisco, California.

1906: Citizens Bank merges with Southern Bank to form Citizens and Southern (C&S) Bank.

1909: Bank of Italy buys its first branch, a struggling San Jose bank.

1927: California regulations allow for branch banking; Giannini consolidates his holdings into the Bank of America of California.

1928: Giannini forms holding company Transamerica.

1929: Bank of America surpasses $1 billion in assets; Blair and Company is purchased.

1930: Giannini consolidates his banking systems into the Bank of America National Trust and Savings Association, which falls under control of Transamerica.

1945: Bank of America becomes the world's largest bank during World War II.

1957: The Federal Reserve forces Transamerica to separate from Bank of America.

1960: The North Carolina National Bank is created.

1968: BankAmerica Corporation is created as a holding company for Bank of America N.T. & S.A.; NCNB Corporation is formed as a holding company for North Carolina National Bank.

1975: BankAmerica's assets reach $60 billion.

1981: BankAmerica begins to experience a loan crisis.

1982: NCNB expands into Florida.

1984: Virginia National Bankshares and First & Merchants Corp. merge to form Sovran Financial Corporation.

1987: BankAmerica begins restructuring efforts.

1990: C&S and Sovran merge.

1991: NationsBank Corporation is formed from the merger of NCNB and C&S/Sovran Corporation.

1992: BankAmerica and Security Pacific Corporation merge.

1997: NationsBank buys Boatmen's Bancshares, Inc., of St. Louis, Missouri.

1998: NationsBank purchases Barnett Banks, Inc.; BankAmerica and NationsBank merge in a $62 billion deal and officially adopt the name Bank of America Corporation soon thereafter.

2001: Kenneth D. Lewis is named chairman and CEO; company focuses on brand recognition.

2004: Bank of America acquires FleetBoston Financial Corporation; total assets pass the $1 trillion mark.

2006: Credit and debit card giant MBNA Corporation is acquired.

2007: Company acquires U.S. Trust Corporation and LaSalle Bank Corporation.

2008: Bank of America buys troubled mortgage giant Countrywide Financial Corporation; company posts its first quarterly loss in 17 years.

2009: Wall Street titan Merrill Lynch & Co., Inc., is acquired for $19.36 billion.

THE FORMATION OF BANK OF AMERICA OF CALIFORNIA AND TRANSAMERICA

The bank grew rapidly; in 1910 it had assets of $6.5 million. By 1920, assets totaled $157 million, far outstripping the growth of any other California bank and dwarfing its onetime benefactor, Crocker National. Further expansion was stymied, however, by the state of California and by the new Federal Reserve system, which did not allow member banks to open new branches. Giannini shrewdly sidestepped this regulation by establishing separate state banks for southern and northern California (in addition to the Bank of Italy) as well as another national bank, and putting them all under the control of a new holding company, BancItaly. Finally, in 1927, California regulations were changed to permit branch banking, and Giannini consolidated his four banks into the Bank of America of California.

With California conquered, Giannini turned to the national scene. He believed that a few large regional and national banks would come to dominate U.S. banking by using branches, and he intended to blaze the trail. He already owned New York's Bowery and East River National Bank (as well as a chain of banks in Italy); next he established Bank of America branches in Washington, Oregon, Nevada, and Arizona, again before branch banking was explicitly permitted.

Federal regulators, objecting to Giannini's attempts to dictate the law, took exception to some of his practices. In response, Giannini created another holding company in 1928, to supplant BancItaly. The new company was called Transamerica, to symbolize what Giannini hoped to accomplish in banking.

Giannini knew he needed a Wall Street insider to help him realize his dream of nationwide branch banking, and he thought Elisha Walker, the head of Blair and Company, an old-line Wall Street investment-banking firm, was just the man. Thus, in 1929, the year Bank of America passed the $1 billion mark in assets, Transamerica bought Blair.

A year later, Giannini consolidated his two banking systems into the Bank of America National Trust and Savings Association, under the control of Transamerica. Sixty years old and in poor health, he relinquished the presidency to Walker, retired for the second time, and went to Europe to recuperate. It was again a short retirement. His stay ended abruptly in 1931, when he received news that Walker was trying to liquidate Transamerica.

DRAMATIC PROXY FIGHT

Giannini headed straight for California, where three-quarters of the bank's stockholders remained. What followed was one of the most dramatic proxy fights in U.S. history. Giannini crisscrossed California, holding stockholder meetings in town halls, gymnasiums, courthouses, and other public spaces. A poor public speaker, he hired orators to drive home the message that Walker and eastern interests, the dreaded "big guys" Giannini had battled against for years, were trying to ruin the bank. The campaign succeeded and the stockholders returned control of the Bank of America to Giannini.

The bank had suffered, though. By the end of 1932, deposits had shrunk to $876 million, from a high of $1.16 billion in 1930. No dividend was paid that year, for the first time since 1905, and the battle had cost Giannini his New York banks. Depositor confidence had to be rebuilt.

Giannini's presence seemed to be just the right thing. By 1936, Bank of America was the fourth largest banking institution in the United States (and the second

largest savings bank), and assets had grown to $2.1 billion. The bank continued to innovate, instituting a series of new loans called Timeplan installment loans. Timeplan included real estate loans, new and used car financing, personal credit loans from $50 to $1,000, home appliance financing, and home-improvement loans, all industry firsts.

As the Bank of America became more influential, Giannini took on bigger and bigger foes, among them the Federal Reserve, Wall Street, the Treasury Department, the Securities and Exchange Commission (SEC), Hans Morgenthau, and J. P. Morgan Jr. Eventually, the enmity Giannini aroused in his war against the American financial establishment cost the bank its chance for nationwide branch banking. The beginning of the end came in 1937, when the Federal Reserve made its first attempt to force Transamerica and Bank of America to separate.

POSTWAR GROWTH

World War II brought tremendous growth to the Bank of America. As people and businesses flocked to California during the war, the bank more than doubled in size: In 1945, with assets of $5 billion, it passed Chase Manhattan to become the world's largest bank.

As California began to rival New York as the most populous state, Bank of America continued to expand. Giannini continued to battle, and win, against the big interests, until his death in 1949. From radical outsider to the leader of what *Business Week* called the "new orthodoxy" of banking—the trend toward serving average consumers—Giannini's was one of the most innovative careers in 20th-century banking.

He was succeeded as president of Transamerica by his son, Lawrence Mario, long a top official at the bank, who continued in his father's tradition. In 1952, however, Lawrence Mario succumbed to lifelong health problems. Following the deaths of the Gianninis, Bank of America slowly made itself over. New chief Clark Beise moved to decentralize operations, encouraging branch managers to assume more responsibility for their branches. This approach paid off with tremendous growth; by 1960, assets totaled $11.9 billion. The bank continued to innovate. In 1959 it was the first bank to fund a small-business investment company. It was also the first U.S. bank to adopt electronic and computerized record-keeping; by 1961, operations were completely computerized. Other new programs included student loans, an employee loan-and-deposit plan that let workers transact bank business through their offices (a response to increased competition from credit unions), and the first successful credit card, BankAmericard, the predecessor of Visa.

In addition, Bank of America stepped up its international presence, becoming one of only four U.S. banks with significant impact on international lending. It also began to pursue wholesale accounts, to supplement its traditional retail base. Finally, in 1957, the Federal Reserve forced Transamerica to separate from Bank of America, an event the two institutions had anticipated.

Bank of America's efforts to become a "department store of finance" in the late 1950s and early 1960s marked the last significant period of innovation in the bank's history until the 1980s. It was a time when the bank strove to sell the widest variety of banking services to the widest possible market. Beise felt there was more room for innovation, saying in 1959 that "there are new frontiers to develop," but warning that "we are constantly fighting against the attitude of entrenched success." It was a battle that the Bank of America lost, as it eventually became a conservative, stodgy, and inflexible institution.

THE FORMATION OF BANKAMERICA CORPORATION: 1968

In 1968 BankAmerica Corporation was created as a holding company to hold the assets of Bank of America N.T. & S.A. and to help the bank expand and better challenge its archrival, Citibank. This came just before banking deregulation, which affected Bank of America more adversely than was predicted. Bank of America's branch banking system was a major problem, since it gave the bank the highest overhead in the banking industry. Through this period the retail division provided 50 percent of the bank's profits. It was not until interest rates exploded in the 1970s that the bank's bulk of low-interest-bearing mortgages became damaging, as it was for many savings and loans.

As the largest bank in the world, the Bank of America was a natural target for groups with statements to make during the 1960s. It became the first major employer in California to sign a statement of racial equality in hiring. At the time, the Bank of America had more than 3,500 minority employees, more than 10 percent of its workforce. The bank also responded to complaints from women's groups by creating a $3.8 million fund for training female employees in 1974, and set itself the goal of a 40 percent female workforce.

By 1970 Bank of America had established a $100 million loan fund for housing in poverty-stricken areas and purchased municipal bonds that other California banks would not touch. This was in keeping with the tradition Giannini had established when he bought rural

school bonds and bonds for the Golden Gate Bridge at a time when no other bank would buy such issues.

A. W. "Tom" Clausen succeeded Rudy Peterson as CEO in 1971. He presided over Bank of America's last tremendous growth spurt; assets jumped 50 percent (to $60 billion) just between 1973 and 1975. Bank of America was the only one of the 20 largest U.S. banks to average 15 percent growth between 1971 and 1978; its seemingly unstoppable growth earned its management great praise during the 1970s.

RESTRUCTURING IN THE EIGHTIES

When Clausen left Bank of America in 1981 to head the World Bank, Bank of America had $112.9 billion in assets. Clausen was replaced by 40-year-old Samuel Armacost. Soon the Bank of America began to fall apart. Energy loans, shipping loans, farming loans (Bank of America was the largest agricultural lender in the world) and loans to Third World countries all started to go bad. Bank of America, whose large deposit base had traditionally made it exceptionally liquid but had also given it trouble in maintaining proper capital reserves, was ill prepared to meet the crisis. Suddenly, the biggest bank in the world had no money. It could not even raise capital in the stock market because its stock price had plummeted at a time when most bank stocks were rising.

Armacost started a general campaign to cut costs. The bank dropped a third of its 3,000 corporate clients, sold subsidiaries and its headquarters building, closed 187 branches, and began to lay off employees, something it had never done before. In 1986 the wounded BankAmerica became the target of a takeover bid from a company half its size. First Interstate Bancorp offered $2.78 billion for the nation's second largest banking group. A few days after this bid was made public in early October, Armacost resigned and was replaced by none other than Tom Clausen, the man many blamed for BankAmerica's troubles in the first place. Clausen resisted the takeover, but Joe Pinola, Interstate's chairman, was determined, and by the end of October had sweetened the deal to $3.4 billion. Clausen was equally determined to prevent BankAmerica's takeover. He rejected First Interstate's bid and battened down the hatches for a hostile assault. In the end, Clausen was able to rally shareholders behind him and thwart First Interstate's plans.

In 1987 BankAmerica set about restructuring its operations. Clausen sold nonessential assets—including the Charles Schwab discount securities brokerage and Bank of America's Italian subsidiary—and refocused the bank's attention on the domestic market. New services, including advanced automated teller machines (ATMs) and extended banking hours, lured California customers back. In addition, the bank went after the corporate business it had neglected in the early 1980s. Clausen cut back substantially on staff, cleaned up the nonperforming loans in Bank of America's portfolio, and hired a number of exceptional managers to execute BankAmerica's new directives. By the end of 1988, the bank was in the black again. Although still plagued by a good deal of exposure to Third World debt, BankAmerica was able to record a profit of $726 million, its first in three years.

By 1989, BankAmerica's recovery was so strong that it was able to declare its first dividend since the fourth quarter of 1985. Industry analysts called the recovery the biggest turnaround in the history of U.S. banking. Retail operations were expanded in Nevada with the acquisition of Nevada First Bank, and in Washington with the purchase of American Savings Financial Corporation by the subsidiary Seafirst Corporation, the largest bank in the Pacific Northwest. During this year, BankAmerica was the first major bank in California to announce that it would open all its branches on Saturdays and extend weekday hours for greater consumer convenience.

ACQUISITIONS AND MERGERS IN THE NINETIES

In 1990 BankAmerica showed further evidence of its recovery by announcing that its revenues exceeded $1 billion for the first time. Industry analysts theorized that the bank had the cleanest loan portfolio of the nation's big banks. Acquisitions included Woodburn State Bank of Oregon, Western Savings and Loan branches in Arizona, and Benjamin Franklin and MeraBank Federal Savings, the largest S&Ls in Oregon and Arizona, respectively. The bank also opened a new international branch in Milan, Italy.

Also in 1990, BankAmerica surpassed Chase Manhattan to become the second largest bank holding company in the nation. In addition, in keeping with the bank's policy of community responsibility, it began an Environmental Program that included activities directed toward saving paper and other materials through recycling and energy and water conservation.

Seeking to expand its operations beyond its branches in seven western states, the bank added branches in two more states with the 1991 acquisitions of ABQ and Sandia Federal Savings banks of New Mexico, and Village Green National Bank in Houston. Another purchase was a subsidiary of GNA Securities that had operated an investment program in the bank's

branches since 1988. The program, called Bank of America Investment Services, offered mutual funds and tax-deferred annuities. In spite of the nation's economic recession at this time as well as higher deposit insurance premiums and higher credit losses and nonaccruals, BankAmerica was able to post its third straight year of record earnings, more than $1 billion.

Expanding services to customers continued with the opening of full-service branches in grocery stores in southern California. In addition, to allow customers access to money anytime and anywhere, the bank opened several hundred new Versateller ATMs for a total of 2,300 in nine states.

After nine months of preparation, the merger of BankAmerica and Security Pacific Corporation became final on April 22, 1992. After the merger BankAmerica became the nation's second largest bank. The joining of the California banks was the largest merger in the history of banking at the time and created an institution with nearly $190 billion in assets and $150 billion in deposits. The merger was part of a national trend of bank consolidation that sought to strengthen troubled and even healthy institutions. For BankAmerica, the merger offered an opportunity to become more efficient and save money, an estimated $1.2 billion annually within the next three years. The merger also helped the bank expand into new markets and geographic locations. By the end of 1992, consumer banking services were provided in ten western states, trust and consumer financial services were provided nationwide, and commercial and corporate banking operations were located in 35 countries worldwide.

Acquisition activity continued with the purchase of Sunbelt Federal Savings, which held 111 branches in 76 cities in Texas; HonFed, the largest thrift in Hawaii; and Valley Bank of Nevada, which made BankAmerica the largest depository institution in that state. However, the persistent national recession, combined with a recession in the state of California, caused a decline in earnings reported for 1992.

Domestic expansion continued in 1993 with the acquisition of First Gibraltar of Texas and with an agreement to make a $1 million equity investment in Founders National Bank, the only African-American-owned bank on the West Coast. Additional overseas expansion occurred when BankAmerica received approval from the People's Bank of China to upgrade its Guangzhou representative office into a full-service branch, the first U.S. bank to have such a branch. Consolidation of consumer and commercial finance units was undertaken, and one year after the merger, the bank had consumer operations in much of the United States, wholesale offices in 37 nations, retail branches in ten western states, and consumer finance company operations in 43 states.

As BankAmerica moved into the mid-1990s, it focused on many of the policies it had begun in the 1980s. Under the leadership of David Coulter, named chairman and CEO in 1996, BankAmerica's strategies included development of new products and services for consumers; geographic diversification into such fast-growing economies as Asia and Latin America, which would enable the bank to better withstand the economic cycles of the domestic market; community investments; environmental programs; and loans to students and those with low income. BankAmerica also continued to hope for changes in laws and regulations that would allow interstate banking and more effective competition with nonbank institutions providing similar financial services. The company got its wish when federal laws began to allow banks to participate in the securities industry. Consequently, BankAmerica purchased investment banking firm Robertson, Stephens & Co. in 1997 for $540 million.

HISTORY OF NATIONSBANK CORPORATION

NationsBank was one of the United States' largest banking and financial companies. Based in Charlotte, North Carolina, the company grew at breakneck speed through the late 1980s and early 1990s to claim a spot as one of the nation's top five financial institutions. Industry analysts credited this phenomenal growth to the company's foundation of bold, aggressive management and thorough, professional planning. They also credited the company's success to the personality and leadership of Hugh L. McColl Jr., who served as NationsBank's CEO from 1983 to 1998 and then as Bank of America Corp.'s chairman and CEO until 2001. McColl's style—a southern-born and bred ex-Marine—contrasted sharply with that of most members of the banking community and contributed to NationsBank's image as one of the mavericks of the banking world.

NationsBank was officially formed on December 31, 1991, with a merger between the $69 billion asset NCNB Corporation and the $49 billion asset C&S/Sovran Corporation. The merger created the fourth largest banking company in the United States. McColl became the first president and CEO of NationsBank, and Bennett A. Brown became the first chairman.

The two companies entered the merger having both completed a decade of rapid growth that was typical of the banking industry in the 1980s. NCNB and C&S/Sovran both followed the common industry pattern of numerous mergers and acquisitions in the 1980s. After

expanding into South Carolina and Florida in the early to mid-1980s, Charlotte-based NCNB took an unprecedented leap forward through a unique expansion into Texas in 1988. The FDIC selected NCNB to manage the restructured subsidiary banks of First RepublicBank Corporation of Texas. Atlanta-based C&S Bank had banking offices throughout Georgia, Florida, and South Carolina. In 1990 this company merged with similarly sized Sovran Financial of Norfolk, Virginia. Sovran had banking offices throughout Virginia, the District of Columbia, and Maryland, as well as in Tennessee and Kentucky. After these two companies merged, the resulting organization established dual headquarters in Atlanta and Norfolk.

THE GROWTH OF NCNB

NCNB traced its illustrious history back to the Commercial National Bank, which was organized by several prominent Charlotte citizens in 1874. Its initial start-up capital was $50,000. A series of mergers with other North Carolina financial institutions in the 1950s ultimately led to the creation of North Carolina National Bank on July 1, 1960. At the time of its formation, North Carolina National had 1,300 employees, 40 offices in 20 North Carolina communities, and assets of $480 million. The bank continued to acquire smaller institutions, and in 1968 it was reorganized under a bank holding company called NCNB Corporation. By 1969 NCNB had grown to 91 offices in 27 North Carolina counties with deposits of more than one billion dollars. Ten years later, it stood as the state's largest bank.

In the mid-1950s, however, when the nation talked about banking in the state of North Carolina, most people were talking about Wachovia Bank and Trust Company, NCNB's archrival. Based in Winston-Salem, Wachovia had offices from the mountains to the coast and exercised considerable political clout in the capital city of Raleigh. Bankers at other institutions stood in envy of Wachovia. Many bankers thrived on the competition, and some, such as Addison Reese at American Commercial Bank, one of NCNB's predecessor institutions, in Charlotte, considered that competition the reason for going to work each morning.

At the time, Reese believed that North Carolina banking was poised for a change, and nothing could stop him from meeting Wachovia's threats. North Carolina's banking laws were more liberal than in most states. They had been on the books since the early 1800s, when a Wilmington, North Carolina, bank appealed to the state legislature for permission to open an office about 90 miles away in Fayetteville. The legislature complied with the bank. Unlike lawmakers in most states, the North Carolina legislature saw no reason to restrict branch banking during the intervening 150 years. In retrospect, many people believe that it was the close competition with backyard rival Wachovia that spurred NCNB's rapid growth.

NCNB broke new ground when it expanded into Florida in January 1982 with its purchase of First National Bank of Lake City, Florida. At the time, it became the first non-Florida bank to expand its retail services into the state. After a quick approval of the purchase by the Federal Reserve Board of Governors, NCNB rapidly purchased several other Florida banks.

In 1986 NCNB benefited from a change in North Carolina's interstate banking laws. With the advent of reciprocal interstate banking in the Southeast, NCNB moved into South Carolina with the purchase of Bankers Trust Company. It acquired Southern National Bankshares of Atlanta in 1985 and Prince William Bank of Dumfries, Virginia, in 1986. NCNB moved into Maryland in 1987 with the purchase of CentraBank of Baltimore. In 1989 NCNB acquired full ownership of First RepublicBank in Texas. During this period of growth, NCNB established several "firsts" in its industry. For example, NCNB was the first U.S. bank to use commercial paper to finance the activities of non-bank subsidiaries; to open a branch in London; to operate a full-service securities company; and to list its common stock on the Tokyo Exchange.

THE DEVELOPMENT OF C&S/SOVRAN

The C&S/Sovran side of the NationsBank puzzle traced its earliest roots back to 1865 and the opening in Virginia of the First National Bank of Richmond. At the time, its customer base included Confederate army commander Robert E. Lee. In 1926 this bank merged with another Richmond bank, Merchants National Bank, forming First & Merchants National Bank, forerunner of First & Merchants Corporation. In 1984 First & Merchants merged with Norfolk-based Virginia National Bankshares to form Sovran Financial Corporation. This amalgamation, the largest banking merger in Virginia's state history, created the state's largest bank. The new name was a variation of the word *sovereign*.

Sovran's management team decided to merge with D.C. National Bancorp, headquartered in Bethesda, Maryland, in 1986. By November 1987, Sovran was moving west by merging with Commerce Union, a 71-year-old bank holding company based in Nashville. Commerce Union's business at the time spanned Tennessee and had a presence in Kentucky. The merger gave Sovran strongholds in both of those states.

Around the time Sovran's foundations were being laid, the Citizens Bank of Savannah, Georgia, opened its doors in the temperate coastal city on November 2, 1887. At the time, the bank had $200,000 in start-up capital. In 1906 it merged with its crosstown rival, Southern Bank of the State of Georgia, to form Citizens and Southern Bank of Georgia. The resulting organization became the state's largest financial institution. It began to spread rapidly across the state of Georgia. Citizens and Southern began opening offices in South Carolina in 1928, but the company sold its operations there in 1940 when it anticipated federal rules preventing banks from owning branches in multiple states. The resulting C&S Bank of South Carolina was rejoined with Citizens and Southern in 1986 when the Georgian giant bought them back. That acquisition, along with the purchase of Landmark Banks of Florida in 1985, helped Citizens and Southern double its size within 18 months during the mid-1980s.

C&S also claimed several firsts in the industry. Among the highlights in C&S history were being the first bank to figure "to the penny" balances, one of the first to offer checking accounts in the South and to issue its own credit card, and the first bank in the nation to offer 24-hour access to its services via ATMs. In 1971 the nation's first ATM was set up in Valdosta, Georgia, under the C&S banner.

In the spring of 1989, C&S was successful in resisting a takeover bid by NCNB. At the time, C&S cited what it considered a low price offer and concerns about NCNB's entry into the then-depressed Texas banking market. Soon thereafter, C&S and Sovran merged in a deal finalized on September 1, 1990.

THE C&S/SOVRAN AND NCNB MERGER

The banking environment, however, was in the midst of tremendous change. Large banks were continuing to consolidate. As a result, smaller banks were under constant pressure to find new ways to improve their efficiency and productivity and reduce their workforces. In addition, the nation as a whole experienced a downturn in the real estate market, an area responsible for much of an average bank's business. The newly merged C&S/Sovran Corporation (the merger was announced in the spring of 1989 and consummated in the fall of 1990) was suffering from the recession in the Southeast, and it had been particularly hard hit by mounting losses on loans in the District of Columbia metropolitan area. Real estate loans made up 32 percent of the bank's $34 billion portfolio at the end of 1990, with Washington, D.C., accounting for 21 percent of the real estate total. C&S/Sovran's stock price had dropped from $35.88 at the close of the first quarter in 1989, when NCNB announced its merger intentions, to $15.63 at the close of the fourth quarter in 1990. Under these circumstances, NCNB renewed its offer to merge with C&S/Sovran.

Prior to reissuing his offer, McColl gathered with his advisers. According to Howard E. Covington Jr. and Marion A. Ellis in the 1993 book *The Story of Nations-Bank: Changing the Face of American Banking,* McColl told Senior Vice-President C. J. "Chuck" Cooley, "I am going to buy C&S/Sovran. I don't know when. I don't know how." He instructed Cooley to hire the best talent available and deliver a complete psychological profile on C&S/Sovran's key players, including Bennett Brown and Dennis Bottoroff. Cooley handled the job himself, and several weeks later, he handed McColl a profile of Brown as well as a profile of McColl himself, as seen by Brown.

Cooley told his boss that the keys to Brown's relationships with people were honesty, sincerity, warmth, and friendliness. To McColl's chagrin, however, each of those traits was opposite of the characteristics that McColl portrayed to Brown. From Brown's vantage point, McColl was arrogant, crude, and ungentlemanly. After hearing Cooley's report, McColl and several other advisers began an intense series of role-playing sessions. McColl was schooled to avoid the use of militaristic terms and other verbal and nonverbal examples of his usual aggressive style. His staff coached him to become softer, more receptive, and friendlier in his approach.

Meanwhile, McColl's confidence was growing as C&S/Sovran's problems continued to multiply. The credit problems in the D.C. area increased, and the bank's board split badly between an Atlanta faction and a Tennessee and Virginia faction. News filtered down to the NCNB leaders that although both factions preferred to remain independent, a merger with NCNB was the second choice among those on both sides. With this knowledge, McColl renewed his merger efforts with Brown.

On June 20, McColl departed Charlotte in the NCNB plane for Atlanta to make Brown a second offer. The two banking leaders sat down in Brown's home to discuss the terms of the deal. Brown's concerns were predictable: He wanted to know about leadership, cuts in personnel and staff, the name of the new bank, and—most important—the price.

McColl supplied the right answers to all of Brown's questions. The merged bank would carry the name Na-tionsBank, which eased concerns about the North Carolina flag flying over Georgia. Shortly after NCNB's Texas acquisitions, the marketing group began experimenting with new names that would better reflect the company's size and geographic diversity, as well as be more acceptable in new markets. At that time, the company began working with the Naming Center in Dallas. The Naming Center enlisted the work of academic linguists who worked with Latin teachers and poets to develop names rather than generating them by computers.

On the list of prospective names was the word *Nation.* Using poster-sized flash cards, the company combined two of them to create the single word *NationsBank.* Everyone was surprised when lawyers determined that the new name was not in use anywhere else in the world, and it soon cleared marketing surveys conducted nationwide. Ironically, NationsBank consistently scored as one of the most recognized and highly regarded names in banking, although it had never been used before. The corporate identity firm of Siegel and Gale in New York then developed a graphic look for the word that would reinforce its characteristics.

As for the issue of leadership, McColl wanted Brown to take the chairmanship, while he retained the title of CEO and president. McColl also pulled a sheet of paper from his coat that illustrated an exchange of 0.75 shares of NCNB stock for each share of C&S/Sovran. That exchange would mean a total payout of $3.99 billion for C&S/Sovran's shareholders. Brown was receptive to the deal, but could not supply McColl with a firm answer.

It was on June 25 that the news about the probable merger broke in the Charlotte community. Even the national media focused on the possibility of this mega-deal between these banks in the South. C&S/Sovran's leadership soon received the second offer with enthusiasm. Among other issues, NCNB had proven the wisdom and success of the large Texas acquisition, and C&S/Sovran was seeking the efficiencies and economies of scale inherent in a merger of this magnitude. The merger was approved by the Federal Reserve on November 29, 1991, and NationsBank officially opened its doors on January 2, 1992. At the time of the union, NCNB was the tenth largest bank in the United States, and C&S/Sovran was the 12th largest. Together, they thrust each other to a position among the top three banking leaders in the United States.

CHARLOTTE HEADQUARTERS FOR NATIONSBANK

The new entity quickly went to work to establish its presence in its chosen corporate headquarters city of Charlotte. NCNB's office buildings jutted into the southern skyline, but as NationsBank the company decided to build a new headquarters building. The result of this goal was the new NationsBank Corporate Center, a pristine 60-story tower designed by architect Cesar Pelli. At the time it was built, it became the tallest building in the Southeast, and NationsBank firmly established itself as one of the nation's financial heavyweights. As tribute to the man who led this building effort, many Charlotte onlookers began to call the new Corporate Center the "Taj McColl."

The new bank had more domestic deposits than New York's Citibank, market capitalization to rival J. P. Morgan & Co., more branch offices than almost any other competitor, and assets of nearly $120 billion. In addition to serving as a leader in the financial world, in the early 1990s NationsBank served as a role model to the larger corporate community as well. Nationwide, it was known as a company that exercised not only sound management practices, but cultural consciousness as well. Under McColl's leadership, NCNB had established flexible hours for working parents and a pretax childcare expense reimbursement fund. Maternity leave was extended to six months, and the concept was expanded to include time off for new fathers. These groundbreaking policies attracted the attention of the *Wall Street Journal,* which in its centennial issue edition in 1989 selected NCNB as one of 12 companies in the world to watch in the future. *Fortune* magazine in a January 1989 issue also chose McColl as one of the previous year's 25 most fascinating businesspeople, the only one selected from the banking industry.

The company's financial strength also served as a resource for the many communities it supported. Charlotte itself was one of the nation's fastest growing metropolitan areas, due largely to the growth and visibility of NationsBank. In 1994, the company had 1,800 branch offices, which made it the second largest branch network in the United States. By providing traditional banking products to retail and corporate customers, as well as investing in innovative products and services, the company's assets had grown to $165 billion.

As the banking industry continued to consolidate and change during the mid-1990s, NationsBank made several key purchases. In October 1993 the company acquired MNC Financial Inc., parent of Maryland National Bank, for $1.39 billion. At the time of the takeover, MNC had total assets of $16.5 billion. In January 1997 NationsBank completed the $9.77 billion acquisition of Boatmen's Bancshares, Inc., a St. Louis, Missouri-based bank with total assets and deposits of $41.2 billion and $32 billion, respectively. McColl commented on the purchase in a 1997 *St. Louis Business Journal* article, claiming that "it brings NationsBank into contact with 100 million Americans, 40 percent of

the population. That's exciting to us. Also, I'm a classical strategist. It denies it to the enemy, the enemy being everyone else." NationsBank then went on to purchase Barnett Banks, Inc., Florida's largest bank, with total assets of $46 billion and total deposits of $35.4 billion. The $14.6 billion deal was completed in January 1998.

THE 1998 BANKAMERICA AND NATIONSBANK MERGER

NationsBank, which had completed more than 70 deals since 1980, made another aggressive move in 1998 when McColl approached BankAmerica's Coulter about merging the two companies. Both McColl and Coulter knew that by joining forces, the combined entity would be the first coast-to-coast banking company in the United States with $572 billion in assets and offices in 22 states. Coulter agreed to a "merger of equals," and on April 13, 1998, BankAmerica announced that it would team up with NationsBank in a $48.7 billion merger. It soon became apparent however, that NationsBank would be the dominant partner. A month prior to the completion of the deal on September 30, 1998, BankAmerica sold Robertson Stephens to BankBoston Corporation because NationsBank owned a directly competitive, and larger, investment banking firm, Montgomery Securities, Inc. NationsBank had acquired the San Francisco-based Montgomery in October 1997 for $1.2 billion.

The merged entity, whose name officially became Bank of America Corporation, took headquarters in Charlotte and served 30 million households in the United States as well as customers in 38 different countries. McColl assumed control of the new company as chairman and CEO. Coulter, however, resigned his presidency in the fall of 1998 amid speculation that he and McColl had come into conflict over some of BankAmerica's previous bad loans and lost earnings. McColl, slated to retire after the deal, had his work cut out for him upon completion of the merger, as he tried to integrate both the BankAmerica and NationsBank combination and the purchases both companies had made just before their merger. Industry analysts began to speculate that perhaps McColl may have taken on more than he could handle with the BankAmerica deal.

During 1999 and into 2000, Bank of America was plagued with integration problems that forced it to post lower than anticipated revenue growth, net income, and earnings. The company cited credit problems and bad loans as culprits in its lackluster financial performance. As such, Bank of America began to restructure in order to streamline operations. Nearly 10,000 jobs were cut, mostly in middle management. The firm also began to refocus on customer service.

McColl retired in April 2001 and left Kenneth D. Lewis to take over as chairman and CEO. Lewis, who had served as president and COO since 1999, began his banking career at NCNB in 1969. Under new leadership, Bank of America turned its efforts to independent growth, which had taken a backseat to deal-making activity for years. "Our priority is organic growth. Our strategy is to deepen, to expand relationships ... and to focus on quality of service," claimed Bank of America's chief financial officer James Hance in a 2001 *American Banker* article. The company also went to work on its brand image, increasing its 2002 advertising budget to $145 million, an increase of 50 percent over the previous year.

By early 2002, Bank of America stood as the largest bank in the United States in terms of deposits. During that year and the next few that followed, the company was the recipient of a spate of bad press stemming from a series of blunders and scandals. In 2002 Bank of America paid nearly $500 million to settle shareholder lawsuits that had been brought accusing it of misleading investors about financial problems that resulted from the NationsBank-BankAmerica merger. The bank in March 2004 agreed to pay $675 million to settle charges it had helped a hedge fund illegally trade mutual fund shares. That same month, Bank of America, in the course of an insider trading investigation, paid $10 million to the SEC for improperly handling e-mails and not disclosing to the SEC that certain requested documents had been destroyed. At the time, this was the largest such fine the SEC had imposed for such infractions. Bank of America in July 2004 paid $69 million to settle a lawsuit brought by Enron Corporation shareholders accusing the bank of participating in a scheme to hide Enron debt via off-balance-sheet maneuvers. Finally, in March 2005 Bank of America agreed to pay $460.5 million to settle a suit initiated by WorldCom Inc. shareholders alleging that the bank had sold now-worthless WorldCom bonds without conducting proper due diligence.

ACQUISITIONS OF FLEETBOSTON, MBNA, U.S. TRUST, AND LASALLE

Despite these embarrassing episodes, Bank of America kept its shareholders happy with steadily increasing earnings and dividends. By 2004 net income had soared to $14.14 billion, nearly double the total for 2000, and the company's total assets surpassed the $1 trillion mark for the first time. In March 2004 Bank of America completed the first of a string of mammoth acquisitions, spending about $47.25 billion for FleetBoston Financial Corporation. FleetBoston, the result of the October 1999 merger of Fleet Financial Group, Inc., and Bank-

Boston Corporation, was the largest bank in New England with nearly 1,500 branches and 3,400 ATMs. Purchasing FleetBoston strengthened Bank of America's position as the nation's largest consumer bank by deposits and expanded its national footprint, providing it with a leading market share for every U.S. region except the Upper Midwest. The integration of FleetBoston, which entailed the elimination of thousands of jobs from the two banks' combined workforces, was completed in 2005, when merger-related cost savings of $1.85 billion were realized. Also in 2005, Bank of America gained a foothold in China's rapidly evolving banking sector by buying a 9 percent stake in China Construction Bank (CCB) for $3 billion. CCB was the third largest commercial bank in China with around $550 billion in assets and $470 billion in deposits. Bank of America also gained an option to increase its stake in CCB to 19.9 percent by the end of 2010.

In January 2006 Bank of America more than doubled its credit-card business and became the largest issuer of general-purpose Visa and MasterCard credit and debit cards in the United States by acquiring Wilmington, Delaware-based MBNA Corporation for $34.58 billion. Following the takeover, Bank of America's card servicing unit had more than 40 million active accounts and nearly $140 billion in outstanding card balances. The MBNA acquisition helped the company achieve record results in 2006 of $21.13 billion in net income, a 28 percent increase over 2005, and $74.25 billion in revenues, a 30 percent increase. By the end of 2006, Bank of America's total assets approached $1.5 trillion.

Bank of America completed two more major deals in 2007. In July the company paid $3.3 billion to acquire U.S. Trust Corporation from the Charles Schwab Corporation. Adding the venerable U.S. Trust, founded in 1853, substantially strengthened Bank of America's private banking business, that sector of the banking world catering to wealthy clients. In October, Bank of America acquired Chicago-based LaSalle Bank Corporation from ABN AMRO Holding, N.V. for $21 billion. Securing LaSalle provided Bank of America with a significant addition to its U.S. retail banking empire as it instantly gave the company the leading market share positions in both Chicago and Michigan, with Chicago being the only major U.S. market in which it had lacked a leading position. LaSalle served 17,000 commercial banking clients and 1.4 million retail customers through 400 bank branches and 1,500 ATMs. Following the LaSalle deal, Bank of America's overall U.S. banking network encompassed around 6,100 branches and 18,500 ATMs.

Also in 2007, as the credit crunch and subprime lending crisis unfolded, Bank of America's investment of

$2 billion in troubled mortgage giant Countrywide Financial Corporation helped to stabilize the credit markets, at least temporarily. Countrywide, the largest mortgage lender in the nation, had been a major originator of subprime and other risky loans during the housing bubble of the first years of the 21st century, and thus by 2007 was struggling amid rising defaults and falling home values. Although Bank of America's mortgage business had been run much more conservatively, the company's overall results for 2007 reflected the negative environment, particularly because of substantial holdings in collateralized debt obligations and structured investment vehicles, two key financial instruments that had been used to fund the mortgage markets. Bank of America was forced to write down the value of these securities by $5.6 billion, and it also had to increase its provision for loan losses from $5 billion to $8.4 billion. Consequently, net income fell for the first time since 2001; the 2007 total of $14.98 billion was 29 percent lower than that of 2006.

BULKING UP FURTHER DURING GLOBAL ECONOMIC CRISIS

Bank of America began 2008 by agreeing to acquire Countrywide outright. The $2.5 billion stock-swap deal closed in July of that year. When the economy deteriorated into a full-blown crisis later in 2008 that particularly undermined the titans of Wall Street, Bank of America after 48 hours of frenetic negotiating agreed to acquire Merrill Lynch & Co., Inc., one of those very titans. The all-stock deal was initially valued at $50 billion, but the plunging value of Bank of America's stock over the course of 2008 slashed the purchase price down to $19.36 billion when the takeover was consummated on January 1, 2009. Although, like the Countrywide acquisition, the Merrill Lynch deal was risky because of the Wall Street firm's billions in troubled assets, it finally provided Bank of America with something it had long coveted, a top-flight investment bank. Even more importantly, Bank of America gained Merrill's "thundering herd" of 16,000-plus stockbrokers, who managed about $1.6 trillion in assets on behalf of their clients. Integrating Merrill's operations were sure to pose a particular challenge, and Bank of America announced plans to eliminate about 35,000 positions from the combined workforces over a three-year period, a reduction of more than 10 percent. An additional 7,500 jobs were be to cut to integrate Countrywide as Bank of America sought to reduce annual expenses companywide by $7 billion.

In the meantime, as part of the financial bailout plan called the Troubled Asset Relief Program, the U.S. government propped Bank of America up through a

$25 billion purchase of preferred shares. In October 2008 Bank of America slashed its quarterly dividend in half to shore up its balance sheet, raised $10 billion in additional capital through a secondary stock offering, and reached a settlement with state attorneys general whereby it agreed to launch a loan modification program for as many as 390,000 borrowers who had taken on subprime and other risky loans originated by Countrywide. The loan modifications had the potential to cost Bank of America more than $8 billion. During the second half of 2008, the company increased its stake in China Construction Bank to just above 19 percent by investing nearly $9 billion more. In the year's fourth quarter, Bank of America posted its first quarterly loss since its predecessor NCNB recorded one in 1991. The company lost $1.79 billion as it had to set aside $8.54 billion for bad loans and wrote down more than $2.5 billion in troubled securities. Provisions for bad loans for the full year totaled $26.83 billion, more than three times the amount for 2007. The net income of just over $4 billion for 2008 was 73 percent below the year-earlier total.

Doubts about Lewis's acquisition spree during the economic crisis, coupled with ongoing pessimism about the health of the overall financial sector, sent Bank of America's stock down 66 percent over the course of 2008. By the time the company announced its dismal 2008 results in mid-January 2009, the stock had fallen a further 24 percent to its lowest level since 1991. Bank of America again slashed its dividend to just a penny (down from 64 cents a year earlier). Unexpected losses of around $15 billion at Merrill Lynch during 2008's fourth quarter had nearly scuttled Bank of America's takeover, but the company had pushed ahead after receiving assurances of further government aid. Thus, two weeks after the completion of the Merrill takeover, Bank of America garnered an additional federal government infusion of $20 billion. The U.S. Treasury also agreed to backstop some $118 billion in toxic assets, most of which came from Merrill's balance sheet.

Although Bank of America, and Lewis in particular, had earned the reputation for carrying out smooth acquisition integrations, the absorption of Merrill Lynch, given the Wall Street firm's level of bad assets as well as the deepening global economic crisis, seemed likely to prove particularly nettlesome. The acquisition of Merrill even had the potential to send Bank of America into insolvency. Some observers believed that further government intervention was inevitable and even speculated that the nascent administration of President Barack Obama needed to nationalize both Bank of

America and Citigroup Inc. in order to successfully overhaul the two bank behemoths' capital structures.

Wendy Johnson Bilas
Updated, Dorothy Kroll; Christina M. Stansell;
David E. Salamie

PRINCIPAL SUBSIDIARIES

American Financial Service Group, Inc.; BA Merchant Services, LLC; Banc of America Advisory Services, LLC; Banc of America Card Servicing Corporation; Banc of America Commercial Finance Corporation; Banc of America Commercial Mortgage Inc.; Banc of America Commercial, LLC; Banc of America E-Commerce Holdings, Inc.; Banc of America Finance Services, Inc.; Banc of America Financial Products, Inc.; Banc of America Investment Advisors, Inc.; Banc of America Investment Services, Inc.; Banc of America Mortgage Capital Corporation; Banc of America Mortgage Securities, Inc.; Banc of America Securities Holdings Corporation; Bank of America Canada; Bank of America Capital Advisors LLC; Bank of America Capital Corporation; Bank of America Mortgage Securities, Inc.; Bank of America Overseas Corporation; Bank of America Singapore Limited; Bank of America, National Association; BankAmerica Acceptance Corp.; BankAmerica International Financial Corporation; BankAmerica International Investment Corporation; BankAmerica Investment Corporation; Countrywide Financial Corporation; LaSalle Bank Corporation; Merrill Lynch & Co., Inc.; United States Trust Company, National Association.

PRINCIPAL OPERATING UNITS

Global Consumer and Small Business Banking; Global Corporate and Investment Banking; Global Wealth and Investment Management.

PRINCIPAL COMPETITORS

JPMorgan Chase & Co.; Citigroup Inc.; Wells Fargo & Company; The PNC Financial Services Group, Inc.; U.S. Bancorp; The Goldman Sachs Group, Inc.; Morgan Stanley; The Bank of New York Mellon Corporation.

FURTHER READING

Bauerlein, Valerie, "Bank of America Can't Resist LaSalle's Allure," *Wall Street Journal,* April 23, 2007, p. C1.

———, "Will BofA Laugh Last? Bet on Countrywide Looks Funny to Some, but Patience May Pay," *Wall Street Journal,* November 29, 2007, p. C1.

Bauerlein, Valerie, and Robert Frank, "Bank of America Targets Ultrarich in U.S. Trust Deal," *Wall Street Journal,* November 20, 2006, p. C1.

Bauerlein, Valerie, and Robin Sidel, "Emerging Colossus: Bank of America Makes Deal for Credit-Card Issuer MBNA," *Wall Street Journal,* July 1, 2005, p. A1.

Bersman, Steve, "BankAmerica: Shake, Rattle, and on a Roll," *Bankers Monthly,* February 1990, pp. 14+.

"BofA's Brash Fight to Build Deposits," *Business Week,* January 17, 1983, pp. 98+.

Bonadio, Felice A., *A. P. Giannini: Banker of America,* Berkeley: University of California Press, 1994, 429 p.

Boraks, David, "B of A, Its Deals Done, Turns Attention to Brand-Building," *American Banker,* August 13, 2001, p. 1.

Brooks, Rick, and Martha Brannigan, "Coulter Quits BankAmerica President Post," *Wall Street Journal,* October 21, 1998, p. A3.

Calvey, Mark, "Executive of the Year: BankAmerica CEO Develops Power Within," *San Francisco Business Times,* January 9, 1998, p. 1.

———, "NationsBank Takes Command," *San Francisco Business Times,* April 17, 1998, p. 1.

Condon, Bernard, "Teflon Bank," *Forbes,* September 20, 2004, pp. 54–55.

Covington, Howard E., Jr., and Marion A. Ellis, *The Story of NationsBank: Changing the Face of American Banking,* Chapel Hill: University of North Carolina Press, 1993, 328 p.

Doherty, Jacqueline, "B of A's Biggest Bet Ever: Big Risks, and Rewards," *Barron's,* September 22, 2008, pp. 27, 29.

———, "Clean Machine: Bank of America Is Poised to Prosper As the Economy Turns," *Barron's,* August 26, 2002, pp. 17–19.

Fitzpatrick, Dan, Deborah Solomon, and Susanne Craig, "BofA's Latest Hit: Treasury to Inject $20 Billion More; Stock at 1991 Level," *Wall Street Journal,* January 16, 2009, pp. C1, C3.

Fitzpatrick, Dan, and Susanne Craig, "BofA to Cut 35,000 Jobs As It Absorbs Merrill Lynch," *Wall Street Journal,* December 12, 2008, p. C1.

Foust, Dan, and David Fairlamb, "Boffo at BofA: CEO Ken Lewis' Hard-Nosed Approach Is Paying Off," *Business Week,* November 11, 2002, pp. 124, 126.

Grant, Linda, and Suzanne Barlyn, "Here Comes Hugh," *Fortune,* August 21, 1995, pp. 42+.

Hansell, Saul, "Biggest Southeast Bank Buying Florida Giant for $15.5 Billion," *New York Times,* August 30, 1997, pp. 1, 36.

———, "Look Out, Wall Street. Beware, Big Banking. Here Comes NationsBank," *New York Times,* July 18, 1993, pp. F1, F6.

———, "Riches in Plain-Vanilla Banking: With Boatmen's Deal, NationsBank Returns to Its Roots," *New York Times,* October 2, 1996, pp. D1, D4.

63

Hawkins, Chuck, "Hugh McColl's Masterwork: So Far, NationsBank Is a Model Merger," *Business Week*, April 27, 1992, pp. 94+.

Hector, Gary, *Breaking the Bank: The Decline of BankAmerica*, Boston: Little, Brown, 1988, 363 p.

———, "It's Banquet Time for Bankamerica," *Fortune*, June 3, 1991, pp. 69+.

———, "More Than Mortgages Ails BankAmerica," *Fortune*, April 1, 1985, pp. 50+.

Holliday, Karen Kahler, "No Guts, No Glory," *US Banker*, June 1997, pp. 31–33, 35–36.

James, Marquis, and Bessie Rowland James, *Biography of a Bank: The Story of Bank of America, N.T. & S.A.*, New York: Harper, 1954, 566 p.

Johnston, Moira, *The Tumultuous History of the Bank of America*, revised ed., Washington, D.C.: BeardBooks, 2000, 417 p.

Karnitschnig, Matthew, Carrick Mollenkamp, and Dan Fitzpatrick, "Bank of America to Buy Merrill," *Wall Street Journal*, September 15, 2008, p. A1.

Levin, Rob, "Birth of a NationsBank," *Business Atlanta*, December 1991, pp. 30+.

Mayer, Martin, "The Humbling of BankAmerica," *New York Times Magazine*, Business World suppl., May 3, 1987, pp. 27–29+.

Mollenkamp, Carrick, "Bank of America Plans Job Cuts of Up to 13,000," *Wall Street Journal*, March 17, 2004, p. A3.

———, "Bank of America to Settle Shareholder Suits," *Wall Street Journal*, February 11, 2002, p. A11.

Mollenkamp, Carrick, and John Hechinger, "Branching Out: Bank of America Bets on Consumer," *Wall Street Journal*, October 28, 2003, p. A1.

Nash, Gerald D., *A. P. Giannini and the Bank of America*, Norman: University of Oklahoma Press, 1992, 162 p.

"NationsBank-BankAmerica—A Coast-to-Coast Pioneer," *American Banker*, April 14, 1998, p. 1.

Nicolova, Rossita, "Birth of National Giant Bank of America Announced," *Kansas City Business Journal*, October 2, 1998, p. 5.

Pollack, Andrews, "BankAmerica's Eastward Push," *New York Times*, April 20, 1991, pp. 33–34.

Rehm, Barbara A., "The Megamergers of 1998: At B of A, Dealmaking Gives Way to Discipline," *American Banker*, October 25, 2001, p. 1.

Rexrode, Christina, and Rick Rothacker, "BofA Sees a 17-Year First: Quarterly Loss," *Charlotte (N.C.) Observer*, January 17, 2009.

Rose, Barbara, "Knowing NationsBank," *Crain's Chicago Business*, May 9, 1994, pp. 1, 52–53.

Rothacker, Rick, "BofA's Ken Lewis Caught in Struggle of His Life," *Charlotte (N.C.) Observer*, January 14, 2009.

Rothacker, Rick, and Christina Rexrode, "BofA's Ken Lewis Faces Growing Pressure over Deals," *Charlotte (N.C.) Observer*, January 19, 2009.

Simon, Ruth, "Bank of America in Settlement Worth Over $8 Billion," *Wall Street Journal*, October 6, 2008, p. A3.

Stewart, Thomas A., "Where the Money Is," *Fortune*, September 3, 2001, p. 153.

Tully, Shawn, "Banker of America," *Fortune*, September 5, 2005, pp. 109–12, 116.

Wayne, Leslie, "C&S/Sovran Merger Set with NCNB," *New York Times*, July 23, 1991, pp. D1, D10.

"The Year's 25 Most Fascinating Business People," *Fortune*, January 2, 1989, p. 32.

Yockey, Ross, *McColl: The Man with America's Money*, Atlanta: Longstreet Press, 1999, 636 p.

Zuckerman, Sam, "B of A Adopting SecPac's Orphan NonBank Units," *American Banker*, April 6, 1993, p. 1.

———, "New Man atop the Pyramid: Can CEO David Coulter Replace BankAmerica's Infighting with Team Spirit?" *Business Week*, January 22, 1996, pp. 76+.

Basic Earth Science Systems, Inc.

———————■———————

633 17th Street, Suite 1645
Denver, Colorado 80202-3625
U.S.A.
Telephone: (303) 296-3076
Fax: (303) 468-9187
Web site: http://www.basicearth.net

Public Company
Incorporated: 1969
Employees: 8
Sales: $7.44 million (2008)
Stock Exchanges: Over the Counter (OTC)
Ticker Symbol: BSIC
NAICS: 211111 Crude Petroleum and Natural Gas
    Extraction

■ ■ ■

Basic Earth Science Systems, Inc., (Basic Earth) is an independent oil and gas exploration and production company involved in both primary and secondary production. The company conducts resource exploitation in difficult geological formations and at wells where the use of alternative technologies increases extractable reserves. As such, Basic Earth applies horizontal drilling, fracture stimulation, or a combination of these technologies, as well as conventional vertical drilling, to oil and gas extraction. Basic Earth's primary assets are located in the Williston Basin, along the border of North Dakota and Montana. At the Banks Prospect site in McKenzie County, North Dakota, Basic Earth owns a 20 percent interest in 13,000 acres, at the western edge

of the plentiful but geologically challenging Bakken oil play. Natural gas production at the Denver-Julesburg Basin in Weld County, Colorado, includes 12 active wells, in which the company owns interests ranging from 2 percent to 52.5 percent, for net ownership of 5.4 wells.

Basic Earth owns minor interests in the South Flat Lake Prospect, in Sheridan County, Montana, and in the TR Madison Unit Prospect in Billings County, North Dakota, both in the Williston Basin, as well as in undeveloped assets at the Christmas Meadows Prospect in Summit County, Utah. Long-producing properties that support cash flow include 23 oil wells (or 20.66 in net ownership) located onshore in south Texas. Overall, Basic Earth owns 1.26 million barrels of oil equivalent in recoverable reserves.

BARTER OF GEOPHYSICAL SERVICES STARTS COMPANY IN HIGH-RISK VENTURES

Founded by G. W. Breuer in 1969, Basic Earth originated as a geophysical services company that exchanged its geological expertise in oil and gas exploration for ownership stakes in properties with potential for oil production. When early high-risk ventures failed to establish Basic Earth as an oil production company, Basic Earth exchanged corporate stock for interests in marginal oil wells in Louisiana in 1973. For a time, Basic Earth provided oilfield services, using stock and promissory notes to purchase oilfield trucking and equipment operations in 1976. Losses, however, prompted Basic Earth to sell those operations in 1980 in order to retire debt. By that time, Basic Earth owned

COMPANY PERSPECTIVES

We are an independent oil and gas exploration company focusing on the fundamentals of company growth and profitability in an effort to enhance shareholder wealth. Our company is comprised of seasoned industry professionals who have been associated with the company for a long time. We are survivors with a management track record in both good times and bad. We have an established production base that generates positive cash flow and profits.

interests in successful oil wells, which established the company's foothold in oil production.

Basic Earth owned substantial interests in oil producing assets in Colorado and Kansas. In Adams County, Colorado, the company owned a 25 percent interest in an oil well producing 1,200 barrels per day. Participation in that well contributed to $6.6 million in revenues in 1979. The company's June 1980 oil discovery near Wichita, Kansas, involved a 12.5 percent interest in production of 480 barrels per day. The August 1980 discovery in Arapahoe County, Colorado, involved a 21.87 percent interest in oil production of 355 barrels per day and natural gas production of 670,000 cubic feet per day. Coupled with high oil prices, participation in these plays facilitated development of revenues that allowed Basic Earth to become strictly an oil and gas production company.

By the end of 1980, Basic Earth decided to parlay its success into a public offering of one million shares of stock, at $15 per share. The company prospectus showed proved developed reserves valued at $40.2 million and proved undeveloped reserves valued at $65.9 million. Such numbers attracted high-profile institutional investors, including pensions for IBM and Bankers Trust. Basic Earth intended to apply proceeds from the $15 million stock offering to pay down debt and to invest in exploratory drilling.

TAX BENEFITS AID GROWTH IN THE EIGHTIES

During the early 1980s, Basic Earth established oil and gas exploration activities in Colorado, Wyoming, and North Dakota, as well as in south Texas. Basic Earth attracted investors by offering tax benefits in the manner in which the company structured the transactions. The investment deals were fruitful for the company as long as oil sold between $35 and $38 per barrel. Then, in

1986, the tax laws changed and the price of oil dropped precipitously. Basic Earth suddenly faced debt repayment disproportionately large for a company of its size. A sudden, dramatic reduction in valuation of oil reserves shortly after the 1980 public offering of stock culminated in a settlement in 1985. By selling vital producing assets, the company paid its $4.2 million in debt over the next six years. The company retained its interests in south Texas and in the Williston Basin in North Dakota. Although the company paid all of its debt, it was paralyzed by a lack of producing assets and cash flow, which impaired its ability to perform exploratory drilling. The final tribulation occurred in 1993, when NASDAQ delisted Basic Earth because it no longer met minimum capitalization standards. Afterward, the company's stock traded over the counter.

BASIC EARTH ESTABLISHES NEW BUSINESS PHILOSOPHY FOR THE NINETIES

Renewal of Basic Earth started with new management and a new approach to business. Ray Singleton became president and chief executive officer of Basic Earth in 1993, after holding positions of consultant/production manager/petroleum engineer at Basic Earth since 1982 and vice-president since October 1989. Rather than risk an extreme reduction in shareholder value if high-stakes ventures fizzled, Singleton chose the secure route of purchasing interests in established oil producing properties. A round of debt financing funded acquisition of these assets, but Singleton intended to use those properties to establish cash flow for new oil exploration. He planned to pay off the debt and turn Basic Earth into an operation that expanded only with available cash. Also, by establishing joint-venture partnerships with geophysicists, Basic Earth reduced initial cash outlays required for new ventures.

In August 1994 Basic Earth obtained a $500,000 loan from Norwest Bank of Colorado to be applied exclusively to well development in the Antenna Prospect in the Denver-Julesburg Basin. Initial projects at the site northeast of Denver involved the recompletion and combination of two existing wells and drilling of two new wells.

In March 1995 Basic Earth completed the acquisition of interests in numerous properties in the bountiful Williston Basin, along the border of Montana and North Dakota. Many of these assets were distressed properties, where recompletion, horizontal drilling, and/or fracture stimulation would be required to extract oil at vertical wells past their peak productive capacity. Sale of some of the company's south Texas properties provided funds for these new projects, and bank debt funded the $800,000 purchase price. Assets in the

KEY DATES

1973: Stock and cash transaction establishes Basic Earth in oil production.

1980: Public offering of stock raises $15 million for oil exploration.

1986: Basic sells key assets after collapse of oil prices leaves company with large debt.

1993: New management and new approach to business begins phase of asset acquisition.

2002: Positive cash flow supports new oil exploration projects.

2008: Basic embarks on its largest capital project at the Wattenberg gas field.

acquisition included 43 producing wells, 15 shut-in wells, and three saltwater disposal properties. Working interest ranged from 5 percent to 50 percent, except for 13 properties in which Basic Earth owned 100 percent working interest. Additional properties with exploration potential would provide 35 percent undivided interest after the first $35,000 in proceeds. The acquisition added more than 200,000 net barrels of oil equivalent to the company's proved reserves, as company-operated wells increased from seven to 37 wells.

The development of distressed properties included the October 1995 recompletion of Richland County, Montana, State #12-16 well, operated by Enserch Exploration. Production increased from nine barrels of oil per day to 147 barrels, and from four million cubic feet (MCF) of natural gas to 112 MCF. In August 2000 Basic Earth purchased a 20 percent interest in properties in Sheridan County, Montana. Activities in that area included recompletion of the Guenther #108 well, where extraction in the Red River formation had been exploited in previous years. Basic Earth's extraction at Guenther targeted the Duperow formation and resulted in production of 75 barrels of oil per day. Basic Earth expected to recomplete two additional nearby wells.

Through modest oil production, Basic Earth gained solvency that would support future growth. Revenue for March 31, 2000, reached $2.19 million with $353,000 in net income. The company finished paying its debt in January 2001 and experienced a highly profitable fiscal year. For the fiscal year ending March 31, 2001, the company reported oil and gas sales of $3 million, garnering net income of $864,000. Singleton succeeded in creating a debt-free company that had positive cash flow. Also, high oil and gas prices facilitated the shift

from acquisition to development as Basic Earth began several exploitation projects.

PROFITABLE AND DEBT-FREE, EXPLORATION PROJECTS ARE PURSUED

Basic Earth embarked on an unprecedented level of drilling activity, which resulted in dry holes and geological obstacles, as well as highly productive wells. In November 2002 the company revived a Canadian subsidiary, Legent Resources Corporation, and initiated exploration projects in the Red River formation of Saskatchewan. These activities failed to procure productive wells and Basic Earth abandoned the projects by mid-2003. Other new projects included two natural gas wells at the 3-D Bright Spot property, in the Wharton County, Texas, Yegua formation. Basic Earth experimented with state-of-the-art 3-D seismic imaging technology at the site, but cost overruns associated with the highly pressurized formation, which prevented resource extraction, led Basic Earth to put activities there on hold in the fall of 2005.

Basic Earth's successful exploration and exploitation projects were located primarily in the Williston Basin. Beginning in August 2004, the Lynn #1 well in Williams County, North Dakota, derived 120 barrels of oil per day and 75 million cubic feet of natural gas per day from the Nisku formation. Production at Lynn #2, in the Rival formation, began in January 2005. The horizontal drilling procured 147 barrels of oil per day before hydraulic stimulation, then stabilized at 100 barrels per day in August 2007, after stimulation. Basic Earth owned an 18 to 20 percent working interest in these projects, operated by Missouri Basin Well Service. Basic Earth planned to apply the hydraulic stimulation model at other properties through further partnerships with Missouri Basin.

Other exploration projects in the Williston Basin included horizontal drilling in the prolific Bakken formation, which extends across the Montana–North Dakota border. The December 2004 exploration at Richland County, Montana, involved dual-lateral horizontal drilling in the Halvorsen 31X-1 well. Hydraulic fracturing at the northern lateral successfully procured 400 barrels of oil per day. Although production was lower than desired, combination with the southern lateral horizontal leg culminated in more profitable returns. The August 2005 completion of the southern leg procured another 250 to 300 barrels of oil per day. Halvorsen 21X-36, a horizontal well completed in early 2006, produced 300 barrels of oil per day. Basic Earth owned a 26 percent working interest in these assets, operated by Headington Oil, L.P.

In June 2005 Basic Earth made its largest acquisition to date, a 20 percent interest in 13,000 acres at the Banks Prospect in McKenzie County, North Dakota. Vertical drilling at State #16-1H began in early 2006, but tests did not suggest the feasibility of investing in hydraulic stimulation. Although Basic Earth viewed this area as having potential for multiple wells, in the fall of 2006, after drilling a third horizontal leg, a shortage of oil rigs and poor test results prompted the company to hold off on activities in this area.

Other exploration and production activities included Basic Earth's newly acquired interest in a Summit County, Utah, property, Table Top Unit #1 at Christmas Meadows Prospect. Drilling at the site commenced in September 2006, in partnership with Double Eagle Petroleum Company. Geological impediments, however, required reassessment, and no further activity was expected until the spring of 2009.

MODEST AND EXTENSIVE INVESTMENTS PROVIDE GROWTH AND STABILITY

Basic Earth further solidified its positive cash flow and profitability through minor investments in productive assets, as well as through a major investment in natural gas exploration and development. In 2007 Basic Earth participated in three horizontal wells at the TR Madison Unit Prospect, in Billings County, North Dakota. Although Basic Earth owned a modest 1.07 percent working interest in these properties, the high level of production at these wells contributed significantly to cash flow. Moreover, the cash gains came with minimum risk and minimum outlay.

After several years of government delay and partnership changes, drilling and production began at Colorado's Antenna Federal property in September 2007. The company's largest single capital investment to date, at $1.7 million, it involved a total of 32 wells, including 16 new wells and 16 well recompletions for secondary extraction. Basic Earth, which held interests ranging from 2 percent to 52.5 percent, and Kerr-McGee Oil and Gas Onshore, which operated the wells, did not encounter problems in drilling or completing the wells.

In mid-2008 Basic Earth acquired two minor working interests in the Bakken horizontal oil play in order to further establish its foothold in this important area of oil exploration and production. Operated by Marathon Oil, the wells were located in Dunn County, North Dakota. Basic Earth held a 1.2 percent working interest in the Paulson 14-9H, a well that produced 387 barrels of oil per day. Basic Earth also owned 1.56 percent of Steffan 14-224, which produced 300 barrels of oil per day.

Although Basic Earth had sidelined its activities in the Banks Prospect, other companies expressed interest in acquisitions and oil exploration in the property because of its proximity to core discovery wells in the Bakken formation. In late 2008 Basic Earth outsourced prospecting in the Banks Prospect to Panther Energy Company, LLC. Panther Energy agreed to drill two horizontal wells and carry Basic Earth for 32.5 percent of its 20 percent interest. Also, Panther earned 67.5 percent of undrilled acreage in the Banks Prospect. Hence, Panther assumed responsibility for managing the 20 partners in the project and for the risk associated with the geological and technological obstacles of the area. Basic Earth retained the rights to participate in additional wells for up to 6.5 percent, depending on distance between wells.

Mary Tradii

PRINCIPAL COMPETITORS

Brigham Exploration Company; Chesapeake Energy Corporation; ConocoPhillips; Continental Resources, Inc.; St. Mary Land and Exploration Company.

FURTHER READING

"Basic Earth Acquires Interest in 2nd Horizontal Bakken Well," *Science Letter,* November 11, 2008.

"Basic Earth Announces Oil Discovery in Kansas," *Wall Street Journal,* June 30, 1980, p. 4.

"Basic Earth Liquidating Trucking Operations of 2 of Its Subsidiaries," *Wall Street Journal,* January 18, 1980, p. 27.

"Basic Earth Science Agrees to Settle Suits over 1980 Offering," *Wall Street Journal,* June 25, 1985, p. 1.

"Basic Earth Science Budget Set," *Wall Street Journal,* February 17, 1981, p. 4.

"Basic Earth Science Set to Offer 1 Million Units," *Wall Street Journal,* December 19, 1980, p. 38.

"Basic Earth Science Systems," *Wall Street Journal,* June 5, 1979, p. 45.

"Basic Earth Science Systems," *Wall Street Journal,* August 13, 1980, p. 7.

"Basic Earth Science Systems Inc.—$864K Net Income in FY 2001," *Market News Publishing,* July 3, 2001.

"Basic Earth Science to Acquire Tanks, Inc.," *Wall Street Journal,* June 10, 1976, p. 14.

Ingersoll, Bruce, "Colorado Concern's 1980 Stock Offering Brings SEC Charges," *Wall Street Journal,* February 15, 1984, p. 60.

Metz, Robert, "Basic Earth's Cut in Reserves," *New York Times,* June 3, 1981, p. D8.

Becton, Dickinson and Company

———■———

1 Becton Drive
Franklin Lakes, New Jersey 07417-1880
U.S.A.
Telephone: (201) 847-6800
Toll Free: (800) 284-6845
Fax: (201) 847-6475
Web site: http://www.bd.com

Public Company
Founded: 1897
Incorporated: 1906
Employees: 28,277
Sales: $7.16 billion (2008)
Stock Exchanges: New York
Ticker Symbol: BDX
NAICS: 325413 In-Vitro Diagnostic Substance Manufacturing; 339112 Surgical and Medical Instrument Manufacturing; 339113 Surgical Appliance and Supplies Manufacturing; 334516 Analytical Laboratory Instrument Manufacturing; 326199 All Other Plastics Product Manufacturing; 541710 Research and Development in the Physical, Engineering, and Life Sciences

■ ■ ■

Becton, Dickinson and Company (BD) develops, manufactures, and markets medical supplies and devices, laboratory equipment, and diagnostic systems for use by healthcare professionals, medical research institutions, clinical laboratories, the pharmaceutical industry, and the general public. The company's operations are ar-

ranged into three worldwide business segments: BD Medical, BD Diagnostics, and BD Biosciences. BD Medical is one of the world's largest suppliers of hypodermic needles and syringes, insulin delivery syringes and pen needles, intravenous (IV) catheters, and prefillable drug delivery systems. Among other products produced by this unit are surgical blades and scalpels, ophthalmic surgical instruments, critical-care monitoring devices, and ACE-brand elastic bandages. BD Diagnostics specializes in products used to safely collect and transport diagnostic specimens for infectious disease testing. BD Biosciences focuses on producing research and clinical tools used in the study of the normal and the disease processes of cells and cell components. These products include fluorescence-activated cell sorters, antibodies for cell analysis, reagent systems, and cell-imaging systems. With operations in the United States and numerous countries around the world, BD derives more than half of its revenue from its international business activities.

FIRST 50 YEARS: STEADY, CONSERVATIVE GROWTH

The company was founded in 1897 by two salesmen, Maxwell W. Becton and Fairleigh S. Dickinson, as a partnership first to sell medical thermometers and syringes (imported from Europe) and then to manufacture them. Expansion into new product lines in the early years came via acquisitions. In 1904 the partnership acquired Philadelphia Surgical Company and Wigmore Company, both of which were makers of surgical, dental, and veterinary instruments. The manufacture of medical bags was added the following

COMPANY PERSPECTIVES

BD is a leading global medical technology company that develops, manufactures and sells medical devices, instrument systems and reagents. The Company is dedicated to improving people's health throughout the world. BD is focused on improving drug delivery, enhancing the quality and speed of diagnosing infectious diseases and cancers, and advancing research, discovery and production of new drugs and vaccines. BD's capabilities are instrumental in combating many of the world's most pressing diseases.

year through the purchase of Comstock Bag Company. One year later, Becton, Dickinson and Company was incorporated in New Jersey and built a manufacturing plant in East Rutherford, for the production of thermometers, syringes, and hypodermic needles.

Even with the company's new plant, Becton, Dickinson continued to rely on European suppliers for some of the products it sold, mainly because of the higher quality of the imports versus those made domestically. Along these lines, the acquisition of New York-based Surgical Supply Import Company in 1913 was completed to gain the company's network of high-quality foreign suppliers. The purchase also helped broaden Becton, Dickinson's product line through such Surgical Supply products as the Asepto bulb syringe.

During World War I, Becton, Dickinson's import supplies were, in large part, cut off, propelling the company deeper into manufacturing its own products. In the midst of the war, the president of Surgical Supply, Oscar O. R. Schwidetzky, who stayed with Becton, Dickinson following the acquisition, developed a new American-made cotton elastic bandage. In 1918 the company conducted a contest among physicians to name the new bandage, out of which emerged the ACE bandage, "ACE" being an acronym for "All Cotton Elastic." Meantime, the slow but steady growth of Becton, Dickinson was evidenced by the company reaching the milestone of $1 million in sales in 1917, two decades after the founding.

Throughout the early decades, the family-run business built a reputation as a maker and marketer of products superior to those of its competitors. Through its product development, and acquisitions, the company kept pace with the latest advances in medical technology and standards. Such was the case with the 1921 purchase of Physicians Specialty Company, which was

headed by Andrew W. "Doc" Fleischer, who like Schwidetzky took a position with Becton, Dickinson following the merger. Fleischer had developed the mercurial sphygmomanometer (an instrument for measuring blood pressure) as well as the binaural stethoscope. In 1924 Becton, Dickinson began making syringes designed specifically for insulin injection, marking the company's first foray into the diabetes care sector. The following year Fairleigh Dickinson received a patent for the Luer-Lok tip, a locking collar that more securely attached a hypodermic needle to a syringe, thereby making injections safer, less painful, and more accurate.

Through the difficult years of the Great Depression, the company's workers retained their jobs by agreeing to a series of voluntary pay cuts. A key development in the World War II years came in 1943 with the acquisition of Multifit, which had been founded by Joseph J. Kleiner eight years earlier. Kleiner had developed a syringe system with interchangeable barrels and plungers. Kleiner's product had a number of advantages, including reduced labor costs, reduced breakage because it was made from a very strong kind of glass, and enhanced convenience for its users. Kleiner also brought to Becton, Dickinson another key concept he was developing called the Evacutainer. Patented in 1949, the Evacutainer used a vacuum system, a needle, and a test tube to draw blood from patients. The device was later renamed the Vacutainer tube, and it marked Becton, Dickinson's entry into the burgeoning field of diagnostic medicine. Also in 1949 the company's first manufacturing facility located outside New Jersey was established in Columbus, Nebraska. Overall revenues reached $16 million by 1950.

POSTWAR EXPANSION INTO A *FORTUNE* 500 COMPANY

Throughout its first 50 years Becton, Dickinson was a conservatively managed, family-run business. The enterprise entered the affluent postwar years with a solid market share in medical supplies and was well prepared for a major expansion. The company recognized that its traditional approach to business would not be appropriate for the future. Therefore, in 1948, the sons of the founders, Henry P. Becton and Fairleigh Dickinson Jr., both astute businessmen, assumed managerial control of the company.

With Dickinson as CEO and Becton serving in a variety of other capacities during the 1950s, Becton, Dickinson gradually expanded its product line. By 1964, more than 8,000 products were being manufactured by Becton, Dickinson, including a broad line of medical supplies of superior diagnostic accuracy. The company divided its business into four operating divisions: medi-

KEY DATES

1897: Maxwell W. Becton and Fairleigh S. Dickinson form partnership.

1904: Philadelphia Surgical Company and Wigmore Company are acquired.

1906: Partnership is incorporated as Becton, Dickinson and Company; factory is built in East Rutherford, New Jersey.

1913: Surgical Supply Import Company is acquired.

1917: Sales reach $1 million.

1918: Company introduces the ACE bandage.

1921: Company acquires Physicians Specialty Company.

1924: Company begins making syringes designed specifically for insulin injection.

1925: Fairleigh Dickinson receives a patent for the Luer-Lok tip.

1943: Multifit, maker of a syringe with interchangeable parts, is acquired.

1948: Henry P. Becton and Fairleigh Dickinson Jr., sons of the founders, assume managerial control of the company.

1949: Company enters diagnostic medicine sector with the patenting of the Evacutainer blood collection device.

1951: International expansion begins with the formation of a Canadian subsidiary.

1955: Baltimore Biological Laboratories is acquired, enlarging the firm's presence in the burgeoning market for disposable medical products.

1962: Company goes public.

1974: Wesley J. Howe is named president and CEO.

1978: Sun Oil Company acquires a 34 percent stake in the company.

1979: Becton, Dickinson and Sun reach agreement on the eventual disposal of Sun's stake.

1980s: Restructuring and disposal of noncore operations.

1986: Headquarters are shifted to Franklin Lakes, New Jersey.

1989: Raymond V. Gilmartin is named CEO.

1994: Clateo Castellini is named chairman, CEO, and president.

1997: PharMingen Inc. and Difco Laboratories Incorporated are acquired.

1998: The Medical Devices Division of the BOC Group is acquired.

1999: Company reorganizes its operations into three business segments: BD Medical Systems (later BD Medical), BD Biosciences, and BD Preanalytical Solutions (later BD Diagnostics); company launches a global brand strategy focusing on the "BD" name.

2000: Edward J. Ludwig succeeds Castellini as CEO.

2006: BD Diagnostics is bolstered with the purchases of TriPath Imaging, Inc., and GeneOhm Sciences, Inc.

cal health, laboratory, animal research and testing, and overseas sales. In the course of an acquisition program, Becton, Dickinson purchased Carworth Inc., the leading producer of laboratory mice; Canton, Ohio-based Wilson Rubber Company, maker of rubber gloves for surgical, industrial, and household use (acquired in 1954); the Bard-Parker Company, manufacturer of surgical blades and scalpels (1956); and several specialized research laboratories. Increasingly, Becton, Dickinson's strongest growth was experienced in the market for disposable items, with the company becoming a leader in this burgeoning area. The 1955 acquisition of Baltimore Biological Laboratories (BBL) was particularly important in this regard as BBL was already making sterile, one-use blood donor kits for the American Red

Cross (with Becton, Dickinson acting as distributor). By 1964, such products as disposable syringes and needles accounted for 60 percent of the company's $70 million in sales.

The new management team also was noted for its attention to international expansion. The first such move came in 1951 with the acquisition of the company's Canadian distributor to create Becton Dickinson Canada, Ltd., its first wholly owned subsidiary and foreign operation. The following year Becton, Dickinson acquired the Mexican firm MAPAD, S.A. de C.V., maker of syringes, needles, and clinical thermometers, and established a manufacturing plant in Le Pont-de-Claix, France. The Brazilian market was next on the expansion list, and Becton, Dickinson began supplying syringes in that country in 1956 and eventually became the number one medical supply company there. In 1963 Becton, Dickinson constructed a disposable syringe plant in Drogheda, Ireland.

The company's need for massive amounts of funding to pay for the conversion from reusable products to sterile disposable products led to a 1962 initial public offering (IPO) of stock at $25 per share. The following year Becton, Dickinson stock began trading on the New York Stock Exchange. By 1970 the company's rapid rate of growth had landed it on the *Fortune* 500 list for the first time.

EARLY SEVENTIES: NEW FDA REGULATION AND NEW MANAGEMENT

During the 1970s, Becton, Dickinson continued to make gains in the medical supplies business, despite increasingly difficult market conditions. The world oil crisis of 1973–74 caused a reduction in petrochemical feedstocks, which, in turn, made medical raw materials difficult to obtain. In addition, the Food and Drug Administration (FDA) planned to adopt the same strict certification standards for diagnostic equipment as it had applied to pharmaceuticals. This would delay the commercial introduction of new products and, with technological advances, expose them to higher rates of obsolescence. Although these conditions lessened Wall Street's interest in companies in the medical industry, Becton, Dickinson remained highly optimistic. With sales figures doubling every five years and with 19 percent of all sales derived overseas, Dickinson declared to shareholders that the company did not fear the impending device regulation, but instead was helping the FDA to formulate its new regulations.

When the FDA's Medical Device Act was enacted, Becton, Dickinson found, to some dismay, that 85 percent of its products were subject to the new regulation. Wesley J. Howe, who succeeded Dickinson as president and CEO in 1974, was confident that the company's products would be able to meet all the new FDA requirements; to be sure, he hired a team of legal and technical experts to guarantee standardization.

Despite growing regulation, the early years of Howe's direction were marked by a continuity of policies; Howe was handpicked by Dickinson and dedicated to the same conservative style of management. To increase efficiency, Howe automated and integrated more of the company's facilities and reduced his staff by 13 percent. To increase his influence, he also replaced 14 of the company's 17 division presidents.

Howe's leadership was proving highly effective. In one area, Becton, Dickinson's marketing approach was particularly effective: targeting insulin users through doctors, diabetes associations, camps, pharmacies, and pharmacy schools. With control of almost 100 percent of the insulin syringe market, Becton, Dickinson saw its sales increase to $456 million in 1975.

LATE SEVENTIES: BOARDROOM INTRIGUE AND TAKEOVER BIDS

This success, however, was greatly compromised in the boardroom by Fairleigh Dickinson, who, despite having relinquished his posts voluntarily, continued to demand managerial control. At the heart of the matter was a conflict between family members determined to maintain control and board members who favored control by a more professional corporate elite. Although Howe remained above this conflict, several other important managers did not; ultimately, Dickinson would order Howe to fire them. In 1977, four board members resigned. With morale an increasingly serious problem, Howe asserted his position. Four new, "unprejudiced" board members were named to the board, and Dickinson was relegated to the ceremonial post of chairman. The power struggle was not over, however.

Dickinson was asked to approach the Salomon Brothers investment banking firm and initiate a study on a company Howe wanted Becton, Dickinson to acquire. When completed, the study warned of numerous problems with the takeover. Howe maintained that Dickinson had sabotaged the study and, when the situation proved unresolvable, ordered Dickinson removed from the payroll.

Dickinson then resorted to another strategy. With 4.5 percent of the company's stock, Dickinson authorized Salomon Brothers to line up additional investors to lead a takeover of Becton, Dickinson. A Salomon agent named Kenneth Lipper approached several companies, including Avon, American Home Products, Monsanto, and Squibb, in an effort to set up a takeover. Becton, Dickinson's attorneys warned Lipper that his action was illegal. Rather than call off the search for buyers, Lipper challenged the attorneys to stop him in court, cognizant that a well-publicized court battle would only gain more attention for his cause.

On January 16, 1978, before Lipper could be stopped, Becton, Dickinson learned that the Philadelphia-based Sun Oil Company had acquired 34 percent of its stock. The transaction lasted only 15 minutes and involved 6.5 million shares at a purchase price of $45 each, well above the trading price of $33. Sun created a special subsidiary called LHIW (for "Let's

Hope It Works") to manage the shares until a controlling majority of shares could be acquired.

The takeover had severe consequences. Like Becton, Dickinson, Sun had just emerged from an important battle against founding family interests. H. Robert Sharbaugh, CEO of Sun, came into strong disagreement over the takeover with the founding Pew family and was eventually forced out of the company. Becton, Dickinson, in the meantime, learned that Sun's purchase had been conducted off the trading floor, in violation of numerous laws. Finally, three Becton, Dickinson shareholders sued Fairleigh Dickinson, complaining that they had been excluded from Sun's tender offer.

The New York Stock Exchange refused to file charges against Salomon and instead turned the matter over to the Securities and Exchange Commission (SEC). At this point, Sun decided to dispose of its interest in Becton, Dickinson and offered to indemnify Salomon against any liabilities resulting from court action. The legality of the takeover was no longer in question. Instead, the question concerned the manner in which Sun should dispose of its Becton, Dickinson shares. With Sun no longer in pursuit of Becton, Dickinson, the only clear beneficiaries of the takeover were the lawyers left to pick up the pieces.

Ironically, Sun and Becton, Dickinson had a common interest in the divestiture. If the 34 percent share were placed on the market in one parcel, share prices would plummet and Sun would lose millions. Becton, Dickinson, on the other hand, opposed summary disposal because large blocks of its shares could fall under the control of still other hostile acquisitors. An agreement was finally reached in December 1979, under which Sun would distribute a 25-year debenture convertible into Becton, Dickinson shares. The unprecedented agreement ensured both a gradual spinoff of Becton, Dickinson shares and the maintenance of stable share prices. Although the agreement was said to have cost Sun an extremely large sum of money, Sun was apparently satisfied.

Fairleigh Dickinson continued to seek injunctive relief from the SEC and remained under attack from Becton, Dickinson shareholders demanding the return of the $15 million profit from the original Sun tender offer. Sun's board at this time was nervously awaiting the response of its shareholders to the costly defense of Salomon Brothers. Around this time, American Home Products made a brief and uncharacteristic hostile bid for 2.5 percent of Becton, Dickinson—by comparison with Sun, a minor incident. Ironically, Sun's debenture scheme prevented any company from gaining greater control of Becton, Dickinson.

RESTRUCTURING AND A REFOCUSING ON THE CORE

The first order of business after this debacle, according to Howe, was to position Becton, Dickinson for future growth. With company profits rising, Howe arranged to reinvest cash on hand into new projects. He reorganized the company into 42 units so that each division's performance could be more accurately scrutinized. Unprofitable operations, such as a computer parts manufacturer, were either sold or closed down. Older products were reassessed and, in some cases, improved; for instance, insulin syringes were redesigned for more accurate dosages. Foreign sales were stepped up, and, despite a negative effect on earnings, an expansion of the product line was carried out. Whereas some new products were added by takeovers, others, such as the balloon catheter, were developed internally.

The expansion had been justified to ensure future viability, but by 1983 bad investments had cost the company $75 million, $23 million alone from a failed immunoassay instrument division. Bad planning caused production stoppages and cost overruns. Howe then came under criticism for failing to invest heavily enough in research and development. With remedial measures in place, the company's financial condition had improved greatly by 1985. That year the company declared an $88 million profit on sales of $1.44 billion. Much of this turnaround, however, came from nonoperating profits resulting from the sale of unprofitable divisions and a reduction in overhead. Howe instituted a new strategy involving slower growth rates and increased productivity. To balance this more modest business plan, Howe allocated a 5.1 percent share of revenue to research and development, particularly for more cost-effective new products, and purchased a 12 percent share of a company that manufactured equipment for synthesizing DNA.

In the late 1980s, Becton faced increased competition on the domestic front, but continued to maintain its estimated 70 percent to 80 percent share of the needle and syringe market. This period also was marked by the company's move into a new corporate headquarters in Franklin Lakes, New Jersey, in 1986 and a transition in leadership. In 1987 Raymond V. Gilmartin was named president of the company, then added the CEO title in 1989, with Howe remaining chairman. Gilmartin had joined Becton, Dickinson in 1976 as vice-president of corporate planning.

INTERNATIONAL EXPANSION AND ACQUISITIONS

Sales increased from $1.71 billion in 1988 to $2.47 billion in 1993 as Becton, Dickinson moved into many new global markets and accelerated new proprietary product introductions. The firm focused expansion efforts on Latin America, the Asia-Pacific region, and Europe. By 1993, international sales contributed 44 percent of annual sales. Howe, who was credited by Robert Teitelman of *Financial World* with reenergizing Becton, Dickinson, retired that year and was supplanted as chairman by Gilmartin.

Becton, Dickinson introduced new drug delivery and blood handling products in the early 1990s that helped reduce healthcare workers' exposure to acquired immune deficiency syndrome (AIDS) and hepatitis. Some of the company's newest diagnostic tests helped researchers and physicians determine when to begin drug therapy for cancer and AIDS patients. In 1993 the firm moved its PRECISE brand pregnancy test from the professional to the over-the-counter market. Becton, Dickinson's investment of 5.6 percent of its 1993 revenues represented a continuing accent on new product introductions.

As criticism of high healthcare costs accelerated in the early 1990s, the wisdom of Howe's shift to more cost-effective new product introductions became evident. Becton, Dickinson positioned its diagnostic tests as accurate, fast ways to reduce healthcare costs by speeding diagnosis and treatment.

In mid-1994 Gilmartin left the company to take the top position at pharmaceutical giant Merck & Co., Inc. Tapped as his successor was Clateo Castellini, who was head of the company's medical unit and had joined Becton, Dickinson in 1978.

Under Castellini, who was born in Italy and had extensive international experience, the company actively expanded its overseas operations in the mid- to late 1990s. Despite the economic turmoil in the region during much of this period, the Asia-Pacific region was the object of much of this growth. In 1995 the company entered into a joint venture in China to produce medical products for the Chinese and other markets. That same year Becton, Dickinson set up a subsidiary in India to construct a manufacturing plant. When it finally opened in 1999, it boasted an annual capacity of more than one billion disposable needles and syringes, making it one of the largest facilities of its kind in Asia. In 1998 Becton Dickinson acquired Boin Medica Co., Ltd., the largest medical supply company in South Korea. The company also began expanding in Latin America, outside of its two strongholds, Mexico and Brazil.

Flush with annual free cash flow of $350 million, Becton, Dickinson earmarked some of the money to buy back shares of its stock to improve earnings per share. The company also made a number of acquisi-

tions, particularly in the late 1990s, a period of consolidation in healthcare across the board, from hospitals to insurance providers to pharmaceutical firms to medical product makers. In 1997 Becton, Dickinson spent $217.4 million on two major acquisitions: PharMingen Inc., a privately held maker of reagents for biomedical research with annual revenues of $30 million; and Difco Laboratories Incorporated, a manufacturer of media and supplies for microbiology labs with sales of $82 million. Six more acquisitions were completed in 1998, the most significant of which was the purchase of the Medical Devices Division of the BOC Group for about $457 million. Among the ten purchases completed in 1999 were Clontech Laboratories, Inc., maker of genetic tests; Biometric Imaging Inc., producer of cell analysis systems for clinical applications; and Transduction Laboratories, manufacturer of reagents for cell biology research.

In the late 1990s Becton, Dickinson was troubled by a spate of lawsuits arising from healthcare workers who had contracted bloodborne diseases using the company's conventional, un-guarded needles and syringes. The suits alleged that safer needles had been available for years but Becton, Dickinson had not been promoting their use. For its part, the company said that it had invested more than $100 million into development of safer products, which were available for its customers to purchase, but it was up to the hospitals and medical centers to make the conversion. By decade's end, a shift to safer needles was clearly underway, in part because of government mandates at the state level.

REORGANIZING AROUND THE BD NAME

The financial results for 1999 were a disappointment, stemming from weaker than expected sales in Europe and emerging markets and from an ailing home healthcare unit, which made such items as ear thermometers and blood pressure monitors. A restructuring was launched in the second half of the year that included the company's exit from certain product lines within the home healthcare sector (a primary exception being ACE bandages). In addition, the company reorganized its remaining operations into three business segments: BD Medical Systems, BD Biosciences, and BD Preanalytical Solutions (later BD Clinical Laboratory Solutions). Becton, Dickinson also began implementing a global brand strategy in which the "BD" name would appear on all of the company's products, either alone or alongside such well-known brands as ACE, Vacutainer, and Tru-Fit. Becton, Dickinson ambitiously aimed to have its new "BD" logo "become as universally recognized worldwide as the Red Cross."

At the beginning of 2000, 20-year company veteran Edward J. Ludwig was named president and CEO of BD, with Castellini remaining chairman. Under Ludwig, the company continued to restructure; in September 2000 it announced the elimination of 1,000 jobs from the company workforce as part of a cost-cutting and profit-boosting drive. At the same time, BD was spending hundreds of millions of dollars on research and development and manufacturing overhauls to produce a new and safer generation of syringes and catheters to meet the requirements of the Needlestick Safety and Prevention Act of 2000, which was designed to prevent the infection of healthcare workers from inadvertent needle jabs. BD Biosciences, which had been built mainly via such late 1990s acquisitions as PharMingen, Clontech Laboratories, Biometric Imaging Inc., and Transduction Laboratories, grew still larger following the January 2001 purchase of Gentest Corporation, a specialist in reagent systems for detecting toxicity in prospective drugs, for $29 million. By 2002 revenues at Becton, Dickinson had surged beyond $4 billion, fueled in part by a 38 percent increase in sales of the new lines of safety-engineered needle-based products.

During the following fiscal year, two of the company's three main units were renamed: BD Medical Systems to BD Medical and BD Clinical Laboratory Solutions to BD Diagnostics. Also that year, BD introduced a glucose-monitoring device for diabetics as it ventured into new territory hoping to capture 10 percent of the $6 billion worldwide market for such devices within five years. Three years later, however, the company was forced to exit from this highly competitive arena after achieving disappointing annual sales of only a little more than $100 million. In the meantime, in July 2004 BD paid $100 million to rival needle-maker Retractable Technologies, Inc., to settle a six-year-old case brought by the Texas firm accusing BD of conspiring to block it from the market. A little more than a year later, BD sold genetic test maker Clontech for $62 million to enable BD Biosciences to concentrate more of its resources on producing clinical and research tools used in the discovery of pharmaceutical drugs. Becton, Dickinson for fiscal 2005 reported record net income of $722.2 million on record revenues of $5.41 billion.

While BD's growth continued to be driven primarily by internally developed products, the company remained open to targeted acquisitions. In February 2006 BD Diagnostics was bolstered with the purchase of San Diego-based GeneOhm Sciences, Inc., for $232.5 million. GeneOhm, founded in 2001, was a pioneer in the development of rapid diagnostic tests for the detection of so-called healthcare-associated infections. Such infections, which were a growing problem around the world, were typically passed between hospital patients via open abrasions, cuts, and incisions. In early 2008 the FDA granted approval for a GeneOhm test for a particularly virulent form of staph infection. Analysts believed this and other GeneOhm offerings had the potential to generate hundreds of millions in annual revenue as more hospitals adopted the tests. In the meantime, BD Diagnostics expanded again in December 2006 by purchasing TriPath Imaging, Inc., for $361.9 million. Based in Burlington, North Carolina, TriPath specialized in the development of molecular tools for cancer screening, diagnosis, prognosis, and therapy monitoring.

Because many of Becton, Dickinson's core products were healthcare staples, the firm was relatively insulated from economic downturns. Its performance during the fiscal year ending in September 2008, as the global economic crisis commenced, supported this contention. Record results were again achieved, including $1.13 billion in net income and $7.16 billion in revenues, with these figures up 27 percent and 12.5 percent from the previous year, respectively. Strong cash flow enabled BD to increase its dividend for the 36th consecutive year and to return another $450 million to shareholders in the form of share repurchases. The company also spent nearly $1 billion on research and development and in capital investments, including the $42.9 million purchase of Cytopeia, Inc., in May 2008. As a producer of advanced flow-cytometry cell-sorting instruments, Cytopeia strengthened BD Biosciences' position in key areas of cell-based research such as cell therapy research, stem cell research, and drug discovery and development. Overall, backed by its production of essential healthcare products, its strong cash flow, and a healthy balance sheet, Becton, Dickinson was confident of emerging from the economic crisis even stronger than when it began.

April Dougal Gasbarre
Updated, David E. Salamie

PRINCIPAL SUBSIDIARIES

Atto BioScience, Inc.; AutoCyte Australia Pty Ltd; AutoCyte NC, LLC; B-D (UK) Ltd.; BD Biosciences, Systems and Reagents Inc.; BD Holding S. de R.L. de C.V. (Mexico); BD Matrex Holdings, Inc.; BD Norge AS (Norway); BD Ophthalmic Systems Limited (UK); BD Rapid Diagnostic (Suzhou) Co., Ltd. (China); BD (West Africa) Limited (Ghana); BDX INO LLC; Becton Dickinson A/S (Denmark); Becton Dickinson Acute-Care Holdings, Inc.; Becton Dickinson AcuteCare, Inc.; Becton Dickinson Advanced Pen Injection Systems GmbH (Switzerland); Becton Dickinson Argentina S.R. L.; Becton Dickinson Asia Limited (Hong Kong); Becton Dickinson Asia Pacific Limited (British Virgin Islands); Becton Dickinson Austria GmbH; Becton Dickinson Benelux N.V. (Belgium); Becton Dickinson Canada Inc.; Becton Dickinson Caribe Ltd. (Cayman Islands); Becton Dickinson Catheter Systems Singapore Pte Ltd.; Becton Dickinson Colombia Ltda.; Becton Dickinson Critical Care Systems Pte Ltd. (Singapore); Becton Dickinson Czechia s.r.o. (Czech Republic); Becton Dickinson del Uruguay S.A.; Becton Dickinson Distribution Center N.V. (Belgium); Becton Dickinson East Africa Ltd. (Kenya); Becton Dickinson Finance B.V. (Netherlands); Becton Dickinson Foreign Sales Corporation (Barbados); Becton Dickinson Guatemala S.A.; Becton Dickinson Hellas S.A. (Greece); Becton Dickinson Hungary Kft.; Becton Dickinson India Private Limited; Becton Dickinson Infusion Therapy AB (Sweden); Becton Dickinson Infusion Therapy B.V. (Netherlands); Becton Dickinson Infusion Therapy Holdings AB (Sweden); Becton Dickinson Infusion Therapy Holdings Inc.; Becton Dickinson Infusion Therapy Systems Inc., S.A. de C.V. (Mexico); Becton Dickinson Infusion Therapy UK; Becton Dickinson Infusion Therapy Systems Inc.; Becton Dickinson Infusion Therapy Holdings UK Limited; Becton Dickinson Insulin Syringe, Ltd. (Cayman Islands); Becton Dickinson Ithalat Ihracat Limited Sirketi (Turkey); Becton Dickinson Korea Holding, Inc.; Becton Dickinson Korea Ltd.; Becton Dickinson Malaysia, Inc.; Becton Dickinson (Mauritius) Limited; Becton Dickinson Medical (S) Pte Ltd. (Singapore); Becton Dickinson Medical Devices Co. Shanghai Ltd. (China); Becton Dickinson Medical Devices Co. Ltd., Suzhou (China); Becton Dickinson Medical Products Pte. Ltd. (Singapore); Becton Dickinson Ltd. (New Zealand); Becton Dickinson O.Y. (Finland); Becton Dickinson Overseas Services Ltd.; Becton Dickinson Pen Limited (Ireland); Becton Dickinson Penel Limited (Cayman Islands); Becton Dickinson Philippines, Inc.; Becton Dickinson Polska Sp.z.o.o. (Poland); Becton Dickinson Pty. Ltd. (Australia); Becton Dickinson (Pty) Ltd. (South Africa); Becton Dickinson Sdn. Bhd. (Malaysia); Becton Dickinson Service (Pvt.) Ltd. (Pakistan); Becton Dickinson Sample Collection GmbH (Switzerland); Becton Dickinson Slovakia s.r.o.; Becton Dickinson (Thailand) Limited; Becton Dickinson Venezuela, C.A.; Becton Dickinson Vostok LLC (Russia); Becton Dickinson, S.A. (Spain); Becton Dickinson (Royston) Limited (UK); Becton, Dickinson A.G. (Switzerland); Becton, Dickinson Aktiebolag (Sweden); Becton, Dickinson and Company, Ltd. (Ireland); Becton, Dickinson B.V. (Netherlands); Becton, Dickinson de Mexico, S.A. de C.V.; Becton Dickinson France S.A.S.; Becton Dickinson GmbH (Germany); Becton, Dickinson Industrias Cirurgicas, Ltda. (Brazil); Becton, Dickinson Italia

S.p.A. (Italy); B-D U.K. Holdings Limited; Becton Dickinson U.K. Limited; Benex Ltd. (Ireland); BioVenture Centre Pte. Ltd. (Singapore; 92%); BTP Immunization Systems, LLC; Cell Analysis Systems, Inc.; Clontech Laboratories UK Limited; Corporativo BD de Mexico, S. de R.L. de C.V.; Critical Device Corporation; Cytopeia; D.L.D., Ltd. (Bermuda); Dantor S.A. (Uruguay); Difco Laboratories Incorporated; Difco Laboratories Limited (UK); Discovery Labware, Inc.; Distribuidora BD Mexico, S.A. de C.V.; Procesos para Esterilizacion, S.A. de C.V. (Mexico); Franklin Lakes Enterprises, L.L.C.; GeneOhm Sciences, Inc.; GeneOhm Sciences Canada Inc.; GeneOhm Sciences Europe, N.V. (Belgium); Healthcare Holdings in Sweden AB; Johnston Laboratories, Inc.; Luther Medical Products, Inc.; Med-Safe Systems, Inc.; Nippon Becton Dickinson Company, Ltd. (Japan); PharMingen; Phase Medical, Inc.; Plasso Technology Limited (UK); Promedicor de Mexico, S.A. de C.V.; Saf-T-Med Inc.; TriPath Imaging; TriPath Imaging Europe bvba (Belgium); TriPath Oncology, Inc.

PRINCIPAL OPERATING UNITS

BD Medical; BD Diagnostics; BD Biosciences.

PRINCIPAL COMPETITORS

Baxter International Inc.; Abbott Laboratories; Covidien Ltd.; Johnson & Johnson; Roche Diagnostics Corporation; Beckman Coulter, Inc.; Boston Scientific Corporation; Siemens Healthcare Diagnostics Inc.

FURTHER READING

"Becton Dickinson Buys PharMingen," *Newark (N.J.) Star-Ledger,* April 13, 1997.

"Becton Dickinson Facelift Unveils New Direction, New Logo," *Health Industry Today,* October 1999, pp. 1, 12.

Celebrating the First One Hundred, 1897–1997, Franklin Lakes, N.J.: Becton, Dickinson and Company, 1997, 152 p.

"Clateo Catellini on Growing a 100-Year-Old Medical-Products Firm in the 1990s," *Business News New Jersey,* March 17, 1997, p. 13.

DeMarrais, Kevin G., "1,000 Jobs to Be Slashed at Becton Dickinson," *Bergen County (N.J.) Record,* September 27, 2000, p. B1.

Krauskopf, Lewis, "Less Pain, More Gain: Becton Hopes Easier Glucose Tester Will Boost Revenue," *Bergen County (N.J.) Record,* January 17, 2003, p. B1.

———, "Navigating in New Waters: Becton Widens View Beyond the Hospital," *Bergen County (N.J.) Record,* December 8, 2000, p. B1.

Middleton, Timothy, "A Shot in the Arm," *Chief Executive,* June 1997, p. 22.

Mosk, Matthew, "Fear of Needles: Care-Givers Demand Safer Hypodermics," *Bergen County (N.J.) Record,* December 10, 1998, p. A1.

Osterland, Andrew, "Becton Dickinson: Time to Check Out," *Financial World,* February 14, 1995, pp. 20+.

Phalon, Richard, *The Takeover Barons of Wall Street: Inside the Billion-Dollar Merger Game,* New York: Putnam, 1981.

———, "Time of Troubles," *Forbes,* September 26, 1983, pp. 80+.

Prial, Dunstan, "Becton Acquiring Biotech Company: GeneOhm Makes Tests for Infections," *Bergen County (N.J.) Record,* January 11, 2006, p. B1.

———, "Becton Bets on New Ideas, Acquisitions," *Bergen County (N.J.) Record,* January 31, 2007, p. B3.

———, "Becton in Talks to Purchase Cancer-Screen Manufacturer: Agrees to Pay $350 Million to Acquire Tri-Path Imaging," *Bergen County (N.J.) Record,* August 17, 2006, p. B3.

Shook, David, "Becton, Dickinson, Rival in Sharp Exchange," *Bergen County (N.J.) Record,* February 13, 2000, p. B1.

———, "Booster for Becton, Dickinson: Future Looking Sharp," *Bergen County (N.J.) Record,* December 16, 1999, p. B1.

Steenhuysen, Julie, "Becton Gives Up on Blood Glucose Monitors," *Newark (N.J.) Star-Ledger,* September 29, 2006.

Taylor, Iris, "Becton, Dickinson Chief to Take Merck Helm," *Newark (N.J.) Star-Ledger,* June 10, 1994.

Teitelman, Robert, "The Devil and the Deep Blue Sea," *Financial World,* June 14, 1988, pp. 30–31.

Tergesen, Anne E., "Team Player: Merck's Gilmartin Is a Regular Guy," *Bergen County (N.J.) Record,* August 14, 1994, p. B1.

Troxell, Thomas N., Jr., "Fighting Back: Clobbered Last Year, Becton, Dickinson Comes Off the Mat," *Barron's,* September 24, 1984, pp. 53+.

———, "Staying Healthy: Becton, Dickinson Bucks the Trend in Health Care, Sees Profits Grow," *Barron's,* December 9, 1985, pp. 60+.

Booz Allen Hamilton Inc.

—■—

8283 Greensboro Drive
McLean, Virginia 22102
U.S.A.
Telephone: (703) 902-5000
Fax: (703) 902-3333
Web site: http://www.boozallen.com

Private Company
Incorporated: 1962 as Booz, Allen & Hamilton
Employees: 20,000
Sales: $4.1 billion (2007)
NAICS: 541611 Administrative Management and General Management Consulting Services; 541618 Other Management Consulting Services

■ ■ ■

Booz Allen Hamilton Inc., a pioneer in the consulting industry, is a leading strategy and consulting firm serving government agencies and institutions. The company provides consulting services, information technology capabilities, and systems engineering and integration expertise to six core markets: defense and national security; homeland security and law enforcement; health; transportation; energy and environment; and financial services. Booz Allen serves the U.S. Departments of Defense, Justice, Labor, Energy, Health and Human Services, Transportation, and Treasury. It performs work for the National Aeronautics and Space Administration, the U.S. Centers for Disease Control and Prevention, the Internal Revenue Service, and the four branches of the U.S. Armed Forces: Air Force, Army, Marine Corps, and Navy. The company operates on a global basis, maintaining a presence in Asia, North America, Europe, Latin America, and the Middle East through 80 offices. The Carlyle Group, a private equity firm, owns a majority interest in Booz Allen, which shed its commercial business, renamed Booz & Company, in 2008.

ORIGINS

Booz Allen Hamilton traces its roots to Edwin G. Booz. A student at Chicago's Northwestern University in the early 1900s, Booz received a bachelor's degree in economics and a master's degree in psychology, upon completion of his thesis "Mental Tests for Vocational Fitness." In 1914, Booz established a small consulting firm in Chicago, and, two years later, he and two partners formed the Business Research and Development Company, which conducted studies and performed investigational work for commercial and trade organizations. This service, which Booz labeled as the first of its kind in the Midwest, soon attracted such clients as Goodyear Tire & Rubber Company, Chicago's Union Stockyards and Transit Company, and the Canadian & Pacific Railroad.

During World War I, Booz was drafted as a private but moved quickly through the ranks by performing personnel work and helping the Army reorganize its bureaus' business methods. Booz left the service in March 1919 as a major in the Inspector General's Office and returned to Chicago to start a new firm, Edwin G. Booz, Business Engineering Service. One of Booz's first clients after the war was Sewell Avery of State Bank &

COMPANY PERSPECTIVES

Booz Allen Hamilton, a leading strategy and technology consulting firm, works with clients to deliver results that endure. Every day, government agencies, institutions, and infrastructure organizations rely on Booz Allen's expertise and objectivity, and on the combined capabilities and dedication of our exceptional people to find solutions and seize opportunities. We combine a consultant's unique problem-solving orientation with deep technical knowledge and strong execution to help clients achieve success in their most critical missions.

Trust Company of Evanston, Illinois, who helped Booz get a loan for his new venture. In return, Booz conducted a bank survey for Avery.

During the early 1920s, Booz's client list grew to include Harris Trust and Savings Bank in Chicago, the Walgreen Company, and Booz's alma mater, Northwestern University. In 1924, Booz changed the name of his firm to Edwin G. Booz Surveys, to more accurately reflect his firm's focus: business surveys and subsequent analysis and recommendations. Unlike other early "efficiency-engineering" consulting firms, Booz adopted a personnel-oriented, applied-psychology approach that included interviewing employees as part of the process of studying the organizational structures of companies.

In 1925, Booz hired his first permanent, full-time assistant, George Fry, another Northwestern alumnus. That year, Business Surveys began working for U.S. Gypsum Company (then under the direction of Sewell Avery), which remained a staple client throughout the decade. Other Business Surveys clients during the latter half of the 1920s included the *Chicago Tribune,* Hart Schaffner & Marx, The Chicago Association of Commerce, Eversharp, Inc., Stock Yards National Bank, and *Chicago Daily News* publisher Walter Strong, who agreed on Booz's recommendation to build a newspaper office across the river from the Civic Opera House.

JAMES ALLEN JOINS THE FIRM IN 1929

In 1929, Booz moved his own office into the new Chicago Daily News Building and hired a third consultant, James L. Allen, who had just graduated from Northwestern. By 1931, Avery was back on Business

Surveys' client list as chairperson of Montgomery Ward, which was losing sales to the new retail operations of Sears, Roebuck and Company. Booz took an office just down the hall from Avery, where he worked full-time and pioneered the "multi-vector" executive appraisal method, which used cross-checking independent criteria in evaluating and hiring managers.

By 1936, Booz had helped push Montgomery Ward back in the black. Informing the company that Avery had been its central problem, Booz resigned from the assignment and returned to his firm's office, where Allen had recently resigned and Booz Surveys itself was in need of organization. By February of that year, Booz had persuaded Allen to return and had hired another consultant, Carl Hamilton. The firm then became a partnership and adopted a new name: Booz, Fry, Allen & Hamilton. The following year, the firm moved into the new Field Building in Chicago, where it would remain for the next 44 years before relocating its headquarters to New York City and taking more modern space for its Chicago operations.

By the late 1930s, the firm's marketing brochure was promising "independence that enables us to say plainly from the outside what cannot always be said safely from within." The firm was also providing executive recruiting services for its clients, which during the late 1930s included the Chicago Title and Trust Company, the University of Chicago, General Mills, and the *Washington Post.* During this period, Booz personally conducted the first study ever of a nationwide institution, the American National Red Cross, which propelled the firm into institutional consulting.

EMPHASIS ON GOVERNMENT AND MILITARY CONSULTING EMERGES: FORTIES

Booz, Fry, Allen & Hamilton entered the 1940s with a significant midwestern client base and a newly established New York branch office. In 1940, the firm expanded into military consulting, when U.S. Navy Secretary Frank Knox, former publisher of the *Chicago Daily News,* hired the company to assess the Navy's preparedness for a major war and to evaluate the Navy's shipyards, telephone systems, and intelligence operations.

After the United States entered World War II, the firm continued to work for the Navy, as well as for the Army and the War Production Board. By 1942, a growing percentage of the firm's billings came from government and military assignments. The firm's increasing interest in work for the government, which Fry denounced as the wrong market for a consulting service,

KEY DATES

1914: Edwin G. Booz establishes The Business Research Service, a consulting business based in Chicago.

1919: After serving in World War I, Booz returns to Chicago and forms Edwin G. Booz, Business Engineering Service.

1924: Booz's consulting practice is renamed Edwin G. Booz Surveys.

1936: The firm changes its name to Booz, Fry, Allen & Hamilton.

1942: The firm, renamed Booz, Allen & Hamilton, relies increasingly on government and military business.

1953: Booz Allen is awarded its first overseas contract.

1962: Shedding its status as a partnership, Booz Allen becomes a private corporation.

1970: Booz Allen converts to public ownership, though returns to private ownership six years later.

1982: Booz Allen develops a strategic repositioning program for AT&T's divestiture.

1994: Booz Allen's sales eclipse $950 million during its 80th anniversary.

1999: Ralph Shrader is elected chairman and chief executive officer.

2004: With $2.7 billion in sales, Booz Allen celebrates its 90th anniversary.

2008: The company spins off its commercial business and sells a majority stake in its government consulting business to The Carlyle Group.

led to friction with Booz and in the midst of the feud a frustrated Allen again left the firm. Fry resigned from the partnership in December 1942 to start his own consulting business, and Allen returned early the following year to a renamed partnership, Booz, Allen & Hamilton, where he was asked to help mold the firm's organizational structure and chair a newly established executive committee.

By war's end, Booz Allen had nearly 400 clients throughout the country being served by offices in Chicago, New York, and a new Los Angeles location. In 1946, Hamilton died, and, the following year, Booz retired, leaving Allen as chairperson of the firm's govern-

ing board. The firm's early postwar work included assignments for S.C. Johnson (known as Johnson Wax) and Radio Corporation of America (RCA), whose chairperson, General David Sarnoff, initially hired Booz Allen to do an organizational survey of RCA. During the late 1940s, Booz Allen also worked for RCA's subsidiary, National Broadcasting Company (NBC), conducting studies of NBC's radio/record division and the young television industry.

Booz Allen's work for the federal government and its military organizations continued in peacetime, and, in 1947, the firm received an Air Force contract to conduct the government's original production management study on guided missiles. Between 1949 and 1955, Booz Allen landed nearly two dozen of these so-called Wright Field assignments, which included a study of Air Force contractors' missile production capabilities.

Booz Allen entered the 1950s as one of only a few management consultant firms in the United States. During the early 1950s, the firm continued to build on its traditional midwestern manufacturing client base, which grew to include Maytag, Parker Pen, Johnson Wax, and Cessna, a small-airplane manufacturer. In 1951, Edwin G. Booz died, leaving behind a pioneering company on the verge of international expansion and diversification.

INTERNATIONAL EXPANSION BEGINS IN THE FIFTIES

In 1953, Booz Allen landed its first international contract, an assignment to study and help reorganize land-ownership records for the newly established Philippine government. About the same time, the firm began helping reorganize the government of Egypt's customs operations and a government-owned Egyptian textile manufacturer. By the mid-1950s, Booz Allen had created an international subsidiary and moved into Italy to conduct studies of a nationalized steel company and state-owned oil company.

In 1955, a group of key Booz Allen partners formed Booz Allen Applied Research, Inc., (BAARINC) as a separate corporate entity. Utilizing the Wright Field studies on missile production as a foundation, BAARINC was designed to launch the firm's diversification into the intelligence arena and was formed around a Booz Allen team of guided missile specialists. BAARINC was soon hired by the federal government to help determine where the Soviet Union was manufacturing missiles and to compile a so-called Red Book, which outlined technical problems Soviets experienced in developing weaponry. During the late 1950s, Booz Allen also worked with the National Aeronautics and Space Administration (NASA), helping to determine the best way to reach the moon—and served on a Navy task force which developed PERT, or the Program Evaluation and Review Technique designed to improve the planning and production of the Polaris submarine missile.

By the close of the decade, Booz Allen was, in the words of a 1959 *Time* article, "the world's largest, most prestigious management consultant firm," having served three-fourths of the country's largest businesses, two-thirds of the federal government's departments, and most types of nonprofit institutions during its first 46 years. During the 1950s, the firm's number of partners grew from 12 to 60, while its total professional staff increased to more than 500, one-third of which were specialists.

CHANGE IN STRUCTURE IN 1962

In 1962, in order to establish profit-sharing and retirement plans for its partners, Booz Allen became a private corporation, and the partnership that had governed the firm legally was dissolved (although the term *partner* continued to be used). That year, James Allen became the new corporations' chairperson and passed the reins of active leadership to Charlie Bowen, who was named president. Between 1962 and 1964, BAARINC acquired two subsidiaries, Designers for Industry (renamed Design & Development) and Foster D. Snell Laboratory. Shortly thereafter, BAARINC also became a Booz Allen subsidiary, bringing to the firm a client list that included IBM, Abbott Labs, United Airlines, and the U.S. Department of the Interior.

During this time, Booz Allen's nonfederal government work included a study on the efficiency of the Nassau County, New York, government and a study of the Chicago public school system. In the corporate arena, Booz Allen helped Johnson Wax expand in Europe, aided Deere & Company in a restructuring, and orchestrated the merger of Rockwell Standard and North American Aviation, resulting in formation of North American Rockwell Corp.

Overseas expansion continued as well, with Booz Allen deployed to evaluate a variety of European industries, including British heavy industry and consumer goods manufacturers and West German and Scandinavian steel producers. Booz Allen was also engaged in a series of assignments for the World Bank to help the governments of Brazil, Argentina, and Venezuela develop steel industries. Moreover, Booz Allen was hired by the Algerian government to help it develop an integrated oil operation which could compete in the world marketplace; similar assignments soon followed in Iran, Abu Dhabi, and Saudi Arabia.

During the Vietnam War, Booz Allen conducted studies for Secretary of Defense Robert McNamara, including a series of feasibility studies involving the so-

called Supersonic Transport plane. Booz Allen also provided the U.S. military with assessments of communications equipment during the firm's first "field work" assignment, in which consultants accompanied military patrols in gathering information on the use of American communications equipment by Vietnamese allies.

By 1969 Booz Allen, the largest consulting firm in the United States, had more than 15 major or project offices on five continents, generating annual revenues of $55 million and earnings of $3.5 million. Having experienced explosive growth during the decade, Booz Allen considered going public, launching a brief debate regarding the ethics of public ownership of a business that stressed confidentiality.

PUBLIC DEBUT IN 1970

The following year, James Allen retired, Bowen was named chairperson and chief executive, and James W. Taylor became president. In January 1970, the firm went public, following the lead of Arthur D. Little, Inc., which had initiated public ownership of large consulting firms a year earlier. The Booz Allen public offering was designed to help the company diversify by giving the firm the ability to acquire specialized companies through stock swaps. Between 1969 and 1972, Booz Allen purchased several small specialty consulting firms. These acquisitions included firms involved in transportation, household chemicals, airport management, real estate, market research, and television advertising testing. The market research, airport, and chemicals operations were later spun off. In 1972, the firm also established a Japanese subsidiary.

During the early 1970s, BAARINC was hired by NASA to assess the ability of a $100 million satellite to orbit the earth for one year. BAARINC predicted the satellite would fail within four days, which it did, building BAARINC's reputation in space systems work and leading to a subsequent assignment to test a redesigned satellite, which met Booz Allen specifications and stayed in orbit for 18 months.

During this time, Booz Allen's government assignments leveled off and then declined, as did commercial work during this "energy crisis" period when consultants became a discretionary budget item for many companies. As a result, Booz Allen's profit margins suffered, and its stock prices slid, as government billings were cut in half and profits from Europe became nearly nonexistent.

In 1973, with the firm in decline, Taylor was asked to resign and Bowen named James Farley as Taylor's successor. Farley formed a cabinet of advisers comprised of unit business heads, and then expanded that team concept with the establishment of a larger operating council, which included the firm's principal managers. The company then made its officers owners, allowing each officer to buy a certain percent of Booz Allen stock. The firm also stepped up its push into international markets, via such avenues as a new Italian subsidiary, and increased its diversification into specialized markets.

$100 MILLION IN SALES BY 1976

In 1976, after four years of gradually buying back its stock, Booz Allen again became a private company in a final buyout that paid outside shareholders $7.75 a share, considerably less than the $24 per share price Booz Allen's stock debuted at earlier in the decade. Farley was named chairperson and chief executive, and John L. Lesher became president. The retirement of Bowen that year marked the close of a quick turnaround for Booz Allen, which saw its billings rise from $54 million in 1972 to $100 million by the end of 1976.

During the mid- and late 1970s, Booz Allen conducted studies of the telecommunications market and the Bell telephone system for AT&T and was engaged in a seven-year assignment for the city of Wichita, Kansas, to help establish a prototype municipal computer information system, which brought the firm national recognition. Booz Allen's expanded work in communications electronics and commercial telecommunications led the firm into new, specialized markets, including communications security, strategic and national command and control systems, and intelligence systems. One result of this increasing technological diversification was a contract to work on the Tri-Service Tactical Communications Program, which involved the coordination of U.S. Army, Navy, and Air Force communications.

In 1978, BAARINC changed its name to Public Management & Technology Center (later becoming known simply as the Technology Center) and refocused its office automation, manufacturing technology, and space systems services, leading to work on the commercialization of space stations. PMTC diversified into new markets, including nuclear survivability, electronic systems engineering, avionics, and software verification and validations, and began offering clients cost containment and flexible pricing options. Key contracts for PMTC during the late 1970s included Navy assignments to help develop the Trident missile and help rebuild Saudi Arabia's navy.

During this time, Booz Allen also helped Chrysler Corporation in its historic turnaround by devising a plan to secure federal loan guarantees for the automaker

and then by serving as a troubleshooter after the federal bailout, monitoring the company's performance for the federal loan guarantee board. Booz Allen also helped orchestrate Hong Kong and Shanghai Banking Corporation's acquisition of Marine Midland after providing HSBC with a comprehensive study of the U.S. banking network.

By 1980, Booz Allen's annual revenues had climbed to $180 million, having more than tripled in a decade, and the company was running a close second in U.S. consulting service billings to Arthur Andersen. The Navy remained one of Booz Allen's principal clients during the 1980s, while Warner-Lambert Company also became an important corporate client, helping to launch the firm into healthcare consulting. Overseas, Booz Allen entered the decade engaged in oil and steel industry work in West Africa, Indonesia, and Nigeria, while also employed in Zambia to help consolidate that country's copper mining industry.

By 1983, recessionary conditions and an oil glut led to a profit slump for Booz Allen. The following year, Farley stepped down from his posts as chairperson and chief executive, returning to client work before becoming president of MONY Financial Services. Before leaving Booz Allen, however, Farley established a firmwide competition to select his successor in what proved to be, according to a 1988 *Forbes* article, a divisive and distracting ten-month process. Ultimately, Michael McCullough, president of PMTC since its 1978 reorganization, was chosen to succeed Farley. Under McCullough, PMTC had remained a bright spot in Booz Allen operations as commercial consulting lagged, generating annual billings of more than $100 million by 1984, while developing information systems for such clients as the U.S. Postal Service and the U.S. House of Representatives.

Also in the early 1980s, Booz Allen provided extensive services to AT&T, helping develop a strategic repositioning program for its divestiture of the local Bell operating companies.

COMMERCIAL WORK DIMINISHES IN THE EIGHTIES

During the mid-1980s, Booz Allen's commercial consulting work began to wane, and rival McKinsey & Company became the powerhouse of general management consulting, and Arthur D. Little grew into a leader in technology consulting. Booz Allen relied increasingly on government work. By 1987, government accounts, with the lowest profit margin in the consulting field, represented nearly one-third of Booz Allen's $340 million in annual revenues at a time when defense spending was increasingly being targeted for budget cuts.

McCullough responded to Booz Allen's mid-1980s slump by restructuring the firm around industries rather than traditional geographic boundaries and emphasizing a multidisciplinary approach to business problems, utilizing technical specialists in tandem with management consulting experts. McCullough's approach at the time was relatively untried, with most firms specializing in either management or technology. In 1989, the company launched a major expansion program of its computer systems integration (CSI) services for commercial clients, in an effort to expand its presence in the commercial computer systems and technology market. Booz Allen entered the commercial systems integration field when CSI was the fastest-growing segment of the consulting industry, and also one of the toughest to crack; Booz Allen had to compete with both computer manufacturers and technology consulting firms.

BOOZ ALLEN IN THE NINETIES

In 1990, William F. Stasior, a senior executive from Booz Allen's technology business, was named president of the firm. The following year, Stasior assumed the additional duties of chairperson and chief executive, after McCullough returned to consulting as a senior partner, having spearheaded a six-year transition from a regional strategy to one increasingly focused on international operations and technology.

In 1991, Booz Allen acquired the major assets of Advanced Decision Systems Inc., a California-based artificial intelligence company, which became a Booz Allen division. By this time, Booz Allen's multidisciplinary approach to business problems had become known in the firm as "Theory P." Named for its emphasis on integrating people and process, Theory P represented a problem-solving approach concerned less with how departments operated independently and more with how they worked together to produce goods and services. This strategy was adopted by other major companies, including Hewlett-Packard, Corning Glass Works, and Ford Motor Company.

During the early 1990s, Booz Allen also began offering its clients a type of corporate war game that simulated competition among companies and served as a business strategy tool. In 1993, Booz Allen was hired by the U.S. Agency for International Development to devise a strategy to lead a consortium of firms in the privatization of civilian and defense industries in 11 newly independent states of the former Soviet Union.

That year, two reports prepared by Booz Allen took center stage in the Delaware Supreme Court. The first, which Paramount Communications had used to inform their decision on whether to be acquired by Viacom

Inc., revealed that Paramount and Viacom together would generate nearly ten times more profit than a Paramount merger with QVC Network Inc., which was also vying to acquire Paramount. In December 1993, the Booz Allen report on possible merger combinations, which included confidential data from Viacom but not QVC, was introduced as evidence in a legal battle between Viacom and QVC over the Paramount acquisition; Paramount sought a reversal of a court decision ruling that it had illegally rejected a QVC offer. Following the Delaware Supreme Court ruling in favor of QVC, Booz Allen prepared a subsequent report with confidential information from QVC, which resulted in the same conclusions as the first study.

GOVERNMENT WORK DRIVES GROWTH IN LATE NINETIES

Booz Allen recorded tremendous physical and financial growth between its 80th and 90th anniversary. When nearly 6,000 employees participated in anniversary celebrations in 1994, the company's sales neared the $1 billion mark. It had taken eight decades for the company to approach the financial milestone, but within a few short years it would increase its volume of business exponentially, as its payroll swelled to 20,000 employees. Numerous major contracts fueled the growth during the company's first wave of expansion, notably projects completed for two federal clients, the U.S. General Services Administration (GSA) and the U.S. Internal Revenue Service (IRS). In 1996, the GSA awarded Booz Allen a $620 million telecommunications contract, the largest contract of its kind. The year also saw a spate of new branch office openings, as the company opened eight new offices in Asia, Europe, the Middle East, and South America to expand its network of satellite locations to 90. In 1998, the company's other major federal contract, its work for the IRS, began, as Booz Allen consultants focused their talents on developing a sweeping transformation program for the 100,000-employee organization. A 250-member Booz Allen team worked on improving the IRS's dismal customer-service reputation, which involved reorganizing the agency, improving its web site, and modernizing its computer systems.

RALPH SHRADER TAKES COMMAND IN 1999

Booz Allen's reliance on business from the public sector became increasingly important under the leadership of Ralph W. Shrader. Appointed chairman and chief executive officer in 1999, Shrader joined Booz Allen in the mid-1970s and played an instrumental role in helping with the AT&T divestiture in the early 1980s. Shrader, who earned his doctorate degree in electrical engineering from the University of Illinois, served as president of Booz Allen's worldwide technology business before being elected to the two most powerful positions at the company. Under his command, Booz Allen increased its dependence on governmental work to an extent that could not be imagined when he first took office.

The demand for the type of services provided by Booz Allen increased substantially following the terrorist attacks in 2001. Government spending increased and a host of new federal agencies charged with tightening security measures emerged, creating needs answered by Booz Allen. "They look at your stuff and say, 'These are significant threats,' and tell you how you should plan on minimizing them," a Booz Allen client said in the July 23, 2004 edition of the *Post and Courier.* The company's entrenched position in the public sector held it in good stead, while its rivals, McKinsey & Company and Boston Consulting Group, who relied more on commercial work, suffered financial declines after 2001. By the time Booz Allen celebrated its 90th anniversary in 2004, its sales had increased to $2.7 billion, nearly tripling during the previous decade, and its payroll swelled to 16,000.

BOOZ ALLEN SPLITS IN TWO IN 2008

Shrader's accomplishments earned the applause of Booz Allen's board of directors. His tenure was extended by another term in 2004, ensuring that he would preside as chairman and chief executive officer until October 2009. One of the most important developments during his second term of office occurred in 2008, when the company allied itself entirely to the public sector. The company spun off its commercial practice as a separate company named Booz & Company, part of an arrangement that saw it sell a majority stake in its government consulting business to The Carlyle Group. A Washington, D.C.-based private equity firm with more than $80 billion worth of assets, The Carlyle Group paid $2.54 billion for its stake.

The government consulting business retained the name Booz Allen Hamilton Inc. and it counted Shrader as its chairman and chief executive officer. "Completing this separation of our two core businesses is an important milestone in our history," Shrader said in the August 1, 2008 issue of *TendersInfo.* "The success of these businesses over many decades and the significant opportunities that lie ahead for both are a tribute to generations of Booz Allen people and clients. Looking ahead," Shrader added, "we are excited about Carlyle's investment and the ability to leverage their experience in our growing U.S. government consulting business, and

we look forward to continuing to collaborate with our Booz & Company colleagues on assignments where our joint capabilities benefit clients." With those words, Booz Allen headed toward its next major anniversary, when the corporate-oriented consulting business founded by Edwin Booz would celebrate its centennial as a government-focused company.

Roger W. Rouland
Updated, Jeffrey L. Covell

PRINCIPAL DIVISIONS

Civil Government; Defense; Energy; Environment; Health; Homeland Security; Intelligence; Law Enforcement; Not-for-Profit/Non-Governmental Organizations; Transportation.

PRINCIPAL COMPETITORS

Accenture Ltd.; BearingPoint, Inc.; McKinsey & Company.

FURTHER READING

Baum, Laurie, "Is Booz Allen Having a Mid-Life Crisis?" *Business Week,* March 9, 1987, pp. 76–80.

Berton, Lee, and Paul B. Carroll, "Booz Allen Plans a Major Expansion in Computer Systems Integration Work," *Wall Street Journal,* January 30, 1989, p. C5.

"Booz, Allen Tells Rich Inside Story," *Business Week,* December 20, 1969, pp. 22–23.

"Booz, Allen Tries to Cure Its Own Ills," *Business Week,* January 20, 1973, pp. 26–28.

Bowman, Jim, *Booz Allen & Hamilton: Seventy Years of Client Service,* New York: Kenner Printing, 1984.

Coy, Peter, "Oh, What a Lovely War Game," *Business Week,* February 1, 1993, p. 34.

Gillies, Andrew T., "Booz Allen's Sweet Spot," *Forbes,* November 25, 2002, p. 190.

"The Instant Executives," *Forbes,* November 15, 1967, pp. 27–41.

Machan, Dyan, "Gladiators' Ball," *Forbes,* December 26, 1988, pp. 130–34.

"Management Experts Thrive on Own Advice," *Business Week,* April 23, 1960, pp. 104–18.

"The New Shape of Management Consulting," *Business Week,* May 21, 1979, pp. 98–104.

Robinson, Christine, "Booz Allen Hamilton Sees Rapid Growth After Sept. 11, 2001," *Post and Courier,* July 23, 2004.

"United States: Booz Allen Hamilton Completes Separation of Core Businesses and Sale of Majority Stake in Government Business to The Carlyle Group," *TendersInfo,* August 1, 2008.

Brenntag Holding GmbH & Co. KG

Stinnes-Platz 1
Mülheim an der Ruhr, 45472
Germany
Telephone: (+49 208) 7828-0
Fax: (+49 208) 7828-698
Web site: http://www.brenntag.com

Private Company
Incorporated: 1874 as Philipp Mühsam AG
Employees: 11,000
Sales: EUR 6.7 billion ($9.1 billion) (2007)
NAICS: 424690 Other Chemical and Allied Products
    Merchant Wholesalers

■ ■ ■

Brenntag Holding GmbH & Co. KG is Europe's largest distributor of industrial and specialty chemicals. Owned by the London-based private-equity firm BC Partners Limited, Brenntag is headquartered in the small German city of Mülheim on the Ruhr River, the country's most industrialized corridor. In addition to its preeminent position in Europe, where 57 percent of its sales originate, Brenntag is also a global leader in the distribution of chemicals, ranking third in North America (31 percent of sales) and first in Latin America (7.5 percent). The company's operations include more than 300 facilities in 64 countries around the world.

19TH-CENTURY ROOTS

Brenntag has been in continuous operation since it was founded in 1874. The early 1870s were a propitious time for establishing new businesses in Germany, which had recently been unified after a series of bloody wars. Germany's nationalistic government was anxious to put an end to centuries of economic stagnation and to assert the country's primacy in Europe.

In this favorable climate, Philipp Mühsam, a young German entrepreneur, founded a small business on the river Spree, the chief artery of Germany's new capital, Berlin. Named after its founder, Philipp Mühsam AG did a flourishing business, first specializing in egg wholesaling and then moving into the trading of canned goods by 1878. By 1879 the firm had entered into the chemical distribution sector, which by the early 1890s had overtaken the original lines as the company core. As the capital city of the largest European country, Berlin was rapidly becoming the showplace of everything modern in the late 19th century, and also the center of the country's new chemical industry. In fact, the modern German chemical industry was by 1900 the most advanced in the world and the first to employ academically trained researchers.

Contributing to Germany's emerging chemical industry became the chief role of Philipp Mühsam AG. By the beginning of the 20th century, its core businesses focused on petroleum as well as on the purchase and distribution of industrial chemicals. Such activities necessitated an international transportation network, which would be upset temporarily during the upheavals of World War I and the subsequent civil unrest. Back on its feet during the 1920s, the company expanded its network under the leadership of Mühsam's successors, and despite the worldwide economic depression of the

COMPANY PERSPECTIVES

Brenntag offers its suppliers and customers innovative ways of working together based on a precise knowledge of production and distribution. As the link between producers and users of chemicals we ensure maximum effectiveness and added value. Our process-oriented logistics solutions enable our suppliers and customers to concentrate on their core businesses and benefit from our know-how and our efficiency.

1930s, the firm remained the largest distributor of petroleum and industrial chemicals in Germany.

WARTIME SHIFT IN PRODUCTION

Because of its clearly Jewish name, Philipp Mühsam AG operated in an increasingly hostile environment once the Nazis came to power. Their lives in danger, the Mühsam family sold the business in early 1937 to the Stinnes family, owners of one of Germany's largest industrial concerns, Hugo Stinnes GmbH. The Mühsam family then immigrated to the United States. Philipp Mühsam AG was not incorporated into the Hugo Stinnes company but remained privately owned by the Stinnes family. In July 1937 the company's name was changed to Brennstoff-, Chemikalien- und Transport AG, but this rather unwieldy name was soon abbreviated, in February 1938, to Brenntag AG. While its traditional operations in petroleum and industrial chemical distribution remained, a new and important branch was added: the allocation of mineral oil byproducts of petroleum, which would be indispensable to the manufacture of cosmetics during the postwar era.

Wartime, however, generated other needs. While raw materials such as petroleum could still be obtained in the vast Nazi-held territories of Eastern Europe during World War II, daily Allied bombing took its toll on Brenntag's business, which during this time consisted wholly of distribution and transportation. By the end of the war, Brenntag AG lay in utter ruin.

POSTWAR RECOVERY

Following the war, Brenntag, still privately held by the Stinnes family, recovered slowly from the turmoil of the war years. A handful of employees remained with the firm when it launched a new beginning with the 1948

relocation of headquarters from Berlin in Germany's eastern zone to the more secure town of Mülheim on the Ruhr, in western Germany. With only 20 employees, the company slowly recaptured its former lead in the chemical transportation industry. Before too long, Brenntag also purchased a number of shipping operations.

Recovery would not have been possible without major currency reform in the western zones in 1948, the unification of the three occupation zones into the Federal Republic of Germany in 1949, and the onset of the Marshall Plan for European economic recovery, which followed unification. Brenntag became decidedly more attuned to the market, especially in the international arena. Management divested the company of its former shares in various manufacturing enterprises, as well as of its shipping business, and concentrated instead on broadening its product lines and increasing its focus on chemical distribution and transportation. Of great urgency in the postwar years was expansion into international markets. Aggressive inroads, most particularly in the biggest and richest market of all, the United States, were made in the 1950s, in the company's first venture on the North American continent. During this time, thousands of tons of industrial chemicals landed in the ports of the Low Countries for transshipment throughout Europe by Brenntag AG. Inroads were also made into Eastern Europe, an area to which Brenntag had had commercial ties for decades. In the following three decades, the Communist countries of the East would constitute a stable but limited market for Brenntag's chemical products. This market would explode in significance and range with the fall of Communism in the late 1980s.

New product lines were developed in the prosperous 1950s, including aromatic petrochemicals for the cosmetics industry, synthetic materials and resins, and chemical solvents, all of which would be purchased and distributed to the major European chemical manufacturers from sources in Europe and overseas.

NEW PARENTAGE IN THE SIXTIES

In 1952 ownership of Brenntag passed into the hands of Otto Stinnes. This member of the Stinnes family ran into financial difficulties in the early 1960s, and Brenntag ended up being sold to the Bank für Gemeinwirtschaft in 1963. A year later this bank sold Brenntag to the largest transportation and distribution company in West Germany, Hugo Stinnes AG, which no longer had any ties with the Stinnes family, for what was considered the immense sum of DM 13 million. With one stroke, Stinnes had plunged into the lucrative industrial chemical distribution market, which

KEY DATES

1874: Philipp Mühsam founds a distribution business in Berlin, initially specializing in egg wholesaling.

1879: Company enters the chemicals trading sector, which soon becomes the core business.

1937: The Mühsam family sells Philipp Mühsam AG to the Stinnes family; company is renamed Brennstoff-, Chemikalien- und Transport AG.

1938: Company name is abbreviated to Brenntag AG.

1948: Headquarters are shifted to Mülheim, Germany.

1964: Brenntag is acquired by Hugo Stinnes AG (later Stinnes AG).

2000: Acquisition of Holland Chemical International makes Brenntag the largest chemical distributor in the world.

2004: Brenntag is acquired by Boston-based private-equity firm Bain Capital, LLC, and renamed Brenntag Holding GmbH & Co. KG.

2006: Bain Capital sells Brenntag to the London-based private-equity firm BC Partners Limited.

complemented its other businesses in the distribution and transportation of raw materials and petroleum, as well as overseas shipping. The transaction represented a major step toward diversifying Stinnes (which altered its name in 1976 to Stinnes AG) as well as toward greatly broadening Brenntag's customer base. By then Brenntag's sales revenues were in the hundreds of millions of dollars; 20 years later, they would exceed a billion. Another advantage of Brenntag's acquisition by Stinnes was the greater financial resources of the parent company, which continued to endow Brenntag with a secure economic base. In 1965 Stinnes AG and Brenntag were acquired by Germany's largest firm, the energy company VEBA AG. Stinnes remained a wholly owned subsidiary of VEBA.

After becoming a member of the Stinnes Group of companies, Brenntag's growth was dramatic. Branch offices were established throughout Germany and the rest of Europe. Out of necessity the company became involved in more than just the buying and selling of a wide array of products, including industrial chemicals, agricultural chemicals, and made-to-order specialty

chemicals. Large investments were also made in fleets of trucks, storage facilities, and tanks, all of which were indispensable in the distribution of Brenntag's products. Sales offices expanding in key geographical areas rapidly transmitted and facilitated customer orders.

EXPANSION AND INDUSTRY CONSOLIDATION IN POSTCOMMUNIST ERA

In the late 1980s, Brenntag underwent tremendous expansion. The fall of Communism in Eastern Europe and the demise of the Soviet Union enabled Brenntag to expand its bases in the East and open new branches in Warsaw, Prague, and even Moscow. With the fall of the Berlin Wall, Brenntag was one of the first West German companies to expand into eastern Germany, opening 15 branches in a year, and establishing Brenntag affiliates in Erfurt, Chemnitz, and the former East Berlin.

In the early 1990s, chemical firms and their suppliers came under increasing scrutiny for their possible roles in polluting and diminishing the world's natural resources. In addition, stringent new environmental laws forced many of these companies out of business, and burdened the remaining ones with enormous cleanup and safety costs. This was just one of many economic factors influencing a shift toward consolidation as a means of rationalization—greater efficiency in the use of financial and other resources.

As *Chemical Week* reported in 1995, the German chemical distribution industry was the largest in Europe, and at its pinnacle was Brenntag, which according to board member Ernst-Hermann Luttmann had experienced 2 percent growth in the preceding fiscal year, its first increase since 1991. The company's more efficient use of resources received much of the credit for this improvement. In Berlin, for instance, Brenntag jointly operated a warehousing venture with Biesterfeld, the second largest chemical distributor in the country. In Nuremberg, Brenntag subsidiary Staub & Co. similarly cooperated with Biesterfeld in its logistical operations. Such cooperation might have seemed strange a few years before, but the new business climate would be characterized by fewer companies possessing more resources and applying more efficient methods, even joining forces with a competitor.

In line with moves toward consolidation, Brenntag shut down several smaller warehouses and brought together a number of its operations. When in 1994 it acquired F & A Wülfing of Gevelsberg, Brenntag closed down two other warehouses in Solingen and Wuppertal. From 1990 to 1995, according to *Chemical Week,* the company had gone from 22 distribution centers in Germany to just 12, six of them operated with partners.

Consolidation of resources did not stop the company from continuing to acquire subsidiaries, and indeed its acquisitions in the 1990s were consistent with the industry-wide trend toward larger companies. Just as Stinnes AG consisted of many companies, Brenntag also came to represent a group of firms specializing in different chemicals and services. For instance, in the same city on the Ruhr where the parent company was located, Brenntag Eurochem GmbH provided made-to-order specialty chemicals.

LATE-CENTURY ACQUISITION SPREE

Among Brenntag's acquisitions in 1997 were Spanish, American, Franco-Belgian, and Swiss companies. With yearly receipts of DM 145 million, Productos Químicos Sevillanos, S.A., of Seville was Spain's second largest chemical distributor; by putting it with its other holdings, Brenntag became the leader in the Spanish market. In 1997 Brenntag also acquired the Franco-Belgian company Bonnave, with cumulative annual sales of DM 165 million in the two countries. This acquisition solidified Brenntag's leadership in the French market, and put it in first place in Belgium as well. Also, Brenntag acquired Christ Chemie AG of Switzerland.

Outside of Europe, Brenntag was most heavily represented in the United States, where Reading, Pennsylvania-based SOCO Chemical, Inc., coordinated all U.S. activities, involving seven U.S. distribution firms with branches in more than 50 locations throughout the country. Even during the recession of the early 1990s, Brenntag's U.S. business fared well, although cost-cutting and streamlining accounted for much of the gain in profitability. In 1997 SOCO acquired Burris Chemical Inc. of Charleston, South Carolina, the largest independent distributor of industrial chemicals in the southeastern United States. Burris also maintained operations in North Carolina and Alabama. SOCO Chemical's name was changed to Brenntag, Inc., in 1998.

As it approached the end of the century, Brenntag offered an increasingly sophisticated and detailed list of chemical products and services to chemical processors. In the increasingly vital environmental area and related fields, a host of Brenntag companies provided recycling services, packaging materials, drying and cleaning assistance, waste hauling, consulting, and marketing. A visit to its web site offered an A-to-Z sampling of the company's wide array of products, from absorbent, acetic acid, and acetone to zinc oxides, zinc stearates, and zinc sulphate. Among the services Brenntag offered in the late 1990s was online tank sensor equipment. When supplies of a chemical fell to a certain point, it registered on the sensor, and it transmitted the information online to the company. This alerted the latter to dispatch a resupply delivery.

Under the leadership of Chief Executive Rients Visser, Brenntag continued its spending spree in 1998. Its purchases of chemical distributors that year included Schuster & Sohn Group of Kaiserslautern, Germany, a firm with annual revenues of DM 80 million ($43.7 million). Brenntag's U.S. position was bolstered via the acquisitions of Milwaukee-based Milsolv Corporation, which generated annual sales of $100 million, and South Plainfield, New Jersey-based Whittaker, Clark & Daniels, Inc., a company concentrating on the distribution of specialty chemicals to the plastics and rubber, coatings, cosmetics, food, and pharmaceutical industries. By the end of the 1990s, Brenntag was generating more than $700 million in revenues a year in the United States, where it ranked number five among chemical distributors.

TO THE GLOBAL TOP

The pressure for Brenntag to make further deals grew stronger in 1999 when the Dutch firms Van Ommeren and Pakhoed NV merged to form Royal Vopak NV, which ranked first in the world among chemical distributors but second in Europe behind Brenntag. The German firm began 2000 by strengthening its position in central and Eastern Europe through the acquisition of Vienna-based Neuber GmbH from Degussa-Hüls AG. Neuber, a concern with sales of DM 420 million ($220 million), was the leading chemical distributor in Austria and Poland and also had strong positions in Croatia, the Czech Republic, Slovakia, and Hungary. Its 19 locations increased Brenntag's European network total to nearly 100.

Of even greater consequence, however, was the November 2000 takeover of Holland Chemical International (HCI) for EUR 288 million ($255 million) plus the assumption of EUR 257 million in debt. The addition of HCI's EUR 1.3 billion in annual sales pushed Brenntag's revenues over the EUR 4 billion mark, making it the largest chemical distributor in the world. The deal was even more significant on a geographic basis. HCI, though based in Amsterdam, generated about 78 percent of its sales in the Americas, whereas three-quarters of Brenntag's sales had come from Europe. HCI had ranked number five in the U.S. market, and the combined U.S. operations of the two firms ranked third. Buying HCI also provided Brenntag with an entry into Canada and the leading positions in both Latin America and Scandinavia, two markets where the firm had been absent. As the second largest chemical distributor in Eastern Europe, HCI served to bolster Brenntag's position in that region as well.

During 2001 Brenntag restructured its enlarged U.S. operations. With the exception of three specialty chemical subsidiaries, the company's remaining 18 U.S. subsidiaries were streamlined into six regional businesses: Great Lakes, Mid-South, Northeast, Southeast, Southwest, and West. In October 2001 Visser retired as chief executive. Promoted to the top from the number two position was Klaus Engel, who had led the integration of HCI into Brenntag. During the following year, Brenntag completed acquisitions of smaller companies in Brazil, Bulgaria, and Spain and also entered into a joint venture with Wilhelm E. H. Biesterfeld GmbH & Co. KG concentrating on the distribution of industrial chemicals. Revenues for 2002 amounted to EUR 4.3 billion ($4.5 billion), while earnings before interest and taxes increased 7.4 percent to EUR 164.4 million.

THE PRIVATE-EQUITY OWNERSHIP ERA

In early 2003 state-owned rail operator Deutsche Bahn AG completed a takeover of Brenntag's parent, Stinnes. Wishing to concentrate on its transportation operations, Deutsche Bahn soon placed Brenntag on the auction block. Private-equity companies emerged as the lead bidders, and in March 2004 the Boston-based private-equity firm Bain Capital, LLC, purchased both Brenntag and another Stinnes unit, the steel-trading unit Interfer, for EUR 1.4 billion ($1.14 billion).

Under Bain's ownership, the newly named Brenntag Holding GmbH & Co. KG strengthened itself through targeted investments in its infrastructure, such as the upgrades of warehouses in Duisburg, Germany, and São Paolo, Brazil, that were completed in late 2004, and via a new string of strategic acquisitions. Purchases in 2005 included specialty chemical distributors in the United Kingdom and Spain as well as Quadra Chemicals, Inc., which bolstered Brenntag's position in the U.S. Pacific Northwest. The company followed up the Quadra purchase with the March 2006 acquisition of Los Angeles Chemical Group of Companies, of Southgate, California, a firm with annual sales of $165 million. These latest deals propelled Brenntag into a market leader in the western United States. In June 2006 the company completed major acquisitions closer to home, purchasing Albion Chemicals Group Ltd., the second largest distributor of industrial and specialty chemicals in the United Kingdom and Ireland with sales of roughly £180 million ($340 million), and Schweizerhall Chemie AG, the leading chemical distributor in Switzerland with revenues of CHF 219 million ($180 million). Also in June 2006, Engel left Brenntag to

become CEO of Degussa GmbH and was succeeded by Stephen R. Clark, the longtime head of the company's North American unit.

Ownership of Brenntag switched again in July 2006 when Bain Capital sold the company to the London-based private-equity firm BC Partners Limited in a deal estimated at EUR 3 billion ($3.8 billion). The change in ownership did not affect Brenntag's strategy of pursuing global growth. Further acquisitions and significant expenditures of capital helped push sales up 9 percent in 2007 to EUR 6.7 billion ($9.1 billion). Profits were also on the rise as earnings before interest, taxes, depreciation, and amortization jumped 14 percent.

In 2008 Brenntag made several more acquisitions of specialty chemical distributors, including Dipol Chemical International, Inc., which specialized in distributing polymers and specialty chemicals in Ukraine, Russia, and the Baltic States. The company gained a foothold in Southeast Asia in September 2008 by entering into an agreement with the French chemical group Rhodia SA to distribute that company's products in Indonesia, Malaysia, the Philippines, Singapore, Thailand, and Vietnam, as well as Australia, India, and Taiwan. Going forward, acquisitions of distributors in Asia and other regions were likely to be pursued, and BC Partners was expected to eventually conduct an initial public offering of Brenntag stock.

Sina Dubovoj
Updated, Judson Knight; David E. Salamie

PRINCIPAL SUBSIDIARIES

Brenntag GmbH; Brenntag International Chemicals GmbH; CVH Chemie-Vertrieb GmbH & Co. Hannover KG; Staub & Co. Chemiehandelsgesellschaft mbH; CVB Albert Carl GmbH & Co. KG Berlin; CVM Chemievertrieb Magdeburg GmbH & Co. KG; Herkommer & Bangerter Vertriebs GmbH; Alliance Chimie Algerie SBA (Algeria); C.N. Schmidt B.V. (Algeria); Brenntag Argentina S.A.; Brenntag Pty. Ltd. (Australia); Brenntag CEE GmbH (Austria); JLC Chemie Handels GmbH (Austria); Brenntag N.V. (Belgium); Brenntag Bolivia SRL; Brenntag Brasil Ltda. (Brazil); Brenntag Bulgaria Ltd.; Brenntag Canada Inc.; Brenntag Chile Ltda.; Brenntag Colombia S.A.; Químicos Holanda Costa Rica S.A.; Brenntag Hrvatska d.o.o. (Croatia); Brenntag CR s.r.o. (Czech Republic); Brenntag Nordic A/S (Denmark); Brenntag Caribe S.A. (Dominican Republic); Brenntag Ecuador S. A.; Brenntag El Salvador S.A.; Brenntag Nordic Oy (Finland); BRENNTAG S. A. (France); Brenntag Maghreb SAS (France); Brenntag Guatemala S.A.; Inversiones

Químicas, S.A. (Honduras); Brenntag Hungária Kft. (Hungary); HCI Hungária Kft. (Hungary); Brenntag India Ltd.; P. T. Brenntag Indonesia; Brenntag S.p.A. (Italy); De Stefani S.r.l. (Italy); Natural World s.r.l. (Italy); Romana Chimici S.p.A. (Italy); SIA Brenntag Latvia; UAB Brenntag Lithuania; Brenntag Mexico, S.A. de C.V.; Brenntag Maroc, S.A.R.L. (Morocco); Alcochim Maroc SARL (Morocco); Brenntag (Holding) N.V. (Netherlands); Brenntag HoldCo B.V. (Netherlands); HCI Central Europe Holding B.V. (Netherlands); HCI U.S.A. Holdings B.V. (Netherlands); Holland Chemical International B.V. (Netherlands); Brenntag Nederland B.V. (Netherlands); C.N. Schmidt B.V. (Netherlands); H.C.I. Chemicals Nederland B.V. (Netherlands); Brenntag Vastgoed B.V. (Netherlands); Biesterfeld Chemiedistributie B.V. (Netherlands); Brenntag Nicaragua, S.A.; Brenntag Nordic AS (Norway); Brenntag Panama, S.A.; Brenntag Peru A.C.; Brenntag Philippines Inc.; Brenntag Polska Sp. z o.o. (Poland); Eurochem Service Polska (Poland); Brenntag Portugal Lda.; Brenntag Puerto Rico, Inc.; S.C. Brenntag S.R.L. (Romania); OOO Brenntag (Russia); Brenntag CEE - Office Beograd (Serbia); Brenntag Asia Pte. Ltd. (Singapore); Brenntag Singapore Pte. Ltd.; Brenntag Slovakia s.r.o. (Slovak Republic); HCI Slovakia s.r.o. (Slovak Republic); Brenntag Ljubljana d.o.o. (Slovenia); Crest Chemicals (South Africa); Brenntag Química S.A. (Spain); Especialidades Puma, S.A. (Spain); Brenntag Nordic AB (Sweden); Christ Chemie AG (Switzerland); Brenntag Schweizerhall AG (Switzerland); Chem-On Vertriebs-AG (Switzerland); Brenntag (Taiwan) Co., Ltd.; Brenntag (Thailand) Ltd.; Alliance Tunisie SARL (Tunisia); Brenntag Kimya Tic. Ltd. Sti (Turkey); Albion Chemicals Group (UK); Albion Colours Ltd. (UK); Albion Distillation Services Ltd. (UK); Albion Plastics Limited (UK); Albion Process Chemicals Ltd. (UK); Albion Solvents Ltd. (UK); Albion Water Treatment Solutions Ltd. (UK); Brenntag (UK) Ltd.; Brenntag Great Lakes, LLC (USA); Brenntag Latin America, Inc. (USA); Brenntag Mid-South, Inc. (USA); Brenntag North America, Inc. (USA); Brenntag Northeast, Inc. (USA); Brenntag Pacific, Inc. (USA); Brenntag Southeast, Inc. (USA); Brenntag Southwest, Inc. (USA); Brenntag Specialties, Inc. (USA); Coastal Chemical Co., LLC (USA); Holanda Venezuela C.A.; Rep. Office of Singapore Pte. Ltd. (Vietnam).

PRINCIPAL COMPETITORS

Univar N.V.; Azelis SA; IMCD Group B.V.; Ashland Inc.; Helm AG.

FURTHER READING

Brenntag: Your Partner in the Market, Düsseldorf: Econ Verlag, 1974.

Burridge, Elaine, "Brenntag Still at the Top," *European Chemical News,* August 1–August 7, 2005, p. 14.

Conroy, Will, "Growing East," *ICIS Chemical Business,* June 9–June 15, 2008, pp. 24–25.

Making Sure the Chemistry Is Right, Mülheim an der Ruhr, Germany: Brenntag AG, 1991.

Milmo, Sean, "Brenntag Buys Degussa-Hüls's Neuber," *Chemical Market Reporter,* January 24, 2000, p. 8.

———, "Brenntag Plans to Purchase HCI Making It Bigger Than Vopak," *Chemical Market Reporter,* September 11, 2000, p. 6.

Seewald, Nancy, "Distribution: Private Equity Changes Face of Chemical Landscape," *Chemical Week,* November 22, 2006, pp. 20–23.

Sinclair, Neil, "Bain Capital Sells Brenntag," *Chemical Market Reporter,* July 31–August 13, 2006, p. 4.

———, "Brenntag Buys Albion and Schweizerhall Chemie," *Chemical Market Reporter,* June 5–June 11, 2006, p. 14.

Whitfield, Mark, "Right Engel," *European Chemical News,* April 26–May 2, 2004, p. 19.

Young, Ian, "Brenntag Enters the U.S. Top Three," *Chemical Week,* April 25, 2001, pp. 26–28.

———, "Brenntag Makes Major Acquisitions in the U.K. and Switzerland," *Chemical Week,* May 31/June 7, 2006, p. 21.

———, "Brenntag Moves to the Top by Buying Holland Chemical," *Chemical Week,* September 13, 2000, p. 9.

———, "Brenntag Shifts Up a Gear," *Chemical Week,* August 16, 2000, pp. 50–51.

———, "Consolidation Benefits Leading Distributors," *Chemical Week,* May 24, 1995, p. 30.

———, "European Firms Are Bulking Up," *Chemical Week,* November 11, 1998, pp. 99–100, 104.

———, "A New Era Opens Up Ahead of Brenntag," *Chemical Week,* November 19, 2003, pp. 37–38.

———, "On the Road to Quality in Europe's Competitive Market," *Chemical Week,* July 22, 1992, pp. 30–32.

———, "Stinnes Agrarchemie Builds Five Centers," *Chemical Week,* February 3, 1993, p. 13.

Bristol Farms

■

915 East 230th Street
Carson, California 90745
U.S.A.
Telephone: (310) 233-4700
Fax: (310) 233-4701
Web site: http://www.bristolfarms.com

Wholly Owned Subsidiary of Supervalu, Inc.
Incorporated: 1982
Employees: 2,200
Sales: $165 million (2007 est.)
NAICS: 445110 Supermarkets and Other Grocery (Except Convenience) Stores; 311811 Retail Bakeries

■ ■ ■

Bristol Farms is a gourmet supermarket chain focused on serving upscale clientele. The company operates 16 stores in California, including more than a dozen units in Los Angeles County. Bristol Farms stocks more than 25,000 items in its stores, offering an extensive and expensive selection of meat, seafood, produce, wine, cheese, bakery, and dairy products. The company also operates a cooking school and it offers catering services. Bristol Farms is owned by Supervalu, Inc., a Minneapolis, Minnesota-based supermarket chain that ranks as the third largest competitor in the United States.

ORIGINS

For Irving Gronsky, Bristol Farms represented the start of a second career, a business launched at a point in his life when many people would have been considering retirement. Before Gronsky opened his first supermarket—a designation he argued did not apply to Bristol Farms—he spent the previous 35 years in the meatpacking business. Gronsky managed his own company, Los Angeles-based Gold Pack Meat Co., which provided a comfortable living, but eventually his interests strayed from his original line of work. Travels abroad, particularly visits to retailing icons such as Harrods in London, England, inspired him to start his own grocery business back home, one that would attempt to emulate the level of service and the quality of prepared food available in Europe's finest supermarkets.

Gronsky opened his first Bristol Farms supermarket in 1982 at the age of 58. The store, measuring 17,800 square feet, was a natural fit for its surroundings, a retail establishment that residents of Rolling Hills Estates greeted enthusiastically. A section of Palos Verdes in southwestern Los Angeles County, Rolling Hills Estates was an affluent community graced with horse paths, high-priced homes, and populated by "frazzled two-income families with more discretionary money than time," as the March 24, 1997 issue of the *Los Angeles Business Journal* characterized Gronsky's target demographic. On Silver Spur Road, in the heart of Rolling Hills Estates' commercial center, Bristol Farms made its debut, offering its well-heeled neighbors a new type of grocery-shopping experience.

"We want customers' trips to the store to be an enjoyable and rewarding experience so they will look forward to their shopping," Gronsky explained in the May 1986 issue of *Supermarket Business.* "We want the atmosphere to be right; we want the little tastings

COMPANY PERSPECTIVES

Bristol Farms' stores have been carefully designed and decorated to create a singular shopping experience that evokes the local area. For example, the Manhattan Beach store features murals depicting the coastal city in the 1930s and the Mission Viejo store evokes images of nearby Mission San Juan Capistrano. In the West Hollywood, Chasen's store they have kept the original high back leather booths that once resided in the world famous Chasen's restaurant. Other design features include stand-alone "shops" with full facades and themed props. The wine area, with its four walls, wine racks, and roof trellis, resembles a specialty wine boutique. Additionally, customer traffic flow is directed through the stylized layout to maximize customer exposure to the full range of Bristol Farms products. Finally, all merchandise is meticulously arranged by what the company calls "merchandising artistry." The produce is hand placed and shelf items are always fully stocked and neatly stacked.

throughout the store. We want the customers to enjoy the store so that at no point during their time in the store are they aggravated in any way." To achieve his goal, Gronsky created a store layout intended to evoke European boutiques, with each department within the store given a sense of individuality and stocked with the finest selection of merchandise he could find. To ensure his customers enjoyed their stay, Gronsky staffed each department with knowledgeable employees, relying largely on full-time workers, which differed from a typical supermarket that relied mainly on part-time employees. Each employee, referred to as an "owner-partner," earned stock in Gronsky's business, and each department manager shared in the business' profits.

THE OPULENCE OF BRISTOL FARMS

A visit to Bristol Farms was akin to walking along a sidewalk of convenience. The store featured ten primary departments (bakery, grocery, meat, produce, deli, cheese, wine and spirits, seafood, floral, and coffee), each operating as a distinct storefront within the store. For the customer, the boutique layout presented the gamut of shopping destinations all within a few paces: the seafood counter sat next to the meat department,

footsteps away from the produce section and dairy case, which abutted the grocery and wine section that was adjacent to the cheese island and coffee counter. Nearly every department offered samples of the merchandise available in its section—kimono-clad Japanese women, for example, offered sushi tastings in the seafood department—giving customers a hint of what each department had available. Bristol Farms, aiming to offer the best food presentation and the best selection, carried more than 25,000 different items, but it did not stock some of the merchandise a consumer would expect at a supermarket. Bristol Farms did not sell dog food, toilet paper, or diapers, for example, but it did offer black truffles at $37.49 an ounce, crab cakes at $17.99 a pound, and an 11-ounce bottle of B.R. Cohn Sonoma Estate Extra Virgin olive oil, which retailed for $69.

EXPANSION STARTS IN 1985

Gronsky knew what his target demographic wanted and consumers responded, flocking to his store on Silver Spur Road. Bristol Farms became a gourmet supermarket that rang up sales and churned out profits primarily because of the extraordinary investment in décor, personnel, and inventory. Expansion of the concept, which Gronsky approached measuredly, was limited to affluent markets, but there was no shortage of wealthy neighborhoods in the greater Los Angeles area. Gronsky opened his second Bristol Farms in tony South Pasadena in November 1985, purchasing a site formerly occupied by a Safeway supermarket. The second store, slightly larger than the Rolling Hills Estates store, measured 22,500 square feet and employed 80 full-time and 30 to 40 part-time workers.

After opening the South Pasadena store, Gronsky offered his thoughts on future expansion in a May 1986 interview with *Supermarket Business*. "I feel that with a store of this type," he said, "it takes at least two years to fine tune it and get all the people to the right spots and get it to a level of excellence where we are satisfied with it." His patience and commitment to detail led to a six-year wait before the third Bristol Farms opened in Manhattan Beach. The store, the largest of the three, measured 33,900 square feet, and featured two new dimensions of Gronsky's business: a cooking school and a catering facility. The 1991 debut of the Manhattan Beach store was the last store opened under Gronsky's ownership, although he continued to lead Bristol Farms for the next four years. When he decided to step aside, the ownership reins passed to other hands, ushering in an era of aggressive expansion that would make Bristol Farms a genuine retail chain.

KEY DATES

1982: Irving Gronsky opens the first Bristol Farms in Palos Verdes, California.

1985: A second store is opened in South Pasadena.

1991: Bristol Farms opens a third store in Manhattan Beach.

1995: Gronsky sells Bristol Farms to two investment firms, Kidd Kamm & Co. and Oaktree Capital Management, L.P.

1996: A fourth store is opened in Woodland Hills.

1997: The Bristol Farms chain expands to six stores with the opening of a unit in Long Beach.

1998: Bristol Farms opens two new stores, one in Mission Viejo and the other in Newport Beach.

1999: The company acquires Chalet Gourmet, a 7,000-square-foot store, and converts it to a Bristol Farms.

2000: Two more store openings increase the size of the Bristol Farms chain to 11 units.

2004: Albertsons, Inc., a supermarket chain based in Idaho, acquires Bristol Farms.

2006: Four new stores are opened, including one in San Diego County and another in San Francisco, during a year in which Minnesota-based Supervalu, Inc., acquires Albertsons and becomes Bristol Farms' new parent company.

2008: The company's 16th store, located in Valencia, is opened.

OWNERSHIP CHANGES HANDS IN 1995

Gronsky sold Bristol Farms for an undisclosed price in 1995. "I pretty much felt it was time to retire," he said at age 71 in the March 24, 1997 issue of *Los Angeles Business Journal*, two years after he sold his company. "There are a lot of places I want to see, a lot of things I want to do. [The] selling of Bristol Farms came at the right time in my life. I was not ready to go forward with an expansion, and Bristol Farms is the kind of company that needs to be expanded."

Expansion was the primary objective of Bristol Farms' new owners in 1995, two investment firms, Beverly Hills-based Kidd Kamm & Co. and Los Angeles-based Oaktree Capital Management, L.P. Both firms embraced expansion wholeheartedly, making their money by acquiring companies, investing in their growth for five or six years, and generating their profits by selling the acquired company or taking it public.

AGGRESSIVE EXPANSION BEGINS IN 1996

The new owners wasted little time before signaling that a new, decidedly more ambitious era in Bristol Farms' history had begun. They recruited Kevin Davis, the senior vice-president of marketing at Ralphs Grocery Company, who had spent 24 years working for the supermarket chain, to lead the charge forward. The first store opened under new management debuted in November 1996 in Woodland Hills, the company's first store in Ventura County. A second store, the chain's fifth unit, opened in Long Beach in February 1997. Further expansion was in the works as the new shepherds of the Bristol Farms concept articulated their vision of the future. "Over the next three to five years," Kurt Kamm said in a March 24, 1997 interview with the *Los Angeles Business Journal*, "we plan to open 15 stores or more." Davis, in the same interview, offered a more expansive view, saying, "We could eventually have as many as 300 high-end specialty stores nationally."

Davis's bold prediction was not realized, at least not in the dozen years that followed his statement, but Bristol Farms did expand at a pace never seen during the Gronsky era. In 1998, the company entered Orange County for the first time, opening two stores, one in Mission Viejo and another in Newport Beach. In June 1999, Davis chose to expand in an atypical fashion, acquiring what many Los Angeles residents considered a Hollywood landmark, a small store that operated under the name Chalet Gourmet. The acquisition was unusual for Bristol Farms because of the size of the outlet. At 7,000 square feet, the Hollywood location was one-third the size of the chain's other stores, but it proved to be one of the company's most successful profit makers.

As Gourmet Chalet was being brought into the Bristol Farms fold, Davis was pursuing expansion in earnest. He announced in mid-1999 that Bristol Farms was looking to raise $25 million in private placements to fund an expansion program. Davis hoped to open four to six stores annually during the ensuing three years, aiming to more than double the size of the chain through acquisitions, conversions, and new development. His objective was bold, setting the stage for the company's first steps outside the greater Los Angeles area. "Once we have 15 to 20 stores in southern California," Davis said in the June 28, 1999 issue of *Supermarket News*, "we'll look at sites in Palm Springs, Phoenix, Las Vegas, and northern California."

Again, Davis's expansion goals were not met. Instead of opening as many as 18 new stores by 2002, the company only opened two new Bristol Farms, completing all the expansion during the period in a matter of weeks at the end of 2000. In November, the company opened a store on the site of the former Chasen's restaurant, a property that enabled Bristol Farms to serve consumers in Beverly Hills and West Los Angeles. In December, the company opened its 11th store, a Bristol Farms in Redondo Beach.

AN EXPERIMENT WITH PRICING IS ABORTED

Failing to expand at his projected pace was not Davis's greatest regret during the period, however. He tinkered with Bristol Farms' pricing structure in an attempt to broaden the company's customer base. Prices were lowered, which, Davis later conceded, was a mistake. "We found we could charge less and increase sales by reaching the masses," Davis explained in the March 3, 2003 issue of *Supermarket News,* "but we also found, after playing with that approach, that it wasn't prudent because we weren't delivering the margins we needed. That's when we realized it's probably better to do less business the right way than to drive top line sales at the expense of margins."

Once Bristol Farms was back on track, the company demonstrated the level of financial performance that had described its success during its first 20 years of existence. By 2003, the 11-store chain's profit margin exceeded 45 percent, a figure far higher than conventional supermarkets posted. Each store averaged $265,000 in sales per week, $65,000 more than the typical supermarket generated with twice the square footage.

ACQUISITION BY ALBERTSONS IN 2004

By every measure, Bristol Farms exuded strength, representing one of the supermarket industry's success stories. The company's glowing reputation presented Kidd Kamm and Oaktree Capital with the ideal conditions to recoup their investment in Bristol Farms, which the investment firms did in 2004 when they sold the company to Albertsons Inc., a Boise, Idaho-based supermarket chain. The sale meant new owners for the gourmet retailer, but not new management. Davis stayed on through the transfer of ownership, continuing to serve as Bristol Farms' president and chief executive officer under the control of Albertsons.

Instead of triggering a period of robust expansion, Davis's pronouncement in 1999 actually led to a moratorium on adding new units to the Bristol Farms

chain. After the addition of the Redondo Beach store at the end of 2000, the company did not open another unit until 2006, but the expansion completed during the year more than made up for the lull in activity. Davis increased the size of the Bristol Farms chain by 40 percent in 2006, opening four new stores. Another store in Los Angeles County was added, a unit in Westchester, but the most significant additions during the year were the stores that expanded the company's operating territory. To the east of Los Angeles, the company opened a store in Palm Desert. To the south, it opened a store in La Jolla, its first presence in San Diego County. To the north, it made its greatest geographic leap, opening a store in downtown San Francisco. By the end of 2006, on the eve of the company's 25th anniversary, Bristol Farms operated 15 supermarkets.

A NEW PARENT COMPANY IN 2006

The Albertsons era of ownership was brief, a relationship cut short after the giant supermarket chain began to struggle financially. Bristol Farms continued to perform at an enviable level, but an ailing parent company was cause for concern. The mood at the company's Carson, California, headquarters brightened in June 2006, when Minneapolis-based Supervalu Inc. came to the rescue. Supervalu acquired Albertsons in a $17.4 billion deal that created the nation's third largest supermarket chain and gave Bristol Farms a new parent company to support its operations. Davis, as he had after the previous change in ownership, remained in charge under Supervalu's ownership.

As Bristol Farms prepared for the future, there was every expectation that the years ahead would witness continued success for the gourmet retailer. Remarkably, the company had managed to retain its identity and its customer base through three changes in ownership, smoothly making the transition each time. The chain's 16th store opened in Valencia, California, in 2008 as the nation's economy began to falter, but Bristol Farms continued to record growing sales, demonstrating a resiliency that pointed to a promising future.

Jeffrey L. Covell

PRINCIPAL COMPETITORS

Whole Foods Market, Inc.; Arden Group, Inc.; Ralphs Grocery Company.

FURTHER READING

"Bristol Farms a Trolley Ride Away in San Francisco," *Progressive Grocer,* November 15, 2006, p. 14.

Coupe, Kevin, "Redefining Convenience: Upscale Bristol Farms Repositions Itself in the Marketplace," *Chain Store Age,* December 2006, p. 36.

———, "'This Is Not a Supermarket!'" *Supermarket News,* May 1986, p. 81.

Ingram, Bob, "Rancho Deluxe," *Supermarket Business,* April 1996, p. 23.

Miller, Lynne, "Bristol Farms Opens Biggest Store to Date," *Supermarket News,* August 14, 2006, p. 28.

Moses, Lucia, "Next Stop for Bristol Farms: Spain," *Supermarket News,* August 7, 2006, p. 34.

Proctor, Lisa Steen, "Gourmet Grocery Chain Bristol Farms on a Rapid Growth Push," *Los Angeles Business Journal,* March 24, 1997, p. 4.

Wilson, Marianne, "Desert Town Embraces Bristol Farms," *Chain Store Age,* June 2007, p. 68.

Zweibach, Elliot, "Bristol Farms Plans Growth; $25 Million in Funds Sought," *Supermarket News,* June 28, 1999, p. 1.

———, "Bristol Farms' President Learns Expansion Lesson," *Supermarket News,* March 3, 2003, p. 24.

———, "Bristol Farms' Upscale Customers Unfazed," *Supermarket News,* May 5, 2008.

Bronco Wine Company

6342 Bystrum Road
Ceres, California 95307
U.S.A.
Telephone: (209) 538-3131
Fax: (209) 538-4634

Private Company
Incorporated: 1973 as JFJ Bronco Winery
Sales: $400 million (2007 est.)
NAICS: 312130 Wineries

■ ■ ■

Bronco Wine Company is a privately held Ceres, California-based company that is one of the largest wine producers in the United States. Bronco is a value wine producer, best known for its Charles Shaw label, sold exclusively through retailer Trader Joe's for $1.99 a bottle, earning it the nickname "Two Buck Chuck." All told, Bronco controls about 60 wine labels, including the popular Forest Glen and Coastal Ridge. The bulk wine company maintains a 35,000-acre vineyard in Central Valley, California, capable of producing 61 million gallons of wine each year, and storage and production facilities in Ceres, Napa Valley, Sonoma Valley, Escalon, and Madera, California. In addition, the company operates its own distribution arm, Classic Wines of California, and generates revenues from providing juice and bottling to other wineries.

Bronco Wine is owned by CEO Fred Franzia with his brother and cousin. The often combative and always driven Franzia is a controversial figure in the California wine community, especially with Napa Valley vintners. He accuses his competitors of overpricing their wines and bamboozling the public into trusting hype over their taste buds. Franzia, on the other hand, prides himself on running a lean and efficient operation, allowing him to slash the prices on his wines, which he maintains are just as good as what the Napa Valley labels have to offer. Reinforcing this contention are the awards Two Buck Chuck has won in blind taste-test competitions against other California wines. Franzia has also upset vintners by buying up Napa Valley labels and selling wines under these labels despite not using Napa Valley grapes. Following a lengthy court battle, Franzia was forced to abandon the practice.

FRANZIA FAMILY, LATE 19TH-CENTURY IMMIGRANTS

Fred Franzia is a third-generation Italian American. His grandfather, Giuseppe Franzia, came to the United States from Genoa, Italy, in 1893 at the age of 22, arriving in New York City and traveling by train to San Francisco. He worked in truck gardens and saved enough money to rent some land in Stockton for farming and in 1906 was able to buy 80 acres of land near Ripon in the San Joaquin Valley. He planted a vineyard to make wine for his own use, and in 1915 he began producing wine for commercial use. Only four years later, however, he would have to stop producing wine because the United States banned all alcoholic beverages, ushering in Prohibition. Franzia's five sons, however, continued to cultivate the vineyard, so that when Prohibition was repealed in 1933 a new business, Fran-

COMPANY PERSPECTIVES

We are committed to growing, producing and selling the finest quality wines of the highest value to our customers.

zia Brothers, was able to produce a large quantity of table wine for sale to Eastern bottlers.

One of the daughters of Giuseppe Franzia, America, married Ernest Gallo, who, with his brother Julio, revolutionized the wine industry by introducing mass production techniques. Franzia Brothers took advantage of this knowledge to begin producing their own branded wines in the mid-1940s. Fred Franzia, in the meantime, was born in 1943. After graduating from Santa Clara University he and other members of the third generation of the Franzia family became involved in Franzia Brothers. Assuming that one day control of the company would pass to his generation, Fred Franzia was shocked in 1973 when his father and uncles sold the winery to Coca-Cola Bottling. He was so incensed over what he considered a poor decision that he refused to even speak with his father for seven years.

BRONCO WINES IS FORMED: 1973

In late 1973 Fred Franzia, his brother, Joseph Franzia, and their cousin, John Franzia, decided to go into business together. In late December 1973 they formed JFJ Bronco Winery, the name possibly drawn from the initials of their first names and an abbreviation of "brothers 'n cousin" to create the "bronco." Other sources maintain that the three Santa Clara University graduates simply used the name of their school's mascot, the Broncos. At the same time, they formed a distributorship, Classic Wines of California. A year later, 1974, the winery began producing its first products, initially generic bulk jug and bag-in-box wines.

In the late 1980s Fred Franzia took advantage of a wine recession to begin acquiring a stable of established brands while simultaneously acquiring acreage in the Central Valley on which to grow the grapes to produce more wine. The strategy proved wise, given that in early 1991 Classic Wines lost its largest customer, the Glen Ellen Winery, which had accounted for more than half of its business. Acquired brands were then used to rebuild that volume as well as to fill out the company's portfolio to include a full range of value and premium wines. Several wineries were acquired, mostly through bankruptcy court sales, in the early 1990s, including Es-

trella River Winery in 1990; Laurier Vineyards in 1991; Grand Cru Vineyards and Hacienda Wine Cellars, Inc., in 1992; Napa Creek Winery and J.W. Morris and Black Mountain Vineyard in 1993; and Salmon Creek Cellars and Rutherford Vintners in 1994. It was during this period that Bronco introduced the Forest Glen brand, which became a top-selling product, its success similar, albeit to a lesser degree, to Two Buck Chuck a decade later.

FRANZIA PLEADS GUILTY TO FEDERAL CHARGES: 1993

While Franzia was conducting this acquisition spree, he also had to contend with legal problems. He and Bronco Wine were caught up in a federal investigation, charged with misrepresenting one million gallons of inexpensive wine blend marketed as premium wine between 1987 and 1992, an industry practice known as "blessing the loads." Franzia opted not to contest the charges after another vintner was sentenced to 18 months in prison for the same crime and another vineyard owner settled his charges by pleading guilty and paying a $1 million fine. Thus, in late 1993 Bronco Wine pleaded no contest and paid a $2.5 million fine, and Franzia pleaded guilty, paid a $500,000 fine, and agreed to step down as chief executive and board member of the company and refrain from grape purchasing for a term of five years. More importantly, he avoided prison, something that the prosecution indicated could have hurt Bronco Wine and unjustly punished partners and employees. Indeed, Franzia's conviction had no lasting impact on Bronco Wine, nor did it chasten him. In 2006 he told *Inc.*, "They tattooed me, so fine. Do I look like I'm worried about it? Does it look like it's killed our company?"

While Franzia was no longer chief executive in the mid-1990s, he continued to direct the company's strategy and court controversy. In 1995 Bronco Wine acquired the Charles Shaw label from a bankrupt Napa Valley winery. The brand had been established by a Chicago investment banker, Charles F. Shaw, who became enamored with the wine industry and in the late 1970s purchased 50 acres in Napa Valley. He planted gamay grapes in cabernet country and in 1979 the Charles F. Shaw Vineyard and Winery began producing a California-style Beaujolais. By the early 1990s the business was failing. Shaw declared bankruptcy and returned to Chicago.

A few years later the Charles Shaw brand fell into the hands of Fred Franzia, who added it to a collection of Napa Valley labels he had gathered over the years, waiting to be put to use if and when needed. In 1986 a federal law had been passed that required brand names

KEY DATES

1973: JFJ Bronco Winery is established.
1974: First wine is offered for sale.
1990: Estrella River Winery is acquired.
1993: Fred Franzia pleads guilty to federal charges of misrepresenting a portion of his wine offerings.
1995: Charles Shaw label is acquired.
2000: Company settles mislabeling charges.
2002: Charles Shaw, popularly known as "Two Buck Chuck," is introduced.
2007: Plans are announced to build Napa Valley bottle-making plant.

to coincide with the regional origin of the wine they contained. Labels in use before July 1986, such as Charles Shaw, however, were exempt, making them valuable to a Central Valley vintner like Bronco Wine which could use the labels for grapes grown there or anywhere else in California. Franzia's willingness to eschew a gentleman's agreement not to take advantage of such a loophole helped to create intense antipathy toward him among Napa Valley winemakers.

He did not help matters in 1996 when an ad for a Bronco Wine label used a picture of a premiere Napa Valley vineyard, the Joseph Phelps Winery. When the winery complained, Franzia had the ads pulled. In the late 1990s the Bureau of Alcohol, Tobacco and Firearms threatened to suspend Bronco's winery permit because the Rutherford Vineyards label the company had acquired was selling wine that came from outside the Napa Valley. In 2000 Bronco settled this matter by agreeing to stop the practice and paying $750,000.

Another wine recession at the start of the new century provided Franzia with further opportunity to grow Bronco on the cheap. In early 2000 the company paid $40 million to Beringer Wine Estate for its Napa Ridge brand and all labeled inventory. It was a move that created much concern in Napa Valley. For several years the Napa Ridge brand had not relied on Napa Valley grapes, but under pressure from other Napa Valley vintners the brand was being phased out until Bronco acquired it. Napa winemakers lobbied the California Assembly to close the federal loophole regarding Napa Valley labels, and later in 2000 the state responded by passing a law that required wine prominently featuring the word *Napa* on its label to contain at least 75 percent Napa grapes. Franzia would take the matter to court.

TWO BUCK CHUCK DEBUTS: 2002

The wine recession also led to a glut of grapes on the market. Aware that California was likely producing too many wine grapes, Franzia allowed much of his acreage to lie fallow. Thus, he had ample room in his storage tanks to procure high-quality grapes at low prices from the 2001 and 2002 harvests, enabling him to produce high-quality wines at value prices. It was at this point that he pulled the Charles Shaw brand out of the drawer and introduced a $1.99 bottle of corked wine in the same kind of 750-millimeter bottles in which the better wines were found. He approached Wal-Mart and Costco about carrying the label, but both declined. Franzia then found a willing retail partner in the Trader Joe's chain of nearly 200 grocery stores, which specialized in gourmet goods at reasonable prices and already carried budget lines of wine. Trader Joe's carried the Charles Shaw label on an exclusive basis. The three vintages—1999, 2000, and 2001—first appeared on the shelves in February 2002, but it was not until the fall that the brand really caught on with consumers, who by the end of the year bought nearly two million cases. The brand also acquired a nickname, "Two Buck Chuck," bestowed upon it by Trader Joe's employees. Given a downturn in the economy, the timing for such an inexpensive wine proved fortuitous. Moreover, consumers embraced the anti-snob appeal of Two Buck Chuck; most could not tell the difference between it and more expensive brands.

Much to the dismay of Franzia's many critics, Bronco Wine was named Winery of the Year by the Unified Wine & Grape Symposium in 2003 and received the same honor in 2004, when Bronco Wine sales, led by Two Buck Chuck, increased to four million cases. Rivals had hoped that Two Buck Chuck had been a mere fad, but it appeared to have carved out a significant niche in the marketplace. The brand proved so popular that it outgrew Bronco's Ceres production facilities, and in 2003 Franzia acquired a winery in Escalon to make up the shortfall in production. Franzia built on the success of Two Buck Chuck by introducing new Charles Shaw wines, including Chardonnay, White Zinfandel, Merlot, Sauvignon Blanc, Shiraz, Cabernet Sauvignon, Valdigue, and Pinot Grigio. Other Bronco wines could be purchased at the $2.99, $3.99, and $5.99 price points. Franzia also hoped to change the restaurant wine business by finding a restaurant partner to offer wine priced under $10 a bottle.

FIVE-BUCK CHUCK DEBUTS: 2000

While growing Bronco Wine through its various value-priced wines, Franzia continued his fight to make use of the word *Napa* in wines that did not contain Napa-grown grapes. The matter made its way to the U.S. Supreme Court, but in 2005 the Court opted, without comment, not to consider the matter. A year later Bronco Wine complied with the state law, agreeing to drop the Napa name from one label while using Napa-grown grapes in two other labels that used Napa in its name. Franzia was not easily deterred, however.

In 2007 he announced plans to build a new glass bottle manufacturing plant in Napa Valley, a move the company portrayed as a way to drastically cut the environmental impact of diesel-fueled trucks that traveled the valley delivering bottle shipments. Skeptics, on the other hand, maintained that Franzia was simply looking for a way to label wine with non-Napa grapes as being "bottled in the Napa Valley," a distinction that would be technically correct but deceiving from a marketing point of view. Franzia also indicated that he wanted to sell a brand of wine that used Napa grapes, vowing that he would price it at less than $5 a bottle. The new "five-buck Chuck" sold under the Napa River label was introduced in 2006.

To make matters worse for Franzia's critics, in 2007 Charles Shaw Chardonnay won the top award at the California State Fair, beating out about 350 other entries in a blind competition. It was also named the best value among all of the more than 3,000 wines entered into the competition. Whether or not Franzia could continue to grow his business on inexpensive wines remained an open question, but his penchant for picking fights and irking his enemies was something that could presumably be counted on for years to come.

Ed Dinger

PRINCIPAL SUBSIDIARIES
Classic Wines of California.

PRINCIPAL COMPETITORS

E. & J. Gallo Winery; Kendall-Jackson Wine Estates, Ltd.; The Wine Group, Inc.

FURTHER READING

Brown, Corie, "Hard Times at the Winery?" *Los Angeles Times,* February 26, 2003, p. F1.

Emert, Carol, "Franzia Takes Aim at Wine Lists," *San Francisco Chronicle,* April 29, 2004, p. F4.

Franson, Paul, "Napa Ridge Winery Gains a Home to Match Its Presence," *Wine Business Monthly,* August 2002.

Haddad, Annette, "Supreme Court Won't Hear Wine Dispute," *Los Angeles Times,* March 22, 2005, p. C2.

Hirsch, Jerry, "Wal-Mart of Wine," *Los Angeles Times,* April 30, 2006, p. C1.

Holland, John, "'2 Buck Chuck' Nabs Top Award," *Modesto Bee,* July 14, 2007.

Locke, Michelle, "'Two Buck Chuck' Maker Takes Aim at Restaurant Wine," *St. Louis Post-Dispatch,* February 17, 2005, p. B06.

Marbella, Jean, "Two-Buck Luck," *Chicago Tribune,* February 25, 2004, p. 3A.

Moran, Tim, "Franzias Take Bronco Winery to the Top Level," *Modesto Bee,* January 9, 2000, p. D1.

Pattison, Kermit, "The Scourge of Napa Valley," *Inc.,* May 2006.

Prial, Frank J., "For $2, a Bottle of Wine and Change," *New York Times,* April 23, 2003, p. F1.

Sinton, Peter, "Bronco Wine's Premium Buy: Rutherford Joins Its Stable," *San Francisco Chronicle,* August 24, 1994, p. B1.

Stein, Joel, "Two Buck Chuck Takes a Bite Out of Napa," *Business 2.0,* September 2007, p. 84.

The Carnegie Hall Corporation

———————■———————

881 7th Avenue
New York, New York 10019-3210
U.S.A.
Telephone: (212) 903-9600
Fax: (212) 903-0765
Web site: http://www.carnegiehall.org

Nonprofit Company
Incorporated: 1960
Employees: 350
Operating Revenues: $34.2 million (2007)
NAICS: 711310 Promoters of Performing Arts, Sports, and Similar Events with Facilities

■ ■ ■

The Carnegie Hall Corporation is a nonprofit corporation charged with managing New York City's famed Carnegie Hall concert hall, which since the late 1800s has showcased the world's greatest orchestras and conductors, soloists, as well as popular singers and musical groups. The facility is actually owned by the City of New York and is leased to the corporation. It is comprised of three halls. The largest venue is the Isaac Stern Auditorium/Ronald O. Perlman Stage, seating as many as 2,800 people. Able to accommodate almost 600, the Judy and Arthur Zankel Hall is a versatile stage located underneath the main hall, used for a wide range of performing and educational events. The more intimate Joan and Sanford I. Weill Recital Hall, seating 268, is used for recitals and chamber music concerts as well as master classes, symposia, and discussions.

Although Carnegie Hall Corporation produces many of the events offered on its stages, it also rents the halls to third-party producers and also offers banquet spaces. In addition, Carnegie Hall sponsors a variety of professional training and school programs, including the Weill Music Institute at Carnegie Hall. The organization is headed by six officers and a board of trustees comprised of about 70 members as well as city, state, and federal representatives.

19TH-CENTURY ORIGINS

The man who supplied about 90 percent of the funds needed to build Carnegie Hall was Scottish-born American industrialist Andrew Carnegie, but the man with the idea of building the hall was 25-year-old Walter Damrosch, the conductor and musical director of the Symphony Society of New York and the Oratorio Society of New York, both of which had been founded by his father in the 1870s. Carnegie and Damrosch met in 1887 aboard a London-bound ship when the 52-year-old Carnegie was on a honeymoon trip and Damrosch was traveling to Europe for a summer of study. Carnegie's young bride, Louise Whitfield, was a socialite with a musical bent and had been a singer in the soprano section of Damrosch's Oratorio society. Growing fond of Damrosch during the voyage and a later visit the young man paid to the newlyweds in Scotland at the end of the summer, Carnegie was receptive to a dream project Damrosch had inherited from his father: opening a world-class concert hall in New York City. Both the Symphony Society and the Oratorio Society had a difficult time finding places to play. The latter, in

COMPANY PERSPECTIVES

For music lovers worldwide, Carnegie Hall is the ultimate musical destination, an international byword for excellence, and an institution whose rich history chronicles the defining moments of so many of the world's most admired and beloved artists. For the leadership of this institution, this legacy provides an enjoyable yet formidable challenge, as we work each season to devise strategies that build upon the past in imaginative ways and create essential new pathways for growth.—Sanford I. Weill, chairman

fact, often resorted to giving performances in piano company showrooms.

Agreeing to help erect a new concert hall in New York City, Carnegie formed a stock company, The Music Hall Company of New York, Limited, in 1889. In the end, he would contribute about 90 percent of the $2 million spent to build the facility. Seven parcels of property were acquired between 56th Street and 57th Street along 7th Avenue. Although close to Central Park, it was still a location that at the time was somewhat remote, the streets not yet paved. For years New York's theater district had been creeping uptown, and when the Metropolitan Opera House opened in 1883 at 39th Street and Broadway it was considered to be far removed from the fashionable part of town, having long been centered in the Union Square area. Twenty years would pass before the modern-day Broadway theater district would begin to take shape. Nevertheless, as the *New York Times* commented in 1889, the new hall was "easily accessible from the 'living' part of the city. Three stations of the elevated railroad are within two to five blocks of the building ... and as the growing of the metropolis is rapidly extending northward and westward the location will soon be the most central that could have been chosen."

OPENING NIGHT PERFORMANCE: 1891

William Burnet Tuthill, a board member of the Oratorio Society, was hired as chief architect and ground was broken on the new six-story hall in 1890. The original design called for three stages: the Main Hall; a 1,200-seat recital hall, located below the Main Hall; and a 250-seat chamber hall adjacent to the Main Hall. Also included were a multitude of assembly rooms, where lectures, readings, receptions, and other events could be

held. Construction of the Carnegie Musical Hall, as it was then called, was completed in the spring of 1891, and the opening night performance was given on May 5, 1891, part of a five-day opening festival. Performances by the Symphony Society and the Oratorio Society were conducted by Damrosch and Russian composer Pyotr Ilyich Tchaikovsky. It was an auspicious start for the new hall, which in some ways upstaged the performers, receiving as it did rave reviews for the quality of its sound and the beauty of its design.

What was not so well received, especially by European artists, was the "Carnegie Music Hall" name, because they associated "Music Hall" with vaudeville. As a result, in 1894 the venue became simply known as Carnegie Hall. Not only did Damrosch's Symphony Society make its home at Carnegie Hall, so too did the rival Philharmonic Society, orphaned for a time after a fire severely damaged the Metropolitan Opera House in 1892. It was the Philharmonic Society that was responsible for one of the early triumphs of Carnegie Hall, one that would help establish it as a world-class concert hall. On December 16, 1893, the Philharmonic presented the world premiere of Antonin Dvorak's "Symphony from the New World" on the main stage of Carnegie Hall. Sitting in the audience was the composer himself. The feuding between the Philharmonic Society and Symphony Society would not end until 1928 when they merged to form the Philharmonic Society of New York. Two years later the orchestra began airing live performances from the Main Hall, something that would carry on for more than 30 years, helping to grow the reputation of both the orchestra and the hall.

Not only did Carnegie Hall quickly build a reputation in the world of classical music, it provided a public forum for such luminaries as Mark Twain, Booker T. Washington, and Winston Churchill (well before he became England's prime minister). Jazz music made its debut as early as 1912, and in the 1930s Benny Goodman and his band used Carnegie Hall to bring public acceptance to swing music. The first folksinger would perform at Carnegie Hall in 1933, and the blacklisted folk group the Weavers gave a memorable performance in 1955. The Beatles made their first New York concert appearance at Carnegie Hall, opening the way for a multitude of rock bands and performers in the years to come.

ROBERT E. SIMONS BUYS HALL: 1925

Andrew Carnegie continued to own the stock company that owned the venue that bore his name until his death in 1919. His wife inherited the property and in 1925 sold it to New York realtor Robert E. Simon, who

KEY DATES

1889: Music Hall Company of New York, Limited is formed by Andrew Carnegie.
1891: Carnegie Music Hall opens.
1894: Name is shortened to Carnegie Hall.
1925: Carnegie's widow sells the building to Robert E. Simon Sr.
1955: Robert E. Simon Jr. agrees to sell Carnegie Hall to real estate developers.
1960: The Carnegie Hall Corporation is formed to lease the facility from the City of New York, which bought it from Simon.
1978: Carnegie Hall is evaluated for renovation.
1986: Renovated Main Hall reopens.
1991: Rose Museum opens.
1995: Composer's Chair is endowed.
2003: Judy and Arthur Zankel Hall opens.
2007: New capital campaign is announced.

pledged to maintain the hall as a performance venue for at least five years. Ten years later his son, Robert E. Simon Jr., assumed management of Carnegie Hall and for a time was able to run it profitably. That situation would begin to change, however, and it became virtually impossible to run a concert hall as a commercial venture. In the mid-1950s Simon offered to sell Carnegie Hall to the New York Philharmonic—the hall's major tenant, booking more than 100 nights a year—for $4 million. By this time, however, another new performance complex was taking shape a few blocks away, Lincoln Center, which would include a Philharmonic Hall (eventually becoming a reality as Avery Fisher Hall). The Metropolitan Opera, whose house was beginning to crumble, had been looking for a new home and the Philharmonic, fearful that Carnegie Hall might be torn down, joined forces with the Rockefeller family and the City of New York to begin development of Lincoln Center. The demise of Carnegie Hall, on the other hand, began to take the shape of a self-fulfilling prophecy.

RESCUING CARNEGIE HALL: 1960

Simon put Carnegie Hall up for sale in 1955, all the while making it clear that any contract could be voided if he was able to find a way to save the facility. He soon found a buyer, a group of developers who wanted to use the site to erect a 44-story office tower. Demolition was set for March 31, 1960. As that date approached there

were some feckless attempts to save the hall, but it was not until violinist Isaac Stern took charge of the Committee to Save Carnegie Hall and brought together money interests and politicians that a viable rescue plan emerged. In April 1960 New York State Governor Nelson Rockefeller signed a pair of bills to save the hall. One of them created the nonprofit Carnegie Hall Corporation to own and operate the hall. The second bill helped to protect Carnegie Hall as well as historical structures across New York State. On May 16, 1960, New York City was given permission to purchase Carnegie Hall for $5 million, and that same day an 18-member board of trustees was named by Mayor Robert Wagner to run the Carnegie Hall Corporation. Investment banker Frederick W. Richmond was named chairman. The hall was subsequently purchased and leased to the corporation. In 1964 Carnegie Hall was honored as a Registered National Historic Landmark.

There was some concern that with the advent of Lincoln Center New York City would not be able to support two major concert halls. Avery Fisher Hall opened in 1962 and the Philharmonic vacated Carnegie Hall. Nevertheless, it became quickly apparent that New York could indeed support two houses. In fact, they fed on one another, stimulating interest in music and creating greater demand for concerts. Later in the 1960s and into the 1970s, Carnegie Hall was also booked for many rock concerts and performances by popular singer-songwriters including James Taylor, benefiting greatly from the prestige factor of performing there. For others, performing at Carnegie Hall was more important personally than just a status engagement. The members of the band Chicago, for example, were classically trained, and found the stage and acoustics so inspiring that they booked Carnegie for a week at a time, giving eight performances in six days, forgoing a chance to play at the much larger Madison Square Garden where they could make more money in a single night.

While popular music bookings helped greatly in paying the bills, the finances of Carnegie Hall remained precarious. That situation would begin to change in the 1970s when the corporation's fund-raising efforts became more organized under the influence of James D. Wolfensohn, an Australian-born investment banker who became treasurer and joined the board of trustees in 1973. He then became chairman in 1979. One of the drains on the corporation's coffers was the rising cost of insurance and utilities related to the 140 artists studios housed in the building. Marlon Brando, Isadora Duncan, and Leonard Bernstein had rented studios, and many of the artists lived in their large studios, some of which were two rooms in size and included bathrooms, paying rents that were far below market rates for accommodations in New York City. In 1977 the corporation announced that new tenants would not be allowed to live in their studios although current tenants could continue the practice. Rent increases were also on the horizon, leading to a well publicized spat between the tenants and Carnegie Hall.

Approaching 90 years old, Carnegie Hall was clearly in need of repair and renovation. In 1978 the trustees commissioned an evaluation of the structure. Completed in 1981 the evaluation led to a nine-phase renovation and expansion plan. To pay for the initiative, the corporation in 1985 launched a $60 million capital campaign. The major portion of the work commenced in May 1986, resulting in the building being shut down for seven months. When the Main Hall reopened it featured new seats, carpeting, fresh paint, a new stage floor, ceiling shell, and a new sound, one that critics and musicians found to be harder in edge than was present in the old hall. Apparently the false ceiling and curtains that had been removed in the restoration had made significant contributions to the hall's famous rich sound. After some study, absorptive panels and other measures were taken to remedy the situation. Aside from this problem, however significant in the short term, the renovation was hugely successful when all of the building phases were completed in time for the centennial season of 1991. Part of the plan included the construction of the 60-story Carnegie Hall Tower, which was able to contribute about 25,000 square feet of new space to the hall, allowing more dressing rooms, a large backstage area, and other much needed accommodations.

Also discovered during the renovation effort was the utter lack of an archive of Carnegie Hall history and events. In 1986 the Carnegie Hall Archives were established and a search of historical materials begun. The material would be used to help create the Rose Museum, which opened in 1991, displaying memorabilia celebrating the history of the hall as well as special exhibits related to current programming.

On a better financial footing, supported by both corporate sponsorships and government funding, Carnegie Hall was able to expand its mission in the 1990s. In 1990 the Professional Training Workshops were established as a way to give younger performers a chance to work with major artists. To present world premieres of new works, the Centennial Commissioning Project was established in 1991, the same year that The Carnegie Hall Jazz Band was formed. In 1995 a Composer's Chair was endowed, bringing notable composers to the hall. In 1995 the Family Concerts series was launched, part of an effort to introduce children to classical music. Also in 1995 primary and secondary schoolteachers were given an opportunity to work with established artists in the Professional Development Workshops.

JUDY AND ARTHUR ZANKEL HALL OPENS: 2007

Further renovations would also be in store. At the end of the 1990s plans were announced to create the Judy and Arthur Zankel Hall beneath the Main Hall, a space that for many years had been the Carnegie Hall Cinema movie theater. In 2003 the new hall opened, restoring the original concept of three different-size halls in one building. In that same year, The Weill Music Institute was established to make use of the three halls in a variety of education programs. In 2007 another capital campaign, $150 million to $200 million in size, was announced, the goal to further renovate backstage areas as well as create more offices, rehearsal, and practice rooms, mostly to the benefit of the education wing. Because of these plans the longtime artist studios would be annexed, and once again the corporation and its tenants were at odds in an emotional, public relations battle.

Garnering a great deal of attention in the fall of 2008 was 96-year-old Editta Sherman, a celebrity photographer who since 1949 had lived in her 800-square-foot, $530 a month studio, where she had photographed numerous notables, including Elvis Presley, Henry Fonda, Paul Newman, and Andy Warhol. She was only one of a handful of artists who held out after the corporation won the legal right to effectively evict the tenants, despite the corporation's pledge to relocate them to similar or better apartments in the area and pay the rent difference for the remainder of their lives. At some point, Carnegie Hall would reclaim the space and move forward with its latest building project. There was every reason to expect that the concert hall and designated landmark, which was itself fortunate to escape the wrecker's ball half a century earlier, was well positioned to maintain its lofty place in the music world for many years to come.

Ed Dinger

PRINCIPAL COMPETITORS

Lincoln Center for the Performing Arts, Inc.

FURTHER READING

"Carnegie Board Named by Mayor," *New York Times,* May 17, 1960.

Esterow, Milton, "Carnegie Hall Looks Confidently to Future," *New York Times,* December 7, 1962.

Freedman, Samuel G., "The Glory of Carnegie Hall," *New York Times,* May 9, 1985.

Herman, Robin, "City Studies Artists' Protests over Rents at Carnegie Hall," *New York Times,* February 26, 1979.

"It Stood the Test Well," *New York Times,* May 6, 1891.

Johnson, Kirk, "Towers Sprouting near Carnegie Hall," *New York Times,* September 9, 1984.

"A New Music Hall," *New York Times,* March 15, 1889.

Rockwell, John, "Carnegie Hall Begins $20 Million Renovation," *New York Times,* February 21, 1982.

"Saving of Carnegie Hall Enabled in Bills Signed by Rockefeller," *New York Times,* April 17, 1960.

Schumach, Murray, "Carnegie Hall to End Its Live-In Studios for Artists," *New York Times,* November 14, 1977.

Shilling, Erik, and Clemente Lisi, "Granny Is Mad As Hall," *New York Post,* December 30, 2008.

Wakin, Daniel J., "Carnegie Hall Plans Major Expansion, Without Its Tenants," *New York Times,* May 22, 2007.

Children's Healthcare of Atlanta Inc.

1600 Tullie Circle NE
Atlanta, Georgia 30329
U.S.A.
Telephone: (404) 785-7000
Fax: (404) 785-7027
Web site: http://www.choa.org

Nonprofit Company
Incorporated: 1998 as Egleston-Scottish Rite Children's
    Health Care System Inc.
Employees: 7,000
Operating Revenues: $198.2 million (2007)
NAICS: 622110 General Medical and Surgical Hospitals

∎ ∎ ∎

Children's Healthcare of Atlanta Inc. is the leading provider of pediatric services in the Atlanta metropolitan area and one of the leading pediatric healthcare systems in the United States. The organization is comprised of two owned hospitals, Scottish Rite at Children's and Egleston at Children's, and one managed hospital, Children's at Hughes Spalding, owned by Grady Health Systems. The organization's 16 neighborhood locations provide primary care, outpatient rehabilitation therapy, sports medicine, orthotics and prosthetics, surgical services, and immediate care for minor injuries and illnesses. *Parents* magazine ranks Children's Healthcare of Atlanta among the nation's top ten hospitals and among the top five in many specialties, including cardiology and orthopedics. Services to children include injury prevention through the Safe Kids Georgia program, and preventive health through scoliosis screening, type 2 diabetes intervention, and weight management education. The Child Protection Center is designed to prevent and identify cases of child abuse and child neglect. Children's Healthcare of Atlanta supports pediatric education, training, and research through partnerships with Emory University School of Medicine and Georgia Technical Institute.

UNITING WITH COMMON CAUSE TO PROMOTE CHILDREN'S HEALTH

Children's Healthcare of Atlanta was formed in 1998 through the merger of Egleston Children's Health Care System and Scottish Rite Medical Center. As changes in healthcare reimbursement policies placed financial pressures on healthcare providers, the hospitals sought to create operating and administrative efficiencies. Initially called the Egleston-Scottish Rite Children's Health Care System, the combination of these pediatric organizations created one of the largest pediatric hospital systems in the United States.

Both of these organizations brought nearly a century of experience in providing healthcare for children. Scottish Rite Medical Center formed in 1915 as the Scottish Rite Convalescent Home for Crippled Children. Founders Forrest Adair, a financier and Scottish Rite mason, and Michael Hoke, M.D., saw the need for a healthcare facility dedicated to disabled children. Mrs. Bertie Wardlaw led several local women in selling pencils to raise funds to equip the 18-bed facility. Scottish Rite accepted poor children who had

COMPANY PERSPECTIVES

Mission: To enhance the lives of children through excellence in patient care, research and education. Vision: To transform pediatric healthcare and be the leading voice for the health of Georgia's children.

undergone surgery at other hospitals and cared for them until they were well enough to go home. In 1918, Scottish Rite broadened its service in conjunction with construction of a new facility, which provided 50 beds and housed an orthopedic surgical facility.

Scottish Rite continued to provide healthcare only for children whose families could not pay for treatment until 1966. That year the hospital began accepting patients from families with the means to pay as well. The organization became the Scottish Rite Children's Medical Center in 1976, when the hospital merged with the Meridian Mark Corporation, owner of an office building housing medical practices, the Wilbur and Hilda Glenn Hospital for Children, and the Scottish Rite Foundation. Scottish Rite moved to north Atlanta at this time.

Throughout its history Scottish Rite distinguished itself in many areas of children's medicine. In 1939, the hospital's medical director, Hiram Kite, M.D., advanced the existing, non-surgical method to correct clubfoot, thus establishing a new standard for such treatment. Later, Scottish Rite became a leader in pediatric emergency and trauma care. The hospital set the standard for 24-hour emergency room patient tracking in 1984 and earned the state of Georgia's commendation as a Pediatric Trauma Unit in 1987. In 1992 Scottish Rite established a network of immediate care centers in order to extend its ability to handle low priority emergencies, such as minor injuries and illnesses, throughout the Atlanta metropolitan area. Doctors at Scottish Rite advanced surgical practice for cerebral palsy as the center's first dorsal rhizotomy surgery, performed in 1992, provided improvements in mobility, posture, and movement to some patients. Scottish Rite gained recognition for its pediatric intensive care units in 1994, when the *Journal of the American Medical Association* noted the facility for producing "best outcomes."

Other areas in which Scottish Rite provided care for children included a program to teach educators and school administrators how to prevent injury and illness among school-age children. Also, the Child Advocacy Center provided psychiatric care for children up to age 21 thought to be victims of sexual abuse.

Egleston Children's Health Care System formed in 1928 with funding from Thomas R. Egleston Jr., whose mother lost four of her five children to childhood diseases. The Henrietta Egleston Hospital for Children opened with 52 beds and treated 605 children the first year in operation. Egleston established itself as a leader in pediatric medicine in several ways. Medical Director M. Hines Robert, M.D., played an instrumental role in establishing the American Board of Pediatrics, formed in 1933 to develop pediatrics as a science and as a practice. In 1956 Egleston became the pediatric teaching hospital for Emory University School of Medicine.

Egleston offered patients leading medical techniques. Doctors at Egleston performed the hospital's first kidney transplant in 1980, and established Georgia's first kidney dialysis program for children in 1982. The first bone marrow transplant occurred in 1984 and the first heart transplant in 1988. Egleston established one of the few medical-psychiatric units for children to be affiliated with a university. The federal government selected Egleston as a primary center for the first pediatric disaster medical assistance team. In 1991 it was the only hospital in Georgia to provide extracorporeal membrane oxygenation, a life-saving heart-lung bypass technique. Doctors performed the first cochlear implant at the hospital in 1992 and the first heart-lung transplant in 1993. That year *Child* magazine listed Egleston as one of the nation's top ten hospitals for children.

Other developments at Egleston involved centers dedicated to specific diseases. The Egleston Cystic Fibrosis Center for adolescents and young adults opened in 1995. The Aflac Cancer Center and Blood Disorders Service of Children's opened in 1995, with $3 million provided by Aflac Inc., a health insurance company based in Columbus, Georgia. *Child* magazine named the Aflac Cancer Center one of the top three pediatric cancer centers in the United States.

HOSPITALS SHIFT FROM COMPETITION TO COLLABORATION THROUGH MERGER

While most cities boasted one or two children's hospitals, Atlanta was unusual for having three such institutions, Scottish Rite, Egleston, and Hughes Spalding Children's Hospital. Changes in health insurers and managed care organizations forced them to become collaborators, and Scottish Rite and Egleston sought to provide complementary services, in order to minimize

KEY DATES

1915: Scottish Rite Hospital for Crippled Children is founded.
1928: Egleston Children's Health Care System is founded.
1998: Egleston and Scottish Rite merge.
1999: Merged entity takes the name Children's Healthcare of Atlanta.
2005: Children's begins public phase of $265 million fund-raising campaign.
2006: Management of Hughes Spalding Children's Hospital begins.
2008: Ten-year vision plan includes unprecedented investment in pediatric research.

redundancy. Nevertheless, they competed for funding and patients. Scottish Rite and Egleston garnered support from the same foundations, though not to the same extent. Both hospitals formed pediatric networks to consolidate the market's potential while checking healthcare costs. In 1994 Scottish Rite established Atlanta's first network of pediatricians and pediatric subspecialists. The Scottish Rite Pediatric Health Alliance supported the administrative functions of more than 350 pediatricians and offered pediatric services to managed care and health insurance companies in Atlanta. Similarly, Egleston formed Children's Rainbow Medical Group, a network of pediatric primary care facilities, opening more than seven satellite offices in the first year and operating a total of 21 offices within the next few years. Scottish Rite opened seven satellite offices.

Both Scottish Rite and Egleston obtained contracts to provide pediatric services at other medical institutions, such as the Promina Health System, with four hospitals in the five-county Atlanta area. In July 1997 Egleston obtained a contract to provide services at two north Atlanta hospitals in Cobb County, pushing Scottish Rite out of one of those hospitals. In 1996, Egleston formed the FamilyPlus health maintenance organization (HMO), but the organization sustained more than $8 million in losses during the first two years.

Competition between Scottish Rite and Egleston did not ease the financial pressures of the new era of managed care, as tighter managed-care and Medicaid reimbursement rates impeded revenues. Also, competition for pediatric patients increased when general hospitals added their own pediatric services. After several

years of occasional, exploratory conversations about the possibility of a merger, in early 1997 Scottish Rite and Egleston began definitive negotiations. An agreement to merge was announced in August 1997 and finalized February 2, 1998. Together the two hospitals created a $425 million, 4,000-employee organization, with 28 satellite clinics and 400 inpatient beds.

Scottish Rite President and CEO James E. Tally, Ph.D., took those positions at the newly formed Egleston-Scottish Rite Children's Health Care System Inc. (ESR Children's Health Care). Under Tally, the organization restructured to eliminate redundant administrative functions, including purchasing and marketing, and to integrate specialized medical services. In September 1999, following extensive market research, ESR Children's Healthcare adopted the name Children's Healthcare of Atlanta.

The merger led to the expansion of prominent medical services as the Aflac Cancer Center opened a unit at Scottish Rite. Through the continued support of Aflac, Inc., and Aflac Field Force, the company's sales associates, the center thrived. Aflac offered a corporate gift of $10 million in December 2001, and Aflac Field Force matched the donation by 2004. In addition, Aflac Field Force donated $30 million in 2002, supporting the endowment of fellowships for future pediatric oncologists and hematologists. Another $3 million provided support to the Family Support Team, which helped teachers, psychologists, social workers, and child life specialists to assist families as soon as diagnosis was made. Support from Aflac allowed Children's to draw the best doctors in the nation to its facility.

Children's developed expertise in several pediatric specialties. In 2001 Children's at Egleston began construction on the Center for Transplantation, GI Diagnostics, and Dialysis. In 2004, doctors at Children's handled the first ABO-incompatible heart transplant to be performed in Georgia.

CHILDREN'S EXPANDS WITH AGREEMENT FOR THIRD PEDIATRIC HOSPITAL

In 2004 Children's initiated plans to raise and spend $344 million for several expansion and renovation projects, in preparation for future population growth in the Atlanta metropolitan area. In 2004 the two hospitals and 16 satellite clinics operated at maximum capacity, with 450,000 patient visits during the year. Moreover, the population of children in Atlanta had increased by 120,000 between 1998 and 2004, and it was expected to grow by another 120,000 children by 2010. Nevertheless, Grady Health System, owner of Hughes

Spalding Children's Hospital in downtown Atlanta, opposed the plans. Grady Health pressed state authorities to deny Children's licenses, referred to as "certificates of need," for construction, citing concern that the expansion would force Hughes Spalding to close, thus denying healthcare to children in and around the downtown area.

In 2004 Children's began an evaluation process to determine the efficacy of managing pediatric services at Hughes Spalding. The hospital's patients came primarily from low income and minority families, and its $8.5 million deficit jeopardized its ability to continue to provide medical services to those populations. Named for attorney and civic leader Hughes Spalding Sr., who recognized the need for healthcare facilities for African Americans able to pay for services but with limited options, the Hughes Spalding Pavilion opened at Grady Hospital in 1952. Initially an adult care facility, the hospital closed for renovations in 1989 and reopened three years later as Hughes Spalding Children's Hospital. By 2004, the 82-bed facility needed to be upgraded, as substandard conditions led to a decline in patient visits. Moreover, the emergency room was frequently engulfed in child abuse and neglect cases.

In addition to community need, Hughes Spalding served targeted areas of medical need. The facility housed the only Poison Center in Georgia and specialty clinics in cerebral palsy and autism; the latter two opened in 1998 and 2002, respectively. A multicultural pediatric clinic opened in 2001. That year Hughes Spalding improved well-child visits by more than 20 percent after installing a computer-based appointment tracking and notification system.

The decision by Children's to manage Hughes Spalding was boosted by a large infusion of funds. To offset losses, Grady agreed to contribute $2 million annually, and Fulton and DeKalb counties and the city of Atlanta together agreed to contribute $2 million annually. The state of Georgia swayed the agreement by adding another $4 million. An $18 million anonymous matching-grant donation, provided further support for saving Hughes Spalding. In December 2005, Children's Healthcare of Atlanta signed an agreement with Grady Health System to manage the hospital.

Children's established a separate affiliate, HSOC, Inc., to manage Hughes Spalding, and the Children's Board of Trustees formed to oversee the combined resources of all three hospitals. HSOC management began in February 2006. HSOC planned to spend $30 million in donations to upgrade the facility, newly renamed Children's at Hughes Spalding. HSOC modernized existing structures and began planning for new building construction. Another priority involved upgrading the emergency care center, which served 50,000 patients annually, though it had never been intended for such use. HSOC more than doubled the space, from 4,300 square feet to 9,000 square feet.

AMBITIOUS FUND-RAISING CAMPAIGN SUPPORTS FURTHER EXPANSION

In April 2005, Children's announced its most ambitious fund-raising campaign to date, to seek $230 million in new donations for expansion. Through its two-year silent phase, the campaign raised $155 million. Large donations included $25 million from the Robert W. Woodruff Foundation and anonymous donors of $10 million and $18 million, the latter earmarked for Hughes Spalding. Another $10 million came from the Marcus Foundation. Children's expected operating revenue and debt to pay for the balance of the $344 million expansion.

In July 2006 Children's increased its fund-raising goal to $265 million. As unreimbursed care continued to rise and patient visits exceeded capacity at peak times, leaders decided that meeting future needs for children's hospital care required additional investment. At Scottish Rite, Children's applied $135.2 million to renovate 95,800 square feet and added 375,900 square feet to accommodate new surgical facilities, including 11 operating rooms.

Significant cost savings generated by the successful integration of Scottish Rite and Egleston allowed Children's to expand its vision toward improvements in pediatric education and research. Through collaboration with Emory University School of Medicine, Children's developed and implemented new strategies for the care of hematology/oncology and cardiac patients. In 2002 the nonprofit began development of a formal Department of Pediatrics. In 2006 Children's established the Center for Pediatric Outcomes and Quality (CPOQ), with Emory University and the Georgia Institute of Technology. Part of a growing research partnership between Children's and Georgia Tech, the CPOQ was integrated into the Health Systems Institute at Georgia Tech. As part of its ten-year plan, Vision 2018, Children's earmarked an unprecedented $430 million from its endowment to fund research.

By March 2008, Children's received $40 million in donations from Aflac and its employees for the Aflac Cancer Center and Blood Disorders Service. The funds supported continued innovations through experimental therapies and lab and clinic research. Every year, the center treated over 325 new cancer patients and tracked more than 2,000 patients with blood disorders, such as hemophilia and sickle cell disease.

Children's announced the development of the Marcus Autism Center, through a partnership with the Marcus Institute. Bernie and Bill Marcus's Marcus Foundation contributed $10 million to the center, located at the Marcus Institute. The Marcus Autism Center provided diagnosis, treatment, and support to children with autism and their families. Furthermore, the partnership enhanced the management of autism and other health problems common to the disorder.

Construction of a new, four-story building at Hughes Spalding began in August 2008. Plans for the facility included the addition of 24 child-friendly inpatient beds, an emergency department, and specialty clinics for asthma, sickle cell disease, and child protection. The facility was expected to open in 2010.

Mary Tradii

PRINCIPAL SUBSIDIARIES

HSOC, Inc.

PRINCIPAL OPERATING UNITS

Children's at Hughes Spalding; Egleston at Children's; Scottish Rite at Children's.

PRINCIPAL COMPETITORS

Emory Healthcare, Inc.; HCA Inc.; Shriners Hospitals for Children; Piedmont Healthcare.

FURTHER READING

"Children's Healthcare of Atlanta Names New CEO to Lead the Not-for-Profit Pediatric Health Care System," *US Newswire*, November 1, 2007.

Grzybowski, Alissa, "Dependent-Care Plan Boosts Retention & Return-to-Work Rates," *Managing Benefits Plan*, June 2007, p. 1.

Hernandez, Andrea V. "Aflac Raises More than $40M for Cancer Center," *Columbus Ledger-Enquirer*, March 20, 2008.

King, Mike, "Two Hospitals, Two Lessons: Management Switch Helps Secure Charity Mission," *Atlanta Journal-Constitution*, September 4, 2007, p. A8.

Miller, Andy, "Children's Hospitals End Spat—Expansion Plans Can Move Ahead," *Atlanta Journal and Atlanta Constitution*, August 14, 2004, p. F1.

Odum, Maria, "Hospital Honors Woman, 90—Scottish Rite Co-founder Treated Her for Polio," *Atlanta Journal and Atlanta Constitution*, September 26, 1990, p. G2.

———, "Scottish Rite Turns 75—Big Bash Attracts 150 Patients and Relatives," *Atlanta Journal and Atlanta Constitution*, September 26, 1990, p. G2.

O'Shea, Brian, "Children's Hospitals Grow Up," *Atlanta Journal-Constitution*, April 3, 2005, p. ZH9.

Palgiery, Jose, "Hospital Begins Expansion," *Atlanta Journal-Constitution*, August 14, 2008, p. D6.

Reid, S. A., "New Egleston Center Is Bringing Health Care Home," *Atlanta Journal and Atlanta Constitution*, March 14, 1996, p. A8.

Robbins, Roni B., "In this Business, There's Room Only for Those Who Put Children at the Top," *Atlanta Business Chronicle*, October 23, 1998, p. 18A.

Saporta, Maria, "Children's Healthcare Boosts Fund-Raising Goal," *Atlanta Journal and Atlanta Constitution*, July 20, 2006.

———, "Children's Healthcare of Atlanta Aims to Improve Pediatric Hospitals," *Atlanta Journal and Atlanta Constitution*, April 26, 2005.

———, "City's Hospitals for Children Look at Closer Ties," *Atlanta Journal and Atlanta Constitution*, May 27, 1993, p. E1.

Smith, Tina, "2 Cobb Hospitals Turning over Pediatric Care to Egleston," *Atlanta Journal and Atlanta Constitution*, July 30, 1967, p. 2.

Williams, Clint, "Growth and Development," *Atlanta Journal and Atlanta Constitution*, January 23, 2001, p. JG9.

Chindex International, Inc.

4340 East West Highway, Suite 1100
Bethesda, Maryland 20814-4450
U.S.A.
Telephone: (301) 215-7777
Fax: (301) 215-7719
Web site: http://www.chindex.com

Public Company
Incorporated: 1981 as U.S.-China Industrial Exchange Inc.
Employees: 1,007
Sales: $103.1 million (2008)
Stock Exchanges: NASDAQ
Ticker Symbol: CHDX
NAICS: 423450 Medical, Dental, and Hospital Equipment and Supplies Merchant Wholesalers

■ ■ ■

Although it maintains its headquarters in Bethesda, Maryland, Chindex International, Inc., operates mostly in mainland China and Hong Kong. The NASDAQ-listed, cross-cultural company maintains two divisions: Medical Products and Healthcare Services. Part of Chindex's original business, the Medical Products Division sells and services capital medical equipment and instrumentation to mainland China and Hong Kong. Products include diagnostic imaging equipment, aesthetic laser products, surgical products, and laboratory and clinical chemistry equipment and consumables. Complementary services include helping hospitals to secure financing and supply chain management for both hospitals and manufacturers. The Healthcare Services Division owns and operates Western-style hospitals in Beijing and Shanghai under the United Family Healthcare banner, as well as a satellite clinic in Shanghai's Pudong district and another Shanghai-area clinic that is under United Family Healthcare management. Additional hospitals are planned in other large Chinese cities, as well as a second hospital in Beijing.

COFOUNDER MOVES TO CHINA: 1979

Chindex was founded in 1981 by longtime CEO Roberta Lynn Lipson and her friend and colleague Elyse Beth Silverberg. Born in New York City, Lipson received a degree from Brandeis University in 1976. It was at Brandeis that she became enamored with China, majoring in East Asian studies. She also learned Mandarin, furthering her studies of the language in Taiwan for a year. After earning an M.B.A. from Columbia Business School in 1977, she was unable to find a job opportunity in China and instead accepted a marketing training position in the United States with the pharmaceutical company Schering-Plough Corporation. In 1979 she was finally able to put her facility with Mandarin to use when she was recruited by Sobin Chemical, Inc., which had long done business in the People's Republic of China and was invited to open a Beijing office.

Lipson moved to China in 1979, the same year that the country's universities began accepting exchange students. One of them was Elyse Silverberg, like Lipson a Long Islander and Chinese enthusiast. Silverberg

COMPANY PERSPECTIVES

Mission: Prosper as a cross-cultural company by providing leading edge healthcare technologies, quality products and services to China's professional communities with pride.

received a degree in Chinese studies and history from the State University of New York at Albany. After a stint as an intern for the National Council for U.S.-China Trade, she took a job with the organization, and then in 1980 joined Lipson at Sobin Chemical.

Having expected a boom in the China market that was not immediately forthcoming, Sobin Chemical elected in 1981 to exit the market. Rather than return to the United States, Lipson and Silverberg stayed, remaining convinced that there was a viable market for Western goods in mainland China. They investigated products made in the United States that had a competitive edge over those made in Japan, the chief competitor in the market, deciding that there was an opening with medical and construction equipment. Medical equipment of all types was especially needed by Chinese hospitals in the wake of the adverse impact of the ten-year Cultural Revolution.

FORMATION OF U.S.-CHINA INDUSTRIAL EXCHANGE INC., OR CHINDEX: 1981

In 1981 Lipson and Silverberg established U.S.-China Industrial Exchange Inc., which became informally known as Chindex, to serve as a market representative for Western manufacturers in China. The business was incorporated in New York State and its headquarters was established in New York City. Although Lipson and Silverberg found that there was indeed a market for medical and construction equipment, they also learned how difficult it was to do business in China, which was fraught with bureaucratic red tape. It took a year for the new company to receive permission to import foreign equipment, and even then they could deal with only the five designated state trading companies.

Business was conducted twice each year during the six-week-long Canton Trade Fair. Taking turns, one of the two partners attended the fair to take orders while the other set up shop in the United States to receive them. All medical equipment for China was acquired by four people working for two of the state trading companies.

Doing business at the fair became a grueling daily routine. Each day one of the partners visited the tables of the trading companies where a stack of handwritten requisitions for imported medical equipment could be found. Not only was the writing, from Chinese hospitals, difficult to read, the names of the products desired were often copied from medical journals, some a decade old. Moreover, the person seeking the equipment never met the person responsible for ordering it, and the person doing the ordering knew nothing about the technology.

With no one available to provide clarification, Lipson and Silverberg often had to guess what it was the hospitals wanted to buy. After copying down the requested items, the one attending the fair then had to book time at the telex office, where she had to curry favor in order to gain access to the mechanical telex machines. A tape would have to be cut, a connection made, and the tape run through the machine. On the other end in New York, the other partner would then have to locate companies willing to fill the orders, assemble quotes, and telex them back to China. The quote would then be presented to the trading company tables at the fair the next morning. If a quote was accepted, the Chindex partner would be given contract papers to complete in the afternoon. The following day, the process began all over again.

At first Lipson and Silverberg dealt only with the trading company representatives, but after a while hospital representatives began attending the trade fair, sitting quietly, never introduced, next to the buyer. Finally after two years, Lipson and Silverberg were permitted to visit Chinese hospitals. Unlike the Western trading companies doing business in China at the time, who were interested in maintaining a relationship only until a contract was signed, at which point they returned home, Lipson and Silverberg took a different approach. They were interested in creating deeper relationships with their customers, to be involved from ordering to installation. As a result, they began conducting seminars to familiarize Chinese physicians with the new medical equipment. Chindex was the first company to bring real-time ultrasound equipment to Beijing. "We had a seminar with 500 obstetricians looking for the first time at a moving fetus on a screen," Lipson recalled in a 2008 interview with *China Business Review.* "We saw professors with tears in their eyes, crying. It was an amazing, moving experience. We had a series of opportunities to expose people to technologies because we were bringing those technologies here." In addition, Chindex brought senior-level Chinese in healthcare and other industries to the United States for the first time.

KEY DATES

1981: Company is founded as U.S.-China Industrial Exchange Inc.
1994: Company is taken public.
1996: Hong Kong subsidiary is formed.
1997: United Family Health Center hospital opens in Beijing.
2002: Name is changed to Chindex International, Inc.
2004: Shanghai hospital opens.
2007: Retail business is phased out.

While Chindex was building trust with the hospitals, it was also importing heavy machinery used in construction, mining, railroads, and port handling, representing such companies as Volvo Construction Machinery Corp. and Euclid-Hitachi Heavy Equipment Inc. The company decided in the early 1990s to become involved in the healthcare business as well.

When Lipson decided to raise a family, rather than give birth in China where the hospital system showed little respect for patients' rights, she flew to the United States. Believing that there was a market for a Western-style birthing center in Beijing, primarily for foreign nationals living in the city, she made plans to open a facility. Finally in 1993 Chindex was permitted to establish the Beijing United Family Hospital. The idea for a birthing center then evolved into a small primary-care hospital that in addition to inpatient maternity services offered outpatient family care. To make the concept a reality, Chindex formed a joint venture with the Chinese Academy of Medical Sciences, which took a 10 percent interest.

GOING PUBLIC: 1994

While United Family Healthcare took shape, Chindex had to contend with a banking credit crunch in China in the early 1990s. Unable to obtain sufficient credit, Chinese hospitals and other companies were forced to cut back on their orders. Installment plan purchasing was an option, but Chindex lacked the deep pockets necessary to acquire capital equipment and be paid over time. In response to the situation they teamed up with their suppliers to create payment plans and also sought help from the Washington, D.C.-based Export-Import Bank, arguing that European suppliers enjoyed the benefit of government assistance. (In 1994 Chindex moved its headquarters from New York City to Be-

thesda, Maryland.) In addition, Chindex went public in August 1994, netting $7.25 million in an initial public offering (IPO) of stock. A portion of those funds were then put to use in providing credit to Chinese customers.

Some of the IPO proceeds were also invested in expanding the operations of Chindex. In early 1995 the company created its first foreign subsidiary, Chindex Holdings International Trade (Tianjin) Ltd., registered in the special economic Tianjin Port Free Trade Zone. The new company was permitted to bypass the foreign trading companies and sell certain products directly to Chinese hospitals in domestic currency. It was also allowed to maintain a distribution center in the country and develop a national sales network. Chindex planned to open several regional sales offices, but instead decided to hire field representatives who worked out of their homes, an innovation in the country. In March 1996 another subsidiary was formed to do business in Hong Kong. Later in the year, in order to provide additional funds for expansion, Chindex completed a secondary offering of stock, netting another $9.8 million.

HOSPITAL OPENS: 1997

After almost four years of effort, much of it devoted to persuading 16 government authorities in China to approve the project, in November 1997 Chindex opened the 43,500-square-foot United Family Health Center in northeast Beijing, where most foreign nationals lived and worked. It was the only government-approved joint-venture hospital in the country. It was housed in an unfinished classroom building, taken over from the Beijing Telecommunications University in March 1996. Plans were also being developed to open more hospitals and satellite clinics under the United Family Health banner.

In 1996 Chindex generated revenues of $22 million, 80 percent of which came from healthcare sales. Because the healthcare side of the business held a great deal more promise than the mature construction equipment market, Chindex decided in 1997 to become a dedicated healthcare company and its other businesses were phased out. Several feeder clinics were established in Beijing in the late 1990s to support the United Family Healthcare operations. In addition, Chindex in 1998 began selling branded healthcare products to China's growing retail pharmacy market, a business that the company expanded aggressively a year later. Also, in late 1998 Chindex opened distribution centers in Tianjin and Shanghai and began offering sales and marketing services to healthcare-related companies looking to do business in China. Chindex ended the decade with sales of $37.13 million in fiscal 1999.

In the early years of the new century, Chindex enjoyed steady growth, with revenues increasing to $56.12 million in 2001. A year later the company changed its state of incorporation to Delaware and U.S.-China Industrial Exchange Inc. was formally renamed Chindex International, Inc. Also in 2002 the company received approval to open a second United Family Healthcare hospital, located in Shanghai. It would open in October 2004. In the meantime, Chindex built up goodwill in the country when it helped China deal with an outbreak of severe acute respiratory syndrome (SARS) in 2003. Lipson and doctors from the Beijing United Family Hospital played an important role in coordinating SARS data and supplying emergency products to the municipal government of Beijing. Although the emergency hurt its profits, Chindex was well positioned to receive favored treatment from a grateful Chinese government.

DISCONTINUATION OF RETAIL DISTRIBUTION: 2007

Net sales topped the $100 million mark for the first time in company history in fiscal 2005, helped in part by the opening of a new primary-care clinic. A year later, Chindex decided to discontinue its retail distribution business, which had consistently lost money since its launch. The business was phased out by the end of 2007, and the unit's distribution and logistics services were taken over by the parent company. As a result of this loss of business, revenues dipped to $90 million in fiscal 2006. A year later revenues regained lost ground, approaching $106 million, due primarily to strong growth in the Healthcare Services Division, which enjoyed a 31 percent increase in sales over the prior year. Continued strong growth in the Healthcare Services Division, which opened clinics in the Shanghai area and the Guangzhou market, led to net sales improving to $130 million in fiscal 2008. A hospital was planned to open in Guangzhou and a second in Beijing in 2010.

Given the scope of the Chinese market, the need for healthcare services and equipment, as well as Chindex's unique position in the country, there was every reason to believe that the company was beginning to scratch only the surface of its potential.

Ed Dinger

PRINCIPAL DIVISIONS

Medical Products; Healthcare Services.

PRINCIPAL COMPETITORS

China Hospitals, Inc.; GE Healthcare; Royal Philips Electronics N.V.

FURTHER READING

Barlyn, Suzanne, "China's Medical Boom," *Time,* October 9, 2008.

Benesh, Peter, "Will Gratitude Add Up to a Rise in Business?" *Investor's Business Daily,* November 18, 2003, p. A09.

Gardner, Bradley, "Healthy Profits," *China International Business,* March 12, 2008.

Hurley, James, "Embracing the China Challenge," *Healthcare Exec,* November 2007.

Johnson, Ian, "MD. Company Finds Success in China," *Baltimore Sun,* June 30, 1996, p. 1D.

Laris, Michael, "The Birth of a Revolution?" *Washington Post,* February 28, 2000, p. F18.

Lipson, Roberta, and Elyse Silverberg, "Roberta Lipson, President and CEO; Elyse Silverberg, Executive Vice President Chindex International Inc.," *China Business Review,* November/December 2008, p. 24.

Nall, Stephanie, "Chindex Shares Expertise with Other US Firms," *Journal of Commerce,* October 1, 1997, p. 5D.

O'Neill, Mark, "Roberta Lipson Has Helped Resuscitate the Mainland Medical Scene," *South China Morning Post,* June 7, 1999.

Pallarito, Karen, "Hurdling a Great Wall," *Modern Healthcare,* November 3, 1997, p. I26.

Salmon, Jacqueline L., "China's Credit Squeeze Hits Home in Bethesda," *Washington Post,* June 19, 1995, p. F10.

Chunghwa Telecom Co., Ltd.

21-3 Hsinyi Road, Section 1
Taipei, 100
Taiwan
Telephone: (+886 2) 2344 5488
Fax: (+886 2) 3393 8188
Web site: http://www.cht.com.tw

Public Company
Incorporated: 1943 as Directorate General of Telecommunications
Employees: 24,138
Sales: $1.53 billion (2007)
Stock Exchanges: NYSE Euronext
Ticker Symbol: CHT
NAICS: 517212 Cellular and Other Wireless Telecommunications; 517110 Wired Telecommunications Carriers

■ ■ ■

Chunghwa Telecom Co., Ltd., is Taiwan's dominant telecommunications company. The company was originally the operational side of the Taiwan telecom regulator Directorate General of Telecommunications and remains the island's dominant provider of long-distance and local fixed-line services. The company also controls the island's core broadband network, holding an 87 percent share. Through subsidiary Hi-net, Chunghwa is the leading provider of Internet access services in Taiwan. Chunghwa also holds the lead in the Taiwan mobile telephone market, with a 35.8 percent market share. Other telecommunications services provided by the company include directory services, data transmission services, and virtual private network (VPN) services. In 2007, Chunghwa launched a $180 million investment program to build an island-wide fiber-optic network, in part to support the group's entry into the digital television market. This investment comes as part of an overall five-year investment program of almost $4 billion to upgrade the group's telecommunications infrastructure. With the Taiwanese telephony market at saturation levels (the country counts more than two telephones per person), Chunghwa has begun looking for growth internationally. The company has been negotiating to form partnerships in Thailand and Vietnam and even, if it succeeds in winning Taiwanese government approval, mainland China. Chunghwa is listed on the NYSE Euronext Stock Exchange and posted revenues of $1.53 billion in 2007. The company is led by CEO and Chairman Shyue-Ching Lu and President Shaio-Tung Chang.

PRE-REVOLUTION TELECOMMUNICATIONS

Chunghwa's history began even before Taiwan broke away from mainland China following the Communist Revolution there. The first propositions to extend telecommunications services from the mainland to the island state came as early as 1874, in order to improve military communications in the face of increasing Japanese military harassment. In July 1877 the government began laying a submarine cable between the Chinese mainland and its island province Taiwan, which the Japanese had claimed as their own.

KEY DATES

1943: Chinese Nationalist government establishes the Directorate General of Telecommunications (DGT).

1949: The DGT is transferred to Taiwan with the Nationalist government.

1969: The DGT launches automated switching throughout its telephone network.

1989: The DGT introduces mobile telephone services.

1996: Taiwan carries out first step in the deregulation of the telecommunications sector, spinning off the DGT's telecommunications operations as Chunghwa Telecom.

2000: Chunghwa's shares are listed on the Taiwan Stock Exchange.

2005: Chunghwa completes its privatization with a listing of its shares on the NYSE.

2008: Chunghwa launches joint venture with Viettel to introduce Internet and other telecom services to Cambodia.

Although this connection was not completed until nine years later, additional lines were started in 1881 for military communications between other Chinese marine bases. These links helped the military to respond to attacks from other foreign armies and domestic warlords. Until these telegraph lines were installed, crucial battlefield communications were delivered on foot and subject to long delays.

Local officials later won grants from the imperial government to establish a public telegraph service, initially linking Shanghai and Tianjin. This line, which included seven switching stations along its route, took eight months to complete.

Because the Chinese language is based on pictographic characters rather than on an alphabet, it was impossible to transmit Chinese words using standard Morse code dots and dashes. Instead engineers developed an ingenious method of dots and dashes that indicated the position and number of strokes of each radical in a given Chinese character. In this way a character could be described with Morse code. In time, this method grew into such a highly efficient shorthand that telegraph operators could transmit messages almost as fast as their English-language counterparts. This same method remains in use in China today.

To help establish this new electronic language, and to assist in the growth of telecommunications in China, the government established a school at Tianjin that it staffed with foreign engineers and teachers.

The network was plagued by frequent outages. Where weather or poor workmanship was not to blame, peasant farmers were usually responsible. Many did not trust those who operated the system, seeing it as an aid to bureaucrats and tax collectors. Others simply did not want the poles on their farmland and others found better uses for the wood and wire. As a result, farmers became a major hazard to the system, taking down what workers spent months putting into place.

In 1890, as officials continued to struggle with telegraphy, the telephone was introduced to China. The first service was set up by a telegraph office in Nanjing connecting 14 customers, all of them government offices. This system and others like it expanded rapidly as businesses and then wealthy residents requested their own lines. Often growth outstripped the capacity of switching offices, forcing Chinese operators to handle hundreds of connections at a single station.

In 1896 China lost a war with Japan and was forced to cede Taiwan to the Japanese government. As a result, the excellent communications network established for the defense of Taiwan was in Japanese hands.

The Japanese military began construction of large telephone networks during 1897 in the areas of China that it occupied, but these were primarily for administrative use. By 1900, however, the Japanese began offering telephone service commercially, including local and long-distance services. At this time there were only about 30,000 telephone customers in all of China, and 80 percent of them were Japanese.

After the establishment of the Chinese Republic in 1911, demand for telephone lines exploded. As more customers requested telephones, the average costs of providing services were reduced, making the telephone affordable to even more customers.

By 1927 every large city in China had Strowger-type switches, which allowed calls to be placed automatically by dialing a customer's number. At this time, telecommunications authorities had completed a major long-distance network connecting more than 7,000 customers in seven provinces. In addition, the government took over international services, which had previously been offered only by foreign companies operating in China. New connections were established from the northeastern city of Shenyang to Germany and France. By 1930 backbone construction of the national telephone network was completed.

Telegraphy, however, was not dead. In 1905 the first wireless telegraph system was installed. While restricted mainly to military applications, the wireless gained widespread commercial application in the late 1920s. A decade later, after the Japanese invasion of Manchuria, the wireless became essential to military operations, as wireline networks were easily and frequently destroyed by enemy action. A wireless telephone service between China and the United States was inaugurated shortly before the outbreak of full-scale war between China and Japan.

CREATION OF THE DIRECTORATE GENERAL OF TELECOMMUNICATIONS IN 1943

The Chinese government evacuated Guangzhou (Canton) to Japanese forces and later moved a thousand miles inland to Chongqing, capital of Sichuan Province. It was here that the ruling Nationalist government reorganized administrative organs, creating a Ministry of Transportation and Telecommunications. Within this ministry, on May 19, 1943, the government established a Directorate General of Telecommunications (DGT), whose mission was to develop telephone and telegraph communications in China.

During World War II China suffered tremendous damage at the hands of the Japanese. So complete was Japan's scorched-earth policy that occupation authorities ordered all telephones impounded and destroyed. In the waning days of the war, as Japan's defeat became inevitable, Japanese authorities on Taiwan ordered the total destruction of the telecommunications network, much of which it had developed over the previous 50 years.

After Japan's surrender in 1945 the DGT inherited a system that was in complete ruin. Even lines that could be salvaged were nearly unusable because they were built with inferior war-grade Japanese wire. Rehabilitation of the network was extremely difficult and costly.

Shortly after the war the Communists under Mao Zedong and the ruling Nationalist faction under Chiang Kai-shek ended their anti-Japanese cooperation. Subsequent hostilities between the parties later escalated into a destructive civil war.

In 1948, amid the battles raging throughout the country, the government's DGT introduced telex service, and telephone subscribership in China peaked at 167,000 customers. The Guomindang, however, began losing to the Communists and in 1949 was forced off the mainland to take refuge on Taiwan. At that time the government had to abandon the entire telecommunications network on the mainland to the Communists.

POST-REVOLUTION GROWTH

Repairs on Taiwan's telephone system began as soon as Chinese control was reestablished on the island in 1945. After 1949, though, with the newly arrived government in exile, thousands of refugees and hundreds of businesses from the mainland, public demands on the network continued to outrun what the service could provide. In 1949 Taiwan had only five international circuits.

The government on Taiwan struggled to arm itself against a final offensive from the mainland. This required highly taxing investments in local industry and infrastructure, which drained commercial financing. With investment prioritized for shipbuilding, steel, and heavy machinery, little was left for modernization of the telephone network.

One major accomplishment, however, was the establishment of rural telephone service along the Taiwanese seacoast. These new rural lines, constructed for military use in 1949, brought telephone service to thousands of farmers. It was not until 1952, however, that reconstruction of the basic network was declared complete.

During the remainder of the 1950s the state-run telecommunications agency struggled to keep its network operating with the most modern technology it could afford. Emphasis was shifted from merely getting lines strung to improving signal quality. In 1957 the company introduced FM-band telegraphy and in the following year it perfected a Chinese-language telegram typewriter. These breakthroughs extended the life of telegraphy in Taiwan and greatly increased telegram traffic.

Gradually, by the mid-1960s, after basic industries had been firmly established in Taiwan, funding for improvements in the telephone network became available. Under government direction, the Taiwanese economy was designed to generate wealth from export earnings. Export-led growth began in certain sectors of the economy during the 1960s and exploded in the early 1970s.

Led by small manufacturers of toys, machinery, and handicrafts, Taiwan's strong growth provided tremendous personal income. This income created further demand for telecommunications services, fueling a period of extremely strong growth for the DGT.

In 1969 the DGT began widespread automated switching, eliminating all operator-connected calling. That year the company also completed construction of a modern satellite communications facility that greatly expanded the capacity for international calls. Microwave communications systems were also established between

Taiwan, the Philippines, and Hong Kong. This had a great effect on Taiwanese commerce, as exporters found it much easier to remain in contact with their customers.

MODERN TELECOMMUNICATIONS PROVIDER IN THE EIGHTIES

By 1971 DGT had nearly 400,000 telephone customers with 600,000 telephones, about twice the number on the entire Chinese mainland. Again, strong demand lowered average costs, making the telephone affordable to even more people.

The DGT placed several thousand public telephones throughout Taiwan during the 1970s. Introduced shortly after World War II, DGT's first public phones collected charges only after a call was completed. In 1955 credit accounts were established. By 1976, however, the company had installed nearly 27,000 standard coin-operated phones and had introduced paging services.

In 1980 the DGT completed an eight-year campaign to bring telephone coverage to all rural areas in China, including many offshore islands. This campaign also helped the company to achieve extremely high rates of growth, averaging 20 percent per year. During the 1970s, as investment in the network averaged a staggering 0.7 percent of the entire nation's gross national product, Taiwan's telecommunications industry moved from developing country levels to those of modern industrial nations. By 1981 the DGT served more than 2.7 million customers with more than 3.7 million telephones.

In 1981 the DGT introduced digital switching, which, in addition to allowing calls to be placed more quickly and accurately, enabled the company to introduce touch-tone service and, later, new vertical services such as call waiting and speed dialing. The company also began direct international dialing, high-speed telex, and data and computer services.

In 1989 the company introduced cellular service and began setting up large networks in each of its major urban markets. By 1992 cellular coverage was extended to the Chungshan Freeway and other trunk highways as well as to remote industrial parks and resorts, such as Sun Moon Lake, Renting National Park, and Snow Dan International Park. Cellular subscription in 1992 exceeded 220,000 customers.

The DGT began installing fiber-optic cable on major long-distance and trunk routes during the late 1980s. These upgrades allowed increases in switching capacity and improvements in signal quality. The fiber-optic backbone had even been extended offshore to Kinmen, Penghu, and Matsu, an island immediately adjacent to the mainland that the Nationalists continued to control.

DEREGULATION IN THE NINETIES

The DGT remained committed to developing Taiwan's telecommunications infrastructure. The company became a major partner in the developing range of trans-Asian and global subsea cabling projects; by the end of the 1990s, the company had joined in on at least 35 such projects, including the world's longest, a cable reaching from east Asia to the United States. The DGT also invested heavily in satellite communications partnerships, including the ST-1 joint venture with Singapore Telecom launched in 1994. By then, the DGT had also installed Taiwan's first "advanced intelligence network," built by AT&T's Taiwan subsidiary, providing for toll-free calls, credit-card calling and telephone voting services. The DGT also controlled the small but growing Internet market in the country, serving as Taiwan's sole Internet access provider.

CONTROLLING THE COUNTRY'S INTERNET

Increasingly, however, the Taiwanese government faced pressure to deregulate its telephone system, amid the wave of deregulation and privatization that swept through the global telecommunications industry from the late 1980s. The government initially was able to resist the pressure to deregulate the domestic market, pointing to the DGT's relatively efficient and modern operations.

By the mid-1990s, the Taiwanese government finally moved to deregulate the market. Internet access became one of the first markets to be opened to private competition, with licenses being handed out as early as 1995. By 1996, the Taiwanese government finally managed to overcome the heated opposition to its proposed deregulation plan. In January of that year, the government succeeded in passing new telecommunications legislation. The Telecommunications Act of 1996 called for the breakup of the DGT into its operations and regulatory components. The latter continued to function as the DGT. The former, however, was spun off as a new and independently operating, state-owned company, Chunghwa Telecom. Former DGT chief Steven Y. Chen was tapped to lead the new company.

PRIVATIZATION IN 2005

Because of its incumbent status, Chunghwa retained its powerful position in the Taiwanese telecommunications market, even as it faced a growing number of competitors. The company's continued de facto monopoly of the fixed-line market provided it with a solid foundation for the expansion of its other operations, including its mobile telephone and Internet access businesses. At the same time, Chunghwa also reaped the benefits of its newfound freedom.

As part of the DGT, the company had been required to submit any new infrastructure investments and projects for government approval. As an independent corporation, Chunghwa, freed from bureaucracy, was able to respond far more rapidly to market developments. The company's hiring practices also benefited from the change. Previously, candidates for DGT jobs were required to pass civil service entrance examinations, often testing on subjects with little or nothing to do with telecommunications. Freed of this constraint, Chunghwa began hiring on an interview-only basis, enabling the company to recruit among the top technology candidates.

This newfound flexibility helped Chunghwa weather the first onslaught of competition, particularly in the all-important mobile telephone market, which was set to explode into the next century. The first competing mobile networks became operational in 1998, and rapidly succeeded in knocking down Chunghwa's market share. By 2000, the group's former monopoly status had been shrunk back to just 50 percent.

Similarly, while Chunghwa maintained its de facto monopoly over the fixed-line market, largely because of the investment required to build a second network on the island, the company's hold over telephone services came under threat as well. In 1998, the Taiwanese government began to make good on its promise to authorize Internet-based telephony services, issuing the first licenses that year. Chunghwa's control of the country's broadband network nonetheless meant that it would retain a share in that market's growth as well. Then, in 1999, the government opened the fixed-line market to competition as well. By 2001, three companies had stepped forward with proposed fixed-line services; all three were slow to start up actual operations, however.

In the meantime, the Taiwanese government's promise to privatize Chunghwa got off to a painfully slow start. Chunghwa's stock was listed on the Taiwan Stock Exchange in 2000, with a secondary offering following over the next several years. However, the government was forced to abort its attempt to attract international investors, through a listing of American depositary receipts on the New York Stock Exchange, due to a lack of strong investor interest. Part of the privatization difficulties came from the global slump in the telecommunications sector, and in the technology sector in general. Chunghwa's privatization was also hampered by the company's own problems. Into the early 2000s, the company's fixed-line operations had begun losing money, while it struggled to maintain its lead in a mobile services market that had reached 100 percent saturation. Indeed, by the middle of that decade, Taiwan could boast of one of the highest mobile penetration rates in the world, with fully two telephones per person.

In response, Chunghwa targeted a number of new telecommunications areas for growth. The booming broadband market provided one outlet, and by 2002, the company had signed up more than 1.2 million high-speed DSL subscribers. By the following year, Chunghwa's control of the broadband network allowed it to launch its own digital television service.

Chunghwa's privatization at last became a reality in 2005, when the Taiwanese government floated 14 percent of its shares on the New York Stock Exchange. The offering, complemented by the sale of another 3 percent to institutional investors, dropped the government's stake in the company below 50 percent for the first time. By the end of 2006, the government had further reduced its shareholding to around 35 percent.

NEW MARKETS FOR THE FUTURE

Chunghwa turned its attention to its future growth strategy. The company entered the 3G (third generation) high-speed mobile telephone race in 2005, becoming the first in Taiwan to launch 3G services. Yet Chunghwa recognized that the saturated Taiwanese market offered little prospect for future growth. Instead, the company announced its plans to develop its operations on an international level.

Thailand became one of the group's first foreign targets, as the company began negotiating a partnership with its counterpart there, TOT. Chunghwa announced its interest in acquiring a stake in TOT from the Thai government. By 2008, Chunghwa had also begun positioning itself in other markets. In Vietnam, the company formed a joint venture with Viettel, operated by the country's military, to launch Internet data and other telecom operations in Cambodia. More controversial, however, was Chunghwa's long-announced interest in entering the mainland Chinese market. For this the company began seeking out a

Chinese partner to introduce 3G mobile services, while also seeking approval from the Taiwanese government, which barred the island's telecom providers from operating on the mainland. Nonetheless, foreign expansion appeared vital for Chunghwa as it fought to maintain its share of its heavily saturated home market.

John Simley
Updated, M. L. Cohen

PRINCIPAL SUBSIDIARIES

A-Kuei Publishing Co., Ltd.; Chief Telecom (Hong Kong) Limited; Chief Telecom Inc.; Chunghwa International Yellow Pages Corporation; Chunghwa System Integration Co., Ltd.; Chunghwa Telecom Global, Inc. (USA); Concord Technology Co., Ltd.; Donghwa Telecom Co., Ltd. (Hong Kong); Era Light Development Co., Ltd.; Glory Network System Service (China) Co., Ltd.; New Prospect Investments Holdings Ltd. (British Virgin Islands); Prime Asia Investments Group Ltd. (British Virgin Islands); Senao International Co., Ltd.; Spring House Entertainment Inc. (BVI) (British Virgin Islands); Spring House Entertainment Inc. (Japan); Spring House Entertainment Inc.; Unigate Telecom Inc.

PRINCIPAL COMPETITORS

Taiwan Mobile Company Ltd.; Far EasTone Telecommunications Company Ltd.; UTStarcom Incorporated Taiwan; Jow Tong Technology Company Ltd.

FURTHER READING

Carrol, Mark, "Asia Loosens Internet Access," *Electronic Engineering Times,* August 7, 1995, p. 68.

Carter, Robert K., "Chunghwa Eyes Bid for 3G Licenses in China," *Wireless Asia,* January–February 2007, p. 8.

———, "Chunghwa Looks to Thailand for Growth," *Telecom Asia,* February 2006, p. 8.

Chung, Oscar, "Leveling the Playing Field," *Taiwan Review,* January 10, 1998.

Clark, Robert, "Taiwan Phone Monopoly Tries to Stamp Out Callback Operators," *Newsbytes,* November 7, 1996.

———, "Thoughts of Chairman Mao," *Telecom Asia,* October 2002, p. 26.

"Singapore & Taiwan in Satellite Deal," *Newsbytes,* September 11, 1995.

"Taiwan Gov't Sells Chunghwa Telecom Stake," *TelecomWeb News Digest,* September 26, 2006.

"Taiwan Spins Off State Telecoms Monopoly," *Newsbytes,* July 3, 1996.

"Taiwan Still Plans to Open Internet Telephony Services to Private Firms by 2001," *East Asian Executive Reports,* November 15, 1998, p. 8.

"Taiwan's Telecommunications: A Profile of Progress," *Telephony,* March 24, 1986.

"Vietnam's Viettel," *Telecom Asia,* July 2008, p. 17.

Wood, Nick, "Chunghwa Eyes China's 3G Market," *Total Telecom Online,* April 17, 2007.

Comerica Incorporated

Comerica Bank Tower
1717 Main Street
Dallas, Texas 75201
U.S.A.
Telephone: (214) 969-6476
Toll Free: (800) 521-1190
Fax: (214) 462-6810
Web site: http://www.comerica.com

Public Company
Founded: 1849 as Detroit Savings Fund Institute
Incorporated: 1871 as The Detroit Savings Bank
Employees: 10,000
Total Assets: $67.55 billion (2008)
Stock Exchanges: New York
Ticker Symbol: CMA
NAICS: 522110 Commercial Banking; 522291 Consumer Lending; 522293 International Trade Financing; 523110 Investment Banking and Securities Dealing; 523120 Securities Brokerage; 523920 Portfolio Management; 523930 Investment Advice; 523991 Trust, Fiduciary, and Custody Activities; 524113 Direct Life Insurance Carriers; 551111 Offices of Bank Holding Companies

∎ ∎ ∎

Comerica Incorporated is one of the 20 largest banking companies in the United States. The firm offers a full range of commercial banking services to individuals and businesses in five states: Michigan, California, Arizona, Texas, and Florida. Select Comerica businesses also operate in other states and in Canada, Mexico, and China. Comerica's operations include about 425 bank branches in its five-state footprint, with more than half located in Michigan. As the culmination of its shift in focus to the faster-growing Sunbelt, Comerica moved its headquarters to Dallas in 2007, after more than a century and a half of being Detroit based, but a significant portion of the bank's revenues and profits are still generated in Michigan. The company remains the second largest bank in Michigan in terms of deposits, trailing only Bank of America Corporation.

BORN IN CRISIS

The Detroit of the mid-19th century was quite different from the modern Motown. The population of only 19,000 traveled on dirt roads; lumber and shipbuilding were the main industries. Similarly, the institution that preceded Comerica gave little hints of its future scale.

The Detroit Savings Fund Institute was created on March 5, 1849. Michigan Governor Epaphroditus Ransom had decreed its founding to provide a safe place for wage earners to invest their savings after a wave of bank failures. Detroit had three other banks at that time, but they were focused on business clients.

The Institute opened for business on August 17, 1849. At the end of its first day, the Institute had $41 in deposits and six customers. By year's end, this increased to $3,287 and 56 customers. Receipts reached $25,000 within two years and the number of customers increased to 300.

Elon Farnsworth, formerly Michigan's attorney general, served as the first president. The Institute was

COMPANY PERSPECTIVES

■

Great Opportunities don't happen by accident. They do happen when a strategy for success is combined with a strong focus on customer service and a clear vision to help people and businesses be successful. That's the Comerica difference.

not a real bank, since it had no shareholders or capital stock. Its managers were unpaid. The Institute hired its first full-time cashier in 1855.

By 1870, the Institute had assets of $1 million. It changed its name to The Detroit Savings Bank in 1871 and reorganized as a corporation.

By 1900, Detroit Savings was a $6 million bank. The new automobile industry was beginning to fuel explosive growth in the area. Detroit's 1906 population of 290,000 would more than triple in the next quarter century.

Detroit suffered with the rest of the country after the stock market crash of October 1929. During a statewide bank holiday and President Franklin D. Roosevelt's national bank holiday, both of which occurred in early 1933, Detroit Savings was forced to temporarily close. In both instances, the bank opened ahead of other Detroit rivals, and individuals and businesses showed their confidence in the bank with a significant influx of deposits into existing and new accounts. In the year following the 1933 bank holidays, savings deposits increased $19 million, or 77 percent, and the number of depositors rose by more than 36,000. Detroit Savings changed its name to The Detroit Bank in 1936.

CREATION OF FUTURE PARTNER: 1933

Another bank was formed in 1933 whose history would one day be linked to that of The Detroit Bank. Manufacturers National Bank of Detroit was created in 1933 by Edsel B. Ford, Henry Ford's son, and continued to hold strong ties to Ford Motor Company.

Beginning with $3 million of Ford money, the bank's assets reached $11 million by the end of its first day in business, August 10, 1933. Unlike Detroit Bank, Manufacturers National focused on mid- and large-sized corporations. It soon bought several other banks in varying degrees of solvency. Manufacturers was originally headquartered in Detroit's historical Penobscot Building,

then the tallest skyscraper in town, but moved to a renovated office building in 1944.

Detroit's factories attracted thousands of workers during World War II. More women began to take teller positions, previously a job mostly held by men. Detroit Bank's president, Joseph M. Dodge, negotiated contracts for the U.S. military and worked on economic restoration programs for the defeated Axis powers. Following the war, Manufacturers bought United States Savings Bank, in 1952, and then merged with Industrial National Bank in 1955.

1956 FORMATION OF DETROIT BANK & TRUST

In 1956 Detroit Bank made a major step forward by consolidating with three other local banks—The Birmingham National Bank, Ferndale National Bank, and Detroit Wabeek Bank and Trust Company—to form The Detroit Bank & Trust Company. The merger, which at the time was the largest corporate consolidation in Michigan history, enabled the bank to gain additional branches both within the city of Detroit and in the surrounding suburbs. At the time of its formation, Detroit Bank & Trust boasted assets of $1 billion.

Detroit Bank & Trust built a new headquarters building, completed in 1964, next to the former Detroit Trust Company building. Manufacturers moved its headquarters to the Renaissance Center in 1977.

The American banking industry changed substantially in the 1970s. Detroit Bank & Trust began offering Master Charge credit cards to its customers in 1971. The following year, the bank installed its first ATM (automated teller machine).

FROM DETROITBANK TO COMERICA

The holding company DETROITBANK Corporation was formed in 1973 to exploit new industry regulations. As a holding company, DETROITBANK could offer more varied types of financial services than its bank subsidiary. It could also offer them in other states, as well as create new out-of-state banks.

A period of bank deregulation in the United States began in 1980. DETROITBANK changed its name to Comerica Incorporated in 1982. The new name was chosen because it seemed national, rather than regional, in scope. The company and its future merger partner Manufacturers National both moved in the 1980s to increase their presence beyond Michigan. Comerica followed its retiring snowbird clients south, forming Comerica Trust Company of Florida, N.A. in 1982, and then

KEY DATES

1849: Detroit Savings Fund Institute is chartered after wave of banking failures.
1871: The Institute becomes a corporation called The Detroit Savings Bank.
1900: Detroit Savings has $6 million in assets.
1933: Edsel B. Ford creates Manufacturers National Bank of Detroit.
1936: Detroit Savings becomes The Detroit Bank.
1952: Manufacturers buys the United States Savings Bank.
1955: Manufacturers merges with Industrial National Bank.
1956: Detroit Bank, The Birmingham National Bank, Ferndale National Bank, and Detroit Wabeek Bank and Trust Company merge to form The Detroit Bank & Trust Company, with assets of $1 billion.
1973: DETROITBANK Corporation is formed as a holding company for Detroit Bank & Trust.
1982: DETROITBANK becomes Comerica Incorporated.
1983: Comerica buys Bank of the Commonwealth.
1988: Comerica begins branch banking in Texas through acquisition of Grand Bancshares, Inc.
1991: Purchases of Plaza Commerce Bancorp and Bank of Industry provide Comerica with its first bank branches in California.
1992: Comerica and Manufacturers merge.
2001: Los Angeles-based Imperial Bancorp is acquired.
2007: Comerica's headquarters are shifted from Detroit to Dallas.

in 1987 it opened a lending office in Texas. Also in 1987, Manufacturers National acquired Illinois-based Affiliated Banc Group, Inc. In the meantime, Comerica expanded its Michigan base by purchasing a hometown rival, Bank of the Commonwealth, in 1983.

SUNBELT EXPANSION

Comerica acquired a Texas bank, Grand Bancshares, Inc., in 1988, through which it gained its first bank branches in that state and was able to offer a full line of banking services. Through 1995, 20 other Texas banks were acquired. By the end of the 1990s, Dallas-based Comerica Bank-Texas ranked as the ninth largest bank

in Texas, with $3.8 billion in assets and 53 branches. It operated in Dallas/Fort Worth, Austin, and Houston.

Comerica's venture into California followed a similar trajectory. The company in 1983 had started a San Jose-based auto financing business, which by 1988 was serving other types of businesses. Comerica acquired its first California bank branches in 1991 with the purchases of Plaza Commerce Bancorp in Silicon Valley and Bank of Industry in Los Angeles. Three additional acquisitions were completed in the mid-1990s. By the end of the decade, Comerica Bank-California had become the state's tenth largest bank, with 30 branch offices serving the San Francisco Bay area, Santa Cruz, Los Angeles and Orange County, and San Diego.

In the Sunbelt states, wrote *USBanker,* "[Comerica's] focus is on lending to small and middle market companies, using products like a state-of-the-art management system to take share from local competitors. Retail customers are basically 'an accommodation.'" Comerica preferred to operate in growing cities with plenty of smaller businesses, particularly industrial ones.

A "MERGER OF EQUALS" IN 1992

Comerica and Manufacturers National merged in 1992. The banks were approximately the same size in assets ($14.3 billion and $12.5 billion, respectively) and employees (7,200 and 6,300), and the combination created the 25th largest bank holding company in the United States. The banks' CEOs promoted the merger to avoid either company being taken over by an out-of-state bank. Manufacturer's CEO Gerald V. MacDonald was picked to head the combined company, which retained the Comerica name as well as the Manufacturers blue trapezoid logo. MacDonald was succeeded in 1993 by Eugene A. Miller, a Comerica veteran since 1955. Also in 1993, Comerica abandoned the Detroit Bank & Trust Building for offices at the corner of Woodward and Larned, which became known as the Comerica Tower at Detroit Center.

Miller restructured the company, eliminating unprofitable enterprises. About 60 out of 348 branches were closed, and 1,800 jobs were cut, mostly through attrition. This reengineering project was dubbed "Direction 2000," and lasted through 1998. Besides hiring a consulting firm, Comerica enlisted the help of its employees, receiving 2,000 suggestions on improving the bottom line.

NEW GROWTH AREAS

One new area of growth was in life insurance sales, a business that states were gradually opening to banks.

Comerica acquired an existing agency, Access Insurance Services, which it renamed. In 1995 the new Comerica Insurance Services began selling life, disability, and long-term care insurance at 274 branch offices in Michigan.

In early 1995 Comerica also expanded its investment business via a merger with Munder Capital Management, based in Birmingham, Michigan. This was combined with Comerica's existing Woodbridge Capital Management and World Asset Management units, which together had $22 billion in assets to Munder's $8 billion. Comerica took a majority interest in the venture. Also in 1995 Comerica bought W.Y. Campbell, a Detroit-based investment banking operation, which became the basis for its capital markets group.

In 1996 Comerica sold two subsidiaries, Comerica Bank-Illinois (formerly Affiliated Banc Group) and John V. Carr & Son, Inc. ABN-AMRO Holdings bought the bank, which Comerica abandoned after determining it could not grow in Illinois.

The Direction 2000 restructuring induced a short-term loss in 1996; the bank, however, was again posting winning numbers in 1997. Comerica began operating in Canada in 1998 to benefit from that country's increasing trade with the states in which Comerica already operated. A Mexican subsidiary had been created in 1997.

The wave of giant banking mergers accelerated in 1998, with BankAmerica Corporation and NationsBank Corporation combining to form Bank of America Corporation, Norwest Corporation joining Wells Fargo & Company, and Banc One Corporation amalgamating with First Chicago NBD Corporation to form Bank One Corporation. The latter deal was particularly significant for Comerica as it brought a strong and newly enlarged retail bank into Comerica's southeastern Michigan home. (The initials "NBD" had stood for National Bank of Detroit, a bank launched in 1933, the same year as Manufacturers' founding, and this bank had a further parallel with Manufacturers: It too was initially capitalized by a Motor City automaker, in NBD's case, General Motors Corporation.) These new superbanks dwarfed Comerica in terms of assets, geographic reach, and range of products. Comerica's keys to survival were a focus on its core markets, innovation, and credit quality.

Miller took over the duties of President Michael Monahan upon his retirement in June 1999. Miller was required by company bylaws to retire at age 65 in 2003; three vice-chairmen—John Lewis, Joseph Buttigieg, and Ralph W. Babb Jr.—were in position in early 1999 to vie to succeed him. Monahan went on to head the Munder Capital Management unit after its president

quit in the fall of 1999. Comerica had been planning to reduce its majority stake in the company. Miller in the meantime had scored a marketing coup by purchasing the naming rights to the new downtown ballpark for the Detroit Tigers in a 30-year deal costing $66 million. Comerica Park hosted its first Major League baseball game in the spring of 2000.

By 2000 Comerica had 11,000 employees, 1,000 of whom worked at its Detroit headquarters; it also had operations in Michigan, Florida, Texas, California, Colorado, Illinois, Indiana, Ohio, Nevada, New York, and Tennessee, as well as Mexico, Canada, and Hong Kong. Seeing a challenging future in spite of his success, Miller told a meeting of the Newcomen Society in October 2000, "Japan has one bank for 1.5 million people. … In the U.S. we have one bank for every 25,000 people, and if you factor in credit unions, it's one for every 10,000. There simply are not enough customers to keep all, or even most, U.S. banks in business."

IMPERIAL TAKEOVER, NEW LEADERSHIP, ORGANIC GROWTH

Miller himself put one more U.S. bank out of business in January 2001 when he saw through to completion Comerica's purchase of Imperial Bancorp in a $1.3 billion stock swap. Acquiring Los Angeles-based Imperial doubled the size of Comerica Bank-California to $14.8 billion, making it the state's fourth largest bank. The acquisition strengthened Comerica's position as a small business lender and as a lender to the technology and life sciences industries. It also sent a clear signal of Comerica's determination to remain independent and not become another bank's latest conquest.

Merger-related and restructuring costs coupled with a significant increase in bad loans stemming from the weakened economy sent Comerica's earnings down 10 percent in 2001, to $710 million. At the beginning of 2002, Babb won the succession sweepstakes and took over as president and CEO. He was named chairman as well in October 2002 upon Miller's retirement. Another increase in bad loans and a goodwill decline at the Munder Capital Management unit pushed Comerica's net income down again in Babb's first year at the helm, to $601 million. The following year, net income began rising again, and Comerica also consolidated its individual state bank charters into the nationally chartered Comerica Bank & Trust, National Association. The latter move enabled Comerica customers, beginning in July 2004, to bank at any Comerica branch in the country.

Comerica's difficulties during the 2001–02 downturn stemmed in large measure from its heavier reliance on commercial banking than its rivals, particularly outside of Michigan. Starting in late 2004, the company began a concerted effort to become more of a full-service bank targeting individuals, small businesses, and middle-market customers. By the end of 2007, Comerica had spent $175 million to open 90 new branches, most located outside Michigan, in California, Arizona, Texas, and Florida. During this period, the number of California branches grew from 42 to 83; Arizona, from one to eight; Texas, from 50 to 79; and Florida, from six to nine. The company preferred organic growth to acquisitions because it wished to avoid the integration issues that takeovers entail. Through 2007, the new branches had generated $1.8 billion in new deposits. In the meantime, in 2006 Comerica sold its controlling stake in Munder Capital Management, though it kept Munder's World Asset Management, Inc., unit, a manager of index portfolios for institutional investors.

2007 HEADQUARTERS MOVE TO DALLAS

Despite the Sunbelt-centered growth efforts, Michigan still accounted for more than half of Comerica's earnings in 2007, and about half of its loans were Michigan originated; the bank also remained in second place in the Michigan banking market in terms of deposits, behind Bank of America Corporation. Nevertheless, with the Michigan economy in a long-term slump principally because of the ongoing problems faced by the Detroit-based automakers, Comerica clearly saw its future growth coming from its southern and western operations. Seeking to accelerate this growth, Comerica in 2007 moved its corporate headquarters to Dallas to be closer to its expanding markets in Texas, California, and Florida. This brought an end to Comerica's more than a century and a half as a Detroit-based company.

During the initial months of the financial and economic crisis that began in 2007, Comerica was hurt not only by its significant exposure to the troubled auto industry but also by its large number of loans to residential real estate developers in California, where the housing market suffered a steep drop-off. Its net income fell 23.2 percent in 2007 to $686 million. The financial crisis also led to the freezing up, in early 2008, of the U.S. market for an investment vehicle known as auction-rate securities. Under pressure from state regulators in Michigan, Comerica was forced to buy back about $1.46 billion of these securities from its customers amid allegations that the company had misled investors about their safety.

Although it managed to stay in the black for 2008, Comerica saw its net income plunge to just $196 mil-

lion, a drop of 69 percent, as it had to set aside increasing amounts of money to cover bad loans. In early 2009 Comerica took further measures in reaction to the deteriorating economic environment, including a workforce reduction of 5 percent, or 570 jobs, a freeze on the salaries of the top 20 percent of its salaried workers, and a slashing of its common stock dividend from 33 cents to 5 cents. The bank also began to significantly slow its pace of new branch openings. Babb was confident that Comerica had sufficient capital to weather the downturn, though he did accept a late 2008 capital injection of $2.25 billion from the federal government as part of the Troubled Asset Relief Program financial bailout plan.

Frederick C. Ingram
Updated, David E. Salamie

PRINCIPAL SUBSIDIARIES

Comerica Bank; Comerica Bank & Trust, National Association; Comerica Insurance Services, Inc.; Comerica Leasing Corporation; Comerica Securities, Inc.; Comerica West Incorporated; Wilson, Kemp & Associates, Inc.; World Asset Management, Inc.; W.Y. Campbell & Company.

PRINCIPAL OPERATING UNITS

Business Bank; Retail Bank; Wealth & Institutional Management.

PRINCIPAL COMPETITORS

Bank of America Corporation; JPMorgan Chase & Co.; Wells Fargo & Company; Citigroup Inc.; Fifth Third Bancorp; KeyCorp; UnionBanCal Corporation; Cullen/Frost Bankers, Inc.

FURTHER READING

Chase, Brett, "Comerica to Ax 1,900 Jobs in Effort to Save $110 Million," *American Banker,* January 23, 1997, pp. 1+.

Child, Charles, "Comerica Goes 'Back to Basics,'" *Crain's Detroit Business,* March 9, 1987, p. 1.

Dodge, Robert, "Comerica Will Buy Grand: Detroit Company Seeks Texas Base," *Dallas Morning News,* March 3, 1988, p. 2D.

Duclaux, Denise, "The $5 Trillion Enigma," *ABA Banking Journal,* October 1995, pp. 107+.

Gallagher, John, "Withdrawn: Comerica to Leave Detroit Headquarters for Dallas," *Detroit Free Press,* March 7, 2007, p. 1A.

Gordon, Jennifer, "As Execs Move, Comerica Seeking a More Even Mix," *American Banker,* March 4, 2008, p. 18.

Henderson, Tom, "Branching Out: Comerica Close to Bringing in Majority of Revenue from Outside Michigan," *Crain's Detroit Business,* October 2, 2006, p. 11.

Hunter, George, "Comerica Picks Triumvirate to Groom for the Top Post," *Detroit News,* March 24, 1999, p. 2B.

Hurst, Nathan, "Comerica Cuts Another 5%," *Detroit News,* January 23, 2009, p. C1.

Klinkerman, Steve, "New CEO Won't Hurry Comerica's Pace Despite Delay in Benefits from Merger," *American Banker,* September 20, 1993, pp. 4+.

———, "The Road Less Taken," *Banking Strategies,* July/August 1998, pp. 14–18.

Mandaro, Laura, "Comerica Joins Stampede to Branch Banking," *American Banker,* February 5, 2003, p. 2.

Marshall, Jeffery, "Buying Munder's Thunder," *USBanker,* June 1997, pp. 51–54.

———, "Sticking to Business," *USBanker,* May 1998, pp. 55–56.

Mazzucca, Tim, "Comerica HQ Shift a Growth Statement," *American Banker,* March 7, 2007, p. 1.

———, "Comerica Plans Further Retail Branch Expansion," *American Banker,* February 16, 2007, p. 2.

———, "Comerica's Retail Plan in the West Gets a Boost," *American Banker,* February 13, 2006, p. 1.

Mehlman, William, "Comerica Seen As Standout Even in 'Worst-Case' Model," *Insiders' Chronicle,* April 18, 1988, pp. 1+.

Merx, Katie, "Acquire and Conquer," *Crain's Detroit Business,* January 15, 2001, p. 1.

———, "Analysts: Comerica's New CEO Will Stay the Course," *Crain's Detroit Business,* October 1, 2001, p. 1.

———, "Despite Fall, Comerica Unlikely Takeover Target," *Crain's Detroit Business,* October 14, 2002, p. 1.

———, "Investors Shy Away As Comerica Banks on Staying Independent," *Crain's Detroit Business,* November 6, 2000, p. 1.

Miller, Eugene A., *Comerica Incorporated: Promises Kept, Promises Renewed,* New York: Newcomen Society of the United States, 2000, 28 p.

Mitchell, Jim, "Hanging Its Star on Texas: Comerica Bank Sees State As Key to Expansion," *Dallas Morning News,* February 14, 1993, p. 1H.

O'Connor, Brian J., "Comerica Customers Get Back $1.46B," *Detroit News,* September 19, 2008, p. C1.

"One for All," *Executive Excellence,* December 1996, pp. 15–16.

Patterson, Gregory A., "Comerica Inc. to Acquire Detroit Bank," *Wall Street Journal,* October 29, 1991, p. A3.

Pepper, Jon, "At 150, Comerica Is a Survivor," *Detroit News,* February 28, 1999, p. 1B.

Preston, Darrell, "Comerica Targets Different Market Than Larger Competitors," *Dallas Business Journal,* January 15, 1990, p. 5.

Promises Kept: The Story of Comerica, 1849–1999, Detroit, Mich.: Comerica Inc., 1999, 120 p.

Reilly, Patrick, "Comerica CEO Miller to Hand Reins to Company Finance Chief Babb," *American Banker,* September 27, 2001, p. 4.

Silvestri, Scott, "Comerica Grows on Its Own Terms: On Road to Expansion, CEO Steers Detroit Firm Clear of Acquisitions," *American Banker,* June 26, 2000, p. 1.

Smith, Joel J., "Why Comerica Checked Out," *Detroit News,* March 7, 2007, p. A1.

Solis, Olivia Carmichael, "Comerica: One Year Later," *Texas Banking,* December 2008, pp. 14–16.

Wethe, David, "Banking Giant Texas-Bound," *Fort Worth (Tex.) Star-Telegram,* March 7, 2007, p. C1.

Yung, Katherine, "Comerica Shares Fall 11% on Poor Quarterly Results," *Detroit Free Press,* January 18, 2008, p. 1E.

———, "Comerica to Cut 570 Jobs in Quarter," *Detroit Free Press,* January 23, 2009, p. 1E.

Zack, Jeffrey, "Rivals Merging, but It's Big Business As Usual at Comerica," *American Banker,* November 6, 1995, pp. 4A+.

Comfort Systems USA, Inc.

777 Post Oak Boulevard, Suite 500
Houston, Texas 77056-3212
U.S.A.
Telephone: (713) 830-9600
Toll Free: (800) 723-8431
Fax: (713) 830-9696
Web site: http://www.comfortsystemsusa.com

Public Company
Incorporated: 1996
Employees: 6,647
Sales: $1.1 billion (2007)
Stock Exchanges: New York
Ticker Symbol: FIX
NAICS: 238210 Electrical Contractors

■ ■ ■

Based in Houston, Texas, and listed on the New York Stock Exchange, Comfort Systems USA, Inc., is a national heating, ventilating, and air-conditioning (HVAC) company with approximately 75 locations in 60 U.S. cities. Comfort Systems is one of several consolidators of the highly fragmented HVAC industry that arose in the 1990s. It focuses on the mid-market, commercial, industrial, and institutional sectors, leaving residential work to others. Having a national footprint, Comfort Systems is able to meet the needs of national accounts, such as big-box retailers, which prefer to deal with a single entity rather than a large number of local contractors, who in many cases are provided by brokers who take a share of the proceeds. As a result, contractors are tempted to concentrate on higher-margin local jobs and give short shrift to the less profitable national accounts. Comfort Systems can also provide consistent service and is large enough to allow project managers to follow national clients to meet their needs in new markets. Comfort Systems offers the full gamut of mechanical design-build services, from project development to post-construction needs.

The company is also a building-control solutions provider, helping clients with all aspects of control system renovations, including the installation of remote monitor and diagnostics systems and the integration of HVAC systems with lighting, closed-circuit television, and access control systems. In addition, Comfort Systems offers HVAC service and maintenance, including a 24-hour call center and 24-hour repair.

FOUNDER'S BEGINNINGS

Incorporated in December 1996, Comfort Systems was one of the consolidation vehicles backed by Steve Harter, whose Notre Capital Ventures made a specialty of the roll-up concept. Harter did not grow up with the goal of becoming a financier. Rather, he was brought up in modest circumstances in rural Carroll County, Ohio, a high school vocational student with lesser aspirations in mind. "I thought I was going to be a carpenter pounding nails on a roof," he told the *Houston Chronicle* in a 1999 interview. As a teenager he was bidding jobs and putting his carpentry skills to use to pay for school expenses and help support his family. When he quickly filled out, becoming six feet, three inches tall, and weighing 245 pounds, he was recruited by his high

COMPANY PERSPECTIVES

To provide the best value HVAC and mechanical systems installation and service, principally in the mid-market commercial industrial and institutional sectors, while caring for our customers, employees and the environment and realizing superior returns for our stockholders.

school football team, whose coach encouraged him to focus on academics and think about college. After graduating from Carrollton High School, he enrolled at Mount Union College, an Ohio liberal arts school where he played offensive tackle on the football team and wrestled, becoming a Division III All-American in both sports as well as an All-American in academics.

Harter was a good enough football player that during his senior year he was drafted by the Memphis Showboats of the United States Football League, a professional football league that during the early 1980s operated in the spring, before running into financial problems and folding. Rather than sign, Harter waited until the National Football League held its draft, but in the meantime he severely injured his knee wrestling, ending any chance at a professional football career. Instead he used the accounting degree he earned at Mount Union in 1984 to take a job with the Houston office of the Arthur Andersen accounting firm.

At Arthur Andersen, Harter became involved in mergers and acquisitions. One of his clients was a Houston consolidator, Allwaste, Inc., involved in environmental services and plant maintenance. After he was with Arthur Andersen for five years, it became apparent that the energetic Harter was not suited in the long run for an accounting career. Arthur Andersen partner Wiley Carmichael encouraged him to become an entrepreneur. Harter then went to work for Allwaste in 1989 as director of mergers and acquisitions. After four years there, Allwaste Chairman R. L. Nelson Jr. reiterated what Carmichael had said, advising Harter that he would be much happier working for himself. Harter had to agree, explaining in the 1999 *Houston Chronicle* interview, "I work better with people than for people."

FORMATION OF NOTRE CAPITAL VENTURES: 1993

Harter was presented with an opportunity to strike out on his own when Allwaste board member Mike Baker

approached him with an idea of starting a venture capital fund that concentrated on roll-ups. In addition to Allwaste, Baker had been involved with the ambulance service consolidator American Medical Response. Houston was, in fact, an incubator for consolidators, offering Harter and Baker several examples to draw upon, including Sysco Corp. in the foodservice marketing and distribution field; Service Corporation International, a funeral service roll-up; and waste management consolidators Browning-Ferris Industries and Sanifill, Inc. In June 1993 Harter and Baker established Notre Capital Ventures, backed by $1 million that was raised mostly from Allwaste executives. Baker provided the reputation needed to get the firm started, but it was Harter who supplied the work ethic behind the new venture capital firm. A year later Baker would leave the country and eventually have no involvement in the fund.

Harter's first roll-up was U.S. Delivery Systems, created in 1993 when he brought together six small business delivery service firms. U.S. Delivery was taken public in 1994, and the proceeds from the stock offering were then used to purchase the founding companies and acquire others. It was a pattern that Harter would repeat several more times, including Physicians Resource Group Inc., an ophthalmology roll-up; Coach USA Inc., a bus company; Home USA, a retailer of manufactured homes; LandCare USA, a landscaper and tree service company; and Comfort Systems.

Some of the industries to target were Harter's idea, such as Coach USA, the result of Harter recognizing while traveling through airports the lack of ground transportation brand names, but he was also approached by others. Comfort Systems came to Harter through Fred M. Ferreira, a cofounder and chief operating officer of Allwaste. "He has always impressed me with his willingness to go anywhere, to do anything," Ferreira told the *Houston Chronicle* in 1999. "Steve knows how to do deals. It's not a financial transaction for him. He's a long-term investor." Indicative of this assessment was Harter taking only a 12 percent stake in the companies he took public, unlike other venture capital firms that took as much as a 75 percent stake. In this way, founders of the individual companies were left with a greater share of equity and remained motivated to grow the business.

With Ferreira serving as chairman and chief executive officer, and Harter taking a seat on the board, Comfort Systems took shape in late 1996 when 12 HVAC companies agreed to join forces. They were Accurate Air Systems, Inc., and Atlas Air Conditioning Co., both of Houston; CSI/Bonneville, Salt Lake City, Utah; Eastern Heating and Cooling Inc., Albany, New

KEY DATES

1996: Comfort Systems is formed.
1997: Initial public offering of stock is completed.
2000: Losses lead to resignation of chairman and CEO.
2002: Company sells 19 subsidiaries.
2005: Granite State Plumbing & Heating is acquired.
2008: Company acquires Delcard Associates, Inc.

York; Freeway Heating and Air Conditioning, Inc., Bountiful, Utah; S.M. Lawrence Co., Inc., Jackson, Tennessee; Quality Air Heating & Cooling, Grand Rapids, Michigan; Seasonair, Inc., Rockville, Maryland; Standard Heating & Air Conditioning, Birmingham, Alabama; Tech Heating and Air Conditioning, Solon, Ohio; Tri-City Mechanical, Inc., Tempe, Arizona; and Western Building Services, Inc., Denver, Colorado. These companies were well established in their markets; their average years in business was 39. Doing business in ten states they combined to generate annual revenues of $167.5 million. All were commercial-industrial contractors, which Ferreira and Harter recognized were generally better managed than residential specialists and did a higher volume of work.

COMPLETION OF PUBLIC OFFERING: 1997

Comfort Systems was taken public on July 2, 1997, netting $68.8 million, of which $45.3 million was used to pay the cash portion of the purchase price of the dozen founding companies. Soon after, Ferreira began looking for national accounts to leverage the scope of the new company. One success was a contract to service Kmart stores in the Northeast, handled by the Albany branch. At the same time, Harter was scouting for further acquisition targets to grow the company. Comfort Systems was not interested in buying out businesses where the owner wanted to retire. Rather, Harter and Ferreira were looking for people who wanted to continue to run and expand their businesses as part of a larger enterprise. By the end of 1997 another 27 HVAC contractors were brought into the fold, adding another $190 million in annual revenues and ten more states of operation.

In 1998 Comfort Systems acquired another 49 companies, which added eight more states. The largest of these deals was the November purchase of Fort

Wayne, Indiana-based Shambaugh & Son, a company that had been around since 1926 and operated out of seven midwest locations. In 1998 Comfort System reported revenues of more than $850 million, but with a full year's contribution from Shambaugh & Son, Comfort Systems was in line to top the $1 billion mark. To help pay down accumulated debt, Comfort Systems conducted a secondary stock offering in 1998 netting $16.4 million. Comfort Systems added a further 19 HVAC contractors in 1999, helping to increase revenues to $1.37 billion for the year and net income to $42.32 million.

CEO RESIGNS: 2000

Comfort Systems had enjoyed rapid growth in the late 1990s, but was not able to fully integrate all of the operations, resulting in problems in 2000. Some of the units did not perform as well as expected and others had trouble executing turnaround efforts. When the company issued a profit warning for the second quarter in August 2000, Wall Street punished the stock and Ferreira stepped down as chairman and CEO, replaced by William F. Murdy, a Notre Capital Ventures associate who had previously served as CEO of LandCare USA. Murdy was deemed better suited than Ferreira in making the transition from the consolidation stage to the operational phase of the company's development, when the internalization of business practices took precedent over entering new markets. As a result, no new companies were acquired in 2000. Although sales increased to $1.6 billion, Comfort Systems posted a $16.85 million net loss, due in large part to a $25.3 million restructuring charge the company recorded.

In 2001 Comfort Systems pared its operations, selling several underperforming subsidiaries. Revenues for the year dipped only slightly, despite the loss of these units and a soft U.S. economy, which adversely affected the remaining businesses. Nevertheless, Comfort Systems returned to profitability in 2002, netting $13.12 million on sales of $1.55 billion. Early in 2002 Comfort Systems made further cuts, selling 19 subsidiaries to Norwalk, Connecticut-based EMCOR Group for $186.25 million plus the assumption of $22.1 million in debt, a move that helped to cut the company's debt load. The largest of the businesses divested was Shambaugh & Son. Comfort Systems was left with 45 subsidiaries with 84 locations in 57 cities. Revenues for the year, as a result, fell to $819.3 million, an amount that was also affected by poor economic conditions. Because of a change in accounting methods, the company also posted a net loss of $209 million.

More subsidiaries were sold and the economy remained stagnant, leading to a decline in revenues to

$785 million and a net loss of $5.58 million in 2003. Conditions improved in some markets in 2004, allowing Comfort Systems to increase revenues 4.6 percent to $819.55 million, albeit the company lost another $10.7 million. Business picked up in 2005, and for the first time in several years Comfort Systems made an acquisition, purchasing Granite State Plumbing & Heating of Manchester, New Hampshire. Granite State contributed about $5 million to Comfort Systems' revenues for the year, which overall improved 15.5 percent to $899.53 million in 2005.

POSITIONING FOR THE FUTURE

Comfort Systems enjoyed an even better year in 2006, when business picked up in a number of locations, resulting in an 18.4 percent increase in revenues to more than $1.05 billion and net income of $28.7 million. The trend continued in 2007 when revenues increased to nearly $1.11 billion and net income to $32.47 million. In addition to internal growth, Comfort Systems benefited from the contributions of a pair of acquisitions: Madera Mechanical in March and Air Systems Engineering in October 2007. Another acquisition followed in August 2008, the purchase of Delcard Associates, Inc., which brought $45 million in annual revenues. Even without this contribution, Comfort Systems was enjoying continued growth in 2008. Because of the nature of the HVAC business, which becomes involved later in construction projects than other building contractors, Comfort Systems did not feel the effects of a troubled economy in the final months of 2008.

Ed Dinger

PRINCIPAL SUBSIDIARIES

Climate Control, Inc.; Comfort Systems USA Energy Services; Comfort Systems USA National Accounts, LLC.

PRINCIPAL COMPETITORS

ACCO Engineered Systems; EMCOR Group, Inc.; Lennox International Inc.

FURTHER READING

Antosh, Nelson, "Comfort Systems Buys Indiana Firm," *Houston Chronicle,* November 17, 1998, p. 3.

Buggs, Shannon, "Comfort Systems Selling Off 19 Units," *Houston Chronicle,* February 13, 2002, p. 1.

Goldberg, Laura, "A Pioneer of 'Poof,'" *Houston Chronicle,* July 18, 1999, p. 1.

Hall, John R., "Comfort Systems USA Announces Acquisition," *Air Conditioning, Heating & Refrigeration News,* January 31, 2005, p. 7.

Mader, Robert P., "Comfort Systems Names New CEO," *Contractor,* August 2000, p. 10.

Mahoney, Thomas A., "Commercial Market Consolidator Heads Toward $800 Million," *Air Conditioning, Heating & Refrigeration News,* October 26, 1998, p. 3.

———, "Consolidator Sees $1.5 Billion in Sales by End of Decade," *Air Conditioning, Heating & Refrigeration News,* December 8, 1997, p. 22.

———, "Fourth Consolidator Will Buy 12 Contractors in Seven States," *Air Conditioning, Heating & Refrigeration News,* April 7, 1997, p. 1.

Perin, Monica, "Head 'em Up, Roll 'em Out," *Houston Business Journal,* October 3, 1997, p. 14A.

Never Settle for Less.

Con-way Inc.

2855 Campus Drive, Suite 300
San Mateo, California 94403
U.S.A.
Telephone: (650) 378-5200
Fax: (650) 357-9160
Web site: http://www.con-way.com

Public Company
Incorporated: 2006
Employees: 27,100
Sales: $4.39 billion (2007)
Stock Exchanges: New York
Ticker Symbol: CNW
NAICS: 484122 General Freight Trucking, Long-Distance, Less Than Truckload

■ ■ ■

Headquartered in San Mateo, California, Con-way Inc. is a leading player in the freight transportation and logistics industry, with an operational base comprised of approximately 500 locations in 17 different countries. The company's workforce of 27,000 people serves customers through three main business units. Its Menlo Worldwide Logistics arm focuses on logistics and transportation management, warehousing, and distribution. Additionally, Con-way Truckload provides full truckload services throughout the United States and Canada. Finally, the company's Con-way Freight business provides less-than-truckload (LTL) services on a local, regional, and transcontinental basis.

PRE-HISTORY: 1929–82

Although Con-way Inc. was formally established in 1983, as Con-Way Transportation Services, the company's roots stretch all the way back to 1929, when Leland James founded Portland, Oregon-based Consolidated Truck Lines.

During its formative years, James's enterprise, which eventually became known as Consolidated Freightways, grew beyond the Portland area and began carrying freight between many of the widely scattered cities of Oregon and Washington.

The onset of the Great Depression sparked a series of ferocious, nationwide rate wars among truckers. In 1935 the federal government stepped into this situation and placed interstate carriers under the general jurisdiction of the Interstate Commerce Commission (ICC), which for years had regulated the railroads. The Motor Carrier Act was indicative of the trucking industry's rapid growth, as the major firms regularly transported goods across state lines and soon would be taking them across the entire country.

By this time Consolidated had established itself as one of the leading truckers in the Northwest, with routes crisscrossing Washington, Oregon, and reaching down to the prosperous cities of California as well. It was not until the advent of World War II, however, that Consolidated enjoyed the remarkable growth that would characterize its history for the coming decades.

With the major railroads overburdened by the demand for war material and personnel, truckers became a more vital part of the country's freight

COMPANY PERSPECTIVES

Guided by our core values, we deliver quality services and innovative solutions to our partners everywhere. We transform vision into reality.

systems. Consolidated added dozens of new terminals throughout much of the western United States, and by the war's end had extended its service as far east as Chicago, the nation's transport hub.

In 1955 Leland James named Jack Snead as president of Consolidated. Snead oversaw the company's rise from regional power to national leadership, not only extending its reach to the Atlantic Ocean but intensively building local service networks in each of the cities along Consolidated's routes.

Another postwar development occurred when Leland James started Freightliner Corp. in Portland to supply Consolidated with the larger, lighter, and more sophisticated trucks and trailers increasingly needed to compete in the maturing freight industry. Freightliner originally built only for its parent company, but in 1951 it signed an agreement with White Motor Corp. of Ohio, under which White would retail Freightliner trucks through its chain of dealerships across the country. The partnership proved successful for the next 25 years.

In 1960 William White succeeded Snead as president. Under his watch, the company's loosely connected units were better integrated and Consolidated committed itself to becoming a specialist in LTL shipment.

After being impacted by union labor costs and oil embargos during the late 1970s, the trucking industry was largely deregulated in 1980 by the administration of President Jimmy Carter. For the first time since 1935, truckers were free to set rates as they pleased, and most analysts predicted another round of frantic mergers and takeovers as the price competition took its toll.

Ray O'Brien, Consolidated's new CEO, took seriously the prospect of renewed rate wars and made a decision to strengthen his hand in trucking while abandoning the manufacturing business. The air freight business also had grown, and by 1980 CF AirFreight had developed from a small forwarder into the number three heavy air freight carrier in North America, with $100 million in annual revenues and an expanding service network.

In 1981 Consolidated announced the sale of Freightliner and its few other remaining manufacturing subsidiaries to Daimler-Benz for about $300 million.

FORMATIVE YEARS: 1983–95

In 1983 Consolidated formed a new business called Con-Way Transportation Services, which focused on providing regional, next-day, short-haul service. Non-union employees benefited from a profit-sharing plan, and put a premium on customer service. Relationship building between drivers and shippers was encouraged, so that the company could better understand customer requirements. Con-Way concentrated on markets where Consolidated's regular business was not active.

Consolidated went on to establish four regional trucking companies during the 1980s. The first, Con-Way Western Express, began operations in May 1983, serving customers in Arizona, California, and Nevada with 120 employees at 11 service centers. Growth of the new business occurred quickly, and in November it acquired Penn Yan Express Inc. in a $3.2 million deal.

In June 1983 Jerry Detter formed Con-Way Central Express, which operated from 11 sites in Illinois, Indiana, Michigan, Minnesota, Ohio, Pennsylvania, and Wisconsin. The company's 43-member workforce utilized a fleet of 46 tractors to provide service to 1,004 sites.

Growth continued through the mid-1980s, culminating in the formation of Con-Way Southern Express in April 1987. With a workforce of 130 people, 100 tractors, and 300 trailers, service was provided from 15 locations. In only a few months time, the new operation expanded significantly, adding nine Georgia-based service centers.

Con-Way Transportation Services ended the 1980s by establishing another new operation. Con-Way Southwest Express came online in November 1989, providing service in Arkansas, Louisiana, Oklahoma, and Texas. With a staff of 150, Con-Way Southwest Express served customers from 15 locations with a fleet of 100 tractors and 200 trailers. It also was in 1989 that Consolidated acquired Emery Air Freight in a deal worth about $242 million.

Progress continued during the early 1990s. In 1991 Consolidated established an integrated logistics company named Menlo Logistics, allowing the company to expand its service offerings.

Con-Way Transportation Services celebrated its tenth anniversary in 1993 and approached the mid-1990s with a workforce of 7,600 people in 32 states. Collectively, they served customers from 302 service

KEY DATES

∎

1929: Consolidated Freightways Inc. is founded by Leland James in Portland, Oregon.

1983: Consolidated forms Con-Way Transportation Services; Con-Way Western Express is founded; Con-Way Central Express is established.

1987: Con-Way Southern Express is formed; Con-Way Southwest Express begins operations.

1989: Consolidated acquires Emery Air Freight for approximately $242 million.

1991: Menlo Logistics is established.

1996: Consolidated Freightways Inc. spins off CF MotorFreight and four other long-haul subsidiaries as a separate company named Consolidated Freightways Corporation; what remains (including Con-Way Transportation Services) becomes CNF Transportation.

2001: CNF combines Vector SCM, Emery Worldwide, and Menlo Logistics into a new organization called Menlo Worldwide.

2003: CNF retires the Emery name; Emery Forwarding changes its name to Menlo Worldwide Forwarding.

2004: CNF sells Menlo Worldwide Forwarding to United Parcel Service for $150 million.

2006: CNF Inc. changes its name to Con-way Inc.; the Con-Way Central, Southern, and Western business names are retired and Con-Way Canada Express becomes Con-way Freight-Canada; company's stock begins trading under the new symbol CNW on the New York Stock Exchange.

centers with a fleet of 13,668 trucks, tractors, and trailers. Con-Way's experience was evident in the 140 million miles its operating companies had recorded.

FORMATION OF CNF: 1996–99

In August 1996, Con-Way Transportation Services formed a new same-day delivery service called Con-Way Now. An important development unfolded in December of that year, when Consolidated Freightways Inc. spun off CF MotorFreight and four other long-haul subsidiaries as a separate company named Consolidated Freightways Corporation. The "old" Consolidated Freightways Inc.—which retained Con-Way Transportation Services,

Emery Worldwide, and Menlo Logistics—was renamed CNF Transportation. The two companies began operating independently on December 3, 1996.

Midway through 1997, Chief Financial Officer Gregory L. Quesnel succeeded Chairman and CEO Donald E. Moffitt as company president, and also assumed the role of chief operating officer. Moffitt retired as CEO in May of the following year, but remained company chairman. At that time, Quesnel took the reins as CEO.

Another development at Con-Way Transportation Services during the late 1990s occurred in April 1998, when Con-Way Western Express and Con-Way Southern Express partnered to offer a coast-to-coast shipping service. It also was around this time that Con-Way Integrated Services was introduced. From a command center located in Chicago, the company provided supply-chain execution services at customer warehouses.

CNF Transportation capped off the 1990s on a high note. In 1999 *Fortune* magazine added the company to its list of the most admired U.S. companies and named it as North America's most admired trucking company. At the decade's end, CNF was a $5 billion enterprise. Its workforce of 35,000 people served approximately 400,000 customers in 200 countries worldwide.

CORPORATE CHANGES: 2000–05

Substantial changes continued at CNF following the dawn of the new millennium. In early 2001 the company announced the completion of a new, 252,000-square-foot, five-story information technology center in Portland. The new structure allowed the company to bring 850 information technology workers together under one roof. Best of all, the center was environmentally friendly, and was supposed to save CNF $65,000 in annual energy costs.

CNF ended 2001 by combining Vector SCM, Emery Worldwide, and Menlo Logistics into a new organization called Menlo Worldwide. More changes occurred in 2003, when CNF retired the Emery name altogether. That year, Emery Forwarding changed its name to Menlo Worldwide Forwarding. It also was in 2003 that Con-Way began offering its customers a no-cost, guaranteed transit time. According to the company, it was the first LTL trucker to offer such a guarantee.

A flurry of important leadership changes occurred at Con-Way Transportation Services in 2004. President Gregory L. Quesnel announced plans to retire in July, ending a 29-year career with the company. CEO Gerald Detter also left the organization, capping off a 40-year career and paving the way for Douglas Stotlar to become CEO in December. At this time, Dr. W. Keith Kennedy served as CNF's chairman.

A major deal occurred in December 2004, at which time CNF announced plans to sell Menlo Worldwide Forwarding to United Parcel Service (UPS) for $150 million. The $1.9 billion operation employed approximately 8,000 people. CNF continued to own and operate Menlo Worldwide Technologies and Menlo Worldwide Logistics.

By 2005 Con-Way Transportation Services had become a $2.2 billion business. That year, a new business unit named Con-Way Truckload commenced operations on January 18. Later that month, parent CNF authorized plans to buy back up to $300 million of the company's common stock.

More leadership changes occurred in 2005. In April, Douglas Stotlar was named president and CEO of Con-Way parent CNF, replacing Chairman W. Keith Kennedy, who had been temporarily fulfilling that role. Following Stotlar's promotion, Con-Way Central Express executive David McClimon was named president of Con-Way Transportation Services in June. Finally, Michelle M. Potter was named president of Con-Way Now.

Physical expansion also occurred at Con-Way in 2005. In November the company announced the opening of new service centers in Woodinville, Washington; Bedford, Pennsylvania; and West Fargo, North Dakota. In addition, the company moved to a larger service center in Tonawanda, New York, in order to better serve the nearby Buffalo market, and also acquired new property near Port Elizabeth in New Jersey. For the year, Con-Way saw its operating income increase 11.2 percent, reaching $2.82 billion. Operating profits surged 34 percent, reaching $331.1 million.

THE NEW CON-WAY: 2006–08

A major milestone was reached on April 19, 2006, when CNF Inc. changed its name to Con-way Inc. The change was accompanied by a $20 million rebranding effort that was expected to take between two and three years. The effort included a new Con-way Freight logo that resembled a signature, which intended to convey the seriousness of Con-way's commitment to its customers. As part of this change, the "w" in the company's name was lowercased.

Operations also were streamlined at this time. The Con-Way Central, Southern, and Western names were retired and Con-Way Canada Express became Con-way Freight-Canada. On May 5 the company's stock began

trading under the symbol CNW on the New York Stock Exchange. It also was in 2006 that APL Logistics teamed with Con-way to offer a new, less-than-container-load overseas freight transportation service named OceanGuaranteed.

By mid-2007 Con-way had grown to include 460 service centers, from which the company served customers in approximately 20 different countries. At this time Con-way acquired Joplin, Missouri-based Contract Freighters. The $750 million deal brought 3,000 new employees to Con-way, along with 2,600 tractors and 7,000 trailers.

There were several other noteworthy deals in 2007. That year, Con-way's acquisition of CFI bolstered the company's truckload freight business. On the international front, Con-way's Menlo business expanded its reach in Asia via the acquisition of Shanghai-based Chic Holdings Ltd., as well as Singapore-based Cougar Holdings Pte Ltd.

In December 2007, a series of customizable tools were unveiled on Con-way's web site, providing customers with more options related to proof of delivery, rate quotes, freight tracking, reports and manifests, and more.

In early 2008 Con-way was recognized by the retail giant Wal-Mart as its 2007 LTL Carrier of the Year. Con-way celebrated 25 years of operations in June. By this time the company's workforce of 20,000 people utilized a fleet of some 8,400 trucks and tractors, along with 25,000 freight trailers, to make approximately 60,000 daily LTL shipments. Working from some 400 different locations, Con-way made about 120,000 daily deliveries and pick-ups.

Developments continued throughout the summer, and in August the company established a new division named Con-way Multimodal. The new truckload brokerage business was a successor to Con-way Truckload Services.

A major reengineering initiative was announced in early December 2008, at which time Con-way Freight revealed plans to close 40 terminals in an effort to save between $30 million and $40 million annually.

Unfortunately, Con-way ended 2008 on a sour note. In the wake of faltering economic conditions, Con-way Freight was forced to lay off 1,450 employees in December. A drop-off in shipping activity reduced the company's business volume to 2003 levels, according to Con-way Freight President John G. Labrie. Nonetheless, at the beginning of 2009, the company seemed well-prepared to face continued challenges from its position of industry leadership.

Paul R. Greenland

PRINCIPAL SUBSIDIARIES

Con-way Freight Inc.; Menlo Worldwide LLC; Transportation Resources Inc.

PRINCIPAL COMPETITORS

FedEx Freight Corp.; UPS Supply Chain Solutions; YRC Worldwide Inc.

FURTHER READING

Carey, Bill, "CNF's New Vision: Transforming CNF into an Operating Company, Future Growth Plans Key for CEO Douglas W. Stotlar," *Traffic World,* September 19, 2005.

———, "Goodbye CNF, Hello 'Conway': Conway Regional Carriers Regroup As Conway Freight As $4.2 Billion Trucking Giant Rebrands," *Traffic World,* April 24, 2006.

"CNF Transportation Rated Among 'America's Most Admired' Companies in Annual Survey by 'Fortune' Magazine," *Business Wire,* February 17, 1999.

"Freight Company Plans to Spin Off Transport Unit," *Wall Street Journal Europe,* August 28, 1996.

Gillis, Chris, "The LTL Evolution," *American Shipper,* November 2008.

"UPS Completes Purchase of Menlo Worldwide Forwarding," *M2 Presswire,* December 20, 2004.

Continucare
Taking personal care of your health and well-being

Continucare Corporation

7200 Corporate Center Drive, Suite 600
Miami, Florida 33126
U.S.A.
Telephone: (305) 500-2000
Fax: (305) 500-2080
Web site: http://www.continucare.com

Public Company
Incorporated: 1996
Employees: 589
Sales: $254.44 million (2008)
Stock Exchanges: American
Ticker Symbol: CNU
NAICS: 621498 All Other Outpatient Care Facilities

■ ■ ■

Continucare Corporation provides primary care medical service in Florida and practice management services to independent physicians. The company operates 18 medical centers in Miami-Dade, Broward, and Hillsborough counties that provide medical care on an outpatient basis. Continucare provides practice management services to 25 medical offices. The company serves more than 30,000 patients, deriving nearly all its revenue from managed care agreements with three health maintenance organizations, Humana Medical Plans, Inc., Vista Healthplan of South Florida, Inc., and Wellcare Health Plans, Inc.

ORIGINS

Charles M. Fernandez made the leap from radio to healthcare when he founded Continucare in February 1996, an abrupt deviation in his career path that also required a cross-country move from Las Vegas to Miami. A finance, accounting, and business major at Florida International University, Fernandez had earned his degree in 1984 and had embarked on a career as a radio executive. Within a decade, he rose to the position of executive vice-president at Las Vegas-based Heftel Broadcasting Corp., a Spanish-language broadcasting company. When he was 34 years old, Fernandez resigned from Heftel to start his own company in the city where he had attended college.

Fernandez set up shop in Miami, using $2 million to purchase management contracts from Health Care Management Partners, Inc., a company based in nearby Fort Lauderdale. Under the terms of the acquired contracts, Continucare began providing a range of services that included clinical development, marketing, financial management, operational oversight, and human resources support. The company's comprehensive mental and physical rehabilitative healthcare programs were provided to general acute care hospitals, psychiatric hospitals, and community mental health centers. By September 1996, an important juncture in the company's development, Continucare had service contracts with six general acute care hospitals, one freestanding psychiatric hospital, 21 community mental health centers, and one outpatient rehabilitative facility.

In September, Fernandez secured the financial support and the medical expertise of arguably the most

COMPANY PERSPECTIVES

Continucare Corporation is a group of physicians and healthcare professionals who believe "old-fashioned" customer service and state-of-the-practice medical care go hand-in-hand. Established in 1996, Continucare is committed to improving the lives of others by providing high quality healthcare services.

important person in Continucare's first decade of business. Phillip Frost, who remained with Continucare longer than Fernandez remained affiliated with the company, earned his medical degree at the Albert Einstein College of Medicine in 1961. Over the course of the next three decades, he distinguished himself as an energetic businessman and doctor, serving as the chairman of the Department of Dermatology at Mt. Sinai Medical Center for more than 20 years and serving in executive capacities at numerous corporations. When Frost joined Continucare as vice-chairman, he was serving as chairman of Whitman Education Group, a provider of career-oriented educational programs, and as chief executive officer and chairman of IVAX Corporation, a pharmaceutical manufacturer he founded in 1987.

PUBLIC DEBUT IN 1996

September also marked Continucare's debut as a publicly traded company. Fernandez chose the most expedient route to public ownership by acquiring a publicly traded company and merging it with Continucare. He acquired Zanart Entertainment Incorporated, a ten-year-old designer, publisher, and marketer of collectible art, sold its assets, and merged it into Continucare, which made Continucare a publicly traded company.

Continucare ended its first year deriving all its revenues from contracts to provide management, staffing, and billing services. In 1997, the company expanded its business by completing a series of acquisitions, beginning with the purchase of its first physician practice. In February, Continucare paid $1.9 million for Norman Gaylis M.D., Inc., one of the largest rheumatology practices in Florida. The month also saw Continucare sign a contract with Bally Total Fitness, the largest commercial operator of fitness centers in the United States. The agreement called for Continucare to operate physical rehabilitation centers in as many as 100 Bally health clubs nationwide. In July, the company

entered the home health services business by purchasing Sunset Harbor Health, a Medicare-certified home health agency licensed in Florida. In August, Continucare agreed to acquire Doctors Health Group, paying $14.5 million for a collection of physician practices. It bolstered its home health services business the following month by purchasing Maxicare, Inc., a home health agency that served customers in Broward County, Florida. As Fernandez built up his business, he also sold some assets. In August, he reached an agreement to sell Continucare's behavioral health management contracts.

ACQUISITIONS IN 1998

The company ended its first full year in business with nearly $14 million in revenues. Fernandez added substantially to the 1997 total by completing further acquisitions in 1998, beginning with the purchase of three healthcare services companies and 11 outpatient primary care centers in April. Continucare acquired SPI Managed Care, Inc., SPI Managed Care of Hillsborough County, Inc., and SPI Managed Care of Broward, Inc., gaining control of companies that provided administrative and healthcare services. The 11 outpatient centers were added to the company's existing 73 outpatient centers and physician practices, significantly adding to Continucare's market presence. "By acquiring this important network of primary care centers," Fernandez explained in an April 9, 1998 interview with *PR Newswire*, "we have not only purchased a direct competitor of Continucare, but have also increased our market share in Florida by 35 percent."

Fernandez showed no signs of slackening the pace of expansion after the acquisitions were completed. In August, he purchased nine physician practices and secured outpatient services agreements with more than 100 physician practices. By the end of 1998, the ambitious acquisition campaign had raised revenues to $64.3 million, more than four times the total generated the previous year, but the year also included a numbing $15 million loss. It was the beginning of turbulent financial times for the provider of outpatient and home care services, a period that forced Fernandez and his successors to scramble for survival.

FINANCIAL TROUBLES IN 1999
AND A CHANGE IN LEADERSHIP

Continucare's revenues shot upward in 1999, as the properties it had acquired were integrated into its operations and began to express their full financial might, but rising sales offered little cause for celebration amid a host of problems suffered by the company. The year ended with a staggering $50 million loss resulting from

KEY DATES

1996: Continucare is incorporated.
1999: CEO Charles M. Fernandez resigns and is replaced by Spencer J. Angel.
2000: Continucare restructures in response to deteriorating financial performance.
2003: Richard C. Pfenniger Jr. replaces Angel as chief executive officer.
2006: Continucare acquires Miami-Dade Health Centers.
2007: The company's first retail outlet, Continucare ValuClinic, opens within a pharmacy in Hollywood, Florida.

"adverse business operations, recurring operating losses, negative cash flow from operations, and significant working capital deficiency," Continucare explained in its annual filing with the Securities and Exchange Commission in 1999.

In the midst of the turmoil, Fernandez stepped aside, resigning as president and chief executive officer in November 1999. His departure made room for the promotion of Spencer J. Angel, who had been serving as Continucare's executive vice-president and chief operating officer for the previous three months. Before joining Continucare, Angel spent three years during the early 1990s working as an associate attorney for Platzer, Fineberg & Swergold, a law firm focused on corporate financial reorganizations. In 1994, he began a two-year stint as president of a payroll service and armored car company, which was followed by two years of service as secretary, treasurer, and director of an auto parts retail and service company. Angel was introduced to the medical field after he left Autoparts Warehouse, Inc., in January 1999 when, for a six-month period, he served as president and chief executive officer of Medical Laser Technologies, Inc., a company that produced digital x-ray archiving and communications systems for cardiac catheterization laboratories.

As the leadership change was being made, Continucare shed some of its troubled assets. Underperforming subsidiaries were sold, including the company's diagnostic division, rehabilitation management division, and physician practice division, which contributed to a 36 percent decline in revenues in 2000. Revenues slipped from $182.5 million to $116.5 million, but the year ended with a $14.1 million profit, an encouraging achievement after the $50 million loss posted the previous year.

The divestitures left Continucare reliant on three business segments as it entered the 21st century. Medical services were provided to patients through staff model clinics, independent physician affiliates (IPAs), and home health agencies. Patients received their care through Continucare-employed physicians, associated IPA physicians, nurses, physical therapists, and nurse's aides. The company's staff model clinics, of which there were 17 in southern and central Florida, were medical centers staffed by physicians employed by Continucare who functioned as primary care physicians practicing in the areas of general, family, and internal medicine. Continucare collected its revenues from staff model clinics by charging a percentage of the monthly premium related to Medicare, Medicaid, or a private medical insurer. The company relied on the same revenue-generating model with its IPAs. Continucare contracted with physicians and physician practices on an independent contractor basis, supplying administrative and operational services. The home healthcare segment was comprised of two home health agencies in Miami-Dade and Broward counties that provided nursing, physical therapy, and nurse's aides to patients in their homes. The company's home health agencies were compensated for their services by Medicare and Medicaid.

RICHARD C. PFENNIGER IS NAMED CHIEF EXECUTIVE OFFICER IN 2003

A new decade ushered in a period of impressive financial performance by Continucare. Much of the financial growth occurred after another change in leadership, a transfer of power that occurred in October 2003, when Angel resigned to pursue other business opportunities. His replacement was Richard C. Pfenniger Jr., an executive with close ties to Phillip Frost, who owned 44 percent of Continucare at the time of the leadership change. Pfenniger, who had spent the previous 18 months sitting on Continucare's board of directors, spent more than a decade at IVAX Corp., the pharmaceutical company founded by Frost. He also had served as chief executive officer of Whitman Education Group, the proprietary education company that counted Frost as its chairman. Pfenniger performed wonders during his six years in charge at Whitman Education, increasing revenues from $47 million to $110 million without the aid of acquisitions and turned a company that was losing more than $3 million a year into a company generating nearly $13 million in net income.

The Pfenniger era began with a strategic retreat. In December 2003, the company announced its decision to sell its home health agencies businesses, which had generated $4.2 million in revenue and had lost $1.8 million in 2003. In a statement published in the December 16, 2003 issue of *Business Wire,* Pfenniger explained the reasoning behind the divestiture. "The disposition of our home health agencies should benefit us in two fundamental ways," he said. "First, the divestiture of these businesses will permit us to focus our resources and efforts exclusively on our core activity of providing primary care medical services. Second, the disposition will eliminate a portion of our business that had historically incurred operating losses and experienced negative cash flow."

SUBSTANTIAL ACQUISITION IN 2006

After taking a step backward, Pfenniger pressed forward, completing two initiatives aimed at expansion that defined his first five years in office. In May 2006, he reached an agreement to acquire Miami-Dade Health Centers (MDHC), one of the largest staff-model medical providers in Miami-Dade County. MDHC, with $80 million in revenues in 2005, operated five medical centers and employed more than 40 physicians, enabling it to serve roughly 18,000 patients. The acquisition was completed in October 2006, making Continucare the largest staff-model medical provider in South Florida and one of the largest in the state. "The addition of MDHC," Pfenniger noted in an October 2, 2006 interview with *Business Wire,* "strengthens our market position as a leading provider of care to Medicare patients and establishes a significant presence in the Medicaid arena, a line of business that we believe possesses attractive growth prospects."

RETAIL OUTLET OPENS IN 2007

The integration of MDHC into Continucare's operations lifted revenues upward. After Pfenniger's first year in charge, revenues in 2004 stood at $101 million, less than the total generated four years earlier, but once MDHC began contributing to the company's business volume, revenues swelled, reaching $217 million in 2007. Net income during the period increased as well, leaping from $6.2 million in 2004 to $10.1 million in 2007. Further financial growth was expected after Pfenniger announced a new line of business for Continucare in late 2006. He decided to launch a retail arm of the company's operations, unveiling the first Continucare ValuClinic a year later in December 2007. The first location, which opened within a Navarro Discount

Pharmacy in Hollywood, Florida, offered treatment for common illnesses, such as the flu, bronchitis, seasonal allergies, and skin infections. Additional locations were slated to open in 2008 as Continucare, having dealt with the financial problems at the start of the decade, embarked toward a promising future, exuding financial stability and growth.

Jeffrey L. Covell

PRINCIPAL SUBSIDIARIES

Continucare Managed Care, Inc.; Continucare Medical Management, Inc.; Continucare Payment Corporation; Continucare Physician Practice Management, Inc.; Sunset Harbor Home Health, Inc.; Continucare Clinics, Inc.; Continucare MSO, Inc.; Continucare MDHC, LLC; CNU Blue 2, LLC.

PRINCIPAL COMPETITORS

Metropolitan Health Networks, Inc.; North Broward Hospital District; Public Health Trust of Miami-Dade County Florida.

FURTHER READING

"Continucare Appoints New Chief Executive Officer," *Business Wire,* October 3, 2003, p. 5049.

"Continucare Completes Acquisition of Miami Dade Health Centers," *Business Wire,* October 2, 2006.

"Continucare Corporation Reports Results for the Year Ended June 30, 1998," *PR Newswire,* October 13, 1998, p. 0091.

"Continucare Opens First ValuClinic Location," *Business Wire,* December 6, 2007.

"Continucare to Acquire First Physician Practice," *PR Newswire,* February 27, 1997.

"Continucare to Acquire Miami-Dade Health Centers," *Business Wire,* May 11, 2006.

"Continucare to Acquire Three Healthcare Services Companies and Large Network of Outpatient Primary Care Centers," *PR Newswire,* April 9, 1998.

"Continucare to Dispose of Home Health Agencies," *Business Wire,* December 16, 2003, p. 5744.

"Continucare to Launch Line of Retail Clinics," *Business Wire,* December 4, 2006.

Danner, Patrick, "South Florida Companies Enjoy Robust Year in 2003," *Miami Herald,* January 2, 2004.

Seemuth, Mike, "Continucare Overstates Profit; Major Shareholder Buys," *Palm Beach Daily Business Review,* May 25, 2005.

Crane Co.

100 First Stamford Place
Stamford, Connecticut 06902-6784
U.S.A.
Telephone: (203) 363-7300
Fax: (203) 363-7295
Web site: http://www.craneco.com

Public Company
Founded: 1855 as R.T. Crane Brass & Bell Foundry
Incorporated: 1865 as North Western Manufacturing Company
Employees: 12,000
Sales: $2.6 billion (2008)
Stock Exchanges: New York
Ticker Symbol: CR
NAICS: 326199 All Other Plastics Product Manufacturing; 332911 Industrial Valve Manufacturing; 332912 Fluid Power Valve and Hose Fitting Manufacturing; 332919 Other Metal Valve and Pipe Fitting Manufacturing; 333311 Automatic Vending Machine Manufacturing; 333319 Other Commercial and Service Industry Machinery Manufacturing; 333911 Pump and Pumping Equipment Manufacturing; 333995 Fluid Power Cylinder and Actuator Manufacturing; 333996 Fluid Power Pump and Motor Manufacturing; 334412 Bare Printed Circuit Board Manufacturing; 334419 Other Electronic Component Manufacturing; 334512 Automatic Environmental Control Manufacturing for Residential, Commercial, and Appliance Use; 334513 Instruments and Related Product Manufacturing for Measuring, Displaying, and Controlling Industrial Process Variables; 334519 Other Measuring and Controlling Device Manufacturing; 335314 Relay and Industrial Control Manufacturing; 336413 Other Aircraft Parts & Auxiliary Equipment Manufacturing; 423720 Plumbing and Heating Equipment and Supplies (Hydronics) Merchant Wholesalers

■ ■ ■

Crane Co. is a diversified manufacturer of engineered industrial products, serving niche markets in fluid handling, aerospace and electronics, engineered materials, controls, and merchandising systems. The company operates from more than 120 locations across 25 countries. From its inception in 1855 as a crude bell and brass foundry run singlehandedly by its founder, Richard Teller Crane, the company grew into an S&P 500 firm with international subsidiaries that generate more than $2.5 billion of sales in fields ranging from transportation to water purification to aerospace to vending machines. The Crane Fund, which was established by Crane Co. in 1914 as a charitable trust benefiting former employees or their dependents in need of assistance, owns about 13 percent of the company's common stock.

LIGHTNING ROD BEGINNINGS

Crane Co.'s roots extend back to Richard Teller Crane's first effort to cast lightning rod tips and couplings in a foundry that he established in Chicago. Born in Paterson, New Jersey, in 1832, Richard Crane moved into the workforce at an early age. By the age of nine,

COMPANY PERSPECTIVES

Our core values of integrity and performance with trust and respect are the basis for the common business system that powers Crane.

Whether evaluating and rewarding people, creating an annual plan, implementing a strategic deployment process, visually managing results in factories and offices, or linking value streams, this common system ensures that all of our businesses are disciplined and focused as one connected body, on achieving our corporate objectives of sustainable, profitable growth and strong free cash flow. We believe that the successful deployment of this powerful system, in concert with strategic acquisitions, is the most important reason behind our ability to grow.

We are united in using the Crane Business System to build a global network of people and solutions with consistent safety, quality, delivery, and cost that generates profitable organic growth, from one side of the globe to the other.

he worked as a cotton mill operator; by 15 he learned brass and bell foundry and brass finishing trades as an apprentice in a Brooklyn foundry; by 21, he had gained further experience in a locomotive plant and several printing press machine shops. He migrated westward in 1855 to join his uncle, Martin Ryerson, who ran a successful lumber business in Chicago. Ryerson lent his young nephew a corner of the Ryerson lumberyard to launch the makeshift foundry, originally called R.T. Crane Brass & Bell Foundry, that would become a multinational company over the ensuing century.

Richard Crane built a 14-by-24 foot wooden shed and secured patterns and brass for couplings and copper for lightning rod tips. The sand that he had turned up excavating the furnace served as raw material for molding. After nearly a year as the sole employee—molder, furnace tender, metal pourer, casting cleaner, and salesman—Crane hired two experts from Brooklyn and started a partnership with his brother, Charles, changing the shop name to R.T. Crane and Brother. Markets quickly expanded beyond Chicago to Wisconsin, Kentucky, and Iowa.

The first substantial order came from P.W. Gates & Co., a Chicago manufacturer of mill equipment and freight cars. Gates's supplier had run out of copper and could not fill an urgent order for journal boxes, the metal containers installed on railroad cars to lubricate axles. After delivering the castings on schedule, Crane won the confidence of Gates & Co. and eventually received all future orders for brass castings.

Following their first big order, the Crane brothers moved to rapidly expand operations and diversify product lines. After building a three-story structure and upgrading production facilities, they began production of engine parts for the emerging railroad business, as well as plumbing and fixtures for new developments in steam power, called "steam warming" at the time. In order to fill a $6,000 contract to supply the new Cook County Court House in Chicago with steam heating, Crane designed and manufactured a wide variety of globe and check valves, pipe fittings, steam cocks, branch tees, and hook plates. Their success won the company a similar contract for the newly constructed Illinois State Penitentiary in Joliet, Illinois, which, in turn, won them further credibility and sustained business in the provision of steam heating supplies. With the onset of the Civil War, the company also became a major government supplier of fittings for saddlery, brass fittings, plates, knobs, spurs, and wagon equipment.

By 1865 the Crane brothers completed construction of an industrial-size factory on Jefferson Street, which enabled them to expand all facets of business operations and manufacture a full line of valves in materials ranging from cast iron to malleable iron and brass. That same year, the company was incorporated and renamed the North Western Manufacturing Company, reflecting its broadening interests.

In 1866 the company printed its first catalog, which contained products as diverse as fire hydrants, ventilating fans, machine tools, water pumps, bung bushings for beer barrels, and steam engines. The advent of the Bessemer smelting process for iron brought low-cost steel to the United States, further assisting Crane in his development of diverse and durable products.

Crane's entry into the elevator business began in 1867, when the company designed an engine with a safety valve to control elevator speed with heavy loads. From the 1870s until the mid-1890s, Crane provided 95 percent of the hoists used in U.S. blast furnaces. In addition, the company established a presence in passenger elevator manufacturing in 1872, spinning off a separate subsidiary called the Crane Elevator Company that remained a major competitor in the field for over three decades. With increased focus on industrial manufacturing, it sold its elevator division in 1895 to a joint venture that eventually became the Otis Elevator Company.

KEY DATES

1855: Richard Teller Crane founds R.T. Crane Brass & Bell Foundry in Chicago.

1865: Company is incorporated and renamed North Western Manufacturing Company, reflecting its broadening interests, including into the production of valves.

1872: Company is renamed Crane Brothers Manufacturing Company.

1884: First company branch operation is opened in Omaha, Nebraska.

1890: Company adopts the name Crane Company.

1918: Expansion outside the United States begins with the establishment of Crane Limited in Canada.

1922: Company name is shortened to Crane Co.

1931: During the Great Depression, Crane suffers its first operating loss.

1936: Company's stock is listed on the New York Stock Exchange.

1951: Crane enters the business of precision aircraft products and flow-control equipment via the acquisition of Hydro-Aire, Incorporated.

1959: Chapman Valve Manufacturing Company is acquired.

1960: Crane expands into water treatment equipment with the purchase of Cochrane Corporation.

1961: Pump maker Deming Company is acquired.

1968: Crane strengthens its position in building products through purchase of Huttig Sash & Door Company.

1969: CF&I Steel Corporation is acquired.

1984: CF&I Steel is spun off to shareholders.

1985: Crane acquires UniDynamics Corporation, which has wide-ranging manufacturing interests, including defense engineering, vending machines, and fiberglass-reinforced plastic panels.

1994: Acquisition of Mark Controls Corporation extends Crane's range into industrial controls.

1999: Huttig Building Products is spun off to shareholders, enabling Crane to focus on its core manufacturing operations.

2001: The Xomox valve business is acquired.

2003: Crane purchases Signal Technology Corporation.

2006: Company's merchandising systems segment is bolstered via the acquisitions of four companies: CashCode Co. Inc., Telequip Corporation, Automatic Products International, and Dixie-Narco Inc.

The year 1871 literally brought a blaze of change, as the company survived the Chicago fire and helped save the city by providing large steam pumps to displace river water to city mains. That same year, Charles Crane retired from the business and sold his share to Richard, making the original founder sole proprietor once again. To emphasize the family heritage after his brother's departure, Richard changed the name to Crane Brothers Manufacturing Company in 1872.

LATE 19TH-CENTURY INNOVATIONS AND GROWTH

In the late 1880s Richard T. Crane contributed to the rise of industrial automation. He pioneered line production in foundries and invented numerous mechanized systems to increase industrial efficiency in its plants. The company developed a steam-powered conveyor system for moving molds and pouring metal. It also fine-tuned the use of multiple-purpose machines, such as a machine that simultaneously bored cylinders, crosshead guides, and crankshaft bearings for steam elevator engines. Other innovations included oil pumps for the lubrication of engine-driven cylinders, an alarm to signal low water levels in steam boilers, a pipe lap joint that set new standards in the industry, and state-of-the art ceiling plates and pipe hangers.

With increased innovation and business volume, the company expanded rapidly. In 1884 a branch operation was opened in Omaha, Nebraska, which proved so successful that another was established in Los Angeles, California, in 1886. Within a few years, branch operations became standard company practice, sprouting up wherever Crane products were in demand. In 1870 a four-story extension was added to the Jefferson Street plant, and in 1881, a second large pipe mill was constructed. By 1880 Crane operated four production facilities employing more than 1,500 workers.

In 1890 the company officially assumed the name Crane Company and became commonly called Crane Co. Crane's business continued to grow rapidly. A new age of increasingly taller buildings demanded greater numbers of pipes, valves, and fittings for water and steam systems with higher performance standards. In addition, commercial electricity depended on massive steam engines, which in turn required stronger and cheaper fluid control equipment. Anticipating the need for new materials and innovative solutions to remain competitive, Richard T. Crane established a chemical laboratory in 1888. The company developed iron castings of uniform tensile strength, a notable achievement for the period. Before long, the rise of large steam power plants outdated even uniform fittings in cast iron, forcing the company to innovate in steel production. In 1907 Crane negotiated for a German steel innovator, Zenzes, to join its staff and supply his coveted patents. By 1910 Crane was producing valves and fittings with minimum tensile strength of 60,000 psi.

During the first decades of the 20th century, Crane invested in metallurgical research that paid off for the company and the industry at large. Experiments designed to test the effects of high temperatures on various metals culminated in a series of papers published in 1912 that became engineering classics. In addition, a number of Crane quality control procedures became industry standards. Crane's inspection of pipe threads using gauges was adopted by the American Society for Testing and Materials, and Crane's practice of tapping and gauging steel flanges eventually served the whole industry as the Pipe Thread Standard.

Crane expanded to East Coast markets with the 1903 acquisition of the Eaton, Cole & Burnham Company in Bridgeport, Connecticut. The company continued to expand its production line, introducing a complete line of air brake equipment, pop safety valves, and drainage fittings, among other products. A 160-acre, electrically powered plant was constructed in Chicago in 1909. After Richard Crane's death in January 1912, his role as president was briefly passed on to the eldest son, Charles R. Crane, and then more permanently transferred to Richard T. Crane Jr. in 1914.

Among the ventures introduced by the new president was an extensive line of practical, decorative bathroom ensembles supported by acquisitions of sizable pottery and enamelware operations and by unprecedented marketing efforts. The copy for a 1925 advertisement in *National Geographic* magazine began, "Your personal taste and appreciation of beauty in form and color can be reflected in the appointments of your bathroom." Among other initiatives to corner the rising bathroom market, Crane retained industrial designer Henry Dreyfuss to conceive an entire fixture line.

INTERNATIONAL EXPANSION FOLLOWING WORLD WAR I

In the years following World War I, Crane established its first operations outside the United States. In 1918 Canadian operations were incorporated as a separate company, Crane Limited, which grew to include Canadian Potteries Ltd., Warden King Ltd., and Crane Steelware Ltd. over the ensuing 20 years. Distribution also expanded to Europe, with the first branch houses established in France in 1918 and in England in 1919. Manufacturing operations were established in those countries in 1925 and 1929, respectively. In the meantime, Crane Co. was adopted as the official name in 1922.

While losses during the Great Depression strained operations, they also prompted replanning and increased efficiency and served to usher the company into World War II as a reliable and flexible supplier. Although Crane reported its first operating loss in 1931, it rebounded within two years to offer shares on the New York Stock Exchange in 1936. After sustained growth during the next decade, the company was ready to supply the U.S. Navy with valves and fittings for the war effort. From a prewar steel valve production capacity of 6,000 tons per year, Crane increased its capacity to an annual rate of 25,000 tons by mid-1942. By supplying the Navy, the Atomic Energy Commission, and new manufacturers of high-octane fuel using catalytic cracking techniques, Crane gained ample experience in designing and manufacturing a wide range of metal-alloy valves and fittings resistant to corrosion, high temperatures, and extreme strain.

POSTWAR GROWTH

Following the war, Crane was able to transfer its war efforts to peace time, meeting increased demands in the petrochemical, chemical, and atomic power industries. With the 1951 acquisition of Burbank, California-based Hydro-Aire, Incorporated, Crane entered the business of precision aircraft products and flow-control equipment, supplying filters and valves to all manufacturers of turbine type aircraft engines. In 1953 Crane developed a household hydronic heating system; it ranked as one of the country's largest manufacturers of residential heating by 1956. In the late 1950s the company shareholders elected a new chairman and chief executive officer, Thomas Mellon Evans, whose strategy was to streamline the distribution network and broaden the industrial product base. A major consolidation of distribution houses and the reorganization of a separate "profit center" resulted in the creation of Crane Supply Company. The October 1959 acquisition of the Chapman Valve Manufacturing Company of Indian Orchard, Massachusetts, significantly expanded domestic valve operations, especially on the East Coast. The following year, the acquisition of the 97-year-old Cochrane Corporation in Philadelphia, Pennsylvania, extended Crane's fluid control line to include steam boilers and water, steam, and wastewater treatment equipment. The Cochrane Division became the nucleus of Crane's growing involvement in the business of pollution control.

By the 1960s, Hydro-Aire catered to the space program with production of life-support and coolant pumps. It also expanded its role in the realm of aerospace by taking the lead in antiskid braking systems, fuel and hydraulic pumps, valves and regulators, actuators, and solid-state components.

Expansion continued through the 1960s. In 1961 the Deming Company, a manufacturer of residential and industrial pumps and water systems, was acquired. Four years later, Crane acquired a highly specialized fluid control company, the Chempump Division of Fostoria Corporation, which specialized in leakproof, trouble-free pump systems for exotic or dangerous fluids.

By the mid-1960s Crane had extended its international operations to Italy, with Crane-Orion, Italy; the Netherlands, with Crane Nederland, N.V.; Spain, with the acquisition of that country's largest valve manufacturer, Fundiciones Ituarte, S.A., and the formation of Crane-FISA, S.A.; Australia, with the new valve plant, Crane Australia Pty., Ltd.; and Mexico. Crane Canada Ltd. and Crane U.K. also made significant acquisitions in 1964 and 1966. Through rising space-age technology, Crane expanded beyond terrestrial boundaries, collaborating with the U.S. Space Team and the Brookhaven National Laboratory's test studies of solar energy, among other projects.

SHORT-LIVED DIVERSIFICATIONS INTO STEEL AND CEMENT

In an effort to improve its position in the area of building products, Crane acquired Huttig Sash & Door Company of St. Louis, Missouri, in 1968, adding milled wood products, windows, and doors to its line. The 1969 acquisition of CF&I Steel Corporation, a vertically integrated steel company, marked an unprecedented diversification into a major industry beyond its existing areas. CF&I provided everything from iron ore, coal,

and limestone to carbon and alloy steel. It represented the largest acquisition in Crane's history and, by 1975, represented the company's single largest business interest. The 1979 acquisition of Medusa Corporation, a cement and aggregates company, added another basic materials industry to Crane's list.

In 1980 Crane began a shift in business strategy away from cyclical basic materials businesses toward a diversified mix that would earn higher returns for shareholders. In February 1984, T. M. Evans resigned as chairman and director of the company, leaving his post to the newly elected Richard Sheldon Evans, son of T. M., who ushered in a major restructuring effort. On July 13 of that year, the company sold its U.S. plumbing division for approximately $9.5 million. One year later, Crane spun off CF&I Steel to its shareholders, and in 1988 shares in Medusa Corporation were made available to its shareholders as well.

While Crane's restructuring involved substantial paring down, it also called for new acquisitions in light-to-medium manufacturing. In 1985 the company acquired UniDynamics Corporation of Stamford, Connecticut, expanding diversification in numerous areas: defense and aerospace contracting, fluid controls, vending machines and coin validators, automation equipment, fiberglass-reinforced plastic and laminated panels, and electronic components.

The late 1980s and early 1990s were marked by management efforts to fine-tune the UniDynamics acquisition; several divisions deemed incompatible with the restructuring plan were sold and appropriate acquisitions were made. In February 1987, 12 Crane Supply plumbing, heating, and air conditioning wholesale distribution branches in southern regions of the United States were sold. Substantial additions were made to the company's U.S. valve line, including valve maintenance and value-added services. In April 1992 Crane's Canadian subsidiary, Crane Canada, Inc., acquired certain assets of Jenkins Canada, Inc., a manufacturer of bronze and iron valves, for approximately $4 million.

The Ferguson Machine Co., the largest supplier of intermittent motion control systems in the world, was established as a division of the Defense and Specialty Systems Group of Crane, and in August 1986 Ferguson acquired PickOmatic Systems of Detroit, a leader in cam-activated mechanical parts handling equipment. Crane's Cochrane Environment Systems division acquired Chicago Heater Company, Inc., a designer, manufacturer, and servicer of deaerators and surface condensers, reinforcing Cochrane's market leadership. Additionally, Huttig Sash & Door Company expanded to become the third largest distributor of wood building products in the industry. Pozzi-Renati Millwork

Products, Inc., was acquired in February 1988, providing Crane with a strong initial entry into the East Coast market; Palmer G. Lewis Co., a distributor of building material, was acquired in June 1988; and Rondel's, Inc., a distributor of doors, windows, and molding, was acquired in April 1993.

Crane Co.'s Hydro-Aire Division was augmented in 1990 by the $40 million acquisition of Lear Romec Corp., a manufacturer of pumps for the aerospace industry. In September of that year the diaphragm pump line of the Crown Pump Company was added to Crane's Deming pump line, increasing Crane's share of the industrial pump market. That same year, a Crane attempt to acquire Milton Roy Co., a manufacturer of metering pumps, was halted by an antitrust suit in which Milton accused Crane of a "greenmail" scheme to manipulate the market in order to acquire Milton stock. Milton repurchased all shares held by Crane for $8.2 million.

SURVIVING RECESSION: EARLY NINETIES

Downturns in residential construction, in defense spending, and in the aerospace industry, paired with weak economies worldwide, strained key Crane divisions in the early 1990s. Hydro-Aire, the leader in electronically controlled antiskid brakes for the aerospace industry, saw declines in profitability of 13 percent and 18 percent in 1991 and 1992, respectively. The April 1993 sale of the precision ordnance business of Unidynamics/Phoenix to Pacific Scientific Company reflected further reduction in Crane's declining defense business. These losses, however, were offset in part by strong increases in revenues at National Vendors for automated merchandising equipment; at Huttig, which served the residential construction industry; and at Kemlite and CorTec, Crane's suppliers of fiberglass-reinforced panels to the transportation industry. R. S. Evans, Crane's chairman and CEO, noted in the 1992 annual report that "one benefit of a diversified business mix is that a recession rarely cuts across all units with equal impact."

Despite the recessionary trends of the early 1990s, Crane was able to increase total operating profit for 1992 by 7 percent and improve productivity, on a sales-per-employee basis, by 6 percent. During 1992 Moody's upgraded the company's senior debt rating from Baa2 to Baa1, while Standard & Poor's reconfirmed the company's A− credit rating on the $100 million senior notes.

LATE 20TH-CENTURY ACQUISITION SPREE

From the fall of 1993 through the spring of 1994 Crane spent $335 million to make five acquisitions. In October 1993 the company spent $25 million for Jonesboro, Arkansas-based Filon, a fiberglass manufacturer that was integrated into the Kemlite unit. Two months later Crane paid $70 million for Burks Pumps Inc. of Piqua, Ohio, a manufacturer of engineered pumps that complemented Crane's Chempump and Deming pump businesses. Added in March 1994 at a price of $77 million in cash and assumed debt of $17 million was EL-DEC Corporation, a Lynnwood, Washington-based maker of aerospace components, including proximity switches and sensing systems, power conversion equipment, fuel flow measurement systems, and integrated modular systems. Crane next won a takeover battle with Tyco International Ltd. for Mark Controls Corporation, a manufacturer of automatic and manually operated valves, specialized electronic and mechanical instruments and controls, regulators, and pneumatic and electronic controllers. Crane acquired Mark Controls in April 1994 for $95 million in cash plus assumed debt of $40 million. The following month Crane, through Huttig Sash & Door, acquired American Moulding and Millwork, of Prineville, Oregon, for $11 million. This acquisition spree increased the company's revenues by 20 percent but also more than doubled its debt, from 27 percent to 60 percent of total capital. Crane's credit rating fell to the bottom of investment grade, Baa3/BBB.

Acquisitions were subsequently put on hold for the remainder of 1994, and only $9.4 million was spent in 1995 to make three minor purchases. Concentrating on consolidating the acquisitions of the previous two years, Crane was able to reduce its debt to total capital ratio to 44 percent by the end of 1995. That year the company posted record net sales of $1.78 billion and net income of $76.3 million.

During the late 1990s Crane continued to perform admirably, with net sales increasing steadily to $2.27 billion by 1998 and net income nearly doubling, reaching $138.4 million by that year. During these boom years in the United States, Crane slowly increased its pace of acquisition, continuing all the while to concentrate on smaller, complementary purchases and to manage the newly acquired companies in a largely hands-off manner. During 1996 Crane completed two acquisitions, the more significant being Interpoint Corporation, a designer and manufacturer of high-density power converters with applications in the aerospace and medical technology industries. Spending $82 million to make five acquisitions in 1997, Crane picked up Sequentia,

Inc.'s transportation products business, which produced fiberglass-reinforced plastic panels for the truck body, trailer, and container market, an operation that was integrated into Kemlite; Polyvend Inc., a maker of snack and food vending machines, which was merged into National Vendors; the nuclear valve business of ITI MOVATS, purchased from Westinghouse; MALLCO Lumber & Building Materials Inc., a leading wholesale distributor of lumber, doors, and engineered wood products that was purchased by Huttig; and Stockham Valves & Fittings, Inc., the largest of the 1997 acquisitions.

Crane accelerated the pace in 1998, completing six acquisitions at a total cost of $224 million. Added to the Crane fold were Environmental Products USA, Inc., a maker of membrane-based water treatment systems; Number One Supply and Consolidated Lumber Company, both of which were integrated into Huttig Building Products; Sequentia Holdings, Inc.; Liberty Technologies, Inc., manufacturer of monitoring products and related services for the nuclear power generation and industrial process markets; and Dow Chemical Company's Plastic-Lined Piping Products division.

Beginning in late 1998 and continuing into mid-1999 Crane fought a losing battle to block B.F. Goodrich Co.'s bid to take over Coltec Industries Inc., a maker of aircraft landing gear that Crane itself wished to acquire. Crane attempted to block the takeover through an antitrust lawsuit but eventually reached an out-of-court settlement that left it without possession of Coltec.

DIVESTING HUTTIG, RESTRUCTURING EFFORTS

At the end of the 1990s Crane continued to find success in its strategy of seeking to dominate selected niche markets. With the company's core businesses lying in manufacturing, Crane's distribution operations seemed increasingly out of place. Huttig Building Products in particular was perhaps a distracting or even detrimental presence in the company's portfolio of businesses as that unit had grown steadily in sales, from about $140 million in the mid-1980s to about $700 million in 1998 (about 31 percent of overall revenues), but had lower profit margins than the manufacturing lines. Evans told the *Wall Street Journal* in June 1999 that "as Huttig becomes a bigger part of Crane, I think it is holding Crane's overall results down." It was with this in mind that Crane in December 1999 spun Huttig off into a separate publicly traded company. With the divestment of Huttig, Crane operated only one distribution business, Crane Supply, which distributed pipes, valves, and

fittings across Canada. Crane also sold its defense systems business late in 1999.

In a further 1999 restructuring, Crane shut down five manufacturing plants and eight other facilities within its fluid handling, aerospace, and controls businesses as it sought to cut its annual operating expenses by $26 million. About 450 jobs were cut from the company's overall workforce of 12,500. In October 1999 the National Vendors vending machine unit was bolstered with the $32.8 million purchase of Stentorfield, Ltd., a Chippenham, England, concern producing hot and cold beverage vending machines for the U.K. and European markets.

The economic downturn that followed the tech-stock crash of 2000–01 hit the manufacturing sector particularly hard, and Crane took both a sales and a revenue hit as a result. Under newly installed CEO Eric C. Fast, who succeeded the retiring R. S. Evans (who remained chairman) in April 2001, Crane restructured once again. The main aim of this overhaul was to create a more centralized organizational structure consisting of fewer and larger units, which would be both stronger and more cost-efficient. Thus, in 2001 several smaller units were internally merged into larger ones; for example, within the aerospace division, Lear Romec was merged into Hydro-Aire, while in engineered materials CorTec was merged into Kemlite. In addition, two peripheral businesses that did not mesh with a large unit were divested—the Crane Plumbing business in Canada (marking the firm's exit from the plumbing sector) and Power Process Control—and the Ferguson industrial machinery unit was transferred to a joint venture with its largest competitor (and this joint venture was then sold to a third party in 2007).

FURTHER ACQUISITIONS AND ASBESTOS LITIGATION

At the same time, Crane continued to seek highly complementary acquisitions and completed seven deals in 2001 at a total cost of $191 million. By far the largest purchase that year came in June when Crane bought the Xomox valve business from Emerson Electric Co. for $145 million. Buying Xomox beefed up Crane's fluid handling unit as it brought onboard a producer of valves and pumps used principally in ships, power and petrochemical plants, and oil and gas refineries. The Cincinnati-based Xomox was also attractive because of its strong global operations, including manufacturing plants in the United States, Mexico, Germany, and Hungary and 22 service centers in the Americas, Europe, and Asia. Crane further strengthened its global operations in this sector by acquiring the Saunders brand of diaphragm valves manufactured in the United

Kingdom and India and the DEPA brand of air-operated diaphragm pumps manufactured in Germany. Among Crane's seven 2002 deals was the $40 million purchase from Tomkins plc of the Florence, Kentucky-based Lasco Composites business. The acquisition of Lasco, a producer of fiberglass-reinforced plastic panels, was particularly significant because it provided Crane's Kemlite unit with an entry into the industrial market.

Like a number of other industrial manufacturers, Crane found itself the defendant in an increasing number of lawsuits brought by claimants alleging personal injury from exposure to asbestos-laden products. The issue cropped up for Crane because the company had until the early 1980s produced industrial fluid handling equipment that included asbestos in its gaskets and rings. As the pending claims against the company ballooned from 2,500 to more than 54,000 between 1999 and 2002, Crane was forced to take an after-tax charge of $73 million in 2002 to increase its litigation reserves. This led to a net loss for the year of $11.4 million. Then in 2004, when pending claims reached 80,000, Crane established an asbestos reserve of $650 million, which was intended to cover the costs of pending and anticipated future claims through 2011. This cost the company a net $252 million after accounting for insurance coverage and taxes, resulting in a 2004 net loss of $105.4 million. In 2007 Crane recorded an additional asbestos liability of $586 million to cover pending and future claims through 2017. A full-year net loss totaling $62.3 million was recorded.

As it contended with this asbestos problem, Crane continued to seek acquisitions to strengthen its operating units, all of which were operating profitably. In May 2003 Crane buttressed its electronics operations by buying Signal Technology Corporation (STC) of Danvers, Massachusetts, for $138 million. STC, which garnered sales of $87 million in 2002, produced power-management products and electronic radio-frequency and microwave-frequency components and subsystems for defense, space, and military communications applications. Crane in January 2004 completed a deal for its aerospace unit, purchasing Woodland Hills, California-based P. L. Porter Co. for $44 million. Porter was a leading manufacturer of motion control products for airline seating.

After recording net income of $136 million in 2005, the year it celebrated its 150th anniversary, Crane Co. enjoyed record profits of $165.9 million the following year on revenues of $2.26 billion. The company completed five acquisitions in 2006 for a total of $283 million, with four of them augmenting the merchandising systems segment: CashCode Co. Inc., producer of banknote validators, storage, and recycling devices used in the vending, gaming, retail, and transportation industries (purchased for $86 million in January); Telequip Corporation, maker of coin dispensers used in supermarkets, convenience stores, and fast-food restaurants ($45 million; June); Automatic Products International, a leading producer of snack vending machines ($30 million; June); and Dixie-Narco Inc., the largest producer of can and bottle vending machines in the world ($46 million; October).

Crane's fifth purchase of 2006 occurred in September, a $72 million deal for Noble Composites, Inc., a manufacturer based in Goshen, Indiana, producing composite panels used in recreational vehicles. Crane followed this deal by buying the composite panel business of Owens Corning in September 2007 for $38 million. This business, also based in Goshen, specialized in fiberglass-reinforced plastics panels for recreational vehicles. In December 2008 Crane acquired the Krombach Group for $69 million in cash and assumed debt. The operations of Krombach, a leading manufacturer of specialty valve flow products for the power, oil and gas, and chemical markets, included headquarters and a manufacturing plant in Germany and foundry, machining, and assembly facilities in Slovenia and China.

Crane's revenues for 2008 were essentially flat compared to the previous year as the global economic crisis began to impact the company's operations. In response to the downturn, the company launched a restructuring involving several facility consolidations and a pretax charge of $40.7 million. The charge reduced Crane's net income for 2008 to $135.2 million. Crane's outlook for 2009 and beyond was somewhat clouded by the uncertainties surrounding the global economy, but the firm entered 2009 with strong liquidity thanks to $232 million in cash and $300 million in revolving credit. Thus, Crane Co. was well positioned to fund internal growth as well as continue pursuing targeted acquisitions.

Kerstan Cohen
Updated, David E. Salamie

PRINCIPAL SUBSIDIARIES

Crane GmbH (Germany); National Rejectors, Inc. GmbH (Germany); NRI Iberica S.A. (Spain); Crane International Holdings, Inc.; Crane Aerospace, Inc.; ELDEC Corporation; ELDEC France S.A.R.L.; Hydro-Aire, Inc.; Crane (Asia Pacific) Pte. Ltd. (Singapore); Resistoflex Plastic Lined System (Shanghai) Co. Ltd. (China); Crane Composites, Inc.; Noble Composites, Inc.; Crane Controls, Inc.; Azonix Corporation; Barksdale GmbH (Germany); Barksdale, Inc.; Dynalco

Controls Corporation; Crane International Trading (Beijing) Co. Ltd. (China); Crane Fluid & Gas Systems (Suzhou) Co. Ltd. (China); Crane Fengqiu (Zhejiang) Pump Co. Ltd. (China; 70%); Crane Nantong Company Ltd. (China; 70%); Crane Ningjin Valve Co. (China); Crane Zhengying Rubber Co. Ltd. (China; 80%); Crane Resistoflex GmbH (Germany); CR Holdings C.V. (Netherlands); Crane Global Holdings S.L. (Spain); Crane Australia Pty. Ltd.; P.T. Crane Indonesia (51%); Crane Process Flow Technologies S.r.l. (Italy); Crane YongXiang (Ningbo) Valve Co. Ltd. (China; 70%); Xomox Hungary Kft.; Xomox International GmbH & Co. (Germany); Crane Holdings (Germany) GmbH; Crane Process Flow Technologies GmbH (Germany); Crane Process Flow Technologies S.P.R.L. (Belgium); Xomox Japan Ltd.; Xomox Korea Ltd.; Crane International Capital S.á.r.l. (Luxembourg); Crane Canada Co.; Crane Ltd. (UK); Crane Merchandising Systems Ltd. (UK); Automatic Products (UK) Limited; Crane Process Flow Technologies Ltd. (UK); Crane Process Flow Tech. (India) Ltd.; Crane Stockham Valve Ltd. (UK); International Couplings B.V. (Netherlands); ELDEC Electronics Ltd. (UK); General Technology Corporation; Interpoint Corporation; Interpoint S.A.R.L. (France); Interpoint Taiwan Corporation; Interpoint U.K. Ltd.; Kemlite Ltd. (UK); MCC Holdings, Inc.; Crane Environmental Inc.; Crane Nuclear, Inc.; Crane Pumps & Systems, Inc.; Xomox Corporation; Flow Technology, Inc.; Signal Technology Corporation; Xomox A.G. (Switzerland); Xomox Chihuahua S.A. de C.V. (Mexico); Xomox Corporation de Venezuela C.A.; Xomox France S.A.; Unidynamics/Phoenix Inc.; Dixie Narco, Inc.; Crane Overseas LLC; Streamware Corporation; Telequip Corporation.

PRINCIPAL OPERATING UNITS

Aerospace & Electronics; Controls; Engineered Materials; Fluid Handling; Merchandising Systems.

PRINCIPAL COMPETITORS

Tyco International Ltd.; Dover Corporation; ITT Corporation; Flowserve Corporation; Precision Castparts Corp.; Goodrich Corporation; Parker Hannifin Corporation; Eaton Corporation; Colfax Corporation.

FURTHER READING

Breskin, Ira, "Crane to Buy Emerson Valve Unit," *Daily Deal,* May 29, 2001.

Campanella, Frank W., "Reshaped Crane: UniDynamics Acquisition Affords It a Profitable Entry into Defense," *Barron's,* May 6, 1985, pp. 59+.

Crane Co., 1855–1975: The First 120 Years, New York: Crane Co., 1975, 44 p.

"Crane Co. to Hasten Restructuring Plan," *Wall Street Journal,* September 14, 1999, p. B6.

Crane, Richard Teller, *The Autobiography of Richard Teller Crane,* Chicago: Crane Co., 1927, 247 p.

Goldstein, Alan, "Milton Roy Co. Repurchases Crane Co. Shares," *St. Petersburg (Fla.) Times,* February 13, 1990.

Haflich, Frank, and Scott Lautenschlager, "CF&I Being Spun Off to Holders," *American Metal Market,* April 4, 1985, pp. 1+.

Hart, Margaret A., and Alan H. Oshiki, "A Horse of a Different Color," *Chief Executive,* January/February 1998, p. 19.

Healy, Peter, "Quiet Giant: Crane, Old-Style Industrial Conglomerate, Celebrates 150 Years," *Stamford/Norwalk (Conn.) Advocate,* May 22, 2005, p. A1.

Henriques, Diana B., *The White Sharks of Wall Street: Thomas Mellon Evans and the Original Corporate Raiders,* New York: Scribner, 2000, 368 p.

Jaffe, Thomas, "The Apple Fell Far from the Tree," *Forbes,* September 25, 1995, pp. 73+.

———, "Daddy Dearest," *Forbes,* September 25, 1995, p. 76.

Lee, Richard, "Crane, Partner Sell Joint Venture," *Stamford/Norwalk (Conn.) Advocate,* December 20, 2007, p. A1.

———, "Crane to Buy N.H. Company for $45M," *Stamford/Norwalk (Conn.) Advocate,* June 13, 2006, p. B6.

Lipin, Steven, and Paul M. Sherer, "Crane, Seeking to Stop Goodrich Deal, Offers Richer Price for Coltec Industries," *Wall Street Journal,* December 15, 1998, p. A3.

"The Questions Evans Left Behind at Crane," *Business Week,* March 12, 1984, pp. 28+.

Trachtenberg, Jeffrey A., "Life Without Father," *Forbes,* March 11, 1985, p. 86.

Vanac, Mary, "Rivals' Moves to Block B.F. Goodrich's Bid for Coltec Were Atypical," *Akron (Ohio) Beacon Journal,* July 18, 1999.

Velocci, Anthony L. Jr., "BFGoodrich, Crane Square Off in Battle to Acquire Coltec," *Aviation Week and Space Technology,* January 11, 1999, p. 447.

Voorhees, Rich, "Crane Takes M&A to the Max," *CFO,* September 1994, p. 31.

Watson, Patricia, *Crane: 150 Years Together,* Stamford, Conn.: Crane Co., 2005, 128 p.

Cyan Worlds Inc.

14617 Newport Highway
Mead, Washington 99021-9378
U.S.A.
Telephone: (509) 468-0807
Fax: (509) 467-2209
Web site: http://www.cyanworlds.com

Private Company
Incorporated: 1987
Employees: 35
Sales: $4 million (2007 est.)
NAICS: 511210 Software Publishers

■ ■ ■

Based in Mead, Washington, Cyan Worlds Inc. is a leading producer of computer games. Among the company's hit titles are the nonviolent adventure games *Myst* and *Riven*, which together have sold more than 12 million copies and won a legion of gaming enthusiasts and admirers.

FORMATIVE YEARS: 1987–90

The origin of Cyan Worlds Inc. can be traced to 1987, when brothers Rand and Robyn Miller established the company as Cyan Inc. Located near Spokane, Washington, operations were initially based inside a two-story garage.

During Cyan's early years, the company introduced a number of whimsical CD-ROM-based games for children, beginning with *The Manhole* in 1989. Other titles included *Cosmic Osmo, The Worlds Beyond the Mackerel, Spelunx,* and *Caves of Mr. Seudo.* In addition to receiving favorable reviews, the company's early offerings received a number of awards. For example, *Manhole* received Best New Use of a Computer honors from the Software Publishers Association in 1988.

BREAKING THROUGH WITH MYST: 1991–93

While Cyan's early products were noteworthy, the company achieved a major breakthrough with the introduction of a nonviolent, first-person adventure game called *Myst* in 1993. Work on this game began in 1991, when the Miller brothers secured financial support from Japan-based Sunsoft and hired artist Chuck Carter and audio engineer Chris Brandkamp.

In a September 24, 1993, *Business Wire* release, the company described *Myst* as "a story of betrayal and adventure brought to life with photo-realistic 3-D graphics, a haunting soundtrack, and mind-bending puzzles that will challenge players ages 14 and up."

Robyn Miller worked with Carter on the game's graphics and animation using a Macintosh computer. Both Miller brothers appeared in filmed portions of the game. In addition, their high-school-aged brother Ryan also provided assistance. Future Chief Financial Officer Chris Brandkamp filled the role of soundman by using a cardboard refrigerator box as a makeshift studio.

In September 1993, Cyan introduced a Macintosh version of *Myst* that sold for $59.95. A PC version was released in February 1994, selling for about the same

COMPANY PERSPECTIVES

Cyan's pursuit of something just beyond what's currently on the shelf has kept it as one of the leading developers of quality entertainment for everyone who has an interest in adventure, intrigue, and exploration.

price. Both titles were distributed through Broderbund Software.

EARLY SUCCESS: 1994–95

While the Miller brothers developed the *Myst* game, they also wrote a related book in order to keep track of the story and characters. *Washington Post* writer James Lileks was eventually hired to flesh out the manuscript. After retaining the Minneapolis, Minnesota-based Lazear Agency, the Millers held an auction for the rights to their book.

In August 1994, a $1 million advance was obtained from Walt Disney Co.'s Hyperion arm in exchange for the rights to three *Myst* novels. By March 1995 sales of *Myst* had exceeded the one million mark and work was underway on *Myst II.* Hyperion planned the release of its first *Myst* novel in tandem with the introduction of *Myst II.*

Cyan's success ultimately led the company to formalize its operations. In mid-1995, the Miller brothers announced they were relocating the company to a 10,000-square-foot building. At this time Robyn was serving as CEO, with a focus on creative development, while Rand, who had spent a decade in the banking industry before cofounding Cyan, filled the role of president. Onetime sound engineer Chris Brandkamp focused solely on his chief financial officer duties.

As the original *Myst* team was tasked with more executive-level responsibilities, it became necessary for them to hire and supervise new talent, making the development of *Myst II* challenging in different ways. After moving to its new quarters, plans were made to increase the company's workforce from 11 to 20 employees.

Heading into late 1995, the Miller brothers contended with the sometimes difficult task of managing their growing enterprise while staying true to their artistic side. The first *Myst* novel, *Myst: The Book of Atrus,* was released in hardcover, and a line of *Myst* merchandise, such as mouse pads and T-shirts, also was introduced.

SUCCESS CONTINUES WITH RIVEN: 1996–99

The development of *Myst II,* which was ultimately given the name *Riven,* cost approximately $15 million, some 33 percent of which was set aside for marketing.

The production of *Riven* was done at an entirely different level than that of the first *Myst* game. Several years before, the Millers hired Richard Vander Wende, production designer for Disney's *Aladdin,* to serve as vice-president and creative director. Compared to *Myst*'s four contributors, *Riven* involved contributions from roughly 50 people, and professional actors were used for the game's filmed sequences. Cyan also had access to better production technology.

Riven debuted on October 31, 1997. Two days after the new game was released, more than 147,000 copies had been sold. By the end of November, sales had reached 474,000 units. Because all Cyan hands were on deck for the development of *Riven,* the company had no other products in the pipeline. Moving forward, Robyn Miller envisioned having multiple creative teams in place so that the development of more than one product could occur simultaneously.

All in all, 1997 was a very successful year for Cyan. The market research firm PC Data named *Riven* as the top-selling game of the year, with *Myst* ranking number two. By this time the company employed a workforce of 23.

On March 6, 1998, *Riven* became the fastest entertainment software application to reach sales of one million copies. That same day, Robyn Miller—who had started two film projects with his brother, Ryan, and several former Cyan employees—announced that he was leaving Cyan to establish a film-focused development company named Land of Point.

Cyan announced plans to introduce an enhanced version of *Riven* on DVD-ROM in August 1998. Instead of the five CD-ROMs required for the previous version of the game, the DVD version was contained on a single disc. In addition to better audio and video quality, a "making of" video also was included.

Cyan celebrated the fifth anniversary of *Myst* by releasing a commemorative edition named *Ages of Myst* in October 1998. Consumers received both *Myst* and *Riven,* along with a hardcover journal, for $49.95.

DEVELOPMENT OF MYST ONLINE: 2000–03

Cyan ushered in the new millennium by hiring former ESPN Chairman and Getty Oil Co. Executive Stuart W.

KEY DATES

1987: Rand and Robyn Miller establish the company inside a two-story garage.

1993: A major breakthrough is achieved with the introduction of a first-person, nonviolent adventure game called *Myst.*

1994: Cyan receives a $1 million advance from Walt Disney Co.'s Hyperion business in exchange for the rights to three *Myst* novels.

1997: *Riven* debuts, selling more than 147,000 copies in its first two days.

1998: Robyn Miller leaves Cyan to establish a film-focused development company named Land of Point.

2001: Cyan releases *Myst: III Exile.*

2003: *Uru: Ages Beyond Myst* and *Uru: Online Ages Beyond Myst* are introduced.

2004: *Myst IV* is released.

2005: After releasing *Myst V: End of Ages,* difficult times cause Cyan to lay off most of its workforce.

2008: Plans are made to develop a version of *Myst* for the Apple iPhone.

Evey as the company's first director of strategic planning. CEO Rand Miller indicated that the addition of Evey would allow Cyan to forge new connections within the entertainment industry.

A new, interactive, Internet-based game—first code-named "Mud Pie," and later "Parable"—was in development by early 2000. Cyan remodeled its facilities in order to accommodate ten additional artists and designers.

In September 2000 a new partnership with Beverly Hills, California-based Creative Artists Agency (CAA) was announced, providing another way for the company to find the right financial and entertainment industry partners for its entertainment products.

Another important development in 2000 was the addition of Susan Bonds, a former Walt Disney Imagineering producer who helped develop Disneyland's Indiana Jones Adventure, as chief design production officer.

Tony Fryman was named as Cyan's president during the early 2000s. With Rand Miller serving as CEO, the company's workforce had grown to include 41

people. Sales of *Myst* then totaled seven million copies, followed by *Riven,* at four million copies.

Cyan released *Myst III: Exile* in 2001. By mid-2002, the company had adopted the new name Cyan Worlds Inc. Following a year's worth of negotiations, Cyan announced that it was partnering with the French entertainment firm Ubi Soft Entertainment to unveil its new product, which was going by the working title *Myst Online,* sometime in 2003.

Unlike previous products, Cyan planned to collect substantial revenues from customers' online play. *Myst Online* would offer users a continuously expanding selection of content. Development costs for *Myst Online* were approximately $12 million. In order to break even, Rand Miller estimated that a base of 100,000 subscribers was needed.

HARD TIMES: 2003–09

In late 2003 Cyan finally unveiled its new product. *Uru: Ages Beyond Myst* was introduced on CD-ROM at leading retailers such as Wal-Mart, and also online under the name *Uru: Online Ages Beyond Myst.*

Moving forward, Cyan hoped *Uru* would build upon the $250 million in revenue generated by its predecessors. However, when subscribers to the online version, which required a broadband Internet connection, proved to be scarce, Ubi Soft pulled it from the market. Plans were formed to use the extensive content developed for the online game to create expansion packs for the traditional version.

In August 2004, Cyan made an investment in a Spokane-based start-up named gamerZunion, which had developed a web site for online game players. That year, the company introduced *Myst IV.* Early the following year, the release of *Myst V: End of Ages,* the final game in the *Myst* series, was announced. After releasing that title in the fall, Cyan intended to shift its focus to new projects.

Unfortunately, after wrapping up development of the final *Myst* title, Cyan laid off virtually all of its employees in September 2005, leaving only Rand and Ryan Miller, as well as President Tony Fryman. The company had seen its sales dwindle in the competitive video game market, which was then dominated by more violent first-person shooter games.

Although *Myst V* found its way to the market, some reviewers criticized the game for lacking the superb graphics and storytelling depth that characterized previous versions.

Better times seemed to be on the horizon in December 2006, at which time Cyan planned to introduce *Myst Online: Uru Live,* a new version of the online game it had attempted to release in 2003. This time, the title was supported by Time Warner Inc.'s Turner Entertainment Co. A staff of 15 people was hired to provide online support to game players, who were required to pay a monthly subscription fee of $9.95. In all, Cyan's workforce had once again grown in size, totaling approximately 40 people.

Myst Online: Uru Live was released by Turner Broadcasting System's broadband entertainment network, GameTap, on February 15, 2007. Unfortunately, GameTap pulled the plug on *Myst Online* in early 2008. Attempts to sell other game ideas to publishers were made, but the efforts were unsuccessful, and the company's workforce was once again reduced. Midway through 2008, Cyan regained the rights to *Myst Online,* and plans were made to maintain the game for a minimal fee.

In addition to developing its own games, Cyan also provided a game testing service for other companies in order to generate a steady stream of revenue. Austin, Texas-based Gamecock Media Group was a leading customer. When SouthPeak Media Group acquired Gamecock, Cyan was forced to lay off 50 employees in late 2008, leaving only a handful of workers in its testing group. In the midst of these difficult times, Cyan's own development initiatives were largely put on hold as the company searched for a new publisher.

One positive development in 2008 occurred in November, when Cyan announced plans to develop a version of *Myst* for Apple's popular iPhone. With its development staff committed to the project, Cyan planned to release the iPhone game during the first half of 2009, and indicated that it would likely sell for about $10.

The sour economic climate of 2009 presented additional challenges for Cyan, in terms of securing funding for new games. However, based on its past success, the company had at least a fighting chance of long-term viability as it moved toward the 21st century's second decade. Indeed, by 2009 Cyan had sold more than 12 million copies of *Myst* and *Riven,* placing those titles among the best-selling video games of all time.

Paul R. Greenland

PRINCIPAL COMPETITORS

Atari Inc.; Electronic Arts Inc.; LucasArts Entertainment Company Ltd.

FURTHER READING

"Broderbund Unveils Myst, a Surrealistic Multimedia Adventure," *Business Wire,* September 24, 1993.

Erickson, Jim, "Success Scary to Myst Makers; Pressure to Sell Rights Raises Questions About Direction," *Seattle Post-Intelligencer,* November 3, 1995.

Evenson, Laura, "'Myst' Muse Leaves Game Company," *San Francisco Chronicle,* March 5, 1998.

Herold, Charles, "The Final Chapter in a Most Influential Series," *New York Times,* October 1, 2005.

"Myst Makers' Company Outgrows Starting Site," *Oregonian,* June 6, 1995.

"Myst Sequel Gets Off to Strong Start; Initial Sales Exceed Expectations; More Than 147,000 Copies of Riven Were Sold; During Its First Two Days of Release," *Spokesman Review,* November 13, 1997.

Sowa, Tom, "Are You Ready for Uru? Mead Video Game Maker Cyan Worlds Goes Underground with New Product," *Spokesman Review,* November 13, 2003.

———, "'Myst' in Future for the iPhone; Version Planned for First Half of 2009," *Spokesman Review,* November 11, 2008.

Daily Journal Corporation

915 East 1st Street
Los Angeles, California 90012-4050
U.S.A.
Telephone: (213) 229-5300
Fax: (213) 299-5481
Web site: http://www.dailyjournal.com

Public Company
Incorporated: 1888 as Daily Court Journal
Employees: 230
Sales: $40.6 million (2008)
Stock Exchanges: NASDAQ
Ticker Symbol: DJCO
NAICS: 511110 Newspaper Publishers

■ ■ ■

Daily Journal Corporation (DJC) is a Los Angeles-based, publishing company focusing mostly on legal newspapers and associated web sites. The flagship publications of the company's stable of 12 newspapers are the *Los Angeles Daily Journal* and *San Francisco Daily Journal,* both of which focus on news of legal importance in their respective markets and include the Daily Appellate Report, which offers case summaries and full text of opinions handed down from the California Supreme Court, the California Courts of Appeal, the U.S. Supreme Court, the U.S. Court of Appeals for the Ninth Circuit, and other major courts. Other newspapers and affiliated web sites include the Los Angeles-based *Daily Commerce,* mostly devoted to real estate matters; the *California Real Estate Journal,* a weekly also published in Los Angeles; the *Daily Recorder,* a Sacramento daily devoted to both legal and real estate news; the *Inter-City Express,* an Oakland, California, newspaper published twice a week, covering legal and real estate news in the Bay Area; the *San Jose Post-Record,* focusing on legal and real estate news and published three days a week; the *Sonoma County Herald-Recorder,* a twice-weekly legal and real estate–focused publication; the *Orange County Reporter,* mostly providing legal and real estate news three days a week; the *San Diego Commerce,* also published three days a week, serving legal and real estate professionals in San Diego County; the *Business Journal,* a Riverside County, California, twice-weekly business publication; and the *Record Reporter* (Arizona), a general news and public record information newspaper published three days a week. In addition, DJC publishes the *California Lawyer,* a legal affairs monthly magazine produced by the State Bar of California and provided free to active members of the State Bar and distributed as well to paying subscribers. Another legal magazine published by the company, *8-K,* is a free magazine sent to corporate officers and counsels.

Other ventures of DJC include information services drawn from its newspaper operations; Court Rules, offering loose-leaf sheets of court rules for state and federal courts in California in multi-volume sets; Local Rules, single volumes of rules for six major California counties; and Judicial Profiles, providing biographical and professional information on California judges. Most of the Daily Journal publications are printed at the company's main printing facility in Los Angeles, although the magazines and some other publications are

COMPANY PERSPECTIVES

The Company publishes newspapers and web sites covering California and Arizona, as well as the *California Lawyer* and *8-K* magazines, and produces several specialized information services. It also serves as a newspaper representative specializing in public notice advertising.

handled by outside contractors. Although a public company listed on the NASDAQ, Daily Journal Corporation is controlled by Chairman Charles T. Munger, a former attorney and longtime key associate (as vice-chairman of Berkshire Hathaway Inc.) of famed investor Warren Buffett.

ORIGIN OF *LOS ANGELES DAILY JOURNAL:* 1888

The oldest of the Daily Journal publications is the *Los Angeles Daily Journal,* established by a printer in 1888 as the *Daily Court Journal.* Five years later it was acquired by Warren Wilson, who, with his son, Douglas, would run the newspaper for almost 60 years. In 1897 Wilson also launched the *Daily Journal* of Denver, which he sold four years later. The California Newspaper Service Bureau, a cooperative of about 60 Los Angeles County community newspapers that specialized in public notice advertising, acquired the *Los Angeles Daily Journal* in 1951. The group manager, Telford Work, became the publisher of the *Daily Journal,* and his 22-year-old son Robert was installed as editor, prompting a revolt in the editorial offices. Not only did the former editor join a rival publication, the six-year-old *Metropolitan News,* and take a number of colleagues with him, the former staffers removed the paper's morgue, depriving the new staff the benefit of previous stories and valuable research material.

The rivalry between the *Daily Journal* and the *Metropolitan News* festered for the next quarter century, and reached a head when the owners of the *News* filed an antitrust lawsuit against the California Newspaper Service Bureau, alleging it monopolized legal advertising in Los Angeles County through the *Daily Journal.* To settle the matter, the community newspapers that owned California Newspaper Service Bureau decided to sell both the *Daily Journal* and its corporate parent. Work failed in his attempt to acquire the paper, which instead was purchased in 1977 by New America Fund Inc., controlled by Charles T. Munger.

Munger was born in Omaha, Nebraska, in 1924, the grandson of a federal judge and son of a lawyer. Although he would not meet fellow Omaha native Warren Buffett until later in life, Munger grew up in a house that would be a stone's throw from where Buffett would one day make his home, and as a teenager he worked in the grocery store owned by Buffett's grandfather. He attended but did not graduate from the University of Michigan and the California Institute of Technology. After a stint during World War II serving as a meteorological officer in the U.S. Army Air Forces, as the Air Force was then known, Munger was able to enroll at Harvard Law School despite the lack of an undergraduate degree. Graduating in 1948 he moved to Los Angeles to join the law firm of Musick Peeler & Garrett, which represented such clients as J. Paul Getty. He later established his own firm, Munger, Tolles & Olson.

Munger met Buffett in 1959, and after Buffett gained control of Berkshire Hathaway in 1962, he persuaded Munger to join him and give up his law career. Munger, agreed, provided he could continue to live in Los Angeles. Thus, Munger became one of Buffett's closest confidants, the one who played devil's advocate and raised doubts about Buffett's stock picks, earning him the memorable descriptive "the abominable no man." He was also credited with playing a major role in Buffett applying more stringent analysis to his investments. In 1978 he became vice-chairman of Berkshire Hathaway. Also in 1962 Munger established an investment counseling firm, Wheeler Munger & Co., and subsequently pursued his own investments separate from Berkshire Hathaway.

MUNGER'S LABOR OF LOVE

Although Munger finally left his law firm as an active partner in 1965 in order to make investments, he remained very much interested in the legal profession. The *Legal Journal* was hardly a major investment for him, but rather a labor of love and a hobby. (When a brash, young Steven Brill, an aspiring legal publisher who would become chief executive officer of American Lawyer Media, dropped in one day to ask for Munger's price for the *Daily Journal,* he was quickly told that Munger would never sell at any price.) Robert Work stayed as the publisher of the *Daily Journal* as well as the *Daily Commerce,* a Los Angeles business publication founded in 1917 that was included in the Daily Journal sale. The *Daily Commerce* would then be edited by Robert Work's son, Bill Work. Nevertheless, Munger played a role in reshaping the *Daily Journal.* A devoted *Wall Street Journal* reader, Munger asked that the *Daily Journal* adopt a similar layout to its front page, which adopted a

KEY DATES

1888: *Daily Court Journal* is founded in Los Angeles.
1893: Warren Wilson acquires publication.
1951: California Newspaper Service Bureau acquires *Daily Journal.*
1977: Charles T. Munger assumes control.
1987: Company is reincorporated in South Carolina as Daily Journal Corporation.
1988: *California Lawyer* begins publishing.
1990: New printing facility opens in Los Angeles.
1996: Daily is sued by Metropolitan News Company for antitrust violations.
1999: Company acquires majority stake in Sustain Technologies Inc.
2002: *Colorado Journal* is closed.
2005: Legal magazine, *8-K*, begins publishing.
2008: Sustain Technologies becomes wholly owned subsidiary.

rigid formula: three major stories related to legal issues or court opinions, brief legal news items and summaries of appellate and Supreme Court opinions, and a profile of a prominent lawyer or judge. In addition, it was Munger who introduced a publishing philosophy that prohibited staff-written editorials, a way to enhance the paper's position as a neutral observer, a reporter rather than an advocate. Munger also brought an infusion of cash, used to purchase a new press and increase the editorial staff.

REINCORPORATION AND EXPANSION

Daily Journal Co. was reincorporated in 1987 under the laws of South Carolina as Daily Journal Corporation. By this time the company had acquired the *Sacramento Recorder* and the *Oakland Inter-City Express.* Renamed the *Daily Recorder,* the *Sacramento Recorder* had been in business since 1911, while the *Inter-City Express* had been serving the Bay Area since 1909. Further assets were added to DJC at a steady pace, either through acquisition or startup. In 1988 *California Lawyer* was launched in conjunction with the State Bar of California. In 1990 the former parent of Daily Journal, California Newspaper Service Bureau, Inc., was brought into the fold, bringing with it the public notice advertising business. In that same year DJC opened a new Los Angeles office and printing facility.

In the 1990s, not only did DJC add to its California holdings, it ventured outside the state as well. In 1992 the *San Diego Commerce* was acquired and subsequently merged with another publication, the *Back Country Trader.* Also in that year the *Washington Journal* was established to cover legal news in Washington state on a weekly basis, and DJC acquired assets from Redloc Infosystems, Inc., to gain online foreclosure information that could be used by the company's string of newspapers. In 1993 the *Desert Business Journal,* serving the business community of Riverside County, California, was acquired and the name shortened to *Business Journal.* A year later the Nevada market was entered with the purchase of *Nevada Supreme Court Reporter,* which was recast as the semimonthly *Nevada Journal.* DJC expanded into Arizona in 1995 with the acquisition of the *Record Reporter,* which focused on real estate news and public record information, and the weekly *Arizona Journal* was also established to serve the state's legal community. In addition in 1995 DJC entered the Colorado market by acquiring The Public Record Corporation, which published the *Code of Colorado Regulations* and the *Brief Times Reporter,* a weekly publication that covered the opinions of the Colorado Supreme Court and Colorado Court of Appeals. It would be supplemented by the launch of another weekly, *Colorado Journal,* which offered a wider purview of state and federal legal matters.

Also added in the years after Munger assumed the chairmanship were the *San Francisco Daily Journal,* established 1893; the *Marin County Court Reporter,* established in the mid-1960s; the *Orange County Reporter,* in business since 1922; the *San Jose Post-Record,* first published in 1910; the *Sonoma County Daily Herald Recorder,* launched in 1899; the monthly *California Real Estate Journal;* and the Court Rules and Judicial Profiles services. Combined these operations generated $20.3 million in revenues in fiscal 1995 (the year ending September 30) and net income of more than $2 million.

LAWSUIT AGAINST DAILY JOURNAL: 1995

With size not only came growing profits but difficulties as well. In August 1995 the company was sued for $4.6 million by Jeffrey Barge, the owner of a Seattle publication, *Washington Law,* who claimed that a Daily Journal executive expressed interest in acquiring his paper, backed out, and then the confidential information he gathered provided an unfair competitive advantage when DJC began the *Washington Journal,* which drove *Washington Law* out of business. The matter would slowly wend its way through the court system, as would another suit, filed in 1996 by perennial rival

Metropolitan News Company. Its lawsuit alleged that DJC used its size to undercut small newspapers on public notice advertising, essentially accusing it of selling below cost as a way to eliminate competition. Hardly one to shy away from a legal scrap, Munger pursued both cases down the line, finally winning both of them in 2000.

In the second half of the 1990s, DJC expanded its operations modestly. In 1997 it established *Antelope Valley Journal,* a weekly real estate–related publication focusing on north Los Angeles County. In that same year the weekly *Ventura Journal* was launched as well, serving a similar function for the Ventura, California area. *House Counsel,* originally a magazine supplement of *California Lawyer,* was spun off as a stand-alone publication in 1998. DJC also ventured into the information systems and services arena in 1999 with the 80 percent purchase of Choice Information Systems, Inc., a Virginia-based provider of technology platforms to fulfill the specific database needs of court systems. The company was renamed Sustain Technologies, Inc., in September 1999. A further 11 percent of Sustain was acquired in 2000. These new businesses helped DJC to inch up to $36.85 million in fiscal 1999, when the company netted $2.12 million.

COLORADO JOURNAL CLOSING: 2002

Business dipped slightly in the early 2000s, falling to $18.5 million in fiscal 2001, primarily due to declines in display and classified advertising revenues. Compounded by the cost of supporting Sustain, DJC posted a net loss of $13.4 million in fiscal 2001. Revenues were essentially flat for the next two years, but the company returned to profitability, netting $1.23 million in 2002 and $2.4 million in 2003. Helping to improve the bottom line was the decision in the fall of 2002 to shut down the *Colorado Journal,* which had experienced declines in advertising revenues and whose subscription base had fallen to 300 readers from about 800. Although *House Counsel* had been profitable, it too was shut down in 2002, recast as the "In-House" section of *California Lawyer.*

In 2005 DJC launched another new publication, *8-K,* a legal magazine aimed at business executives, mailed to more than 13,000 U.S. corporate officers and California corporate counsels. In 2008, the company acquired the remaining interest in Sustain, which became a wholly owned subsidiary. Revenues improved to more than $40.6 million in fiscal 2008, and net income grew to $7.1 million. Compared to Munger's other investments, with and without Buffett, these amounts were hardly staggering, but DJC was a steady producer. It was also a pet project for Munger, but now that he was well into his 80s the future of DJC was far from certain.

Ed Dinger

PRINCIPAL SUBSIDIARIES

Sustain Technologies, Inc.

PRINCIPAL COMPETITORS

Hearst Communications Inc.; Metropolitan News Company; Thomson West.

FURTHER READING

Davis, Ann, "Meet Mr. Munger: Shrewd Investor with Odd Investment," *Wall Street Journal,* November 19, 1997, p. B1.

DiEdoardo, Chris, "Daily Journal Target of Suits," *San Diego Daily Transcript,* May 1, 1997, p. A1.

Fletcher, Amy, "Law Newspaper Calls It Quits Due to Decline in Readers, Ads," *Denver Business Journal,* September 30, 2002.

Goldman, Lea, "The Daily Defendant," *Forbes,* December 11, 2000, p. 64b.

Grant, Linda, "The $4-Billion Regular Guy," *Los Angeles Times,* April 7, 1991, p. 36.

Lenzner, Robert, and David S. Fondiller, "The Not-So-Silent Partner," *Forbes,* January 22, 1996, p. 78.

Oliver, Myrna, "It's the Law!" *Los Angeles Times,* July 1, 1985, p. 1.

Sanders, Lisa, and Larry Light, "The Legal Woes of a Legal Publisher," *Business Week,* June 23, 1997, p. 8.

Debenhams plc

One Welbeck Street
London, W1G 0AA
United Kingdom
Telephone: (+44 20) 7408 4444
Fax: (+44 20) 7408 3366
Web site: http://www.debenhamsplc.com

Public Company
Founded: 1778 as Flint & Clark
Incorporated: 1905 as Debenhams Limited
Employees: 27,400
Sales: £2.34 billion ($4.27 billion) (2008)
Stock Exchanges: London
Ticker Symbol: DEB
NAICS: 452110 Department Stores; 454111 Electronic Shopping

∎ ∎ ∎

Debenhams plc is one of the United Kingdom's longest continuously operating clothing and goods retailers and one of the largest as well. The company operates more than 140 traditional department stores across the United Kingdom and Ireland under the Debenhams name plus ten small-format Desire by Debenhams stores. In the U.K. market, Debenhams ranks as the second largest department store chain. There are also around 50 international franchised Debenhams stores in the following 17 countries: Bahrain, Cyprus, the Czech Republic, Dubai, Iceland, India, Indonesia, Jordan, Kuwait, Moldova, the Philippines, Qatar, Romania, Russia, Saudi Arabia, Turkey, and the United Arab Emirates.

The typical Debenhams store encompasses some 80,000 square feet of selling space and includes the following departments: women's wear, menswear, children's wear, lingerie, accessories, health and beauty, and homeware. Private-label brands, such as Debut, Maine New England, Red Herring, and Thomas Nash, account for more than 70 percent of the stores' sales. Customers are also able to purchase much of the Debenhams product range through the company's online store.

Founded in 1778, Debenhams operated as an independent company until a hostile takeover by The Burton Group plc in 1985. Three years later, Debenhams regained its independence when it was "demerged" from The Burton Group, which subsequently changed its name to Arcadia Group plc. A private-equity consortium took Debenhams private again in 2003. Then, in 2006, Debenhams was listed on the London Stock Exchange for a third time and began a new era of independence.

18TH-CENTURY ORIGINS

The first incarnation of what would later become known as Debenhams started in 1778 as Flint & Clark, a partnership between Thomas Clark and a man named Flint. The partners operated a draper's store in London's West End at 44 Wigmore Street with a stock that included expensive fabrics, ribbons, bonnets, gloves, and parasols. The Debenham name came into the picture in 1813 when the ownership of the shop changed to a partnership between Clark and William Debenham. Born in 1792, Debenham had previously served as an

COMPANY PERSPECTIVES

Debenhams is a leading department store group with a strong presence in womenswear, menswear, homeware, health and beauty, accessories, lingerie and childrenswear. Our exclusive own brands, including Designers at Debenhams, differentiate Debenhams from its competitors.

apprentice at the wholesaling operations of a Nottingham hosiery manufacturer. He invested £500 for his share of the equal partnership Clark & Debenham.

As Clark & Debenham became a London fixture, the company expanded to operate stores elsewhere in London and in other parts of the United Kingdom as well. The first store outside London, opened in Cheltenham in 1818, was an exact replica of the original store at Wigmore Street. Over the years, additional changes in ownership occurred. In 1837 Clark retired, and Debenham went into partnership with two of his employees, William M. Pooley and J. Smith. The business then operated as Debenham, Pooley & Smith until 1851 when Pooley and Smith retired. Debenham then brought his son William Debenham Jr. into a new partnership that also included Clement Freebody, the elder Debenham's brother-in-law, and was thus called Debenham & Freebody.

Throughout its first 100 years Debenhams had grown to include not only a number of stores but also its own manufacturing operations, producing the company's own clothing designs. In this capacity, Debenhams would build a strong, and somewhat exclusive, reputation; among its customers, Debenhams counted none other than Queen Victoria. William Debenham Jr.'s brother Frank was instrumental in another growth initiative: the establishment of a Debenhams wholesaling operation that sold cloth and other items to dressmakers and other leading retailers.

EARLY 20TH-CENTURY SHIFT TO DEPARTMENT STORES

The company continued to build its reputation into the 20th century, especially with the opening of the first Debenhams department store in 1905. In the same year, the company incorporated as Debenhams Limited. Debenhams converted its other stores to the department store format over the next decades. The company also expanded beyond its own stores, purchasing Marshall &

Snellgrove in 1919 and Knightsbridge retailer Harvey Nichols in 1920. The Harvey Nichols name, featured in Debenhams stores and in its own stores, grew to become an exclusive, high-end label. In 1927 Ernest Debenham, son of Frank Debenham, sold his shares in the company, which ended the involvement of the Debenham family in the business. A year later the ever expanding Debenhams went public, listing its shares on the London Stock Exchange, just in time for the Great Depression.

In the post–World War II years Debenhams found itself playing catch-up in a marketplace featuring rising stars, such as Marks and Spencer. One problem was the company's structure, which owed more to its 18th-century roots than to the modern commercial era. Although the company had continued to add new stores, each of its stores remained more or less independent while grouped under the Debenhams name. Purchasing, warehousing, and other functions were performed at individual locations, rather than through a centralized source. In addition, the positioning of some of the company's stores placed them in direct competition with other Debenhams stores, cannibalizing sales. Once a leader in the London department store market, Debenhams was soon outpaced by Marks and Spencer, among others.

Beginning in the 1950s, however, Debenhams began building a new, stronger, and more centralized management. The company took steps to streamline its operations, particularly in its purchasing program, reducing these expenses while strengthening consistency among the Debenhams stores themselves. The process of transforming Debenhams into a modern firm continued into the 1960s, particularly with the 1966 introduction of centralized buying at all the company's stores. In 1976 Debenhams purchased the historic Browns department store at Chester. The company a year later rebranded nearly all of its stores across the United Kingdom under the Debenhams banner. The only exceptions were Browns and Harvey Nichols.

By the 1980s Debenhams operated about 65 department stores. It also had attempted an expansion, buying the Hamley toys retail chain. This acquisition was resold soon after, although the Debenhams stores continued to feature Hamley toys. Nonetheless, Debenhams was facing difficulties. The recession initiated by the oil crisis of the early 1970s had had lasting effects on the British economy, which continued in its slowdown into the 1980s. Debenhams revenues were slipping, as was its share price, making the company a ripe target for the hostile takeover rage of the 1980s.

KEY DATES

1778: The draper's store Flint & Clark is established in London's West End at 44 Wigmore Street.

1813: William Debenham buys into the business, which is renamed Clark & Debenham.

1818: First store outside London opens in Cheltenham.

1837: Upon Clark's retirement, Debenham leads the new partnership Debenham, Pooley & Smith.

1851: With another partnership change, the company begins operating as Debenham & Freebody.

1905: Company opens its first department store and incorporates as Debenhams Limited.

1927: Involvement of Debenham family in the business ends.

1928: Company goes public for the first time, with a listing on the London Stock Exchange.

1977: Nearly all of the various stores operated by the company across the United Kingdom are rebranded under the Debenhams name.

1985: Debenhams is taken over by The Burton Group plc.

1997: Company opens its first international location, in Bahrain, via a franchise agreement.

1998: Debenhams is demerged from Burton and its stock again trades on the London Stock Exchange.

2003: Baroness Retail Limited, a consortium led by CVC Capital Partners, Texas Pacific Group, and Merrill Lynch Global Private Equity, acquires Debenhams and takes it private.

2006: An IPO returns Debenhams to public ownership and its third listing on the London Stock Exchange.

BURTON GROUP ERA: 1985–98

That bid came in 1985, when The Burton Group plc, an operator of such clothing chains as Burton Menswear, Evans, Dorothy Perkins, and Top Shop, launched a takeover of Debenhams. The department store company, independent for more than 200 years, fought to regain control, including seeking a white knight in competing retailers. In the end, however, The Burton Group won control of Debenhams for a price of nearly $900 million. Ralph Halpern, Burton's CEO,

brought in the American John Hoerner, seconded by Terry Green, to revitalize the ailing Debenhams chain.

Hoerner and Green took Debenhams on a restructuring program, closing stores, reducing departments, cutting back on sales events, and introducing a series of company-owned brand names. Much of the new management team's efforts went toward repositioning Debenhams, which had slipped in prestige to the lower end of the market, toward a mid-range store concept.

By the end of the 1990s Debenhams was on its way to recovery, both in sales and profits. The Burton side, however, had run into difficulties, with a number of decisions made by the high-flying Halpern proving costly to the company. When Halpern resigned in 1990, his position was taken over by John Hoerner. The following year, Hoerner named Terry Green as CEO of the Debenhams operation. Green continued to expand the store-owned range of brands, bringing that number to around 40, each targeted to different market segments and product categories, by the mid-1990s. As Debenhams regained its profit and sales momentum, the company slowly began to seek new store openings. In addition, the Harvey Nichols unit was sold in 1991.

The United Kingdom was hit by a new extended recession during the early 1990s. As the effects of that economic crisis began to diminish in the second half of the decade, The Burton Group featured the successful Debenhams department store chain on the one hand and its portfolio of clothing retail chains, mostly struggling, on the other. In 1997 Hoerner announced that The Burton Group would "demerge" from the Debenhams chain, restoring the department store group to independence as a public company.

1998: INDEPENDENT AGAIN

This move was taken at the beginning of 1998 at a cost of some £65 million. John Hoerner surprised analysts by remaining with the less profitable Burton Group. Terry Green remained as the Debenhams chief executive.

Restored to independence and once again listed on the London Stock Exchange, Debenhams featured more than 90 department stores, 118 restaurants, a growing wedding gift service, and a vibrant range of proprietary as well as internationally recognized brands. The company also had taken the first steps toward an international presence, entering a franchise agreement with the Middle East's MH Alshaya Group. The first Middle East location had opened in 1997 in Bahrain, followed soon thereafter by locations in Kuwait and Dubai.

Debenhams continued to expand its U.K. presence as well. In 1998 and 1999 the company embarked on an ambitious expansion plan, calling for the opening of 17 new stores and the modernization of some ten existing stores. Debenhams closed out its first year of regained independence with rising profits and rising revenues.

Green left the company in September 2000 to take over the reins at rival mid-market retailer BHS. Green's successor was Belinda Earl, who had joined The Burton Group in 1985 as a merchandiser and later worked closely with Green on his turnaround of Debenhams, particularly the successful development of private-label brands. Earl continued her predecessor's modernization program and put in place an even more ambitious growth trajectory aiming to ultimately increase the store count to 150. She also placed an emphasis on improving customer service at the stores, especially through the deployment of personal shoppers. A concurrent project was the tailoring of the product range at individual stores to suit local markets.

For the fiscal year ending in August 2002, Debenhams enjoyed solid results: same-store sales were up 4.6 percent, a 5 percent increase in pretax profits to £153.6 million, and an increase in sales from £1.6 billion to £1.7 billion. Plans were in place to increase the store total to 120 by 2007 and for £430 million in capital spending over a three-year period, including the construction of a new distribution center in Peterborough. Additional franchised stores overseas were also in the works, including the first Debenhams in Asia.

2003–06: PRIVATE-EQUITY ERA

In 2003 Debenhams was swept up in the private-equity buyout spree and became the subject of a five-month takeover battle between two consortiums of private-equity houses. In the end, Baroness Retail Limited, a consortium led by CVC Capital Partners, Texas Pacific Group, and Merrill Lynch Global Private Equity, prevailed with an offer of £1.7 billion ($2.9 billion). When the deal was completed in December 2003, Earl stepped down as chief executive. Taking the leadership mantle was Rob Templeman, who had previously overseen two other British retailers while they were under private-equity ownership, Homebase and Halfords.

The leveraged takeover increased Debenhams' debt load by £1.1 billion to £1.4 billion. This debt was reduced initially through a concerted cost-cutting effort and later through the £500 million raised when about two dozen store properties were sold and then leased back. In the summer of 2005, however, the debt ballooned back up to £1.87 billion following a refinancing that enabled the company's private-equity owners to nearly double the £600 million in equity they had invested in Debenhams. At the store level, in the meantime, Templeman increased the number of sales in order to clear out slow-moving merchandise and keep the cash flowing to service the debt load. Some critics felt that such actions were harming the stores' image by giving them more of a promotional feel.

Nevertheless, Templeman was able to report a more than doubling of pretax profits for fiscal 2005 to £238.6 million, and sales that year surpassed the £2 billion mark. Since 2003 Debenhams' share of the U.K. department store market had increased from 15 percent to nearly 19 percent. The company also opened its first smaller-format Desire by Debenhams stores. These outlets, about a tenth the size of a traditional Debenhams, were created for towns unable to support a full-sized store. Another 2005 development was the purchase of eight former Allders stores, which were later converted into Debenhams outlets.

THIRD PERIOD OF PUBLIC OWNERSHIP

The positive results for 2005 set the stage for Debenhams' third period of public ownership. In May 2006 the company was once again listed on the London Stock Exchange through an initial public offering (IPO) that valued the firm at £1.68 billion. Proceeds from the IPO were used to reduce the debt load to £1.11 billion. Templeman remained at the helm and continued to aggressively expand the firm's retailing footprint. In 2006, nine department stores in the Republic of Ireland were purchased from Roches Stores, which expanded the Debenhams chain to Galway, Waterford, and Limerick. Five new department stores were also opened in 2006, bringing the store total to nearly 140. By this time, Debenhams had increased its projected chain total to 240.

As the economic environment deteriorated in 2007 and 2008, Debenhams remained solidly profitable and was gaining market share in key clothing categories. Investors, however, were increasingly leery about heavily leveraged companies, and Debenhams was certainly in that category given its £1 billion pile of debt. By October 2008, the company's shares had fallen 68 percent over the previous 12 months. At this time, a higher priority was placed on slashing this debt burden, and among the measures enacted was a halving of the dividend. In January 2009 Debenhams took the further step of hiring an outside financial adviser to recommend ways to revise its capital structure. At the same time, despite the global financial and economic crisis and its own debt issues, Debenhams was not reining in its growth ambitions. The company opened new flagship stores in Liverpool and at the Westfield London shopping center in 2008 and had another 20 stores in its pipeline through the year 2013, including the first Debenhams in Newcastle upon Tyne, a 125,000-square-foot flagship store.

M. L. Cohen
Updated, David E. Salamie

PRINCIPAL SUBSIDIARIES

Debenhams Retail plc; Debenhams Group Holdings Limited; Debenhams Retail (Ireland) Limited; Debenhams Properties Limited.

PRINCIPAL COMPETITORS

John Lewis Partnership plc; Marks and Spencer Group p.l.c.; NEXT Retail Ltd.; House of Fraser Limited; Arcadia Group.

FURTHER READING

Bevan, Judi, "Burton's Flying Ringmaster," *Daily Telegraph* (London), July 13, 1997, p. 4.

Braithwaite, Tom, "Debenhams Pledges to Reduce £1bn Debt Pile," *Financial Times,* April 16, 2008, p. 21.

Braithwaite, Tom, and Fiona Harvey, "Debenhams to Halve Dividend After Setback," *Financial Times,* October 22, 2008, p. 21.

Buckley, Sophy, "Profit Is Up, Debts Are Down, Now Debenhams Is Set to Be Talk of Town," *Financial Times,* January 19, 2006, p. 21.

"Burton Claims Takeover of Debenhams," *WWD,* August 5, 1985, p. 35.

Churchill, David, "Separate but Together: Focus on the Structure of Debenhams Department Store Group," *Financial Times,* April 29, 1985, p. 10.

Cope, Nigel, "Debenhams Plans New Stores," *Independent* (London), April 28, 1998, p. 21.

———, "Debenhams to Be Spun Off As Burton Regroups," *Independent* (London), July 9, 1997, p. 17.

Corina, Maurice, *Fine Silks and Oak Counters: Debenhams, 1778–1978,* London: Hutchinson, 1978, 200 p.

Gilbert, Nick, "The Top Man and His Plan," *Independent on Sunday* (London), July 13, 1997, p. 3.

Hall, James, "Debenhams Gets Buyout Offer, Leading to Talk of More Bids," *Wall Street Journal Europe,* May 13, 2003, p. A4.

Isaac, Debra, "What's in Store for Debenhams," *Management Today,* September 1984, pp. 42+.

Killgren, Lucy, "Once-Robust Shop Drops in Estimation: Debenhams Has Been Left in the Shade by Rivals," *Financial Times,* March 17, 2007, p. 14.

Koenig, Peter, "Debenhams Gets a Brand New Image," *Independent on Sunday* (London), December 14, 1997, p. 2.

Larsen, Peter Thal, "Debenhams Stays Bullish," *Independent* (London), October 28, 1998, p. 23.

Osborne, Alistair, "Debenhams to Recruit 6,000 More Staff," *Daily Telegraph* (London), April 28, 1998.

"Permira Cedes Debenhams to Rivals," *Daily Deal,* October 24, 2003.

Pickard, Jim, and Elizabeth Rigby, "Debenhams Plans £500m Sale and Lease Back on Its Freehold Properties," *Financial Times,* February 5, 2005, p. 3.

Potter, Ben, "Debenhams Passes High Street Test," *Daily Telegraph* (London), April 28, 1998.

Raghavan, Anita, "Debenhams Bid Is Sweetened by CVC, Texas Pacific Group," *Wall Street Journal,* October 23, 2003, p. C5.

Rigby, Elizabeth, "Flip or Flop? The Inside Story of a Private Equity Deal," *Financial Times,* August 6, 2007, p. 9.

Sakoui, Anousha, and Tom Braithwaite, "Debenhams Examines Refinancing," *Financial Times,* January 23, 2009, p. 19.

Smith, Alison, "Earl's Style Is Wearing Well As Debenhams Is Back in Fashion," *Financial Times,* July 23, 2002, p. 22.

Smith, Peter, "Now Templeman Works His Retail Magic at Debenhams," *Financial Times,* August 2, 2004, p. 21.

Sullivan, Ruth, "Debenhams Boss Is Hard Act to Follow," *Financial Times,* September 14, 2000.

"A Tale of Two Retailers," *Economist,* April 29, 2006, p. 61.

Vitorovich, Lilly, "Debenhams to Relist in London with Aim of Raising $1.25 Billion," *Wall Street Journal Europe,* April 21, 2005, p. 17.

DESERET MANAGEMENT CORPORATION

Deseret Management Corporation

60 East South Temple, Suite 575
Salt Lake City, Utah 84111-1016
U.S.A.
Telephone: (801) 538-0651
Fax: (801) 538-0655
Web site: http://www.deseretmanagement.com

Private Company
Incorporated: 1966
Employees: 4,000
Sales: $1.2 billion (2007 est.)
NAICS: 551112 Offices of Other Holding Companies

■ ■ ■

Deseret Management Corporation (DMC) is a Salt Lake City, Utah-based holding company that houses for-profit operating companies owned by The Church of Jesus Christ of Latter-day Saints (LDS), commonly known as the Mormons, which receives all profits of DMC. The independently run operating companies, each maintaining their own board of directors, include Beneficial Financial Group, Bonneville International Corporation, Deseret Book Company, Deseret News Publishing Company, Hawaii Reserves Inc., Temple Square Hospitality Corporation, and Zions Securities Corporation. The oldest of the operating companies is Deseret News Publishing Company, publisher of the Salt Lake City daily newspaper the *Deseret Morning News,* as well as *Mormon Times* and the weekly *Church Times.* Long known as Beneficial Life Insurance Company, Beneficial offers a variety of financial services

and products in addition to life insurance. Bonneville is Deseret's media company, the owner and operator of a Salt Lake City television station, and radio stations in Salt Lake City, Chicago, Cincinnati, Los Angeles, Phoenix, Seattle, St. Louis, and Washington, D.C.

Other assets include advertising agency Bonneville Communications, and Bonneville Satellite Company, provider of domestic and international satellite services through a Salt Lake City teleport facility. Deseret Book Company includes two publishing units, Deseret Book Publishing and Covenant Communications, as well as two retail units, Deseret Book Retail and Seagull Book & Tape. It also operates Excel Film, which produces and distributes family-oriented movies consistent with a Mormon viewpoint. Another DMC company, Hawaii Reserves, Inc., manages Mormon-owned commercial and residential properties in Oahu, Hawaii. Temple Square is a Salt Lake City hospitality business, handling receptions, dinners, and other events at two venues. Finally, Zions Securities is a real estate company, primarily involved in the management of about 1.75 million square feet of office space and more than 1,100 apartment units in Salt Lake City, as well as properties located in several other states. DMC has been headed by Chief Executive Officer Rodney H. Brady since 1996.

FORMATION OF DESERET MANAGEMENT: 1966

"We belong to a church that believes in work," said Mormon member Donna Marriott, the wife of J. Willard Marriott Jr., hotel magnate, in a 1991 interview with the *Arizona Daily Star.* From the time Brigham

COMPANY PERSPECTIVES

Deseret Management Corporation (DMC) is a corporate holding company whose purpose is to oversee the commercial companies affiliated with The Church of Jesus Christ of Latter-day Saints and to provide appropriate services to its subsidiaries and to its ownership.

Young and his followers settled in the Great Salt Lake Valley in 1847, the Mormons proved industrious. Indicative of this attitude was the word *Deseret* as the name of their provisional state. Drawn from the Book of Mormon, Deseret meant "land of the honeybee." The beehive became an apt symbol for the Mormons because it embodied such traits as industry, thrift, self-reliance, and perseverance. The beehive would also become the centerpiece of the Utah State Seal and the state flag. Deseret would also be applied to many of the businesses established by LDS, and was a natural choice for a name when the church decided in 1966 to form a holding company to house many of its businesses, resulting in Deseret Management Corporation.

In the 1800s a large number of Christian sects in the United States grew out of mainstream Christianity, but only a few of these stood the test of time: Christian Science, Jehovah's Witnesses, Seventh-Day Adventists, and The Church of Jesus Christ of Latter-day Saints. LDS was founded in Ohio in the 1830s by Joseph Smith Jr. Because of financial reasons he and his followers moved to Missouri, but due to religious persecution they were forced to move again to Nauvoo, Illinois, where Smith was assassinated in 1844. The new head of the church, Brigham Young, then led the Mormons on a 1,300-mile journey that ended in the Great Salt Lake Valley, a place so desolate that he believed his people would finally be free of persecution. Immediately they began creating a community and economy, an experience that would make LDS very comfortable with business. In fact, many of the church's future leaders would first enjoy successful business careers. Although they were seemingly isolated in Utah, the area's economy would soon be stimulated by the California gold rush of 1849, which brought miners through the territory, many of whom elected to stay rather than continue on to the gold fields. Twenty years later, the building of the transcontinental railroad, the two ends of which met at Promontory Summit, Utah, provided a second economic stimulus.

DESERET NEWS BEGINS PUBLISHING: 1850

The oldest Deseret Management asset, the *Deseret News* was first published in June 1850, edited by Willard Richards. It was the first newspaper established between the Missouri River and San Francisco. A weekly, it was initially intended to serve as the voice of the State of Deseret and the church. Early on, lack of paper was a serious problem. It cost far too much to have paper shipped from St. Louis, requiring that the Mormons create their own paper industry. An English convert and trained papermaker was brought to Utah and the people were encouraged to donate rags for his use. Without the proper equipment, the resulting product was poor, however. A paper machine was imported, and in 1860 a state-of-the-art paper mill was acquired to assure the newspaper of a ready supply of paper.

In 1851 *Deseret News* adopted a larger size and came out twice a month. Three years later it reverted to a weekly but remained the same size, and in 1855 became an eight-page quarto. A semiweekly version was introduced in 1865, followed two years later by a daily called the *Deseret Evening News.* For a time, all the daily, semiweekly, and weekly versions coexisted. The *Deseret News* name was not adopted until 1920. Two years later the first Sunday edition was published.

Also in the 1800s Deseret Book Company took shape. The company traced its origins to 1886 when George Q. Cannon, an elder, established George Q. Cannon and Sons Company in Salt Lake City to publish and retail books as well as publish a magazine he started 20 years earlier, the *Juvenile Instructor* (printed on the *Deseret News* press), a publication he hoped would provide a wholesome alternative to the "cheap novels" that he believed were having a "pernicious influence" on young people. Shortly before his death in 1900, Cannon sold the business to *Deseret News* and it was renamed Deseret News Bookstore. The *Juvenile Instructor* was sold to the Deseret Sunday School Union, an organization established by Cannon to help educate young people on the LDS faith that also operated a bookstore. In 1919 Deseret News Bookstore and Deseret Sunday School Union bookstore were merged and the combination was named Deseret Book Company. A year later the two bookstores were closed and the operations consolidated in a single location. Although *Deseret News* owned 70 percent of the business, the Deseret Sunday School Union managed the bookstore until 1932. At that point Deseret Book was incorporated as a for-profit company. In 1948 *Deseret News* bought the remaining interest, making Deseret Book a subsidiary, a relationship that continued until 1966 when both became subsidiaries of DMC.

KEY DATES

1850: *Deseret News* begins publication.

1900: *Deseret News* acquires bookstore, renamed Deseret Book Company.

1905: Beneficial Life Insurance Company is founded.

1922: Zions Securities Corporation and KZN radio station are founded.

1949: KSL Television is established.

1952: *Deseret News* and *Salt Lake Tribune* create joint operating agreement.

1964: Bonneville International Corporation is formed.

1966: Deseret Management Company is established as holding company.

1975: Bonneville Communications is started.

1985: Zions Securities divests Hawaii land holdings.

1993: Hawaii Reserves, Inc., is established.

1999: Bookcraft, Inc., is acquired.

2003: *Deseret News* converts to morning publication.

2006: Covenant Communications and Seagull Book & Tape are acquired.

2008: Los Angeles radio station KSWD-FM is acquired.

BENEFICIAL LIFE INSURANCE: 1905

Other businesses that became part of DMC also took shape in the early decades of the 1900s. Beneficial Life Insurance Company was established in 1905 to aid widows and orphans at the behest of Church President Heber J. Grant, who had lost his father as a child and knew firsthand the travails such people endured. He served as president of the company for the first 27 years. Also during Grant's tenure as church president, real estate company Zions Securities Corporation was formed in 1922 to manage some properties that the church had acquired, including land in Hawaii, where LDS missionaries had been visiting since 1850. Zions would acquire additional properties in Hawaii, divesting them in 1985. Hawaii Reserves, Inc., would then be formed in 1993 to succeed Zions as the manager of the church's Hawaii properties.

Through *Deseret News,* LDS also became involved in radio. In 1922 the company established one of the United States' first radio stations, KZN, operating out of a tin shack erected atop the Deseret News Building. The first broadcast featured church President Grant

speaking. In 1924 the radio station became a separate company and a year later changed its call letters to KSL, referring to Salt Lake. KSL broadcast its performance of the Mormon Tabernacle Choir in July 1929, establishing a weekly tradition that would carry into the next century. KSL launched Utah's first FM radio station shortly after the end of World War II, and in 1949 KSL Television began broadcasting.

In 1964 KSL expanded beyond Salt Lake City, acquiring the KIRO television and radio stations in Seattle. A few months later a new company was formed to hold the church's media assets, Bonneville International Corporation. (The prehistoric body of water that created the Great Salt Lake Valley was called Lake Bonneville, named after the army captain who first surveyed the area in 1836.) In the meantime, Deseret Book had also become involved in film production in 1947, forming Deseret Film Productions. This company was mostly used to record LDS General Conference talks, a task that in the 1950s was taken over by KSL-TV, which began covering General Conferences, and Deseret Film Production was phased out.

NEWSPAPERS SHARE EXPENSES: 1952

Other postwar changes were in store for *Deseret News,* which was struggling financially, as was the *Salt Lake Tribune* and the *Salt Lake Telegram,* which was also owned by the *Tribune.* In 1952 *Deseret News* and the *Tribune* entered into a joint operating agreement. While the two publications maintained editorial independence, they shared the cost of printing, advertising, and circulation, which would be handled by Newspaper Agency Corp., 50 percent-owned by both papers. *Deseret News* discontinued its Sunday editions, instead delivering the *Sunday Tribune* to its readers for several years. *Deseret News* also acquired the *Salt Lake Telegram* from the *Tribune,* easing competition in the afternoon market, and well into the 1960s the newspaper was printed under the *Deseret News and Salt Lake Telegram* nameplate.

All the enterprises that were brought together under the DMC umbrella in 1966 continued to operate independently. In that same year, Bonneville completed its first acquisition since being formed two years earlier, purchasing a New York City FM radio station broadcasting from the Empire State Building, WMXV. Also in the 1960s Bonneville added KBIG-FM in Los Angeles and KMBZ-AM and KLTH-FM in Kansas City, and created a Washington News Bureau to provide its media properties with content related to government and politics. In 1975 the company formed Bonneville Communications, which was responsible for advertising services related to domestic and international broadcasts of General Conferences and the performances of the Mormon Tabernacle Choir. Additional media properties were also acquired in the 1970s: KOIT-FM and KOIT-AM in San Francisco, and sister Dallas stations KZPS-AM and KZPS-FM. Other stations would later be added in Chicago and Phoenix. Deseret Book Company, in the meantime, began publishing LDS fiction in 1979, after years of focusing on commentary and inspirational titles by church leaders.

Chief Executive Officer Rodney H. Brady, who had served for the previous nine years as president and CEO of Bonneville International, took charge of DMC in 1996. A Utah native and graduate of the University of Utah, from which he received a bachelor's degree in accounting and a master's of business administration, Brady was a man of inherent ambition and varied background. After a church-mandated missionary stint to the United Kingdom in the early 1950s he earned a doctorate in business administration from Harvard University, followed by three years serving in the U.S. Air Force. He then became partners with one of his Harvard professors and started a management consulting firm, working for *Fortune* 500 firms. In the early 1970s he served in the public sector, joining the Nixon administration as an assistant secretary for administration and management for the U.S. Department of Health, Education and Welfare. He next served as a top executive at a pharmaceutical firm and in 1978 fulfilled a longtime goal of running a college, becoming president of Weber State in Ogden, Utah, a post he held until joining Bonneville.

Under Brady's stewardship of DMC, the operating companies continued to grow in their own directions. Before he left Bonneville he sold the Seattle television station, and over the next few years the company was reshaped further, mostly due to the 1996 Telecommunications Act that increased the number of radio stations a company could own in a market from four (two AM and two FM stations) to eight. Bonneville elected to concentrate its radio holdings and divested its holdings in Dallas, Kansas City, Phoenix, New York, and Seattle. By 1998 the reconfigured portfolio included three radio stations in Chicago; four in San Francisco; three in Washington, D.C., and another three in nearby Arlington, Virginia; and single stations in Los Angeles and St. George, Utah. In 1999 Deseret Book Company made news of its own, acquiring Bookcraft, Inc., an independently owned LDS book publisher, founded in 1942. The result was a behemoth of the LDS publishing world, one that would grow larger in 2000 with the addition of new and former imprints to increase further the number and variety of titles the company had to offer.

DESERET NEWS BECOMES MORNING PAPER: 2003

Early in the new century *Deseret News* and the *Tribune* fell out over the terms of their half-century-old joint operating agreement. Long owned by the Kearns family and then the McCarthy family, the *Tribune* became a subsidiary of Tele-Communications Inc. in 1997, and two years later it was acquired by AT&T Corp. Under that owner, the morning paper enjoyed a much higher circulation than the *Deseret News*. The *Deseret News* not only attempted to acquire control of Newspaper Agency Corp., which managed the joint operating agreement, but it also was eager to switch from afternoon to morning publication. Resolution to the conflict began to emerge in early 2001 when MediaNews Group Inc. completed the $200 million purchase of the *Tribune*. Under the conditions of the joint operating agreement *Deseret News* had the right to veto any *Tribune* ownership, and the two parties worked out an agreement that allowed *Deseret News* to switch to morning publication if it paid the equipment costs associated with the conversion. In 2003 the change to the mornings was made and the newspaper began publishing under the name the *Deseret Morning News*.

Deseret Book named its first woman chief executive, Sheri L. Dew, in 2002. Under her leadership the company expanded its operations in 2004 with the acquisition of Excel Entertainment Group, a distributor of LDS-oriented films. The company started out in 1995 as a music distributor, but enjoyed greater success when it began distributing films in 2000. With the backing of Deseret Books, Excel expected to significantly strengthen its film business. Deseret Books grew further in late 2006 when it acquired publisher Covenant Communications and sister bookstore company Seagull Book & Tape, both of which would be operated as independent enterprises.

Bonneville International also made some moves. In 2006 it paid $77.5 million for a Phoenix radio station, KKFR-FM. A year later it traded three FM radio stations in San Francisco for four radio stations in Cincinnati and three Seattle stations owned by Entercom Communications. In 2008 KSWD-FM in the Los Angeles market was acquired as well at a cost of $137.5 million.

Ed Dinger

PRINCIPAL SUBSIDIARIES

Beneficial Financial Group; Bonneville International Corporation; Deseret Book Company; Deseret News Publishing Company; Hawaii Reserves Inc.; Temple

Square Hospitality Corporation; Zions Securities Corporation.

PRINCIPAL COMPETITORS

Clear Channel Communications, Inc.; Salt Lake Tribune; Thomas Nelson, Inc.

FURTHER READING

"Business Important in Mormon Past, Present Church Leadership Follows Commercial Careers," *Arizona Daily Star,* June 30, 1991, p. 10A.

DeMoss, Jeff, "Salt Lake City Deal Pairs Religious Media Provider, Distributor," *Ogden (Utah) Standard-Examiner,* November 16, 2004.

Goddard, Connie, "Deseret: Growing with the Mormons," *Publishers Weekly,* November 15, 1991, p. 48.

Kratz, Gregory P., "Meeting Every Goal," *Deseret News,* April 1, 2001, p. M1.

Lindsey, Robert, "The Mormons; Growth, Prosperity and Controversy," *New York Times,* January 12, 1986, p. A19.

McCann, Sheila R., "Salt Lake City Newspapers Seek Appropriate Cooperative Solutions," *Salt Lake Tribune,* October 30, 2000.

Moses, Lucia, "Shaky Peace in Salt Lake City," *Editor & Publisher,* January 8, 2001, p. 12.

Nii, Jenifer K., "Deseret Book Buys 2 Top Competitors," *Deseret Morning News,* December 29, 2006, p. A01.

"Planning for the Future Boom," *Nation's Business,* June 1975, p. 53.

DXP Enterprises, Inc.

———————— ■ ————————

7272 Pinemont
Houston, Texas 77040
U.S.A.
Telephone: (713) 996-4700
Fax: (713) 996-4701
Web site: http://www.dxpe.com

Public Company
Incorporated: 1913 as Southern Engine and Pump Co.
Employees: 1,594
Sales: $543.2 million (2008)
Stock Exchanges: NASDAQ
Ticker Symbol: DXPE
NAICS: 423830 Industrial Machinery and Equipment
    Merchant Wholesalers

■ ■ ■

Houston, Texas-based DXP Enterprises, Inc., is a distributor that divides its business between two segments: MRO (maintenance, repair, and operating) products and Electrical Contractor. The MRO segment serves its customers as a single source for fluid handling equipment, power transmission equipment, bearing, general mill, safety supply, and electrical products. Additional services provided include system design, fabrication, installation, repair, and maintenance. DXP also offers its SmartSource integrated supply program, on an outsource basis taking full or partial responsibility for a customers' purchasing, accounting, and onsite warehousing of MRO products. Industries served include General Manufacturing, Oil and Gas, Petrochemical, Mining,

Food and Beverage, Pulp and Paper, Construction, Service and Repair, Wood Products, Chemical, and Municipal. The Electrical Contractor segment distributes such electrical products as wire conduit, wiring devices, electrical fittings and boxes, wire nuts, fans and fuses, switch gear, tape, lugs, signaling devices, and batteries. Warehousing and sales are handled at a facility located in Memphis, Tennessee. All told, DXP serves more than 40,000 customers in 36 states and one Canadian province. DXP is a public company listed on the NASDAQ. Longtime Chairman and Chief Executive Officer David R. Little owns 35.7 percent of the company, either personally or through a family trust.

EARLY 20TH-CENTURY ORIGINS

The roots of DXP reach back to 1908 when Charles A. Leavens formed a company in Houston to provide irrigation pumps for growing cotton and to service the cotton gins used for textile production. In 1913 the business was incorporated as Southern Engine and Pump Co. (SEPCO). Over the years the company expanded the products it sold and serviced, especially industrial pumps and gas turbine compressors, and moved beyond cotton to serve other industries, such as the oil and gas sector which emerged as a major factor in Texas in the early decades of the 1900s.

In 1979 Southern Engine was rechartered as Sepco Industries, Inc. David Little gained a controlling interest in the company in 1986. He had started with the company in 1975 as a staff accountant and worked his way up through the ranks, serving as controller, vice-president of finance, and president. Under his leadership

COMPANY PERSPECTIVES

Over the years, we have strengthened our ability to support our customers by acquiring a diverse group of companies with a powerful corporate focus on product expertise, technical services and MROP supply chain management.

Sepco began adding products and services, mostly through acquisition. In 1987 Sepco bolstered its industrial pump business by acquiring Shoreline Supply Company, which expanded the company's footprint in Texas, Louisiana, and New Mexico. Bearing and transmission equipment were then added to the mix in the early 1990s with the purchase of T.L. Walker Bearing Co., Jackson's Industrial Supplies, and Cunningham Bearing Co.

REORGANIZATION OF SEPCO: 1994

By 1994 Sepco included five product divisions. The company was reorganized into three product groups with all subsidiaries operating under the SEPCO name. They included Sepco's Pump Group, which housed Southern Engine and Pump Co.; Sepco's Valve & Automating Group, the new name for the Wesco Equipment, Inc., subsidiary; and Sepco's Bearing & Power Transmission Group, which combined the operations of T.L. Walker Bearing Co., Jackson's Industrial Supplies, and Cunningham Bearing Co. Sepco then expanded into Arkansas in 1995 through the acquisition of Bayou Pump Company. A year later Austin Bearing Company was added, strengthening Sepco's position in the southern Texas power transmission distribution business.

After Sepco netted $2 million on sales of $111 million in 1995, Little decided to take the company public in 1996, accomplished through a reverse merger with a shell company, Newman Communications Corp., a former producer and distributor of books-on-tape and other audio products. Newman had been cofounded in 1981 by Hal Newman and his friends, married couple Grady Hesters and Linda Olsen, when audiobook distribution was a market in the early stages. Hal Newman handled distribution operations in Albuquerque, New Mexico, while his partners took care of the direct-mail operations where they lived in San Mateo, California. Filling a niche, the company grew quickly, becoming a major player in audiobook marketing and publishing. The company went public in 1984 and

was listed on the NASDAQ. Audiobook distribution proved to be a capital intensive business, a large amount of money needed to maintain high levels of inventory. In 1986 the company's lender became concerned about Newman's poor cash position and began putting pressure on the company. When a major account returned a large amount of fully refundable stock, Newman quickly found itself in a death spiral. The lender canceled credit lines while demanding payment on the balance. Layoffs were also demanded, which only served to prevent Newman from generating the sales needed to pay off the debt. Soon the company was being dismantled for liquidation. Hesters and Olsen would acquire some of those assets and have much better luck with a second audio company they founded, The Audio Partners, Inc.

NASDAQ LISTING: 1997

A decade after the demise of Newman, the shell of its public company remained. Little learned of its existence through a Dallas financial firm, Halter Financial Group, headed by financier Tim Halter. To engineer the reverse merger and take Sepco public, a new parent company called Index Inc. was created. Index then acquired Newman and changed its name to DXP Enterprises, Inc. Initially listed on the NASDAQ bulletin board, DXP moved to the NASDAQ Small Cap Market in the summer of 1997. Having saved on the cost of conducting an initial public offering (IPO) of stock, DXP was still able to raise funds through a secondary stock offering as well as use its public stock as currency for further acquisitions.

DXP completed a pair of acquisitions in 1997, paying $5.2 million in cash and stock and assuming $7.7 million in debt and liabilities for Pelican State Supply Co. Inc. and Strategic Supply Inc. The moves not only opened up territories, but added safety and general mill product lines. Based in Baton Rouge, Louisiana, Pelican State added $14 million in revenues and took DXP into the Baton Rouge market. A subsidiary of Strategic Distribution, Strategic Supply brought with it about $50 million in annual sales as well as seven new states and 24 cities for DXP, and the rudiments of what would become the SmartSource integrated supply program. Two more acquisitions followed in 1998. In February, San Antonio-based Tri-Electric Supply, an electrical supply distributor, was added at a total cost of about $7.8 million. Not only did Tri-Electric add $16 million in revenues, it laid the foundation for DXP's Electrical Contractor segment, providing an excellent complement to MRO business. Later in the year, DXP added to the new segment by purchasing virtually all of the assets of Memphis, Tennessee-based Lucky Electric & Supply,

KEY DATES

1908: Company is founded in Houston by Charles A. Leavens.
1913: Business is incorporated as Southern Engine and Pump Co.
1979: Company recharters as Sepco Industries, Inc.
1986: David R. Little gains majority control.
1996: Company goes public as DXP Enterprises, Inc., in a reverse merger.
1998: Electrical contractor segment is added.
1999: Valve and valve automation division is sold.
2001: Tri-Electric is sold.
2007: DXP acquires Precision Industries, Inc.

Inc., an electrical supply wholesaler. Also in 1998 DXP acquired most of the assets of M.W. Smith Equipment, Inc., a Longview, Texas-based pump and compressor specialist. As a result of these acquisitions, DXP increased annual revenues to $203.44 million in 1998 and net income to $2.9 million.

SALE OF VALVE ASSETS: 1999

Rapid growth did not come without complications, however. Integrating the technologies of acquisitions with the corporate infrastructure proved especially nettlesome, leading DXP to develop a team to visit potential acquisitions and anticipate any problems with integrating systems and processes. Work began on consolidating the various operating systems and DXP also decided it needed to refine its business model, and as a result in 1999 it divested its valve and valve automation division. Not only did this sale erode total revenues, DXP had to contend with the impact of falling oil prices which suppressed sales to oil and gas customers. As a result, revenues decreased to $179.9 million in 1999 and the company recorded a loss of $118,000.

In response to business conditions, DXP in 2000 consolidated its warehouse and customer service functions in Houston. DXP also curtailed its acquisition strategy, focusing instead on internal growth. In other moves, the company opened a Houston distribution center to serve as its Ballistic Distribution Center, and in May 2000 DXP launched an Internet business component, which initially offered general mill and bearing power transmission equipment.

Although the oil and gas industry showed improvement in 2000, DXP's revenues continued to slide to

$182.6 million and the company lost a further $7.45 million. A slowing economy hurt the company in 2001, forcing further consolidation. Tri-Electric was sold, due to what the company called inconsistencies in the target market, as well as a general decline in the construction business for electrical contractors. While revenues continued to fall, to $174.3 million in 2001, DXP was able to return to profitability, netting $929,000 in 2001.

DXP finally consolidated its operating systems in 2002, bringing together five systems into just one operating and financial system used by all locations. The savings helped the company to remain profitable. Although a poor economy continued to cripple business, as sales fell another 15.1 percent to $148.1 million, DXP was able to post net income of $1.62 million in 2002. Increased demand for products used in offshore energy production helped to slightly improve revenues in 2003. For the year, DXP netted $2 million on total revenues of $150.7 million. Business continued to pick up in 2004, when DXP was also able to once again pursue external growth, acquiring James S. Kone and Company, a move that opened up the Texas panhandle to DXP. Revenues for the year improved to $160.6 million and net income increased to $2.78 million.

DXP continued its momentum in 2005, when it expanded its presence in the Rocky Mountain region with the acquisition of Rocky Mountain Compressor, Inc. In August 2005, DXP added Houston-based PMI, a pump remanufacturer, the addition of which allowed DXP to hasten delivery of certain pumps to its customers. At the end of the year, DXP also acquired R.A. Mueller, Inc., a Cincinnati, Ohio-based fluid transfer, mixing, and metering company doing business in Ohio, Indiana, Kentucky, and West Virginia. These acquisitions, in addition to better business conditions in oil and gas and other industries, helped drive revenues to $185.4 million and net income to $5.5 million in 2005.

YEAR OF STRONG GROWTH: 2006

Growth, both internal and external, continued in 2006. The company more than doubled its Houston fabrication facility in order to increase its ability to offer pumps and pump packages. DXP also purchased a pair of west Texas companies, Production Pump and Machine Tech, pumping equipment companies that served oilfield, pipeline, and municipalities. Later in the year, Odessa, Texas-based Safety International was acquired, bolstering DXP's safety products business in the Texas panhandle area as well as safety and environmental consulting and training services. Also in October 2006, DXP purchased Houston-based Gulf Coast Torch and Regulator, a full-service welding supplies distributor. A month later, DXP added to its safety products business serving the energy and mining sectors by acquiring Farmington, New Mexico-based Safety Alliance. These additions along with improved economic conditions and escalating energy prices, resulted in a 51 percent surge in revenues for DXP in 2006, when the company recorded sales of $279.8 million and net income of $11.9 million.

The upward trend continued in 2007 for DXP, which took advantage of the good conditions to complete several more acquisitions. In May 2007 it paid $10 million in cash for Delta Process Equipment, Inc., a Denham Springs, Louisiana-based supplier of industrial and municipal pump equipment, serving markets in Louisiana, Florida, and Tennessee. Later in 2007 DXP paid $106 million in cash for Precision Industries, Inc., an Omaha, Nebraska, family-owned business that brought with it $250 million in annual revenues, in a single stroke essentially doubling DXP in size. A national industrial distributor, Precision offered abrasives and cutting tools, bearings, power transmission, electrical products, fasteners, fluid power, hand and power tools, janitorial products, linear products, lubrication, material handling, pipes, valves and fittings, rubber products, and safety products. Like DXP it had become something of a consolidator, completing several acquisitions since 2001. Also in the fall of 2007, DXP acquired Indian Fire & Safety, adding to its safety products and services to the New Mexico and Texas markets. With a partial contribution for the year from Precision Industries, DXP increased revenues to $444.5 million

and net income to $17.3 million in 2007. Sales in 2008 were well ahead of the pace set the year before, with revenues totaling $543.2 million through three quarters compared to $275.7 million the previous year. In September 2008 the board of directors approved a two-for-one stock split, indicative of a company poised for further growth.

Ed Dinger

PRINCIPAL SUBSIDIARIES

SEPCO Industries, Inc.; Pelican States Supply Company, Inc.; Global Pump Services and Supply, LLC; Precision Industries; Pump-PMI LLC; R.A. Mueller, Inc.

PRINCIPAL COMPETITORS

Industrial Distribution Group, Inc.; MSC/J&L Metalworking; MSC Industrial Direct Co., Inc.

FURTHER READING

Elliott, Alan R., "Katrina Recovery Effort Pumps New Business to Equipment Supplier," *Investor's Business Daily,* September 22, 2005, p. A06.

Harper, Doug, "Technical Difficulties," *Industrial Distribution,* March 1999, p. 102.

"Integrate Supply Drive Mergers," *Industrial Distribution,* July 1997, p. 16.

Murphy, Anne, "Company Profile: True Value," *Inc.,* January 1995.

Pybus, Kenneth R., "90-Year-Old Sepco Industries Goes Public via Merger," *Houston Business Journal,* September 2, 1996.

Eisai Co., Ltd.

4-6-10 Koishikawa, Bunkyo-ku
Tokyo, 112-8088
Japan
Telephone: (+81 813) 38175120
Fax: (+81 813) 38113077
Web site: http://www.eisai.co.jp

Public Company
Incorporated: 1955
Employees: 10,700
Sales: ¥734.3 billion ($6.67 billion) (2007)
Stock Exchanges: Tokyo
Ticker Symbol: 4523
NAICS: 325412 Pharmaceutical Preparation Manufacturing; 325411 Medicinal and Botanical Manufacturing

■ ■ ■

Eisai Co., Ltd., is one of Japan's leading pharmaceutical companies, and counts among the global top 25, with annual revenues of ¥734.3 billion ($6.67 billion) in 2007. A substantial proportion of these sales are generated by just two drugs, the Alzheimer's treatment Aricept (39.6 percent of sales), and the proton pump inhibitor AcipHex/Pariet (24 percent of sales). Both drugs, however, are approaching their patent expiration dates, in 2010 and 2013, respectively. With no advanced-stage drugs in its pipeline, Eisai has been acquiring drugs and drug companies, including MGI Pharmaceutical in 2008, and Morphotek in 2007, both based in the United States. In 2006 Eisai acquired four drugs already on the market from Ligand Pharmaceutical. These purchases underscore the importance of the U.S. market to Eisai's turnover profile. Since 2005 the United States has become Eisai's single largest market, contributing 45 percent of sales, compared to 43 percent from Japan. Since that year, however, Eisai has launched a new strategy targeting increased expansion into developing markets, especially into China and India. Eisai is listed on the Tokyo Stock Exchange but remains controlled by the founding Naito family. Haruo Naito, grandson of the company's founder, is its CEO and president.

FOUNDED AS A RESEARCH LABORATORY IN 1936

Eisai began as a research laboratory founded by Toyoji Naito and a number of partners in 1936. Called the Sakuragaoka Research Laboratory, the group's research initially turned toward developing vitamin preparations. In 1941 Naito led the creation of a new company, Nippon (or Nihon) Eisai Co., in order to launch the production of pharmaceuticals. For this, the company opened a factory in Honjo-machi, in Saitama Prefecture. By 1944 Eisai had absorbed the operations of the Sakuragaoka Research Laboratory.

Eisai changed its name to Eisai Co. Ltd. in 1955. By then, the company had completed a number of successful product launches. These included Neophyllin, a cardiotonic, introduced in 1950; Sampoon, a contraceptive, launched in 1951; and Methaphyllin, an ulcer treatment introduced in 1953. Nevertheless, the company's most important product introduction at this time was its Juvela, a vitamin E formulation made avail-

COMPANY PERSPECTIVES

Corporate Philosophy: We give first thought to patients and their families, and to increasing the benefits health care provides.

able in both tablet and injection form.

Vitamins and vitamin-related pharmaceuticals were to play a major role in Eisai's product development over the next decade. In fact, most of the group's successful formulations were derived from vitamins during the early years of its growth. Into the 1990s, vitamin-based preparations continued to account for some two-thirds of the group's sales.

Eisai's jump-start into the Japanese pharmaceutical market's big leagues nonetheless began during the 1960s, following the company's public offering in 1961. Backed by its listing on the Tokyo Stock Exchange, the group sought new product areas. In the early 1960s, for example, the company began producing bulk pharmaceuticals for the veterinary sector.

The arrival of Naito's son Yuji as company president in 1966 launched the next phase of Eisai's growth. One of the youngest players in Japan's pharmaceuticals sector, Eisai used its relative newcomer status to its advantage, launching an ambitious marketing-based expansion drive that caught its more established competitors off-guard. Part of the group's growth was accredited to its aggressive recruitment policies. These included paying higher-than-average wages in order to attract Japan's top talent; at the same time, the company instituted Western-style management training initiatives, including sending many of its employees to business schools in the United States. Yuji Naito's own son, Haruo, and the company's future CEO, earned an M.B.A. from the Kellogg School of Management at Northwestern University in 1974.

A new vitamin E–derived formulation, Juvela Nicotinate, was among the first to receive the benefits of Eisai's marketing initiatives. Launched in 1967, the product, a microcirculation activator, brought new success for the company. The launch was supported as well by the opening of the company's new manufacturing facility, Kawashima Industrial Park, in 1966.

OVERSEAS EXPANSION IN THE SEVENTIES

Into the 1970s, the company achieved several new sales successes. These included the launch of Sahne, a

vitamin-based cream, in 1973, and Neuquinon, a metabolic cardiotonic prescribed for mild congestive heart failure, also derived from vitamin E, launched in 1974. The following year, the company released a natural vitamin E tablet, Juvelux. By the end of the decade, Eisai's product line had expanded again, with the introduction of the vitamin B12-based formulation for treatment of peripheral neuropathies. Into the 1980s, Eisai's product line included Selbex, an ulcer treatment introduced in 1984, and a vitamin K2 formulation. The relative lack of depth of the company's product portfolio earned the company the perception that its growth was derived as much from its extensive marketing capacity as from its capabilities for developing new pharmaceuticals.

Nonetheless, Eisai's marketing investments had enabled the company to achieve strong growth, both within the Japanese market and abroad, through the 1970s and 1980s. The company's first move into foreign markets came in 1970, when Eisai launched a sales subsidiary for its prescription drugs in Indonesia. Three years later, Eisai added sales subsidiaries in Malaysia and the Philippines as well. Eisai then established a holding company for its Asian-region subsidiaries in Singapore in 1979. Other subsidiaries in the region followed, including Taiwan in 1987, Thailand in 1989, and Hong Kong in 1991. This expansion was accompanied by the opening of a production facility, in Bogor, Indonesia, completed in 1987.

By then, the company had dipped its toe into the U.S. market as well, opening a sales subsidiary in California in 1981. Toward the end of the decade, Eisai's attention turned to Europe. The company set up its first subsidiary in that market in London in 1988, followed by the creation of a subsidiary in Germany one year later. Through the 1990s, Eisai established operations in most of the major European markets, including France, Italy, the Netherlands, Spain, and Switzerland.

Despite this international expansion, Japan remained Eisai's dominant market by far, accounting for more than 90 percent of its revenues in the early 1980s. While the launch of Selbex in 1984, and then the allergy treatment Azeptin in 1986, helped the company maintain its growth through the decade and even claim a place among the top five drug companies in Japan by the 1990s, Eisai's portfolio remained, in the words of one analyst, "unimpressive." Into the 1990s the company's drug portfolio was increasingly viewed as aging and lacking innovation.

Eisai had been taking steps both to increase its industrial strength while expanding its research capacity in the hope of developing new drug formulations. The

KEY DATES

1936: Toyoji Naito founds the Sakuragaoka Research Laboratory in Japan.
1941: Nippon Eisai Co. is founded as a pharmaceutical production company, which takes over the Sakuragaoka laboratory in 1944.
1955: The company adopts the name Eisai Co., Ltd.
1981: Eisai enters the United States with a sales subsidiary in California.
1987: Company establishes a research facility in Boston.
1997: Two blockbuster drugs, Aricept and Pariet, are launched.
2006: Four existing drugs are acquired from Ligand Pharmaceuticals.
2007: Morphotek, a biopharmaceutical company based in Pennsylvania, is acquired.
2008: Eisai pays $3.9 billion to acquire MGI Pharmaceutical, based in Minnesota.

company added a new factory in Misato in 1981. This was followed by the launch of a chemicals production subsidiary, and the opening of a dedicated factory in Kashima in 1984. At the same time, Eisai expanded its main Kawashima Industrial Park complex with the addition of a third factory there in 1986.

RESEARCH FOCUS IN THE EIGHTIES

This manufacturing expansion was accompanied by an increase in research spending by the group. In 1980 the company established a new research laboratory in Kawashima. This laboratory was soon complemented by the opening of another research facility in Tsukuba in 1982.

Leading this new research investment drive was Haruo Naito, soon to take over the company's CEO position in 1988. In the mid-1980s, Naito had been looking to establish a research and development (R&D) facility for the company in Europe. In 1986, however, Naito was contacted by Yoshito Kishi, a Harvard University professor who had been developing a means to synthesize a powerful toxin found in the *Halichondria okadai* sea sponge, native to Japan's southern coast. Naito immediately recognized the importance of the

toxin as a potential cancer treatment, and agreed to establish a new research laboratory in Boston. The new facility opened the following year.

Eisai quickly expanded its U.S. operations, adding a production and sales subsidiary in New Jersey in 1988. In 1992 that state became the home of a new research laboratory, as well as the group's U.S. headquarters, established as Eisai Corporation of North America. In the meantime, Eisai had made good on its promise to form a research base in Europe, opening a laboratory in London in 1992. At the same time, Eisai continued to build its sales base, adding a subsidiary in Suzhou, China, in 1996, then entering South Korea the following year.

Eisai's investment in research began to pay off toward the middle of the 1990s, as a number of its formulations entered late-phase clinical trials. By 1995 the company had launched its vitamin K2-based osteoporosis treatment, Glakay (alternatively, Gla-K). Other drugs in the pipeline included Cepock, the first antibiotic developed in-house by Eisai, targeting resistant bacteria; and Imigran, for the treatment of migraines, which the company had been developing in partnership with Glaxo. The company's Boston laboratory had also been developing a new drug for the treatment of septic shock.

GLOBAL BESTSELLERS AT THE START OF THE 21ST CENTURY

While these drugs showed varying degrees of promise, Eisai's pipeline in the mid-1990s contained two additional molecules. The first was a proton pump inhibitor, called Pariet, which proved highly effective in killing the ulcer-causing *Helicobacter pylori* bacteria in the stomach, while having reduced side effects compared to similar treatments. In 1997 Eisai received approval to launch sales of Pariet to the Japanese market. By 1999 the company had also gained U.S. Food and Drug Administration approval to market the drug, which was renamed AcipHex for the U.S. market.

For this launch, Eisai formed a marketing partnership with industry heavyweight Pfizer Inc. As a result, AcipHex/Pariet quickly became a bestseller for Eisai, particularly after the company received approval to market the drug for other disorders, such as GERD (gastroesophageal reflux disease), in Europe and the United States. In that latter market, AcipHex also became the first drug approved as a seven-day treatment for *H. pylori* infections.

By then, the company was also riding the success of a second new drug, an acetylcholinesterase (AChE) inhibitor for the treatment of Alzheimer's disease, which the company marketed under the brand name Aricept. Once again, Eisai teamed up with Pfizer, ensuring the new drug's successful launch. The company initially rolled out the new drug to the German, U.K., and U.S. markets, but quickly expanded sales on a global basis. Eisai backed its success in the United States with the opening of a new production and R&D facility, located in North Carolina's Research Triangle Park, in 1997.

The success of AcipHex and especially Aricept helped transform Eisai into one of the world's top 25 pharmaceuticals companies. In the United States alone, the group's sales topped $1 billion, marking one of the fastest growth rates in the history of the pharmaceuticals industry there. Encouraged, the company spun off its nonpharmaceuticals operations, which included the production of pharmaceuticals machinery, as well as its food additives and chemicals division, refocusing itself as a pure-play pharmaceuticals company.

SEARCHING FOR NEW SUCCESS AFTER 2010

By the midpoint of the first decade of the 2000s, however, Eisai was forced to revise its growth strategy. Both Aricept and AcipHex were approaching their patent expiration dates: Aricept in 2010 and AcipHex in 2013. Yet these two drugs alone accounted for more than 65 percent of the group's total revenues. In the meantime, Eisai's pipeline had more or less stalled since the mid-1990s; the few company preparations that reached the market failed to repeat the blockbuster successes of Aricept and AcipHex.

In response, Eisai adopted a new strategy, called the "Dramatic Leap Plan," and began targeting acquisitions as a means of expanding its drug portfolio and pipeline. The company made a first step in 2006, buying four oncology drugs already on the market, including Ontak, Targretin, and Panretin, from Ligand Pharmaceuticals. The following year, the group made its first outright acquisition, paying $325 million to buy Exton, Pennsylvania-based Morphotek. That company had two highly promising anti-cancer drugs in the early clinical trial phase.

Eisai continued to seek further extensions to its portfolio, and in 2008 the company agreed to pay $3.9 billion to acquire oncology and critical-care specialist MGI Pharmaceutical, based in Minnesota. That company's portfolio included its strong-selling Aloxi, an anti-nausea chemotherapy treatment, as well as Dacogen, used to treat bone marrow diseases.

Although analysts remained skeptical that these purchases would be enough to cushion the loss of the Aricept and AcipHex patents, the analysts were more enthusiastic about another prong of Eisai's strategy: that of boosting its presence in developing markets, particularly in China and India. In the meantime, the company continued to roll out new drugs, such as Humira, a treatment for rheumatoid arthritis, launched in 2008. Eisai hoped to discover the next blockbuster drug to ensure its place among the global pharmaceutical giants well into the 21st century.

M. L. Cohen

PRINCIPAL SUBSIDIARIES

Eisai (Thailand) Marketing Co., Ltd.; Eisai Asia Regional Services Pte. Ltd. (Singapore); Eisai China Inc.; Eisai Clinical Research Singapore Pte. Ltd.; Eisai Corporation of North America (USA); Eisai Europe Ltd. (UK); Eisai Food & Chemicals Co., Ltd.; Eisai Inc. (USA); Eisai London Research Laboratories Ltd. (UK); Eisai Machinery U.S.A. Inc.; Eisai Manufacturing Ltd. (UK); Eisai Medical Research Inc. (USA); Eisai Pharmaceuticals India, Pte. Ltd.; Eisai Research Institute of Boston Inc. (USA); Eisai Taiwan Inc.; KAN Research Institute, Inc.; MGI PHARMA, Inc. (USA); Morphotek, Inc. (USA); PT Eisai Indonesia; Sanko Junyaku Co., Ltd.; Sannova Co., Ltd.

PRINCIPAL COMPETITORS

Takeda Pharmaceutical Company Ltd.; Ajinomoto Company Inc.; Teijin Ltd.; Astellas Pharma Inc.; Daiichi Sankyo Company Ltd.; Daito Corp.; Otsuka Pharmaceutical Company Ltd.; Chugai Pharmaceutical Company Ltd.

FURTHER READING

Ajima, Shinya, "Eisai to Acquire U.S. Bio Venture Morphotek for $325 Million," *Knight-Ridder/Tribune Business News*, March 22, 2007.

Breitstein, Joanna, "Eisai's New Leadership," *Pharmaceutical Executive*, May 2005, p. 72.

D'Silva, Jeetha, "Japan Pharmaceutical Eisai Plans Research, Manufacturing Hub in India," *Economic Times*, January 10, 2005.

Jack, Andrew, "Drug Groups Win Alzheimer's Appeal," *Financial Times*, May 2, 2008, p. 4.

"Japanese Drug Major Eisai Plans Production in India," *Economic Times*, February 4, 2007.

"Japanese Firm to Buy Bloomington, Minn.-based Marketer of Cancer Drugs," *Knight-Ridder/Tribune Business News*, December 11, 2007.

Kelly, Tim, and Deborah Orr, "Out of Pfizer's Shadow," *Forbes Global*, April 23, 2007, p. 28.

Koberstein, Wayne, "Eisai Rises in the West," *Pharmaceutical Executive*, February 2003, p. 36.

Prial, Dunstan, "Eisai Sees Hope for Breast Cancer Treatment in Lowly Sea Sponge," *Knight-Ridder/Tribune Business News*, December 20, 2005.

Evergreen Solar, Inc.

138 Bartlett Street
Marlboro, Massachusetts 01752
U.S.A.
Telephone: (508) 357-2221
Fax: (508) 357-0747
Web site: http://www.evergreensolar.com

Public Company
Incorporated: 1994
Employees: 400
Sales: $69.89 million (2007)
Stock Exchanges: NASDAQ
Ticker Symbol: ESLR
NAICS: 334413 Semiconductor and Related Device
    Manufacturing

■ ■ ■

Evergreen Solar, Inc., is a relatively small, but growing manufacturer of silicon-based solar panels. With headquarters in Marlboro, Massachusetts, a 2008-built plant in nearby Devens, and a joint-venture factory in Germany, the company's proprietary String Ribbon technology makes it one of the industry's leaders in the efficient consumption of polysilicon, a primary and often costly component of solar cells. Evergreen's highly automated process turns solid blocks of silicon into wafers, configures them into solar cells, then assembles the cells into flat panels, each of which weighs about 50 pounds, looks like a large storm window, and produces up to 200 watts of power. The company's solar systems are sold primarily in Germany and the United States.

STAKING OUT A NICHE

Evergreen Solar, Inc., was formed in Waltham, Massachusetts, in 1994 by Mark Farber (president and CEO), Richard G. Chleboski (chief financial officer), and Jack I. Hanoka (chief technology officer). The trio plotted their venture around a kitchen table the summer after losing their jobs in 1993 when Mobil Oil sold its solar division. By November they had secured some start-up funds from a private investor and soon set up shop in a cramped, former plumbing-supply garage, intent on mass manufacturing solar electric panels for residential, commercial, and industrial applications around the world.

At the time, the solar industry had been around for 25 years and still had not produced the technology necessary to make solar power commercially viable on a large scale, despite being dominated by giant corporations with deep pockets such as Mobil, Exxon, and Texas Instruments. Evergreen's founders were convinced that they had found the key to low-cost high-volume solar panel manufacturing. They licensed the so-called String Ribbon Technique from its inventor, Professor Emanuel Sachs of the Massachusetts Institute of Technology.

Unlike conventional methods of making silicon wafers, which involve sawing blocks of silicon into thin slices, Evergreen's proprietary process pulled two strings vertically through a shallow pool of molten silicon, causing the silicon to form a sheet, or ribbon, about as thick as a business card between the two strings. The ribbon solidified at room temperature, was cut into six-inch strips, or wafers, and turned into solar cells.

COMPANY PERSPECTIVES

Evergreen Solar, founded in 1994, develops, manufactures and sells solar power products, primarily solar panels, that provide reliable and environmentally clean electric power throughout the world. The three markets the Company serves are: wireless power, rural electrification and grid-connected applications. The Company expects to exploit its proprietary and patented technology to produce distinctive products, to reduce manufacturing costs through lower materials use and streamlined processes, and to manufacture internationally for global market penetration.

In December 1995, Evergreen won an award for its string-ribbon technology from the Swiss Academy of Engineering Sciences, garnering recognition for creating high quality crystalline silicon wafers without the cost and waste of sawing solid blocks. The process used 50 percent less silicon than conventional technology. In 1996, the company secured $5.6 million in private financing and a $1.5 million grant from the U.S. Department of Energy's Commercialization Ventures Program.

BECOMING A PLAYER

After two years of research and a successful six-month pilot program, Evergreen in March 1997 completed its first production line for manufacturing photovoltaic (solar electric) panels. The company started limited commercial production in the last quarter of 1997, and shipped its first batch of solar panels to supply electricity to 130 rural schoolhouses in Bolivia. For the year, Evergreen had won $3.2 million worth of new contracts, including a $1.37 million research grant from the federal government to work on thinner, wider, and more efficient silicon ribbons. The company ended 1997 with 42 employees, revenues of $100,000, and a net loss of $3.1 million.

With solar energy generally costing about three times more than conventional electricity from a city's power grid, government subsidies for solar energy companies and consumers were important for Evergreen and its 21 global competitors. In March 1998, a year after President Bill Clinton launched an initiative to add solar systems to one million commercial and residential roofs nationwide by 2010, local electric utility and solar energy companies in Massachusetts formulated plans to install solar systems on the roofs of 100,000 buildings in New England by 2010. Evergreen ended 1998 with a $2.5 million net loss.

In December 1999, Evergreen inked a five-year strategic marketing and distribution agreement with Kawasaki Heavy Industries, Inc. The deal made Kawasaki the exclusive marketing partner in Japan, the largest and most heavily subsidized solar power market in the world at the time. Kawasaki also acquired an 11.5 percent stake in Evergreen with a $5 million equity investment. With product revenues still only accounting for 8.2 percent of total revenues for the year, Evergreen finished 1999 with a $2.9 million net loss.

GAINING MOMENTUM IN THE 21ST CENTURY

The year 2000 was a big one for Evergreen on the financial front. In February, the company obtained $18 million in its fourth round of private equity financing. The company also announced plans to relocate to a new plant in nearby Marlboro, Massachusetts, in order to ramp up full-scale commercial production of its solar energy products. On November 2, Evergreen became part of a wave of new energy technology companies entering the market with its own initial public offering (IPO) on the NASDAQ of three million shares of stock priced at $14 apiece. The stock rose 36 percent and closed the day at $19. The offering raised $42 million in gross proceeds for the company.

As reported by Evergreen in March 2001, annual product revenues for fiscal 2000 more than doubled to $419,000. Research revenues shrank from $2.1 million to $1.8 million for the same period and the company's net loss grew to $5.2 million. In April 2001, Evergreen's new 56,000-square-foot manufacturing and headquarters facility in Marlboro began operating around-the-clock. In June, the company shipped its first new product that featured a wider, more efficient ribbon. December brought distribution agreements with Solar Century Holdings Ltd., a marketer and distributor of photovoltaic products in the United Kingdom, and with Hutton Communications for the U.S. market.

According to annual financial reports released in February 2002, the company's 2001 net loss soared to $12.5 million, but product revenues more than tripled to $1.5 million, mostly from sales to Germany, Japan, and other foreign markets. In October 2002, Evergreen secured a $3 million, three-year research grant from the U.S. Energy Department's National Renewable Energy Laboratory to improve solar cell manufacturing techniques. Also in the fall of 2002, after reaching highs over $20 since its IPO in 2000, Evergreen's share price dipped below $1.

KEY DATES

1994: A trio of former Mobil Solar Energy executives forms company to manufacture solar panels.

1997: Company's Waltham, Massachusetts, facility begins pilot production of solar panels.

1999: Evergreen breaks into Japanese market with marketing deal with Kawasaki Heavy Industries, Inc.

2000: Company goes public, raises $42 million in offering.

2001: Full production begins at new Marlboro, Massachusetts, manufacturing plant and headquarters.

2005: Evergreen forms EverQ in Europe with Germany's Q-Cells AG.

2006: Production begins at EverQ plant in Thalheim, Germany; EverQ adds third equal partner.

2007: EverQ plant in Germany expands.

2008: Devens plant opens in July; contractual backlog grows to almost $3 billion.

Evergreen's annual product revenues for 2002, reported in March 2003, again more than tripled to $5.3 million, but the company continued to lose about $1 million a month. In May 2003, Evergreen shareholders approved plans to raise $29.5 million of private-equity funding by selling 43.2 million shares of preferred stock to a group of institutional investors. The company used the proceeds for a second manufacturing line at its Marlboro facility, which enabled it to quadruple production capacity. December brought a change of leadership at the top. Richard M. Feldt became CEO, president, and director, and cofounder Mark Farber moved to the position of vice-president of marketing and business development.

PARTNERING ABROAD

Increased production volumes and selling activities resulted in continued growth of product revenues to $7.7 million in 2003, as reported in March 2004, but the net loss for the year reached $15.2 million. The company's revenue growth, however, continued to be hampered by limited manufacturing capacity. Like other solar system manufacturers at the time, Evergreen was benefiting from all-time high crude oil prices, a worldwide increase of government subsidies for solar

energy, and a concurrent shortage of solar products. Producers everywhere were selling everything they could make. In August 2004, with its future seeming to hinge on the ability to increase production enough to meet demand, Evergreen again raised funds for expansion by selling $18 million worth of stock to preferred shareholders.

In January 2005, Evergreen announced the formation of EverQ, a joint venture with Germany's Q-Cells AG, one of the world's largest producers of solar cells, to build a 30-megawatt solar panel manufacturing plant in Thalheim, Germany, near Berlin. Evergreen's annual financial report for 2004, released in February, showed net losses of $22.3 million on $23.5 million in revenue. In November 2005, Norway's Renewable Energy Corporation ASA (REC), the world's largest manufacturer of solar-grade silicon and multicrystalline wafers, became a 15 percent stakeholder in EverQ, with Evergreen retaining 64 percent and Q-Cells 21 percent. The transaction included a seven-year commitment from REC to supply solar-grade silicon to EverQ and Evergreen.

January 2006 brought great news for the solar industry, including Evergreen, although it was struggling to meet demand. California regulators approved the largest U.S. solar-power subsidy ever, a $2.5 billion ten-year initiative to install 3,000 megawatts of solar panels on the state's homes, businesses, farms, schools and public facilities. The company's 2005 financial results, posted in February 2006, showed product revenues nearly doubled to $43.6 million, while net losses shrank to $17.3 million. In April 2006, Evergreen's new EverQ manufacturing plant in Thalheim, Germany, began making volume shipments of finished solar modules to the company's ever increasing list of customers. In June, Evergreen, Q-Cells, and REC all became equal partners in EverQ. EverQ also announced new polysilicon supply agreements that called for the joint venture to substantially boost its solar panel production capacity.

BOOKING THE FUTURE

The big story of 2006 for Evergreen, however, actually began in November 2005, when the company signed a $70 million contract for solar panels with PowerLight Corp. The company followed with two more supply contracts in February 2006, one for $100 million with S.A.G. Solarstrom AG, and another for $88 million with Global Resource Options. March brought a $125 million agreement with Donauer Solartechnik, and a $200 million deal with SunEdison LLC was signed in

July. In October, Evergreen inked a four-year $100 million contract with Mainstream Energy LLC, registering its sixth large long-term agreement in a year's time, representing a total of almost $700 million in sales through 2011.

Evergreen's joint venture in Europe began showing dividends by the end of 2006, as annual revenues more than doubled to $103.1 million, according to February 2007 company figures. Construction of a second EverQ plant in Germany, with a capacity of 60 megawatts, was underway when Evergreen in February announced plans for a third factory. In April, the company said it would build a second Evergreen plant in the United States, a $150 million project funded in part with a $44 million financing package of state government grants, low-interest loans, and a low-cost, 30-year lease of state-owned property. In May, Evergreen raised $117 million to help finance the construction project in a public offering of 15 million shares priced at $8.25 each.

In June 2007, company officials announced that Devens, Massachusetts, had been chosen as the site of Evergreen's second U.S. manufacturing facility creating 350 new jobs, an amount that doubled the company's number of employees. August brought an expansion of annual manufacturing capacity at EverQ's flagship plant in Germany from 30 megawatts to 100 megawatts, and in October, plans to build an 80-megawatt EverQ plant in Bitterfeld-Wolfen, Germany were made public .

Financial results for the last quarter of 2007, reported in January 2008, showed the company making its first profit ever, a net income of $788,000 compared to a net loss of $3.7 million for the same quarter in 2006. However, annual financial results released in February showed only $58.3 million in revenues for 2007, a 43 percent decrease that the company attributed in part to not including EverQ revenues in its report. Royalty revenue and marketing and selling fees from EverQ in 2007 amounted to $11.5 million. February 2008 also saw the company raising over $150 million in a public offering of 16 million common shares at $9.50 apiece to finance ongoing manufacturing capacity expansion projects.

MAINTAINING THE MISSION

With first-phase construction still in progress, the company broke ground on an 80-megawatt expansion of its Devens facility in April 2008, and said it would hire 350 more employees. The move would double the plant's workforce to 700 and bring the total number of employees in Massachusetts to 1,000 by 2009. Evergreen's contractual backlog increased $1 billion in

May, when the company signed two long-term sales contracts for its Devens plant, a $750 million, five-year deal with German-based Ralos Vertriebs GmbH, and another pact with an unnamed U.S.-based installer. The news caused Evergreen stock to surge 23.5 percent to $11.23.

In June 2008, Evergreen announced plans to build a $35 million to $50 million parts plant in Midland, Michigan. The company also signed two long-term sales contracts for its U.S. plant worth $600 million with solar-products makers GroSolar and Wagner & Co. Solartechnik GmbH. The company raised another $325 million to finance construction projects with a sale of senior notes in July. Concurrent with the official opening of its Devens plant on July 16, Evergreen announced the biggest deal in the company's history, a $1.2 billion sales contract with Germany's IBC Solar AG. The agreement increased the company's contract backlog to $2.9 billion.

On September 16, shares plummeted nearly 28 percent to a three-year low of $4.56 after news broke that Evergreen would probably have to write off $39.5 million due to a complicated financial transaction with the freshly bankrupted Lehman Brothers Holdings Inc. With the signing in October of two more long-term sales contracts, one of them with a top-tier Japanese trading company, 100 percent of the Devens facility's 160 megawatts of annual manufacturing capacity was committed from 2010 and beyond.

Things went from bad to worse in October 2008 as the financial world was rocked by a global credit crisis and solar stocks plunged with the broader market on continued recession fears. Evergreen sued Lehman Brothers seeking to recover its losses, but a U.S. bankruptcy court denied the request in early November. Having traded between $2.92 and $18.85 over the past year, company stock hovered just above $2 in mid-November.

Despite being able to sell as many solar panels as production capabilities allowed well into the near future, it appeared in the fourth quarter of 2008 that Evergreen's all-out drive to expand manufacturing capacity to meet demand and attain profitability could be derailed by a general global financial meltdown. With the economies of the top solar markets of Germany, Japan, and the United States in recession, and downturns expected in consumer demand and government subsidies, Evergreen faced great challenges finding the capital required to stay the course. However, there was also the possibility that the company would be well positioned to benefit from new energy and environmental policies promised by newly elected President Barack Obama.

Ted Sylvester

PRINCIPAL SUBSIDIARIES

Evergreen Solar GmbH (Germany).

PRINCIPAL COMPETITORS

Energy Conversion Devices, Inc.; First Solar, Inc.; JA Solar Holdings Co., Ltd.; Kyocera Solar, Inc.; LDK Solar Co., Ltd.; Solarfun Power Holdings Co., Ltd.; SunPower Corporation; Trina Solar Limited.

FURTHER READING

Ailworth, Erin, "Evergreen Solar Opens New Production Facility in Devens; Company Also Snags $1.2b Pact, Its Biggest," *Boston Globe,* July 16, 2008, p. C1.

Bodor, Jim, "Evergreen Solar Sees Bright Future," *Worcester Telegram & Gazette,* October 9, 2000, p. E1.

———, "Solar Push Benefits Evergreen; Calif. Plan Creates Homeowner Incentives," *Worcester Telegram & Gazette,* August 11, 2004, p. E1.

"CEO Interview: Mark Farber—Evergreen Solar Inc. (ESLR)," *Wall Street Transcript,* January 15, 2001.

"CEO Interview: Richard Feldt—Evergreen Solar Inc. (ESLR)," *Wall Street Transcript,* September 27, 2004.

Dick, Amanda, "From Solar Cell to Solar Panel; Robots, Employees Team at New Plant," *Worcester Telegram & Gazette,* July 16, 2008, p. D2.

Esposito, Andi, "Module Demand Fuels Expansion at Evergreen," *Worcester Telegram & Gazette,* February 23, 2007, p. 9.

"Evergreen Solar (ESLR) Comments on Public Offering with Lehman (LEH) As Lead Underwriter," *StreetInsider.com,* September 15, 2008.

"Evergreen Solar Introduces New ES-A Series String Ribbon Solar Panels at InterSolar 2008 in Munich, Germany," *Science Letter,* July 8, 2008.

Fitzgerald, Jay, "Solar Co. Sues Lehman, Barclays," *Boston Herald,* October 22, 2008, p. 23.

Gage, Jack, "High Energy Stocks; Demand for Energy Has Made It the Hottest Industry on Wall Street," *Forbes,* June 16, 2008.

"German Q-Cells Raises Stake in EverQ to 33.3 Pct," *German News Digest,* June 6, 2006.

LaPedus, Mark, "Solar-Cell Fab Capacity Rising," *Electronic Engineering Times,* March 6, 2006, p. 12.

Luttrell, Martin, "Evergreen Solar Tied to Lehman; Bankrupt Company Underwrote Stock," *Worcester Telegram & Gazette,* September 16, 2008, p. D1.

Monahan, John J., "Have Sun, Will Electrify: Evergreen Opens Solar Panel Plant in Marlboro," *Worcester Telegram & Gazette,* May 24, 2001, p. A1.

"Richard Chleboski, Co-Founder, CFO of Evergreen Solar," *Corporate Financing Week,* April 8, 2005.

Senyak, Sierra, "Bright Ideas for Power; Marlboro Company Uses New Methods to Lower Costs of Solar Energy," *Sunday Telegram Worcester,* December 29, 2002, p. E1.

"Solar Stocks Mostly Lower; Evergreen Solar Bucks Trend," *AFX Asia,* May 22, 2008.

Syre, Steven, "A Case of Bad Timing," *Boston Globe,* February 7, 2008, p. E1.

Valigra, Lori, "Evergreen's Goal: Plugging in the Sun Start-Up Seeks to Tap into Vast Potential of Solar Energy Field," *Boston Globe,* January 18, 1998, p. C4.

Exactech, Inc.

---■---

2320 Northwest 66th Court
Gainesville, Florida 32653-1630
U.S.A.
Telephone: (352) 377-1140
Toll Free: (800) 392-2832
Fax: (352) 378-2617
Web site: http://www.exac.com

Public Company
Incorporated: 1985
Employees: 214
Sales: $124.2 million (2007)
Stock Exchanges: NASDAQ
Ticker Symbol: EXAC
NAICS: 339113 Surgical Appliance and Supplies
Manufacturing

■ ■ ■

Exactech, Inc., is a Gainesville, Florida, company that develops and manufactures orthopedic implant devices used to repair or replace hip, shoulder, and knee joints damaged by injury or disease. Exactech also offers bone cement and cement spacers, and makes the AcuDriver air-driven impact hand piece used to remove bone cement and failed prostheses. In addition, the company makes and markets biologic products for the healing and regeneration of bone and wound tissue; some of the products are produced by outside companies. Internationally, Exactech does business through subsidiaries in Canada, China, France, and the United Kingdom. Through a North Carolina-based subsidiary,

Altiva Corporation, Exactech is also involved in spinal implants and instrumentation. The company chairman and chief executive officer, William Petty, is a cofounder and a practicing orthopedic surgeon.

COMPANY FOUNDED: 1985

Exactech was founded in 1985 by William Petty, his wife Betty, and Gary J. Miller, a bioengineer. Both William Petty and Miller were members of the University of Florida College of Medicine faculty. After receiving his education from the University of Arkansas and completing his residency at the Mayo Clinic in Rochester, Minnesota, Petty joined the faculty at the University of Florida College of Medicine in 1975 while practicing as an orthopedic surgeon. In 1981 he became chairman of the Department of Orthopaedic Surgery at the school. Petty also served as a consultant for orthopedic companies. Over the years he became increasingly concerned about the rising cost of healthcare and the adverse impact it might have on the type of products he and his fellow orthopedic surgeons might have to treat patients. He and his wife, who had been an English major in college, decided to start a product development company for musculoskeletal treatments. From his work with orthopedic companies, he was convinced he could do better at running a medical device company, one that could use the input of professors and private practitioners to develop less expensive but higher quality products.

To be in charge of research and development, the Pettys recruited Gary Miller, an adjunct associate professor in the College of Veterinary Medicine's Small

COMPANY PERSPECTIVES

Founded in 1985 by an orthopaedic surgeon and a biomedical engineer, Exactech is committed to making every day *A Great Day in the O.R.*—for the surgeon, the operating room staff and above all, for the patient. It's the driving force behind everything we do.

Animal Surgical Sciences Division. Miller had enrolled at the University of Florida as a mechanical engineering major, specializing in machine design. His interests would change when he began working in the school's new biomechanics laboratory. Convinced that the human body was the ultimate machine, he switched to the biomechanics program, which was so new that Miller was able to essentially create his own curriculum. He then received a degree in biomechanics from the Massachusetts Institute of Technology, which was in the vanguard of the biomechanics field. He returned to the University of Florida to complete his doctorate in the field and become a professor at the school. Like William Petty, he too would serve as a consultant to orthopedic companies.

FIRST PRODUCT: NOVEMBER 1987

In November 1985 the Pettys and Miller incorporated Exactech in the state of Florida. William Petty served as chairman and chief executive officer, Betty Petty was secretary and treasurer of the corporation, and Miller was vice-president for research and development. Miller began designing the company's first orthopedic product, and in July 1986 he also joined William Petty at the Department of Orthopaedic Surgery, becoming an associate professor and director of research and biomechanics. Two years after incorporation, Exactech in November 1987 introduced its first product, a cemented hip implant system. A few years later, in June 1990 the company began marketing a porous-coated hip implant system that eliminated the cement. Instead, the coating on the prosthesis allowed bone to grow into the device to secure it in place.

After three years, Exactech was a profitable business and moved beyond development and marketing to begin handling manufacturing for itself. For 1991 sales totaled $2.4 million and net income was more than $300,000. Also in 1991, William Petty, who continued to head the Department of Orthopaedic Surgery, edited a book, *Total Joint Replacement*. In 1992 the company enjoyed

its first international sale. Sales improved to $3.72 million in 1992, $4.7 million in 1993, and $5.36 million in 1994, while net income never t pped $418,000. International sales were spurred in 1993 by the addition of a distributor in Korea.

Although it was a company focused mainly on hip repair or replacement, Exactech was making plans to expand its purview, hard at work on a total knee replacement system in collaboration with the Hospital for Special Surgery in New York City, as well as a team of physicians and biomechanists. In February 1995 the system, branded Optetrak, was introduced to the market. It was available with a cruciate ligament sparing femoral component or a posterior-stabilized femoral component, both of which came either cemented or porous coated. Sales of the knee system helped Exactech to increase revenues to $9.1 million and earnings to $830,000 in 1995.

COMPANY GOES PUBLIC: 1996

To raise capital for further growth, Exactech filed for an initial public offering (IPO) of stock in 1996. The offering was completed in June of that year, netting nearly $12.7 million for the company. Later in the year, Exactech received clearance from the U.S. Food and Drug Administration (FDA) to market a new hip product, the AuRA Total Hip System, which would not begin to have an impact on the balance sheet until the following year. Exactech also licensed technology in 1996 for a modular revision hip system, the development of which was soon launched. Through the sale of its available hip and knee products, Exactech grew sales to $13.8 million and net income to more than $1.5 million in 1996. International sales to eight countries (Argentina, Australia, Colombia, Greece, Italy, Korea, Spain, and Turkey) contributed about $2.1 million or 15.4 percent of revenues.

Revenues increased 28 percent to $17.65 million in 1997, due primarily to the knee implant products and the growing importance of international sales, which improved 44 percent to more than $3 million, compared to a 25 percent increase in domestic sales. The growth in hip product sales began to sag, however. The line needed to be updated and enhanced, but Exactech lacked the resources to simultaneously develop hip products and knee products.

Hence, Exactech was in the market for diversification, to add new products to generate more cash flow to fund expanded development efforts. It launched a new venture with the University of Florida Tissue Bank, Inc., to develop and market biologic bone repair material. In March 1998 the company introduced Opteform, a

KEY DATES

∎

1985: Company is founded.
1987: First product is introduced.
1992: First international sale is completed.
1996: Company is taken public.
1999: Exactech is named to *Forbes'* list of 200 Best Small Companies.
2006: Sales top $100 million.
2008: Altiva Corporation is acquired.

biologic bone grafting and repair material provided by Regeneration Technologies, Inc., a private company recently spun off by the Florida Tissue Bank. Later that same year Exactech diversified further, acquiring the AcuDriver assets from Synvasive Technologies for $375,000. The air-driven AcuDriver device helped surgeons performing implant surgery to save time and money by removing bone cement and failed prostheses with a quick, high-energy blow to a target spot. In other important developments in 1998, Exactech was granted ISO 9001 certification, allowing it to display the CE (Conformité Européene, or European Conformity) marking on products sold in Europe, and also received regulatory approval to sell its knee products in Japan.

HONORED AS A "BEST SMALL" COMPANY: 1999

The new products helped Exactech to increase sales to $24 million in 1998 and almost $33 million in 1999, and net income to $2.13 million in 1998 and $3.17 million in 1999. More important, money became available to upgrade the hip products. In the fall of 1999 Exactech began the full-scale marketing of the first component in an updated version of the hip implant system, the AcuMatch C-Series. The initial offering was the cemented femoral stem, which provided greater stability and lowered the risk of dislocation. The company was also recognized for its performance in 1999 by being named to *Forbes* magazine's 200 Best Small Companies list. A year later it would achieve the same honor for a second time.

More AcuMatch products received FDA clearance in 2000, including the acetabular component and modular femoral hip prosthesis. Later in the year Exactech reached an agreement with a German firm, aap Implantate AG, for the exclusive rights to distribute a number of implant products in the United States, including a hip compression screw system, a variety of

large- and small-cannulated screws, and a tibial nail sold under the Biorigid name. Also that year, Exactech signed a research agreement to work with Kentucky-based Focal Inc. on applying that company's surgical sealant, FocalSeal, to orthopedic surgical products.

Sales approached $42 million in 2000 and net income increased to $4.2 million. The international business continued to grow at a strong pace, and management believed that much of the company's future growth was linked to international sales, especially in Asia. "In many Asian cultures," William Petty told *Investor's Business Daily* in 2000, "having excellent knee flexion is important because there's a lot of squatting and sitting on the floor." The major obstacle to increasing sales in the market was the lack of qualified surgeons to implant Exactech products. As Asian countries began "to emphasize the importance of orthopedic medicine," Petty explained, "it will be a very attractive market." A major step in exploiting this opportunity came in 2001 when Exactech and InVigor Biotechnology created a Hong Kong–registered joint venture called Exactech Asia Ltd. to sell hip and knee products in China and Taiwan.

A number of other developments took place in 2001. The company began marketing a new modular hip stem in February, and in that same month gained the exclusive right to market Cemex bone cement in the United States. The company also strengthened its South America business by establishing a distributorship in Brazil. Revenues increased to $46.6 million in 2001 and $59.3 million in 2002, when Exactech also began distributing the Link hip and knee systems and surgical instruments of Germany's Waldemar Link GmbH & Co. and its U.S. subsidiary, Link America, Inc., products that were complementary to what Exactech had to offer. Because of a costly legal dispute with Regeneration Technologies that was resolved in 2001, net income dipped to $3.46 million in 2001, but rebounded to a record $5.3 million in 2002.

In the first decade of the 2000s, Exactech sought to make improvements to its hip implant systems, expand its knee product line, and enter the shoulder replacement market. In addition, it established an acquisition strategy to augment organic growth. The first step in this effort took place in October 2003 when the company acquired a 16.7 percent interest in Charlotte, North Carolina-based Altiva Corporation at a cost of $1 million. Altiva was an early stage company looking to carve out a niche in the spinal products market. Exactech also received an option to acquire all of Altiva at a specified price.

Revenues improved at a steady pace, reaching $71.23 million in 2003, $81.8 million in 2004, and

$91 million in 2005, while net income ranged between $6.5 million and $7.3 million. Helping to drive these sales increases were such new products as a bone paste and a preformed cement hip spacer. A new shoulder replacement system introduced to the market in 2005 helped the company to maintain the momentum. Revenues topped the $100 million mark in 2006 and continued to grow in 2007, when sales reached $124.2 million and net income approached $8.5 million.

DAVID PETTY BECOMES PRESIDENT: 2007

In late 2007 David W. Petty, the 41-year-old son of William and Betty Petty, was named president, ensuring a large measure of continuity as the company grew. He had been with Exactech from the beginning. In fact, he was the first person hired, joining the company in 1988 after graduating from the University of Virginia. Three years later he left for a stint with the Arthur Andersen accounting firm, but returned in 1993 and held a number of management positions before becoming president.

At the start of 2008 Exactech exercised its option and acquired Altiva, the deal valued at $25 million. A month later Exactech solidified its position in two key markets, Japan and France, when a wholly owned distribution subsidiary opened in Japan and plans were announced to acquire the French distribution subsidiary France Medica SAS. The transaction was completed in April 2008. Later in the year Exactech released the latest addition to its hip system, the Novation Crown Cup, which offered greater strength and stability. It would also serve as the platform for additional cup (acetabular) products, which would become increasingly important because an aging population and longer life spans were expected to make hip replacement surgeries more commonplace. It would also ensure that Exactech, as long as it retained its technological edge, would enjoy steady growth for years to come.

Ed Dinger

PRINCIPAL SUBSIDIARIES

Altiva Corporation; Exactech Asia, Ltd.; Exactech (UK), Ltd.

PRINCIPAL COMPETITORS

Biomet, Inc.; DePuy Inc.; Zimmer Holdings, Inc.

FURTHER READING

Cariaga, Vance, "Gainesville, Florida Chief Gets an Up-Close Look at His Industry," *Investor's Business Daily,* August 28, 2000, p. A12.

"Exactech Buys Local Spinal-Device Firm," *Charlotte Business Journal,* January 3, 2008.

Lau, Gloria, "The Aging of America Keeps This Firm Busy," *Investor's Business Daily,* December 31, 2002, p. A05.

———, "Size Doesn't Matter at Orthopedic Device Maker," *Investor's Business Daily,* June 21, 2004, p. A09.

Mitseas, Catherine, "Traditions of Excellence," *Florida Trend,* October 15, 2003, p. 91.

Petty, William, ed., *Total Joint Replacement,* Philadelphia: Saunders, 1991.

Rigsby, G. G., "New Hip Implant Could Be Cost-Cutter," *St. Petersburg Times,* November 11, 1993, p. 3B.

Fiesta Mart, Inc.

5235 Katy Freeway
Houston, Texas 77007-2210
U.S.A.
Telephone: (713) 869-5060
Fax: (713) 569-6197
Web site: http://www.fiestamart.com

Wholly Owned Subsidiary of Grocers Supply Co.
Incorporated: 1972
Employees: 5,900
Sales: $1.1 billion (2008)
NAICS: 445110 Supermarkets and Other Grocery (Except Convenience)

■ ■ ■

Fiesta Mart, Inc., is the leading chain of international foods grocery stores in Texas, with 33 stores in Houston, 15 stores in Dallas, and two stores in Austin. Although the company serves the Hispanic grocery market primarily, Fiesta Mart offers fresh and packaged foods for people from diverse cultural backgrounds. Located in multiethnic neighborhoods, Fiesta Mart stores provide an extensive array of exotic fresh fruit, vegetables, meat, and seafood, in addition to mainstream American choices. Prepared meals at Fiesta Mart stores appeal to the variety of customer tastes as well. Aesthetically, Fiesta Mart caters to Hispanic tastes, with a festive atmosphere of bright colors in a south-of-the-border style. Frilly piñatas hang from the ceiling and Mexican and Latin-style music plays in the background. Fiesta Mart operates 17 Beverage Mart liquor stores, located near the grocery stores.

FOUNDERS PROVIDE INTERNATIONAL SPECIALTY GROCERIES

Donald Bonham and O. C. Mendenhall opened the first Fiesta Mart, on Fulton Street, in 1972. Bonham conceived the idea of a grocery store catering to the Hispanic market after several years of employment in Latin American countries. He worked for the Interamerican Development Bank in Chile, where he organized food supply and distribution systems for a grocery store chain. Also, he farmed in Guatemala and Belize. When Bonham returned to Houston, he found it remarkable that no grocery store served the city's large population of Hispanic people. He formed a partnership with Mendenhall, who brought in-store management experience to the enterprise. As a child, Mendenhall's family owned and operated a grocery store in Seiling, Oklahoma, and he himself started a chain of grocery stores with outlets in Oklahoma and Kansas.

In deciding the name for the store, the story goes that Bonham and Mendenhall saw a "Fiesta" sign on a vacant building, purchased it, and hung it on the exterior wall of the Fulton Street building. The name fit the concept Bonham had as a grocer serving an urban, Hispanic neighborhood. In Latin America he observed shopping as a social event. Fiesta Mart, accordingly, provided an atmosphere conducive to lingering. He al-

COMPANY PERSPECTIVES

We are proud to have been able to bring you the highest quality meat, grocery, fresh produce and seafood departments, world class delicatessens, beer and fine wines, as well as a variety of international and specialty foods and products. Our approach is a simple one, by blending our variety of product selection and our special brand of customer service with an authentic "Fiesta" atmosphere, we provide a unique grocery shopping experience for you, our customer.

lowed independent vendors to sell goods, such as blankets, toys, audio equipment, in kiosks outside the store. Also, Fiesta Mart staged carnivals, with rides and games, in the parking lot.

Bonham's former business associates provided the supply of fresh and packaged foods for the specialty Hispanic market. The 30,000-square-foot store carried ingredients common to Latin American cuisines, such as corn husks for tamales and dried chili peppers. Fresh fruit included guava, sapote, breadfruit, mango, plantains, yucca, and malanga, and vegetables included jicama, chayotes, and cactus leaves. Meats used in Mexican and other Latin American cuisines included *cabrito* (goat meat), tripe, pork ears, and pig's feet. Fiesta Mart offered a wide array of fresh fish and seafood. The store carried brand-name package goods familiar to immigrant customers, such as La Costeña canned refried beans, Bimbo bakery products, and Jarritos soft drinks. The Beverage Mart liquor store, which began operation in 1974, catered to Hispanic tastes by highlighting imported alcoholic beverages.

Although neither Bonham nor Mendenhall were Hispanic, they used every tool available to attract the diverse population. Fiesta Mart advertised in Spanish-language publications and hired bilingual staff and Hispanic managers. As the Fulton Street neighborhood attracted immigrants from Vietnam, Korea, India, and Africa, Fiesta Mart began to offer ethnic foods for these customers. Soon market shelves carried everything from Korean pickled cabbage, to Indian chutneys, to African bark teas. Thai and African American food sections evolved as Fiesta Mart opened stores in multiethnic areas serving those populations. Success with international foods allowed the chain to grow to 12 stores by the end of fiscal 1987.

NEW DEPARTMENTS EXPAND FIESTA MART CONCEPT

During the mid-1980s, Fiesta Mart opened larger stores that encompassed many departments providing specialty foods or serving the low-income customers that patronized the stores. In 1983, Fiesta Mart opened its first tortilleria, which produced fresh corn tortillas, a staple of the Hispanic diet. The company offered fresh, machine-made tortillas in one dozen, two dozen, and 100-count packages. Products include corn tortilla chips, tostadas, red pepper tortillas, and flour tortillas. Initially, Fiesta Mart introduced tortilla bakeries at stores with at least a 40 percent Hispanic customer base. However, the tortillerias attracted both Hispanic and non-Hispanic customers, who willingly waited in line for hot tortillas. The tortilleria department, at approximately 550 square feet, opened in nine of the 12 Houston stores by 1987.

The typical Fiesta Mart customer earned less than $20,000 per year and supported school-age kids, and the company introduced products attractive to these patrons. Fiesta Mart offered electronics in off-brands at low prices, and displayed bulk-sized detergent on pallets. The larger stores offered regular deals on apparel, such as T-shirts for $1, blouses for $3, and vinyl, leather-look jackets at $4.

Fiesta Mart launched a new design for stores opening in 1987. The company developed different departments in the store, each with a unique look. Fiesta Mart hoped the style would promote browsing and inspire increased sales. For instance, a new 78,000-square-foot store that opened in June 1987 included a coffee nook near the bakery. The design included a low mirror ceiling that reflected the wood and tile in that area of the store. Also, the bakery offered made-from-scratch pastries.

In 1988, Fiesta Mart began offering food under its own private label, thus adding to its low-cost options. Fiesta Mart brand products included milk, eggs, meat, carbonated beverages, pizzas, pasta, rice, cereal, dressings and spreads, and paper goods. Canned goods included beans, tuna, and vegetables. Snack items included chips, cookies, and crackers.

As a market providing specialty and low-cost goods, Fiesta Mart succeeded, even during economic downturns. While other stores closed, Fiesta Mart expanded. By 1989, Fiesta Mart generated $400 million in sales from its 16 Houston grocery stores and eight Fiesta Beverage Mart liquor stores. Apparel accounted for approximately $25 million in sales. Part of the company's success in catering to international tastes showed itself in produce, which accounted for 14 to 17 percent of store sales.

KEY DATES

■

1972: The first Fiesta Mart opens on Fulton Street in Houston.

1983: Fiesta Mart introduces in-store tortilla bakery with great success.

1989: Fiesta Mart experiments with an upscale hypermarket in suburban south Houston.

1992: Fiesta Mart enters Austin market with two stores.

1994: Fiesta Mart opens four stores in Dallas area.

1998: Conoco gas stations are added to several Fiesta Mart stores.

2004: The death of founder leads to sale of Fiesta Mart to Grocers Supply Co.

2008: Grocers Supply's acquisition of Carnival brand adds 11 stores to Fiesta Mart.

EXPERIMENTING WITH SUBURBAN UNITS AND SUPERSTORES

As Fiesta Mart saturated the multiethnic areas of Houston's urban neighborhoods, growth expanded toward the suburbs. Fiesta Mart retained its identity as an international foods market, but adapted the store concept to local preferences. In November 1989 Fiesta Mart ventured to the outskirts of Houston for the first time, when the company opened a hypermarket prototype in Webster, Texas, near the Johnson Space Center. Construction of the 185,000-square-foot store, anchored in a shopping center that included a Wal-Mart, cost approximately $20 million. Fiesta Mart brought vendor kiosks indoors, offering leased space along the inside front wall of the store. A 60,000-square-foot open balcony provided space for two leased stores. In addition to groceries, the store offered general merchandise, with stable and revolving sections. Apparel, housewares, paper goods, and bath and body departments remained stable. New departments included The Yogurt Zone, a yogurt and fruit bar, and a bakery featuring customized cake decorating. Fiesta Mart provided sushi through a leased concession.

In an extraordinary move, Fiesta Mart installed a hydroponic garden to grow organic produce to sell in the store. Cultivation in the five-story, 8,000-square-foot garden included tomatoes, cucumbers, spinach, watercress, five kinds of lettuce, and numerous herbs. The vegetables grew in a rich mineral medium with a constant flow of water. A glass wall separated the garden

from the produce department; customers could not enter the garden space, but it created a beautiful, natural backdrop.

The move into a suburban area required changes in the produce department at Fiesta Mart. Fiesta Mart welcomed a different ethnic mix by providing foods for Chinese and Japanese residents. Asian produce additions included kabocha squash, loquat, tamarind, and lemongrass. Fiesta Mart expanded the available produce common to American tastes, such as peaches, berries, and broccoli, while playing down Hispanic produce. Certain produce displays, such as garlic and citrus fruit, remained extensive in all stores, regardless of ethnic mix.

The hypermarket in Webster drew customers from nearby consulates, the National Aeronautics and Space Administration, and the local neighborhoods. After an initial grand opening rush, the store stayed busy but struggled to meet overhead costs. In 1991, Fiesta Mart reduced the sales floor by 45,000 square feet and leased the space to SportsTown. However, parking problems and intense grocery store competition prevented the hypermarket from achieving profitability. By the end of 1993, Fiesta Mart closed the store. Another suburban store, in Deerbrook, closed in 1992. In reorienting itself to the multiethnic demographic, Fiesta Mart purchased four stores in the Houston area from AppleTree Markets and began exploring markets in north Texas.

With 22 stores operating in the Houston area, Fiesta Mart expanded to Austin and Dallas. The company opened two stores in Austin in early 1992, an 85,000-square-foot store in north Austin and a 60,000-square-foot store in south Austin. Austin was an attractive market for Fiesta Mart because of the large population of immigrants from Central and South American countries. Also, the University of Texas attracted an ethnically diverse population of students. In mid-1992, Fiesta Mart began planning for at least eight stores in the Dallas and Fort Worth area, primarily in central city communities. Fiesta Mart opened four stores in late 1993 and four in 1994. The company eliminated general merchandise and focused on its strength in perishable ethnic foods, keeping floor space between 40,000 and 60,000 square feet.

COMPETITION PROMPTS ADDITION OF SHOPPING CONVENIENCES

During the 1990s, competition among grocery stores sparked a rivalry of one-stop shopping conveniences. At the north Austin store, Fiesta Mart opened an authentic Mexican taqueria in late 1992. The taqueria featured tortillas freshly prepared on a 60-foot tortilla machine.

Menu items included enchiladas, quesadillas, fajitas, and tacos served in a traditional style, without the load of melted cheddar cheese found in Tex-Mex food. Mexican drinks included a sweet rice drink and hibiscus-flavored water. Colorful wall tiles and wood tables with pink, purple, and red formica tops reminded customers of taquerias in Mexico. The 1,250-square-foot space seated up to 32 customers.

Other efforts to compete with other supermarkets included an experiment with the introduction of pharmacies. Through a 1994 lease-space contract, Medicine Shoppe International opened at five Houston stores. In 1996 Fiesta Mart increased sales through an integrated approach to selling housewares, by placing gadgets in relevant food aisles, such as can openers near canned goods and coffee pots and mugs in the coffee aisle. Also, Fiesta Mart sold cookware appropriate to Hispanic foods, including tortilla warmers, located in the bread section. Cast aluminum enamel caldera pots, used for cooking menudo (a soup made with tripe, pig's feet, and hominy), could be found in the meat department.

In 1998 Fiesta Mart signed a ground-lease agreement with Conoco to open gas stations at six stores. Fiesta Mart agreed to build payment kiosks and small convenience stores near the gasoline pumps, and Conoco operated the stations. In an effort to retain Hispanic patronage, Fiesta Mart entered into a lease space agreement with CCC Global Communications in 2002. CCC planned to sell bundled local and long-distance telephone service popular with Hispanics. CCC would potentially open kiosk service and payment centers at 43 of the 50 Fiesta Mart grocery stores and at all 16 Fiesta Beverage Mart stores.

By 2002 Fiesta Mart operated 52 stores, 35 in Houston, 15 in Dallas, and 2 in Austin. The company began exploring the possibility of opening a store in Waco, Texas, at a location vacated by Winn-Dixie. Closure of the Winn-Dixie would have left the residents of the neighborhood, inhabited by many Hispanics, without a grocery store. In the midst of a revival of Hispanic businesses, the 25th Street corridor attracted Hispanics to relocate from other parts of the city. Local activist and former Mayor LaNell McNamara lobbied Fiesta Mart to open the store in order to preserve the neighborhood. Fiesta Mart opened in July 2002, drawing 15,000 customers per week, including people from other areas of Waco who were interested in the international products. Fiesta Mart planned to install a tortilleria and other specialty departments. The store helped advance development of the area by drawing more Hispanic residents to the neighborhood.

Nevertheless, Fiesta Mart sold the Waco store to an independent grocery store chain in 2005.

In February 2002 Fiesta Mart announced it would close its south Austin store after two years in operation. The closure was prompted by an unsatisfactory lease agreement and lower than expected sales. The location and size of the store were never optimal.

DEATH OF FOUNDER PROMPTS SALE OF COMPANY

Bonham died in April 2003, prompting the August 2004 sale of the company to Grocers Supply Co., a wholesale distributor. Fiesta Mart was the largest customer of Grocers Supply, which wanted to ensure that it would retain Fiesta Mart's business, with revenues estimated at $1.1 billion. At the time of the sale, Fiesta Mart operated 34 stores in Houston, 15 stores in Dallas, 1 store in Austin, plus 17 Beverage Mart liquor stores. Employees, who owned approximately 34 percent of the company, were pleased with the acquisition by Grocers Supply, founded in 1923 as a retail grocer.

Grocers Supply could not risk losing its biggest customer to a large retail chain that handled its own grocery distribution. With revenues of $1.5 billion, the company distributed goods to more than 700 stores in Texas and Louisiana.

Grocers Supply maintained normal operations throughout the Fiesta Mart chain, retaining CEO Louis Katolodis. Indeed, the company expanded the chain in July 2008, when Grocers Supply purchased 37 grocery stores owned by Minyard Food Stores, Inc. Fiesta Mart took over 11 of the 23 stores operated under the Carnival and Save and Sac brands. Nine of the stores were transferred to the Fiesta Mart brand. Fiesta Mart retained the Carnival brand and two Carnival stores continued business as usual. Grocers Supply planned to sell the remaining 26 stores to independent grocers. The acquisition provided Fiesta Mart with additional market share in north Texas, with seven stores located in the Dallas–Fort Worth area and one in Austin. After the closure of two stores in Houston, the acquisition brought the number of Houston stores to 33.

Mary Tradii

PRINCIPAL COMPETITORS

Albertsons LLC; H.E. Butt Grocery Company; The Kroger Co.; Randall's Food and Drugs L.P.; Safeway, Inc.; Wal-Mart Stores, Inc.

FURTHER READING

Abram, Lynwood, "D. Bonham, Co-founded Fiesta Mart," *Houston Chronicle,* April 8, 2003, p. 14.

Bennet, Stephen, "Fiesta Steps Out of Inner City; By Opening Its Biggest Store Yet, Fiesta Aims to Cash In on Projected Growth South of Houston," *Progressive Grocer,* November 1989, p. 49.

Breyer, Michelle, "Fiesta Mart Will Shutter Its South Lamar Location; Slow Sales, Lease Dispute Prompt Grocer to Close 1 of 2 Austin Sites," *Austin American-Statesman,* February 18, 2003, p. D1.

"CCC Global Corp.—Signs Strategic Agreement with Fiesta Mart," *Market News Publishing,* February 28, 2002.

Copeland, Mike, "Fiesta Mart Reportedly Wants to Open in Departing Waco, Texas, Winn-Dixie," *Waco Tribune-Herald,* May 16, 2002.

———, "Fiesta Mart's Market Share Obscures Huge Impact on Diverse Neighborhood," *Waco Tribune-Herald,* February 28, 2005.

———, "Neighborhood Grocery Store Fiesta Mart Sold to Independent Chain," *Waco Tribune-Herald,* March 3, 2007.

Elder, Laura, "Fiesta Atmosphere: Conoco Partners with Grocery Chain to Build Stations," *Houston Business Chronicle,* May 22, 1998, p. 4.

Elson, Joel, "Housewares, Grocery Mix Sparks Fiesta Sales," *Supermarket News,* May 13, 1996, p. 54.

"Fiesta Mart Will Open Austin Stores in '92," *Supermarket News,* April 8, 1991, p. 13.

"Fiesta to Open First Neighborhood Store," *Houston Chronicle,* May 21, 1986, p. 4Business.

"Founder of Fiesta Supermarket Chain Dies at 76," *Houston Chronicle,* October 4, 1997, p. 32.

Hamstra, Mark, "Fiesta: A Taste of Mexico and Beyond," *Supermarket News,* September 15, 2003, p. 20.

Harper, Roseanne, "Fiesta Mart Launches Cooking Show," *Supermarket News,* September 28, 1992, p. 42.

———, "Fiesta Mart Taco Stand Has the Spice of Mexico," *Supermarket News,* March 22, 1993, p. 37.

———, "Fiesta's Mexican Program Expands, Spices Up Sales," *Supermarket News,* September 6, 1993, p. 45.

Hassell, Greg, "Party's Over for NASA Fiesta—Huge, Landmark Store Closing at the End of the Year," *Houston Chronicle,* December 4, 1993, p. 1Business.

Hem, Brad, and David Kaplan, "Retail: Fiesta to Shut Store As Road Widening Eats into Parking," *Houston Chronicle,* November 2, 2007, p. 1.

Hisey, Peter, "Ethnic Food Flavors Fiesta Mart; Houston Chain Poised to Open Hypermarket-Size Unit," *Discount Store News,* September 4, 1989, p. 3.

Hughes, Bob, and Kevin Coupe, "As a New Houston Fiesta Mart the Bakery Lets 'Em Linger," *Supermarket Business,* July 1987, p. 17A.

Kaplan, David, and Nancy Sarnoff, "Grocers Supply Bags Fiesta; Wholesaler Set to Announce Purchase of Chain It Serves," *Houston Chronicle,* August 26, 2004, p. 1.

Lenius, Pat Natschke, "Fiesta Mart Increasing Ethnic Prepared Foods," *Supermarket News,* December 16, 1991, p. 40.

Mejia, John, "Fiesta Mart Tries 'Melting Pot' Marketing," *Supermarket News,* July 30, 1990, p. 28.

Natschke, Patricia, "Tortillerias Everyone Likes," *Supermarket News,* February 9, 1987, p. 40.

Schlachter, Barry, "Ethnic-Oriented Houston Grocery Chain Is Bought by Supplier in Defensive Move," *Fort Worth Star-Telegram,* August 27, 2004.

———, "Fiesta Mart Parent Buys 37 Grocery Stores from Minyard," *Fort Worth Star-Telegram,* July 24, 2008.

Smith, J. B., "Waco, Texas, Ethnic-Food Mart Popular with Former Winn-Dixie Customers," *Waco Tribune-Herald,* August 11, 2002.

Warmbrodt, Zachary, "Carnival Brand Unlikely to Survive After Stores' Sale," *Dallas Morning News,* July 26, 2008.

Williams, Mina, "Fiesta Harvest Hydroponic Crop," *Supermarket News,* September 11, 1989, p. 42.

Zoeller, Janice, "Fiesta Mart Is in Pact to Add Medicine Shoppe Pharmacies," *Supermarket News,* July 4, 1994, p. 6.

Zweibach, Elliot, "Fiesta Mart to Enter Dallas Market," *Supermarket News,* June 22, 1992, p. 6.

Fluxys SA

Ave. des Arts 31
Brussels, B-1040
Belgium
Telephone: (+32 02) 282 72 11
Fax: (+32 02) 230 02 39
Web site: http://www.fluxys.net

Public Company
Incorporated: 2002
Employees: 998
Sales: EUR 433.04 million ($636.2 million) (2007)
Stock Exchanges: NYSE Euronext Brussels
Ticker Symbol: FLUX
NAICS: 221210 Natural Gas Distribution; 488320
   Marine Cargo Handling

■ ■ ■

Fluxys SA provides natural gas transport services as the exclusive operator of Belgium's natural gas transport and transit grid. The company's gas transmission services also include hub and dispatching services. Fluxys plays a crucial role in positioning Belgium as a major hub in the European gas transit market. The company provides 18 entry points to the Belgian grid, enabling the flow of natural gas from the major European gas-producing markets, including Russia, the United Kingdom, Norway, and the Netherlands. Fluxys also holds stakes and otherwise participates in a number of European interconnector partnerships, particularly the Balgzand (Netherlands)-Bacton (UK) interconnector. Fluxys's control of the Zeebrugge LNG Terminal and the Zee-

brugge Hub make it a major player in the European natural gas terminal sector. The company provides off-load services for liquefied natural gas (LNG) tankers, with a total storage capacity of 380,000 cubic meters of LNG. The Zeebrugge Terminal then provides regazification services in order to inject the natural gas into the grid. The Zeebrugge Hub, operated through subsidiary Huberator, serves as a short-term gas trading facility, providing a range of trading services. Fluxys was formed through the breakup of formerly state-owned Distrigaz into its commercial sales and infrastructure components in 2002. Fluxys is listed on the NYSE Euronext Brussels stock exchange and is led by CEO and Chairman Sophie Dutordoir. Suez-Tractebel remains the company's major shareholder, with more than 57 percent in 2007. In that year, Fluxys posted sales of EUR 433 million ($636 million).

BELGIAN GAS MONOPOLY FROM 1929

The Imperial Continental Gas Association, a U.K.-based company, played a central role in the development of Europe's gas transmission network in the early decades of the 20th century. In 1929, the company backed the creation of a Belgian gas transmission company called Distrigaz.

By 1932, Distrigaz had succeeded in building its first 143-kilometer pipeline. The company initially focused on the transportation of gas generated in Belgium's coke ovens. Before long, the increasingly vital interests of the gas transmission sector to the country's economic growth led the Belgian government to take

COMPANY PERSPECTIVES

Fluxys plays a vital role in supplying natural gas to industrial customers, power stations and households in Belgium and in transmission of natural gas to other European countries.

control of Distrigaz. Over the next decades, Distrigaz expanded the country's gas transport and transit grid, and related infrastructure.

The post–World War II economic and industrial boom years quickly saw demand outstrip the supply of coke gas. By then, discoveries of major new natural gas fields, in Europe and elsewhere, promised a more plentiful and easier to produce gas supply. Belgium, however, proved to have no natural gas resources of its own. As a result, Distrigaz's efforts were directed to establishing connections to gain access to the production of natural gas fields beyond Belgium's borders.

One of the company's first natural gas supply agreements came in the early 1960s, after a significant natural gas field was discovered in Slochteren, Netherlands. The discovery of the field close to the Belgian border permitted Distrigaz to establish its first large-scale supply contract. The company constructed the infrastructure to connect the Slochteren field to the Belgian grid, and by 1966 had begun transiting the Dutch natural gas.

LNG TERMINAL IN THE SEVENTIES

Natural gas demand increased significantly in Belgium and other European markets during the 1960s and 1970s. Distrigaz adopted a new strategy of developing multiple natural gas supply agreements. In this way, the company sought to maintain a stable supply of what had become a vital part of the country's power grid. The discovery of vast natural gas fields beneath the Sahara Desert in Algeria led to negotiations between that country's Sonatrach and Distrigaz. In 1975, the Algerian government signed a 20-year, 100 billion cubic-meter supply agreement.

Distrigaz soon followed the Sonatrach agreement with a supply contract with Norway's Ekofisk. That deal, signed in 1977, gave Distrigaz access to the recently discovered natural gas fields off the Norwegian coast. Distrigaz then moved to expand its transmission network, extending its grid with a new pipeline and infrastructure into Belgium's southern and western regions.

In 1976, the Belgian government, in part to ensure the supply of natural gas for the country's own needs, authorized Distrigaz to build an LNG terminal facility at the Zeebrugge port. The terminal, initially slated for a capacity of 135,000 cubic meters, was to become the largest and most modern LNG terminal in Europe. The project also included regazification facilities, allowing the company to inject the LNG deliveries into its natural gas grid.

Construction of the project began in 1978, with the formation of a manmade peninsula. By 1982, construction of the LNG terminal itself was underway. The Zeebrugge terminal received a further boost in 1986, when the site was chosen by the Norwegian government as the entry point for the Zeepipe project. The Zeepipe was an underwater pipeline connecting the Troll and Sleipner gas fields to the European continent, and represented a major step forward in enabling natural gas to compete economically with coal, oil, nuclear power, and other fuel sources. Norway agreed to ship ten billion cubic meters of natural gas per year into the European continent, establishing Zeebrugge as a major entry point even before the completion of its LNG terminal. The Zeebrugge terminal at last received its first tanker in 1987.

EUROPEAN HUB IN THE NINETIES

Distrigaz had made a foray into the technological services sector during the 1980s, establishing a subsidiary providing international pipeline and transmission consulting services. At the end of the decade, however, the company decided to refocus its operations around a new strategy of developing its Belgian operations into a major European natural gas hub. Motivating this decision was the coming unification of the European trade market, slated for 1992. The creation of the European Union was also expected to result in the liberalization of the gas market, putting an end to the dominance of state-owned monopolies.

Following the launch of construction of the Zeepipe, Distrigaz undertook a number of complementary infrastructure extensions. The company built a new pipeline providing an entry point into the Belgian market from Luxembourg. At the same time, the company completed a new 145-kilometer pipeline connecting Zeebrugge to Blaregnies, on the French border. Construction of the Zeepipe was completed in 1993, with the pipeline extension to France entering service in 1995. Distrigaz had positioned itself to provide transport and transit services for Norway's natural gas throughout most of southern Europe.

KEY DATES

1929: Distrigaz is formed to transmit coke gas in Belgium.

1966: Distrigaz signs first large-scale natural gas transmission agreement.

1977: Distrigaz launches the construction of the Zeebrugge LNG terminal.

1986: The Zeebrugge terminal begins operations.

1993: The completion of the Zeepipe provides Distrigaz with access to the Norwegian gas fields.

1998: Interconnector pipeline is completed, connecting the United Kingdom to the Zeebrugge complex.

2002: Distrigaz is broken up and Fluxys is created to take over its gas transmission infrastructure and terminal operations.

2007: Fluxys and Gazprom of Russia announce agreement to build a gas storage facility in Belgium.

The United Kingdom represented another major European natural gas source in the mid-1990s. In 1992, Distrigaz joined the Interconnector consortium, proposing to build a new subsea pipeline linking Bacton, in England, to the Zeebrugge terminal. The pipeline also featured reverse flow capabilities, in order to allow European gas suppliers access to the U.K. market, where gas prices remained higher than on the continent. Construction of the pipeline began in 1996 and was completed in 1998. As part of the Interconnector project, the company launched construction of an additional pipeline connecting Zeebrugge to Eynatten, on the German border. This new pipeline held added importance, giving the company access not only to the German market, but especially to the Russian supply as that company emerged as one of the world's single largest suppliers of natural gas.

INDEPENDENT INFRASTRUCTURE SPECIALIST IN THE 21ST CENTURY

The differences in gas prices between the European continent and the United Kingdom quickly stimulated a market in short-term trading. This brought Distrigaz the opportunity to further enhance its strategy to become the major European natural gas hub. In 1998 the company set up a new subsidiary, Huberator, which specialized in providing natural gas trading services.

The company's LNG terminal operations had in the meantime been steadily expanding as well, as the company added a second and then a third reservoir, complete with regazification capacity, to the terminal complex. Distrigaz continued to seek new gas supply sources in its ambition to transform the Zeebrugge complex into Europe's leading gas transmission hub. The company bid for a new pipeline connecting the gas fields in Norway; in the end, however, the Norwegian government chose France instead.

By the early 2000s, the European Union had established new rules governing the gas utilities market. Under the new regulations, the individual markets were required to break up their gas monopolies. As a result, in 2002, Distrigaz hived off its transmission, transport, and LNG terminal operations into a separate company, called Fluxys. The reformed Distrigaz then became wholly focused on gas sales and related commercial operations. Fluxys was taken public, listing on the Euronext Brussels stock exchange. The majority of Fluxys's shares remained controlled by Suez-Tractebel, which held more than 57 percent of the company.

In 2003, Fluxys took the first steps toward a new expansion of its LNG terminal, when it signed agreements to provide twice its existing capacity to a customer consortium starting in 2007. The contract became the starting signal for the construction of the company's fourth reservoir, boosting its capacity to 380,000 cubic meters by the time of its completion in 2008.

Fluxys also put into place a strategy for confronting the full liberalization of the European gas market. In 2002, the company acquired Gas Management Services Ltd. in the United Kingdom, a provider of natural gas shipping services, as well as related software and communications technologies. The company expected to gain access to the U.K. and other European markets. The following year, Fluxys announced its decision to invest EUR 700 million in infrastructure upgrades through 2011.

Part of this investment went toward expanding transmission capacity over the Interconnector pipeline into the United Kingdom, as that country was expected to become a net importer of natural gas starting in 2005. Also in 2003, Fluxys became a minority partner in a new Interconnector project launched by the Netherlands' Gastransport Services, linking the Netherlands and the United Kingdom. In the meantime, the company's LNG terminal moved to switch from a negotiated tariff system to regulated tariffs in keeping with European Union rules. As a result, the Zeebrugge facility's rates were reduced, enabling the site to become still more competitive as it sought to claim the leading position in the European market.

Fluxys continued to raise its total investment objectives into the second half of the decade. By 2006, the company had announced plans to invest some EUR 1.35 billion through 2015. These investments included an additional EUR 400 million investment, announced in 2006, to expand its transmission capacity, in part to woo the Russian gas market. The expansion appeared to have succeeded: in March 2007, Fluxys and Russia's Gazprom announced their agreement to develop a gas storage facility in Belgium, principally for gas from Gazprom's Nord Stream pipeline. Both the pipeline and the gas storage facility were expected to be completed by 2012.

Fluxys's investment program appeared likely to expand again. In December 2007, the company began investigating the feasibility of doubling the Zeebrugge LNG terminal's capacity by 2016. In the meantime, the company maintained an active expansion program. At the end of 2008, the company's list covered some 20 projects, including a number of new pipelines, and the upgrade and expansion of other parts of its transmission infrastructure. Fluxys remained focused on becoming the leading natural gas transmission player in the European market.

M. L. Cohen

PRINCIPAL SUBSIDIARIES

APX Gas Zeebrugge BV (42%); BBL Company VOF (20%); Belgian Pipe Control SA (25%); Fluxys BBL BV; Fluxys LNG Sa (93.2%); Fluxys NL BV; Gas Management Services Ltd.; Huberator SA (90%); Segeo SA (75%).

PRINCIPAL COMPETITORS

Petrobras Distribuidora S.A.; RWE AG; Repsol YPF S.A.; SONATRACH; E.ON AG; ENI S.p.A.; Gazprom Russia Joint Stock Co.; Centrica PLC; Gaz de France; ENDESA S.A.; TRACTEBEL S.A.; Electrabel S.A./NV.

FURTHER READING

"Backing Its Own Future," *Gas Connections,* August 7, 2003, p. 6.

"Belgian Distrigas Split into Distrigas, Fluxys," *World Gas Intelligence,* December 5, 2001, p. 1.

"Belgian Gas Pipeline Operator Fluxys to Invest EUR 400 Mln to Meet Rising Demand," *Poland Business News,* June 27, 2006.

"Belgian System Operator Fluxys and Its French Counterpart GRT Gaz Have Agreed to Develop a Shared Electronic Platform for Capacity Trading on Both Pipeline Networks," *Gas Connections,* July 10, 2008, p. 7.

"Belgium Plans Grid, LNG Boost," *World Gas Intelligence,* December 19, 2007, p. 3.

"Belgium's Fluxys Takes Stake in New Interconnector," *Gas Connections,* November 20, 2003, p. 4.

"EIB Lends EUR 400 Million to Develop Fluxys Gas Infrastructure," *TendersInfo,* December 3, 2008.

"Fluxys Aims for Grid Capacity Boost," *Gas Connections,* September 6, 2007, p. 6.

"Fluxys Buys UK Gas Services Firm," *Gas Connections,* November 21, 2002, p. 12.

"Gasunie in New Link Deal with Fluxys," *Utility Week,* November 28, 2003, p. 11.

"Gazprom, Fluxys in Storage Pact," *Gas Connections,* March 8, 2007, p. 1.

"GdF-Suez Envisages Greater Independence for Fluxys," *Gas Connections,* September 28, 2006, p. 6.

"Suez Raises Distrigas Stakes," *Gas Connections,* September 14, 2006, p. 1.

FreightCar America, Inc.

———— ∎ ————

2 North Riverside Plaza, Suite 1250
Chicago, Illinois 60606
U.S.A.
Telephone: (312) 928-0850
Toll Free: (800) 458-2235
Fax: (312) 928-0890
Web site: http://www.freightcaramerica.com

Public Company
Incorporated: 1901 as Cambria Steel Company
Employees: 576
Sales: $817.02 million (2007)
Stock Exchanges: NASDAQ
Ticker Symbol: RAIL
NAICS: 336510 Railroad Rolling Stock Manufacturing

∎ ∎ ∎

FreightCar America, Inc., is the leading manufacturer of aluminum-bodied railcars in North America. The company's BethGon railcar, designed to carry coal, is the industry's best-selling brand of aluminum-bodied railcar, having led the market virtually since its introduction in 1986. FreightCar America supplies its railcars, which include a broad range of aluminum-bodied and steel-bodied railcars, to shippers, railroads, and financial institutions. The company's manufacturing operations are located in Danville, Illinois, and Roanoke, Virginia.

ROOTS IN CAMBRIA COUNTY, PENNSYLVANIA

For more than a half-century, the assets that formed the foundation of FreightCar America were part of the Bethlehem Steel Company, the Bethlehem, Pennsylvania-based conglomerate that once ranked as the second largest steel producer in the United States. In its heyday, the company added to its prowess in the steel industry by diversifying into a number of different areas such as shipbuilding and mining. It delved into the design and production of railcars in 1923 when it acquired the non-steel-producing assets of Midvale Steel and Ordnance Company, a company that had entered the railcar business by acquiring Cambria Steel Company, which built its first freight car in 1901.

In Johnstown, Cambria County, Pennsylvania, the business begun by Cambria Steel Co. gradually matured under the ownership of Bethlehem Steel. Over the course of several decades, the plant acquired in 1923 developed into a designer and producer of a full line of covered and open-top steel railcars. The operation became known as Bethlehem Steel's Freight Car Division, or FCD. In the years leading up to FCD becoming FreightCar America's predecessor, two developments occurred. In 1974, the Johnstown facilities, which built hopper cars, gondola cars, ore cars, flatcars, mine cars, and special purpose cars, were outfitted with state-of-the-art equipment that ushered in the age of mass production. Once the new equipment was installed, FCD was able to produce 50 cars in a 24-hour period. In 1986, FCD introduced what would be the division's flagship railcar, the aluminum-bodied

COMPANY PERSPECTIVES

FreightCar America—the home of the aluminum railcar—is proud of its heritage of building and designing railcars. And we have good reason. FreightCar America has been manufacturing quality railcars since 1901. The generations of employees responsible for creating its reputation for quality have made FreightCar America the largest North American manufacturer of aluminum railroad freight cars used to haul coal. FreightCar America uses its design knowledge, enhanced production facilities, and unequaled experience in aluminum railcar building to expand its product line and provide cost benefits to customers.

BethGon. Within a decade, more than 25,000 BethGon cars would be produced in Johnstown.

INDEPENDENCE IN 1991

By the time the BethGon railcars were introduced, Bethlehem Steel was no longer an industry titan. The company's strength had begun to wane, and the onetime giant moved inexorably toward collapse, eventually declaring bankruptcy in 2001 before disappearing entirely from the steel industry two years later. Before the company foundered, it attempted to cure its ills by shedding assets and focusing all its energies on its core steel business. The strategy led the company to put FCD up for sale in 1990, creating a business opportunity that one industry veteran, Thomas M. Begel, dismissed immediately. When a colleague asked him if he was interested in buying Bethlehem Steel's railcar division, Begel said, "Not a chance, no way in the world," according to the June 6, 1994 issue of *Forbes*.

Begel had good reason to eye FCD's sale with disdain. He had spent the previous decade dealing with the nightmarish cyclicality of the railcar business. During the 1980s, Begel served as chairman and chief executive officer of Chicago's Pullman Standard, a railcar manufacturer that fell victim to the railcar glut of the late 1970s and early 1980s. At the time, railcars were marketed as tax shelters, which fueled extraordinary demand throughout the industry. "Every dentist had to own a couple freight cars," Begel recalled in the June 6, 1994 issue of *Forbes*. From the typical annual production of 60,000 railcars, industry production swelled to 85,000 in 1980 as industry capacity skyrocketed to 150,000 railcars per year. When provi-

sions in the tax code that made railcar ownership attractive were removed in 1981, the market was left in ruins, with roughly 400,000 railcars, a six- or seven-year supply, up for sale and unwanted.

Begel, as the head of Pullman Standard, looked at the saturated market and he decided to retreat. In 1984, he sold the company's railcar manufacturing assets and began building a new company with a new orientation. He began acquiring other manufacturing properties, turning Pullman Standard into a producer of truck trailers, airline seats, and other products. In 1987, he resigned from the company, sold his Pullman Standard stock, and began looking for a new business to acquire. After his experience with Pullman Standard, nothing was more unappealing than acquiring a railcar manufacturing business.

Begel's immediate negative reaction to the availability of FCD soon turned to excitement. He reconsidered the prospect after surveying the industry he had fled in 1984. The number of freight cars in the United States had dropped from 1.8 million to 1.2 million. The number of freight car manufacturers in the country, which had totaled 23 in 1980, had been winnowed down to fewer than six manufacturers a decade later. Industry manufacturing capacity had checked itself, declining from 150,000 cars per year to 50,000 railcars per year. The nation's fleet of railcars, Begel observed, was getting older; railroads increasingly were asking more of the existing fleet. He sensed an imminent increase in demand, which led him to embrace what he had earlier shunned. In 1991, he led an investment group that included his own company, TMB Industries, and Toronto, Canada-based Onex Corp., that acquired FCD in December for roughly $50 million. For the purchase price, Begel gained ownership of two plants—one devoted to fabrication, the other devoted to assembly—that were capable of generating $200 million in annual sales. He named the Johnstown-based company Johnstown America Corp., a manufacturing operation that later would be known as FreightCar America, Inc.

NEW OWNERSHIP AND BRIGHT PROSPECTS

At the former FCD, whose payroll had shrunk to fewer than ten employees at one point, Begel injected vitality. He invested more than $5 million in new machinery, organized the workforce into teams, and implemented a quality-improvement program that required Johnstown America workers to enroll in a two-day training program. The increase in demand occurred as he had expected: In 1993, industry freight car deliveries increased from 25,000 to 35,000 before reaching 45,000

KEY DATES

1901: Railcar production begins in Johnstown, Pennsylvania, with the formation of Cambria Steel Co.

1923: Bethlehem Steel Company acquires the Johnstown-based, railcar manufacturing operations established by Cambria Steel Co.

1986: Bethlehem Steel's Freight Car Division (FCD) introduces the aluminum-bodied BethGon, a railcar that will dominate the coal-carrying market.

1991: FCD is sold to an investor group led by Thomas M. Begel and renamed Johnstown America Corp.

1995: Johnstown America acquires manufacturing operations in Danville, Illinois.

1999: The railcar operations in Johnstown and Danville are sold to management.

2004: Johnstown America leases manufacturing operations in Roanoke, Virginia, and changes its name to FreightCar America, Inc.

2005: FreightCar America completes its initial public offering of stock in April.

2007: FreightCar America announces it will close its Johnstown plant.

in 1994. In Johnstown, production volume followed the industry trend, increasing from 4,500 in 1992 to 10,000 in 1994. The company's sales shot upward as a result, rising from $205 million in 1992 to $469 million in 1994. Early investors in the company realized the financial rewards of Begel's vision, quintupling their money. "We've created something out of nothing, and we've all made a lot of money out of it," Begel said in the June 6, 1994 issue of *Forbes.* "I love these nuts-and-bolts kind of businesses."

For Begel, all was well in the railcar industry, but he knew the capricious business could show its ugly side with debilitating speed. As a hedge against the cyclical nature of Johnstown America's line of work, Begel began diversifying, essentially doing what he had done at Pullman Standard except for exiting the railcar industry. In 1995, he purchased Truck Components Inc., a manufacturer of iron castings and wheel-end components, and Bostrom Seating, Inc., another supplier to the motor carrier industry. The year also saw him expand his railcar business by acquiring Freight Car Services, which added manufacturing operations in

Danville, Illinois. He had hoped to create a transportation conglomerate immune to the wild swings of the railcar market, but his strategy backfired.

DERAILED IN THE MID-NINETIES

Oversupply again crippled the railcar industry in the mid-1990s. The behavior of TTX Co., the purchasing cooperative for the country's 12 largest railroads, exemplified the industry's downturn. The company, whose orders had accounted for nearly half of Johnstown America's sales in 1994, informed Begel it had no need for a single car in 1996 or in 1997, sending Johnstown America's production volume plummeting. Begel struggled just to make the interest payments on the junk bonds he used to complete the acquisition of Truck Components and Bostrom System, which amounted to quarterly, $8 million interest payments. "We're stymied right now," Begel said in the March 10, 1997 issue of *Crain's Chicago Business,* "this is just a terrible time for the railroad freight car industry."

Begel struggled through the period, eventually deciding to take essentially the same course of action as he had taken with Pullman Standard. In 1999, he sold a majority interest in the railcar business to its management for $100 million, separating it from the operations that made wheel components, iron castings, truck and bus seats, drive axles, and gearboxes. Johnston America was split in two, with the truck components business, which generated nearly half of the company's $966 million in sales in 1998, cast off as an independent company with a different name. Johnstown America emerged as the corporate title for the railcar operations, a company headed by John E. Carroll Jr., who had served as the railcar unit's president under Begel's command.

Carroll, who had led the purchasing group that acquired the railcar operations, suffered through the same anemic conditions that had plagued Begel. Johnstown America lost money for four consecutive years at the beginning of the new century, making the start of his leadership tenure a painful period that was exacerbated by ongoing squabbles with the company's union workers. Prospects brightened midway through the decade, as the bright side of the cyclical railcar industry showed its face, with the Carroll-led management team plotting the construction of aluminum railcars to satisfy the nation's increasing demand for coal. The company boosted production capacity by leasing a freight car construction and repair shop from Norfolk Southern in Roanoke, Virginia, where it planned to hire 400 employees within the ensuing 30 months to build aluminum railcars.

PUBLIC DEBUT IN 2005

In December 2004, the company changed its name from Johnstown America to FreightCar America in anticipation of its imminent initial public offering (IPO) of stock. In April 2005, it completed its IPO, selling 8.5 million shares at $19 per share, which raised roughly $85 million in net proceeds.

FreightCar America recorded the best financial performance in its history following its IPO. Between 2004 and 2005, revenues soared from $482 million to $927 million, the increase fueled by a wave of orders for aluminum-bodied railcars, which accounted for an overwhelming percentage of the company's business. The good news continued in 2006, a banner year for FreightCar America that included reaching a significant milestone. In December, the company delivered a Beth-Gon II high-capacity gondola to NRG Energy Inc., the 100,000th aluminum-bodied railcar shipped by the company since the introduction of the BethGon railcar 20 years earlier. The shipment to NRG Energy was one of 2,695 railcars being built for the Princeton, New Jersey-based company, just one of several sizable contracts that pointed to a promising future for Freight-Car America. The company also signed an agreement with TXU Generation Development Co. at the end of 2006 to build more than 7,600 railcars for delivery in 2008 and 2009. FreightCar America ended the year with record-high totals in revenues and net income, posting $1.4 billion in sales and $128 million in profits.

NEW LEADERSHIP IN 2007 AND THE END OF AN ERA

As FreightCar America neared its 20th anniversary as an independent company, it held sway as the largest producer of aluminum-bodied railcars in North America based on the number of railcars delivered. In 2007, two significant events occurred against the backdrop of declining industry production volumes and pricing pressures. The downturn led to a substantial decline in revenues for the year, as sales shrank from $1.4 billion to $817 million. The burden of contending with the constant market fluctuations was handed to a new chief executive officer during the year after Carroll resigned to pursue other business interests. Christian Ragot, who was promoted from the post of chief operating officer, took his place, becoming FreightCar America's new president and chief executive officer in April 2007.

As Ragot took the helm and plotted the company's future course, his primary objective was to restructure his operations to guard against industry downturns. In December 2007, an integral part of his plan was announced when FreightCar America revealed its intention

to close down its Johnstown manufacturing operations. Deemed a higher-cost facility in comparison to the Danville and Roanoke plants, the Johnstown plant had been a source of labor problems for years. "Although we entered into decisional bargaining with the union representing our Johnstown employees regarding labor costs at the Johnstown facility," Ragot explained in the January 2008 issue of *Railway Age*, "we and the union did not reach an agreement that would have allowed us to continue to operate the facility in a cost-effective way." FreightCar America kept its administrative offices in Johnstown, but moved forward without any manufacturing presence in its hometown, ending a more than century-long legacy of railcar production in Cambria County.

Jeffrey L. Covell

PRINCIPAL SUBSIDIARIES

JAC Intermedco, Inc.; JAC Operations, Inc.; Johnstown America Corporation; Freight Car Service, Inc.; JAIX Leasing Company; JAC Patent Company; FreightCar Roanoke, Inc.

PRINCIPAL COMPETITORS

Trinity Industries, Inc.; National Steel Car Limited; The Greenbrier Companies, Inc.; American Railcar Industries, Inc.

FURTHER READING

Caliri, Lois, "FreightCar America Hopes to Get Back on Track by Capitalizing on Coal Demand," *Roanoke Times,* January 14, 2005.

Flint, Jerry, "A Market Cleared," *Forbes,* June 6, 1994, p. 53.

"FreightCar America Closing Johnstown Plant," *Railway Age,* January 2008, p. 14.

Gallagher, Thomas L., "FreightCar America Settles Suit," *Traffic World,* November 21, 2008.

"Johnstown Seeks to Acquire Transcisco," *Railway Age,* May 1995, p. 18.

Murphy, H. Lee, "A Railcar Maker Is Running Out of Track," *Crain's Chicago Business,* March 10, 1997, p. 4.

Piatek, Shawn, "FreightCar America President to Step Down in April," *Tribune-Democrat,* November 3, 2006.

"TMB Bets Big on Johnstown," *Railway Age,* January 1992, p. 60.

Vantuono, William C., "Rebirth at Roanoke," *Railway Age,* July 2005, p. 29.

Welty, Gus, "Johnstown Makes Its Mark," *Railway Age,* September 1993, p. 71.

Wooley, Scott, "Derailed," *Forbes,* August 26, 1996, p. 14.

GeoResources, Inc.

110 Cypress Station Drive, Suite 220
Houston, Texas 77090-1629
U.S.A.
Telephone: (281) 537-9920
Fax: (281) 537-8324
Web site: http://www.georesourcesinc.com

Public Company
Incorporated: 1958 as GeoResources Exploration Inc.
Employees: 61
Sales: $40.1 million (2007)
Stock Exchanges: NASDAQ
Ticker Symbol: GEOI
NAICS: 211111 Crude Petroleum and Natural Gas Extraction

■ ■ ■

GeoResources, Inc., is a Houston, Texas-based energy company that primarily develops and operates oil- and gas-producing properties located in the Gulf Coast of Texas and Louisiana, the Permian Basin of Texas, the Rocky Mountain region of Colorado and Wyoming, and North Dakota's Williston Basin. The northern half of the company's activities are conducted through the G3 Operating, LLC, Denver-based subsidiary, which in addition to its focus on North Dakota, where more than 90 wells are in operation, also pursues acquisition opportunities in Montana, Utah, Colorado, Kansas, and Michigan. Southern region activities are handled by Southern Bay Operating, LLC, which also provides the corporate headquarters for GeoResources. Southern Bay operates oil and gas properties in Texas and Louisiana. Southern Bay also has oil and gas interests located in New Mexico, Oklahoma, and Alabama, and maintains offices in Odem and Midland, Texas, and Church Point, Louisiana. All told, at the end of 2007 GeoResources had pro forma reserves of about 15.7 million barrels of oil equivalent, and about 146,000 net developed acres and more than 59,000 net undeveloped acres in Colorado, Louisiana, Montana, North Dakota, Texas, and Utah. GeoResources is a public company listed on the NASDAQ.

BEGINNINGS IN URANIUM MINING

GeoResources was incorporated in 1958 as Geo-Resources Exploration Inc. by Rollin C. Vickers and associates, its original business uranium mining. Born in upstate New York, Vickers earned a bachelor of arts degree in geology from Cornell University in 1950. To pursue his postgraduate education Vickers enrolled at Syracuse University, earning a master of science degree in geology in 1952. He focused on hard rock and minerals, but his master's thesis, "A Radioactive Study of the Sedimentary Rocks of Central New York State and a Description of the Methods and Apparatus Used," also indicated an interest in uranium. Vickers then earned his doctorate in economic geology and mining from the University of Wisconsin, graduating in 1957. A year later he teamed up with colleagues and others to form GeoResources. One of the partners, attorney Milton R. Litman, was responsible for the incorporation and the completion of other necessary paperwork. Vickers

COMPANY PERSPECTIVES

GeoResources' business strategy includes the acquisition of oil and gas reserves, along with field re-engineering, development, exploitation and exploration activities, intended to increase estimated quantities of proved reserves, and increase production and share values.

became the president and chairman of the new company.

GeoResources began mining uranium in the Moorcroft, Wyoming region. The only customer for yellow cake uranium produced from uranium ore was the U.S. government, which for national security reasons controlled this key material used in nuclear weaponry, stockpiling supplies of it. It became apparent that soon the government's need for uranium would diminish—indeed, the United States stopped purchasing yellow cake in the early 1960s—and GeoResources began looking for other mining activities. It acquired manganese interests in western Montana as well as the Reymert Silver Mine in Arizona, established in the 1880s in Pinal County by Norwegian immigrant James DeNoon Reymert. GeoResources acquired the silver operation from a bankrupt company and would operate the mine sporadically, depending on the price of silver. When the Hunt brothers attempted to corner the silver market in the late 1970s and early 1980s, resulting in skyrocketing silver prices, the Reymert assets were especially valuable, but once the silver bubble burst, the mine reverted to its status as a minor asset for GeoResources. It also produced some revenues by harvesting commercial rock.

More significant business pursued by GeoResources was the mining of leonardite, primarily used as a drilling mud additive by oil and gas well drillers. Named after North Dakota's first state geologist, Dr. A. G. Leonard, it was a minor form of coal, between peat and sub-bituminous. Leonardite was used in concert with products high in humic acid, which was used as a drilling mud thinner. A South American substance, quebracho, had been the prevalent drilling mud thinner until World War II when import restrictions led to the use of leonardite. After the war it became even more widely used, mostly employed in warmer climes, such as the Gulf Coast. U.S. companies would also take GeoResources' leonardite overseas, in particular to Mexico and the Pacific Rim. The opportunity to become involved in leonardite came to GeoResources through Kenneth

Koenen, a board member and classmate of Vickers at the University of Wisconsin. Another friend in Koenen's circle of geologists worked for the Great Northern Railway, which owned reserves of leonardite in Williston, North Dakota.

MOVE TO WILLISTON: 1964

GeoResources acquired the leonardite reserves and moved its operations to Williston, where in 1964 it built its first leonardite processing plant. Williston was also the center of oil and gas exploration activity in North Dakota, providing GeoResources with a ready customer base. Although Vickers had no training in oil and gas exploration, now that he was living in Williston and serving the industry it was natural for him to become interested and involved in the energy field.

In 1969 GeoResources began participating in oil and gas exploration and production projects. It enjoyed some success and lined up investors for private placements of stock. Because it was inefficient and expensive to arrange these private placements, the company soon decided to make an initial public offering (IPO) of stock. In October 1971 the company was reincorporated as GeoResources, Inc., and taken public. The company's stock then began trading as an over-the-counter stock on the new electronic system implemented earlier that year by the National Association of Securities Dealers. Called the National Association of Securities Dealers Automated Quotations, the new system would be known by the acronym NASDAQ.

In addition to the funds generated by the IPO, GeoResources' drilling activity was supported by the leonardite business, which for many years was a cash cow. GeoResources continued to maintain its other minor mining interests, but it was nonetheless a company very much dependent on the price of oil and gas. When commodity prices were high, the demand for leonardite was high as well, and the company's exploration activities also became more lucrative. GeoResources enjoyed a growth spurt in 1977 when an OPEC oil embargo led to higher crude oil prices and increased domestic exploration and drilling activity. Oil and gas revenues reached $1.89 million in 1980 and leonardite revenues totaled $874,000. A year later oil and gas revenues improved to $2.85 million and leonardite sales increased to more than $1.1 million. By that time, the price of oil was beginning to soften, however. GeoResources was able to continue to post record results through 1983, but commodity prices fell and the entire energy industry collapsed.

KEY DATES

1958: GeoResources Exploration Inc. is founded in Wyoming by Rollin C. Vickers to mine uranium.

1964: Leonardite processing plant opens in Williston, North Dakota.

1969: GeoResources becomes involved in oil and gas exploration and development.

1971: Company goes public.

1980: Vickers resigns as president but remains chairman.

1983: Vickers's son, Jeffrey Vickers, assumes presidency.

1996: Rollin Vickers retires.

2002: Subsidiary Western Star Drilling Company becomes operational.

2007: GeoResources merges with Southern Bay Oil & Gas, L.P. and Chandler Energy, LLC.

VICKERS STEPS DOWN: 1980

In the meantime, there were changes at the top ranks of GeoResources. In 1980 Vickers stepped down as president, although he retained the chairmanship, a position he would hold for several more years. After that he would stay on as a director until his retirement at the end of 1996. Vickers turned over day-to-day control of GeoResources in 1980 to Lonnie W. Mollberg and his management team. They were not well trained in the oil and gas industry, however, and soon Vickers was looking for an experienced hand to step in. He found it in his son, Jeffrey P. Vickers.

The younger Vickers had been born in Wisconsin when his father was still in graduate school. Growing up in Wyoming he became interested in mining and enrolled at the University of North Dakota to study mining. With the advent of the oil embargo he decided that the oil and gas industry offered greater opportunities, and so he changed his major to geological engineering with a petroleum engineering option. After graduating in 1978 he went to work as an associate petroleum engineer in the Williston Basin for Amerada Hess Corporation. Jeffrey Vickers had never planned on joining his father's company. Moreover, at the time he completed his degree there were no openings at GeoResources. When he joined the company in 1981 he served as drilling and production manager, responsible for providing technical assistance to the drilling operations as well as overseeing the entire program. He became a director of the company in June 1982, and then at the start of 1983 assumed the presidency.

Jeffrey Vickers was soon faced with a difficult business environment to navigate. With the collapse of the oil and gas industry in 1983, GeoResources entered a period of severe belt tightening. The company consolidated its operations in Williston, where in 1982 it had constructed a larger leonardite processing plant and it was at least less expensive to maintain an office there than in larger cities. To stay in business, everyone in the home office also had to take on multiple tasks. To make matters worse, the previous management team had taken on debt in 1981 to fund exploration and production activities. Despite the conditions, GeoResources hung on, unlike many companies in the energy sector, and managed to pay off its debt without defaulting. The company did not, however, enjoy any growth through the decade.

By the start of the 1990s, GeoResources' business was split equally between its leonardite and oil and gas segments. That balance would change over the next few years, as oil and gas revenues took on greater importance. In 1994, for example, leonardite contributed $758,000 to the company's total revenues of $2.45 million. A year later, overall revenues increased to $2.9 million, while leonardite's contribution amounted to $704,000, the result of lower demand and lower average price per ton.

FALLING PRICES HURT COMPANY: 1998

GeoResources enjoyed steady growth in the mid-1990s. Revenues peaked in 1997 at $4.2 million, resulting in net income of $766,265. Another drop in oil and gas prices led to a difficult 1998, however. Revenues fell to $2.38 million and the company reported a net loss of $1.6 million. About 35 oil wells were shut down and not brought back into production until the second quarter of 1999 when prices finally began to rebound. As a result, GeoResources returned to profitability at the end of the decade, posting a profit of $481,552 on sales of $3.34 million.

Business continued to improve for GeoResources in the new century. Revenues improved to $5.11 million and net income to $1.41 million in 2000. Leonardite sales were essentially flat, however, accounting for only $676,000. To support the company's oil and gas exploration activities, GeoResources formed a contract drilling subsidiary, Western Star Drilling Company, and in 2001 acquired a drilling rig rated to 8,000 feet, which was then retrofitted for use by Western Star. Contract drilling operations commenced in 2002.

Eroding commodity prices led to declining revenues for GeoResources in 2001 and 2002, dipping below $4 million. As prices firmed up, revenues improved to $4.84 million in 2003 and net income increased to $446,563. Steady growth followed over the next three years, with revenues increasing to $5.53 million in 2004, $7.2 million in 2005, and $8.9 million in 2006. Net income during this period reached a high of $2.18 million in 2005. In the meantime, the Williston leonardite processing plant was damaged by a fire in May 2005. Because leonardite was no longer a core activity, GeoResources began looking to sell its leonardite assets.

Jeffrey Vickers was also thinking about merging GeoResources with another company in order to facilitate further growth. The legal counsel for GeoResources was aware of an energy client in Houston, Southern Bay Oil & Gas, L.P., that was also looking to expand its footprint and might be interested in the northern assets that GeoResources had to offer as well as its status as a public company. Founded in December 2004, Southern was headed by Frank A. Lodzinski, a certified public accountant with more than three decades of oil and gas industry experience. Over the years he had developed several oil and gas companies in the Gulf Coast area, building up their reserves and successfully selling or merging the companies to the benefit of shareholders. Lodzinski had also been involved in a limited way in the Rocky Mountains and was attracted to the region because of its reserve potential and long-term production possibilities. Hence, he was looking to join forces with companies similar in size to Southern who could provide the expertise in the Rockies he lacked. GeoResources was an ideal candidate, as was Denver-based Chandler Energy, LLC, established in 2000 by Collis P. Chandler III to conduct oil and gas exploration and production in the Rockies and Michigan.

MERGER RESULTS IN NEW GEORESOURCES: 2007

In late 2006 a deal was reached between GeoResources, Southern Bay, and Chandler, completed in April 2007. Because GeoResources was a public company, it acquired the two other companies in a $78 million stock transaction. At the same time Southern Bay and Chandler brought in $20 million in new capital to fund expansion plans. Lodzinski took over as CEO and president of the new GeoResources, which also moved its headquarters to Houston. Vickers stayed with the company in Williston but soon left. Some of the longtime assets of GeoResources were also divested. The Reymert Silver Mine was sold, and the leonardite operation was sold to plant employees, who conducted business under the Leonardite Products LLC name.

Even as the merger was being completed, GeoResources was positioning itself for the future, paying $82 million for properties in the Giddings Field of Texas, backed by GE Energy Financial Services, which also made $27 million available to develop the properties. In addition, GeoResources used its financial wherewithal to launch an ambitious development drilling program to take full advantage of escalating oil and gas prices. Although the three companies that comprised the new GeoResources were together for only part of the year, revenues increased to more than $40 million and net income totaled $3 million. A year later, through three quarters, GeoResources posted revenues of $75.74 million, well ahead of the previous year's $21 million, and net income of $17.8 million. Falling oil and gas prices curbed growth later in the year. Even so, GeoResources remained a fast-growing business. Lodzinski made it clear to *Oil and Gas Investor* in a November 2007 interview that he planned to run GeoResources as he had other ventures in his career: "Our strategy with GeoResources is to, again, build the company over the next three or four years, then realize profit through market liquidity or through a merger or sale."

Ed Dinger

PRINCIPAL SUBSIDIARIES

G3 Operating, LLC; Southern Bay Operating, LLC.

PRINCIPAL COMPETITORS

Abraxas Petroleum Corporation; Brigham Exploration Company; Devon Energy Corporation.

FURTHER READING

"General Electric Co.: Unit Joins Two Firms to Buy Energy Reserves," *Wall Street Journal,* May 9, 2007, p. C6.

"GeoResources Explores for, Develops Oil, Gas in the Williston Basin," *Oil & Gas Journal,* October 27, 2003, p. 41.

Stell, Jeannie, "Rockies Rookies," *Oil & Gas Investor,* November 2007, p. 24.

"Williston Firm Acquiring Two Private Oil and Gas Companies," *Bismarck Tribune,* September 18, 2006, p. 1b.

Witte, Brian, "Low Oil Prices Hurt N.D. Producers," *Grand Forks Herald,* June 1, 1998, p. 4.

Georgia-Pacific LLC

133 Peachtree Street, Northeast
Atlanta, Georgia 30303-5605
U.S.A.
Telephone: (404) 652-4000
Fax: (404) 749-2454
Web site: http://www.gp.com

Wholly Owned Subsidiary of Koch Industries, Inc.
Incorporated: 1927 as Georgia Hardwood Lumber Company
Employees: 50,000
Sales: $2.14 billion (2007 est.)
NAICS: 321211 Hardwood Veneer and Plywood Manufacturing; 321212 Softwood Veneer and Plywood Manufacturing; 321213 Engineered Wood Member (Except Truss) Manufacturing; 321219 Reconstituted Wood Product Manufacturing; 327420 Gypsum Product Manufacturing; 322110 Pulp Mills; 322121 Paper (Except Newsprint) Mills; 322130 Paperboard Mills; 322291 Sanitary Paper Product Manufacturing; 326140 Polystyrene Foam Product Manufacturing; 326199 All Other Plastics Product Manufacturing

■ ■ ■

Georgia-Pacific LLC is a leading manufacturer and distributor of paper-based consumer products, pulp, paper, packaging, building products, and related chemicals. Overall, it ranks as the second largest U.S. forest products company, trailing International Paper Company. The company holds the number one position worldwide in tissue products, producing paper towels, paper napkins, and bath and facial tissue under such brands as Quilted Northern, Angel Soft, Brawny, Mardi Gras, Sparkle, and Vanity Fair. Its Dixie business is the leading North American brand of disposable tableware, including plates, cups, and cutlery made of paper, plastic, and foam. Other Georgia-Pacific units produce bleached paperboard used in foodservice items; kraft paper used to make grocery and other paper bags as well as brown wrapping paper; containerboard used to make corrugated boxes and other packaging products; various pulps used to produce a variety of products; and building products, including plywood, oriented-strand board and other wood panels, lumber, and gypsum wallboard. Unlike many other major forest products firms, Georgia-Pacific does not own any timberlands, having sold its timber holdings in 2001. Since December 2005 Georgia-Pacific has been a wholly owned subsidiary of Koch Industries, Inc., one of the largest privately held companies in the United States.

EARLY DECADES OF GEOGRAPHIC AND OPERATIONAL EXPANSION

Although its operations in the 21st century range widely, the company's beginnings were in lumber distribution. Georgia Hardwood Lumber Company began operation in 1927 in Augusta, Georgia, as a hardwood lumber wholesaler with $12,000 in start-up funds provided by its founder, Owen R. Cheatham. During its first decade in business, the company began lumber manufacturing in addition to its wholesaling activities. Cheatham focused on expanding the

COMPANY PERSPECTIVES

At Georgia-Pacific, we believe in creating long-term value for our company, customers and business partners. Our 50,000 employees are guided by Market Based Management principles, which are based on integrity and compliance. These principles challenge us to achieve world-class excellence by constantly finding new and better ways to manufacture products and support the needs of our customers.

company's milling capabilities in the southern United States (the company was operating five sawmills in the South by 1938), a strategy that allowed it to become the largest supplier of lumber to the U.S. Army during World War II.

The company's 1947 purchase of Bellingham Plywood Company, operator of a plywood mill in Bellingham, Washington, coincided with plywood's growing popularity in the construction industry and gave the company a strong competitive advantage. To help fund the $1.1 million acquisition, Cheatham took his company public, netting $700,000 from the sale of 100,000 shares of common stock at $8.20 per share. Additional plywood mills in Washington and Oregon were purchased in 1948, as well as another plywood plant in 1949, to support this growing business area. The company changed its name in 1948 to Georgia-Pacific Plywood and Lumber Company to reflect more accurately its geographic and operational expansion. The following year the company's stock began trading on the New York Stock Exchange.

In 1951 the company changed its name again, to Georgia-Pacific Plywood Company. Cheatham gradually developed a reputation as an industry maverick. Over the next six years, he conducted a $160 million timberland-acquisition program in the western and southern United States. To finance this program, he borrowed heavily from banks and insurance companies expecting that the proceeds gained from the timber in the future would more than cover the required return on their investment. In order to be closer to these newly purchased resources, the company moved its headquarters from Georgia to Olympia, Washington, in 1953, and then again to Portland, Oregon, the following year.

Over the next decade, Cheatham used his financing model several times to acquire additional forest acreage and manufacturing facilities, including Coos Bay

Lumber Company (Coos Bay, Oregon) and Hammond Lumber Company (Humboldt County, California) in 1956. That same year the company's name was changed, for the third time since its founding, to Georgia-Pacific Corporation. Subsequent purchases of Booth-Kelly Lumber Company (Springfield, Oregon) in 1959 and W.M. Ritter Lumber Company in 1960 took the company to the number three position in its industry.

The company's unorthodox approach to growth was evident in other areas as well. It opened a kraft pulp and linerboard mill in Toledo, Oregon, in 1957, and its first resin adhesive plant at Coos Bay, Oregon, in 1959. The latter manufacturing operation was intended at first to supply the resin required for the company's plywood-production business but gradually grew large enough to supply resin to other plywood manufacturers as well. Georgia-Pacific was also one of the first manufacturers to use wood byproducts rather than timber in pulp production. The company continued to pioneer in the development of plywood products, eventually shifting away from the traditional use of Douglas fir to a process using less expensive southern pine. This wood previously had been considered inappropriate for use in plywood because of its high resin content.

During the 1960s, Georgia-Pacific embarked upon another series of acquisitions by buying several lumber and paper companies across the country. These included Crossett Lumber Company (Crossett, Arkansas) in 1962; Puget Sound Pulp and Timber Company (Bellingham, Washington), Vanity Fair Paper Mills (Plattsburgh, New York), St. Croix Paper Company (Woodland, Maine), and Fordyce Lumber Company (Fordyce, Arkansas) in 1963; Bestwall Gypsum Company (Paoli, Pennsylvania) in 1965; and Kalamazoo Paper Company (Kalamazoo, Michigan) in 1967. With the purchases of Puget Sound Pulp and Timber and Vanity Fair Paper, Georgia-Pacific entered the tissue business. After building its first corrugated-container plant in Olympia in 1961, the company added a series of additional manufacturing facilities for lumber, paper, and chemical products over the course of the rest of the decade.

STRUGGLES IN THE SEVENTIES

Upon Cheatham's death in 1970, Robert B. Pamplin, who had worked with Cheatham since the company's inception, became chairman and CEO. This transition was virtually seamless because Pamplin had effectively been running the company since 1960, when the founder suffered a debilitating stroke. Although Georgia-Pacific's building-products business benefited from the housing boom of the early 1970s, its paper and pulp interests struggled because of low prices and

KEY DATES

1927: Owen R. Cheatham founds Georgia Hardwood Lumber Company in Augusta, Georgia, as a hardwood lumber wholesaler.

1938: After expanding into lumber manufacturing, the firm operates five sawmills in the South.

1947: Expansion to the West Coast begins with the purchase of a plywood mill in Bellingham, Washington; company goes public.

1948: The company's name is changed to Georgia-Pacific Plywood and Lumber Company to better reflect the geographic and operational expansion.

1949: Company stock begins trading on the New York Stock Exchange.

1951: The company is renamed Georgia-Pacific Plywood Company.

1956: The company's name is changed to Georgia-Pacific Corporation.

1957: Company expands into pulp and paper sector with the opening of a kraft pulp and linerboard mill in Toledo, Oregon.

1963: Georgia-Pacific expands into the tissue business with the acquisitions of Puget Sound Pulp and Timber Company and Vanity Fair Paper Mills.

1972: A Federal Trade Commission consent order forces the company to divest 20 percent of its assets, which are spun off as Louisiana-Pacific Corporation.

1982: Headquarters are relocated to Atlanta, Georgia.

1990: Great Northern Nekoosa Corporation is acquired.

1997: Timber operations are split off into a separate operating group, the Timber Company, with its own common stock.

2000: Fort James Corporation is acquired for $7.7 billion in stock and cash plus the assumption of $3.3 billion in debt.

2001: Georgia-Pacific sells four fine-paper mills to Domtar Inc. for $1.65 billion; Timber Company is merged into Plum Creek Timber Company, Inc., marking Georgia-Pacific's exit from the timber business.

2004: Company sells its building products distribution business.

2005: In a $21 billion deal, Koch Industries, Inc., acquires the company, which becomes a wholly owned Koch subsidiary under the name Georgia-Pacific LLC.

sluggish demand. To bolster its manufacturing operations, the firm expanded production of two new building materials, polyvinyl chloride (PVC) and particleboard, the former through a joint venture with Permaneer Corporation. Georgia-Pacific opened its own PVC manufacturing plant in 1975. When the cost of oil increased soon afterward, however, the company's prices for its PVC-molding products proved to be too high to compete effectively with wood moldings, resulting in significant losses.

It was also during this period that the firm was required by the Federal Trade Commission (FTC) to defend its acquisition of 16 small firms in the South that supplied the company with 673,000 acres of the southern pine used to make plywood. Charging that the acquisitions tended to create a monopoly, the FTC issued a consent order in 1972 that forced Georgia-Pacific to divest 20 percent of its assets. This step resulted in the formation of a spinoff company called Louisiana-

Pacific Corporation. The order also prohibited the firm from acquiring any other softwood plywood companies and imposed restrictions on timberland purchases in the South for five years and on plywood mill acquisitions for ten years.

A slump in the housing industry in 1973 and 1974 depressed the company's lumber and plywood business. Georgia-Pacific continued to post record profits, however, largely because of the growth of its chemical, pulp, and paper operations. These areas experienced slowdowns as well by the middle of the decade. Nevertheless, the company moved forward in its long-range program to increase manufacturing capacity across the board. It expanded through vertical integration into the production of additional chemicals derived from wood wastes, such as chlorine, phenol, and methanol. The 1975 acquisition of New Orleans-based Exchange Oil & Gas Corporation enabled the company to become more self-sufficient by developing its own reserves of important raw materials required for the operation of its chemical plants.

In 1976 President Robert Flowerree succeeded Pamplin as chairman and CEO. A 25-year Georgia-Pacific veteran, Flowerree had been instrumental in taking the company into the chemical business. He was also considered to be more cautious than his predecessors. Under his leadership, the firm expanded its building products to include roofing materials, which it began to produce in a converted paper mill.

By 1978, the company was drawing three-quarters of its sales from the southern and eastern United States. This shift away from the West was instrumental in the decision to move the headquarters of the firm back to Georgia, specifically to Atlanta, 150 miles away from its original location. The relocation, completed in 1982, caused many employees to leave the company, and several senior executives chose to retire rather than make the move. This shift left the firm vulnerable at a critical time, particularly in the growing chemical area.

TURNAROUND IN THE EIGHTIES

The early 1980s brought with it another housing slump, but Georgia-Pacific was able to use its chemical business to maintain overall growth. Its plywood products, however, were slowly losing competitive ground to new and less expensive materials, such as waferboard and oriented-strand board, which were being manufactured and sold aggressively by such firms as Louisiana-Pacific and Potlatch Corporation. Until then, Georgia-Pacific had not placed significant emphasis on these materials, with only one plant producing waferboard and another producing oriented-strand board. Most of its capital expenditure was directed instead toward upgrading existing facilities and buying timberlands.

In 1982 T. Marshall Hahn Jr., who had succeeded Flowerree as president in 1976, became COO. When he became chairman and CEO one year later, following Flowerree's early retirement, he faced several serious problems. Demand for paper was strong, but only in the area of higher-quality products, not in the basic linerboard and kraft paper sectors in which Georgia-Pacific concentrated. Although an upturn in the construction industry augured well for the company's building products business, the high interest rates on the debt the firm had used to fund expansion severely limited its freedom to take advantage of opportunities in that area. Furthermore, its chemical business, once the firm's star division, fell on hard times as sales dropped significantly. This business was spun off through a 1984 management-led leveraged buyout that created the new

firm Georgia Gulf Corporation, and Exchange Oil & Gas was sold for $180 million in 1985. The company retained its specialty chemicals business, which continued to deliver good returns.

Hahn instituted a series of measures designed to get the company back on its feet. These included reviewing the health of its assets, improvement of cost controls and productivity, and continued investment in areas such as the pulp and paper business, which could insulate the company from future economic calamities and provide a hedge against cyclical upturns and downturns in the various industries in which the company operated. In 1984 Georgia-Pacific acquired a containerboard mill in Monticello, Mississippi, several corrugated container plants, and 275,000 acres of forest from St. Regis Corporation. It converted two paper plants to the production of higher-margin products, such as lightweight bleached board and white paper used by copiers and computer printers. It also successfully expanded a wood products mill in South Carolina and a plant in Florida to produce lattice and fencing materials, which were in heavy demand.

In 1986 the company entered the premium bathroom tissue market with the introduction of Angel Soft bath tissue. By the end of 1987, Georgia-Pacific's tissue and towel operation, combined with its production of containerboard, kraft, and fine papers, enabled the company to achieve higher profitability in paper products than in wood products for the first time in its history, despite tough competition from major consumer products companies such as The Procter & Gamble Company. Other elements of Hahn's turnaround strategy included further decentralization of the company's operations, which forced plant managers to compete with each other for capital funds, and the addition of several building materials distribution centers nationwide to capitalize on the growing trend toward remodeling and do-it-yourself projects.

During the last years of the decade, the company made further acquisitions. These included U.S. Plywood Corporation and selected assets of the Erving Distributor Products Company in 1987 and Brunswick Pulp & Paper Company and American Forest Products Company in 1988. Its most controversial purchase, however, commenced in 1989 with an offer to buy Great Northern Nekoosa Corporation of Norwalk, Connecticut, a competing producer of pulp, paper, containerboard, lumber, and plywood.

1990 ACQUISITION OF GREAT NORTHERN NEKOOSA

Originally incorporated in 1898 as the Northern Development Company but soon renamed Great

Northern Paper Company, the predecessor to Great Northern Nekoosa had begun producing newsprint in 1900. By 1924 it was manufacturing corrugated paper and a decade later began a gradual transition from wrapping paper to business paper production. The company expanded its pulp and paper operations over the next 40 years. In 1970 the Great Northern Paper Company and the Nekoosa Edwards Paper Company merged to become Great Northern Nekoosa Corporation. Great Northern Nekoosa acquired several firms subsequently to enhance the company's manufacturing and distribution capabilities, including Heco Envelope Company in 1973; Pak-Well in 1975; Leaf River Forest Products in 1981; Barton, Duer & Koch and Consolidated Marketing, Inc., in 1982; Triquet Paper Company in 1983; Chatfield Paper Company in 1984; J&J Corrugated Box Corporation and Carpenter Paper Company of Iowa in 1986; Owens-Illinois's forest products company in 1987; and Jim Walter Papers in 1988. By 1989, Great Northern Nekoosa was operating 55 paper mills and paperboard converting plants, 83 paper distribution centers, one plywood plant, and two sawmills.

Great Northern Nekoosa was a particularly attractive candidate for acquisition because of its depressed stock price. Georgia-Pacific saw the combination of the two companies as an opportunity to achieve economies of scale and other cost savings. In Hahn's opinion, the acquisition would enable Georgia-Pacific to add manufacturing capability at less expense than by building its own plants. On the other hand, Great Northern Nekoosa viewed Georgia-Pacific's $3.74 billion bid as a hostile takeover attempt. It tried to halt the proposed buyout with a series of lawsuits and an extensive search for another buyer. All of these measures failed, however, and the purchase was completed in March 1990. Georgia-Pacific assumed a significant amount of debt as a result, pushing the total cost of the takeover to $5.4 billion, but was able to eliminate part of the burden through the subsequent sale of several mills and some timberland to Tenneco, the John Hancock Mutual Life Insurance Company, and the Metropolitan Life Insurance Company.

With its hard-fought acquisition of Great Northern Nekoosa complete, Georgia-Pacific held market leadership positions in containerboard, packaging, pulp, and communication papers and was a major producer of related products, such as tissue, kraft paper, and bleached board. The most significant threat to the company's continued growth would be the economy's effects on its key business areas. Although the firm's diversification into paper and pulp manufacturing was intended to help it survive cyclical downturns in lumber and housing construction, its new business areas were also highly cyclical in nature, with peaks and valleys lagging only months behind those occurring in lumber and housing.

Paper prices fell soon after Georgia-Pacific closed the Great Northern Nekoosa deal, but true to plan, the declining paper market was offset by record profits in the company's building products division, which posted profits of $432 million in 1990 despite low levels in housing starts. Georgia-Pacific was also able to reduce a significant amount of the $8 billion debt it was saddled with following the Great Northern Nekoosa purchase, thanks to the company's healthy cash flow. Despite these favorable signs, net income fell to $365 million in 1990, down from $661 million in 1989.

Prices of Georgia-Pacific shares on the New York Stock Exchange fell almost 50 percent in 1990 in response to investors' fears that the company might be acquiring too much debt. To ease this concern, the company took out a two-page ad in national magazines to convey the message that the company had significant cash flow to pay down its debt and had laid the groundwork for a strong future.

Despite Georgia-Pacific's intentions, profits took a dive in 1991 when the bottom dropped out of both the building materials and pulp and paper markets. The company reported a net loss of $151 million, compared to profits of over $3 million the preceding year. Georgia-Pacific continued to rely on its substantial cash flow to reward shareholders and reduce debt in 1991.

In 1991 the company also reorganized its building products division along product lines, as opposed to its previous method of management along geographical lines. It also completed the expansion of its Ashdown, Arkansas, paper mill with the addition of the world's largest and fastest paper machine. A. D. (Pete) Correll, who joined Georgia-Pacific's paper division in 1988 after being wooed from his position at the Mead Corporation, was elected president and chief operating officer.

COST-CUTTING INITIATIVES

Despite its continuously healthy cash flow and record-breaking profits in its building products division, the company posted losses again in 1992. In response to the recession, which continued to affect Georgia-Pacific's key businesses, management chose to focus on keeping costs down and reducing debt. Georgia-Pacific did this by paring down its "nonstrategic" assets, selling its Butler Paper distribution operations (acquired as part of its purchase of Great Northern Nekoosa) to Alco Standard Corporation in 1993 and its roofing manufacturing business to Atlas Roofing Corporation the following year. Also divested in 1994 was its envelope manufacturing business (another Great Northern inheritance), which evolved into Mail-Well, Inc. (later renamed Cenveo Inc.). Proceeds from these sales went to further reduce the company's debt.

By the time that Correll succeeded Hahn as Georgia-Pacific's chairman and CEO during 1993, the company's financial outlook had begun to look brighter. Housing starts were on the rise again, and lumber production remained far below demand. Lumber prices began rising to record highs in October 1993. Georgia-Pacific had grown to become the largest supplier of building lumber in the United States and was perfectly poised to benefit from improvements in the economy. The pulp and paper market, meanwhile, started a strong recovery in 1994, enabling the company to return to profitability after two years in the red. The improving conditions led the firm during 1994 to launch a two-year, $1.75 billion capital improvement program, focusing primarily on expanding its strongly performing engineered wood products operations. Surging pulp and paper prices enabled Georgia-Pacific to post record profits of $921 million on record revenues of $14.31 billion in 1995. The pulp and paper market began to enter another slump, however, late that year.

While the market was still surging, Correll launched a number of initiatives aimed at making Georgia-Pacific the most cost-efficient company in the industry. A major restructuring of the building products distribution operation, aiming at cutting costs and increasing sales, began in 1994. This led to the announcement in mid-1995 that 60 of Georgia-Pacific's 130 building products distribution centers would be closed by early 1997. Later in 1994 the company launched the Mill Improvement Program to cut costs and increase efficiency at the firm's 14 large pulp and paper mills. A little more than two years later, the mills had each identified cost savings of $20 million to $40 million per year. Finally, in mid-1995 the building products manufacturing operation launched Operation Complete, eventually identifying nearly $200 million in cost savings and productivity improvements at the 140 facilities of that company unit.

LATE 20TH-CENTURY DEAL-MAKING

Georgia-Pacific used some of its profits from the heady results of 1995 to bolster its gypsum wallboard capacity. It paid about $350 million in early 1996 to acquire nine wallboard plants from Domtar Inc., based in Montreal, Canada. Moving quickly to counter the effects of the sliding paper prices, Correll, in May 1996, launched a three-year effort to reduce overhead costs by $400 million. The effort included a hiring freeze and an early retirement program for salaried employees. In late 1996,

Georgia-Pacific announced that it would sell a number of operations based in Martell, California, including 127,000 acres of timberland, a sawmill, and a particleboard plant, to Sierra Pacific Holding Co. The $320 million deal closed in early 1997.

Seeking to increase its overall market value and to free its timber operations from the financial gyrations of its wildly cyclical pulp, paper, and building products businesses, Georgia-Pacific, in December 1997, split off its timber operations into a separate operating group with its own common stock. Georgia-Pacific Corporation essentially became a holding company for two operating groups, Georgia-Pacific Group (all operations other than the timber operations) and the Timber Company (the timber operations), with two classes of common stock for the two groups. The preexisting common stock was redesignated as the common stock of Georgia-Pacific Group, while company shareholders received shares of newly created Timber Company stock.

The late 1990s were also noteworthy for two significant acquisitions. In June 1998, Georgia-Pacific acquired Indianapolis-based CeCorr Inc. for about $190 million plus the assumption of $92 million in debt. CeCorr produced corrugated sheets at 11 sheet feeder plants, with the sheets sold to other firms for conversion into corrugated containers. CeCorr was the leading independent maker of corrugated sheets in the United States with 1997 revenues of $282 million. In mid-1999, Georgia-Pacific acquired Unisource Worldwide, Inc., for about $850 million plus the assumption of $785 million in debt. This acquisition was secured through an unsolicited offer that bested a previously agreed upon bid by UGI Corporation. Based in Berwyn, Pennsylvania, Unisource was a leading North American distributor of printing and imaging paper and supplies, with revenues for the fiscal year ending in September 1998 of $7.42 billion. Georgia-Pacific thus returned to the paper distribution sector it had been involved in briefly, and more modestly, when it owned Butler Paper from 1990 to 1993.

Also in 1999, Georgia-Pacific combined its commercial-tissue business with Wisconsin Tissue, the commercial-tissue unit of Chesapeake Corporation. The resulting joint venture, Georgia-Pacific Tissue, LLC, was 95 percent owned by Georgia-Pacific and 5 percent by Chesapeake and was managed by Georgia-Pacific. As part of the deal, Chesapeake received $755 million in cash from Georgia-Pacific. The joint venture, kept separate from Georgia-Pacific's consumer-tissue operations, focused on selling paper towels and tissues to institutions. Meantime, the Timber Company during 1999 sold 194,000 acres of timberlands in northern California for about $397 million and 390,000 acres in

Maine and 440,000 acres in New Brunswick, Canada, for about $92 million.

2000 AND 2001: ENTER FORT JAMES, EXIT TIMBER

Seeking to gain a more significant presence in the consumer market as a hedge against the wild cycles of its core paper, pulp, packaging, and building products operations, Georgia-Pacific, in November 2000, acquired Fort James Corporation for about $7.7 billion in stock and cash plus the assumption of $3.3 billion in Fort James debt. Fort James's key products included Brawny paper towels, Quilted Northern bathroom tissue, Vanity Fair napkins, and Dixie plates, cups, and cutlery. Based in Deerfield, Illinois, the company had been formed in August 1997 through the merger of James River Corporation of Virginia and Fort Howard Corporation. Fort James had posted profits of $516.5 million in 1999 on revenues of $6.8 billion. The addition of Fort James made Georgia-Pacific the number one tissue maker in the world. To placate antitrust authorities and complete the transaction, however, the company had to agree to sell its commercial-tissue unit, Georgia-Pacific Tissue, LLC, because of the commercial-tissue operations it was gaining from Fort James, which included the Preference and Envision brands. In March 2001 the unit was sold to Svenska Cellulosa Aktiebolaget SCA for $852 million, with Georgia-Pacific paying Chesapeake $237 million to cover deferred capital gains and for its equity interest in the venture.

Continuing its drive to focus more on consumer products, Georgia-Pacific announced in March 2001 that it would close its pulp mill in Bellingham, Washington. Then, in August, the firm sold four fine-paper mills to Domtar Inc. for $1.65 billion in the largest divestiture in company history. This left Georgia-Pacific with four white paper mills and two pulp mills. The company was looking to unload the pulp mills as well as its specialty chemicals unit. In June, meanwhile, the firm announced it would close three gypsum plants and reduce its gypsum wallboard production by 45 percent in response to industry-wide overproduction that was driving prices down. A divestment even larger and more significant than the sale to Domtar came in October 2001 when Georgia-Pacific completed the merger of the Timber Company into Plum Creek Timber Company, Inc., in a transaction valued at about $4 billion. This marked the exit of Georgia-Pacific from the timber business.

Late in 2001, Georgia-Pacific entered into talks with Willamette Industries Inc. regarding a possible joint venture of the companies' building products businesses or the sale of Georgia-Pacific's building products operations to the other firm. Willamette was seeking a way to extricate itself from a hostile takeover bid from Weyerhaeuser Company, but early in 2002 Willamette backed away from a transaction with Georgia-Pacific and agreed to a merger with Weyerhaeuser.

Part of Willamette's concern about a deal with Georgia-Pacific was the possibility of exposing itself to asbestos liabilities. In 1965 Georgia-Pacific had acquired Bestwall Gypsum, which made some gypsum products containing asbestos, which can cause lung disease and other diseases. Georgia-Pacific's use of asbestos was discontinued in 1977, and the firm had manufactured no products containing the substance since then. Lawsuits began to be filed against Georgia-Pacific in the mid-1980s, but it was not until late 2001, when large jury awards began making headlines and several major companies had been forced into bankruptcy because of their asbestos liabilities, that the issue began to seriously affect Georgia-Pacific. From early December 2001 to late January 2002, the company's stock lost more than one-third of its value as a result of investor concern about the firm's asbestos liability. Acting to halt the crisis, Correll announced that the firm would take a fourth quarter 2001 charge of $350 million for anticipated asbestos claims through 2011. The move was intended to quantify the company's asbestos risk and show that Georgia-Pacific was nowhere near the brink of bankruptcy. Correll emphasized that a third-party study had shown that the company's total liabilities through 2011 were expected to amount to less than $1 billion.

A COMPANY BREAKUP, ABANDONED

Whether these moves would be sufficient to lay to rest the asbestos concerns remained to be seen, but Georgia-Pacific in any event continued its drive to emphasize its consumer products side while also seeking to shave its high debt load, which stood at $12.2 billion in early 2002. Then in May 2002 the board of directors approved plans for what promised to be another seminal event in the firm's history. Wishing to separate its highly cyclical building products business from its more profitable consumer products operations, Georgia-Pacific announced that it intended to spin off its consumer products, packaging, and pulp and paper businesses into a separate public company. A slimmed-down Georgia-Pacific would then be left as a specialist in building products and would also have to carry the asbestos liability.

This plan was never carried out, however, as the company was forced to announce a delay in its implementation later in 2002 because of weakness in the capital and equity markets, a sharp decline in the firm's stock price, and the poor performance of the business products unit. By early 2003 the plan was shelved altogether. In the meantime, Georgia-Pacific in November 2002 sold a controlling 60 percent stake in the Unisource paper distribution unit to the private-equity firm Bain Capital, L.L.C., for more than $800 million. A pretax loss of $298 million connected with this sale coupled with an additional $315 million charge for anticipated asbestos claims sent Georgia-Pacific into a net loss of $735 million for 2002.

Georgia-Pacific returned to profitability in 2003, when strong cash flow enabled it to pare its debt burden by nearly $900 million to $10.6 billion. Debt was slashed by nearly $2 billion more during 2004 in part through a string of divestments, including the sale of the firm's building products distribution business, its founding business, for $808 million. The company also sold its nonintegrated pulp operations to Koch Industries, Inc., for $520 million in cash and $73 million in assumed debt. The assets sold to Koch included pulp mills in Brunswick, Georgia, and New Augusta, Mississippi, producing fluff pulp, used in disposable diapers and baby wipes, and market pulp used to make postage stamps and coffee filters. Revenues for 2004 remained virtually unchanged from the previous year because of the divestments, but net income more than doubled to $623 million thanks to the strong performance of its consumer products operations.

2005 ACQUISITION BY KOCH INDUSTRIES

In December 2005 Georgia-Pacific was acquired by Koch Industries for $13.2 billion in cash plus the assumption of $7.8 billion in debt. Based in Wichita, Kansas, Koch was an industrial conglomerate managing an array of businesses, including oil refining, operating petroleum pipelines, cattle ranching, and manufacturing fibers and chemicals. Still headquartered in Atlanta following the purchase, the newly named Georgia-Pacific LLC operated as a wholly owned subsidiary of Koch. It also regained responsibility for the pulp operations it had sold to Koch the previous year. Correll remained company chairman only through June 2006, when he retired. Taking over as president and CEO upon the deal's completion was Joseph W. Moeller, a Koch veteran who had been Koch's president and COO.

As the subsidiary of a deeply pocketed private company, Georgia-Pacific was well positioned to grow both internally and through acquisitions. The company was able to pursue certain deals that might have been avoided previously because of their potentially negative impact on the price of its stock. By late 2007 Koch had invested about $2 billion in Georgia-Pacific, including

the completion of three acquisitions. In July 2006 the firm's Dixie unit was bolstered via the purchase of Insulair Inc., a producer of premium insulated paper cups and lids based in Vernalis, California. Georgia-Pacific acquired five wood products mills in the southern United States from International Paper Company in April 2007 for $237 million. In September 2007 the company acquired a containerboard mill in Brewton, Alabama, from Smurfit-Stone Container Corporation for roughly $355 million. Other investments during this period included capacity upgrades at two tissue mills and one gypsum wallboard mill.

In addition to seeking growth opportunities, which continued under Moeller's successor as president and CEO, James Hannan, who took over in November 2007, Georgia-Pacific was also pursuing efficiency improvements, particularly through Koch's market-based management philosophy. Georgia-Pacific and other Koch companies operated independently under this homegrown free-market philosophy that essentially encouraged employees to think like entrepreneurs, to constantly question themselves and their colleagues.

Sandy Schusteff
Updated, Maura Troester; David E. Salamie

PRINCIPAL SUBSIDIARIES

Georgia-Pacific Cellulose, LLC; Georgia-Pacific Chemicals LLC; Georgia-Pacific Consumer Products LP; Georgia-Pacific Kemrock International Private Limited.

PRINCIPAL OPERATING UNITS

Dixie; Georgia-Pacific Building Products; Georgia-Pacific Gypsum; Georgia-Pacific Packaging; Georgia-Pacific Paper; Georgia-Pacific Professional.

PRINCIPAL COMPETITORS

International Paper Company; The Procter & Gamble Company; Kimberly-Clark Corporation; Boise Cascade Holdings, L.L.C.; Weyerhaeuser Company; MeadWestvaco Corporation; USG Corporation.

FURTHER READING

Bell, John, "Georgia-Pacific's Paper Profits," *Journal of Business Strategy,* May/June 1997, pp. 36–40.

Berman, Dennis K., and Chad Terhune, "Koch Industries Agrees to Buy Georgia-Pacific," *Wall Street Journal,* November 14, 2005, p. A3.

Berman, Phyllis, "Brawny—Lucky, Too; Georgia-Pacific's Slow Comeback," *Forbes,* February 2, 2004, p. 60.

"The Best of Everything," *Forbes,* March 15, 1977.

Bond, Patti, "Georgia-Pacific Chief Slams Analysts," *Atlanta Journal-Constitution,* January 25, 2002, p. F1.

———, "Georgia-Pacific Puts Down New Roots," *Atlanta Journal-Constitution,* July 22, 2000, p. F1.

———, "GP Sells Unisource Stake," *Atlanta Journal-Constitution,* August 15, 2002, p. F3.

———, "Reinventing Georgia-Pacific Is Correll's Big Mission: Bold Move into Tissue, Paper Towels Wins Praise," *Atlanta Journal-Constitution,* November 4, 2001, p. E1.

Brannigan, Martha, "Georgia-Pacific Delays Its Plans for a Breakup," *Wall Street Journal,* September 13, 2002, p. A6.

Brooks, Rick, "Georgia-Pacific Is No Longer a Paper Tiger," *Wall Street Journal,* July 18, 2000, p. B8.

Calonius, Erik, "America's Toughest Papermaker," *Fortune,* February 26, 1990, pp. 80+.

DeGross, Renee, "Georgia-Pacific to Cut 1,100 Jobs," *Atlanta Journal-Constitution,* October 5, 2005, p. C1.

———, "G-P's New Owner Reveals Executive Team," *Atlanta Journal-Constitution,* January 4, 2006, p. C3.

———, "$21 Billion Acquisition: New Era for Georgia-Pacific," *Atlanta Journal-Constitution,* November 15, 2005, p. A1.

De Lisser, Eleena, "Georgia-Pacific Plans New Class of Stock Tied to Its Profitable Timber Business," *Wall Street Journal,* September 18, 1997, p. C27.

Deogun, Nikhil, and Dean Starkman, "Georgia-Pacific Nears Buying Fort James," *Wall Street Journal,* July 17, 2000, p. A3.

Ferguson, Kelly H., "Georgia-Pacific: Deals, Debt, and Redirection," *Pulp and Paper,* March 1994, pp. 34–35.

Fisher, Daniel, "Mr. Big," *Forbes,* March 13, 2006, pp. 100+.

Foust, Dean, "Georgia-Pacific Turns Paper into Gold," *Business Week,* August 15, 1988, p. 71.

Gold, Jackey, "Culture Shock: Georgia-Pacific's Hostile Bid for Great Northern Nekoosa Changes the Game," *Financial World,* February 20, 1990, pp. 56+.

"G-P Adding Tissue, Toweling Capacity," *Pulp and Paper,* July 2006, p. 8.

"G-P Focusing Closely on Needs of Major Customers, Increasing Product Values," *Pulp and Paper,* July 2007, p. 6.

"G-P's Tissue Reshuffle Will Shut Four Machines," *Pulp and Paper,* November 2005, pp. 6–7.

Grillo, Jerry, "Corporate Citizen," *Georgia Trend,* May 2006, pp. 20+.

Grimes, Ann, "Plum Creek Timber Agrees to Buy Georgia-Pacific Unit in Stock Deal," *Wall Street Journal,* July 19, 2000, p. A6.

Hagerty, James R., "No-Nonsense Paper Firm Bets on 'Calming Sandalwood': Georgia-Pacific, Tired of Commodity-Price Gyrations, Focuses on Branding," *Wall Street Journal,* December 14, 1999, p. B4.

Hahn, T. Marshall, *Georgia-Pacific Corporation: "The Growth Company,"* New York: Newcomen Society of the United States, 1990, 18 p.

Harte, Susan, "Accepting the Challenges with Confidence: Correll Faces Unprecedented Demands As He Takes the Reins at Georgia-Pacific," *Atlanta Constitution,* December 1, 1993, p. D1.

Henderson, Barry, "Critics' Choice: Georgia-Pacific Is Poised for a Rebound After Panned Purchase," *Barron's,* August 23, 1999, pp. 19–20.

"Is Georgia-Pacific Pruning at the Top?" *Business Week,* November 15, 1982, p. 38.

Kempner, Matt, "New Era at Georgia-Pacific: A Change in Philosophy; Koch Stresses Entrepreneurship," *Atlanta Journal-Constitution,* March 4, 2007, p. E1.

Kimelman, John, "Knock on (Composite) Wood: Georgia-Pacific Is Poised for a Sharp Cyclical Recovery," *Financial World,* July 19, 1994, pp. 36–37.

"Koch Industries to Acquire Georgia-Pacific in $48 Per Share Cash Transaction," *Pulp and Paper,* December 2005, p. 6.

Mitchell, Cynthia, "Leading Georgia-Pacific Out of the Woods," *Atlanta Journal-Constitution,* July 20, 1997, p. D4.

Monroe, Doug, *The Maverick Spirit: Georgia-Pacific at 75,* Lyme, Conn.: Greenwich Publishing Group, 2001, 240 p.

Norvell, Scott, "Southern Comfort for a Timber Giant," *New York Times,* March 23, 1993, p. 6.

Pamplin, Robert B., *Heritage,* New York: Mastermedia, 1994, 520 p.

Reier, Sharon, "New Math vs. Old Culture," *Financial World,* March 22, 1988.

Ross, John R., *Maverick: The Story of Georgia-Pacific,* Portland, Ore.: Georgia-Pacific Corporation, 1978, 318 p.

Saporta, Maria, "Next Chief Envisions More Acquisitions for G-P," *Atlanta Journal-Constitution,* October 11, 2007, p. C2.

Scredon, Scott, and Rebecca Aikman, "Georgia-Pacific Bets on Paper to Smooth Out Its Swings," *Business Week,* April 15, 1985, pp. 120+.

Terhune, Chad, "Brawny's Lumberjack Man Tagged for a Makeover," *Wall Street Journal,* February 13, 2002, p. B1.

———, "Georgia-Pacific Hopes Its Streak of Bad Luck Will End," *Wall Street Journal,* January 28, 2002, p. B3.

———, "Georgia-Pacific Says Asbestos Charge Will Result in Net Loss for Fourth Period," *Wall Street Journal,* January 25, 2002, p. A5.

Thomas, Emory, Jr., "Georgia-Pacific May Embark on a Spending Spree," *Wall Street Journal,* December 12, 1994, p. B4.

"Unrest at Georgia-Pacific," *Business Week,* November 24, 1980, pp. 147+.

Walker, Tom, "Ga.-Pacific to Sell Unit, Decrease Debt Load," *Atlanta Journal-Constitution,* March 13, 2004, p. F1.

Wiegner, Kathleen K., "A Tale of Two Companies," *Forbes,* March 6, 1978.

Wilbert, Tony, "G-P Has Loss for 2nd Year in a Row," *Atlanta Journal-Constitution,* January 22, 2003, p. D1.

———, "G-P in Black for Full Year, 4th Quarter," *Atlanta Journal-Constitution,* February 4, 2004, p. D1.

————, "How Does G-P Stack Up? Countering Public Image a Challenge," *Atlanta Journal-Constitution,* April 5, 2003, p. F1.

————, "The Paper-Towel Chase: G-P's Brawny Has No. 1 Bounty in Its Sights," *Atlanta Journal-Constitution,* October 15, 2003, p. D1.

Gifts In Kind
International

---

333 North Fairfax Street
Alexandria, Virginia 22314
U.S.A.
Telephone: (703) 836-2121
Fax: (703) 549-1481
Web site: http://www.giftsinkind.org

Private Company
Incorporated: 1984
Employees: 25
Operating Revenues: $748.32 million (2007)
NAICS: 813219 Other Grantmaking and Giving Services

■ ■ ■

Based in Alexandria, Virginia, the nonprofit organization Gifts In Kind International accepts product and service donations from approximately 450 companies and distributes them to roughly 100,000 certified charities throughout the world. In 2007 Gifts in Kind received and placed approximately $750 million in donations. The charity is considered one of the top four most efficient organizations of its kind in the United States, according to *Forbes* magazine.

FORMATIVE YEARS: 1984–89

The inspiration behind Gifts In Kind International can be traced to the fall of 1983, when United Way of America received $12 million in office equipment donations from 3M Company. In addition to various United Way agencies, the donated typewriters and copiers also benefited the United Negro College Fund and Junior Achievement.

3M's generosity ultimately resulted in funding from Lilly Endowment Inc. to establish a new independent organization named Gifts In Kind Inc., the purpose of which was to encourage corporate donations to nonprofit organizations.

Gifts In Kind was established on March 13, 1984, with former American Telephone & Telegraph Co. President William M. Ellinghaus serving as chairman. Among the organization's founders was Susan Corrigan, who served as its president and CEO for many years.

After rounding out its board of directors with executives from leading companies, Gifts In Kind began carrying out its mission with a staff of four employees, two of whom were full-time. During its first year the organization distributed $17 million worth of products from ten companies.

Gifts In Kind took further steps to formalize its operations in 1985. That year, a national survey was conducted in order to better understand the needs of the organizations it served. In addition to developing and implementing formal policies and strategies, it was decided that donations would be channeled largely through the network of community organizations served by the United Way. The year ended on a successful note. Product donations doubled from the previous year's level, reaching $35 million and benefiting some 17,000 different U.S. nonprofit organizations.

In 1986 Gifts In Kind received nearly $44 million in donations from 32 companies, including Levi Strauss,

COMPANY PERSPECTIVES

Gifts In Kind receives donations from thousands of large and small companies, including half of the *Fortune* 100 technology, retail, and consumer corporations. We distribute these donations to more than 100,000 community charities across the United States and throughout the world.

Lotus Development Corp., J. C. Penney, Gillette, and Avon. In addition, a three-year partnership was forged with Apple Computer, resulting in the donation of approximately 300 computers.

By this time the organization carried out its mission on the strength of a five-member staff that included four full-time employees. Gifts In Kind covered its operational expenses in several ways. In addition to charging donation recipients an administrative fee to offset distribution costs, the United Way began sponsoring Gifts In Kind with an annual grant. Another highlight from 1986 was the development of the organization's very first three-year strategic plan.

Heading into the late 1980s, Gifts In Kind continued to grow in sophistication. Benefiting the organization was the expertise of its board members, on whom it relied to provide advice in matters of administration, marketing, financial planning, inventory management, community affairs, and more.

As evidence of Gifts In Kind's growth, the organization began using ten warehouses to process donations and repackage them into smaller quantities for approximately 40,000 charities. Additionally, several companies began relying upon Gifts In Kind for the management of their product giving programs.

An unfortunate situation emerged in 1988, when the U.S. Treasury Department proposed regulatory changes that threatened tax breaks for companies that made inventory-related donations. In the wake of this uncertain development, donations fell to $23 million for the year. Gifts In Kind's efforts helped to prevent the Treasury Department from implementing its proposal.

After clearing this hurdle, donations swelled to $53 million in 1989. That year, Gifts In Kind changed its name to Gifts In Kind America. When earthquakes impacted California and Hurricane Hugo left devastation in its path, the organization did its part to help by contributing to relief efforts. By this time donations were received from approximately 134 different

companies. Awareness was generated by several marketing initiatives, including a public service announcement campaign.

NEW PROGRAM DEVELOPMENT BEGINS: 1990–95

During the early 1990s, Gifts In Kind began developing campaigns that were focused on specific social problems. One successful effort was Clothe & Comfort USA, which collected clothing for homeless individuals. One factor in the organization's growth was a major increase in the number of donor companies, which skyrocketed to 471, up from 134 in 1989.

Gifts In Kind continued to find ways to increase efficiency and reduce operational costs. One example was a partnership with the National Private Truck Council and the American Trucking Association Inc. to develop CONNECT, a national volunteer transportation network that provided free shipping. These and other efforts resulted in the *NonProfit Times* naming Gifts In Kind America as the nation's fastest-growing and most cost-efficient charity.

By 1991 Gifts In Kind America had distributed $300 million worth of donations since its establishment seven years before. The Pew Charitable Trusts bestowed a $230,000 grant upon the organization that year, providing funding that was used to computerize many aspects of its operation.

Significant progress continued in 1992, when Gifts In Kind America was chosen as the most efficient of the nation's largest 100 charities by *Money* magazine. That year, product donations rose nearly 30 percent, reaching a record $45 million. Highlights included $10 million in clothing and personal care product donations made through the organization's Clothe & Comfort program.

Product donations soared even higher in 1993, rising 71 percent to a record $77 million. The organization attributed this increase to its growing donor base, which included 206 new corporate donors that year.

During the early 1990s, one major theme at Gifts In Kind America was the establishment of new programs. In 1993 these included a family healthcare initiative named Healthy from the Start, a home and neighborhood redevelopment program called Housing America, a software donation partnership with the Software Publishers Association, and the development of the organization's Transportation & Logistics Center, which provided nonprofit entities with low-cost transportation management services.

More new programs were established in 1994. In addition to introducing the Youth Education & Sports

KEY DATES

1984: Gifts In Kind Inc. is established.

1989: Gifts In Kind changes its name to Gifts In Kind America.

1992: *Money Magazine* names Gifts In Kind America as the most efficient of the nation's largest 100 charities.

1996: Gifts In Kind America changes its name to Gifts In Kind International.

2000: Since the organization's inception, the value of distributed donations totals approximately $2.5 billion.

2001: Aid for 9/11 disaster recovery initiatives.

2005: Product donations valued at $27 million are provided to victims of Hurricanes Katrina and Rita.

2008: Gifts In Kind hosts its first corporate giving conference.

program, Gifts In Kind America developed its Recycle Technology program to encourage the donation of used computer equipment. Explosive growth continued that year, with 249 new corporate donors pushing product donations past the $118 million mark.

INTERNATIONAL FOCUS: 1996–2000

A major development unfolded during the mid-1990s. In 1996 Gifts In Kind America changed its name to Gifts In Kind International, which was a more accurate reflection of the organization's worldwide impact.

In April 1996, Gifts In Kind International made its official debut in Canada. To mark the occasion, the organization established the Technology Learning Centre at the Toronto, Ontario, Canada-based Dovercourt Boys' and Girls' Club. One major highlight of the event was the participation of His Royal Highness Prince Charles, Prince of Wales. In addition to Gifts In Kind International's new Toronto office, the organization also established a London office. To mark the occasion, a special event was held at St. James Palace.

Significant progress continued in 1997. Gifts In Kind International became the official charity of SOFT-BANK COMDEX that year, and a number of corporate heavyweights joined its donor base, including Adobe Systems, Hearst Corp., Reader's Digest Association, and Simon & Schuster. Leading retailers such as United

Retail Group and Eddie Bauer became part of the organization's Retail Donation Partner program. In addition, the Recycle Technology program distributed 20,000 used computers. Following six years of 42 percent average annual growth, 18,500 donations were received, totaling $288 million.

The Chronicle of Philanthropy named Gifts In Kind International as the nation's 13th largest charity in 1998. Highlights that year included the implementation of a new information management system. A ten-year strategic plan was implemented in 1999, calling for further international growth. In keeping with this plan, and with support provided by The Bill & Melinda Gates Foundation, new programs were implemented in Taiwan, Singapore, Mexico City, Hong Kong, Colombia, and Brazil.

Gifts In Kind International concluded the 1990s by distributing approximately $343 million in donated products to some 50,000 different charities. Among these donations were home furnishings from ExecuStay by Marriott, which partnered with Gifts In Kind International to develop a program named Sharing with Our Communities. The initiative benefited shelters in approximately 15 major cities with gently used kitchen products, bed and bath items, electronics, and more. Marriott's generosity continued into the early 2000s, as the organization revealed plans to donate some 100,000 mattresses over the course of three years.

Remarkable progress had been achieved by the dawn of the new millennium. Since inception, the value of product donations distributed by Gifts In Kind International totaled approximately $2.5 billion. In 2000 alone, about $456 million in product donations were received. That year, donations included more than 6,400 gallons of latex paint from ICI Paints to the Alabama Council on Human Relations and Indianapolis, Indiana-based Rehab Resource Inc.

DISASTER RELIEF: 2001–07

During the early 2000s, Gifts In Kind International continued to build upon the international growth that occurred during the late 1990s. The organization added new affiliates in Latin America, Australia, South Korea, Asia, and Europe in 2001. That year, $676 million in product donations were distributed. In the wake of the September 11 terrorist attacks against the United States, Gifts In Kind International did its part by assisting disaster recovery initiatives in both Washington, D.C., and New York City.

By 2002, some 200,000 nonprofit entities were benefiting from the efforts of Gifts In Kind International. A key development that year was the establishment of technology labs in roughly seven cities worldwide. In fact, technology became a central focus of the organization during the first decade of the 2000s. For example, when the company's research revealed that new technology was sorely needed by the nonprofit community, it partnered with Microsoft, IBM, Adobe, Hewlett-Packard, and other leading technology companies to improve the situation.

On the strength of 340 new donors and donation programs at approximately 44 percent of *Fortune* 500 companies, product and service donations reached $786 million in 2003. That year, Gifts In Kind International worked in partnership with the Toy Industry Foundation to develop The Toy Bank, a philanthropy program designed to provide disadvantaged children with new toys.

In keeping with its record for responding swiftly to unfortunate situations, Gifts In Kind International reached out to help victims of several disasters during the middle of the first decade of the 2000s. In 2004 the organization assisted individuals affected by the tsunami in Southeast Asia, providing approximately $1.3 million in product donations.

A major leadership change occurred in 2005 when founder and CEO Susan Corrigan retired. Barry R. Anderson filled the role until the organization hired Richard Wong. That same year, $27 million worth of products were provided to victims of Hurricanes Katrina and Rita. The organization quickly opened 31 donation and relief centers in the U.S. Gulf area and provided more than 280 truckloads of goods. Among the items donated by the corporate community were approximately 700 new refrigerators from Sears and Maytag, valued at nearly $800,000.

Product donations reached the $850 million mark in 2005, and totaled nearly $900 million in 2006. By this time Gifts In Kind International was serving a network of roughly 150,000 nonprofit organizations. In addition to its efforts to promote giving as a central component of corporate social responsibility initiatives, Gifts In Kind International partnered with The Home Depot in 2007 to establish The Framing Hope Product Donation Program, which helped to connect local charitable organizations with nearby Home Depot stores.

HELPING IN HARD TIMES: 2008–09

In 2008 the organization held its first corporate giving conference in Alexandria, named Innovation in Product Giving: Creating Value for Business & Community. In September, Barry Anderson was again chosen to serve as interim president and CEO following the departure of Richard Wong.

In 2009 Gifts In Kind International found itself operating in a dire economic climate. In order to help the network of nonprofit organizations that it served, new programs named Charity Stimulus Package and Operation Rescue Charity were established. After a quarter of a century, the organization had firmly established itself as a leader in the nonprofit sector. Moving forward, it seemed well-positioned to weather the difficult economic times and continue to help the charities upon which so many people depended.

Paul R. Greenland

PRINCIPAL COMPETITORS

The National Association for the Exchange of Industrial Resources.

FURTHER READING

Amato-McCoy, Deena M., "In-Kind Gifts Keep on Giving," *Chain Store Age,* July 2008.

"Evolution of the World's Leading Charity in the Field of Philanthropy," Alexandria, Va.: Gifts In Kind International, 2002.

"Gifts In Kind International Establishes Formal Canadian Presence, Opens Technology Learning Centre with Prince of Wales," *Canada NewsWire,* April 26, 1996.

"National Retail Institute Giving Survey Shows Retailers Are Committed & Active Corporate Citizens; Money, Merchandise & Volunteers Are Favored Ways to Contribute," *PR Newswire,* January 8, 1998.

Google™

Google, Inc.

1600 Amphitheatre Parkway
Mountain View, California 94043
U.S.A.
Telephone: (650) 253-0000
Fax: (650) 253-0001
Web site: http://www.google.com

Public Company
Incorporated: 1998
Employees: 20,123
Sales: $16.59 billion (2007)
Stock Exchanges: NASDAQ (GS)
Ticker Symbol: GOOG
NAICS: 541512 Computer Systems Design Services;
514191 Online Information Services

■ ■ ■

Google, Inc., operates the world's largest Internet search engine, Google.com, which continuously downloads the entire World Wide Web and uses the information to produce an updated link graph. By mid-2008, its indexing system revealed the existence of one trillion unique URLs (web page addresses), and indicated that several billion new individual pages were being created each day. In addition to its leadership status in the area of web searching, Google also is the gateway to billions of images, as well as news headlines, books, maps, phone book listings, stock quotes, satellite imagery, e-mail, free software applications, and more.

Because Google is available in many languages, and is accessible via both personal computers and wireless devices, it has become one of the world's most recognizable brands. In fact, just as the Kleenex and Xerox brand names became synonymous with facial tissue and photocopying, respectively, Google has become synonymous with web searching. For this reason, the *Oxford English Dictionary* listed the word *Google* as a verb in mid-2006.

GRADUATE STUDENTS CONCEIVE GOOGLE AT STANFORD

Google, Inc., the developer of the award-winning Google search engine, was conceived in 1995 by Stanford University computer science graduate students Larry Page and Sergey Brin. Their meeting at a spring gathering of new Ph.D. computer science candidates launched a friendship and later a collaboration to find a unique approach to solving one of computing's biggest challenges: retrieving relevant information from a massive set of data.

By 1996 this collaboration had produced a search engine called BackRub, named for its unique ability to analyze the "back links" that point to a given web site. Continuing to perfect the technology in 1998, Page and Brin built their own computer housing in Larry's dorm room, a business office in Sergey's room, and Google had a new home. The next step was to find potential partners who might want to license their search technology, a technology that worked better than any available at the time. Among the contacts was David Filo, a friend and Yahoo! founder. Filo encouraged the two to grow the service themselves by starting a search engine company.

COMPANY PERSPECTIVES

Google's mission is to organize the world's information and make it universally accessible and useful.

BACKRUB BECOMES GOOGLE

The name "Google" was chosen from the word *googol*, a mathematical term coined by Milton Sirotta, nephew of American mathematician Edward Kasner, for the number represented by 1 followed by 100 zeros. A googol, or google, represented a very large number and reflected the company's mission to organize the immense, seemingly infinite, amount of information available on the World Wide Web.

Unable to secure the financial support of the major portal players of the day, cofounders Page and Brin decided to make a go of it on their own. They wrote a business plan, put their graduate studies on hold, and searched for an investor. They first approached Andy Bechtolsheim, founder of Sun Microsystems, and friend of a Stanford faculty member. Impressed with their plans, Bechtolsheim wrote a check to Google Inc. for $100,000. The check, however, preceded the incorporation of the company, which followed in 1998.

Shortly after its incorporation, Google Inc. opened its new headquarters in the garage of a friend in Menlo Park, California. Their first employee was hired: Craig Silverstein, who later became Google's director of technology. By this time, Google.com was answering 10,000 search queries a day. Articles about the new web site with relevant search results appeared in *USA Today* and *Le Monde*. In December, *PC Magazine* named Google to its list of Top 100 Web Sites and Search Engines for 1998.

GOOGLE SIGNS ITS FIRST COMMERCIAL SEARCH CUSTOMER

With the number of queries growing to 500,000 a day, and the number of employees growing to eight, Google moved its offices to University Avenue in Palo Alto in February 1999. With interest in the company growing as well and Google's commitment to running its servers on the Linux open source operating system, Google signed on with RedHat, its first commercial customer.

By early June, Google had secured $25 million in equity funding from two leading venture capital firms in Silicon Valley: Sequoia Capital and Kleiner Perkins

Caufield & Byers. Staff members from the two investors joined Google's board of directors. Joining as new employees were Omid Kordestani from Netscape, who became Google's vice-president of business development and sales; and University of California–Santa Barbara's Urs Hölzle, who became Google's vice-president of engineering. Having again outgrown their work space, the company moved to the Googleplex, its headquarters in Mountain View, California.

Google continued to expand in many ways. AOL/Netscape selected Google as its web search service, helping push daily traffic levels to more than three million. The Italian portal Virgilio and the United Kingdom's leading online entertainment guide, Virgin Net, signed on as well. *PC Magazine* awarded Google its Technical Excellence Award for Innovation in Web Application Development and included it in several of its "Best of" lists. *Time* magazine named Google to its Top Ten Best Cybertech list for 1999.

THE GOOGLE CULTURE EVOLVES

Although the company grew rapidly, it still maintained a small company feel. The Googleplex helped nurture an atmosphere of innovation and collegiality with its exercise balls, lava lamps, workout room, grand pianos, and visiting dogs. Sophisticated computer equipment was originally set up on wooden doors supported by sawhorses. Charlie Ayers, former cook for the Grateful Dead, was hired as company chef. Twice-weekly street hockey games were held in roped-off areas of the parking lot and weekly staff meetings were held in the open space among employees' desks.

Improvements to the search engine itself came in the introduction of the Google Directory, which was based on Netscape's Open Directory Project, and the ability to search via wireless devices. Thinking globally, Google also introduced ten language versions for search users.

In May 2000 Google received a Webby award for Best Technical Achievement for 2000 and a People's Voice Award for Technical Achievement. The following month, Google introduced its billion-page index and, with 18 million search queries per day, officially became the world's largest search engine.

GOOGLE LAUNCHES KEYWORD-TARGET ADVERTISING PROGRAM

A number of clients in the United States, Europe, and Asia began signing up to use Google's search technology on their own web sites. By launching a keyword-targeted advertising program, Google added another source of

KEY DATES

1995: Google founders Sergey Brin and Larry Page meet at Stanford University.

1997: BackRub, the precursor to the Google search engine, is founded.

1998: Google is incorporated and moves into its first office in a Menlo Park, California, garage.

1999: Google moves its headquarters to Palo Alto, California, and later to Mountain View, California; Red Hat becomes Google's first commercial customer.

2000: *Yahoo! Internet Life* magazine names Google the Best Search Engine on the Internet; Google becomes the largest search engine on the Web and launches the Google Toolbar.

2001: Google acquires Deja.com's Usenet archive and launches Google PhoneBook; Dr. Eric Schmidt joins Google as chairman of the board of directors and is later appointed CEO.

2002: Google launches the Google Search Appliance, AdWords Select, the 2001 Search Engine Awards, and Google Compute.

2004: Company occupies its new "Googleplex" headquarters campus in Mountain View, California; conducts initial public offering, selling 19.6 million shares of common stock for $85 each on the NASDAQ.

2008: DoubleClick Inc. is acquired; Google celebrates its tenth anniversary.

revenue. On June 26, the company's reputation was further solidified with the announcement of a partnership with Yahoo! Other partners adding Google to their sites were China's leading portal NetEast and NEC's BIGLOBE in Japan. In an effort to extend its keyword advertising to smaller businesses, Google introduced AdWords, a self-service advertising program that could be activated with a credit card. Google Number Search was launched, making wireless data entry easy and faster. Other awards received included the addition to *Forbes'* Best of the Web Round-Up, *PC World*'s recognition as "the Best Bet Search Engine," and the *WIRED* Readers Raves award for Most Intelligent Agent on the Internet. *PC Magazine UK* also honored Google with its Best Internet Innovation award.

By December, Google was answering more than 60 million searches per day. The Google Toolbar, a highly popular innovative browser plug-in, was introduced in late 2000. Searches could be generated from a Google search box and by right-clicking on text within a web page and highlighting keywords in results.

Reaching the 100-million search mark per day in 2001, Google acquired the assets of Deja.com and integrated all the data in Deja's Usenet archive dating back to 1995 into a searchable format. Google PhoneBook was launched, providing publicly available phone numbers and addresses as search results. By early 2001 Google was powering search services at Yahoo! Japan, Fujitsu NIFTY, and NEC BIGLOBE, the top three portals in Japan, as well as U.S. corporate sites such as Procter & Gamble, IDG.net, Vodaphone, and MarthaStewart.com. Dr. Eric E. Schmidt joined Google in May as chairman of the board and eventually became CEO. Schmidt had previously served as chairman and CEO of Novell and CTO of Sun Microsystems.

The list of search services customers continued to grow throughout 2001 with the addition of Sprint and Handspring. By mid-year, Google powered 130 portal and destination sites in 30 countries, with advertising programs attracting more than 350 Premium Sponsorship advertisers and thousands of AdWords advertisers. Click-through rates were delivered four to five times higher than click-through rates for traditional banner ads. Country domains were offered in the United Kingdom, Germany, France, Italy, Switzerland, Canada, Japan, and Korea, with users selecting Google's interface in nearly 40 non-English languages.

By the beginning of the fourth quarter of 2001, Google announced an achievement that had eluded many other online companies: profitability. With the appointment of Schmidt as new CEO, cofounders Larry Page and Sergey Brin became president, products, and president, technology, respectively. Google was awarded another Webby for the new Best Practices category.

Cingular Wireless and more than 300 of Sony's corporate web sites were linked to Google by mid-2001. The new Google Image Search index was launched with 250 million images. Google Zeitgeist, from the German *Zeit* (time) + *Geist* (spirit), meaning the general intellectual, moral, and cultural climate of an era, published results of search patterns, trends, and surprises. On a monthly, weekly, and sometimes daily basis, the Google Zeitgeist page was introduced to reflect lists, graphs, and other tidbits of information related to Google user search behavior.

In September, Google purchased the technology assets of Outride Inc., and partnered with Universo Online (UOL) to provide access to millions of UOL users throughout Brazil and Latin America. On the global scene, Google launched a new tabbed home page interface on Google.com and 25 international sites. The Arabic and Turkish languages were added and the Google Toolbar launched versions in five new languages. Lycos Korea came onboard as well.

By the end of 2001, Google had increased the size and scope of searchable information available through the Google search engine to three billion web documents, including an archive of Usenet messages dating back to 1981. Google News Headlines was added and Google Catalog Search enabled users to search and browse more than 1,100 mail-order catalogs. New sales offices were opened in Hamburg, Germany, and Tokyo, Japan.

THE GOOGLE SEARCH APPLIANCE IS INTRODUCED

In January 2002 Google announced the availability of the Google Search Appliance, an integrated hardware/ software solution that extended the power of Google to corporate intranets and web servers. AdWords Select—an updated version of the AdWords self-service advertising system, with new enhancements, including cost-per-click-based pricing—also was launched.

More honors were received in 2002, including "Outstanding Search Service," "Best Image Search Engine," "Best Design," "Most Webmaster Friendly Search Engine," and "Best Search Feature" in the 2001 Search Engine Watch Awards. Expansion of global capabilities continued with the launching of interface translation for Belarusian, Javanese, Occitan, Thai, Urdu, Klingon, Bihari, and Gujaratie, bringing the total number of interface language options to 74. Google Compute offered a new toolbar feature to access idle cycles on Google users' computers for working on complex scientific problems. Folding@home, a nonprofit research project at Stanford University aimed at understanding the structure of proteins in order to develop better treatments for certain illnesses, was the first beneficiary of this effort. Google Web APIs service enabled programmers and researchers to develop software that accessed billions of web documents as a resource in their applications. Awards in mid-2002 included Google's founders, Brin and Page, being named to *InfoWorld*'s list of "Top Ten Technology Innovators" and receiving an M.I.T. Sloan eBusiness award as the "Student's Choice."

A multi-year agreement with AOL was announced to provide results to AOL's 34 million members and millions of visitors to AOL.com. Under the agreement, Google's search technology began powering the search areas of AOL, CompuServe, AOL.com, and Netscape. Google Labs was launched, providing users with access to Google's latest and evolving search technologies. Seven new interface languages were introduced, including traditional and simplified Chinese, Catalan, Polish, Swedish, Russian, and Romanian. Global expansion continued with a new office opening in Paris to complement existing international offices in London, Toronto, Hamburg, and Tokyo. The 2002 Google Programming Contest, launched in early 2002, announced its first winner of $10,000 for the creation of a geographic search program that enabled users to search for web pages within a specified geographic area.

In September 2002, Google News was unveiled, providing users with access to some 4,000 news sources. The following month a new office opened in Sydney, Australia. Google rounded out the year with the introduction of Froogle, which eventually was renamed Google Product Search.

In early 2003 Google acquired blogger-software creator Pyra Labs. Another acquisition followed in April, at which time the company snapped up Applied Semantics and gained technology that strengthened its company's AdSense service. Google capped off the year by introducing Google Print. Eventually renamed Google Book Search, the new service allowed the inclusion of small book excerpts in search results.

GOING PUBLIC

In March 2004, the company occupied its new "Googleplex" headquarters campus in Mountain View, California. During the first half of the year, Google began offering trial use of its free Gmail service. Available by invitation only, it gave users one gigabyte of storage for their e-mail as well as the ability to use Google tools to search through old messages. Some privacy advocates were concerned about the new advertising-supported service, which generated ads based on keywords found in e-mail messages. In addition, they pointed out the ability of law enforcement agencies to "profile" users by analyzing the content of their e-mail, along with Google search results.

Another major development occurred in August, when Google conducted its initial public offering (IPO), selling 19.6 million shares of common stock for $85 each through a Dutch auction on the NASDAQ. Two months later, a new office was established in Dublin, Ireland, and a short message service named Google SMS was introduced, allowing users to send text search queries via their mobile devices. In addition, the company rolled out Google Desktop Search, which allowed the use of Google technology to look for files on one's own computer. Finally, Google acquired the digital mapping company Keyhole, which provided the foundation for its Google Earth service. The year concluded with the formation of a new research and development facility in Tokyo.

New service introductions continued in 2005, beginning with the rollout of Google Maps in February. This new service was enhanced with satellite views and directions two months later. The introduction of Google Earth followed in June, providing web searchers with a mapping service based on satellite imagery. Later in the year, Google Analytics was unveiled, providing tools for measuring web site traffic.

EXPANSION AND ACQUISITIONS

During 2005, Google also continued to expand its global reach. This was evident by the establishment of a new research and development complex in China, the formation of an office in Mexico City, and the acquisition of the São Paulo, Brazil-based search technology firm Akwan Information Technologies. By this time, Google also had research and development centers located in India, Japan, and Switzerland.

In 2006 Google made giant strides in its effort to put more information into the hands of Internet users. Free searchable books became available for downloading and printing in August of that year. While Google determined that the books it offered were in the public domain, the company was challenged by organizations such as the Association of American Publishers, as well as the Authors Guild, on the grounds of copyright infringement.

Shortly after the introduction of books, Google News became more robust when an archival function was added to the service, allowing users to search articles dating back some 200 years. In December, a new tool called Patent Search came online, providing an index of roughly seven million U.S. patents.

Other significant developments during 2006 included plans to construct a large research center in Ann Arbor, Michigan, which would house approximately 1,000 employees, as well as the acquisition of the popular online video site YouTube. In addition, Google introduced free web-based productivity software applications named Docs & Spreadsheets.

Google kicked off 2007 by making Gmail available to all users on Valentine's Day. Throughout the year, the company continued its physical expansion. In January, plans were announced for a new $600 million data center in Lenoir, North Carolina, which would employ approximately 210 people. Faced with the need for ad-

ditional room, Google subleased property from Gap Inc. later in the year, providing an additional 180,000 square feet of workspace in San Bruno, California.

In March 2008, Google completed its acquisition of the online advertising company DoubleClick Inc., finalizing a $3.1 billion deal that had been announced in April 2007. Several major developments followed, beginning with the introduction of the company's Chrome open source web browser in September. That same month, Google's Android operating system was introduced on T-Mobile's new G1 phone, along with an Android Market that offered related applications. This development enabled Google to compete with Apple's iPhone and related App Store.

Google ended 2008 by celebrating its tenth anniversary. The company moved forward with Eric Schmidt as its CEO. Although it faced dire economic conditions, which had a negative impact on advertising revenues, Google seemed prepared to weather the storm successfully.

Carol D. Beavers
Updated, Paul R. Greenland

PRINCIPAL SUBSIDIARIES

@Last Software Inc.; @Last Software Ltd. (UK); AdScape Media (Canada) Inc.; AdScape Media Inc.; Advertising and Marketing Limited (Turkey); Aegino Limited (Ireland); allPAY GmbH (Germany); Android Inc.; Applied Semantics Inc.; At Last Software GmbH (Germany); bruNET GmbH (Germany); bruNET Holding AG (Germany); bruNET Schweiz GmbH (Switzerland); dMarc Broadcasting Inc.; Endoxon (Deutchland) GmbH (Germany); Endoxon (India) Private Ltd.; Endoxon Ltd. (Switzerland); FeedBurner Inc.; Ganji Inc.; Google Airwaves Inc.; Google Argentina S.R.L.; Google Australia Pty Ltd.; Google Austria GmbH; Google Belgium NV; Google Bermuda Limited; Google Bermuda Unlimited; Google Brasil Internet Ltda (Brazil); Google Canada Corporation; Google Chile Limitada; Google Czech Republic s.r.o.; Google Denmark ApS; Google Finland OY; Google France SarL; Google FZ LLC (United Arab Emirates); Google Germany GmbH; Google Holdings Pte. Ltd. (Singapore); Google India Private Limited; Google Information Technology Services Limited Liability Company (Hungary); Google International LLC; Google Ireland Holdings; Google Ireland Limited; Google Israel Ltd.; Google Italy s.r.l.; Google Japan Inc.; Google Korea LLC. (South Korea); Google Limited Liability Company - Google OOO (Russia); Google LLC; Google Mexico S. de R.L. de C.V.; Google Netherlands

B.V.; Google Netherlands Holdings B.V.; Google New Zealand Ltd.; Google Norway AS; Google Payment Corp.; Google Payment Hong Kong Limited; Google Payment Ltd. (UK); Google Payment Singapore Pte. Ltd.; Google Poland Sp. z o.o.; Google Singapore Pte. Ltd.; Google South Africa (Proprietary) Limited; Google Spain S.L.; Google Spectrum Investments Inc.; Google Sweden AB; Google Sweden Tecnique AB; Google Switzerland GmbH; Google UK Limited; GrandCentral Communication Inc.; GreenBorder Technologies Inc.; Ignite Logic Inc.; ImageAmerica Aviation Inc.; Image-America Inc.; Jaiku Ltd. (Finland); JASS Inc.; JG Productions Inc.; JotSpot Inc.; Kaltix Corporation; Leonberger Holdings B.V. (Netherlands); Liquid Acquisition Corp. 2; Neotonic Software Corporation; Neven Vision Germany GmbH; Neven Vision KK (Japan); Nevengineering Inc.; Orkut.com LLC; Peakstream Inc.; Picasa LLC; PiFidelity Holding Corporation; PiFidelity LLC; Postini Canada Holding Co.; Postini Switzerland GmbH (Switzerland); Postini UK Limited; Postini Inc.; Scott Concepts LLC; Scott Studios LLC; SkillSet LLC; Skydocks GmbH (Germany); The Salinger Group LLC; Tonic Systems Pty. Ltd. (Austria); Tonic Systems Inc.; Transformic Inc.; Upstartle LLC; Urchin Software Corporation; Where2 LLC; YouTube LLC; ZipDash Inc.

PRINCIPAL COMPETITORS

Ask.com; GoodSearch.com; MSN; Yahoo! Inc.

FURTHER READING

Blumenstein, Rebecca, et al., "Beyond Global," *Wall Street Journal,* March 21, 2002, p. B6.

Cummings, Betsy, "Beating the Odds," *Sales & Marketing Management,* March 2002, pp. 24–29.

Helft, Miguel, "Google at 10: Searching Its Own Soul," *New York Times,* November 8, 2008.

Swisher, Kara, "Beneath Google's Dot-Com Shell," *Wall Street Journal,* January 21, 2002, p. B1.

Wildstrom, Stephen H., "Google's Gmail Is Great—But Not for Privacy; Oodles of Storage, Wide Open to Law Enforcement Snoops," *Business Week,* May 3, 2004.

Greyston Bakery, Inc.

104 Alexander Street
Yonkers, New York 10701-2535
U.S.A.
Telephone: (914) 375-1510
Toll Free: (800) 289-2253
Fax: (914) 375-1514
Web site: http://www.greystonbakery.com

Private Company
Incorporated: 1982
Employees: 130
Sales: $9.8 million (2007 est.)
NAICS: 311812 Commercial Bakeries

■ ■ ■

Greyston Bakery, Inc., is a for-profit company that supports nonprofit goals. Not only does the Yonkers, New York, company provide employment opportunities to disadvantaged people—many of whom have been homeless, drug dependent, or convicts—it also turns over its profits to the Greyston Foundation, which provides low-income housing, operates affordable child-care centers and health clinics, and supports other social programs. The 23,000-square-foot bakery produces wedding and specialty cakes, brownie and cookie crumbles used in specialty ice creams, and brownies and other dessert bars. Since the late 1980s Greyston has been a supplier of brownie bits to premium ice-cream maker Ben & Jerry's. Other industrial baking offerings include yellow and chocolate round and layer cakes, custom baking, and custom flavor development. The bakery is Kof-K

Kosher certified. Greyston has entered the retail business as well, launching the Do Goodie line of brownies in 2008.

The bakery has also garnered a great deal of press attention for its use of an open hiring system. Job applicants are asked no questions about their work history and references are not checked. People are simply placed on a waiting list. When a job becomes available the first person on the list, based on date of application, is called in to serve a two-week apprentice program. The bakery allows no absences during this period, and if apprentices are late more than once, they are dismissed. Many people are unable to make this cut; others disappear as soon as they receive their first paycheck, and about 80 percent leave before the end of their first year. However, still others have been able to make the best of the opportunity and turn their lives around. The bakery promotes from within, allowing dedicated workers to climb the ranks to greater levels of responsibility. Greyston Bakery has ties to a Zen Buddhist meditation group, which originally launched the business for the benefit of its seminary monks and students.

FOUNDER, 1939 BROOKLYN BORN

The man behind Greyston Bakery was Roshi Bernie Glassman, born Bernard Tetsugen Glassman in Brooklyn, New York, in 1939. His parents were Jewish immigrants, his father from Russia and his mother from Poland. Both of them had socialist leanings, imbuing Glassman with a sense of social responsibility. In the late 1950s he enrolled at the Brooklyn Polytechnic Institute to study engineering. It

COMPANY PERSPECTIVES

We don't hire people to bake brownies; we bake brownies to hire people.

was there that he also took a course on religions and became interested in Zen Buddhism. After receiving his degree in 1960, he went to work as an aeronautical engineer for McDonnell Douglas Corporation in Los Angeles, California, concentrating on interplanetary flights. He continued his education at the University of California at Los Angeles, earning a master's degree in 1968 and a Ph.D. in applied mathematics in 1970. He also continued to study Zen Buddhism. In 1968 he began personal studies with Taizan Maezumi Roshi and helped in the development of the Los Angeles Zen Center. In the same year that Glassman received his doctorate in aeronautical engineering, he was also ordained as a Buddhist monk. Glassman continued his aeronautical career, and was involved in drawing up plans for a Mars mission, but in 1976 decided to devote his life to developing the Los Angeles Zen Center.

In 1980 Glassman was dispatched to New York City by Maezumi Roshi to establish the Zen Community of New York. The interreligious Zen practice center, established in the Bronx, offered scheduled meditation, workshops, seminars, and classes. As abbot of the associated temple of the Zen Community of New York, Glassman launched a full-time, comprehensive training program, the Greyston Seminary, named after the Greyston mansion in the wealthy Riverdale section of the Bronx that housed the seminary. In order to provide an income for his three dozen monks and students, he decided to start a business in which they could pursue "meditation in action" (meditation conducted through daily activities) while earning a livelihood. Initially they tried catering, but Glassman knew of the successful Tassajara Bakery operated by the Zen Center of San Francisco, and he sent three monks to learn the business as well as to bring back recipes.

All told, creating the new bakery took about a year. Using $300,000 in borrowed funds, the operation was set up in a rented facility, a former lasagna factory damaged by fire, a few blocks north of Riverdale. Rather than concentrate on breads, like the Tassajara Bakery, Greyston Bakery, as it was named, elected to focus on higher-margin baked goods. It became operational in December 1982. Greyston Café was also established in Riverdale to provide a retail outlet for the baked goods, but the bakery primarily looked to take advantage of its

location to do a wholesale business with the many restaurants, gourmet shops, and department stores found in nearby Manhattan and upscale Westchester County.

LANDING THE FIRST COMMERCIAL CUSTOMER

Greyston started out making cakes and cookies and soon landed its first commercial customer, the Neiman Marcus department store. A month after opening, the bakery began offering muffins and scones. Brownies, blondies, and walnut coffee cakes were then added. To round out the bakery line, bread, rolls, chiffon cakes, and tarts were introduced as well. After being in business for six months, Greyston was barely able to meet the needs of its 100 regular customers, including Bloomingdale's, the Guggenheim Museum, the Dean & Deluca specialty stores, and several prominent hotels. Quickly outgrowing its facility, Greyston moved its operations to a new Yonkers facility after a year.

In 1986 Glassman decided to become more socially active, in keeping with his upbringing, and established the Greyston Family Inn, a nonprofit service organization devoted to the issue of homelessness, a problem that was especially acute in Yonkers, which was saddled with the country's highest per-capita rate of homelessness. The Riverdale Greyston mansion was sold and the Zen Buddhists moved into the community, establishing a new headquarters in an old convent in Yonkers. An apartment complex was acquired to provide affordable housing for single-parent homeless families and, as part of the effort to address homelessness, Glassman believed that employment opportunities should be made available as well. Minority managed Greyston Builders was established to renovate the building that would become the Greyston Family Inn, and Greyston Network was established to provide career counseling as well as day care and help with managing personal finances.

BEGINNING OF JOB-TRAINING PROGRAM: 1987

A job-training program in the bakery was established in 1987 by the Greyston Family Inn, the first step in the open hiring policy of Greyston Bakery and a move away from seminary monks and students serving as the workforce. Backed with funds from the Yonkers Private Industry Council, the pilot program was intensive, including several months of classroom and laboratory instruction, and stints working in different stations of the bakery, a far cry from the two-week apprentice program that would become a major component of the open hiring policy that would follow.

KEY DATES

1982: Greyston Bakery opens in Yonkers, New York.
1983: Bakery moves to larger facility.
1987: Bakery establishes "open hiring" policy.
1993: Greyston Foundation is established, funded by bakery profits.
1997: Julius Walls Jr. is named chief executive.
2003: New bakery plant opens.
2008: Do Goodie line of brownies is introduced.

The community was not especially receptive to Glassman's idea, however. Many residents mistakenly believed that Zen Buddhism was a modern cult and not an ancient religion, and they opposed the sale of an empty public school that was to be renovated to become the Greyston Family Inn. It was not until 1991 that the project finally opened. Along the way, Glassman became more politically astute, for example, adding African Americans to the board of directors where once there had been none.

FIRST PROFITABLE YEAR: 1991

Greyston Bakery, although respected for its goods in New York City, did not make money. The operation had outstripped the business skills of Glassman, who brought in Jef Hoeberichts, an adviser to the company, to take charge. A major step in turning the bakery into a profitable concern was taken in 1988 when it began producing baked crumbles, such as small brownie pieces, that were mixed into ice cream. At the founding meeting of Social Ventures Network, organized by socially minded corporations, Ben Cohen, cofounder of the Ben & Jerry's ice-cream company, agreed to purchase Greyston brownies for inclusion in Ben & Jerry's fudge-brownie ice cream. The deal helped Greyston Bakery achieve its first profit in 1991.

The Greyston Foundation was established in 1993 to develop and run community programs funded by the proceeds of the bakery. The bakery enjoyed steady growth, so that by the autumn of 1995 it was operating 24 hours a day. In 1996 Glassman became less directly involved in the Greyston operations, founding the Zen Peacemaker Order, an umbrella organization for ministry and social activism, in which Greyston Bakery and related Greyston entities were members.

Greyston Bakery was again in the red by the mid-1990s. To lead a turnaround, in 1997 a new president and chief executive officer was named, Julius Walls Jr.,

an African American. A former certified public accountant, and Brooklyn-born like Glassman, Walls had worked for a chocolate manufacturing company and had started his own company, Sweet Roots, Inc., which offered the only chocolate bar made from only African-sourced cocoa, sold under the Sweet Roots name. It was through the cocoa business that he met Glassman and began doing business with Greyston Bakery. Walls became a volunteer in 1993 as part of an effort to present the bakery's cookies to the White House. Two years later he became director of marketing on a consulting basis. Early in 1997 he agreed to become the bakery's director of operations and later in the year became chief executive. In 1998 he called the employees of the bakery together and told them that if they were to keep their jobs, the business needed to reduce waste in order to turn a profit. Through a group effort, the operation became leaner, and by the end of the year the business was once again turning a profit.

NEW PLANT OPENS: 2003

Greyston enjoyed steady growth into the new century, reaching $5 million in sales in 2003. Again, demand outstripped the capabilities of the plant, and $9 million was raised to build a new plant. Financial backers included the city of Yonkers Industrial Development Agency and Community Development Agency; the U.S. Department of Housing and Urban Development; the Nonprofit Finance Fund; KeyBank; and the F.B. Heron, Enterprise, and Calvert foundations. Designing the new facility was Maya Lin, renowned for her design of the Vietnam Veterans Memorial. Opened in September 2003, the state-of-the-art, 23,000-square-foot bakery was three times larger than the old facility. It was also able to receive kosher food certification, creating further sales opportunities. The extra production capacity allowed for a return to the retail business. The Greyston Café and Bakery was opened by the Greyston Foundation in Yonkers in 2003 to serve as a restaurant and outlet for the baked goods. It also provided further opportunities for "hard-to-employ" workers. The foundation was willing to absorb some losses until the operation established itself, but after 15 months the foundation was unable to provide further support and the business was shut down.

The new plant allowed Greyston to introduce several new products in 2004, including a "decadent" line of extra-rich chocolate cakes and other cakes, and a line of dessert bars, including brownies with nuts, blondies, lemon bars, peanut butter bars, pecan bars, and "magic" bars that combined brownies, coconut, chocolate chips, and other ingredients. The new products helped drive sales close to the $17 million mark in 2007.

A year later, Greyston introduced its first product intended for the retail trade, the Do Goodie line of individual brownies, which included four varieties: Chocolate Fudge, Walnut Fudge, Espresso Bean, and Brown Sugar Blondie. Endorsed by Ben Cohen and Jerry Greenfield of Ben & Jerry's, the product was able to find a number of retailers willing to carry it. Part of the marketing appeal of the line was the assignment of all profits to the Greyston Foundation to support housing, child care, healthcare, and employment for the underprivileged. While Greyston Bakery was still very much a small company, it was clearly one with a large heart and a great deal of public goodwill and commercial potential.

Ed Dinger

PRINCIPAL COMPETITORS

Horizon Food Group, Inc.; Interstate Bakeries Corporation; Sara Lee Food & Beverage.

FURTHER READING

Archer, Rick, "Poised to Raise More Dough," *Fairfield County (Conn.) Business Journal,* April 26, 2004, p. Y14.

Austin, Charles, "A Blend of Baking and Meditation," *New York Times,* July 10, 1983, p. A1.

Bramson, Constance Y., "And Zen There Were Goodies from Greyston Bakery," *Harrisburg (Pa.) Patriot-News,* December 10, 1986, p. C1.

Charkes, Juli Steadman, "Bakery's 'Open Hiring' Offers Anyone a Chance," *New York Times,* November 26, 2006, p. 6L.

Field, Elizabeth, "Zen Bakery Begins Training Program," *New York Times,* October 18, 1987.

Goldman, Ari L., "Cookies, Civic Pride and Zen," *New York Times,* December 23, 1991, p. B6.

Gupta, Udayan, "Blending Zen and the Art of Philanthropic Pastry Chefs—Buddhist Monk Puts the Poor to Work, and Houses Them with the Profit," *Wall Street Journal,* January 2, 1992, p. 12.

Hlotyak, Elizabeth, "Recipe for Success: Triple the Capacity," *Westchester County (N.Y.) Business Journal,* October 6, 2003, p. 2.

Perman, Stacy, "A New Model for Community Service," *Business Week Online,* May 25, 2007.

Stewart, Barbara, "In the Hood: Jobs for the Poor," *New York Times,* February 23, 2003, p. 14WC.1.

GT Solar International, Inc.

———————— ■ ————————

243 Daniel Webster Highway
Merrimack, New Hampshire 03054
U.S.A.
Telephone: (603) 883-5200
Fax: (603) 595-6993
Web site: http://www.gtsolar.com

Public Company
Incorporated: 1994 as GT Equipment Technologies, Inc.
Employees: 305
Sales: $244.05 million (2008)
Stock Exchanges: NASDAQ
Ticker Symbol: SOLR
NAICS: 333295 Semiconductor Machinery Manufacturing

■ ■ ■

GT Solar International, Inc., through its subsidiary, GT Solar Incorporated, is a leading manufacturer of machines used by the photovoltaic (PV) industry to make solar energy systems. GT Solar designs, manufactures, assembles, programs, and installs machines and turnkey fabrication lines for the production of solar wafers, cells, modules, and panels. With headquarters and an assembly plant in Merrimack, New Hampshire, a facility in Missoula, Montana, and two offices in China, the company outsources the bulk of its manufacturing, focusing on the major proprietary components and final assembly. Its key products, photovoltaic wafer fabrication machinery and silicon furnaces, are mostly destined for the Asian market and used by such global solar products suppliers as LDK Solar, Yingli Green Energy, BP Solar, Top Green Energy Technologies, and Soltech.

A SMOOTH TAKEOFF

Kedar Gupta and Jonathan Talbott founded the company that became GT Solar International, Inc., in Nashua, New Hampshire, in 1994 with $1,000 between them and a shared passion for the solar industry. Gupta, the "G," and Talbott, the "T," in "GT," were both working for Ferrofluidics Corp. when they started getting requests from solar companies. When their employer showed no interest in expanding the company's focus from the semiconductor industry to include solar energy, the pair saw a golden opportunity to start their own business selling machines that enabled other companies to make solar wafers, cells, and panels.

Gupta and Talbott quit their jobs and created their own company, GT Equipment Technologies, Inc. At first, they worked out of their home basements. Gupta served as president and chief executive officer and Talbott assumed the positions of chief operating officer and vice-president of sales and marketing. The start-up company was without a source of venture capital or loans, but Gupta and Talbott were very well connected from their work at Ferrofluidics, where they had succeeded in taking that company's system equipment division from a 5 percent share to more than 60 percent worldwide.

By the time GT Equipment officially opened its 16,000-square-foot Nashua facility as a manufacturing and technology company offering a variety of

COMPANY PERSPECTIVES

GT Solar Incorporated is an industry leader globally providing essential technology, turnkey manufacturing and equipment solutions across the photovoltaic supply chain, enabling the establishment of successful photovoltaic businesses.

semiconductor and photovoltaic equipment, it already had one customer and a $650,000 order, with a 35 percent advance deposit. The founders later said they were surprised that customers and suppliers accepted CODs and 60- to 90-day terms from a start-up company. In the early years, the company's growth was based entirely on advance orders. In 1995, the company posted revenues of $870,000.

SMALL, BUT GROWING FAST

With sales offices in Oregon, Texas, and Japan, and a backlog of $13 million by July 1997, GT Equipment opened an additional 3,000-square-foot manufacturing plant in Bedford, New Hampshire, to keep up with demand. From the start, the company outsourced the bulk of its manufacturing, and focused on the key proprietary components and final assembly. Its initial phenomenal growth landed the enterprise the 20th slot on *Entrepreneur* magazine's 1997 list of the fastest-growing new small businesses in the country.

In early 1998, GT Equipment created a subsidiary, GT Solar Technologies, Inc., and began to manufacture, sell and distribute heat exchanger method (HEM) silicon furnaces, a state-of-the-art crystal growing technology acquired in a licensing agreement with Crystal Systems, Inc., of Salem, Massachusetts. The furnaces were designed to melt polysilicon and grow multicrystalline ingots used in the production of solar wafers, and ultimately solar cells. In April 1998, GT Solar announced its first multiple unit sale of HEM furnaces to ScanWafer AS in Norway. In the same year, the company received its first significant investment, a $500,000 loan through the state Small Business Development Fund.

January 1999 brought more orders for HEM furnaces from customers in the United States and Europe, and in July, GT Solar received a multimillion-dollar contract to supply Maharishi Technology Corporation, based in the Netherlands, with turnkey wafer and solar cell production lines, which included

HEM multicrystalline wafer and cell processing technology. The deal also tapped GT Solar for installation, training, and support services for the project. The company ended the year with 45 employees.

BUILDING MARKET PRESENCE

In January 2001, GT Solar inked a deal to sell an undisclosed number of multicrystalline silicon growing furnaces to Maryland-based BP Solar, at the time the world's largest manufacturer of photovoltaic systems. The month also brought a $4.5 million contract for the sale of crystal growers and laser cutting systems with ASE Americas, a Massachusetts-based manufacturer of photovoltaic wafers, cells, and modules.

In late November 2001, GT Equipment signed a five-year contract, worth over $70 million, to license its latest feedstock production technology to Germany-based SolarWorld AG. The GT Equipment technology, which cut the cost of producing solar electricity by as much as 20 cents a watt, was an integral part of a project initiated by Deutsche Solar, a subsidiary of SolarWorld, to put an end to the chronic shortage of silicon feedstock for solar cell production. GT Equipment closed 2001 with about $20 million in revenues.

In January 2002, with the number of employees up to 85 from 70 the year before, GT Equipment bought a 19.75-acre lot for $800,000 in Merrimack to build a $3 million, 60,000-square-foot facility. In March, the company received a $5 million investment from RBC Capital Partners, the private equity group of the Royal Bank of Canada, to finance the project and help the business develop new products and expand further into European markets.

GT Equipment exports to eight countries, namely France, India, Norway, Algeria, Japan, Italy, Germany, and Ukraine, accounted for 70 percent of its business. In April 2002, the company added China to the list with a $6 million deal to install a turnkey photovoltaic wafer fabrication line for Yingli New Energy Resources Co., Ltd., of Baoding, China. On October 12, the company moved into its new factory and headquarters in Merrimack, New Hampshire. In November, Yingli added a turnkey photovoltaic cell fabrication line to its order. With an annual growth rate of 40 percent for the previous three years, GT Equipment finished 2002 with equipment and services revenues of $29 million.

RIDING OUT THE STORM

The year 2003 was a down one for the company. Records revealed only one announcement in October that GT Solar received an order for a 2004 installation

KEY DATES

1994: Kedar Gupta and Jonathan Talbott start GT Equipment from their basements with $1,000.

1997: *Entrepreneur* magazine cites company as 20th fastest-growing new small business in the United States.

1998: GT Solar Technologies, Inc., a subsidiary, is created to expand solar energy offerings.

2002: Company penetrates Asian market with new business in China.

2006: Private equity firm GFI Energy Ventures acquires majority interest in GT Equipment; GT Equipment is renamed GT Solar International, Inc.; subsidiary becomes GT Solar Incorporated; GT Solar adds polysilicon reactors to its equipment line.

2008: Public offering falls flat; share price slides significantly with global economic downturn.

of a turnkey photovoltaic module assembly line at Romag Limited in Newcastle, United Kingdom. Revenue for the year dropped to only $9.5 million, which prompted Fleet Boston Financial to yank its $2 million line of credit, which nearly bankrupted the company. CEO Gupta responded by cutting his own, then other top executives' salaries, followed by salary cuts in middle management while the company paid down its debt and searched for new financing and more sales contracts.

GT began to rebound in mid-2004. In June, the U.S. Department of Energy awarded the company a $100,000 Small Business Innovation Research grant for continued development of methods aimed at lowering the cost of solar energy. In August, GT Solar inked its biggest contract to date, a $14 million contract to install a turnkey crystal silicon wafer manufacturing line at Taiwan-based Green Energy Technology Inc., a subsidiary of Tatung Company. In September, GT Equipment expanded its upper management team by hiring Tom Zarrella for the newly created position of president and chief operating officer.

By October 2004, the company said it had record bookings of $21 million in its third quarter, a 500 percent increase over the same quarter of 2003. In November, the company signed a $9.5 million deal with Yingli for directionally solidified silicon (DSS) furnaces, the company's technologically advanced multi-crystal silicon ingot growth furnaces. GT Equipment closed the

year with a financing package of $9.5 million from Wells Fargo.

NEW OWNERS, NEW NAME

GT Equipment continued its dramatic turnaround in 2005, driven by the success of its subsidiary, GT Solar. Uncertainty surrounding the supply and price of oil, and increased government incentives in certain countries for solar energy, generated a record growth of 150 percent in revenues for the company in the fiscal year that ended March 31, 2005. As of June 2005, the $38 million booked by the company for fiscal 2005 had far exceeded the nearly $23 million for all of fiscal 2004. Employment also grew at a record pace, as the workforce went from 35 to 80 in an 18-month period.

In August 2005, the floodgates to the Chinese market opened for GT Solar with a $33 million contract to create a wafer fabrication turnkey line for solar energy applications for LDK Solar Hi-Tech Co., Ltd., of Jiangxi Province. In December, GT Solar received a record 100-unit order for DSS multi-crystal silicon ingot growth furnaces from LDK. The deal brought GT Solar's total sales for 2005 in the Chinese market to $80 million.

In January 2006, GT Equipment announced that GFI Energy Ventures, LLC, a Los Angeles-based investor group, acquired a majority interest in the company for an undisclosed amount. The transaction also included a significant, but undisclosed, investment from Angelino Group, another Los Angeles-based private equity firm focused on high-growth investments in the energy sector.

For fiscal 2006, which ended March 31, 2006, company documents showed annual revenues of $58 million and a total of 120 employees. In August, GT Equipment Technologies, Inc., changed its name to GT Solar International, Inc., to reflect the company's primary focus on solar energy. The name of the company's wholly owned subsidiary, GT Solar Technologies, Inc., was changed to GT Solar Incorporated. In December, the company expanded its presence in China by creating a wholly owned foreign enterprise, GT Solar Co., Ltd., with offices in Shanghai and Beijing. Cofounder and CEO, Dr. Kedar Gupta, 59, retired from the company on December 31, 2006. Tom Zarrella remained in a top leadership position as company president.

NEW PRODUCT: POLYSILICON REACTORS

In 2006, GT Solar created its Polysilicon Division, located in Missoula, Montana, and entered the polysilicon production equipment market. In addition to supplying polysilicon production equipment, known as polysilicon reactors, the division was also set up to provide facility design, engineering, and installation services.

In March 2007, GT Solar landed its first order for polysilicon reactors in a $49 million deal with Siberia-based Nitol Group. In April, GT Solar announced that overall sales had risen 30 percent a year for five years in a row, and the company needed to hire 80 more employees and double the size of its manufacturing plant. It also elevated Thomas Zarrella to president, chief executive officer, and director of its parent company, GT Solar International, Inc.

Sales of photovoltaic equipment really took off in the summer of 2007. In June, the company landed a $39.5 million contract for polysilicon reactors and converters with China-based Jiangsu Shunda Electronic Materials and Technology. In July, GT Solar signed a $40.7 million deal to sell a turnkey line of equipment capable of making solar wafers, cells, and modules with Soltech, S.A., in Patras, Greece. July also brought a deal with LDK Solar for solar reactors and the company's largest single contract to date, a two-year $171 million sale of DSS450 furnaces, capable of producing 400-kilogram to 450-kilogram silicon ingots, to China-based Glory Silicon Energy Co., Ltd.

In November 2007, GT Solar secured a $56 million follow-on deal with Yingli to supply it with DSS450 furnaces, and before the year ended, the company broke ground on a multi-phase construction project intended to add 60,000 square feet to its Merrimack headquarters over the next two to three years. GT Solar's exports to the Asian market continued to grow in March 2008 with a $200 million contract to supply polysilicon reactors to DC Chemical Co., Ltd., of South Korea. April brought a $91 million contract for polysilicon reactors and converters with The Silicon Mine B.V., of the Netherlands.

GOING PUBLIC IN DIFFICULT ENVIRONMENT

On July 7, 2008, GT Solar International, Inc., filed documents with the Securities and Exchange Commission for an initial public offering (IPO) on the NASDAQ under the symbol SOLR. It was expected to raise about $500 million with the sale of 30.3 million shares at an estimated price of $15.50 to $17.50 each. The stage seemed set for a successful market debut. Demand for GT Solar's equipment had skyrocketed and the company's revenue had quadrupled to $244 million in fiscal 2008, which ended March 31, while net income

rose to $36 million, compared with a 2007 net loss of $18 million.

On July 24, 2008, the company raised $499.95 million from the sale of shares priced at $16.50 each, which made it the largest IPO ever by a U.S. solar company. It peaked at $17.50 but closed the trading day at $14.59. On the second day of trading, shares slid 14 percent to $12.59 when the company issued a statement that LDK Solar, which accounted for 62 percent of GT Solar's revenue in fiscal 2008, had signed a contract with China-based rival JYT Corp. Although GT Solar was expected to do better, its fate appeared no better or worse than most of the rest of the market, especially solar energy stocks, which had been in retreat from March rally levels since late May, due in large part to tumbling oil prices and a looming recession.

In August 2008, in its first financial report since going public, GT Solar reported net income of $5.14 million on revenue of $57.1 million for the first quarter of fiscal 2009, which ended June 28, compared to a year earlier loss of $5.03 million on revenues of $15.4 million.

The fall of 2008 brought more sales contracts with Asia. In September, repeat customer LDK Solar ordered $32 million worth of polysilicon reactors from GT Solar. In October, the company signed a $46.8 million polysilicon production equipment and services agreement with Taiwan-based Top Green Energy Technologies, Inc. The order brought the company's contractual backlog to more than $1.4 billion, according to November company reports for the second quarter of fiscal 2009, which ended September 27, 2008. Revenues for the quarter increased 71 percent to $140.2 million, as compared to $81.8 million for the same quarter a year earlier.

As 2008 came to a close, GT Solar appeared healthy in many ways despite a global credit crisis and financial meltdown in the fall that caused company shares to lose more than 80 percent of their value. While an impending global economic recession threatened the security of the company's impressive backlog of orders as customers could be forced to push back delivery dates, the company was also uniquely positioned, as a maker of the machines needed to make solar energy products, to benefit from new energy and environmental policies, including the promotion of solar energy, promised by the incoming administration of President Barack Obama.

Ted Sylvester

PRINCIPAL SUBSIDIARIES
GT Solar Incorporated.

PRINCIPAL DIVISIONS

Polysilicon Division.

PRINCIPAL COMPETITORS

JYT Corp. (China); Amtech Systems, Inc.; Applied Materials, Inc.; centrotherm voltaics AG (Germany); MEMC Electronic Materials, Inc.; Mitsubishi Electric Corporation (Japan); OTB Group B.V. (Netherlands).

FURTHER READING

Brooks, Dave, "N.H. Remains a Leading High-Tech Exporter," *New Hampshire Business Review,* August 3, 2007, p. 23.

Cowan, Lynn, "GT Solar a Bellwether for 'Green' IPOs—Machine Producer Could Give a Boost to Eco-Offerings," *Wall Street Journal,* July 21, 2008, p. C5.

————, "GT Solar Falls 12% in a Blow to IPO Issues," *Wall Street Journal,* July 21, 2008, p. C5.

"Former Ferrofluidics Execs Know the Value of Having a Good Reputation," *New Hampshire Business Review,* July 4, 1997, p. 4.

Gelsi, Steve, "GT Solar's IPO Weighs In at $500 Million," *MarketWatch,* July 9, 2008.

Harlin, Kevin, "Capital Goods Maker for Solar Energy Steps into Sunlight," *Investor's Business Daily,* July 22, 2008.

Kennedy, Eileen, "Department of Commerce Gives Export Certificate to Nashua, N.H., Tech Firm," *Nashua (N.H.) Telegraph,* October 1, 2002.

————, "Investors Acquire Majority Ownership of Merrimack, N.H., Energy Equipment Maker," *Nashua (N.H.) Telegraph,* January 10, 2006.

————, "Merrimack, N.H.-based Firm Works to Help Lower Cost of Solar Energy," *Nashua (N.H.) Telegraph,* June 30, 2004.

Leighton, Brad, "Nashua, N.H., Solar-Energy Equipment Maker Gets $5 Million Cash Infusion," *Nashua (N.H.) Telegraph,* March 23, 2002.

Marzloff, Karen, "GT Equipment Technologies," *Business NH Magazine,* September 1, 1998, p. 13.

Morrison, Todd, "Founder of GT Solar Retires at 59," *Nashua (N.H.) Telegraph,* December 17, 2006.

O'Brien, Andrea, and Elizabeth Ward, "High-Tech Firm Leverages Growth with Grants, Venture Capital," *New Hampshire Business Review,* August 9, 2002, p. C1.

Sanders, Bob, "GT Solar Fends Off IPO Class Action Suits," *New Hampshire Business Review,* August 29, 2008, p. 1.

Smith, Ashley, "Solar Power Firm in Merrimack, N.H., Looks to Go Public," *Nashua (N.H.) Telegraph,* July 9, 2008.

Harley Ellis Devereaux Corporation

26913 Northwestern Highway, Suite 200
Southfield, Michigan 48034
U.S.A.
Telephone: (248) 262-1500
Toll Free: (866) 237-7359
Fax: (248) 262-1515
Web site: http://www.harleyellis.com

Private Company
Incorporated: 1946 as Harley, Ellington and Day
Employees: 600
Sales: $70.5 million (2007)
NAICS: 541310 Architectural Services

■ ■ ■

Harley Ellis Devereaux Corporation (HED) is an architecture and engineering firm offering a range of services that guide projects from planning and design through to construction. Services offered by the company include strategic planning, program management, real estate service, sustainable design, quality review, and construction services. HED serves clients in more than 40 states through seven offices, catering to the needs of corporations, major colleges and universities, hospital systems, government and civic institutions, and research centers. Through four subsidiaries, HED offers specific services. Spectrum Strategies offers planning, consulting, and management services. Crime Lab Design specializes in designing facilities for the forensic community. GreenWorks Studio functions as HED's sustainable design business. HED Build offers construction services.

ORIGINS

After 100 years, one vestige of HED's inception remained, the surname of its founder, Alvin E. Harley. The son of a farmer, Harley was born in Portage La-Prairie, in the Canadian province of Manitoba, in 1884. At the age of six, he and his family moved east to the neighboring province of Ontario, where Harley landed his first job as a draftsman while he was a teenager. After three years of working for a man named Herbert Matthews, Harley was determined to become an architect, a profession, his employer advised, that would be best pursued in the bustling metropolis of Detroit.

Harley heeded Matthews' advice, arriving in Detroit in 1903 at the age of 19. He found work as a draftsman and apprentice working under the supervision of two of the country's most influential architects, Albert Kahn and George D. Mason. After five years of learning the trade, Harley was ready to start his own firm and convinced a colleague at Mason's office, Norman Atcheson, to join him. The pair formed Harley and Atcheson in 1908, remaining partners for five years, during which time the number of buildings constructed in Detroit more than doubled. Buoyed by hospitable market conditions, the two entrepreneurs fared well, designing, among other projects, the Globe Theater, a 650-seat vaudeville theater, and the Henry Clay Hotel.

Harley dissolved the partnership in 1912 and remained on his own for more than 20 years. During the period, he dabbled in the design of commercial and

COMPANY PERSPECTIVES

We have an obligation to do work that aspires to greatness. This demands an energetic vigilance, where well-explored ideas lead to thoughtful solutions. We must comprehend balance and beauty, function and economy, science and society and know when each is being served well. We must advocate for inspired design, lasting value, environmental stewardship, and consistently deliver these qualities in all that we do. Above all, our work must be clearly responsive to our clients' needs.

industrial buildings, but he primarily focused on residential designs, finding a lucrative market in the Detroit suburbs of Grosse Pointe and Bloomfield Hills, home to wealthy automobile executives. The demand for sprawling, upscale homes dropped off with the onset of the Great Depression, which forced Harley to seek help by joining forces with another architect also feeling the sting of the harsh economic climate.

HARLEY AND ELLINGTON: A LASTING PARTNERSHIP BEGINS IN 1933

Unlike Harley and Atcheson, the partnership between Harley and Harold S. Ellington endured for years, representing the first meaningful chapter in HED's history. A Chicago native two years Harley's junior, Ellington earned a bachelor's degree in civil engineering in 1908 from what became the Illinois Institute of Technology. Ellington worked as a chief engineer for the Standard Concrete Construction Company after earning his degree, spending his days designing reinforced concrete structures for buildings, bridges, and breweries. In 1912, he moved to Detroit after being hired as the plant and construction engineer for the Stroh Brewing Company. The prohibition on the sale of alcohol, which took effect in Michigan in 1917, forced Ellington to find a different line of work, prompting him to form partnerships with other architects and engineers. When his primary partner died in 1932, Ellington was left alone to navigate the turbulent waters of the Great Depression. For help, he turned to Harley, proposing a merger of their practices. The two men, both in their late 40s at the time, united their firms in 1933, creating Harley and Ellington, Architects and Engineers.

A FOUNDATION BUILT ON BREWERIES

The complementary skills of the two partners, Ellington, an engineer, and Harley, an architect, proved to be a winning combination. The partnership benefited especially from Ellington's contributions because of his experience with breweries. The end of Prohibition in 1933 provided a wealth of business for Harley and Ellington, representing more than 50 percent of the firm's business in the years leading up to World War II. Work on breweries also led the firm outside of Michigan for the first time, when the two partners designed a stock house for the Eichler Brewing Company in New York City in 1936. The first steps beyond state boundaries were followed quickly by geographic expansion into Boston, Massachusetts; Washington, D.C.; Cincinnati, Ohio; Newark, New Jersey; and Windsor, Ontario. By the time the United States entered World War II, Harley and Ellington was deriving more than 40 percent of its annual revenue from outside Michigan.

During the 1940s, the most significant development was the arrival of a third principal partner. Clarence E. Day, a Detroit native, had started his own practice in 1915, focusing his work on designing residences. He courted the same clientele as Harley had served, designing homes for wealthy executives in Grosse Pointe and Bloomfield Hills. He started working with Harley and Ellington in 1937, beginning a professional relationship that led to a merger of the two firms in 1943, which marked the birth of Harley, Ellington and Day. The firm incorporated in 1946 and became a leader in the design of civic and cultural buildings as its brewery business, which had served as its mainstay for decades, petered out. The higher education market filled the void created by the loss of brewery revenue, providing ample business for Harley, Ellington and Day. The firm was the chief architect for the University of Detroit, designed the General Service Building at the University of Michigan, and designed the Richard Cohn Building at Wayne State University. The 1950s also saw the firm take on two of the largest projects in the country, the Army Finance Center at Fort Benjamin Harrison in Indiana, a two-million-square-foot building, and the State Department Building in Washington, D.C., a 2.6-million-square-foot structure.

The end of the 1950s marked the last decade the three principals were in power. Day retired in 1959, while Harley and Ellington transitioned into semiretirement the following year, staying on as consultants during the change in leadership. Ellington died in 1964 and Day died the following year. Harley, after a half-century of leading the firm he founded, lived to the age of 92, passing away in 1976.

KEY DATES

1908: Harley Ellis Devereaux is founded by Alvin Harley and Norman Atcheson.

1933: Alvin Harley and Harold Ellington merge their practices.

1936: The firm works on its first project outside Michigan, a stock house in New York City designed for Eichler Brewing Company.

1961: New leadership necessitates a new name, Harley, Ellington, Cowin and Stirton.

1969: The firm, renamed Harley Ellington Associates, moves its headquarters from Detroit to nearby Southfield.

1991: Dennis King is named president of the firm.

2000: A merger with Ellis/Naeyaert/Genheimer Associates creates HarleyEllis Corp.

2006: A merger with Fields Devereaux Architects and Engineers creates Harley Ellis Devereaux Corporation.

2008: The firm celebrates its centennial.

DIVERSIFICATION IN THE SIXTIES

New leadership brought a new name to the firm. Operating as Harley, Ellington, Cowin and Stirton, the name adopted in 1961, the firm expanded into new practice areas during the decade. The firm designed numerous recreation centers, libraries, city halls, and police stations in Michigan. It delved into designing military buildings such as dormitories, hospitals, and armories and, perhaps most important, began courting healthcare companies as clients. The firm's business was rounded out by its continued reliance on higher education work, particularly at the University of Michigan, and on the mausoleum and cemetery market, which had been a staple of the firm's diet since Harley's early years. At the end of the 1960s, the firm moved its headquarters from downtown Detroit to Southfield, just north of the city, and it changed its name to Harley Ellington Associates, a corporate title adopted to avoid the necessity of any name changes in the future.

Harley Ellington Associates, the name that was supposed be permanent, was used for only four years. In 1970 the firm decided to merge with Pierce, Wolf, Yee and Associates. The merger took three years to complete, resulting in the new corporate title of Harley Ellington Pierce Yee Associates in 1973. During the decade, an energy management-consulting practice was added to the firm's services, as it increasingly turned to industrial and automotive clients for business. The end of the decade marked the arrival of Dennis King, who was hired as a project manager in 1979 and elected a principal partner two years later.

THE KING ERA

King, who would lead the firm toward its centennial, earned a bachelor's degree in architecture from the University of Michigan. He rose quickly through the ranks of the firm's project management practice, witnessing a decade of spirited financial growth. Although the firm had diversified into new practice areas during the 1960s and 1970s, the years were bleak financially, comparatively stagnant after the firm's vibrant performance during the 1950s. The 1980s put an end to the financial malaise, as Harley Ellington Pierce Yee Associates tripled its revenues during the decade. The firm leaned heavily on its healthcare area, which completed more than 250 medical projects during the decade, and it enjoyed a thriving higher education business, designing new chemical and biological science buildings for Indiana University and the University of Michigan.

Dennis King took control of the firm in 1991, becoming its sixth president. During his tenure, he grappled with determining the fate of the firm, sensing as the 1990s progressed that the firm faced a dilemma. Michigan-based architecture and engineering firms were losing ground to firms located elsewhere according to rankings provided by *Engineering News-Record*. He realized the firm had two choices: either scale back its services and focus on niche markets or expand aggressively to develop more comprehensive capabilities and geographic diversity. King opted for the second choice, choosing to become a consolidator in his industry, which led to two important mergers in the years leading up to the firm's centennial.

MERGER WITH ELLIS/NAEYAERT/GENHEIMER ASSOCIATES IN 2000

King, who changed the name of the firm to Harley Ellington Design in 1995, began discussions with one of his competitors at the end of the decade. Founded in 1962, Ellis/Naeyaert/Genheimer Associates practiced in the same areas as Harley Ellington (healthcare, higher education, corporate, government, research, and automotive) but it was noted more for its engineering capabilities than its architectural talents. The Troy, Michigan-based firm, led by CEO James Page, began talking with Harley Ellington in early 1999. "When

Dennis King and I got together and shared our visions, they were very compatible," Page explained in the September 27, 1999 issue of *Crain's Detroit Business.* "It was to be a provider of a wider range of services to our clients and new clients."

The proposed partnership, uniting one firm known primarily as an architect with a firm known primarily as an engineer, harkened back to the partnership between Alvin Harley and Harold Ellington, one an architect, the other an engineer. Negotiations for the merger continued throughout 1999, resulting in the formation of HarleyEllis Corp. in 2000, a firm that counted King as its chairman and Page as the managing principal in charge of daily operations. Combined, the two firms boasted annual revenues of $40 million generated by 300 employees.

MERGER WITH FIELDS DEVEREAUX ARCHITECTS AND ENGINEERS IN 2006

King's next move on the expansion front was his boldest move, adding greatly to his firm's prominence on a national level. Several years after completing the merger with Ellis/Naeyaert, King began talking with a Los Angeles-based firm, Fields Devereaux Architects and Engineers. The two firms had worked together on a $150 million crime lab located on the campus of California State University. With offices in Las Vegas and California offices in Los Angeles, San Diego, Riverside, and Bakersfield, Fields Devereaux was led by J. Peter Devereaux, who presided over a growing business that generated roughly $20 million in revenue in 2004. King pursued Fields Devereaux to give his firm greater exposure outside the Midwest. "The Midwest is not the aggressively growing part of our country," he said in the August 29, 2005 issue of *Crain's Detroit Business.* "For us to grow our organization, we need to go further and further from home."

The merger was completed in January 2006, creating a firm named Harley Ellis Devereaux Corporation with 500 employees in four states and revenues that were expected to reach $70 million. King became chairman and chief executive officer of the combined company, while J. Peter Devereaux assumed the responsibilities of president. The merger likely was not the last move that King or his successors would engineer, but the deal marked the conclusion of activity at the end of the firm's first century of business. HED celebrated its 100th anniversary in 2008 with Alvin Harley's name still in its corporate title and still bearing the characteristics of the firm he established in 1908.

Jeffrey L. Covell

PRINCIPAL SUBSIDIARIES

Spectrum Strategies; Crime Lab Design; GreenWorks Studio; HED Build.

PRINCIPAL COMPETITORS

SmithGroup, Inc.; Skidmore, Owings & Merrill LLP; A. Epstein and Sons International, Inc.

FURTHER READING

"Harley Ellington Pierce Yee Associates Inc.," *Building Design & Construction,* October 1995, p. 12.

Mercer, Tenisha, "Architectural, Interior-Design Companies Exchange Stock," *Crain's Detroit Business,* September 21, 1998, p. 5.

Smith, Jennette, "Architect Firms to Unite," *Crain's Detroit Business,* September 27, 1999, p. 3.

———, "HarleyEllis, Calif., Firm Plan Merger," *Crain's Detroit Business,* August 29, 2005, p. 1.

———, "State Firms Broaden Footprints," *Crain's Detroit Business,* January 22, 2007, p. 12.

H Harman International

Harman International Industries, Incorporated

—■—

400 Atlantic Street, Suite 1500
Stamford, Connecticut 06901
U.S.A.
Telephone: (203) 328-3500
Fax: (203) 328-3951
Web site: http://www.harman.com

Public Company
Founded: 1953 as Harman-Kardon Inc.
Incorporated: 1980
Employees: 11,694
Sales: $4.11 billion (2008)
Stock Exchanges: New York
Ticker Symbol: HAR
NAICS: 334310 Audio and Video Equipment Manufacturing

■ ■ ■

Harman International Industries, Incorporated, manufactures and markets a wide range of high-end, high-fidelity audio products and electronics systems for consumer and professional markets. Well-known brands sold by the company include JBL, Infinity, Harman/Kardon, Mark Levinson, and Becker. Harman is also a major producer of audio, electronics, and so-called infotainment systems for automobiles, supplying such products to a number of automakers around the globe. Its automotive group, which generates more than 70 percent of the firm's overall revenues, includes several German automakers—such as Audi AG, Daimler AG, and Volkswagen AG—among its key customers;

Germany therefore accounts for more than 42 percent of overall sales. Harman secures about 15 percent of its sales elsewhere in Europe and roughly 22 percent at home in the United States.

Harman International was incorporated in 1980 by Dr. Sidney Harman, a politician, philosopher, entrepreneur, and one of the founding fathers of the stereo industry. He formed the enterprise to purchase the JBL loudspeaker unit operated by the mammoth Beatrice Foods Company conglomerate. The roots of the company that Harman created in 1980, though, reach back to a venture that Harman himself launched in the 1950s. Indeed, Harman purchased the JBL division as part of a plan to regain control of the company that he had started and, over the course of nearly three decades, built into a respected developer and manufacturer of cutting-edge, high-fidelity stereo gear.

COMPANY FOUNDING

The predecessor to Harman International was founded in 1953 by Sidney Harman and Bernard Kardon. Both Harman and Kardon were engineers by training; the "Dr." in Harman's title, interestingly, refers to a Ph.D. in social psychology that he earned at the Union Institute of New York. The two friends were working together during the early 1950s as engineers at the Bogen Company, which was then the top manufacturer of public-address systems. High-fidelity technology that was emerging at the time had caught Harman's interest, and he tried to persuade his superiors at Bogen to become more involved in the burgeoning field.

COMPANY PERSPECTIVES

Harman International is a worldwide leader in the manufacture of high-quality, high-fidelity audio and electronic products for automotive, consumer and professional use. For more than 50 years, our legendary brands have taken a leading role in the creation and innovation of progressive technologies, from the world's first car radio in 1948 to today's most revolutionary infotainment systems. Our commitment to quality and innovation can be found everywhere, from theaters and stadiums to homes and automobiles, and continues to redefine the boundaries of technology and entertainment. Through internal development and a series of carefully selected acquisitions, we have built up a broad range of renowned brands and products in our principal markets, and a substantial and experienced digital engineering capability.

But the companies of Harman International don't just develop new technologies; they also have the infrastructure to manufacture and distribute them. This gives us an advantage over our competitors by enabling us to share and combine valuable resources and research.

Bogen showed little interest in Harman's desire to pioneer high-fidelity equipment for the home. Thus, in 1953, Harman and Kardon left the company to form their own enterprise: Harman-Kardon Inc. Drawing from their $10,000 in funds, the pair developed an advanced stereo system that could be used to play records at home. When their friends heard the system, they were amazed. "We knocked the hell out of them; they were trembling with Shostakovich's Fifth," Harman recalled in the September 1989 *Regardies—The Business of Washington.* "Nobody had heard anything like that in his living room," Harman added.

Harman and Kardon were not alone in their quest for the ultimate home sound system. Several European companies—H. H. Scott and Fisher, for example—were both selling amplified home sound systems at the time. The systems developed by Harman-Kardon, however, differed from the competition in that they were designed with aesthetic appeal, as well as cutting-edge sound. Importantly, Harman-Kardon was the first company to put an amplifier, preamp, and radio tuner in a single unit that actually looked like a piece of furniture, rather than a commercial amplifier. That innovation is credited with bringing high-fidelity to the masses. It also gave the entrepreneurs an edge in the marketplace that would allow them to pursue their goal of developing continually better home stereo equipment.

HARMAN AT THE SOLO HELM

Kardon retired in 1956 and Harman bought his share of the blossoming enterprise. Harman sold part of his company in 1962. For several years thereafter, Harman-Kardon, under Sidney Harman's control, operated as the flagship division of an enterprise that owned other high-fidelity operations, including the 1969-acquired JBL, a firm founded by James B. Lansing in 1946 that had helped to pioneer the loudspeaker industry. From the mid-1960s into the 1970s, Harman built his stereo company into a leading contender in the high-fidelity industry. At the same time, the innovative and intriguing Harman was involved in a number of other pursuits.

Among the most notable sidelines was his interest in higher education. Beginning in the early 1970s Harman became president of Friends World College, an experimental Quaker school in Long Island that was a sort of school-without-walls. Harman had also been heavily involved in the civil rights movement, and even cofounded and taught at a highly respected "free school" in Virginia (officials in the county had shuttered the local public schools and opened all-white academies to circumvent U.S. Supreme Court integration rulings).

Among Harman's top business ventures during the 1970s was a manufacturing plant in Tennessee that produced automobile side-view mirrors. Harman's management of that plant demonstrated how effectively he was able to mix his interests in education and business. In an effort that became known as the "Bolivar Experiment," Harman applied the principles that he taught at the Friends World College to the manufacturing plant. His attempt to enhance worker satisfaction and productivity by creating an employee-oriented work environment earned him recognition as a pioneer in the field of participatory management. Furthermore, his management strategies were considered a driving force in the success of Harman-Kardon during the 1960s and 1970s.

By the mid-1970s Harman-Kardon was a powerhouse in the U.S. stereo industry. Importantly, the company profited by pioneering the concept of separate components; instead of selling stereo systems as integrated units, Harman-Kardon began selling separate

KEY DATES

■

1953: Sidney Harman and Bernard Kardon found Harman-Kardon Inc. to develop high-fidelity equipment for the home.

1956: Kardon retires, leaving Harman in solo control.

1969: Company acquires the loudspeaker maker JBL.

1977: After accepting a government post, Harman sells the company to Beatrice Foods Company.

1980: Harman acquires Beatrice's audio equipment assets, which center on the JBL brand, and organizes them as Harman International Industries, Incorporated., based in Washington, D.C.

1981: Purchase of Cleveland Electronics (renamed Harman Motive) moves the company into the automotive stereo sector.

1983: The Infinity consumer loudspeaker business is acquired.

1985: Harman International regains the rights to the Harman-Kardon brand.

1986: Company goes public.

1995: Harman acquires Becker GmbH, a leading German maker of automotive radios and electronics, and the Mark Levinson line of high-end electronics products.

1998: Restructuring of consumer products unit is launched.

2001: Company supplies its first integrated infotainment systems for BMW 7 Series automobiles.

2007: Kohlberg Kravis Roberts & Co. and Goldman Sachs Group, Inc.'s private-equity arm agree to acquire Harman for $8 billion, but the deal later collapses; Dinesh Paliwal is named CEO.

2008: Company founder Sidney Harman retires; Harman International shifts its headquarters to Stamford, Connecticut.

receivers, speakers, amplifiers, and other pieces that buyers could purchase separately and wire together to tailor their own home sound system. By 1976 the company was generating an amazing $136.5 million in annual sales and churning out a healthy $9.1 million in annual profits.

THE BEATRICE INTERREGNUM, 1977–80

Meanwhile, Harman continued to pursue additional interests, including politics. Indeed, in 1976 newly elected President Jimmy Carter appointed Sidney Harman to the post of undersecretary of commerce. Harman accepted the job and in 1977 sold his 25 percent stake in Harman-Kardon to Chicago-based corporate behemoth Beatrice Foods Company. Harman pocketed $100 million from the sale and went on to achieve notable successes in the Carter administration. Beatrice, in contrast, mismanaged its Harman-Kardon subsidiary (one of 200 under the Beatrice umbrella) and promptly ran it into the ground.

Beatrice sold some portions of the business and neglected what was left. By 1980 only about 60 percent of the organization of which Harman-Kardon had been a part before Sidney Harman exited remained. The original Harman-Kardon division, in fact, had been sold to a Japanese company named Shin Shirasuna, which was later absorbed by the giant Hitachi group of companies. Basically, all that was left of Harman's original company was JBL (a loudspeaker business) and some international distribution companies. Although Beatrice had damaged it, JBL remained a respected manufacturer of high-end professional speaker systems.

REACQUISITION BY THE FOUNDER

Sidney Harman, from his station in Washington, D.C., watched from the corporate sidelines as Beatrice drove his company toward ruin. Near the end of the Carter administration, Harman became determined to regain control of the enterprise and restore its former glory. In 1980 Sidney Harman and a group of investors paid $55 million for what amounted to about 60 percent of the assets of the company that Harman had sold in 1977. Harman established a bare-bones headquarters in Washington, D.C., and began streamlining and organizing the newly created Harman International Industries, Incorporated to compete in the 1980s.

Many electronics industry insiders doubted the wisdom of Harman's decision to jump back into the now-hypercompetitive stereo equipment industry. Some critics also wondered if he lacked the vision to compete in the rapidly evolving, increasingly global electronics industry. The primary culprit in the downfall of many U.S. electronics and related equipment manufacturers was intense overseas competition, particularly in Japan. U.S. companies had ceded the bulk of their domestic market share to the Japanese, and pressure on such companies as Harman International was intensifying.

Despite gloomy predictions, Harman proceeded during the 1980s and early 1990s to build Harman International Industries into a powerhouse in the niche for high-end consumer and professional audio equipment. He achieved that growth largely by acquiring smaller companies, reorganizing their management and operations, and allowing them to run relatively autonomously using his style of management. The strategy eventually proved to be hugely successful, and Harman International became known as one of the few large U.S. audio-equipment producers to prosper during the 1980s and 1990s.

Harman credited the prosperity of his companies to the success of a strategy that emphasized three tactics: (1) all of the company's products were built in factories that it owned, rather than purchased from companies that contracted to manufacture the goods for Harman; (2) Harman International vigorously marketed all of its products globally; and (3) the company honored its employees and treated them with respect. The success of that three-pronged strategy was evidenced by one of Harman's first acquisitions, Cleveland Electronics, a producer of original-equipment automotive stereo speakers that he purchased in 1981 and renamed Harman Motive. When Harman bought the small company from United Technologies Corporation, it was generating sales of about $8 million per year. Before the end of the decade, however, the division was churning out $100 million in annual revenues.

ACQUISITION SPREE AND RESTRUCTURING

Just as important as management strategy was a string of acquisitions throughout the 1980s that pushed Harman International's sales from about $80 million in 1981 to more than $200 million by 1986, and then to more than $500 million by 1989. Notable among Harman's early acquisitions were two completed in 1983—UREI, a manufacturer of professional amplifiers, and the Infinity consumer loudspeaker business—the latter of which added another true high-end speaker brand to the firm's product lineup. Of greater significance was the purchase in 1985 of the original Harman-Kardon operation from Shin Shirasuna. That buyout represented one of the few acquisitions of a Japanese electronics company by a U.S. firm during the 1980s. Harman International went public in 1986 with a stock offering on the New York Stock Exchange. Cash from that sale was used, among many other purchases, to buy Soundcraft, a U.K. producer of professional mixing boards, in 1988, and Salt Lake City digital electronics producer DOD Electronics Corp. in 1990.

By 1990 the Harman organization had grown into a loose conglomeration of several autonomous companies, each of which catered to a specific niche in the high-end audio equipment industry. Most of Harman's goods, though, were marketed under the venerable JBL, Infinity, or other top brand names. Harman's sales topped $550 million in 1990 and net income was shy of $15 million. Although Harman International achieved growth and much success during the 1980s, it became clear to Sidney Harman that major changes had to be initiated if the company was going to compete successfully in the 1990s. That concern was reflected in a disappointing $19.8 million loss experienced by Harman International in 1991, during the recession.

Harman moved away from his family in Washington—interestingly, Harman's wife (a Democrat from California) was elected to Congress in 1992—and moved to California to get closer to his operations. He sent the president of the company packing and, at the age of 70, took control of Harman's day-to-day operations. He merged the 21 scattered divisions into five units and eliminated duplicate departments and operations. He used the cash saved by that effort to intensify marketing efforts. Harman also adopted a new strategy of marketing the company's products through mass retail channels such as Circuit City, because he believed that the consumer market was shifting away from ultra-high-end, "audiophile" products to more mainstream, value-oriented audio devices.

Harman did not give his age a second thought. "[I'm] flat out uninterested in being retired," he said in the March 1, 1993, *Los Angeles Times*, adding, "I don't give a damn how old I am. I can run the pants off everybody working in this place." He was also unfazed by critics who believed the company would be unable to compete in the mainstream audio markets, which were dominated by low-cost giants in Asia.

Harman International bucked criticism with its performance during the early and mid-1990s. The company focused on growing existing operations, but also continued its aggressive acquisition drive. Sales jumped from $604 million in 1992 to $862 million in 1994, while net income rose from $3.5 million to $25.6 million. Harman also continued to streamline and consolidate, reducing its entire operation to just three divisions: professional, automotive, and consumer.

Harman sustained the pursuit of its assertive growth agenda in late 1994 and early 1995. It purchased Becker GmbH (a leading German maker of automotive radios and electronics), for example, and took over the respected Mark Levinson and Proceed lines of U.S. high-end electronics. The company also established Harman China (a unit charged with marketing and distributing Harman products to that massive market) and opened an "Advanced Technology Center" that was designed to focus on developing critical digital audio technologies. Those and other efforts contributed to a rise in sales to $1.17 billion in 1995 (fiscal year ending in June), about $41.2 million of which was netted as income.

AUTOMOTIVE DIVISION ON THE RISE

One of the noteworthy developments of the second half of the 1990s was the increasing importance of Harman's automotive division. New agreements to supply original-equipment audio systems for a wider array of car models propelled the automotive division's share of overall revenues from less than 25 percent in 1994 to nearly 50 percent by decade's end. After discontinuing an agreement with Ford Motor to exclusively supply that automaker with JBL brand audio systems, Harman reached deals to supply Toyota, Peugeot, and others with JBL equipment. By the end of the 1990s, DaimlerChrysler had become Harman's largest customer, accounting for nearly one-quarter of total company sales. Daimler-Chrysler was offering Infinity audio systems in most of its Chrysler, Dodge, and Plymouth models and Becker audio and navigation systems in a number of Mercedes-Benz automobiles. Leveraging its experience as an automotive audio system supplier, Harman in 1996 began producing audio systems and loudspeakers for personal computer manufacturers. That year, the firm started supplying JBL Professional brand speakers to Compaq Computer Corporation for its new line of Presario personal computers.

In November 1998 Harman shook up its top management team. Although Sidney Harman relinquished the CEO position, he remained intimately involved in the firm's activities as executive chairman. Bernard Girod, who had served as the company president since 1994, was named CEO, while Gregg Stapleton, the head of the automotive division, was promoted to president and COO.

Around the time of this shakeup, Harman International launched a restructuring program aimed at turning around its troubled consumer division. Trying to boost its market share, Harman over the previous few years had increased the number of consumer products it was producing. As part of the restructuring, the company cut its product lines from 2,000 to just 200, dropping dozens of unprofitable or marginally profitable products. Harman also shut down its manufacturing plant in El Paso, Texas, as well as additional facilities in Sunnyvale, California, and Nagoya, Japan, and it rationalized its distribution system by dropping two big-box discounters and hundreds of low-volume specialty audio dealers. Its relationships with two key customers, electronics retail giants Best Buy and Circuit City, were revamped and strengthened by marketing its Infinity speakers primarily to Circuit City and its JBL line to Best Buy.

Restructuring charges totaling $66.4 million slashed net income for the fiscal year ending in June 1999 to just $11.7 million, but Harman rebounded with record profits of $72.8 million a year later. Sales also began to grow again after stagnating in the late 1990s. Fiscal 2000 revenues totaled a record $1.68 billion, up 12 percent from the previous year. In addition to a 12 percent increase in sales to automobile manufacturers, Harman doubled its sales of computer audio systems as its list of clients grew to include Apple, Dell, Compaq, and IBM.

PUSH INTO INFOTAINMENT SYSTEMS

At the beginning of the 21st century, Harman pushed further into the automotive sector by beginning to offer what it called integrated infotainment systems for cars. These dashboard-mounted systems combined into one unit audio, video, navigation, voice recognition, telecommunications, and climate-control capabilities, which could be operated via a control panel installed between the driver's and front passenger's seats. Harman viewed this technology as a potentially high-growth area and one through which it could increase the amount of revenues it generated per vehicle it supplied. As was typical with cutting-edge automotive features, Harman's first contracts were for high-end models. Thus, it began shipping integrated infotainment systems for the BMW 7 Series in the fall of 2001 and for the Mercedes-Benz E Class in February 2002.

By fiscal 2005, Harman International was supplying these systems for Mercedes-Benz, BMW, Porsche, Audi, Renault, and Land Rover models. It also kept pace with the latest electronics gear, offering rear-seat DVD players, the ability to connect portable music players to the audio systems, and wireless capability enabling music to be downloaded from a personal computer in a home to the car in the driveway. Through such innovations, Harman's automotive division continued to be the company's driving force as its sales to automobile manufacturers reached around 64 percent of overall sales by fiscal 2006. Revenues that year soared to $3.24 billion. Its record net income of $255.3 million for 2006 was more than four times the total from five years earlier. During this same period, Harman's stock more than tripled in price.

COLLAPSED TAKEOVER AND THE FOUNDER'S RETIREMENT

The stock jumped even higher in April 2007 when Harman agreed to be acquired by Kohlberg Kravis Roberts & Co. (KKR) and Goldman Sachs Group, Inc.'s private-equity arm in a $120-per-share buyout offer that valued the firm at $8 billion. This private-equity buyout fell apart that fall, however. As the credit crunch that arose soon after the deal's announcement quickly brought an end to the private-equity buyout boom, the takeover partners cited financial setbacks at Harman as a reason not to complete the deal. Executives at Harman strongly disagreed with this rationale, but in October 2007 the two sides reached an agreement to terminate the takeover that called for KKR and the Goldman Sachs unit to purchase $400 million in Harman convertible debt securities.

In July 2007, as the takeover drama unfolded, Dinesh Paliwal was brought onboard as president and CEO. Paliwal joined Harman after 17 years of executive experience at Swiss engineering giant ABB Ltd., where he had served as head of the firm's North American unit and as president of global markets and technology. While occasionally butting heads with the company founder, who remained chairman, Paliwal quickly initiated a number of important moves.

At a company that had never shuttered a major facility in its more than half a century of operations, the new CEO garnered the board's assent on the shutdown of four of Harman's 12 U.S. plants as part of an efficiency drive. A portion of the firm's manufacturing capacity was thus shifted during fiscal 2008 from higher-cost U.S. facilities to lower-cost plants overseas, including a newly built, state-of-the-art, automotive audio and infotainment systems plant in Suzhou, China, located near Shanghai. Production capacity was doubled at existing plants in Mexico and Hungary as well. Restructuring costs totaling $46 million associated with the plant closures contributed to a two-thirds drop in net income for fiscal 2008 to $107.8 million. Extremely high engineering costs stemming from a record 13 contracts to supply infotainment systems to luxury automakers also factored into this downturn.

In May 2008 Paliwal brought onboard two executives with a great deal of international experience as the new CFO (Herbert K. Parker) and the new head of the automotive division (Klaus Blickle). These executives were expected to play key roles in expanding Harman's presence beyond the developed countries of Germany and the United States into such emerging markets as Brazil, Russia, India, and China. Just two months later, Paliwal's grip on the company reins were strengthened further when Sidney Harman retired and Paliwal added the board chairmanship to his duties. Later in 2008, further evidence of a new era at Harman International surfaced in the form of a headquarters relocation from the founder's base in Washington, D.C., to Stamford, Connecticut, near Paliwal's home. In September 2008 Harman opened an engineering center in Bangalore, India, in support of its expansion in South Asia. As the global economic crisis began affecting Harman's operations to the tune of an 8 percent drop in sales for the first quarter of fiscal 2009, the company had launched a two-year effort to cut annual operating costs $400 million.

Dave Mote
Updated, David E. Salamie

PRINCIPAL SUBSIDIARIES

AKG Acoustics GmbH (Austria); AKG Acoustics Limited (UK); Amek Systems and Controls Ltd. (UK); Amek Technology Group Limited (UK); Becker Automotive (Pty) Ltd. (South Africa); Becker Service und Verwaltungs GmbH (Germany); BSS Audio (UK); C Audio (UK): Crown Audio, Inc.; Digital Audio Research Limited (UK); Fosgate, Inc.; Harman Audio de Mexico S.A. de CV; Harman Becker Automotive Electronic Systems Suzhou Co. Ltd. (China); Harman Becker Automotive Systems GmbH (Germany); Harman Becker Automotive Systems Holding GmbH (Germany); Harman Becker Automotive Systems, Inc.; Harman Becker Automotive Systems Italy S.r.l.; Harman Becker Automotive Systems Japan KK; Harman Becker Automotive Systems Korea, Inc.; Harman Becker Automotive Systems Manufacturing Kft (Hungary); Harman Becker Automotive Systems (Michigan), Inc.; Harman Becker Automotive Systems S.A. de C.V. (Mexico); Harman Becker Automotive Systems (Wisconsin), Inc.; Harman Becker Media Drive Technology GmbH (Germany); Harman Becker Optical Components Technology Shenzhen Co. Ltd. (China); Harman Belgium NV; Harman Consumer Finland OY; Harman Consumer Scandinavia A/S (Denmark); Harman International snc (France); Harman Consumer Nederland, B.V. (Netherlands); Harman Consumer UK; Harman de Mexico S.A. de C.V.; Harman Deutschland GmbH (Germany); Harman Europe EEIG (UK); Harman Financial Group LLC; Harman France snc; Harman Holding GmbH & Co. KG (Germany); Harman International Industries Limited (UK); Harman International Japan Co. Ltd.; Harman International Singapore Pte. Ltd.; Harman JBL (Suzhou) Ltd. (China); Harman Kardon, Incorporated; Harman Management GmbH (Germany); Harman Motive (UK); Harman Music Group, Incorporated; Harman Navis, Inc.

(Korea); Harman Pro North America, Inc.; Harman Pro UK; Harman Software Technology International Beteiligungs GmbH (Germany); Harman Software Technology Management GmbH (Germany); Harman UK Limited; HBAS International GmbH (Germany); HBAS Manufacturing, Inc.; Infinity Systems, Inc.; innovative Systems GmbH Navigation-Multimedia (Germany); ISAS Gesellschaft fr innovative Anwendungs-Software GmbH (Germany); ISGPAS General Purpose Applications Systems GmbH (Germany); JBL Incorporated; Lexicon, Incorporated; Madrigal Audio Laboratories, Inc.; MARGI Systems, Inc.; QNX Software Systems Co. Canada; QNX Software Systems GmbH (Germany); QNX Software Systems GmbH & Co. KG (Germany); QNX Software Systems K.K. (Japan); QNX Software Systems, Inc.; QNX Software Systems International Corporation (Canada); QNX Software Systems (Vancouver), Inc. (Canada); Son-Audax Loudspeakers Limited (UK); Soundcraft Electronics (UK); Studer Digitec snc (France); Studer Japan Ltd.; Studer Professional Audio AG (Switzerland); Studer UK; Total Audio Concepts Ltd. (UK); Trinity Bay Sdn Bhd (Malaysia).

PRINCIPAL OPERATING UNITS

Automotive; Consumer; Professional.

PRINCIPAL COMPETITORS

Bose Corporation; Pioneer Corporation; Foster Electric Company, Limited; Panasonic Corporation; Polk Audio, Inc.; Klipsch Group, Inc.; Royal Philips Electronics N.V.; Boston Acoustics, Inc.; Bowers & Wilkins; Altec Lansing Technologies, Inc.; Yamaha Corporation; Sony Corporation; Denon Brand Company; Onkyo Corporation.

FURTHER READING

Abrahms, Doug, "Big Quake Didn't Shake Great Year for Harman," *Washington Times,* August 20, 1994, p. D5.

Anthes, Gary H., "Strategy: Make Here, Sell Abroad; Harman International Reverses Conventional Business Wisdom," *Washington Business Journal,* March 30, 1987, pp. 1+.

Berman, Dennis K., "Unusual Buyout Offers a Piece to Shareholders," *Wall Street Journal,* April 27, 2007, p. A1.

Burgess, John, "Harman Profits in Electronics Market Abroad," *Washington Post,* June 6, 1988, p. F5.

Cho, David, "$8 Billion Buyout of D.C. Firm Collapses," *Washington Post,* September 22, 2007, p. A1.

Cimilluca, Dana, and Dennis K. Berman, "KKR, Goldman Cancel $8 Billion Harman Deal," *Wall Street Journal,* September 22, 2007, p. A3.

"Dr. Feelgood," *Economist,* March 16, 2002, p. 68.

Epstein, Gene, "Back in Tune: Harman International Looks Sharp After Some Flat Years," *Barron's,* October 18, 1999, pp. 24, 26.

Greenberg, Manning, and Doug Olenick, "Turning Up the Volume," *HFD–The Weekly Home Furnishings Newspaper,* December 20, 1993, pp. 112+.

"Harman International Seems Likely to Reach Another High Profits Note," *Barron's,* January 19, 1976, pp. 62+.

Harman, Sidney, *Mind Your Own Business,* New York: Currency/Doubleday, 2003, 196 p.

Heath, Thomas, "Harman, 89, to Retire After Five Decades at Stereo Firm Helm," *Washington Post,* May 30, 2008, p. D1.

——, "Harman International Sold for $8 Billion," *Washington Post,* April 27, 2007, p. D1.

——, "Harman to Move District Staff to Connecticut," *Washington Post,* January 29, 2008, p. D1.

Heath, Thomas, and David Cho, "Harman, Former Suitors Find Closure Through Cash," *Washington Post,* October 23, 2007, p. D1.

Hudgens, Dallas, "Washington's Other Mr. Speaker: At 79, Sidney Harman Still Puts Sound Management Theories to Practice," *Washington Post,* March 23, 1998, p. F14.

Kaplan, Fred, "Sidney Harman," *Regardies: The Business of Washington,* September 1989, p. 94.

Killian, Linda, "California, Here We Come," *Forbes,* November 23, 1992, pp. 146+.

Knight, Jerry, "Harman Still Upstages His Competition," *Washington Post,* December 8, 2003, p. E1.

Koehler, Ron, "Sidney Harman Talks Success," *Grand Rapids Business Journal,* November 10, 1986, p. 5.

La Franco, Robert, "Loudspeaker Envy," *Forbes,* August 9, 1999, p. 68.

Loomis, Carol J., "An Old Hand in a Strange New World," *Fortune,* February 4, 2008, pp. 114–16+.

Lublin, Joann S., "Harman's New Chief Finds His Voice," *Wall Street Journal,* September 25, 2008, pp. B1, B6.

McTague, Jim, "Ticket to Ride," *Barron's,* December 2, 2002, pp. 19–20.

Peltz, James F., "HII Founder Seeks to Pump Up Volume," *Los Angeles Times,* March 1, 1993, p. D2.

Schneider, Greg, "A Man of Many Epiphanies: Sidney Harman Is Driving His Company in a New Direction—Again," *Washington Post,* March 5, 2001, p. E1.

Segal, David, "The Hi-Fi Manufacturer That Listens Well; D.C.'s Harman International Stays Close to the Customer," *Washington Post,* September 4, 1995, p. F10.

Wayne, Leslie, "Notes at Harman: Sweet and Sour," *New York Times,* July 2, 1990, p. D4.

We're Hertz. They're Not.

The Hertz Corporation

225 Brae Boulevard
Park Ridge, New Jersey 07656-0713
U.S.A.
Telephone: (201) 307-2000
Toll Free: (800) 654-3131
Fax: (201) 307-2644
Web site: http://www.hertz.com

Public Company
Incorporated: 1967
Employees: 29,350
Sales: $8.69 billion (2007)
Stock Exchanges: New York
Ticker Symbol: HTZ
NAICS: 532111 Passenger Car Rental; 532412 Construction, Mining, and Forestry Machinery and Equipment Rental and Leasing

■ ■ ■

With about 8,000 locations in 147 countries, The Hertz Corporation ranks as the largest general use car rental brand in the world. In addition, the company's Hertz Equipment Rental Corp. business is a world leader, serving customers from approximately 375 locations in the United States, Canada, France, Spain, and China. The oldest company in the car rental industry, Hertz has experienced many changes in ownership since its founding.

INDEPENDENT VENTURE TO CORPORATION: 1918–66

The origins of Hertz date back to 1918, when Walter L. Jacobs, a 22-year-old car salesman with a fleet of a dozen Ford Model Ts, started a small car rental business in Chicago. Within five years, Jacobs had expanded his operations so that the business was generating annual revenues of about $1 million through a fleet of 600 cars. In 1923, Jacobs sold the company to John Hertz, the head of Yellow Cab and Yellow Truck, although Jacobs remained with the company, serving as its chief operating officer. Hertz held the DriveUrSelf System, to which he would add his name, for three years before including it as part of his deal to sell Yellow Truck to General Motors Corp.

General Motors kept the thriving business until 1953 when it was sold to the Omnibus Corporation. The following year Omnibus changed its name to The Hertz Corporation and went public on the New York Stock Exchange, where the company's shares would remain until 1967. In 1954, the newly public Hertz acquired Metropolitan Distributors, a pioneer in New York truck leasing and the largest truck rental business at the time, with a fleet of 4,000 trucks. The purchase was made for $6.75 million in cash. Walter Jacobs, who was president of Hertz until his retirement in 1960, commented at the time that the acquisition "rounds out Hertz operations by providing in New York City the largest single truck rental operation in existence." Leon C. Greenbaum, the president of Metropolitan, became vice-chairman of the Hertz board of directors. The acquisition brought the total Hertz fleet to 15,500 trucks and 12,900 passenger cars.

COMPANY PERSPECTIVES

Our mission is to be the most customer focused, cost efficient vehicle and equipment rental/leasing company in every market we serve. We will strengthen our leading worldwide positions through a shared-value culture of employee and partner involvement by making strategic investments in our brand, people and products. The focus of everything we do will be on continuously improving shareholder value.

By 1960, the market for rental cars was rapidly expanding, reflecting the expansion of air travel among the general consumer market and the growth of the travel industry as a whole. Despite the influx of new firms into the industry, Hertz retained the number one position throughout the 1960s. Much of its success was attributed to the expertise and guidance of rental car veteran Walter Jacobs, who was recognized as being "the maven of the car rental business," knowing how to buy and sell cars expertly in order to build and maintain a profitable rental car fleet.

THE RCA AND UAL YEARS: 1967–87

In 1967, ownership of Hertz was altered again in a merger/stock swap deal. The new association was with Radio Corporation of America (RCA). Hertz became a wholly owned subsidiary (though the company operated as a separate entity with its own management and board of directors), and Hertz stockholders received RCA stock in return. Leon Greenbaum, who was chairman of Hertz by this time, became a director of RCA.

The relationship with RCA continued until 1985, when RCA decided to focus on its more traditional product lines and sold Hertz to UAL, Inc., owner of United Airlines, the largest airline in the country. UAL ostensibly planned to combine Hertz with its airline and its Westin Hotel Co. subsidiary in order to position itself as the most formidable travel corporation in the world. The deal was expected to face federal government antitrust scrutiny, but it did not, and once closed, Hertz joined the three leaders in their respective competitive industries. Since UAL, Inc., also invested in travel agencies, it clearly meant to overlap nearly all travel services "from reservation to check-in to baggage handling," according to Richard J. Ferris, chairman of UAL. One unique aspect of the deal, according to some analysts,

was that during a time of great leveraged buyouts, the acquisition of Hertz did not involve any investment bankers. In the meantime, UAL was concerned that it might find itself the target of a takeover.

In 1987, UAL changed its name to Allegis, Inc. Later that year, as predicted, Allegis was involved in hostile takeover attempts, as several investor groups believed that the conglomerate would be worth more if it were disassembled. Frank A. Olson, the chairman and CEO of Hertz, was named to those positions at Allegis. As part of a restructuring plan in which UAL (the Allegis name was dropped) divested itself of its non-airline holdings, Hertz was sold again. In a $1.3 billion deal that was completed in December 1987, Allegis sold Hertz to the Park Ridge Corporation, an investor group made up of Ford Motor Company executives as well as some from Hertz, formed expressly to acquire Hertz. In the buyout, Ford obtained 80 percent of the equity, and Hertz management received the remainder. Of the $1.3 billion in necessary capital, $520 million was provided by Ford while the balance was borrowed. Ford later sold 31 percent of its investment to Commerzbank of Germany and Volvo of Sweden. After UAL's transition, Frank Olson gave up the chairman and CEO positions of that company, although he remained a member of the board of directors.

OWNERSHIP CHANGES IN THE LATE EIGHTIES

After the sale, there was some speculation that Ford eventually might want to take Park Ridge public, a move that had proved profitable in other leveraged buyouts at the time. Buyout groups would make an acquisition, hold it for a short time, and then sell shares to the public at a sizable profit. More importantly for Ford, the buyout was undoubtedly good strategy. Hertz had been buying 65,000 vehicles a year from Ford domestically and 15,000 overseas. In fact, Ford's share of Hertz's vehicle orders, about 50 percent, would increase and thereby help Ford maintain its market share even though Hertz would still buy cars from other makers. Although auto sales to rental car companies were not particularly profitable (since rental cars generally had a low profit margin), Ford thought the move would allow it to keep rivals, namely Chrysler, out and preserve its strong relationship with the rental companies.

At the same time it was completing its takeover of Hertz via Park Ridge, Ford was also trying to keep a distance from some serious legal problems being faced by the car rental company. In August 1988, Hertz was involved in a dispute involving charges for repairs that

KEY DATES

∎

1918: Walter L. Jacobs starts a car rental business in Chicago with a fleet of 12 cars.

1923: Jacobs sells the company to John Hertz, head of Yellow Cab and Yellow Truck.

1927: Jacobs sells his Hertz DriveUrSelf System and Yellow Truck to General Motors.

1950: Hertz begins European operations.

1954: Omnibus Corporation acquires Hertz and takes it public on the New York Stock Exchange.

1960: Walter L. Jacobs retires.

1967: Hertz becomes a subsidiary of Radio Corporation of America (RCA).

1985: UAL, holding company of United Airlines, acquires Hertz.

1987: Hertz is sold to Park Ridge Corporation, an investor group affiliated with Ford Motor Company.

1988: Volvo North America Corporation becomes an investor in Park Ridge.

1991: Hertz Technologies subsidiary is established.

1994: Ford buys out the Park Ridge investors, and Hertz becomes a subsidiary of Ford.

1997: Hertz is spun off as a public company.

2001: Ford acquires full ownership of Hertz for $710 million.

2005: Ford sells Hertz to Merrill Lynch Global Private Equity, Clayton Dubilier & Rice, and the Carlyle Group for $5.6 billion in cash and $10 billion in debt.

2006: Hertz Global Holdings files its IPO, offering 88.24 million shares for $15 each.

2008: The company celebrates its 90th anniversary.

resulted from collisions with Hertz vehicles. It was charged that Hertz, in some instances, had claimed for damages when repairs were not made and, in other instances, paid discounted wholesale rates for car repairs, while charging the retail rates to the parties involved. Although it was noted that such rental car companies as Avis, Budget, and Alamo also followed the practice of charging retail repair costs, according to *Business Week,* Hertz failed to disclose to those concerned that they would be billed for repairs at "prevailing retail rates." Hertz agreed to pay $13.7 million in restitution and $6.35 million in fines, "the largest fine ever imposed upon a corporation in a criminal consumer fraud case,"

according to Andrew J. Maloney, U.S. attorney for the Eastern District of New York.

In addition to this historic legal settlement, Hertz's parent company, Park Ridge Corporation, faced change in 1988 as well. The Volvo North America Corporation, a subsidiary of AB Volvo of Sweden based in Rockleigh, New Jersey, became an investor in Park Ridge, paying $100 million in cash to Ford in exchange for a 20 percent interest in the joint venture. Park Ridge Corporation was then merged into The Hertz Corporation so that the investors, who retained their equity positions, owned the company directly.

INCREASED COMPETITION IN A COMMODITY-BASED MARKET

Meanwhile, the competitive battle between the major car rental companies continued to rage. In January 1992, Hertz and Avis, Inc., reached a settlement after Hertz brought suit against its competitor, accusing it of false advertising. Avis had received the Alfred Award given to the "best car rental company" by Gralla Publications' *Corporate Travel.* Hertz's suit questioned the validity of the magazine's readers poll. In the settlement, Avis was enjoined from further advertising its receipt of the Alfred Award.

In another legal battle, a federal judge in New York City upheld a newly enacted city ordinance that prohibited all rental companies from imposing "resident-based" rates, but at the same time barred the city from putting the law into effect. Specifically, Hertz and others were charging residents of the boroughs of Manhattan, the Bronx, Brooklyn, and Queens higher rates when cars were rented locally. The U.S. Court of Appeals later reversed the U.S. District Court ruling and remanded the case for trial. Later, in 1994, the state of New York sued Hertz and other rental car companies for refusing to rent vehicles to licensed drivers between the ages of 18 and 25. The judgment in this case eventually went against Hertz in 1997, the same year that Hertz agreed to pay somewhere between $4 million and $6 million in refunds to customers who had purchased their unregulated rental car insurance in Texas.

Competition remained fierce among the top five car rental companies in the early 1990s, and many analysts likened the ensuing price wars to those of the airline and hotel industries, whose markets complemented the rental car business. The rental sector was becoming increasingly a commodity market, meaning that there were more rental cars available than customers. In addition to price cutting, Hertz offered various promotional strategies to expand its product base. One strategy, for example, allowed customers to earn mileage in the frequent flyer programs of such airlines as American, Northwest, United, and U.S. Air, as well as to gain points in Marriott's Honored Guest program. Another involved removing mileage limits in the United States in 1995 and expanding its "Rent It Here/Leave It There" program in Europe. In 1994, in the aftermath of the O. J. Simpson murder trial, Hertz abruptly canceled Simpson's sponsorship, begun in 1975, in favor of its new "Not Exactly" campaign.

Improvements to the actual Hertz rental fleet were also made in the mid- and late 1990s. In 1995, Hertz introduced Rockwell-built vehicle navigation system units, a technology it named NeverLost, to many of its mid- and full-size cars. In 1996, it increased safety features, adding anti-lock brakes and airbags in most of its cars, and teamed with Shared Technologies Cellular to offer cellphone rental.

Hertz also began to diversify. In 1991, for example, the company established Hertz Technologies, a wholly owned subsidiary involved in the telecommunications services business. Four years later, it launched Hertz Insurance Replacement Entity (HIRE), later renamed Hertz Local Edition, a subsidiary specializing in providing vehicles to the insurance community and auto dealers. In 1996 the company expanded its used-car sales business, adding lots with 50 to 60 cars in almost 40 U.S. cities. The year also marked Hertz's foray onto the Internet with the introduction of its informational web site, www.hertz.com. By 1997 the site would become interactive, offering rate quotes and the possibility of checking on availability, as well as booking, confirming, and canceling reservations online.

Adding to the competition among rental car companies, the big three automakers raised their acquisition costs for cars, no longer subsidizing fleet purchases beginning in 1992. At the time, Hertz was purchasing approximately 70 percent of its domestic fleet and one-third of its European fleet from Ford. For three successive years, Hertz's holding costs rose about 30 percent per year, for a compounded impact in excess of 100 percent. The higher cost of cars meant that rental companies had to keep their vehicles longer (from three to six or nine months). Despite this hardship on revenue, the environment for rentals in the United States continued to improve steadily, a byproduct of an American boom in travel; throughout most of the 1990s, the rental car industry averaged an 11 percent increase per year on rentals.

Eroding profits became a problem for Hertz and its competitors. Squeezed between spiraling car costs and competitive pricing, the industry as a whole posted losses of $150 million in 1995. Car rental companies, including Hertz, responded by raising rates several times

beginning in 1993, and by cost-cutting, weeding out unprofitable locations, and limiting excess inventory. Yet Hertz managed to remain profitable throughout the early and mid-1990s. Its revenues for 1994 were $2.1 billion; in 1995, that figure rose to $2.27 billion.

CONSOLIDATION TREND

By the mid- to late 1990s, the $14 billion car rental industry was undergoing a transition toward consolidation and public ownership. In 1994, Ford bought Commerzbank A.G.'s 5 percent stake in Hertz, thereby raising its own stake to 54 percent and acquiring control of Hertz. It then purchased the 46 percent of the company owned by Volvo and the company's management. In 1997, with Hertz enjoying 29 percent of the car rental market, Ford floated about one-fifth of its shares.

Although Hertz was eclipsed in 1995 by Enterprise as the rental car company enjoying the largest number of U.S.-based rentals, Hertz held its own through the remainder of the 1990s, in terms of profit, and kept its position as the largest car rental company worldwide. In fact, beginning in 1993, Hertz enjoyed a six-year string of record earnings. In 1999 it recorded revenues of $4.7 billion, an increase of more than 11 percent over the $4.2 billion garnered in 1998. Craig Koch, who became company president in 2000, attributed the 1999 record performance to strong demand, improved car rental pricing, and continuing cost efficiency.

FORD SECURES FULL OWNERSHIP

Hertz ushered in the new millennium by expanding its global footprint. In April 2000, the company announced plans to open a new branch in Syria. Around the same time, cell phone service for overseas travelers was expanded, allowing customers to rent phones in Asia, Australia, Africa, the Middle East, and Europe. During the first half of the year, Hertz also acquired the French construction equipment rental company Locenergie, as well as the Spanish equipment rental company Caprisa SA. In October, new services were introduced in Yemen, and at the Beirut International Airport.

In the fall of 2000, Ford Motor Co. offered to acquire all of the outstanding shares of Hertz that it did not already own for $30 per share. In early 2001, the company ultimately agreed to a higher offer of $35.50 per share. The $710 million deal was concluded on March 9, at which time Hertz became a wholly owned subsidiary of Ford. Subsequently, shares of Hertz ceased trading on the New York Stock Exchange on March 12.

Developments continued in 2002, at which time a luxury car rental service named the Hertz Prestige Collection was introduced. That year, the company became the first major industry player to establish a presence in China when it opened branches in Shanghai, Beijing, and Guangzhou. That year, the company recorded a $150 million loss on sales of approximately $5 billion. After becoming Online Travel Corp.'s exclusive car rental provider in 2003, Hertz forged a three-year partnership with Air France, in which the airline's passengers received benefits such as more competitive car rental rates.

INDEPENDENT ENTERPRISE

By late 2005 Hertz remained the largest daily car rental company in the world, serving customers from approximately 7,400 locations in about 150 countries. In September, Ford agreed to sell Hertz to Merrill Lynch Global Private Equity, Clayton Dubilier & Rice, and the Carlyle Group for $5.6 billion in cash. Factoring in $10 billion in debt, the overall deal, which was finalized in December, was worth about $15 billion.

In July 2006, parent Hertz Global Holdings Inc. filed for an initial public offering (IPO) of its common stock from which the company hoped to generate up to $1 billion. Three weeks before the filing, the company took out a $1 billion loan that was used to pay its new owners a special dividend. On July 19, former Tenneco Inc. Chairman and CEO Mark P. Frissora was named CEO of Hertz, becoming the first car rental industry outsider to hold that position at the company. Hertz Global Holdings announced its IPO on November 16, offering 88.24 million shares for $15 each.

In early 2007 Hertz sold its car rental operations in Eksjo, Jonkoping, and Nassjo, Sweden, to the Jonkoping, Sweden-based automotive dealer Claes Nybergs Bil. By this time, Hertz's Reservations Centers took roughly 40 million calls per year and made approximately 30 million customer reservations.

In 2008 Hertz celebrated its 90th anniversary. In honor of the special milestone, the company planned a variety of promotions throughout the year. At this time, growth continued in Hertz's equipment rental business. Toward the latter part of the year, the company opened its doors in Shanghai, China. In order to take advantage of growth in that country's construction, manufacturing, industrial, and shipbuilding industries, Hertz Equipment Rental Corp. planned to offer cranes, excavators, area lifts, and more.

In December 2008 Hertz unveiled a new car-sharing business. Beginning in Park Ridge, New Jersey, and New York City, Connect by Hertz allowed customers to rent cars by the hour and avoid a variety of fees associated with traditional rentals. Reservations could be made online, and customers used special cards to access vehicles, which were parked in specially designated lots. In order to appeal to a younger demographic, rental offerings included vehicles such as the Mini Cooper and Toyota Prius. The new service allowed Hertz to compete with Zipcar, which had been offering a similar service for about eight years.

Despite the challenging economic climate of 2009, Hertz seemed well positioned to weather the storm. With its 100th anniversary looming in the distance, the company approached the 21st century's second decade from a position of industry leadership.

John A. Sarich
Updated, Carrie Rothburd; Paul R. Greenland

PRINCIPAL SUBSIDIARIES

Hertz International Ltd.; Hertz Equipment Rental Corp.; Hertz International RE Ltd. (Ireland).

PRINCIPAL COMPETITORS

Avis Budget Group Inc.; Enterprise Rent-A-Car Co.; United Rentals Inc.

FURTHER READING

Buder, Leonard, "Hertz Admits Use of Fraud in Bills for Auto Repairs," *New York Times,* August 5, 1988.

Cano, Debra, and James F. Peltz, "The Siege of Alamo," *Los Angeles Times,* April 20, 1996, p. D1.

Cole, Robert J., "United Airlines Set to Buy Hertz from RCA in $587 Million Deal," *New York Times,* June 18, 1985.

Dickson, Martin, "Ford to Take Full Ownership of Hertz and Raise Payout," *Financial Times* (London), April 15, 1994, p. 23.

Durbin, Dee-Ann, "Ford Concludes $5.6B Hertz Sale; Group of Buyers to Take on $10B in Debt," *Record,* December 22, 2005.

Flynn, George, "Jury Clears Hertz in Lawsuit over Insurance Dispute," *Houston Chronicle,* February 19, 1998, p. A21.

"Ford to Raise Hertz Stake to Total 54 Percent," *New York Times,* February 15, 1994, p. D3.

Halper, Mark, "Hertz Mulls Outsourcing Rescue," *Computerworld,* June 22, 1992.

Harler, Curt, "How Hertz Makes Its Call Center #1," *Communications News,* November 1992.

"Hertz Corp. Plans Acquisition Here," *New York Times,* December 4, 1954.

"The Hertz Corporation," Park Ridge, N.J.: Hertz Corporation, January 1993.

"Hertz Is Doing Some Body Work—On Itself," *Business Week,* February 15, 1988.

"Hertz Warns That Car Rental Fees Could Rise," *New York Times,* November 11, 1992.

"IBM Reaches Pact with Hertz," *Wall Street Journal,* March 31, 1993.

"Judge in New York Upholds Law Barring Surcharge by Hertz," *Wall Street Journal,* April 1, 1992.

Magenheim, Henry, "Car Rental Firms Expect a Boost from Air Fare Restructuring," *Travel Weekly,* May 11, 1992.

McDowell, Edwin, "Pricing Plans Shift at Hertz and Alamo," *Wall Street Journal,* May 5, 1992.

Miller, Lisa, "Rental Car Industry Merger Trend Could Hurt Consumers," *Kansas City Star,* January 19, 1997, p. F4.

Moskowitz, Milton, et al., eds., *Everybody's Business: A Field Guide to the 400 Leading Companies in America,* New York: Doubleday, 1990.

Ross, Philip E., "Volvo to Get 20% of Hertz Parent," *New York Times,* June 23, 1988.

Ruggless, Ron, "Operators Woo Foreign Tourists with Hertz's Help," *Nation's Restaurant News,* April 12, 1993.

Salpukas, Agis, "Ford Leads Group Deal for Hertz," *New York Times,* October 3, 1987.

Sherefkin, Robert, "Hertz Rental Cars Getting Rockwell Navigational System," *Crain's Detroit Business,* August 28, 1995, p. 25.

"SPECIAL REPORT: Hertz Marks 90 Years with Deals," *Travel Trade Gazette UK & Ireland,* October 10, 2008.

Thomas, Charles M., "Hertz Pays Record Fine: Pleads Guilty to Defrauding Consumers," *Automotive News,* August 8, 1988.

Yung, Katherine, "Big Three Exiting Car Rental Business," *Detroit News,* January 15, 1997, p. B1.

Hornbeck Offshore Services, Inc.

103 Northpark Boulevard, Suite 300
Covington, Louisiana 70433
U.S.A.
Telephone: (985) 727-2000
Fax: (985) 727-2006
Web site: http://www.hornbeckoffshore.com

Public Company
Incorporated: 1997 as Hornbeck-Leevac Marine Services, Inc.
Employees: 1,092
Sales: $338.97 million (2007)
Stock Exchanges: New York
Ticker Symbol: HOS
NAICS: 483211 Inland Water Freight Transportation; 483111 Deep Sea Freight Transportation; 483113 Coastal and Great Lakes Freight Transportation

∎ ∎ ∎

Hornbeck Offshore Services, Inc., is a marine transportation operator serving the oil and gas industry in the Gulf of Mexico, the northeastern United States, and Puerto Rico. Hornbeck Offshore is primarily focused on operating a fleet of offshore supply vessels (OSVs) in the Gulf of Mexico. The company operates a fleet of 47 OSVs, nearly half of which were built according to the specifications of its proprietary designs. Hornbeck Offshore also operates a fleet of 17 oceangoing tugs and 21 oceangoing tank barges, which provide marine transportation services in the Gulf of Mexico, the northeastern United States, and Puerto Rico. Horn-

beck Offshore, in its support of offshore exploration and drilling activities, serves major energy companies such as Chevron Production Company, Shell Oil Company, BP America Production Company, and ConocoPhillips Company.

THE ENTREPRENEURIAL HORNBECK FAMILY

The Gulf of Mexico was home to two companies that operated under the name Hornbeck Offshore Services, Inc., one company the entrepreneurial creation of a father and the other company the entrepreneurial creation of his son. The father, Larry D. Hornbeck, formed his company in 1981, establishing a marine transportation and services company that quickly grew into a formidable competitor in the Gulf of Mexico. No novice when he started Hornbeck Offshore Services, Hornbeck had spent more than a decade at Sealcraft Operators, Inc., before striking out on his own. Sealcraft, a publicly traded company, operated as a specialty OSV concern, conducting its business on a worldwide basis. He served as the company's president, chief executive officer, and chairman from 1969 to 1980, honing the skills that he would bring to his own company.

Larry Hornbeck shaped his start-up venture into a notable player in the Gulf of Mexico, becoming the president, chief executive officer, and chairman of a company that the offshore oil and gas industry turned to frequently. He took Galveston, Texas-based Hornbeck Offshore Services public, which gave him access to capital that enabled him to build up his fleet of supply, tug supply, crew, and specialty service vessels. In 1991,

COMPANY PERSPECTIVES

Our mission is to be recognized as the energy industry's marine transportation and service company of choice for our customers, employees and investors through innovative, high quality, value-added business solutions delivered with enthusiasm, integrity and professionalism with the utmost regard for the safety of individuals and the protection of the environment.

he welcomed his son, Todd M. Hornbeck, into the business, asking for his help in matters related to business strategy and development. Together, father and son engineered the boldest move in Hornbeck Offshore Services' history, completing the $46 million acquisition of 17 vessels from Oil & Gas Rental Services, Inc., in 1994. Hornbeck Offshore Services, a $48-million-in-sales company before the acquisition, grew 33 percent, becoming the second largest operator in the Gulf of Mexico, trailing only New Orleans-based Tidewater, Inc.

The battle between the two titans of the Gulf of Mexico lasted only a few short years, ending on the most amicable of terms. In 1996, Larry Hornbeck and Tidewater's chief executive officer, William O'Malley, decided to merge their businesses. Tidewater emerged as the surviving entity after the merger. Larry Hornbeck was named to the company's board of directors and his son made the move as well, accepting a position as the marketing director of the company's Gulf of Mexico operations in March 1996. Todd Hornbeck remained with Tidewater a little more than a year before deciding, as his father had decided 15 years earlier, to form his own company.

TODD HORNBECK FORMS HIS OWN COMPANY IN 1997

The younger Hornbeck established his offshore service vessel company in Mandeville, Louisiana, forming Hornbeck-Leevac Marine Services, Inc., in June 1997. He served as the company's president, secretary, and chief operating officer, and as a director. The same month of its formation, the company acquired two tugs and one tank barge from Sun Oil Co.

From the inception of his business, Todd Hornbeck approached the marine transportation service business in a distinguishing fashion. He assembled a team of in-house naval architects to develop new generation OSVs based on the company's proprietary designs. The new

class of OSVs was developed to address the specific challenges of deepwater operations, featuring enhanced capabilities that strengthened the appeal of the Hornbeck-Leevac fleet to oil and gas customers, which included global behemoths such as Shell Oil Company, Chevron Production Company, and ConocoPhillips Company.

CUSTOM-MADE FLEET

OSVs built according to Hornbeck-Leevac's specifications featured double-bottomed and double-sided hulls. They contained two to three times the dry bulk capacity and deck space of conventional 180-foot OSVs. They contained three to ten times the liquid mud capacity of conventional OSVs. They contained two to four times the deck tonnage of conventional OSVs. Hornbeck-Leevac-designed OSVs were equipped with advanced dynamic positioning systems, which enabled the vessels to maintain position within a minimal variance, and they used a unique hull design and integrated rudder and thruster system to improve the vessels' manageability.

Hornbeck-Leevac's fleet of OSVs, which expanded with the first shipment of the company's new breed of vessels in November 1998, primarily served the oil and gas industry. The company's vessels offered service to exploratory and developmental drilling rigs and production facilities, transporting deck cargo such as pipe, drummed material, and equipment. The OSVs also transported liquid mud, potable and drilling water, diesel fuel, dry bulk cement, and personnel to and from shore bases and offshore rigs. The company's role as the conduit between sea and shore meant its business was dependent largely on the demand for oil and gas and the level of exploration and drilling taking place. Aside from its OSV activities, the company conducted business through a subsidiary named Leevac Marine, LLC, which operated tugs and tank barges in New York harbor, Puerto Rico, and the Gulf of Mexico. Hornbeck-Leevac's tug and tank barge business served major oil companies, refineries, and oil traders, transporting "dirty" and "clean" petroleum products. Dirty products consisted primarily of crude oils, residual crudes and feedstocks, heavy fuel oils, and asphalts. Clean products included gasoline, home heating oil, diesel fuel, and jet fuel.

FLEET EXPANSION: 1999–2002

During its first five years in business, Hornbeck-Leevac's fleet of OSVs and tugs and tank barges expanded steadily. The company acquired four vessels from Maritrans Operating Partners LP in March 1999. The vessels

KEY DATES

1997: Todd Hornbeck establishes Hornbeck-Leevac Marine Services, Inc.

2002: Hornbeck-Leevac Marine Services changes its name to Hornbeck Offshore Services, Inc.

2004: The company completes its initial public offering of stock.

2005: In a secondary offering of stock, Hornbeck Offshore collects $205 million in net proceeds.

2007: Revenues reach a record high of $338.9 million.

2008: Hornbeck Offshore acquires its fourth multipurpose supply vessel.

were put into service in the Caribbean, where Hornbeck-Leevac transported dirty and clean petroleum products from refineries and distribution terminals in Puerto Rico to the Puerto Rico Electric Power Authority and to utilities located on neighboring islands. In June 2000, the company announced a new vessel-construction program to build six OSVs according to proprietary design specifications. In May 2001, Hornbeck-Leevac purchased a fleet of nine oceangoing tugs and nine oceangoing tank barges from the Spentonbush/Red Star Group. In April 2002, the company unveiled plans for another new vessel-construction program, declaring its intention to build eight additional deepwater OSVs. The physical expansion completed during the period fueled electric financial growth, lifting revenues from $6.6 million at the end of its first year in business to $92.5 million in 2002.

HORNBECK-LEEVAC BECOMES HORNBECK OFFSHORE SERVICES IN 2002

As revenues neared the $100 million mark, Todd Hornbeck paid homage to his father, who had left Tidewater's board in 2000 and joined his son's company as a director in 2001. Midway through 2002, Todd Hornbeck announced he was changing the name of his company, choosing Hornbeck Offshore Services, Inc., as a new corporate title. The reemergence of the name of the original Galveston-based company also prompted a new name for the company's tug and tank barge subsidiary, as Leevac Marine, LLC, was cast away in favor of Hornbeck Offshore Transportation, LLC. "These name

changes will allow us to operate under a common identity across each of our operating divisions and facilitate the markets' identification with each of our services under one name and logo," Todd Hornbeck explained in the June 3, 2002 issue of *Market News Publishing*. "In addition, this should address any confusion to our customers, vendors, and investors regarding the similarity in the name of one of our shipyard vendors, Leevac Industries, LLC."

With a new name for his company, Hornbeck looked to complete the next evolutional step in its development. In July 2002, he filed with the U.S. Securities and Exchange Commission (SEC) for Hornbeck Offshore's initial public offering (IPO) of stock, hoping to raise $126 million from Wall Street. The proceeds from the IPO were to be used to build more OSVs—the company operated 11 OSVs at the time of the filing with ten additional vessels either planned or under construction—but Hornbeck Offshore's debut in the public sector hit a snag. In October 2002, the company canceled its IPO, citing bleak market conditions, and forcing Hornbeck to "investigate other strategic growth opportunities," as he said in the October 15, 2002 issue of the *Daily Deal*. He pressed ahead without the infusion of capital, acquiring five 220-foot deepwater OSVs from Candy Marine Investment in July 2003, which expanded the company's OSV fleet to 20 vessels.

PUBLIC DEBUT IN 2004

After backing away from Wall Street in 2002, Hornbeck returned in 2003, determined to take his company public. In November 2003, he filed with the SEC for an IPO, hoping to attract investor interest in his fleet of 22 OSVs, 12 tugs, and 16 tank barges. "If they pull the trigger on it," an analyst said in the November 2003 issue of *Workboat*, "that means they got a fair price. If the market is soft, they won't proceed ... that's just being smart business owners." Hornbeck pulled the trigger, but when the company sold six million shares at $13 per share in March 2004, the offering price was at the bottom of the proposed price range. Instead of the $126 million IPO he had hoped for in 2002, he had to settle for the $78 million he secured in the stock offering.

Hornbeck Offshore, which had moved its headquarters from Mandeville to Covington, Louisiana, soon enjoyed a far more positive reception from the investment community. Hurricanes Katrina and Rita sparked feverish interest in offshore service companies, sending share prices skyrocketing upward. During the period of heightened interest, Hornbeck was able to sell 6.1 million shares at $35.35 per share, netting him

$205 million in proceeds that he earmarked for the purchase of new supply boats, tank barges, and tugs.

RECORD-SETTING FINANCIAL PERFORMANCE: 2005–07

As Hornbeck Offshore neared the end of its first decade in business, the company was enjoying energetic growth. Initially, the company had relied on its tug and tank barges business for support while it gradually assembled a fleet of new generation OSVs. By 2003, the company's OSV fleet had become the major contributor to its financial growth, no longer taking a back seat to the tugs and tank barges in operation. Sales rose robustly as the company's fleet of OSVs earned the business of oil and gas operators in the Gulf of Mexico, leading to a 38 percent jump in revenue in 2005, when sales reached $182.6 million. Hornbeck Offshore followed the banner year with even better performance in 2006, when sales leaped 50 percent to $274.5 million and net income doubled to $75.7 million.

By the end of Hornbeck Offshore's tenth year in business there was much to celebrate. The company's proprietary designs had been used to construct 22 new generation OSVs, accounting for nearly half of the 47 OSVs it had in operation. The company's tug and tank barge business, which had begun a decade earlier with fewer than five tugs and tank barges, had expanded to comprise a fleet of 17 tugs and 21 tank barges. Financially, the company's anniversary year concluded with new records being set: sales swelled to $338.9 million and net income increased to $94.7 million.

Looking ahead, Hornbeck saw considerable promise in the deployment of multipurpose supply vessels (MPSVs), which typically were 400-foot-long vessels. "We believe that the worldwide demand for highly specialized equipment like our MPSVs is rapidly expanding and is currently being serviced by a relatively few foreign flagged vessels," he explained in the June 18, 2007 issue of *New Orleans CityBusiness.* "For this reason, we believe that the high-end ultra-deepwater MPSV niche is still undersupplied and that more of such vessels are required for the post-2009 market, particularly in the Gulf of Mexico." Toward that end, Hornbeck Offshore began its second decade of business with the purchase of its fourth MPSV in 2008, a small facet of

the company's business that was expected to increase in stature in the years ahead.

Jeffrey L. Covell

PRINCIPAL SUBSIDIARIES

Hornbeck Offshore Services, LLC; Hornbeck Offshore Transportation, LLC; Hornbeck Offshore Operators, LLC; Energy Services Puerto Rico, LLC; HOS-IV, LLC; Hornbeck Offshore Trinidad & Tobago, LLC; HOS Port, LLC.

PRINCIPAL COMPETITORS

Tidewater, Inc.; Crowley Maritime Corporation; SEACOR Holdings Inc.

FURTHER READING

Dulle, Tracy, "Hornbeck Offshore to Acquire Superior Achiever," *Offshore,* February 2008, p. 24.

Hocke, Ken, "Hornbeck to Make Second Stab at IPO," *Workboat,* November 2003, p. 27.

"Hornbeck Buys Five Vessels," *Oil Daily,* July 8, 2003.

"Hornbeck Gives Investors Underwater Option," *IPO Reporter,* August 5, 2002.

"Hornbeck Launches Initial Public Offering," *America's Intelligence Wire,* March 29, 2004.

"Hornbeck Offshore Service," *Daily Deal,* October 15, 2002.

"Hornbeck Offshore Services Inc.," *Houston Business Journal,* May 16, 1994, p. 41.

"Hornbeck Resigns from Tidewater Board," *Workboat,* November 2000, p. 20.

"Hornbeck to File IPO," *Oil Daily,* July 23, 2002.

"Hornbeck-Leevac Changes Name to Hornbeck Offshore Services, Inc.," *Market News Publishing,* June 3, 2002.

"Offshore Oil Supply Co. Sells Shares for New Vessels," *Corporate Financing Week,* October 17, 2005, p. 9.

Rouffignac, Ann, "Hornbeck Offshore Purchases Fleet of Service Vessels for $46 Million," *Houston Business Journal,* November 18, 1994, p. 3.

"Tidewater Earnings Down; Hornbeck May Go Public," *Workboat,* September 2002, p. 16.

"Up to the Challenge," *Exploration + Processing,* Winter 2005, p. 50.

Webster, Richard A., "Class-Action Suit Overshadows Record Year for Covington-Based Hornbeck Offshore Services," *New Orleans CityBusiness,* June 18, 2007.

HUMANA.

Guidance when you need it most

Humana Inc.

——————■——————

The Humana Building
500 West Main Street
Louisville, Kentucky 40202-2946
U.S.A.
Telephone: (502) 580-1000
Toll Free: (800) 448-6262
Fax: (502) 580-3677
Web site: http://www.humana.com

Public Company
Incorporated: 1961 as Heritage House of America Inc.
Employees: 22,000
Sales: $25.29 billion (2007)
Stock Exchanges: New York
Ticker Symbol: HUM
NAICS: 524114 Direct Health and Medical Insurance
　　　Carriers

■ ■ ■

One of the largest publicly traded health insurers in the United States, Humana Inc. has about 11.5 million people enrolled in its health plans across the country and in Puerto Rico. The largest concentrations of Humana health-plan members are in Florida, Texas, and Kentucky, with these three states comprising more than 22 percent of the total membership. More than 70 percent of the company's premium income is derived from government programs, including Medicare Advantage plans, Medicare stand-alone prescription drug plans, Medicaid, and health plans for the U.S. military services. For commercial employers and individuals, Hu-

mana offers health maintenance organization (HMO) and preferred provider organization (PPO) plans, as well as specialty products, including dental, vision, and supplemental health and life benefits plans.

BEGINNING WITH NURSING HOMES IN THE SIXTIES

In 1961 two lawyers in Louisville, Kentucky, built a nursing home, pledging $1,000 apiece with four friends. Wendell Cherry and David A. Jones—cofounders of that first home, Heritage House—were soon approached with other offers to buy and build nursing homes. Expansion was rapid in the first seven years, and the two men added facilities in Kentucky, Virginia, and Connecticut. With the establishment of Medicare and Medicaid in the mid-1960s, the industry grew quickly. Slightly ahead of the pack in what was to become the most rapidly expanding sector of the nation's economy, Jones and Cherry reincorporated their venture in 1961 and sold stock for seven years to finance further growth. Extendicare Inc., as the group was known, grew to more than 40 facilities, becoming the nation's largest nursing home company.

As Medicare spawned a nursing home glut and stocks suffered, Extendicare experimented with alternatives. There was a brief and unfortunate diversification into mobile home parks between 1969 and 1971, which the company quickly unloaded. Extendicare acquired its first hospital in late 1968, realizing it could apply the same business practices it had developed for operating nursing homes. Within two years, the company had acquired nine more hospitals. The

COMPANY PERSPECTIVES

As the leader in health benefits innovation, Humana is delivering guidance and consumer-oriented options for individuals and employer groups who seek the best possible health care outcomes through choosing, financing and using their health benefits with confidence.

hospitals proved so successful that Extendicare sold all of its nursing homes in 1972.

HOSPITALS BECOME FOCUS IN THE SEVENTIES

With a focus entirely on hospitals, the company's name was changed to Humana Inc. in January 1974. Some of the features that distinguished Humana from other hospital chains early on were its nonconforming management decisions, the refusal to overpay in buying hospitals, the refusal to manage hospitals it did not own, and rigid cost-control measures well-enforced through the company's centralized management. These methods became much discussed: first because they seemed remarkable in the industry; later because of complaints by some physicians about over-control. For example, Humana's efforts to ensure reimbursement included the insistence on a specific payment-plan agreement before patients were discharged.

The cost controls eventually became one of Humana's greatest assets. Between 1975 and 1980, Humana grew quickly and achieved economies of scale, like other hospital chains, by making bulk purchases of supplies and equipment. Unlike some competitors, however, Humana remained very centralized, operating all patient-billing and data-collection out of its home office in Louisville. Freed from the distraction of managing hospitals it did not own—also unlike most competitors—Humana concentrated on strict productivity and profitability goals.

DOUBLING SIZE THROUGH 1978 ACQUISITION OF AMERICAN MEDICORP

As the nation's third largest hospital-management chain in 1978, Humana committed a bold act: It acquired the number two chain, American Medicorp, Inc. This purchase doubled Humana's size and extended its debt. Having used leveraged debt with confidence for some

time during its expansion, Humana was faced with a debt that one company official claimed was "nearly 90% of capital."

Cofounders Jones and Cherry, chairman and president, respectively, remained untroubled because 45 percent of hospital revenues were coming from government-guaranteed Medicare and Medicaid. The two men also saw the hospital business as recession resistant, even though Humana suffered from low-occupancy rates at some of its facilities during these years.

Meanwhile, Humana unloaded unprofitable hospitals. While the healthcare industry was burgeoning into the second largest industry in the United States, Humana alone was honing its cost controls. Between its own growth and government-subsidized medical care, the industry in general had not yet felt the need for cost efficiency.

To build its medical reputation, Humana established a Centers for Excellence program in 1982 for the purpose of specialty care. This included centers for neuroscience, diabetes, spinal injuries, and artificial-heart research and surgery. The artificial-heart projects, which were undertaken partly for the publicity they generated, helped push Humana's name into public view. In 1982 Humana had 90 hospitals, primarily in the Sun Belt states. Humana also leased and operated the University of Louisville's teaching hospital, where Jefferson County, Kentucky, citizens without the ability to pay for hospital care received inpatient treatment for no charge; state, city, and county governments covered the costs.

During the following years the healthcare industry's overexpansion and the government and private insurers' cost-containment efforts began to clash. Here, Humana's tradition of tight cost controls helped, but the industry reeled from severe changes. Industry-wide hospital occupancy rates dropped below 50 percent from a high of 80 percent just three years earlier. From the onset of federal policies in 1983, with private insurers following suit, the industry changed drastically.

OFFERING HEALTH PLANS IN 1984

Early in 1984, Humana launched Humana Health Care Plans, to offer insurance plans with attractively low premiums and punitive deductibles for patients who used rival hospitals. Competitors soon imitated this vertical integration. Humana banked on a 70 percent referral rate from its managed healthcare business, thus ensuring a healthy occupancy rate for its hospitals. Two years into the venture, however, Humana discovered its plan was seriously flawed.

KEY DATES

1961: David A. Jones and Wendell Cherry build and begin running a nursing home in Louisville, Kentucky.

1968: The company, now known as Extendicare Inc., is operating seven nursing homes in three states.

1969: Company acquires its first hospital.

1972: Extendicare divests its nursing homes to focus solely on hospitals.

1974: Company is renamed Humana Inc.

1978: Humana doubles in size with the acquisition of American Medicorp, Inc.

1984: Company enters the insurance business with the launch of Humana Health Care Plans.

1993: Humana spins off its hospitals to concentrate on health insurance.

1995: Acquisition spree includes purchase of EMPHESYS Financial Group, Inc.

1997: Company acquires Physician Corporation of America (PCA) and ChoiceCare Corporation.

1998: Humana agrees to be acquired by United HealthCare Corporation, but the deal later falls through.

2002: "Consumer-directed" Smart products for commercial employers are introduced.

2004: Humana assumes responsibility for the South region of the U.S. military's Tricare program.

2006: Company makes major push into the Medicare Advantage and Medicare Part D segments.

The premiums had been underpriced, missing costs by at least 20 percent. It was assumed policyholders would use Humana hospitals, but in 1986, as losses began to mount, it was found that only 46 percent of Humana's Care Plus group-plan members were using its facilities. The deductibles offered to lure users to their hospitals were not sufficient; independent physicians could recommend any hospital to their patients, and did. Because policyholders were not restricted in their choice of physician, there was no guarantee that they would be referred to Humana facilities by independents. In fact, by this time, a rancor had developed between medical professionals and the business forces behind the cost wars. Humana had incurred further animosity because of its strict business policies. Jones himself contended that in 1986 doctor resentment had resulted

not only in patients being steered to other hospitals but also in strategies to bypass Humana's deductibles for use of other facilities. Doctors would, for instance, claim that a standard admission was an emergency.

Humana addressed these problems by campaigning to change doctors' perceptions of the company and preventing the use of outside hospitals by enforcing stricter procedures. These procedures included requiring doctors to speak with a health-plan nurse and to accept the Humana hospital recommended for use. Refusal to follow this process would prevent reimbursement. (This type of tightly managed plan would become typical of HMO plans of the 1990s.) Humana also trimmed the number of policies it offered and avoided cities where the company was not a dominant presence.

In 1987, with founders Jones and Cherry still at the helm, Humana worked to right its insurance plans. Net income had plunged nearly 75 percent between 1985 and 1986. Humana adjusted its insurance plans and underwent restructuring. It closed clinics and purchased several HMOs. That same year, Medicare ceased its practice of prepayment and started requiring bills before all reimbursements. This meant a significant slowing of cash flow for Humana. It was followed by further government cost-reimbursement strictures that directly affected Humana. Public pressure to contain the cost of healthcare was growing.

By 1988, Humana had greatly reduced losses caused by its insurance operations and seemed intent on recovery. By 1989, after five years of losses, Humana's health-plan division made $4 million, its first operating profit. Raising premiums up to 25 percent, reducing its markets from 50 to 17, operating only where it had a strong hospital presence, and ensuring that patients were sent to its hospitals, Humana began to rebound by the end of the 1980s. Humana, which continued to move counter to the industry while competitors increased their debt loads through leveraged buyouts, saw its debt-to-capital ratio reach an all-time low of 37 percent in 1990.

In October 1990 Humana announced that it had agreed to acquire Chicago-based Michael Reese Health Plan Inc. and Michael Reese Hospital and Medical Center. At the time of the agreement, Michael Reese was one of the largest private academic medical centers in the United States. Michael Reese Health Plan had 240,000 members; Humana had five times as many members. In 1991 cofounder Cherry died.

COMPANY SPINS OFF HOSPITALS IN 1993

By the early 1990s Humana's healthcare plans, primarily managed care plans (HMOs and PPOs), had grown into a $2 billion business with 1.7 million plan participants. Although dogged by a series of charges (overcharging patients for services, using misleading sales tactics, seeking improper Medicare expense reimbursements) that brought ongoing negative publicity, the company's health plan division was much healthier than the hospital side. With its hospitals continuing to post declining profits because of industry-wide cost-containment efforts and falling admissions of full-paying patients (those not covered through government-sponsored plans), Humana decided in 1993 to stake its future on managed healthcare plans. In March of that year, the company spun off the hospital division, including 76 Humana hospitals (most of the company's total), into a new and separate company called Galen Health Care, Inc. Within six months of the spinoff, Galen merged with Columbia Hospital Corp. (later merged into HCA Inc.).

Humana emerged with $685 million in cash and long-term debt of only $21 million (Galen took on most of Humana's pre-spinoff debt). The company thus went on a spending spree. In 1994 Humana spent $180 million to acquire Group Health Association, a 125,000-member HMO in Washington, D.C., and CareNetwork, an HMO in Milwaukee. The company in October 1995 acquired EMPHESYS Financial Group, Inc., for $650 million. Green Bay, Wisconsin-based EMPHESYS was a leading provider of health insurance in the small group market, with 1.3 million members, and the tenth largest commercial group health insurer. Thus by the end of 1995 Humana had boosted its overall plan membership to 3.8 million and its revenues to $4.7 billion.

By mid-1996, however, it appeared that Humana had grown too fast. Amid skyrocketing costs, Humana was forced to abandon 13 unprofitable markets. The largest of these was Washington, D.C., and the company sold Group Health Association to Kaiser Permanente in January 1997; in only two years of ownership, Humana had suffered losses of $100 million attempting to turn around the money-losing Group Health HMO. Also sold was Humana's 30,000-member health plan in Alabama. As part of this restructuring, Humana recorded a $200 million pretax charge for the second quarter of 1996, leading to net income for the year of only $12 million, compared to $190 million for the previous year. Also, Jones, still serving as company chairman and CEO, forced out longtime President Wayne T. Smith and CFO W. Roger Drury. Gregory H. Wolf, who had been senior vice-president of sales and marketing and had come to Humana from EMPHESYS, where he had been president and COO, took over as president of Humana in September 1996. He added

the CEO title in December 1997, with Jones remaining chairman.

Wolf set about resurrecting Humana's image by improving relations with both doctors and patients. He abandoned the use of gag clauses in HMO contracts with doctors, clauses that forbade doctors from discussing the financial arrangements or patient-care policies of the HMO. On the patient side, Humana targeted improvements in basic customer service, answering phone calls faster, mailing out identification cards more quickly, and expediting claims handling.

ACQUISITIONS AND AN ABORTED MERGER

Humana made two significant acquisitions in late 1997. In September the company acquired Physician Corporation of America (PCA) for $290 million in cash and the assumption of $121 million in debt. PCA had a total of 1.1 million members in its HMOs, with 324,000 in Florida alone where Humana already had 1.1 million members. Humana also gained large plans in Texas and Puerto Rico. In October 1997 Humana bought ChoiceCare Corporation for about $250 million in cash. ChoiceCare managed the largest HMO in the Cincinnati area, which had about 250,000 members.

Meanwhile, Humana continued to restructure its operations by shedding additional noncore operations. During 1997 the company sold its last remaining hospital and its pharmacy benefits management subsidiary. In August 1997 Humana announced it would sell its HMO in California. By early 1998 it had committed to selling all of its Humana health centers. After enjoying an acquisitions-aided increase in revenues to $8.04 billion and a rebound in net income to $173 million in 1997, Humana was positioned in mid-1998 as a 6.2 million member group with the number one or number two position in 14 of the major markets in which it operated.

Then, on May 28, 1998, Humana agreed to be bought by Minneapolis-based United HealthCare Corporation in a stock swap initially valued at $5.5 billion. The deal promised to create the largest managed healthcare company in the United States, with annual revenues of $28 billion and 10.4 million full-paying HMO and PPO members (and overall membership of more than 19 million), exceeding the nine million of Kaiser Permanente. In August 2008, however, United HealthCare's stock plummeted after the company disclosed it was taking a $900 million restructuring charge. The stock dive sharply lessened the value of the deal to Humana shareholders, and Humana walked away from the merger.

During 1999 Humana and other health insurers faced a difficult environment in which medical costs were continuing to rise, employers were demanding tougher terms on contracts, and Medicare reimbursements were falling. Earnings were consequently disappointing for the first two quarters of the year, leading to Wolf's resignation. Jones was named interim CEO. Early in 2000, Humana announced charges for 1999 totaling nearly $500 million mainly in connection with a write-down in the value of the poorly performing PCA. During 2000, Humana sold PCA's workers' compensation unit as part of its exit from that sector and also divested its Medicare supplement business. The 1999 charges pushed the company into a net loss of $382 million on revenues of $10.11 billion.

RESTRUCTURING AND NEW INITIATIVES UNDER NEW CEO

In February 2000 Michael B. McCallister was named Humana president and CEO. McCallister, a 26-year company veteran, had most recently served as a senior vice-president. He had played a key role during Jones's period of interim leadership when the company began to turn its fortunes around with changes to its pricing, specifically by increasing the premiums of its health plans to match their increasing, underlying costs. During 2000 the company continued to restructure by exiting from a number of unprofitable markets. It also agreed to pay a $14.5 million fine to the U.S. government to settle allegations it had submitted false Medicare payment information.

While continuing its efforts to bring costs under control, Humana in 2001 also increased its membership rolls by more than one million mainly through the acquisition of a contract that nearly doubled the company's participation in Tricare, the U.S. Department of Defense's health benefits program for active-duty and retired military personnel and their dependents. Humana had participated in Tricare since 1996. Following a government restructuring of the program, Humana in 2004 assumed responsibility for Tricare's South region, which covered about 2.9 million beneficiaries in ten southern states. That year, the company derived about 17 percent of its premiums and administrative services fees from its Tricare contract.

In the meantime, Humana in 2002 introduced a revolutionary approach to reining in medical costs with the debut of its "consumer-directed" Smart products for commercial employers. These plans harnessed Internet-based guidance tools to cut costs by providing employees with direct incentives to rein in medical spending. Early results for these plans were positive as they did indeed reduce the typical double-digit annual increases in costs by a considerable amount. Employers, however, were somewhat slow to adopt the Smart plans. By 2007, about 16 percent of Humana's commercial members, or 564,700 members, had coverage through a Smart plan.

Keeping an eye on its own bottom line, Humana late in 2002 announced the closure of three customer service centers and the resulting elimination of 2,300 jobs, or about 17 percent of its workforce. Despite an associated charge of $85.6 million, the company still managed to post 2002 net income of $142.8 million, a 22 percent increase over the previous year. Revenues increased 10 percent to $11.26 billion. Humana further diversified its plan offerings that year, launching HumanaOne, the firm's first product aimed at the individual health insurance market. The company hoped to tap into what it saw as a growing market given the increasing number of Americans without employer-provided insurance. By the end of 2003, more than 50,000 individuals in 14 states had signed up for the plan.

During this period, Humana also sought targeted acquisitions to bolster specific geographic and product areas. In April 2004 the company purchased Ochsner Health Plan of Louisiana for $157.1 million, gaining a new market in New Orleans for its commercial and Medicare lines of business. Humana expanded its Medicare business via the February 2005 acquisition of CarePlus Health Plans of Florida for roughly $445 million. CarePlus had more than 50,000 Medicare Advantage members in South Florida. In April 2005 company cofounder Jones retired from his position as chairman. Succeeding him was his son, David A. Jones Jr., a board member since 1993 who also ran a Louisville venture-capital firm called Chrysalis Ventures, LLC. Later in 2005, Humana agreed to pay $40 million to settle a class-action lawsuit that had been brought against it and other managed healthcare companies by more than 700,000 doctors who claimed the companies had systematically underpaid them for services they had provided under the insurers' plans.

BIG MEDICARE PUSH

The passage of the Medicare Modernization Act of 2003 brought sweeping changes to the government-administered healthcare program, including an expansion of the Medicare Advantage program and the January 2006 launch of a voluntary Medicare prescription drug plan known as Part D. Humana settled on a plan to aggressively expand its Medicare business. The company rolled out a significant marketing effort to quickly become one of the two largest players in the stand-alone Medicare prescription drug program, signing up more than 3.5 million seniors by the end of 2006. At the same time, Humana leveraged Part D into a major boost for its position in the Medicare Advantage program. The company offered individuals a better deal on drug premiums when they signed up with Humana for both Medicare Advantage and Part D or when Part D enrollees added Medicare Advantage to their Humana coverage. Through such initiatives, Humana between 2005 and 2007 was able to increase its Medicare Advantage enrollment from a little more than 550,000 to more than 1.1 million. By 2007, the company's government segment, which included Medicare, Medicaid, and military services plans, accounted for more than eight million of Humana's total medical membership of 11.4 million.

Humana further strengthened its diversified operations through two fourth-quarter 2007 acquisitions in the area of specialty benefits. CompBenefits Corporation, based in Atlanta and purchased for $369.1 million, provided dental and vision coverage to more than 4.8 million members in 22 states, primarily in the South and Midwest. Minnetonka, Minnesota-based KMG America Corporation, acquired in a $192.4 million deal, was a provider of long-duration insurance benefits including supplemental health and life benefit plans covering costs associated with cancer and other critical illnesses.

Strong revenue growth from its government segment, particularly the increased Medicare business, helped push revenues up 18 percent in 2007 to a record $25.29 billion and net income up more than 70 percent to another best-ever total of $833.7 million. During 2008 Humana completed several more strategic acquisitions, including the October purchase of PHP Companies, Inc., for around $252.9 million. The acquisition of PHP, which operated as Cariten Healthcare, added 73,500 commercial and 46,900 Medicare Advantage members to Humana's existing business in Tennessee. The financially turbulent economy of 2008 led Humana to post $108.3 million in losses from its investment portfolio during the third quarter, and net income for the first nine months of the year was consequently down 20 percent compared to the same period in 2007. The investment losses were one factor in the company stock's 50 percent drop in value during 2008. Also adding to investors' concerns about Humana and other health insurers was the election of Barack Obama to the U.S. presidency. The Obama administration was expected to increase regulation of the insurance industry and also push cost-cutting initiatives that were likely to dent insurers' profits. At the same time, however, promotion of universal health coverage by House and Senate Democrats was expected to provide opportunities for insurers to expand their businesses,

and Humana, as a major player in the government healthcare sector, was well placed to be one of the main beneficiaries.

Carol I. Keeley
Updated, David E. Salamie

PRINCIPAL SUBSIDIARIES

ALABAMA: CompBenefits of Alabama, Inc. ARKANSAS: American Dental Providers of Arkansas, Inc.; DELAWARE: American Tax Credit Corporate Georgia Fund III, L.L.C. (58.2%); CompBenefits Corporation; CompBenefits Direct, Inc.; DefenseWeb Technologies, Inc.; Dental Health Management, Inc.; Emphesys, Inc.; Health Value Management, Inc.; Humana Innovation Enterprises, Inc.; Humana Military Healthcare Services, Inc.; Humana Military Pharmacy Services, Inc.; Humana Pharmacy, Inc.; Humana Veterans Healthcare Services, Inc.; HumanaDental, Inc.; KMG Capital Statutory Trust I. ENGLAND & WALES: Humana Europe, Ltd. FLORIDA: CAC-Florida Medical Centers, LLC; CarePlus Health Plans, Inc.; CompBenefits Company; CompBenefits Dental and Vision Company; CPHP Holdings, Inc.; HUM-e-FL, Inc.; Humana Health Insurance Company of Florida, Inc.; Humana Medical Plan, Inc.; OHS, Inc.; Ultimate Optical, Inc. GEORGIA: CompBenefits of Georgia, Inc.; Humana Employers Health Plan of Georgia, Inc. ILLINOIS: CompBenefits Dental, Inc.; Dental Care Plus Management, Corp.; INFOCUS Technology, Inc.; The Dental Concern, Ltd. KENTUCKY: CHA HMO, Inc.; CHA Service Company; Humana Active Outlook, Inc.; Humana Health Plan, Inc.; Humana Insurance Company of Kentucky; Humana MarketPOINT, Inc.; Humco, Inc.; Preservation on Main, Inc.; The Dental Concern, Inc.; 516-526 West Main Street Condominium Council of Co-Owners, Inc. LOUISIANA: Humana Health Benefit Plan of Louisiana, Inc.; Humana Health Plan Interests, Inc. NEW YORK: Humana Insurance Company of New York. NORTH CAROLINA: American Dental Plan of North Carolina, Inc. OHIO: Humana Health Plan of Ohio, Inc. PUERTO RICO: Healthcare E-Commerce Initiative, Inc.; Humana Health Plans of Puerto Rico, Inc.; Humana Insurance of Puerto Rico, Inc.; Humana MarketPOINT of Puerto Rico, Inc. SOUTH CAROLINA: Kanawha Insurance Company. TENNESSEE: Kanawha Healthcare Solutions, Inc. TEXAS: CompBenefits Insurance Company; DentiCare, Inc.; Corphealth Healthcare, Inc.; Corphealth, Inc.; Corphealth Provider Link, Inc.; Emphesys Insurance Company; Humana Health Plan of Texas, Inc.; Texas Dental Plans, Inc. UTAH: Humana Medical Plan of

Utah, Inc. VERMONT: Managed Care Indemnity, Inc. VIRGINIA: KMG America Corporation. WISCONSIN: CareNetwork, Inc.; Humana Insurance Company; Humana Wisconsin Health Organization Insurance Corporation; HumanaDental Insurance Company.

PRINCIPAL COMPETITORS

UnitedHealth Group Incorporated; Aetna Inc.; CIGNA Corporation; Blue Cross and Blue Shield Association; WellPoint, Inc.; Kaiser Foundation Health Plan, Inc.; Universal American Corp.

FURTHER READING

Benmour, Eric, "Bullish on Wolf," *Business First of Louisville,* September 29, 1997.

———, "Humana Breakup Leaves Competitors Seeing Double," *Business First of Louisville,* September 7, 1992, pp. 1+.

Britt, Russ, and Dinah Wisenberg Brin, "Humana's Net Sinks amid Portfolio Woes," *Wall Street Journal,* October 28, 2008, p. B6.

Burton, Thomas M., "United Health, Humana Deal Is Terminated," *Wall Street Journal,* August 10, 1998, p. A3.

Burton, Thomas M., and Steven Lipin, "United HealthCare to Acquire Humana," *Wall Street Journal,* May 29, 1998, pp. A3, A10.

Carrns, Ann, "Humana Posts Loss, Expects a Turnaround," *Wall Street Journal,* February 10, 2000, p. B21.

———, "Humana to Sell Unit and Take a Big Charge," *Wall Street Journal,* January 4, 2000, p. B2.

———, "Humana to Slash Work Force by 17%, Partly on Closings," *Wall Street Journal,* December 6, 2002, p. B2.

———, "Humana's Chief Executive Steps Down After Two Quarters of Earnings Setbacks," *Wall Street Journal,* August 4, 1999, p. B15.

Castro, Janice, "Earning Profits, Saving Lives: Humana Offers Proof That Health Is a Sound Investment," *Time,* December 10, 1984, pp. 84+.

Cook, James, "We're the Low-Cost Producer," *Forbes,* December 25, 1989, pp. 65+.

Coolidge, Carrie, "Heal Thyself: Humana Experiments with Fixing Health Care," *Forbes,* November 26, 2007, pp. 137–38.

Deveny, Kathleen, "How Humana Got a Painful Black Eye," *Business Week,* July 21, 1986, p. 108.

Deveny, Kathleen, and John P. Tarpey, "Humana: Making the Most of Its Place in the Spotlight," *Business Week,* May 6, 1985, pp. 68+.

Dorfman, John R., "Batting .857," *Forbes,* October 25, 1982, pp. 145+.

Foust, Dean, "Vital Signs at Humana," *Business Week,* July 12, 2004, pp. 56, 58.

Freudenheim, Milt, "Humana Bets All on Managed Care," *New York Times,* May 20, 1993, pp. D1, D6.

———, "Humana Buys Health Plan in Cincinnati," *New York Times,* June 6, 1997, p. D3.

Fuhrmans, Vanessa, "Bedside Manner: An Insurer Tries a New Strategy—Listen to Patients," *Wall Street Journal,* April 11, 2006, p. A1.

Galuszka, Peter, "Humana, Heal Thyself," *Business Week,* October 14, 1996, pp. 73, 76.

Gleckman, Howard, "Plan A: Hook Them with Part D," *Business Week,* January 30, 2006, p. 96.

Gold, Jacqueline S., "Humana: Spin Doctors," *Financial World,* July 6, 1993, p. 17.

Greene, Jan, "Humana Gets Happy," *Hospitals and Health Networks,* May 5, 1997, pp. 34+.

"History of Humana," Louisville, Ky.: Humana Inc., 1997.

Howington, Patrick, "David Jones Ends Era As Co-founder, Chief," *Louisville Courier-Journal,* April 26, 2005, p. 1A.

———, "Five Years Later, McCallister 'Walks on Water' at Humana," *Louisville Courier-Journal,* April 17, 2005, p. 1D.

———, "Humana Builds Individual Sales," *Louisville Courier-Journal,* July 13, 2003, p. 1E.

———, "Young Executive Fuels Turnaround at Humana," *Louisville Courier-Journal,* September 21, 1997.

Johnsson, Julie, "David Jones: Reinventing Humana for the 1990s," *Hospitals,* May 20, 1991, pp. 56+.

Kertesz, Louise, "Life After Restructuring: Humana Redefines Self After Shedding Hospitals, Clinics," *Modern Healthcare,* April 20, 1998, pp. 114+.

Miller, Susan R., "Humana May Be Just What PCA Needs," *South Florida Business Journal,* June 6, 1997, pp. 1+.

Phillips, Stephen, "Humana Regains That Healthy Glow," *Business Week,* May 22, 1989, pp. 127+.

Racanelli, Vito J., "Humana Frailty," *Barron's,* January 10, 2000, p. 13.

Rubenstein, Sarah, "Humana Cuts Forecast, Shares Tumble," *Wall Street Journal,* March 13, 2008, p. A14.

Schiller, Zachary, "Humana May Be Wearing Too Many Hats," *Business Week,* June 8, 1992, p. 31.

Schiller, Zachary, Susan Garland, and Julia Flynn Siler, "The Humana Flap Could Make All Hospitals Feel Sick," *Business Week,* November 4, 1991, p. 34.

Sharpe, Anita, and Deborah Lohse, "Acquisition-Hungry Humana Is Back in the Hunt Again," *Wall Street Journal,* November 17, 1998, p. B4.

Shinkman, Ron, "Humana's Buying Spree: Firm Makes Acquisition Comeback with Three New Deals," *Modern Healthcare,* June 9, 1997, p. 12.

Stern, Gabriella, "Humana Copes with Medicare Probe, Financial Woes," *Wall Street Journal,* June 15, 1992, p. B3.

Tompkins, Wayne, "Seasoned Insider Will Lead Humana," *Louisville Courier-Journal,* February 4, 2000, p. 11B.

Ward, Sandra, "Hidden Handicap?" *Barron's,* May 10, 1999, pp. 19–21.

Interbond Corporation of America

3200 Southwest 42nd Street
Hollywood, Florida 33312
U.S.A.
Telephone: (954) 797-4000
Toll Free: (800) 432-8579
Fax: (954) 797-4047
Web site: http://www.brandsmartusa.com

Private Company
Incorporated: 1977
Employees: 2,600
Sales: $1.03 billion (2007)
NAICS: 443111 Household Appliance Stores; 443112 Radio, Television, and Other Electronic Stores; 443120 Computer and Software Stores

■ ■ ■

Interbond Corporation of America, which conducts its business under the name BrandsMart USA, operates a chain of eight consumer electronics stores in Florida and Georgia. In Florida, BrandsMarts are located in Miami, Sunrise, Deerfield Beach, and West Palm Beach. In Georgia, the stores are located in Atlanta, Kennesaw, and Stockbridge. BrandsMart offers a vast selection of products, including appliances, computers, televisions, cameras, car stereos, telephones, and home theater components. Each store carries more than $8 million in merchandise and generates roughly $130 million in annual sales.

ORIGINS

Success for BrandsMart did not come by blanketing the nation with retail outlets. It took more than 20 years for the company to approach a stature that rightly could be described as a retail chain, if four stores constituted a chain. More than two decades passed before the company's operating territory stretched beyond 50 miles. The company celebrated its 30th anniversary presiding over only two major markets: South Florida and the greater Atlanta, Georgia, area. Instead of impressing industry onlookers with its size, BrandsMart earned recognition for doing what it did very well, distinguishing itself by sheer effectiveness. BrandsMart achieved preeminence in two categories that defined success in the retail industry, sales per store and sales per square foot, making the family behind the business, the Perlmans, esteemed figures within the hotly contested retail sector of the consumer electronics business.

Robert Perlman opened his first store north of Miami in 1977. The store, which would collect more than $1.5 billion in sales before it was closed, represented the only source of income for BrandsMart for the next dozen years. Featuring a 28,000-square-foot showroom, the company's flagship store was smaller than the other units to follow, but it attracted a wealth of business from surrounding Dade County. During the 1980s, the store set the precedent for the handful of stores that were established in the decades ahead: Offer an enormous selection of products at attractive prices, run the business with minimal overhead, and reap the rewards of market dominance. Products, roughly 80,000 items, were stacked along a racetrack layout describing the perimeter of the showroom. Certain product

KEY DATES

∎

1977: Robert Perlman opens his first BrandsMart in Miami, Florida.
1990: A second store opens near Fort Lauderdale.
1992: BrandsMart opens its third store in Deerfield Beach.
1995: The company's flagship store in Miami is replaced with a new store.
2000: A fourth BrandsMart opens in Kendall.
2001: A fifth store debuts in West Palm Beach.
2004: The company's first out-of-state store opens in a suburb of Atlanta.
2006: The company's third store in Georgia opens in Stockbridge.
2008: Design work begins on the company's ninth store.

categories, such as big-screen televisions, camcorders, and car audio, were presented to the customer in a boutique-like approach, housed in separate alcoves or soundproof rooms. The price range of the products stocked in a BrandsMart reflected the diversity of the inventory, stretching from under $100 to $44,000.

BrandsMart coupled a profusion of offerings with proficient management, squeezing maximum profits from the Miami store through efficient operations. Robert Perlman's son, Mike Perlman, had risen to the post of vice-president by the end of the 1980s, serving as one of the company's few executives in a streamlined organization. "We have three buyers and a vice president—that's it," Mike Perlman said in the June 3, 1991 issue of *Discount Store News.* "Our sales staff talks directly to the appropriate buyer daily by computer, so everyone is up-to-date on what to sell, what prices to sell at, and so on. We don't drop many balls." By operating as such, BrandsMart enjoyed admirable success with its lone store, generating nearly $100 million in annual sales from the Miami location by the end of the 1980s.

A SECOND STORE OPENS IN 1990

The start of the 1990s saw the company switch to expansion mode for the first time. For the location of his second store, Robert Perlman chose the Fort Lauderdale suburb of Sunrise, 30 miles north of Miami. The store, featuring a 55,000-square-foot showroom, became an anchor tenant in the Sawgrass Mills mall, one of the largest malls in the nation when it opened in

1990. With the addition of the second store, sales were expected to reach $200 million by the end of 1991, an ideal time for such retailers as BrandsMart. The company, along with a handful of other competitors such as the New Jersey-based Tops chain and the nation's largest consumer electronics retailer, Minnesota-based Best Buy, were redefining success in the industry. "The balance of power in the consumer electronics market," *Discount Store News* observed in its June 3, 1991 issue, "seems to be turning toward true power retailers: low-cost providers who offer massed out selection, product depth, and appropriate but unobtrusive service levels."

BrandsMart, the "power retailer," suddenly became more aggressive as it entered the 1990s. After waiting 13 years to open their second store, the Perlmans waited only two years to open their third store. The third location, in Deerfield Beach north of Fort Lauderdale, opened in late 1992, giving the company another property capable of generating $100 million in annual sales. After tripling the size of their business in two years, the Perlmans hinted for the first time about expanding beyond southeastern Florida, revealing a desire to export their successful retail concept into another major market. "There aren't too many major markets left in the United States," Mike Perlman said in the June 3, 1991 issue of *Discount Store News,* "but Atlanta is relatively understored, and that's a great market. I could see someone moving in there and giving Circuit City a run for its money ... let's just say that we're looking at it."

REPLACING ORIGINAL STORE: 1995

Befitting their cautious approach to expansion, the Perlmans' exploration of opportunities in Atlanta took more than a decade. Meanwhile, in their stronghold in South Florida, the Perlman team looked to strengthen their formidable presence. In 1995, they replaced their original BrandsMart with a new store, the largest store they had ever constructed. Situated several blocks away from the original site, the new Miami store was a 185,000-square-foot facility with an 88,000-square-foot showroom, more than three times the size of the original store's showroom. "We'll never build one this big again," Mike Perlman vowed in the May 15, 1995 issue of *Discount Store News.* The new store featured an expanded housewares selection and, for the first time, included onsite foodservice by Miami Subs Inc., a 180-unit sandwich chain.

When the new flagship store opened, BrandsMart was generating $320 million in revenue, a total that was expected to increase significantly once the Perlmans completed expansion plans announced in 1995. They planned to open two more stores in South Florida by 1998, a store in Kendall, south of Miami, and a store in West Palm Beach, 60 miles north of Miami. The father-and-son team was in the midst of negotiating real estate deals when the new flagship store opened, but neither project moved forward as planned. Site selection for the Kendall store proved to be an arduous search and a legal battle erupted over the West Palm Beach store, stalling expansion as the Perlmans dealt with a transfer of power under undesirable circumstances. In 1996, Robert Perlman was convicted of tax evasion and sentenced to ten months in federal prison, effectively handing the reins of command to Mike Perlman.

EXPANSION STALLS IN THE LATE NINETIES

Mike Perlman led the search for a suitable location south of Miami in an area referred to as South Dade County. He had hoped to have the new store opened by 1998, but years were spent trying to find a location with enough space for the store and for parking. Eventually, a suitable location was found in Kendall on a site formerly occupied by a Home Depot. The store, the company's fourth unit, opened in 2000, answering the needs of a growing population in the greater Miami area. "Over the last 20 years with the increase in traffic," Perlman explained in the April 13, 2000 edition of *Knight-Ridder/Tribune Business News,* "it has become increasingly difficult for people from South Dade who want to shop at our original North Dade store to get there."

For Perlman, any frustration at the slow process of opening the Kendall store was eclipsed by the struggle to open the West Palm Beach store. BrandsMart had reached an agreement to acquire 18 acres of land on Palm Beach Lakes Boulevard for $5.5 million in 1997, but a protracted battle with the owner of the land, Joseph Della Ratta, ensued. In November 1998, the company sued Della Ratta, alleging he had backed out of the deal because he had received a better offer from another retailer. The two parties eventually resolved their dispute in early 2000, when BrandsMart acquired the 18-acre plot for $5.5 million.

A MARKET WINNER

Construction of a 120,000-square-foot store in West Palm Beach began in August 2000, ending a three-year wait for the company's foray into Palm Beach County. Frustrations ebbed and gave way to excitement, as BrandsMart, about to become a five-store chain, exerted considerable sway in the consumer electronics market in South Florida. As a three-store operation at the end of

the 1990s, the company generated $395 million in sales, averaging more than $130 million in sales per store. In comparison, the nation's largest consumer electronics retailer, Best Buy, which operated 360 stores in 40 states, averaged $37.5 million in sales per store. Another much larger rival, Circuit City, averaged $17.3 million in sales per store. BrandsMart controlled 26 percent of the South Florida market as a three-store operation, a market share that was expected to increase to 40 percent by the time the West Palm Beach store opened, when sales were expected to reach $550 million. The store opened in June 2001, giving BrandsMart market dominance along a 50-mile swath of coastline stretching from Deerfield Beach in the north to Kendall in the south.

BRANDSMART EYES GEORGIA

After a quarter-century devoted to building its business in South Florida, BrandsMart was ready to make the most ambitious geographic leap in its history. The company began plotting its entry into the Atlanta market in earnest, more than a decade after Mike Perlman had discussed the possibility in an interview with *Discount Store News.* Expansion plans crystallized in late 2003, when a site was selected in the Atlanta suburb of Doraville. The company purchased 16.6 acres occupied by a former General Motors parts distribution facility, as Perlman revealed his intention to open between four and six stores in the Atlanta area in the coming years.

RAPID EXPANSION IN GEORGIA

BrandsMart, a company that expanded with caution in Florida, exhibited a decidedly more aggressive demeanor in Georgia. The company's first out-of-state store opened in Doraville in September 2004. Over the course of the next two years, two more stores opened in the greater Atlanta area, a store in Kennesaw and a store in Stockbridge, giving the company a total of eight stores in a two-state operating territory.

With eight stores under its control, BrandsMart was able to surpass the $1 billion mark in sales after its Stockbridge store opened in late 2006, an impressive achievement for a company of its size. The volume of business reflected a retailer that led the nation in sales per store and sales per square foot, making it a model for competitors in its industry to emulate. In the years ahead, the company was not expected to embark on a far-flung expansion spree. The precedent set in South Florida—dominate a market with a cluster of stores—was being followed in Georgia, where a ninth store was being planned in 2008. The store was being designed to meet criteria established by the U.S. Green Building

Council, which would make it the first LEED-certified retail superstore in Atlanta. The store was expected to be built near the Mall of Georgia in Gwinnett, northeast of Atlanta, enabling BrandsMart to approximate the market dominance it enjoyed in South Florida.

Jeffrey L. Covell

PRINCIPAL COMPETITORS

Best Buy Co., Inc.; Circuit City Stores, Inc.; Sears, Roebuck and Co.

FURTHER READING

"BrandsMart Caps the Year with Opening of Monster Flagship," *Discount Store News,* December 9, 1996, p. 5.

Cohen, Karen-Janine, "Hollywood, Fla.-based Electronics, Appliances Retailer to Open Atlanta Store," *South Florida Sun-Sentinel,* October 3, 2003.

DeGross, Renee, "Discounter BrandsMart Eyes Atlanta," *Atlanta Journal-Constitution,* March 22, 2003, p. F2.

Heller, Laura, "BrandsMart's New Prototype Underscores Chain's Strength," *DSN Retailing,* May 8, 2000, p. 7.

Hisey, Pete, "BrandsMart Means Selection," *Discount Store News,* June 3, 1991, p. 33.

Newkirk, Margaret, "Florida Retail Chain Plans Doraville Store," *Atlanta Journal-Constitution,* September 30, 2003, p. D1.

Owers, Paul, "BrandsMart Building West Palm Store," *Palm Beach Post,* August 25, 2000, p. 1D.

———, "BrandsMart Set to Build in West Palm," *Palm Beach Post,* April 15, 2000, p. 1D.

Pearson, Michael, "Big-Box Goes Green," *Atlanta Journal-Constitution,* February 21, 2008, p. J1.

Salisbury, Susan, "New BrandsMart Pulls in Crowds," *Palm Beach Post,* June 29, 2001, p. 1D.

IRIS International, Inc.

———————■———————

9172 Eton Avenue
Chatsworth, California 91311
U.S.A.
Telephone: (818) 709-1244
Toll Free: (800) 776-4747
Fax: (818) 700-9661
Web site: http://www.proiris.com

Public Company
Incorporated: 1979 as International Remote Imaging
   Systems, Inc.
Employees: 308
Sales: $84.03 million (2007)
Stock Exchanges: NASDAQ
Ticker Symbol: IRIS
NAICS: 334516 Analytical Laboratory Instrument
   Manufacturing

■ ■ ■

IRIS International, Inc., is an in vitro diagnostics company whose products analyze particles and living cell forms using flow imaging technology, particle recognition, and automation. IRIS's primary focus is on providing devices that perform urinalysis tests, embodied in the company's flagship line of iQ analyzers, which are fully automated analyzers for urine microscopy and chemistry. The company's products increase the consistency of test results and reduce the time spent by laboratory technicians in completing a urinalysis. Through its sample processing division, IRIS makes centrifuges and blood analyzers. The company's products are sold in more than 50 countries.

INDUSTRY PIONEER: FRED DEINDOERFER

Before IRIS was established there was no automated way to perform a urinalysis, one of the three standard profile tests administered to every patient admitted to a hospital. Blood chemistry and blood cell count had been automated years earlier, but a urinalysis had to be performed manually by a technician who smeared a specimen on a glass slide and examined it under a microscope. Developing automated instrumentation for analyzing urine had been impossible because of the complexity of urine, the principal reason urinalysis was effective in diagnosing diseases. Blood was a simple substance in comparison to urine, which contained bacteria, yeast, red and white blood cells, skin cells, and numerous other crystals and particles. Consequently, the estimated 90 million tests performed annually had to be done by hand, a burdensome chore a chemical engineer named Fred Deindoerfer sought to ease through automation.

Deindoerfer, who earned his doctorate degree from the University of Pennsylvania, delivered innovation to the analytical instrument industry. He began his career at American Hospital Supply Corp., where he helped establish an intravenous solutions business. He left the industry giant in 1974 to start his own company, International Diagnostic Technology, which represented his first success as a pioneer in the analytical instrument industry. Through International Diagnostic Technology,

COMPANY PERSPECTIVES

With our commitment to offering complete urinalysis we have succeeded in developing an unprecedented array of new instruments and workcells that will benefit any size laboratory with both true image morphology and walkaway capability, for the highest level of diagnostic accuracy and workflow efficiency.

Deindoerfer developed the first commercial fluorescent system for analyzing hormones, drugs, and antibodies in the body, but, as he would experience with IRIS, a pioneering achievement did not automatically translate into financial success.

IRIS INCORPORATES IN 1979

International Diagnostic suffered financially early in its development. In 1978, Deindoerfer decided the best solution for the company's pressing cash woes was to sell the business to a larger company. He found a buyer in the West German firm Boehringer Ingelheim, which purchased International Diagnostics for $7 million. Deindoerfer remained with his entrepreneurial creation for another two years. During this period, his attention began to stray to another project, the development of an automated microscope, one of the most formidable obstacles blocking the development of automated urinalysis systems. In 1979, he and several other scientists who formed a private development group invested $130,000 and secured $400,000 from other investors to incorporate International Remote Imaging Systems, Inc., the name IRIS International operated under for 25 years.

In Chatsworth, California, part of the City of Los Angeles, work began on developing a way to automate the various steps involved in analyzing urine. By the early 1980s, significant progress had been made, putting the company on the verge of gaining clearance from the U.S. Food and Drug Administration (FDA) to market its system. International Remote's sophisticated technology incorporated a variety of scientific disciplines into the design of its automated intelligent microscope (AIM), using image analysis, electro-optics, and microprocessors. AIM, the integral component of the company's IRIS system, took rapid-fire (20 frames per second), stop-action photographs of urine sandwiched between two planes of flowing liquid and then analyzed the specimen with a microprocessor.

The commercial release of the IRIS system represented a significant breakthrough in the healthcare industry. Although not fully automated—it automated chemical analysis but required a technician to complete the microscopy component of urinalysis—the device developed by Deindoerfer and his colleagues was remarkable. An IRIS urinalysis took an average of three to four minutes to complete, half the time of a conventional test. There were two problems with the invention, however, flaws that would keep International Remote's financial growth in check for decades. The IRIS system was large, measuring five feet high by five feet long, essentially requiring its own room within a healthcare facility. More problematic was the price of the system, with the machine selling for between $75,000 and $80,000 during the early 1980s. Deindoerfer hoped to have an IRIS system in 20 percent of the largest 3,000 clinical laboratories in the United States by the late 1980s, but he fell far short of the goal primarily because of the price of his invention.

DIVERSIFICATION IN THE MID-NINETIES

As the years passed, International Remote subsisted on a trickle of business. Demand for an automated urinalysis system was limited. A hefty machine with a hefty price tag, the IRIS system was beyond the budgetary means of community hospitals, most urban hospitals, and all except the largest reference laboratories. An IRIS system was most likely to be found in one of the country's largest teaching hospitals, giving the company little chance to thrive financially. In an attempt to bolster its sales volume, International Remote completed two acquisitions in the mid-1990s. Norwood, Massachusetts-based StatSpin Technologies was purchased, giving the company business that would later constitute its Iris Sample Processing division. StatSpin manufactured a line of small centrifuges that separated blood, urine, and other specimens into components for manual analysis. The acquisition proved a prudent purchase, accounting for 20 percent of International Remote's annual sales by the end of the decade. The company's second acquisition was an unmitigated disaster.

IRIS FALTERS IN THE LATE NINETIES

Witness to the debacle was John A. O'Malley, a 30-year veteran of the healthcare and medical device industry. An International Remote board member beginning in 1988, O'Malley came out of retirement in 1998 to become the company's new chief executive officer. His first days in office were depressing ones, time spent deal-

KEY DATES

1979: Backed by $430,000, IRIS is incorporated as International Remote Imaging Systems, Inc.

1996: International Remote acquires StatSpin Technologies.

2000: Research and development spending is doubled as the company tries to improve its flagship product.

2002: Cesar M. Garcia, appointed chief executive officer in 2003, joins International Remote as an executive vice-president.

2003: Renamed IRIS International, the company introduces iQ 200, a new line of analyzers.

2006: IRIS acquires Leucadia Technologies, Inc.

2007: Revenues reach a record high of $84 million.

ing with the company's imprudent purchase of Perceptive Scientific Instruments, a genetic analysis business. International Remote borrowed a substantial sum to complete the acquisition, expecting to enjoy a substantial flow of revenues from the purchased business, but the revenues never materialized. Consequently, International Remote recorded a series of quarterly losses that stretched into the third quarter of 1999, when the company lost $1.4 million, the worst quarterly performance in its 22-year history. In response, the company's stock value plunged, dropping from $12 per share in 1996 to $1 per share in 2001. "That almost took us under," O'Malley said in the September 10, 2001 issue of the *Los Angeles Business Journal.*

A SEARCH FOR A BETTER PRODUCT

Perceptive Scientific's assets were liquidated in 2001, but the removal of a thorn in the company's side did not resolve its perennial dilemma. The company's automated urinalysis machines were prohibitively expensive, selling for up to $175,000 in 2001. During the previous seven years, the company had sold roughly 400 units, a volume of business that O'Malley wanted to increase significantly. He doubled the amount spent on research and development, realizing that the growth of his company depended on reducing the price of its products. "The way to grow is to provide systems that are economically justifiable," he said in the September 10, 2001 issue of the *Los Angeles Business Journal.*

As O'Malley marshaled his forces to search for a solution, International Remote entered into a period of

leadership flux. Cesar M. Garcia was hired as executive vice-president in January 2002, joining the company he would soon lead. Garcia, who earned his bachelor's degree in industrial engineering from the University of Puerto Rico, began his career in 1974 working for a subsidiary of Bayer USA. He remained within the Bayer organization for the next 20 years, leaving in 1994 to serve as vice-president of Datascope Corporation, a manufacturer of medical devices for cardiology, anesthesiology, and critical monitoring. In 1998, he began a three-year stint as vice-president of Cytometrics Incorporated, a manufacturer of noninvasive medical devices for point-of-care diagnostics. Garcia joined International Remote after several months of serving as president of Primera LLC, a Philadelphia-based management consulting company.

One year after Garcia joined the company, Kshitij Mohan arrived as International Remote's new president and chief executive officer. Mohan's appointment as International Remote's new leader in January 2003, which enabled O'Malley to move up to the position of chairman, was intended to help the company introduce a new line of products that had been under development, the line of products developed under O'Malley's watchful eye. In Mohan, the company gained a seasoned veteran well versed in the intricacies involved in the product rollout set to occur. Mohan had served as the director of the FDA's Office of Device Evaluation during the 1980s, overseeing the testing of medical devices. He had spent a dozen years at Baxter International Inc., serving as the vice-president of research and technical services for the healthcare products manufacturer. He had also served as senior vice-president and chief executive officer of Boston Scientific Corporation, a manufacturer of cardiovascular and other medical devices.

NEW PRODUCT LINE DEBUTS IN 2003

The long wait for a more inexpensive, more technically advanced urinalysis system ended in August 2003, when International Remote introduced its iQ 200 analyzer. In the months leading up to the release of the new flagship product Mohan, and Garcia, who was promoted to the post of president in June 2003, doubled the company's U.S. sales force and established a European subsidiary and network of distributors that covered 18 countries. The greatly expanded sales and distribution infrastructure reflected management's commitment to the iQ 200 platform, a desktop analyzer priced more than $50,000 below previous models that, for the first time, offered fully automated urinalysis capabilities. The new system automated the chemistry component of the test, detecting glucose, nitrates, and proteins, and, unlike previous models, automated the microscopy component of a urinalysis, which detected tiny particles such as blood cells and yeast. Smaller, less expensive, and more sophisticated than anything previously offered by International Remote, the iQ 2000 promised to deliver long-awaited financial growth to the Chatsworth-based company.

One month after releasing the iQ 200, the company announced it was changing its name, choosing IRIS International, Inc., as its new corporate title. "We have reached a number of milestones and a new name is a natural next step in our rapid evolution as a global company," Mohan explained in the September 10, 2003 issue of *PrimeZone Media Network.* "IRIS is well-known and highly regarded within our industry. We believe that 'IRIS International' has a ring of familiarity and also reflects our growing international presence. It will further strengthen our brand and recognition among our customers and within the investment community," he said.

SURGING FINANCIAL GROWTH

By the end of September 2003, there was strong evidence of the commercial appeal of iQ 200. In 2002, the company sold 50 of its larger, more expensive analyzers. During the first two months of iQ 200's availability, 41 units were delivered. As the encouraging news buoyed spirits at the company's headquarters, another change in leadership occurred when Mohan resigned in November 2003, having never settled comfortably in the Los Angeles area. "This commute back and forth was getting to me," Mohan said in the November 20, 2003 issue of *PrimeZone Media Network,* referring to his frequent trips to his permanent home in Potomac, Maryland. "I was operating out of a little apartment." Mohan's sudden departure prompted the promotion of Garcia to the post of chief executive officer, a change in leadership that typically was sufficient to make Wall Street wary, but IRIS's stock fared extremely well. By the beginning of 2004, the company's stock value had increased threefold, trading at more than $6 per share, reflecting a level of enthusiasm among the investment community that had not been seen since 1997.

With iQ 200 accounting for the bulk of the company's business, sales and profits increased at an unprecedented pace. After waiting nearly 30 years to capitalize on the potential of an automated urinalysis system, the company was reaping the rewards of the work begun in 1979 by Fred Deindoerfer. By mid-2005, the company's stock was trading at nearly $20 per share. By the end of the year, it had shipped 564 iQ 200

machines, eclipsing the number of units it had sold during the previous 20 years. In 2006, IRIS fleshed out its business with the purchase of Leucadia Technologies, Inc., a molecular diagnostics company that was renamed Iris Molecular Diagnostics. The lifeblood of the company continued to be its urinalysis analyzers, however, which drove sales upward. IRIS began the decade generating $28 million in revenue, the result of more than 20 years of growth. During the ensuing seven years, the company nearly tripled its volume of business, recording $84 million in revenue in 2007. The commercial success of the iQ 200 platform fueled confidence that the years ahead would see IRIS firmly establish itself as a leader in the medical device industry.

Jeffrey L. Covell

PRINCIPAL SUBSIDIARIES

Iris Diagnostics France; Iris Deutschland GmbH (Germany); Iris Molecular Diagnostics; Iris Sample Processing.

PRINCIPAL DIVISIONS

Iris Diagnostics; Iris Sample Processing.

PRINCIPAL COMPETITORS

Sysmex; Roche Diagnostics Corporation; Siemens Healthcare Diagnostics Inc.

FURTHER READING

"Cesar M. Garcia Joined International Remote Imaging Systems Inc.," *IIE Solutions,* September 2002, p. 12.

Darmiento, Laurence, "Growth Challenge Lures Health Veteran," *Los Angeles Business Journal,* January 13, 2003, p. 23.

———, "Returning Attention to Core Business Aids Medical Firm," *Los Angeles Business Journal,* September 10, 2001, p. 40.

———, "'Significant Transition' at Urinalysis Company Pleases Investors," *Los Angeles Business Journal,* January 5, 2004, p. 13.

"International Remote Imaging Systems Announces Promotion of Cesar Garcia to President and Chief Operating Officer," *PrimeZone Media Network,* June 16, 2003.

"International Remote Imaging Systems to Become Iris International, Inc.," *PrimeZone Media Network,* September 10, 2003.

Reeves, Amy, "Its Theme Song: Urine the Money," *Investor's Business Daily,* May 16, 2005, p. A8.

Wiegner, Kathleen K., "Focusing In," *Forbes,* July 4, 1983, p. 142.

Ito En Ltd.

———————■———————

47-10 Honmachi 3-chome, Shibuya-ku
Tokyo, 151-8550
Japan
Telephone: (+81 03) 5371 7111
Fax: (+81 03) 5371 7184
Web site: http://www.itoen.co.jp/eng

Public Company
Incorporated: 1966 as Frontier Tea Corporation
Employees: 4,959
Sales: ¥328.07 billion ($2.97 billion) (2007)
Stock Exchanges: Tokyo
Ticker Symbol: 2593
NAICS: 311920 Coffee and Tea Manufacturing; 722213 Snack and Nonalcoholic Beverage Bars

■ ■ ■

Ito En Ltd. is Japan's leading producer of green tea and tea-based soft drinks, as well as other beverages including fruit juices, vegetable juices, mineral water, and coffee. A pioneer in producing canned green tea drinks, Ito En has built up the leading share of the canned and bottled green tea market in Japan, through its Oi Ocha (It's tea time) brand. The company's green tea beverage sales account for nearly 52 percent of its total revenues, while the company's packaged tea leaves and tea bags add nearly 9.5 percent. The company also sells its teas in the United States, under the Teas' Tea, Sencha Shot, Dr. Andrew Weil, and other brands. In addition, Ito En is a major producer of raw tea, controlling some 20 percent of the crop in Japan. The company also operates

a tea processing plant in Australia, sourcing tea through a network of local farmers. Ito En was the first company in Japan to import oolong tea leaves from China, and produces a line of bottled Chinese teas, which contribute 4.3 percent to group sales. Additionally, Ito En operates a small number of Ito En Tea Garden tea shops, primarily in Japan, as well as a flagship tea shop and restaurant on New York's Madison Avenue.

In addition to tea-based beverages, Ito En produces fruit and vegetable drinks, under the Jujitsu Yasai and Ichinichibun no Yasai brands. These drinks add 18.6 percent to the group's sales. Coffee, under the W brand, adds more than 6 percent, while black tea, functional foods, and other products, including barley teas, contribute 9.7 percent to the company's sales. In 2008 Ito En entered the mineral water market, acquiring the license for the Evian brand for the Japanese market. The company also owns Florida-based Mason Distributors Inc., which distributes vitamins and other functional food supplements, as well as a majority stake in the Tully's Coffee chain of coffee shops in Japan. While the vast majority of Ito En's turnover comes from its Japanese home base, the company expects to benefit from the rising interest in the United States in the purported health benefits attributed to green tea. Ito En Ltd. is listed on the Tokyo Stock Exchange and is led by President Hachiro Honjo. In 2007 the company's total revenues reached ¥328.07 billion ($2.97 billion).

GREEN TEA PACKAGING PIONEER IN 1966

One of Japan's traditional beverages, tea—and specifically green tea–has played a prominent role in much of

COMPANY PERSPECTIVES

ITO EN's management is based first and foremost on the principle of "Always Putting the Customer First." "Customer" is used in this context in a very broad sense, and refers collectively to six types of stakeholders—consumers, shareholders, retailers, suppliers, financial institutions and local communities. In line with this principle and its core management policies, ITO EN strives to develop close, direct relationships with each of these groups by maintaining dialog at as many points of contact as possible. Through this approach based on grass-roots communication, we aim to achieve constant innovation by always asking ourselves how we can better meet the needs of our customers ... on the principle of "Always Putting the Customer First."

Japanese secular and ceremonial life. A variety of health benefits has also long been attributed to green tea, enhancing its appeal. The quickening pace of Japanese life in the 1960s introduced a growing demand for new packaging methods and sales channels for the green tea market. This demand led to the creation of a new company, Frontier Tea Corporation, which was founded in Shizuoka City in 1966 in order to package tea leaves. In addition to loose tea, the company became one of the first to develop its own line of bagged teas.

By 1968 the company had begun to expand beyond the Shizuoka Prefecture. This led to the opening of a new sales and distribution center in Yokohama, in the Kanagawa Prefecture. The following year, the company changed its name to Ito En Ltd. By 1971 the company prepared to extend its operations to the national level, and in that year moved its headquarters to Tokyo. At the same time, the company invested in developing its own processing capacity and technologies, in order to ensure consistent quality and flavor of its teas.

Packaging played a major role in Ito En's success in the 1970s and into the 1980s. The company's emphasis on developing innovative packaging techniques, methods, and materials began as early as 1972, when the company debuted a new method for vacuum packing its teas. At the same time, the group brought in new high-speed wrapping machinery, which had been invented by Switzerland's Industriel Gesellschaft. Into the middle of the decade, the company expanded its

production and distribution capacity, adding a new and larger plant in Shizuoka Prefecture.

By the end of the decade, Ito En had begun to build its reputation as one of Japan's leading green tea brands. The company's brand image was further enhanced with the opening of its first specialty tea shop, called Chajuttoku, in 1977. The success of the first Yokohama City location led the company to launch a full-scale rollout of the tea-shop chain.

Ito En also expanded its product range during this period, becoming in 1979 the first Japanese company to import oolong tea from China. Sales of this product line remained comparatively small, just over 4 percent of revenues in the early 21st century. Nonetheless, the new product provided the group with a training ground for its entry into the canned soft-drinks market. In 1981 the company launched its first canned drink, an oolong tea. The launch also provided the company with access to the highly important vending-machine market as the demand for ready-made and easy-to-drink beverages soared in Japan.

LAUNCH OF CANNED GREEN TEA

Packaging a green tea beverage remained a more challenging prospect, however. The tea's subtle flavor, as well as the wide variety in quality of raw leaves, made it extremely difficult to achieve a fresh-brewed flavor in a canned tea drink. Yet Ito En turned its packaging and processing research capacity to the problem. By 1985 the company had perfected its brewing method, which it called the "T-N (Tea & Natural) Blow." In that year, the company launched its new canned green tea drink, Canned Sencha.

The success of the new drink, which won an award for "Outstanding Product of the Year" from the *Nihon Keizai* newspaper, encouraged Ito En to step up its research and development capacity. In 1987 the company unveiled its Central Research Institute, in Shizuoka.

NEW BRAND NAME: OI OCHA

It was marketing, not technology, that laid the groundwork for Ito En's next success. In 1989 the company decided to relaunch its green tea beverage under a new brand name: Oi Ocha. Translatable as "it's tea time" or "tea please," the brand built upon a common, everyday phrase, quickly capturing consumer attention. Before long, Oi Ocha had become one of the most recognized brands in Japan, propelling Ito En into the leadership of the country's green tea market.

KEY DATES

1966: The company is founded as Frontier Tea Corporation in Shizuoka, Japan, and begins marketing green tea.

1969: Name is changed to Ito En Ltd.

1979: Ito En becomes first company in Japan to import oolong tea from China.

1985: Ito En perfects a new canned green tea beverage, Canned Sencha.

1989: Canned Sencha is rebranded as Oi Ocha, which becomes a major green tea brand in Japan.

1992: Ito En goes public on the Tokyo Stock Exchange.

2002: Flagship tea shop in New York City is opened.

2006: Ito En acquires vitamin-distributor Mason Distributors in Florida.

2007: Tully's Coffee chain of coffee shops in Japan is acquired.

2008: Ito En gains the Japanese distribution rights to the Evian mineral water brand.

In 1990 the success of the Oi Ocha launch helped propel the company's sales past the ¥50 billion mark for the first time. By 1995 the company's sales had topped ¥100 billion (approximately $900 million).

NEW MARKETS IN THE NINETIES

Buoyed by Oi Ocha's sales success, Ito En went public in 1992, and took up new headquarters in the Shibuya-ku district of Tokyo. The company also went in search of new markets. Geographically, Ito En had targeted an entry into the U.S. market, initially to serve the large Japanese population there. As a result, the company's first U.S. subsidiary was created in Hawaii in 1987.

In 1994 Ito En entered Australia as well, setting up a subsidiary in that market, which had been emerging as an important source for traditional Japanese crops, such as buckwheat. The rapid growth of green tea consumption in Japan, fueled in part by a growing body of research pointing to the health benefits of a number of substances contained in green tea, sent Ito En searching for new sources of raw tea. While most of Japan's tea imports came from China, these leaves were considered of an inferior quality to domestically grown tea.

Instead, Ito En began working with farmers in Murrindindi Shire, in Victoria, Australia, starting in 1996. By 1999 the company had built up agreements with a network of growers to establish up to 100 hectares (247 acres) of green tea over the next several years. Ito En in turn launched construction of a tea processing plant in Myrtleford, Victoria, that year. The first shipments of Australian tea finally reached Japan in 2004. By then, Ito En itself had entered the tea farming sector, establishing its own tea gardens in Miyakonojo, in Miyazaki Prefecture. This move was part of Ito En's "Program for Revitalizing Tea-Growing Regions" in order to counteract the decline of the Japanese agriculture market in face of the country's continued urbanization and the aging of its population.

In the meantime, Ito En had also been broadening its operations into other product categories. In 1992 the company launched a line of fruit and vegetable drinks, called Jujitsu Yasai, or "vegetables galore." The new line aimed to make vegetable-based beverages more palatable by combining them with fruit juices. The launch into fruit juices was soon joined by an entry into the coffee sector, as the company debuted its "W" brand of coffee. For this, Ito En built its own coffee-roasting plant in Shizuoka. The new product lines provided the inspiration for the rollout of a new retail format. In 1996 the company opened its first Natural Station shop, in Shinjuku, selling fresh-squeezed fruit and vegetable cocktails, as well as fresh coffee.

TARGETING HEALTHY GROWTH IN THE 21ST CENTURY

Ito En added a new green tea packaging factory in Fukushima in 1996. At the same time, the company had readied the launch of a new breakthrough in green tea packaging. In that year, the company patented a new type of polyethylene terephthalate (PET) bottle, called Natural Clear, making it possible to package green tea in a plastic bottle for the first time. The company continued to develop packaging innovations, introducing the first PET bottles that could be heated in 2000. Another innovation, introduced in 2008, housed the dry green tea powder in the bottle cap, releasing it into the mineral water contained in the bottle only when the tea was ready to be consumed.

The surge in interest in so-called functional foods in Japan and elsewhere helped stimulate Ito En's own growth. By 2001 the company's revenues had topped the ¥200 billion mark. Ito En itself played an active role in attempting to establish green tea's health credentials. In 1997 the company joined a clinical study being carried out by the M.D. Anderson Cancer Center at the University of Texas.

The huge health foods industry in the United States led Ito En to expand its presence in that market in the first decade of the 2000s. The company created a new subsidiary in New York in order to produce and distribute its teas and beverages in the United States. The company developed a new brand, Teas' Tea, for this market. The launch was supported by the opening of a flagship tea shop in New York City, on Madison Avenue, in 2002.

In 2005 Ito En applied to the U.S. Food and Drug Administration (FDA) for permission to make health claims for its green tea products in the United States. This effort received a setback, however, when the FDA, after reviewing the clinical research on the subject, found no evidence of green tea's effectiveness in preventing certain diseases, including cancer.

Undeterred, Ito En continued to pursue growth in the functional foods market. In 2004 the company launched a new 100 percent vegetable drink for the Japanese market, Ichinichibun no Yasai (literally "a day's worth of vegetables"), which promised to meet the government guidelines for daily vegetable consumption. Ito En also rolled out a number of variations of its Oi Ocha flagship, including the stronger-tasting Koi Aji, in 2004.

In the United States, Ito En teamed up with well-known health expert Dr. Andrew Weil to launch a new line of green tea-based beverages under the Dr. Andrew Weil for Tea brand in 2007. By the end of that year, Ito En had also entered the mainstream distribution channels in the United States for the first time, placing its products all across the country in such store chains as Wal-Mart and Kroger.

Ito En had also completed a series of acquisitions. In 2006 the company acquired Mason Distributors Inc., based in Florida, a distributor of vitamins and other health supplements. The following year, the company bought majority control of the Tully's Coffee chain in Japan. These acquisitions were followed by that of the license for the Evian mineral water brand, acquired in 2008, allowing Ito En to add its first operations in that beverage category as well. With revenues of nearly ¥330 billion ($3 billion) in 2007, Ito En had grown into one of Japan's leading beverage champions.

M. L. Cohen

PRINCIPAL SUBSIDIARIES

Fujian New Oolong Drink Co., Ltd. (China); Ito En (North America) Inc. (USA); Ito En Australia Pty. Ltd.; Ito En Kansai-Chagyo, Ltd.; Ito En Sangyo Ltd.; Ito En (USA) Inc.; Mason Distributors, Inc.; Ningbo Shunyi Tea Products Co., Ltd. (China); Okinawa Ito En, Ltd.; Tully's Coffee Japan Co., Ltd.

PRINCIPAL COMPETITORS

Japan Tobacco Inc.; Asahi Breweries Ltd.; Morinaga Milk Industry Company Ltd.; QP Corp.; Meiji Seika Kaisha Ltd.; Kaneka Corp.; Snow Brand Milk Products Company Ltd.; Ezaki Glico Company Ltd.

FURTHER READING

Honjo, Yosuke, "More Than Green Tea," *Beverage World,* October 15, 2007, p. 34.

"Ito En Makes Plastic with Tea Leaves, Antibacterial Power," *AsiaPulse News,* August 14, 2003.

"Ito En + Andrew Weil, M.D. = One Healthy Drink!" *Tea & Coffee Trade Journal,* June 2007, p. 60.

"Ito En Set to Acquire 51% Stake in Tully's Coffee Chain Operator," *Kyodo News International,* October 26, 2006.

"Ito En Set to Launch Tea Garden Operations," *Kyodo New International,* May 11, 2005.

"Ito En Tea Shop Ranked As NYC's Best Tea Emporium," *Gourmet Retailer,* November 13, 2007.

"Japan Firm Ito En Completes Green Tea Plant in Australia," *Kyodo News International,* October 19, 2004.

"Japanese Set Up $5M Plant in Victoria," *Tea & Coffee Trade Journal,* March 1999, p. 10.

"Japan's Ito En Aims for Green Tea Health Claim Permission in US," *AsiaPulse News,* August 24, 2005.

Johnsen, Michael, "Mason Vitamins," *Drug Store News,* July 17, 2006, p. 31.

"Just What the Doctor Ordered," *Beverage World,* July 15, 2007, p. 16.

"New Cup Coffee Container from Ito En," *Cosmetics & Toiletries & Household Products Marketing News in Japan,* April 25, 2008.

"Tea Lovers Turning to New Leaf," *Business Asia,* September 13, 1999, p. 9.

"Unique Green Tea Beverage," *Cosmetics & Toiletries & Household Products Marketing News in Japan,* October 25, 2008.

Jaiprakash Associates Limited

———————————■———————————

JA House, 63 Basant Lok, Vasant Vihar
New Delhi, 110 057
India
Telephone: (+91 011) 2614 1540
Fax: (+91 011) 2614 5389
Web site: http://www.jilindia.com

Public Company
Incorporated: 1972 as Jaiprakash Associates Private Ltd.
Employees: 25,000
Sales: INR 39.85 billion ($943.9 million) (2008)
Stock Exchanges: Mumbai
Ticker Symbol: 500888
NAICS: 551112 Offices of Other Holding Companies; 237990 Other Heavy and Civil Engineering Construction; 327310 Cement Manufacturing

■ ■ ■

Jaiprakash Associates Limited (Jaypee Group) is one of India's largest conglomerates. Its publicly listed flagship company is one of India's leading civil engineering and construction companies with particular expertise in the construction of hydroelectric dams and power plants. The company's engineering division has also expanded strongly into the construction of expressways and other highways, including the 165-kilometer Yamuna Expressway and the contract to build the 1,047-kilometer Ganga Expressway. In addition to its civil engineering and construction business, Jaypee has developed a strongly integrated range of operations. Through Jaypee Cement, the company is India's fourth largest cement producer, with an annual capacity of nine million metric tons per year, and plans to expand capacity to more than 30 million metric tons by 2011. In addition to building hydropower facilities, Jaypee has also entered the private power generation sector, through its control of Jaiprakash Hydro-Power Limited. That company had a total generation capacity of more than 1,800 megawatts in 2008, while participating in projects to add more than 3,000 megawatts into the next decade. Jaypee is also active in real estate development and hospitality sectors, notably through the construction of the Jaypee Greens Golf Resort and the ownership of three five-star hotels. In December 2008, Jaypee restructured its operations, merging most of its integrated companies holdings into Jaiprakash Associates Limited. Jaypee is led by founder and Chairman Jaiprakash Gaur, and his son and CEO Manoj Gaur. Jaypee Group's sales neared INR 40 billion ($950 million) in 2008.

FROM CIVIL SERVANT TO CIVIL ENGINEERING IN 1972

Jaiprakash Gaur earned a degree in civil engineering at the University of Roorkee in 1950, then began a career as a civil servant with the Uttar Pradesh government. As the most populous state in the young Indian nation, Uttar Pradesh offered strong opportunities for private initiatives. Gaur's interest soon turned to the private sector as well, and by 1957 he had established a contracting business in Kota. The following year Gaur left the civil service, starting his own civil engineering contracting firm. Gaur's operations grew strongly, and in 1972

COMPANY PERSPECTIVES

Vision: As a group, we are committed to strategic business development in infrastructure, as the key to nation building in the 21st century. We aim to achieve perfection in everything we undertake with a commitment to excel. It is the determination to transform every challenge into opportunity; to seize every opportunity to ensure growth and to grow with a human face. Mission: Our solitary Mission is to achieve Excellence in every sector that we operate in—be it Engineering & Construction, Cement, Real Estate or Consultancy.

he incorporated the company as a partnership, Jaiprakash Associates.

Jaiprakash emerged as a leading construction and engineering group in India. The company developed particular expertise in the design and construction of hydroelectric dams, as the Indian government sought to harness the country's many rivers as a renewable and economical source of power.

Over the next decades, Jaiprakash participated in many of the country's landmark infrastructure projects. These included the Veerbhadra Barrage, the Karjan Concrete Gravity Dam, the Vadgam Saddle Dam, and the Chamera Concrete Gravity Dam. The company also participated in Stages I and II of the construction of the Lakhya Earthen Dam. Jaiprakash also completed a number of industrial projects, such as the Vishakhapatnam Steel Plant. Nonetheless, hydropower installations remained the group's main focus. Through the end of the century, Jaiprakash grew into one of the leading companies in its sector, involved in as many as 13 simultaneous hydropower projects, spanning six states as well as across the border in Bhutan.

CEMENTING ITS POSITION IN 1983

Jaiprakash Gaur was joined by son Manoj Gaur in the early 1980s, which sparked the company's first diversification efforts. Unlike the case of many of India's fast-growing conglomerates, which often established widely diversified businesses, the expansion of the Gaur family's business interests took on a more integrated form. One of the group's first extensions beyond civil engineering brought the company into the hospitality market, through the construction of two five-star hotels,

the Siddharth and Vasant Continental, established in 1980.

On the other end of the spectrum, the growing company entered the market for construction materials, establishing a new company, Jaypee Rewa Cement Plant, in Madhya Pradesh in 1983. By 1986, that subsidiary had commenced production, with an initial capacity of one million metric tons per year. At that time, the family merged Jaiprakash Associates and Jaypee Rewa into a single entity, renamed Jaiprakash Industries Ltd. (JIL). Over the next decade, the company established one of India's strongest cement brands, supported by its own limestone mining operations. By 1992, the company had completed an extension of the original Rewa complex, opening a second plant and raising its total output to 2.5 million metric tons per year.

Manoj Gaur took the leadership role in expanding the group's cement operations. In 1995, the company created a new subsidiary, Bela Cement Co.; by the following year, the Bela plant had launched production, boosting the group's total capacity by another 1.5 million metric tons per year. With an eye toward further expansion, JIL transferred control of the two Rewa cement plants to its Bela cement subsidiary. That company was then renamed Jaypee Cement. By then, it represented some 50 percent of Jaiprakash Industries' total revenues.

Nonetheless, in 2000, Jaiprakash Group announced its interest in selling a 49 percent stake in Jaypee Cement to an outside investor. A number of major international cement groups, including Italcementi, Lafarge, Blue Circle, and Cemex, expressed interest in acquiring the stake. Yet Jaiprakash soon changed course, and launched a new expansion of its cement operations. In 2002, for example, the company completed construction of a cement blending facility in Sadva, with an annual capacity of 600,000 metric tons. This facility was followed by a one million-ton-per-year grinding facility in Tanda, Faizabad, in 2004. By then, the importance of Jaypee Cement to the group as a whole was underscored when the Jaiprakash family launched a restructuring of its holdings, merging Jaypee Cement and Jaiprakash Industries into a single company, Jaiprakash Associates.

TARGETING THE TOP FOR 2011

The year 2006 marked a new milestone for Jaypee Cement, as it completed the acquisition of the ailing state-owned company UP State Cement Corporation. That company added more than two million metric tons to Jaypee's annual capacity, raising its total to nine million metric tons per year. The UP State Cement purchase also gave Jaypee three new cement production plants, at Churk, Chunar, and Dala.

KEY DATES

1958: Jaiprakash Gaur founds a civil engineering contracting business in Uttar Pradesh, India.

1972: Gaur reincorporates his company as a partnership, Jaiprakash Associates.

1986: The company commissions its first cement plant, in Rewa, which forms the basis for Jaypee Cement.

1992: Jaypee Cement adds a second cement plant in Rewa; the company forms Jaiprakash Hydro Power Ltd. to enter the hydroelectric power generation market.

1995: Bela Cement Co. is founded as the company's third cement plant.

2005: Jaiprakash Hydro Power becomes the first private hydropower company to list on the Mumbai Stock Exchange.

2008: Jaypee Group restructures its operations, merging most of its subsidiaries into Jaiprakash Associates.

At the same time, Jaypee proceeded with construction of a three million metric ton cement plant in Himachal Pradesh, expected to be ready for production by 2007. In the meantime, Jaypee remained on the lookout for acquisitions. Opportunity came again soon after the UP acquisition, when the company agreed to purchase Guarat Anjan Cement, a company then in the process of building its 1.2 million metric ton cement plant in Kutch, in Gujarat. The purchase was of added strategic importance, allowing Jaypee to enter the western Indian market for the first time, and, especially, to gain access to the export market through the Kutch seaport. Also in 2006, Jaypee Cement launched construction of another greenfield cement plant, a 1.5 million metric ton facility in Sidhi, near Rewa.

Jaypee continued to expand its cement position into the second half of the first decade of the 2000s, as the booming growth of India's economy stimulated demand. The company began revising its targets upward, from 15 million metric tons, to 26 million metric tons, and finally to more than 30.5 million metric tons by 2011. Among the initiatives taken to meet this goal was a joint venture created with the Steel Authority of India (SAIL) to establish two new cement plants, both with a capacity of more than two million metric tons per year. By the end of 2008, Jaypee Ce-

ment had established itself as the third largest cement producer in India.

HYDROPOWERED EXPANSION IN THE 21ST CENTURY

Jaiprakash Group, later known as Jaypee Group, had in the meantime begun exploring other areas of expansion. In 2000, for example, the company moved into the real estate development sector, in part as an expansion of its existing hospitality operations. For this, the company acquired a 438-acre golf resort and sports complex project originally launched by Sterling Resorts. The company renamed the project Jaypee Greens Golf Resort. The success of this project led the group to launch a still more ambitious development project, a 1,160-acre "integrated township," complete with residential homes, medical and educational facilities, a commercial center, and two golf courses. That project, called Jaypee Greens Noida, got underway in 2007.

By then, Jaypee had been developing another major pole of operations: power generation. This effort began in the early 1990s, when the Indian government, in a new effort to develop the country's hydroelectric power capacity, announced its intention to allow the development of private sector hydroelectric power plants. Jaiprakash recognized the opportunity to extend its longstanding expertise in the hydropower construction sector, and in 1992 created subsidiary Jaiprakash Hydro Power Ltd. In that year, the company received authorization for its first power generation facility, a 300-megawatt facility at Baspa. That project was completed in 2003.

The successful implementation of the Baspa plant led Jaypee to take its power generation arm public, and in 2005 Jaiprakash Hydro Power became the first hydroelectric company to go public in India. By then, the company had a number of other power generation projects in the works, including the 400-megawatt Vishnu Prayag plant. That project was completed in 2006 and established the company as India's largest private hydroelectric power producer. By the end of 2008, the company had completed several other power plant projects, raising its total output to nearly 1,900 megawatts. By then, the company had several new plants under construction, including a 2,000-megawatt project on the Lower Siang, expected to be completed by 2014.

At the same time, Jaypee Group began to venture beyond the hydroelectric sector, launching its first thermal power developments in 2008. The company began developing a 1,320-megawatt coal-based complex in Nigrie. Then, in May 2008, the group acquired Bina

Power Supply, part of the Aditya Birla Group, which held the authorization to build a 1,000-megawatt site in Bina, Madhya Pradesh. Meanwhile, the company had also begun looking into alternative and renewable fuel sources. In 2008, the company built its first wind farms, with a total capacity of less than 60 megawatts. Also that year, the company commissioned a municipal solid waste power plant in Chandigarh.

The success of its various operations led Jaypee to restructure its holdings again at the end of 2008. As part of that effort, the company merged a number of its subsidiaries, including Jaypee Cement, Jaypee Hotels, and others, directly into Jaiprakash Associates. The move was expected to develop significant operating synergies and cost reductions for the group. As the company turned toward the beginning of the next decade, Jaypee Group had established itself as a strongly focused and integrated conglomerate, not to mention a major force driving the Indian economy.

M. L. Cohen

PRINCIPAL SUBSIDIARIES

Bhilai Jaypee Cement Limited (74%); Bokaro Jaypee Cement Limited (74%); Gujarat Anjan Cement Limited (99.88%); Gujarat Jaypee Cement & Infrastructure Limited; Himalayan Expressway Limited; Jaiprakash Hydro-Power Limited (63.34%); Jaiprakash Power Ventures Limited (80.56%); Jaypee Cement Limited; Jaypee Ganga Infrastructure Corporation Limited; Jaypee Hotels Limited (72.18%); Jaypee Infratech Limited (98.96%); Jaypee Karcham Hydro Corporation Limited (100%); Jaypee Powergrid Limited (74%); JPSK Sports Private Limited (61.70%); Madhya Pradesh Jaypee Minerals Limited (70%).

PRINCIPAL COMPETITORS

Tata Sons Ltd.; NTPC Ltd.; Larsen and Toubro Ltd.; National Projects Construction Corporation Ltd.; IVRCL Infrastructures and Projects Ltd.; Nagarjuna Constructions Company Ltd.; GMR Infrastructure Ltd.; Hindustan Construction Company Ltd.; Punj Lloyd Ltd.; Gammon India Ltd.

FURTHER READING

Choudhary, Sanjeev, "Jaypee Buys Bina Power from Aditya Birla Group," *Economic Times,* May 23, 2008.

———, "Jaypee Eyes 5MT Cement Unit in Middle East," *Economic Times,* December 8, 2007.

———, "Jaypee Group May Partner Houston Airport System," *Economic Times,* December 4, 2007.

———, "SAIL Ties up with Jaypee for Cement Unit," *Economic Times,* July 12, 2007.

Guarie, Misra, Shekhar Jha Mayur, and Joji Thomas Philip, "Jaypee Group, Future Join the Telecom Rush," *Economic Times,* September 29, 2007.

Jayaswal, Rajeev, "Jaypee Leads Race for ICICI's 45% Stake in Prize Petro," *Economic Times,* March 19, 2008.

"JPA Gives Nod for Amalgamation of Four Arms," *Financial Express,* December 23, 2008.

Mathew, James, "Jaypee Acquires UP Cement's Assets with Rs 459-crore Bid," *Economic Times,* January 31, 2006.

———, "Jaypee Group to Acquire Gujarat Anjan Cement," *Economic Times,* May 2, 2006.

JDA Software Group, Inc.

14400 North 87th Street
Scottsdale, Arizona 85260-3649
U.S.A.
Telephone: (480) 308-3000
Toll Free: (800) 438-5301
Fax: (480) 308-3001
Web site: http://www.jda.com

Public Company
Founded: 1985
Employees: 1,500
Sales: $390.3 million (2008)
Stock Exchanges: NASDAQ
Ticker Symbol: JDAS
NAICS: 511210 Software Publishers

■ ■ ■

JDA Software Group, Inc., is a Scottsdale, Arizona-based software maker that provides many of the world's top companies with comprehensive, integrated software programming to manage their businesses. JDA's customized programs provide its retail, manufacturing, and distribution clients with high-performance, money-saving business applications. JDA designs and installs its software programs for clients in 60 countries worldwide, allowing sophisticated tracking from raw material purchases to finished products and services.

CANADIAN ROOTS: SEVENTIES

JDA Software traces its roots to a similarly named company founded in Calgary, Alberta, in 1978. James D. Armstrong formed JDA Software Services using his initials, and was a maverick in the little-known field of retail software programming. Armstrong designed an effective merchandise tracking software and soon became one of Canada's leading IBM-based midrange software providers.

Armstrong sold the business in 1985 and moved south of the Canadian border to Ohio where, with partner Frederick Pakis, he formed a new company: JDA Software Group, Inc., in Cleveland. The founders' vision was similar to the Canadian venture: to sell quality, packaged software and to provide consulting services to the retail industry, which had become increasingly automated. Businesses needed sophisticated software to manage the vast amount of information generated by sales, returns, and inventory levels.

JDA's primary product, Merchandise Management System, operated on an IBM AS/400 platform and compiled data so users could make sound decisions about products, margins, inventory, and efficiency. The company's first big contract came in 1987 from a Phoenix, Arizona-based automotive dealer. To serve this new client better, JDA's management—Armstrong as chief executive and Pakis as president—and its handful of employees packed up and moved to Arizona.

Newly settled in Scottsdale, within the greater Phoenix metropolitan area, JDA Software had no trouble finding new clients for its business software. As word spread about JDA's software capabilities, the firm began signing local, regional, and national clients.

COMPANY PERSPECTIVES

JDA Software Group, Inc., is focused on helping companies realize real supply chain and revenue management results—fast. JDA Software delivers integrated merchandising as well as supply chain and revenue management planning, execution, and optimization solutions for the consumer-driven supply chain and services industries. Through its industry leading solutions, leading manufacturers, distributors, retailers and services companies around the world are growing their businesses with greater predictability and more profitability.

GROWTH AND EXPANSION: NINETIES

The company's first acquisition came from sibling JDA Canada with the purchase of DSS (distributed store system) software, comprised of in-store and data warehousing tracking systems, in 1994. DSS's capabilities allowed the American JDA to segue into open-platform products using either DOS- or Windows-based operating systems. The move proved prescient as JDA's reputation for comprehensive, flexible products grew, as did its revenues, which climbed to almost $50 million for 1995.

The next year, JDA was ready to take the plunge and become a publicly traded company. On March 16 the company made its initial public offering (IPO) on the NASDAQ of 3.1 million shares at $13 each. The company, which boasted a number of high profile clients like Gucci, Helzberg Diamonds, Laura Ashley, Staples, and Sunglass Hut, planned to use the offering's $40 million in proceeds to expand its product line and to cover the costs of acquiring the original JDA firm founded in Canada.

With the two JDA companies combined, Armstrong oversaw a rapidly expanding workforce and growing international clientele. He relinquished day-to-day operations to Brent Lippman in 1997, who came on board as COO. Armstrong remained CEO and with cofounder Pakis became co-chairman of the board. The company also launched its Windows-based data warehousing software package, Retail IDEAS, and in-store system (Win/DSS) for retail management, both of which could be professionally installed and customized by JDA specialists. JDA's growth caught the eye of *Forbes* magazine, which named it one of the nation's top 200 small companies in November 1997. Annual sales topped $61 million as JDA sought additional space for its burgeoning operations, which included JDA University, a training facility for students to learn JDA's unique software programs.

Acquisitions continued to bolster JDA's holdings and management technology: LIOCS Corporation in 1997 and Michigan-based Arthur enterprise software designer in 1998. Each gave clients including Cabela's (sporting goods), CompUSA (computers), The Limited (apparel), Planet Hollywood (restaurants), Sony (electronics), Starbucks (beverages), and Wolf Cameras (photography) fast, easy access to merchandising information to manage their businesses and optimize profitability.

In the third quarter of 1998 JDA stumbled and announced it would not meet expectations; the company actually went into the red and by January 1999 changes were underway. The company canceled a proposed joint venture with Baan Company and replaced CEO Lippman with Armstrong. By the fourth quarter of 1999, JDA was back on track, having invested heavily in research and development (R&D) and signing several big-name clients including Joan & David and Estée Lauder. The company then partnered with the California-based Blue Martini Software to offer fully integrated merchandising solutions for both brick-and-mortar stores and Internet companies. JDA finished 1999 with sales of just under $100 million and a workforce of about 1,200.

THE NEW MILLENNIUM: 2000–03

By the dawn of the new century, JDA Software was poised to become an international powerhouse. Its proprietary software was firmly established throughout the United States and Canada, but the firm would settle for nothing less than worldwide domination. As JDA moved forward, cofounder Pakis left his post as co-chairman and moved on to different pastures. At the helm, Armstrong moved forward with expansion plans, paying $20.5 million for the Texas-based Intactix International, Inc., in April, followed by the $20 million acquisition of Marietta, Georgia-based E3 Corporation in 2001. Both buys increased JDA's business-to-business (B2B) solution clients by the thousands, including a slew of new international clients in nearly two dozen countries including Australia, Chile, Japan, Mexico, and the United Kingdom.

Also in 2001 came the purchase of Accrue Software Inc.'s Vista sales software assets, and a joint venture with J.D. Edwards Canada, Ltd., (a division of J.D. Edwards & Company) to unite their software programs for a Quebec-based liquor distributor. J.D. Edwards, maker of

KEY DATES

1978: James D. Armstrong founds JDA Software Services in Calgary, Alberta.

1985: The Canadian JDA software business is sold and JDA Software Group, Inc., is formed in Ohio.

1987: Landing a major Arizona client, the new company moves its operations to Scottsdale, Arizona.

1994: The firm buys DSS from JDA Canada to develop open-platform products.

1996: JDA goes public on the NASDAQ in March and buys its Canadian counterpart.

1998: JDA acquires Comshare's Arthur retail software unit.

2000: The company purchases Intactix, a Texas-based merchandise planning and B2B software firm.

2001: JDA acquires E3 Corporation and its optimization software, adding 500-plus new clients.

2006: The company acquires Manugistics to increase its demand management and logistics capabilities.

2008: JDA partners with Management Dynamics Inc. to deliver supply chain solutions.

2009: Virgin Stores SA signs on with JDA for custom management and inventory software programs.

the OneWorld Internet-based enterprise software package, integrated JDA's Portfolio package (launched the year before) to create a customized merchandising program. Sales for 2001 reached $206.9 million, up 20 percent from 2000's $171.7 million.

By 2002 JDA continued to tweak its offerings and signed new "Tier 2" retail clients (those with sales from $100 million to $5 billion), including Brooks Brothers, CVS Corporation, Dollar Tree Stores, Galyan's Trading Company, Kmart Corporation, Rite Aid, and Royal Ahold, N.V. With more than 40 customizable merchandising programs, JDA offered its clients time-saving, profit-maximizing packages and a herd of programmers and specialists to install, troubleshoot, and maintain the systems.

In 2003, Armstrong again stepped down as CEO, but remained chairman. Hamish Brewer, who had served as the company's president since 2001 and had been with the company in various positions since 1994, was named chief executive. Brewer had his hands full with a sluggish economy and soft information technology market. Eyeing the future, JDA moved ahead with acquisitions, including content management software maker Engage, Inc., for $3.5 million and workforce management software firm Timera Texas, Inc., for $14.1 million. The company managed to finish the year with revenues of $207.4 million, down from 2002's $219.5 million, but a respectable showing in the weak software market.

REGROUPING FOR THE FUTURE: 2004 AND BEYOND

As the software market slowly recovered, JDA executives were cautiously optimistic. The company invested in an additional 136,000 square feet of office space in Scottsdale and upped its R&D spending to develop new products and broaden the scope of its established applications. Research and development expenditures for 2004 accounted for 24 percent of revenues, up 5 percent from two years earlier, amounting to $52.8 million of the year's $216.9 million. While 2005's revenues dipped slightly to $215.8 million, the company was on track to come back with a vengeance.

A major acquisition came in 2006 with the $212 million purchase of Manugistics Group, Inc., a demand management, pricing optimization, and transportation/logistics applications firm. Manugistics significantly broadened JDA's supply chain solutions and spurred major growth in this segment, especially with Tier 1 (sales in excess of $5 billion) clients including Coca-Cola Enterprises, Heinz, Kraft Foods, and Tyson. Despite the ups and downs of the economy, JDA's market share increased as its supply and demand software took off and revenues leapt to $277.5 million for the year. Other new clients drawn to JDA's increasingly sophisticated software packages included Black & Decker, Continental Airlines, Inc., and Thomson Holidays Ltd.

The company announced a strategic alliance with Management Dynamics Inc., a global trade management software firm, in 2008. The partnership added to JDA's growing supply chain and information services. Next came the announced merger of JDA and i2 Technologies, creating a supply chain software powerhouse, big enough to cause headaches for such towering competitors as SAP AG and Oracle Corporation. In December 2008, however, the planned $346 million acquisition was called off after i2's stock plummeted to nearly half its value.

As i2's fortunes seemed questionable, JDA's annual revenues had climbed to $390.3 million for 2008, up slightly from the previous year's $373.6 million. Not wasting time on what might have been with the i2 merger, JDA moved forward in 2009, signing Virgin Stores SA as a new client to provide customized management and inventory applications for its music outlets.

Nelson Rhodes

PRINCIPAL OPERATING UNITS

Retail Enterprise Systems; In-Store Systems; Collaborative Solutions.

PRINCIPAL COMPETITORS

AC Nielsen Corporation; i2 Technologies, Inc.; IBM Corporation; Microsoft Corporation; Oracle Corporation; Retek Inc., SAP AG; Workplace Systems International.

FURTHER READING

Amato-McCoy, Deena M., "An Enterprise Plan," *Chain Store Age,* November 2006, pp. 56+.

Beerens, Marie, "JDA Helps Optimize Supply-Demand Chain," *Investor's Business Daily,* June 12, 2007, p. B08.

Bonasia, J., "JDA Escapes Sales Slump by Meeting Demand for Packaged Software," *Investor's Business Daily,* March 25, 2002, p. A06.

Calandra, Bob, "Live Wires," *Sporting Goods Business,* February 4, 1998, pp. 84+.

Hoffman, William, "Going It Alone," *Traffic World,* January 12, 2009, p. 16.

———, "Then There Was One," *Traffic World,* August 18, 2008, p. 17.

"J.D. Edwards & Company," *Market News Publishing,* June 11, 2001.

"JDA Co-Founder Resigns," *Business Journal (Phoenix),* September 1, 2000, p. 45.

"JDA, i2 Technologies Merger Scrapped," *Traffic World,* December 15, 2008, p. 15.

"JDA Software and Management Dynamics Inc. Form Strategic Alliance to Drive Improvements in Global Trade Management," *Traffic World,* February 21, 2008.

"JDA Software Buys Intactix," *Business Journal (Phoenix),* April 14, 2000, p. 66.

"JDA Software Group," *Washington Business Journal,* September 14, 2001, p. 34.

"JDA Software Group, Inc.," *Business Journal (Phoenix),* June 28, 1996, p. 64B.

"JDA Software Group, Inc." *Drug Store News,* October 25, 1999, p. 65.

"JDA Software Profit Tumbles As Software Sales Sink," *America's Intelligence Wire,* July 24, 2006.

"JDA's E3 Proves Collaborative Technology Generates Value," *Drug Store News,* November 19, 2001, p. S28.

Maiello, Michael, "Hard Luck Software," *Forbes,* November 24, 2003, p. 11.

Netherton, Martha, and Ken Brown, "JDA Software Searching for More Space," *Business Journal (Phoenix),* January 23, 1998, pp. 1+.

"New Win/DSS from JDA," *Computer Dealer News,* June 23, 2000, p. 50.

Rolwing, Rebecca, "JDA Software Group Looks to Triple Revenue," *Business Journal (Phoenix),* July 5, 1996, p. 13.

Shinkle, Kirk, "JDA Software Group Inc.: Helping Stores Manage Is Software Firm's Goal," *Investor's Business Daily,* July 27, 2001, p. A10.

Smith, Tom, "JDA Preps Major Product Update," *InternetWeek,* June 20, 2002.

———, "Retail Software Vendor JDA," *InternetWeek,* October 8, 2002.

———, "Retail Systems Vendor JDA to Beat Expectations," *InternetWeek,* April 9, 2002.

Stedman, Craig, "Baan, JDA Software Scrap Retail Venture," *Computerworld,* January 11, 1999, p. 14.

Teichgraeber, Tara, "JDA Expands Product Reach," *Business Journal (Phoenix),* July 6, 2001, p. 16.

———, "JDA Software Brings Out 'Portfolio' for Retailers," *Business Journal (Phoenix),* June 30, 2000, p. 9.

———, "Senior Management Team Members Added at JDA," *Business Journal (Phoenix),* November 10, 2000, p. 24.

Trebilcock, Bob, "Top 20 Supply Chain Management Software Suppliers," *Modern Materials Handling,* July 1, 2008, p. 33.

John B. Sanfilippo & Son, Inc.

1703 North Randall Road
Elgin, Illinois 60123-7820
U.S.A.
Telephone: (847) 289-1800
Fax: (847) 289-1843
Web site: http://www.jbssinc.com

Public Company
Incorporated: 1959
Employees: 1,500
Sales: $541.8 million (2008)
Stock Exchanges: NASDAQ
Ticker Symbol: JBSS
NAICS: 311911 Roasted Nuts and Peanut Butter
    Manufacturing

■ ■ ■

John B. Sanfilippo & Son, Inc., is the nation's second largest distributor of full-line nut products, after the Planters division of Kraft Foods, Inc. Nestled in suburban Chicago, Sanfilippo processes, packages, markets, and distributes thousands of nut and snack products under several brands, including the very popular Fisher, as well as Evon's, Sunshine Country, Flavor Tree, and Texas Pride. In addition, Sanfilippo also sells and packages numerous private-label products for companies across the nation.

ORIGINS IN PECAN SHELLING

Sanfilippo started as a small pecan shelling operation in Chicago, early in the 20th century. At the time, pecan shelling was a cottage industry, with hundreds of small shellers supplying larger processors, distributors, and retail channels. Chicago, the center of the pecan shelling industry, had as many as 70 pecan-shelling businesses by the time of the Great Depression. Manual shelling was typically performed by the large immigrant population, and one such sheller was Gaspare Sanfilippo, of Sicily. By the time Sanfilippo's Sicilian-born son, John, was ten years old, he too worked as a pecan sheller.

Individual pecan shellers processed about 45 pounds of shelled pecans a day, earning around $6 for their labor. By 1922 the Sanfilippos were able to open their own pecan shelling business in a storefront on Chicago's Division Street. The company's output climbed to 40,000 pounds per month and the first Sanfilippo processing facility was built in 1929. For the next 40 years Sanfilippo supplied a customer base of retail nut shops, distributors, and several large candy and other confectionery manufacturers. Pecan shelling remained their sole source of revenue.

John Sanfilippo's son Jasper entered the family business at the age of nine. In the early 1950s, when John fell ill, Jasper took a one-year leave of absence from college to manage the business. After college, Jasper rejoined his father and, in 1959, they changed the name to John B. Sanfilippo & Son. Operations moved to a new building located on Montrose Avenue on the northwest side of Chicago.

The company began to diversify its product line as the pecan shelling industry began to change. The introduction of new machinery made it possible to shell greater quantities of pecans; the growth of national

COMPANY PERSPECTIVES

John B. Sanfilippo & Son, Inc., is an in-house sheller, processor, packager, marketer and distributor of shelled and in-shell nuts which are sold under a variety of private labels and under the company's Fisher, Evon's, Flavor Tree, Sunshine Country and Texas Pride brand names. The company also markets and distributes, and in most cases, manufactures or processes a diverse product line of food and snack items including peanut butter, candy, natural snacks, trail mixes, extruded corn snacks and sesame sticks.

distribution channels in the years following World War II made it possible for a single sheller to serve a wider area. The increased competition in turn led processors and consumers to demand higher product consistency and quality. Many of the smaller shelling operations began to disappear as the industry consolidated into fewer, larger nut processors.

JASPER TAKES THE REINS

Jasper took leadership of the company after John's death in 1963, a year in which the company's sales topped $300,000. Jasper was soon joined by his brother-in-law, Mathias Valentine. Sanfilippo stepped up its diversification, entering distribution deals with almond, walnut, and peanut shellers. The company organized a network of brokers to sell its products, marketing to bakeries, candy manufacturers, and other confectioners. Sanfilippo also moved into retail sales, packaging its products under the "Prairie State" brand name.

The company enjoyed modest success through the 1960s. Everything changed in 1974 when H.H. Evon Company of Chicago, which distributed nutmeats throughout the Midwest under the Evon's brand name, went bankrupt. Evon defaulted on its $90,000 debt to Sanfilippo. Rather than demand a cash payment, Sanfilippo agreed to acquire the Evon brand name, as well as the company's small fleet of delivery trucks and its midwest distribution business. Sanfilippo dropped its Prairie State brand and began to market the bulk of its products under the Evon name. The fleet of trucks allowed Sanfilippo to initiate the store-to-door distribution of its products beyond Chicago.

With the acquisition of the assets of Evon, Sanfilippo entered a new era of sustained growth. At the same time, quality and consistency became even more vital for

the company in view of increasing consumer sophistication and the growth of national brands such as Planters and Fisher Nuts. Differences in growing and storage conditions and variable shelling, roasting, and packaging processes among its many suppliers affected not only the taste and appearance of their products, but also the size grading. Since Sanfilippo sought greater control of the handling and quality of its raw products, the company moved toward a vertical integration of its production process.

GROWTH AND MODERNIZATION: 1980–94

In 1980 Sanfilippo constructed a modern pecan processing facility, designed by Jasper, in Elk Grove Village in Illinois. The company also moved its corporate headquarters to a 135,000-square-foot processing complex, which took two years and $9 million to build. The new plant incorporated the latest technological advances, including a high degree of automation, allowing Sanfilippo to control the full range of its manufacturing processes, from processing to packaging to distribution. The move also cut costs and raised the profit margins in its processing operations.

The company's growth continued throughout the 1980s. In 1984 Sanfilippo entered the bulk foods market with its acquisition of Midwest Nut & Seed Company, helping propel sales to $56 million. As business increased, Sanfilippo had to expand its distribution facility in Elk Grove. Before the end of the decade, the plant was expanded twice, first in 1985 and again in 1989, to a total of 300,000 square feet. Sales for 1985 had reached almost $79 million and were well on their way to the $100 million mark when the company constructed a 200,000-square-foot production and warehouse facility in Bainbridge, Georgia, in 1987. The new plant featured complete continuous-line shelling, blanching, processing, and packaging capabilities, with a production capacity of 120 million pounds per year. It became the first and only peanut plant in the world capable of performing the entire production process.

In 1990 sales had swelled to $152 million and the company began to think about marketing its products internationally. The following year, 1991, brought sales of $161 million with production reaching 103 million pounds of peanuts, 37 million pounds of walnuts, pecans, and other nut products, and an additional 38 million pounds of other snack items. These goods were shipped to more than 6,000 retail, wholesale, foodservice, industrial, and government customers across the country. Its expansion and exploration of overseas markets, however, had left Sanfilippo with nearly $60 million in debt and a high debt-to-equity ratio.

KEY DATES

■

1922: The Sanfilippo family opens a pecan shelling business in Chicago.

1929: The company's first processing facility is built in Chicago.

1959: The company name is changed to John B. Sanfilippo & Son after John's son Jasper joins the business full-time.

1963: John Sanfilippo dies and son Jasper takes over the business.

1974: Sanfilippo buys the bankrupt H.H. Evon Company and its distribution network.

1980: A new processing facility is built in Elk Grove Village, Illinois.

1984: Sanfilippo enters the bulk nut market by acquiring Midwest Nut & Seed Company.

1987: A new production and warehouse facility is built in Bainbridge, Georgia.

1991: Sanfilippo goes public on the NASDAQ at $12 per share.

1993: The company acquires the Gustine, California-based Crane Walnut Orchards.

1995: Sanfilippo signs with Supervalu to produce nuts for its Preferred private-label nut brands, and buys Procter & Gamble's top peanut brand, Fisher Nuts.

1998: Sanfilippo begins making foreign-language labels in French, Spanish, Dutch, and German.

2000: Fisher Nuts becomes the official peanut for the Chicago Cubs baseball team.

2004: Fisher becomes the official peanut of the Chicago White Sox and New York Mets.

2007: Sanfilippo moves to a new headquarters/production facility in Elgin, Illinois.

2008: Jasper Sanfilippo Sr. steps down as chairman, leaving the business to sons Jasper Jr. (COO, president) and Jeffrey (CEO, chairman).

Nevertheless, as the industry continued to consolidate, Sanfilippo planned an aggressive expansion plan, beginning with an initial public offering (IPO) on the NASDAQ.

Sanfilippo went public in 1991 with an offering of $12 per share and raised $22 million. Part of the proceeds were used to pay down debt and $4.2 million was spent to acquire the San Antonio, Texas-based Sunshine Nut Company and its popular "Sunshine Country" and "Texas Pride" brands. Next came the construction of a new 50-acre, $11.2 million facility in Selma, Texas, to house Sunshine's operations. Sanfilippo completed a second stock offering for $14.25 per share, adding $31.5 million to its coffers.

With its debt-to-equity ratio substantially lowered and newly available credit worth nearly $60 million, the company began implementing its expansion plan, spending $9.5 million for a full-scale, in-shell processing facility in Garysburg, North Carolina. The company followed this move with the $3.2 million cash purchase of California-based Crane Walnut Orchards in 1993, making it a major player in each of the five major nut types and the country's largest fully integrated supplier. Sales for 1993 reached $200 million, and an agreement with Procter & Gamble in 1994 to handle part of its Fisher nut line was a harbinger of good things to come.

NUTS AND MORE: 1995–97

During its expansion, Sanfilippo invested heavily in upgrading its existing plants. The Elk Grove facility's shipping and receiving capacity was increased by an additional 475,000 square feet, while another plant was built in Arlington Heights, Illinois, for $5.3 million. Sanfilippo also spent $9.7 million redesigning its recently acquired California walnut facility, while each of the company's existing facilities were retrofitted with updated technology.

Much of Sanfilippo's production technology was designed, invented, and even patented by its in-house industrial engineers. For the walnut plant, the engineering team adapted its pecan-shelling technology to crack each walnut, as opposed to the industry practice of using rollers for mass-cracking, while the company had also built the nation's largest refrigerated storage house to slow the deterioration of nutmeat. In its Arlington Heights plant, Sanfilippo designed a fully automated production system, including a computer-controlled roasting system capable of processing up to 4,000 pounds per hour.

Expansion, coupled with a sluggish economy and declining retail sales, resulted in a sharp drop in earnings in the mid-1990s. Revenues also took a hit, rising only slightly, while an excessive peanut inventory forced the company to take a $1 million write-down.

Sanfilippo's problems turned out to be temporary, however; by 1995 the company closed two major deals to solidify its number two industry position. In May the company announced a ten-year agreement with Supervalu Inc.'s subsidiary Preferred Products Inc., to supply all of its private-label Supervalu nuts, peanut butter, and coconut products. At the time, Sanfilippo processed and/or packaged for 100 other private labels, a market that had grown increasingly important as consumer demand for name-brand products slowed. Nevertheless, Sanfilippo's Evon's brand continued to provide the majority of its revenues, and the company made plans to push deeper into name-brand retail sales.

A further boost to the company came with the fall 1995 acquisition of nearly all assets of Procter & Gamble's Fisher Nut business. Fisher, with 1994 sales of $62 million, represented nearly 5 percent of the market, compared with Sanfilippo's 1.7 percent and Planters' leading 37 percent position in the $1.3 billion market.

Aside from nuts, Sanfilippo's product line included peanut butter, dried coconut and fruit, seeds, snack mixes, crackers, sesame snacks, chocolate and other candies, as well as branded items such as Tootsie Rolls and Jelly Belly jelly beans. Approximately 55 percent of the company's nearly $209 million in 1994 sales was generated through its consumer products, another 31 percent came from industrial sales, and the remainder from contract manufacturing, government, and foodservice channels, with exports making up the smallest percentage of its business.

Sanfilippo's customers included the U.S. Department of Agriculture's Agricultural Stabilization and Conservation Service, the U.S. Department of Defense's Personnel Support Center, national franchises such as McDonald's, as well as airlines, hospitals, universities, schools, and retail restaurants. While the company's products were distributed nationwide, the bulk of Sanfilippo's sales were concentrated in 11 midwestern states and distributed by its own 60-truck fleet. By 1997 Sanfilippo operated ten state-of-the-art processing and packaging facilities in Illinois, Georgia, Texas, North Carolina, and California, and a distribution facility in Nevada.

MOVING FORWARD: 1998–2005

Sanfilippo stepped up its international production by creating foreign-language labels for clients in Canada and Europe in 1999. While the Canadian labels were in French, the "Eurolabels" covered French, Spanish, Dutch, and German labeling. Domestically, the company had been experimenting with packaging sizes and shapes, coming up with Fisher Snack & Serve Nut Bowls, which proved a favorite with retailers and customers alike. Both the new labeling and packaging helped spur sales, which reached $319 million for 1999. The new Nut Bowl line went on to win several industry awards, while Sanfilippo scored another major coup in 2000 when its Fisher brand became the official peanut supplier for the Chicago Cubs baseball club.

In 2001 Sanfilippo acquired Navarro Pecan Company, a Corsicana, Texas-based firm that was one of the United States' largest pecan shellers. Additionally, Sanfilippo continued to reinvent itself by launching new products, such as Fisher peanut butter and healthier snacks under the "Fisher Nature's Nut" brand in 2001 and a "Basics" line of low-priced nut products in 2002. Consumers responded favorably to the new brands, with annual sales topping $341 million for 2001 and a small climb to $343 million in 2002. Like most companies, however, Sanfilippo struggled somewhat after the September 11, 2001, terrorist attacks on the United States, but was able to maintain modest increases in sales, income, and share pricing. The year 2003 brought more robust sales ($409 million), the arrival of nut products by the case to compete with the Sam's Club and Costco warehouse chains, and an advertising campaign capitalizing on its Chicago roots.

After the success of its Chicago Cubs affiliation, Sanfilippo continued the baseball-themed product placement by scoring agreements with the Chicago White Sox, New York Mets, and Minnesota Twins to become the official peanut supplier at their home stadiums in 2004 and 2005. Sales for these years reflected the company's increased exposure, with $521 million in 2004 and $582 million for 2005. Meanwhile, in the company's boardroom, Jasper Sanfilippo remained chairman of the board but had turned over operations of the family business to his sons, Jasper Jr. (COO, president, treasurer) and Jeffrey (CEO). Other key players included Jasper Sr.'s brother-in-law Mathias Valentine and his son Michael (CFO), both board members and major shareholders in the company.

MOVING TO ELGIN: 2006 AND BEYOND

By 2006 Sanfilippo found itself struggling on several fronts. Not only were nut prices soaring, the economy was weakening and consumer demand falling amid health concerns about cholesterol and the fat content of nuts. The company was also in a heated battle with the city of Elgin, Illinois, and its park district, over a chunk of land where Sanfilippo wanted to build a new processing facility and headquarters. Company woes were exacerbated by poor year-end figures, with sales falling $2 million from 2005's $582 million to 2006's $580 million. While the $2 million loss in sales was not horrendous, the net loss of $6.5 million from 2005's profit of $37.1 million was a major misstep.

Sanfilippo bounced back after winning use of the Elgin land; construction on the new HQ was completed in 2007. The company moved into the state-of-the-art million-square-foot facility in September and set its sights on the future. Although the company finished the year with sales hitting only$540.9 million (due in part to costs of the move and new facility), Sanfilippo returned to profitability with income of $2.3 million.

In 2008 Sanfilippo continued to struggle as the economy worsened. Late in the year, there was a changing of the guard as Jasper Sr. turned over his duties as chairman of the board to son Jeffrey, and became chairman emeritus. Jeffrey and brother Jasper Jr. had their work cut out for them, as year-end sales were up slightly to $541.8 million, but the company suffered its second consecutive loss—$6 million. As the end of the decade arrived, companies across the nation and worldwide fought to stay afloat in the volatile economy.

Despite its difficulties, Sanfilippo had much going for it: It remained the second largest nut producer in the United States, and served a loyal customer base of nearly 10,000. It remained an independent, highly successful firm, able to compete against huge, global rivals. Sanfilippo's position as a technological leader in the industry, coupled with its integration of the entire production process, would enable the company to not only survive but thrive in the coming years.

M. L. Cohen
Updated, Nelson Rhodes

PRINCIPAL COMPETITORS

Diamond Foods, Inc.; Kraft Foods, Inc. (Planters); Ralcorp Holdings, Inc.

FURTHER READING

Alva, Marilyn, "John B. Sanfilippo & Son Inc.," *Investor's Business Daily*, November 14, 2003, p. A06.

Canning, Kathie, "New Headquarters Can Handle 'Lots of Nuts,'" *Private Label Buyer*, November 2008, pp. 11+.

Crown, Judith, "Local Nut Tycoon Emerges from His Shell," *Crain's Chicago Business*, August 3, 1992, pp. 3+.

Cummins, Kevin, "Nut Firm Cracks an IPO," *Crain's Chicago Business*, November 11, 1991, p. 53.

Demetratakes, Pan, "From Soap to Nuts: When Sanfilippo Bought Fisher Nut Co. from Procter & Gamble," *Food Processing*, July 1996, pp. 55+.

Keri, Jonah, "Sanfilippo Runs Up, Etches New Pattern," *Investor's Business Daily*, July 15, 2003, p. B08.

Murphy, H. Lee, "Nuts! Airline Ban, Planters Pressure Squeeze Sanfilippo," *Crain's Chicago Business*, November 16, 1998, p. 47.

———, "Ready to Reap Gains from Bumper Crops," *Crain's Chicago Business*, November 15, 1999, p. 26.

Richardson, Patricia, "Tough Nut to Crack," *Crain's Chicago Business*, March 13, 2000, p. 62.

Rogers, Paul, "Peanut Better," *Snack Food*, June 1995.

———, "Shell Game," *Snack Food*, September 1995.

Samuels, Gary, "Nuts to Planters!" *Forbes*, January 17, 1994.

"Sanfilippo & Son to Buy Navarro Pecan Company," *Candy Industry*, September 2001, p. 12.

King's Hawaiian Bakery West, Inc.

———————■———————

19161 Harborgate Way
Torrance, California 90501
U.S.A.
Telephone: (310) 533-3250
Toll Free: (800) 800-5464
Fax: (310) 533-8732
Web site: http://www.kingshawaiian.com

Private Company
Incorporated: 1977
Employees: 278
Sales: $60 million (2007 est.)
NAICS: 311812 Commercial Bakeries; 311813 Frozen Cakes, Pies, and Other Pastries Manufacturing; 722211 Limited-Service Restaurants

■ ■ ■

King's Hawaiian Bakery West, Inc., is best known for its Original Hawaiian Sweet Round Bread, which the company produces at its baking facility in Torrance, California. The company distributes its sweet bread throughout the United States, relying on food brokers to facilitate sales in 29 states. King's Hawaiian Bakery, whose products are found in the bakery sections of retailers such as H.E. Butt Grocery Company, Safeway Inc., and Albertsons LLC, markets a range of bakery products that include loaves of bread, dinner rolls, and sandwich rolls. The company's bread is available in four flavors: Hawaiian Sweet, Honey Wheat, Savory Butter, and 100% Whole Wheat. King's Hawaiian Bakery also owns two restaurants located in Torrance, King's Hawai- ian Bakery & Restaurant and The Local Place Bakery & Café. The company is led by CEO Mark Taira, the son of founder Robert Taira.

ORIGINS

Centuries before Robert Taira's parents emigrated from Japan to Hawaii, Portuguese sailors weighed anchor at the archipelago, using the island chain as a stopping point during their long journey across the Pacific Ocean. Their frequent visits introduced the islands' residents to a staple of the sailors' diet, a soft and sweet bread whose crust quickly hardened, providing a protective cover that preserved the bread during long voyages. The Portuguese sweet bread found a receptive audience on land, becoming a part of the Hawaiian diet that a young Robert Taira first enjoyed while working on a sugarcane plantation in Hilo on the island of Hawaii. Made by plantation workers of Portuguese descent, the round loaves became Taira's passion.

Born in Hilo in 1923, Taira was one of 11 children raised in a family with modest means. He began working at a sugarcane plantation at the age of 13, an experience that not only introduced him to Portuguese sweet bread but also inculcated a work ethic that occasionally was expressed in an entrepreneurial fashion. At the plantation, he grew his own vegetables and sold them to his fellow workers. To defray the transportation costs involved in attending school, he drove a school bus on a part-time basis. By the time he was 19 years old, Taira managed his own transportation company.

When World War II broke out, Taira joined the U.S. Army. He served as an interpreter for Allied forces

COMPANY PERSPECTIVES

The King's Hawaiian Brand is the global leader in the fast growing Hawaiian food category. Our people are recognized as the most skilled, empowered and highly motivated in the industry.

occupying Japan, a stint that proved inspirational. While in Japan, he became convinced a business selling Western bakery products would thrive once hostilities ceased, which prompted him to enroll in the Chicago Institute of Baking when the war ended. Taira was graduated in 1949, but his dream of starting a bakery in Japan, inspired during a war, was shattered by the outbreak of another war. The start of the Korean War dissuaded Taira from launching a business in Japan, forcing him to begin his professional baking career in his hometown of Hilo.

FIRST BAKERY OPENS IN 1950

Taira borrowed $382 from his father to open his own business, establishing a bakery and coffee shop in 1950 that operated under the name "Robert's Bakery." He enlisted the help of his brother-in-law, Tokihiko Shimabukuro, and began experimenting with the sweet bread recipe he had learned from the Portuguese family that had lived on the sugarcane plantation. Eventually, he came up with his own variation—the creation of the Original Recipe King's Hawaiian Sweet Bread—that kept the bread soft for nearly two weeks. The recipe and the business became a Hilo favorite. After its first year in business, Robert's Bakery collected $60,000 in sales.

Never one to check his ambition, Taira began considering expanding his business once it had proved successful. In 1961, he opened a larger bakery and coffee shop in Honolulu on the island of Oahu. He established the business on King Street and named the business after its location, hanging a sign on the storefront that read "King's Bakery." The name of Honolulu's newest business quickly became ingrained in the minds' of the island's residents, as queues of patrons flocked to King Street, enabling Taira to eclipse his efforts in Hilo. Within five years, King's Bakery was recording $750,000 in annual sales.

King's Bakery attracted island residents as well as tourists. King Street, situated near Waikiki and Diamond Head, proved an ideal location for Taira's thriving business, introducing sweet bread to mainlanders who were not content with sampling the delicacy

only while on vacation. Taira was inundated with requests for his "Hawaiian" sweet bread from the continental United States, which he responded to by shipping his bread, frozen, via mail order. The sideline mail-order business flourished, eventually developing to a point where Taira was shipping 100 loaves daily through the mail. Taira, who initially thought the Japanese market offered the greatest opportunity for success, began to think of the continental United States as his prime market.

ACROSS THE PACIFIC OCEAN IN 1977

Taira made the boldest move in his life in 1977. He decided to establish a physical presence on the mainland, a bold enough move on its own, but instead of merely opening a retail bakery he decided to build a multimillion-dollar production plant equipped with the most advanced automated baking machinery available. The plant, a $3.7 million, 25,000-square-foot facility, opened in Torrance, California, in 1977, marking the birth of King's Hawaiian Bakery West, Inc., and triggering the first faltering steps in Taira's career.

The enormous investment in automated, state-of-the-art machinery caused maddening problems from the first day the Torrance plant became operational. The bread, primarily made by hand in Hawaii, could not be made with the automated equipment at first. Processing the rich and sticky dough was a chore the machinery struggled mightily with, forcing Taira to shut down production while he searched for a solution. He spent three months making adjustments on the equipment before the loaves began to taste consistently like the hand-mixed bread made in Hawaii, but his difficulties did not end once production problems were resolved. Taira's sales force, limited in size, did not maintain vigilant contact with supermarket store managers, who served as the omnipotent gatekeepers determining the success or failure of food products. Sales suffered as a result, but a remedy was found when Taira began marketing his sweet bread through food brokers, who provided the crucial link to branch managers, ensuring Original Hawaiian Sweet Bread succeeded on retailers' shelves.

Once the company made the necessary adjustments following its ambitious foray across the Pacific, it began to hit its stride. Taira, always looking for a new challenge, ventured out of the Los Angeles market in 1978 and began distributing his products to the Chicago market, known as a "bread town" in the baking industry. By the following year, he had begun to generate a profit, ending a two-year period of struggling with growing pains. During the critical transition period,

KEY DATES

1950: Robert Taira opens his first bakery in Hilo, Hawaii.

1961: Taira opens a larger bakery in Honolulu on King Street.

1977: Taira establishes a modern production plant in Torrance, California.

1986: Taira's son, Mark Taira, takes control of the business.

1988: The company opens a restaurant in Torrance named King's Hawaiian Bakery & Restaurant.

1993: The last of the company's Hawaii-based operations are closed.

2004: A new, 150,000-square-foot production plant opens in Torrance.

2007: King's Hawaiian Bakery celebrates 30 years of business in Torrance.

Taira's son, Mark Taira, joined the company, beginning an apprenticeship of sorts that saw him take on every job within the bakery. In his early 20s at the time, Mark Taira divided his time between working at the bakery and attending the University of Southern California, where he studied business in preparation for taking command of the family firm.

MARK TAIRA TAKES CONTROL IN 1986

The father-and-son team presided over encouraging growth during the 1980s. The business, which had generated in excess of $3 million in annual sales before the move to Torrance, was collecting $10 million in annual sales midway through the 1980s. There was talk of establishing a plant in South Carolina to support distribution in the East Coast, but the company never committed to the project. It did build another plant in Torrance, however, using the two facilities to penetrate 50 markets in the country. Mark Taira took control of King's Hawaiian Bakery in 1986, assuming the duties of chief executive officer while his 63-year-old father took on the role of the company's chairman.

King's Hawaiian Bakery ceased to maintain a physical presence in Hawaii by 1993. The Tairas had decided their business would be a Torrance-based business well before the last of their Hawaiian operations shut down in 1993. In 1988, they opened a restaurant in Torrance, King's Hawaiian Bakery & Restaurant, a dining facility

that abutted a bakery. The restaurant served a blend of Hawaiian cuisine, offering breakfast, lunch, and dinner. A second dining establishment, The Local Place Bakery & Café, followed, offering similar cuisine in a more casual setting. The Local Place, which offered cakes and pastries, served breakfast and lunch, featuring noodles, rice bowls, sandwiches, and hamburgers.

Robert Taira, having essentially created the market niche in which his company competed, held sway as an innovator and market leader during his lifetime. In 2003, five months shy of his 80th birthday, he passed away, succumbing to a battle with cancer. Behind him, he left a legacy of success that had made the Hawaiian bread segment "big enough that many consumers now consider it in the same breath as rye or sourdough products," according to the June 2003 issue of *Snack Food & Wholesale Bakery.*

NEW PRODUCTION PLANT IN 2004

During Robert Taira's last months, his son was presiding over a massive expansion project that testified to the commercial appeal of the brand created a half-century earlier. A new headquarters facility and manufacturing plant was being constructed in Torrance, but for a brief period, Mark Taira considered moving the company's operations elsewhere. "Nevada was very tempting," he said in the April 2004 issue of *Snack Food & Wholesale Bakery.* "We really looked at going out of state, but there is still a lot of family involved in our business." The new facility opened in 2004, a 150,000-square-foot plant that doubled the manufacturing capacity of the company's two older production plants. The new plant involved three years of planning, a project that incorporated the latest innovations in automated machinery. The plant featured robotic pan handling, robotic palletizing, and a warehouse management system that monitored every aspect of production. "One of the most wonderful things from an operations standpoint is that we're able to get all of this feedback from our equipment," Taira said in the April 2004 issue of *Snack Food & Wholesale Bakery.* "If something goes down, it tells you what's wrong. The computers tell you when to maintain your equipment. They tell you what product you are making and what temperatures—everything that you need to know to run your operation efficiently. That's one of the biggest accomplishments on the equipment side of the industry."

With the completion of the new plant, King's Hawaiian Bakery was able to consolidate production and its main offices, which had been spread across three sites, into one location. From its concentrated perch, the company faced a future of promise, sitting atop a $60-

million-in-sales business that controlled its market niche. The Original Hawaiian Sweet Round Bread brand and its signature orange packaging enjoyed widespread recognition among consumers throughout the nation, ensuring that the years ahead would continue to see solid financial performance from the Taira family business.

Jeffrey L. Covell

PRINCIPAL SUBSIDIARIES

King's Hawaiian Bakery & Restaurant; The Local Place Bakery & Café.

PRINCIPAL COMPETITORS

Flowers Foods, Inc.; Interstate Bakeries Corporation; Sara Lee Food & Beverage.

FURTHER READING

"King's Hawaiian Founder Passes Away," *Snack Food & Wholesale Bakery,* June 2003, p. 12.

"King's Hawaiian Markets Mini Sub-Style Sandwich Rolls," *Meat & Deli Retailer,* May 2008, p. 10.

"King's Hawaiian Restaurants Debut Six Single-Serve Entrees," *Quick Frozen Foods International,* April 1999, p. 168.

Malovany, Dan, "The King's New Castle," *Snack Food & Wholesale Bakery,* April 2004, p. 26.

McTaggart, Jenny, "Sweet Breads Get a New Look," *Progressive Grocer,* June 1, 2003, p. 98.

Pacyniak, Bernard, "Baker Brings Bits of Paradise to the Mainland," *Bakery Production and Marketing,* April 24, 1999, p. 60.

"Three More Asian Bowls from King's Hawaiian," *Quick Frozen Foods International,* January 2001, p. 87.

Wantuck, Mary-Margaret, "A Baker's Dozen? A Baker's Millions!" *Nation's Business,* March 1984, p. 77.

KMG Chemicals, Inc.

9555 West Sam Houston Parkway South, Suite 600
Houston, Texas 77099-2168
U.S.A.
Telephone: (713) 600-3800
Fax: (713) 600-3850
Web site: http://www.kmgchemicals.com

Public Company
Incorporated: 1992 as Water Point Manufacturing, Inc.
Employees: 118
Sales: $154.4 million (2008)
Stock Exchanges: NASDAQ
Ticker Symbol: KMGB
NAICS: 325998 All Other Miscellaneous Chemical
   Product and Preparation Manufacturing

■ ■ ■

KMG Chemicals, Inc., is a Houston, Texas-based public company that through its subsidiaries produces and distributes a number of specialty chemicals serving niche markets. The KMG-Bernuth, Inc., unit produces wood preservative chemicals, pentachlorophenol (penta) and creosote, used to treat utility poles, marine pilings, railroad crossties, and construction timbers. KMG-Bernuth also offers animal health products, including insecticidal cattle ear tags and other protective insecticides and chemicals to eliminate parasites in livestock and poultry. Another subsidiary, KMG Electronic Chemicals, Inc., supplies the acids, solvents, and other chemicals needed to produce semiconductors. Operations are maintained in Colorado as well as Italy.

KMG has grown over the years by pursuing a disciplined acquisition strategy that focuses on mature, niche chemicals, ones that larger companies are willing to discard in order to focus on new chemicals with higher margins and rapid growth potential. The chemicals that interest KMG have also reached a point in their life cycle when the market has receded, leading to the exit of many competitors and resulting in a stable and predictable, albeit smaller, niche market. KMG is able to take over these lines, establish a strong market position, reduce costs, improve operating efficiencies, and thus, create a healthy profit stream. Chairman David L. Hatcher owns more than 60 percent of the company.

DAVID HATCHER ACQUIRES KMG CHEMICALS: 1984

David Hatcher is the man responsible for the growth of KMG. He had been involved in the wood-treatment business through KMG and its affiliates since 1980. KMG itself was launched in the 1970s to distribute a single chemical, penta, about 95 percent of which was produced by Reichold Chemical Company. Hatcher acquired KMG in a leveraged buyout in late 1984, only to be informed four months later that Reichold was shutting down its penta plant and abandoning the niche. Saddled with considerable debt, Hatcher found himself in a precarious position. Convinced that there was still a market for penta, he decide to produce penta himself to fill the needs of his existing customer base. While building a plant, Hatcher was able to keep KMG afloat by importing penta from a German supplier, which at the time was the world's only source for the

COMPANY PERSPECTIVES

The Company has grown by acquiring and optimizing stable chemical product lines and businesses with established production processes. Its current operations are focused on the electronic chemicals, wood treatment and agricultural chemical markets. By applying management expertise and operating cost efficiencies, the Company expands profitability and extends the economic life of its mature chemicals.

chemical. Although he lost money for two consecutive years, Hatcher survived until KMG's own plant opened in Mexico in early 1986 and began producing penta.

KMG remained a one-product company for the next five years, as Hatcher ran a lean operation and paid down his debt. In 1991 he seized an opportunity to add a second specialty chemical when the family firm of Bernuth-Lembcke Co. elected to divest its creosote distribution business, selling the German-produced chemical that was used to treat railroad ties and utility poles. Like penta, the market for creosote was not growing but was stable. KMG took the name KMG-Bernuth, Inc. Hatcher would look for other chemicals that also fit this mold to drive further growth. In 1993 he zeroed in on a penta derivative—sodium penta, used to prevent mold in sawmill lumber—acquiring this product line from Rhône Poulenc. Hatcher would devote countless hours scouring for similar "orphan" chemicals.

REVERSE MERGER TAKES COMPANY PUBLIC: 1996

In order to tap the equity markets to fund further growth, Hatcher took KMG public in 1996 through a reverse merger with a Dallas company called Water Point Manufacturing, Inc. Water Point had been incorporated in Texas in 1992 by 32-year-old Mark A. Hope, director of operations for Dr. Pepper/Seven Up. He had tried to persuade his employer to start a branded drinking water that relied on vending machines which purified and dispensed tap water for customers who brought their own bottles. The idea was to dramatically cut distribution and packaging costs by placing the machine in supermarkets and other retail locations.

When Dr. Pepper/Seven Up rejected the idea, Hope quit and started Water Point with seed money provided by a Fort Worth, Texas-based venture-capital firm. In 1993 he signed a deal to use the Canada Dry trademark on his vending machines. At the end of the year he took Water Point public, raising $10.1 million, and began a rapid expansion program, one made necessary by the terms of his 20-year agreement with Canada Dry's parent, Cadbury Beverages Inc., which called for the installation of 1,250 Canada Dry vending machines in two years. Hope ramped up deployment of the machines, but the cost of assembling and installing each unit totaled about $6,000. He managed to roll out about 700 machines before running into financial difficulties. The company posted major losses, the price of Water Point stock was reduced to pennies, and in 1995 Hope resigned and the company lapsed into bankruptcy. A liquidation followed in the summer, and the Water Point vending operations were sold off, as was the corporate entity to Hatcher in 1996. To merge with KMG operations, Water Point changed its name to KMG-B Inc. Without assets it then acquired KMG-Bernuth. In December 1997 KMG-B was renamed KMG Chemicals, Inc.

When KMG ended fiscal 1997, it recorded net sales of $19.5 million and net income of $2.7 million. Hatcher, in the meantime, continued his search for orphan chemicals, an effort that was constantly met with rejection, he told *Chemical Week* in 2002. "I'm kissing all the toads looking for one prince," he said. Although he did not find any new product lines in the remaining years of the 1990s, he did acquire the creosote assets and long-term contracts from AlliedSignal Inc., making KMG the second largest supplier of creosote in the United States. The new business helped to increase sales in 1998 to nearly $22.7 million and net income to $3.2 million. A year later sales grew to $36.4 million and net income to $3.75 million.

PURCHASE OF MSMA PRODUCTS: 2000

Adverse market conditions caused a dip in revenues in 2000 to $33.74 million. Consolidations among utilities caused a reduction in the demand for utility poles, in turn depressing the demand for wood-treatment products. To make matters worse, the price of diesel oil spiked. Diesel oil was used to dissolve penta in order to produce wood-treating solutions, and because of the extra cost, a competing treatment product, CCA, a water-dissolved wood preservative, became a more cost-competitive product. Nevertheless, KMG was able to increase net income slightly, to almost $3.9 million. During 2000 the company also positioned itself for further growth by acquiring the MSMA herbicide products business from Zeneca AG Products for $2.3

KEY DATES

1984: David Hatcher acquires KMG, a pentachlorophenol (penta) distributor.
1986: Penta plant opens in Mexico.
1991: Creosote business is acquired.
1996: KMG is taken public through reverse merger with Water Point Manufacturing, Inc.
2000: MSMA herbicide product lines are acquired.
2003: Rabon insecticidal product lines are acquired.
2005: The penta business of Occidental Chemical is acquired.
2008: KMG Electronic Chemicals, Inc., is formed through acquisition of Air Products and Chemicals, Inc.

million, providing KMG with a new revenue stream and a foothold in agricultural chemicals. The chemicals added were monosodium and disodium methanearsonic acid herbicides, used on genetically modified cotton crops. Income from the MSMA products helped to offset a continued erosion in sales of wood-treating chemicals and increased net sales in fiscal 2001 to $35.8 million.

KMG's next acquisition was completed in early 2003 when the company added the Rabon insecticidal product lines of Boehringer Ingelheim Vetmedica Inc. (BIV) to become more involved in the animal health business. The Rabon insecticide line contained the active ingredient tetrachlorvinphos, and was used to protect poultry and domestic livestock from flies and other pests. It was available as a powder or oral larvicide. In 2004 KMG purchased the Revap insecticidal product line from BIV, a liquid spray that also relied on tetrachlorvinphos as its active ingredient. In addition to branching out into animal health, KMG did not lose sight of its wood-treatment business. In December 2003 it acquired the penta distribution assets of Wood Protection Products, Inc. Next, in June 2004 KMG acquired the creosote distribution business of Trenton Sales, Inc., in the process gaining a long-term supply agreement with Lufkin Creosoting Company, which was affiliated with Trenton Sales. As a result of these acquisitions, KMG grew revenues to $43.6 million in fiscal 2004.

Shortly before the close of fiscal 2005, in June 2005 KMG added to its penta business by acquiring certain assets from Occidental Chemical Corp. used in the manufacture and sale of the chemical. The timing proved fortuitous for KMG, which was the only North

American manufacturer and distributor of penta. A few months later hurricanes Katrina and Rita struck the Gulf Coast and Florida, laying waste to utility poles. The need for new poles meant an increased need for penta. Demand was so strong that KMG expanded its Mexican penta plant to add 30 percent more capacity. The extra sales helped KMG to improve sales from $59.2 million in fiscal 2005 to $71 million in fiscal 2006. Net income also increased from $3 million to almost $3.8 million.

ACQUISITION OF INSECTICIDE BUSINESS: 2006

In 2006 KMG once again dealt with BIVto acquire that company's U.S.-based animal insecticide business, adding a number of products and assets, including the top-selling brand of insecticidal ear tags for cattle; a line of liquid and dust formulations of insecticides for cattle, swine, poultry, other animals, and their habitats; and a Kansas manufacturing plant and warehouse, as well as a staff experienced in product development and regulatory matters. The new business played a major factor in KMG increasing revenues to $86.2 million and net income to $8.85 million in fiscal 2007.

Far from content, KMG initiated a five-year plan in 2007 to grow sales to $250 million. Although he stayed on as chairman, Hatcher stepped down as president and chief executive officer, turning over day-to-day control to J. Neal Butler, who was also a member of the board of directors. He had been groomed for the post since 2004 when he joined KMG as chief operating officer. At the time, he was a well-seasoned executive, having held a number of sales and product management positions at Diamond Shamrock and Fermenta ASC, followed by senior management posts with Zeneca Agrochemicals and ISK Biosciences. Just prior to joining KMG, Butler had served as president and CEO of Naturize BioSciences.

FORMATION OF KMG ELECTRONICS CHEMICALS: 2007

KMG took a major stop in achieving its ambitious sales goal in late 2007 when for $74.6 million it acquired the high-purity process chemicals business of Allentown, Pennsylvania-based Air Products and Chemicals, Inc.; the products were used in the manufacture of semiconductors. The deal also brought with it a 215,000-square-foot production facility and warehouse in Pueblo, Colorado, and a plant and warehouse near Milan, Italy, but more importantly it provided KMG with entry into a new market: electronic chemicals. The assets were housed in a new subsidiary, KMG Electronic

Chemicals, Inc. In one stroke KMG effectively doubled its business. With contributions from KMG Electronic Chemicals for only part of the year, KMG increased revenues to $154.4 million.

In order to grow further, KMG would have to continue to make acquisitions, primarily due to the types of products on which the company focused. Because the markets were mature, there was little opportunity for organic growth, although there were some international opportunities to exploit, especially in Europe and the Middle East, and the Far East for electronic chemicals. The company was especially hopeful that it could find "hidden gems" in the electronic chemicals market, where such corporate giants as BASF, Honeywell, General Chemical, and Mitsubishi Gas Chemical were likely to shed mature product lines. KMG also looked to new markets in which to ply its strategy, such as agricultural chemicals and surface preparation chemicals for use in industrial applications. In short, there was no lack of acquisition prospects, and there was an excellent chance that KMG would exceed its five-year goals.

Ed Dinger

PRINCIPAL SUBSIDIARIES

KMG-Bernuth, Inc.; KMG Electronic Chemicals, Inc.

PRINCIPAL COMPETITORS

Arch Chemicals, Inc.; Koppers Holdings Inc.; Perstorp AB.

FURTHER READING

Blanchfield, Lindsey, "KMG Chemicals Knocks on Wood," *Chemical Market Reporter,* June 19–June 25, 2006, p. 36.

"KMG Starts Mexico Chlorophenol Plant," *Chemical Market Reporter,* August 24, 1998, p. 29.

Penn, Monica, "The Right Chemistry," *Houston Business Journal,* January 12, 1998.

Scheraga, Dan, "KMG Seeks 'Orphan Chemicals' As Part of Strategy for Growth," *Chemical Market Reporter,* January 12, 1998, p. 16.

Seewald, Nancy, "KMG Chemicals," *Chemical Week,* December 20, 2000, p. 25.

———, "KMG: On the Hunt for 'Hidden Gems,'" *Chemical Week,* October 6, 2008, p. 49.

Wren, Worth, Jr., "Water Point Systems Founder Resigns amid Crisis," *Fort Worth Star-Telegram,* March 4, 1995, p. 1.

L. Foppiano Wine Co.

12707 Old Redwood Highway
Healdsburg, California 95448
U.S.A.
Telephone: (707) 433-7272
Fax: (707) 433-0565
Web site: http://www.foppiano.com

Private Company
Incorporated: 1933 as Foppiano Wine Company
Employees: 20
Sales: $6.8 million (2007)
NAICS: 312130 Wineries

■ ■ ■

L. Foppiano Wine Co. is a wine company based in the Russian River Valley in Sonoma County, California, where it was established in the late 19th century. Family-owned and -operated, the company markets its red and white wines under the names Foppiano Vineyards, Fox Mountain, and Riverside Farm, selling its product line in all 50 states. Its leading varieties are Petite Sirah, Pinot Noir, Cabernet Sauvignon, and Merlot, but the company also produces Cabernet Franc, Chardonnay, Sauvignon Blanc, and Sangiovese. Foppiano Wine exports its wines to a dozen countries in Europe, the Caribbean, and Asia. The company's 200-acre property in Healdsburg contains 140 acres of vineyards and a tasting room. The company produces 75,000 cases of wine annually.

FAMILY DYNASTY BEGINS IN LATE 19TH CENTURY

The fate of generations of Foppiano family members was determined when Giovanni Foppiano decided to leave his native Genoa in 1855 to seek his fortune in California. Giovanni left Italy, boarded a ship headed to New York City, and found his way to California via Panama, ready to join the chase for gold in the northern part of the state. He arrived in California at the end of the seven-year gold rush, one of more than 300,000 gold seekers who flocked to the region in search of riches. Foppiano did not find his trove of gold, but the pursuit of his dream did give him a new home. In 1864, he settled in Healdsburg, in the heart of what later became Sonoma County wine country.

Foppiano eventually turned his attention from prospecting to working in the vineyards. He married and raised a family, becoming the father of ten children. In 1896, 41 years after his arrival in California, he purchased a winery named Riverside Farm and launched his career as a vintner, starting what would become one of the oldest, family-run wineries operating in the 21st century. His decision to enter the wine-making business marked the beginning of the Foppiano legacy in the California wine industry, a heritage that would involve generations of Giovanni Foppiano's descendants, beginning with one of his sons, Louis A. Foppiano (Louis A.), who was 19 years old when his father purchased Riverside Farm.

Foppiano Wine, as a family-owned-and-managed business, was susceptible to intrafamilial conflicts affecting its operation, but the company progressed for more

COMPANY PERSPECTIVES

Few wineries have Foppiano's extensive history, and are still family owned and operated. Since 1896, when Giovanni Foppiano bought the Riverside Farm on Old Redwood Highway, the Foppianos have been a part of the wine industry, calling the Russian River Valley "home." The Russian River Valley holds a prominent position in not only the California wine industry, but is also recognized as a world-class wine grape growing region for Pinot Noir. The Foppiano family has been growing Pinot Noir since the beginning in their vineyard adjacent to the Russian River on its eastern shore. Cool morning fog creates ideal microclimatic conditions for their excellent Pinot Noir.

than a century without a family fight making headlines. There was one incident, however, and it occurred relatively early in its development, with the company's future hanging in the balance.

A FOPPIANO COUP

By 1900, Louis A. had earned his father's confidence. He was put in charge of sales and marketing for the family business, a job that largely entailed bringing the wine to the customers. Using a horse-drawn wagon, Louis A. would make the trek to San Francisco, a city enriched by the gold craze that had captivated his father. One of the main stops on his route was in North Beach, a section of the city teeming with Italian immigrants. Louis A., who married the sister of one of his North Beach customers, would dispense his family's wine to customers who brought their own jugs to be filled.

Louis A. followed his routine for a decade, ensuring customers in San Francisco and outlying areas received a steady supply of bulk wine. That supply of wine almost ran dry after a father-and-son clash that ended a relationship and nearly ended the Foppianos' involvement in wine making. The particulars of the argument were not made public, but when Louis A. and his father disagreed over a business matter, Giovanni Foppiano threatened to sell the winery. Louis A. responded by secretly securing a loan from his wife's family—Foppiano Wine customers in North Beach—and purchasing the family business. The surreptitious move destroyed their relationship; the two did not speak to each other until just before Giovanni Foppiano died.

PROHIBITION

Louis A. took responsibility for all aspects of the family business after his confrontation with his father. Foppiano Wine grew steadily during the ensuing decade, but the most formidable of all obstacles loomed ahead. The Volstead Act, the popular name for the National Prohibition Act, went into effect in California in 1919, making the sale, manufacture, and transportation of alcohol for consumption illegal. Prohibition, for obvious reasons, forced Louis A. to make profound changes in the way the family business operated. He turned to farming other crops, keeping his vineyards in place, but planting prunes, apples, and pears in between his rows of vineyards. He did not curtail his wine-making activities entirely, however. He continued selling small quantities of wine out of the back door of the winery until his death in 1925, a clandestine aspect of the winery's business made public when U.S. Treasury agents raided Foppiano Wine in 1927 and dumped 100,000 gallons of wine in a nearby creek.

THIRD GENERATION TAKES POWER IN 1925

Louis A.'s death in 1925 marked the ascension of the third generation of the family to a position of power. Louis J. Foppiano (Louis J.) was born the year his father and grandfather parted ways, and he began working in the vineyards at age seven. His father's death thrust him into the role of winemaker, a position he gained "by title, not by skills," as he said in his September 1996 interview with *Wines & Vines*. In his interview, he explained how Foppiano Wine operated before Prohibition and how he learned the nuances of his new responsibilities as Foppiano Wine's winemaker. "There were no wine schools then," he said. "You just talked to the old winemen and got all the information you could, then went back to the winery and tried it. Most of what we produced was red. The red grapes—Zinfandel, Petite Sirah, and Carignane, with a little Alicante—were bottled either as Burgundy or Barberone. The difference was strictly in the color. You'd look at a tank of wine and if it was heavy and dark it was Barberone. The wines had to be dark and have a lot of body to sell."

Louis J. would have to wait eight years before he could put his wine-making skills to the test. Prohibition dragged on, but in 1932 he became convinced the ordeal was coming to an end. "You could tell Repeal was on the way," he recalled in the October 1993 issue of *Wines & Vines*. "When Al Smith ran for president in 1928 he was for Repeal, and when Roosevelt was elected four years later, we were sure. As soon as it looked certain, we steamed and soaked the tanks and got ready."

KEY DATES

■

1896: Giovanni Foppiano acquires a winery, Riverside Farm, in Healdsburg, California.

1910: Giovanni Foppiano's son, Louis A. Foppiano, acquires the family business.

1925: The third generation of family leadership, led by Louis J. Foppiano, takes control of the business during Prohibition.

1933: After a 14-year moratorium on wine making at the family estate, production resumes when Prohibition is repealed.

1941-45: Increased production makes Foppiano Wine the second largest bottler of wine in Sonoma County.

1966: After 70 years of producing jug wines, the company begins producing cork-finished varieties.

1975: White wine production is increased dramatically in response to changing consumer preferences.

1981: Foppiano Wine introduces Riverside Farm, a brand created to market lower-priced wines.

1985: Louis J. Foppiano's son, Louis M. Foppiano, takes control of the family business.

1986: The Fox Mountain label is introduced, a brand that later will be reserved for all the winery's white wines.

1996: The Foppiano Vineyards label is converted to a 100 percent red wine brand.

1999: The fifth generation of the Foppiano family, Paul Foppiano, joins the company.

2007: Foppiano Wine opens its wine library to give consumers access to small quantities of its Petite Sirah dating back to the 1992 vintage.

The fruit trees were ripped from the vineyards and Foppiano Wine was ready for business when Prohibition ended in December 1933. The winery produced 83,000 gallons of wine during its first year back in business, and recorded welcomed growth in the years to follow. In 1937, Foppiano Wine became one of the first Sonoma County wineries to bottle wine under its own winery label. The winery enjoyed a surge of business in 1939 when supplies of imported wine from Europe were cut off because of World War II, which created a boom period for California winemakers. When the United States entered the war two years after its start, business

only improved. Foppiano Wine was sending five to six rail tank cars each week to the eastern United States, supplying bulk wine at a rate that caused annual production to rise to 800,000 gallons. The winery became the second largest bottler of wine in Sonoma County as a result, a stature Louis J. leveraged to acquire the Sotoyome Vineyard abutting his family's property. The purchase doubled the size of the family's estate, giving it 200 acres of property.

FROM JUGS TO CORKS IN THE SIXTIES

Louis J., nowhere near passing the reins of command to the next generation, led the family business throughout the postwar period. One of the most important developments during his tenure occurred in 1966, when Louis J. began to steer the winery away from the jug wines that had been its mainstay for the previous 70 years. He purchased new oak barrels and tanks, stainless steel tanks, and other new equipment, which he used to move Foppiano Wine into the premium category of the wine market. New grape varieties were planted such as Cabernet Sauvignon and Pinot Noir, as jug wines were replaced with the increasingly popular cork-finished varieties. The transition culminated in the release of the first vintage-dated bottling from the winery in 1969.

The fourth generation of the Foppiano family joined the business as the winery began to compete in the premium segment. Louis M. Foppiano (Louis M.) joined the winery on a full-time basis in 1970 as a 23-year-old, and was named director of sales and marketing two years later, the same year his younger brother Rod Foppiano was named winemaker. The brothers, joined by their sister, Susan Foppiano Valera, as hospitality manager, helped their father adjust to changing consumer tastes. White wines became increasingly popular during the 1970s, and Foppiano Wine responded nimbly to the market trend, converting its annual production, which was 97 percent red varieties, to 70 percent white wines by 1975.

THE FOURTH GENERATION TAKES CONTROL IN 1985

In the 1980s, the Louis J. era of control ended after a remarkably long run. In 1985, after 60 years of leading the company, he handed day-to-day managerial responsibilities to Louis M., one year after his other son, Rod Foppiano, died after a long battle with cancer. The last years of the Louis J. era saw Foppiano Wine introduce a new label, Riverside Farm, a brand released in 1981 to market the winery's lower-priced wines. In 1986, with Louis M. at the helm, the company introduced another label, Fox Mountain, the name of the family hunting retreat in Mendocino County. Fox Mountain made its debut with special vintages of Cabernet Sauvignon and Chardonnay.

Although Louis J. was no longer in charge of the family business, he continued to be actively involved in monitoring its operation. On most days, he could be found riding around in his pickup truck, checking on the estate's vineyards. He was privy to a major brand transition in the 1990s, as the Foppiano family decided to set aside the Foppiano Vineyards brand exclusively for red wines. The company began making the conversion in 1995 in preparation for its centennial the following year. Fox Mountain became the label for all the winery's white wines and Foppiano Vineyards became a 100 percent red wine brand in 1996, when centennial celebrations were attended by three generations of Foppiano family members.

A SECOND CENTURY BEGINS

Louis J. lived to see Foppiano Wine thrive in the 21st century. His grandson, Rod Foppiano's son, Paul Foppiano, represented the fifth generation of the family involved in the wine business. After an apprenticeship at Sausal Vineyard, Paul Foppiano joined the family business in 1999, becoming vineyard manager with Raul Guerrero, who had learned the craft from Rod Foppiano. Working with his uncle and his aunt, Paul Foppiano continued the work begun by his great-great-grandfather Giovanni Foppiano, playing a vital role in ensuring the winery's signature wine, a Petite Sirah,

lived up to the high standards established by the generations before him. In a nod to the importance of Petite Sirah to the heritage of the Foppianos, the company opened its wine library in 2007 to give consumers access to small quantities of its Petite Sirah dating back to the 1992 vintage. Although Sonoma's Russian River Valley was best known for Pinot Noir and Chardonnay, Foppiano Wine had built its reputation on Petite Sirah, a hallmark of its past that promised to figure prominently in its future, perhaps under the leadership of Paul Foppiano.

Jeffrey L. Covell

PRINCIPAL SUBSIDIARIES

Foppiano Vineyards.

PRINCIPAL COMPETITORS

E. & J. Gallo Winery; Sebastiani Vineyards, Inc.; Kendall-Jackson Wine Estates, Ltd.

FURTHER READING

Boyd, Gerald D., "Rock 'N' Roll Winemaker," *San Francisco Chronicle,* May 9, 2001, p. WB6.

Hinkle, Richard Paul, "Foppiano at the Century Mark," *Wines & Vines,* September 1996, p. 19.

———, "Recollections of Repeal," *Wines & Vines,* October 1993, p. 16.

Mauro, Rich, "Foppiano Offerings Show How Well Petite Sirahs Age," *Colorado Springs (Colo.) Gazette,* November 7, 2007, p. F4.

La Doria SpA

Via Nazionale 320
Angri, I-84012
Italy
Telephone: (+39 081) 5166111
Fax: (+39 081) 5135991
Web site: http://www.ladoria.it

Public Company
Incorporated: 1954
Employees: 700
Sales: EUR 406.6 million ($597.3 million) (2007)
Stock Exchanges: Borsa Italiana
Ticker Symbol: LD
NAICS: 311421 Fruit and Vegetable Canning; 311423
    Dried and Dehydrated Food Manufacturing

■ ■ ■

La Doria SpA is Italy's largest producer of canned tomato products, and one of the country's leading food manufacturing companies, focusing primarily on the canned vegetable and fruit juice segments. The company's "red line" of tomato-based products accounts for nearly 30 percent of group sales. In Italy, where La Doria commands a 50 percent share of the all important canned tomato market, the company markets its products under the popular La Doria brand. Other Italian brands include the La Romanella canned fruits and vegetables line, and the Vivi G line of fruit-based drinks. Italy accounts for less than 28 percent of La Doria's total revenues, which topped EUR 406 million (approximately $600 million) in 2007. The Northern European and especially the U.K. markets represent the major source of the company's revenues, at nearly 63 percent of sales. The company's U.K. operations are conducted through its 51 percent stake in LDH (La Doria) Ltd., which in addition to the company's tomatoes, vegetables, and fruits lines, also markets canned seafood and other products for the U.K. private-label sector. More than 80 percent of La Doria's revenues are generated through the private-label channel, and the company counts many of Europe's leading supermarket chains, including Tesco, Sainsbury, Carrefour, and Auchan as its customers. The majority of La Doria's production takes place in its five factories in Angri, Sarno, Fisciano, Faenza, and Lavello, Italy. La Doria is listed on the Borsa Italiana's Star Segment. The founding Ferraioli family owns more than 70 percent of the company, and Antonio Ferraioli serves as the group's chief executive officer.

FAMILY BUSINESS IN 1954

While it is difficult to imagine Italian cuisine without the tomato, its introduction into Italian cuisine is relatively recent, dating from the European discovery and colonization of South America. Italy's climate proved highly adapted to growing tomatoes, which soon became not only an important crop, but also one of the single most important ingredients of Italian cooking. The Agro Nocerino Sarnese area, near Naples in the province of Salerno, became one of the most prominent centers of tomato cultivation. The region's production turned especially toward the San Marzano tomato variety, popularly known as the plum tomato, which

COMPANY PERSPECTIVES

The Group's Mission: Customer satisfaction. Our Group pays close attention to the needs of our clients in every market. Thanks to our 50 years of experience and our high-level of flexibility, we are able to satisfy almost any type of need, through customised recipes, packaging and service.

Effective and efficient. Our objective is to make our manufacturing processes as effective and efficient as possible. Global vision. Our production is local, typical of the "Made in Italy" brand, but our Group exports to approximately 40 countries throughout the world.

proved especially useful in the preparation of tomato-based sauces.

The introduction of modern grocery and then supermarket formats in Italy, particularly after World War II, gave rise to a new demand for the canning of tomatoes and other fruits and vegetables on an industrial scale. This demand encouraged the Ferraioli family, led by Diodata Ferraioli, to invest in canning equipment. The family launched their company in 1954. An important ingredient to the company's success during this period was its recognition of the potential for developing its own brand. The introduction of the La Doria brand proved a quick success, and before long La Doria had become one of Italy's major packaged tomato brands.

The slow growth of Italy's economy compared to other European markets in the meantime had driven large numbers of Italians across the border into France and elsewhere to seek employment. This immigration wave was to have a profound impact on the European kitchen, as other European markets discovered and rapidly embraced Italian pasta and pizza. La Doria quickly recognized the potential for expansion into these new markets, and by the early 1960s had put into place a small export model. Unlike in Italy, where the company focused on the branded segment, La Doria instead focused its foreign growth as a supplier of private-label products for the fast-growing European supermarket groups.

Italy's temperate climate also made the country a major source of a variety of other fruits and vegetables as well. In the 1970s, La Doria decided to diversify its operations, and launched its own lines of canned fruits

and vegetables, as well as packaged fruit juices. These were sold under the La Doria brand, as well as a new brand, La Romanella, in Italy. At the same time, La Doria expanded its product offering to the private-label sector, both in Italy and abroad. Indeed, international markets came to represent the company's vast majority of the group's fruits and vegetables sales; by the 1990s, more than 90 percent of the sales in this category were generated outside of Italy. The United Kingdom, Germany, and the Scandinavian markets became the company's major international markets.

PUBLIC OFFERING IN 1995

In the meantime, La Doria had invested in developing a highly modern production base. By adopting state-of-the-art technologies, the company was able to build a strong position in the Italian market through the 1970s and into the 1980s. By the end of the century, the La Doria brand had become the dominant Italian canned tomato brand, commanding a 50 percent share of the market. The company also became a prominent partner to the fast-growing supermarket giants in the United Kingdom, Germany, and elsewhere in Europe.

Toward the end of the 1980s, La Doria took the strategic decision to double its production capacity. The company carried out a new modernization program at its main Angri production facility. The enlarged production capacity enabled La Doria to expand its range of products as well. At the same time, La Doria began developing sales to other markets, including Japan and other Asian markets. The company's sales rose strongly as well, reaching ITL 113 billion in 1992, then topping ITL 167 billion in 1994.

La Doria set its sights on stepping up its growth into the new century. The unification of the European trade zone, and the dropping of import tariffs among member nations in particular opened up new expansion opportunities for the company. In order to raise the capital for its expansion, La Doria went public in 1995, listing its shares on the Borsa Italiana. The Ferraioli family nonetheless retained control of the company, holding more than 70 percent among the various family members, and nearly 80 percent including the shares held by La Doria itself.

ACQUIRING SCALE FOR THE 21ST CENTURY

The public offering enabled La Doria to launch its first acquisition the following year, with the purchase of a 24.75 percent stake in Delfino SpA. That company specialized in the production of tomato sauces. La Doria

KEY DATES

1954: Diodata Ferraioli founds a company producing canned tomatoes in Angri, Italy, launching the La Doria brand.

1960s: La Doria begins exporting to the European markets, primarily to the private-label sector.

1970s: La Doria expands its production to include canned fruits and vegetables, and juices.

1995: La Doria goes public on the Borsa Italiana.

1997: La Doria establishes a U.K. joint venture with Gerber Foods.

1998: La Doria acquires Italian tomato canner Pomagro.

1999: Heinz becomes a partner in La Doria's U.K. operations, which becomes LDH (La Doria) Ltd.

2004: La Doria acquires Italy's Panafrutta and its subsidiary Confruit, as well as a stake in Eugea Mediterranea.

2005: La Doria raises its stake in Eugea to 80 percent.

2007: Heinz exits LDH, selling its stake to John West Foods.

also began seeking expansion beyond Italy. The company's target fell especially on the United Kingdom, which represented one of the country's most important markets outside of Italy. In 1997, La Doria reached an agreement with the United Kingdom's Gerber Foods International. Gerber had long been one of the leading U.K. producers of canned foods, and in the 1950s had begun importing canned goods into the United Kingdom from other markets.

Gerber and La Doria established a joint venture, Gerber La Doria, and began importing La Doria's canned tomatoes and other Italian foods for the U.K. private-label sector. Soon after, however, Gerber decided to refocus its U.K. operations onto the fruit juice sector. As a result, La Doria joined a management buyout of the U.K. operation, with La Doria taking a majority stake.

La Doria then sought a new partner for the U.K. operation, and by 1999 had reached an agreement to bring Heinz into the venture. As a gesture of commitment to the U.K. business, Heinz bought a 20 percent stake. The U.K. company was then renamed LDH (La Doria) Ltd. The partnership with Heinz provided a major boost for LDH, which gained greater access to

the U.K. supermarket sector, particularly the market's major players including Tesco, Sainsbury, and Waitrose. By 2000, LDH claimed to control some 50 percent of the U.K. private-label canned tomatoes market.

By then, La Doria had taken steps to expand and rationalize its production capacity. In 1998, the company acquired Pomagro Inc., a smaller canned tomato producer based in Fisciano, Italy. The addition of Pomagro brought La Doria a new production facility of more than 56,000 square meters. The purchase of Pomagro also allowed La Doria to negotiate its expansion despite the increasingly stringent European quota levels.

La Doria completed a new expansion of its production capacity in 2000, buying a 195,000-square-meter production plant in Sarno from Star SpA. La Doria than converted the factory to the production of an expanded line of canned tomato specialties. The company invested in redeveloping the plant's operations, especially its packaging capacity. At the same time, the group added the production of metal containers, needed for both the Sarno plant's production and at its other locations. The expansion of the Sarno site, which lasted into 2002, came as part of a EUR 36 million capital expenditure program put into place by La Doria two years earlier.

La Doria continued to look for new growth opportunities into the middle of the decade. In 2004, the company completed two new acquisitions, starting with an 80 percent stake in Sanafrutta SpA. That company in turned owned 100 percent of Confruit G Spa, which operated a canning facility in Faenza, in northern Italy, for that region's fruit and vegetable specialties. In 2005, La Doria acquired an additional 10 percent of Sanafrutta, then merged both Sanafrutta and Confruit G into its own operations.

Confruit G also brought La Doria a 24.52 percent share in Eugea Mediterranea, a producer of canned tomato products, as well as fruit purees and juices. In 2005, La Doria boosted its stake in Eugea Mediterranea to 80 percent; Eugea's farmer-suppliers retained most of the remaining shares in the company. The addition of Eugea Mediterranea allowed La Doria to increase its total tomato production by nearly one-third, to 4,000 tons per year.

These acquisitions enabled La Doria to strengthen its export operations. By 2007, international sales represented more than 70 percent of the company's total revenues, which topped EUR 400 million ($600 million) that year. La Doria had also achieved a strong balance among its various product categories. Where its "red line" accounted for 50 percent of its sales in the early 1990s, this category generated less than 30 percent of the group's total sales. In the meantime, the company's canned fruit and canned vegetables production had grown to 27.5 percent and 19.3 percent, respectively. The remaining 24 percent included the canned seafood and other products produced by LDH in the United Kingdom.

In 2007, LDH's shareholding structure changed again, when Heinz, as part of its exit of the canned seafood sector, sold its 20 percent share of the company to John West Foods. By then, La Doria had begun exploring new international frontiers, launching exports of its products to the New Zealand and Australian markets. While representing only a small part of La Doria's total sales, these markets nonetheless grew strongly, achieving a growth rate of some 70 percent through 2008, and becoming one of the few bright spots for the company as its overall sales were hit by the global economic crisis that year. By then, La Doria had become one of Italy's leading canned food producers and a major provider to the European private-label sector.

M. L. Cohen

PRINCIPAL SUBSIDIARIES

Eugea Mediterranea S.p.A. (89.46%); LDH Foods (Hellas) Idt (Greece); LDH Foods S.L. (Spain); LDH (La Doria) Ltd (U.K.; 51%); Pomagro s.r.l.; Tec Trading s.r.l. (51%).

PRINCIPAL COMPETITORS

Parmalat S.p.A.; Unilever Bestfoods Italia S.p.A.; Kraft Foods Italia S.p.A.; Sterilgarda Alimenti S.p.A.; Apofruit - Soc. Coop.arl; CoInd Scarl; Zuegg S.p.A.; Fratelli Sacla S.p.A.; Fruttagel ScpA; Antonio Petti Fu Pasquale S.p.A.

FURTHER READING

Dempsey, Karen, "Heinz Working with La Doria As It Enters the Canned Tomato Market," *Grocer,* July 29, 2000, p. 52.

Falconio, Guidoni, "Crisi: La Doria Soffre, Iesm Resiste," *Il Denaro,* October 9, 2008.

"La Doria Posts Slight Revenue Increase," *just-food.com,* March 21, 2006.

Pritchard, Bill, and David Burch, *Agri-Food Globalization in Perspective,* London: Ashgate Publishing, 2003.

Verzura, Enrico, "Gruppo La Doria, Boom in Oceania," *Il Denaro,* November 21, 2008.

LDK Solar Co., Ltd.

Hi-Tech Industrial Park
Xinyu, Jiangxi 338032
China
Telephone: (+86 790) 686-0171
Web site: http://www.ldksolar.com

Public Company
Incorporated: 2005
Employees: 6,253
Sales: $524.0 million (2007)
Stock Exchanges: New York
Ticker Symbol: LDK
NAICS: 334413 Semiconductor and Related Device
  Manufacturing

■ ■ ■

Founded in 2005 by a very young Chinese entrepreneur, LDK Solar Co., Ltd., is a world-leading manufacturer of low-cost multicrystalline solar wafers, a key component of solar cells, which convert sunlight into electricity. The company is headquartered in Xinyu City, in China's southeastern Jiangxi Province, with offices in Hong Kong and Sunnyvale, California. With a sprawling manufacturing factory operating at maximum capacity and the largest polysilicon production facility of its kind in the world under construction, LDK supplies wafers to solar energy product makers throughout Asia, Europe, and North America.

FROM SAFETY HELMETS TO SOLAR WAFERS

When LDK Solar Co., Ltd., was founded by Xiaofeng Peng in his native Jiangxi Province in mid-2005, China was just beginning to emerge on the world stage as a manufacturer of photovoltaic solar energy products. Just 29 years old at the time, Peng was already running another very successful business, Liouxin Industrial Group, which he had founded in 1997 in Suzhou. The company, which had 12,000 employees, made personal protective equipment, such as gloves and safety helmets. After traveling to Europe and the United States in 2003 in search of ideas to import to China, Peng concluded that green energy was potentially big business.

At first, Peng considered making solar energy panels, but instead decided to focus his new business on the production of low-cost solar wafers, a key ingredient used to produce solar cells. Unlike the competition, LDK established a model for low-cost wafer production that utilized a combination of virgin and recycled polysilicon, which the company harvested from semiconductor industry scrap.

With $30 million of his own money and $80 million from Hong Kong banks, Peng began building high-tech factories in Xinyu City next to land still tilled by farmers with water buffalo. In August 2005, LDK ordered $33 million worth of silicon wafer production machinery from New Hampshire-based GT Solar Technologies, a maker of equipment for the photovoltaic and semiconductor industries.

BECOMING A GLOBAL PLAYER

The installation of the GT-made furnaces, which were used to bake raw silicon into multicrystalline ingots that were then sliced into wafers, was complete by February 2006. LDK made its first commercial shipment of solar

COMPANY PERSPECTIVES

LDK Solar Co., Ltd., is a manufacturer of multicrystalline solar wafers, which are the principal raw material used to produce solar cells. LDK sells multicrystalline wafers globally to manufacturers of photovoltaic products, including solar cells and solar modules. In addition, the company provides wafer processing services to monocrystalline and multicrystalline solar cell and module manufacturers. LDK's headquarters and manufacturing facilities are located in Hi-Tech Industrial Park, Xinyu City, Jiangxi Province, in the People's Republic of China. The company's office in the United States is located in Sunnyvale, California.

wafers in April 2006, and by the end of the second quarter, the company had turned a profit. By August 2006, LDK had added corporate offices and research and development centers in the Chinese cities of Suzhou, Shanghai, and Hong Kong, as well as in Sydney, Australia, and Sunnyvale, California.

In October 2006, the firm announced plans to increase annual manufacturing capacity of solar wafers from 100 megawatts to 1,000 megawatts by 2010 (1,000 megawatts of solar energy is enough to power 300,000 houses). In pursuit of that goal, the company sought venture capital funds prior to a planned initial public offering (IPO) of stock in the United States. Before the year was over, at least four investment companies, including CDH Investments and JAFCO Asia, invested more than $100 million in LDK. The company ended 2006 with a net income of $30.2 million on sales of $105.4 million.

By the end of March 2007, LDK had expanded its annual wafer production capacity to about 215 megawatts. In the first quarter of 2007, according to financial data released in May, LDK reported a net income of $24.5 million on $73.4 million in sales. That compared to a loss of $440,000 and no revenue in the same quarter of 2006.

A RISING STAR

On May 14, 2007, LDK filed documents with the U.S. Securities and Exchange Commission (SEC) for an IPO of company stock on the New York Stock Exchange (NYSE) under the symbol LDK. On June 1, 2007, the company raised $469.4 million from the sale of 17.38 million American Depositary Shares at an opening price

of $27 each, which made it the largest U.S. IPO of a mainland Chinese company on the NYSE since 2004. Share price peaked at $30.15 but closed the trading day at $27.20. LDK Chairman and CEO Peng retained an 83 percent stake. The company's market debut was considered a disappointment only because it came two weeks after the IPO of China Sunergy Co., Ltd., which surged 51 percent on its first day of trading.

In the summer of 2007, with the price of polysilicon at an all-time high, LDK announced plans to build two polysilicon production factories next to its wafer plant. The move, expected to cost more than $1 billion, was designed to reduce costs and alleviate the company's exposure to a chronic industry-wide shortage of refined silicon. In July, LDK won regulatory approval for its expansion project from the Development and Reform Commission of Jiangxi, a local top-ranking economic regulator in the province. The company then announced plans to purchase polysilicon reactors and other production equipment from GT Solar.

In August 2007, LDK reported a net income of $28.7 million on sales of $99.1 million for the second quarter of fiscal 2007. As the company broke ground on construction of the largest polysilicon production facility of its kind in the world, it also announced multiyear contracts to supply solar wafers to two Taiwan-based companies, a $516 million deal with Chuan-Yi Investment Corporation and a $495 million agreement with Neo Solar Power Corp.

In September 2007, *Forbes* magazine identified LDK founder Xiaofeng Peng, with his $3.25 billion stake in the two-year-old company, as China's richest solar entrepreneur. It also reported that China had risen to the world's number three producer of solar cells, after Germany and Japan, and identified LDK as one of the companies leading the surge. In late September 2007, after it landed multiyear, multimillion-dollar, fixed-price contacts with Taiwan-based Solartech Energy Corp. and Mosel Vitelic Inc., LDK saw its share price rise to a year-high $76.75, almost triple its June listing price.

RIDING CHOPPY WATERS

LDK began a tumultuous fourth quarter on October 3, 2007, when it became public that a financial controller had left the firm after making allegations the company misrepresented its inventory and financial results. LDK denied the charges the next day, but by October 8 shares had fallen more than 50 percent to $37.50. The stock rebounded some the next day when LDK raised its revenue forecast for the third quarter but as it stood on October 12, the firm's market capitalization had dropped from $7 billion to about $4.8 billion.

KEY DATES

2005: Chinese entrepreneur, 29-year-old Xiaofeng Peng, founds solar wafer business in Jiangxi Province.

2006: Company makes first commercial shipments of solar wafers in April.

2007: LDK begins trading on the New York Stock Exchange in June; firm breaks ground in August on the largest polysilicon production facility of its kind in the world; stock falls 50 percent on allegations of inventory accounting fraud in October.

2008: Securities and Exchange Commission clears LDK of wrongdoing in inventory accounting practices in April; company becomes the world's largest producer of solar wafers in August.

2009: Polysilicon production projects are put on hold for six months in January.

LDK received another blow on October 22, the same day LDK Chairman and CEO Xiaofeng Peng was named the sixth richest person in China, when Goldman Sachs initiated coverage of the company's shares with a "sell" rating. Share price fell 14 percent on the news despite another same day announcement of a three-year wafer supply contract with China-based Canadian Solar Inc. The deal marked the company's fifth contract in a month for a total of $1.35 billion in new sales.

On December 1, 2007, company CEO Peng was named "The Most Admired Entrepreneur of 2007" at the Annual Meeting of Chinese Management. A week later the company signed a ten-year contract with Germany-based Q-Cells AG that provided up-front payments to help LDK finance its polysilicon production expansion plan. Shares closed at over $58 on the news.

Shares of LDK surged 22 percent on December 18, 2007, after the company said an independent investigation by its audit committee found no material errors in its silicon inventory levels. Delayed third-quarter financial results, released the next day, showed that sales had increased over 400 percent, but shares fell back 20 percent when the company's gross profit margin shrank due to rising polysilicon prices. By the end of 2007, LDK had secured nine long-term wafer supply contracts during the year and expanded and diversified its customer base, with more than 75 percent of revenues

coming from outside China, up from 20 percent in 2006.

NEW DEALS IN 2008

LDK began 2008 with a January acquisition of a 33.5 percent stake of Jiangxi Sinoma New Material Co., Ltd., a Xinyu-based manufacturer of crucibles, equipment used in the manufacture of polysilicon crystals. LDK continued to build its catalog of long-term wafer supply contracts in February through an eight-year deal with Korea-based Hyundai Heavy Industries Co., Ltd.

In April 2008, the company signed a ten-year wafer supply agreement with India-based Moser Baer Photo Voltaic Ltd., a six-year deal with Silcio S.A. Greek, and a four-year pact with Arise Corporation of Canada. April also brought news that LDK was moving forward on the construction of the world's largest polysilicon plant with a $1 billion contract with Fluor Corp. for engineering, procurement, and construction management services.

Financial details were not disclosed but LDK continued to ink wafer supply deals that called for advanced payments and included market-based pricing linked with take-or-pay provisions. In May 2008, the company signed a five-year contract to supply solar wafers to Germany's Qimonda AG. June brought orders from Chinese companies: a five-year wafer supply pact with Jiangxi Solar PV Corp. and a ten-year supply contract with repeat customer Canadian Solar. July brought a ten-year supply contract from Europe with Belgium-based Photovoltech.

GAINING MOMENTUM

LDK continued to experience substantial revenue growth in the second quarter of 2008, as reported by the company in August. Net sales were up 89.2 percent from the first quarter to $441.7 million and net income tripled to $149.5 million. The results smashed all expectations and the news sent company stock up 20 percent to around $40 a share.

In August 2008, the Chinese media declared LDK the world's largest producer of solar wafers. As of June 30, the report said, LDK's silicon wafer production capacity surpassed Norway-based Renewable Energy Corp. (REC). LDK's April to June wafer sales also topped REC's, according to the report.

Orders continued to roll in as the company signed five more multiyear wafer supply contracts from mid-August to mid-September 2008. LDK renewed and expanded agreements with repeat customers Hyundai, Solartech, and Q-Cells, and added new contracts with

India-based XL Telecom & Energy Ltd. and Japan-based Sumitomo Corporation.

In September 2008, the company received official approval for construction of its polysilicon manufacturing plant and expansion of its wafer production facilities from the Jiangxi Provincial Development and Reform Commission. The company planned to finance its multimillion-dollar expansion, in part, with proceeds from $192.4 million raised in a late September secondary offering of 4.8 million American Depositary Shares.

WEATHERING THE ECONOMIC DOWNTURN

By the start of the fourth quarter of 2008, however, LDK's stock and that of the rest of the solar industry began reeling from the impact of the global financial crisis and the collapse of the crude oil market. Not even the extension of solar tax credits through 2016 by the U.S. Congress in early October could stem the tide. LDK share price fell from $51.26 on August 29 to $33.12 on October 1.

The global financial crisis took its toll on LDK Chairman Peng's personal fortune as well. In October 2008, he was again at the top of China's Hurun Energy Rich List for the second consecutive year, but his personal assets had shrunk by $1.95 billion to $3.95 billion. The Hurun Report also named Peng "The Most Respectable Young Entrepreneur of China."

In October 2008, the company finished building its smaller, 1,000-ton-per-year polysilicon plant and reiterated that construction of its larger, 15,000-metric-ton polysilicon factory was on track. In late October 2008, LDK closed a seven-year deal to supply wafers to Italy-based Helios Technology. In mid-November, the firm signed BP Solar International to another multiyear wafer supply contract. Part of the deal called for BP Solar to provide a minimum of 1,600 mega-tons (MT) of silicon to LDK during the contract period.

Compared to the second quarter, net sales for the third quarter of 2008, as reported by the company on November 17, were up 22.7 percent to $541.8 million. Net income was down to $88.4 million from $149.5 million. However, the company posted a third-quarter profit of 77 cents per share, and easily beat the 71 cents per share expected by analysts. LDK stock rose on the news but on November 19, share price fell with the broader market and hit an all-time low of $9.95. That low point prompted LDK Chairman Peng to tell the *Wall Street Journal Asia* the following day: "Our business will not be immune to the current global economic downturn."

LOWERING EXPECTATIONS

CEO Peng also expressed confidence in his company's prospects. LDK had signed 16 long-term wafer supply agreements in 2008 and had reached an annualized wafer production capacity goal of 1.2 gigawatts by the end of the third quarter.

As 2009 began, LDK was still trying to find its footing in a very uncertain market. In mid-January, the company was forced to lower its fourth-quarter revenue guidance by $130 million and its revenue guidance for 2009 by $600 million. Even with the plunge in the price of polysilicon from $400 per kilogram to $150 per kilogram, the company also announced that it had started polysilicon production at its first 1,000 MT plant on January 14 and expected full production in the second quarter. On January 19, LDK also said that its 16,000 MT plant was operational and would be in full production by the end of the year.

While LDK's order catalog for 2009 and well beyond was booked solid, in January the company began to get requests for shipment delays due to tight credit markets and the growing global recession. Yet with a strong leader at the helm in Xiaofeng Peng, prospects for increased profit margins due to the drop in silicon costs, and the promises of the governments of China and the United States to promote alternative energy solutions to environmental and economic problems, this still very young company appeared well positioned to ride out the storm and shine brightly when the clouds finally cleared.

Ted Sylvester

PRINCIPAL SUBSIDIARIES

Jiangxi Sinoma New Material Co., Ltd. (33.5%).

PRINCIPAL COMPETITORS

Renewable Energy Corporation ASA (Norway); MEMC Electronic Materials, Inc. (USA); SolarWorld AG (Germany); ReneSola Ltd (China); PV Crystalox Solar plc (UK); Kyocera Corporation (Japan).

FURTHER READING

Alpert, Bill, "China's Solar Boom Loses Its Luster," *Barron's,* October 8, 2007, p. 22.

Anand, Shefali, Carolyn Cui, and Laura Santini, "LDK Solar Sinks Behind a Cloud," *Wall Street Journal Asia,* October 22, 2007, p. 23.

Bogoslaw, David Solar, "Stocks Get Their Day in the Sun," *BusinessWeek Online,* January 3, 2008.

Chernova, Yuliya, "Former LDK Controller Says His Doubts Began in May," *Dow Jones News Service,* November 6, 2007.

————, "LDK Investors Criticize Company's Communication," *Dow Jones News Service,* October 25, 2007.

————, "LDK Solar's Accounting Puzzles Even an Accounting Expert," *Dow Jones News Service,* March 17, 2008.

"China Solar Firm in Nasdaq Dream," *SinoCast China Financial Watch,* August 2, 2006, p. 1.

Cui, Carolyn, "LDK Ex-Officer Provides More Claims Against Firm," *Wall Street Journal,* October 13, 2007, p. B3.

Flannery, Russell, "China's Bright Light; China's LDK Solar," *Forbes Asia,* September 3, 2007, p. 84.

Groom, Nichola, "Solar Stocks Soar on Outlook for U.S. Subsidies," *Reuters News,* April 4, 2008.

"Inventory Allegations Only Paint a Partial Picture—LDK," *China Business Newswire,* October 23, 2007.

"LDK Solar Down on Report; Financial Controller Out," *Reuters News,* October 3, 2007.

"LDK Solar Wins Expansion Approval from Regulators," *SinoCast China IT Watch,* July 18, 2007, p. 1.

"Polysilicon Price May Drop in 2010," *China Chemical Reporter,* November 16, 2008.

Reeves, Amy, "With Supplies Short, Chinese Solar Firm to Manufacture Own Silicon," *Investor's Business Daily,* September 14, 2007.

Spencer, Jane, "China Solar Stocks Shine in U.S., but Some Could Be Overheated," *Wall Street Journal Asia,* May 23, 2007, p. 21.

Legal & General Group Plc

One Coleman Street
London, EC2R 5AA
United Kingdom
Telephone: (+44 20) 3124 2000
Fax: (+44 20) 3124 2500
Web site: http://www.legalandgeneralgroup.com

Public Company
Founded: 1836 as The Legal & General Life Assurance Society
Incorporated: 1920 as The Legal & General Assurance Society
Employees: 10,067
Total Assets: £277.57 billion ($552.37 billion) (2008)
Stock Exchanges: London
Ticker Symbol: LGEN
NAICS: 524113 Direct Life Insurance Carriers; 524114 Direct Health and Medical Insurance Carriers; 524126 Direct Property and Casualty Insurance Carriers; 525110 Pension Funds; 525910 Open-End Investment Funds; 525920 Trusts, Estates, and Agency Accounts; 525990 Other Financial Vehicles; 551112 Offices of Other Holding Companies

■ ■ ■

Legal & General Group Plc is one of Great Britain's largest insurance concerns. Although it also writes home, disability, travel, and other nonlife policies; offers investments products such as pensions, unit trusts, and individual savings accounts (ISAs) to individuals; and provides investment-management services to institutional and retail customers, life insurance has always stood at the core of its operations. In fact, it sold nothing but life insurance until after World War I. In the early 21st century, about 85 percent of Legal & General's operating profits came from its domestic operations, with the remainder generated from subsidiaries in the United States, France, and the Netherlands.

FOUNDED IN 1836 BY SIX LAWYERS

The Legal & General Life Assurance Society was founded in 1836, when British life insurance was just beginning to thrive. At that time, rapid population increases in Great Britain and a surge in real personal income were creating favorable conditions for the life insurance industry. Between 1834 and 1836, 310 joint-stock life insurance companies were created, of which Legal & General turned out to be one of the most durable. Its founders were six prominent London lawyers—Sergeant John Adams, Basil Montagu, W. C. L. Keene, Kenyon S. Parker, J. H. R. Chichester, and George Leake Baker—who convened their first board meeting in a legal office at 18 Lincoln's Inn Fields in June 1836. At that meeting, Adams was elected as chairman and the company's initial capitalization was set at £1 million, a goal it reached through sale of stock in 1839. The first board of directors was set at 24 members, raised to 30 at the next meeting, and shares were limited to members of the legal profession.

In October 1836 Legal & General accepted its first policy, for the solicitor Thomas Smith. Although the

COMPANY PERSPECTIVES

It has been said that insurance can claim to be the first real financial service in that it was the first to bring the benefits of financial planning and risk-sharing within the reach of everyone. In the case of Legal & General this has certainly been a consistent aim. We have sought over many years to progressively extend our services and product range in various areas of insurance—often introducing new ideas and concepts in the process. For many years, too, we have played an increasingly strong role in underpinning economic, industrial and scientific progress; this is typified today, not only by Legal & General insuring massive new projects such as satellites in space, but also by backing financially the effective transfer of infant technologies to larger-scale production and commercial use.

As well as running a business, we believe we have social responsibilities—that we should function as a profitable enterprise and also play a part in the cultural and social life of the community. It is for this reason that we have developed within Legal & General, again over a period of years, a conscious and sustained programme of sponsoring and other contributory activities.

society carefully screened each applicant for insurance, Smith proved not to be a good risk: he died four years later and his policy of £1,000 was paid after the society had received only about £177 in premiums. That fall, the firm appointed six provincial agents, including one in Edinburgh, and within its first year of business it accepted more than 100 policies.

Legal & General began to lend money to both corporate and individual customers soon after its founding. In 1841 it lent £20,000 to the Stockton and Hartlepool Railway, and in 1852 it authorized £60,000 worth of credit to the Regent Canal Company. A request from the Great Western Railway in 1846 for a loan of £65,000 was, however, turned down. A substantial number of London aristocrats also took out loans from the firm at this time, more likely than not to cover gambling debts.

Legal & General expanded throughout the rest of the 19th century. In the 1850s it entered the real estate business, investing heavily in the development of

Birkenhead, near London, and the transformation of Belvedere Estate into a residential area in 1860. To serve its growing core life insurance business, Legal & General established its first office outside London, in Manchester, in 1889. By the end of the century, the firm's total assets exceeded £2 million and it was the second largest insurance company, in terms of capitalization, in Great Britain doing only ordinary life business.

EXPANSION OVERSEAS FOLLOWING WORLD WAR I

Legal & General emerged from World War I intact, despite four years of paying an unusually high number of claims because of war casualties and the influenza epidemic of 1918. In 1920 the society incorporated and dropped the word *Life* from its name. The company began writing fire and accident policies, a business that immediately proved successful; the new popularity of automobile and airplane travel created a huge demand for accident insurance. In 1929 the restriction of society membership to those in the legal profession was lifted. The Great Depression's effect on the world economy in the 1930s was scarcely felt by the British insurance industry. In fact, historian G. Clayton pointed out in his *British Insurance* that, if anything, widespread pessimism in bad times tended to increase the demand for insurance.

Legal & General expanded overseas and by acquiring other companies. In 1931 it opened a life insurance office in Johannesburg. In 1933 it strengthened its pensions operations when it acquired the London-based pensions business of New York-based Metropolitan Life Insurance, after restrictions placed on U.S. insurance companies in the wake of the 1929 stock market crash made it unprofitable for Met Life to continue its British business. The next year Legal & General further strengthened its position both at home and abroad by acquiring Gresham Life Assurance and Gresham Fire and Accident. The Gresham mergers were particularly important for their long histories of doing business overseas. Gresham's fire insurance business in Australia provided a base from which Legal & General would begin to penetrate the Australian market in 1948.

World War II put a tight squeeze on the British insurance industry. Men and money fueled the war effort; the firms were asked to contribute the former by releasing employees devoted to generating new business and the latter by buying up low-interest government bonds, often selling securities paying higher yields in order to do so. Fire insurance claims skyrocketed as German bombs fell on England. Legal & General was among the many firms forced to relocate offices outside London for the duration because of the bombing. After

KEY DATES

1836: Six prominent London lawyers form the Legal & General Life Assurance Society.

1920: Society incorporates and drops the word *Life* from its name; it soon thereafter begins writing fire and accident policies.

1933: Legal & General acquires the London-based pensions business of Metropolitan Life Insurance.

1956: Company enters the Australian life insurance market.

1971: Company establishes pensions-management and unit-trust subsidiaries.

1979: Company is reorganized under a new parent company, Legal & General Group Plc.

1981: Government Employees Life Insurance Company, later renamed Banner Life Insurance Company, is acquired.

1984: The Dutch branch of the Unilife Assurance Group is acquired.

1989: Legal & General acquires William Penn Life Insurance Company of New York.

1996: Company divests its commercial general insurance business.

1998: Company sells its Australian life insurance subsidiary.

1999: Legal & General agrees to be acquired by National Westminster Bank Plc, but the deal later falls through.

2001: As part of a string of alliances, Legal & General enters into a distribution partnership with Barclays PLC.

2008: Company acquires the life insurance business and unit-trust management arm of Nationwide Building Society.

several temporary relocations, the company ended up at a former school at Kingswood in Surrey. Its head office remained in Kingswood after the return of peace, and later its central computer was located there as well.

Once the war ended, the firm picked up where it had left off in 1939. In 1947 it began writing fire and accident policies in South Africa, as well as life insurance policies. In 1956 the company added life insurance to its nonlife business in Australia. Back home, the firm added marine insurance in 1949, using Andrew Weir & Company as its agent. In 1960 it acquired Andrew Weir's marine subsidiary, British Commonwealth Insurance.

From just after World War II through the late 1960s, Legal & General ranked behind Prudential as Great Britain's second largest life insurance company when measured by total sums insured, maintaining about 10 percent of the market. It grew substantially early in the decade, and total assets reached the £1 billion mark by 1970. The 1960s, however, were not without contention for the firm: In 1966 angry shareholders complained when Legal & General failed to raise its dividend and the firm's directors did not adequately explain why. Rumors circulated in the financial press over the next year that Legal & General would "go mutual," with the shareholders selling out to the policyholders, but at its 1967 annual meeting the firm declared that the firm would not change hands.

INTERNATIONAL EXPANSION

After a reorganization of the executive office in 1970, increasing international expansion of operations marked the decade for Legal & General. In 1972 it entered into cooperation agreements with three European insurance companies: Colonia of West Germany, La Paix of France, and Reale Mutuale of Italy. In 1973 it joined with the West German firm Cologne Reinsurance Company to purchase Victory Insurance, Britain's second largest reinsurance company. Legal & General took the majority interest and subsequently bought Cologne's minority stake. In the same year, it sold off Gresham Life Assurance but retained most of its overseas businesses. Between 1974 and 1976, it signed cooperation agreements with AGO Holding (later part of AEGON of the Netherlands), Assubel of Belgium, Ireland's Life of Eire, Vadoise Vie of Switzerland, and Nippon Life. In 1976 Legal & General merged its South African general insurance business with that of Norwich Union under the name Aegis Insurance Company. The company also took some domestic actions during the 1970s. In 1971 it introduced a pensions-management subsidiary and set up the Tyndall Fund-Unit Assurance Company to gain a foothold in the unit-trust field. In 1973 Legal & General acquired the real estate developer Cavendish Land.

At the end of the decade, Legal & General underwent a major reorganization. It separated its British insurance operations, its international operations, and its investment-management activities into three distinct subsidiaries. The new parent company, called Legal & General Group Plc, became a noninsurance company. The move was made to give Legal & General greater financial flexibility and to differentiate its activities more clearly.

After this reorganization, Legal & General ventured into the U.S. market in 1981 when it acquired Government Employees Life Insurance Company for $140 million. It changed the Washington, D.C.-based company's name to Banner Life the next year. In 1984 it acquired Unilife Netherlands, the Dutch subsidiary of the Unilife Assurance Group, and added it to the newly established Legal & General Netherlands. At the same time, however, not all of Legal & General's overseas ventures were working out. The firm decided to terminate its general insurance businesses in France and Australia in 1981. In 1987 Legal & General sold its 45 percent stake in Aegis Insurance, joining the trend among British companies toward divesting South African holdings because of declining profitability, shareholder pressure, and worries over political instability in that country.

The late 1980s were marked by Legal & General's attempt to bolster its U.S. operations amid some difficulty at home. Throughout much of the decade, the performance of Legal & General's pension fund asset management was embarrassingly poor. In 1987 the amount of assets managed by its investment arm shrank from £12.5 billion to £11 billion after the U.S. stock market crash. To remedy the situation, the firm lured David Prosser from his position as chief of the Coal Board's pension fund in January 1988 to head its investment-management operations. In Prosser's first year, the investment division's asset pool increased to over £14 billion, and in March 1989 Legal & General strengthened its position in the U.S. market when it acquired William Penn Life Insurance Company of New York from Continental Corporation, a U.S. insurance concern, for $80 million.

Legal & General also expanded in another direction when it reached a cooperative agreement with Kyoei Mutual Fire and Marine Insurance Company of Tokyo in 1989. The agreement gave the company greater access to the Japanese market. At the same time, it provided more business from Kyoei's industrial clients moving into the unified European market.

LATE 20TH-CENTURY DEVELOPMENTS

In the 1990s Legal & General continued to tinker with its various operations as it was guided by Prosser, who was named group chief executive in 1991. The same year, that company exited the reinsurance business by selling Victory to Nederlandes Reassurantie Group Holding N.V. Legal & General in 1995 entered into a joint venture with Woolwich Building Society to provide Woolwich customers with a variety of general insurance policies, including homeowner's insurance.

Also in 1995, Legal & General's Australian subsidiary joined with Australian insurer SGIO Insurance to acquire SGIC, the insurance operations of the South Australian government, for AUD 170 million (£80 million). Through this transaction, Legal & General gained SGIC's life insurance business as well as an investment management contract for the South Australian government's third-party insurance pool. The company sold its commercial general insurance business to Guardian Insurance in 1996 and the following year began offering banking services in the United Kingdom after securing a banking license in June. The first service offered by this new venture was an instant access deposit account service, which was launched in July 1997.

Historically conservative in nature and thus usually capable of avoiding entanglement in scandals, Legal & General nonetheless found itself in the 1990s in the midst of an ongoing pensions selling scandal. In early 1994 Lautro, an organization that self-regulated the U.K. life insurance industry, fined Legal & General a then-record £400,000 for failing to meet standards set by Lautro. The main charge, which the company did not dispute, was that some of its direct sales agents had persuaded thousands of customers to leave lucrative occupational retirement plans and instead purchase personal pensions from Legal & General. Other life insurance companies were also implicated in the scandal, which was estimated to have wronged as many as half a million people in the late 1980s and early 1990s. In response, Legal & General established the new post of director of compliance in April 1994. Moreover, in March 1997 the company unveiled a pensions guarantee, which promised to pay individuals the pension they would have received had they retained their occupational retirement scheme. In July 1998 Legal & General set aside more than £600,000 ($1 billion) to compensate victims of the scandal.

Lacking a leading share of an increasingly competitive market undergoing consolidation, Legal & General withdrew from the Australian life insurance market in mid-1998 by selling its subsidiary in that nation to Colonial Limited for AUD 892 million (£339 million). Back home, in the meantime, amid the continuing consolidation of the financial services industry, most notably the purchase of insurance companies by banks, Legal & General became the object of takeover rumors in late 1997 and early 1998, but the company insisted that it was large enough and strong enough to remain independent. In March 1998 Legal & General announced that its new business had increased 40 percent in fiscal 1997 compared to the previous year, while its pretax operating profits had risen 20 percent, to £349.6 million ($583.8 million).

In September 1999 Legal & General reversed course from its independent stance when it agreed to be acquired by National Westminster Bank Plc (NatWest) in a cash-and-stock deal valued at around £10.75 billion ($17.3 billion). Like other similar deals, it was pursued mainly for its potential cross-selling opportunities, notably the selling of Legal & General's insurance and savings offerings through NatWest's extensive network of bank branches. The market reacted negatively to the deal, however, as many observers concluded that the offering price was too high. NatWest's share price almost immediately fell sharply, leaving the bank itself vulnerable to a takeover. Bank of Scotland soon came forward with a hostile takeover offer, and NatWest in early October was forced to drop its offer for Legal & General to concentrate on fending off this bid. Legal & General thus continued on its path of independence. (NatWest eventually was swallowed by the Royal Bank of Scotland Group plc.)

ALLIANCE-LED GROWTH STRATEGY

In the wake of the failed NatWest merger, Legal & General eventually decided to access bank customers via alliances. Thus, in early 2001, the company entered into a partnership with Barclays PLC, the fourth largest bank in the United Kingdom, through which Legal & General was able to begin selling life insurance, pensions, and mutual funds through Barclays' more than 1,700 branches. Shortly thereafter, Legal & General partnered with another U.K. banking firm, Alliance & Leicester plc, to begin offering individual savings accounts (ISAs), unit trusts, and single premium bonds through the bank's 300 branches.

During 2002 Legal & General sold two marginally profitable, noncore businesses, its banking and mortgage units, to Northern Rock plc for £131 million ($200 million). As part of the deal, the two companies agreed to extend an existing partnership by enabling Legal & General to begin selling Northern Rock's mortgage and deposit products to its customers under the insurer's brand. Legal & General had been selling its long-term savings products to Northern Rock customers. To strengthen its balance sheet and thereby position itself for further organic growth, Legal & General in the fall of 2002 successfully raised £788 million ($1.2 billion) through a rights issue. Although the company posted a 13 percent increase in new business during 2002, in part stemming from strong contributions from the Barclays and Alliance & Leicester alliances, its operating profits fell 7 percent as Legal & General was forced to increase its reserve by £140 million ($215 million) because annuity customers were living longer than

predicted. Its funds under management, which totaled £116.3 billion ($187.2 billion) by the end of 2002, remained essentially unchanged over the course of the year because of an ongoing downturn in global equity markets.

Over the next couple of years, Legal & General continued to pursue growth in its home market by entering into additional alliances, including one with supermarket operator J Sainsbury plc. The company performed strongly in 2004 as operating profits increased 4 percent despite another reserve increase of £240 million ($460 million), again tied to increased longevity of annuitants. In March 2005 Legal & General reduced its presence in homeowners insurance by selling Gresham Insurance Company to Barclays. At the end of 2005, Prosser retired after more than 14 years as group chief executive. He was succeeded by Tim Breedon, the deputy chief executive who had previously headed the firm's fund management arm.

Breedon immediately launched a thorough review of Legal & General's capital and cash flow position. The review, completed in late 2006, revealed that the company's strong position had left it with about £1 billion ($1.96 billion) in surplus capital. Over the next two years, these funds were conveyed back to stockholders through a share-buyback program. Under Breedon, Legal & General also returned to acquisition mode, purchasing the life insurance business and unit-trust management arm of Nationwide Building Society in February 2008 for around £293 million ($569 million). Nationwide also agreed to a distribution deal through which it began selling Legal & General products via its branches to its 11 million customers. Nationwide was the largest of the United Kingdom's building societies (a type of member-owned financial institution) and the nation's second biggest savings provider.

During the first nine months of financially chaotic 2008, Legal & General more than tripled its pension-fund buyout business, bolstering its position as the largest pension insurer in the United Kingdom. Because of its almost exclusive concentration on its home market, however, Legal & General was particularly vulnerable to the weaknesses in the U.K. economy; sales of individual protection policies fell 13 percent during this nine-month period as individuals tightening their belts and concerned about stock market volatility shied away from putting their money into the long-term savings products in which Legal & General specialized. Mortgage-related products, such as mortgage insurance, also fared poorly as the U.K. housing market went into a tailspin. Breedon nevertheless remained confident that the company's solid foundation would enable it not only to weather the financial storm but also to gain business at the expense of weaker rivals. In addition, Legal & General was pursuing opportunities for additional growth overseas, including joint ventures to provide insurance products through banks in India and the Gulf States.

Douglas Sun
Updated, David E. Salamie

PRINCIPAL SUBSIDIARIES

Legal & General Finance PLC; Legal & General Resources Limited; Legal & General Assurance Society Limited; Legal & General Insurance Limited; Legal & General Investment Management Limited; Legal & General Assurance (Pensions Management) Limited; Legal & General Pensions Limited; Legal & General Partnership Services Limited; Legal & General (Portfolio Management Services) Limited; Legal & General Property Limited; Legal & General (Unit Trust Managers) Limited; LGV Capital Limited; Legal & General (France) SA; Legal & General Bank (France) SA; Legal & General International (Ireland) Limited; Legal & General Nederland Levensverzekering Maatschappij NV (Netherlands); Banner Life Insurance Company Inc. (USA); William Penn Life Insurance Company of New York Inc. (USA); First British American Reinsurance Company (USA); First British American Reinsurance Company II (USA); First British Bermudan Reinsurance Company (Bermuda).

PRINCIPAL COMPETITORS

Prudential plc; Aviva plc; AXA; Friends Provident plc; Standard Life plc; Scottish Widows plc; Paternoster UK Limited.

FURTHER READING

Adams, Christopher, "L&G Exits from Australian Life Market," *Financial Times,* May 28, 1998, p. 24.

Bolger, Andrew, "Banking on the Giant at the Top of the L&G Beanstalk," *Financial Times,* September 11, 1999, p. 22.

———, "Ruthless Legal & General Casts Shadow over Assurers," *Financial Times,* September 11, 2002, p. 23.

Brown-Humes, Christopher, "L&G Insists on Independence," *Financial Times,* September 12, 1997, p. 23.

———, "L&G Wants to Stay Independent," *Financial Times,* March 13, 1998, p. 27.

———, "Legal & General New Business Increases 40%," *Financial Times,* January 16, 1998, p. 22.

———, "Pensions Guarantee Unveiled by L&G," *Financial Times,* March 21, 1997, p. 8.

Clayton, G., *British Insurance,* London: Elek Books, 1971, 381 p.

Croft, Jane, and Andrea Felsted, "Barclays to Stop Selling L&G General Insurance," *Financial Times,* February 4, 2005, p. 22.

———, "Legal & General Acquires Nationwide Arm in £285m Deal," *Financial Times,* February 8, 2007, p. 20.

Felsted, Andrea, "Breedon Steps into a Big Pair of Shoes," *Financial Times,* December 19, 2005, p. 23.

Felsted, Andrea, and Chris Hughes, "L&G on Course to Return £1bn," *Financial Times,* March 15, 2007, p. 19.

Felsted, Andrea, and Maggie Urry, "L&G Reassures on Its Position in Spite of Turmoil," *Financial Times,* October 17, 2008, p. 20.

Felsted, Andrea, and Sundeep Tucker, "Breedon to Succeed Prosser at L&G," *Financial Times,* May 27, 2005, p. 20.

Fleming, Charles, "Life Insurer Goes for Growth: Legal & General's Chief Seizes Opportunity in Troubled Times," *Wall Street Journal Europe,* October 11, 2002, p. M1.

Leigh-Bennett, E. P., *On This Evidence,* London: Baynard Press, 1936, 121 p.

Smith, Alison, "L&G and Woolwich in Insurance Venture," *Financial Times,* July 17, 1995, p. 17.

———, "L&G Looks to Develop Banking Services," *Financial Times,* March 15, 1996, p. 26.

———, "L&G Shake-Up to Benefit Investors," *Financial Times,* November 17, 1995, p. 19.

———, "Record Lautro Fine for Legal & General," *Financial Times,* March 1, 1994, p. 1.

Tait, Nikki, "A $170m Joint Buy for L&G," *Financial Times,* November 21, 1995, p. 23.

Taylor, Catherine, "Barclays and Legal & General Form Distribution Alliance," *Wall Street Journal Europe,* January 17, 2001, p. 12.

———, "Legal & General Sheds Banks," *Wall Street Journal Europe,* July 5, 2002, p. M2.

———, "NatWest Drops Bid for Legal & General," *Wall Street Journal Europe,* October 7, 1999, p. 27.

Williams, Trevor, "UK's Legal & General Predicts Sour Results," *Journal of Commerce,* February 11, 1991, p. 10A.

Liquidity Services, Inc.

1920 L Street NW, 6th Floor
Washington, D.C. 20036-5004
U.S.A.
Telephone: (202) 467-6868
Toll Free: (800) 310-4604
Fax: (202) 467-5475
Web site: http://www.liquidityservicesinc.com

Public Company
Incorporated: 1999 as Liquidation.com, Inc.
Employees: 533
Sales: $198.6 million (2007)
Stock Exchanges: NASDAQ
Ticker Symbol: LQDT
NAICS: 541990 All Other Professional, Scientific, and Technical Services; 421490 Other Professional Equipment and Supplies Wholesalers

∎ ∎ ∎

Liquidity Services, Inc., (LSI) is a Washington, D.C.-based company that specializes in the online wholesale liquidation of excess inventory, damaged items, customer returns, and end-of-life-cycle equipment from corporate and government sellers. The company serves more than 375 large corporate sellers, including *Fortune* 500 retailers, and about 1,000 government agencies, including the U.S. military. More than one million buyers are registered with LSI auction marketplaces. The company receives a percentage of the sale price (15 to 25 percent) from the seller and a buyer premium fee (5 to 10 percent). To maximize prices, items are broken into lots for bidding. Buyers are mostly resellers, such as discount retailers, import-export firms, and refurbishers. All participants are screened by LSI to make sure they are legitimate and qualified. The names of sellers are kept confidential, and if requested, LSI will remove trademarks. To prevent the fraudulent return of merchandise to retailers, all labels are also removed.

LSI's flagship auction marketplace is Liquidation.com, which helps corporation and federal government agencies to sell salvage, surplus, and wholesale items. GovLiquidation.com focuses on the sale of surplus assets and scrap materials from the federal government, primarily the U.S. Department of Defense. Another site, GovDeals.com, sells surplus and confiscated items for state and local governments, school boards, and public utilities. LSI also does business in Europe through LiquiBiz.com under the auspices of subsidiary Liquidity Services Europe. Finally, the goWholesale industry portal connects advertisers with wholesale buyers. Product categories include apparel, aerospace parts and equipment, consumer electronics, scientific equipment, and technology hardware.

Aside from hosting the auction marketplaces, LSI generates revenues through value-added services, including marketing, warehousing, shipping, and the collection of payments. Buyers and sellers can also tap into LSI databases to check on the price of items as well as the status of bids, shipping, and money owed. LSI also handles fund disbursement dispute mediation and title transfer. LSI operates six distribution centers in six strategic locations: Cranberry, New Jersey; Plainfield, Indiana; Dallas, Texas; Las Vegas, Nevada; and Fullerton and Sacramento, California. The company's European

COMPANY PERSPECTIVES

Liquidity Services, Inc., (LSI) is a leading online auction marketplace for wholesale, surplus and salvage assets.

subsidiary maintains distribution centers in Stafford, England, and Schwaig, Germany. LSI is a public company listed on the NASDAQ. The company's chairman and chief executive officer, William P. Angrick III, is the largest shareholder, owning nearly 30 percent.

REGISTRATION OF LIQUIDATION.COM: 1994

The Liquidation.com domain name was registered in 1994 by William F. Burke. Born and raised in California, Burke and his wife, weary of earthquakes, moved to the eastern shore of Maryland in 1987. A self-described serial entrepreneur who started his first business at the age of 14, Burke began selling Eastern Shore distressed properties for institutional owners in the early 1990s at a time when the real estate market was especially weak. In newspaper advertisements he often used the word *liquidation,* so that when he learned about the Internet and the chance to register domain names, he acquired liquidation.com in August 1994. A month later he was using it as part of his efforts to sell real estate, this in the days before graphic interfaces such as Netscape began to make the World Wide Web accessible to a wider audience. Instead, Burke had to rely on usenet, e-mail, and arcane Unix mainframe computer commands. Because of the Internet aspect to his business, Burke latched onto the "hybrid" name, launching a company called Hybrid Liquidation Service.

In 1996 Burke hired a software developer to design a real estate auction web site. He continued to sell real estate in a conventional manner over the new liquidation.com web site, but in 1998 he began receiving inquiries from people interested in selling business goods on a liquidation basis on the site, prompting Burke to change tack and reposition liquidation.com as a business-to-business auction web site. Although not fully developed, the revamped web site began doing business in November 1998, making it, according to Burke, the first online business-to-business liquidation auction service in the world. In the first month Burke claimed to have sold $80,000 worth of business goods, an amount that totaled $200,000 the second month, and reached $1 million the fourth. The auction list

posted on the site was wide ranging, including aircraft, antiques, art, apparel, electronics, estate items, real estate, and wholesale liquidation items.

BURKE AND ANGRICK MEET: 1999

Reading about the lavish sums of money being invested in Internet ventures at the time, Burke decided to seek funding for liquidation.com. In January 1999 he placed an ad on his web site as well as in the *Wall Street Journal,* seeking "One sophisticated investor; Internet Liquidation Auction; $10,000,000.00 Equity Position." He received numerous replies, including one from William P. Angrick III. The son of the ombudsman of the state of Iowa, Angrick earned an undergraduate degree from the University of Notre Dame and became a certified public accountant in 1990. He then enrolled at the Kellogg School of Management at Northwestern University. Upon graduation in 1995 Angrick went to work as an investment banker at the Baltimore, Maryland, office of Deutsche Bank Alex. Brown, a major underwriter for the initial public offerings (IPOs) of growth firms, becoming vice-president of the Consumer and Business Services Investment Banking Group. In this capacity, he told Sharon McLoone of *Washingtonpost.com* in 2008, "I had a front row seat to observe all of the exciting new ventures being created in the early stages of e-commerce, including Amazon.com, Trademarketplace and eBay." He said that he spotted an opportunity to apply the Internet to the reverse supply chain market, in other words, returns.

While retailers were willing to invest heavily on supply chains, they had over the years neglected the back end, making little provision for selling returned items, excess stock, and outdated merchandise. Without the mechanism to make a market, they disposed of these goods for an extremely small percentage of the original investment. Angrick's idea was essentially to apply the eBay Internet auction model on a wholesale basis, matching up sellers of surplus goods with buyers for the benefit of both. Not only would sellers receive higher returns and hand off most of the burden in completing the transaction to someone else, the buyers would be able to more efficiently search for merchandise and have some assurance of quality and timely delivery.

Given his interest in conducting wholesale liquidation auctions online, it was not surprising that Angrick took notice of Burke's ad. Angrick did not have $10 million to invest, but indicated that he had the contacts and ability to raise capital. Thus, in July 1999 he invested $100,000 of his own money to acquire a stake in Hybrid Liquidation Service, which in November 1999 was incorporated in Delaware as Liquidation.com,

KEY DATES

1994: Domain name liquidation.com is registered.
1998: Web site liquidation.com begins doing business.
1999: Liquidation.com, Inc., is incorporated in Delaware.
2000: Liquidation.com, Inc., becomes operational.
2001: Contract to sell surplus military items is won; name is changed to Liquidity Services, Inc.
2003: U.K. web site goes live.
2006: Company is taken public.
2008: Geneva Group is acquired.

Inc. In multiple interviews since this time, Angrick has neglected to mention Burke's contribution to the creation of LSI and claims that he cofounded Liquidation.com, Inc., with others and supplied $100,000 in "seed capital." Cached versions of the liquidation.com web site, however, list Burke as a "founder" and other people as "cofounders." They included Angrick's former Northwestern roommate, Jaime Mateus-Tique, who after graduate school had gone to work for the management consulting firm of McKinsey & Co. Other cofounders included Benjamin R. Brown, who became director of technology, and James Holmes, executive vice-president of software development. Angrick would take over as chairman and CEO of the company, while Burke's vice-president title would change on a regular basis, sometimes in charge of industry alliance, government surplus, and at one point the head of "Customer Experience."

RAISING START-UP FUNDS: 2001

In January 2000 the company raised $1 million from angel investors. Through Mateus-Tique, Liquidation.com then landed an investment of $11.2 million from Europtaweb, the Internet holding company controlled by Bernard Arnault, head of luxury goods giant LVMH Moët Hennessy Louis Vuitton SA. As a result, the company also opened a Paris office, followed by one in Munich, Germany. (While the Munich office fared well, the Paris office did not, and was eventually closed.)

By that time the dot-com bubble was beginning to burst and many Internet companies were being forced to close their doors. In interviews Angrick has claimed that Liquidation.com under his leadership made some crucial decisions that prevented it from suffering a similar fate. While many Internet start-ups of the period had eagerly

accepted funding from venture capitalists but gave up control of the company, LSI was more cautious, he maintained, and chose to husband its resources. After the company relocated to downtown Washington, D.C. (taking over, at a discount, the former campaign office of presidential candidate Al Gore, after that operation moved to Nashville, Tennessee), in order to be closer to a higher-quality pool of talent, Angrick and Mateus-Tique again became roommates, sharing a nearby 300-square-foot studio apartment. Perhaps of even greater importance was the decision to hire software engineers to build an online marketplace infrastructure that met the specific needs of wholesalers rather than settle for readily available generic auction software. "We had to question what was more important: to be first to market or have a system that effectively services this unique marketplace," Angrick explained in a 2008 interview with Wholesalecentral.com. The choice of the latter, he claimed, would prove to be a competitive advantage by providing a better customer experience.

Burke, in an interview conducted by the author in December 2008, offered a different picture, however. He depicted a company that was spendthrift, not frugal, led by an inexperienced management team, whose members had hardly, if ever, attended an auction. Because sellers were permitted to pull items if they were not happy with bid levels, liquidation.com generated a meager amount of fees, prompting the company to consider hiring salespeople to find buyers at the prices the sellers wanted, in effect thinking of a brokerage and sourcing model rather than an online auction house approach.

The company's burn rate of available cash was so high, according to Burke, that the company was only months from ruin in 2001. A major turning point for LSI came in May 2001 when Burke's Government Surplus team won the company's first contract with the Defense Reutilization and Marketing Service, a Defense Department agency responsible for the disposal of excess military property, then valued at about $23 billion. LSI won a seven-year contract to dispose of such items as computers, electronics, office supplies, equipment, aircraft parts, clothing, and textiles. According to Burke, Angrick had been far from supportive of the effort, repeatedly telling him during the pre-bid phase to stop "wasting your time on that stupid government contract."

Within days of winning the Defense Department contract, Burke was dismissed for cause. Burke claimed that he was fired because he had refused to lie, at Angrick's behest, to the board of directors about the company's precarious financial position. Burke claimed that as a result of his firing he lost more than 2.4 million shares of stock, bought back by the company for "pennies" as permitted by the terms of his employment contract. It was also a move that Burke said "tilted the balance of controlling shares" to Angrick. Burke would take the matter to court, but was unsuccessful in his attempts for legal redress.

ADOPTION OF LIQUIDITY SERVICES NAME: 2001

In November 2001 Liquidation.com Inc. changed its name to Liquidity Services, Inc. (LSI). Through its two auction marketplaces, Liquidation.com and Govliquidation.com, LSI posted revenues of $16 million in fiscal 2002 and turned profitable. In 2003 LSI leveraged its success selling surplus items for the Pentagon to win a comparable contract with the British defense ministry. The U.K. auction web site began operating in November 2003, two months after fiscal 2003 closed. For the year, revenues improved to $60.7 million and LSI netted $2.8 million.

Business continued to grow in fiscal 2004, when LSI launched the wholesale industry portal www.goWholesale.com. Revenues for the year increased to $75.9 million and net income topped $5.2 million. Two weeks after the close of the year, LSI raised $20 million in an institutional round of financing from ABS Capital Partners, a private equity firm. The money was used to pay a special dividend to the holders of capital stock. To spur further growth LSI bid on the Defense Department scrap metal contract and in calendar 2005 was awarded the contract to auction off scrap metal and building materials from 55 U.S. military bases, starting in August of that year. This extra business helped to drive revenues to $89.4 million in fiscal 2005 and net earnings to $4.1 million.

After the end of fiscal 2005, in November 2005, LSI filed for an $86.3 million IPO of stock. The offering was completed in February 2006 and shares began trading on the NASDAQ and quickly increased in value. More good news followed a month later when LSI won a contract to sell certain assets of the U.S. military on German bases. Later in 2006 the company launched www.LiquiBiz.com to serve as an English- and German-language auction marketplace for European corporations and government agencies. When the year came to a close, LSI reported a 65.3 percent increase in revenues to $147.8 million, while net income approached $8 million.

Early in fiscal 2007 LSI paid $10.1 million for the wholesale unit of STR Inc., a California-based reseller of overstocked items and products returned by customers to discount retail stores and wholesale buyers. It was an area that held a great deal of promise for LSI, given the "no-questions-asked" policy adopted by many retailers that resulted in higher returns in almost every category of merchandise. The addition of STR assets also helped LSI become less dependent on its military surplus business. The improved product mix helped LSI increase revenues 34.4 percent to $198.62 million in fiscal 2007. Net income also topped $11 million.

ACQUISITION OF GENEVA GROUP: 2008

LSI completed another acquisition in fiscal 2008, one that broadened its international platform. It paid $17 million for the Geneva Group, U.K.-based companies involved in the marketing of returned, salvaged, and overstocked merchandise from the country's retailers and manufacturers, mostly consumer electronics, technology equipment, and durable goods. Also in 2008 LSI grew its product mix by adding a new category, store fixtures and equipment sold by retailers, convenience stores, and government agencies. Customers included small retailers, convenience stores, supermarkets, restaurants, bakeries, and delis as well as remanufacturers.

Revenues continued to grow in fiscal 2008 and the number of registered buyers reached the one million mark. In the fall of 2008 the hard-hit economy led to an extremely difficult retail climate as the all important holiday season approached. For LSI, however, it meant good business. "Maybe a year ago," Angrick told the *Christian Science Monitor* in 2008, "retailers would have been willing to muddle through this but in this era, they are slashing their positions and moving aggressively even before we have gotten to Thanksgiving." He added, "For some it's no longer a matter of improving their return on investments, it's a matter of survival."

Ed Dinger

PRINCIPAL SUBSIDIARIES

Surplus Acquisition Venture, LLC; Government Liquidation.com, LLC; Liquidity Services Limited; DOD Surplus LLC; Liquidity Services, GmbH; Liquidity Services Asia Limited; Liquidity Services Co., Ltd.

PRINCIPAL COMPETITORS

Buxbaum Group; ICON International, Inc.; International Monetary Systems, Ltd.

FURTHER READING

"Burke Living Well with 'liquidation.com,'" *Ocean Pine Gazette,* January 22, 1999.

Heine, Christopher, "Buyers & Sellers Win with Liquidation. com," *Wholesalecentral.com,* February 1, 2008.

McCarthy, Ellen, "Online Auctioneer Files for $86.3 Million IPO," *Washington Post,* November 21, 2005, p. D5.

McLoone, Sharon, "Local Liquidator Flourishes in a Tight Market," *Washingtonpost.com,* July 10, 2008.

Richardson, Kari, "Supply Chain Gains," *Kellogg World,* Winter 2005.

Scherer, Ron, "Consumers Close Their Wallets," *Christian Sci-ence Monitor,* November 17, 2008.

Sowinski, Lara L., "Going Forward with Reverse Logistics," *World Trade,* February 2003, p. 28.

Torres, Nichole L., "Beyond Their Years," *Entrepreneur Magazine,* November 2003.

Walker, Leslie, "Bidding for the Leftovers," *Washington Post,* September 4, 2003, p. E1.

Woellert, Lorraine, "Liquidity Services: Sell It Again, Sam," *Business Week,* June 4, 2007, p. 64.

macrovision®

Macrovision Solutions Corporation

2830 De La Cruz Boulevard
Santa Clara, California 95050
U.S.A.
Telephone: (408) 562-8400
Fax: (408) 567-1800
Web site: http://www.macrovision.com

Public Company
Incorporated: 1983
Employees: 450
Sales: $155.7 million (2007)
Stock Exchanges: NASDAQ (GS)
Ticker Symbol: MVSN
NAICS: 541512 Computer Systems Design Services

■ ■ ■

Headquartered in Santa Clara, California, Macrovision Solutions Corporation develops and markets technologies that are used to protect and distribute digital content, including movies, television programs, games, and music. The company serves its customer base, which includes motion picture studios, consumer electronics firms, and cable and satellite companies, from about 13 offices worldwide. Macrovision holds roughly 4,100 patents.

FORMATIVE YEARS: 1983–89

Macrovision's roots date back to 1983, when A. Victor Farrow and John O. Ryan established the company in California. A native of Naples, Italy, Farrow graduated

from San Jose State University in 1964 with a B.S. degree in accounting and finance and went on to establish a CPA firm two years later, which he eventually sold.

Only three years after Macrovision was formed, the market was ripe for the company's copy protection technology, which most industry leaders considered to be the most reliable. Invented by cofounder John Ryan, Macrovision's technology used electronic pulses to interfere with a VCR's automatic gain control, thereby distorting an illegally copied movie's picture and rendering it non-viewable. In addition to protecting videotapes, Macrovision's technology also could be used to protect pay-per-view movies and regular television broadcasts.

Midway through 1986, videotape piracy was causing the motion picture industry to lose approximately $1 billion annually. In addition to small video stores that purchased one legitimate copy of a movie and then made multiple illegal copies for rental use, home users also were contributing to the entertainment industry's losses.

From 1980 to 1985, the number of U.S. homes with videocassette recorders (VCRs) swelled from one million to 25 million, and some industry observers estimated that as many as 20 percent of VCR owners used their equipment to make illegal copies of movies. Operating from its offices in Torrance, California, Macrovision had secured contracts with many leading studios by the mid-1980s, including Disney, MCA Home Video, CBS-Fox, and MGM. By 1986 Macrovi-

COMPANY PERSPECTIVES

The result of deploying Macrovision's solutions is a simple end user experience to discover, acquire, manage and enjoy digital content.

sion technology was used to protect roughly half of the 80 million movies released on videotape each year.

By the late 1980s Macrovision's technology was pervasive enough that so-called video stabilizers, which allowed one to bypass copy protection when recording between two VCRs, began appearing on the market. This prompted legal action by Macrovision, which was ultimately successful at removing the devices from the marketplace.

EARLY GROWTH: 1990–96

Progress continued at Macrovision during the early 1990s. In August 1990, Joe Swyt was named president. By September 1991, the Macrovision AntiCopy Process had been used to protect 400 million videotapes. The company's technology, which was used at more than 75 different facilities throughout North America, resulted in estimated annual savings of about $160 million for the entertainment industry.

Building on its success during the previous decade, by the early 1990s Macrovision had added HBO, New Line, Warner Brothers, and Paramount to its customer base.

On June 4, 1992, Macrovision bade farewell to cofounder A. Victor Farrow, who died following an illness that had forced him to relinquish his position as company chairman midway through the previous year.

Heading into the mid-1990s, Macrovision was focused on the advent of digital televisions, digital VCRs, and MPEG-2 digital video disc players. As part of an effort to prevent digital piracy, the company agreed to include its Intellectual Property Protection System in these types of electronic devices at no cost to manufacturers.

A major leadership development unfolded in mid-1995, when President Joe Swyt resigned to establish a company named MediaPhysics. He was temporarily succeeded by Bill Krepick, who was appointed president and chief operating officer. At this time, cofounder John Ryan remained at the helm as chairman and CEO.

By the mid-1990s, Macrovision's headquarters were based in Mountain View, California, with international

offices in Tokyo and London. In November 1995, the company established a new communications subsidiary named Command Audio Corp. Former Giga-tronics President and CEO Donald F. Bogue was tapped to fill those same positions with the new company.

PREPARING FOR THE DIGITAL AGE: 1997–2000

In early 1997 Macrovision added Universal Home Entertainment to its customer base. The company went public in March of that year via an initial public offering (IPO) of 2.35 million shares of its common stock, which began trading on the NASDAQ National Market under the symbol MVSN. It was around this time that the company reincorporated in the state of Delaware.

On the new product front, new advancements during the late 1990s included an authentication signature system aimed at providing copy protection for digital video discs (DVDs). In addition, Macrovision invested $1.5 million in Digimarc Corp., a developer of digital watermarking technology, which made it possible to include "invisible" copyright data on digital video, including DVDs. The company ended 1997 with annual revenues of $20.3 million.

Macrovision added a number of significant new customers in 1998. In August, the company announced that it had signed a multiyear deal with DreamWorks SKG to protect the company's videos in 17 different countries. The following month, a new multiyear agreement with Paramount Home Video, which covered all of the company's DVDs made in Canada and the United States, also was announced.

A major development unfolded in October 1998, when Congress passed the Digital Millennium Copyright Act. In addition to making the illegal duplication of movies a federal offense, the act recognized Macrovision's technology as the industry standard.

It was at this time that Macrovision established a new division that sought to develop copy protection technology for computer software, especially video games. In early 1999 the company sponsored a study conducted by Merrill Research & Associates that placed the value of illegally copied personal computer CDs at $1 billion.

After acquiring a near 20 percent stake in C-Dilla Ltd. in early 1998, Macrovision secured full ownership in the company in mid-1999 for $12.8 million. The company rounded out 1999 by increasing its investment in Digimarc, bringing the total amount to $3.5 million.

The new millennium was accompanied by a flurry of developments at Macrovision. In January 2000 the

KEY DATES

1983: A. Victor Farrow and John O. Ryan establish Macrovision.

1986: Macrovision technology protects roughly half of the 80 million movies released on videotape each year.

1992: A. Victor Farrow dies.

1997: Macrovision goes public and begins trading on the NASDAQ National Market under the symbol MVSN.

2008: The company acquires Gemstar-TV Guide International Inc. in a deal worth $2.8 billion; Macrovision agrees to sell its software and games units.

company made a $4 million investment in TTR Technologies Inc. This was followed by a $750,000 investment in AudioSoft three months later. Midway through the year Macrovision forged a deal with electronics manufacturer Philips to include its copy protection technology in digital set-top boxes.

In late August Macrovision acquired San Jose, California-based GLOBEtrotter Software Inc., which became a wholly owned subsidiary. GLOBEtrotter provided large companies with software asset management products, and also supplied licensing technology to the software industry.

Another acquisition followed in October 2000, when Macrovision snapped up the assets of U.K.-based Productivity through Software plc. That same month, Macrovision upped its stake in Digimarc Corp. via a $21.8 million investment. The company also benefited from a five-year extension of its agreement with Paramount Home Entertainment Inc.

CONTINUED GROWTH: 2001–03

Macrovision began 2001 by signing a long-term copy protection agreement with Artisan Entertainment Inc. Midway through the year, the company furthered its expansion into China by opening a new office in Hong Kong. By this time, some 75 percent of the DVDs distributed by Motion Picture Association of America member studios were protected by Macrovision's technology. In fact, the company's copy protection had been used on approximately three billion videotapes, 500 million DVDs, and 60 million digital set-top boxes.

Macrovision acquired the technology- and intellectual property-related assets of AudioSoft Inc. in July,

and MediaDNA Inc. in September. By this time, some 200 manufacturers of DVD players and DVD-ROM drives were incorporating the company's protection technology into their devices. An important leadership change occurred that October, when cofounder John Ryan stepped down as CEO and was succeeded by William Krepick. Ryan remained with the company as chairman.

In early 2002 Macrovision forged new multiyear contracts with both DreamWorks SKG and Twentieth Century Fox Home Entertainment, which involved the protection of the studios' videotapes and DVDs throughout the world. Another agreement was established that year with Warner Home Video, and the company announced plans to buy back as many as five million shares of its common stock, of which some 51 million shares were outstanding.

Developments continued during the latter part of the year as Macrovision partnered with Websense to develop technology for locating pirated music files on corporate and government computer networks. The company rounded out the year by acquiring Midbar Technologies Ltd. in November, in a deal worth approximately $17.8 million.

Capitalizing on growth opportunities in the music industry, which was suffering from widespread CD copying among consumers, Macrovision kicked off 2003 by establishing a new music technology division that combined its technology with Midbar's. By April of that year, some 100 million music CDs had been protected by Macrovision's technology.

Macrovision furthered its growth via the $5.7 million acquisition of TTR Technologies Inc. Around the same time, the company reorganized its business into two main units. These included the Entertainment Technologies Group, which was comprised of its former Music Technology and Video Technology divisions, as well as the Consumer Software division's SafeDisc business. In addition, Macrovision's new Software Technologies Group was formed from what had been its SafeCast business and Enterprise Software division. The company ended the year with record net revenues of $128.3 million, up from $102.3 million in 2002.

ACQUISITIONS AND DIVESTITURES: 2004–08

Developments continued in 2004 as Macrovision renewed agreements with Columbia House and Twentieth Century Fox Home Entertainment during the early part of the year. In July, Macrovision acquired InstallShield Software Corp. in a $76 million cash deal. This was the first of many acquisitions that would occur into the latter part of the decade.

In mid-2005, Macrovision snapped up San Francisco-based Zero G Software Inc. for $10.6 million. That deal was followed by the acquisition of Trymedia Systems Inc., which also was based in San Francisco, for approximately $34 million. Acquisitions continued in early 2006, at which time Macrovision acquired the New York-based software company eMeta Corp. in a $35 million deal.

In early 2007, Macrovision acquired the San Mateo, California-based software enterprise Mediabolic. This was followed by the $45 million acquisition of Blu-ray disc security technology from San Francisco-based Cryptography Research Inc. in November. The following month, the $82 million acquisition of All Media Guide Holdings Inc. was completed, giving Macrovision one of the largest databases of entertainment information (details about music, movies, and video games) in the world.

Macrovision capped off 2007 by announcing plans to acquire Gemstar-TV Guide International Inc. The $2.8 billion deal, which added a leading video and entertainment information provider to the Macrovision family, was completed in May 2008.

During 2008 Macrovision agreed to sell its software and games units. The software operation was sold to Thoma Bravo LLC for approximately $200 million. In addition, the assets of online game technology company TryMedia were sold to RealNetworks Inc. Another divestiture followed in October 2008, when Macrovision agreed to sell the *TV Guide* print magazine to Beverly Hills-based OpenGate Capital. The following month, the company also sold its eMeta business to Atypon Systems Inc.

Macrovision ended 2008 with a major deal. On December 18, the company announced that it had agreed to sell TV Guide Network, including TV Guide Online, to Allen Shapiro and One Equity Partners for $255 million. Another significant deal—the sale of Macrovision's horse racing wagering channel, TVG Network—was planned for 2009.

From its roots as a developer of copy protection technology for videotapes, Macrovision headed into the 21st century's second decade on strong footing. The company had evolved into a provider of numerous technologies for protecting and distributing many forms of digital content, and seemed well positioned for continued success.

Paul R. Greenland

PRINCIPAL SUBSIDIARIES

All Media Guide Holdings Inc.; All Media Guide LLC; Deterrence Acquisition Ltd. (UK); Gemstar-TV Guide International Inc.; Macrovision Corp.; Macrovision Europe Ltd. (UK); Macrovision GmbH (Germany); Macrovision International Holding LP (Cayman Islands); Macrovision International Holdings Inc.; Macrovision International Licensing SARL (Switzerland); Macrovision Israel Ltd.; Macrovision Japan KK; Macrovision Japan YK; Macrovision Korea Co. Ltd. (South Korea); Macrovision Licensing & Holding B.V. (Netherlands); Macrovision Ltd. (UK); Macrovision Service LLC; Macrovision Taiwan Ltd.; Macrovision UK Ltd.; Mediabolic Inc.; Moodlogic Inc.; Moodlogic Ltd. (Switzerland).

PRINCIPAL COMPETITORS

Intertrust Technologies Corp.; Microsoft Corporation; RealNetworks Inc.

FURTHER READING

"A. Victor Farrow," *San Francisco Chronicle*, June 23, 1992.

Gillott, Roger, "Video Industry Has New Weapon in War Against Pirates," *Associated Press*, July 8, 1986.

"Macrovision Completes Initial Public Offering of 2,350,000 Shares of Common Stock," *Business Wire*, March 13, 1997.

"Macrovision Forms Music Technology Division," *Medialine*, January 1, 2003.

"Macrovision Reorganizes into Two Primary Business Units; Entertainment and Software Focus Reflects Digital Convergence," *Business Wire*, June 17, 2003.

Magazine Luiza S.A.

Rua de Comércio, 1924, Centro
Franca, São Paulo 14400-660
Brazil
Telephone: (55 16) 3711-2068
Fax: (55 16) 3724-1723
Web site: http://www.magazineluiza.com.br

Private Company
Incorporated: 1966
Employees: 11,417
Sales: $1.52 billion (2007)
NAICS: 442110 Furniture Stores; 443111 Household Appliance Stores; 443112 Radio, Television, and Other Electronic Stores; 452111 Department Stores (Except Discount Department Stores)

∎ ∎ ∎

Magazine Luiza S.A. owns one of the largest retail chains in Brazil. Although often classified as a department store chain, it does not carry clothing and is best known for its appliance and furniture stock. Like its chief competitors, Magazine Luiza relies heavily on installment plan purchases. It provides credit at affordable rates and also offers financial services such as personal loans and insurance policies to customers otherwise deemed too poor to qualify. Magazine Luiza is considered one of the best companies to work for in Brazil.

SERVING BRAZIL'S RANK AND FILE: 1957–2002

The department store chain got its start in 1957, when Luiza Trajano Donato and her husband, Pelegrino Jose Donato, founded a store in Franca, São Paulo. It was called, in its early years, A Critaleira for its large windows, but after it started to grow in size, customers in a poll voted to rename it for Luiza. (In French, *magazine* is a store or shop.) Magazine Luiza did not begin to spread out to other cities until the 1980s, when it expanded by purchasing small chains. A niece of the Donato couple, Luiza Helena Trajano Rodrigues, started working summers at the original store when she was 12 and became a full-time saleswoman when she was 18. She became chief executive of Magazine Luiza in 1991.

Almost immediately, the younger Luiza greatly expanded the business, which was always profitable after losing money in 1992, a year of recession. Throughout its history, Brazil had been characterized by an unusually large disparity between rich and poor. Magazine Luiza was one of the first large retailers to extend credit to shoppers below middle-class level. Following in the footsteps of a bigger chain, Casas Bahia, it required borrowers to return to the store of purchase each month to make a payment in person. The captive customer then often made more purchases. Magazine Luiza added to the traffic by offering deep discounts on big ticket items during its periodic sales.

Luiza Helena also changed the enterprise's management structure, establishing a holding company to administer other businesses that had been acquired by the founders, including real estate ventures and

KEY DATES

1957: Luiza Trajano Donato and her husband open a store in Franca, São Paulo.

1991: A niece, Luiza Helena Trajano Rodrigues, becomes chief executive of the chain.

1992: Luiza Helena establishes a virtual store that offers the chain's wares on computer.

1994: Magazine Luiza introduces its annual "Fantastic Liquidation" post-Christmas sale.

1997: The retail chain has raised its scope to 97 stores.

2004: Magazine Luiza has 235 stores in six Brazilian states.

2005: Magazine Luiza sells a 12 percent stake in the company to a U.S.-based private equity firm.

2007: The retailer purchases 28 store sites in São Paulo.

2008: The chain enters the city of São Paulo for the first time, opening at least 44 stores.

automobile dealerships. She created a board to direct Magazine Luiza's day-to-day operations and authorized veteran store managers and sales representatives to establish prices and extend credit. "That was the turning point," a consultant told Todd Benson of the *New York Times* in 2004. "Most companies only look to change when things aren't going well. Magazine Luiza was doing just fine, but Luiza Helena sensed that she had to try something new to stay ahead of the curve."

Magazine Luiza's dynamic leader instituted a profit-sharing program for its employees in 1997. This policy not only enhanced sales by motivating personnel but also contributed to profits by making employees responsible for securing payments. Of the retail chain's BRL 495.4 million (about $460 million) in revenue in 1997, credit sales accounted for 65 percent. Net profits more than doubled over the previous year. There were 92 stores at the end of 1997, of which 54 were in São Paulo.

Luiza Helena was also a pioneer in the use of computers to stimulate sales, long before Internet shopping became an everyday reality. She established the chain's first virtual store in 1992 in order to present its wares by means of computer banks that displayed catalogs and videos. Without merchandise to stock, these stores of no more than 200 square meters were cheap to establish. By 2002 they were accounting for 8 percent of Magazine Luiza's annual sales. By late 2007,

when there were 60 of these stores, they accounted for 13 percent of annual sales, and 950,000 people were registered. Customers were spending an average of BRL 485 (about $265).

By this time the virtual stores were linked by high-speed computers to a portal housing the company's database, with home delivery of merchandise guaranteed within 48 hours. There was free Internet service and the opportunity to enroll in numerous courses, including cooking classes and an introduction to computer training. Magazine Luiza had an alliance, LuizaCred, with Unibanco, one of Brazil's largest banks, that allowed visitors to pay utility bills to an onsite teller.

GROWING IN SIZE AND AMBITION: 2002–07

Magazine Luiza made five acquisitions in 2002 and 2003. The following year it purchased Lojas Arno, a 51-store chain in Rio Grande do Sul, Brazil's southernmost state. This transaction raised its number of stores to 235 in six states. The chain was also opening new stores at a breathtaking pace, one almost every two weeks. In 2005 Luiza Helena introduced as the chain's slogan, "Be happy!"

Magazine Luiza's annual "Fantastic Liquidation" day long, January post-Christmas sale, dating from 1994, was one of the chain's big draws. Some three million persons were expected to take part in the 2006 event, which offered discounts as large as 70 percent. According to a newspaper account filed from Campinas, São Paulo, 400 people were waiting at 5 A.M. for the doors at one store to open an hour later. The regional manager said that Magazine Luiza expected to earn as much in sales in the single day as it normally did for a week. He said the main products purchased were television sets, DVDs, and refrigerators. One couple, after enduring a wait of three days, purchased a refrigerator, stove, air purifier, washing machine, vacuum cleaner, microwaves, pots and pans, and a "sanduicheira."

Magazine Luiza sold a 12 percent stake in the business in 2005 to Capital Group, a U.S. private equity firm, for $50 million. In 2006 the retail chain formed a partnership with Google that allowed it to exhibit videos about its merchandise on YouTube. By this time the retailer was directing 15 percent of its online advertising budget to a search link tied to Google's portal. The producer of these videos was also translating into Portuguese the chain's training manuals. There were 120 videos by the end of 2007, and Magazine Luiza's marketing department was planning on 500 in 2008, some of them to appear on digital cameras, digital television sets, and MP3 cellphones.

THE BIG PUSH INTO SOUTH AMERICA'S LARGEST CITY: 2008

Magazine Luiza had 397 stores in seven states serving 12 million customers at the beginning of 2008, when it launched a three-year, BRL 150 million (about $85 million) expansion plan that would put the department store chain in the greater São Paulo metropolitan area for the first time. The foundation for this leap forward was the retailer's acquisition the previous year of 28 store sites formerly occupied by Kolumbus, a furniture chain that had gone out of business.

The entry into São Paulo, about 250 miles from company headquarters in Franca, was planned and executed with the precision of a military operation. A number of executives spent almost a year in the city, visiting potential sites able to meet certain standards. They had to be in areas where families had income of about BRL 1,500 a month (about $840, typical of three-quarters of Magazine Luiza's customers); near to large banks drawing in a large number of people; and close to rival mass market stores. Company executives also visited the homes of potential customers in the vicinity to observe the kind of purchasing decisions that they were making.

Fourteen contractors were put to work building the first 50 stores, starting at the beginning of 2008. Two thousand people were hired to receive orientation training before working in the stores. First they watched videos on the history of the company and attended lectures given by motivational speakers. After two weeks they were sent to Magazine Luiza stores in other cities for another two weeks of practical training before taking up their posts. "Graduation" ceremonies included a two-hour address by Luiza Helena, who was treated like a rock star. By the end of September, 44 of the planned 50 stores had been completed.

As the world economic downturn began to bite, Luiza Helena told a meeting of businesspeople that the first days of November had been the worst for retail purchases in a long time. To stimulate sales, she introduced Sunday shopping in Magazine Luiza stores in the interior of São Paulo that were normally closed on that day. In a video to her employees explaining the crisis, she told them not to panic and said no jobs would be lost if everyone met goals.

Magazine Luiza's chief executive was proud of her company's standing as one of the best places to work in Brazil. The retail chain believed in promoting from its own ranks and offered employees scholarships covering up to 70 percent of tuition. An open door policy included a telephone line to headquarters. Internal communication included Portal Luiza and a weekly program from Rádio and TV Luiza. Salaries were supplemented by commissions on sales, and managers who met their goals could, in many cases, earn an annual bonus of BRL 25,000 (about $14,000). Mothers with children under ten years received a monthly stipend of BRL 200 (about $112).

Each Monday morning at 7:45 A.M., Magazine Luiza employees took part in a Japanese-style motivational ceremony to start the workweek. They held hands and sang the national and company anthems, "crooning enthusiastically," according to Benson, "like worshippers at an evangelical service." New employees introduced themselves to the others, those celebrating birthdays received presents to a "Happy Birthday!" chorus, and there was a group prayer before dismissal. Employees, though, were also expected to know the monthly target for sales and be familiar with weekly promotions, and to address themselves to customer complaints.

A publicity campaign was based on popular radio stations, posters in public transport, and ads in free papers and evangelical newspapers (one of which had two million readers, according to its editors). This was supplemented by telemarketing and mailings of discount coupons. As a result, two-thirds of the residents in one São Paulo neighborhood said they were familiar with Magazine Luiza, even though the chain had yet to make its appearance in the city.

A distribution center, Magazine Luiza's sixth, occupying the equivalent of five soccer fields was constructed in Louveira, about 40 miles from São Paulo. This giant warehouse stocked some 100,000 different products and accommodated about 80 trucks each day. Magazine Luiza had the following departments: babies; health and beauty; bed, table and bath; toys; movies and photos; appliances; electronics, games; sports and leisure; computers; furniture; telephones; and kitchen utensils.

With the advance of the São Paulo project in late 2008, Magazine Luiza was likely to vault to second place among nonfood retailers in Brazil, trailing only Casas Bahia. Luiza Helena also had plans to take the chain to Rio de Janeiro and northeastern Brazil within the next two years. LuizaCred had a total of more than BRL 1 billion ($562 million) in outstanding loans. LuizaSeg, or Consórcio Luiza, the company's insurance joint venture with Cardif, an arm of the French bank BNP Paribas, had issued 723,000 policies.

The heir apparent to the management of Magazine Luiza was Luiza's son, Frederico, director of sales and marketing. He entered the company in 2000 as director of e-commerce, then studied business administration in São Paulo before postgraduate work in finance at the

University of California at Berkeley. Magazine Luiza, which had been talking about possibly going public as far back as 2004, broached the subject again in 2008, but the ensuing world financial crisis of late 2008 made this prospect problematic in the near future. A potential problem for Luiza was the high level of debt it had assumed, rated at 85 percent of its assets by the Brazilian business magazine *Exame*.

Robert Halasz

PRINCIPAL COMPETITORS

Arthur Lundgren Teçidos S.A.-Casas Pernambucanas; Casas Bahia Comercial Ltda; Globex Utilidades S.A.

FURTHER READING

Alves, Cristina, and Germano Oliveira, "Trajano diz que Magazine Luiza chegara ao Rio e defende gasto público menor," *O Globo de Brasil*, November 26, 2007.

Benson, Todd, "Courting the Poor, a Retailer Rises to No. 3 in Brazil," *New York Times*, July 14, 2004, pp. W1+.

"Em São Paulo, descontos de até 70%," *O Globo de Brasil*, January 6, 2007.

"Expansão," *Exame*, August 27, 2008, pp. 140–42, 144, 146.

Ramiro Gonçalves, Marilucia, "Magazine Luiza," *Exame*, Melhores Empresa para Socé Trabalhar, 2008 issue, p. 147.

Rodrigues, Lino, "Luiza aporta no YouTube," *O Globo de Brasil*, December 5, 2007.

Vasconcellos, Carlos, "Ni virtual ni real," *AméricaEconomía*, January 2002, p. 25.

Viveiros, Ulisses de, et al., "Marketing Global Powers," *Chain Store Age*, December 1996, supplement, pp. 20B–21B.

Mammoth Mountain Ski Area

1 Minaret Road
Mammoth Lakes, California 93546
U.S.A.
Telephone: (760) 734-0745
Toll Free: (800) 626-6684
Fax: (760) 934-0603
Web site: http://www.mammothmountain.com

Wholly Owned Subsidiary of Starwood Capital Group Global L.L.C.
Incorporated: 1955
Employees: 2,600
Sales: $15.1 million (2007 est.)
NAICS: 713920 Skiing Facilities; 721110 Hotels (Except Casino Hotels) and Motels

■ ■ ■

Mammoth Mountain Ski Area is California's most popular ski resort, and the second leading ski resort in the United States. The company comprises the ski slopes of Mammoth Mountain and June Mountain, high in the Sierra Nevada range. The slopes cover some 3,500 acres, at elevations up to 11,500 feet. The company owns and operates the hotels Tamarack Lodge and Mammoth Mountain Inn and Resort. It also manages real estate in the town of Mammoth Lakes through a joint venture with the Canadian resort operator Intrawest. Other ventures operated by Mammoth Mountain Ski Area include Mammoth Snowmobile Adventures, Sierra Star Golf Club, and Mammoth Mountain Bike Park. Long run by founder Dave Mc-

Coy and his family, since 2005 Mammoth Mountain has been majority owned by Starwood Capital Group Global, L.L.C. Intrawest also owns 15 percent of the company.

A MOUNTAIN ADVENTURER

Mammoth Mountain Ski Area was founded by Dave McCoy. McCoy skied the area as a young man, and developed the ensuing ski resort business almost by happenstance. He did not set out to create an immensely popular recreation area that turned into a multimillion-dollar business. He simply loved the area, loved to ski, and gradually took steps that allowed others to enjoy Mammoth Mountain with him.

McCoy was born in 1915 in El Segundo, California. His father initially worked for Standard Oil, but later worked as a construction contractor, building California highways. Mr. and Mrs. McCoy and their young son moved all around the state, seldom staying anywhere for more than a few months. The family sometimes lived in tent camps, if there was no rental housing available.

At the beginning of the Great Depression, McCoy's parents separated. For a time, young McCoy lived with his grandparents in Wilkeson, Washington. He was unhappy there, however, and eventually made his way back to California. He had learned to ski in Washington, and he made a pair of wooden skis in his high school shop class. After graduating, he moved to the town of Bishop, California, 40 miles south of Mammoth Lakes. He worked for the Los Angeles Department of Water and Power as a hydrologist. His job

COMPANY PERSPECTIVES

Mammoth is committed to fulfilling the dreams of our guests by providing world-class recreation and California mountain lifestyle experiences.

entailed surveying snow in order to predict how much snow melt would flow to Los Angeles, 300 miles south of the Sierra Nevadas. He skied into remote areas for work, and for entertainment pursued ski racing. He was California's top ski racer in 1937.

A HOBBY BECOMES MORE PERMANENT

With his passion for skiing and love of the mountains, McCoy nevertheless did not set out to make a living off his hobby. He and some friends built a rope tow on McGee Mountain in the late 1930s out of a rope pulley and parts from an old Ford Model A car. McCoy married in 1941. His hydrologist salary did not stretch very far. One day McCoy asked his wife to set out a cigar box at the base of the rope tow and ask users to donate 50 cents. At the end of the day, the couple had made $15. McCoy recalled being pleased with the money, but thinking it would never be enough to live on.

McCoy asked for a bank loan in 1941 of $85 in order to purchase another ski lift for the slope on McGee. Then he received a permit from the National Forest Service to set up portable rope tows on Mammoth Mountain. The mountain, a dormant volcano, received heavy snowfall every year. Other local developers did not think much of Mammoth's potential as a ski area. The snow was too dense, and the area was close to the San Andreas Fault, and so plagued with earthquake activity. However, McCoy's reputation as a ski racer and racing coach brought skiers up from Los Angeles. Mammoth was a six- or seven-hour drive from the city, but this was not too far for car-oriented Los Angeles residents to travel for a snowy weekend. In 1946, McCoy put up his first permanent rope tows on Mammoth. Although other ski areas had more amenities, including chair lifts, Mammoth continued to grow in popularity. From a few hundred skiers a weekend in the 1940s, the area was seeing thousands by 1950. Mammoth had greater capacity than Squaw Valley, which was much more developed.

The mountain land was owned by the federal government, managed by the National Forest Service. In the 1950s, the Forest Service began asking entrepreneurs to develop skiing in the Sierra Nevadas. McCoy had no money to invest. Nevertheless, the Forest Service granted him a permit in 1953. It seemed that no one else was interested in developing Mammoth. It was stormier, wetter, and at higher altitude than other promising ski areas. McCoy was the only taker. Then a wealthy acquaintance offered to lend him the money to install a chair lift. Although McCoy had no collateral, no way to pay his investor back, the deal was done on a handshake.

McCoy and friends installed the chair themselves, doing all the hard labor. It took two years. The first chair lift opened on Thanksgiving Day in 1955. So many skiers were enticed by the new lift that thousands waited in line two or more hours for a ride up. McCoy was able to pay back his loan and install new lifts, averaging about one a year. Although McCoy had suffered a horrific multiple fracture of his left leg in 1942, he was still an incredible skier and a famed coach. Many of the champion ski racers of the 1950s and 1960s trained under McCoy at Mammoth. This did much to spread the word about the ski area.

UPS AND DOWNS

Mammoth Mountain continued to be very popular with California skiers. McCoy made additional improvements year by year, and the ski area drew more and more visitors, despite some setbacks. Mammoth Mountain was usually heavily snowy, with good skiing weather lasting from Thanksgiving all the way through the Fourth of July. The mountain could be temperamental as well. Through the winter of 1958 to 1959, for example, there was hardly any snow on Mammoth through late December. Other seasons, the snow itself kept people from making it to Mammoth. Weekend snowstorms could keep potential skiers from being able to drive into the mountains.

Consequently, the development of the ski area was not smooth. Still, when conditions were good, skiers came, and McCoy invested the profits into new facilities. McCoy built a ski lodge in 1953. He added lifts, expanded the lodge, and made other improvements mostly as suggested to him by visitors. McCoy made a major improvement in 1967 when he bought a gondola from a Swiss company, so that skiers could reach the very top of Mammoth. Typical of McCoy's luck and style, the multimillion-dollar purchase of the gondola was done on a handshake, and all went well.

The gas shortage of 1973 to 1974 could have proved disastrous for Mammoth Mountain. The ski area depended on drivers making their way up from distant Los Angeles. With gas rationed and expensive, car traffic

KEY DATES

1941: Dave McCoy begins putting portable tow ropes on Mammoth.
1953: Forest Service grants McCoy permit to develop Mammoth as ski area.
1955: Mammoth Mountain Ski Area is incorporated.
1967: New gondola takes skiers to the top of Mammoth Mountain.
1985: Company buys neighboring June Mountain.
1992: Mammoth invests in snowmaking system.
1996: Intrawest buys part interest in Mammoth.
2003: Village at Mammoth opens.
2005: Company is acquired by Starwood Capital.

could have stopped. Yet Mammoth Mountain was so popular that dedicated skiers managed to drive up anyway. They stayed longer, or packed more people into each vehicle. Most importantly, they continued to come.

Mammoth Mountain expanded its amenities throughout the 1980s. In 1980, McCoy purchased the Mammoth Mountain Inn. This was a hotel at the base of the ski area that had not been doing well. McCoy's management was able to make the inn profitable. In 1985, he bought a neighboring ski area, June Mountain. McCoy's dream was to link the two ski areas, which were eight miles apart. June Mountain was only a quarter of the size of Mammoth, but it played into McCoy's long-term plans.

By the mid-1980s, Mammoth Mountain was hosting crowds of up to 21,000 skiers on weekends. It held the record as busiest ski area in the United States. The ski area boasted over 30 lifts. It featured every kind of ski run, from shallow beginner slopes to some of the most challenging runs around. The ski area brought in an estimated $20 million annually just from lift passes, not including revenue generated by the hotels.

The area drew dedicated skiers in spite of factors that might have scared crowds away. When Mount St. Helen's, in Washington, erupted in 1980, the Mammoth Lakes area was struck by four heavy earthquakes in 48 hours. Numerous small earthquakes followed. Geologists noted troubling changes in the area, and in 1982 the U.S. Geological Survey issued a hazard notice because of the quakes and the potential for an eruption. In 1984, the mountain was hit by a 5.7-magnitude quake while a crowd of some 20,000 people skied or stood in line for lifts. Amazingly, the skiers were un-

fazed, and the day continued calmly. It seemed that nothing could knock the popularity of Mammoth.

BUILDING A SNOW MACHINE

A years-long drought began to cut back on available ski days in the Mammoth area beginning in the late 1980s. The area had an average annual snowfall of more than 300 inches, and some years it received up to 600 inches. However, the snow lessened in the late 1980s, and in the 1990 to 1991 season, the area had only received 50 inches of snow by March. Investors stepped in with offers to buy the ski area from McCoy and family. McCoy was not interested in selling.

Instead, he began a huge construction project, installing a snowmaking system. The system was expected to cost $10 million, and it involved digging a 28-million-gallon reservoir. McCoy managed to build the system for only $5 million, employing not only friends but also volunteers from the town. The ski area was vital to the economy of the region, and everyone counted on the development continuing. The snowmaking system was a success, able to provide snow for about 10 percent of the resort's skiable land.

Now able to provide snow for skiers no matter what the skies brought down, McCoy pumped money into other amenities. In the early 1990s, the Mammoth Mountain Inn underwent a $2 million renovation. Some lifts were upgraded, and development in the town of Mammoth Lakes, at the base of the mountain, continued.

INTRAWEST INVESTMENT

McCoy had fended off many offers to buy Mammoth Mountain over the years. By the time he passed his 80th birthday, though, he was willing to listen to outside interests. In 1996, McCoy made a deal with a Canadian ski area development firm called Intrawest. Intrawest bought 240 acres of real estate in the town of Mammoth Lakes, plus 33 percent of the non-voting stock in Mammoth Mountain. By 1997, Intrawest's share in Mammoth Mountain had increased to 52 percent. The developer embarked on a ten-year plan to build condominiums, hotels, and shops in the town's North Village area, transforming the ramshackle ski town into a world-class resort destination. The overall cost for the plan was estimated at $350 million. Intrawest helped develop a golf course, which opened in 1999, and worked with the town of Mammoth Lakes to provide better air access to the area's small airport. This was a huge change to the town, which had had only a dozen residents when McCoy first visited in the 1930s.

TRANSFORMATION AND SALE

By the early 2000s, Mammoth Lakes looked much different than it had a decade earlier. Intrawest's investment in the ski area and surrounding town now bore a price tag of $1 billion. Real estate prices in Mammoth Lakes had skyrocketed, so that housing tripled in value, leaving it out of reach of many ordinary citizens. Much more linked the town and the ski area, so that non-skiers or light skiers could also be drawn to Mammoth. The year 2003 saw the completion of the new "Village at Mammoth," a combination shopping mall/condominium complex. A $15 million gondola carried visitors between the Village and the ski slopes. An Intrawest spokesman told the *New York Times* (January 24, 2003) that the typical skier spent "less than four hours a day on the mountain." Intrawest, therefore, aimed to find things to occupy skiers for the rest of their time.

Development continued after Mammoth Mountain changed hands in 2005. The McCoy family sold their interest in the ski area to the investment group Starwood Capital in a deal valued at $365 million. A few months later, Intrawest pared down its interest in Mammoth Mountain to 15 percent, leaving Starwood with the remaining 85 percent.

Starwood Capital Group was run by Barry Sternlicht, who had formerly run Starwood Hotels. Starwood Hotels had taken various hotel properties and pushed them into a stable of fine lodging brands including Westin, Sheraton, and the upscale boutique hotel chain W. Although Starwood Capital Group was unaffiliated with Starwood Hotels, it too had a history of luxury hotel management. It owned the Crillon hotel in Paris, and was in the midst of launching a new upscale hotel chain that would combine lavish style with environmental consciousness.

The new ownership agreement left Intrawest's Rusty Gregory as chief executive of Mammoth Mountain. Starwood and Intrawest had a separate agreement to develop Intrawest's real estate in Mammoth Lakes. By the time Starwood took over, Mammoth Mountain had blossomed into not only the leading ski resort in California and one of the busiest in the United States, but also the operator of a golf course, bike park, and snowmobile adventure company. Mammoth Mountain also owned and managed lodges and inns on Mammoth Mountain and at nearby June Mountain.

The new owners went forward with plans to build a luxury hotel, as well as to develop residences along the golf course that would entail so-called fractional ownership, akin to a time share. In 2008, the Mammoth Lakes airport opened to commercial air flights. This began as only one flight a day from Los Angeles, but the developers hoped that soon Mammoth Mountain would be able to draw skiers from the East Coast and Midwest. Still, 90 percent of the resort's skiers were from within California. With Mammoth's significant upgrades, it seemed on the path to becoming a bigger draw for holiday crowds from across the country.

A. Woodward

PRINCIPAL COMPETITORS

Vail Resorts, Inc.; Aspen Skiing Co.; Booth Creek Ski Holdings, Inc.

FURTHER READING

Auer, Tonie, "$1B Investment Planned for California Ski Resort," *Commercial Property News,* April 5, 2007.

Barlow, Zeke, "Flights Start Coming into Mammoth Today," *Ventura County Star,* December 18, 2008.

Buchanon, Leigh, "How I Did It," *Inc.,* December 2008, p. 118.

Carlson, Lee, "Ah, McCoy, You're at It Again," *Skiing,* January 1994, p. 30.

Clark, Brian E., "California Ski Resorts Unveil Renovations, New Amenities, More Activities," *San Diego Union-Tribune,* November 25, 2002.

Dugard, Martin, "Changing of the Guard," *Snow Country,* November 1997, p. 53.

Forstenzer, Martin, "Intra-Town Squabble," *Mountain Sports & Living,* January/February 1999, p. 15.

"Gold in Those Ski Hills," *America's Intelligence Wire,* October 17, 2005.

Johnson, William Oscar, "A Man and His Mountain," *Sports Illustrated,* February 25, 1985, p. 58.

Lambert, Melissa, "2001: A Ski Odyssey," *Skiing,* December 1997, p. C6.

Lee, Denny, "Whose Mountain Is It Anyway?" *New York Times,* January 24, 2003, p. F1.

Nelson, Janet, "Bound for Slope and Trail," *New York Times,* November 13, 1988, p. A15.

Sanders, Peter, "Sternlicht Makes Another Move in Luxury Hotels," *Wall Street Journal,* October 18, 2006, p. D14.

"Ski Resorts Viewed As New Real Estate Play," *Investment Dealers' Digest,* October 17, 2005.

"Town on Shaky Ground Is Seeing a Turnaround," *New York Times,* August 16, 1998.

Webster, Donovan, "Dave McCoy Holds His Ground," *Skiing,* February 1996, p. 74.

MARINER ENERGY, INC.

Mariner Energy, Inc.

One Briar Lake Plaza, Suite 2000
2000 West Sam Houston Parkway South
Houston, Texas 77042
U.S.A.
Telephone: (713) 954-5500
Fax: (713) 954-5555
Web site: http://www.mariner-energy.com

Public Company
Incorporated: 1983 as Trafalgar House Oil & Gas USA
Inc.
Employees: 233
Sales: $874.72 million (2007)
Stock Exchanges: New York
Ticker Symbol: ME
NAICS: 211111 Crude Petroleum and Natural Gas
Extraction

■ ■ ■

Mariner Energy, Inc., is an oil and gas exploration and development company operating in the Gulf of Mexico and west Texas. The company pursues projects that range from high-risk exploration projects to low-risk development projects. Mariner Energy has 836 billion cubic feet equivalent (Bcfe) of proved reserves. In west Texas, where it operates in an 80,000-acre region, the company obtains 46 percent of its proved reserves. Roughly 15 percent of its proved reserves are located in the deep waters of the Gulf of Mexico, where it holds interests in 57 blocks. Mariner Energy's Gulf of Mexico shelf properties account for 39 percent of its proved

reserves. The balance of the company's proved reserves are tilted slightly toward natural gas, which accounts for 54 percent of its 836 Bcfe. Oil, condensate, and natural gas liquids account for 46 percent of its proved reserves.

ORIGINS

Roughly a decade after it was founded, Mariner Energy discovered its calling, carving a niche for itself in the deep waters of the Gulf of Mexico. Once the company moved into the "deepwater Gulf," it gained a new identity, taking on the characteristics that would define its success. Founded in 1983 as Trafalgar House Oil & Gas Co., the company began plotting its foray into the deepwater Gulf in 1992, when it operated under the name Hardy Oil & Gas USA Co.

Hardy Oil & Gas explored opportunities in the deepwater Gulf for two years before taking on its first project. The company drilled its first deepwater well, Mustique, in 1994, beginning a new chapter in its corporate life. The new strategy hinged on acquiring and exploiting small discoveries that the major operators in the region—subsidiaries and affiliates of industry giants such as Shell Oil Co., Chevron Corp., and Exxon Corp.—considered to be too small to meet their strategic criteria.

As a small independent concern, Hardy Oil & Gas was an early entrant into the deepwater Gulf. The region soon would be abuzz with small independent companies looking to feed off what the major oil and gas explorers cast aside. In 1993, there were 56 leases in the deepwater Gulf operated by independent companies, a figure that would skyrocket to 1,202 by the end of the

COMPANY PERSPECTIVES

We are a growth company and strive aggressively to increase our reserves and production from our existing asset base as well as through expansion into new operating areas. Our management team pursues a balanced growth strategy employing varying elements of exploration, development, and acquisition activities in complementary operating regions intended to achieve an overall moderate-risk growth profile at attractive rates of return under most industry conditions.

decade, as small companies flocked to the region, seeking to potentially double their reserves with one exploration well. By the end of the 1990s, independent companies were spending three times as much money as the major explorers on acquiring deepwater leases, with industry observers estimating that independent companies owned more than 40 percent of the active leases in the deepwater Gulf.

NEW OWNERS IN 1996

As might be expected, the independent companies in the deepwater Gulf became ventures of interest to those wanting to share in the fortunes that could be made. For Hardy Oil & Gas, the interest it received from one investor had a profound effect on its existence, becoming the single-most important event during its first quarter-century of business. In 1996, Enron Corporation, the giant Houston, Texas-based energy conglomerate, decided it wanted to take a stake in the region, and it selected Hardy Oil & Gas as its acquisition target. The deal was completed in April, when a group of Hardy Oil & Gas employees, led by Robert Henderson, formed Mariner Energy and purchased Hardy Oil & Gas. Concurrently, Enron, through its Joint Energy Development Investments Limited Partnership (JEDI), purchased a 96 percent interest in Mariner Energy for $185 million, installing Henderson as the new company's chairman, chief executive officer, and president.

FROM EXPLOITATION TO EXPLORATION

With the backing of Enron, Mariner Energy added a new dimension to its business. The company made the leap from exploitation to exploration in 1996, seeking to increase its reserves by making its own discoveries in

the deepwater Gulf. At first, the company targeted fields in the range of five million to 15 million barrels of oil equivalent before gradually becoming more ambitious and taking on projects with up to 75 million barrels of reserves. Mariner Energy recorded encouraging success as an explorer, hitting eight discoveries out of 15 exploration wells drilled by the end of the 1990s.

Mariner Energy's new approach of building reserves through the drillbit did not bring an end to the company's original practice of acquiring discoveries. "As larger companies consolidate," Henderson said in the December 2000 issue of *Oil and Gas Investor*, "their minimum thresholds rise in terms of reserve sizes. When they shed assets, that means more opportunities for us to acquire their small discoveries." By the end of the 1990s, Mariner operated three exploitation projects, Pluto, Aconcaqua, and Devils Tower. The company acquired the Pluto project when BP Plc, Chevron, and BHP Petroleum (Americas) Inc. farmed out the discovery of 20 million barrels of oil equivalent in 2,900 feet of water in the Gulf. Subsequently, Mariner Energy developed the field. The company purchased Aconcaqua and Devils Tower at a U.S. Minerals Management Service lease sale, acquiring the properties in 1998. A fourth exploitation project was added in August 2000, when Mariner Energy agreed to acquire Shell Exploration and Production's 50 percent working interest in the King Kong development project, located in 3,900 feet of water in the Green Canyon blocks roughly 150 miles southeast of New Orleans.

CAUGHT IN A MAELSTROM

The combination of exploitation and exploration served Mariner Energy well. The company used subsea technology to develop midsize fields that were purchased from asset-shedding industry giants or discovered through low-cost exploration efforts, relying on its two areas of activity to record admirable financial performance. The company filed with the U.S. Securities and Exchange Commission (SEC) for an initial public offering (IPO) of stock, ready to use its success to gain an infusion of capital from Wall Street. Revenues climbed to $121 million and profits reached $21 million in 2000. There was every indication that all was well at the company's suburban Houston headquarters, but profound problems were brewing not too far away that would make 2000 the last year any sense of normalcy existed at Mariner Energy for the next half-decade. The company's owner, Enron, was headed toward collapse, a spectacular demise that would ensnare Mariner Energy in one of the most notorious scandals in U.S. business history.

Systemic accounting fraud forced Enron to declare bankruptcy in December 2001, the largest bankruptcy

KEY DATES

1983: Mariner Energy is incorporated as Trafalgar House Oil & Gas Co.
1994: The company, operating as Hardy Oil & Gas USA Co., drills its first well in the deep waters of the Gulf of Mexico.
1996: Hardy Oil & Gas becomes Mariner Energy when Enron Corp. acquires the company.
2001: In the wake of Enron's bankruptcy, Mariner Energy is put up for sale.
2004: Mariner Energy is acquired by Acon Investments and Riverstone Holdings.
2006: Mariner Energy merges with Forest Oil Corp., more than doubling its reserves.
2007: Revenues reach a record high of $874 million.

at that time in U.S. business history. Revelations of accounting malfeasance abounded in the months before and after Enron's collapse, including highly publicized stories that focused on Mariner Energy. Of all Enron's private investments, Mariner Energy was the most overvalued, typifying the creative and illegal way Enron's management inflated profits to keep its stock value increasing.

As it was later revealed, Mariner Energy was a subject of heated debate among Enron's upper management in the months leading up to the conglomerate's bankruptcy. Members of the Risk Assessment and Control Group (RAC), an internal watchdog group at Enron, had argued that the value of Mariner Energy was grossly inflated. Energy Capital Resources (ECR), another Enron unit, calculated the value of Mariner Energy, estimating that Mariner Energy was worth $350 million. RAC argued that Mariner Energy was worth closer to $150 million, but Enron's upper management dismissed RAC's objections, recording the gains accumulated from the company's original investment as operating income for Enron. "Mariner was referred to as a honey pot where people would go to when [fiscal] quarters were tough," a former RAC employee said in the September 22, 2002 edition of the *Houston Chronicle*. "Everyone knew that Mariner would turn out to be whatever they wanted it to be."

In stature, Mariner Energy was exceptionally small compared to Enron. Enron, with a payroll of 22,000, posted $101 billion in revenues in 2000, the same year the 80-employee Mariner Energy celebrated $121 mil-

lion in revenues. Mariner Energy did not cause Enron's failure—it represented merely a case in point of widespread misconduct—but Enron threatened to cause Mariner Energy's failure. Of a host of problems that resulted from Mariner Energy's relationship with Enron, its inability to complete its IPO was one effect assessed by Henderson. "The last thing they would have wanted to do was to take us public because that would have meant a write-off," he said in the September 22, 2002 edition of the *Houston Chronicle*. Mariner Energy's problems ran deeper, however, presenting daunting challenges to Henderson's successor. Henderson resigned in mid-2001 before the full extent of the disaster was made public, replaced by Scott Josey, one of two executives recruited by Enron CEO Jeff Skilling to head Energy Capital Resources, the Enron unit responsible for calculating Mariner Energy's value.

SCOTT JOSEY TAKES THE HELM IN 2001

Josey faced a public relations nightmare. There was nothing wrong with Mariner Energy, but its reputation had been severely damaged because of its affiliation with Enron. "It was a perfectly healthy oil and gas drilling company, but Enron had abused it, systematically inflating its value to meet earnings targets," the September 10, 2007 issue of *Business Week* observed. Bankers shunned Mariner Energy after Enron declared bankruptcy, giving it little access to credit. The company was up for sale to compensate Enron creditors, but the stigma of Enron made the oil and gas industry wary. Desperate for cash, Josey sold half of the company's proven reserves for $200 million, as he redirected drilling efforts to less risky inland projects, making Mariner Energy less of a deepwater-focused company. The company's payroll shrank to 40 employees. "Even though Mariner wasn't bankrupt, it got treated like it was," Josey explained in the January 2006 issue of *Oil and Gas Investor*. "People were hesitant to do business with Mariner and banks didn't want to stay with it because they were the same banks that had significant exposure to Enron. Mariner was guilty by association."

NEW OWNERS IN 2004

Mariner Energy hung in limbo for month after month, unable to access capital and remaining on the auction block with no suitors expressing interest. Salvation arrived when two private equity funds operated by Acon Investments LLC and Riverstone Holdings made a bid to acquire Mariner Energy. "We were originally contacted in mid-2003 by Acon, which has an affiliation with Texas Pacific Group," Josey explained in the February 2006 issue of *Oil and Gas Investor*. "They had heard about Mariner, knew we were owned by Enron, and were looking for oil and gas opportunities. They invited Riverstone into the partnership." Enron sold Mariner Energy in March 2004 for $271 million, giving Riverstone Holdings a 67 percent stake and Acon Investments a 33 percent stake in Mariner Energy. "We threaded a needle to emerge from Enron," Josey recalled in the September 10, 2007 edition of *Business Week*. "I still view it somewhat like a miracle."

2006 MERGER WITH FOREST OIL

Mariner Energy's situation improved dramatically once it completely escaped the pall hanging over Enron. In late 2005, a deal of great significance began to take shape when Mariner Energy and Denver, Colorado-based Forest Oil Corporation discussed merging their Gulf of Mexico assets, a complex transaction that would make Mariner Energy a publicly traded company once it was completed. In March 2006, Forest Oil spun off its Gulf of Mexico assets into a separate company, aptly named Spinco, that subsequently merged into Mariner Energy. The deal more than doubled Mariner Energy's reserves to 615 Bcfe, adding Forest Oil's shallow-water assets that further distanced Mariner Energy from its historical roots in the deepwater Gulf.

As Mariner Energy completed its first quarter-century of business, the company was recording vibrant financial growth. Between 2005 and 2007, its revenues soared from $199 million to $874 million. Net income during the period jumped substantially as well, rising from $40.4 million to $143.9 million. The company, after years of being hamstrung by the Enron debacle, was on the rise, making it on *Business Week*'s annual list of "Hot Growth Companies" in 2007. "Mariner's story is kind of like the Yellow Brick Road," Josey remarked in the January 2006 issue of *Oil and Gas Investor*. "It starts out okay, it gets bad pretty fast, but it turns out well in the end."

Jeffrey L. Covell

PRINCIPAL SUBSIDIARIES

Mariner Energy Resources, Inc.; Mariner Gulf of Mexico LLC.

PRINCIPAL COMPETITORS

Chesapeake Energy Corporation; BP P.l.c.; Royal Dutch Shell P.l.c.

FURTHER READING

"Enron's Fish Story," *Business Week*, February 25, 2002, p. 39.

Fletcher, Sam, "Mariner Cites Gas Find in the Gulf," *Natural Gas Week*, October 18, 1999, p. 2.

Gosmano, Jeff, "Forest Spins Off Then Merges Gulf Business with Mariner's Assets," *Oil Daily*, September 13, 2005.

Hindo, Brian, "Surviving Enron and Thriving," *Business Week*, September 10, 2007, p. 61.

"Mariner Cancels IPO," *Oil Daily*, November 7, 2002.

"Mariner Energy LLC, Houston, Has Been Purchased by Affiliates of Private-Equity Funds Acon Investments LLC and Carlyle/Riverstone Global Energy and Power Fund II," *Oil and Gas Investor*, April 2004, p. 124.

"Mariner to Buy King Kong Stake," *Oil Daily*, August 2, 2000.

Maxwell, Taryn, "Mariner's Josey Talks About Enron," *Oil and Gas Investor*, January 2006, p. 127.

———, "The Steadfast Mariner," *Oil and Gas Investor*, February 2006, p. 41.

Perin, Monica, "Two Houston Companies Plan to Make Public Stock Offerings," *Houston Business Journal*, October 1, 1999, p. 8A.

Rice, Harvey, "The Fall of Enron," *Houston Chronicle*, September 22, 2002, p. 35.

Wetuski, Jodi, "Small Companies, Big Plans," *Oil and Gas Investor*, December 2000, p. 70.

Martin's Super Markets, Inc.

———————◼———————

760 West Cotter Street
South Bend, Indiana 46613
U.S.A.
Telephone: (574) 234-5848
Toll Free: (800) 910-7079
Fax: (574) 234-9827
Web site: http://www.martins-supermarkets.com

Private Company
Incorporated: 1947
Employees: 3,100
Sales: $462 million (2008 est.)
NAICS: 445110 Supermarkets and Other Grocery (Except Convenience) Stores

◼ ◼ ◼

Martin's Super Markets, Inc., owns and operates 20 grocery stores in north central Indiana and southwestern Michigan. Ranging from 47,000 to 75,000 square feet in size, Martin's stores feature a full range of groceries and a delicatessen, with some also incorporating a Starbucks coffee counter, a pet supply store, a pharmacy, and/or a gas station. The family-owned firm maintains strong ties to the communities and customers it serves, and continues to perform well against intense competition from larger regional and national chains. In addition to its own stores, Martin's also manages several Sav-A-Lot limited-inventory groceries for Supervalu, Inc., of Minnesota.

BEGINNINGS

The first Martin's store was opened on September 15, 1947, by Martin Tarnow and his wife, Alice Jane. Both born in 1917, they married in 1936 and the first of their two daughters was born a year later. Martin Tarnow had worked in a grocery from the age of ten, and later was employed by the makers of Singer sewing machines and Studebaker automobiles. Looking to earn money for their daughters' college education, the couple took $100 in savings and borrowed $9,000 to stock a small "mom and pop" grocery, which was housed in a 20-by-40-foot storefront. Martin Tarnow's tasks included butchering meat, while Jane operated the cash register and attended to the store's decor.

The Tarnows moved their operation into a larger space in 1951, and several years later they bought a second store some 25 miles away in Dowagiac, Michigan, which Jane would manage. In 1961 another grocery was added in nearby Elkhart, Indiana, and the following year the South Bend store was relocated to a new, larger building. By this time they had given up the Dowagiac store.

In 1964 the Tarnows' daughter Nancy married Bob Bartels, who had trained as an engineer. The young couple moved to Rhode Island after his employer transferred him there, but he was soon lured back to Indiana by an offer to manage a Martin's grocery. Complementing his in-laws' talents for merchandising and customer service, Bartels would work on improving the financial and managerial side of the operation. Over the next decade the firm gradually added more locations.

COMPANY PERSPECTIVES

Pledging service and value to customers and community since 1947.

In 1977 Martin and Jane Tarnow stepped back from running the company full-time, and Bob Bartels became the firm's president. He quickly boosted the pace of expansion, adding four new stores in 1979. In 1985 the Tarnows retired for good, though Martin would retain the title of chairman emeritus.

The firm's expansion plans were ramped back during the year when four stores in relatively distant Hammond, Indiana, were sold, leaving operations centered in South Bend, Elkhart, and the adjacent town of Mishawaka. During the year Martin's also built a central baking plant at its South Bend flagship store that allowed it to add items including decorated cakes at every location, and in 1986 a program to gradually renovate all of its stores was begun.

INTRODUCTION OF LARGER STORE FORMAT: 1989

Martin's 12th grocery opened in South Bend's Erskine Plaza in 1989. At 50,000 square feet, it was larger than the chain's 30,000–35,000 square foot average. A year later an outlet with a similar footprint replaced an older unit in Elkhart. Future stores would follow this template.

The larger store size allowed for inclusion of more products and enhancement of popular services such as video rentals, with nonfood items making up about 6 percent of sales. Competition in the supermarket industry was heating up as the firm went toe-to-toe with national chains including Kroger, and it used a combination of print, radio, and television ads to get its message out, as well as in-store merchandising.

In January 1992 the company took over a Felpausch grocery in Elkhart after the larger chain pulled out of northwest Indiana, closing a smaller nearby outlet in the process. Martin's had five stores in the city out of a total of 13.

Like other grocers, the company was constantly refining its offerings to find the broadest appeal, tweaking each location to suit its particular customer mix. Martin's also attracted business in innovative ways with programs such as one begun in 1980, in which it chartered buses to take senior citizens from area retirement homes to its stores. The seniors were offered shopping aids including motorized wheelchairs, and Martin's employees rode back with them to help carry their purchases inside. Some 1,500 trips were chartered each year. The firm also was actively involved in supporting charitable organizations in the communities it served, frequently through in-kind donations.

Many of Martin's employees were recruited from the large student population in South Bend (home to the University of Notre Dame), as well as from area high schools, and the company was a member of Education First, a coalition that promoted finishing school before seeking full-time employment. To retain employees the firm actively promoted from within, offered generous benefits, and paid 75 percent of tuition for full-time employees to take up to two college classes at a time. As a result, its turnover rate was significantly lower than the industry averages of 17 percent for full-time employees and 82 percent for part-timers.

PREFERRED CUSTOMER CARD DEBUTS IN 1993

In 1993 Martin's unveiled the Preferred Customer Card, which could be used to debit the cost of purchases from a patron's checking account and also helped generate data about buyer preferences. Store upgrades were continuing, and in 1994 the firm's flagship location in South Bend was expanded by a fifth to 51,000 square feet. New additions included video rentals, flowers, a pizza bar, and a deli café, with most areas of the store enhanced in the $2.5 million makeover. The expansion was facilitated in part by a decision to move the company's central bakery out of the store to a separate location.

As Americans' eating habits evolved to include more prepared take-away meals, grocers shifted their focus to this area. Martin's hired a chef to create dishes that would be prepared in its delicatessens for reheating at home, and some locations began to offer such specialty foods as sushi, Panini sandwiches, and more. The firm's popular Side Door Deli concept would eventually be incorporated into every store.

In 1995 Martin's announced it would build new stores in Valparaiso and Logansport, Indiana, and in early 1996 another was announced for the north side of Elkhart. That summer the Logansport grocery opened, but plans for the Valparaiso location were eventually dropped.

In the spring of 1997 the company bought three stores from bankrupt South Bend-based Van Camps Supermarkets in a three-way deal that also involved creditor Supervalu, Inc. One was closed after a new

KEY DATES

1947: Martin and Jane Tarnow open a small grocery store in South Bend, Indiana.

1961: First store opens in Elkhart.

1964: Son-in-law Bob Bartels joins firm as store manager.

1977: Tarnows reduce involvement in management; Bob Bartels takes charge.

1979: Four stores open as Martin's boosts pace of expansion.

1985: New central baking plant is built; Hammond, Indiana, stores are sold; Tarnows retire.

1993: Preferred Customer Card is introduced.

1997: Three Van Camp's stores are purchased; Niles, Michigan, location opens.

1999: First Starbucks coffee counter is added; firm takes over Elkhart Sav-A-Lot.

2002: Five stores add pharmacies; first Martin's Fuel Center opens.

2007: Firm moves its wholesale, private-label food business to Spartan Stores, Inc.

Martin's was completed nearby, while the others were rebranded. In the fall another new store opened a few miles north of South Bend in Niles, Michigan. The 50,000-square-foot outlet included a Side Door Deli and a branch of the Valley American Bank & Trust.

In August 1998 company namesake Martin Tarnow died at the age of 80, and his wife Jane passed away the following spring at 82. Asked by a reporter why his company was successful, Martin Tarnow had replied, "Personality, low prices and clean stores," and the company continued to follow his philosophy after its founders' passing. By that time, Martin's had 17 stores and employed 2,500.

In 1999 the firm opened a new store in Elkhart that replaced a smaller location nearby. The larger store had a Side Door Deli that also incorporated a Starbucks coffee counter, while the smaller location was refitted as a Sav-A-Lot grocery, which Martin's would operate after the inventory of a closed Sav-A-Lot was moved in to fill it. While an average Martin's carried some 40,000 different items, the limited-inventory, discount-priced Sav-A-Lot offered a mere 1,500. Martin's officials stated that they were operating the Sav-A-Lot in part to study the different market segment it served.

Several Martin's stores boasted Paw Mart departments, an enhanced version of the pet food aisle that of-fered a wider range of products. The firm had earlier started a Pet Club, whose members received discounts on purchases, and some 10,000 had joined.

In 2000 Martin's bought a Plymouth, Indiana, Miller's Super Valu store, rebranded it, and added popular departments including a bakery and flower shop. Grocery competition was growing increasingly fierce, with Wal-Mart having opened supercenters in Elkhart, South Bend, and Mishawaka in 1999, and other national retail chains such as Kmart and Target adding food aisles. During the year the company's flagship store dropped video rentals and its Side Door Deli switched from Seattle's Best to Starbucks coffee. Many of the firm's other stores subsequently added Starbucks counters as well.

ADDING PHARMACIES, GAS STATION TO THE MIX: 2002

In the summer of 2001 Martin's moved further into Michigan by opening a store in St. Joseph, about 40 miles north of South Bend. Plans were underway to add pharmacies in selected outlets, and the following year they appeared in five locations that did not have drugstores nearby. PRS Pharmacy Services of Pennsylvania set up the operations and secured the necessary licensing.

During 2002 Martin's also opened a gas station adjacent to a store in Elkhart, which offered discounts based on purchases made with preferred customer cards. The cost of the gas operation was put at $300,000, and four others were added over the next several years.

The firm's Erskine Plaza store in South Bend was enlarged in 2002 to become its largest to date, expanding into an adjacent space that had been vacated by a shuttered CVS. The $4.5 million makeover boosted it from 56,000 to 75,000 square feet. A pharmacy, bank, Side Door Deli, and Starbucks were added, and many departments were expanded. Other new additions included international and kosher foods. The renovated store opened the following year.

The company added a third Michigan location in August 2003 when it bought a D&W grocery store in Stevensville, near St. Joseph. It was reopened as a Martin's in September with a pharmacy, deli, and Starbucks.

In 2006 Martin's expanded its central bakery in Mishawaka by 13,000 square feet to keep up with expansion and growing customer demand. Two new stores opened during the year, as well, one in Goshen and the other in Mishawaka. The latter was a newly built 71,000-square-foot superstore in a new shopping plaza, which replaced a location the firm had converted from a Thrifty Mart in the 1980s. The plush store featured the usual departments as well as a special kitchen for cooking classes. More natural and organic foods would also be offered.

By that year, Bob Bartels was serving as the firm's chairman, and his son Robert Jr. (known as Rob) was president and CEO. The younger Bartels had worked in the family business since 1989 in a variety of positions. Annual sales were estimated at upwards of $300 million, and the company employed nearly 3,000.

In April 2007 Martin's switched its contract for many wholesale and private-label food products to Michigan-based distributor/retailer Spartan Stores, Inc. The company had long sourced such goods from Roundy's, but made the change after abandoning a brief affiliation with Nash Finch, having purchased nonfood items from Spartan since 2005. Martin's business, which Nash Finch had valued at $153 million per year, would make it Spartan's largest customer among the 350 independent grocers it served in Michigan, Indiana, and Ohio.

In 2008 Martin's began offering free generic prescription antibiotics to customers with a preferred customer card. The program had proven popular with other grocers around the country. The firm had 20 stores, 17 of them in Indiana and three in Michigan.

More than 60 years after Martin and Jane Tarnow opened their first small grocery, Martin's Super Markets, Inc., had grown into a chain of 20 stores in north central Indiana and southwestern Michigan. The family-owned firm continued to follow its founders' philosophy of offering friendly customer service, quality goods, and low prices, and was holding its own against fierce competition from Kroger, Wal-Mart, and others.

Frank Uhle

PRINCIPAL COMPETITORS

The Kroger Co.; Wal-Mart Stores, Inc.; Meijer, Inc.; Spartan Stores, Inc.; Aldi Group; Jewel-Osco; Supervalu, Inc.; Target Corporation.

FURTHER READING

Bennett, Stephen, "Martin's Puts More in the Store," *Progressive Grocer,* January 1990, p. 84.

Dodson, Paul, "Martin's Founder: 'Run the Store for the Customer,'" *South Bend Tribune,* August 23, 1998, p. B1.

———, "Martin's to Open 'Nearly New' Store," *South Bend Tribune,* May 4, 1994, p. C6.

Elliott, Carol, "Martin's Opening First Gas Station on Elkhart's West Side," *South Bend Tribune,* May 17, 2002, p. B10.

Martin, Jennifer, "Businesses Feted for Being Disabled-Friendly," *Tribune Business Weekly,* March 15, 1995, p. 2.

"Martin's Co-Founder Dies at Age 80," *South Bend Tribune,* August 18, 1998, p. B2.

Prescott, Heidi, "David vs. Goliath," *South Bend Tribune,* June 10, 2001, p. B1.

———, "A Makeover for Martin's," *South Bend Tribune,* August 13, 2006, p. F1.

———, "Martin's Acquiring D&W of Stevensville," *South Bend Tribune,* August 13, 2003, p. B8.

———, "Martin's Expands Its Bakery," *South Bend Tribune,* January 12, 2006, p. C8.

———, "Pet Specialty Store Opens in Martin's," *South Bend Tribune,* February 17, 1999, p. B8.

———, "Waking a Tired Store," *South Bend Tribune,* March 21, 2003, p. B8.

Schreiber, David, "Felpausch Pulls Out of County," *Elkhart Truth,* January 7, 1992.

———, "Supermarkets Reach Agreement," *Elkhart Truth,* March 13, 1997, p. A1.

"Spartan Expands Distribution," *Grand Rapids (Mich.) Press,* April 26, 2007, p. C1.

Tarnowski, Joseph, "Breaking into Pharmacy," *Progressive Grocer,* April 15, 2005, p. 110.

Mastellone Hermanos S.A.

Encarnación Ezcurra 365
Buenos Aires, C.F.
Argentina
Telephone: (54 11) 4311-6206
Toll Free: (0800) 888-0800 (in Argentina)
Fax: (54 11) 4313-5458
Web site: http://www.laserenisima.com.ar

Public Company
Incorporated: 1973
Employees: 5,000
Sales: ARS 2.1 billion ($677.42 million) (2007)
NAICS: 311421 Fruit and Vegetable Canning; 311511 Fluid Milk Manufacturing; 311512 Creamery Butter Manufacturing; 311513 Cheese Manufacturing; 311514 Dry, Condensed, and Evaporated Dairy Product Manufacturing; 311520 Ice Cream and Frozen Dessert Manufacturing

∎ ∎ ∎

Mastellone Hermanos S.A., best known by its chief brand, La Serenísima, is Argentina's leading company for the manufacture of dairy products. La Serenísima dominates the sale of milk in the nation and is so well known and admired in Argentina that it ranks as a national symbol of quality. Its sales are particularly strong in the greater Buenos Aires metropolitan area. The company owns a large industrial complex in General Rodríguez, Buenos Aires, and six plants elsewhere. Although a public company, Mastellone Hermanos's shares are not quoted on any exchange.

THE FIRST HALF-CENTURY

Antonino Mastellone was born in southern Italy in 1899 to a family long involved in cheesemaking. As a young man he was employed in the most prestigious Italian cheese factory of the era. He immigrated in 1925 to Argentina, where he took up his trade and summoned his younger brother José. The brothers moved to General Rodríguez in the province of Buenos Aires, in 1927 and began making mozzarella and ricotta, then almost unknown in Argentina, from milk that they bought from local dairies. Antonino took the train at the break of day into the city of Buenos Aires, some 30 miles away, where he sold the day-old cheese at a market or by going house to house. At noon he returned to make cheese for the next day's sales.

By 1935 José was no longer in the business, but another younger brother, Pascual, had followed the first two to Argentina and was making deliveries from the enterprise's first van to pizzerias in La Boca, a heavily Italian Buenos Aires neighborhood. The cheeses were bearing the name of La Serenísima (Most Serene), an allusion to La Serenissima, the name of a squadron of Italian aviators who, during World War I, flew over Vienna, capital of enemy Austria-Hungary, where they dropped pamphlets that urged peace. It was not until 1942, however, that Antonino, Pascual, and two partners registered the enterprise under this name. Production was still entirely artisanal, although by 1950 the business was selling 600 kilos (1,320 pounds) of cheese a day.

Antonino Mastellone was able to buy out his partners in 1949, but he died of lung cancer less than

COMPANY PERSPECTIVES

Mission: To be nationally and internationally recognized for the competitiveness, the quality of its products and customer attention.

three years later, leaving the business to his three sons in equal proportion. In practice, the firm came under the leadership of the elder, Pascual, who, like his father, never drank milk because it made him feel ill. Pascual worked long hours and did not take a vacation for the first ten years.

By 1960 La Serenísima's production was 50 times greater than ten years earlier. Having outstripped the capacity of its own facilities, it had begun buying smaller dairy processors. The course of the enterprise changed dramatically, however, in 1960 or 1961, when the city of Buenos Aires banned milk that had not been pasteurized. Moreover, all milk, formerly sold in metal cans, would have to be bottled. La Serenísima borrowed the use of a pasteurization plant and began processing the production of about 300 neighboring dairies. A rusty old bottling plant in disuse was located in Mar del Plata, purchased, and restored. On the day after New Year's 1962, the company was ready with the first bottled milk on the market. In 1967, when the province of Buenos Aires also banned unpasteurized milk, La Serenísima's output reached 100,000 liters a day. The company included a dozen trucks and its own laboratory to control and verify the quality of the milk.

La Serenísima's milk output had, by 1971, reached between 800,000 and one million liters daily. Later in the decade Mastellone Hermanos was actually importing powdered milk from the European Economic Community because of low cost and easy credit. To market the product, the company obtained the unique privilege of a waiver exempting it from the law that prohibited the import of milk powder. Mastellone then sold fluid milk from reconstituted powder very cheaply and without any pertinent declaration of origin.

La Serenísima was outstripping its competitors in the 1970s by collecting milk in bulk to reduce costs and converting delivery to the customer from bottles to a form that not only cut the weight, size, and expense of the retailed product but also reduced damage from shattering. Rival companies such as Usina Láctea La Armonía S.A., Utilaca S.A., Granja Iris S.A., Tamberos Unidos de Cañuelas Agropecuaria S.A., Industrias Lácteas Teubuco S.A., and José y Ramón Marzol S.A. were

swallowed up by the Mastellone Hermanos juggernaut between 1978 and 1981. (What had been Mastellone Hermanos Sociedad Colectiva, a partnership, became a corporation, Mastellone Hermanos S.A., in 1973.)

To maintain its technical leadership, the company sent agronomists to advise its dairy suppliers. Con-Ser S.A., majority owned by Mastellone, had at its disposal 2,000 delivery vehicles, repair shops for these vehicles and refrigeration equipment, rectifiers, and a fuel depot. The company introduced, in 1984, Ultra, the first milk in Argentina for lactose intolerant people. Four years later, it introduced to the market probiotic milk and other probiotic dairy products.

DOWNSIZING IN A TROUBLED DECADE: 1990–2000

In 1990 Mastellone Hermanos was a group with five dairy products subsidiaries, a food products subsidiary, and one, added in 1988, that raised, fed, and sold hogs. Besides Con-Ser, it also held a majority stake in six other corporations. Two of these, both processors of dairy products, were almost entirely owned by Mastellone. Two others were also related to dairy, while, of the last two, one was engaged in insurance and the other in the purchase and sale of auto parts. Yet the enterprise was in deep difficulty, having fallen in arrears to thousands of creditors, including almost 2,000 dairies. Its total debt was estimated at almost $50 million, much of it related to the construction of a powdered milk plant in Villa María, Córdoba.

Mastellone Hermanos saved itself by means of a strategic alliance with French-based Group Danone, the world's largest processor of dairy products. This group entered the Argentine market in 1994 by means of Danone S.A., a joint venture with Mastellone that marketed yogurt, dairy desserts, and cheese spreads under the La Serenísima brand name. Danone S.A. had a majority of the market in these products in 1998, when it had sales of $236 million. That year the partners opened a $57 million plant producing 200,000 metric tons a year of yogurt, custard, dairy desserts, and cheese spreads in Longchamps, Buenos Aires. With 40,000 square meters of floor space, it was the largest dairy products industrial complex in Latin America and the second largest of this kind in the world.

Meanwhile, Pascual Mastellone had his eye on Brazil, where in 1996 his company acquired a majority stake in a firm named Leitesol Indústria e Cómercio, S.A. Two years later, when this firm came almost completely under Mastellone's control, it was marketing the La Serenísima brand and held 5 percent of milk powder sales in Brazil. During this period Mastellone

KEY DATES

∎

1925: Antonino Mastellone, a young Italian cheese-maker, immigrates to Argentina.

1942: Four partners, including the Mastellone brothers, register the business as La Serenísima.

1962: La Serenísima begins pasteurizing its milk and selling it in bottles instead of metal cans.

1973: The enterprise becomes a corporation under the Mastellone Hermanos name.

1994: Mastellone begins an alliance with French-based Group Danone.

1999: The firm sells its part in two joint ventures to Danone and takes in a minority partner.

2004: Mastellone's creditors agree on a restructuring plan for its $329 million debt.

built a new $80 million plant in the General Rodríguez complex, introduced organic milk to the Argentine market, added iron sulfate to fluid and powdered milk, yogurt, and dairy desserts, and launched an Ultra line of pasteurized milk promising a refrigerated shelf life of 25 days without nutritional loss. It was planning to open a large cheesemaking plant in Trenque Lauquen, Buenos Aires, to challenge the lead of rival SanCor Cooperativas Unidas Ltda. in sales of this product.

To maintain his company's leadership in its field and invest in further expansion for this purpose, Pascual Mastellone sold 15 percent of the shares in Mastellone Hermanos to Dallpoint Investments in 1998 for $48 million. Dallpoint, represented in Argentina by Greenwich Investments, consisted of eight foreign institutional investors. Six months later, Dallpoint purchased another 18 percent of Mastellone's shares for an additional $55 million. Meanwhile, also in 1999, Mastellone collected about $120 million more by selling its stake in the Danone and Lácteos Longchamps joint ventures to its French partner. The following year Mastellone also sold Group Danone 51 percent of Logística Serenísima S.A., its distribution arm, for $174 million.

STILL STRUGGLING, BUT STILL NUMBER ONE: 2001–08

The money earmarked for further investments was needed almost immediately to service Mastellone Hermanos's growing debt, as Argentina's economy fell into deep recession. After world milk prices fell precipitously in 1999 and 2000, the company's financial problems

became even more serious. When the Argentine government defaulted on its own debt at the end of 2001, the peso, which had been maintained at par with the U.S. dollar, dropped to 30 cents in value. Mastellone's dollar denominated debt tripled, reaching $329 million, a sum on which it could not meet interest payments. The company sold its Buenos Aires headquarters in 2003. Its creditors agreed on a restructuring plan in 2004.

In spite of these problems, Mastellone Hermanos could point to some achievements in the first decade of the new century. It opened plants in Los Varillas, Córdoba, and the province of San Luis in 2000. The following year it introduced Actimel, a line of products intended to strengthen natural defenses against diseases, and Dananino, a concentrated milk with fruit pulp added. In 2004 it introduced Finlandia cheese and began exporting butter to the European Union, and in 2006 it added milk fortified with vitamin C to its products. A national poll that ranked food and beverage brands by reputation put La Serenísima first, even before Coca-Cola. During this period the company also launched a nondairy product, the fruit juice line Crecer.

As Argentina's economy improved, Mastellone Hermanos, in 2005, surpassed its 1998 sales for the first time. It was aided by growing world demand for dairy products; between 2001 and 2007, the price of powdered milk rose from $1,000 to over $4,500 a metric ton (although the Argentine government promptly captured much of this bonanza to finance a fund subsidizing the dairy trade).

Nevertheless, Mastellone Hermanos was not in a good position to exploit this opening. Because the company had been favored, and protected against foreign competition, by one Argentine government after another, it was expected to supply the home market first, even though pricing agreements limited what it could charge the consumer. Accordingly, although the industry as a whole sent about 30 percent of its production abroad, Mastellone earmarked only 15 percent of its own production to more lucrative markets beyond the national borders. Squeezed between rising costs for buying milk from dairy farmers, paying its workers, and meeting its energy needs, and limits on passing these costs on to the consumer, Mastellone Hermanos lost money in 2006, 2007, and almost certainly 2008, although in the latter case the company was still waiting for payments due to it in compensation for accepting restraints on what it could charge retail customers.

Mastellone was producing and marketing about 50 products in 2008, including butter and various lines of milk, cheese, cream, and desserts. The largest of its seven facility sites was in General Rodríguez, where its industrial complex of 109,000 square meters was the largest in the Argentine dairy industry. This city, although it had about 100,000 inhabitants, bore some of the earmarks of a classic company town, since 3,000 worked for Mastellone and another 1,200 were closely tied to the firm. The company was processing 4.8 million liters of milk a day. Some 1,100 trucks and vans were traveling 75 million kilometers a day to bring its products to 79,000 points of sale throughout Argentina from Logística La Serenísima's strategically located ten depositories.

At 78 years old, Pascual Mastellone was still firmly in charge of the company in 2008. None of his three sons had shown interest in following a career in the business.

Robert Halasz

PRINCIPAL SUBSIDIARIES

Frigorífico Rydhands S.A.; Leitesol Indústria e Comércio, S.A. (Brazil); Marca 4 S.A.; Marca 5 Asesores en Seguros S.A.; Mastellone Hermanos do Brasil Comercial e Industrial Ltda. (Brazil); Mastellone San Luis, S.A.; Promas, S.A.; Puraláctea, S.A.

PRINCIPAL COMPETITORS

Danone Argentina S.A.; Milkaut S.A.; Molfinos Hermanos S.A.; Nestlé Argentina S.A.; SanCor Cooperativas Unidas Ltda.

FURTHER READING

Ancery, Paula, "Las 200 marcas que más admiran los argentinos," *Clarín,* January 23, 2005.

Bertello, Fernando, "Se agrava la crisis en el sector lechero," *La Nación de Argentina,* November 13, 2008.

"Danone se asoció a Mastellone en la distribución de lácteos," *El Cronista,* September 13, 2000.

"Mastellone—A Success Story," IPR Strategic Information Database, November 22, 1998.

"Mastellone: El arte de la convocatoria," *Apertura,* May/June 1990, pp. 54–60, 62.

"Mastellone: El empuje de General Rodríguez," *Apertura,* August 2006, pp. 74–75.

"Mastellone se quedó sin el postre," *El Cronista,* April 13, 1999.

"Qué hay detrás de la crisis láctea," *Apertura,* May 2007, pp. 72, 74–75.

Tomás, Juan Pedro, "Udder Improvement," *Latin Trade,* May 2006, p. 24.

Medical Action Industries Inc.

800 Prime Place
Hauppauge, New York 11788-4759
U.S.A.
Telephone: (631) 231-4600
Toll Free: (800) 645-7042
Fax: (631) 231-3075
Web site: http://www.medical-action.com

Public Company
Incorporated: 1977
Employees: 703
Sales: $290.5 million (2008)
Stock Exchanges: NASDAQ
Ticker Symbol: MDCI
NAICS: 339113 Surgical Appliance and Supplies Manufacturing

■ ■ ■

Medical Action Industries Inc. is a Hauppauge, New York-based developer, manufacturer, and distributor of disposable products used in surgery. The company divides its business among six categories: Patient Bedside Utensils, including bedpans, washbasins, soap dishes, service trays, and medicine cups; Minor Procedure Kits and Trays; Containment Systems for Medical Waste; Operating Room Disposables and Sterilization Products, including towels, drapes, isolation gowns, surgical headgear and shoe covers, and instrument protection; Dressings and Surgical Sponges; and Laboratory products, including petri dishes, specimen containers, culture tubes, measures, beakers, and vials. End users of the products have expanded to include dental and veterinary offices, outpatient surgery centers, long-term care facilities, and laboratories. Manufacturing and warehouse-distribution facilities are maintained in Arden, North Carolina; Clarksburg, West Virginia; Gallaway, Tennessee; and Northglenn, Colorado. A general office is also maintained in Shanghai, China, which procures raw materials and certain products. Medical Action is a public company listed on the NASDAQ.

FORMATION OF COMPANY: 1977

Operating out of a small office with just two employees, Medical Action Industries was founded in Farmingdale, New York, by Joseph R. Meringola in 1977. After earning a science degree from C.W. Post College of Long Island University in 1964, he went to work as a medical supplies salesman. He eventually decided to manufacture his own medical supplies rather than sell someone else's products. His concept was to initially focus on a single product, and then build a distribution infrastructure and industry reputation around it that would allow him in time to add other product lines. That first product, which he had successfully sold for others, was laparotomy (lap) sponges.

Made of gauze and disposable, lap sponges were used in surgery to absorb blood as well as act as a buffer between medical instruments and the skin. Although a simple product, consistent quality and precision were the key attributes to a successful brand. The sponges, which were intended for use within the body cavity, had to be free of contaminants, and the unit count, five to a package, had to be accurate every time. Surgeons could

COMPANY PERSPECTIVES

In today's Medical arena, there is no room for imperfection. That's why Medical Action dedicates every working day to meticulous attention to detail under stringent quality controls. We never accept average during the design, manufacture, packaging and delivery of our products. Because we understand that superior performance begins with getting it … Right. From the Beginning.

not be put in a position of guessing how many lap sponges they left in a body when the patient was closed up. (Rather than have a group of employees tasked with quality control, Medical Action would make everyone in a product group responsible for the finished goods.) Meringola knew that once he was able to establish a reputation for producing dependable lap sponges, customers would remain extremely loyal.

CHINA RELATIONSHIP BEGINS: 1980

Lap sponges were a low-priced item and Meringola faced stiff competition in the field. In order to shave off pennies from the price he turned to the People's Republic of China in 1980 to manufacture his products, making connections through a Chinese agent in New Jersey who had contacts in the Communist country. Meringola succeeded in lowering his costs, but he also had to contend with some nettlesome problems dealing with Chinese partners, including defective goods and unreliable deliveries. Nevertheless, the company did well enough that Meringola was able to add the more profitable disposable operating room towels to the product mix and take Medical Action public, completing a stock offering in 1985.

Sales reached $21 million and earnings $900,000 in fiscal 1988 (for the year ending March 31, 1988), but a year later Medical Action had to contend with a number of problems with its China-sourced products, including lint, uneven bleaching, and shoddy sewing. Although sales improved to $26 million in fiscal 1989, earnings dipped to $491,000 because of these manufacturing shortcomings. In order to gain greater control over quality, Medical Action sought a stake in a Chinese textile plant, an effort that generally required a great deal of patience when working with Chinese bureaucrats. In 1989, however, the government cracked down on dissidents, resulting in the Tiananmen Square massacre.

Dozens of U.S. companies left the country, but Medical Action remained. The Chinese, eager to retain investors, quickly approved the company's deal to buy an interest in a textile plant.

Another development related to China in 1989 had an adverse effect on Medical Action. The U.S. Commerce Department reclassified operating room towels as general textiles, thus making them subject to import quotas and cutting off supplies of the product for months at a time. As a result, Medical Action's revenues fell to $24.2 million in fiscal 1990 and the company reported a loss of $514,000. Although sales rebounded to the $26 million level in fiscal 1991, Medical Action lost a further $118,000. In an effort to ensure more reliable deliveries, Meringola built a plant in Asheville, North Carolina, where, in addition to lap sponges and operating room towels, the company produced gauze sponges and dry burn dressings. Also helping in turning around the company's fortunes was the increasing demand for its disposable products because of the AIDS epidemic and the general fear of infectious diseases. Medical Action returned to profitability in fiscal 1992, netting $344,000 on sales of $27 million. A year later sales improved to $33.34 million and net earnings increased to $1.3 million.

COMPANY HURT BY RECALL: 1993

Medical Action was poised to enjoy an ever better fiscal 1994 when it suffered a setback in July 1993. A customer informed the company that mold had been found in some of the lap sponges the customer had received. Although tests revealed that the mold, *Pyronema domesticum,* was not harmful and had caused no illnesses, the sponges marked sterile were anything but, and in August shipments of the products were halted in a voluntary recall. Providing some cold comfort was that the mold would soon be found in the sponges of competitors, which had also been sourced from China. As a result, Medical Action instituted a more strenuous sterilization method, and shipments resumed in less than a month. The impact on the balance sheet was significant: Net income fell below $400,000 on revenues of $36.5 million.

To gain some diversity and drive sales, Medical Action instituted an acquisition program in 1994. The first deal, which closed in August of that year, was the purchase of the disposable products business of QuanTech, Inc., including a sterile surgical-light handle cover, needle counters, instrument pouches, magnetic instrument drapes, and other operating room items. The addition of these products helped to mitigate somewhat the lingering effects of the lap sponge recall, as well as

KEY DATES

1977: Joseph R. Meringola founds company.
1980: Company begins association with People's Republic of China.
1985: Company is taken public.
1993: Contaminated products are voluntarily recalled.
1994: An acquisition strategy is adopted.
1997: Joseph Meringola is succeeded as chairman and CEO by brother Paul Meringola.
2001: Company acquires some assets of Medi-Flex Hospital Products, Inc.
2006: Medegen LLC is acquired.

declines in the sale of gauze products in fiscal 1995, when net sales slipped to $35.1 million and the company posted a loss of nearly $200,000.

Early in 1996 Medical Action completed its second acquisition, adding some of the sterilization packaging, monitoring, and contamination control products of Lawson Mardon Medical Products, Inc. They included biohazard bags, sterilization pouches, sterility maintenance covers, laboratory specimen bags, and sterilization monitors used in operating rooms as well as physicians' offices. A pair of further acquisitions followed in 1997. Most of the specialty packaging business of Dayhill Corporation was acquired in October of that year, adding a variety of collection and containment bags, including biohazard bags, autoclave bags, laboratory transport bags, sponge counting bags, and ziplock bags. A month later the inventory of the ATI PyMaH line of sterilization pouches were acquired from 3M Healthcare, bolstering Medical Action's U.S. leadership position in the sterilization packaging products business.

The year 1997 was also noteworthy because a succession plan was put into effect, in which Joseph Meringola was replaced as chairman of the board and chief executive officer by his younger brother, Paul D. Meringola. The younger Meringola had been with the company since the early 1980s and had served as president and chief operating officer since 1982.

ACQUISITION OF SAGE PRODUCTS: 1998

In January 1998 Medical Action completed another acquisition, picking up the sponge counter product lines of Sage Products, Inc. The new line made a modest contribution to fiscal 1998, which ended three months

later. Net sales for the year increased to $54.64 million, compared with $46 million in fiscal 1997. Net income also increased from $971,000 to a record $1.68 million in fiscal 1998. To close the decade, Medical Action paid $8.3 million for the disposable instrument kits and trays and other product lines of Acme Healthcare, the medical products division of Acme United Corporation. The end of the 1990s also saw Medical Action make significant progress in introducing its wound care products in Latin America.

Because of these positive developments, the company improved revenues to $57.5 million in fiscal 1999 and net income grew to $1.92 million. The Acme Healthcare assets were fully integrated in fiscal 2000 and Medical Action forged important new relationships with hospital purchasing alliances and distributors, such as the $56 million, three-year deal to supply operating room towels, lap sponges, and sterilization packaging to Novation, the parent company of hospital buying groups VHA and the University HealthSystem Consortium. Hence, Medical Action enjoyed another strong year, netting $3.24 million on revenues of nearly $71 million in fiscal 2000.

At the start of fiscal 2001 Medical Action announced that it was again in the market for acquisitions, a strategy driven in large part by consolidation within the healthcare industry. Nothing came of the effort until November 2001, well into fiscal 2002, when the company added certain products of Medi-Flex Hospital Products, Inc., including sterile kits for the inserting of intravenous catheters and sterile procedure trays that contained the components needed for the maintenance of large catheters inserted into the chest cavity. A pair of acquisitions followed in calendar 2002. In June the specialty packaging and collections systems for the containment of infectious waste and sterilization products were purchased from MD Industries, including chemotherapy waste collection bags, biohazard safety bags, water-soluble laundry bags, patient belonging bags, and equipment dust covers. Next, in October 2002, Medical Action acquired the BioSafety Division of Maxxim Medical Inc. at a cost of $20.5 million, adding many of the same collection and containment bags, but the focus this time was on sharps containment systems.

COMPANY'S LARGEST DEAL, PURCHASE OF MEDEGEN LLC: 2006

Medical Action made no further acquisitions for the next four years. In the meantime, revenues increased steadily, topping $100 million in fiscal 2003 and $150 million in fiscal 2006. Net income also kept pace, growing from $8.2 million to $11.5 million during this same period. Then, in October 2006 Medical Action completed the largest acquisition in its history when it paid $80 million for Scottsdale, Arizona-based Medegen LLC, maker of such patient utensils as washbasins, bedpans, and urinals. The deal brought with it two plants in Colorado and Tennessee that possessed plastic blow and injection molding capabilities, and $100 million in annual sales. Not only did Medical Action gain access to new customers, to whom it could cross-sell other product lines, the production capabilities of the new plants provided an opportunity to make some components in-house. Added size also gave the company critical mass both in terms of buying power but also in its national distribution footprint.

The contribution of the Medegen assets helped increase net sales to $217.33 million in fiscal 2007 and net income to about $13 million. A year later revenues increased to $290.53 million and net income improved to $13.2 million. Going forward, Medical Action planned to acquire more companies while also investing in product development, the goal being to achieve 10 percent growth each year by organic means and another 15 percent through acquisitions.

Ed Dinger

PRINCIPAL SUBSIDIARIES

Medegen Medical Products, LLC.

PRINCIPAL COMPETITORS

Becton, Dickinson and Company; Covidien Ltd.; Medline Industries, Inc.

FURTHER READING

"The Action at Medical Action," *Business Week,* December 14, 1992.

Birmingham, John, "One Founder's Far Eastern Foray," *Venture,* June/July 1989, p. 79.

Braly, Damon, "Industry Facing Lap Sponge Shortage Following Medical Action Recall," *Health Industry Today,* October 1992, p. 1.

"Gimme Five: Soaking It In," *Long Island Business News,* July 6, 2001, p. 5A.

Grugal, Robin M., "After Lengthy Dry Spell, Med Firm Back on Prowl," *Investor's Business Daily,* November 6, 2001, p. A12.

"Medical Action Rebounds After Recall," *Newsday,* June 7, 1996, p. A67.

"Medical Action Sets $100 Million Goal," *Long Island Business News,* September 18, 1998, p. 36A.

"New Lines Cure Ills at Medical Firm," *Crain's New York Business,* January 18, 1993, p. 15.

Solnik, Claude, "Thriving Medical Suppliers in Long Island on Acquisition Spree," *Long Island Business News,* August 8, 2003.

Verespej, Mike, "Medical Action Boosts Capacity with Purchase of Medegen Unit," *Plastics News,* September 18, 2006, p. 8.

Meijer, Inc.

2929 Walker Avenue NW
Grand Rapids, Michigan 49504-9428
U.S.A.
Telephone: (616) 453-6711
Fax: (616) 791-2572
Web site: http://www.meijer.com

Private Company
Incorporated: 1934
Employees: 67,000
Sales: $13.9 billion (2007 est.)
NAICS: 452910 Warehouse Clubs and Supercenters

■ ■ ■

Meijer, Inc., is a fast-growing regional chain of grocery supercenters, headquartered in Grand Rapids, Michigan. Established in 1934 by Hendrik Meijer, the company remains a family business run by the founder's namesake grandson, Hendrik "Hank" Meijer. With revenues approaching $14 billion for its 180-plus stores in Michigan, Ohio, Indiana, Illinois, and Kentucky, Meijer has more than challenged its rivals Wal-Mart, Target, and Kroger by giving its customers no-nonsense low prices. In return, customers in the Midwest have remained increasingly loyal to Meijer and its ever growing product line. What makes Meijer such an overwhelming success is simple: Its stores are open 365 days a year, 24 hours a day and each store has 40 or more departments selling everything from applesauce and flour to pants and coats to lawn furniture and zinc oxide. Customers can also get prescriptions filled,

shoes repaired, and their gas tanks filled, all in one place.

EARLY HISTORY: 1907–37

Hendrik Meijer immigrated from the Netherlands to the United States in 1907, settling in Michigan. In 1914 he opened a barbershop, expanding it to a double storefront by 1923. When the Depression hit, Meijer had trouble finding a tenant to rent the new space in his Greenville, Michigan, location. He decided to open a grocery store, hoping to cover the building rent and operating costs from store profits. With $328.76 of goods bought on credit, Hendrik and his son Fred, stocked the goods and began selling food to their customers in 1934, competing with a grocer across the street and some 20 other competitors in town.

Hendrik and Fred traveled far and wide seeking the best goods for their grocery store at the lowest prices. In keeping with the needs of Americans in the 1930s, Meijer's goal was to help customers save money. To speed shoppers' progress through the store, Fred built a space designed to display 12 handheld baskets. Above the baskets was a handwritten sign inviting customers to take one and help themselves. This "self-service" innovation of 1935 increased the number of customers Meijer could serve, thus aiding the growth of the business. By 1937 Hendrik had doubled the size of his original store.

GROWTH AND EXPANSION: FORTIES TO EARLY SIXTIES

As the grocer across the street from the original Meijer store mowed his neatly kept lawn, Hendrik noticed the

COMPANY PERSPECTIVES

Meijer is a Grand Rapids, Michigan-based retailer that operates 185 supercenters throughout Michigan, Indiana, Illinois, Ohio, and Kentucky. As the inventor of the "one-stop shopping" concept, Meijer stores have evolved through the years to include expanded fresh produce and meat departments, as well as pharmacies, comprehensive electronics departments, garden centers, and apparel offerings. Additional information and the ability to shop online can be found at www.meijer.com.

more trampled path to the front door of his shop, called "Thrift Mart," with pride. In 1942 Meijer opened a second store, and with the help of wife Gezina, daughter Johanna, and Fred, the grocery businesses prospered throughout the rest of the decade. In the 1950s the family built four new stores and opened a supermarket chain in western Michigan. After a fire leveled Meijer's first Greenville store, the company relocated to a new headquarters in Grand Rapids, Michigan.

Meijer had more than ten stores in operation in Grand Rapids, Muskegon, and Holland, Michigan, by the late 1950s. By 1961 there were 14 supermarkets and a legion of loyal customers. To keep its market share and attract new customers, Meijer initiated a rather bold marketing campaign to combat the proliferation of trading or green stamps, closing all of its stores on a Monday to lower hundreds of prices. Heavily advertised in local and regional newspapers, the gambit proved successful with customers viewing stickers comparing Meijer's newly lowered prices and competitors' costs allowing for stamps. While its rivals offered double- and triple-coupon or stamp savers, Meijer increased sales and showed customers it would always be the true "supermarket."

In 1962 the company opened its first Thrifty Acres Discount Department Store, a combination food/retail item store similar to a hypermarket that had opened in Belgium the previous year. Within two years Meijer had three Thrifty Acres built, with two more in the planning stages. These large capacity discounters increased Meijer's lead in the retail segment. The growth of Meijer was overshadowed, however, by the death of founder Hendrik at age 57 in 1964. Fred continued the company's expansion after his father's death, planning to take Meijer's brand of retailing throughout Michigan.

FROM STATE TO STATE: MID-SIXTIES TO 1987

In the late 1960s Meijer ventured outside of Michigan with plans for its first supermarket in Ohio. Its one-stop shopping theme, which the company claimed to have pioneered, gave customers the chance to buy not only food but a variety of retail items including garden and pet supplies, small appliances, jewelry, sporting goods, clothing, and home décor items. Growth remained steady through the 1970s with more than 20 stores, some set up with gasoline pumps as well. Although Meijer planned to build more retail/gas station combination stores, its plans were stalled by a 1978 law prohibiting a business from selling both gasoline and alcohol unless it was in a village, town, or municipality with a population of fewer than 3,000 residents.

By the 1980s Meijer's hypermarket concept had caught on. Nationally, retail giants such as Kmart and Wal-Mart dominated; locally, competitors increased advertising and low-price wars. As more stores increased their square footage and challenged Meijer in the discount retail segment, the company was forced to become more aggressive in its advertising to retain customers. In 1984 the company bought 880 inches of page space in the *Grand Rapids Press;* by December 1985 Meijer had increased space to 2,800 inches.

The company also introduced in-store delis, bakeries, and fresh meat and fish departments in the mid-1980s, promoting the changes under the slogan "Rediscover Meijer's." In February 1987 Meijer marched into the Columbus, Ohio, market, and immediately claimed a 20 percent slice of the market with one store. Flush with this success, Meijer planned to open another unit in Columbus, then others in outlying areas to compete with wholesale club stores popping up in the region.

CHANGING DIRECTION: 1988–89

A major change in Meijer's practices occurred when the company announced it would keep most of its Michigan and Ohio stores open 24 hours beginning in March 1988. A total of 43 of 46 stores were designated round-the-clock units, departing from the previous policy of closing Meijer stores for Thanksgiving, Easter, Christmas Day, and a half-day on Christmas Eve. Disgruntled employees sent a letter to Fred Meijer, requesting he reconsider the change and allow workers to spend holidays with families and friends. Meijer declined to reverse the new policy.

In an effort to sell alcohol in its Michigan stores, Meijer pushed passage of a state bill to change the ten-year-old law prohibiting the sale of alcohol and gasoline

KEY DATES

1934: Hendrik Meijer opens a grocery store adjacent to his barbershop in Greenville, Michigan.

1935: Meijer gives his customers "self-serve" baskets to use in the store.

1942: A second grocery store opens in Michigan.

1962: The company launches a new retail outlet called Thrifty Acres Discount Department Store.

1964: Founder Hendrik Meijer dies suddenly at age 57.

1984: Meijer initiates an aggressive newspaper marketing campaign in Grand Rapids.

1988: Many Meijer stores begin staying open 24 hours per day.

1989: Meijer debuts an electronic checking system in its stores.

1990: Doug and Hank Meijer become co-chairmen of the family business.

1992: Meijer enters the wholesale/warehouse foods market with SourceClub.

1999: Fred Meijer steps down as CEO, but remains on the company's board.

2002: Hank Meijer takes the reins as chief executive, in addition to his duties as co-chairman of the company.

2007: Meijer begins an $18 million renovation of its regional distribution center in Lansing, Michigan.

2008: The company introduces private-label organic foods and groceries by the case.

2009: Meijer's "Simply Give" holiday program raises more than $287,000 for Michigan food pantries.

from the same location. The bill would allow gas pumps on a site where liquor was sold, provided the shopping center had 50,000 square feet of space or an inventory of at least $250,000. Opponents included the Associated Food Dealers of Michigan and the Package Liquor Dealers Association. The latter group believed the bill was discriminatory and served the interests of only the big chains.

Meijer had reason enough to compete at any level possible; by 1988 the company, still unknown outside its Michigan/Ohio retail segment, ranked 42nd in *Fortune* magazine's Top 400 Private Companies. Fred Meijer, son of the founder, had an estimated wealth of more than $400 million. After 50 years in business, company sales were estimated at $2 billion. Meijer proved a serious challenge to any small retailers in its markets and could even go up against mega-retailers Kmart and Wal-Mart.

As the 1980s came to a close, there were 53 regional Meijer stores and the company put $20 million into the construction of its tenth distribution center, its largest to date, near Detroit. Another innovation was an electronic checking system in early 1989. The "Meijer 1 Card" allowed customers to withdraw from their checking accounts automatically, with no paperwork or identification verification necessary. Patrick Gavin, vice-president of pharmacy, service, and retail technology, stated in the *Grand Rapid Press* that Meijer would be "the first in the world to set up a paperless software system through its cash registers." The company and banking institutions could save money, up to a total of $1.75 per check on processing fees.

By mid-1989 sales for the entire Meijer chain were estimated at $65 million per week, bringing the annual sales figure to approximately $3 billion. Store sales were not the only indicator of Meijer's success, however; each new Meijer store cost $18 million to put up and Meijer was opening up to five per year during the 1980s. The company researched expansion possibilities in new markets such as Toledo, Ohio, and both South Bend and Indianapolis, Indiana.

In keeping with its growth, Meijer decided to make a historic advertising shift, moving from Grand Rapids' Johnson & Dean to Southfield, Michigan-based W.B. Doner & Company. Near Detroit, Doner had national marketing expertise, something Meijer looked for in a changing marketplace. Johnson & Dean had had the Meijer account for 33 years, a record time period in advertising, producing 200 radio and 150 television ads per year.

Part of Meijer's new image concerned environmental awareness. Ahead of general sentiment and two months after Wal-Mart advertised a similar stance, Meijer initiated an environmental awareness program in late 1989. In-store posters, grocery bags, and shopping cart signs stated, "We Care About the Earth We Share." Response was positive and Meijer's management looked for other ways to show its support of "green" or Earth-friendly causes.

THE NINETIES AND BEYOND

Early in 1990, as it had done 30 years earlier, Meijer once again led its peers in a major change by abandoning double-coupon promotions. The company drew on founder Hendrik Meijer's steady, practical approach to retailing, concentrating on the simplicity of rock-bottom pricing instead of gimmicks. New Meijer ads touted the simplicity theme with the slogan, "Meijer: The store built on common sense."

Store openings in the early 1990s included ten new Meijers in Michigan and seven for Ohio in the Dayton and Toledo markets. Wal-Mart began competing with Meijer in its Ohio market with the construction of a new distribution center. Industry analysts noted Meijer's traditionally loyal customer base as a hedge against Wal-Mart's aggressive growth. In 1990 Fred's sons, Doug and Hank, were named co-chairmen of Meijer, with their father remaining chief executive.

The company continued growing as a premier discount retailer in the Midwest, maintaining a low profile yet high profit margins. With sales at $3 billion, Meijer led the hypermarket supercenters field. Still, Fred Meijer's vision of an expanding network of supercenters throughout the Midwest was still in its infancy. Another step in the right direction was the opening of a state-of-the-art retail store in South Bend, Indiana, followed by a second store a few years later.

In 1998 Meijer opened its first store in Louisville, Kentucky, with four additional stores planned before the end of the year. The family's riskiest expansion site, however, would be Chicago, where the company planned to open ten new supercenters, beginning in 1999, the same year Fred Meijer stepped down as CEO, after serving in the post for 17 years. His replacement, Jim McLean, a management executive since 1986, took the reins of the company with a sophisticated strategy to take on Wal-Mart and newer rival Target in the Chicagoland area. One newly introduced innovation was an express self-checkout lane for Chicagoans with just a few items, designed to attract frugal shoppers in a hurry.

GROWTH AND CAUTION IN THE 21ST CENTURY

In the early 2000s Meijer looked for ways to differentiate itself as the supercenter playing field became increasingly crowded. While Kmart Corporation's closure of underperforming stores was good news to Meijer, the second phase of Kmart's restructuring was not; many of its remaining units were expanded and remodeled as SuperK stores, mirroring the variety and scope of Meijer's supercenters. Target had also unveiled plans of its own for SuperTarget centers. Meijer answered with a restructuring in 2002, and a change in top management as Hank Meijer was named CEO and his father Fred was appointed chairman emeritus. Hank took his new

duties seriously and hit the ground running, trying a different format for new stores in Michigan, Ohio, and Illinois; adding more international and ethnic foods to Meijer's 162 stores; and implementing a new tracking system to better monitor trucking operations.

By the middle of the first decade of the 2000s Meijer was consistently ranked in the top 20 of *Forbes* magazine's annual Largest Private Companies listing. While there seemed to be little to stop Meijer's continued expansion, even the Michigan-based giant began to slow down as the economy took a turn for the worse. Meijer hit its zenith employee-wise in 2002 with more than 83,000 workers, a number it maintained for a year until belt-tightening and cost-cutting measures whittled the number to 75,000 for 2004 and 2005, then down to 70,000 in 2006, and finally 67,000 in 2007. Revenues, however, maintained their health with a slow climb upward: $11.9 billion for 2004 and 2005, $12.5 billion for 2006, and a solid leap to $13.9 billion in 2007.

Several innovations helped Meijer weather the economic storm, such as free generic antibiotics and prenatal vitamins from its pharmacies, introducing a private-label organic food line, slashing gas prices (ten cents per gallon) for customers with Meijer credit cards, and even offering alternatives to gas such as ethanol and bio-diesel fuel. The company also undertook an $18 million expansion of its Lansing, Michigan, regional distribution center, the overhaul of dozens of older stores, and the opening of new stores in Michigan, Indiana, Kentucky, and Illinois. Since arriving in Chicago only a few years earlier, Meijer had proven its mettle by opening more than a dozen stores in the Windy City and its suburbs, managing to thrive amid the double threat of Wal-Mart and the middle-upper-class favorite, Target.

In 2008 Meijer continued to expand its services by offering consumers large-quantity discounts like Costco and Sam's Club (selling select groceries by the case but without a membership fee), a 5 percent bonus discount off their next shopping trip with a purchase of $100 or more, expanded online shopping services (including Pea Pod–like personal shoppers), launching meal plans complete with coupons, and even introducing its own line of prepaid phones, all available at the company's 185 stores.

As the decade headed to a close and the nation fell deeper into a recession, customers counted on Meijer for its huge selection of groceries, housewares, health and beauty items, clothing, and gas products, but more for the company's longstanding tradition of low-low prices. While other retailers struggled in the volatile economy,

Meijer remained at the top of the regional supercenter chains, gaining ground on rivals Wal-Mart and Target.

Frances E. Norton
Updated, Thomas Derdak; Nelson Rhodes

PRINCIPAL COMPETITORS

Albertsons LLC; Dominick's Finer Foods; The Kroger Co.; Target Corporation; Ultra Stores, Inc.; Wal-Mart Stores, Inc.

FURTHER READING

Cipriano Pepperl, Jo-Ann, "Meijer: Serving Customers an Array of Choices," *Greater Lansing Business Monthly,* February 1, 1992.

Couretas, John, "Most Meijer Stores to Open 24 Hours," *Grand Rapids Press,* February 6, 1988.

DeNitto, Emily, "Meijer Breaks Store-Wide 'Earth Friendly' Program," *Supermarket News,* November 6, 1989.

"Don't Just Drop Stamps—Give Customers Something Better," *Progressive Grocer,* February, 1963.

Duff, Mike, "Meijer Enters Louisville Market," *Discount Store News,* May 11, 1998, pp. 3, 130.

Gallagher, Julie, "How Low Can You Go?" *Supermarket News,* December 15, 2008.

Halverson, Richard C., "Meijer to Enter New Markets," *Discount Store News,* March 9, 1998, pp. 1, 83.

———, "Meijer to Re-Enter Cincy After Hills, Ames Exit," *Discount Store News,* June 17, 1991.

Kaplan, Rachel, "Meijer Ads Heat Up Grand Rapids Market," *Supermarket News,* January 20, 1986.

Kelly, Mary Ellen, "Traditional Columbus Chains Brace for Superstore Assault," *Discount Store News,* February 16, 1987.

"Longtime Super Store Meijer Poised for Growth After Completion of DC," *Discount Store News,* December 19, 1988.

"Meijer Eliminates 350 Positions," *MMR,* September 22, 2003, pp. 2+.

"Meijer Faces Challenge from Wal-Mart Thrust," *Discount Store News,* July 16, 1990.

"Meijer Finds Right Combination for Midwest," *Discount Store News,* July 17, 1989.

"Meijer Leads Field As Hyper/Supercenter Challengers Take Aim," *Discount Store News,* July 22, 1991.

"Meijer Units Sport New Look," *MMR,* May 27, 2002, p. 1.

Miller, Lynne, "Starbucks Brews Deals with Meijer, Giant Eagle," *Supermarket News,* June 30, 2003, p. 33.

Moukheiber, Zina, "Squeezing the Tomatoes," *Forbes,* February 13, 1995, p. 55.

Muller, Joann, "Meijer First Store to Cut Double Coupons," *Detroit Free Press,* February 20, 1990.

Power, Denise, "Meijer's, a Hypermarket Chain, Ramps Up Self Checkout," *Daily News Record,* September 9, 1998, p. 8.

Radigan Lohr, Mary, "Meijer Inc. Switching to Detroit-Area Ad Agency," *Grand Rapids Press,* August 8, 1989.

———, "Meijer Stores to Use Electronic Checking System," *Grand Rapids Press,* March 12, 1989.

Stall, Sam, "Grocery Rivals Continue Store-Upgrade Spree," *Indianapolis Business Journal,* December 22, 2008, pp. 8+.

Strnad, Patricia, "Hypermarket Pioneer Changes Tack," *Advertising Age,* September 25, 1989.

———, "Meijer Hyper in Midwest Markets," *Advertising Age,* February 15, 1988.

———, "Meijer Shapes Ads on Common Sense," *Advertising Age,* April 16, 1990.

"Supercenters Drive Star Performance," *Retail Merchandiser,* July 2002, pp. 24+.

Tarnowski, Joseph, "Mining with Meijer," *Progressive Grocer,* December 1, 2002, pp. 40+.

Yue, Lorene, "Family Member Takes Helm of Retailer Meijer Based in Walker, Mich.," *Detroit Free Press,* February 5, 2002.

Mondragón Corporación Cooperativa

Paseo Jose Maria Arizmendiarrieta No. 5
Mondragón, E-20500
Spain
Telephone: (+34 943) 77 93 00
Fax: (+34 943) 79 66 32
Web site: http://www.mcc.es

Cooperative Company
Incorporated: 1956
Employees: 104,000
Sales: EUR 16.37 billion ($22.12 billion) (2007)
NAICS: 522120 Savings Institutions; 236210 Industrial Building Construction; 333210 Sawmill and Woodworking Machinery Manufacturing; 333512 Machine Tool (Metal Cutting Types) Manufacturing; 333513 Machine Tool (Metal Forming Types) Manufacturing; 333613 Mechanical Power Transmission Equipment Manufacturing; 335314 Relay and Industrial Control Manufacturing; 335999 All Other Miscellaneous Electrical Equipment and Component Manufacturing; 336399 All Other Motor Vehicle Parts Manufacturing; 445110 Supermarkets and Other Grocery (Except Convenience) Stores; 524113 Direct Life Insurance Carriers

∎ ∎ ∎

Mondragón Corporación Cooperativa (MCC) is one of the world's largest cooperative groups, with more than 250 companies—half of which are cooperatives—and more than 100,000 employees in 18 countries. With total sales of nearly EUR 16.5 billion ($22 billion), combined with banking assets of more than EUR 12 billion, MCC is the leading company in Spain's Basque region, and the seventh largest company in all of Spain. MCC groups its operations into four major divisions: Industrial, including consumer goods, industrial components, and capital goods subdivisions; Retail Distribution; Financial; and Knowledge. The Industrial division includes Fagor Electrodomesticos, a leading producer of white goods and other appliances, and its counterpart Fagor Industrial; furniture producers, including Danona, Domusa, and Eredu; Orbea bicycles; Wingroup camping and fitness equipment; automotive components and systems, through Fagor Ederlan Taldea and others; and the Danobat group of machine tool and industrial equipment manufacturers, among many others.

The Distribution division features Spain's largest domestically owned retail group, Eroski, which includes more than 1,600 stores, including 84 hypermarkets, 700 supermarkets, as well as the If chain of perfumeries, more than 200 travel agencies, as well as Cash & Carry stores, and restaurants and cafeterias. Other MCC retail operations include the Forum Sport sportswear and sporting goods stores, and Erkop, specialized in goods and services for the agro-industrial sector. MCC Financial division has long played a central role in the company's success, and includes its own bank, Caja Laboral-Euskadiko Kutxa (the People's Workers Bank), as well as the group's Lagun Aro pension fund and insurance operations. The last division, Knowledge, remains another strategically important part of both the group's expansion and cooperative principles. This divi-

COMPANY PERSPECTIVES

MONDRAGON is the embodiment of the cooperative movement that began in 1956, the year that witnessed the creation of the first industrial cooperative in the town in Gipuzkoa of the same name; its business credo is contained in its Corporate Values: Cooperation. Participation. Social Responsibility. Innovation. MONDRAGON's Mission combines the core goals of a business organisation competing on international markets with the use of democratic methods in its business organisation, the creation of jobs, the human and professional development of its workers and a pledge to development with its social environment. In terms of organisation, MONDRAGON is divided into four areas: Finances, Industry, Retail and Knowledge. Today, MONDRAGON is the foremost Basque business group and the seventh largest in Spain.

sion includes the company's various research and development facilities, as well as its vocational schools and training academies, including its own business and management training operations. MCC also operates its own university, the University of Mondragón, with three campuses and nearly 4,000 students. As noted, only half of MCC's subsidiaries operate as cooperatives. The group's international operations, in particular, many of which are operated as joint ventures with local partners, are structured as limited liability companies. Even in Spain, salaried employees make up a growing percentage of MCC's workforce. In this way, MCC has successfully negotiated the challenges of operating within a global market. Nonetheless, the company has managed to retain its cooperative identity and maintain its commitment to its founding principles. MCC is led by Chairman Juan Maria Otaegui.

REVIVING THE BASQUE ECONOMY IN POST–CIVIL WAR SPAIN

The Basque region's experience with the cooperative movement reaches back to the 19th century; into the period prior to the Spanish civil war, one of the region's larger employers was a firearms manufacturer, Alfa. Yet the Basque people's largely anti-fascist stance led to the devastation of much of the region's economy, and to

a general lack of investment from the Franco regime after the war.

The development of the future Mondragón Corporación Cooperativa (MCC) had its roots in the arrival of a newly ordained priest, Don José Maria Arizmendiarreta (often shortened to Arizmendi), in Mondragón in 1941. Then 26 years old, Arizmendi was confronted with the region's wholly inadequate educational system, and massive unemployment. Very quickly Arizmendi extended his duties from the religious sphere into the social area. Arizmendi's activism later earned him the nickname as "the Red Priest."

Recognizing the need to develop stronger educational opportunities for the community, Arizmendi founded his own school, Eskola Politeknikoa, in 1943. That school provided vocational training, but also became an important stepping-stone to university for many of its students.

Arizmendi recognized the importance of creating not only educational opportunities, but employment opportunities as well. Arizmendi also began developing his own corporate model, based on a set of principles borrowed from the cooperative movement. A main feature of Arizmendi's model was its intention of building an egalitarian, democratically organized structure.

Arizmendi's chance came when five students, whom he had helped enroll into university, returned to Mondragón with their engineering degrees. Led by Arizmendi, the five bought a nearby stove-making business, and transferred its operations to Mondragón in 1956. Taking letters from the last names, they named the company Talleres Ulgor. The company then took on a legal status as a cooperative, which provided the closest legal form for accommodating Arizmendi's corporate principles. The company's initial production focused on paraffin-based stoves and heaters.

The Franco regime's isolationist industrial policies provided Ulgor, which later became the internationally successful Fagor group, with its first opportunities. The company quickly recognized that Spain represented something of a captive market, since all goods sold were required to be produced in Spain. The company understood that by producing high-quality goods, it could easily gain a strong share of the national market. As a result, Ulgor grew rapidly through the end of the decade. The company at first produced appliances under licenses from foreign brands. Before long, however, Ulgor developed its own product development operations, eliminating the need to pay licensing fees.

Ulgor's growth quickly provided a motor for the development of the region's industrial infrastructure. From the start, Ulgor encouraged the creation of a

KEY DATES

1943: Don José Maria Arizmendiarreta founds a vocational school in Mondragón, in the Basque region of Spain.

1956: Under Arizmendi's leadership, five former students acquire a stove-making workshop and establish the first Mondragón cooperative, Ulgor.

1959: The Mondragón cooperative movement forms its own bank, Caja Laboral, and its own pension fund, Lagun Aro.

1966: Several Mondragón cooperatives, including Ulgor, join together to found Ularco (later Fagor).

1969: The Mondragón movement expands into distribution, creating the Eroski retail group.

1985: Ularco changes its name to Fagor, which becomes the main brand for its household appliances and tools as well.

1988: The Mondragón movement adopts new Basic Principles and reorganizes as Mondragón Corporación Cooperativa (MCC).

1997: Fagor Industrial launches production commercial refrigeration systems with new factory in Lucena.

2005: Fagor Industrial launches international manufacturing expansion, with new factories in Turkey, Mexico, Poland, and elsewhere.

2007: MCC's sales near EUR 16.5 billion.

number of new cooperatives, founded in order to produce parts and materials for Ulgor's production.

DEVELOPING A COOPERATIVE GROUP IN THE SIXTIES

These cooperatives too operated along the principles established by Arizmendi. Among these was a policy of establishing capital accounts for its members, instead of providing them with shares in their respective companies. Approximately 10 percent of business profits were placed into these accounts, available to members only if they left the cooperative. Instead, workers received dividends from the interest generated by the capital accounts. In this way, the bulk of a company's profits were used for the company's expansion.

The rising assets in the capital accounts inspired Arizmendi to suggest that the growing cooperative movement create its own bank. This led to the establishment of the Caja Laboral Popular (or, People's Worker Bank), in 1959. Based on the credit union model, the Caja Laboral developed savings account services both for cooperative members and the general public. The Caja Laboral then became the cornerstone for the Mondragón cooperative movement's rapid growth through the 1960s, providing a financial foundation that would have otherwise been unavailable to the cooperatives themselves.

Caja Laboral quickly became the central coordinating body for the cooperative movement, a position it would hold through the 1980s. The cooperative movement by then had extended its financial operations into other areas as well. In the late 1950s, the Franco government, in a move to slow the growth of the cooperative movement, decided that since cooperative members were technically "owners," they were not eligible for the social security and welfare benefits generally provided to workers. Confronted with this crisis, the Mondragón movement decided to establish its own pension fund, Lagun Aro, in 1959. From this experience, the movement also added its own insurance arm, Lagun Aro Vida, as well.

By the 1960s, many of the future MCC group's operations had been established. These included Fagor Industrial, created in 1960 as a division of the Ulgor's appliance operations; Fagor Arrasate, created in 1957 to produce presses, sheet-metal cutting and processing equipment, tool and die systems, and other machinery needed for the group's production arms; Onapres, focused on production presses, in 1961; Soraluce, producing radial drilling machines, in 1962; and Rochman, created in 1958, as a packaging company. The cooperative movement branched out into furniture as well, adding Danona in 1962, metal furniture specialist Eredu in 1963, and office furniture company Coinma, in 1964, among others.

While the cooperative movement itself created most of its growing list of companies, it also absorbed a number of existing Basque-region companies. Such was the case of Orbea, a bicycle manufacturer located in that village, which had originally been founded as a family company, before converting to a cooperative in 1960, then joining the Mondragón group in 1964.

From the start, the various cooperative companies had operated as separate business units. Into the mid-1960s, however, Caja Laboral, by then functioning as the central coordinating body, encouraged companies to begin grouping together, in order to pool their administrative, logistics, and other functions. One of the first of these groupings was Ularco, created in 1966 through the combination of five cooperatives, including

Ulgor, Arrasate, the metal foundry Ederlan, gas stove and heater company Copreci, and Fagor Electronica. Ularco, which later evolved into the larger Fagor group of companies, grew steadily following the merger, and by the mid-1970s had grown to more than 3,500 employee-members.

FORMING A CENTRAL BODY IN 1988

The Mondragón movement's commitment to quality not only enabled the group to establish major positions in the Spanish market, it also provided a strong foundation for the development of the group's international expansion. Exports became the driver of this growth, and by 1970 accounted for 11 percent of the group's total revenues, a remarkable total considering the hostility that lingered between the Franco regime and the other European markets until the 1970s. In the meantime, the Mondragón cooperatives' total revenues had achieved impressive growth. In 1960, the group's total sales had reached ESP 150 million. By 1970, that total had topped ESP 7 billion.

The movement's educational efforts remained an important component of its growth. By the early 1960s, the movement's original vocational school had evolved into a full-fledged university. By 1962, the group had also founded its own polytechnical school. Other educational initiatives included a university-level teacher training college and a business management school. At the same time, the group also developed its own network of research and development centers, fueling its own product innovation. These educational and research operations later formed the group's Knowledge division.

The Mondragón movement entered new territory at the end of the 1960s, when it launched its own retail distribution wing, Eroski, in 1969. That group soon became one of the powerhouses of the cooperative movement. By the end of the century, Eroski had become the single largest Spanish-owned retail company in Spain, with a network of more than 1,600 stores.

The movement's evolution toward a modern centralized structure had its roots in the 1970s. By the middle of that decade, the cooperative movement counted more than 40 companies within its network. A number of companies had begun to follow the merger model pioneered by Ularco; other cooperatives joined together into regional groupings. However, the long economic crisis in Spain—begun with the Arab oil embargo in the early 1970s, exacerbated by the transition to a democratic, free-market model following the death of Francisco Franco, and continuing until well into the 1980s—tested the strength of many of the movement's cooperatives.

At the same time, the Mondragón group was forced to recognize that Spain's joining the European Union spelled the end of an era of relatively strong market protection. By the early 1980s, the cooperative movement understood that it needed to adapt its own structure and principles to meet the coming onslaught of globalization. In order to brace itself for the arrival of the giant multinational groups into the Spanish market, the Mondragón group redeveloped a number of its businesses, especially its Ularco flagship. That company established a new brand name, Fagor; by 1985, the Fagor brand had been rolled out as the main brand for all of the cooperative's household appliance lines. The creation of the single brand played an important role in the group's success in expanding its sales, and later production, onto a truly international scale.

By the end of the 1980s, the Mondragón movement decided to transform its entire organizational model. Following a series of congresses, the movement formulated a new set of overriding Basic Principles for the entire cooperative group, replacing the former set of individual charters. A new central coordinating body was then established, called Mondragón Corporación Cooperativa (MCC), which adapted a more pyramid-based management structure. One of the first steps of the new MCC was to draft a dramatic reorganization of the group's businesses, replacing the regional model with one based on business sectors. Toward this end, the group drafted a new divisional structure, grouping its operations into its Financial, Industrial, Distribution, and Knowledge divisions.

For some, the creation of MCC represented an end to the business model established by Arizmendi. A number of cooperatives broke away from MCC, forming the Grupo Ulma cooperative. Yet the decision to establish MCC became the single most important factor behind the cooperative movement's success, and indeed survival, into the next century.

GLOBAL OPERATIONS IN THE 21ST CENTURY

MCC's sales topped the equivalent of EUR 1.2 billion in 1987. Just five years later, the company's sales had climbed to nearly EUR 2.5 billion, and would more than double again before the end of the decade. Much of this growth came as a result of the revitalization of the Spanish economy, following its entry into the European Union. This in turn opened a whole new range of expansion opportunities for MCC, as it began establishing a series of international sales subsidiaries through the decade.

The company's own operations grew as well. In 1989, for example, the group added Wingroup, a producer of fitness and camping equipment, both through its own brand names and for the original equipment manufacturer and private-label channels. Wingroup later became one of the drivers for MCC's decision to develop manufacturing operations in lower wage markets, as the group established manufacturing joint ventures in such markets as China, Thailand, Mexico, India, and Turkey. The company's retail operations grew as well, adding a sportswear and sporting goods format, Forum Sport, in 1991. In that year, also, Grupo Eroski opened its first hypermarket, later building a chain of 84 hypermarkets throughout Spain. Into the next century, the group's range of retail businesses grew to include the If perfumery chain, as well as restaurants and cafeterias, and a network of 200 travel agencies. Eroski also expanded its retail operations to include holdings in southern France.

In-house development also provided a source of growth. By the 1990s, MCC had become a prominent partner to the European automotive industry, providing a variety of parts, components, and systems, through subsidiaries such as Matrici. In 1996, that company began developing its own specialized welding and assembly operations, which were then spun off as Matrici Sistemas e Ingenieria in 2000.

Fagor Industrial also grew strongly. In 1997, that unit launched production of commercial refrigeration equipment at a new factory in Lucena, in the Cordoba region of Spain. The success of that product line soon led the group to boost its global reach. For this, the company turned to developing international partnerships, setting up three new factories in Turkey, Poland, and Mexico between 2005 and 2006. By 2008, Fagor Industrial's manufacturing network included ten factories, including five in Spain, as well as plants in France and Italy.

Noteworthy was that, while the majority of the group's Spanish subsidiaries remained based on the cooperative model, the company's international operations took on a decidedly more capitalistic face. This was in part because in many of the group's new operating markets, the cooperative model either did not exist or was not sufficiently developed to support the group's operations. Even MCC's Spanish operations had come to include a growing number of non-cooperative businesses, usually joint ventures formed with foreign partners. Within the MCC cooperatives themselves, the percentage of non-member employees, originally limited to no more than 10 percent of the workforce, had also been rising steadily, with some companies receiving authorization to employ non-members up to 40 percent of their payroll.

While these changes exposed the group to criticism that it had turned its back on at least some of its original principles, MCC had nonetheless displayed the flexibility that permitted it not only to survive, but to thrive into the highly competitive, heavily globalized economy. MCC's growth remained strong, building its total sales to nearly EUR 8.5 billion by 2002. Just five years later, MCC's total turnover had nearly doubled, reaching EUR 16.4 billion ($22 billion) at the end of 2007. With more than 100,000 employees, more than 250 companies, and operations spread over 18 countries, Mondragón had grown into one of the world's largest and most dynamic cooperative enterprises.

M. L. Cohen

PRINCIPAL SUBSIDIARIES

Alecop; Alkargo S.Coop; Ampo; Aurrenak; Batz; Becker; Berriola S. Coop; Caja Laboral; Caja Laboral Gestión; Danobat Group S.Coop; Danona S.Coop; Domusa S.Coop; Grupo Eroski; Fagor Electrodomésticos; Fagor France S.A.; Fagor Industrial S.Coop; Fagor Mastercook S.A.; Geyser Gastech S.A.; Ihardun Multimedia; Lagun Aro; Lagun Aro Vida; Seguros Lagun Aro; Shanghai Minidomésticos Cookware (China); Wingroup S.Coop.

FURTHER READING

Burns, Tom, "Basque Co-op Changes Its Culture," *Financial Times,* June 17, 1994, p. 26.

Gomez Damborenea, Pedro, "Basque Co-operative Group MCC Aims to Wrest Market Share While Sticking to Its Social Guns," *Europe Intelligence Wire,* September 26, 2004.

———, "Mondragon to Open 12 New Plants in China," *Europe Intelligence Wire,* July 7, 2004.

Huet, Tim, "Can Coops Go Global?" *Dollars & Sense,* November–December 1997, p. 16.

"MCC Looks for Various Ventures in India," *Financial Express,* November 10, 2006.

"MCC to Decrease Investments by 25% in 2002," *Expansion,* June 18, 2002.

"Mondragon Asked into Car-Parts Production," *America's Intelligence Wire,* June 8, 2006.

"63 Cooperatives Join Ategi Internet Retailer," *Expansion,* August 13, 2002.

White, David, "Mondragon Helps Itself to Success," *Financial Times,* June 10, 1997, p. 29.

Whyte, William F., "The Mondragon Cooperatives in 1976 and 1998," *Industrial and Labor Relations Review,* April 1999, p. 478.

Morgan's Foods, Inc.

———————— ■ ————————

4829 Galaxy Parkway, Suite S
Cleveland, Ohio 44128-5955
U.S.A.
Telephone: (216) 359-9000
Fax: (216) 359-2110
Web site: http://www.morgansfoods.com

Public Company
Incorporated: 1925 as Stark Provision Company
Employees: 2,147
Sales: $96.3 million (2008)
Stock Exchanges: Over the Counter (OTC)
Ticker Symbol: MRFD
NAICS: 722211 Limited Service Eating Places

■ ■ ■

Morgan's Foods, Inc., is a Cleveland, Ohio-based company that at the end of 2008 operated 94 franchised restaurants in Pennsylvania, Ohio, New York, West Virginia, Illinois, and Missouri. Operations include 70 Kentucky Fried Chicken (KFC) units, six Taco Bell restaurants, 13 units co-branded with KFC and Taco Bell; three restaurants that combine the Taco Bell and Pizza Hut brands; one KFC and Pizza Hut combination, and one KFC and A&W Restaurant combination. Once listed on the American Stock Exchange, Morgan's Foods' stock is traded on an over-the-counter basis. Nevertheless, it remains one of the largest publicly held KFC franchisees. Chairman and Chief Executive Officer Leonard R. Stein-Sapir and his family own more than one-quarter of the company.

FOUNDER, POSTWAR ENTREPRENEURIAL WUNDERKIND

The man who began Morgan's Foods' was William A. Morgan Jr., born in Butler, Pennsylvania, in 1929. Like many entrepreneurs of his generation, Morgan learned the rudiments of business by delivering papers as a child. Enrolled at Grove City College in the late 1940s and majoring in business administration, he would pay the bills by working at a funeral home and soon recognized a business opportunity. Taking notice of returning servicemen, whose discharge papers had been provided to them in laminated, protective sleeves, Morgan began laminating obituaries for funeral directors to offer to the family of the deceased. According to his own obituary published in the *Butler Eagle,* "He was soon making more money than the college professors and made enough to buy two new cars, put himself through college and buy his first restaurant in 1953, Dight's Diner, on Washington Street, at the age of 21."

Morgan added to his restaurant interests by opening the Wonder Boy Drive In. Then, in 1955, he became the fifth KFC franchise holder when he added carryout service to his diner. Morgan opened more restaurants in western Pennsylvania and eastern Ohio, each of which combined a coffee shop, dining room, and KFC carryout. By 1970 Morgan owned a chain of 52 such operations, and he also delved into the automatic car wash business. Morgan decided to retire in 1970, the same year he was commissioned a Kentucky Colonel, and sold his restaurants to Canton, Ohio-based Sugardale Foods. Two years later, however, Morgan grew weary of retirement and bought a former shirt factory,

KEY DATES

1925: Stark Provision Company is incorporated.
1926: Stark is renamed Sugardale Provision Co.
1953: William A. Morgan Jr. acquires first restaurant.
1955: Morgan becomes Kentucky Fried Chicken franchisee.
1970: Morgan sells restaurant chain to Sugardale.
1976: Morgan's Restaurants Inc. is formed.
1986: Name is changed to Morgan's Food's, Inc.
1997: Franchise licenses are renewed.
2004: Restructuring program is initiated.

converting it into a professional office complex. He pursued other real estate development projects as well as charitable work until his death at the age of 78 in November 2008.

Sugardale Foods traces its heritage to 1920 when a meatpacking operation was established in Canton. Five years later the company was incorporated as Stark Provision Company, and in 1926 adopted the name Sugardale Provision Co. It was not until 1967 that the business became known as Sugardale Foods. In 1976 restaurant operations broke away from Sugardale as Morgan's Restaurants Inc.

FARINA ACQUIRES COMPANY: 1977

In 1977 businessman James V. Farina acquired Morgan's Restaurants, which at the time included 22 KFC units and eight full-service restaurants. As an independent enterprise, Morgan's Restaurants did not fare well as it attempted to diversify beyond its profitable KFC business. For seven straight years the company lost money, due mostly to its involvement in the Royal Castle hamburger chain, similar to New York City's White Castle chain but one that struggled and eventually folded. To make matters worse, the company lost its food processing plant due to fire. In 1981 several new backers brought an infusion of $1.5 million in cash and gained majority control. More managerial missteps followed, however. In another attempt to diversify, Morgan's Restaurants entered the coin-operated electronic videogames business, leading to another name change in 1982, when Morgan's Restaurants became MorTronics, Inc. Most of the video game business was conducted in Colorado and Southern California. The company did not do well in this venture, either, and was

forced to exit it in 1985. With the company's focus entirely on the restaurant sector, MorTronics changed its name to Morgan's Foods, Inc., in 1986. Along the way, Farina fell out with the new owners and was ousted as chairman in 1983.

Even while the company was pursuing the videogame business it continued to acquire KFC restaurants, which totaled 45 in Pennsylvania, Ohio, New Jersey, and West Virginia by the end of 1986. While KFC had always been profitable, Morgan's Foods was never satisfied with concentrating on these assets. In October 1987 the company acquired 11 franchised Sizzler Restaurants located in the Chicago area. Morgan's Foods held high hopes for the inexpensive, buffet-style steak house concept, hoping to open more units in the Chicago market. One unit was opened but, less than two years later, another new management team was installed and quickly moved to sell the Sizzler restaurants.

STEIN-SAPIR TAKES CHARGE: 1989

Taking over as chairman and chief executive officer was Leonard Stein-Sapir. He had been one of the 1981 investors, and in 1989 he and another director invested $2 million to acquire a further stake in Morgan's Foods. A native of Cleveland, Stein-Sapir earned an undergraduate degree in economics from the Wharton School of the University of Pennsylvania as well as law degrees from Case Western Reserve University and Georgetown University. Prior to joining Morgan's Foods he had served as chairman of Record Data Inc., a title agency and appraisal company, which he sold to TRW Inc. in 1985.

After selling the 12 Sizzler restaurants to Midwest Restaurant Concepts Inc., Stein-Sapir was able to refinance his bank loans in the fall of 1990. Although his plan at the time was to focus on core KFC assets, his options on growth were limited. There was no opening for more KFC restaurants in the company's markets, nor could he obtain new licenses. In order to create shareholder value, as a result, he took the company back into the table-service category in the summer of 1992 with the acquisition of Toronto, Canada-based Prime Restaurant Group Inc., which operated six restaurants and franchised 67 under its four concepts. They included the flagship operation, East Side Mario's, an Italian restaurant with a New York Little Italy feel, offering wood-fired pizzas, pastas, as well as burgers, steaks, ribs, and seafood. Other Prime concepts were Casey's, a roadhouse eatery offering grilled food and sandwiches;

Lime Rickey's, a 1950s-era diner; and Pat and Mario's, a more upscale eatery focusing on northern Italian cuisine.

East Side Mario's was the key format for Morgan's Foods, which planned to open 25 of the Italian restaurants in Ohio by the end of 1997. To help support this plan, the company in July 1995 sold 24 KFC restaurants in central Pennsylvania and New Jersey to Kazi Foods of Los Angeles in order to pay down debt. Two years later, however, Morgan's Foods would be shifting directions again. The East Side Mario's venture was limited to six units and not performing especially well. The parent company of the concept, Dallas-based East Side Mario's Corp., had not offered much marketing support, and even though it was sold to Wilshire Group Inc. in February 1997, it was not certain that significant enough changes were going to be made to improve sales performance. Eventually Morgan's Foods filed a $20 million lawsuit against East Side Mario's, alleging deceptive trade practices and failure to support franchisees.

RENEWAL OF KFC FRANCHISE AGREEMENTS: 1997

While Morgan's Foods was severing its relationship with East Side Mario's, Stein-Sapir again returned his attention to the always profitable KFC business. In 1997 Morgan's Foods remodeled most of the restaurants, and also renewed all of its franchise agreements for 20 years. In addition, the company began to pursue co-branding opportunities, combining KFC operations with other concepts, such as Taco Bell. The first "2n1" operation with a KFC and Taco Bell sharing the same roof opened in Youngstown, Ohio, in May 1997. Helping to finance the opening of these "2n1" restaurants was fresh funding from Captec Financial Group Inc. of Ann Arbor, Michigan. The co-branded units proved popular with customers, resulting in significant sales increases. It was also more economical for Morgan's Foods to shoehorn a Taco Bell into an existing KFC restaurant than to open a freestanding Taco Bell, which cost as much as $700,000 compared to about $75,000 to install a Taco Bell inside a KFC. Thus, the company found a relatively easy way to boost sales at many of its KFC units.

In the late 1990s Morgan's Foods looked to expand its KFC and Taco Bell holdings as well as Pizza Hut, because all three of those concepts, owned by Tricon Global Restaurants Inc., were being refranchised and company-owned units were being made available for sale to outside companies. In fiscal 1999 Morgan's Foods acquired four KFC restaurants in the Erie, Pennsylvania, market, and two units each in Jamestown, New York, and St. Louis, Missouri. In addition, the company built

a new KFC restaurant in Boardman, Ohio. In fiscal 1999, which ended at the close of February 1999, Morgan's Foods posted revenues of $40.6 million and a loss of $1 million, the third consecutive year the company was in the red.

In May 1999 Morgan's Foods significantly expanded its holdings by signing a $33.7 million deal with KFC and Taco Bell to acquire 55 restaurants, including 26 KFCs in the Pittsburgh, Pennsylvania, market; eight KFCs in Wheeling, West Virginia; nine KFCs in St. Louis, Missouri; and 12 Pittsburgh Taco Bells. Moreover, 11 of the KFC restaurants also offered a Taco Bell menu. Later in 1999 Morgan's Foods sold four of its five remaining East Side Mario's restaurants to the parent company of Steak and Ale. When the fiscal year came to a close in February 2000, the company increased revenues to $63.6 million and narrowed its net loss to $346,000.

LAST EAST SIDE MARIO'S: 2001

In fiscal 2001 the last East Side Mario's unit was sold and five KFC restaurants were also closed. Although revenues improved to $78.1 million for the year, Morgan's Foods continued to lose money, recording a net loss of more than $1.54 million. During the year the company hired an investment banking adviser to help evaluate options to improve shareholder value, but in the end no action was taken and Morgan's Foods returned to profitability in fiscal 2002, when the company netted $600,000 on sales of $85 million.

Revenues dipped to $83.3 million in 2003 and $81.7 million in 2004, and once again Morgan's Foods recorded net losses of $1.1 million and $1.3 million, respectively. In fiscal 2005 the company voluntarily delisted from the American Stock Exchange, unable to meet exchange requirements. Instead, shares in the company were traded on an over-the-counter basis. Later in 2004 Morgan's Foods initiated a restructuring program, which included the closure of unprofitable restaurants, the elimination of some positions, management reassignment, and pay cuts in the managerial ranks. The company began to turn around, aided in large measure by better product promotions provided by the franchisers. As a result, Morgan's Foods netted $3.44 million on revenues of $87.5 million in fiscal 2006. A year later, revenues improved to $91.25 million and net income increased to $3.53 million. Net income fell to $414,000 in fiscal 2008 despite an increase in sales to $96.3 million. The performance was strong enough, however, to persuade GE Capital Solutions, Franchise Finance to provide $12.6 million to refinance existing loans for Morgan's Foods in May 2008, setting the stage for improved profitability and greater growth.

Ed Dinger

PRINCIPAL SUBSIDIARIES

Morgan's Restaurants of Ohio, Inc.; Morgan's Restaurants of Pennsylvania, Inc.; Morgan's Restaurants of West Virginia, Inc.; Morgan's Foods of Missouri, Inc.; Morgan's Restaurants of New York, Inc.; Morgan's Tacos of Pennsylvania, Inc.

PRINCIPAL COMPETITORS

Carrols Restaurant Group, Inc.; Chick-fil-A, Inc.; Valenti Management Inc.

FURTHER READING

Byard, Katie, "Morgan's Foods Says Chicken Is Its Game," *Akron Beacon Journal,* September 11, 1989, p. B1.

————, "Restaurant Business Lures Farina Back," *Akron Beacon Journal,* July 6, 1985, p. B6.

————, "Sizzler Owner Losses Set at $5.25 Million," *Akron Beacon Journal,* April 20, 1989, p. E1.

Canedy, Dana, "Aimed at Family Dining Morgan's Foods Pins Hopes on New Restaurant Chain," *Cleveland Plain Dealer,* November 6, 1993, p. 1E.

Carlino, Bill, "Morgan's Foods Corrals Prime Restaurant Group," *Nation's Restaurant News,* July 6, 1992, p. 3.

Datzman, Cynthia, "Morgan's President Keeps Eye on Present," *Crain's Cleveland Business,* November 2, 1987, p. 2.

Gleisser, Marcus, "Morgan's Foods Inc. to Buy Canadian Group," *Cleveland Plain Dealer,* June 24, 1992, p. 2F.

Hardin, Angela Y., "Hungry for Turnaround," *Crain's Cleveland Business,* June 16, 1997, p. 34.

"William A. Morgan Jr.," *Butler (Pa.) Eagle,* December 2, 2008.

National Jewish Health

1400 Jackson Street
Denver, Colorado 80206-2761
U.S.A.
Telephone: (303) 388-4461
Toll Free: (800) 222-5864
Web site: http://www.nationaljewish.org

Nonprofit Company
Founded: 1899
Employees: 1,600
Operating Revenues: $149.6 million (2008)
NAICS: 622310 Specialty (Except Psychiatric and Substance Abuse) Hospitals

■ ■ ■

National Jewish Health is considered the best medical center for the care of respiratory ailments in the United States, and it is on the leading edge of research in asthma, allergies, immunology, and chronic pulmonary diseases. With only a 46-bed hospital, National Jewish Health operates primarily as an outpatient care facility; agreements, however, with other Denver-area hospitals supplement inpatient care when necessary. Through the Disease-Specific Care Management service, National Jewish provides patients with tools for controlling health conditions from home, thus reducing the need for in-hospital visits. National Jewish provides advanced diagnostic techniques, including state-of-the-art imaging technology, tissue comparisons, and genetic information, to address general and individual factors that contribute to ill health. Wellness programs include the Tobacco Quitline, a smoking cessation coaching service, and Fit-Logix, a weight-loss support program. Activities at National Jewish are supported by patient services, charitable donations, and research grants. Doctors and scientists at National Jewish have made important discoveries in AIDS, lupus, asthma, and numerous respiratory and immunological disorders.

PIONEER IN CARE FOR TUBERCULOSIS PATIENTS

National Jewish Health was the first of several facilities in Denver to serve indigent people with tuberculosis (TB). During the late 1800s and early 1900s, hundreds of people traveled to Colorado in the belief that the dry, sunny climate would relieve symptoms of the respiratory disease, then known as consumption. Unfortunately, most people afflicted with TB came from overcrowded city slums, so they arrived in Denver without resources for living, let alone medical care. Frances Wisebart Jacobs offered food and medical care to the consumptives living on the streets of Denver. Nevertheless, with many people dying on the streets, she found her efforts to be inadequate. Known for her benevolence as the "Mother of Charities," Jacobs and Rabbi William Friedman, gathered funds from Denver's Jewish community to establish a hospital for consumptives unable to pay for medical treatment. In November 1889 a plan emerged to build a hospital that would care for poor people with respiratory diseases, regardless of their religious background.

Although construction on the building was completed in 1893, the hospital did not open until

COMPANY PERSPECTIVES

Our mission since 1899 is to heal, to discover and to educate as a preeminent health care institution. We serve by providing the best integrated and innovative care for patients and their families, by understanding and finding cures for the diseases we research; and by educating and training the next generation of health care professionals to be leaders in medicine and science.

1899 because of an economic recession. Jacobs had died in 1892, so Rabbi Friedman persuaded Louis Anfenger, founder of the Denver chapter of the International Order of B'nai B'rith, to become involved in the project. In turn, Anfenger persuaded the national B'nai B'rith organization to assume responsibility for the hospital. With funding from Jewish supporters nationwide, the aptly named National Jewish Hospital for Consumptives opened in November 1899. In December National Jewish admitted its first ten patients. The institution operated under the motto, "None may enter who can pay—none can pay who enter."

Initially, National Jewish treated only patients exhibiting an early onset of symptoms, because they were most likely to respond well to treatment. With facilities for 150 patients, hospital stays were limited to six months. Healthcare at National Jewish emphasized nutrition, bed rest, and fresh air, and patients frequently slept on balconies, combining bed rest with the fresh air. Because malnutrition associated with poverty was considered a contributing factor in contracting TB, National Jewish provided patients with abundant nutritious foods, including meat, eggs, and milk produced at a nearby farm that had been donated to the hospital in 1912. Eventually, National Jewish extended the stay allowed at the hospital, and patients spent three to five years in recovery. As patients healed, the hospital prepared them for a return to normal life, including vocational education that would support an economically sufficient living.

EDUCATION AND RESEARCH CONTRIBUTE TO TB TREATMENT AND PREVENTION

As TB continued to ravage urban populations, National Jewish became involved in research to find a cure. In 1919 the hospital hired Harry J. Corper, M.D., to oversee a new research department. Dr. Corper succeeded in establishing the importance of immunology in understanding TB when he developed a new method of culturing TB, on an Irish potato rather than in guinea pigs. By separating tubercle bacillus from a host mammal, Corper learned that the bacteria could sustain itself up to 30 years outside a human body, enduring hot and cold extremes of weather.

In order to prevent the spread of TB among impoverished children likely to contract the disease, National Jewish opened the Hofheimer Preventorium in 1920. The preventorium provided opportunities for adequate fresh air, exercise, and nutrition to keep healthy children well. Children stayed at the preventorium for three to four years. Over the next 22 years the operation provided care to 730 children. In 1932 National Jewish established a school for children who were chronically ill and unable to keep pace with regular classroom instruction. The accredited school, later named the Kunsberg School, provided full educational instruction for kindergarten through eighth-grade children.

Providing education to future generations of TB healthcare providers became a new priority at National Jewish. Beginning in 1925 the Colorado Medical School employed the newly renamed National Jewish Hospital at Denver as its resident-doctor training hospital for TB and chest medicine. During the 1940s National Jewish initiated a partnership with the University of Colorado to provide in-hospital instruction for basic and advanced nursing courses specific to care for TB patients. After World War II, the United Nations World Health Organization employed National Jewish as an international training site for TB control.

At this time National Jewish updated its methods of TB treatment. In 1946 the release of streptomycin made chemotherapy available as a treatment for TB. A new holistic approach to TB involved psychiatric care for long-term patients. Under Research Director Gardner Middlebrook, research and hospital care became oriented to new drug therapies. Middlebrook showed how isoniazid adapted to individual physiology, and he developed methods for using the drug based on different requirements and dosages for each patient. The emphasis on drug therapies changed the dynamic of patient care, as extensive bed rest became unnecessary, and the focus shifted to exercise.

RANGE OF CARE EXPANDS

As treatments improved and widespread use of penicillin reduced the incidence of TB, National Jewish shifted its healthcare concern to other diseases. In 1946 National

KEY DATES

1893: Construction on 60-room, 100-bed tuberculosis hospital is complete.

1899: National Jewish Hospital for Consumptives opens with support of national Jewish organization B'nai B'rith.

1919: Hospital establishes a research center.

1925: Resident-doctor training begins in conjunction with Colorado Medical School.

1932: National Jewish establishes a school for chronically ill children.

1969: Pay-for-service begins, but National Jewish continues to serve those who cannot pay.

1978: National Asthma Center merges with National Jewish.

1980s: National Jewish establishes expertise in immunology.

1990s: Financial losses and changes in managed care plans spark shift to outpatient care.

1996: Disease-Specific Care Management is launched.

1998: *U.S. News & World Report* ranks National Jewish the top respiratory hospital nationwide.

2002: National Jewish initiates Tobacco Quitline and other preventive health programs follow.

2007: Ten-year strategic growth plan focused on diagnostic and preventive medicine is launched.

Jewish opened the Cardiopulmonary Physiology Laboratory. Within a few years, the center hired the necessary staff to perform heart surgery, until then available only in the eastern United States. National Jewish was among the first hospitals to receive research grants from health insurance companies and the federal government to obtain equipment and hire staff capable of performing heart catheterizations during the 1950s. National Jewish contributed several innovations to the science of open-heart surgery. In the area of respiratory care, National Jewish created the first large inpatient hospital for adult asthmatics in the country. By 1960 about one-half of the patients at National Jewish were TB patients, about one-third were asthma patients, and the balance were heart patients.

The hospital treated many respiratory diseases, including emphysema, bronchitis, and cystic fibrosis, as well as lung infections, such as sarcoidosis, silicosis, and bronchiectasis. National Jewish expanded its commitment to respiratory illness with a $1.25 million investment in a basic research laboratory focused on chest medicine. The five-story facility was thought to be the largest, most up-to-date research center of its kind in the world. Innovations at the center included a technique for diagnosing asthma appropriate to the clinical setting. To reflect increased activity in research, National Jewish Hospital at Denver became National Jewish Hospital and Research Center.

FOCUS ON IMMUNOLOGY

As National Jewish increasingly emphasized treatment of lung diseases, including asthma in children, the hospital closed its cardiology clinic in 1968 and began to develop a staff focused on clinical immunology. By 1970 the basic science department comprised nine independent scientists dedicated to the study of human and animal biology. The department offered postdoctoral training and National Jewish offered clinical research positions to medical students and research fellows. Areas of research included chest medicine, chest surgery, children's chest diseases, and asthma and allergy clinics.

National Jewish's progress during the 1970s featured research into new treatments for asthma. Physicians addressed problems associated with physical resistance to treatment and with developing effective treatments specifically for individual issues. For instance, theophylline in combination with other drugs was the focus of several clinical studies. Research conducted at this time provided the basis for asthma treatments that would evolve later.

In 1978 National Jewish expanded its pediatric asthma care facilities by merging with the National Asthma Center, which had been founded in 1904 as the Jewish Consumptives Relief Society. Later, as the Children's Asthma Research Institute and Hospital, the institution was responsible for the discovery of Immunoglobulin E, known as the allergy antibody, which further established immunity problems as a physical basis for asthma. The merger of the two organizations created the largest inpatient treatment facility for pediatric and adult asthma patients worldwide. National Jewish became one of the world's leading medical centers involved in the study and treatment of chronic respiratory, allergic, and immune system disorders.

During the 1980s National Jewish scientists and doctors made two important discoveries that changed the way researchers viewed the immune system as it detects foreign organisms and defends the body from infection. The first discovery involved identifying and isolating one of two genetic codes that produce the human T-cell receptors, molecules responsible for generating an immune response in the form of antibodies. The other discovery was of superantigens, bacterial or viral toxins that stimulate T-cell activity to the point of harming the body, such as attacking the body's own cells. This new knowledge about T cells facilitated research in HIV. Such discoveries placed National Jewish among the worldwide leaders in immunology research. Hence, in 1985 the institution changed its name to National Jewish Center for Immunology and Respiratory Medicine.

FINANCIAL PROBLEMS PROMPT TRANSITION FROM INPATIENT TO OUTPATIENT CARE

The movement to reduce healthcare costs through managed care and self care prompted National Jewish to reevaluate its methods of patient care. Although National Jewish initiated a pay-for-service policy in 1969, the hospital provided care based on ability to pay and continued to provide care to those who could not pay. During the late 1980s and early 1990s, however, the hospital faced rising costs that outpaced revenue increases.

The cost of healthcare at National Jewish related to the long hospital stays for patients with respiratory illness, an average of 21 days compared to six days at other hospitals. Hence, outpatient care became the means to reduce costs during the 1990s. Under new President Lynn Taussig, National Jewish launched a day treatment program for children in 1995 and adult day treatment in 1996. Not only did outpatient care allow clients to spend the evenings in the more relaxed surroundings of their home or a local hotel, the program enabled National Jewish to maximize the hospital's ability to care for people with respiratory diseases.

In 1996 National Jewish implemented the Disease-Specific Care Management service for asthma patients and patients with chronic obstructive pulmonary disease. Supported by managed care plans, the service covered nearly three million members in five states by 1998. The service generated $3 million in revenues in its second year. Moreover, emergency room visits were reduced from 366 to 106 visits annually, and 202 days of inpatient hospital care were reduced to 47 days annually. By 2001 the program covered more than 7,500 patients in 40 states.

PREVENTION AND WELLNESS BECOME FOCUS OF EXPANSION IN EARLY 2000S

Although National Jewish experienced great success in attracting research grants, with more than 100 research doctors bringing in more than $25 million annually, and gained recognition as one of the leading hospitals for research and care for patients with pulmonary and immunological diseases, the institution became pigeonholed as a hospital for specialized care. Indeed, in 1998 *U.S. News & World Report* named National Jewish the top hospital in the nation for respiratory disease. Hence, the hospital did not attract patients in need of general care.

To counter the public's narrow perception, National Jewish initiated a marketing program. The first step involved a name change, from National Jewish Center for Immunology and Respiratory Medicine to National Jewish Research and Medical Center in 1998. An advertising campaign sprang from market research that revealed consumers to be more interested in images of wellness than sickness. Hence, print ads carried images of healthy activity, such as a man and a boy walking hand-in-hand; the tagline stated, "We are the warm sun holding your hand."

Fundraising efforts supported expansion of research and healthcare programs at National Jewish at this time. Alberto Vilar, who had been a patient at National Jewish, donated $25 million for a 113,000-square-foot biomedical research facility. A special fundraising campaign garnered $20 million for the addition of a 90,000-square-foot six-story tower. The hospital's research space increased 30 percent, allowing National Jewish to attract new research grants, which increased from $34 million in 2000 to $42.5 million in 2005. Clinic space was expanded by 100 percent, supporting an increase in clinic visits by 62 percent, from 15,664 visits in 2000 to 25,312 in 2005. New patient revenues reached $40 million in fiscal 2005.

ADOPTION OF TEN-YEAR STRATEGIC PLAN

Dr. Michael Salem became chief executive officer of National Jewish in 2005. Under Salem, National Jewish adopted a ten-year strategic plan in 2007 to create multiple streams of revenue, beyond the unpredictability of research grants and charitable donations. The core of the strategic plan involved the application of state-of-the-art biomedical technology to develop "personalized medicine," in which genetics and patient information were combined to customize a targeted, accurate diagnosis and treatment program.

Components of the "Science Transforming Life" approach to medicine included the Institute for Advanced Biomedical Imaging, which opened in 2008. The institute upgraded National Jewish's imaging capabilities with the latest PET (positron emission tomography),

CT (computed tomography), and MRI (magnetic resonance imaging) technology. The Integrated Bioinformation and Specimen Center held a repository of blood and tissue samples, frozen at minus 80 degrees centigrade, which researchers could use to learn about the genetic patterns of illness. Under David Schwartz, M.D., one of the leading experts on the genetics of pulmonary diseases, the Center for Genetic and Therapeutics planned to develop tests for evaluating genetic indicators of physical tendencies. A related program included the Molecular Diagnostics Laboratory, which opened in early 2008, led by Praveen Ramamoorthy, Ph.D. Part of National Jewish's Advanced Diagnostic Laboratories, the center focused on determining the appropriate medication for individual patients based on genetics.

National Jewish continued to perform research for a variety of respiratory ailments. One study concerned the impact that certain kinds of bacteria have on chronic asthma patients and whether the use of antibiotics is effective in curing the bacterial infection. National Jewish was chosen by Nutra Pharma to test a rapid diagnostic test kit for TB. In conjunction with 23 organizations nationwide, National Jewish received part of a $27 million grant from the National Heart, Lung and Blood Institute. The funds were to be applied to a comprehensive study of chronic obstructive pulmonary disease, in which National Jewish and Brigham and Women's Hospital of Boston, Massachusetts, would be the two coordinating centers.

Expansion at National Jewish involved the development of new products and services as well as of satellite offices throughout the Denver metropolitan area. Preventive health programs included the Tobacco Quitline, started in 2002. By the end of 2007 the program had expanded to five states and employed 80 coaches. At nearby Rose Medical Center, National Jewish provided pulmonary consulting services and staff at the hospital's intensive care unit. Satellite offices opened in Littleton, Highlands Ranch, and Englewood, Colorado, where National Jewish provided care for pediatric allergy/immunology, pulmonology, rheumatology, and/or sleep disorders. In January 2008 National Jewish launched FitLogix, a weight-loss support program that provided 15 coaching sessions over the course of a year. In the area of self care, National Jewish introduced the Family Air Care Indoor Allergens and Mold Test Kit. The product allowed people with asthma and allergies to test their homes' environments for irritants that could exacerbate their illness.

In July 2008 National Jewish changed its name to resonate with the focus on preventive healthcare and personalized medicine. The new name, National Jewish Health, represented a move beyond the typical view of a hospital (treating illness rather than wellness), as well as beyond its areas of specialization. National Jewish reestablished a cardiology unit and planned to establish services for lung cancer and related medical specialties. The overall goals of National Jewish's strategic plan involved increasing research grants by $60 million and increasing staff with 100 physicians and research scientists. National Jewish sought to double the number of annual patient visits to 70,000 by 2012.

Mary Tradii

PRINCIPAL DIVISIONS

Division of Allergy and Clinical Immunology (Adult); Division of Cardiology (Adult); Division of Environmental and Occupational Health Sciences; Division of Mycobacterial and Respiratory Infections; Division of Pediatric Allergy and Clinical Immunology; Division of Pediatric Behavioral Health; Division of Pediatric Clinical Pharmacology; Division of Pediatric Pulmonary Medicine; Division of Psychosocial Medicine (Adult); Division of Pulmonary and Critical Care Medicine (Adult).

PRINCIPAL COMPETITORS

Cleveland Clinic; Johns Hopkins Hospital; Massachusetts General Hospital; Mayo Clinic; University of California–San Diego Medical Center.

FURTHER READING

Algeo, David, "National Jewish Cuts Staff, Costs: Effort Aims to Restore Financial Health," *Denver Post,* July 29, 1997, p. C01.

Anfenger, Milton Louis, *The Birth of a Hospital: The Story of the Birth of National Jewish Hospital in Denver, Colorado,* Denver: National Jewish Hospital, 1942.

Boyle, Salynn, "Internet TB Site Could Revolutionize Consulting Practices," *Tuberculosis & Airborne Disease Weekly,* December 28, 1998.

Braly, Damon, "National Jewish Center Launching Disease-Management Message," *Health Management Technology,* September 1995, p. 20.

Brand, Rachel, "National Jewish Grows Upward, Hospital Is Halfway Through Building a Six-Story Tower," *Rocky Mountain News,* May 11, 2006, p. 5B.

Bunn, Dina, "National Jewish Hospital Campaign Promotes Wellness," *Rocky Mountain News,* September 27, 1998, p. 4G.

Conklin, Michele, "Creative Medicine; National Jewish Broadens Patient Care, Revenues with National Market," *Rocky Mountain News,* October 18, 1998, p. 3G.

Davis, Joyzelle, "Hospital Takes Deeper Breadth: National Jewish Invests in Customized Diagnosis," *Rocky Mountain News,* January 19, 2008, p. 1.

———, "National Jewish Changes Its Name: Switch Signals Hospital's Focus on Prevention," *Rocky Mountain News,* July 11, 2008, Business sec., p. 3.

Fitzharris, Mary, and Jeanne Abrams, *A Place to Heal: The History of National Jewish Center for Immunology and Respiratory Medicine,* Denver: National Jewish Center for Immunology and Respiratory Medicine, 1989.

Fletcher, Amy, "National Jewish's New Deal," *Denver Business Journal,* June 1, 2001, p. 10A.

Fong, Tillie, "National Jewish to Hunt for Bacteria-Asthma Link," *Rocky Mountain News,* June 9, 2006, p. 21A.

Hicks, Wayne, "National Jewish Trims Staff, Emphasizes Outpatient Care," *Denver Business Journal,* January 4, 1991, p. 4.

Jones, Rebecca, "A Century of Care: People Touched by TB Plan Reunion to Celebrate National Jewish Hospital's Centennial," *Rocky Mountain News,* July 15, 1999, p. 4D.

"National Jewish Health Launches Family Air Care Indoor Allergens and Mold Test Kit," *Immunology Weekly,* October 22, 2008, p. 263.

"NIH Awards Funds to Develop Tuberculosis Treatments," *AIDS Weekly Plus,* November 4, 1996.

"100 Years of National Jewish," *Rocky Mountain News,* December 10, 1999, p. 83A.

Perrault, Michael, "$24 Million Gift Largest in Hospital's 92 Years: National Jewish Plans to Build 5-Story Addition," *Rocky Mountain News,* July 13, 2001, p. 1B.

Toll, William, "Pisco, Seraphine Eppstein," *Encyclopedia Judaica,* edited by Michael Berenbaum and Fred Skolnik, Vol. 16, 2nd ed., Detroit: Macmillan Reference USA, 2007, pp. 185–86.

Wood, Ron, "Jewish Hospital in National Spotlight," *Cincinnati Post,* April 27, 2005, p. A12.

Nordex AG

Bornbarch 2
Norderstedt, D-22848
Germany
Telephone: (+49 40) 300 30 1000
Fax: (+49 40) 300 30 1101
Web site: http://www.nordex-online.com

Public Company
Incorporated: 1985
Employees: 2,000
Sales: EUR 747.0 million ($1.1 billion) (2007)
Stock Exchanges: Frankfurt
Ticker Symbol: NDX1
NAICS: 333611 Turbine and Turbine Generator Set Unit Manufacturing

■ ■ ■

Nordex AG is one of the world's leading developers and manufacturers of wind turbines. Based in Rostock, Germany, Nordex focuses on the market for large-scale turbines. The company's range includes 1.5 megawatt and 2.3 megawatts turbines, as well as the world's largest serial production turbine, capable of generating 2.5 megawatts. Altogether, Nordex boasts a global installed base of more than 3,600 wind turbines, with a total generating capacity of more than 4.6 gigawatts. However, Nordex has been forced to play catch-up, as competitors such as REpower Systems AG have moved into the advanced prototype testing phases of a newer five-megawatt turbine design.

Nordex's operations span the design and engineering of turbines, as well as the manufacturing of nacelles (the enclosures that house such items as the generating components and gearbox) and rotor blades, and turnkey wind farm development services. The company operates manufacturing facilities in Germany, China, and, since 2008, in the United States. Nordex operates sales subsidiaries in France, Greece, Poland, Sweden, the United Kingdom, and elsewhere. Nordex itself is a holding company for two primary divisions, Nordex Energy BV, which oversees most of the company's European and North American operations, and Nordex Energy GmbH, which includes the group's manufacturing operations in China. Nordex is listed on the Frankfurt stock exchange and is led by CEO Thomas Richterich and Chairman Yves Schmitt. Founder Carsten Pedersen is the company's sales director. In 2007 Nordex's revenues neared EUR 750 million ($1.1 billion).

FROM BLACKSMITH TO TURBINE PRODUCER IN 1985

The founding of Nordex stemmed from Denmark's role as a wind power industry pioneer in the late 1970s and early 1980s. With limited natural energy resources of its own, Denmark had been hard hit by the Arab oil embargo and resulting surge in global oil prices during the 1970s. The need to ensure the country's energy supply led to the search for alternative energy sources. Although nuclear energy represented one potential direction, the country's population proved hostile to this technology. As a result, the Danish government launched an effort encouraging the development of renewable energy sources.

COMPANY PERSPECTIVES

As developers and manufacturers of wind turbines, we concentrate on our core competencies. In addition to the overall technical design, our know-how also lies in the development of rotor blades with a length of up to 45 metres and in the integrated electrical and control technology for wind turbines.

Wind power quickly emerged as the major direction for this effort. The government helped stimulate the growth of a domestic wind power industry, providing a number of incentives, including funding a substantial percentage of wind turbine installations. Private ownership of wind farms was also actively encouraged. Although a number of individuals, especially farmers, installed their own wind farms, the privately owned wind farms and turbines were generally acquired through the creation of ownership cooperatives. In this way, some 80 percent of the country's total installed generating capacity was owned by the private sector through the 1990s.

The expertise gained in developing wind turbines also placed Denmark at the forefront of the global industry. The country's wind turbine producers quickly switched from an older two-blade rotor model to a more powerful three-blade model. This technological advantage placed the Danish manufacturers in a strong position to respond to the sudden surge in interest in wind farming that took place in California at the beginning of the 1980s. The Danish companies were able to rapidly sell their products to the California market, setting the groundwork for the country's continued dominance of the sector. Into the next century, five of the world's top ten wind turbine producers were Danish.

The wind turbine industry also generated work for a large number of component and parts suppliers. One of these suppliers was Flemming Pedersen, who operated a metalworking shop in the town of Give. Into the early 1980s, Pedersen began supplying towers and other fittings to the country's turbine manufacturers.

Pedersen was joined by his son, Carsten Pedersen, born in 1963. The younger Pedersen studied at the Herning Technical School, then completed a machine fitter's apprenticeship at his father's shop, before going on to complete a three-year business school program. Returning to Give, Carsten joined his father's business.

By the mid-1980s, the Pedersens' work on building structures for other companies' wind turbines had spurred them to try building their own turbine. This led to the completion of a 65-kilowatt turbine. Inspired, Carsten Pedersen, joined by his younger brother Jens, decided to launch their own wind turbine company. This led to the founding of Nordex in 1985, and the hiring of the company's first engineer. Carsten Pedersen became the company's managing partner.

MOVING TO GERMANY IN THE NINETIES

From the start, Nordex decided to focus on building bigger and more efficient turbines. The company worked on improving the output of its turbines. Just two years after its founding, Nordex succeeded in establishing a new milestone for generating capacity in the industry, when it launched serial production of a 250-kilowatt turbine.

The Danish market, however, remained limited in size. The large number of strong players in that country also forced the industry to seek growth on the international market. Neighboring Germany, the largest single economy in Europe, provided an obvious expansion target for Nordex and other Danish wind turbine producers. Germany's attractiveness became all the more powerful following the institution of new regulations encouraging the development of the country's wind power capacity in 1990.

Nordex's move into Germany came in 1991, when the company established a sales subsidiary there, Nordex Energieanlagen GmbH. Nordex quickly added a production component in Germany as well, launching construction of its first factory there in Rerik in 1992. At the same time, Nordex continued to develop its technology and by 1995 had debuted a new one-megawatt turbine. In this, the company claimed to have been first to break the one-megawatt barrier.

During the 1990s Nordex shifted more of its operations to Germany, in part to take advantage of fiscal incentives provided for the wind power industry by the German government. Germany's wind power industry also boasted an increasingly strong design and engineering component. As a result, Nordex transferred much of its own turbine development program to Germany during the decade.

Rising competition also caused the company to seek stronger financial backing. This led the company to Germany's Balcke-Dürr, a leading player in nuclear and other power technologies. Balcke-Dürr acquired a 51 percent stake in Nordex in 1996, then increased its shareholding to 75 percent by 1998. The company then took on a new name, Nordex Balcke-Dürr. Throughout

KEY DATES

1985: Carsten and Jens Pedersen found Nordex in Denmark to produce wind turbines.

1987: Nordex becomes the first in the world to produce a 250-kilowatt turbine.

1991: Nordex launches sales subsidiary in Germany, which opens a production facility the following year.

1996: Balcke-Dürr of Germany acquires 51 percent of Nordex (raised to 75 percent in 1998).

2001: Nordex AG goes public on the Frankfurt stock exchange.

2006: Company opens first of two new production facilities in China.

2008: Nordex announces plans to build a $100 million factory in Arkansas.

this period, Carsten Pedersen remained the company's managing partner.

With its powerful parent, Nordex Balcke-Dürr registered a major increase in production. Part of this came through the acquisition of a license for a new generation of wind turbines, developed by Germany's pro + pro Energiesysteme, with a capacity of 1.5 megawatts. In 1997 Nordex Balcke-Dürr became one of a number of companies, including Jacobs Energie (the future REpower Systems) to acquire the license to produce turbines incorporating pro + pro's design.

PUBLIC LISTING IN 2001

The success of the 1.5 megawatt design enabled Nordex Balcke-Dürr to record a new milestone in 1999. In that year, the company installed its 1,000th turbine. Nordex Balcke-Dürr's success with the pro + pro design also led the company into a cooperative effort with both that company and Jacobs Energie to work toward the development of a five-megawatt turbine. The achievement of that goal was expected to mark a turning point for the wind power industry, making wind power energy cost-effective for the first time. The five-megawatt turbine was also considered an important step for the deployment of offshore wind farms, considered by many to be the future of the wind power industry. Nordex Balcke-Dürr's success with the 1.5-megawatt turbine, however, had placed Jacobs Energie under pressure, leading to that company's merger with pro + pro and a related company, BWU-Brandenburgische Wind- und Umwelttechnologien, forming REpower Systems.

This merger became part of a larger consolidation of the German, and ultimately international, wind power market at the dawn of the 21st century. Nordex itself took part in this trend, adding the operations of Südwind Energy, also in Germany. This company added its own turbine production, while also extending Nordex's capabilities in turnkey construction of wind parks, as well as their maintenance and service. In 2000 Babcock-Borsig, which had long been struggling financially (and ultimately collapsed in bankruptcy in 2002), restructured its operations, regrouping all of its wind power businesses into a single company, called Nordex AG.

Although no longer part of REpower's five-megawatt turbine project, Nordex controlled the technology of its own next step. By the end of 2000 Nordex had become the first in the industry to launch series production of a 2.5-megawatt turbine. Nordex was taken public in 2001, with a listing on the Frankfurt stock exchange. This move marked the first time a wind turbine manufacturer had completed an initial public offering (IPO) in Germany. The Pedersen family remained involved with the company. Carsten Pedersen took the role of sales director, while Flemming Pedersen sat on the board of directors, and Jens Pedersen joined his older brother in Nordvest, an investment vehicle controlled by the Pedersen family, which in turn held nearly 10 percent of Nordex.

Following its IPO, Nordex opened a new factory in Germany for the production of rotor blades. In this way, the company expected to bring the production of some 30 percent of its rotor blades needs in-house. Nordex invested in other technologies as well, backing the creation of natcon7, a company focused on developing automation and information systems for the wind power industry.

NEW MARKETS IN THE 21ST CENTURY

Nordex emerged as one of the world's top-ten wind power groups in the new century. In support of this achievement, the company opened a series of sales subsidiaries throughout Europe and elsewhere, including Australia, New Zealand, and China. Into 2001 the company established sales offices in the United States and United Kingdom as well. Nonetheless, into the new decade, Germany and Denmark still accounted for some 60 percent of the group's total sales. Germany alone accounted for nearly half of the group's revenues, which neared EUR 273 million ($220 million) in 2001.

Nordex set out to adjust this balance into the new decade, setting into motion a plan to boost the share of international orders to more than 60 percent by the middle of the decade. Toward this end, Nordex targeted an expansion into the Chinese market, where it established its own production facilities, both for turbine and rotor blade production, by 2003. As such, Nordex became the first of the Western turbine producers to begin manufacturing directly for the Chinese market.

France became another important market for Nordex during the decade, as the French government set into motion an ambitious program to expand the country's wind power generation capacity. Nordex's 2.5-megawatt turbine provided the company with a strong edge in penetrating that market. Ireland too became an important market for Nordex, starting with an order to supply ten turbines for the Kings Mountain wind farm near Sligo in 2002.

By 2003 the company had sold its 2,000th turbine. In that year, too, Nordex dipped its toe into the important offshore wind farm sector, installing its first offshore turbine. However, that year proved a difficult one for the company, as its order book slumped by some 70 percent. At the same time, weaknesses in the company's operating model—including the launch of serial production in 2002, which resulted in high inventory rates, as well as mistakes made in estimating the cost of a number of its projects—had led the group into losses. The company's financial difficulties in turn caused it to lose a number of major orders.

In response, Nordex replaced its top management, including CEO Dietmar Kestner, with Thomas Richterich taking over that role. Nordex developed a new order-driven production model, while also carrying out a streamlining program to achieve greater operating efficiency. By 2004 the company's new orders had once again begun to build, and by 2006 Nordex had once again achieved profitability.

FULLY INTEGRATED OPERATOR TOWARD 2010

By then, Nordex had launched a new generation of turbines, the N90, which boasted 2.5 megawatts of generating power, while the longer, 90-meter rotor blades enabled the turbine to operate effectively in low-wind settings. Nordex had also begun to distinguish itself from many of its competitors by instituting a fully integrated operating model. As such, the company became one of only a few in its sector to be able to offer a full range of integrated services, including project development, marketing and financing, and especially wind farm system planning services.

At the same time, Nordex continued expanding its production capacity in order to meet the surge in global demand. The group invested in expanding its Rostock, Germany, production capacity. Nordex also boosted its presence in the Chinese market, building new factories for rotor blade production and for the company's multi-megawatt turbine designs. The latter factory launched production in 2006, while the rotor blade facility began production the following year.

Nordex's revenues rose accordingly, nearing EUR 750 million ($1.1 billion) by the end of 2007. The company turned its sights toward boosting sales to the U.S. market, announcing its decision to establish a new U.S. headquarters in Chicago. In October 2008, despite the gloomy economic climate as the global economy entered a deep recession, the company unveiled plans to begin construction of a new $100 million production facility in Jonesboro, Arkansas, with production expected to begin by 2010. As one of the leaders in the global wind power industry, Nordex appeared to have the wind in its sails.

M. L. Cohen

PRINCIPAL SUBSIDIARIES

Nordex (Baoding) Wind Power Co. Ltd. (China); Nordex (Dongying) Wind Power Equipment Manufacturing Co. Ltd. (China); Nordex (Yinchuan) Wind Power Equipment Manufacturing Co. Ltd. (China; 50%); Nordex Energy BV (Netherlands); Nordex Energy GmbH (Germany); Nordex Energy Iberica SA (Spain); Nordex France SAS; Nordex Hellas Monoprosopl EPE (Greece); Nordex Italia s.r.l (Italy); Nordex Polska Sp. z.o.o. (Poland); Nordex Sverige AB (Sweden); Nordex UK Ltd.; Nordex USA Inc.; Xi'an Nordex Wind Turbine Co. Ltd. (China; 40%).

PRINCIPAL DIVISIONS

Nordex Energy BV; Nordex Energy GmbH.

PRINCIPAL COMPETITORS

Babcock Borsig AG; GE Energy; REpower Systems AG; Siemens Solarparc AG; Vestas Wind Systems A/S.

FURTHER READING

"Nordex to Cease Wind Machine Production in Denmark," *Advanced Materials & Composites News,* March 3, 2003.

"Plummeting Nemax 50 Puts Heat on Eu450m Nordex IPO," *Euroweek,* March 23, 2001, p. 19.

Truini, Joe, "Nordex to Manufacture Wind Turbines in Ark.," *Waste News,* November 24, 2008, p. 5.

"United States: Nordex to Open Wind Turbine Plant in Arkansas," *TendersInfo,* October 25, 2008.

Northern Trust Corporation

50 South LaSalle Street
Chicago, Illinois 60603-1006
U.S.A.
Telephone: (312) 630-6000
Fax: (312) 630-1512
Web site: http://www.northerntrust.com

Public Company
Incorporated: 1889 as The Northern Trust Company
Employees: 10,918
Total Assets: $79.24 billion (2008)
Stock Exchanges: NASDAQ
Ticker Symbol: NTRS
NAICS: 522110 Commercial Banking; 523920 Portfolio Management; 523930 Investment Advice; 523991 Trust, Fiduciary, and Custody Activities; 551111 Offices of Bank Holding Companies

■ ■ ■

Serving corporations, institutions, and affluent individuals, Northern Trust Corporation is a leading provider of investment management, asset and fund administration, fiduciary, and banking services in the United States. On the corporate and institutional side, Northern Trust serves mainly large and midsized corporations and financial institutions from its principal branches in Chicago, London, Singapore, and Toronto, with additional offices in New Jersey, Ireland, the Channel Islands, the Netherlands, China, and Australia. Considered one of the largest providers of personal trust services to wealthy Americans, the bank serves individuals via a network of 85 offices in 18 states with overseas locations in London and Guernsey. Over nearly a century and a quarter, Northern has provided steady and safe investment services, in the process earning the nickname "Gray Lady of LaSalle Street," so named for the solid-granite headquarters on Chicago's LaSalle Street established in 1906. From its earliest days, Northern Trust cemented its sterling reputation through its association with such Chicago luminaries as department store pioneer Marshall Field and the meatpacking Armour family.

BYRON SMITH FOUNDS COMPANY IN 1889

The Northern Trust Company was founded by Byron Laflin Smith. Formerly associated with Hide and Leather Bank and then Merchants Savings, Loan and Trust Company, Smith left the banking industry in 1885 to devote more time to family business matters. Over the next four years, however, he was frequently called upon by relatives and friends for advice about planning estates and setting up trusts. As the demand from wealthy Chicagoans for his services increased, he decided in 1889 to open a new type of bank.

Because of the previously chaotic nature of banking throughout the United States, Chicago was ripe for a different kind of financial institution. During the 19th century the banking industry was unregulated; it lacked any centralized control over bank charters; and individual banks issued hundreds of different paper notes, which flooded the local area and were of questionable value. In 1887 the Illinois state legislature,

COMPANY PERSPECTIVES

■

Throughout our history, Northern Trust has led the financial services industry by aligning our efforts with our guiding principles. Today, these shared principles continue to unite Northern Trust's partners around the globe.

Service: Northern Trust has a relentless drive to provide exceptional service—not just for our clients, but for our partners and communities. We set new standards. Skillfully execute. Deliver more. It's what we're known for. Regardless of what we're providing—technology, solutions or our time—we are passionately and personally committed to delivering above and beyond.

Expertise: In everything we do, expertise has always been at Northern Trust's core. We know what we do well, and focus sharply on those things. We expand our knowledge and capabilities with an eye on the future. We hire and support talented professionals to help deliver creative solutions. Our expertise is why we've been a trusted advisor for five generations, and will continue to be for generations to come.

Integrity: Northern Trust has a heritage of acting with the highest ethics. The utmost honesty. And unfailing reliability. We have the wisdom earned through generations of relationships. The stability to weather change and uncertainty. And the insight to understand that diversity makes us stronger. For nearly 120 years, our integrity has remained intact. And we have no intention of that changing.

sensing the potential danger, enacted banking laws that regulated state bank charters and the administration of trusts.

This was the predicament that led Smith to open The Northern Trust Company on August 12, 1889. In one room on the second floor of the Rookery Building, which still stands on the corner of Adams and LaSalle streets, a staff of six opened seven accounts and handled $137,981 of deposits during the first day's business. By the beginning of the new year, the bank had taken in over $1.5 million in deposits.

Smith provided 40 percent of the bank's original capitalization of $1 million, and counted such businessmen and civic leaders as Marshall Field, Martin A. Ryer-

son, and Philip D. Armour among the original 27 shareholders. Intimately acquainted with the operations of the bank, these men would personally examine Northern's assets and records at each year's end. On December 31st, they would assemble in the banking room, count all the bank's cash and securities, and greet the new year.

Northern became the first bank in Chicago to advertise its services, first by direct mail and then by ads in the daily newspapers and Chicago City Directory. Smith reasoned that spending significant amounts of cash on newspaper advertising and becoming the first bank in the city to hire an advertising agency would help build confidence in Northern's conservative approach to banking.

During the 1893 Columbian Exposition, held in Chicago to commemorate the 400th anniversary of the arrival of Columbus in the new world, Congress had authorized another Chicago bank to open a branch on the fairgrounds. The exposition had been open for only eight days when the bank failed, and Northern was asked to operate the branch. The exposure bolstered Northern's reputation and increased its international recognition. Despite the panic in the financial industry because of bank closures and industrial insolvencies across the United States in 1893, which, in turn, led to a general economic decline for several years, Northern's fortunes continued to improve. By 1895 deposits totaled $10.5 million.

EARLY 20TH-CENTURY GROWTH

Declaring its first dividend in July 1896, Northern began to grow rapidly. In 1906 the bank constructed its own building in the center of Chicago's financial district at 50 South LaSalle Street. The architecture of the bank building received so much attention that its cornerstone was used to measure the height of all buildings in Chicago. Much fanfare also surrounded the fact that the banking offices were the first in Chicago equipped with "manufactured air," an ancestor of modern air conditioning, and that its telephone system was at the forefront of technology for the era.

The business climate began to change dramatically in the early years of the 20th century, and Northern was forced to reassess some of its longstanding policies. Since its founding, the bank had made only collateral loans, but aware that this policy stymied growth, the board of directors approved Northern's purchase of commercial paper in 1912. After the Federal Reserve System was created a year later, reducing the chance of the money panics that plagued the banking industry during the 19th century, Northern joined the system and began to

KEY DATES

1889: Byron Laflin Smith founds The Northern Trust Company to provide banking services to affluent individuals and organizations in Chicago.
1906: Bank moves into a new headquarters building in Chicago at 50 South LaSalle Street.
1969: Northern opens an office in London.
1971: Bank expands into Florida and sets up Northern Trust Corporation as a holding company.
2005: Northern Trust completes the largest acquisition in its history, the $494 million purchase of the London-based Financial Services Group of Baring Asset Management.

provide unsecured lines of credit to its most reputable customers. Within a brief period, commercial banking become one of the most important sectors of Northern's business.

A new era was on the horizon when Byron Smith died in March 1914 and his son, Solomon A. Smith, took over the reins of the bank. World War I started in August 1914, and stock and bond prices dropped markedly, even though the dollar gained in value against European currencies. When the United States finally entered the war in 1917, Northern acted as a depository for the Alien Property Custodian Act and held over $500 million in enemy assets. During and immediately after the war, Northern sold nearly $30 million in war bonds for the Liberty Bond and Victory Bond campaigns.

Immediately after the war, the U.S. economy muddled through a short period of inflation and slow growth. By 1922 the Roaring Twenties was in full swing, a time when public confidence in the economy was at its highest, and throughout the nation investors were enticed into highly speculative markets. On October 23, 1929, however, the flamboyant decade of the 1920s came to a sudden halt; the stock market crash led to a spectacular drop in prices, employment, and production. Banks were hit particularly hard. What had previously been regarded as sound loans could not be collected, and panicking depositors withdrew their funds from banks. As these troubles swept across the country, one bank after another closed.

THRIVING ON SOLID REPUTATION DURING GREAT DEPRESSION

By mid-1932 the economy had reached its lowest point ever, and public confidence, especially in the banks, had all but faded away. Two days after his inauguration on March 6, 1933, Franklin D. Roosevelt closed all the banks in the United States. When they reopened a short time later, there was a great deal of uncertainty as to what might occur. Fortunately, the people in line outside Northern's bank offices were there to deposit money instead of withdraw it. In fact, so much money was deposited during the first day that cash had to be stacked in huge piles on the floor.

Northern's conservative policies had served it well during the 1920s. Because it had refused to involve itself in highly dubious stock or bond speculations and had passed up the opportunity for rapid earnings growth, Northern was able to pay its depositors their money whenever they wanted it. It was therefore no fluke that public confidence in Northern ran high; more than 10,000 new accounts were opened at the bank in the early 1930s. In 1929 deposits amounted to $56 million; by 1935, deposits had soared to over $300 million. In 1929 there were 335 banks within Cook County; in 1935 there were only 95 left. Northern Trust was one of the few banks in Chicago that survived the Great Depression without the need for any government assistance.

Near the end of the Great Depression, Northern started to expand its effort to solicit commercial business, particularly in the Midwest. By 1941 nearly half of all the bank's commercial accounts were drawn from outside the Chicago metropolitan area. During World War II, Northern once again took part in the government's war bond drives, and also provided loans for manufacturing war materials under special government programs. The war created more opportunities for the bank; all sectors of its business expanded, and by 1945 Northern Trust had doubled in size.

EXPANDING SERVICES IN POST–WORLD WAR II ERA

The years after World War II brought even greater prosperity to the bank as it continued to expand its services. Still under the direction of Solomon Smith, management at the bank became more aware of electronic data processing and how this new technology would revolutionize the banking industry. During the 1950s, Northern was at the forefront of developing numerous automated banking services, including fully automated financial statements for trust clients, the very first in the industry.

When Solomon Smith died in 1963 and his son, Edward Byron Smith, assumed leadership of the bank, assets totaled more than $1 billion. Near the end of the decade, Northern became the first state-chartered bank from Illinois to open an office outside the United States. Illinois banking laws were revised in order to allow state-chartered banks to open offices abroad, yet strangely prohibited opening branches within the state. Northern's new London office, which opened in 1969, helped expand the bank's services to European customers. The Northern Trust International Banking Corporation, a New York subsidiary created to handle currency transactions for financial institutions abroad, was also established the same year.

The 1970s ushered in dramatic changes not only for Northern Trust but also for the banking industry as a whole. Deregulation had two far-reaching effects: First, financial institutions were allowed to pay their depositors interest rates that were competitive with other market rates. Consequently banks began to lose depositors to money-market funds offering higher interest rates. Second, many corporations discovered that the commercial paper market was a cost-efficient method of borrowing short-term funds, and thus banks lost their most stable and most profitable earnings asset. As a result of these changes, Northern, like many other banks, was forced to search for new markets.

During the late 1960s, the creation of the Eurodollar market provided U.S. banks with the opportunity to grant foreign loans at a much lower risk than what was ordinarily expected. In 1973 the availability of dollars skyrocketed when the Organization of Petroleum Exporting Countries (OPEC) oil cartel inflated its prices for a barrel of crude oil, and many nations that depended on OPEC oil watched helplessly as their dollar reserves were depleted. The United Nations and many world governments, in order to prevent less developed countries from becoming even poorer, encouraged banks to recycle what came to be known as "petrodollars," by granting loans to these countries. As speculation rose in financial circles as to the prospects of crude oil increasing to $100 a barrel, the more needy nations demanded more bank credit.

When oil prices dropped suddenly in the early 1980s, many South American nations realized they could not pay off their enormous bank loans. Northern suffered uncharacteristically high losses, but through aggressive and astute management, loan reserves, and write-offs, the bank was able to restore its asset quality.

SUN BELT–CENTERED EXPANSION

In 1971 Northern acquired Security Trust Company, located in Miami, Florida. Additional trust operations were established in Palm Beach, Sarasota, and Naples. In 1982 Northern expanded its services in the state of Florida from trust operations to include a full range of financial services. In 1990 the bank administered trust assets worth over $5 billion in South Florida alone. In 1974 Northern established a trust operation in Arizona, and expanded in 1986 to include full financial services. In 1988 a trust subsidiary was created with offices in San Francisco, Los Angeles, and Santa Barbara, California. In 1989 the acquisition of Concorde Bank in Dallas, Texas, provided Northern with access to business opportunities in one more state. By the end of 1993, the bank had more than 40 offices in five states.

The bank created a holding company in 1971, Northern Trust Corporation, for the purpose of future expansion within the state of Illinois. In 1981, when the state finally permitted Illinois banks to acquire banks in Cook and the surrounding counties, Northern immediately took advantage of the law and acquired O'Hare International Bank in Park Ridge, First Security Bank in Oakbrook, and First National Bank of Lake Forest.

With offices in five states, Northern Trust provided many personal financial services, including investment management, securities custody, estate planning and administration, and tax preparation. The bank provided master trust and custody services to foundations, endowments, corporations, and pooled investments worldwide. Northern's cash management and commercial banking services were provided to corporations and financial institutions to help manage cash collections, control cash disbursements, and create information systems needed for the growing complexity of clients' needs.

When Edward Byron Smith retired in 1979, he was succeeded by E. Norman Staub, followed a few years later by Philip W. K. Sweet, and then by Weston Christopherson. When company veteran David W. Fox took over in 1989, he was only the seventh chief executive in the bank's existence. This stability, in both leadership and financial policy, enabled Northern Trust to weather some difficult moments in its history and develop into one of the most trustworthy banks in the United States.

Northern Trust ventured somewhat belatedly into mutual funds in the early 1990s, launching its Benchmark Funds for institutional customers in 1992 (which were later renamed Northern Institutional Funds) and its no-load Northern Funds for individuals two years later. In October 1995 Northern acquired RCB International, Inc., an international provider of institutional investment management services based in Stamford, Connecticut. RCB was later renamed Northern Trust Global Advisors, Inc. Also in 1995 Fox retired and was succeeded as CEO and chairman by William A. Osborn, who had been president and COO.

During the mid- to late 1990s, Northern gradually expanded its core personal banking operations. In reflection of the bank's overriding focus on retirement services, its expansion continued to center on the Sun Belt states, thus following its hometown clients to their retirement destinations. This wave of growth was accomplished in part through a series of moderate-sized acquisitions, including the 1995 purchases of Beach One Financial Services, Inc., of Vero Beach, Florida, and Houston-based Tanglewood Bancshares, Inc.; the 1996 buyout of Dallas's Metroplex Bancshares, Inc.; and the 1998 purchase of Denver-based Trustbank Financial Corp. At the same time, Northern Trust began to more aggressively pursue "underserved" wealthy clients closer to home, within the Rust Belt. It thus set up offices in Milwaukee and the affluent Detroit suburb of Bloomfield Hills in 1998 and in Cleveland as well a year later. Also in 1999, Northern went after newly minted tech millionaires by establishing an office in Seattle, Microsoft Corporation's home base. By 2000 Northern Trust's personal banking network encompassed about 80 offices in a dozen states.

The bank thrived in the second half of the 1990s even as the banking industry continued to consolidate and create ever larger giants. Northern Trust posted earnings growth of at least 14 percent each year from 1995 to 1999. By 2000 the bank's total assets had grown to more than $36 billion. This figure was a far cry from J.P. Morgan & Co., whose assets at this time totaled more than $350 billion. However, Northern Trust's $333 billion in assets under management, a figure fueled in part by a long-running bull market, nearly equaled that of the New York-based banking giant. In another contrast with traditional commercial banks, which typically derive the bulk of their income from interest on loans, Northern garnered more than 70 percent of its income from the fees it charged its customers for various services.

EARLY 21ST-CENTURY GROWTH AT HOME AND ABROAD

In the early 21st century, Northern Trust continued to expand its personal banking network, opening up offices in Nevada and Missouri in 2000 and then in 2003 venturing into the Atlanta market via the purchase of the wealth management firm Legacy South, Inc. Also in

2003, Northern entered the potentially lucrative though highly competitive Northeast market by setting up offices in New York City and Stamford, Connecticut. This initiative continued with the opening of an office in Boston in 2005, the same year an office opened in Minneapolis as well. By this time, Northern was operating in close proximity to more than 40 percent of the millionaires in the United States.

Northern's foray into the Northeast was aided by its January 2003, $123.8 million acquisition of Deutsche Bank AG's index-based asset-management business, which was centered in New York City. The acquired unit was one of the leading providers of indexing services for mutual funds and other clients in the United States, with $75 billion in assets under management. In indexing, also known as passive investing, the investment vehicle attempts to mimic the moves of a stock market index. This acquisition occurred at a time when Northern Trust's earnings were being undermined by a decline in fee income stemming from stock market doldrums. The bank consequently launched a cost-cutting program that involved a workforce reduction of 7 percent, or 700 employees, the closure of five personal banking branches, and the divestment of a retirement consulting business in Atlanta. The aim was to slash annual operating expenses by $75 million.

Another key development of the early 21st century was a concerted push to become a global player, particularly on the corporate and institutional side. With Northern's key corporate customers becoming increasingly multinational, the bank was forced to follow its clients overseas or risk losing their business. Thus, by the end of 2004 Northern Trust was serving corporate and institutional clients in 39 countries from its Chicago headquarters and from nine foreign offices. It ranked as the ninth largest asset manager worldwide, with $572 billion in global assets under management, an 89 percent increase over the figure for year-end 2002. It was the custodian of more than $1 trillion in overseas pension, government, and other institutional funds.

Northern Trust cemented its position as a global player in March 2005 by completing the largest acquisition in the bank's history, the £261.5 million ($494 million) purchase of the London-based Financial Services Group of Baring Asset Management, a unit of the Dutch firm ING Groep N.V. This deal added $123 billion of assets to the $1 trillion Northern was already administering outside the United States. It also significantly bolstered Northern's capabilities in several areas where they had been lacking, including hedge-fund, private-equity, and real-estate administration.

Northern followed up the Baring deal with further overseas growth initiatives, including adding an office in

Melbourne, Australia, to the bank's network of Asia-Pacific branches in Singapore, Japan, Hong Kong, China, and India. By 2007 Northern was generating one-third of its revenues outside the United States. That year the bank's net income increased 9 percent to $726.9 million, its assets under custody grew 17 percent to $4.14 trillion, and its assets under management jumped 9 percent to $757.2 billion. Highlighting its position as a bedrock financial institution, Northern Trust's 2007 dividend payment was its 111th consecutive year of dividends paid.

At the beginning of 2008, Frederick H. Waddell was named CEO of Northern, succeeding Osborn, who remained chairman. Waddell, a 32-year company veteran who was promoted from the position of president, had previous stints as head of the bank's wealth-management group and its corporate and institutional services business. The new leader took over at an inauspicious time, right in the midst of the severe global economic crisis. Northern's position as a trust bank reduced its exposure to potential losses from bad loans, but the plummeting global stock markets cut into its fee income. Northern posted a net loss for the third quarter of 2008 thanks to $561.5 million in pretax charges it was forced to take to shore up its money-market funds and pay back clients who had lost money in a securities-lending program. Some major clients, including the University of Washington and a BP Corporation pension plan, had sued Northern, claiming that its investment activities had involved "inappropriate" levels of risk, claims Northern denied. Although these developments dented Northern Trust's reputation for providing steady, safe investment services, the bank remained well capitalized. It further shored up its capital base by participating in the U.S. government's program to bolster the banking system through capital injections. The U.S. Treasury Department purchased $1.57 billion in Northern Trust preferred stock and related warrants in November 2008.

Thomas Derdak
Updated, David E. Salamie

PRINCIPAL SUBSIDIARIES

The Northern Trust Company; Norlease, Inc.; MFC Company, Inc.; The Northern Trust Company, Canada; Nortrust Nominees, Ltd. (UK); The Northern Trust Company U.K. Pension Plan Limited; Northern Trust Guernsey Holdings Limited (99%); The Northern Trust International Banking Corporation; Northern Trust Cayman International, Ltd. (Cayman Islands); The Northern Trust Company of Hong Kong Limited (99.99%); Northern Trust Fund Managers (Ireland)

Limited; Nortrust Nominees (Ireland) Limited; Northern Trust Property Services (Ireland) Limited; Northern Trust Management Services Limited (UK); Northern Trust Global Investments Limited (UK); The Northern Trust Scottish Limited Partnership (U.K.; 99%); Northern Trust Luxembourg Capital S.A.R.L.; Northern Trust (Ireland) Limited; Northern Trust GFS Holdings Limited (Guernsey; 99%); Northern Trust International Fund Administration Services (UK) Limited; Northern Trust Fiduciary Services (UK) Limited; Northern Trust Fiduciary Services (Guernsey) Limited (99%); Northern Trust Fiduciary Company (Guernsey) Limited; Trafalgar Trust Company (Guernsey) Limited; Northern Trust International Fund Administration Services (Guernsey) Limited (99%); Northern Trust Partners Scotland Limited (UK); Northern Operating Services Private Limited (India; 99%); Northern Trust Investments, National Association; Northern Trust Holdings Limited (UK); Northern Trust European Holdings Limited (UK); Northern Trust Luxembourg Management Company S.A. (99.99%); Northern Trust, NA; Realnor Properties, Inc.; Realnor Special Properties, Inc.; Realnor Hallandale, Inc.; Northern Annuity Sales, Inc.; Northern Trust Bank, FSB; Northern Trust Holdings L.L.C.; Northern Investment Corporation; Northern Trust Securities, Inc.; Northern Trust Services, Inc.; Nortrust Realty Management, Inc.; The Northern Trust Company of New York; Northern Trust Global Advisors, Inc.; NT Global Advisors, Inc. (Canada); Northern Trust Global Advisors, Limited (UK); The Northern Trust Company of Connecticut; Northern Trust Global Investments Japan, K.K.; The Northern Trust Company of Delaware.

PRINCIPAL OPERATING UNITS

Corporate and Institutional Services; Personal Financial Services.

PRINCIPAL COMPETITORS

State Street Corporation; The Bank of New York Mellon Corporation; Bank of America Corporation; Brown Brothers Harriman & Co.; JPMorgan Chase & Co.; Citigroup Inc.; The Goldman Sachs Group, Inc.; Morgan Stanley.

FURTHER READING

Ackermann, Matt, "As Rivals Merge, Northern Trust CEO Stresses Organic Growth," *American Banker,* December 20, 2006, p. 1.

———, "For Northern Trust CEO, Megadeal Is Not an Option," *American Banker,* January 30, 2008, p. 11.

———, "Loss for Northern Trust," *American Banker,* October 23, 2008, p. 5.

Arndorfer, James B., "Northern Trust Is Following the Money into New Markets," *Crain's Chicago Business,* December 6, 1999, p. 29.

Bailey, Jeff, "Northern Trust Names As Chairman Jewel Cos.'s Ex-Chief," *Wall Street Journal,* December 4, 1984.

———, "Northern Trust Strategy to Spur Growth Stresses Its Profitable Trust Operations," *Wall Street Journal,* April 19, 1984.

Bernard, Tara Siegel, "Northern Trust Works on Bottom Line," *Wall Street Journal,* May 21, 2003.

Carter, Adrienne, "Northern Trust's New Wanderlust," *Business Week,* April 11, 2005, p. 92.

Daniels, Steve, "Blue-Blood Bank," *Crain's Chicago Business,* June 2, 2003, p. A99.

———, "Northern Brakes Branch Expansion," *Crain's Chicago Business,* May 3, 2004, p. 6.

———, "Northern Gets Ready to Take a Bow in NY," *Crain's Chicago Business,* February 10, 2003, p. 3.

———, "Northern Trust Raises the Ax," *Crain's Chicago Business,* May 19, 2003, p. 3.

———, "Northern's Latest Calling: London," *Crain's Chicago Business,* February 6, 2006, p. 2.

———, "Staying the Course at Northern," *Crain's Chicago Business,* October 29, 2007, p. 1.

Fox, David W., *The Northern Trust Company: Celebrating 100 Years, 1889–1989,* New York: Newcomen Society of the United States, 1989, 20 p.

Fox, Pimm, and A. J. Hesselink, "Northern Trust Will Purchase Services Unit of ING's Baring," *Wall Street Journal,* November 23, 2004, p. C3.

Gruber, William, "Gray Lady Likes New Money, Too," *Chicago Tribune,* February 19, 1998, Business sec., p. 1.

Healy, Beth, "CEO Must Juice Up Northern's Lights," *Crain's Chicago Business,* March 20, 1995, p. 1.

Kulikowski, Laurie, "Northern Trust, Completing Deal, Is Not Done Abroad," *American Banker,* March 31, 2005, p. 2.

Lubove, Seth, "Snowbird Bank," *Forbes,* February 19, 1990, pp. 64+.

McGee, Suzanne, "A Bedrock-Solid Bank," *Barron's,* November 5, 2007, p. 29.

McMurray, Scott, "Northern Star," *Institutional Investor* (International ed.), December 1997, p. 149.

Merrick, Amy, "Northern Trust, Shunning Mergers, Stays True to Roots," *Wall Street Journal,* October 9, 2000, p. B6.

Miller, James P., "Northern Buying Baring Business: $480 Million Deal Targets Europe," *Chicago Tribune,* November 23, 2004, Business sec., p. 3.

———, "Northern Plans Big Charge," *Chicago Tribune,* September 30, 2008, News sec., p. 24.

"Northern Trust Opts to Build, Not Buy," *ABA Bank Journal,* March 1990, pp. 54–55.

O'Donnell, Thomas, "A Bank of Choice," *Forbes,* September 24, 1984, p. 58.

Progress of the Northern Trust Company, Chicago: Northern Trust Company, 1949, 35 p.

Reed, Robert, "Northern Trust Marks Changing of the Guard," *Crain's Chicago Business,* May 7, 1990, p. 51.

Rieker, Matthias, "Northern Trust: Cuts About Focus, Not Markets," *American Banker,* June 24, 2003, p. 1.

Ringer, Richard, "Old Gray Lady of LaSalle Street Is Getting a Facelift: With California Strategy and Ad Campaign, Northern Trust Is Changing Its Image," *American Banker,* October 30, 1987, pp. 24+.

Samuels, Gary, "Snowbird Bank," *Forbes,* November 4, 1996, p. 52.

Stangenes, Sharon, "Northern Lights Up: Trust Power Emerges," *Chicago Tribune,* July 4, 1993, Business sec., p. 1.

Strahler, Steven R., "The Bill Comes Due for Osborn," *Crain's Chicago Business,* March 14, 2005, p. 1.

———, "Enron Crash Shines Light on Northern," *Crain's Chicago Business,* October 13, 2003, p. 4.

Yerak, Becky, and James P. Miller, "Northern Trust CEO to Give Up Exec Role," *Chicago Tribune,* October 17, 2007, Business sec., p. 1.

NTD Architecture

9655 Granite Ridge Drive, Suite 100
San Dimas, California 91773
U.S.A.
Telephone: (858) 565-4440
Fax: (858) 569-3433
Web site: http://www.ntd.com

Private Company
Incorporated: 1953 as Neptune & Thomas Associates
Employees: 300
Sales: $43 million (2007 est.)
NAICS: 541310 Architectural Services

■ ■ ■

NTD Architecture is focused on the education and healthcare markets, employing a staff of 300 architects, engineers, interior designers, and support personnel. To a lesser degree, the firm plans and designs public sector projects. For healthcare clients, NTD Architecture provides a range of services, including strategic planning, master planning, programming, and specialty consulting in women's health, cancer treatment, and emergency room services. In the education market, the firm designs elementary and secondary (K–12) projects, ranking as the third largest firm in the nation in the K–12 market. NTD Architecture also has extensive experience in projects for institutions of higher learning, including designing facilities for private and public universities, colleges, and community colleges. NTD Architecture maintains seven offices, operating through five California offices in San Diego, Los Angeles, Auburn, Visalia, and Salinas, and through two Arizona offices in Phoenix and Tucson.

POST–WORLD WAR II BEGINNINGS

NTD Architecture, which operated under four different names during its first half-century of business, evolved through the organic growth of its practice and through a series of mergers with other architectural practices. Despite a history of blending its business with other businesses, the firm never strayed far from the strategic focus established by its founders, Donald E. Neptune and Joseph F. Thomas.

With Neptune and Thomas at the helm, NTD Architecture enjoyed a pedigree that put it among the elite in its industry. The industry's national association, the American Institute of Architects (AIA), contained a coterie of architects who had earned the utmost respect of their peers, the AIA College of Fellows. Fewer than 2 percent of all registered architects in the United States were elected to fellowship in the AIA, an honor designated by the post-nominal letters FAIA. Both Neptune and Thomas were FAIA, having made, in the estimation of a jury of peers, outstanding contributions to their profession through design excellence and the advancement of the industry's aesthetic and scientific practices.

Neptune, born in 1916 in San Diego, studied at the University of California, Berkeley. Johnson, born in 1915 in Oak Hill, West Virginia, completed his education at Duke University. After honing their skills while working for others—Thomas, for instance, was

COMPANY PERSPECTIVES

NTD employs a unique approach to the programming and design of projects in which the clients' leadership will become participants in the planning and design of the project. The process is called Esquisse, from a French word meaning "to sketch or outline." NTD's Esquisse process is an intensive, onsite work session in which the client's leadership and professionals work directly with the design team in programming, planning, and designing their project. During the Esquisse process, the NTD project team sets-up on a site convenient for the client (usually within the client's current facility) where they create a "mini design studio" or Esquisse workroom. The clients and users, those who will use the proposed facility, are invited to work directly with the project team to identify issues and goals related to the project. They actively participate in the design process while realistically considering budget, schedule, and volume issues.

employed as a staff architect by the state of California—the two men formed a partnership when they were in their late 30s. In 1953, they formed Neptune & Thomas Associates (NTA), establishing the firm in Pasadena, California.

Neptune and Thomas, who earned FAIA status while working together (the AIA College of Fellows was formed in 1952), established the business orientation their successors would follow in the decades ahead. They bid for work on projects to construct hospitals, schools, colleges, and universities, designing Upland High School, Glendora High School, Arcadia Community Hospital, the Tri-City Hospital in Oceanside, California, and the Pasadena City Schools administration building, among other projects. The work completed during NTA's first decade of business established the two practice areas the firm would focus on for the decades to follow: healthcare and education.

SAN DIEGO OFFICE OPENS IN 1965

The company achieved much of its growth after the leadership tenures of Neptune and Thomas. The most significant physical expansion that occurred during the firm's era as NTA was the opening of an office in San Diego in 1965. The office opening marked the first time

the firm expanded, giving it a presence in the city that later served as its headquarters location.

After its first expression of organic expansion, it was nearly a 25-year wait before NTA expanded through a merger. In 1989, the firm merged with Davis-Duhaime Associates, which prompted NTA to change its name to Neptune Thomas Davis (NTD). Founded in 1971, Davis-Duhaime Associates was led by Bill Davis, an AIA-registered architect whose practice represented an ideal addition to the education-related business of the former NTA. With the acquisition of Davis-Duhaime Associates, the newly constituted NTD gained a range of comprehensive capabilities to attract public school districts as clients. Davis-Duhaime Associates had expertise in public education funding programs, extensive master-planning skills, and offered an array of demographic mapping and architectural services.

STRENGTHENING THE HEALTHCARE BUSINESS: 1994

With the acquisition of Davis-Duhaime Associates, the balance of the firm's practice tilted toward the education side. The firm's next major merger with another architectural practice reduced the disparity between NTD's education and healthcare business. In 1994, NTD asked Jordan Knighton, an AIA-registered architect, to join the firm's fold, an offer Knighton accepted. Although the merger did not engender a name change, it did give NTD another office, the third office for the 41-year-old firm. Knighton was based in Auburn, California, a small community northeast of Sacramento. The merger represented NTD's greatest leap geographically, giving it a presence in the northern reaches of the state. It also gave the firm Knighton's expertise in designing highly technical medical facilities, a practice that lessened NTD's reliance on school design for its financial sustenance.

A decade passed before NTD made another move on the merger front, but the lull in activity preceded a transaction of enormous importance. NTD, which had earned much of its reputation by designing buildings for high schools, colleges, and universities, greatly bolstered its involvement in the healthcare market with a merger in 2004. The merger with Jordan Knighton had given more weight to the firm's healthcare business, but after NTD's path crossed with the practice established by Ronald A. Stichler, the firm became a leading force in the healthcare market, substantially strengthening its capabilities and broadening its geographic presence.

THE STICHLER GROUP

AIA-registered Stichler started his own practice in 1980, forming the business under the name The Stichler

KEY DATES

1953: NTD Architecture is founded as Neptune & Thomas Associates in Pasadena, California.

1965: The firm opens a second office in San Diego, California.

1989: After merging with Davis-Duhaime Associates, the firm changes its name to Neptune Thomas Davis.

1994: An office in Auburn, California, becomes the firm's third office after acquiring the practice of Jordan Knighton.

2004: A merger with a specialist in healthcare design, The Stichler Group, Inc., creates NTDStichler Architecture.

2006: The firm opens an office in Tucson, Arizona.

2007: The firm merges with a specialist in community college design, Spencer/Hoskins + Associates; company shortens name to NTD Architecture.

2008: An office in Salinas, California, is established.

Design Group, Inc. Basing his operations in San Diego, Stichler focused on designing complex healthcare facilities, initially relying on the support of a small staff of five employees. His practice grew quickly as he concentrated on courting large institutional clients such as healthcare giant Kaiser Permanente, an approach that differed from the speculative projects undertaken by his peers, who preferred to work with developers. "Our marketing plan was totally different from most of our colleagues," Stichler said in the February 10, 1997 edition of the *San Diego Business Journal.*

As Stichler's practice grew, he demonstrated a willingness to take on projects in unfamiliar markets, developing a business with far greater geographic diversity than his crosstown rival, NTD. By 1987, he had begun to design facilities for clients located outside California. By 1991, he had made his first leap into international markets, taking on a project in Australia. By 1997, after establishing offices in Arizona and Texas, Stichler's $12-million-in-revenue firm was designing an entire city on the outskirts of Kuala Lumpur, the capital of Malaysia. Stichler's firm, which employed nearly 100 architects, mechanical engineers, structural engineers, interior designers, construction managers, and financial specialists, was handling every aspect of the $600 million, mixed-use, commercial and residential project. The firm was designing the project's high-rise

buildings, its roads and bridges, and its plumbing and electricity.

Although the Malaysian project exhibited an impressive range of capabilities, Stichler's firm gained prominence by designing facilities for the healthcare market in the United States. In the greater San Diego area, the firm designed Sharp Mary Birch Hospital for Women, Pomerado Hospital, and the A.B. and Jessie Polinsky Children's Center. Outside of San Diego, it left its mark as well, contributing to the design and space planning for more than 20 cancer facilities throughout the country during the 1990s. In 2001, The Stichler Group, Inc., as it was then known, designed what healthcare providers in California referred to as a "bedless hospital." The firm created a $91 million Outpatient Medical Center in Otay Mesa, California, just north of the Mexican border. The facility offered a full range of diagnostic, treatment, and surgical services, rivaling the capabilities of a hospital.

SAN DIEGO'S LARGEST ARCHITECTURE FIRM: 2004

After more than 20 years of building his practice into a leader in the healthcare market, Stichler decided to sell his business, creating an ideal opportunity for NTD. Negotiations for the merger began in 2003, when NTD's president and chief executive officer, Jon A. Baker, looked to create more of a balance between the firm's healthcare and education businesses. "NTD has always been a healthcare and education specialist," Baker said in the March 1, 2004 issue of the *San Diego Business Journal.* "Our education practice has grown so much, but our healthcare work has slowed and we didn't have as much healthcare as we wanted." The Stichler Group, although it had downsized to 75 employees and two offices, promised to bolster NTD's healthcare business substantially.

The merger was completed in February 2004, combining NTD, the third largest architecture firm in San Diego with the city's sixth largest firm, The Stichler Group. The new entity, ranking as San Diego's largest architecture firm, was named NTDStichler Architecture, a company with 300 employees and four offices, which included an office in Phoenix, Arizona, the first out-of-state office for the former NTD.

SPENCER/HOSKINS + ASSOCIATES JOINS THE FOLD IN 2007

Baker identified additional acquisition candidates as he led NTDStichler forward. In early 2007, after opening an office in Tucson the previous year, he began negotiations with two architects who had been with the firm when it operated under the name Neptune & Thomas Associates. Jim Spencer and Steve Hoskins left the firm in 1980 to start their own practice, Spencer/Hoskins + Associates. The partners focused on design work for community colleges after they gained their independence, building a practice during the ensuing 25 years that represented an attractive addition to NTD-Stichler's education business. Spencer and Hoskins merged their 16-employee practice with NTDStichler in March 2007. "This merger," Baker noted in the April 2, 2007 issue of the *San Diego Business Journal,* "will strengthen our community college service and enhance our relationship with the market."

Baker did not wait long before completing his next deal. In July 2007, a sixth office was added to the firm's operations through the acquisition of the architectural division of Quad Knopf, which provided engineering, environmental planning, geographic information systems, land development, and landscape architectural services. The division operated out of a seven-person office in Visalia, California, giving NTDStichler greater ability to serve clients in the central region of the state.

NTDSTICHLER ARCHITECTURE BECOMES NTD ARCHITECTURE

Before celebrating its 55th anniversary, the Baker-led firm changed its name, the first name change not precipitated by a merger. In September 2007, NTD-Stichler Architecture shortened its name to NTD Architecture. Projects the firm completed during its anniversary year included a sample of its staple diet: education and healthcare facilities. In September 2008, NTD Architecture finished three projects, beginning with Willow Grove Elementary School in San Diego County, a 63,500-square-foot school designed to accommodate 750 students. In the Blue Ridge Unified School District in Lakeside, Arizona, NTD Architecture's design of the district's new junior high school came to fruition when construction of the 127,000-square-foot facility was completed. In Glendale, Arizona, NTD Architecture completed work on a new lobby at Banner Thunderbird Medical Center, part of a $289 million expansion project awarded to the firm two years earlier. The year also included the establishment of an office in Salinas, California.

After 55 years in business, NTD Architecture had firmly established itself in its two principal markets. The firm's capabilities in the education and healthcare markets had evolved to a point where it occasionally stepped beyond the traditional role of an architect. NTD Architecture, for example, had assisted rural hospitals in securing U.S. Department of Housing and Urban Development funding and it had lobbied on behalf of school districts to obtain funding from the state. "We do whatever it takes to make sure our clients get results," Baker said in the Fall 2007 issue of *Furniture & Interiors.* He also suggested the aggressive expansion that occurred between 2004 and 2008 had not concluded. "We are also looking at alternatives to expand our practice into the Midwest," he told *Furniture & Interiors,* offering a glimpse into NTD Architecture's future. "That might be the result of a merger or acquisition," he added.

Jeffrey L. Covell

PRINCIPAL COMPETITORS

Austin Veum Robbins Partners, Inc.; HMC Architects; Anshen+Allen Architects, Inc.

FURTHER READING

Dorich, Alan, "Making a Mark: NTD Architecture's Interiors 'Break Out of the Everyday Mold,'" *Furniture & Interiors,* Fall 2007, p. 100.

Harman, Liz, "At Stichler U., the Specialty Is a Degree Called Success," *San Diego Business Journal,* February 10, 1997, p. 1.

Jackson, Mandy, "Merger Creates San Diego's Largest Architectural Firm," *San Diego Business Journal,* March 1, 2004, p. 21.

Mowad, Michelle, "NTDStichler Architecture Expands Services with Opening of Visalia Office," *San Diego Business Journal,* July 16, 2007, p. 33.

———, "Welcome Back," *San Diego Business Journal,* April 2, 2007, p. 36.

Schweizer, Andrew, "NTD Architecture Gets Contract to Design High School in Escondido," *San Diego Business Journal,* July 28, 2008, p. 36.

Weidemann, Liz, "Executive Profile: Jon Baker," *San Diego Business Journal,* April 2, 2007, p. 38.

Nypro, Inc.

101 Union Street
Clinton, Massachusetts 01510
U.S.A.
Telephone: (978) 365-9721
Fax: (978) 368-0236
Web site: http://www.nypro.com

Private Company
Incorporated: 1955 as Nylon Products Corporation
Employees: 18,000
Sales: $1.16 billion (2008)
NAICS: 326199 All Other Plastics Product Manufacturing; 333511 Industrial Mold Manufacturing

■ ■ ■

Nypro, Inc., is a leading global injection-molding firm whose services range from design and mold-making to packaging and distribution. The Clinton, Massachusetts-based company has nearly 50 operations in 16 countries. About half of its 18,000 employees work in China, although it also has a major presence in the United States, Europe, and Mexico. Nypro produces plastic parts for companies in the healthcare, consumer electronics, consumer products, and packaging industries, with a roster of *Fortune* 500 clients that includes Procter & Gamble, Eli Lilly, Abbott Laboratories, and Gillette. In 1999 longtime owner Gordon Lankton sold his stake back to the company and created an employee stock ownership plan, which grants shares to all of its workers and buys them back when they depart.

BEGINNINGS

Nypro was founded as Nylon Products Corporation in 1955 by Nick Stadtherr and molding industry veteran Fred Kirk. The Clinton, Massachusetts-based firm found steady work producing price tag fasteners for clothing, turning out millions each day for Avery Dennison. In its first year the firm recorded sales of $174,000.

In 1962 the ailing Stadtherr sold his stake to Gordon Lankton, a 1954 Cornell University mechanical engineering graduate. Born in Illinois, Lankton had settled on the East Coast after a stint in the Army and learned injection molding while working for DuPont and Stanley Tools. After buying half of the company for $280,000, he took the role of general manager. The 40-employee Nypro had annual sales of $785,000.

In 1964 Lankton helped inaugurate a profit-sharing program that paid each employee an annual bonus, which was given out in the form of silver dollars. In 1969 he was made president and in 1971 he bought the remaining half of the firm for $750,000 from Kirk, who felt it was growing too big to be managed properly. Sales stood at about $4 million.

At this time a U.S. economic slowdown caused a significant drop in orders, and the firm's president decided changes needed to be made in the way Nypro operated. In 1972 Lankton, who after his 1956 Army discharge had traveled for nine months through Europe, the Middle East, and Asia by motorcycle, unveiled a plan to begin adding molding plants near clients that were taking manufacturing abroad. Key to the idea was standardization, with quality guaranteed no matter where the parts were produced.

COMPANY PERSPECTIVES

Our Mission: To serve our customers with integrated, innovative and environmentally sound manufacturing solutions, built on Nypro's global plastics leadership, creating value for our team members, communities and shareholders.

Nypro also vowed to explore new product areas, in particular looking toward the recession-proof healthcare industry. Over the next few years the firm would upgrade its technology by adding robotic machines and developing "clean rooms" where injection molding could be performed to healthcare standards. Lankton had noticed that manufacturers liked to have the full attention of a supplier, and the firm began to share production and even cost data, which allowed customers to continuously monitor product quality and gave them the ability to quickly make changes.

PUERTO RICAN PLANT LAUNCH: 1973

Its new strategy in place, in 1973 Nypro opened a molding facility in Puerto Rico and then added another in France the next year, followed by one in Taiwan in 1976. The company's early foreign efforts were not without problems, however, and in France lack of familiarity with the country taught it a powerful lesson. When a contract producing disposable lighter parts for Gillette proved unprofitable and losses mounted to $700,000 per year, Lankton reluctantly decided to lay off workers. However, his decision was opposed by the French government labor board, and when the employees union vowed to block any attempt to remove equipment, Nypro abandoned the plant and its machines. The valuable molds were transported out under cover of darkness and moved to Ireland, where production resumed. The experience taught Lankton the importance of having a local partner that knew the laws and customs of a country, and he subsequently sought to operate foreign units as joint ventures.

As the firm expanded, its molding facilities were set up in an unusually independent fashion. Plant managers reported to a board of eight Nypro employees from other units, including a general manager. There was no direct oversight by the company, although if financial reports were not good the firm would contact the plant's chairman and direct that person to take action.

This system also helped share information among the different plants, which developed a healthy rivalry.

In the late 1970s, at the request of the Clinton schools, Nypro began to train high school students in plastics technology at its plant, and in 1980 the Nypro Institute was established in partnership with two area colleges to train both employees and interested outsiders. Lankton's willingness to train non-employees was surprising to some, but he strongly believed that improving the industry as a whole would benefit his firm. During this period the company's first clean room became operational, and its Clinton headquarters and molding operation were moved into the former home of Bigelow Carpet Mills, which had been built in 1854.

Nypro's Puerto Rican operation had become its most profitable unit in the mid-1970s, but early in the next decade it began losing money and the firm began edging toward bankruptcy. The company was serving about 800 clients at this time, some with annual orders as low as $10,000, and in 1983 Lankton decided to concentrate on ones worth $1 million per year or more, telling his sales staff that if existing customers could not be brought to that level in two years, they should be dropped. Setting up a molding project had certain fixed costs, and after it began jettisoning small accounts to concentrate on larger product runs, the firm returned to profitability.

In 1986 Nypro began making Vistakon's new Acuvue lens molds, single-use plastic pieces that were produced to an extremely fine tolerance of six microns. Over the next decade the firm would ship 2.5 billion of them with no rejects and no late or missed shipments. For fiscal 1987, which ended in the summer, sales hit $72.2 million and the company had earnings of $1.2 million. Although Nypro was privately held, many of its competitors were publicly owned; for transparency's sake, the firm had begun to issue a detailed annual financial report.

In the late 1980s Nypro ramped up the pace of forming joint partnerships abroad. In most cases they were 50-50 deals, with neither partner holding controlling interest, a condition Lankton believed fostered better cooperation. These included Nycosa (S) Pte of Singapore, owned jointly with Swiss firms UHAG Uebersee Handel AG and Netstal-Maschinen AG, founded in 1988.

SALES TOP $100 MILLION IN 1989

Nypro's sales reached the $100 million mark for the first time in 1989, with some 40 percent of revenues coming from abroad. The company employed 1,500 and had ten plants that were located in Massachusetts, Georgia,

KEY DATES

1955: Fred Kirk and Nick Stadtherr found injection-molding firm in Massachusetts.

1962: Gordon Lankton buys Stadtherr's stake in company.

1971: Lankton purchases remainder of Nypro from Kirk.

1973: Firm begins global expansion with plant in Puerto Rico.

1974: Lankton starts offering ownership stakes to key employees.

1980: Nypro Institute is established to offer plastics technology training.

1989: Annual sales top $100 million.

1997: Stake in Kentucky-based DJ, Inc., gives Nypro a presence in auto industry.

1999: Lankton announces he will transfer ownership of firm to its employees.

2006: Annual sales top $1 billion.

Iowa, North Carolina, California, Puerto Rico, Ireland, Singapore, and Hong Kong. Only the Massachusetts, Puerto Rico, and one of two North Carolina plants were wholly owned, with the rest joint ventures. Major items produced at this time included blood analysis product components, computer diskette shells, and videocassettes, with top customers including Abbott Laboratories, Johnson & Johnson, Sony, and IBM.

During 1989 a plant was set up in Thailand, and in 1990 a Russian operation was added in partnership with Rottel AG of Switzerland and Micromaschina of Moscow, after Lankton had been talked into going there to investigate business conditions. In 1991 the firm added a Canadian plant in Toronto and in 1992 a new subsidiary, Nymedex, was opened in Clinton to make plastic components such as IV valves for the medical industry. The firm was constructing an 82,000-square-foot, $10 million facility near Chicago that would allow it to better serve Abbott, which included a 20,000-square-foot technical center for making and testing molds.

In 1993 Nypro's Singapore joint venture was doubled in size and a technology center created there to facilitate future Asian expansion. The year 1994 was a busy one, with new additions including a joint-venture plant in Shenzhen, China, that the firm later took full ownership of; two new joint-venture operations in Mexico; a 50-50 venture in Turkey; an 83 percent stake

purchased in Philips Plastics of Wales; and a 94,000-square-foot plant opened in Oregon to serve Hewlett-Packard. Sales topped $197 million, and a profit of $10.8 million was recorded. The firm's initiative to reduce the number of customers had borne fruit, as it worked with only about 75 companies, half of which accounted for $1 million or more in orders per year.

In 1973 Lankton had begun granting key personnel ownership stakes in the firm, and by the early 1990s his own position had dropped to 70 percent, with some 100 employees having become shareholders. The firm's Clinton workforce stood at 900, making Nypro the town's largest employer.

Growth continued in 1995 as the company's Asheville, North Carolina, plant was doubled in size; it bought a 50 percent stake in Technology Products, Inc., of Colorado; set up a 50-50 joint venture with FAL Industries, Ltd., in Bangalore, India; and acquired an 80 percent stake in a Singapore mold maker. Nypro also bought a 100,000-square-foot plant in Dothan, Alabama, from videotape and computer disc maker Sony Magnetic Products, Inc., which would continue to be the location's main customer.

The following year saw another Chinese joint venture formed with government-owned Tianjin Electronics Industries Group near Beijing, and in 1997 the firm started operations in the Dominican Republic and bought Kentucky-based DJ, Inc., a 25-year-old injection-molding firm with $81 million in annual sales. DJ employed 1,000 at plants in Kentucky and Texas and primarily served the auto industry, which Nypro had little presence in.

In 1998 the company formed a 50-50 joint venture in Germany; started a mold-making shop in Hong Kong; opened a plant in Turkey; and completed a $5 million clean room operation in Clinton. Sales for the fiscal year topped $458 million.

LANKTON GIVES FIRM TO EMPLOYEES IN 1999

In January 1999 Gordon Lankton, age 68 and with no family members interested in succeeding him, announced his intention to transfer ownership of Nypro to its employees. The first beneficiaries would be some 2,500 American and Puerto Rican workers, who were 18 or over and had worked a year for the company or one of its 80 percent-owned joint ventures. The long-established profit-sharing plan would be kept in place, and Lankton planned to give Nypro's foreign workers stakes while legal issues in each country were sorted out. To effect the transfer, he would sell the firm all but 5 percent of the total and an employee stock ownership plan (ESOP) would be enacted to distribute the rest. Nypro was one of the 50 largest ESOP companies of more than 10,000 in the United States.

Although there were corporate tax advantages for an ESOP, setting it up cost nearly $500,000 in legal fees and administrative effort to implement. Nypro had borrowed the money to buy Lankton's shares from a consortium of insurance companies, and as the loan was paid down over the next 12 years the full 95 percent would be given out. An employee would be fully vested within five years, and after they left or retired the company would buy the stock back. Its value would be set each year by investment bank Bear Stearns & Co. based on the price of similar publicly traded companies. Lankton's motivation for the ESOP, in addition to his strong desire to reward Nypro's employees, was a belief that the firm could be damaged if it was sold or went public.

During 1999 the company also was restructured into several regional groups in an effort to better operate as a global organization; established an automotive products group to help boost the $60 million it did in this sector; announced plans to expand its Singapore operation with an $18 million upgrade that included new metal-molding technology; and began work on a new $6 million Mexican plant.

In late 2000 Nypro won a contract from Medisys to produce a new retractable-needle syringe, and in 2001 it bought two Chinese molding operations; acquired a French plant; started a joint venture in Hungary; opened new plants in Puerto Rico and Ireland; closed a Georgia facility; and made cuts to its Alabama operation. At year's end Gordon Lankton stepped back to the title of chairman and Nypro North America head and 14-year company veteran Brian Jones took the title of president, later adding the duties of CEO. An Office of Chairmen was created, which Lankton would share with two others, although he would continue to work full-time for the firm. When not traveling to Nypro's many plants (which he visited once each year), he arrived at 6 a.m. to oversee his vast operation, and usually worked six full days per week.

Growth continued in 2002 with a new joint venture in Mexico and another to mold and decorate items in China; a new plant in India; acquisition of Advance Dial Company's Mexican and U.S. assets; purchase of a stake in Minnesota-based Profile Plastics, Inc.; and a $10 million expansion in Clinton that included a clean room and a 105,000-square-foot, $8 million technical center on a former ball field bought from the city.

NUMBER OF EMPLOYEES TOPS 10,000 IN 2002

For fiscal 2002 Nypro had sales of $730 million and profits of $45 million, while worldwide employment reached 10,000 for the first time. The firm had 40 plants in 12 countries and made nearly 60 percent of sales through its overseas operations, the first time they had exceeded those of the United States. Half of sales were from the computer, telecommunications, and electronics industries, with the firm's two top customers Dell Computer and cellphone maker Nokia. Products for the healthcare industry had fallen from 50 percent a few years earlier to just 20 percent of the total.

Although many others in its industry were struggling as manufacturing volume fell to its lowest point since the end of World War II, Nypro continued to grow. Its revenue mix had shifted from 90-plus percent injection molding in the mid-1990s to include 40 percent value-added services such as painting and assembly.

During 2003 the firm expanded its operations in China, opened a mold-making shop in Russia, and entered a 50-50 joint venture in Finland. The following year it sold controlling interest in an Iowa plant to Native Alaskan–owned Sealaska Corp., which helped position it to win more government contracts. A 100,000-square-foot Intesys Technologies plant in Mexico was purchased in 2004, while a new facility opened in Brazil in an industrial park where that country's cellphone production was centered.

Nypro was aggressively cutting costs through the use of lean manufacturing techniques, as new challenges including short product life cycles, industry consolidation, and increasing global competition threatened profitability. During the year the firm closed a plant in Colorado that made automotive parts and moved its work to Kentucky; cut jobs in the United Kingdom; closed a plant in Ireland; and laid off 30 in Clinton, including two vice-presidents, while asking other executives to take pay cuts.

In 2005 a new plant opened in China and the firm boosted its involvement with Sealaska; bought out the joint venture stake of DJ, Inc.; acquired several product lines from Millipore Corp.; and added an online plastics technology program with Fitchburg State College. The company was looking to seek more patents for its technology, having obtained only one in five decades of operation.

On December 1 Nypro celebrated its 50th anniversary with 18½ hours of live webcasts from 23 of its 66 plants in 12 of the 18 countries it operated in. In Clinton, Chairman Lankton gave a speech and the local high school band marched through the aisles of the factory. The date coincided with the point when the firm's average annual revenues would reach $1 billion, marking another milestone in its evolution.

That year Nypro had more than 15,000 employees, more than half of them in China, and the majority of its sales came from value-added services rather than molding. One example of the firm's new approach was a fragrance product made for Dial Corp. which it molded, assembled, filled, packed, and shipped.

ESOP BENEFITS EXTEND TO FOREIGN WORKERS: 2005

As it celebrated 50 years in business, the firm also began rolling out ESOP benefits to its foreign employees. Although they were not actually vested with ownership, they would receive a payment upon retirement equivalent to what the stock appreciation would have been. Share value had quintupled since the ESOP was begun, and about 40 employees had retired as millionaires. Nypro was the sixth largest ESOP in the United States.

In February 2006 CEO Brian Jones abruptly departed, citing philosophical differences, and Vice-President and COO Theodore Lapres III was named acting president. In the summer the 18-year company veteran was also made CEO.

During the year Nypro added auto parts manufacturing in China; opened its fifth plant in Mexico; shuttered plants in Finland, Wales, Kentucky, and Texas; sold its less than two-year-old Brazilian operation; downsized in the Dominican Republic; disposed of a small U.S. robot-making unit; and sold a stake in its Alabama plant to Sealaska. The firm was seeking to focus on operating larger plants with multiple capabilities to serve an even smaller group of major customers. In 2006 Gordon Lankton also opened a $3 million museum near Nypro headquarters to display a collection of Russian religious icons that he had collected on more than 40 trips to that country.

In 2007 the company began U.S. production of a new product for Eli Lilly, the insulin pen, which could keep records of doses and was expected to be hugely popular with diabetics. The firm also began expanding operations in North Carolina and Clinton, where it would spend $15 million to add two new clean rooms that would create 100 jobs.

In 2008 Nypro expanded medical product manufacturing in China, India, Ireland, Hungary, and Mexico. Sales of healthcare products were again approaching 30 percent of the total, and the firm was

looking to double clean room capabilities over the next several years. Its life sciences unit was also sold to Roush Enterprises during the year.

For fiscal 2008, sales topped $1.16 billion. Nypro was focusing on the healthcare, consumer products, electronics, and packaging products markets, and seeking clients that generated more than $10 million in sales per year. The firm's largest customer accounted for $200 million in revenues.

In its second half-century, Nypro, Inc., was continuing the pattern of growth and innovation established by longtime owner and CEO Gordon Lankton. The employee-owned firm was working to broaden the range of molding and allied services it offered, and appeared well-positioned to face the challenges that lay ahead.

Frank Uhle

PRINCIPAL SUBSIDIARIES

Nypro operates 49 companies in 16 countries, many of them joint ventures.

PRINCIPAL COMPETITORS

Berry Plastics Corp.; Newell Rubbermaid, Inc.; Illinois Tool Works, Inc.; Aptar Group, Inc.; Rexam Plc; Letica Corp.; Siegel-Robert, Inc.

FURTHER READING

Antosiewicz, Frank, "Nypro Finishes Expansions in N.C., Ireland," *Plastics News,* October 13, 2008.

———, "Nypro Works to Keep Edge," *Plastics News,* May 13, 2002, p. 4.

Bregar, Bill, "Taking Chances Takes Lankton to Top," *Plastics News,* June 19, 2000, p. 53.

Donker, Peter P., "A Global Concern," *Worcester Telegram & Gazette,* June 15, 1997, p. E1.

———, "Nypro Continues Its Habit of Rapid Growth," *Worcester Telegram & Gazette,* October 8, 1996, p. E1.

———, "Nypro Molds Winning Formula," *Worcester Telegram & Gazette,* August 25, 1991, p. E1.

Earls, Alan R., "Keeping the Customer Ecstatic," *Computer-World,* February 21, 1994, p. 80.

Esposito, Andi, "Lapres Named Nypro Chief," *Worcester Telegram & Gazette,* July 21, 2006, p. E1.

———, "Nypro ESOP About to Start," *Worcester Telegram & Gazette,* February 26, 1999, p. E1.

———, "Succession Plan on Track at Nypro, Inc.," *Worcester Telegram & Gazette,* October 15, 2001, p. E1.

———, "World of Good," *Worcester Telegram & Gazette,* December 2, 2005, p. E1.

Ferris, Roger M., "Gordon B. Lankton: Nypro's Evolution from Regional to Global Molder," *Plastics Engineering,* March 1, 1997, p. 24.

Halmesmaki Lahti, Rachel, "Nypro in Midst of Good Times," *Worcester Telegram & Gazette,* February 19, 1989, p. 10E.

Lauzon, Michael, "Nypro Buying Automotive Molder DJ Inc.," *Plastics News,* March 10, 1997, p. 1.

McLaughlin, Mark, "An Odyssey to the Big Time," *New England Business,* April 1, 1989, p. 17.

Nugent, Karen, "Nypro Takes Stock of Ideas," *Worcester Telegram & Gazette,* February 25, 2005, p. F30.

Pryweller, Joseph, "Nypro Slates Two More Plants for China," *Plastics News,* February 3, 2003, p. 1.

Sheridan, John H., "Gordon Lankton's Global Vision," *Industry Week,* April 3, 1995, p. 37.

Toloken, Steve, "Nypro Cutting Jobs, Pay, Plant," *Plastics News,* April 12, 2004, p. 3.

———, "Nypro Taps Emerging Markets," *Plastics News,* October 13, 1997, p. 1.

Verespej, Mike, "Nypro Expanding Medical Capability in Mexico," *Plastics News,* February 11, 2008, p. 1.

Odfjell SE

Conrad Mohrsv. 29
PO Box 6101 Postterminalen
Bergen, N-5892
Norway
Telephone: (+47 55) 27 00 00
Fax: (+47 55) 28 47 41
Web site: http://www.odfjell.com

Public Company
Incorporated: 1916 as Rederiet Odfjell
Employees: 3,487
Sales: $1.09 billion (2007)
Stock Exchanges: Oslo
Ticker Symbol: ODF
NAICS: 483111 Deep Sea Freight Transportation

■ ■ ■

Odfjell SE is a world-leading specialist provider of deep-sea transportation, storage, and related services for the global chemicals industry. The Bergen, Norway-based company operates through two primary divisions: Parcel Tankers and Tank Terminals. Parcel Tankers is by far the company's largest division, accounting for 97 percent of the group's revenues of $1.09 billion in 2007. This division oversees the operations of Odfjell's fleet, which counted 94 vessels at the end of 2008. The company also has in place an advanced newbuilding program, with more than 15 vessels expected for delivery by 2010. Altogether, the company's fleet offers a capacity of more than three million deadweight tons (dwt) for chemicals and other liquids, including both organic and nonorganic liquids, such as vegetable oils. Odfjell's fleet operates at a global level, and includes a number of joint-venture operations for specific markets, such as China and Germany.

The smaller Tank Terminals division oversees three wholly owned tank terminal operations in Rotterdam, Netherlands, and Houston, Texas. The company also participates in a number of tank terminal joint ventures in China, Iran, Oman, Singapore, and South Korea. In addition to storage services, the Tank Terminals division provides distillation and decontamination services. Odfjell was founded as part of the Storli group of companies; the founding Odfjell family remains active in the company as shareholders, with Bernt Daniel Odfjell serving as the company's chairman of the board. Terje Storeng is the group's CEO and president.

WORLD WAR I ORIGINS

The Odfjell family's involvement in the shipping industry dates to at least the dawn of the 20th century. Brothers Abraham and Frederik Odfjell both took to sea, eventually becoming ship captains. Abraham earned his ship captain's certificate at the age of 20 in 1901. Norway's neutrality during World War I provided new opportunities for the country's shipping industry. In 1916 the Odfjell brothers decided to go into business together, founding the shipping company Rederiet Odfjell. That company became one of a number of companies founded by the Odfjell family during the period. These companies later formed the basis of a larger group, Storli.

COMPANY PERSPECTIVES

Mission Statement: Odfjell shall be a leading, preferred and profitable global provider of transportation and storage of bulk liquid chemicals, acids, edible oils and other special products. We shall be capable of combining different modes of transportation and storage. We shall provide our customers with reliable and efficient services. We shall conduct our business to high quality, safety and environmental standards.

Dry cargo was the central focus of the company's operations for most of its early history. In the years leading up to World War II, however, Storli began developing an interest in the growing market for transportation of liquids, in particular chemicals and liquefied gases.

The chemicals and liquids transport sector grew strongly in the years following World War II. The massive increase in demand for both organic and inorganic chemicals on an international basis set the stage for the growth of specialized shipping vessels and equipment. Storli became one of the first to recognize the potential of the market, and invested in building up its chemicals shipping capabilities.

Few regulations governed the shipping of chemicals in the 1950s. Because there was at the time no means of shipping fluids in bulk, chemicals were shipped in drums aboard ships that had been designed originally for other types of cargo. The low barrier to entry into the market encouraged a large number of shippers to begin converting their fleets for the shipping of chemicals. Yet these early means of chemicals shipping quickly proved inadequate to the task of handling the often highly hazardous chemicals. By the mid-1950s, the global community had begun putting into place the first international standards governing the chemicals shipping market, helping to limit the sector's appeal.

A major breakthrough, however, came through the efforts of another Norwegian, Jacob Stolt-Nielsen, who had come up with a design for subdividing a ship's hold into separate tanks, each with its own piping and safety systems. In this way, chemicals not only could be transported more safely, but also in bulk, significantly cutting the cost of shipping. The Odfjell family was quick to recognize the importance of the new vessel design, called the parcel tanker, and became one of the pioneers of this sector. Rather than converting existing vessels, the company invested in building a fleet of purpose-built parcel tankers. In this way, Storli was

counted among the world leaders in the parcel tanker category by the end of the 1960s.

BUILDING A PARCEL TANKER FLEET THROUGH THE SEVENTIES

Through the 1960s, Storli built up a fleet of 15 parcel tankers. A number of these were also equipped to carry liquefied gas. The company's vessels at the time remained for the most part on the smaller side, at less than 10,000 dwt. Nonetheless, the company was among the first to add stainless steel tanks—greatly expanding the range of chemicals it could carry—while also helping to pioneer double-hull techniques to protect the cargo as well as provide some environmental safeguards.

The company confirmed its commitment to the chemicals shipping sector by 1968, when it abandoned its remaining dry cargo business to focus wholly on the fluids handling market. Also during the 1960s, Storli added its first tank storage facilities. The company had also begun developing a small operation offering various support services, such as a distillation unit, set up in 1963. This business initially focused on decontaminating customers' liquid bulk shipments; over time, however, the distillation business became involved in providing processing, upgrading, and end-product production services for the chemical industry.

Storli had also built up a partnership with Denmark's Westfal-Larsen, forming the chemicals shipping joint-venture Odfjell-Westfal-Larsen, in 1963. That partnership remained in place until the late 1980s, when Westfal-Larsen exited the chemicals shipping sector altogether. The linkup with Westfal helped Storli/Odfjell expand its fleet to 24 vessels, including 14 outfitted with stainless steel tanks, by 1972. This enabled the company to outpace perennial rival Stolt-Nielsen.

The company's early investment in the sector enabled it to weather the more difficult climate of the 1970s. The chemicals shipping industry had undergone a dramatic expansion during the 1960s. This expansion came to a sudden halt during the 1970s. The rise in fuel prices in particular threatened the cost-effectiveness of the industry, while the increasing stringent safety regulations put into place by the international community helped raise the barrier for entry. As a result, the parcel tanker operators were encouraged to invest in larger vessels (with a capacity of 30,000 dwt or more) outfitted with stainless steel tanks and more technologically advanced safety systems.

In partnership with Westfal, Storli invested in adapting its fleet to the new conditions, despite the difficult market. Indeed, the slump in international trade

KEY DATES

1916: Frederik and Abraham Odfjell found a shipping company, Rederiet Odfjell, later part of the Storli group.

1959: The Odfjells become pioneers of the parcel tanker market.

1986: The company goes public as Skibsaksjeselskapet Storli.

1998: Storli changes its name to Odfjell SE.

2000: Number two Odfjell merges with number four Seachem Tankers to become the industry leader.

2003: Odfjell is fined $42.5 million after pleading guilty to price-fixing and bid-rigging.

2007: Odfjell forms a tank terminal joint venture in Hebei Province in China.

during the late 1970s resulted in an oversupply of vessels. Storli's position as a market leader nonetheless enabled the company to endure in the rough economic times. The company's continued investments also provided it with a solid foundation to take advantage of a new shipping boom in the 1980s.

PUBLIC OFFERING IN 1986

Storli remained entirely controlled by the Odfjell family, now represented by cousins Dan and Abraham Odfjell. In 1980, however, the two cousins agreed to divide up their holdings, including reorganizing their shipping operations into two new companies. Abraham Odfjell reformed his share of the company into JO Odfjell, which then placed its operations into a joint venture, JO Tankers, with Sweden's Johnson Line. JO Odfjell later acquired full control of JO Tankers, which remained a major competitor through the 1990s.

Dan Odfjell in the meantime maintained the shipping Skibsaksjeselskapet Storli company. In 1980 the company and its longtime partner Westfal-Larsen brought their various joint-venture holdings together into a single company. The two companies set up a co-owned facility, the Baytank tanker terminal, in Houston, Texas, in 1983, expanding their tank terminal operations. That terminal soon grew to include more than 90 tanks, including 31 stainless steel tanks. The Odfjell family also acquired interests in tank terminals elsewhere in the world, including a number of South American locations, which were brought into the company's larger network of operations.

The booming shipping market encouraged Storli to invest in the continued expansion of its fleet. As part of that effort, the company went public in 1986, listing its shares on the Oslo stock exchange. The Odfjell family nonetheless maintained majority ownership of the company. Although Storli remained the holding company's name, its operations were best known under its Odfjell Tankers name. As a result, in 1998 Storli decided to change its name, becoming Odfjell SE.

The end of the 1980s saw a major expansion of Odfjell's fleet size, in part because of Westfal's decision to exit the chemicals shipping business in 1989. Storli then bought Westfal's fleet, which included the nine vessels it owned outright, as well as four vessels owned as part of the Odfjell-Westfal joint-venture partnership. At the same time, Odfjell launched its own fleet expansion effort, acquiring five new vessels in 1989.

The importance of the Persian Gulf to the international chemicals market led Odfjell to seek a partner in the region. In 1990 the company agreed to establish a joint venture with the National Shipping Company of Saudi Arabia (NSCSA), selling that company the nine ships Odfjell had acquired from Westfal. These were then placed into a new company, National Chemical Carriers (NCC). Odfjell then became the operator and marketer of the NCC fleet.

MEGAMERGING INTO THE LEAD IN THE 21ST CENTURY

During the economic recession of the early 1990s, Odfjell instituted a strategy of "safeguarding its market share." In this respect, the joint venture with NSCSA took on a highly strategic importance. From this solid base of operation, Odfjell then set out to boost its position in the global market. For this, the company stepped up its newbuilding program, placing orders at several Kvaerner-controlled shipyards for six 37,500 dwt vessels in 1991.

By the middle of the decade, as the world economy once again began to rise, Odfjell extended its initial order with two more vessels. The company continued to add to its newbuilding orders, and by the end of the decade had taken delivery on a total of 16 vessels. At the same time, the company also carried out a number of purchases of secondhand vessels. The extension of the company's fleet in particular enabled the company to claim a greater share of the deep-sea segment.

By 1998 the company's fleet included nearly 50 deep-sea tankers. In another expansion, Odfjell entered a joint venture with Germany's Hoyer to operate a tank container business from the Rotterdam, Netherlands, port. The joint venture grew into one of the world's largest by the middle of the next decade. Odfjell, however, decided to sell its stake in 2004, citing a lack of synergy with its core operations. In another expansion move, Odfjell boosted its tank terminal operations, buying the Botlek tank terminal facility in Rotterdam in 2000.

Despite the expansion of its fleet, Odfjell had temporarily slipped back to the number two position at the start of the 21st century. The company soon rectified this situation, however. In 2000 the company announced its decision to merge with the market's number four player, Seachem Tankers, a London-based company controlled by Greece's Ceres Hellenic Shipping Enterprises Ltd. The "megamerger" created a new industry heavyweight, with nearly $700 million in revenues and control of some 26 percent of the total market. The merger came, however, amid an ongoing consolidation of the global chemicals shipping sector, spurred on by several years of depressed profits across the industry.

The result was a reduction in the industry to a small handful of large-scale players, including Odfjell, Stolt-Nielsen, Tokyo Marine, and JO Tankers. In the first decade of the 2000s the chemicals industry began to chafe under the tightening hold of the majors over the global shipping market. By 2003 Odfjell and the others found themselves charged with bid-rigging and price-fixing as part of an industry cartel. As a result, Odfjell's CEO and vice-president at the time pleaded guilty and were sentenced to serve time in prison. The company itself was slapped with a $42.5 million fine.

JOINT VENTURES AND EXPANSION

Despite this setback, Odfjell's growth remained strong throughout the first decade of the 2000s. By 2004 the company had added operations along the Brazilian coast, through the Flumar joint venture and its four vessels. The company's South American operations included a 50-50 joint venture with Chile's CSAV, operating two vessels. The company had also formed a European joint venture with Ahrenkiel, of Germany, with eight tankers in operation. Through the second half of the decade, Odfjell's expansion brought the company to China, where it established a number of partnerships, largely to serve the domestic market. These partnerships included a joint venture in 2007 with Dalian Port Co. to build and operate a tank terminal in the Caofeidian Industrial Zone, in Hebei Province.

Odfjell continued to expand its fleet as well. In 2006, for example, the company bought five chemicals tankers, including four secondhand vessels, paying $130 million to boost its total fleet to 95 vessels. At the same time, the company had embarked on an ambitious new-build program, with ten new ships on order at the end of the decade. Odfjell remained one of the leading names in the global chemicals shipping industry.

M. L. Cohen

PRINCIPAL SUBSIDIARIES

Flumar Ltda (Brazil); Odfjell Ahrenkiel (Germany; 50%); Odfjell Terminals (Dalian) Ltd (China); Odfjell Terminals (Houston) Inc. (USA); Odfjell Terminals (Jiangyin) Co. Ltd (China); Odfjell Terminals (Korea) Co. Ltd (South Korea; 50%); Odfjell Terminals (Rotterdam) B.V. (Netherlands); Odfjell Tankers AS; Odfjell Terminals BV (Netherlands); Odfjell y Vapores (Chile); Oiltanking Odfjell Terminal & Co. LLC (Oman).

PRINCIPAL DIVISIONS

Parcel Tankers; Tank Terminals.

PRINCIPAL COMPETITORS

Stolt-Nielsen SA; A.P. Møller-Maersk A/S; TUI AG; Alghanim Industries; Louis Dreyfus S.A.S.; ThyssenKrupp Services AG; Suhail Bahwan Group (Holding) L.L.C.; Dr August Oetker KG; Danzas Group; Hapag-Lloyd AG.

FURTHER READING

Boswell, Clay, "Deep-Sea Chemical Shipping Faces Rough Waters," *Chemical Market Reporter,* November 19, 2001, p. 14.

Burridge, Elaine, "Brussels Drops Antitrust Probe of Chemical Shipping Markets," *Chemical Week,* May 12, 2008, p. 5.

———, "Odfjell Acquires Five Chemical Tankers," *ICIS Chemical Business,* October 2, 2006, p. 43.

———, "Odfjell Boosts European Fleet," *European Chemical News,* April 11, 2005, p. 14.

Dela Cruz, Roderick T., "Norwegian Shipping Company Bullish on RP," *Manila Standard,* September 9, 2008.

Frank, Jerry, "Chemical Tanker Giants Face Cartel Charge," *Lloyds List,* April 11, 2003.

———, "Odfjell Waits on Outcome of Brussels Investigation," *Lloyds List,* May 6, 2003.

Milmo, Sean, "Odfjell Acquires the Botlek Tank Terminal in Rotterdam," *Chemical Market Reporter,* April 24, 2000, p. 5.

"Norwegian Heritage—Global Vision," *Fertilizer International,* May 2000, p. 54.

"Odfjell Feels the Heat," *European Chemical News,* February 16, 2004, p. 15.

"Odfjell Spends Big in Rotterdam," *Chemical Business Newsbase,* March 5, 2007.

"Oiltanking, Odfjell to Form JV in Oman," *Chemical Week,* August 3, 2005, p. 14.

Ramesh, Deepti, "Odfjell Plans Storage Venture in China," *Chemical Week,* August 29, 2007, p. 16.

Stene, Trygve, *Entry Barriers and Concentration in Chemicals Shipping,* Bergen: SIØS-Centre for International Economics and Shipping, Foundation for Research in Economics and Business Administration, 2000.

"Stolt and Odfjell Face Antitrust Charges in Europe," *Chemical Week,* April 11, 2007, p. 7.

Tree, Ken, "Odfjell: Leader of the Seas," *AllBusiness.com,* November 1, 2004.

Young, Ian, "Shipping Megamerger Makes Tidal Waves," *Chemical Week,* June 14, 2000, p. 37.

——, "Storli Builds Storage and Shipping Network," *Chemical Week,* August 27, 1997, p. 58.

OfficeMax Incorporated

263 Shuman Boulevard
Naperville, Illinois 60563
U.S.A.
Telephone: (630) 438-7800
Fax: (630) 438-2452
Web site: http://www.officemax.com

Public Company
Incorporated: 1988
Employees: 36,000
Sales: $9.08 billion (2007)
Stock Exchanges: New York
Ticker Symbol: OMX
NAICS: 453210 Office Supplies and Stationery
Stores

■ ■ ■

OfficeMax Incorporated is North America's third largest office supply chain. The company's OfficeMax, Retail unit operates nearly 1,000 stores in the United States, Puerto Rico, and the U.S. Virgin Islands, selling office supplies and paper, technology products, and office furniture. In addition, print and document services are offered via OfficeMax Impress sites, which are located within the company's stores. OfficeMax also has a retail presence in Mexico, via a joint venture in which it has majority ownership. Through OfficeMax, Contract, the company serves large corporations and government entities, as well as midsized businesses in the United States, Canada, New Zealand, and Australia.

1988: HUMBLE BEGINNINGS

The OfficeMax concept was hatched by entrepreneurs Michael Feuer and Robert Hurwitz. Feuer, who became the driving force behind the chain's growth, had been nurturing the idea during more than 17 years of service with Fabri-Centers of America, a 600-store retailer in Cleveland. By his early 40s, Feuer had risen to the executive ranks. Nevertheless, he was frustrated by his inability to run the company as he believed it should be operated. "At age 42 I was bored and, like many executives, I also suffered from the Frank Sinatra syndrome—I wanted to do it my way," Feuer recalled in the September 1993 issue of *Corporate Cleveland.* "I had always claimed that if we could just cut through all the nonsense—for example, the 20 to 25 percent of time most executives spend on CYB (covering your butt)—and do it my way, we could make millions."

Feuer finally jumped ship and, despite other excellent corporate job offers, decided to start his own enterprise. He and Hurwitz decided that they did not want to fund the start-up with bank debt or venture capital because they did not want to forfeit control of the operation. Consequently, they scrambled to raise capital from friends and family. They eventually found 50 investors, including several doctors and lawyers, who were willing to contribute a total of $3 million. The sum was paltry compared to other retail start-up businesses at the time, but the pair thought that they could parlay the cash into a winning enterprise.

Feuer and Hurwitz launched their enterprise on April Fool's Day in 1988. On that day, they laid out on a sheet of paper their concept for a new type of office

COMPANY PERSPECTIVES

Every company can claim to be a leader. We earn the distinction from those who matter most: our customers. By partnering with our customers, understanding their needs and exceeding their goals, they succeed and so do we. From corporations on Wall Street to homes on Main Street we deliver the unrivaled service and unmatched expertise that gives our customers the edge.

products store. Their goal was to create a large business supplies discount store that was an exciting place to shop, and which offered professional and friendly service, as well as prices between 10 and 30 percent less than those found in more traditional office supply retailer shops. The main goal was to bypass all of the middlemen, such as wholesalers and distributors. Achieving that goal, they reasoned, would allow them to effectively replace mom-and-pop office supply stores, much as supermarkets had replaced small grocers years earlier.

OfficeMax was fighting an uphill battle from the start. In May, an office supplies industry trade paper published a list of 15 start-up companies that were trying to crack into the business; OfficeMax was 14th on the list by asset size. The start-up team knew that it had to keep expenditures at an absolute minimum to compete. Feuer and Hurwitz rented office space in a 500-square-foot brick warehouse that had barely any heat or air-conditioning. The space was equipped with a few pieces of inexpensive office furniture, a coffee machine, and a copier (the copier and coffee machine could not be operated at the same time, however, because the fuse would blow). They decided not to invest in a fax machine until it became absolutely necessary.

OfficeMax started out with a skeletal staff of seven people, not including the founders. Their requirements for potential employees were simple: They had to be hard workers with open minds, big hearts, and plenty of enthusiasm. They also had to be willing to work for very little money. Feuer and Hurwitz attracted the workers by promising them part ownership in the company if they stuck with it, and by offering them the chance to go further, faster, and to have more fun than they had ever had in any other job. From the beginning, Feuer made it clear that OfficeMax would be operated differently from the bureaucracies from which most of the

team members had come. There would be no secrets, criticism and praise would be swift and frank, and everyone would cooperate as a team.

Thus, OfficeMax was up-and-running without a single store or any other operation that could bring in any money. The founders hoped that they would be able to get manufacturers to fund their inventory, but they soon found that few big companies were eager to do business with a meager upstart. To overcome such hurdles, the team got together every morning and created a game plan for the day on a blackboard. They flew by the seat of their pants and used every trick they could conjure to get what they needed. Importantly, the company was able to get an unsecured line of credit from a local Cleveland bank. The bank granted the line of credit under one condition: that the founders agree never to use it.

Feuer and Hurwitz were able to take their "line of credit" to big suppliers such as Xerox and convince them to fund their inventory on credit, sometimes for a full year or more. Indeed, the OfficeMax team learned early that the only way to get the cooperation of potential suppliers was to act as though OfficeMax was much bigger than it really was. They dealt with suppliers as though OfficeMax was a soon-to-be major chain with 20, 50, or even 300 stores going up in the near future, suggesting that if those suppliers wanted to secure a place with OfficeMax tomorrow, they would have to cooperate today. To the founders' surprise, most companies played along. Those that did not often regretted it, as OfficeMax quickly became the leading customer for many major office equipment and supplies manufacturers.

1988–90: GOING FROM ONE STORE TO 30 IN TWO YEARS

OfficeMax opened its first store just 90 days after the founders had created their business blueprint on April Fool's Day. Observers were surprised that the team had managed to find space, hire and train a store staff, and hone a store concept in just three months. The first OfficeMax was opened on July 5, 1988, at the Golden Gate Shopping Center in the Cleveland area. The only advertising for the grand opening was a newspaper ad two days prior to the store's opening. Nevertheless, the store had sales of $6,400 on its first day.

After only six months in operation, the store was breaking even (before corporate overhead). That feat was accomplished partly as a result of the grueling hours put in by the team. Feuer, for instance, worked at the corporate office from 7:00 A.M. to 7:00 P.M. He would then race home, shower, put on casual clothes, and drive

KEY DATES

■

1988: Company is founded by Michael Feuer and Robert Hurwitz.

1990: Company merges with Office World; Kmart invests $40 million in OfficeMax.

1991: Kmart purchases 92 percent of outstanding shares and becomes company's owner.

1992: Company purchases Office Warehouse and Bizmart.

1994: Company conducts largest IPO in industry history; launches FurnitureMax, CopyMax, and OfficeMax Online.

1995: Second stock offering eliminates Kmart's ownership.

1996: Company opens Mexico City superstore.

1997: Company opens more stores in Mexico and its first store in Japan.

1998: Company opens its first urban-targeted OfficeMax PDQ store and opens stores in Brazil.

2000: Gateway invests $50 million in company and becomes its exclusive computer provider.

2001: Hewlett-Packard replaces Gateway as company's computer provider; company closes 50 stores.

2003: Boise Cascade Corp. acquires OfficeMax for $1.15 billion and adds OfficeMax to its Boise Office Solutions group.

2004: Boise Cascade sells its non-office-supply assets to Madison Dearborn Partners for $3.7 billion and changes its name to OfficeMax Incorporated; OfficeMax terminates six employees in connection with a $3.3 million wrongful billing scandal.

2005: CopyMax is renamed OfficeMax Print and Document Services.

2006: The company announces a $100 million turnaround initiative and restructures its contract business.

2008: In the wake of difficult economic conditions, OfficeMax suspends payment of quarterly cash dividends on its common stock.

out to the store to observe the customers and employees. When a customer left the store without purchasing anything, Feuer was known to chase after the person and ask if OfficeMax had failed in any way. That type of thinking was later reflected in OfficeMax's intensive customer-satisfaction orientation. For example, the company began requiring that all customer complaints be resolved to the customer's satisfaction within 24 hours.

Enthused by the quick success of the first store, Feuer and Hurwitz hurried back to the original investment group and raised additional capital for expansion. They dumped the cash into an aggressive growth program that had OfficeMax operating 13 stores in Ohio and Michigan less than 12 months after opening the first outlet. Sales had climbed to an impressive $13 million annually and, more important, the stores were operating at a profit. The success was so quick that it worried Feuer, who was convinced that the company's accounting system was messed up and that OfficeMax could easily be teetering on the edge of bankruptcy.

Shortly before OfficeMax had opened its first store, a similar office superstore venture called Office World had started in Chicago. The business was funded heavily by retailer Montgomery Ward, but despite hefty financial backing, the effort had lost $10 million in the span of a few years. Thus, when Montgomery Ward approached OfficeMax about the possibility of a merger between OfficeMax and Office World, Feuer and Hurwitz were hesitant. They eventually warmed up to the idea, however, and the resulting agreement brought seven new stores to their chain, as well as the resources of several deep-pocketed venture capital firms. OfficeMax, for its part, only had to give up two of the ten seats on its board.

By the summer of 1990, following the Office World merger, OfficeMax was operating a total of 30 stores. After once again going back to its investment group, the company was banking an impressive $33 million in cash. The cost-conscious founders finally decided that it was time to move into a better headquarters facility, one that featured separate men's and women's restrooms, for example. The rest of the money was put to use funding an aggressive expansion plan that would, the company hoped, add 20 more stores to the chain within a year. Despite healthy gains and a bright future, however, a development in 1990 threatened to quash OfficeMax and its competitors.

Feuer and Hurwitz had perceived the threat years earlier. Finally, their fears were realized when mass discount merchant Kmart announced plans to roll out an office supplies superstore dubbed Office Square. OfficeMax executives realized that the new venture, backed by Kmart's massive bank account and retailing savvy, could literally crush start-ups such as OfficeMax. Feuer and Hurwitz, refusing to ignore the threat, began trying to initiate talks with Kmart. The talks centered on an outright purchase of OfficeMax by Kmart. Feuer and Hurwitz, however, were hesitant to give up control of their company. The two companies finally agreed to a plan whereby Kmart invested $40 million in OfficeMax in return for a 22 percent ownership share.

EARLY NINETIES: LIFE WITH KMART

Fortunately for the founders, Kmart turned out to be OfficeMax's greatest ally, rather than its worst enemy. Feuer and Hurwitz were allowed to maintain total control of the company, and Kmart smartly became a silent financial partner. With its new bankroll, OfficeMax intensified its expansion efforts and quickly met the goals that it had set with Kmart executives. Both companies were so pleased with the arrangement that Kmart decided to up the ante in 1991. It purchased 92 percent of the outstanding shares from the original investors and became the owner of OfficeMax. The net result was that OfficeMax was sitting on a mountain of cash and had virtually no long-term debt. Furthermore, Feuer and Hurwitz were still firmly in control of the company.

The deal could not have been sweeter for Office-Max, which was suddenly positioned to launch a bid to dominate the national business supplies superstore segment. That was exactly what the company did. During the next 18 months the company began opening new OfficeMax outlets at a feverish pitch. More importantly, the company purchased the 46-store Office Warehouse chain and the 105-outlet Bizmart chain, and eventually integrated those stores into the OfficeMax organization. As a result of store additions and acquisitions, OfficeMax was operating 328 stores in 38 states, coast-to-coast, by the end of 1993. Sales for that year climbed to $1.41 billion, from just $245 million in 1991, while net income increased to $1.08 billion (OfficeMax's first positive annual net income).

Although cash was a major ingredient in the company's recipe for growth, its shrewd operating strategy was just as important for success. Indeed, throughout its expansion, OfficeMax maintained its customer focus. It also adapted the format of its stores to capitalize on the huge growth in the small and home-based business markets, which became the dominant industry trend during the early 1990s. In addition, OfficeMax managed to implement cutting-edge information and distribution systems that allowed such top mega-discounters as Kmart and Wal-Mart to thrive. By the mid-1990s, OfficeMax was efficiently operating nearly 400 stores and several distribution centers, and stocking more than 6,000 brand-name office products,

business machines, computers and related electronic devices, software, and other goods.

With Kmart's financial backing and the OfficeMax team's successful operating strategy, the company sustained its growth rate in 1994. By the end of the year, the company was operating 388 stores in 40 states and Puerto Rico. Importantly, the end of 1994 marked a huge change for the company. Late in that year its well-heeled parent, Kmart, sold out. Kmart's investors had been pressuring Kmart to sell its side interests and refocus its resources on the hyper-competitive general merchandise discount industry. Kmart's directors stooped to the pressure and decided to bail out of the OfficeMax venture. OfficeMax completed the largest initial public offering (IPO) in the history of the retail chain industry when it sold 35.7 million shares at a price of $19 per share, bringing in the $678 million that allowed Kmart to reduce its ownership interest. A subsequent offering in July 1995 entirely eliminated Kmart's ownership share.

GOING PUBLIC WITHOUT KMART

Thus, after growing by leaps and bounds with the help of Kmart, OfficeMax was suddenly on its own again as a publicly held enterprise. For 1994, OfficeMax posted $1.81 billion in sales, $30.4 million of which was netted as income. As Hurwitz had removed himself from day-to-day operations at OfficeMax following the stock sale, Feuer stepped up expansion plans in 1995, hoping to boost OfficeMax's 11 percent share of the U.S. office supplies superstore market. By 1995, OfficeMax became the second largest business superstore in the nation (behind Office Depot), and was gunning for the number one slot.

Meanwhile, OfficeMax launched related ventures beginning in 1994, including FurnitureMax, a chain of discount office furniture stores, and CopyMax, a chain of copy-service centers. Both of the new store concepts were designed to be connected to existing OfficeMax stores and to serve as add-on profit centers. In 1995, the company debuted its TriMax stores, which consisted of an OfficeMax superstore flanked by a FurnitureMax and a CopyMax. The company also initiated a computer service called OfficeMax Online (which later became OfficeMax.com) that was designed to enable customers to purchase OfficeMax products online from their home or office computers.

A period of tremendous expansion for OfficeMax began in 1996. At its annual shareholder's meeting, the company announced a major expansion into Southern California, an area where its rivals, Office Depot and

Staples, were well established. Additionally, the company made its first international foray by opening a superstore in Mexico City with venture partner Grupo Oprimax. This store was followed by more store openings in Mexico, and the company's success in that country was phenomenal. CEO Feuer told *Discount Merchandiser* in 1998, "We went in with very modest expectations, but they have been more fully realized than anticipated. The volume in Mexican stores is equal or better than in the U.S." The company also began testing a smaller format store called Office PDQ, aimed at urban markets, and formed a joint venture with Jusco Co., Ltd., to open OfficeMax stores in Japan.

During 1997, Staples and Office Depot attempted a merger that was ultimately blocked by the Federal Trade Commission (FTC). While its two main competitors were focused on merger plans and court battles, Office-Max took the opportunity to expand even further, opening a total of 150 stores in 1997 alone. This growth earned the company, for a time, the long-coveted number one position in the market. Despite the large number of openings, the company still suffered a gap in sales. Even though it had the most stores, the company's sales volume fell below $4 billion in 1997, as compared with Office Depot's $6.7 billion and Staples' $5.2 billion. Feuer attributed the gap to the company's relative youth in the market. He planned to make up the numbers in part by focusing on the copy center portion of the business, which had a very high profit margin. In 1998 the company turned its focus to increasing the productivity of its store base, primarily by reducing its inventory of computers, an area that had been disastrous in terms of profitability.

DIFFICULT TIMES

By 2000, the company had eliminated computers completely, instead forming a partnership with Gateway. Under their agreement, Gateway would install Gateway stores inside OfficeMax superstores. The Gateway operations would be staffed by Gateway employees. Gateway also invested $50 million in OfficeMax. However, the deal was scrapped in 2001, with Hewlett-Packard replacing the flagging Gateway as OfficeMax's computer supplier.

The year 2000 was challenging for OfficeMax. The company's profits continued to fail to keep pace with its expansion, and the company underwent a major restructuring, which Feurer called "deliberate suffering." It installed a new integrated computer system and revamped its distribution system, a move that it hoped would ultimately save the company several million dollars a year. It also changed its purchasing policies to be more in line with what its customers actually bought,

rather than what vendors provided incentives for it to sell.

These measures helped, but in 2001 the company was faced with the decision to close stores. In January of that year, OfficeMax announced plans to close 50 stores, resulting in the loss of 1,200 jobs, and take a one-time after-tax charge of $69 million. The company ended the year with a $133.2 million loss.

Difficult times continued for OfficeMax in 2002. In the midst of tough economic conditions, the company shuttered another 29 stores and began to implement cost-cutting measures. That year, OfficeMax saw its revenues fall to $4.6 billion, down from $5.1 billion the previous year, and it recorded a loss of $309.5 million.

By early 2003 conditions had improved at OfficeMax. The company returned to profitability, and adopted more of a retail format at its stores, as opposed to a warehouse approach. A $37.5 million initiative to spruce up 250 of its older stores also was announced, and plans were made to expand the profitable CopyMax service. OfficeMax once again turned its eye toward expansion, and revealed plans to open between ten and 15 stores. In addition to new domestic sites, the company looked toward international markets, including Mexico.

ACQUIRED BY BOISE CASCADE

A major development unfolded in August 2003, at which time the paper and lumber products company Boise Cascade Corp. agreed to pay $1.15 billion for OfficeMax. The deal was concluded in December, and Boise Cascade added OfficeMax to its Boise Office Solutions group. OfficeMax remained the third-leading industry player, but was in a much better position to compete with Office Depot and Staples. Namely, the company benefited from the addition of Boise's commercial business, while Boise benefited from Office-Max's retail operations.

Progress continued with the company's effort to transform its stores. In early 2004 Boise Office Solutions revealed plans to close some 45 OfficeMax locations by the year's end. However, 200 locations were slated for remodeling, and about 15 were targeted for relocation. In addition, a new 3,000-square-foot concept store called OfficeMax Express opened in Chicago.

Boise's transformation from a paper and lumber company into a pure-play office supply chain was completed during the last half of 2004. In August the company announced the $3.7 billion sale of its name; its headquarters in Boise, Idaho; plants, pulp/paper mills, and distribution centers; and more than 2.3 million acres of land to Boise Cascade LLC, a new enterprise that had been established by the Chicago-based equity firm Madison Dearborn Partners.

Following the completion of the deal, Boise Cascade Corp. changed its name to OfficeMax Incorporated on November 1, 2004. Former Boise Chairman and CEO George J. Harad was named as OfficeMax's executive chairman. In addition, former Boise Office Solutions President and CEO Chris Milliken was elected to those same positions at OfficeMax. Former OfficeMax President and Chief Operating Officer Gary Peterson, who had been serving as president of Boise Office Solutions' retail operations, continued in the same capacity. In addition, Michael Rowsey was appointed as president of the company's contract business.

2004–07: MAKING IMPROVEMENTS

OfficeMax experienced difficult times during the middle of the first decade of the 2000s. In late 2004 a supplier's allegations regarding irregular billing led to an internal investigation of the company's accounting practices. Ultimately, OfficeMax terminated six employees in connection with a $3.3 million wrongful billing scandal that had been going on for two years. The situation required the company to restate its income for the first three quarters of 2004, and delayed its fourth-quarter earnings report. In the wake of these difficulties, and coupled with weak financial performance, Gary Peterson and Chief Financial Officer Brian Anderson left the organization in January 2005, and Chris Milliken resigned in February.

In early 2005 OfficeMax adopted a new name for its CopyMax business, which became OfficeMax Print and Document Services. Locations were planned for inclusion in all 50 of the new retail stores that OfficeMax planned to open by the year's end. In addition, a presence for the business was slated for OfficeMax's distribution centers, in order to handle print jobs for large contract customers.

In May 2005, former ShopKo CEO Sam Duncan was named as OfficeMax's CEO. Following three quarters of losses, the company quickly moved forward with efforts to improve the situation. In January 2006, OfficeMax announced it would shutter 110 U.S. stores, five Canadian locations, as well as a building materials factory. However, 70 new stores also were planned, pushing the company's domestic store total to 887.

In early 2006 OfficeMax announced a $100 million turnaround initiative that called for a stronger focus on small business customers, its profitable Print and Docu-

ment Services business, as well as its ink-refill program. The company also restructured its contract business by consolidating the management structure of the division's sales force.

OfficeMax's turnaround efforts proved to be successful. By October, the value of the company's shares had increased nearly 90 percent since the beginning of the year. Progress continued in 2007 as the company made in-store improvements, such as the addition of digital signage in high-traffic areas. OfficeMax also forged a partnership with Bermuda-based VistaPrint, which allowed customers to design business cards and other items at OfficeMax locations and have orders shipped to the store or their home.

AN UNCERTAIN FUTURE

In 2008 OfficeMax announced a partnership with Safeway Inc., in which about 300 of its private-label school and office supply products would be offered in more than 1,600 Safeway stores. By the year's end, OfficeMax operated a chain of more than 1,000 stores and employed a workforce of more than 30,000 people.

Following other cost-cutting efforts taken throughout the year, in December the company suspended payment of quarterly cash dividends on its common stock. Chairman and CEO Sam Duncan estimated this would save OfficeMax about $45 million annually. While the future remained to be seen, the company's efforts gave it at least a fair chance of weathering the storm.

Dave Mote
Updated, Lisa Whipple; Paul R. Greenland

PRINCIPAL OPERATING UNITS

OfficeMax Contract; OfficeMax Retail.

PRINCIPAL COMPETITORS

Corporate Express US Inc.; Office Depot Inc.; Staples Inc.

FURTHER READING

"As Staples, Office Depot Battle FTC, OfficeMax Expands Its Concepts," *Discount Store News,* July 7, 1997, p. 80.

Baird, Kristen, "OfficeMax Plan May Supply 900 More Local Jobs," *Crain's Cleveland Business,* July 31, 1995, p. 1.

Bartalos, Greg, "'Til the Cows Come Home," *Barron's,* June 11, 2001, p. 35.

Berdon, Caroline, "Great Expectations: As Sam Duncan Swings to the Rescue at OfficeMax, the Industry Collates into Two Schools of Thought on a Prospective Turnaround at the Company," *Office Products International,* June 2005.

"Big Name in Office Game Is Diversity," *Discount Store News,* August 9, 1999, p. 50.

"Boise Exits Paper; Closes $3.7-Bil Deal," *Pulp & Paper,* December 1, 2004.

Brandt, John R., and Michael Feuer, "Taking It to the MAX: How Did Michael Feuer Take a Start-Up Company to $1.5 Billion in Revenue in Just Five Years?" *Corporate Cleveland,* September 1993, p. 16.

Carpenter, Dave, "OfficeMax Chief Resigns in Scandal," *Associated Press,* February 15, 2005.

Cotlier, Moira, "OfficeMax to Close 50 Stores," *Catalog Age,* March 15, 2001, p. 7.

Einhorn, Cheryl Strauss, "Maximum Markdown," *Barron's,* December 18, 2000, pp. 23–24.

———, "Promises Kept," *Barron's,* February 5, 2001, p. 14.

Garvey, Martin J., "Gateway Takes Aim at the Business PC Market," *Informationweek,* February 28, 2000, p. 30.

"Gateway to the Future," *Discount Merchandiser,* April 2000, p. 23.

Hanover, Dan, "Honey, I—Shrunk—the Store," *Chain Store Age,* January 1999, pp. 40–45.

Harrison, Kimberly P., "OfficeMax to Launch New Unit: Company to Test Concept of Furniture Showroom," *Crain's Cleveland Business,* November 14, 1994, p. 1.

Howes, Daniel, "Kmart Plans to Sell Rest of Stake in Office-Max," *Detroit News,* June 27, 1995, p. E1.

"HP Replaces Gateway at OfficeMax," *Client Server News,* May 21, 2001.

Johnson, Jay L., "The FTC Shuffle: Two Losers, One Winner," *Discount Merchandiser,* August 1997, p. 19.

———, "OfficeMax: On a Fast Track," *Discount Merchandiser,* March 1998, pp. 32–34.

Kemp, Ted, "Staples Chases Small Biz," *Internetweek,* November 13, 2000, p. 11.

King, Angela G., "OfficeMax Stock Shines for Openers," *Detroit News,* November 3, 1994, p. E1.

Liebeck, Laura, "Staples, OfficeMax Look Abroad," *Discount Store News,* January 6, 1997, pp. 6, 88.

Marcial, Gene G., "Officemax May Be Hunter—or Prey," *Business Week,* November 25, 1996, p. 154.

"Market Slows, but Still Grows," *DSN Retailing Today,* August 7, 2000, p. 40.

Nottingham, Nancy, "Office Superstore Opens Today on West End," *Billings Gazette,* June 15, 1995, p. D5.

"Office Superstore Chains Plan 9 Million Sq. Ft. of New Space in '98," *Discount Store News,* March 23, 1998, pp. 6, 67.

"Office Superstore Expansion in High Gear," *Discount Store News,* October 20, 1997, pp. 5, 77.

"Office Supply Chains Foresee Continued Expansion," *Discount Store News,* July 13, 1998, p. 86.

"OfficeMax Boosts Expansion," *Chain Store Age,* November 1996, p. 43.

"OfficeMax Plans California Blitz," *Discount Store News,* June 3, 1996, p. 3.

"OfficeMax Reveals Plans at Shareholders Meeting," *Discount Store News,* May 25, 1998, p. 3.

"OfficeMax to Close 50 Stores, Cut 1,200 Jobs," *Futures World News,* May 7, 2001.

"OfficeMax to Offer On-Line Custom Printing," *DSN Retailing Today,* May 21, 2001, p. 6.

Pascale, Moira, "The Price Is Right ... or Is It?" *Catalog Age,* February 1999, p. 6.

Radcliff, Deborah, "Back-to-School.com," *Computerworld,* August 23, 1999, p. 40.

Russell, John M., "OfficeMax Breaks Loose," *Small Business News–Cleveland,* September 1994, p. 16.

Shingler, Dan, "Hurwitz Trading Paper for Pillows," *Crain's Cleveland Business,* April 11, 1994, p. 1.

"Speculation over OfficeMax Suitor Points to Staples, Hints at Antitrust," *Discount Store News,* October 26, 1998, p. 6.

"Staples to Sell 63 Units to OfficeMax, FTC to Decide on Acquisition," *Discount Store News,* April 1, 1997, p. 6.

Swanson, Sandra, "Office-Supply Vendors to Offer E-learning," *Informationweek,* August 21, 2000, p. 40.

Thompson, Chris, "OfficeMax Sees Profits Stack Up for Pending IPO," *Crain's Cleveland Business,* September 12, 1994, p. 3.

Troy, Mike, "Accessories Rise to Demands of Evolving Office Environs," *Discount Store News,* April 5, 1999, pp. 19–20.

———, "'98 Writing Instrument Sales Script Strong Outlook for '99," *Discount Store News,* February 22, 1999, pp. 41–44.

———, "Office Suppliers Scurry to Revamp Financials," *Discount Store News,* October 25, 1999, pp. 5, 63.

———, "OfficeMax Is the Biggest, Now It Has to Prove It's the Best," *Discount Store News,* November 17, 1997, pp. 31–39.

———, "OfficeMax Looks for Improvement Before It's Too Late," *DSN Retailing Today,* November 6, 2000, pp. 37–38.

———, "OfficeMax Names Peterson President, Gateway In-Store Pact First Challenge," *Discount Store News,* March 6, 2000, pp. 5, 87.

———, "OfficeMax Reorganizes," *DSN Retailing Today,* March 19, 2001, pp. 1, 8.

———, "OfficeMax Unveils New Prototypes," *Discount Store News,* August 10, 1998, pp. 10, 118.

———, "OfficeMax's Actions Draw Shareholder Lawsuits," *DSN Retailing Today,* May 8, 2000, pp. 10, 144.

———, "The Rx That Delivers the Max," *Discount Store News,* December 8, 1997, pp. 75–76.

———, "Softened Office Supply Market Gives Big Three Cause for Pause," *DSN Retailing Today,* April 2, 2001, pp. 8, 74.

———, "Store Closings Imminent for Office Superstore Channel," *DSN Retailing Today,* January 1, 2001, p. 6.

Opus Corporation

10350 Bren Road West
Minnetonka, Minnesota 55343
U.S.A.
Telephone: (952) 656-4444
Fax: (952) 656-4529
Web site: http://www.opuscorp.com

Private Company
Incorporated: 1953 as Rauenhorst Construction Company
Employees: 2,000
Sales: $2.2 billion (2007)
NAICS: 236220 Commercial and Institutional Building Construction; 236210 Industrial Building Construction; 237210 Land Subdivision

■ ■ ■

Opus Corporation ranks as one of the largest design-build construction firms in the United States. The company is involved in eight areas of expertise: office, industrial, retail, multifamily, government, institutional, higher education, and sustainable development. Opus ranks as the second largest office developer, the eighth largest industrial developer, and as the tenth largest design-build firm. Through five regional operating companies, the company offers its clients a full range of services, including real estate development, architecture and engineering, construction and project management, property management, and financial services. During its existence, Opus has completed roughly 2,500 projects representing nearly 250 million square feet of space. The company operates 26 offices in 16 states and the Canadian province of Ontario.

SIMPLE BEGINNING, SOLID CONSTRUCTION: FIFTIES AND SIXTIES

Gerald Rauenhorst founded his own construction business in 1953. The farm boy from Olivia, Minnesota, earned a degree in economics from St. Thomas University in St. Paul, and one in civil engineering from Wisconsin's Marquette University, where he taught for a year. Rauenhorst put in another two years as a construction engineer before striking out on his own. His first solo project, which got off the ground thanks to a loan from his brother, was the construction of the Zion Lutheran Church in his hometown of Olivia. Rauenhorst Construction built a number of other buildings for religious organizations during its first years of operation.

In 1957, Rauenhorst moved his business out of the breezeway of his suburban Minneapolis home into a small Bloomington office building and, by renting out the adjacent office space, established a leasing business.

By 1960, Rauenhorst Construction held a solid position in the Twin Cities design-build market. The next year, two significant developments occurred. One was the completion of the company's first "turnkey" project: the design, engineering, and construction of a 157,000-square-foot office and manufacturing facility for The Toro Company. Secondly, the company purchased 200 acres of undeveloped land in the southwest Minneapolis suburbs. Shortly thereafter,

COMPANY PERSPECTIVES

Opus' unique design-build approach teams architects, engineers, construction and property management professionals to devise the best space solution for our clients. Ours is a collaborative approach that allows us to customize projects to meet clients' needs on time and on budget. Our approach provides a single-source solution, taking total responsibility for every aspect of a building project, from concept through final occupancy. Decisions are made in real time, working with clients from the very beginning, simultaneously offering design, testing and pricing options.

Rauenhorst contracted to build Control Data's headquarters on the property and thus launched what would be Rauenhorst Construction's first business park development, Normandale Center Industrial Park. The growing company built itself new headquarters in 1963 and changed its name to Rauenhorst Corporation in 1965.

CHANGING SKYLINES

In the 1970s, Rauenhorst Corporation moved beyond the Twin Cities, opening an office in Milwaukee in 1972 and one in Chicago in 1978. The decade was also marked by the construction of the company's first office tower. Construction volume for the privately held company was an estimated $75 million in 1977. In addition, the regional developer had more than 500 construction projects newly contracted or in progress, totaling in excess of $250 million. The company concentrated its efforts on smaller growing cities spread throughout the eastern two-thirds of the nation.

A 1970s diversification drive was less successful. Rauenhorst tried manufacturing concrete walls and floor planks as well as fiberglass parts, toys, and heavy equipment. Losing money on such efforts, the company dropped the businesses by mid-decade.

Rauenhorst, meanwhile, had another more engaging concept in mind. He envisioned a suburban development encompassing ponds and green space, commercial and industrial facilities, and housing, all served by a dual roadway system to cut down pollution from exhaust fumes. In 1974, the company broke ground on Opus II, located on some prime property at the convergence of three major thoroughfares less than ten miles from the center of downtown Minneapolis.

Just as the ambitious project was started, an economic recession hit, creating some uneasy days. "As it happened, even the timing worked out to Rauenhorst's ultimate advantage. The recession reduced the competition for one thing. And more important, when the upturn finally occurred Opus II was well underway and ready to meet the rejuvenated demand for commercial and industrial building," wrote William Swanson in a 1977 *Corporate Report Minnesota* article.

About the same time, Rauenhorst delegated responsibility for the real estate and construction ends of the business, in effect moving the company from an entrepreneurial to a corporate structure and creating more time for his many family and community commitments.

Rauenhorst Corporation opened an office in Phoenix in 1980. Then, reflecting the ongoing growth and expansion, the company changed its name to Opus Corporation in 1982. The same year, the company moved into new headquarters located in the Opus II mixed-use development project and purchased a Florida-based construction company, creating a presence in the southeastern United States. During the early 1980s, the company reorganized based on its geographic locations.

Opus Corporation's entry into the downtown Minneapolis market in 1984, via the development of a 25-story tower, depicted the changes taking place within the company. "Five years ago, the Minnetonka-based firm was known as a builder of sound if unimaginative, one story warehouse, manufacturing plants and office buildings in suburban Minneapolis, Milwaukee and Chicago," wrote Eric Wieffering for *Minneapolis/St. Paul CityBusiness* in 1985.

The Minneapolis endeavor, the company's first speculative project in a highly competitive downtown market, moved the company into a new submarket, an accomplishment Rauenhorst pointed to with pride. In the early 1970s, architects were both derisive and threatened by Rauenhorst's design-build niche. The developer had moved outside the norm of the day by taking on all elements of a project: finance, design, and construction. By the mid-1980s, according to a 1987 *Minneapolis Star Tribune* profile by Sharon Schmickle, the two ends of the spectrum were "barely distinguishable" from one another. Rauenhorst paid more attention to design, and architectural firms had begun adding engineering and construction services.

"Rauenhorst and company continue to exploit one distinguishing feature of the design-build approach: the ability to move quickly. Opus can start a project as soon as it finds a tenant and finance it later because it maintains lines of credit backed by its real estate assets," wrote Schmickle.

KEY DATES

1953: Gerald Rauenhorst undertakes first solo construction project.

1957: Rauenhorst Construction moves into first headquarters.

1961: Company completes its first "turnkey" project.

1972: Company expands beyond Twin Cities metropolitan area.

1982: Company changes name to Opus Corporation.

1984: Opus builds first office tower in major downtown market.

1988: Company decentralizes into regional operating companies.

1992: Opus is named developer of the year by industry association.

1999: Gerald Rauenhorst's son, Mark Rauenhorst, takes over leadership of the company.

2003: Opus enters the residential housing market.

2007: Mark Rauenhorst is named chairman of Opus.

Founder and Chairman Gerald Rauenhorst was the driving force for his company's long-term growth as others handled the day-to-day operations. William Tobin served as president and COO. He had succeeded longtime employee and board Vice-Chair Robert Dahlin.

MIXED REVIEWS: LATE EIGHTIES THROUGH MID-NINETIES

By 1987, Opus had created more than 1,000 buildings. Annual construction surpassed $200 million, placing the company among the top 100 in *Engineering News-Record's* ranking of leading U.S. contractors.

Opus decentralized in 1988, forming a holding company, Opus U.S. Corp., for the regional operating companies. Mark Rauenhorst, son of the founder, was named president and COO of the holding company in 1990. The younger Rauenhorst joined Opus in 1982, after earning a degree in finance and an M.B.A. and gaining seven years of work experience outside the family business. Opus further decentralized operations in 1990 by creating Opus Architects and Engineers, Inc., as a subsidiary of Opus U.S. Corp. The entity provided architectural and engineering services to affiliate companies.

"Rauenhorst describes the overall operation as 'opportunistic,' adding that 'we are always looking for the right opportunity for development,'" wrote Barbara Knox for *Corporate Report Minnesota* in 1990. Speculative industrial development represented a major piece of Opus U.S. Corp.'s business. Keith Bednarowski served as chairman and CEO of the company, which was based in Minnesota but operated primarily outside the state.

Opus weathered a late 1980s industry downturn and in 1991 ranked among the top 15 developers in the United States, producing a combined construction volume of more than $300 million. The company received its industry's highest honor in 1992: Developer of the Year by the National Association of Industrial Office Properties (NAIOP).

Nevertheless, Opus faced challenges in the early 1990s. Internally, the company was moving toward the succession of one generation of leadership to the next. Three of Gerald Rauenhorst's sons, including Mark, held top management positions. Externally, the Tampa and Phoenix markets were in a downturn, prompting workforce layoffs in those regions. A new affiliate, Opus Investments, Inc., was formed to acquire, develop, and remarket distressed properties. The Chicago market, on the other hand, was growing, and Opus had long-established customers and a high rate of repeat business.

In 1995, the *National Real Estate Investor* ranked Opus the nation's largest developer, based on 8.3 million square feet under construction nationwide. Gerald Rauenhorst, over four decades, had guided his business from a one-wheelbarrow operation to a national design-build and real estate concern. His accomplishment was no small feat in an industry hit by four or five downturns during his many years in business.

In fact, during the 1990s Opus was still feeling the pinch of the late 1980s Minneapolis office glut. Wieffering wrote for *Corporate Report Minnesota* in 1995, "Gerald Rauenhorst made his name and fortune in the suburbs southwest of Minneapolis by guessing where the people were going to be, and buying land in advance of their arrival. Once he brought his company, Opus Corporation, to downtown Minneapolis in the early 1980s, he applied the same strategy. Though the results have so far been mixed, it's one reason why Opus owns more potential development sites in downtown Minneapolis than anyone else."

In 1998, Opus lost a two-year legal battle with the city of Minneapolis over some of that property. The city condemned an Opus-owned site on the Nicollet Mall for a subsidized development slated to be built by a competitor.

Concurrently, Gerald Rauenhorst prepared for his eventual exit from the business, something he had been planning for since the mid-1980s. In addition to bringing in the best personnel he could find, Rauenhorst added four outsiders to the seven member board of the holding company and relinquished more control to the management team lead by Bednarowski. In a 1996 *Star Tribune* article, Sally Apgar reported that Bednarowski was "also charged, say insiders, with helping to educate the next generation."

CONSTRUCTION AHEAD: LATE NINETIES INTO THE 21ST CENTURY

As a merchant builder, Opus had sold almost everything it built. During 1998, the company changed gears, raising nearly $250 million from investors for two real estate investment funds. "'It's an unbelievable mechanism,'" Tom Crowley of Chicago-based Heitman Financial told Dirk Deyoung in a 1999 *Minneapolis/St. Paul CityBusiness* article. "Opus is already one of the most respected, well-capitalized developers in the nation. Now it's building a 'great machine' that can efficiently swallow, digest and eventually divest the huge volume that it manufactures, he said. 'It's a perfect strategy for Opus.'"

On another front, Opus pushed to win more national accounts. Local or regional projects compromised much of the company's business due to the limitations of its decentralized structure. A national accounts group was created in the late 1990s to pursue clients, pull together resources from the regional offices, and assist the regional companies in taking current customers to the multiple development level.

Gerald Rauenhorst retired as chairman of the company in 2000, although he remained on the board of directors. Bednarowski succeeded him as chair, and Mark Rauenhorst was named president and CEO. *National Real Estate Investor* had named Gerald Rauenhorst one of the 40 most influential people in real estate in 1998, and over the years, Rauenhorst had received frequent recognition for his principled conduct in business and for his contributions to his community.

SECOND GENERATION OF LEADERSHIP BEGINS IN 1999

Mark Rauenhorst began building his legacy as he led his father's company to its 50th anniversary and spearheaded the company's growth during the beginning of its second half-century of business. During his first decade in charge, Rauenhorst took control of a company that had yet to generate $1 billion in annual revenue and guided it past the $2 billion mark, quashing any

fears of a problematic transfer of power from father to son. The successful start to his era of leadership earned the full confidence of Opus's executive ranks, including his father's esteem. In 2007, Rauenhorst replaced Bednarowski as chairman, giving him the three most powerful titles in the organization: president, chief executive officer, and chairman.

DIVERSIFICATION FUELS GROWTH

Rauenhorst fueled Opus's financial growth by expanding geographically and by steering the company into new areas of construction. The company's physical expansion occurred primarily during his first five years as chief executive officer. Opus opened eight new offices during the period, establishing a physical presence in California, Kansas, Missouri, Pennsylvania, and in the Canadian province of Ontario. His expansion into new areas of construction faltered on some occasions, notably the company's entry into the military housing market in 2003. "We seriously thought we could do a good job in that sector and use some of our core competencies," Rauenhorst reflected in an August 16, 2007 interview with *Finance and Commerce Daily,* "but after we got into it, we learned a little more and found out it wasn't the best fit and stepped back."

Opus recorded considerably more success in its entry into the residential and sustainable development markets. The company began focusing on the residential building market in 2003. "It's a bid deal for us," Rauenhorst noted in the October 13, 2003 edition of the *Star Tribune.* Examples of its first projects included a $110 million, 327-unit, condominium complex in downtown Minneapolis and a 39-story, 285-unit condominium development also located in downtown Minneapolis. The company's sustainable development efforts, which focused on highly efficient, environmentally friendly projects, resulted in more than three million square feet of development space certified by Leadership in Energy and Environmental Design (LEED), a green building rating system developed by the U.S. Green Building Council. Prominent projects completed by the company's sustainable development team included a condominium tower in Seattle, a six-story office building in Addison, Texas, and a nine-story office building in Washington, D.C.

50 YEARS AND BEYOND

Looking ahead, Rauenhorst envisioned continued expansion. "Our growth plans are aggressive in light of the long-term, sustainable kinds of growth," he explained in the August 16, 2007 edition of *Finance and*

Commerce Daily Newspaper. "We're probably going to add a few cities, but not as many cities as we did during that time period of eight to 10 years ago—but we're going to see growth in the cities that we're already in." He added, "Our hottest markets now are in Arizona and Southern California; Washington, D.C., is very busy and Chicago has seen a strong renaissance for us." The one uncertainty clouding the company's future was the bleak economic forecast at the end of the decade, portending deleterious conditions that would test Rauenhorst's leadership skills as he attempted to maintain Opus's ranking as one of the country's largest builders.

Kathleen Peippo
Updated, Jeffrey L. Covell

PRINCIPAL SUBSIDIARIES

Opus East L.L.C.; Opus North Corporation.; Opus Northwest L.L.C.; Opus South Corporation; Opus West Corporation; Opus Architects & Engineers, Inc.; Opus Properties, L.L.C.; Opus Northwest Management, L.L.C.; Opus North Management Corporation; Opus West Management Corporation; O.R.E. Development Corporation (Canada).

PRINCIPAL COMPETITORS

The Structure Tone Organization; Lincoln Property Company; Brookfield Properties Corporation.

FURTHER READING

Apgar, Sally, "Opus Corp. Heading Down a New Path: Multiple Transitions Pending," *Minneapolis Star Tribune,* October 19, 1992, p. 1D.

———, "Setting the Stage," *Minneapolis Star Tribune,* February 5, 1996, p. 1D.

Bloomfield, Craig, "Opus Targets National Accounts," *Commercial Property News,* November 1, 1999.

Deyoung, Dirk, "Opus Raises $250M As Part of Strategic Shift," *Minneapolis/St. Paul CityBusiness,* January 8, 1999, pp. 1+.

Diaz, Kevin, "Minnesota Supreme Court Lets City's Target Store Deal Stand," *Minneapolis Star Tribune,* November 3, 1998, p. 1A.

Knox, Barbara, "Mark Rauenhorst: Moving Up in His Father's Company," *Corporate Report Minnesota,* September 1990, p. 82.

Levy, Melissa, "Gerald Rauenhorst Retires As Chairman of Opus," *Minneapolis Star Tribune,* April 11, 2000, p. 3D.

Messelt, Todd, "Rauenhorst Looking to the Future at Minnesota-Based Opus Corp.," *Finance and Commerce Daily Newspaper,* August 16, 2007.

Mundale, Charles I., "The Opus Culture," *Corporate Report Minnesota,* January 1983, p. 154.

St. Anthony, Neal, "With Downtown Condos, Opus Turns to Residential Development," *Minneapolis Star Tribune,* October 13, 2003, p. 1D.

Schmickle, Sharon, "Opus Chief's Business Dealings Reflect the Man," *Minneapolis Star Tribune,* August 31, 1987, p. 1M.

Sundstrom, Ingrid, "New Opus President Says Firm Will Continue to Expand," *Minneapolis Star Tribune,* March 25, 1991, p. 2D.

Swanson, William, "Rauenhorst's Song of the Suburbs," *Corporate Report Minnesota,* July 1977, pp. 29–31, 64–68.

Wieffering, Eric, "Opus' Interests in Downtown Development," *Corporate Report Minnesota,* February 1995, pp. 8–10.

———, "Opus Makes Its Mark on Downtown," *Minneapolis/St. Paul CityBusiness,* August 28, 1985, pp. 34, 36.

———, "Opus Not Telling Plans for Powers," *Minneapolis/St. Paul CityBusiness,* August 28, 1985, p. 34.

Parallel Petroleum Corporation

1004 North Big Spring, Suite 400
Midland, Texas 79701
U.S.A.
Telephone: (432) 684-3727
Fax: (432) 684-3905
Web site: http://www.parallel-petro.com

Public Company
Incorporated: 1979
Employees: 43
Sales: $116.03 million (2007)
Stock Exchanges: NASDAQ
Ticker Symbol: PLLL
NAICS: 211111 Crude Petroleum and Natural Gas
    Extraction

■ ■ ■

Parallel Petroleum Corporation is an independent oil and gas company operating primarily in the Permian Basin in west Texas and New Mexico, the Fort Worth Basin in northern Texas, and the onshore Gulf Coast area in southern Texas. Parallel Petroleum focuses on acquiring and developing mature oil and natural gas reserves. To a lesser extent, the company explores for new oil and natural gas reserves. Parallel Petroleum has proven reserves of 43.8 million barrels of oil equivalent.

ORIGINS

During Parallel Petroleum's first 30 years of business, it never strayed far from its two core areas of operation. At various times in its history, the company ventured beyond its principal areas of activity, extending its presence into Oklahoma, Utah, and Colorado, but it mainly restricted its exploratory and drilling efforts to the Permian Basin in western Texas and southeastern New Mexico and the Yegua/Frio/Wilcox gas trend in southeastern Texas.

Of the two areas, the Permian Basin initially was more important to Parallel Petroleum, serving as its headquarters location and its only region of activity. The Permian Basin, which included a 75,000-square-mile region, ranked as one of the world's thickest deposits of rocks from the Permian geologic period. During the 1930s and 1940s, when the Permian Basin enjoyed its most productive period as a source of oil and natural gas, it supplied one-fourth of the world's oil supply, its acreage littered with drilling rigs, oil derricks, and infrastructure to support the frenzy of activity taking place within the basin. The economic stimulus provided by the exploration and drilling efforts created scores of boomtowns in west Texas, as thriving communities emerged overnight to support the oil companies flocking to the Permian Basin. The wealth engendered by the rush to find oil spread across more than two dozen counties, but two locations more than any others came to serve as the headquarters for oil production activities in the basin, Odessa and Midland. The Midland Basin, the largest component of the Permian Basin, became the home of a new oil and gas company in 1979, a small, independent venture name Parallel Petroleum.

When Parallel Petroleum opened its offices in Midland in November 1979, decades had passed since oil production activity in the Permian Basin had peaked.

COMPANY PERSPECTIVES

Our primary objective is to increase the value of our common stock by increasing reserves, production, and net cash provided by operating activities. We attempt to reduce our financial risks by dedicating a smaller portion of our capital to high risk projects, while reserving the majority of our available capital for exploitation, development drilling and acquisition opportunities. Positions in long-lived oil and natural gas reserves are given priority over properties that might generate more net cash provided by operating activities in the early years of production, but which have shorter reserve lives.

Major discoveries were rare, but the company's strategy did not hinge on finding new sources of oil. Instead, Parallel Petroleum focused its efforts on generating drilling prospects for producing properties, attempting, in essence, to best the efforts of a property's previous owner. The company was small; a dozen years after its founding, Parallel Petroleum employed five full-time workers and generated less than $3 million in annual sales. Yet its size did not factor into its ability to achieve success. The company intended to acquire previously developed properties and, through technology, efficiency, and expertise, extract oil and gas from properties deemed expendable by larger energy companies. Parallel Petroleum, in essence, intended to live off the scraps of others, and it found decades worth of viable opportunities in the once-fecund Permian Basin.

LONGTIME LEADER: LARRY C. OLDHAM

For nearly 15 years, Parallel Petroleum remained focused principally on the Permian Basin, primarily concentrating on crude oil drilling. The region was familiar ground to the company's most influential leader, the only founder who remained with the company after its fledgling years. Larry C. Oldham, in his mid-20s when he helped organize Parallel Petroleum, earned his undergraduate degree in business from West Texas State University four years before becoming Midland's newest entrepreneur. He spent his first year after college working for the giant accounting and consulting firm KPMG Peat Marwick before serving a three-year stint at Dorchester Gas Company. When Parallel Petroleum was founded, Oldham became a director of the company and served as its executive vice-president. He was named

president of the company in October 1994, one year after Parallel Petroleum made a definitive shift in its strategic focus.

FROM EXPLOITATION TO EXPLORATION

Although the company did not end its involvement in the Permian Basin the year before Oldham took the helm, it did turn its attention to the southeast. In 1993, the company entered the Yegua/Frio/Wilcox gas trend, located in Jackson and Wharton counties between Houston and Victoria. Parallel Petroleum began acquiring 3-D seismic data pertaining to the gas trend, data that it scrutinized before plotting its most prudent moves for exploration and drilling activities. It represented a riskier move than its involvement in the Permian Basin—any time an oil and gas company added the word *exploration* to its business strategy the odds of failure ratcheted up—but Parallel Petroleum moved headlong into the "play." The drilling program in Yegua/Frio/Wilcox commenced in 1994, the year Oldham was named president, and during the next five years the company acquired 800 square miles of 3-D seismic data covering the region. Based on its study of the data, the company participated in more than 160 gross wells in Yegua/Frio/Wilcox, an aspect of its business that overshadowed all others, becoming its "main bread and butter," according to a Parallel Petroleum spokesperson quoted in the August 2001 issue of *Oil and Gas Investor*.

More willing to take on risk, the company also exhibited greater ambition than it had during the 1980s. In 1999, Parallel Petroleum formed a joint-venture company with Baytech Inc., naming the subsidiary First Permian LLC. Through First Permian, Parallel Petroleum strengthened its position close to home, using the joint-venture company (30.6 percent owned by Parallel Petroleum) to acquire assets in the Permian Basin owned by Firm Oil and Chemical Company. The acquisition included interests in properties, both operated and non-operated, that gave First Permian a stake in more than 800 wells in the basin.

A CHANGE IN STRATEGY IN 2002

As Oldham guided Parallel Petroleum into the 21st century, he ordered a significant change in the company's operating strategy. In the wake of his decision, the company recorded the greatest growth in its history, increasing its proven reserves by a factor of 13 and recording a tenfold increase in its annual revenues. The impressive growth occurred after Oldham decided to scale back the company's exploration efforts in Yegua/Frio/Wilcox, where Parallel Petroleum had drilled four dry holes between October 2001 and mid-2002. The

KEY DATES

1979: Parallel Petroleum is incorporated.
1993: The company shifts its focus to the Yegua/Frio/Wilcox gas trend.
1999: Parallel Petroleum helps establish First Permian LLC.
2002: The company lessens its involvement in the Yegua/Frio/Wilcox gas trend and concentrates on acquiring mature properties in the Permian Basin.
2007: After six years of acquiring properties in the Permian Basin, Parallel Petroleum's annual revenues climb above the $100 million mark for the first time.

decision ended the company's decade-long emphasis on the Yegua/Frio/Wilcox gas trend and returned its focus to its historical roots in the venerable Permian Basin.

The change in strategy was facilitated, in part, by significant changes at the company's joint-venture subsidiary, First Permian. The properties purchased by First Permian in 1999, 22 producing properties for $92 million, were sold in April 2002. Oldham used the proceeds from the sale of the properties to fund Parallel Petroleum's expansion in west Texas, employing an "acquire-and-exploit" strategy that would see it purchase properties and enhance their production. "We are in a mature basin, but maturity is in the eye of the beholder," Oldham said in the June 24, 2002 edition of *Odessa American,* announcing Parallel Petroleum's push into the Permian Basin. "I still believe that we, as independents, are definitely in a growth industry as far as buying older properties and enhancing those properties, especially since all the larger companies are selling their assets and laying off all their people."

Oldham used the money from the First Permian sale to pay for the expansion in west Texas and he used First Permian personnel to help orchestrate the expansion. Nearly tripling its payroll, Parallel Petroleum hired ten new employees, eight of whom were executives at First Permian involved in the enhancement, exploitation, and drilling of First Permian's oil and gas properties.

2002–08: RAPID EXPANSION FUELS FINANCIAL GROWTH

With a fresh supply of cash and a new team of executives, Parallel Petroleum embarked on what would be the most aggressive acquisition campaign in its history. The tone of the campaign was set by the company's first deal, the purchase of producing properties in Andrews County in the Permian Basin. Owned by Texland Petroleum for the previous eight years, the properties consisted of 128 wells on nine contiguous leases covering 3,640 acres. Parallel Petroleum paid $46.1 million for working interests in the properties that ranged from 22 percent to 85 percent. The acquisition more than tripled the company's reserves, increasing reserves from 3.5 million barrels of oil equivalent to 12.7 million barrels of oil equivalent.

Further acquisitions followed, as Oldham focused on the Fullerton Field in Andrews County. He referred to the Fullerton Field as Parallel Petroleum's "cornerstone asset," in the October 12, 2004 edition of *Odessa American,* saying, "that's our cookie cutter." In September 2004, he purchased $15.3 million worth of properties in the Fullerton Field from Chevron USA. The following month he paid Kaiser-Francis Oil Co. $5.6 million to increase Parallel Petroleum's interests in the Lineberry and Grogan leases in the Fullerton Field, by which point the company had spent $67 million during the previous two years on oil and gas properties primarily in Andrews County.

Oldham pressed forward in the Permian Basin, methodically building up the company's presence in Andrews County. In October 2005, he negotiated a purchase agreement with ten private parties to acquire producing properties in Andrews and Gaines counties in a 6,500-acre area. For $44.5 million, he gained 6.4 million barrels of oil equivalent, which represented a 29 percent increase in Parallel Petroleum's reserves. For 2006, Oldham announced $103 million of capital spending, money that would be spent making Parallel Petroleum the most active oil and gas company in Andrews County.

As Parallel Petroleum neared its 30th anniversary, the company was growing by leaps and bounds. By completing well workovers, water or carbon dioxide injections, or infill drilling, the company was fully developing mature oil and gas properties and reaping the financial rewards of its efforts. Between 2001 and 2008, Parallel Petroleum's proved reserves swelled from 3.2 million barrels of oil equivalent to 43.8 million barrels of oil equivalent. The enormous increase in its reserve volume delivered vibrant financial growth, as the company's revenues rose sharply under the acquire-and-exploit strategy adopted in 2002. Between 2002 and 2008, Parallel Petroleum's revenues increased from $12.1 million to $116 million, offering tangible proof that Oldham's approach was serving the company well.

In the years ahead, the company's disciplined yet aggressive acquisition strategy promised to serve it well.

Jeffrey L. Covell

PRINCIPAL SUBSIDIARIES

Parallel L.P.; Parallel L.L.C.

PRINCIPAL COMPETITORS

Abraxas Petroleum Corporation; Brigham Exploration Company; Anadarko Petroleum Corporation.

FURTHER READING

Breaux, Julie, "Midland, Texas-based Oil Company Looks to Expand in Permian Basin," *Odessa American,* June 24, 2002.

———, "Parallel Petroleum Co.'s Permian Basin Exploits Prove Profitable," *Odessa American,* November 16, 2004.

———, "Parallel Petroleum Solidifies Leases in Andrews County, Texas," *Odessa American,* October 12, 2004.

Coghlan, Kelly, "Parallel Finds Unparalleled Success in Southeast Texas Gas Field," *Oil Daily,* May 11, 2000.

Haines, Leslie, "Producing the Permian," *Oil and Gas Investor,* May 2004, p. 39.

"Parallel Buys Permian Assets," *Oil Daily,* October 18, 2005.

"Parallel Petroleum Corp.," *Oil and Gas Investor,* September 2006, p. S91.

"Parallel Petroleum Corp.," *Oil and Gas Investor,* August 2001, p. 2S18.

"Parallel Triples Reserves," *Oil Daily,* December 23, 2002.

"United States: Parallel Petroleum Acquires Additional Interest in Diamond M," *TendersInfo,* June 28, 2008.

Pathmark Stores, Inc.

2 Paragon Drive
Montvale, New Jersey 07645-1718
U.S.A.
Telephone: (201) 571-4453
Toll Free: (866) 443-7374
Fax: (201) 571-8667
Web site: http://www.pathmark.com

Wholly Owned Subsidiary of Great Atlantic and Pacific Tea Company, Inc. (A&P)
Incorporated: 1993
Employees: 26,000
Sales: $4.05 billion (2007)
NAICS: 445110 Supermarkets and Other Grocery (Except Convenience) Stores

■ ■ ■

Pathmark Stores, Inc., is a leading grocer in the northeastern United States, with 144 grocery stores within a 100-mile radius of its New Jersey headquarters. Pathmark operates urban and suburban stores in New York, New Jersey, Pennsylvania, and Delaware, including several stores in New York City and Philadelphia. Pathmark operates small, neighborhood stores, at 20,000 square feet, midsize stores, and discount supercenters of more than 60,000 square feet. In addition to primary groceries, frozen foods, and paper goods, the merchandise mix includes natural and organic products, fresh prepared foods and bakery items, general merchandise, such as kitchenware, as well as its own private label brand foods. Pathmark serves customers of diverse ethnic minorities, so its stores offer a wide range of ethnic foods. Many stores provide separate pharmacy and bank operations.

PATHMARK FOUNDINGS

The Pathmark chain arose out of the Wakefern cooperative formed in 1947 by independent New Jersey grocers who felt the need to organize to compete with large food chains. Some members of the cooperative agreed to operate their stores under the Shop-Rite name. Wakefern was both a wholesale and a retail operation. Among its members was a subgroup called Supermarkets Operating Co. Formed in 1956 by Alex Aidekman, Herb Brody, and Milt Perlmutter, the company opened new Shop-Rites and in 1963 branched into nonfood retail by acquiring Crown Drugs.

Supermarkets Operating Co. and General Super Markets, another subgroup within Wakefern, merged in 1966 to become Supermarkets General Corp., with Perlmutter as president. Supermarkets General operated 75 Shop-Rite stores in New Jersey, New York, Connecticut, Delaware, and Pennsylvania at the end of 1966, with annual sales of about $420 million. It was achieving high volume by opening large stores in densely populated areas and keeping prices low on both nationally branded goods and private label items.

In 1968 Supermarkets General left the Wakefern cooperative and renamed its Shop-Rite stores Pathmark. Although Supermarkets General had other holdings, including the Genung's department store chain and Rickel Bros.' home centers, the Pathmark business was its major operation. These units included not only

COMPANY PERSPECTIVES

The name Pathmark was established in 1968 by its founding fathers, Herb Brody, Milton Perlmutter and Alex Aidekman. This new company would provide a "path" for easy, one-stop shopping, and be the "mark" of one of the most successful supermarket retailers in the United States.

The company was a pioneer in the "supercenter" concept, which combined traditional grocery and perishable items with expanded offerings on nonfoods, including small appliances. Pathmark was the first supermarket company in the Northeast to operate its stores 24 hours each day, 7 days a week. Also, the company was among the first in the Northeast to utilize scanning registers at the checkout.

supermarkets (33 of which had a drug department with a pharmacy) but 11 freestanding drugstores and 11 gasoline stations.

Pathmark's 81 supermarkets were accounting for about 85 percent of Supermarkets General's sales and 80 percent of its earnings in 1969. The number of Pathmark supermarkets had reached 91 in October 1971, and there were also 24 Pathmark gas stations and 14 Pathmark drugstores. In May 1972, 94 of the 96 supermarkets began operating around the clock, seven days a week. Pathmark pioneered in the use of computer scanners at checkout counters, introduced by the chain in 1974.

After a period of relative stagnation, in 1977 Pathmark opened the first of its "Super Centers," huge discount grocery stores that also offered health and beauty aids, small appliances, and videotape rentals. These 50,000-square-foot units were being created in large part by renovating and expanding the existing stores. At the end of the year Pathmark had full-line pharmacies in 81 of its 103 supermarkets, horticulture departments in 64, bakery departments in 60, and "mini-bank branches" in 13. In its annual report, Supermarkets General claimed its sales per store were the highest in the industry. "Pathmark does more than three times the business in a store only 33% larger than the industry average," the report said.

In its 1978 annual report, Supermarkets General claimed Pathmark had become the top supermarket chain in the New York metropolitan area, with a 15 percent market share. Twelve of its 109 outlets had

become Super Centers. In all, Pathmark sales volume in 1978 came to $1.8 billion and the chain contributed 82 percent to corporate profits. About 60 percent of the volume was generated in stores opened, enlarged, or substantially remodeled during the past three years. Perlmutter died in 1978 and was succeeded by Brody as chief executive officer of Supermarkets General.

Pathmark's supermarket sales reached $2.8 billion in 1982, when it was the nation's tenth largest supermarket chain. Of the 121 units, 62 were Super Centers. Barnes & Noble minibookstores were located in 27 Pathmark supermarkets and cheese shops were located in 19. In addition, the company had 13 freestanding Pathmark drugstores. Pathmark continued to dominate Supermarkets General's sales and operating profits, with 87 and 83 percent of the corporate total, respectively. Pathmark opened Manhattan's first superstore, a 42,600-square-foot unit, in Peck Slip, near Chinatown, in 1983. The chain was still number one in the New York metropolitan area in 1985, with a 12.5 percent market share, according to a telephone survey.

PRIVATE COMPANY, 1987–93

To foil a takeover bid by Dart Group Corp., management took Supermarkets General private in a $2.1 billion 1987 leveraged buyout, in which Merrill Lynch Capital Markets Inc. received 55 percent of the shares and the Equitable Life Assurance Society of the U.S., 30 percent, with management retaining 10 percent for itself. Servicing the debt ($1.6 billion in early 1990, half of it in junk bonds) soon proved a problem.

Although corporate sales reached $6 billion in fiscal 1989, the 51-unit Rickel subsidiary was performing poorly and the 142 store Pathmark grocery chain had slipped to third place in the New York area. Many of the Pathmark units had become, according to a *Forbes* article, "unkempt, dirty, and outmoded." Pathmark, the story went on to say, "continues to stock scores of the dreary no-frills offerings customers have shunned for years." Merrill Lynch sacked Chief Executive Kenneth Peskin, replacing him with Jack Futterman. The only bright spot for the parent company was its 66-unit Purity Supreme division, consisting of Massachusetts grocery and convenience store chains acquired in 1984. This division was sold in 1991 for about $265 million. (Supermarkets General's department stores had been sold in 1986.)

Supermarkets General lost money in every fiscal year between 1988 and 1993 and sales volume every fiscal year between 1989 and 1993. In fiscal 1993 it lost a record $617 million on sales of $4.34 billion, mainly reflecting a $600 million write down of goodwill (the

KEY DATES

1947: The Wakefern grocers' cooperative forms.

1956: The establishment of Supermarkets Operating Corporation (SOC) stimulates founding of the ShopRite chain.

1966: General Supermarkets forms through the merger of SOC and General Supermarkets.

1968: Parent Supermarket General renames Shop-Rite stores to Pathmark.

1972: Pathmark is a leader in 24 hours a day, seven days a week grocery shopping.

1974: Pathmark pioneers use of checkout scanners.

1977: Pathmark opens its first discount supercenter.

1989: Supermarket General averts hostile takeover, but going private through a leveraged management buyout leads to five years of losses.

1993: Supermarket General takes the Pathmark Stores name and speeds development of a larger supercenter format.

1994: Pathmark adjusts to changing tastes by adding an upscale line of private label foods.

1995: Pathmark sells freestanding pharmacies in lieu of in-store pharmacy development.

1997: Intense competition leads to decline in same-store sales and net losses.

2000: Pathmark undergoes Chapter 11 bankruptcy and reorganization; small store prototype is introduced in Queens, New York.

2004: Larger store format accommodates fresh foods, prepared meals, and bolder interior décor.

2007: A&P acquires Pathmark Stores.

premium paid in excess of assets) in the 1987 buyout. The company's interest payments, averaging between $160 million and $180 million a year on its debt, were hampering its efforts to modernize its stores and thereby keep in pace with its competitors. Pathmark consisted at this time of 146 supermarkets, 33 freestanding drugstores, and 7 distribution/processing facilities.

Supermarkets General sought in March 1993 to take Pathmark public, but backed off in the face of insufficient investor interest. Instead, in an October 1993 corporate reorganization, Supermarkets General Corp., a subsidiary of Supermarkets General Holdings Corp., changed its name to Pathmark Stores, Inc., and

in essence recapitalized $1.3 billion in outstanding debt. The company thereby lowered its interest costs, reportedly from about 13 to 9 percent of revenues, and thus increased cash flow. This allowed the company to step up capital investment in Pathmark. Rickel was spun off at this time and was sold in 1994.

PATHMARK STORES, 1993–97

Pathmark was putting its hopes for the future on stores even bigger than the traditional Super Centers. The Pathmark 2000 format, first introduced in 1992, called for units as large as 64,000 square feet. By early 1995 there were 27 such stores, some new, some converted from other Pathmark outlets. They emphasized perishables such as produce, seafood, baked goods, flowers, and delicatessen items, as well as health and beauty aids with a selection to rival that of drugstore and discount competitors. These goods all had higher profit margins than packaged groceries. Pathmark 2000 stores also offered a customer service desk for product returns, video rentals, film processing, and UPS mail delivery, and restrooms with changing tables for mothers with babies in diapers. By the end of May 1996, 44 such stores were in operation and, by February 1997, 53 were in operation.

Pathmark also added to its private label products in 1994 by introducing an upscale line called Pathmark Preferred to its generic No Frills brand and its mid-tier Pathmark brand. At this time Pathmark's more than 3,300 private label items were accounting for about 24 percent of the chain's sales. In late 1995 a Pathmark on Long Island launched Chef's Creations, a program offering a menu of about 40 entrees, side dishes, and salads made in store each day by a team of chefs. Pathmark, in late 1996, introduced Chef's Creations To Go, fresh, prepackaged meals for takeout, offering a choice of eight entrees and side dishes in microwavable containers. An outside manufacturer was preparing these meals to Pathmark's specifications.

By the summer of 1994 Pathmark had won its way back into the favor of New Yorkers, according to one survey that found it to be the city's most popular supermarket chain. A total of 17 percent of city residents were shopping at Pathmark regularly, and more than half of those who said they did so cited its low prices. The top ranking chain in Brooklyn, the Bronx, and Staten Island, Pathmark was operating 17 superstores in New York City.

Pathmark was honored in 1995 as Pharmacy Chain of the Year by the magazine *Drug Topics,* the first time a supermarket retailer had won the award. All of its 142 supermarkets had pharmacies except six that were located in shopping centers with lease restrictions. According to the company, Pathmark was the leader in filling prescriptions in the metropolitan New York area and was participating in more than 200 major insurance plans. Prescriptions accounted for nearly 7 percent of Pathmark's sales volume in 1994. Futterman, still the company's chief executive officer, was himself a registered pharmacist.

In June 1995, however, Pathmark reduced its pharmacy operations by selling 30 of its 36 freestanding drugstores to Rite Aid Corp. for $60 million. These outlets had accounted for $145 million in sales in fiscal 1995, about 3.5 percent of the company-wide total. A company executive said that although the 30 stores had earned satisfactory profits, Pathmark had decided to concentrate its pharmacy efforts in the supermarkets, which he said were more efficient and attractive to customers. Pathmark's remaining drugstores, six Connecticut ones featuring deeply discounted prices, were subsequently closed during 1995–96.

Construction began in August 1997 on Pathmark's controversial $14.5 million supermarket in Manhattan's East Harlem. This 53,000-square-foot unit was the first large supermarket in Harlem and had been bitterly opposed by owners of neighborhood food stores. This Pathmark was expected to generate hundreds of construction jobs as well as 200 in-store jobs and would include a pharmacy and a Chase Manhattan Bank branch. Pathmark was planning its biggest Bronx store in 1998: a 55,000-square-foot unit on ten acres in the blighted area east of Crotona Park.

Supermarkets General cut its loss in fiscal 1994 to $17 million on net sales of $4.21 billion. It had its first profitable year in 1995 since fiscal 1987, earning $10 million in net income on $4.21 billion in net sales. Pathmark's supermarket sales came to $3.84 billion and $3.79 billion, respectively.

In 1996, Supermarkets General had net income of $77 million on sales of $3.97 billion. Pathmark's supermarket sales came to $3.85 billion. In 1997, the parent company had a net loss of $20 million on sales of $3.71 billion. This result included a charge the company took for the upcoming sale of 12 unprofitable Pathmark stores, most of them in southern New Jersey. Pathmark's supermarket sales came to all but $9 million of the corporate total. Same-store supermarket sales decreased 2.8 percent from the previous fiscal year, primarily due to heavy competition. James Donald, Futterman's successor as chief executive officer, laid off more than 200 employees at Pathmark's Woodbridge, New Jersey, headquarters in March 1997.

In addition to Pathmark's corporate headquarters, Pathmark had, in 1997, distribution facilities for dry groceries and meat, dairy, and deli products in Woodbridge; a distribution facility for frozen food in Dayton, New Jersey; one for dry groceries in North New Brunswick, New Jersey; and one for general merchandise (healthcare and beauty products, pharmaceuticals, and tobacco) in Edison, New Jersey. It had processing facilities for delicatessen products in Somerset, New Jersey, and for banana ripening in Avenel, New Jersey. Pathmark's stores ranged from 26,000 to 66,500 square feet in size. All but five were either Pathmark 2000 or Super Center stores, and all but seven contained in-store pharmacy departments.

In October 1997 Pathmark announced that C&S Wholesale Grocers of Brattleboro, Vermont, would take over its distribution facilities and become the chain's supplier for substantially all groceries and perishables. Pathmark was expected to receive perhaps $50 million from the deal, part of which would be used to pay down its debt of $1.47 billion.

MERCHANDISING INITIATIVES AND BANKRUPTCY PRIME PATHMARK FOR ACQUISITION

With operations streamlined to the grocery store market, Pathmark expressed interest in being bought by another company. Meanwhile, Pathmark sought to improve its strengths as a low price leader and urban, ethnic grocer. In 1997 Pathmark promoted its Smart Price program, which lowered prices on 5,000 grocery and frozen food items. New stores opened in underserved areas of New York City, including the long-awaited store in Harlem and a Pathmark 2000 store in Queens. Pathmark introduced a community store prototype, at 20,000 square feet. In 2000 two community stores opened in Queens, followed by one in Germantown, in Philadelphia, in 2000.

Shortly after Royal Ahold canceled its planned acquisition of Pathmark, due to Federal Trade Commission restrictions, Pathmark began planning for a prepackaged bankruptcy. Saddled with $75 million interest expense annually, Pathmark entered Chapter 11 proceedings in September 2000. The bankruptcy affected bond holders but not vendors and creditors, allowing the company stores to continue operations as usual. Within a month, Pathmark emerged with its debt reduced from $1.5 billion to $500 million.

Restructuring provided Pathmark with the opportunity to expand the chain and improve operations. In 2001 the company purchased six stores from Grand Union in New Jersey and began construction on three new stores. In 2003 new lead management, by longtime Pathmark executives Eileen Scott and Frank Vittano, prompted several changes. Pathmark invested in technology to improve productivity, and installation of self-scan checkout equipment improved the flow of customer traffic. Pathmark updated its merchandise mix, adding natural and organic foods and offering fresh baked goods made from prepackaged dough. The company expanded its fresh and ethnic foods sections. Renovations involved updating with bold colors.

Pathmark obtained funds for further improvements when The Yucaipa Companies LLC invested $150 million in August 2005. Under new CEO John Stadley, Pathmark refined its merchandising program. Stadley further expanded the perishables and organics sections, applying the motto, "Go Fresh, Go Local." He moved general merchandise from the edges to the interior of the store to improve sales, and he updated the interior with lighting techniques and distinctive product departments. Named for icons of the East Coast, these departments included the Tribeca Baking Company and the Chesapeake Seafood Company. A new store prototype added a prepared foods section; Bella Care offered casual dining with quality meals, gourmet desserts, and an espresso bar.

Despite these changes, sales stagnated, hovering at $4 billion between 2001 and 2006. Moreover, the company continued to operate at a loss. Nevertheless, Pathmark's stronghold in urban markets made it an attractive acquisition target. When Pathmark agreed to be acquired by A&P in 2007, industry analysts said the acquisition could facilitate profitability for both companies through annual cost savings of $100 million. Success of the combination depended upon correctly honing the merchandising mix to demographic needs of different store formats and locations.

Robert Halasz
Updated, Mary Tradii

PRINCIPAL COMPETITORS

Acme Markets, Inc.; Stop & Shop Supermarket Company; Wakefern Food Corporation.

FURTHER READING

"Ahold Terminates Pathmark Deal," *Food Institute Report,* December 20, 1999.

Brookman, Faye, "Big Stores Winning Food Fight in NY," *Crain's New York Business,* August 29, 1994, pp. 3, 17.

———, "Into the Future with Pathmark 2000," *Women's Wear Daily,* February 3, 1995, p. 6.

"Changing the Rules," *Forbes,* June 15, 1967, p. 54.

Dowdell, Stephen, "Pathmark Introduces Upscale Private Label," *Supermarket News,* August 29, 1994, pp. 29, 32.

Fink, James, "Tops Parent Extends Reach to New York City Market," *Business First of Buffalo,* March 15, 1999, p. 3.

Fiorilla, Paul, "Pathmark Searches for New Leadership," *Business News New Jersey,* May 29, 1996, pp. 4+.

Fitzgerald, Beth, "Pathmark Will Shed 12 Sites and 300 Jobs," *Newark Star-Ledger,* March 27, 1997, p. 59.

Garry, Michael, "Preparing for the Millennium," *Progressive Grocer,* May 1995, pp. 82, 85–86, 88.

Jacobson, Greg, "Pathmark Prototype," *MMR,* October 8, 2007, p. 53.

Lo Bosco, Maryellen, "Pathmark Unit in Harlem Set to Appeal to Demographics," *Supermarket News,* May 3, 1999, p. 135.

May, Roger B., "Supermarket Shopping in Wee Hours, or Any Old Time, Is Tested by a Chain," *Wall Street Journal,* May 24, 1972, p. 11.

Morgenson, Gretchen, "Can Bankers Sell Groceries?" *Forbes,* October 30, 1989, pp. 54, 56.

Murray, Barbara, "Ethnic Foods a Staple at NYC Pathmark," *Supermarket News,* April 24, 2000, p. 111.

———, "Pathmark Opens Its First Community Store in NY," *Supermarket News,* November 22, 1999, p. 31.

Nagle, James J., "Anticipating Consumerism," *New York Times,* October 24, 1971, Sec. 3, pp. 5, 12.

"Pathmark Emerges from Bankruptcy; Sets Goals," *Supermarket News,* September 25, 2000, p. 1.

"Pathmark to Open Nine New Stores," *Drug Store News,* March 5, 2001, p. 6.

Quint, Michael, "Pathmark to Sell Rite Aid New York City Drugstores," *New York Times,* June 22, 1995, p. D2.

Rosendahl, Iris, "Well Done, Pathmark!" *Drug Topics,* April 24, 1995, pp. 65–66, 68.

Springer, Jon, "A&P, Pathmark's Discuss Long-Awaited Merger," *Supermarket News,* March 5, 2007, p. 12.

———, "A&P to Touch Up Pathmark Stores," *Supermarket News,* January 14, 2008, p. 12.

———, "On the Mark; Amid Merger Speculation, Pathmark's New Leadership Looks for a Turnaround," *Supermarket News,* July 17, 2006, p. 12.

"Supermarkets General Presents New Plan to Recapitalize Debt," *Wall Street Journal,* August 24, 1993, p. B8.

Turcsik, Richard, "Pathmark Launches Campaign to Regain Low-Price Position," *Supermarket News,* April 21, 1997, p. 99.

———, "Pathmark's Wild Ride," *Progressive Grocer,* September 2000, p. 47.

Weber, Joseph, "What Put Pathmark in Such a Pickle?" *Business Week,* February 26, 1990, pp. 68, 71.

"Yucaipa to Invest $150 Million in Pathmark," *Refrigerated Transporter,* April 1, 2005.

Zwiebach, Elliot, "C&S to Take Over Pathmark's Distribution," *Supermarket News,* October 13, 1997, pp. 7, 71.

———, "Pathmark's Trailblazing Ways; Speculation Is Rife That the New Jersey-based Chain Is a Prime Acquisition Target. However, the New Executive Team Is Managing for the Long Term," *Supermarket News,* August 25, 2003, p. 10.

Potash Corporation of Saskatchewan Inc.

Suite 500
122 - 1st Avenue South
Saskatoon, Saskatchewan S7K 7G3
Canada
Telephone: (306) 933-8500
Toll Free: (800) 667-0403 (Canada); (800) 667-3930
    (USA)
Fax: (306) 933-8877
Web site: http://www.potashcorp.com

Public Company
Incorporated: 1975
Employees: 5,003
Sales: $9.45 billion (2008)
Stock Exchanges: Toronto New York
Ticker Symbol: POT
NAICS: 212391 Potash, Soda, and Borate Mineral Mining; 212392 Phosphate Rock Mining; 325311 Nitrogenous Fertilizer Manufacturing; 325312 Phosphatic Fertilizer Manufacturing

■ ■ ■

Potash Corporation of Saskatchewan Inc. (PotashCorp) is the leading integrated fertilizer company in the world, while also producing related industrial and animal feed products. The company ranks as the world's largest producer of potash, the second largest nitrogen producer, and the third largest producer of phosphate. Potash and phosphate are mined for their essential nutrients, potassium and phosphorus, which are used in making fertilizer; nitrogen, which is produced from anhydrous ammonia synthesized from natural gas, steam, and air, is also a key fertilizer ingredient. Potassium is used to increase crop yields, raise the food value of certain plants, and aid in resisting diseases leading to crop failure. Phosphorus, which is instrumental in the process of plant photosynthesis, is necessary for the normal growth of either an animal or plant, and is an essential ingredient for its maintenance and repair. Nitrogen, essential to the synthesis of amino acids, is tied closely to crop yield and the production of plant RNA and DNA.

PotashCorp operates five potash mines and has mineral rights at another in its home province of Saskatchewan, which contains the world's largest deposits of potash; it also operates an additional potash mine in New Brunswick. More than 60 percent of the firm's gross profits stem from its potash operations. The company also operates four nitrogen production facilities, three in the United States and one in Trinidad, and has two main sites, in North Carolina and Florida, where it mines phosphate ore and produces phosphate products. The primary destination for its potash, nitrogen, and phosphate products is the stable North American market. In addition, PotashCorp exports large quantities of its potash to China, India, Brazil, and Southeast Asia.

Through an aggressive acquisition policy, the company has been able to make its presence felt throughout the world. Two important acquisitions, Texasgulf and White Springs Agricultural Chemicals, both bought in 1995, have enabled Potash Corporation of Saskatchewan to build a flexible phosphate business able to provide a diversified mix of products. The 1997

COMPANY PERSPECTIVES

Committed to seeking earnings growth and minimizing volatility, we employ a Potash First strategy, focusing our capital—internally and through investments—to build on our world-class potash assets and meet the rising global demand for this vital nutrient. By investing in potash capacity while producing to meet market demand, we create the opportunity for significant growth while limiting downside risk.

We complement our potash operations with focused nitrogen and phosphate businesses that emphasize the production of high-margin products with stable and sustainable earnings potential.

acquisition of Arcadian Corporation provided the company with its presence in nitrogen fertilizer, industrial, and feed products. Starting in 1998, Potash-Corp also purchased minority stakes in several overseas fertilizer businesses, including Israel Chemicals Limited, Sociedad Química y Minera de Chile S.A., Jordan-based Arab Potash Company, and the Chinese firm Sinofert Holdings Limited.

EARLY HISTORY

Potash Corporation of Saskatchewan Inc. was established on February 4, 1975, by what is called an Order-In-Council of the Canadian government. Private potash companies had been operating in Saskatchewan since the mid-1950s, but the federal government of Canada had failed to reach any agreement with those companies that would guarantee not only increased production capacity of potash but also a greater degree of benefit and ownership for the people living in Saskatchewan province. Created to function as a commercial provincial crown corporation to produce and market potash, the firm actually began its life as a functioning producer during the 1976–77 fiscal year. By the end of that time, the company had acquired two mines, the Duval Mine and the Sylvite Mine, renamed the Cory Division and Rocanville Division, respectively, and had increased its production capacity from zero to the second largest producer in the North American market with over 540,000 metric tons. The corporation had established a network of 16 distribution warehouses, 15 of which were located in the United States, and had started to market all its foreign sales through Canpotex Limited, a marketing agency set up by all the potash

firms operating in Saskatchewan for the sole purpose of promoting the sale of potash outside the North American market. Profits of $890,000 were made on sales of just over $22 million, and more than 1,100 people were employed by the company.

PotashCorp initially started its operations in five geographically distinct areas within the province of Saskatchewan, which possesses about half of the world's known reserves of potash. In addition to the Cory Division and the Rocanville Division, the company purchased the Alwinsal mine, the Allan mine, and the large potash reserves at Esterhazy, which significantly increased its holdings. The raw ore of potash, comprised of approximately 50 percent sodium chloride, 45 percent potassium chloride, and 5 percent clay, is found in naturally occurring potash beds ranging from eight to 25 feet thick in Saskatchewan. Discovered during the early 1940s as oil companies drilled for oil to fuel the Allied war effort against Germany and Japan, the potash beds are located between 3,000 and 7,000 feet below the earth's surface. Found to be a highly effective ingredient to enhance crop yields, potash was soon used in fertilizer products. By the late 1970s, PotashCorp had grown so large that it accounted for 40 percent of Saskatchewan's total production capacity. Most impressively, company sales had skyrocketed from $22 million in 1977 to over $312 million by the end of fiscal 1979–80.

SUFFERING THROUGH AN ECONOMIC DOWNTURN

Unfortunately, during the early 1980s PotashCorp faced one of the most difficult periods in its short history. Company sales had plummeted to $188 million in 1982, due largely to the deteriorating conditions of the North American market. The U.S. government initiated a comprehensive program to cut grain inventories across the country by reducing the total amount of planted acreage and, when combined with a lengthy drought, sharply reduced the application of potash products. Fertilizer consumption within the United States dropped 23 percent from 1980, while other fertilizer producers managed to capitalize on PotashCorp's lost market share by taking advantage of American freight deregulation and lower levels of oceangoing freight. At the same time, foreign markets such as Brazil and Indonesia were oversupplied with potash products, thus lowering prices and revenues for the company.

PotashCorp's management responded by implementing a major cost reduction program, which included production reductions, inventory reductions, intermittent shutdowns, and employee layoffs. In addition, management reduced the amount of capital

KEY DATES

1975: Potash Corporation of Saskatchewan Inc. (PotashCorp) is created as a commercial provincial crown corporation to produce and market potash.

1976-77: Company acquires its first potash mines.

1989: PotashCorp is privatized and becomes a publicly traded company.

1995: Company becomes the world's third largest phosphate producer via the acquisitions of Texasgulf, Inc., and White Springs Agricultural Chemicals, Inc.

1997: PotashCorp gains a major presence in nitrogen production and becomes the world's leading integrated fertilizer company with the $1.14 billion purchase of Arcadian Corporation.

2008: Company enjoys record net income of $3.5 billion on record sales of $9.45 billion.

budgeted for lower-priority programs and research and development activities. By the end of fiscal 1985, sales had increased only slightly to $197 million, and net income for the company was reported at a loss of $49 million.

The bad news for PotashCorp continued into 1986. The slight increase in sales, initially interpreted as a sign of more promising economic indicators by company management, was misleading. In 1986 sales fell to $155 million, and losses were reported at $103 million, the worst financial record in the company's history. In contrast to the period between 1975 and 1981, when planted acres, prices, and agricultural land values were on the rise and potash consumption was growing at an average rate of 6.3 percent in the United States alone, the period between 1982 and 1985 brought with it falling prices and land values and a reduction in planted acreage, resulting in a drop of potash consumption that totaled 2.5 percent per year. Compounding the company's problems was the U.S. farm policy, which withdrew more than 75 million acres out of production. The use of potash-based fertilizers for corn and soybeans, the two most essential crops for potash consumption, decreased dramatically across the United States because of its farm policy. Thus, in the U.S. market, potash prices fell to an all-time low.

There was a bright light on the horizon for the company, however. Through its association with Canpo-

tex Limited, the marketing agency selling potash to overseas customers, offshore sales of 4.2 million metric tons surpassed the previous record of two million metric tons set in 1980. Markets in Asia and Oceania were growing at a quick pace, and exceptionally strong sales records were being set in China, Japan, Korea, Indonesia, Malaysia, and Australia. In fact, PotashCorp signed a contract with the Chinese government to deliver more than 550,000 metric tons of potash, the largest contract arranged through Canpotex for a single customer.

GROWTH AND RESURGENCE

A dramatic reversal of fortunes occurred during the late 1980s. By 1988, revenues increased to $368 million, while net income was reported at $106 million. The cost-cutting measures initiated by company management during the early and mid-1980s began to show their rewards. Daily, monthly, and yearly production records were broken at the company's five facilities in Saskatchewan, while production costs were held to a minimum. Record tonnage was sold to China, Korea, Malaysia, Taiwan, Argentina, Chile, and Italy, and prices began to improve over the levels of the mid-1980s. The use of potash began to increase within the U.S. market, largely because more acreage was used for planting than in the previous four years.

In 1989 the decision was made to privatize PotashCorp. The most significant event in the company's history came when the Province of Saskatchewan sold approximately 35 million shares in an initial public offering (IPO) of PotashCorp company stock on the Toronto and New York stock exchanges.

By 1991, PotashCorp reported an increased net income of 78 percent over the previous year, while revenue from overseas sales jumped 18 percent during the same time. In September 1991 the company purchased Florida Favorite Fertilizer, Inc., an American-based full-range fertilizer company with facilities in Florida, Georgia, and Alabama. Florida Favorite's production of blended, granulated, and solution-mixed fertilizers significantly improved PotashCorp's presence in the U.S. fertilizer market. In addition, the company acquired Horizon Potash, a potash producer based in Carlsbad, New Mexico, for the purpose of strengthening its market share as the world's leading potash supplier.

During the early 1990s, PotashCorp was affected by the march of international events. The Gulf War, and the subsequent elimination of Iraq as a threat to peace in the Middle East, led to an increased demand for potash in the region. Jordan and Israel, two of the world's leading suppliers of potash, increased their production. Nonetheless, PotashCorp was able to make significant inroads into the regional market as the demand for its fertilizer products increased.

More importantly, however, to the worldwide demand for potash was the fall and dissolution of the U.S.S.R. in the latter part of 1991. As the various republics within the former Soviet Union became politically independent, the Commonwealth of Independent States (C.I.S.) was established. Two of these newly independent republics, Russia and Belarus, included the most important potash-producing regions in the world. As the Russian economy made the transition from state-owned companies to private businesses, which involved a major decrease in the production of potash, the difficulties that ensued included a dramatic drop in potash consumption throughout Eastern Europe, especially those countries formerly associated with the Soviet bloc. Russia and Belarus, traditional suppliers to all of Eastern Europe, attempted to shift more of their sales to markets located in Latin America and Asia, which were normally supplied by other producers, such as PotashCorp. However, the loss of captive markets, the difficulties involved in the change to a market economy, and the lack of an efficient infrastructure (such as usable railroad lines), hampered companies in Russia and Belarus from effectively competing with PotashCorp at the time. Consequently, PotashCorp's global market share remained stable, but management recognized the need for expanding its product line.

GROWING AND DIVERSIFYING VIA ACQUISITION

By 1993, under the direction of Charles Childers, who had been hired by the Saskatchewan provincial government in 1987 to help improve the fortunes of Potash-Corp, the company began to reap rewards from a carefully conceived strategic plan. Childers was the driving force behind an aggressive acquisitions policy that expanded PotashCorp's market share. One of the most important of these purchases was the 1993, $111.8 million acquisition of Potash Company of America, which operated a mine, mill, and port facility in New Brunswick as well as a mine and mill in Saskatchewan at Patience Lake. PotashCorp thus gained the ability to ship its products from both the west and east coasts of Canada. In addition, the company began to develop and market more intensely its industrial applications for potash, including the manufacture of detergents, soaps, glass and ceramics, textiles and dyes, chemicals and drugs, and recycling materials. Some of the more innovative industrial potash products were an ice melt, lawn and garden items, and a water softener named 1 Softtouch. Sales for 1993 were reported at $374.3 million.

In 1994 PotashCorp's sales jumped 59 percent, to a record of $597 million. For the first time since 1988, the worldwide consumption of potash had increased over the previous year. Part of this increased demand resulted from the consolidation and closure of numerous inefficient mines in Eastern Europe, Belarus, and Russia, and the growing disruption of supply and consumption patterns in those countries caused by the continuing social, political, and economic upheaval. At the same time, as income levels began to rise in Asia and Latin America, the demand for more and better food, and more fertilizer, increased. As the world's largest potash producer, PotashCorp increased its production to send record amounts of tonnage to Malaysia, Thailand, New Zealand, Argentina, China, and India. Stronger markets and more stable prices in both Europe and Brazil helped add to the company's increased sales volume.

With the acquisition of Texasgulf, Inc., in April 1995 for $832.6 million, PotashCorp engaged in a major product shift. Texasgulf, a leader in the production of phosphate rock and phosphate chemicals, conducted its operations in Aurora, North Carolina, and owned the largest vertically integrated phosphate mine and chemical processing facility in the world. While most of its sales came from phosphate fertilizer, the company also produced a large line of phosphate-based products such as animal feed supplements and purified phosphate acid for industrial use. Attracted by Texasgulf's stability during downturns in the fertilizer market, management at PotashCorp saw the acquisition as an important step in reducing the volatility inherent in relying on a single market: potash. The purchase of Texasgulf doubled PotashCorp's assets, and its number of employees. Following the takeover, Texasgulf was renamed PCS Phosphate Company, Inc. PotashCorp's position in phosphate was boosted in October 1995 through the purchase of White Springs Agricultural Chemicals, Inc., from Occidental Chemical Corporation for $291.5 million. The addition of White Springs, which ran a phosphate mine and two chemical plant complexes in northern Florida, made PotashCorp the third largest producer of phosphate fertilizer in the world. By the end of fiscal 1995, sales at PotashCorp had increased dramatically to $906.9 million.

As the economies of Russia and Eastern European nations began to stabilize, and the political and social tumult subsided, Russia and Belarus improved their infrastructures and increased potash production and sales to the worldwide markets. In order to protect itself from future reductions in demand and prices because of Russian competition, PotashCorp decided to buy Arcadian Corporation, the largest producer of nitrogen fertilizer products in North

America. Arcadian, based in Memphis, Tennessee, was purchased in March 1997 for $1.14 billion in cash and stock. Arcadian's nitrogen operations included facilities in Georgia, Iowa, Louisiana, Nebraska, North Carolina, Ohio, and Tennessee as well as a large-scale operation in Trinidad. The acquisition of Arcadian, which was renamed PCS Nitrogen, Inc., increased the importance of PotashCorp as a world fertilizer supplier, because the company completed its consolidation of the three primary fertilizer nutrients: potash, phosphate, and nitrogen. PotashCorp ranked as the largest integrated fertilizer producer in the world, and its revenues topped $2.3 billion.

OVERSEAS INVESTMENTS AND NEW LEADERSHIP

Late in 1996, while the Arcadian deal was still pending completion, PotashCorp reached a deal with BASF AG to acquire a controlling stake in Kali und Salz AG, the sole potash producer in Germany. The German government, however, blocked the takeover because of concerns it would limit competition in that nation's potash market. Undeterred, PotashCorp remained in the hunt, buying the Cassidy Lake potash mine in New Brunswick and a 9 percent stake in Israel Chemicals Limited (ICL) in 1998. ICL owned Dead Sea Works, the fifth largest potash exporter in the world. In 1999 PotashCorp attempted to purchase control of ICL's parent company but was thwarted by a rival bid. It nevertheless retained its minority stake in ICL.

In July 1999 Childers stepped aside as CEO while remaining chairman. Taking over as top executive was William J. Doyle, a 35-year veteran of the fertilizer industry who had spent a dozen years playing a key role as a member of PotashCorp's senior management team. Doyle took over at a difficult moment when nitrogen prices had fallen sharply over a two-year period thanks to a global glut of nitrogen fertilizers, a decrease in corn acreage planted, and grain prices at 25-year lows. Phosphate prices were also down as global production capacity was on the upswing. PotashCorp reacted to these trends by reducing its operations, shutting down nitrogen plants in Iowa and Nebraska, a phosphate feed plant in Virginia, and its phosphate terminal in Jacksonville, Florida. Charges for these closures totaled $55.7 million. The company also wrote down the value of its nitrogen operations by $526.6 million, resulting in a net loss for 1999 of $412 million. Net sales that year fell 11 percent to $2.06 billion.

PotashCorp rebounded in 2000 with net profits of $198 million thanks to a turnaround in nitrogen prices and record potash sales. The company struggled the next two years, however, as wild swings in crop prices made farmers reluctant to commit to spending money on fertilizer and tough weather conditions disrupted sowing and harvesting around the world. Another net loss totaling $126.3 million was recorded in 2003 following further plant shutdowns, including nitrogen plants in Tennessee and Louisiana and a phosphate facility in North Carolina, that resulted in charges amounting to $264.2 million.

In the meantime, PotashCorp gained a greater global footprint through a series of equity investments. In October 2001 the company spent $131 million for an 18 percent stake in Sociedad Química y Minera de Chile S.A. (SQM), a Chilean specialty fertilizer producer. After making additional investments, Potash-Corp held a 32 percent stake in SQM by 2007. In October 2003 PotashCorp secured another foothold in the Middle East by purchasing a 26 percent stake in Arab Potash Company (APC) for $178 million. Based in Jordan, APC held the rights to extract potassium chloride from the mineral-rich waters of the Dead Sea. It was one of the world's lowest-cost potash producers because it extracted the potash using simple evaporation in crystallization ponds. Finally, in two transactions completed in July 2005 and February 2006, PotashCorp bought a 20 percent interest in Sinofert Holdings Limited, a subsidiary of Sinochem Corporation. Sinofert was a major vertically integrated fertilizer company and a key potash distributor in China, the largest fertilizer market in the world.

A SPECTACULAR BOOM AND POSSIBLE BUST

Potash Corporation of Saskatchewan's dominating position in fertilizer, particularly potash, began to pay off handsomely in 2004, the first of five straight years of record profits. Fueling demand for potash and other fertilizer ingredients was the increasing pressure to boost grain yields that stemmed in particular from rising incomes in such rapidly developing nations as China and India. Consumers in these countries were using their higher incomes in part to increasingly consume more beef, pork, and chicken, ratcheting up demand for feed grains. Potash prices shot up, and PotashCorp was able to quickly ramp up production, resulting in astounding growth by 2008: net income of $3.5 billion, a more than 11-fold increase over 2004's total, on sales of $9.45 billion.

By the end of 2007, PotashCorp had plans in place for a huge investment of around $5 billion in its potash mines in Saskatchewan and New Brunswick. The goal was to increase its potash operational capacity by more than 50 percent by the end of 2012 to 15.7 million metric tons a year. Still riding the boom, PotashCorp in

July 2008 announced that it intended to invest an additional $1.6 billion to further boost its capacity to 18 million metric tons by year-end 2012. These expansion projects were expected to result in the creation of nearly 15,000 direct and indirect jobs. Meanwhile, Potash-Corp's soaring stock peaked in June 2008 at CAD 246.29 a share; the company's market value at that time of approximately CAD 76 billion made it the most valuable company on the Toronto Stock Exchange.

The global economic meltdown, however, soon sent the stock in the opposite direction as demand for potash, nitrogen, and phosphate severely weakened. The stock fell to as low as CAD 61.81 per share in December 2008 before rebounding above CAD 100 by early January 2009. PotashCorp announced in December its intention to cut its 2009 potash production by two million metric tons to match the decline in market demand. Although the global economic turmoil threatened to bring PotashCorp's string of record full-year results to an end in 2009, the company's long-range prospects remained quite bright. The company was continuing with its ambitious plans for increased potash capacity, leaving it well positioned to benefit from future increases in demand for fertilizer that were sure to follow from increased demand both for food, stemming from global population growth, and for feed grains, stemming from increased consumption of meat.

Thomas Derdak
Updated, David E. Salamie

PRINCIPAL SUBSIDIARIES

AA Sulfuric Corporation (USA); Augusta Service Company, Inc. (USA); Canpotex Bulk Terminals Limited; Chilkap Resources Ltd.; Inversiones El Boldo Limitada (Chile); Inversiones El Coigüe S.A. (Chile); Inversiones El Roble Limitada (Chile); Inversiones El Sauce Limitada (Chile); Inversiones PCS Chile S.A.; Inversiones RAC Chile Limitada; Minera Saskatchewan Limitada (Chile); PCS Administration (USA), Inc.; PCS (Barbados) Holdings SRL; PCS (Barbados) Investment Company Ltd.; PCS (Barbados) Shipping Ltd.; PCS Cassidy Lake Company; PCS Cassidy Lake Limited; PCS Chesapeake LLC (USA); PCS Chile I LLC (USA); PCS Chile II LLC (USA); PCS Fosfatos do Brasil Ltda. (Brazil); PCS Hungary Holding Limited Liability Company; PCS Industrial Products Inc. (USA); PCS Joint Venture, Ltd. (USA); PCS Jordan LLC (USA); PCS L.P. Inc. (USA); PCS LP LLC 2 (USA); PCS Nitrogen Ammonia Terminal Corporation I (USA); PCS Nitrogen Ammonia Terminal Corporation II (USA); PCS Nitrogen Delaware LLC (USA); PCS Nitrogen Fertilizer, L.P. (USA); PCS Nitrogen Fertilizer Limited (Trinidad); PCS Nitrogen Fertilizer Operations, Inc. (USA); PCS Nitrogen, Inc. (USA); PCS Nitrogen LCD Corporation (USA); PCS Nitrogen Limited (Trinidad); PCS Nitrogen Ohio, L.P. (USA); PCS Nitrogen Payroll Corporation (USA); PCS Nitrogen Trinidad Corporation (USA); PCS Nitrogen Trinidad Limited; PCS Phosphate Company, Inc. (USA); PCS Purified Phosphates (USA); PCS Sales (Canada) Inc.; PCS Sales (Indiana), Inc. (USA); PCS Sales (Iowa), Inc. (USA); PCS Sales (USA), Inc.; PCS USA LLC (USA); Phosphate Holding Company, Inc. (USA); Potash Corporation of Saskatchewan (Florida) Inc. (USA); Potash Corporation of Saskatchewan Transport Limited; PotashCorp Finance (Barbados) Limited; Potash Holding Company, Inc. (USA); RAC Investments Ltd. (Cayman); Texasgulf Aircraft Inc. (USA); TG Corporation (USA); White Springs Agricultural Chemicals, Inc. (USA).

PRINCIPAL COMPETITORS

The Mosaic Company; RUE Production Amalgamation Belaruskali; JSC Silvinit; JSC Uralkali; Office Chérifien des Phosphates Group; Yara International ASA; K+S Aktiengesellschaft; Agrium Inc.; CF Industries Holdings, Inc.; Koch Industries, Inc.; Terra Industries Inc.; Sinofert Holdings Limited; Arab Potash Company Limited; Intrepid Potash, Inc.; Companhia Vale do Rio Doce.

FURTHER READING

Ebner, David, "Once-Mighty Potash Falls Hard," *Globe and Mail,* October 3, 2008, p. B1.

———, "Potash Corp. Profit Warning Caps Wild Year," *Globe and Mail,* December 19, 2008, p. B5.

———, "Potash Corp. Pulls 'the Trigger' with Commitment to N.B. Mine," *Globe and Mail,* July 21, 2007, p. B7.

Elliot, Ian, "Agriculture Hit Hard As Budget Is Slashed in Canada," *Feedstuffs,* March 13, 1995, pp. 3, 7.

Etter, Lauren, "Fertilizer Firms Accused of Price Fixing," *Wall Street Journal,* September 16, 2008, p. B7.

Freeman, Alan, "Germany Rejects Potash Corp.'s Bid for Kali und Salz," *Globe and Mail,* July 23, 1997, p. B7.

Fritsch, Peter, "Potash to Pay $1.18 Billion for Arcadian," *Wall Street Journal,* September 3, 1996, p. A3.

Geer, John, F., "Mixed Marriage," *Financial World,* October 21, 1996, pp. 46–47.

Greenshields, Vern, and Jenni Mortin, "Crown Corporation Series," *Saskatoon (Saskatchewan) Star-Phoenix,* February 24, 1982, p. C1.

Henry, Brian, "Potash Corporation Emerges As a Fertilizer Major," *Chemical Marketing Reporter,* September 9, 1996, pp. 3, 36.

Hoffman, John, "Strong Potash Fundamentals Bode Well for Profitability at PotashCorp," *Chemical Market Reporter,* October 4, 2004, p. 20.

Ip, Greg, "Potash Corp. Building Empire," *Globe and Mail,* September 4, 1996, p. B1.

"A Jewel from the Crown," *Saskatchewan Business,* May/June 1995, pp. 8+.

Johnson, Dexter, "PCS Is Stopped in Its Attempt at Potash Buy," *Chemical Market Reporter,* July 28, 1997, pp. 1, 16.

Kennedy, Peter, "Potash Looks to Dead Sea for Growth," *Globe and Mail,* July 12, 2003, p. B5.

Kirschner, Elisabeth, "Elf Aquitaine to Sell Stake in Phosphate Firm," *Chemical and Engineering News,* March 13, 1995, p. 8.

Lazo, Shirley A., "Riding High Profits, Potash Lifts Dividends," *Barron's,* August 15, 1994, p. 37.

Martin, Paul, "Doyle Prepares PCS for New Growth," *Saskatchewan Business,* February 2000, pp. 15–17.

McFarland, Janet, "Potash CEO Rides Boom in Food Prices," *Globe and Mail,* May 8, 2008, p. B1.

Muirhead, Sarah, "Potash Corporation Announces It Will Buy Texasgulf," *Feedstuffs,* March 13, 1995, p. 3.

Paulson, Joanne, "PotashCorp to Cut Production," *Saskatoon (Saskatchewan) Star-Phoenix,* December 11, 2008, p. C9.

Philips, Elizabeth, "Chuck's Stake," *Saskatchewan Business,* May 1990, pp. 22+.

Plishner, Emily S., "PCS's 'Superb Acquisition': Texasgulf for $835 Million," *Chemical Week,* March 15, 1995, p. 9.

Robinson, Allan, "Potash Unit Pleads Guilty to U.S. Environmental Charge," *Globe and Mail,* September 11, 2002, p. B3.

Tan, Kopin, "On Fertile Ground," *Barron's,* November 6, 2006, p. 36.

Williams, Nicole, "PotashCorp Remains a Bright Spot in the Saskatchewan Economy," *Regina (Saskatchewan) Leader-Post,* November 27, 2008, p. D5.

RadioShack Corporation

300 RadioShack Circle
Fort Worth, Texas 76102-1964
U.S.A.
Telephone: (817) 415-3011
Fax: (817) 415-2647
Web site: http://www.radioshack.com

Public Company
Incorporated: 1960 as Tandy Corporation
Employees: 35,800
Sales: $4.25 billion (2007)
Stock Exchanges: New York
Ticker Symbol: RSH
NAICS: 443112 Radio, Television, and Other Electronics Stores; 443120 Computer and Software Stores; 443130 Camera and Photographic Supplies Stores; 451120 Hobby, Toy, and Game Stores; 454111 Electronic Shopping; 334210 Telephone Apparatus Manufacturing; 334290 Other Communications Equipment Manufacturing; 335929 Other Communication and Energy Wire Manufacturing; 811211 Consumer Electronics Repair and Maintenance; 811212 Computer and Office Machine Repair and Maintenance; 811213 Communication Equipment Repair and Maintenance

∎ ∎ ∎

RadioShack Corporation, known as Tandy Corporation from its founding in 1960 until the early 2000s, is one of the largest consumer electronics retailers in the United States. Forming the company's core operation are the 5,800 RadioShack stores located throughout the country. The stores feature a broad array of brand-name and private-label consumer electronics products and accessories, including wireless and residential telephones, flat-panel televisions, DVD players, computers, direct-to-home satellite systems, home entertainment and wireless accessories, digital cameras, radio-controlled cars and other toys, and general- and special-purpose batteries. RadioShack also operates around 700 wireless phone kiosks, comprising Sam's Club kiosks located within Sam's Club warehouse stores and Sprint Nextel kiosks located in shopping malls; three manufacturing plants in the United States and China that produce electronics products, most of which are sold in company stores; and a network of service centers that repair consumer electronics products and personal computers (PCs). The company holds a minority interest in a joint venture with Grupo Gigante, S.A. de C.V., that operates around 180 RadioShack-branded stores in Mexico.

EARLY HISTORY

Founder Charles Tandy's talent for marketing became evident when he took over the leather store his family had operated since 1919. He began to expand into the hobby market. Subsidiary locations had to be found as mail-order and direct sales increased. In 1960, as scouts and campers all over the country made moccasins and coin purses from Tandy leathercraft and hobby kits, the Tandy Corporation was established and began trading on the New York Stock Exchange.

As good as business was, it could not satisfy Tandy's passion for retailing. By the early 1960s, he began look-

COMPANY PERSPECTIVES

Today, RadioShack offers a retail service concept unlike any other specialty consumer electronics retailer. Through its convenient and comfortable neighborhood stores, knowledgeable sales associates help customers get the most out of their technology products. RadioShack's legendary force of knowledgeable and helpful sales associates has been consistently recognized by several independent groups for providing the best customer service in the consumer electronics and wireless industries.

ing for a way to diversify. In 1963 Tandy purchased RadioShack, a virtually bankrupt chain of electronics stores in Boston that had been founded in 1921. Within two years, Tandy was making a profit on a company that had nearly $800,000 in uncollectibles when he took over. Ten years after starting with nine Boston outlets, the Tandy Corporation was opening two RadioShack stores every working day.

By all accounts, Charles Tandy was a modest man from Fort Worth, who stayed in his original office and answered his own phone until the day he died. While his CB radio moniker was "Mr. Lucky," Tandy's success was, according to analysts, due to more than just luck. They gave much more credit to three key marketing strategies that Charles Tandy developed and implemented.

First, Tandy stressed the importance of gross profit margins. Popular wisdom said a chain store's profits lay in cutting prices to yield a high sales volume. Tandy thought differently. As far as he was concerned, cutting the profit margin cut the profit. He decided to maintain market prices but reduce RadioShack's 20,000 item inventory to the 2,500 best-selling items.

Second, Tandy kept RadioShack prices competitive. He eliminated a whole spectrum of middleman costs by limiting stock to private-label items. At first, the company established exclusive contracts with manufacturers, but as RadioShack grew, more items were designed and manufactured by associates or subdivisions of the Tandy Corporation. In the late 1980s, Tandy still manufactured about half of the products sold in its RadioShack stores. Twenty-five North American and six overseas manufacturing plants produced everything from simple wire to sophisticated microchips, and RadioShack's Realistic brand name,

which dated back to the 1950s, had achieved nationwide recognition.

Charles Tandy's strategy of pairing high profit margin with high turnover and of in-house marketing and distribution more than proved itself. The gross profit margin on sales for the RadioShack division was consistently above 50 percent.

Even as he consolidated his inventory, Tandy was keenly aware that buyers must be conscious of a company's presence. "If you want to catch a mouse," Tandy was fond of saying, "you have to make a noise like a cheese." Thus another Tandy strategy was to go all out on advertising. Especially in the early years, as much as 9 percent of the corporation's gross profits went straight back into advertising. For years, RadioShack's newspaper ads and flyers were not only frequent but also flamboyant. Bold type and huge letters proclaimed a never-ending series of "super sales."

The third arm of Charles Tandy's strategy was, in the words of one company official, to "institutionalize entrepreneurship." Tandy Corporation and RadioShack employees were living testimony that hard work and impressive sales earn their own rewards. Store managers, division vice-presidents, and Charles Tandy himself regularly earned eight or ten times their relatively modest salaries through bonuses based on a percentage of the profits they had a direct hand in creating; this policy spawned some 60 homegrown millionaires.

As RadioShack's electronics line grew increasingly central to Tandy, the family leather business became an anomaly. Finally, in 1975, the leather line and a related wall and floor-covering business were spun off into separate companies.

LEADERSHIP TRANSITION

When Charles Tandy died suddenly in 1978, at the age of 60, pundits and insiders alike wondered if the corporation could survive without its workaholic director and his individualistic marketing philosophy. Philip North, a director of the company and Tandy's administrative assistant and boyhood friend, stepped in as interim president and CEO of Tandy Corporation.

By his own admission, North knew virtually nothing about the technical side of RadioShack's product line. "All I know about electronics is that the funny end of the battery goes into the flashlight first," he told *Fortune* magazine. North knew plenty, however, about his late friend's retailing style. Analysts credited him with keeping the corporation's strong management team together during the adjustment period after Tandy's death.

KEY DATES

1960: Tandy Corporation is established and begins trading on the New York Stock Exchange.
1963: Tandy buys the RadioShack chain.
1977: Company begins selling personal computers.
1985: Scott-McDuff and Video Concepts are acquired.
1988: GRiD Systems Corporation is acquired.
1991: Computer City chain is launched.
1992: Incredible Universe retail concept debuts.
1993: Company sells most of its manufacturing operations.
1995: Video Concepts is closed down.
1997: McDuff's and Incredible Universe chains are shuttered; RadioShack forms alliance with Sprint.
1998: Computer City chain is sold to CompUSA.
2000: Tandy Corporation changes its name to RadioShack Corporation.
2004: RadioShack takes over the operation of more than 500 wireless kiosks located within Sam's Club warehouse stores and begins developing Sprint-branded (later Sprint Nextel), mall-based wireless kiosks.

During these years, North increasingly called on the expertise of John Roach, a man whose scientific and computer background had attracted Charles Tandy's attention. Within a few years of hiring Roach as the manager of Tandy Data Processing, Tandy had made Roach vice-president of distribution for RadioShack. Two years later, in 1975, Roach became vice-president of manufacturing. Roach was then appointed RadioShack's executive vice-president immediately after Tandy died, becoming RadioShack division's president and chief operating officer in 1980, and CEO in 1981. When North retired in July 1982, Roach became chairman as well.

ENTERING COMPUTER MARKET

Roach's major contribution was in masterminding Tandy's entry into the computer market. Before Charles Tandy's death, Roach had talked him into venturing into the preassembled computer market. The sale of 100,000 computers between September 1, 1977, and June 1, 1979, kept RadioShack comfortably in the black even as the bottom dropped out of the CB radio market.

As Roach moved up the corporate structure, he intensified investment in computers. In 1982, less than a year after becoming CEO, Roach was singled out as "the best of the best" by *Financial World*, which lauded Roach as "the driving force at the front-running company in the red-hot personal computer race."

Within a short time, however, there were rumblings that the driving force in this hot race might have been burned. By 1984, RadioShack's impressive 19 percent market share had plummeted to under 9 percent. According to some critics, one of Tandy's problems resulted from Charles Tandy's policy of limiting RadioShack to private-label items, preferably manufactured by one of Tandy's subsidiary divisions. As software and applications software poured out for Apple and IBM-compatible systems, fewer and fewer serious computer users were willing to limit themselves to software designed exclusively for RadioShack's TRS-80, or "Trash-80," as some sneeringly referred to it. In fact, Tandy found that even a superior machine could not overcome the software handicap. Officials at the company were shaken to find their 1983 Model 2000 would not sell, even though it was three times as fast as IBM's own PC, because it was unable to run half of the available IBM software.

In addition, RadioShack's marketing strategies had a vulnerable side. Company policy was to let other retailers test the waters with items such as stereos, CB radios, and "fuzz buster" radar detectors. Then Tandy would take over a significant part of the market by introducing a house brand it advertised intensively. It was not always possible, however, to know what would boom and when. When the VCR market exploded in the mid-1980s and RadioShack simply did not have stock on hand, the same time the computer market was drying up, both sales and revenues fell at an alarming rate.

SHIFT TO IBM-COMPATIBLE COMPUTERS

That crisis led Tandy to modify its marketing policy. In 1984 the company introduced two new computers that were fully IBM-compatible and exchanged the TRS label for Tandy. RadioShack management then set about underselling its Big Blue competitor. Such price competition was a departure from previous marketing strategy, but because Tandy's own in-house manufacturing divisions still produced virtually all the components, from wire to plastic boards to microchips, Tandy was able to keep profits up.

While it never regained its initial share of the PC market, Tandy between 1985 and 1990 consistently held first place among IBM-compatibles. Tandy regained its place in the computer market by offering the buyer significant savings over IBM and other compatibles. At the same time, Roach also oversaw a wholesale revamping of the company's image. Ordinary RadioShack stores were given a facelift. To overcome the reluctance of serious business customers to take a computer shelved next to a CB or electronic toy seriously, Roach established a series of specialized RadioShack Computer Centers, providing a level of support and service that earned a "Hall of Fame" award from *Consumer's Digest* in 1985.

Tandy continued to pour money into research and development to ensure that the company would not be left behind again by new developments in the computer field. In 1988 it acquired GRiD Systems Corporation, an innovator in the burgeoning laptop computer market. GRiD's ability to manufacture and market field automation systems using laptop computers opened a whole new area of expansion into government and *Fortune* 1000 marketing companies. Sales in GRiD's first year as a Tandy subsidiary exceeded expectations and helped underscore Tandy's image as a leader in PC technology by introducing innovations such as handwriting recognition and removable hard disc drive cartridges. In 1989 Tandy acquired the European marketing operations of Victor Microcomputer and Micronic, two respected microcomputer manufacturers. Merged under the name Victor Technologies Group, Tandy used the subsidiary to market GRiD products throughout Europe.

Tandy continued to maintain a high profile in the consumer electronics market outside of computers. In the late 1980s, the company put special emphasis on becoming a major force in both manufacturing and retailing cellular phones and home computers, which it saw as a major consumer product of the 1990s. Extensive efforts also went into the development of more business-oriented technology, including multimedia applications and digital recording. The latter resulted in the development of an erasable and recordable compact disc that commanded a great deal of interest in the electronics industry.

In many ways, during the 1980s, the Tandy Corporation had simply expanded on Charles Tandy's philosophies. The company centered its manufacturing and marketing firmly around computers and consumer electronics, which it retailed primarily through its RadioShack outlets. Nonetheless, there were some significant deviations from Charles Tandy's views during the late 1980s. In 1985 the company entered the name-brand retail market with the acquisitions of Scott-McDuff and Video Concepts, two electronic equipment

chain stores. The 290 stores organized under the Tandy Brand Name Retail Group did not follow the RadioShack policy of selling exclusively private-label brands. Other subsidiaries in the Tandy Marketing Companies also began to develop broader distribution channels. Memtek products, which included the Memorex brand of audio and video tapes, became available virtually everywhere such products were sold.

Tandy also made an effort to sell its computers outside of RadioShack stores. In 1985 the company edged into broader markets by offering its computers on college campuses, at military bases, and through special offers to American Express cardholders. In 1988 Tandy test-marketed its 100SX computer line through 50 Wal-Mart stores. The company also announced plans to develop new computers with Digital Equipment Corporation (reselling the finished product under the DEC name) and to supply PCs to Panasonic (which would be sold under the Panasonic name).

Some RadioShack dealers saw Tandy's move to broaden its computer distribution as a potentially lethal threat. Many RadioShack dealers depended on their computer business for a significant portion of sales and doubted whether they could survive if customers began to shop around, looking for the same Tandy products for less elsewhere. In August 1988 a small group of dealers formed the RadioShack Dealers Association and began considering a class-action suit against Tandy.

Tandy's foundation at the time was its retail outlets. However, beyond remodeling its 7,000 RadioShack stores and refining retail strategies, by the late 1980s, Tandy's own success had left its retail divisions with little room for growth. In 1989 Tandy posted record earnings. Business at RadioShack stores, however, continued to decline, while sales in Tandy's subsidiaries GRiD, Memtek, Lika, and O'Sullivan Industries grew over 50 percent.

INCREASING FOCUS ON RETAIL

In the early 1990s, with its nonretail segment growing steadily, Tandy turned its attention to boosting its retail division. Leading the way were its McDuff and Video Concept Stores, which experienced an average of 14 percent same-store sales growth in 1989 and 1990. Tandy began a rapid expansion project, more than doubling the number of stores to 380 by the fall of 1991.

RadioShack, however, continued to feel the effects of a soft consumer electronics market. Tandy responded by closing its RadioShack Computer Center chain and by instituting an extensive marketing strategy that emphasized the high quality of both RadioShack products and service. In June 1991 Tandy announced plans to open Computer City, a new chain of computer superstores that was the first to offer IBM, Hewlett-Packard, Apple, Compaq, and Tandy computers, accessories, and software all under one roof. With its new 1000RL, a home computer system developed specifically for family use, Tandy went head-to-head against IBM for the home computer market, betting that this industry segment would grow 10 percent annually in the 1990s.

Also in 1991 Tandy opened the Edge in Electronics, a chain of upscale consumer electronics "boutiques" designed to complement RadioShack's moderately priced goods. Its biggest new foray into consumer electronics retail, however, came with the 1992 launch of Incredible Universe, an elaborate 160,000-square-foot consumer electronics mini-mall, complete with child-care centers, karaoke contests, a recycling center, and a restaurant. According to Tandy literature, Incredible Universe was patterned after "Disney's famous theme-park style of customer service. The store experience is called 'the show,' employees are known as 'cast members' and customers are the 'guests.'" Its $9 million inventory included everything from ten brands of computers to 300 different television sets to more than 40,000 music and video titles.

The company took an enormous risk with opening Incredible Universe. Industry analysts predicted that each new store would have to turn over a volume of $100 million annually to remain profitable. Tandy committed itself entirely to the new venture. In 1993 it restructured its entire operations to focus on retailing and, in a bold move, sold most of its manufacturing operations. Victor, Tandy, and GRiD were sold to AST Research, Inc., for $201 million. O'Sullivan Industries, its successful furniture manufacturing arm, was spun off to raise $350 million. Memtek Products was sold to Hanny Magnetics for $128 million, and plans were made to sell Lika's manufacturing facilities for cash and notes.

Tandy then devoted its energies to polishing its image and expanding its base as an electronics retailer. Incredible Universe became a separate division and plans were announced to open 50 units by 2000. Computer City, which posted over $600 million in annual sales in its second year of operation, announced plans to open 20 new stores by the end of 1994. RadioShack improved service in its 6,500 locations and hired the agency Young & Rubicam to design a new advertising campaign that featured the slogan "You've got questions. We've got answers." The chain also changed its merchandise mix, most notably paring back its offerings in the increasingly low-margin PC sector and bolstering higher margin lines such as private-label batteries and electronics parts. RadioShack also put increased emphasis on such hot areas as cellular telephones and direct satellite systems. For the first time since the early 1980s, RadioShack posted eight straight months of in-store sales growth. The Tandy Brand Name Retail Group's McDuff's and Video Concepts stores grew to become two of the biggest home appliance and electronics appliance retailers in the southeastern and south central United States. In less than two years, Tandy had transformed itself from a longstanding supplier and retailer of consumer electronics into a high-image conglomeration of electronics "superstore" chains.

REFOCUSING ON RADIOSHACK

The "new" Tandy proved to have a short shelf life, however; by decade's end the company would transform itself again. In the brutal environment for consumer electronics retailers in the late 1990s, with fierce competition from archrivals such as Best Buy and Circuit City and from general retailers such as Kmart and Wal-Mart, which were increasingly selling basic electronics goods, Tandy was forced to shed one after another of its chains.

Video Concepts was shuttered in 1995, along with 49 McDuff's stores. In late 1996 Tandy announced that it would close the remainder of the McDuff's chain; the entire Incredible Universe chain, which lost an estimated $130 million from 1993 to 1996; and 21 of its 113 Computer City outlets. The latter was operating in the red as well. While the divestments took place in 1997, Tandy took restructuring charges of $230.3 million in 1996, leading to a net loss for the year of $91.6 million on sales of $6.29 billion. The company completed a further retrenching move in mid-1997 when it sold a 20 percent stake in Computer City to a group of computer retailing executives, who took charge of running the chain.

Meanwhile, the RadioShack chain was continuing to be revitalized under the leadership of Leonard Roberts, who took over the presidency in mid-1993, having previously led turnarounds of Arby's and Shoney's Inc. In 1997 RadioShack began forming strategic alliances with key players in the electronics, telecommunications, and computer industries. The first was with Sprint Communications Company, which began operating "Sprint Communications Stores" within RadioShack outlets offering a full range of telecommunications products and services, including long-distance and wireless services. The "store within a store" concept was extended to the computer arena the following year through an alliance with Compaq Computer Corporation, which launched "Compaq Creative Learning Centers" featuring PCs and accessories. The Compaq brand became the exclusive computer brand found in RadioShack stores. The Compaq alliance later evolved into one with Hewlett-Packard Company following the latter firm's 2002 takeover of Compaq. A byproduct of these alliances was that entire sections of RadioShack stores were overhauled with the help of outside partners, reducing Tandy's share of the remodeling costs.

The increasing influence of Roberts was shown by his promotion to president of Tandy Corporation in March 1997. One year later, Roach announced that he would retire at the end of 1998, with Roberts becoming chairman, president, and CEO of Tandy. Also in 1998 Tandy bought back the Computer City stake it had sold, then sold Computer City to CompUSA Inc. for $211 million. It could now be said, as Roberts put it at the 1998 annual meeting, "Tandy is RadioShack, RadioShack is Tandy."

The "store within a store" strategy was clearly paying dividends as RadioShack had become the number one seller of telecommunications products in the country by 1998. The chain had two major categories of business: the longstanding electronics parts and accessories and telecommunications. Further alliances followed. In May 1999 RadioShack entered into a partnership with Thomson Multimedia, owner of the RCA brand, to create a new "store within a store" called the RCA Digital Entertainment Center, where RCA brand televisions, VCRs, camcorders, DVD players, digital cameras, and audio products were displayed within RadioShack stores. In November of that same year, an alliance with Microsoft Corporation was formed to create the Microsoft Internet Center @ RadioShack, which featured dial-up and broadband Internet access as well as related products and services. Microsoft also agreed to invest $100 million in the e-commerce web site that RadioShack launched in October 1999, www. radioshack.com.

RADIOSHACK CORPORATION IN THE EARLY 21ST CENTURY

The newly streamlined and focused Tandy Corporation posted its best results in years in 1999: net income of $297.9 million on sales of $4.13 billion. Tandy Corporation changed its name to RadioShack Corporation in May 2000, the culminating move in a successful refocusing on its RadioShack core. That year was the company's most profitable in its history as it earned $369 million on sales of $4.79 billion.

RadioShack in 2001 continued to pursue additional "store within a store" concepts and also expanded further into the wireless field when a portion of its stores began offering Verizon Wireless phones, accessories, and services. Late in the year, however, the firm retrenched after concluding that its recent initiatives had moved RadioShack too far down the road toward becoming a generalist electronics retailer; the small size of its typical store (about 2,300 square feet) made it impossible for RadioShack to compete head-on with sector leader Best Buy and its 20-times-larger superstores. Hence, in December 2001, RadioShack announced its exit from a number of product categories, including commercial electronics parts, car stereos, security systems, pagers, and larger televisions. The company also cut back on the number of computer models it carried, exited from the commercial installation business, and shuttered 35 underperforming stores. In addition, RadioShack and Microsoft ended their strategic alliance during 2002. RadioShack stores began placing an increased emphasis on three of their most profitable categories: wireless, accessories, and batteries. By the end of 2002, these categories accounted for about 55 percent of the stores' revenues.

In important developments from 2004, RadioShack made a deeper commitment to the wireless category by taking over the operation of more than 500 kiosks selling wireless products and services that were located within Sam's Club warehouse stores and by launching the development of Sprint-branded, mall-based wireless kiosks. The latter were later rebranded under the Sprint Nextel name following Sprint Corporation's 2005 acquisition of Nextel Communications. By the end of 2007, RadioShack was operating more than 700 of the two types of wireless kiosks in total, and these kiosks were responsible for about 7 percent of the company's sales, or nearly $300 million.

In the meantime, Roberts, who had spearheaded the company's refocusing around the RadioShack stores, stepped aside as CEO in May 2005 while remaining chairman. Longtime RadioShack executive David J. Edmondson, who had served as company president since 2000, was named the new CEO. At the end of 2005 RadioShack stores stopped selling Verizon Wireless products and services and began offering Cingular Wireless service instead. RadioShack also extended its agreement to sell Sprint Nextel products and services.

Disappointing sales within the increasingly competitive wireless product category were a key factor in a sharp decline in earnings for the fourth quarter of 2005. RadioShack subsequently launched a major restructuring program in February 2006 that included the eventual shuttering of nearly 500 stores and the closure of distribution centers in Mississippi and South Carolina. Also in February 2006, Edmondson resigned under pressure after published reports revealed that he had falsified the educational credentials he had listed in his résumé and biography. After a period of interim leadership, Julian Day was brought onboard as chairman and CEO in July 2006. Day was touted for the turnaround skills he had shown during stints as a senior executive at supermarket giant Safeway Inc. and as CEO of Kmart Holding Corporation.

After RadioShack, for the first time in its history, posted a net loss through the first three quarters of 2006, cost-cutting efforts implemented by Day helped generate much better results for the fourth quarter, and the company was able to eke out full-year net income of $73.4 million on sales of $4.78 billion. This trend continued in 2007, when net income more than tripled to $236.8 million. Sales dropped to $4.25 billion, however, as same-store sales fell 8.2 percent. The maturing of the wireless industry and its increasingly competitive nature was one of the prime challenges facing RadioShack given that the firm generated one-third of its sales within the wireless category. At the same time, overall sales of consumer electronics were slowing, and the small size of RadioShack stores precluded any significant presence within two hot electronics categories: large-screen televisions and notebook computers. Some signs of a rebound were evident in 2008, however, as same-store sales for company-owned stores and kiosks increased 3.4 percent during the first nine months of the year. Part of this surge was attributable to strong sales of digital television converter boxes. Many U.S. consumers needed these devices to enable their older televisions to receive broadcast signals following the June 2009, federally mandated changeover from analog to digital television broadcasting. Other strong categories during 2008 included GPS devices, video gaming, prepaid wireless phones, and upgrade activations for AT&T wireless service (formerly Cingular Wireless). In October 2008 the company launched a nationwide electronics trade-in program that enabled consumers to recycle select categories of technology products in exchange for a RadioShack gift card.

Maura Troester
Updated, David E. Salamie

PRINCIPAL SUBSIDIARIES

Tandy Finance Corporation.

PRINCIPAL COMPETITORS

Best Buy Co., Inc.; Circuit City Stores, Inc.; Wal-Mart Stores, Inc.; Target Corporation; Sears Holdings Corporation; Amazon.com, Inc.; AT&T Inc.; Cellco Partnership; Sprint Nextel Corporation; T-Mobile USA,

Inc.; Staples, Inc.; Office Depot, Inc.; OfficeMax Incorporated.

FURTHER READING

Anderson Forest, Stephanie, "Promises, Promises at Tandy," *Business Week,* January 20, 1997, pp. 28–29.

———, "Radio Shack Looks Like a Palace Now," *Business Week,* May 13, 1996, pp. 153–54.

———, "Thinking Big—Very Big—at Tandy," *Business Week,* July 20, 1992, pp. 85–86.

Biesada, Alexandra, "Incredible Gamble," *Financial World,* June 9, 1992, pp. 49–51.

Clark, Don, and Carlos Tejada, "Microsoft, Tandy Announce Internet Partnership," *Wall Street Journal,* November 12, 1999, p. B5.

Dorman, Shirleen, "RadioShack Plans a Face-Lift for Most Stores," *Wall Street Journal,* September 18, 2008, p. B4.

Faison, Seth, "'Incredible Universe' Seeks a Big New York Bang," *New York Times,* November 17, 1994, p. D1.

Farman, Irvin, *Tandy's Money Machine: How Charles Tandy Built Radio Shack into the World's Largest Electronics Chain,* Chicago: Mobium Press, 1992, 464 p.

Goldgaber, Arthur, "Tandy: Out of Juice," *Financial World,* June 17, 1997, p. 26.

Halkias, Maria, "Retailer Begins to Recharge," *Dallas Morning News,* February 27, 2008, p. 1D.

Heller, Laura, "Next Wave for RadioShack," *Discount Store News,* April 3, 2000, pp. 1, 44.

———, "RadioShack Inks Two Wireless Deals," *DSN Retailing Today,* October 25, 2004, pp. 5, 68.

———, "RadioShack Provides Foundation for Tandy Turnaround," *Discount Store News,* January 4, 1999, pp. 31–32, 34.

———, "RadioShack to Pare Back Select Categories," *DSN Retailing Today,* January 7, 2002, pp. 3, 44.

———, "RadioShack's New CEO Unveils Growth Plans," *DSN Retailing Today,* June 27, 2005, pp. 1, 48.

———, "Visionary Offers New Perspective," *Discount Store News,* May 24, 1999, pp. 60, 87.

Hulock, Jim, Todd Mason, and Scott Ticer, "Burned by Superstores, Tandy Is Fighting Fire with Fire," *Business Week,* October 28, 1985, pp. 62+.

Landy, Heather, "A Brighter Day Ahead: RadioShack Is Looking to the New CEO for a Turnaround," *Fort Worth (Tex.) Star-Telegram,* July 24, 2006, p. C1.

———, "RadioShack CEO Quits," *Fort Worth (Tex.) Star-Telegram,* February 21, 2006, p. A1.

Mason, Todd, "Radio Shack Puts on the Pinstripes," *Business Week,* September 1, 1986, p. 66.

———, "Tandy Finds a Cold, Hard World Outside the Radio Shack," *Business Week,* August 31, 1987, p. 68.

McWilliams, Gary, "RadioShack CEO Agrees to Resign," *Wall Street Journal,* February 21, 2006, p. A3.

Miller, Annetta, "Shufflin' at the Shack," *Newsweek,* June 7, 1993, p. 44.

Palmer, Jay, "From RadioShack to RadioShanty: There's No Quick Fix in Sight," *Barron's,* July 17, 2006, p. 14.

Palmeri, Christopher, "RadioShack Redux," *Forbes,* March 23, 1998, pp. 54–56.

"Radio Shack's Rough Trip," *Business Week,* May 30, 1977, p. 55.

Ramstad, Evan, "Inside Radio Shack's Surprising Turnaround," *Wall Street Journal,* June 8, 1999, p. B1.

———, "Tandy to Shed Incredible Universe Chain," *Wall Street Journal,* December 31, 1996.

Roberts, Leonard H., *RadioShack Corporation: A Story of Extraordinary Growth,* New York: Newcomen Society of the United States, 2001, 24 p.

Spagat, Elliot, "RadioShack's Revamp Runs on Batteries," *Wall Street Journal,* June 25, 2002, p. B5.

Spector, Mike, "Former Kmart CEO to Become RadioShack Chairman, CEO," *Wall Street Journal,* July 7, 2006, p. B5.

Strauss, Lawrence C., "A New Day at RadioShack," *Barron's,* March 26, 2007, pp. 25–26.

"Tandy Corp. Aims to Get Some Respect," *Business Week,* September 12, 1983, pp. 94+.

West, James L., *Tandy Corporation: Start on a Shoe String,* New York: Newcomen Society in North America, 1968, 24 p.

"Why Hotshot Tandy Suddenly Sounds So Humble," *Business Week,* May 21, 1984, pp. 45+.

REpower Systems AG

Überseering 10 / Oval Office
Hamburg, D-22297
Germany
Telephone: (+49 40) 555 50 900
Fax: (+49 40) 555 50 90 39 99
Web site: http://www.repower.de

Public Company
Incorporated: 2001
Employees: 1,005
Sales: EUR 678.15 million ($999.2 million) (2007)
Stock Exchanges: Frankfurt
Ticker Symbol: RPW
NAICS: 333611 Turbine and Turbine Generator Set
  Units Manufacturing

■ ■ ■

REpower Systems AG is a leading developer and manufacturer of wind power generation systems. The Hamburg, Germany-based company operates on a global level, with subsidiaries in Australia, Canada, China, France, Greece, India, Italy, Japan, Portugal, Spain, the United Kingdom, and the United States. Through its own technology, REpower has developed a range of wind turbines for the onshore and offshore market, with power generation capacities from 1.5 megawatts to an industry-leading five megawatts. The group's 5M five-megawatt turbine, developed specifically for the offshore market, also boasts the world's largest rotor diameter of 126.5 meters. In addition to direct sales, REpower licenses its technology to third parties.

The company also provides a full range of after-sales services.

With more than 1,000 employees, REpower generated sales of EUR 678 million ($999 million) in 2007. Sales outside of Germany represented approximately 65 percent of this total. In Germany, the company's market share nears 11 percent. The company was the subject of a bidding war in 2007, between Areva and Suzlon Energy. The latter company, the leading wind generation operator in India, ultimately succeeded in gaining more than 87 percent of REpower's shares. Suzlon founder Tulsi Tanti is REpower's chairman, with Per Hornung Pedersen serving as CEO. REpower is listed on the Frankfurt stock exchange.

MID-NINETIES BEGINNINGS

REpower Systems resulted from the 2001 merger of three prominent players in the young German wind power industry. Jacobs Energie, pro + pro Energiesysteme, and BWU-Brandenburgische Wind- und Umwelttechnologien had all been founded in the early 1990s to exploit the newly emerging technologies for generating energy from the wind. All three companies were initially supported by investment capital and project development assistance from Regenerative Energien Denker & Dr. Wulff KG, a company founded in 1995 and later renamed as Denker & Wulff.

Jacobs Energie was the oldest of the companies. By 1994 Jacobs had become one of the first to develop a 500-kilowatt (0.5-megawatt) turbine, marking a new step toward establishing wind power as a cost-effective, renewable energy source. By 1996 Jacobs had perfected

COMPANY PERSPECTIVES

Our driver is to be the leading technical force in the wind industry. That does not mean adopting a new and different approach to everything. To us, it means optimising our wind turbines down to the very last detail, thus guaranteeing our clients the technical edge in terms of performance and reliability.

its turbine technology, raising output to 600 kilowatts. In that year, Jacobs reached a licensing agreement with BWU, which had been founded by Denker & Wulff earlier in the year. The licensing partnership eventually helped raise Jacobs's turbine output to 750 kilowatts.

In 1997, however, pro + pro, founded that year as a Denker & Wulff protégé, introduced groundbreaking technology for a new turbine type with a potential of generating up to 1.5 megawatts of power. Rather than build the turbine itself, pro + pro sought licensing partners. The first to sign up was Jacobs Energie, which became the first to launch construction of the first MD70 prototype. Pro + pro also sold licenses to the MD70 design to Nordex AG, Fuhrländer, and Husumer Schiffswerft.

In the meantime, BWU had been progressing with its own technology, resulting in the launch of full-scale production of the BWU 1000/57, the first wind turbine to break the one-megawatt barrier, in 1998. The following year BWU also launched serial production of its smaller BWU 48/600-750 series.

MERGING FOR STRENGTH IN 2001

Pro + pro's project faced a setback in 1999 when Husumer Schiffswerft went bankrupt. Jacobs Energie quickly took up the slack, however, taking over the former Husumer shipyards. The site became Jacobs Energie's main production facility, a position it was to retain under REpower Systems as well. In its new quarters, Jacobs Energie was able to extend the pro + pro design to its full 77-meter rotor capacity, introducing the first 1.5 megawatt turbine. The company launched full-scale production of that model in 2000. A unique feature of the MD77 was its ability to generate power even in low-wind locations.

Jacobs Energie faced bruising competition from Nordex and Fuhrländer. Both companies owned the license to pro + pro's technology, and had begun

marketing turbine designs highly similar to that of Jacobs Energie. The company responded by launching a new effort to improve its technology and boost the output of the MD series to an industry-leading two megawatts.

Toward this end, Jacobs Energie, BWU, and pro + pro decided to merge their operations in 2001, forming REpower Systems Group. As part of the merger, Denker & Wulff became a subsidiary of REpower. By the following year, REpower had completed the integration of its merged operations. The company then went public, listing its shares on the Frankfurt stock exchange. The new company established itself among the leading players in the fast-growing and highly competitive German wind power generation sector.

INTERNATIONAL FOCUS

REpower had by then recognized the necessity of establishing itself on an international level. This was the case in part because of the relatively small size of the German market especially its offshore market, expected to play a major role in the future growth of the wind power industry. Meanwhile, the German market had become crowded not only with domestic rivals, but also with an increasing number of large-scale foreign companies.

REpower's first move into the international market came at the beginning of 2002, when the company reached a licensing and distribution agreement with Japan's Meidensha Corporation. Partnerships quickly emerged as an important part of REpower foreign growth strategy. By July 2002 the company had entered the Australian market, forming a joint venture with Australia's Notus Energy. Similarly, a new joint venture brought the company into Canada, with the creation of REpower Wind Corp., before the end of the year.

Other joint ventures followed, as the company teamed up with Greek construction major Diekat to enter that market in 2003. The company also established itself in the United Kingdom, forming a partnership with Peter Brotherhood Ltd. and establishing REpower UK in Scotland.

The company's turbine sales grew strongly during this period. By the end of 2002, REpower had sold more than 500 of its MD 70/77 turbines. Soon after, the company successfully connected a new generation turbine, the MM82, another two-megawatt turbine, to the power grid. This launch helped back the company's strong sales growth, including an entry into France following the purchase of 11 turbines by that country's electricity monopoly, EDF. Soon after, REpower entered Italy as well, backed by the sale of 19 turbines to that market.

KEY DATES

1994: Jacobs Energie of Germany develops 0.5-megawatt wind power turbine, which is subsequently licensed to BWU.

1997: Jacobs Energie acquires the license for pro + pro's new 1.5-megawatt turbine design.

1999: Company takes over former Husumer Schiffswerft shipyards.

2001: Jacobs, pro + pro, and BWU merge to form REpower Systems.

2002: REpower goes public with a listing on the Frankfurt stock exchange.

2003: REpower begins development of new 5M turbine, the world's largest with a capacity of five megawatts.

2007: Suzlon of India wins takeover battle and acquires 87 percent of REpower.

MEGAWATT CHAMPION IN 2006

REpower had been developing a major new breakthrough in wind turbine technology. Development of the company's next generation turbine began in 2003. By September 2004 the company unveiled an onshore prototype for the 5M, the world's largest wind turbine, with a rotor diameter of 126.5 meters, and a total weight of 290 metric tons. The nacelle (the enclosure that houses such items as the generating components and gearbox) of the 5M alone was said to be the size of a detached house.

By November REpower had completed the construction of the first 5M test site, in Brunsbüttel, Germany, connecting the turbine to the power grid. The success of the 5M marked a new industry milestone, becoming the first wind power turbine to reach an output of five megawatts. The 5M represented a major step forward toward the cost-effectiveness of wind power as a significant energy source.

The 5M's true destination, however, was to equip the offshore market. In order to prove the turbine's capability, REpower launched development of its first offshore test site, called Beatrice, located some 25 kilometers off the Scottish coast in 44 meters of water. Construction of that site lasted until August 2006.

REpower continued to make strong advances in sales of its smaller turbines, which included a new two-megawatt design, the MM92, which had entered the prototype phase in 2005. The company entered the Portuguese market, forming a joint venture with that country's Martifer Energia in 2005. Martifer also became a shareholder in REpower as well, increasing its stake from an initial 9 percent to a 25 percent stake by June 2005.

By then, REpower had boosted its share of the German wind power market to nearly 10 percent. The company was also able to claim the leading share of the French wind power industry by 2005, a position solidified in 2006 with an order for 140 wind turbines placed by EDF. REpower's prominence also attracted the attention of another investor, as the French nuclear power plant giant Areva became the company's single largest shareholder.

NEW OWNERS IN 2007

REpower's 5M turbine quickly became the major motor for the company's future growth. In October 2006, the company signed a contract to supply turbines for Germany's first offshore wind farm, Borkum West, expected to be connected to the power grid by 2008. In order to supply its growing number of orders for the 5M, REpower began construction of a second manufacturing facility, in Osterönfeld, Germany, in December 2006.

REpower's technology had attracted interest farther abroad. The company's entry into the United States market came in 2006, when that country's enXco placed an order for 56 of REpower's turbines. Soon after, REpower reached an agreement to form a joint venture with China's Honiton Energy Ltd. and North Heavy Industry Corp., becoming the first Western wind power group to enter the Chinese market. The company also began exploring another potentially vast market in 2006, when it formed a licensing partnership with India's Essar Group.

In 2007 REpower found itself at the center of a takeover battle. In January of that year, Areva announced its intention to acquire majority control of REpower, launching a takeover offer worth EUR 105 per share. The French company's ambitions were soon thwarted, however, when Indian wind power leader Suzlon Energy launched a counteroffer. By May of that year, Suzlon, which had also been buying REpower shares on the open market, won the battle, finally raising its offer to EUR 168 per share. Suzlon founder and billionaire Tulsi Tanti then became REpower's chairman, as the Indian group acquired more than 87 percent of REpower.

The takeover battle was unable to distract REpower from its own steady expansion. In March 2007 the company reached an agreement to provide six of its 5M turbines for the proposed Thornton Bank offshore wind farm, the first in Belgium. The company also formed a consortium with Galp Energia, successfully bidding for a massive 400-megawatt project tendered by the Portuguese government.

In December 2007 REpower commissioned its new production facility, dedicated to the production of the 5M nacelles, in Bremerhaven, Germany. The group also expanded its manufacturing capacity that year through the creation of a joint venture, Abeking & Rasmussen Rotec, with PowerBlades GmbH, to build an offshore rotor blade manufacturing facility in Bremerhaven. That site launched production in April 2008.

NEW ORDERS SURGE

The expansion of its production capabilities came amid a surge in new orders as REpower's 5M turbine surpassed its initial power generation expectations. New orders included an agreement to supply wind turbines with a total power of up to 690 megawatts to the United States, placed at the end of 2007. In May 2008 REpower led a consortium in a successful bid for a contract to build a 954 megawatt wind farm in Quebec, Canada, becoming part of one of the largest wind farm projects in the world. By then, however, REpower had also launched negotiations with RWE Innogy, in Germany, to supply turbines for as much as 1,900-megawatts total capacity over the next several years. In another success, the company received an order for turbines with a capacity of 263 megawatts for an Italian-French wind farm project led by Italy's ENEL.

The strong expansion of installed turbine bases also led REpower to boost its service component, supported by an increasingly global network of subsidiaries. REpower also sought to boost its services operations at home in Germany. By 2008 it had gained a nearly 11 percent share of the German market, which remained the company's single largest, generating 35 percent of its total revenues of EUR 678.15 million ($999.2 million) in 2007. In support of this business, the company acquired Schaumann GmbH & Co., gaining control of its fleet of vehicles. In this way, the company boosted its response time, claiming that its service technicians were

able to reach nearly all of its German turbine installations within two hours. REpower's leading-edge technology had made it a major force in the global wind power market in the new century.

M. L. Cohen

PRINCIPAL SUBSIDIARIES

REpower Australia Pty Ltd.; REpower Diekat (Greece; 50%); REpower Espana S.L.; REpower Italia S.r.l.; REpower North (China) Co. Ltd.; REpower Portugal–Sistemas Eolicos S.A.; REpower S.A.S. (France); REpower Systems AG Beijing Office (China); REpower UK Ltd.; REpower USA Corp.

PRINCIPAL COMPETITORS

Babcock Borsig AG; GE Energy; Nordex AG; Siemens Solarparc AG; Vestas Wind Systems A/S.

FURTHER READING

Chaudhary, Archana, "Wind Turbine Maker Sells Shares to Pay Debt," *International Herald Tribune,* December 20, 2007, p. 22.

De Vries, Eize, "REpower: Suzlon Wins Takeover Battle," *Renewable Energy Today,* July 1, 2007.

Leahy, Joe, "Suzlon Private Equity Sell-off Could Fund REpower Deal," *Financial Times,* November 24, 2008, p. 20.

"Olympian Task for REpower," *Modern Power Systems,* May 2006, p. 37.

"REpower Bid: Areva Wants to Settle for Less," *Financial Express,* April 17, 2007.

"REpower, Denker & Wulff Sell Eastern German Wind Farms," *Renewable Energy Today,* July 7, 2005.

"REpower in License Agreement with Essar Group for Entry into India," *Financial Express,* March 23, 2007.

"REpower Inaugurates Operation of Prototype Turbine," *Renewable Energy Today,* February 11, 2005.

Ross, Ian, "Winds of Change Stall Project," *Northern Ontario Business,* September 2003, p. 7B.

"Suzlon Pips Areva with $1.33bn Offer," *Financial Express,* February 9, 2007.

Riverbed Technology, Inc.

199 Fremont Street
San Francisco, California 94105
U.S.A.
Telephone: (415) 247-8800
Fax: (415) 247-8801
Web site: http://www.riverbed.com

Public Company
Incorporated: 2002 as NBT Technology, Inc.
Employees: 623
Sales: $236.4 million (2007)
Stock Exchanges: NASDAQ
Ticker Symbol: RVBD
NAICS: 511210 Software Publishers

∎ ∎ ∎

Riverbed Technology, Inc., develops hardware and software that accelerates performance across wide-area networks. The company sells appliances under the name Steelhead, which consist of its Riverbed Optimization System, a proprietary software program embedded on a general purpose hardware computing platform. Customers, primarily large corporations, use Steelhead to ensure employees at branch offices can readily access and share data and applications. Steelhead reduces application protocol inefficiencies, network protocol inefficiencies, and bandwidth requirements. Riverbed sells its products on a global basis, serving more than 3,500 customers.

FOUNDERS: KENNELLY AND MCCANNE

Riverbed's founders, Jerry M. Kennelly and Steven McCanne, possessed distinct and complementary skills that enabled their start-up venture to clear two important hurdles. The first challenge was to develop technology that could captivate the marketplace, the task embraced by McCanne, and the subsequent challenge was to capitalize commercially on the technology, the chief responsibility assumed by Kennelly. The partnership—not the first time Kennelly and McCanne worked together—proved effective, as Riverbed established its footing during its first five years in business and embarked toward a promising future.

In the thriving community of high-technology companies rooted in northern California, chief executive officers commonly were young, technically gifted executives, but Kennelly did not fit the stereotype. He was 51 years old when he helped start Riverbed, having spent the previous three decades not as an engineer, but as a specialist in finance and sales. Kennelly studied literature at Williams College before earning his master's degree in business from New York University's Stern School of Business. Beginning in the 1970s, he worked in finance departments at Motorola and Hitachi. He joined Hewlett-Packard in 1980, serving as worldwide sales and marketing controller for the company's Tandem Computers division. In 1988, he left Hewlett-Packard to serve as finance director for Oracle Corporation's U.S. operations, a two-year stint that ended when he joined Sybase, Inc., an infrastructure software company. After serving in several financial and operational positions at Sybase, Kennelly joined another infrastructure software

COMPANY PERSPECTIVES

Riverbed's award-winning Steelhead WDS appliances address all of the issues that affect application performance over the WAN, dramatically improving the performance of applications that companies and knowledge workers rely on every day—including file sharing, e-mail, backup, document management systems, IT tools, as well as ERP and CRM solutions. With Riverbed, any of these applications can be accelerated somewhere between 5 and 50, and even up to 100 times faster. In very simple terms, the impact for companies is the difference between having dial-up and having broadband. Suddenly, the impossible becomes possible, just like that.

company, Inktomi Corporation, serving as its chief financial officer for the six years leading up to Riverbed's formation.

"In a way it's good I am not a technical founder," Kennelly said in a December 17, 2007 interview with *Financial Week.* "I'm not in love with the code. All I care about is winning—getting the development right by the customers' requirements. It gives me a liberated place from which to run the company." What Kennelly lacked in technological expertise, his partner, McCanne, more than compensated for, giving Riverbed a chief technology officer who was hailed by *MIT Technology Review* as one of the top 100 young innovators in the world in 2002. "Steve McCanne's a rock star," one of Riverbed's principal investors said in the January 17, 2003 issue of *Byte and Switch.*

Nearly 20 years Kennelly's junior, McCanne spent his academic career at the University of California, Berkeley. He earned a bachelor's degree in electrical engineering and computer science and a doctorate degree in computer science at the Berkeley campus before joining the university's faculty. McCanne taught computer science at Berkeley until 1998, when he cofounded FastForward Networks, a network infrastructure company that developed Internet broadcasting technology. He remained with FastForward Networks until it was acquired two years after its inception. The company, its value inflated in the midst of the hyperbolic dot-com era, sold for $1.3 billion, the price paid by Inktomi. After the acquisition, McCanne joined Inktomi, where, as chief technology officer, he worked alongside the company's chief financial officer, Kennelly.

RESEARCH AND DEVELOPMENT BEGINS IN 2002

Kennelly and McCanne worked together for two years at Inktomi before setting out on their own. They founded Riverbed in May 2002, incorporating the company as NBT Technology, Inc.; both executives loved to fish, which prompted the name change to Riverbed one year after the company was incorporated. Their focus was on wide-area networks (WANs), specifically on how to improve the performance of applications shared over WANs. In a local-area network (LAN), such as a group of computers located within an office, applications performed as much as 100 times faster than they did over a network of geographically dispersed locations, such as the branch offices of a corporation. Through Riverbed, Kennelly and McCanne were aiming to help WANs function as efficiently as LANs by developing software to accelerate the transmission of applications such as e-mail, Microsoft Office, Windows file sharing, and design software.

The market potential for WAN optimization solutions was promising. Large corporations (Riverbed estimated there were more than four million remote offices of U.S.-based companies alone) spent substantial percentages of their information technology budgets to combat the poor performance of WANs. They built and operated local data centers throughout their operating territories to ensure critical data was readily accessible by their employees. Instead of costly, redundant data centers, Riverbed intended to offer software as a solution, answering the need for accelerated WAN performance at a fraction of the cost of building and operating scores of data centers.

Riverbed operated purely as a research-and-development company for its first two years, existing as a company without a product and without any ability to generate revenue. It did have the ability to lose money, however, racking up more than $4 million in losses while McCanne worked on developing the technology Kennelly would bring to market. During this initial, incubating stage of the company's existence, it relied on the financial support of venture capital (VC) firms, beginning with $6.6 million in funding it received in 2002 from Accel Partners, a VC firm focused on networking and software, and Lightspeed Venture Partners, a VC firm focused on early-stage investments. The two firms threw their financial might behind Riverbed based on McCanne's reputation as a technological wizard, a reputation that would be put to the test once he developed a product for Riverbed to sell.

KEY DATES

2002: Riverbed is incorporated as NBT Technology, Inc., by Jerry M. Kennelly and Steven McCanne.
2003: The company changes its name to Riverbed Technology, Inc.
2004: Riverbed begins shipping its first Steelhead appliances.
2005: An office in Singapore is opened to serve as the headquarters for the company's operations in the Asia Pacific region.
2006: Riverbed completes its initial public offering of stock.
2007: The company records its first annual profit.
2008: RiOS 5.0 is released.

SHIPPING THE FIRST PRODUCT: 2004

After toiling in Riverbed's San Francisco offices looking for a way to optimize WANs, McCanne achieved success, developing the company's signature product, Steelhead, another nod to the founders' passion for fishing. The product, powered by the Riverbed Optimization System, or RiOS, began shipping in May 2004, precisely two years after the company's formation. Steelhead attacked the challenge of delivering LAN-like performance to WANs in several ways, including performing scalable data referencing. The technology allowed Steelhead appliances to decompose the structure of data and to find similarities among the bytes transmitted over WANs. Instead of sending data in byte form, which resulted in redundancy, Steelhead transmitted a data reference, thereby significantly reducing the amount of bytes being transmitted. "About 70 percent to 90 percent of WAN traffic is repetitive and can be redundant," a Riverbed executive told *Networkworld* (December 14, 2004). "This feature removes bytes from the WAN."

Steelhead appliances were available in five models, priced at between $6,000 and $40,000. For the money, customers, according to Riverbed's claims, enjoyed transmission speeds that were five to 50 times faster than without utilizing Steelhead, sometimes as much as 100 times faster, which made a Steelhead-supported WAN as efficient as a LAN. By the end of 2004, 68 companies had purchased Steelhead, enabling McCanne and Kennelly to collect their first stream of revenue. Riverbed generated $2.5 million in revenue during the ab-

breviated year, and prospects for the future were exceedingly bright. JMP Securities, which estimated the market for WAN optimization technologies at $200 million in 2004, projected a market worth between $2 billion and $4 billion by 2007.

RAPID INITIAL GROWTH

Once Steelhead began shipping, it was time for Kennelly's talents to shine. McCanne's technical work was not completed. Improvements in Steelhead and RiOS would be ongoing, beginning with the release of Version 1.1 in October 2004 that featured a central management console. Yet the moment had come for Kennelly to monetize the value created by McCanne. Toward that end, Riverbed announced the establishment of operations in the Asia Pacific region in March 2005. Multinational companies in Asia were particularly aware of the performance problems that occurred across WANs in their region because the high latency inherent in satellite and transoceanic networks severely degraded the throughput of applications. Riverbed stepped in to provide a solution to their problems, opening an office in Singapore that served as the regional headquarters for branch offices that were slated to be established in China, India, and Australia.

As Kennelly expanded Riverbed's sales and distribution operations, revenues swelled. In 2005, the company's first full year with a marketable product, sales jumped from $2.5 million to $22.9 million. Net income was nonexistent, however, as expenses outpaced revenue growth, resulting in a loss of $9.8 million in 2004 and $17.4 million in 2005. The cost of building up a sales and marketing force impeded the company's chance to turn a profit, but Kennelly was more concerned about increasing Riverbed's customer base and its sales total. He wanted to turn to Wall Street to gain the capital to finance further expansion, and the progress achieved during the first half of 2006 convinced him the time was right for Riverbed's public debut. During the first half of 2006, the company's losses widened, totaling $10.3 million, but revenues increased by a factor of six, reaching $31.8 million. As preparations were being made for the company's initial public offering (IPO) of stock, Riverbed was serving more than 1,000 customers.

PUBLIC DEBUT IN 2006

Riverbed completed its IPO on September 20, 2006, when 8.8 million shares were sold. The response from investors was cause for celebration at the company's San Francisco headquarters. Shares increased 57 percent during their first day of trading, closing at $15.30 per share, which made Riverbed's public debut one of the most successful IPOs of the year. The company raised $87.5 million from the offering, giving Kennelly the funds to continue his expansion campaign.

FIRST ANNUAL PROFIT IN 2007

Riverbed celebrated its fifth anniversary in 2007. The company's stock value rose to $52.81 per share toward the end of the year, an enormous increase from the IPO price of $9.75 per share roughly a year earlier, but the biggest cause for celebration during the year was the company's financial performance. Revenues skyrocketed 162 percent in 2007, reaching $236.4 million. More impressive, the company posted its first annual profit, turning a nearly $16 million loss in 2006 into a $14.7 million gain.

As Riverbed prepared for the future, the road ahead offered an opportunity for vibrant growth provided the company was able to keep pace with competitors such as Cisco Systems, Juniper Networks, and F5 Networks. Kennelly was ready for the challenge, exuding confidence in a February 5, 2008 company press release. "With the majority of the global workforce working outside of headquarter offices," Kennelly said, "we believe that wide area data solutions can significantly improve productivity while allowing companies to consolidate expensive equipment and services, saving billions of dollars for companies worldwide. Our competitive leadership in this market remains unchanged and we are leveraging our unique software architecture to enter into attractive new markets." To aid him in his efforts to increase Riverbed's customer base, Kennelly turned to Version 5.0 of RiOS, which was released in 2008. With the introduction of RiOS 5.0, Riverbed became the first vendor to provide application-level protocol optimization for Microsoft Exchange 2007, a technological edge Kennelly intended to exploit as he pressed forward.

Jeffrey L. Covell

PRINCIPAL SUBSIDIARIES

Riverbed Technology Limited (UK); Riverbed Technology Sarl (France); Riverbed Technology Pte. Ltd. (Singapore); Riverbed Technology GmbH (Germany); Riverbed Technology Pty Ltd. (Australia); Riverbed Technology Korea, Inc.; Riverbed Technology Limited (Hong Kong); Riverbed Technology K.K. (Japan); Riverbed Technology B.V. (Netherlands); Riverbed Technology India Private Limited; Riverbed Technology International, Inc.; Riverbed Technology AG (Switzerland); Riverbed Technology SL (Spain); Riverbed Technology Canada LTD; Riverbed Technology South Africa (Proprietary) Limited; Riverbed Technology S.r.l. (Italy); Riverbed Technology Limited (New Zealand); Riverbed Technology AB (Sweden); Riverbed Technology Sdn. Bhd. (Malaysia); Riverbed Technology S. de R.L. de C.V. (Mexico).

PRINCIPAL COMPETITORS

Cisco Systems, Inc.; Juniper Networks, Inc.; BlueCoat Systems, Inc.; F5 Networks, Inc.

FURTHER READING

Dubie, Denise, "Get to Know Riverbed," *Networkworld,* December 14, 2004.

"Former Inktomi CFO Heads NBT Technology," *San Francisco Business Times,* September 24, 2002.

Hawn, Carleen, "Beans to Bytes: Ex-CFO Scores As Tech Top Exec," *Financial Week,* December 17, 2007.

"IPO Spotlight: Riverbed Technology," *Europe Intelligence Wire,* September 15, 2006.

Maitland, Jo, "NBT Technology," *Byte and Switch,* January 17, 2003.

"NBT Technology Raises $6.6 Million in Series A Financing," *Silicon Investor,* January 7, 2003.

"Networking—Riverbed Technology—Angling for Success in the Optimisation Market," *Computing,* June 2, 2005, p. 32.

"Riverbed Technology Launches Asia Pacific Operations," *Asia Africa Intelligence Wire,* March 1, 2005.

"Riverbed Technology Leaps in IPO," *Europe Intelligence Wire,* September 21, 2006.

"United States: Riverbed Extends Lead in WDS Market with Launch of RiOS 5.0 Software," *TendersInfo,* March 19, 2008.

Ross Stores, Inc.

4440 Rosewood Drive
Pleasanton, California 94588-3050
U.S.A.
Telephone: (925) 965-4400
Fax: (925) 965-4388
Web site: http://www.rossstores.com

Public Company
Incorporated: 1957
Employees: 39,100
Sales: $5.98 billion (2007)
Stock Exchanges: NASDAQ
Ticker Symbol: ROST
NAICS: 448140 Family Clothing Stores

■ ■ ■

Ross Stores, Inc., is the second largest off-price retailer in the United States, trailing only The TJX Companies, Inc. The company operates more than 900 Ross Dress for Less stores in 27 states, mainly in the West and South, and roughly 50 dd's Discounts stores in California, Florida, Texas, and Arizona. Although Ross operates one of the largest chains of its kind in the country, it reached this stature late in its corporate life. When the chain was purchased in 1982 by a group of investors that included Mervin Morris, founder of the defunct Mervyn's chain, it included only six units in the San Francisco Bay area. During the ensuing decade, the chain grew robustly under the stewardship of Stuart Moldaw and Don Rowlett who converted the junior department stores to off-price retail units, the first of

their kind in California, sporting the name Ross Dress for Less. During the early 21st century, Ross Dress for Less stores offered brand and designer name apparel, accessories, and footwear for the entire family, as well as home accessories, at prices 20 percent to 60 percent below the prices charged by competing department stores and specialty shops. The dd's Discounts chain, which was launched in 2004, offers more modestly priced assortments of items within these same categories, at prices 20 percent to 70 percent below those charged by mid-market department stores and discount stores. About one-quarter of Ross Stores' outlets are located in California, making that state by far the company's most important market. More than 10 percent of the outlets are sited in the firm's second and third largest markets, Texas and Florida, respectively.

ORIGINS

The roots of the Ross retail chain stretch back to 1957, when the first Ross junior department store opened. Yet the first definitive year in the company's history occurred nearly 30 years after its birth. In 1982, the year that separated the two distinct eras in Ross's history, two men with a wealth of experience in the off-price retail industry purchased the Ross enterprise when the chain comprised six junior department stores in the San Francisco Bay area. With these six stores, acquired with the help of venture capital partners, the two entrepreneurs made no mistake about their intentions, quickly developing a retail empire that would boast 107 stores three years later, 156 stores by the end of the 1980s, and nearly 300 stores by the mid-1990s. The orchestrators of this rapid expansion that erased three

COMPANY PERSPECTIVES

Our mission is to offer competitive values to our target customers by focusing on the following key strategic objectives: Achieve an appropriate level of recognizable brands, labels and fashions at strong discounts throughout the store. Meet customer needs on a more local basis. Deliver an in-store shopping experience that reflects the expectations of the off-price customer. Manage real estate growth to compete effectively across all our markets.

decades of sleepy growth were Stuart Moldaw and Donald Rowlett.

Moldaw, who became chairman of Ross following the August 1982 acquisition, was not new to the off-price retail scene. Prior to his involvement with Ross, Moldaw founded Pic-A-Dilly, an off-price retail chain, Country Casuals, and The Athletic Shoe Factory. Rowlett, who was selected as the new president of Ross, was no novice either, having created and developed F.W. Woolworth's off-price subsidiary, J. Brannam, into a 36-unit chain. Together, these two retail veterans had visions of creating a powerful off-price retail chain in an area of the country where the off-price concept was virtually nonexistent. Elsewhere, particularly along the East Coast and in the Midwest, off-price retail stores were enjoying burgeoning popularity during the early 1980s, but in California they were conspicuous by their absence, at least as Moldaw and Rowlett saw it. Considering the pace at which Moldaw and Rowlett expanded the Ross chain shortly after acquiring it, the two were intent on pioneering the concept in California and saturating markets before rival off-price chains recognized the opportunities that existed in the state.

MOLDAW AND ROWLETT ERA

Success was realized from the changes instituted by Moldaw and Rowlett, the first of which was recasting the six-unit chain as a different type of retailer. The two shifted the chain's focus away from its junior orientation to create an off-price format stocking branded apparel for men, women, and children, as well as domestics merchandise, shoes, and accessories at sharply reduced prices. Once the stores were dedicated to attracting a broader customer base and outfitted with a broader merchandise selection, Moldaw and Rowlett made their second decisive move by quickly adding to their store count. Two Ross Dress for Less stores were opened in

the fall of 1982 and 18 stores the following year, more than tripling the size of Ross in little more than a year.

Much of the physical growth recorded during the first full year of Moldaw's and Rowlett's leadership was accomplished by acquiring existing stores in strip malls and freestanding locations abandoned by other retailers. This acquisition strategy would continue to be used by the company as its geographic scope of operations broadened, severing the chains that had fettered it to northern California for three decades. By the end of 1983, Ross Dress for Less stores were situated in southern California and the first store beyond the state's borders—a store in Reno, Nevada—was opened, touching off a march across the map that in a few short years would extend the company's presence from coast to coast.

Early in 1984, plans called for the establishment of 20 stores in California, Arizona, Washington, and Oregon, but by the end of the year Ross had opened twice as many, including stores in Utah, Texas, and Oklahoma. Much of the growth during the year was realized from the acquisition of 15 stores from the Handyman division of Edison Brothers Stores, which added Ross Dress for Less stores in Texas and Oklahoma. The Handyman deal, completed in July, was concluded in the same month that Ross's corporate headquarters were moved to a 494,000-square-foot facility in Newark, California, which also served as the company's distribution center.

From this location in Newark, the company's expansion would be plotted into the 1990s, as the number of stores, each stocking a list of brand and designer names that rivaled most department stores and specialty stores, increased exponentially. Although its merchandise compared favorably with the selection offered by department stores and specialty stores, Ross charged substantially less than traditional retailers, selling its merchandise for as much as 60 percent below competitors' prices. The enormous savings lured customers to Ross's stores, convincing management, in turn, that the only obstacle checking the company's financial growth was the number of stores it operated. More stores meant more revenue and greater profits, so Moldaw and Rowlett focused their efforts on expansion, making an initial public offering of stock in 1985 to help fund the opening of additional stores. At the time of the public offering, there were 107 Ross Dress for Less stores, an impressive number given the company's total store count of six three years earlier, and an extensive operating territory the company could call its own. After entering Washington, Utah, Arizona, Texas, and Oklahoma in 1984, Ross expanded into new markets in Colorado, Florida, Georgia, New Mexico,

KEY DATES

■

1957: First Ross junior department store opens.
1982: Stuart Moldaw and Donald Rowlett purchase the Ross chain, which then consists of six stores in the San Francisco Bay area; the pair begin converting the units to off-price Ross Dress for Less stores.
1983: Rapid expansion begins with the opening of 18 more stores.
1985: Company goes public to fund further expansion.
1992: Sales surpass the $1 billion mark for the first time.
2001: A new push into the southeastern United States begins.
2004: Headquarters are moved to Pleasanton, California; Ross launches the dd's Discounts chain.
2006: Ross Stores acquires the leasehold rights to 46 former Albertsons supermarkets in California, Florida, Texas, Arizona, Colorado, and Oklahoma.

and Oregon in 1985. By the end of the year, sales were up an encouraging 79 percent, swelling to $375.9 million.

1986 SETBACK

The company's record-setting growth in 1985, which included the addition of 41 stores, was followed by an equally impressive 1986, when 39 stores were opened and new markets were penetrated in Maryland, North Carolina, and Virginia. By this point, there were 121 Ross Dress for Less stores scattered throughout 16 states, 40 percent of which had been open for less than a year. Fueled by this new growth, annual sales shot past the $500 million mark by the end of 1986 and future revenue growth seemed assured as expansion plans were laid for the company's penetration into new markets. In 1986, however, the company suffered its first major setback when it was forced to shutter 25 unprofitable stores located primarily in Texas and Oklahoma, where anemic economic conditions crimped Ross's profits. For the year, Ross reported a crippling $41.4 million loss, $39.4 million of which stemmed from the closures in Texas and Oklahoma.

On the heels of this downturn, the company lost one of its two chief architects when Rowlett resigned

from the company in 1987. It was not long, however, before Ross gained a new architect to rebuild the company and carry it into the 1990s. Following Rowlett's departure, a company veteran, Norman A. Ferber, who was serving as Ross's executive vice-president of merchandising, marketing, and distribution, was appointed as Ross's president and chief operating officer. Less than a year later, in January 1988, Ferber was also named Ross's CEO, taking charge of the company as it was undergoing a series of changes to quickly restore its profitability.

Responding to the $40 million loss in 1986, Moldaw and Ferber drastically cut back on expansion in 1987, opening only 11 stores and situating those stores in markets where Ross Dress for Less stores were already located or in close proximity. The days of adding one new state after another to the company's geographic fold were over. Instead of trying to dot the country with store after store, Ross executives focused their expansion in three principal markets, the West Coast, the Washington area, and Florida, and devoted more time to developing a profitable merchandising strategy. Hoping to rescue their company from the red, company officials eliminated the domestics departments in Ross stores and added cosmetics and fragrance departments. Additionally, executives added "high-end" clothing to Ross's merchandising mix, upgrading their inventory with items such as men's sport coats and women's silk dresses.

By the end of 1987, management could point to positive results. For the year, Ross recorded an $11.5 million gain after the more than $40 million loss the year before. Encouraged by their initial success, Moldaw and Ferber continued to refine Ross's merchandising strategy as the 1980s progressed. By 1989, 95 percent of the company's 140 stores contained full cosmetic and fragrance departments staffed with beauty consultants, one of the new and decidedly upscale features adopted by Ross as it repositioned itself for consistent profitability. In the chasm separating discount stores and traditional department stores, off-price retailers occupied the middle ground, but as the 1990s neared Moldaw and Ferber were tipping the balance toward the department store end of the scale by adopting the trappings of more upscale retail outlets. Like many off-price chains, Ross had never divided, or "departmentalized," its retail floor space into merchandise categories to any great extent, but as the company entered the 1990s chrome and wood partitions were used with increasing frequency to delineate various departments. Among the other changes reshaping the chain was a refocused inventory strategy, as Ross Dress for Less stores began stocking less variety of merchandise while boosting their supply of preferred lines, creating a narrower and deeper inventory for stores to stock.

STEADY EXPANSION IN THE NINETIES

With these changes came a renewed commitment to expand the chain. In 1989, when Ross ranked as the third largest off-price retailer in the country, company officials announced plans to open 100 to 150 stores during the ensuing five years. As the early 1990s progressed, the chain went a long way toward achieving this ambitious goal. In 1990, 29 new stores were opened, giving the company a total of 185 stores in 18 states by the end of the year and opening up new markets in Philadelphia and in Boise, Idaho. Another 20 stores were opened the following year, as annual sales jumped from $804 million to $930 million, and another 23 stores were added to the chain in 1992, when sales eclipsed the billion-dollar mark, reaching $1.04 billion.

Upon reaching this milestone, Moldaw and Ferber began test marketing a "Home Accents" department, which featured picture frames, china, ceramic ware, and crystal. The concept was introduced in 20 stores early in 1992 and quickly registered sufficient success to warrant its incorporation into other existing Ross Dress for Less stores. With 223 stores by the end of 1992, the company planned to put Home Accents departments in nearly all of its existing locations before the close of 1993, giving it a high-profit-margin vehicle to fuel its financial growth in the years ahead. By the end of 1995, only ten of the company's 292 stores did not contain Home Accents departments. By this time another new department, Bed and Bath, had been launched in 1994. This department featured bed and bath linens and accessories, and by 1997 the rollout of Bed and Bath had been completed throughout the entire chain. In 1996, meantime, a small line of sporting goods, such as basketballs and handheld weights, were added to Ross stores.

Entering the mid-1990s, Ferber, who was named chairman in 1993, was focusing the chain's growth in existing markets. Twenty stores were opened in 1993, another 32 stores in 1994, and 17 stores in 1995, with each successive wave of openings giving Ross a more entrenched market position. With 292 stores by the end of 1995, Ross was collecting nearly $1.5 billion a year in sales, having experienced considerable financial growth during the previous decade. Equally impressive was the company's profitability, which had been strengthened substantially by the changes adopted in the wake of Ross's mid-1980s debacle. In 1995, the company earned more than $43 million, with the average sales per square foot climbing to $230 from an average of $214 in 1991.

That the company recorded this increase during a national recession which crippled many retailers throughout the country boded well for its future, fueling confidence that the "new" Ross was well-positioned to reap the rewards of a recovering economy. As the company prepared for the late 1990s, it hired new management to lead it toward its future. Effective September 1996, Michael Balmuth, Ross's executive vice-president of merchandising, became the company's CEO, replacing Ferber, who stayed on as chairman. Balmuth had joined Ross in 1989 as senior vice-president and general merchandise manager.

Under Balmuth's leadership in the late 1990s, Ross continued to grow steadily within its existing markets and further expanded the nonapparel offerings of its stores. In 1997 an additional 17 stores were opened and revenues were just a shade under $2 billion. Average sales per square foot rose to $285, a 24 percent increase over the figure for 1995. Profits reached a record $117.5 million. Store openings increased to 26 in 1998 and 29 in 1999, bringing the store count to 378 by the end of the latter year. Continuing its steady growth, Ross posted revenues of $2.47 billion, profits of $150.1 million, and average sales per square foot of $300 for 1999. The late 1990s saw the company test and then begin a chainwide rollout of maternity and fine jewelry departments. By the end of the 1990s, more than 16 percent of overall revenues were derived from the sale of nonapparel goods. Another key initiative in the late 1990s was an aggressive expansion of the company's buying staff to broaden its market coverage and gain additional opportunities to purchase closeout merchandise.

EARLY 21ST CENTURY: ACCELERATING GROWTH AND LAUNCH OF DD'S DISCOUNTS

In 2000, 31 more Ross Dress for Less stores opened, boosting the number of units to 409. The company then accelerated its pace of expansion, adding more than 50 stores each year over the next three years. This growth phase included a concerted push into the southeastern United States. In 2001 Ross reentered the Georgia and North Carolina markets and entered South Carolina for the first time. The company moved into Alabama a year later and then into Louisiana and Tennessee in 2003, broadening its reach to 25 states. The expansion in the Southeast was supported by the opening of a new distribution center in Fort Mill, South Carolina, in July 2002. Ross's distribution center in Carlisle, Pennsylvania, buttressed another key growth region around this time, the mid-Atlantic states. The company also positioned itself for further growth in its western stronghold by opening a new 1.3-million-square-foot distribution center in Perris, California, located about 70 miles southeast of Los Angeles. This facility, which began operating in September 2003, replaced the center in Newark. During 2004, Ross sold its Newark property and moved its corporate headquarters to a leased facility in Pleasanton, California, also in the San Francisco Bay area.

The more rapid pace of expansion helped push revenues to nearly $4 billion by fiscal 2003. Ross then ambitiously launched a new retail chain to provide itself with a second vehicle for future growth. During the second half of 2004, the company opened the first ten dd's Discounts stores, all located in California. Averaging about 26,000 square feet in size, slightly smaller than the typical Ross Dress for Less outlet, the dd's stores featured similar categories as those found in the original chain with a similar off-price positioning, but the focus was on lower-cost labels typically sold in mid-market department stores and discount stores. Whereas the typical Ross Dress for Less customer had a household income of around $50,000, dd's Discounts targeted households with incomes of about $30,000. Another contrast centered on site selection. Ross Dress for Less stores were generally located in newer, high-volume power centers, whereas the dd's stores were opened in smaller, older, strip-mall shopping centers. Encouraged by the early performance of the new concept, company executives believed that dd's Discounts had the potential to eventually become a 500-unit, nationwide chain; their vision for the flagship Ross chain was even grander: 1,500 stores from coast to coast.

In addition to the ten dd's stores, the company added 71 net new Ross Dress for Less locations during fiscal 2004, including the first Mississippi store, as revenues increased 8 percent to $4.24 billion. Ross Stores continued on the same path in 2005, opening 75 net new Ross stores and adding ten more dd's Discounts outlets in California. Solid same-store sales growth that year of 6 percent helped propel overall revenues up 17 percent to almost $5 billion. Ross added a fourth distribution center in 2005, purchasing a 685,000-square-foot warehouse in Moreno Valley, California, near the city of Riverside. At the same time, Ross Stores implemented a number of initiatives to improve the efficiencies of its entire supply chain.

While adding 57 Ross Dress for Less outlets and six dd's Discounts stores to its retailing network in 2006, Ross Stores late that year acquired the leasehold rights to more than 40 former Albertsons supermarkets in California, Florida, Texas, Arizona, Colorado, and Oklahoma. During 2007 about half of these locations were converted into Ross Dress for Less units, while the other half began sporting the dd's Discounts banner. This purchase provided the basis for a larger growth spurt in 2007 encompassing 67 new Ross Dress for Less and 26 new dd's outlets. Among the openings were the first dd's sites in Florida, Texas, and Arizona.

As the economic climate deteriorated in 2007, Ross Stores still managed to post solid results for the year, including eking out a 1 percent increase in same-store sales, an overall increase in revenues of 7 percent to just shy of $6 billion, and an 8 percent increase in profits to $241.6 million. Company officials were disappointed, however, in the performance of the new dd's stores located outside California, and they thus decided to curtail growth of that chain in other states until they could gain a handle on what went wrong. Other than this one exception, Ross appeared to be thriving in the economic downturn as increasingly value-conscious consumers sought bargains. Through the first nine months of fiscal 2008, same-store sales were up 3 percent, overall revenues had increased 10 percent, and profits surged 25 percent. The company was less optimistic about the 2008 holiday season, however, and anticipated a decline in same-store sales for the final quarter of fiscal 2008. Expansion plans nevertheless remained on track as nearly 70 more Ross Dress for Less and five dd's stores debuted during the year, though none of the new Ross units were located in a new state and all the dd's were sited in California, indicating a more cautious growth strategy.

Jeffrey L. Covell
Updated, David E. Salamie

PRINCIPAL SUBSIDIARIES

Ross Procurement, Inc.; Ross Merchandising, Inc.; Ross Dress for Less, Inc.; Retail Assurance Group, Ltd. (Bermuda).

PRINCIPAL COMPETITORS

The TJX Companies, Inc.; Wal-Mart Stores, Inc.; Kohl's Corporation; Target Corporation; Sears Holdings Corporation; Burlington Coat Factory Warehouse Corporation; J.C. Penney Company, Inc.; The Men's Wearhouse, Inc.; Goody's Family Clothing, Inc.; Stein Mart, Inc.; The Dress Barn, Inc.; Loehmann's Holdings Inc.; Charming Shoppes, Inc.

FURTHER READING

"Balmuth Named CEO of Ross Stores," *Daily News Record,* June 11, 1995, p. 10.

Carmichael, Aja, "Ross Thrives in Slowdown, but Some Doubts Remain," *Wall Street Journal,* May 14, 2008, p. B5A.

Clark, Ken, "Off-Price Apparel Chains Struggle to Keep Up," *Chain Store Age,* March 2000, pp. 92, 96.

"Dressing More for Less," *Retail Merchandiser,* July 2002, p. 48.

Emert, Carol, "Ross Is Dressed for Success," *San Francisco Chronicle,* March 19, 1997, p. D1.

Gilbert, Les, "Ross Doing Well in Coast with Off-Price Format," *Footwear News,* July 23, 1984, p. 66.

"Going Public Should Help Ross Reach Coast-to-Coast," *Discount Store News,* August 5, 1985, p. 18.

Kahn, Hal, "Ross Stores Inc. CEO to Resign in September," *Knight-Ridder/Tribune Business News,* May 31, 1996.

Krein, Pamela, "Ross Stores to Close 25 Money-Losing Units in Southwest," *Discount Store News,* March 16, 1987, p. 39.

Lau, Gloria, "Know Thy Customer," *Forbes,* July 7, 1997, p. 76.

MacIntosh, Jean, "Refocused Strategy Puts Off-Pricer Ross Stores Right on the Money," *Daily News Record,* October 27, 1988, p. 6.

Meek, Pamela, "Ross Goes Further Upscale in Prototype," *Discount Store News,* September 25, 1989, p. 1.

Moin, David, "Ross Stores Plans to Grow Spin-Off Chain," *Women's Wear Daily,* February 13, 2007, p. 21.

Paris, Ellen, "A Touch of Class," *Forbes,* February 5, 1990, p. 148.

Radwell, Steven, "Dayton Hudson Sells Its Four Plum Stores," *Daily News Record,* February 22, 1984, p. 1.

Razzano, Rhonda, "Ross Stores Realigns Mix, Redirects Strategies: Off-Price Recovers from Oil Patch Setback," *Chain*

Store Age Executive with Shopping Center Age, May 1989, p. 25.

"Ross Unveils Aggressive Plan: 25 New Stores Set for 1994," *Discount Store News,* March 7, 1994, p. 6.

Ruben, Howard, "Ross Stores Plays the Off-Price Game," *Daily News Record,* February 14, 1984, p. 10.

Rutberg, Sidney, "Ross Stores Loss Fails to Chill Optimism," *Women's Wear Daily,* June 25, 1987, p. 6.

Sarkar, Pia, "Ross Buying Albertson's Store Sites," *San Francisco Chronicle,* October 11, 2006, p. C1.

Scardino, Emily, "Ross Stores' dd's Comes into Focus," *DSN Retailing Today,* March 22, 2004, pp. 4, 43.

Steen, Margaret, "More Are Dressing for Less: Ross Stores Thrives amid Slump," *San Jose (Calif.) Mercury News,* December 31, 2002, p. 1C.

Strasburg, Jenny, "High Hopes for Low Prices: Ross Appeals to Bargain Hunters with dd's Discounts," *San Francisco Chronicle,* August 14, 2004, p. C1.

———, "Ross Shuffles Its Top Execs," *San Francisco Chronicle,* February 9, 2005, p. C1.

Strom, Shelly, "Retailer Plans Expansion," *Santa Clara (Calif.) Business Journal,* June 16, 2000, p. 3.

Tanaka, Wendy, "Ross Is Boss," *San Francisco Examiner,* February 7, 1997, p. B1.

Torres, Blanca, "Ross Reports Higher Profit, Big Plans," *Walnut Creek (Calif.) Contra Costa Times,* March 22, 2007, p. C1.

Young, Kristin, "Ross to Open in Atlanta Area," *Women's Wear Daily,* March 7, 2001, p. 13.

Young, Vicki M., "Ross Picks Peters As New President," *Women's Wear Daily,* July 17, 2000, p. 23.

SafeNet Inc.

4690 Millennium Drive
Belcamp, Maryland 21017
U.S.A.
Telephone: (410) 931-7500
Fax: (410) 931-7524
Web site: http://www.safenet-inc.com

Private Company
Incorporated: 1983
Employees: 1,043
Sales: $263.1 million (2007 est.)
NAICS: 334290 Other Communications Equipment
    Manufacturing

■ ■ ■

Based in Belcamp, Maryland, SafeNet Inc. is a leading information security company. In addition to government agencies such as the U.S. Departments of Defense and Homeland Security, as well as the Internal Revenue Service, corporations including Adobe, Bank of America, Cisco, and Microsoft rely on SafeNet's encryption technologies to protect intellectual property, communications, and digital identities.

FORMATIVE YEARS: 1983–92

SafeNet's roots date back to April 1983, when the company was established as Industrial Resource Engineering (IRE). Operating from a basement office in Timonium, Maryland, the company's founders included a computer security specialist named Anthony A. Caputo, as well as two former National Security Agency (NSA) employees. Alan Hastings had served as a cryptographic scientist with the NSA, and Doug Kozlay had worked as a manager within the agency.

Measured progress continued at IRE during its first few years of operation. During this time, the founders developed a system that encrypted messages transmitted via telephone lines. The company's customer base eventually grew to include Citibank, American Telephone and Telegraph Co., the Bank of Montréal, and Lawrence Livermore National Laboratory.

By 1987 IRE's revenues totaled $290,000. The following year, sales increased to $886,560. By 1989 the company employed a workforce of 11 people. IRE ended the 1980s by making its initial public offering (IPO) and becoming a publicly traded enterprise. At this time, Caputo was serving as company chairman, while Kozlay served as president and Hastings held the title of vice-president.

Moving forward into the 1990s, IRE went head to head with competitors that offered similar technologies. In particular, the company faced strong competition from the makers of modems and computers. However, IRE's efforts were successful. In 1991 the company sold $2.1 million worth of its products, which included encryption devices as well as cards equipped with encryption chips, that users inserted into special card readers.

In early 1992 IRE secured a $1.5 million order from Citibank for its X.25 network system. The contract called for the implementation of the company's technology at the bank's main computer centers, as well

COMPANY PERSPECTIVES

Today, SafeNet offers the broadest range of products and solutions of any security company in the world, protecting critical business data, communications and digital identities through a full spectrum of encryption technologies, hardware, software, and chips.

as 250 branches throughout the New York area. IRE secured another major deal during the year when the U.S. Treasury Department chose the company's technology to protect its computerized bill payment system.

Another major deal in 1992 came in the form of a $35 million subcontract with Computer Science Corp., which involved developing electronic locks for 240 military complexes. IRE rounded out the year with a workforce of 25 people.

EARLY GROWTH: 1993–96

During the early 1990s, IRE was recognized as the fastest-growing publicly traded company in the state of Maryland. Following that distinction, in mid-1993 IRE Chairman and CEO Anthony Caputo was named Maryland Entrepreneur of the Year by *Inc.* magazine, Ernst & Young, and Merrill Lynch. By this time Wachovia Bank and the Internal Revenue Service had become IRE customers.

New developments continued during the mid-1990s. In October 1994 the company acquired Chantilly, Virginia-based Connective Strategies Inc., a maker of products used for connecting computers to communications networks.

On the new product front, IRE unveiled its AX400 secure pocket modem in September, giving laptop users a 14.4 kbps modem that also included an encryptor and a random password generator. Another mobile device was introduced in mid-1995, when IRE introduced its AX200 Encrypting Token. Small enough to fit inside one's shirt pocket, the device generated a one-time password that remote users could use for secure computer network access.

Another noteworthy development during the mid-1990s was IRE's $4 million acquisition of Regensdorf, Switzerland-based Gretag Data Systems AG from AT&T International Inc. Following the deal, Gretag adopted the new name Gretacoder Data Systems AG.

INTERNATIONAL EXPANSION: 1997–99

New product introductions continued during the late 1990s. In January 1997, plans for the introduction of a low-cost communications chip were announced. The new product combined IRE's hardware encryption with technology from Norwood, Massachusetts-based Analog Devices Inc., and provided affordable security for conducting business over the Internet and other computer networks.

By 1997 IRE's customer base had grown to include the Bank of Sweden, the Post Office Savings Bank of Singapore, the Bank of New York, and Chase Manhattan Bank. On the government front, the Federal Bureau of Investigation also had joined the company's client roster.

Despite all of its progress, IRE had failed to show a profit since 1992. In order to turn things around, Internet visionary Vinton G. Cerf was added to the company's board to provide the organization with strategic advice.

It was around this time that IRE embarked upon a path of strong international growth. The company's products became available in Japan and the Asia/Pacific region through a distribution agreement with Tokyo-based Kanematsu Corp. in March. Three months later, IRE forged distribution agreements with eight partners in Latin America in order to better serve the liberalized economies there.

One major setback in 1997 was the loss of a $10 million contract with MCI Communications. However, in mid-1997 IRE signed a $4 million network security technology deal with Bethesda, Maryland-based Lockheed Martin Information Systems & Technologies. The contract called for Lockheed to buy and resell IRE's products, including one named SafeNet.

IRE ended the year with a net loss of $3.6 million on revenues of $16 million, compared to a net loss of $7.1 million on revenues of $14.3 million in 1996.

International progress continued in early 1998. At that time IRE forged a three-way strategic alliance that allowed the company to make stronger inroads in Japan. The alliance involved Osaka Media Port, which agreed to market IRE's SafeNet products in Japan, as well as Mitsubishi Corporation, which planned to rely on the other two firms' technology and services to protect a virtual private network (VPN) connecting Mitsubishi offices throughout the world via the Internet. By encrypting the data that is transmitted, VPNs allow private, secure communication and information access on public networks including the Internet.

KEY DATES

1983: Industrial Resource Engineering (IRE) is established in a Timonium, Maryland, basement.
1989: IRE becomes a publicly traded enterprise.
1999: Deloitte & Touche includes the company on its Technology Fast 500 list.
2000: IRE changes its name to SafeNet Inc. and begins trading on the NASDAQ under the symbol SFNT.
2007: Vector Capital acquires SafeNet for $634 million, and the company becomes a privately held enterprise.

More activity occurred in Japan in August 1999. Building upon a relationship that had begun the previous year, the think tank Nomura Research Institute announced that it would expand its use of IRE's VPN products and services. By this time IRE was providing companies and governments with around-the-clock VPN management via its SafeNet/Trusted Services offering.

In keeping with the company's efforts to ensure the interoperability of its VPN solutions, IRE became a charter member of Cisco Systems Inc.'s Security Associate Program in September 1999.

Developments continued to unfold through the end of the year. In December IRE announced that it had issued one million new shares of common stock, which it planned to sell to a select group of investors for $15 million. That same month, Deloitte & Touche added the company to its Technology Fast 500 list in recognition of strong growth. Over the course of only five years, IRE had seen its revenues grow 579 percent. At the decade's end, the company's workforce had expanded to approximately 150 people.

GROWING THROUGH ACQUISITIONS: 2000–05

A major change occurred following the dawn of the new millennium. On July 25, IRE's shareholders okayed plans to change the company's name to SafeNet Inc. The new name was more in line with the organization's VPN-related technology.

Throughout the year, strong growth continued to occur in IRE's VPN business. For the quarter ending September 30, 2000, sales of its VPN-related products were up 193 percent compared to the same period in 1999. IRE rounded out the year by officially adopting its new name on November 1. On that date, the company began trading on the NASDAQ under the symbol SFNT.

SafeNet hit the ground running in 2002. In January, the company snapped up Pijnenburg Securealink Inc. in a deal worth $15.1 million. The following month, the company shuttered operations of its Greta-Coder Data Systems subsidiary.

Developments continued to unfold at a rapid pace in 2003. In February, SafeNet acquired the Santa Clara, California-based security technology company Cylink Inc. for approximately $35 million. Established around the same time as SafeNet, Cylink provided encryption technology for wide-area networks, and shared a similar customer base. The following month, SafeNet parted with $890,000 and nearly $6.1 million in stock to acquire Raqia Networks Inc.

More deals occurred later in the year. In October SafeNet agreed to acquire the Irvine, California-based authentication technology provider Rainbow Technologies Inc. in a stock deal worth $455 million. In addition to $70 million in government-related business, the deal with rainbow bolstered SafeNet's product base with new consumer-related anti-piracy software.

On the international front, SafeNet agreed to acquire the OEM Products Group business of Finland's SSH Communications Security Corp. for approximately $14 million in November.

In March 2004 SafeNet completed its acquisition of Rainbow Technologies. The deal, which tripled the company's revenue base, was especially significant because it transformed SafeNet into the seventh largest information security firm in the world.

In mid-2004, the company established a Networking Business Unit to supply its SafeNet chips to original equipment manufacturers. It was around this time that the company made several key changes in the executive suite. Senior Vice-President and Chief Financial Officer Carole Argo was named president and chief operating officer, while Ken Mueller, who had served as chief financial officer of Microsoft Business Solutions, was named chief financial officer.

By 2004 SafeNet's workforce had grown to include some 800 employees who served approximately 5,000 customers worldwide. In September the company agreed to acquire the Minnesota-based access and authentication software company Datakey Inc. The $11.6 million deal was finished in mid-December.

SafeNet continued to grow via acquisitions during the middle of the first decade of the 2000s. In April

2005, the Amsterdam, Netherlands-based digital rights management solutions provider DMDsecure B.V. was acquired. The $9.6 million deal bolstered SafeNet's offerings in the area of digital content protection, including solutions for audio, video, and gaming.

A $20.5 million cash and stock deal unfolded when SafeNet snapped up Morristown, New Jersey-based MediaSentry Inc., which provided the motion picture and recording industries with anti-piracy and business management services.

SafeNet concluded 2005 with another major deal, when it acquired data encryption software and hardware security module developer Eracom Technologies AG for about $25 million in cash.

CHALLENGING TIMES: 2006–07

Midway through 2006, SafeNet's stock moved from the NASDAQ National Market to the new NASDAQ Global Select Market. The company faced a very difficult situation in October of that year, when Chairman and CEO Anthony A. Caputo and President and Chief Operating Officer Carole Argo tendered their resignations. These key departures occurred in the wake of investigations by the Securities and Exchange Commission, as well as the U.S. Attorney for the Southern District of New York, into alleged backdating of stock options. For the interim, the company named independent director Walter W. Straub as chairman and CEO.

Following a $150 million contract from the U.S. Department of Defense (DOD) in 2006, SafeNet announced the largest contract in the company's history in early 2007. Specifically, SafeNet's Mykotronx Inc. subsidiary received a contract worth as much as $400 million to help DOD update its encryption technology.

While the DOD contract was good news, SafeNet continued to contend with several challenges. In addition to the stock option situation, the company faced the possibility of being delisted from the NASDAQ in early 2007 after failing to file its quarterly and annual earnings report on time. A solution emerged when the San Francisco-based private equity firm Vector Capital acquired SafeNet for $634 million. Following the deal, SafeNet became a private company on April 12, at which time the company's shares ceased trading on the NASDAQ.

With a new board of directors, SafeNet moved forward with Chris Fedde as president and chief operating officer. Chairman and interim CEO Walter Straub stepped down. There were no immediate plans to fill the CEO position. While there were many positive factors

associated with the deal, a number of analysts claimed that the Vector offer was too low. Subsequently, some shareholders sued SafeNet, claiming that the company had breached its fiduciary duties with them.

SECURITY LEADER: 2008

After pleading guilty to stock option fraud in October 2007, former Chief Financial Officer Carole Argo was sentenced to six months in prison and fined $1 million in January 2008.

SafeNet continued in a positive direction in early 2008, at which time the company acquired the Redwood City, California-based enterprise data protection and privacy solutions provider Ingrian Networks Inc.

At the year's end, SafeNet claimed to offer the world's largest range of security products and solutions for protecting digital identities, communications, and business data. After its start as a basement-based business, the company had evolved into a global enterprise with approximately 1,100 employees, annual revenues of around $270 million, and some 10,000 customers. Moving forward, SafeNet seemed well-positioned for success during the 21st century's second decade.

Paul R. Greenland

PRINCIPAL SUBSIDIARIES

353 Patent LLC; Caro Kann Corp.; Cylink Communications B.V. (Netherlands); Cylink France SARL; Cylink International Corp. (Cayman Islands); Digital Spread Spectrum Technologies Inc.; IRE Secure Solutions Inc.; iVea Corp.; Mykotronx Inc.; Nihon SafeNet KK (Japan); Pijnenburg Securealink Inc.; Pijnenburg Securealink USA Inc.; Rainbow Information Technologies (Taiwan) Co. Ltd.; Rainbow Information Technology Co. Ltd. (China); Rainbow Technologies C.I. L.P. (Cayman Islands); Rainbow Technologies GmbH (Germany); Rainbow Technologies International GmbH (Switzerland); Rainbow Technologies Ltd. (UK); Rainbow Technologies North America Inc.; Raqia Acquisition Corp.; RNBO Corp.; SafeNet (Australia) Pty Ltd.; SafeNet Asia Limited (Hong Kong); SafeNet B.V. (Netherlands); SafeNet Brasil Ltda. (Brazil); SafeNet BVI Ltd. (British Virgin Islands); SafeNet Canada Inc.; SafeNet China Ltd.; SafeNet Consultancy Ltd. (UK); SafeNet France SARL; SafeNet Information Technologies Pvt. Ltd. (India); SafeNet Japan KK; SafeNet Pte. Ltd. (Singapore); SafeNet Systems Pvt. Ltd. (India); SafeNet Technologies B.V. (Netherlands); SafeNet UK Limited; Seguridad Informatica SafeNet,

S. de RL de CV (Mexico); SFNT Finland Oy; Wyatt River Software Inc.

PRINCIPAL COMPETITORS

Aladdin Knowledge Systems Ltd.; Cisco Systems Inc.; Juniper Networks Inc.

FURTHER READING

Balluck, Kyle, "Information Resource Engineering Renamed SafeNet," *Newsbytes,* July 25, 2000.

"Former Chief Financial Officer of SafeNet, Inc. Sentenced to 6 Months in Prison for Securities Fraud in Connection with Backdating of Stock Options," New York: U.S. Department of Justice, United States Attorney, Southern District of New York, January 28, 2008, http://www.usdoj.gov.

Hirsh, Stacey, "SafeNet Sold, Goes Private," *Baltimore Sun,* April 13, 2007.

"IRE Chairman Is Chosen Maryland Entrepreneur of the Year," *PR Newswire,* July 6, 1993.

"IRE Named to Deloitte & Touche's 'Fast 500' List of Nation's Fastest-Growing Technology Companies," *Business Wire,* December 7, 1999.

Kleiner, Kurt, "City Computer Firm Codes Federal Files for a Profit," *Baltimore Business Journal,* July 17, 1992.

Mook, Ben, "San Francisco-based Equity Firm Offers $634M Buyout for Belcamp-Based Safenet Inc.," *Daily Record,* March 6, 2007.

Pierpont, J. B., "Computer Security Company Readies Initial Public Offering," *Baltimore Business Journal,* May 22, 1989.

"SafeNet Is Roiled by Options Inquiry," *New York Times,* October 19, 2006.

Smitherman, Laura, "Options Fraud Admitted," *Baltimore Sun,* October 6, 2007.

Salzgitter AG

—•—

Eisenhüttenstraße 99
Salzgitter, 38239
Germany
Telephone: (+49) 5341 21-01
Fax: (+49) 5341 21-2727
Web site: http://www.salzgitter-ag.de

Public Company
Incorporated: 1957
Employees: 25,606
Sales: EUR 10.19 billion ($13.97 billion) (2007)
Stock Exchanges: Xetra Frankfurt Berlin Bayerische Borse
Ticker Symbol: SZG
NAICS: 331111 Iron and Steel Mills; 333993 Packaging Machinery Manufacturing; 423510 Metal Service Centers and Other Metal Merchant Wholesalers

■ ■ ■

Salzgitter AG is one of Europe's leading steel technology groups, with annual production of rolled steel and tubes of more than seven million tons. The company's Steel Division, one of Europe's five largest steel producers, manufactures such products as flat steel, steel plate, sheet piles, and components for roofing and cladding. The Tubes Division is a global leader in such areas as large-diameter tubes, welded line pipes, cold-finished tubes, and seamless stainless-steel tubes. Salzgitter diversified in 2007 with the acquisition of a majority stake in Klöckner-Werke AG, which was housed within a newly formed Technology Division. Klöckner specializes in the production of packaging and filling machinery for the food and beverage industries, while also producing specialty machinery for companies in the plastic processing, shoe manufacturing, and confectionary industries. About 48 percent of Salzgitter's sales are generated in its home market, with roughly 23 percent originating elsewhere in Europe, 10 percent in Asia, and 9 percent in North and South America. The German state of Lower Saxony, where the company is based, holds a stake of just over 25 percent in Salzgitter, a vestige of the state's purchase of the firm in 1998 to keep it from falling into foreign hands.

EARLY HISTORY

In the 1930s it was known that vast deposits of iron were present around Salzgitter in the German federal state of Lower Saxony. Their potential capacity was estimated at 1.5 billion tons from exploratory boring carried out in the 1920s. The disadvantage with this ore, however, was that it contained a high proportion of silicic acid. It was only with the development of new metallurgical engineering processes that this acidic ore could be smelted successfully.

Projects such as smelting the ore deposits in the Salzgitter region were given priority in the Four Year Plan embarked upon by Nazi Germany in 1936 with the aim of creating a self-sufficient economy, and making possible German industrial self-reliance, even in the case of war. Together with the iron ore deposits, the site of Salzgitter as a location for iron works was favored because of its central position; the relatively rapid and economical connections that could be made with existing transport routes such as the railway, inland canals,

COMPANY PERSPECTIVES

Salzgitter AG enjoys one of the richest traditions among Germany's conglomerates. Its future focus is set firmly on steel and technology. Through internal and external growth, the Salzgitter Group has become an innovative power in the international steel industry. We aspire to rank and to remain among the best in steel and in technology.

Our workforce and our management alike are committed to achieving this goal. To guide them on their way, they have developed a corporate mission comprising their vision of themselves, their principal aims and corporate philosophy.

Putting this corporate mission into practice and realizing the aims and the corporate philosophy it embodies is a demanding task, yet it is one to which every individual employee feels bound. Our corporate mission and corporate philosophy are signposts to the ambitious goals the Salzgitter Group has set itself. We accept a commitment to honor and abide by the letter and the spirit of the law and by ethical values.

and motorways; and the infrastructure already in place in the region. The National Socialist economic planning also relied on the premise that the steel companies of the Ruhr River basin would support the project and participate in its operation. Negotiations between Hermann Göring, Adolf Hitler's right-hand man, and the representatives of the steel industry failed, however, as the latter regarded this enterprise as a competitor. Finally the state took on the building of the works, and the Reichswerke AG für Berg- und Hüttenbetriebe Hermann Göring (the Hermann Göring Imperial Iron and Steel Works) were founded in 1937.

Other installations were built in quick succession, and by April 1945 six coke furnace batteries, ten blast-furnaces, three blenders, six converters, three Siemens-Martin tilting furnaces, and two electric arc furnaces were in operation. Total raw steel capacity amounted to 1.8 million tons a year.

At the same time as the building up of Reichswerke, as it was known, housing for workers was constructed on a massive scale. In 1942 the town of Salzgitter was enlarged by the incorporation of 29 surrounding parishes and the special building of housing for the workers. Before the start of World War II, the

workforce was partly recruited and, partly, compulsorily enlisted by the state to work in Salzgitter. During the war, the German workforce was increasingly replaced by workers forcibly recruited from the German-occupied countries, especially those in Eastern Europe. Eventually prisoners of war as well as prisoners from concentration camps were forced to work and live in inhuman conditions at Reichswerke. The state used criminal methods to control this workforce. The number of victims was very high. This chapter in Salzgitter's history was brought to an abrupt end with the occupation of the iron and steel works by Allied forces on April 10, 1945.

The number of people living in the Salzgitter area had grown from 20,000 in 1933 to 117,000 by 1944. By the same year, Reichswerke and its subsidiaries were employing 66,177 people.

POSTWAR DISMANTLING AND RECONSTRUCTION

In the Treaty of Potsdam, the victorious Allied powers stipulated that the German armaments industry should be dismantled as a part of the war reparations. A plan that had been reworked numerous times for the British and U.S. zones contained a list of 682 installations to be dismantled wholly or in part. Of these, 72.7 percent fell within the British zone. Reichswerke was included on the list of 116 plants to be dismantled, which was handed to the chief minister of Lower Saxony on October 16, 1947.

The structure of the economy of the Salzgitter industrial region was geared to one line of production, because of the presence of Reichswerke. The closing down of the iron and steel works, Reichswerke's main pillar, created deep conflicts of a social and political nature. In the mid-1950s, unemployment in Salzgitter was reported at 35 percent, in Lower Saxony at 19.8 percent, and in West Germany as a whole at 12.2 percent. Under such conditions, the inhabitants of this industrial region and the Reichswerke workforce fought against the dismantling of the Reichswerke and for the preservation of their jobs. The clashes with the police and with the occupying British forces came to a head in March 1950. Workers who remained gathered at the plants that were to be demolished. Drilling machinery was destroyed and explosive devices torn out of the boreholes; workers ripped out the fuses or sat down on foundations, prepared to be blown up.

The end of the dismantling of German industrial capacities in the respective Western-occupied zones of what was West Germany was accelerated by the general changing conditions in postwar Germany. In Reichswerke's case, the resistance of a whole region, and in

KEY DATES

■

1937: Nazi-led Germany forms the Reichswerke AG für Berg- und Hüttenbetriebe Hermann Göring to build a steelworks at Salzgitter, Lower Saxony.

1942: Town of Salzgitter is enlarged by the incorporation of surrounding parishes; wartime workforce of Reichswerke is increasingly comprised of forced laborers and prisoners of war.

1945: Allied forces seize Reichswerke.

1947: The partial dismantling of the Salzgitter steelworks commences.

1953: Control of the Reichswerke complex is transferred to the West German government, which begins reconstruction.

1955: The former Reichswerke company is reorganized as Aktiengesellschaft für Bergbau und Hüttenbetriebe; steelworks are transferred to the affiliated Salzgitter Hüttenwerke AG.

1970: Salzgitter Hüttenwerke, subsidiary of government-owned Salzgitter AG, merges with Ilseder Hütte to form Stahlwerke Peine-Salzgitter AG.

1989: The West German government sells Salzgitter to Preussag AG.

1992: Stahlwerke Peine-Salzgitter is renamed Preussag Stahl AG; steel plate manufacturer Walzwerk Ilsenburg GmbH is acquired.

1998: The German state of Lower Saxony in partnership with Norddeutsche Landesbank acquires Preussag Stahl from Preussag AG; Preussag Stahl is taken public as Salzgitter AG.

2000: Tubular steel product specialist Mannesmannröhren-Werke AG is acquired.

2007: Salzgitter gains majority control of Klöckner-Werke AG, specializing particularly in packaging and filling machinery for the beverage industry; revenues surpass EUR 10 billion.

particular of the workforce and the management, played a special role in combating the policy of dismantling pursued by the Allied occupying forces. In January 1951 the three Western Allied high commissioners announced the end of all dismantling. The reconstruction of the iron and steel works began on March 25, 1953.

The companies belonging to the Reichswerke complex were released from the control of the Allied High Command on an order given on June 27, 1953. The powers to run and the responsibility for reorganizing the Reichswerke complex were handed over to the West German government. In the course of the restructuring ordered by the government, the Reichswerke AG für Erzbergbau und Eisenhütten was liquidated and its fixed assets transferred to the companies established in the industrial region. The mining plants, including buildings and equipment, became the property of the Erzbergbau Salzgitter AG, while the plants belonging to the iron and steel works were transferred to the Salzgitter Hüttenwerke AG. The Aktiengesellschaft für Bergbau und Hüttenbetriebe, formerly Reichswerke, was formed in 1955, comprised of a number of affiliated companies.

CONSOLIDATION AND EXPANSION IN THE FIFTIES AND SIXTIES

The economic development of the Aktiengesellschaft für Bergbau und Hüttenbetriebe was marked in the 1950s by the consolidation of the individual companies and the group's further expansion. In January 1960 the group had a share of at least 50 percent in 41 companies, and out of those it had a 100 percent holding in 34 companies. At the end of the 1950s the pig iron and steel production sector reported healthy figures. Peak profits reached in the business year 1959–60 were surpassed in 1960–61. By contrast, in mining and other raw material businesses, turnover and profits diminished on increased mining. Until the mid-1960s the group's board of directors focused attention on measures that concentrated on mining and production in the most competitive plants. That meant in particular restructuring in the steel sector, the uniting of several shipyards into one company, and intensified efforts to increase profitability in individual companies. The director intended to get rid of interests in businesses whose viability could not be restored in the long term. By the mid-1960s the following groups had been formed within the government-owned Salzgitter AG: mining, raw materials, processing, industrial planning, trade, and transportation.

In 1968 Hans Birnbaum was elected chairman of the board. Under his leadership a reorganization of the Salzgitter group was set in motion. Beginning in November 1972, the structure of the group was redivided into three business areas by the uniting of companies that until then had been split into different groups with other related businesses. The first business area embraced the group's steel interests and the delivery and services companies associated with it. The second business area's main focus was on the shipbuilding and railway carriage-building side. The third business area grouped together the remaining companies in the Salzgitter concern, notably the machine construction, steel construction, and building materials sectors.

1970 CREATION OF STAHLWERKE PEINE-SALZGITTER

Priors to the restructuring, the Salzgitter group had taken over the shares jointly held by Peine and Salzgitter in the Industrie-Aktiengesellschaft. After the plan of creating Nordstahl AG from the combination of Salzgitter Hüttenwerke, Klöckner-Werke AG, and the Ilseder Hütte had collapsed in the spring of 1969, Stahlwerke Peine-Salzgitter AG had been formed from the April 1970 merger of Salzgitter Hüttenwerke and Ilseder Hütte. The latter had been founded in 1858 in Peine, a town about 20 miles northwest of Salzgitter. Originally an ore mining concern before later beginning to manufacture pig iron at Groß Ilsede, Ilseder Hütte gained a steelworks via the 1880 acquisition of Peiner Walzwerk, founded in 1872. Salzgitter AG, parent of Stahlwerke Peine-Salzgitter, was in possession of a network of interconnecting companies.

The Salzgitter group consolidated to give it a sustained presence in the various fields of steel production. The two iron and steel works became so closely bound that in the end a single, modern, and efficient steel group developed. Salzgitter AG had become the third largest steel producer in West Germany.

When Birnbaum took over the position of chairman of Salzgitter AG, one of his objectives was to diversify the group's interests through an intensified reworking of the company. His attempt failed in part. As a result, the shares in Büssing Automobilwerke AG had to be ceded to the Gutehoffnungshütte Aktienverein (GHH) in 1971. In return, however, Salzgitter AG took over the GHH shareholding in the Howaldtswerke-Deutsche Werft AG (HDW) shipyard. In the group's plans for the 1970s, the consolidation of the steel and shipbuilding sectors were a main priority on the one hand, while on the other it was also endeavoring to adapt these sectors to the changing market conditions. Therefore in 1970 the steel-girder construction firm Noell in Würzburg was taken over, the Hildesheim foundry Kloth-Senking was acquired in 1973, and a shareholding in the Sachsgruppe acquired. A new shipbuilding program was elaborated at the end of the decade. It concerned not only the further consolidation of HDW and the preservation of the largest possible number of jobs in Hamburg and Kiel, but also activities outside shipbuilding. Incinerating plants, desalination plants,

and water purification plants as well as energy-saving systems and products, for example in the processing of liquid gas, were also created in the HDW capacity.

The emphasis on steel interests took into account a development that had been put in place at the end of the 1960s: the decline in iron ore mining. The ore in the Salzgitter district is mined from depths of between 300 meters and 1,200 meters. The ore had a relatively small iron content. Further, the price of foreign ore was constantly falling.

A particularly important chapter in Salzgitter AG's history concerns its exports to the East. Business with the East was of great importance to West Germany. The 1970s, apart from 1977, saw constant growth and an export surplus. The share of West German exports to the East had for years fluctuated around the 6 percent mark. This was not the case for Salzgitter. Between 20 percent and 35 percent of its total export turnover was derived from trade with the Eastern European states. In 1977 alone, Salzgitter AG received three large orders from the Soviet Union with a total value of DEM 605 million. Other products, and in particular rolled products, also found takers in the Eastern area and here again above all in the Soviet Union. In the business year 1988–89, the share of export turnover to Eastern Europe still represented 12 percent.

With the appointment of Ernst Piepers to chairman of the board on August 1, 1979, the group's policy continued to be pursued along the same lines, but a fourth area of activity was introduced, embracing general contracting and engineering for industrial plants as well as consulting engineering.

At the beginning of the 1980s the individual fields of business were rationalized or extended. At that time a crisis existed in the steel and shipbuilding industries, badly affecting the Salzgitter group. At the end of the 1980s, it was possible to distinguish a clear upturn in business.

As a result of the rationalization and automation of the group's business, as well as the growing importance of the high-tech fields of business, the number of employees decreased steadily through the decades, from approximately 82,000 in 1963–64 to 56,800 in 1971–72 to 39,000 in 1988–89. The latter year was the most successful in the company's history, with net profits of DEM 2.5 billion.

1989–98: THE PREUSSAG ERA

Late in 1989 the West German government sold Salzgitter AG to Preussag AG for DEM 2.5 billion. This move gave Preussag, another Lower Saxon company based in

Hannover with a workforce of 26,000, a wide ranging collection of industrial activities, including steel, ship and carriage construction, information technology, trade, distribution, and energy. In 1992 the core of Salzgitter's steel operations, Stahlwerke Peine-Salzgitter, was renamed Preussag Stahl AG.

The early 1990s were marked by overcapacity in the steel industry throughout Europe. German steelmakers were particularly vulnerable because steel prices in that country were the highest in Europe. Preussag Stahl, which ranked as the third largest German steelmaker, posted losses large enough to push Preussag AG itself into the red. Preussag Stahl returned to profitability in the 1994–95 fiscal year thanks in part to a restructuring effort that involved large capital outlays to upgrade its manufacturing facilities and job cuts totaling some 1,500.

In the meantime, following the 1990 reunification of Germany, an agency called the Treuhandanstalt was set up to privatize the former state-owned businesses of East Germany. In 1992 Preussag Stahl purchased from the Treuhandanstalt the steel plate manufacturer Walzwerk Ilsenburg GmbH, which was based in Ilsenburg, about 30 miles southeast of Salzgitter across the former East–West border in the state of Saxony-Anhalt. Walzwerk Ilsenburg, producer of about 480,000 metric tons of coated sheet in 1990, pushed Preussag Stahl's share of the European Community market for laminated steel sheet to 13 percent. Walzwerk Ilsenburg traced its origins back to the 1595 founding of the copper mill Ilsenburger Kupferhammer.

Also during this period Preussag Stahl allowed local historians to turn one of the former barracks on the property of the Salzgitter complex into a memorial to the Drütte concentration camp. The barrack was restored to the way it would have appeared during World War II when slave laborers were housed there. In May 2000 an executive at Salzgitter told the *Wall Street Journal Europe* that his company was the first "to do something like this, to have a [concentration camp] memorial right in the middle of a live production site."

1998 EMERGENCE AS THE PUBLIC FIRM SALZGITTER AG

Preussag Stahl remained profitable into 1998 with its revenues reaching DEM 3 billion ($1.75 billion), but it faced the prospect of increased competition from the looming merger of the German steel giants Krupp and Thyssen, which later became ThyssenKrupp AG in March 1999. Preussag AG at this same time was in the process of transitioning into a services group centered on tourism specialist TUI and the shipping company

Hapag-Lloyd AG. As it gradually divested itself of its once-core industrial holdings, Preussag began exploring a sale of its steel unit in late 1997. (Preussag AG was later renamed TUI AG.)

The Austrian steelmaker Voest-Alpine Stahl AG stepped forward with a bid of about DEM 1.27 billion, and a deal was nearly agreed upon in early 1998. However, Gerhard Schroeder, then prime minister of Lower Saxony (and the future chancellor of Germany), pressured Preussag AG into breaking off its talks with Voest-Alpine as he moved to keep the Salzgitter steelmaking operations from falling into foreign hands and possibly being forced into job cuts by its new owner. Schroeder then quickly engineered the purchase of Preussag Stahl by the state of Lower Saxony in partnership with the publicly owned bank Norddeutsche Landesbank. The purchase price for this politically controversial deal was DEM 1.06 billion ($580 million), about DEM 200 million less than what Voest-Alpine had been offering. In June 1998 Lower Saxony and Norddeutsche Landesbank placed 60 percent of the shares in Preussag Stahl on the Frankfurt stock exchange through a public offering, with the newly public company emerging as Salzgitter AG. Lower Saxony retained a stake of about 25 percent, and Norddeutsche Landesbank kept a significant interest as well. The operations of Salzgitter, under the leadership of chief executive Hans-Joachim Selenz, remained centered on its steelworks in Salzgitter, Peine, and Ilsenburg, which collectively were producing about five million metric tons of steel each year.

Early in 1999 Salzgitter entered into talks with Luxembourg-based Arbed S.A. about a merger to create the largest steelmaker in Europe. These talks collapsed, however, after Salzgitter's managers and workers expressed skepticism about a deal that would have essentially ceded control of the company to Arbed. Selenz resigned after being criticized for not having kept workers sufficiently apprised of the talks' progress. After a period of interim leadership, Wolfgang Leese was named the new chief executive.

Around this same time, numerous German companies were facing pressure to contribute to a government–industry fund to compensate surviving slave laborers from the Nazi era. Salzgitter had initially balked about cooperating with this effort arguing, with some justification, that it had no legal ties to the Nazi-era entity that had operated on the premises at Salzgitter. Indeed, most of the slave laborers at the site had been forced to work on mining activities, and Preussag AG had retained any mining-related assets that could be traced to the Nazi-era Salzgitter operations. Nevertheless, in early 2000, after months of negotiations, Salzgitter agreed to contribute DEM 5.3 million (EUR 2.7 million) to the fund.

EARLY 21ST-CENTURY ACQUISITIONS

In October 2000 Salzgitter considerably expanded its steel tubular product capacities by acquiring Mannesmannröhren-Werke AG (MRW) from Mannesmann AG. Based in Mülheim an der Ruhr, MRW and its holdings and joint ventures produced a wide range of products, including large-diameter pipes, welded line pipes, and cold-finished tubes. One of the joint ventures, Vallourec & Mannesmann Tubes S.A., specialized in seamless steel tubes and was a partnership with the French firm Vallourec S.A. Salzgitter also inherited MRW's 20 percent stake in Vallourec itself. MRW became the central piece of Salzgitter's newly formed Tubes Division. In July 2001 Salzgitter restructured its operations into five largely independent divisions: Steel, Trading, Services, Processing, and Tubes.

Booming global demand for rolled steel and tubular products, particularly from China, helped push Salzgitter to record levels of both net income and sales by 2005: EUR 842 million ($993 million) and EUR 7.15 billion ($8.43 billion), respectively. In June 2005 Salzgitter sold its share in the Vallourec & Mannesmann Tubes joint venture to Vallourec S.A., booking EUR 162.6 million in proceeds in the process. Salzgitter recorded an additional EUR 907 million in proceeds from its August 2006 sale of its minority stake in Vallourec S.A. The latter gain propelled the company's 2006 net income up to EUR 1.51 billion ($1.99 billion). As the steel boom continued, sales increased a further 18 percent, to EUR 8.45 billion ($11.12 billion).

Flush with cash and seeking further opportunities for growth but unwilling to pay the high prices steel-industry takeovers were commanding and also seeking a counterweight to the cyclicality of its core business, Salzgitter elected to diversify with its next significant move. In July 2007 the company purchased an 83 percent stake (later raised to 86 percent) in Klöckner-Werke AG, based in Duisburg. Klöckner specialized in the production of packaging and filling machinery for the food and beverage industries, while also producing specialty machinery for companies in the plastic processing, shoe manufacturing, and confectionary industries. Another reason for Salzgitter's attraction to Klöckner was the latter's highly global reach; its manufacturing operations, for instance, included eight production plants in Germany, two in the United States, and one each in Mexico, Brazil, India, and China. Klöckner's annual revenues were nearly EUR 1 billion.

Klöckner-Werke formed the centerpiece of the newly formed Technology Division. This division was bolstered via the April 2008 acquisition of SIG Beverages from the SIG Group of Switzerland. Buying SIG Beverages filled in a hole in the Klöckner-Werke operations as the SIG unit produced PET blow-molding bottle-related machinery. The acquired unit's main operations were based in Germany, in Hamburg and Neuss, and its 2007 revenues totaled around EUR 150 million. As it was pursuing this diversification effort, Salzgitter was also in the midst of a major investment program to strengthen its core steel business through upgrades and modernizations of its three main facilities in Salzgitter, Peine, and Ilsenburg. A total of EUR 1.4 billion was earmarked to be spent on this program through 2012. After pushing its revenues over the EUR 10 billion mark in 2007, Salzgitter continued to post record results through the first nine months of 2008 but then began to feel the effects of the global economic and financial crisis, which seemed certain to halt the firm's upward momentum. Nevertheless, in late 2008 Salzgitter gained further prestige when it was added to the DAX-30, Germany's leading stock market index.

Gerd Henniger, translated from the German
by Philippe A. Barbour
Updated, David E. Salamie

PRINCIPAL SUBSIDIARIES/DIVISIONS

Salzgitter Mannesmann GmbH; STEEL DIVISION: Salzgitter Stahl GmbH; Salzgitter Flachstahl GmbH; Peiner Träger GmbH; Ilsenburger Grobblech GmbH; Salzgitter Europlatinen GmbH; Salzgitter Bauelemente GmbH; HSP Hoesch Spundwand und Profil GmbH. TRADING DIVISION: Salzgitter Mannesmann Handel GmbH; Salzgitter Mannesmann Stahlhandel GmbH; Stahl-Center Baunatal GmbH; Salzgitter Mannesmann International GmbH; Salzgitter Mannesmann International (USA) Inc.; Salzgitter Mannesmann International (Canada) Inc.; Salzgitter Handel B.V. (Netherlands); Hövelmann & Lueg GmbH; Universal Eisen und Stahl GmbH. TUBES DIVISION: Mannesmannröhren-Werke GmbH; Mannesmannröhren Mülheim GmbH; Salzgitter Großrohre GmbH; Mannesmann Fuchs Rohr GmbH; Salzgitter Mannesmann Precision GmbH; Mannesmann Präzisrohr GmbH; Mannesmannrohr Sachsen GmbH; Vallourec Précision Etirage S.A.S. (France); Mannesmann Robur B.V. (Netherlands); Mannesmann DMV Stainless GmbH. SERVICES DIVISION: DEUMU Deutsche Erz- und Metall-Union GmbH; SZST Salzgitter Service und Technik GmbH; Verkehrsbetriebe Peine-Salzgitter

GmbH; Hansaport Hafenbetriebsgesellschaft mbH (51%); Salzgitter Mannesmann Forschung GmbH; Salzgitter Mannesmann Altersversorgung Service GmbH; "Glückauf" Wohnungsgesellschaft mbH; Salzgitter Magnesium-Technologie GmbH; Salzgitter Information und Telekommunikation GmbH; GESIS Gesellschaft für Informationssysteme mbH; TELCAT MULTICOM GmbH; TELCAT KOMMUNIKATIONSTECHNIK GmbH; Salzgitter Automotive Engineering GmbH & Co. KG; Salzgitter Hydroforming GmbH & Co. KG. TECHNOLOGY DIVISION: Klöckner-Werke AG (86.1%); KHS AG (86.1%); Klöckner DESMA Elastomertechnik GmbH (86.1%); Klöckner DESMA Schuhmaschinen GmbH (86.1%); Klöckner Hänsel Processing GmbH (86.1%); RSE Grundbesitz und Beteiligungs-AG (96.2%).

PRINCIPAL COMPETITORS

ArcelorMittal; ThyssenKrupp AG; Klöckner & Co. AG; Tetra Laval International S.A.

FURTHER READING

Atkins, Ralph, "Preussag May Float Steel Subsidiary," *Financial Times,* November 20, 1997, p. 28.

———, "Schroder's Steel Workers Happy to Go Their Own Way," *Financial Times,* August 22, 1998, p. 2.

Bowley, Graham, "German State Beats Rival to Preussag Arm," *Financial Times,* February 6, 1998, p. 27.

———, "Lower Saxony to Hold 25% of Salzgitter After Sale," *Financial Times,* May 19, 1998, p. 34.

Buchanan, Sandra, "Salzgitter Gathers Pace," *Metal Bulletin Monthly,* December 1999, pp. 84–87.

Cornwell, Rupert, "Salzgitter's Heart of Steel Is Strengthened by Surgery," *Financial Times,* July 23, 1986, p. 16.

Fuhrmans, Vanessa, "German Steelmaker Can't Escape Ties to the Nazi Past: Salzgitter Joins Fund to Compensate Slaves," *Wall Street Journal Europe,* May 15, 2000, p. 1.

Goodhart, David, "The Marriage of an Odd Couple Gets a Blessing from the State: The Union of Germany's Preussag and Salzgitter," *Financial Times,* October 3, 1989, p. 29.

Köhl, Christian, "Salzgitter Gets Mannesmann Tubes Unit," *American Metal Market,* May 31, 2000, p. 2.

———, "Salzgitter Swims Against the Flow," *Metal Bulletin Monthly,* July 2002, pp. 15–17.

———, "Salzgitter to Join Slave Labor Funds," *American Metal Market,* February 17, 2000, p. 4.

———, "Smaller but Wiser?" *Metal Bulletin Monthly,* November 2006, p. 10.

Ruch, Matthias, "Salzgitter Aims for Diversification," *Financial Times,* August 16, 2006, p. 22.

"Salzgitter Buys SIG Bottle Biz," *Plastics News,* January 21, 2008, p. 3.

Zwick, Steve, "Salzgitter AG's New Chapter," *Iron Age/New Steel,* November 1998, p. 76.

SanCor Cooperativas Unidas Ltda.

———■———

Teniente General Ricchieri 15
Sunchales, Santa Fe S2322FYA
Argentina
Telephone: (54 3493) 428-000
Fax: (54 3493) 421-158
Web site: http://www.sancor.com

Cooperative
Founded: 1938 as Cooperativas Unidas Limitada Fábrica
    de Manteca
Employees: 5,300
Sales: $564.7 million (2008)
NAICS: 311511 Fluid Milk Manufacturing; 311512
    Creamery Butter Manufacturing; 311513 Cheese
    Manufacturing; 311514 Dry, Condensed, and
    Evaporated Dairy Product Manufacturing; 524113
    Cooperative Life Insurance Organizations

■ ■ ■

SanCor Cooperativas Unidas Ltda., a union of about 60
Argentine cooperatives representing about 1,600 dairy
farms, is the second largest of the nation's processors
and distributors of dairy products. Some 16 industrial
facilities process well over a billion liters of milk a year,
distributing to the nation's wholesalers, supermarkets,
and other shopkeepers fresh and powdered milk, butter,
cream, cheese, whey, and other dairy products. SanCor
also exports its products to about 35 other countries and
has subsidiaries in Brazil and the United States.

FIFTY YEARS OF STEADY GROWTH

Argentina's temperate climate and well-watered, fertile
pampas make it one of the best areas in the Americas
for raising dairy cows and marketing the products
derived from their milk. The provinces of Santa Fe and
Córdoba are particularly well suited for this activity. In
1938, 16 cooperatives of dairy farmers banded together
to form Cooperativas Unidas Limitada Fábrica de Man-
teca, or United Cooperatives Butter Factory. This facility, in Sunchales, Santa Fe, which remains SanCor's
headquarters, was completed in 1940. By then many
more dairy cooperatives had joined the founding group,
which took the SanCor name for the two provinces of
Argentina's dairy heartland and embarked on a broader
agenda for its members.

SanCor, in 1943, began processing fresh milk in
Sunchales and opened a second plant in Brinkmann,
Córdoba, for exported butter. A year later, the cooperative completed a third butter plant in Devoto, Córdoba.
By 1946 SanCor included 206 associated cooperatives
and was selling dairy products abroad as well as in
Argentina. In 1947 it erected its first cheese production
unit, in Gálvez, Santa Fe. An underground area there
had the capacity to store two million kilos (about 1,100
tons) of cheese for ripening. Another butter plant was
put into operation in 1949 in Coronel Charlone, Buenos Aires.

SanCor was taken over by the authoritarian government of President Juan Perón in 1947 and remained
under its control until Perón's fall from power in 1955.
It opened a New York office in 1953 to facilitate its

COMPANY PERSPECTIVES

To optimize the value of the milk produced by our associated milk producers and maximize their benefits, while fulfilling at the same time our consumers' expectations and managing our operations in such a flexible way that they lead to the development of the people involved in our cooperative system and the communities where we have a presence.

international commercial activities. In 1956, when SanCor completed another butter factory in San Justo, Santa Fe, it also opened sales offices in the city of Buenos Aires and other principal Argentine cities. SanCor began to turn out pasteurized milk, in 1962, in Sunchales, where in the following year it erected its first facility for powdered milk. In 1968 the cooperative implemented its system of providing products to exclusive concessionaires.

SanCor began to expand, in 1970, its line of fresh products by adding yogurt, flan (custard), and dairy desserts similar to flan. It also added mayonnaise. In 1974 the cooperative ranked 27th in revenue among reported Argentine enterprises. It was 31st in 1980 and 22nd in 1985, just ahead of Mastellone Hermanos S.A., its main competitor. In 1986 the cooperative established a Brazilian subsidiary, SanCor do Produtos Alimenticios Ltda., in São Paulo. Industrial La Carlota, opened in 1989, was designed specifically to serve the export market.

The 1980s was a difficult decade throughout Latin America, as companies, and entire nations, struggled to pay off debts incurred in the previous decade. In Argentina, the end of the 1980s saw a crisis marked by hyperinflation. In the dairying sector, Mastellone Hermanos almost went under. SanCor lost many of its members when it lowered the prices it was paying farmers for milk. It even had to suspend payments for several months.

FINDING PARTNERS FOR FURTHER EXPANSION: 1990–2004

Argentina, in the first half of the 1990s, opted for economic liberalization, including extensive deregulation and privatization, the lapse of all price controls, and the end of almost all subsidies. The companies manufacturing dairy products sought to halt—and if possible, reverse—the rising price of the milk delivered to them. One method was to seek milk supplies from dairies

outside traditional areas, even importing powdered milk in large quantities. This action, however, was not successful, owing to a loss in quality of the products derived and to the ability of larger, more efficient farms to adjust the mix of their output by slaughtering their cattle or using their land to raise more crops instead of delivering more milk.

SanCor, in 1995, launched a $200 million, five-year investment plan. That year it opened a plant in San Guillermo, Santa Fe, to process 250,000 liters of milk per day into blue cheese, Camembert, and Port Salut. Other facilities arising from this plan were a cream and pasteurized milk facility in Chivicoy, Buenos Aires, receiving 450,000 liters of milk per day; a specialty cheese factory in Bainearia, Córdoba, converting 250,000 liters of milk a day; a dehydration plant in Morteros, Córdoba; and a highly automated distribution center by the Pan American Highway.

A severe economic recession during the last years of the 1990s resulted in a fall in sales for SanCor's chief brands. Increasingly. Despite the problem of obtaining financing from Argentina's troubled banks, the cooperative looked inreasingly to exports, which represented about one-fifth of its sales, for growth. A U.S. subsidiary, SanCor Dairy Corporation, was established in 2000. Also that year, SanCor formed a joint venture with the Danish-Swedish company Arla Foods amba to produce 500,000 metric tons a year of whey from cheese, selling 85 percent of the output in international markets. The processing plant commenced operations in 2002 in Porteña, Córdoba. In 2008 SanCor announced that it would invest $37 million for the expansion of this plant.

In 2004 SanCor established another joint venture with Daily Partners Americas Argentina S.A. to market fresh dairy products in Argentina and export powdered milk and cheese under the SanCor label. DPAA was an alliance of Nestlé S.A. and Fonterra Cooperative Group New Zealand. The joint venture was called UTE (Unión Transitaria de Empresas).

SanCor's plan for surviving the economic crisis also rested on emphasizing products that offered high added value to the basic raw material. In 2001 the cooperative introduced SanCor Bio Salud, the first line of dairy products specifically developed for medicinal use. It also premiered two new yogurt lines, SanCor Natur (with fruit) and SanCor Vida (flavored), which corresponded to different segments of the market, and it reintroduced UAT, an ultrahigh-temperature milk in two varieties, both low-fat in different degrees. UAT was fortified with vitamins A and D. It had a half-year shelf life without refrigeration.

KEY DATES

1938: Sixteen Argentine dairy cooperatives unite to establish a butter factory.

1943: Now a cooperative under the SanCor name the group begins processing fresh milk.

1963: SanCor builds its first facility for producing powdered milk.

1970: SanCor has added yogurt, flan, other dairy desserts, and mayonnaise to its products.

1986: SanCor establishes a subsidiary in Brazil.

1995: The cooperative launches a five-year, $200 million investment plan.

2000: SanCor forms a joint venture with Arla Foods, a big Danish-Swedish company.

2004: The cooperative establishes another joint venture with two foreign partners.

2006: A loan from Venezuela saves SanCor from having to sell a majority stake to pay down debt.

SURVIVING THE CRISIS: 2004–08

As 2001 ended, Argentina, no longer able to support its currency on a par with the U.S. dollar, defaulted on its debts, which reduced the value of the peso to 30 cents. For years Argentine exporters had been complaining that dollarization made it difficult to sell its products abroad at a price competitive with those of neighboring countries with weaker currencies, such as Brazil and Chile. SanCor's exports were less expensive, but it was having trouble servicing its dollar denominated debt from its earnings in much reduced pesos. In 2004, the International Finance Corporation agreed to refinance SanCor's $29 million in loans from this body.

This accord still left SanCor with the need to restructure a debt that reached $167 million in 2006. Adecoagro LLC, a farming company, offered $120 million for 62.5 percent of the shares. The prospect of selling the cooperative to a company majority owned by foreigners provoked public outrage. SanCor was rescued by President Hugo Chávez of Venezuela, who extended a loan of $135 million in exchange for ten years' delivery of powdered milk and technical aid for Venezuela's own dairy industry. The cooperative allotted $80 million of this sum to pay down debt and the rest for working capital.

In fiscal 2006 (the year ended June 30, 2006), SanCor processed 1.5 billion liters of milk, more than 15 percent of the national production. The domestic market accounted for three-quarters of its sales, with the leading customers for its products being so-called concessionaires (32 percent) and supermarkets (24 percent). Fluid milk, powdered milk, and cheeses accounted for 81 percent of this total. In the export market, Algeria was the main destination (30 percent), followed by Venezuela (15 percent).

SanCor, in 2006, consisted of some 60 cooperatives embracing about 1,600 dairy producers. Sixteen industrial complexes were processing about 4.5 million liters of milk per day into butter, cream, refrigerated milk, powdered milk, sterilized milk (UAT), *dulce de leche* (a caramel spread made by boiling milk and sugar), whey, special formulas, and yogurt, flan, and other dairy desserts. There were also two depositories for allowing cheese to mature and a plant fractioning milk into powder. The cooperative had five sales offices, nine commercial offices, and a distribution center supplying 270 exclusive distributors and over 140 independent wholesale customers as well as 1,500 supermarkets and 60,000 other retailers.

Chávez was doing more for SanCor than the Argentine government, which was collecting a large amount of taxes from the cooperative's exports of powdered milk. The price of this product had soared from $1,000 per metric ton in 2001 to more than $4,500 in 2007. However, the government and the dairy companies had agreed that sums greater than $2,770 per ton from exports would be directed to a fund created to subsidize dairy farms and agribusinesses. This levy was in addition to longstanding export taxes on dairy products ranging from 5 to 10 percent. The dairy products processors found little relief in domestic sales, complaining that the retail price of milk, which was also subsidized by the state, did not take into account the rising price of raw milk from dairy farmers.

By 2008 the Argentine dairy products industry accounted for nearly $6 billion a year in sales. However, there were fears that production would fall because the expansion of soybean planting, stimulated by the high demand of China, was crowding out not only other crops but land for livestock raising. Rural associations claimed that ten million hectares (near 25 million acres) had been converted to cropland since the mid-1990s.

By late 2008 the dairy products processors had succeeded in obtaining a 15 percent reduction in their payments to the government. SanCor reported a profit of ARS $163.6 million ($52.77 million) in fiscal 2008. As the calendar year began to draw to a close, the international financial crisis threatened to reduce the market for exports.

The cooperative—or more correctly, cooperative of cooperatives—had more than strictly business objectives. It sponsored a youth movement, published a magazine, and had created a bank, insurance company, and meat-packing plant. It provided technical assistance on every facet of running a dairy farm, including milk quality control, new milking techniques, genetic improvement and artificial insemination of the herd, advice on financing equipment, and the sharing of farm machinery. A foundation under the SanCor name was dedicated to promoting cooperativist ideals.

SanCor's system of government was based partly on equal representation for each cooperative and partly on representation according to volume of production. Executive authority was wielded by an administrative council, an enforcement commission, and a steering committee.

Robert Halasz

PRINCIPAL SUBSIDIARIES

Amplicampo Inversora S.A.; Aproagro S.A.; Arla Foods Ingredients S.A. (50%); Coop Publicidad S.C.; Estable-cimiento San Marco S.A.; El Homero S.C.; Integral Insumos S.C.; SanCor do Brasil Produtos Alimenticios Ltda. (Brazil); SanCor Cooperativa de Seguros Ltda.; SanCor CUL/DPAA UTE Unión Transitoria de Empresas (50%); SanCor Dairy Corporation (USA); SanCor Medicina Privada S.A.; SODECAR S.A.

PRINCIPAL COMPETITORS

Compañia Regional de Lácteos (Corlasa); Danone Argentina S.A.; Mastellone Hermanos S.A.; Milkaut S.A.; Nestlé Argentina S.A.

FURTHER READING

Casaburi, Gabriel C., *Dynamic Agroindustrial Clusters,* New York: St. Martin's Press, 1999, pp. 104–07, 117–18, 143.

"La crisis no impide a SanCor lanzar nuevos productos," *Redacción económia,* December 2001, p. 36.

Lacunza, Sebastián, "Argentina: Dairy Farmers Butt Heads with President Fernandez," *Global Information Network,* January 11, 2008.

"Qué hay detrás de la crisis láctea," *Apertura,* May 2007, pp.72, 74–75.

"Quién es quién?" *INFOBAE Diario,* March 9, 2007.

Square Enix Holdings Co., Ltd.

Shinjuku Bunka Quint Building
3-22-7 Yoyogi, Shibuya-ku
Tokyo, 151-8544
Japan
Telephone: (+81-3) 5333-1555
Fax: (+81-3) 5333-1554
Web site: http://www.square-enix.co.jp

Public Company
Incorporated: 1975 as Eidansha Boshu Service Center
Employees: 2,973
Sales: ¥147.51 billion (2008)
Stock Exchanges: Tokyo
Ticker Symbol: 9684
NAICS: 511210 Software Publishers

■ ■ ■

Square Enix Holdings Co., Ltd., is the holding company for a group of businesses involved in video game development and publishing and ancillary entertainment ventures. Square Enix develops and distributes games for game consoles, personal computers (PCs), and handheld game machines, organizing its gaming business into off-line and online segments. Offline games account for ¥41.5 billion of the company's ¥147 billion in total sales and online games account for ¥12 billion of the total. The company generates ¥6.5 billion from the development of mobile telephone content, marketing games designed for mobile telephones as well as ring-tones and wallpapers. Square Enix operates a publishing arm that produces comic magazines, comic books, and game-related books, collecting ¥11 billion from such efforts. Through its Taito Corporation subsidiary, Square Enix owns arcade facilities that generate ¥69 billion of its total annual revenues. Square Enix is best known for its role-playing video games *Dragon Quest* and *Final Fantasy.* The company operates on a global basis, but derives nearly 85 percent of its revenue from sales in Japan.

Square Enix was the result of a marriage between two of Japan's leading video game producers, Square Company, Ltd., and Enix Corporation. The two software companies united in 2003, but before they sought each other's help in competing in the hotly contested video game market by merging, each company fought the battle on its own. Each company conducted its business in a different way, possessing distinct skills that made the 2003 merger a synergistic union, a business combination that was greater than the sum of its parts.

ENIX CORP.

Of the two predecessor entities, Enix Corp. was the older company, a business formed in September 1975 under the name Eidansha Boshu Service Center. Initially, the company published *manga,* or print cartoons, a multibillion-dollar business in Japan. In 1982, the year the company changed its name to Enix Corp., it diversified into the gaming market, using a PC game programming contest to provide the content it would market.

COMPANY PERSPECTIVES

To spread happiness across the globe by providing unforgettable experiences. This philosophy represents our company's mission and the beliefs for which we stand. Each of our customers has his or her own definition of happiness. Square Enix provides high-quality content, services, and products to help those customers create their own wonderful, unforgettable experiences, thereby allowing them to discover a happiness all their own.

The 1982 contest, which awarded a trip to the United States to attend AppleFest '83 in San Francisco, greatly influenced Enix Corp.'s development. It set the precedent for Enix Corp. as a publisher, not a developer—the company looked outside its organization for content—but more significantly, the contest attracted the talent that would give Enix Corp. its greatest commercial success. One of the contestants, Yuuji Horii, submitted *Love Match Tennis,* a game that became one of Enix Corp.'s first titles released for the PC. Another contestant, Koichi Nakamura, earned his trip to San Francisco with *Door Door,* a game that became one of Enix Corp.'s best-known PC titles before being released for the Nintendo video game console. What Enix Corp. gained from the work of the two contest winners was cause for celebration, but the company gained far more than two successful titles. By staging the contest, Enix Corp. attracted the individuals who would create a blockbuster, a video game infinitely more popular than *Love Match Tennis* or *Door Door.*

Horii, Nakamura, and three other winners of the contest in 1982 formed the team that would develop *Dragon Quest,* a role-playing game (RPG). Released in Japan in 1986, *Dragon Quest* was a spectacular commercial success, eventually selling more than 30 million copies worldwide as the initial release developed into a series. The game became Enix Corp.'s most profitable franchise in the years leading up to its merger with Square Co.

Dragon Quest demonstrated the financial rewards of relying on outside developers, and Enix Corp. used it as a blueprint, outsourcing the production of additional games to other developers by paying them royalties. The company published other, less successful titles, completed its initial public offering (IPO) of stock in 1991, and began publishing *manga* in its own magazine,

Monthly Shonen Gangon. During the 1990s, the company kept its video game business growing by fostering relationships with developers, enabling it to release titles for fourth-, fifth-, and sixth-generation game consoles as the battle between hardware makers Sony Corp. and Nintendo Company Ltd. for market share occurred. In 1997, Enix Corp. thrust itself into the middle of the battle when it announced it would release games for both the Sony PlayStation and Nintendo 64 consoles, which led to a significant rise in its stock value because one of its chief rivals, Square Co., had committed itself to developing games exclusively for the Sony PlayStation.

SQUARE CO.

As Enix Corp. made its rise from a *manga* publisher to the publisher of *Dragon Quest,* Square Co. made its rise from the hallways of a power-line construction company to the publisher of *Final Fantasy.* Square Co. was founded in September 1983 by Masafumi Miyamoto, whose father owned Den-Yu-Sha Electric Company, a power-line construction company. Miyamoto started his venture as a computer game software division within his father's company, an odd mix of businesses that continued until the division was spun off as a separate company in September 1986, the date Square Co. regarded as the date of its inception.

Before Square Co. became a separate company, Miyamoto had set an important precedent for his company, much like Enix Corp.'s contest in 1982 had sent it down the road as a publisher. Instead of relying on others to create content, Miyamoto wholly embraced the role of the developer, perhaps more than any of his peers at the time. During the first half of the 1980s, video game development typically was the work of one programmer, but Miyamoto envisioned greater efficiency and possibilities by assembling graphic designers, programmers, musicians, and storywriters to work together on a project. Using his collaborative model, Square Co. entered the console market in December 1985, releasing *Thexder* for the Nintendo Entertainment System (NES), the predecessor to the Nintendo 64. Several unsuccessful titles followed until Miyamoto was inspired by the stunning success of a game released by Enix Corp. *Dragon Quest* propelled Miyamoto in a direction that led to the development of *Final Fantasy,* which was released in 1987, one year after the debut of *Dragon Quest.* Designed by Hironobu Sakaguchi, *Final Fantasy* realized enormous success in the market, selling 24 million copies before Square Co. united with Enix.

KEY DATES

1975: Enix Corp. is founded as Eidansha Boshu Service Center.

1982: Eidansha Boshu enters the video game business and changes its name to Enix Corp.

1983: Square Co. is created as a division of a power-line construction company, Den-Yu-Sha Electric Company.

1986: Enix Corp. releases *Dragon Quest*.

1987: Square Co. releases *Final Fantasy*.

1991: Enix Corp. completes its initial public offering of stock.

2003: Square Co. and Enix Corp. merge, becoming Square Enix Co., Ltd.

2005: Square Enix acquires Taito Corporation.

2008: The company implements a holding company structure, forming Square Enix Holdings Co., Ltd., to control the Square Enix group of companies.

INDUSTRY CONDITIONS LEADING INTO THE 21ST CENTURY

The years leading up to the merger between Enix Corp. and Square Co. represented a difficult period for game developers and publishers. The increasing sophistication of consoles, PCs, mobile telephones, and handheld devices drove game development costs upward, adding significant financial pressures to companies battling it out in a fiercely competitive industry. The cost of developing a game, less than ¥100 million during the late 1990s, increased to more than ¥500 million as the 21st century began, with some titles requiring as much as ¥2 billion to develop.

To improve their chances of commercial success, some game makers looked for help from each other, including three of Japan's most important game publishers, Namco Ltd., Enix Corp., and Square Co. The three companies employed a common Japanese tactic, particularly within the country's banking industry, of exchanging equity shares in each other's companies, a practice known as "cross-shareholding." In April 2001, Namco Ltd., Enix Corp., and Square Co. agreed to cross-hold shares in each other's companies, a move that gave each company between 4 to 5 percent stakes in its competitors. In July 2001, the agreement led to the first collaboration among the three firms when they announced they would run an online games distribution

operation together and jointly develop a means for delivering games to mobile telephones.

2003 MERGER CREATES SQUARE ENIX

For Enix Corp. and Square Co., the cross-shareholding agreement was a prelude to a far deeper bond between the two companies. In November 2002, the companies announced their intention to merge into a single company on April 1, 2003. Each company was struggling in the months leading up to the announcement, suffering from problems a corporate marriage was intended to fix. Square Co. posted a ¥16.5 billion loss in 2002 primarily because of the commercial failure of the release of *Final Fantasy* as a film. Enix Corp. had recorded profits consistently, but the company suffered from a dearth of popular titles and had failed to release new products on schedule. The proposed merger sought to create a stronger competitor in the gaming market by joining a publisher with a developer, a company that would be led by Square Co.'s president, Yoichi Wada, and operate under the name Square Enix Co., Ltd., "We are going on the offensive with this merger," Wada said in the November 27, 2002 edition of the *Financial Times*. The merger was completed on schedule. Enix Corp., with 140 employees and ¥21.8 billion in sales united with Square Co., which employed 891 workers and generated ¥40.2 billion in sales, creating ¥63.2-billion-in-sales Square Enix.

GROWTH THROUGH ALLIANCES

The first five years of Square Enix's existence witnessed robust financial growth, as the company more than doubled its annual volume of business. Acquisitions and alliances with competitors in its industry fueled the revenue growth, creating a company with nearly $1.5 billion in sales by the end of the decade. Square Enix formed numerous partnerships during the period, but several deals stood out from the rest. In 2003, just after the merger was completed, Square Enix formed a partnership with chipmaker Intel Corporation. The two companies agreed to work together to improve online and offline gaming capabilities for PCs, mobile telephones, and personal digital assistants (PDAs). In 2006, Square Enix joined forces with PopCap Games, a developer and publisher of "casual" games, gaining the distribution and marketing rights for PopCap's titles in the Japanese market. Several months later, in early 2007, Square Enix announced a licensing agreement with Epic Games, a Cary, North Carolina-based game development company. Under the terms of the agreement, Square Enix paid for the right to use Epic Game's

Unreal Engine 3, the company's core technology, in the development of Square Enix games.

TAITO CORP. ACQUIRED IN 2005

By far the most significant event in the years immediately following the merger was the acquisition of Taito Corporation. Square Enix purchased the company, a developer of arcade machines and an operator of arcade facilities, in December 2005, initially operating Taito as a separate company before integrating it as a wholly owned subsidiary in March 2006. The acquisition added a new business segment to Square Enix's operations, a segment it referred to as "Amusement," and it provided an enormous boost to the company's annual business volume. By 2007, Taito accounted for 43 percent of Square Enix's annual sales, ranking as the company's largest business segment.

As Square Enix looked to the future, the company was enjoying a period of encouraging growth. Annual sales climbed steadily in the years following the merger, increasing from ¥63 billion in 2004 to ¥147 billion in 2008. The company stood as a formidable competitor, particularly in the RPG segment of the game market, continuing to reap financial rewards from additions to its two most popular series of titles, *Final Fantasy* and *Dragon Quest*. The company changed its structure in 2008, implementing a holding company system. Square Enix Holdings Co., Ltd., was created to control the group of Square Enix companies with Square Enix Co., Ltd., becoming a subsidiary of the holding company. Organized as such, the company pursued its mission of providing entertainment to consumers in Asia, Europe, and North America, seeking, in its words, to "spread

happiness across the globe by providing unforgettable experiences."

Jeffrey L. Covell

PRINCIPAL SUBSIDIARIES

Square Enix Co., Ltd.; Taito Corporation; SG Lab Inc.; StyleWalker, Inc.; Smile-Lab Co., Ltd.; Community Engine Inc.; Digital Entertainment Academy Co., Ltd.; Square Enix, Inc. (USA); Square Enix Ltd. (UK); Square Enix (China) Co., Ltd.

PRINCIPAL COMPETITORS

Electronic Arts Inc.; Konami Corporation; Nintendo Co., Ltd.

FURTHER READING

"Enix, Square to Merge in April," *Asia Africa Intelligence Wire,* November 26, 2002.

"Game Software Makers Enix, Square to Merge in April," *Asia Africa Intelligence Wire,* November 26, 2002.

"Intel and Square Enix Work Together to Improve Gaming Experience," *EDP Weekly's IT Monitor,* November 3, 2003, p. 1.

"Japan's Namco, Enix, Square Founders to Cross-Hold Shares," *AsiaPulse News,* April 24, 2001, p. 677.

Nakamoto, Michiyo, "Enix Captures Square in All-Share Bid," *Financial Times,* November 27, 2002, p. 17.

"Online Games Joint Venture to Aid Sony," *Screen Digest,* July 2001, p. 201.

"PopCap Games Partners with Square Enix," *Wireless News,* September 10, 2006.

Shimbun, Asahi, "Enix, Square Merger Sign of the Times for Game Makers," *Asia Africa Intelligence Wire,* November 28, 2002.

"Square Enix Inks Licensing Pact with Epic Games," *Wireless News,* January 28, 2007.

SunTrust Banks Inc.

P.O. Box 4418
Atlanta, Georgia 30302-4418
U.S.A.
Telephone: (404) 588-7711
Toll Free: (800) 786-8787
Fax: (404) 827-6001
Web site: http://www.suntrust.com

Public Company
Incorporated: 1985
Employees: 30,000
Total Assets: $174.8 billion (2008)
Stock Exchanges: New York
Ticker Symbol: STI
NAICS: 551111 Offices of Bank Holding Companies;
522110 Commercial Banking

■ ■ ■

SunTrust Banks Inc., with total assets of about $175 billion and deposits of about $116 billion, as of September 2008, ranks as one of the largest banking organizations in the United States. In a city that had seen its large financial institutions overtaken, SunTrust remains the only major banking company with headquarters in Atlanta. The holding company's subsidiaries serve a range of consumer, commercial, corporate, and institutional clients. Primary businesses include deposit, credit, trust, and investment services. Its retail branch and ATM network operates in the Southeast and Mid-Atlantic regions. Other businesses include mortgage banking, insurance, brokerage, investment management, equipment leasing, and capital market services. Vast

holdings in Coca-Cola Inc., long at the heart of the bank's stability, became a point of contention in the early 2000s, as shareholders and analysts looked for higher returns on investment. Unfortunately, the riskier activities of the nation's financial institutions led to widespread government intervention in 2008.

A CENTURY OF TRUST COMPANY

SunTrust traces its roots to the Trust Company, a bank founded in Atlanta in 1891. Trust Company would remain a major institution in the city for the next century, though since the formation of SunTrust in 1985 and the full name change of all company institutions that went into effect in 1995, little remains of the old company's history.

At the time of Trust Company's founding in the last decade of the 19th century, Atlanta was well on its way to becoming a leading commercial center. From the devastation wrought by the Civil War and Sherman's burning of the city, Atlanta had emerged much like its symbol, the phoenix, a bird that rejuvenates itself periodically through immersion in fire. By the 1890s, as Atlanta took on the nickname "The Gate City," a druggist named Asa Candler had developed a sweet brown carbonated drink destined to place the city squarely on the commercial map.

The drink was Coca-Cola, and in 1919 the Woodruff family purchased the Candlers' interest in the company. The patriarch of the clan, Ernest Woodruff, had become president of Trust Company, in which capacity he served from 1904 to 1922. With the family's acquisition of the company, Woodruff in 1919

COMPANY PERSPECTIVES

Atlanta-based SunTrust enjoys leading market positions in some of the highest growth markets in the United States and also serves clients in selected markets nationally.

took Coca-Cola public, using Trust Company as underwriter. In return, Trust Company received $110,000 worth, in 1919 dollars, of Coca-Cola stock. This investment would form the heart of the company's fortunes over the century that followed.

Although Woodruff left his position as bank president in 1922, the link between Trust Company and Coca-Cola was formed. Ultimately Ernest's son Robert took his place at the helm of Coca-Cola, a position he would hold into the 1980s. During his long career, Woodruff left a heavy imprint on Atlanta in the form of numerous donations by the foundation named for him. His family, however, had made a strong and abiding mark on Trust Company: "From them evolved the bank's steady, glitz-eschewing philosophy," according to Rob Chambers of the *Atlanta Journal and Constitution.*

That philosophy, along with its mother lode of Coca-Cola stock, ensured steady growth for Trust Company through the ups and downs of the mid-20th century. By the 1970s, Trust Company had adopted as its logo a "big blue T," with an advertising campaign that centered around that nickname. From the image projected by the bank, the operative term in "Trust Company" was "Trust."

The company's stability would become a particularly noteworthy facet in years to come, as one by one of its competitors were swallowed by the giants from North Carolina, NationsBank and Wachovia. The former absorbed Bank South and Citizens & Southern (C & S), while the latter took over First Atlanta. Georgia Federal, National Bank of Georgia, Fulton Federal, and numerous other former competitors likewise disappeared; only Trust Company remained apart. When Trust Company, too, ceased to exist, it would not be through acquisition, but through transformation from within.

TRUST COMPANY PLUS SUNBANKS EQUALS SUNTRUST: 1985

In 1984, Trust Company announced its intention to merge with another bank. A year later, reciprocal

interstate banking laws between Georgia and Florida became effective, and on July 1, 1985, Trust Company formally merged with Orlando-based SunBanks. It was an auspicious beginning; starting with $16 billion in assets, the new company ended the year with $19.4 billion.

In 1985, SunTrust also acquired two banks with total assets of $130 million. It would continue to make such acquisitions, some smaller and some larger, throughout the coming years. In 1986 SunTrust took on the $5 billion Third National Corporation of Nashville. With this acquisition, the bank had offices in a wide swath from Miami to the mountains of Tennessee, as well as a tiny foothold in Alabama through Third National, which became SunTrust Banks of Tennessee Inc.

The year 1986 was also pivotal in that it saw the formation of the subsidiary SunTrust Securities. In addition, the company created "The SunTrust Vision," a statement of principles that would remain in effect for years to come. As the mid-1980s became the late 1980s, the company's reputation grew. During the first half of 1987, SunTrust posted the highest earnings in the industry, and later that year *American Banker* named it "Top Performing Regional Bank Holding Company." In 1988, it acquired two Mellon Bank trust subsidiaries in Florida and was added to the Standard & Poor's 500 Index.

In the energetic, sometimes volatile, business climate of the 1980s, the bank faced serious challenges as well. When it entered the Tennessee market in 1986, the area had seemed a promising one, particularly since Saturn and other automakers had begun moving production facilities there. Nevertheless, the local real estate market experienced a sudden and severe downturn, which according to SunTrust's own literature might have had an extremely adverse effect on the company if not for its "quick action to confront this problem." With spreading repercussions from the crisis in savings and loan institutions, 1989 was not a good year for banking. The increased leveraging of companies in preceding years became a matter of concern, as did real estate lending practices. In 1990, the federal government required substantial increases in deposit insurance premiums.

Again, however, SunTrust's foundation, its Coca-Cola stock and its conservative principles, stood it in good stead. The company had obtained stock in Columbia Pictures Entertainment during Coke's short-lived ownership of that entertainment company, and in 1989 SunTrust realized a $10 million windfall from the sale of Columbia common stock. Also in that year, it began consolidating its regional banking subsidiaries

KEY DATES

1891: Trust Company bank is founded in Atlanta, Georgia.

1919: The bank underwrites Coca-Cola public offering in return for stock.

1985: Trust Company merges with SunBanks located in Orlando, Florida.

1986: Merger with a Nashville, Tennessee-based bank expands reach in the Southeast.

1992: Coca-Cola investment tops $1 billion.

1998: SunTrust makes largest acquisition to date.

2004: Bank accomplishes long-awaited entry into the Carolinas.

2008: Holding company sells preferred securities to U.S. government.

from a high of 53; within six years, the company had reduced this number to just 29.

With the approaching retirement of its first chairman, Bob Strickland, the company in 1990 instituted a plan of succession. Joel Wells became chairman and James B. "Jimmy" Williams became president and CEO. In 1991 Williams became chairman while remaining CEO, and Phil Humann was named to the position of president.

NEW NAME, SAME BANK

In 1992, the year the company's investment in Coca-Cola passed the $1 billion mark, SunTrust introduced an initial group of six mutual funds as the STI Classic family of funds. The next year, *Euromoney* magazine rated SunTrust Banks Inc. the 14th best bank in the world on the basis of its stability and solid performance. Likewise in 1994 several STI Classic Funds earned national recognition for their strong performances. By that point, STI had made available to the public a total of 18 different funds. Also in 1994, the company formed SunTrust Capital Markets and inaugurated a series of growth initiatives to increase revenue and core earnings.

In 1994 and 1995, the company took steps to consolidate all subsidiaries under the SunTrust brand name. Up until then, for instance, the Georgia subsidiary had continued to operate under the Trust Company name with the "big blue T" logo. In Florida, moreover, where a number of local bankers took pride in the fact that the 1992 devastation wrought by Hur-

ricane Andrew had not presented a major setback to SunBanks, the sun was finally setting.

In a bittersweet 1996 profile, the *Wall Street Journal* reported on one tangible consequence of SunTrust's decision to bring all its banks together under one brand name, which went into full effect in 1995. With the end of SunBanks came the removal of a major Miami landmark, the large orange sign, 12 feet high and 88 feet across, on the bank's Brickell Avenue tower. According to the bank's marketing manager, Karen Dorscher, "Every time they'd shoot a movie in Miami, we'd see the orange sign," which had appeared in *True Lies* with Arnold Schwarzenegger and in the Sylvester Stallone movie *The Specialist*. Bank officials arranged to have more than 100 small cubes cut from the big orange "S," and they sent these, engraved with the inscription "a piece of history," to local leaders and journalists. With more pieces left over from the "S," Dorscher told the *Journal*, "I took the leftovers to my son's day care, and they built things with it."

FOCUS ON THE INFORMATION AGE: 1995

SunTrust Banks was likewise in a building mode, with a heightened focus on technology. In 1995, it instituted "PC Banking," a personal computer-based home banking service. Offered through an agreement with Intuit Inc., makers of the popular financial management software package Quicken, PC Banking made SunTrust only the second financial institution in the Southeast to offer online banking. The company also took steps in the area of in-store banking. SunTrust's Georgia subsidiary in 1995 entered into an agreement with Publix Super Markets to offer in-store banking facilities throughout the state. The bank's Chattanooga affiliate, part of the Tennessee subsidiary, signed a similar agreement with Winn-Dixie stores.

Another area of technological development for SunTrust in the mid-1990s was enhanced automated teller machine (ATM) service. The company offered statement printing, coupon and stamp dispensing, and check cashing at its ATMs. For some time SunTrust had its Telebank 24 service in place, a 24-hour automated banking system available by phone, and it expanded its offerings through this system to include investment information and other types of services. At the level of the client/server systems connecting its branches and subsidiaries, until 1995 SunTrust had three platforms in operation; in that year, it introduced a single platform to link its intranet.

Technological advancements also allowed the company to present its commercial customers with a number of services. SunTrust in 1995 became the first bank in the United States to offer its corporate customers information access by means of both CD-ROM and an online connection. SunTrust also applied new technologies to an upgrade of its wholesale lockbox service and to assisting customers in receiving fax copies of check images directly through a PC. This would in turn introduce heightened levels of security. In conjunction with Antinori Software Inc., SunTrust developed an automated system to safeguard against fraudulent checks. It also began offering one of the nation's first image-based systems designed to assist in processing damaged checks.

BETTER WITH COKE?

As SunTrust approached the new millennium as the 19th largest bank in the United States, aspects of its operation would have been unrecognizable to the bank's founders from the 1890s. Nonetheless, two themes remained constant: the significance of its relationship with Coca-Cola, and the conservative attitude of stable, managed growth instilled by the Woodruff family.

Noting that James B. Williams sat on the Coca-Cola board and that Coke Chairman Roberto Goizueta (who died in the summer of 1997) sat on the SunTrust board, the *Atlanta Journal and Constitution* in June 1997 profiled the strong bond between the bank and the soft-drink maker. A large portion of the "trust and other business" at the bank, according to market analyst John W. Mason, "stems from wealthy officers and shareholders of Coca-Cola. ... Most of the public and the media doesn't understand that seventy-five to 100 percent of the bank's business comes from thirty percent, even twenty percent of its customers."

A central facet of SunTrust's financial picture continued to be its Coca-Cola shares. By 1997, nearly eight decades after Ernest Woodruff paid the bank's underwriting fee in Coke stock, the original $110,000 had grown to a value of $3.3 billion. The shares, numbering 48.3 million, had grown by $2 billion since the beginning of 1992.

This sizable nest egg, the Atlanta paper noted, "helps keep the bank stock pricey and beyond reach of unwanted suitors except those with the deepest of pockets." In other words, one key factor underlying SunTrust's continued independence from the North Carolina superbanks, which made it by 1997 the sole Atlanta-based financial institution, was its stock in Coca-Cola. Furthermore, in the four years since 1993, SunTrust had bought back more than 39 million of its own shares at a cost in excess of $1 billion and had plans to buy more of the 216 million shares still outstanding. This further decreased its potential vulnerability to takeover and increased earnings per share.

NEW FORMULATION: 1998–2006

Less tangible but no less real was the cautious mentality that had governed SunTrust from its origins. On March 21, 1998, Williams retired and President L. Phillip Humann assumed his role as chairman and CEO, but the *Journal and Constitution* predicted no significant change of direction. Of Williams and Humann, Summerfield K. Johnston, Goizueta's successor as chairman of Coke and a director at SunTrust, said, "They're not the same people, but they've been in lock-step for a number of years. They're both conservative, thorough bankers."

The bank's slow-growth strategies, however, could be a liability in a climate increasingly governed by the most aggressive competitors. According to the Atlanta paper, Wall Street analysts "continued to express concern that SunTrust Banks is becoming a lost lamb as a relentless round of acquisitions is creating ever-larger wolves in the banking industry." The article noted that SunTrust had purchased Nashville-based Equitable Securities in September 1997, "but hasn't acquired a bank of consequential size since its purchase of Third National ... in 1986."

Still, Williams and Humann appeared to be in agreement in their refusal to let the strategies of competitors such as NationsBank determine their own response to events. Jon R. Burke of Burke Capital Partners observed, "They've been miraculously good at not being reactive. ... And they've retained a community focus."

Humann faced both highs and lows early in his tenure. During 1998, he led SunTrust in its largest acquisition to date: the $9.5 billion purchase of Richmond-based Crestar Financial Corp. He also had to "preside over an embarrassing earnings restatement after the Securities and Exchange Commission said the company's reserves were too high," David Boraks recounted for *American Banker* in September 2002.

The new leader did not wait long to shake up the company internally. In 1999, he initiated a drive to increase efficiency, and in 2000 the company moved to centralize operations.

In 2001, SunTrust engaged in a three-month proxy campaign, incurring about $15 million in after-tax expenses, in a failed attempt to acquire Wachovia Corp. Despite a higher offer from SunTrust, Wachovia shareholders accepted a buyout offer from Charlotte, North Carolina-based, First Union Corp. SunTrust, seeking to gain a foothold in the Carolinas, made an unsolicited $14.7 billion bid for Winston-Salem, North Carolina-based Wachovia and its banking network and regional retail brokerage.

The new Wachovia claimed the top spot in deposit share in the SunTrust territory of Virginia and Georgia.

BB&T Corp., also in Winston-Salem, was the largest independent bank remaining in the Carolinas, but according to *American Banker* a SunTrust BB&T combination was unlikely. Other smaller banks occupied the region.

"With or without Wachovia, we are well into executing a business strategy and sort of restructuring that we started putting in place a couple years ago," Humann, SunTrust chairman and CEO, said in an August 2001 *American Banker* article. "It emphasizes high-growth, high-profit lines of business." Humann also said SunTrust could organically grow in its Southeast strongholds.

Humann's strategy had already put its mark on the company. Since January 2000, SunTrust had cut more than 2,300 jobs, consolidating its "27 separately chartered banks under a single corporate structure," according to *American Banker's* David Boraks. The July 2001 deal with Citigroup Inc. for the institutional business of investment bank Robinson-Humphrey Co., however, helped stabilize the employee count. The $10.4 million cash acquisition of the Atlanta-based company strengthened SunTrust's corporate advisory operations, but a bid for the firm's retail brokerage offices in the Southeast was rejected.

SunTrust acquired the Florida branch network of Columbus, Ohio-based Huntington Bancshares, Inc., in February 2002. Competition in the Southeast's retail banking business continued to intensify, driven by financial institutions' desire to claim a share of some of the wealthiest and fastest-growing markets in the country.

To distinguish itself from larger players and regain the feel of a community bank, Humann returned some autonomy to local markets. Growth in profits from lending had been lagging well behind those from fees.

SunTrust's efforts to enter the Carolinas finally paid off in 2004. Referring to SunTrust's bid for National Commerce Financial Corp. of Memphis, Humann told investors and analysts the deal would make "the best footprint better," *American Banker* reported in June 2004. In addition to providing entry into the Carolinas, National Commerce would enhance SunTrust's presence in Georgia, Tennessee, and Virginia. Wachovia, meanwhile, pursued an Alabama bank with branch networks in key National Commerce locations.

SunTrust closed the $7 billion deal for National Commerce in October, elevating its standing to the eighth largest U.S. banking company in terms of assets. National Commerce, a pioneer of in-store banking, had built a partnership with Wal-Mart and developed expertise in new branch expansion.

In-store retail banking locations afforded a less costly and more flexible option than the stand-alone brick-and-mortar branch site. By April 2005, SunTrust operated about 350 in-store branches.

A two-decade old rumor regarding the sale of Sun-Trust persisted into the middle of the first decade of the 2000s. In actuality, the last big Atlanta-based bank had limited purchase potential, according to *Atlanta Journal-Constitution.* Its sheer size demanded a hefty price tag and sale of its Coca-Cola Inc. holdings was burdened with capital gains tax.

TROUBLE AHEAD: 2007–08

Coca-Cola's second largest shareholder donated about $4 million in shares to one of its charitable trusts, the *Knight-Ridder/Tribune Business News* reported in February 2007. SunTrust avoided capital gains due to appreciation by giving the stock to its Mid-Atlantic Foundation in Richmond. The bank supported causes such as children's charities, healthcare research, the arts, and education.

In May, SunTrust President and CEO James M. Wells III announced the sale of 4.5 million shares, or 9 percent of its stake in Coca-Cola. Part of the proceeds were tapped for repurchase of some of its own stock.

Coca-Cola stock had traded in the $60 range at the end of 1997, but during the first decade of the 2000s the stock generally traded in the low $40 range. Some investors and analysts had been calling for sale of the stock and a move toward investments with greater gains.

Wells had succeeded Humann in January 2007, at the time pledging to pare expenses. He deepened the cuts in May, setting a goal of $530 million in annual costs by the end of 2009, according to *American Banker.* SunTrust, moreover, was evaluating business lines with an eye toward optimizing returns. News of job cuts came in August 2007.

Toward the end of the year, SunTrust was looking at a spate of failing investments and a spike in loan defaults. "Beyond the immediate bad news, the disclosures clearly signaled the end of SunTrust's long-touted reputation as a bank that guarded its performance by taking fewer risks and making smarter bets on loans than its rivals," Valerie Bauerlein wrote for the *New York Times.*

SunTrust was challenged on at least two fronts. The overheated housing market driving the economy had collapsed, taking mortgage-backed securities with it. In addition, the Federal Reserve had cut interest rates, dampening loan profits for banks.

In 2008, the level of nonperforming assets held by U.S. banks continued to rise. Reserves as a percentage against total loans also trended up. Yet, when measured against nonperforming loans, bank reserves were losing ground. SunTrust was among banks with "credit reserves below their level of nonperforming loans," *American Banker* reported in May. Troubled loans held the potential of moving into chargeoffs, should banks fail to find a payment solution with their customers.

Federal regulators moved to shut down failed banks, reminiscent of the savings and loan crisis of the 1980s. The Federal Deposit Insurance Corporation (FDIC) sold the deposits, and other assets, to solvent financial institutions, among them SunTrust. The action served to boost the confidence of investors in banks given an "implied endorsement" by the FDIC, the *American Banker* explained in September.

The U.S. government intervention into the faltering financial system continued to evolve during the later months of 2008 as economic conditions deteriorated. In October, SunTrust announced plans to sell $3.5 billion in preferred stock to the U.S. government, through the U.S. Treasury's $250 billion bank stabilization and loan stimulation program.

Wells found himself defending the stock sale in November, as some lawmakers raised questions regarding the bailout. "Contrary to the quotes coming out of Washington, this is not free money that was given to banks," Wells told investors and analysts. The government expected a 5 percent annual return on the investment. As for future lending activity, Wells said, "We don't know exactly how it will go, but we're trying to be balanced and sensible and not do anything radical in the meantime," *American Banker* reported.

In December 2008, SunTrust's competitor Wachovia, taken down by the mortgage-backed securities crisis, awaited a sale to Wells Fargo & Co. SunTrust, meanwhile, moved to take full advantage of the Treasury's Capital Purchase Program, seeking approval to sell the remaining $1.4 billion in preferred securities for which the bank was eligible.

Judson Knight
Updated, Kathleen Peippo

PRINCIPAL SUBSIDIARIES

SunTrust Bank; SunTrust Mortgage, Inc.

PRINCIPAL COMPETITORS

Bank of America Corp.; BB& T Corp.; Wachovia Corp.

FURTHER READING

Bauerlein, Valerie, *Wall Street Journal,* December 21, 2007, p. C2.

Boraks, David, "At SunTrust These Days It's 'Better' Not 'Bigger': Carolina Demographics Still a Lure, CEO Says," *American Banker,* September 16, 2002, p. 1.

———, "SunTrust: No Deal 'Anytime Soon': CEO Says No Regrets About Pushing Hard in Failed Bid for Wachovia," *American Banker,* August 9, 2001, p.1.

———, "Two Deals Close: Let the Integrations Begin," *American Banker,* October 4, 2004, p. 23.

Chambers, Rob, "Enterprise: Coca-Cola Long an Important Part of SunTrust," *Atlanta Journal and Constitution,* June 8, 1997, p. H10.

———, "A New Leader for SunTrust: But No Switch in Direction," *Atlanta Journal and Constitution,* February 11, 1998, p. E1.

Davenport, Todd, "Reserves Being Built; Will They Stand Up?" *American Banker,* May 5, 2008, p. 1.

Davis, Paul, "Deeper Cuts Cool Deal Talk Around SunTrust," *American Banker,* May 16, 2007, p.1.

Dobbs, Kevin, "An Inferred Blessing in Post-Failure Asset Sales," *American Banker,* September 8, 2008, p. 1.

Donsky, Paul, "Bailout 'Not Free Money': SunTrust Chairman Hopes to Use Government Funds to Increase Lending Activity in a Way That's 'Balanced and Sensible,'" *Atlanta Journal-Constitution,* November 8, 2008, p. C1.

———, "SunTrust May Buy Back Securities: Deal Would Cost Bank $500 Million," *Atlanta Journal-Constitution,* September 9, 2008, p. C1.

———, "SunTrust Will Sell Stock to Government: $3.5 Billion Sale Will Help Bank Weather Economic Turndown and Buy Competitors," *Atlanta Journal-Constitution,* October 28, 2008, p. C1.

———, "U.S. to Buy $3.5 Billion Stake in SunTrust," *Knight-Ridder/Tribune Business News,* October 27, 2008.

Fajt, Marissa, "Ruling for Buyers Upheld in S&L Case," *American Banker,* October 7, 2008, p. 20.

Harris, Doug E., "Updated Commodity Law Was a Victory for Bank Regulators," *American Banker,* February 9, 2001, p. 13.

Moyer, Liz, "Head to Head with SunTrust for Third Time in Three Years," *American Banker,* June 22, 2004, p.1.

Paul, Peralte C., "So Far, No Partner Has Been Lured by ... Stubborn SunTrust," *Atlanta Journal-Constitution,* April 9, 2006, p. Q1.

———, "A SunTrust Shift?" *Knight-Ridder/Tribune Business News,* February 2, 2007.

———, "SunTrust Shines in Hot Retail Climate," *Atlanta Journal-Constitution,* April 19, 2005, p. C1.

St. Anthony, Neal, "Minnesota Law Firm Brings AIG Good News," *Minneapolis Star Tribune,* December 9, 2008, pp. D1, D6.

"SunTrust Banks to Cut 2,400 Jobs," *New York Times,* August 21, 2007.

"SunTrust Settles Escrow Suit," *Wall Street Journal,* February 26, 1996.

"SunTrust's Earnings for 4th Quarter Rose Despite Its Expenses," *Wall Street Journal,* January 10, 1996, p. B4.

Tippett, Karen L., "Florida Journal: Signing Off: SunTrust Preserves Plastic," *Wall Street Journal,* February 28, 1996, p. F2.

Taschen GmbH

Hohenzollernring 53
Cologne, D-50672
Germany
Telephone: (+49 221) 201 80 0
Fax: (+49 221) 25 49 19
Web site: http://www.taschen.com

Private Company
Incorporated: 1981
Employees: 150
NAICS: 511130 Book Publishers

■ ■ ■

Taschen GmbH is one of the world's leading specialist publishers of art books. The Cologne, Germany-based company had played a major role in modernizing and democratizing the art book format, producing a number of popular and popularly priced series of books on contemporary artists, photography, design, film, and other subjects. In addition to its low-priced art books, Taschen also produces a wide range of high-end and highly eclectic works. These include a series of folio-size books (called XXL by the company), including *SUMO,* at more than 60 pounds claimed to be the heaviest book published in the 20th century, which presents a retrospective on the work of photographer Helmut Newton. In 2004 the company released *GOAT,* in a similarly XXL-sized format detailing the life and career of the boxer Muhammad Ali.

In addition to its Cologne headquarters, Taschen operates subsidiaries in France, Hong Kong, Japan, Spain, the United States, and the United Kingdom. The company, which originated as a comic-book store in the early 1980s, also operates a small number of flagship bookstores, in Paris; New York; Hollywood and Beverly Hills, California; London; and Cologne. The company's most recent store opened in Brussels, Belgium, in December 2008. Taschen remains a private company led by founder Benedikt Taschen, and his wife Angelika (née Muthesius) Taschen. The company does not release its financial details.

COMIC BOOK ORIGINS IN THE EIGHTIES

Benedikt Taschen grew up as the youngest child of five in Cologne, Germany. Both of Taschen's parents were physicians, and his siblings were much older than he. As a result, as Taschen told the *Observer* in 2001: "Nobody played with me. ... Neither parents nor siblings. Though my brother-in-law Ulli did. He was an art and music fan."

This early exposure to art and popular culture led Taschen to become an avid comic book fan at an early age. He quickly developed a penchant for collecting as well, building not only an impressive collection of comic books, but also more specialized collections, such as drawings of Donald Duck made by Disney artist Carl Banks. By the age of 12, Taschen had extended his passion for collecting into the commercial range, launching his own mail-order catalog.

Taschen chose not to seek a university education, and instead, at the age of 18, opened his own comic book store in Cologne. The small shop was packed full

COMPANY PERSPECTIVES

∎

Our company credo: to democratize "great" books and make them affordable and accessible all over the world at unbeatable prices.

of both new comics and collector's items. Soon after, the shop also boasted a more ambitious venture: the publication of its own comic book, *Sally Forth,* created by Wallace Wood.

Publishing quickly captured more of Taschen's interest, and by 1981 he had launched his first catalog. For this, he was joined by a group of partners, including Ludwig Könemann, who handled distribution; Michael Kriegeskorte, who took charge of design and production; and Hubertus Röder, who oversaw the business end. By 1982 the company had grown enough to move into a new three-story headquarters, from which it launched a number of successful titles, such as *Ray Banana.*

Despite this early success, the company soon found itself struggling, after a number of titles failed to find an audience. By 1984 the company had more or less run out of funds, and depended on Taschen's parents and other relatives for a cash lifeline.

DISCOUNT ART BOOK PIONEER

Taschen decided to try a different approach, and in 1984 he took a chance and purchased 40,000 copies of an English-language art book on René Magritte that had been remaindered. Taschen purchased the books for $1 per copy, borrowing the money from his family, and promptly sold them all for DM 10 (approximately $3) per book. The experience encouraged Taschen to convert his publishing business to focus on art books.

In this, Taschen proved to have a natural talent. By the end of the year, he had purchased the publishing rights to a book of photographs by Annie Leibovitz, correctly recognizing that she was soon to emerge as one of the world's best-known photographers. Another successful venture was the purchase of the publishing rights to *New York,* by Reinhart Wolf, the original edition of which had been priced at DM 168. Yet Taschen was in the process of inventing the discount art book formula that became the company's hallmark. Taschen priced the Wolf book at just DM 30, and the book quickly became a bestseller in its category.

Taschen then set out to develop its own original catalog. With the help of editor Ingo F. Walther, the company prepared a new series of "Basic Art" books. The series presented well-known artists in a high-quality but low-priced format—in the United States, each title of the series was priced at just $9.98—unheard of at the time. The first in the series, *Picasso,* became an instant strong seller for the company.

MULTILINGUAL PUBLISHING MODEL

This success led the company to develop a unique publishing and distribution model that enabled it to drive down its costs in order to maintain a low pricing structure. A major factor in the group's early success was its decision to develop a multilingual publishing model. The company typically printed a first run of a new book in German; if sales were successful, the book would then be rolled out in as many as 20 different languages.

Another important step in the group's developing distribution model came with the decision to print art books featuring text in English, German, and French. The decision greatly expanded the scope of distribution for each title; by generating large volumes, the company was able to reduce its production costs. As a result, the company released large-scale art books at greatly reduced prices.

Taschen also broke out of traditional art book sales channels, which remained limited to bookstores and museums, and proved willing to sell books to a wide variety of retail outlets, including department stores and supermarkets. At the same time, the company broke with the traditional publishing industry again when it imposed a minimum on the level of customers' orders and instituted a no-return policy.

By the end of the 1980s, Taschen's distribution model had enabled it to develop a worldwide market for its books. The company also moved into the high-end of the art book market. In 1989, for example, the company launched a two-volume retrospective of the works of Vincent van Gogh, in honor of the upcoming 100th anniversary of the painter's death. Priced at just $60—easily one-third of the typical price of similar works—the van Gogh became another company bestseller.

HEAVYWEIGHT IN THE NINETIES

Taschen moved to new headquarters, a large mansion in Cologne, in 1990. The company emerged as a major force on the cutting edge of the international art and design markets, forming relationships with such noted contemporary artists as Jeff Koons, Philippe Starck, and H. R. Giger. The interest in contemporary art led the

KEY DATES

■

1981: Eighteen-year-old Benedikt Taschen opens a comic book store in Cologne, Germany, and publishes his first comic book title, Wallace Wood's *Sally Forth.*

1984: Focus is switched to art books after 40,000 remaindered copies of a Magritte book sell successfully.

1985: Taschen debuts its discount "Basic Art" series, pioneering the market for low-priced art books.

1994: Under the editorial direction of Angelika Muthesius, Taschen publishes the first in a series of best-selling interior design books.

1999: Taschen releases *SUMO,* claiming it to be the heaviest book published in the 20th century.

2000: Company opens a store in Paris.

2007: Taschen opens a store in Hollywood, which becomes the group's U.S. headquarters.

2008: Taschen opens two new stores, in London and in Brussels.

company to launch the successful low-priced Icon series featuring both established and emerging contemporary artists.

Design became an important fixture as well in the company's catalog into the early 1990s. Much of this impetus came from Angelika Muthesius, who had earned a Ph.D. in art history from the University of Heidelberg before joining the company as an editor in 1988. Under her guidance, the group released its first design-oriented book, *Twentieth Century Furniture Design.* In the early 1990s Muthesius pioneered a series of interior design books that went on to become some of the company's strongest sellers. Muthesius's role within Taschen became still more prominent when she married Benedikt Taschen in 1996.

Taschen continued to broaden its catalog through the 1990s, often raising eyebrows with its penchant for erotica, or borderline pornography, depending on the viewer. The strong sales of the company's catalog overall enabled the company to take risks elsewhere, as Taschen continued to innovate through the decade. One of the group's higher-profile projects was its launch of a series of folio-sized books, dubbed XXL by the company. Among the first in this series was Gilles Néret's *Erotica universalis,* released in 1995.

By 1999 the company had taken the XXL format to a logical next step, creating what it claimed was the heaviest book to be published in the 20th century, a 460-page retrospective of the work of fashion photographer Helmut Newton. The volume, appropriately titled *SUMO,* stood two-and-a-half-feet tall and weighed in at 66 pounds. Accompanied by a support designed specifically for the project by Philippe Starck, the edition, initially priced at $1,500, quickly sold out, and saw its value rise nearly tenfold over the next decade. The success of *SUMO* encouraged the company to launch several new XXL volumes, including the massive *GOAT* (Greatest Of All Time), on the life and career of Muhammad Ali, released in 2004.

INTERNATIONAL PRESENCE IN THE 21ST CENTURY

The dawn of the 21st century witnessed further expansion of Taschen's catalog, with the debut of the company's first book on the cinema. That work, dedicated to the 1959 Billy Wilder film *Some Like It Hot* (reportedly Benedikt Taschen's favorite motion picture), was published in 2001. The success of that volume led the company to develop a permanent film series, with subjects including the works of Stanley Kubrick and Marilyn Monroe and the *Godfather* movies.

In other areas, Taschen also developed a series of works treating web design and other online topics. The company extended its design interests to include corporate design, launching the trilingual *Package Design Now!* in 2008. Another popular Taschen series involved retrospectives, such as a book incorporating photographs from legendary nudist magazine *Jaybird.* In 2007 the company released *Fifty Years of Slightly Slutty Behavior,* featuring 1970s-era pornographic film star Vanessa del Rio. Other titles included in the company's catalog included a retrospective of the National Football League and the "twin" volumes *The Big Breast Book* and *The Big Penis Book.*

Taschen by then had also been expanding the international side of its operations. The company had created a subsidiary in New York to oversee its sales in the United States, which had become the group's largest market since the early 1990s. In 1998 Taschen opened an office in Madrid, Spain. This was followed by the creation of a subsidiary in Tokyo in 1999.

In addition to establishing sales and distribution subsidiaries, Taschen had also begun developing an international retail presence. The company drew on its relationship with Philippe Starck to design a new series of retail stores, starting with Cologne. By 2000 the company had added Paris to this list, then opened a

Beverly Hills store in 2003. Taschen's New York store opened briefly in SoHo at the end of 2005, but permanently opened only about a year later, in 2006. In 2007 the company opened a store in Hollywood, which then became the site of the group's U.S. headquarters. Additional Taschen stores opened in London in October 2008 and in Brussels in December that same year. Under the guidance of Benedikt and Angelika Taschen, Taschen had grown into one of the world's most recognizable international publishing houses.

M. L. Cohen

PRINCIPAL SUBSIDIARIES

Taschen America Inc.; Taschen Deutschland GmbH; Taschen España SA; Taschen France SA; Taschen Hong Kong; Taschen Japan KK; Taschen UK Ltd.

PRINCIPAL COMPETITORS

Phaidon Press Ltd.; Rizzoli SpA; Harry N. Abrams Inc.; Thames & Hudson Ltd.; De Agostini S.p.A.; Farrar Straus and Giroux L.L.C.; Axel Springer Verlag AG; Bonnier AB.

FURTHER READING

Berens, Jessica, "A Passion for Taschen," *Observer* (London), November 4, 2001.

Bernhard, Brendan, "Sex & Beauty, Art & Kitsch," *LA Weekly,* September 19, 2002.

Bing, Jonathan, "A Passion for H'wood Coffee-Table Tomes," *Daily Variety,* December 4, 2002, p. 4.

Brown, Laura, "Agent Provocateur," *W,* August 2003, p. 96.

Georgiades, William, "The Passions of Taschen," *New York,* January 22, 2007, p. 16.

Golden, Reuel, "The Man Who Made Photo Books Sexy," *Photo District News,* December 2000, p. 40.

Mazin, Cécile, "L'editeur Allemand Taschen se Taille une Librairie à Bruxelles," *Actualités,* December 11, 2008.

Palmeri, Christopher, "Germany's Publishing Heavyweight," *Business Week,* May 3, 2004.

"Taschen's First UK Store," *Design Week,* October 9, 2008, p. 5.

Taylor, Sally, "Art Books at Pocket Prices," *Publishers Weekly,* December 28, 1992, p. 33.

Tzortzis, Andreas, "Inspired, and Made Rich, by Art," *International Herald Tribune,* October 24, 2005, p. 10.

Tate & Lyle PLC

Sugar Quay
Lower Thames Street
London, EC3R 6DQ
United Kingdom
Telephone: (+44 20) 7626 6525
Fax: (+44 20) 7623 5213
Web site: http://www.tateandlyle.com

Public Company
Incorporated: 1921
Employees: 6,488
Sales: £3.42 billion ($6.79 billion) (2008)
Stock Exchanges: London
Ticker Symbol: TATE
NAICS: 311311 Sugarcane Mills; 311312 Cane Sugar Refining; 311221 Wet Corn Milling; 311999 All Other Miscellaneous Food Manufacturing; 325193 Ethyl Alcohol Manufacturing; 325199 All Other Basic Organic Chemical Manufacturing

■ ■ ■

Formed in 1921 by the merger of two family-run sugar refiners founded in the mid-19th century, Tate & Lyle PLC is one of the world's leading processors of cane sugar, cereal sweeteners (mainly those made from corn, such as high-fructose corn syrup), and starches. The company produces the sugar-based sweetener sucralose and sells it under the brand name Splenda to food companies around the world, who use it to sweeten more than 4,000 products. Splenda, in contrast to Tate & Lyle's core low-margin sugar business, generates strong profits as it is responsible for more than 20

percent of the firm's operating profits but only about 4 percent of its revenues. The company also produces other food and industrial ingredients, including citric acid and ethanol, as well as various byproducts that arise in the carbohydrate production process, such as molasses, from the production of sugar, and corn oil, from the making of starch. From its base in the United Kingdom, Tate & Lyle maintains a network of more than 50 production facilities throughout Europe, North and South America, and Southeast Asia.

HENRY TATE AND ABRAM LYLE: 19TH-CENTURY ORIGINS

Henry Tate was born in Liverpool in 1819, the seventh son of a Unitarian clergyman. At age 13, he was apprenticed to his older brother Caleb, a grocer, and at age 20 he set out on his own. By age 36, he owned a chain of six grocery shops and began to look for other profitable ventures. In 1859 Tate became the partner of Liverpool sugar refiner John Wright and began to learn about sugar.

Use of sugar at the time was burgeoning in Great Britain, where decreasing prices led to a steady increase in consumption. New uses were being developed for sugars, including jams, condensed milk, and desserts, which made it a staple on British tables.

In 1869 Tate, a man who liked to be his own boss, dissolved his partnership with Wright and, with sons Alfred and Edwin, formed Henry Tate & Sons. He began building his new refinery in Liverpool in 1870. By 1878, the business had grown so much that Tate opened a second refinery on the Thames, which specialized in

COMPANY PERSPECTIVES

Tate & Lyle's vision is to create the world's leading renewable ingredients business. We aim to achieve this by building a consistent portfolio of distinctive, profitable, high-value solutions in products and services for our customers.

making sugar cubes using a process developed on the continent. His 250 employees at that refinery worked 60-hour weeks in 12-hour shifts.

If Henry Tate was successful in sugar, that was not true of all sugar producers, most of them family firms like his own. At the end of the 18th century, about 120 sugar refiners in Great Britain had supplied the growing need for sugar. By 1882, that number had been reduced to 26, and there were only 16 by 1900. The changing business climate for sugar producers, however, did not deter Abram Lyle III.

Lyle, born in 1820, had gone from his father's cooperage into shipping, like Tate setting up a business with his sons. The story goes that he got into the sugar business when he accepted a cargo of sugar in lieu of payment and had to find something to do with it. In 1881 Lyle bought Odam's and Plaistow Wharves on the Thames and began to build his own sugar refinery, which would form the foundation of Abram Lyle & Sons.

Lyle got off to a rocky start. An especially large continental sugar beet crop in 1882 severely depressed the price of sugar. At the same time, the cost of construction for his refinery soared well over the estimates. Lyle was forced to adopt severe personal measures, including taking his children out of school, to get his fledgling business off the ground.

Lyle's policy at his Plaistow Wharf refinery was to produce a few types of sugar as cheaply as possible. He specialized in Golden Syrup, a low-price sugar product designed to resemble honey (packaging that highlighted a bee motif enhanced the identification). It was said that the poor of the industrialized cities of England lived on bread and cheap sugar products such as Golden Syrup and treacle.

Although both their refineries were on the Thames, Henry Tate and Abram Lyle never met. However, the two firms seemed to have had a tacit understanding: Lyle never produced sugar cubes and Tate never produced syrup. When Lyle died in 1891, he left his sons firmly in charge of his business, as Tate did when he died eight years later.

In 1903 Sir William Henry Tate, the founder's oldest son, made a significant change in his father's company by taking it public, perhaps because one of his brother's widows wanted to withdraw her share of the investment. Only 17 shareholders, the majority of them family members, originally invested in the company.

By 1914, both concerns were successful family-run businesses. With the outbreak of World War I, however, they faced a very difficult situation. Between 60 percent and 90 percent of the sugar refined at the two Tate factories and at Lyle's Plaistow Wharf had been raw beet sugar, primarily from Germany and Austria. That supply was quickly cut off, and U-boats threatened cane shipments from regular suppliers in the West Indies, Peru, and Mauritius. In 1914 the government took control of sugar refining, confiscating the Lyles' supplies of raw sugar and portioning out supplies of all incoming sugar to the country's sugar producers. Government wartime policy allowed companies the same profit as they had averaged on granulated sugar for the three preceding years. Because granulated sugar was not the major product of either company, this formula was a blow.

Both companies faced other hardships during the war years, including an inability to replace crucial supplies such as the charcoal used as a filter during sugar manufacture, and overworked staffs of women who replaced the soldiers. Both the Tates and Lyles survived, though.

CREATION OF TATE & LYLE IN 1921

In 1918 Ernest Tate, the son of Henry Tate's oldest son William, approached second-generation brothers Charles and Robert Lyle about combining the two firms. The products of the two companies were complementary, and there would be advantages in being able to purchase in larger lots and exchange technical expertise.

Tate was probably motivated by two factors: Although his company had a greater refining capacity, it also made a lower profit per ton of sugar processed and a lower total profit. Also, the Tates saw a coming dearth of family leadership. Although the two founders were virtually the same age, the second- and third-generation Tates were much older than the Lyles and only one grandson, Vernon, was coming into the firm. The Lyles, on the other hand, had two active second-generation brothers and four family members in the firm from the third generation.

KEY DATES

1859: Henry Tate forms partnership with sugar refiner John Wright.

1869: Tate dissolves his partnership and starts his own sugar refining firm, Henry Tate & Sons.

1881: Abram Lyle III buys Odam's and Plaistow Wharves on the Thames and begins building his own sugar refinery, the foundation of Abram Lyle & Sons.

1903: Henry Tate & Sons becomes a publicly traded firm.

1921: Henry Tate & Sons and Abram Lyle & Sons merge to create Tate & Lyle.

1936: The government combines British beet sugar companies into British Sugar Corporation, effectively excluding Tate & Lyle from the domestic beet sugar industry.

1937: Company forms West Indies Sugar Company to buy sugarcane plantations in Jamaica and Trinidad.

1940: World War II sugar rationing begins, cutting back Tate & Lyle's production.

1949: Facing threat of nationalization, Tate & Lyle launches "Mr. Cube" campaign, which helps keep the firm independent.

1953: Tate & Lyle buys 50 percent interest in Rhodesian Sugar Refineries.

1959: Canada & Dominion Sugar Company (later renamed Redpath Industries) is acquired.

1976: Manbré and Garton, the only other British cane sugar refiner, and Refined Syrups and Sugars, based in the United States, are acquired.

1985: Several U.S. beet sugar factories are acquired, forming basis of the Western Sugar Company.

1988: Staley Continental, a major U.S. corn wet milling firm, is acquired in hostile takeover; U.S. sweetener maker Amstar Sugar is acquired and is later renamed Domino Sugar.

1991: Australia-based Bundaberg Sugar is acquired.

1998: Tate & Lyle becomes the leading producer of citric acid in the world by purchasing the citric acid business of Haarmaan & Reimer.

2000: Bundaberg is divested; Tate & Lyle buys out the minority shareholdings in Staley and Amylum.

2001: Company sells Domino Sugar.

2002: Divestment of Western Sugar completes exit from the U.S. sugar market.

2004: Tate & Lyle restructures its sucralose agreements with Johnson & Johnson subsidiary McNeil Nutritionals, becoming the sole global manufacturer of sucralose and gaining the worldwide rights to market Splenda-branded sucralose as an ingredient to food and beverage manufacturers.

2007: Divestments include Redpath and five European starch plants.

Negotiations began in the autumn of 1918 and dragged on until the spring of 1921, although the actual stumbling blocks in the negotiations were minor. Perhaps the most important deterrent was that the Tates and Lyles had different ideas about management. Whereas the Tates hired people to handle purchasing, sales, and management, the Lyles handled those positions themselves. Philip and Oliver Lyle, grandsons of Abram III, were said to dislike the Tates on principle.

The advantages of a merger finally outweighed the objections, and the two companies became Tate & Lyle in 1921, with Charles Lyle as the first chairman, to be succeeded by Ernest Tate. The actual mechanics of the merger were complicated, especially because Tate's was a public company and Lyle's was privately owned. The merger was designed to form a 50/50 partnership.

Despite agreements between managements and an exchange of personnel between plants, however, fraternization between Tates and Lyles was slow. Even 15 years after the merger, old Tate employees were reluctant to mingle with the Lyle group and vice versa.

EARLY CHALLENGES FOR THE NEW FIRM: POST–WORLD WAR I ERA

The first challenge the newly amalgamated company faced was to respond to the postwar economy. The end of World War I meant a growing worldwide demand for refined sugar—in West Africa, in fact, sugar cubes were used as currency after the war. Tate & Lyle invested in sugarcane-producing land in Africa (an experiment that was later transferred to local government control after political upheavals), expanded capacity with new refining techniques, and became a leader in the distribution of brand-name goods instead of bulk commodities.

Tate & Lyle also became involved in the effort to develop a homegrown sugar industry so Britain would not have to face the supply crisis precipitated by World War I. The company invested heavily in the Bury Group, which was set up to develop a beet sugar industry in Britain.

However, the government also had its eye on beet sugar production. In 1933 national quotas for beet sugar products were established. The government was soon prepared to go even further. In 1936 existing beet sugar companies were combined into the British Sugar Corporation under the supervision of a Sugar Commission. The Bury Group received £1.4 million in British Sugar Corporation shares in exchange for its assets; this money was distributed to its shareholders, including Tate & Lyle.

The company was effectively excluded from the beet sugar industry at home. With the money from the transaction, Tate & Lyle looked for new sources of sugarcane to offset the loss. In 1937 Tate & Lyle formed the West Indies Sugar Company to buy property in Jamaica and Trinidad. The company also built a new central processing center in Frome, Jamaica.

By this time, however, a new crisis was at hand with the opening of hostilities leading to World War II. Sugar rationing began in mid-February 1940 and limited each citizen to three-quarters of a pound of sugar a week, later reduced to one-half pound. That meant a huge reduction in Tate & Lyle production. The directors, still primarily immediate family members, decided to keep both the London and Liverpool refineries open despite the drop in production. Plaistow made Golden Syrup, which was in great demand because of its low price. The Thames facility continued to make sugar cubes, although wartime shortages meant that the quality was lower. Both London factories were hit hard by bombs and required substantial repairs. By 1942 over half of the employees in both refineries were women.

POSTWAR ERA: FIGHTING TO REMAIN INDEPENDENT, EXPANDING ABROAD, DIVERSIFYING

The end of the war again meant increased demand and an abundant workforce, but it was not long before government intervention in the sugar industry became a

direct threat to the company. In 1949, with Socialists in power, it looked as if the government was ready to expand from its base in beet sugar and directly nationalize Tate & Lyle. To avoid becoming a subsidiary of British Sugar, the company enlisted the support of other sugar producers and took its case directly to the people with its "Mr. Cube" campaign. The little square cartoon character told homemakers, "State control will make a hole in your pocket and my packet," and "If they juggle with SUGAR they'll juggle with your SHOPPING BASKET!" The pressure held off the threat to the company's independence, which was further relieved when the Socialists were defeated in 1951.

Tate & Lyle may have been independent, but in the postwar world the company could not function freely. The U.S. Sugar Act of 1948 set the price of sugar there to protect its own sugar industry. The act also admitted Cuban sugar under a preferential tariff and regulated other imports under a quota system, thus severely limiting Tate & Lyle's expansion in the United States.

Other industry regulations followed. In 1951 the Commonwealth Sugar Agreement, an agreement suggested by the British West Indies Sugar Association (which included Tate & Lyle interests in Jamaica and Trinidad) specified quotas and prices for imported sugar in Great Britain. The agreement was monitored by the Sugar Board to provide fixed quantities of sugar at reasonable prices, and it did provide a stability in the industry that Tate & Lyle welcomed.

The 1950s saw Tate & Lyle begin to branch out into related ventures. In 1951 the company established Tate & Lyle Technical Services to emphasize research and development. That company in turn spawned Tate & Lyle Enterprises, an agricultural planning service to help foster agricultural ventures, especially in the developing world.

The company continued to acquire interests in sugar, buying a 50 percent stake in Rhodesian (later Zimbabwe) Sugar Refineries in 1953. Another major subsidiary, Canada & Dominion Sugar Company (later Redpath Industries), was acquired in 1959, giving Tate & Lyle a new foothold in the beet sugar industry and a better opportunity to serve the large U.S. market (beet sugar imports were not regulated under the same quotas as cane imports). When the United States slashed Fidel Castro's Cuban sugar quotas in the early 1960s for political reasons, Tate & Lyle took advantage of additional quotas for Caribbean cane sugar by buying Belize Sugar Industries. In 1964 the company diversified into a related area when it bought United Molasses. In 1967, as a member of a European consortium, Tate & Lyle expanded its interests in beet sugar outside of

Britain by investing in the Say beet sugar factories in France.

Redpath Industries and United Molasses brought with them business areas outside of Tate & Lyle's traditional concerns. Subsidiaries of Redpath manufactured automotive parts and vinyl siding for homes, and United Molasses included shipbuilding capacity.

Tate & Lyle's diversification and expansion abroad proved to be the right course when Great Britain joined the European Economic Community (EEC) in 1973. One provision of membership that directly affected the company was the EEC's sugar quotas. Traditional suppliers of cane sugar would continue to supply the EEC with specific annual quotas of raw cane sugar, both to assure British producers of an adequate supply and to protect the economies of developing countries dependent on sugar. The EEC Sugar Protocols guaranteed annual quotas of raw sugar from the African, Caribbean, and Pacific producers. These agreements, embodied in 1975 in the Lomé Convention, completely insulated the EEC from the world price of sugar and tightly controlled sugar trading.

Another provision of membership that affected Tate & Lyle was the EEC's subsidization of beet sugar production. Locked out of the beet sugar market at home by government-controlled British Sugar, Tate & Lyle was never satisfied with the EEC's subsidization, as it provided substantial incentives for the beet sugar industry to overproduce and decreased the market for Tate & Lyle's cane products.

Nonetheless, EEC membership had little impact on the company at first. An acute world shortage of sugar in 1975 meant sugar reached all-time high prices. In 1976 Tate & Lyle was able to expand both at home and abroad, purchasing the last remaining independent British sugar refiner, Manbré and Garton (which specialized in starches and glucose), Amylum of Belgium, and Refined Sugars in the United States (which finally gave it a foothold in the U.S. market). However, when sugar prices fell dramatically in 1978 at the same time that worldwide sugar production rose 14 percent, Tate & Lyle's earnings plummeted 62 percent in one year.

RESTRUCTURING AND REVIVAL IN THE EIGHTIES

That same year Lord Jellicoe became the first non-Tate or Lyle to fill the chairmanship of the company, and Tate & Lyle began a policy of retrenchment because of "a trading climate which [was] unlikely to become easier in the near future," according to Jellicoe. Because of the "crisis of overcapacity" since membership in the EEC,

the company closed its Liverpool refinery in 1981 to help reestablish a better balance between supply and demand. The Liverpool refinery had been in operation for more than 100 years, and some workers there were the third generation of their families to work for the company. Tate & Lyle also introduced cost-cutting measures at the Thames refinery and terminated the production of starches and glucose. Finally, the company put a new organizational structure in place, marked by a smaller number of chief executives who had clear lines of responsibility and were held personally accountable for the performance of their divisions.

With unprofitable areas of the business gone and a reinvigorated management team in place, Tate & Lyle worked to regain a position of leadership. In the early 1980s, Tate & Lyle took another step, recognizing that sugar was not the only sweetener consumers wanted. High-fructose corn syrup had become an extremely important product early in the 1970s. Corn syrup not only used the bumper corn crops of the United States, but also was easier to use in soft drinks and many types of packaged goods. In 1981 Tate & Lyle's Redpath Industries entered a joint venture with John Labatt to produce high-fructose corn syrup for the soft-drink industry. Redpath withdrew from the venture, called Zymaize, two years later, but Tate & Lyle was convinced that they would have to compete in the industry to stay on top of sweeteners. In 1985 Tate & Lyle reentered the beet sugar processing business by acquiring several U.S. beet factories; seven midwestern factories began operating as the Western Sugar Company.

As the decade went on, Tate & Lyle bought controlling interests in other foreign sugar producers, including the Alcântara and Sores refineries in Portugal, and developed new sugar technology with a microcrystalline process at the Plaistow plant to provide new types of sugar for packaged foods and industry. It also expanded some of its profitable nonsugar interests with the acquisition of Vigortone, a U.S. producer of animal feed, in 1984 and of Heartland Building Products, a producer of vinyl siding, in 1987. The Heartland acquisition put Tate & Lyle among the top five vinyl siding manufacturers in North America. At the same time, Tate & Lyle began another strong public relations effort to counteract a trend toward decreased consumption of sugar in developed countries because it had been implicated as a cause of dental cavities, obesity, diabetes, and hyperactivity.

Three major developments in the late 1980s promised to keep the reinvigorated firm at the forefront of the sweetener industry. In June 1988 Tate & Lyle purchased Staley Continental, a major corn wet milling business in the United States. The $1.48 billion hostile takeover gave the company 25 percent of the U.S. high-fructose corn syrup market. Tate & Lyle's aggressive new chairman, Neil Shaw (who took over in 1986 after serving as group managing director, beginning in 1980), immediately began restructuring the company to fit with Tate & Lyle by selling Staley's foodservice division. Staley Continental was later renamed A. E. Staley Manufacturing Company.

In October 1988, after resolving antitrust problems by selling the refining interests of Refined Sugars, Tate & Lyle acquired another major U.S. sweetener business, Amstar Sugar, which produced the Domino brand, for $305 million. Amstar was renamed Domino Sugar in 1991.

Finally, Tate & Lyle announced its development of sucralose, a calorie-free sweetener made from sugar that could compete with aspartame (marketed as Nutrasweet). This discovery was developed in a joint venture with the U.S. company Johnson & Johnson to ensure approval for its use in the United States. The approval process, however, proved slower than anticipated, with final ratification from the U.S. Food and Drug Administration not coming until 1998.

GLOBAL OPERATIONS, GLOBAL CHALLENGES

The early 1990s saw Tate & Lyle expand still further, with the biggest prize being Bundaberg Sugar, which was secured in mid-1991 through another hostile takeover. The addition of the Queensland, Australia-based Bundaberg significantly increased the Asia-Pacific interests of Tate & Lyle. The year 1991 also saw Tate & Lyle make its first venture into the newly emerging markets of Eastern Europe through an investment in the Kaba Sugar Factory of Hungary. In April 1991 Stephen Brown was hired by Shaw as group managing director and heir apparent. Formerly with Alcan Aluminum Ltd. of Montreal, Brown was named chief executive in April 1992, with Shaw remaining nonexecutive chairman. "Differences in management style," however, led to Brown's departure in March 1993. Shaw returned to his previous roles of chief executive and executive chairman.

Tate & Lyle extended its global reach in the mid-1990s as the sugar markets in more and more countries were opened to foreign operators. The firm acquired companies or interests in companies in Slovakia, the Czech Republic, Saudi Arabia, Zambia, Namibia, Botswana, China, and Vietnam. In Mexico, Tate & Lyle in 1995 acquired a 49 percent interest in Occidente, the fourth largest sugar group in that nation. Profits suffered during the mid-1990s, however, in part because of difficulties with some of the operations in emerging

markets, some of which were initially unprofitable. Ventures into Ukraine and Bulgaria were abandoned altogether. Another problem was the high-fructose corn syrup operation of A. E. Staley, which was hurt by low prices in the U.S. market caused by sector overcapacity. In 1992 Larry Pillard was hired away from Staley competitor Cargill, Incorporated to run Staley, and Pillard improved the situation by turning Staley into the lowest cost competitor and by finding additional markets for the company's products. Through his efforts at Staley, Pillard emerged as the new heir apparent to Shaw and was named group chief executive in November 1996.

During 1996 Tate & Lyle made its first inroads into the starch and citric acid sectors of India through an investment in Bharat Starch Industries Ltd. and a citric acid joint venture with Bharat. The following year Tate & Lyle became the first foreign firm to enter into a joint sugar venture in India by investing in a new cane sugar plant in Chilwaria being built by Simbhaoli Sugar Mills Ltd. Tate & Lyle became the leading producer of citric acid in the world in 1998 by purchasing the citric acid business of Haarmaan & Reimer, a subsidiary of Bayer AG, for $219 million. This business was renamed Tate & Lyle Citric Acid. In June 1998 Shaw retired from his position as chairman after his long tenure of transformative leadership. His successor was David Lees, a former chief executive of U.K. industrial giant GKN plc who had continued to serve as nonexecutive chairman of that firm.

Pillard and Lees faced fresh challenges as the 20th century drew to a close. Falling sugar prices around the world put severe pressure on profits. The situation was particularly dire in the United States, where strong beet and cane crops had pushed sugar prices down, forcing Tate & Lyle's U.S. sugar operations into the red. The decline in world sugar prices also turned Bundaberg, the Australian firm acquired in 1991, into a loss-making operation. In starch, Staley's high-fructose corn syrup operations suffered from both declining prices of fructose and increasing raw material costs. By March 2000 Tate & Lyle's stock price had fallen to its lowest level since 1989 following a series of warnings about lower than expected profits.

DIVESTMENT OF UNDERPERFORMING UNITS

In response to this dire situation, Tate & Lyle began divesting itself of underperforming assets. During the second half of 2000, Bundaberg was sold to Belgium-based Société Financière des Sucres for $247 million and several other smaller sell-offs were completed. Another important move for the longer term was the purchase in

June 2000 of the minority shareholdings in Staley and Amylum. By taking full control of these companies, Tate & Lyle could create global businesses in the areas of cereal sweeteners and starch and achieve significant cost savings in the process. In August 2000 Tate & Lyle entered into a joint agreement with du Pont to develop bio-based polymers. Further divestments came in 2001, including the sale of the company's interest in Zambia Sugar. Having concluded that the outlook for an improvement in the U.S. sugar market was bleak, Tate & Lyle placed its U.S. sugar operations up for sale. By mid-2001 preliminary agreements had been reached to sell Tate & Lyle North American Sugars, which did business as Domino Sugar, to an investment group led by brothers Adolfo and J. Pepe Fanjul, and to sell Western Sugar to the Rocky Mountain Sugar Growers Cooperative. The former deal closed in November 2001, while the latter was consummated the following April. The divestments continued in 2003 with the sale that March of United Molasses Company and UM Canada to Westway Holdings Corporation.

At the end of 2002, Pillard left Tate & Lyle to become executive chairman of the Swedish packaging group Tetra Laval. The outgoing chief executive received kudos for his stewardship of the company through a key period of transformation. By disposing of a number of unprofitable sugar businesses, particularly those based in the United States; reducing operating costs, especially within the Amylum cereal sweetener and starch business; and placing greater emphasis on more profitable, value-added products, Pillard left Tate & Lyle in an improved state of health. Results for the fiscal year ending in March 2003 supported this conclusion as pretax profits jumped 18 percent to £187 million ($288 million) despite a 20 percent drop in sales. Pillard also managed to chop the company's net debt load by more than half, leaving it at a more manageable £471 million ($725 million).

VALUE-ADDED PRODUCT PUSH

After a brief period of interim leadership, Iain Ferguson was hired on as chief executive in May 2003. Ferguson took over after a quarter of a century at the Anglo-Dutch consumer products giant Unilever, where he had served as a senior vice-president. At Tate & Lyle, he continued his predecessor's emphasis on pursuing value-added product opportunities. Thus in April 2004 the company realigned its sucralose agreements with Johnson & Johnson subsidiary McNeil Nutritionals, LLC. Tate & Lyle became the sole global manufacturer of sucralose by acquiring McNeil's sucralose manufacturing plant in Alabama as part of a £70 million ($134 million) deal. Tate & Lyle gained the worldwide rights to market sucralose as an ingredient to food and beverage manufacturers under the brand name Splenda. The company assumed responsibility for supplying McNeil with sucralose for the latter's Splenda retail and foodservice business. At the time of this realignment, demand for the no-calorie sugar-based sweetener was surging, particularly because of the low-carb diet craze that was sweeping the United States, and by early 2005 Splenda was being used to sweeten more than 4,000 food and beverage products worldwide. To keep up with its customers' demands, Tate & Lyle doubled the production capacity of the Alabama plant by 2006. Further capacity came online early the following year with the opening of a new, £100 million plant in Singapore.

Also in 2004, Tate & Lyle and du Pont created a new U.S. joint venture to produce the industrial ingredient Bio-PDO from a renewable resource, corn sugar. This bio-based, biodegradable ingredient was designed as a replacement for certain nonrenewable, petrochemical-based ingredients used in cosmetics, liquid detergents, antifreeze, and textiles, including du Pont's specialty polymer Sorona. Production of Bio-PDO began in June 2007 with the opening of a $100 million production facility in Loudon, Tennessee. In the meantime, in July 2004 Tate & Lyle subsidiary A. E. Staley agreed to pay $100 million to settle a long-running U.S. civil lawsuit alleging the firm had conspired with its rivals to control high-fructose corn syrup prices.

In November 2004, in the first of a string of acquisitions of food ingredients firms around the world, Tate & Lyle purchased full control of the South African firm Dolcré Food Ingredients (Pty) Ltd., which was promptly renamed Tate & Lyle South Africa. The acquired company was the largest importer of fructose in South Africa and that nation's sole distributor of Splenda sucralose. Tate & Lyle acquired the Italian firm Cesalpinia Foods, producer of natural flavorings, gums, and stabilizers for food manufacturers, late in 2005, and then a month later bought Continental Custom Ingredients Inc. (CCI), which specialized in dairy stabilizers and emulsifiers with additional expertise in beverage flavors and vitamin and mineral fortification. CCI, based in Sycamore, Illinois, with satellite operations in Mexico and Canada, was renamed Tate & Lyle Custom Ingredients Inc.

Following the European Union's announcement of a new regulatory framework for the sugar industry that included a slashing of sugar prices, Tate & Lyle booked a £272 million ($487 million) charge for the impairment of its European sugar assets. This charge reduced pretax profits for the year ending in March 2006 to just

£42 million. In addition, the company subsequently halted production of sugar from beets based on the impact of the new regulations and elected to divest more of its low-margin, commodity-based businesses. Tate & Lyle sold its Canadian sugar-processing business (Redpath) in April 2007 and its Mexican sugar business that December. In mid-2008 the company sold its international sugar trading business to Bunge Limited. Five primarily wheat-based starch plants located in the United Kingdom, Belgium, France, Spain, and Italy were sold to Syral SAS for EUR 310 million ($440 million) in October 2007. While further reducing its dependence on the volatile commodities of sugar and wheat, Tate & Lyle continued to beef up its value-added operations with the June 2007 purchase of an 80 percent stake in G.C. Hahn & Co. Limited, a leader in dairy and convenience food stabilizers. Founded in 1848 with its headquarters and primary operations in Lübeck, Germany, Hahn operated additional facilities in the United Kingdom and the United States, and had sales offices in 22 countries.

After profits rebounded in fiscal years 2007 and 2008, Tate & Lyle in September 2008 warned of a significant hit to profits stemming from a delay in the installation of new technology at its wet corn-milling plant in Loudon, Tennessee. At the same time, in the deteriorating economic climate, food and drink makers were launching fewer products, which had the potential to undercut the growth prospects for Splenda. Also in September 2008, a U.S. judge ruled against Tate & Lyle in a lawsuit it had filed accusing Chinese makers of sucralose with patent infringement. This decision had the potential to open up Splenda to generic competition. This latest news sent Tate & Lyle's stock down to a four-year low, while the price of the stock had been halved over the previous two years. Splenda was a key component of Tate & Lyle's attempts to shore up its earnings as the sweetener was responsible for more than one-fifth of operating profits while comprising just 4 percent of sales. Nevertheless, Splenda was far from the company's only value-added business, and Tate & Lyle's future prospects were brightened by a 30 percent jump in operating profits at its North American food and industrial ingredients division during the first half of fiscal 2009.

Updated, David E. Salamie

PRINCIPAL SUBSIDIARIES

G.C. Hahn & Co. Limited; Cesalpinia UK Limited; Orsan SA Limited (80.4%); Tate & Lyle Holdings Limited; Tate & Lyle Industrial Holdings Limited; Tate & Lyle Industries Limited; Tate & Lyle International Finance PLC; Tate & Lyle Investment Services Limited; Tate & Lyle Investments Limited; The Molasses Trading Company Limited; United Molasses (Ireland) Limited (50%); Tate & Lyle ANZ Pty Ltd (Australia); G.C. Hahn & Co. (Australia) Pty Ltd; Tate & Lyle Molasses Belgium NV; Tate & Lyle Management & Finance Limited (Bermuda); Tate & Lyle Brasil SA (Brazil); Anglo Vietnam Sugar Investments Limited (British Virgin Islands; 75%); Orsan Guangzhou Gourmet Powder Company Limited (China; 51%); Hycail Oy (Finland); France Melasse SA (66.6%); Société Européenne des Mélasses SA (France; 66.6%); G.C. Hahn & Co. Stabilisierungstechnik GmbH (Germany); Tate & Lyle Molasses Germany GmbH; Cesalpinia Germany GmbH; Tate & Lyle Insurance (Gibraltar) Ltd; Tate & Lyle Greece SA (99%); Tate & Lyle Asia Limited (Hong Kong); Tate & Lyle Gadot Manufacturing (Israel; 65%); Cesalpinia Food SPA (Italy); Tate & Lyle Molasses Italy SrL; The Mauritius Molasses Company Limited (66.7%); Continental Colloids Mexicana SA (Mexico); Mexama, SA de CV (Mexico; 65%); Tate & Lyle Mexico SA de CV; Tate & Lyle Morocco SA; Companhia Exportadora de Melaços (Mozambique); Tate & Lyle Netherlands BV; Tate & Lyle Molasses Holland BV (Netherlands); Tate & Lyle Holland BV (Netherlands); Tate & Lyle Norge A/S (Norway); Alcântara Empreendimentos SGPS, SA (Portugal); Tate & Lyle Açucares Portugal, SA; Tate & Lyle Molasses Portugal Ltda; Tate & Lyle Singapore Pte Ltd; Tate & Lyle South Africa; Tate & Lyle Molasses Spain SA; Caribbean Bulk Storage and Trading Company Ltd (Trinidad); Tate & Lyle Custom Ingredients Inc. (USA); Tate & Lyle Ingredients Americas, Inc. (USA); Staley Holdings Inc. (USA); Tate & Lyle Finance, Inc. (USA); Tate & Lyle LLC (USA); Tate & Lyle Holdings (US) LLP; Tate & Lyle Sucralose, Inc. (USA); TLI Holdings Inc. (USA); Nghe An Tate & Lyle Sugar Company Limited (Vietnam; 80.9%).

PRINCIPAL DIVISIONS

Food & Industrial Ingredients, Americas; Food & Industrial Ingredients, Europe; Sucralose; Sugars.

PRINCIPAL COMPETITORS

Associated British Foods plc; Béghin-Say; Südzucker AG; Cargill, Incorporated; Corn Products International, Inc.; Archer Daniels Midland Company; Ag Processing Inc.; Nordzucker AG.

FURTHER READING

Bream, Rebecca, and Maggie Urry, "Pillard Leaves Tate for Tetra," *Financial Times,* June 15, 2002, p. 16.

Carolan, Michael, "Ruling in Splenda Case May Hit Tate & Lyle's Margins," *Wall Street Journal,* September 24, 2008, p. B3.

Carolan, Michael, and Monica Mark, "Tate & Lyle Warns of Flat Profits," *Wall Street Journal,* September 19, 2008, p. B5.

Chalmin, Philippe, *The Making of a Sugar Giant: Tate and Lyle, 1859–1989,* translated from the French by Erica E. Long-Michalke, Chur, Switzerland: Harwood Academic, 1990, 782 p.

El-Rashidi, Yasmine, and Deborah Ball, "Tate & Lyle Is in Sticky Spot: Patents for Splenda Sweetener to Start Expiring Next Year," *Wall Street Journal,* May 19, 2005, p. B2.

Freedman, Michael, "Sweet Stuff: Iain Ferguson Has British Icon Tate & Lyle Growing Again," *Forbes,* January 31, 2005, pp. 98–100.

Howard, Susanna, "Splendid Sales Boost Splenda," *Wall Street Journal Europe,* December 2, 2004, p. A4.

Hughes, Chris, and Lucy Warwick-Ching, "'Natives Restless' with Tate Management," *Financial Times,* September 29, 2007, p. 14.

Hugill, Antony, *Sugar and All That …: A History of Tate & Lyle,* London: Gentry Books, 1978, 320 p.

Mintz, Sidney W., *Sweetness and Power: The Place of Sugar in Modern History,* New York: Viking Penguin, 1985, 274 p.

Oram, Roderick, "Sweet Success Beckons in Newly Opened Markets," *Financial Times,* November 30, 1995, p. 35.

Perez, Marvin G., "Investment Group to Buy Producer of Domino Sugar," *Wall Street Journal,* July 26, 2001, p. C15.

Urry, Maggie, "Executive Euphoria Fed by the Sweet Taste of Success," *Financial Times,* November 5, 2004, p. 23.

——, "A Food Lover Aiming for Weightier Profits," *Financial Times,* May 30, 2003, p. 23.

——, "New Products Sweeten Sugar Group," *Financial Times,* August 13, 2005, p. 23.

——, "Survivors of the Sugar Shake-Out Look Forward to Sweeter Times," *Financial Times,* August 11, 2008, p. 18.

——, "A Sweet, Starchy Taste That Soon Turned Sour," *Financial Times,* May 9, 1997, p. 28.

——, "Tate & Lyle Escapes U.S. Sugar Market," *Financial Times,* June 8, 2001, p. 29.

——, "Tate & Lyle Hit by U.S. Ruling on Sucralose Patents," *Financial Times,* September 24, 2008, p. 24.

——, "Tate & Lyle Sees Its Hopes Melt Away," *Financial Times,* March 9, 2000, p. 30.

Watkins, Mary, "Tate Poaches Unilever Man," *Financial Times,* March 25, 2003, p. 26.

Wiggins, Jenny, "Atkins Diet Fad Helped Create False Dawn for Tate & Lyle's Sweetener," *Financial Times,* January 24, 2007, p. 19.

Ukrop's Super Markets Inc.

———————— ■ ————————

600 Southlake Boulevard
Richmond, Virginia 23236-3922
U.S.A.
Telephone: (804) 379-7300
Fax: (804) 794-7557
Web site: http://www.ukrops.com

Private Company
Incorporated: 1937
Employees: 6,000
Sales: $607.3 million (2007 est.)
NAICS: 445110 Supermarkets and Other Grocery (Except Convenience) Stores

■ ■ ■

Ukrop's Super Markets Inc. is the leading independent supermarket group in the central Virginia region, and has long been admired as one of the most innovative supermarket groups in the United States. Based in Richmond, Ukrop's operates a chain of 27 supermarkets. The company has long differentiated itself from its competitors through its extensive range of fresh and fresh-cooked foods, prepared in its own central kitchen; the company stores also operate their own restaurants. In addition, Ukrop's First Market Bank joint venture, in partnership with National Commerce Financial Corporation, operates full-service banking branches in 25 of the company's stores, as well as ten stand-alone branches. Other Ukrop's operations include the small format Joe's Market store, named after the company's founder Joseph Ukrop, in Richmond. Uk-

rop's remains a privately owned, family-run business, led by brothers James and Robert Ukrop.

ORIGINS IN THE THIRTIES

As a supermarket chain, Ukrop's began modestly, a characteristic that would describe the company's existence during its first half-century of business. The first store, started by husband and wife Joe and Jacquelin Ukrop, opened in 1937 in Richmond, Virginia. Located on Hull Street, the first store belied the grandeur of the Ukrop's that would follow in its wake, measuring 16 feet wide and 32 feet long. In their garage-sized store, the Ukrops made $23 in their first day's sales, a total that thrilled Joe Ukrop.

The store survived the last years of the century's most devastating economic crisis, eventually becoming a fixture in the Richmond area. Despite the success of the store, Joe and Jacquelin were in no hurry to open a second store. Instead, the Ukrops were content with running a single store and leading a simple life. Devout Baptists, the Ukrops raised their children according to their faith, closed the store on Sundays, and sold no alcohol. Jacquelin cooked lunch for the employees, and Joe frequently lent a hand to neighboring farmers, closing the store when the demands of harvest season required his help. The Ukrops demonstrated no interest in parlaying the success of one store to finance the establishment of another store. In fact, 26 years separated the opening of the first store from the debut of the second Ukrop's, time enough for the Ukrops' children to mature and take an active role in the leadership of the family business.

COMPANY PERSPECTIVES

Vision: To be a world class provider of food and services. Purpose: To create great shopping and working experiences by sharing our passion for food in a fun and dynamic atmosphere.

A SECOND STORE AND A SECOND GENERATION IN THE SIXTIES

James Ukrop joined the business at his father's side in 1960 and began laying the seeds for the company's first expansion. A second store opened three years later, beginning an initial expansion spree that brought the store count to five by the time James's younger brother Robert joined the family business. When Robert Ukrop joined the company in 1972, serving as manager of two Richmond stores, Ukrop's controlled 7 percent of the grocery market in Richmond. By comparison, the market leader, Safeway, commanded 35 percent of the market, far outdistancing the independent and privately owned Ukrop organization. When Robert Ukrop joined the company, however, his brother, who served as chief executive officer, and his father, who served as chairman, were ready to begin another major expansion drive. In addition to new stores, the company purchased a bakery as part of its 1970s expansion program. The success of the bakery taught the Ukrops the efficiencies that they could achieve through a central production site, which served as a key lesson in later years when the company reached the defining moment in its history. By 1981, after a steady stream of new store openings, Ukrop's had closed the distance on its much larger rivals, laying claim to 26 percent of the market.

Ukrop's command of the Richmond market was impressive, especially in light of the company's insistence on remaining closed on Sundays and refusing to sell beer or wine. Observers credited the company's unwavering focus on details, which was a byproduct of the Ukrops' signature trait: its attention to customers. Providing superior service enabled the company to differentiate itself from the deep-pocketed national chains with units in the Richmond area. "The people that know them, know them as a company that runs superb foods stores," explained Bill Bishop, a food-retailing analyst, to *Marketing News* in a June 5, 1989 interview. "I think that far and away the most important thing that Ukrop's does is to put their customer number one," Bishop continued, noting "A lot of people say that, but

it's not done all that frequently, and they do that." Robert Ukrop reiterated the importance of customer service, explaining to the *Richmond Times-Dispatch* in a June 12, 1996 interview: "Our goal isn't to keep our eye on the market share, but to take care of our customers. People keep score, but that is not what is driving our business. The numbers will take care of themselves if we keep our eyes on our customers."

Perhaps as important as the company's focus on customer service was its extensive investment in employee training and its interest in developing an environment conducive to retaining its employees. As with customer service, Ukrop's success in providing an enjoyable atmosphere for its "associates" came not from articulating such a goal, but through execution, from actually achieving such a goal. The chain refused to sell wine or beer because the Ukrops were devout Baptists, but the chain remained closed on Sundays in deference to its employees. "If you want to be the best place to shop, you have to be the best place to work," Robert Ukrop remarked to *Marketing News* in a June 5, 1989 interview, referring to the longstanding policy of closing the stores on Sundays. Ukrop's ability to compete against an onslaught of national chains was attributable, so industry pundits theorized, to the chain's focus on the fundamental aspects of business. Many retailers proclaimed a commitment to customer service and employee morale, but far fewer actually succeeded in realizing their commitment. By all accounts, Ukrop's delivered on its commitment, presenting Richmond shoppers with an attractive alternative to the swarm of grocery stores in their area.

The distinction in consumers' minds was strong enough to make Ukrop's the largest grocery store operator in Richmond. By the late 1980s, the company controlled 30 percent of the metropolitan region's grocery sales, enabling it to collect nearly $275 million in annual sales. Expansion since the 1960s, pursued at a measured pace, had increased the store count to 19 by the end of the 1980s, with two more stores in the offing. Although the company was frequently presented with requests to open stores beyond the greater Richmond area, the Ukrop family resisted more far-flung geographic expansion. "We have an advantage being local," Robert Ukrop was quoted as saying in the June 5, 1989 issue of *Marketing News,* adding "We live here, we have friends here. We're able to put our arms around our business."

PREPARED FOODS DEBUT IN 1989

Despite the family's reluctance to penetrate other markets, it was preparing a bold move in another direction. Remarkably, Ukrop's had achieved its market

KEY DATES

1937: Joseph and Jacquelin Ukrop open a grocery store on Hull Street in Richmond, Virginia.

1960: The Ukrops' son, James Ukrop, joins the family business.

1963: A second store is opened.

1972: James Ukrop's brother, Robert Ukrop, joins the company.

1989: A line of prepared foods debuts.

1994: The company launches a $125 million expansion program.

1997: The company opens its first store outside of Richmond.

2000: The company's annual sales surpass $500 million.

2001: Ukrop's opens a small-format Joe's Market in Richmond.

2004: Ukrop's announces plans to open its first store in Roanoke, an event that finally occurs in 2007.

2006: Ukrop's opens a second store in Lightfoot, area of Williamsburg.

2009: After closing the Roanoke store, Ukrop's is forced to close the Lightfoot store as well.

explained in the October 1997 issue of *Progressive Grocer.* "We needed it out of one place. Bakery gave us some experience with manufacturing and logistics. We learned that some things are better done centrally." By relying on a single, large kitchen, the chain saved money on equipment and staff, possessed greater control over food quality, and could more precisely supply each store with an accurate supply of food items.

Out of a 10,000-square-foot kitchen, Ukrop's began experimenting with proprietary recipes, concentrating on what it referred to as "homestyle" foods. On Halloween 1989, the company's prepared foods line debuted, featuring ten items that included twice-baked potatoes, lasagna, and macaroni and cheese. It took approximately three years for the kitchen operation to begin generating a profit, but the company's persistence paid off. By 1994, the roster of prepared foods had swelled to a rotating list of 125 items that included chilled soups, grilled chicken breasts, spoon bread, cobblers, meat loaf, and various potato salads. Ukrop's foray into prepared foods became the talk of the industry, accounting for nearly 15 percent of the chain's total sales and adding further incentive to shop at Ukrop's. "They are not the flashiest ... but what they do, they do very well," a retail consultant remarked in the April 11, 1994 issue of *Supermarket News.* "It wasn't duck a l'orange," the consultant added, "It was very middle America. They obviously know who their customers are."

dominance without the hallmark quality that underpinned its success at the century's end. The company's greatest contribution to grocery store innovation came from research conducted during the mid-1980s, which revealed that changing consumer demographics and lifestyles indicated a growing demand for convenient, restaurant-quality food. The Ukrops decided to tap into the demand and further differentiate themselves from competitors. The result was one of the grocery industry's most lauded success stories of the late 20th century.

Based on their experience with a central bakery, the Ukrops decided to construct a central kitchen to prepare and chill food, which consumers could then reheat. For those few grocers who offered prepared foods at the time, the common method was to prepare the food items separately at each store. Ukrop's approach ran counter to the norm and received much criticism, but a combination of past experience and financial constraints predicated the reasoning behind establishing a central kitchen. "We realized, from a kitchen point of view, that we couldn't produce out of [each store]," Robert Ukrop

EXPANSION IN THE NINETIES

By 1994, with the prepared foods business a confirmed success, Ukrop's began to show signs of a more aggressive approach to expanding the chain. There were 22 stores in operation, generating an estimated $420 million in sales. After doubling the size of the central kitchen, the company purchased two buildings in Richmond in 1994 with a combined 393,000 square feet of space to serve as the future site for the expanded and consolidated bakery and fresh food preparation operations that supplied the chain. Company executives also began charting the chain's expansion beyond Richmond for the first time, looking at sites to the northwest and southeast in Charlottesville and Williamsburg, Virginia. In charge of overseeing the company's expansion was 47-year-old Robert Ukrop, who was named president in August 1994, succeeding his 57-year-old brother James Ukrop, who added the title of vice-chairman and continued to serve as chief executive officer. The company also had six new sites targeted in Richmond, as it readied itself for an unprecedented pace of expansion.

Ukrop's expansion and renovation program began in earnest in 1996, financed for the first time in the company's history by taking on debt. The $125 million program, perceived as a preemptive strike against mounting competition, included relocating stores, expanding existing stores, and adding new locations. The new store openings included the August 1997 debut of a store in Fredericksburg, Virginia, a 63,000-square-foot store that represented the company's first major move beyond the Richmond area. A greater geographical leap followed a month later, when the company's 26th store opened in Charlottesville. Meanwhile, as executives focused on growth, the company's market performance continued to improve despite the distractions of expansion. In 1997, the chain's market share increased to 37.6 percent, keeping the company well in the lead amid intensively competitive conditions.

Midway through the company's expansion and renovation program, management duties among the Ukrop family evolved one more step. Family patriarch Joseph Ukrop was named chairman emeritus in 1998, making room for the appointment of James Ukrop as chairman and the promotion of Robert Ukrop to chief executive officer.

By the end of the decade, the company's expansion program was winding down. Between 1996 and 2000, four new stores were opened, three stores were relocated, and four existing stores were expanded, but the company's expansion activity was expected to diminish as it entered the 21st century. Although the company was reluctant to divulge specifics, analysts predicted three new stores would open by 2005.

One area of the company that was expected to expand in the new century was Ukrop's foray into health-oriented departments within its stores. In November 1999, the company opened its first full-blown health-focused store, which featured a store-within-a-store format. The concept integrated in-store pharmacies with wellness/patient centers that included large natural and organic foods departments staffed by a registered dietitian. The extension of the format chain-wide was expected in the decade ahead, as company executives confirmed that the "whole-health" approach was a major focus for the future.

HOLDING ON IN THE 21ST CENTURY

Ukrop's continued to roll out new services into the new century. In 1997, the company formed a joint-venture partnership with National Commerce Financial Corporation to open bank branches within the company's stores. By the middle of the first decade of the 2000s, that partnership, called First Market Bank, had opened 25 in-store bank branches and another ten freestanding branches. In addition to operating as full-service banks, the First Market chain provided cross-marketing opportunities; bank customers could earn as much as $50 in free groceries each quarter, for example. Ukrop's also embraced the coffee shop trend, adding Starbucks outlets to five of its stores. The company's pharmacy and wellness center program also became a feature throughout much of the chain. As the first decade of the 2000s neared its end, 23 stores offered pharmacy services, and 20 stores featured full-scale wellness centers.

The group's commitment to health also extended to its food aisles. In 2000, the company launched its own line of organic products, called Full Circle. The following year, the company debuted a new health-oriented, smaller store format, called Joe's Market, which featured upscale gourmet and organic foods, as well as pharmacy services. The company opened the first Joe's Market in Richmond in 2001. The company later rolled out a new line of Joe's Market–branded products in its supermarkets as well. That opening came ahead of the death of the company's founder, as Joseph Ukrop died at the end of 2002. Wife Jacquelin died in 2005.

By then, Ukrop's had finally made progress toward its goal of expanding the chain. In 2004, the company announced plans to open its first Roanoke-area store as part of the proposed Ivy Market mall. The developer of that project, however, hit multiple construction delays. In the end, the Roanoke store only opened in June 2007. That complex was one of the group's most ambitious to date, featuring 58,700 square feet, and included a two-level, 200-seat restaurant, an underground parking garage, as well as space for conferences, meetings, and private parties. By then, the company had opened a new store in Williamsburg, a 53,000-square-foot building in the newly developing Lightfoot area.

The Roanoke opening soon hit a snag, as construction of the rest of the Ivy Market mall stalled. With no other retail neighbors, Ukrop's was unable to attract the necessary customer traffic to make the store a success. By 2008, Ukrop's sent out a message to customers, pleading with them to help the company keep the store open. Despite a 10 percent increase in traffic, the company, by then confronted with the collapsing U.S. economy, was finally forced to shut the store at the end of the year.

By then, Ukrop's had been fighting to hold on to its market share elsewhere as well, as it saw its leadership position shrink from year to year through the first decade of the 2000s. In 2006, the company launched a new promotion, called "Consistent Low Prices" (CLP), negotiating with its suppliers in order to provide for longer-term pricing guarantees on some 10,000 items. In 2008, as fuel prices soared past $4 per gallon, the company launched its "fuelperks!" program, providing discounted gasoline prices of as much as 10 cents per gallon for every $50 of groceries purchased in the company's stores. However, these promotions were not enough to shield the company from the bruising effects of increasing competition from the major chains, and the collapse of the U.S. economy. By January 2009, after closing the Roanoke store, the company was forced to announce its decision to close its youngest Williamsburg store as well. Ukrop's, while remaining one of Virginia's retail powerhouses, braced itself for the latest economic storm.

Jeffrey L. Covell
Updated, M. L. Cohen

PRINCIPAL SUBSIDIARIES

First Market Bank Inc.; Ukrop's Dress Express Inc.; Ukrop's Food Group Inc.

PRINCIPAL COMPETITORS

Wal-Mart Stores Inc.; Ahold USA Inc.; Winn-Dixie Stores, Inc.; The Kroger Co.; The Great Atlantic & Pacific Tea Company, Inc.

FURTHER READING

Coupe, Kevin, "'We're Going to Fight,'" *Progressive Grocer,* July 1994, p. 52.

"50 Movers and Shakers," *Supermarket News,* November 25, 2002, p. 16.

Frederick, James, "Ukrop's Breaking New Ground in Merging Pharmacy," *Drug Store News,* August 28, 2000, p. 13.

Gilligan, Gregory J., "Ukrop's Supermarket Chain Continues Dominance of Richmond, Va., Area," *Knight-Ridder/Tribune Business News,* June 11, 1997.

———, "Virginia-Based Ukrop's Super Markets Inc. Gains Market Share," *Knight-Ridder/Tribune Business News,* June 12, 1996.

Hammell, Frank, "Ukrop's Journey, Outward and Inward," *Progressive Grocer,* October 1997, p. 108.

Harper, Roseanne, "Ukrop's Acquires 2 Sites to Boost Bakery Output," *Supermarket News,* August 22, 1994, p. 19.

Kincaid, Jenny, "Ukrop's Closing a Store in Williamsburg," *Roanoke Times,* January 1, 2009, p. C8.

Kramer, Louise, "Down-Home Pat," *Supermarket News,* April 11, 1994, p. 29.

McTaggart, Jenny, "Store of the Month: New Frontier," *Progressive Grocer,* October 1, 2007.

Perman, Stacy, "Indie Grocery Stores Beat Back the Bigs," *Business Week Online,* November 8, 2006.

"Personal Touch, Traditional Values Help Family Grocery Beat 'Giants,'" *Marketing News,* June 5, 1989, p. 6.

Tanner, Ronald, "A New Dimension in Marketing," *Progressive Grocer,* May 1987, p. 133.

"Turning 70," *Progressive Grocer,* October 1, 2007.

"Ukrop's Celebrates 70 Years in Business," *Progressive Grocer,* August 7, 2007.

"Ukrop's Clings to Top Grocery Spot," *Richmond Times-Dispatch,* June 13, 2008.

"Ukrop's Cuts Gas Discount," *Convenience Store News,* January 6, 2009.

"Ukrop's Debuts Joe's Market," *Supermarket News,* August 6, 2001, p. 4.

"Ukrop's Gears up for First Va. Store Opening," *Gourmet Retailer,* June 26, 2007.

"Ukrop's to Close Its Lightfoot Store," *Daily Press,* December 31, 2008.

Vosburgh, Robert, "There's a Whole Lotta Health Goin' on at Ukrop's," *Supermarket News,* September 12, 2005, p. 10.

Valve Corporation

10500 NE 8th Street, Suite 1000
Bellevue, Washington 98004
U.S.A.
Telephone: (425) 889-9642
Fax: (425) 827-4843
Web site: http://www.valvesoftware.com

Private Company
Incorporated: 1996
Employees: 160
Sales: $10.5 million (2007)
NAICS: 511210 Software Publishers

■ ■ ■

Headquartered in Bellevue, Washington, Valve Corporation is a leading developer of entertainment software and technology. The company has sold more than 20 million copies of popular computer games, including *Half-Life, Half-Life 2, Day of Defeat, Team Fortress, Counter-Strike,* and *Portal.* Valve claims that its games enjoy an 80 percent share of the personal computer online action game market.

Besides game development, Valve also offers a video game engine called Source, as well as a digital content distribution platform called Steam, which has a subscriber base of approximately 15 million people and offers approximately 242 downloadable games.

FORMATIVE YEARS: 1996–98

Valve's roots stretch back to 1996, when the company was established as Valve LLC by Gabe Newell and Mike Harrington. Prior to starting their own company, the cofounders worked as operating system developers for Microsoft Corporation in Redmond, Washington.

Newell, who eventually bought Harrington's stake in Valve, attended Harvard University. However, future Microsoft CEO Steve Ballmer, who at the time was in charge of the software developer's sales, convinced him to drop out and join Microsoft. Newell was the 271st employee to join Microsoft, which eventually would employ more than 28,000 people. Over the course of his 13-year career, he served as lead developer for the first three versions of the Microsoft Windows operating system.

Video game development was more or less new territory for Valve's founders. During the 1980s, Harrington had contributed to some sports-related videogames for Dynamix. Although Newell had no such experience, he made a significant financial contribution to the company. After cashing in his Microsoft stock options, Newell used $15 million to establish Valve.

Despite the founders' computer industry experience, getting Valve off the ground was no easy task. "We got no credibility for having been at Microsoft for a number of years," Newell explained in the February 26, 1999 issue of the *Puget Sound Business Journal.* "Everyone was nice, but it was clear they were thinking, 'You developed operating systems and now you think you can develop games?'"

When Harrington in Newell started Valve, the videogame industry was dominated by a growing number of first-person shooter games. The partners read numerous reviews of these games and had many

COMPANY PERSPECTIVES

Today, Valve is composed of just over 160 of the industry's best artists, programmers, and writers. In the company's 12-year history, it has risen from "unlikely new entry" to industry leader, producing a string of best selling and critically acclaimed PC products and technologies.

conversations with game players and members of the press to identify areas in which its competition was lacking.

Ultimately, they discovered that the market was hungry for a game with a more extensive storyline than typical first-person shooter titles. This led to the development of a new game called *Half-Life.* Some of the code used to create the new title came from the popular game *Quake,* which Valve licensed from Id Software. Id also had created the popular game *Doom.*

A big break came when Harrington and Newell arranged a meeting with Ken Williams, CEO of Bellevue, Washington-based Sierra Online Inc., who agreed to publish *Half-Life.* In mid-2008 Valve acquired Australia-based TF Software Pty. Ltd., along with the popular Internet-based, first-person action game *Team Fortress.*

After Valve developed the game at a cost of more than $1 million, *Half-Life* hit the market in November 1998. The game sold more than 500,000 copies in only eight weeks, exceeding a pre-established lifetime sales goal of 180,000 copies. By this time, Kirkland, Washington-based Valve's workforce included about 30 people.

EARLY GROWTH: 1999–2004

Adding to *Half-Life*'s appeal was the fact that Valve made it easy enough for casual game players to understand. The game's popularity ultimately resulted in "Best PC Game Ever" honors from *PC Gamer* in the publication's November 1999 issue.

Like other leading videogame companies had done, Valve allowed gamers to modify the code behind its games, resulting in the creation of modified versions (called "mods") with new scenery and other details. This approach allowed game developers to identify new sources of talent. For example, Valve ended up hiring two programmers from Australia who had created a popular *Quake* mod called *Team Fortress,* to which Valve

acquired the rights. In 1990 a college student from Vancouver, British Columbia, created a *Half-Life* mod called *Counter-Strike* in partnership with a New Jersey high school student. Valve acquired the rights to that title in 2000, and added its creators to the company payroll.

Moving forward, Valve began work on a multiplayer problem-solving game called *Team Fortress II,* which it planned to offer as an expansion pack for *Half-Life.* The company had released *Team Fortress Classic* in April 1999.

By early 2001, *Half-Life* and *Team Fortress* had each sold approximately 2.5 million copies throughout the world. Led by CEO Gabe Newell, Valve's 45-member workforce moved forward with efforts to make its popular title available for new videogame systems such as the Xbox and PlayStation 2. In October, *Half-Life* was once again named "Best PC Game Ever" by *PC Gamer.*

In April 2003, the company forged a strategic partnership with Activision Inc., in which Activision secured exclusive worldwide publishing rights to several Valve games, including a new World War II multiplayer action game called *Day of Defeat.*

Valve had sold more than eight million games worldwide by mid-2003. At this time, gamers everywhere were eagerly anticipating the release of *Half-Life 2,* which was planned for a December rollout. However, a major setback occurred in October, when the source code for the new game was stolen by hackers and posted onto the Internet.

Gabe Newell suspected that someone had been illegally accessing his e-mail account beginning in September. In time, it was discovered that keystroke recording software had been installed on some of Valve's computers, allowing hackers to steal passwords and other information. This unfortunate situation caused Valve to delay *Half-Life 2*'s release.

The company published a special e-mail address to collect tips and leads from disappointed gamers in its attempt to identify the source of the code theft, which was dubbed as one of the worst in the videogame industry's history.

A major development in the *Half-Life 2* saga occurred in mid-2004, when the Federal Bureau of Investigation announced that it had made arrests in several countries. Gabe Newell credited the online gaming community for helping to track down the criminals. Following the code theft setback, *Half-Life 2* was released in November 2004. The new release received multiple awards and high accolades for its storyline and high-quality graphics.

KEY DATES

1996: The company is formed as Valve LLC by Gabe Newell and Mike Harrington.
1998: Valve establishes itself as a leading game developer via the introduction of the breakthrough game *Half-Life.*
2005: Sales reach approximately $70 million.
2008: Orange County, Calif.-based Turtle Rock Studios is acquired; Steam, Valve's online distribution service, has 15 million customers and offers approximately 242 downloadable games.

GENERATING STEAM: 2005–07

Success continued in 2005 as *PC Gamer* again bestowed "Best PC Game Ever" honors upon *Half-Life* in its April issue. In May of that year, the company reached an out-of-court settlement with Vivendi-Universal Games in a lawsuit it had filed in August 2002. Valve's lawsuit centered on the alleged unauthorized distribution of its games to cyber cafés. Following the settlement, Vivendi-Universal stopped distributing Valve's games, and was required to pull the company's titles out of stores by August 31.

The company's legal dispute also involved Vivendi-Universal's opposition to Valve's online distribution service, Steam, which allowed customers to download games directly from the company, as opposed to buying the packaged Vivendi-Universal version.

At this time Valve considered the possibility of distributing its games exclusively via Steam. As evidence of the online distribution model's potential, Valve competitor Electronic Arts revealed plans to roll out its own digital distribution system, EA Downloader.

Valve's sales reached approximately $70 million in 2005, doubling the previous year's total. In addition, the company's operating profit reached $55 million. By this time Steam had three million subscribers. Profit margins for games sold via Steam exceeded 80 percent, compared to the 36 percent margin for retail game sales. Heading into 2006, Valve had sold approximately four million copies of *Half-Life 2,* for which some 100 mods had been created.

In early 2007 Valve announced plans to begin selling its games in packages that could be used on multiple platforms. Two of these packages were planned in partnership with Electronic Arts' EA Partners. The first

was a personal computer game package dubbed The Black Box, which included *Half-Life 2: Episode 2, Team Fortress 2,* and *Portal.* A similar collection, named The Orange Box, was planned for the personal computer, Xbox 360, and PlayStation3. That collection included everything offered in The Black Box, as well as the original *Half-Life 2* and *Half-Life 2: Episode One.*

Significant progress continued in the online gaming sector during 2007. Midway through the year, the company's Steam platform included a base of 13 million subscribers and offered approximately 150 downloadable games. Each month, Steam experienced an average of approximately seven billion player minutes. Valve bolstered the platform's growth via offerings such as guest passes and free weekends, which allowed potential customers to experience what Steam had to offer.

INDUSTRY LEADER: 2008–09

Valve kicked off 2008 by acquiring Orange County, California-based Turtle Rock Studios. As part of the deal, the company added the highly anticipated game *Left 4 Dead* to its lineup.

At this time, the market for downloadable video games was dominated by Valve, with its Steam offering, as well as competitor GameTap. Steam offered roughly 15 million customers approximately 242 downloadable games. Customers were able to buy games, but the software remained within the Steam system, and only one version could be played at any given time. One new source of competition emerged when the online retail powerhouse Amazon.com introduced its Amazon Software Download store, which planned to offer digital video game products.

Valve placed a heavy emphasis on play-testing. Instead of waiting to show players polished versions of future games, the company instead brought players into the mix during the very early stages of development, in order to secure their feedback as soon as possible.

In mid-2008 Valve released the Steamworks Software Development Kit, a free suite of software publishing and development tools. The company also announced that it was partnering with Novint Technologies Inc. to make its games more realistic. Specifically, Valve made several of its games compatible with a computer interface device called the Novint Falcon, which allowed players to feel things such as weapon recoil, vehicle movement, and force feedback while playing. Among the games that were compatible with the Falcon were all Orange Box selections, as well as *Counter-Strike: Source, Team Fortress 2, Portal,* and titles within the *Half-Life 2* series. In order to take advantage of the new feature, customers were required to download an update from Steam.

By 2008 Valve had sold more than 30 million copies of its games. The company continued to hold an estimated 80 percent share of the market for computer-based action games. In addition to its Bellevue, Washington-based headquarters, the company also operated from an office in Irvine, California.

In recognition of Valve's efforts to create widescreen-compatible video games, the company was recognized with a Field of Vision award from the Widescreen Gaming Forum in October 2008.

In 2009, Valve held a position of industry leadership that it expected to continue into the second decade of the 2000s. Over the course of nearly 15 years, the company had developed a strong lineup of popular video games as well as a loyal customer base.

Paul R. Greenland

PRINCIPAL COMPETITORS

Activision Blizzard Inc.; Electronic Arts Inc.; Take-Two Interactive Software Inc.

FURTHER READING

Baker, Sharon, "A Charmed Half-Life," *Puget Sound Business Journal,* February 26, 1999.

Barret, Victoria Murphy, "It's a Mod, Mod Underworld," *Forbes,* December 12, 2005.

Hopkins, Nic, "Hackers Delay Launch of Vivendi Computer Game," *Times* (London), October 8, 2003.

WellCare Health Plans, Inc.

8725 Henderson Road
Tampa, Florida 33634
U.S.A.
Telephone: (813) 290-6200
Toll Free: (866) 530-9491
Fax: (813) 262-2802
Web site: http://www.wellcare.com

Public Company
Incorporated: 2002 as WellCare Group, Inc.
Employees: 3,000
Sales: $3.76 billion (2006)
Stock Exchanges: New York
Ticker Symbol: WCG
NAICS: 524114 Direct Health and Medical Insurance
Carriers

∎∎∎

WellCare Health Plans, Inc., a health maintenance organization (HMO), is a provider of managed care services for government-sponsored healthcare programs. The company focuses on managing the healthcare received by recipients of Medicaid and Medicare. Medicaid, managed by state governments, provides healthcare to low-income and disabled persons. Medicare, administered by the federal government, provides healthcare to individuals who are age 65 or older. WellCare offers a variety of Medicaid and Medicare plans, including healthcare plans for families, children, the elderly, blind and disabled individuals, as well as prescription drug plans. The company operates in nine states and provides stand-alone Medicare prescription drug plans in all 50 states. WellCare ranks as the largest operator of Medicaid managed care plans in Florida. The company's plans are marketed under a variety of names, including WellCare, Staywell, Health-Ease, PreferredOne, and Harmony Health.

ORIGINS

As a corporate title, WellCare Health Plans, Inc., first appeared in July 2004, but the assets owned by the newly named company entered the healthcare industry years earlier. The oldest of the assets, a company known as Well Care HMO, was founded in 1985 by a group of Tampa, Florida, physicians, establishing the first building block used to create WellCare Health Plans. The business was purchased by Dr. Kiran Patel in 1992, and under Patel's guidance, began offering Medicaid managed care services two years later. In 2000, Well Care HMO began offering Medicare managed care services.

Another WellCare Health Plans building block was formed the same year Well Care HMO expanded into the Medicare sector. In May 2000, HealthEase of Florida, Inc., was created to acquire the business of Tampa General Health Plan, Inc., which included the company's HMO license and 5,900 Medicaid members. One month after its formation, HealthEase greatly expanded its membership rolls when it acquired nearly 100,000 Medicaid participants from rival Humana, Inc.

HealthEase and Well Care HMO composed the Florida operations owned by WellCare Health Plans. Its presence outside Florida was secured through another building block: The WellCare Management Group, Inc.

COMPANY PERSPECTIVES

Our vision: To be the leader in government sponsored healthcare programs in partnership with the members, providers, governments, and communities we serve.

A publicly traded holding company, WellCare Management provided managed care services in New York and, after the acquisition of Yale New Haven Health Plan in 1995, in Connecticut.

BUSINESSES UNITE IN 2002

The building blocks operated as separate companies, but they did share a link. The Florida operations—Well Care HMO and HealthEase—operated as a closely held business, the owners of which were the majority stockholders of WellCare Management, the company that provided managed care services in New York and Connecticut through two subsidiaries. The connection between the two entities became a solid, inseparable bond in 2002 when Soros Private Equity Investors LP entered the picture, an investment group that served as the catalyst for the formation of WellCare Health Plans. Fantastic financial growth ensued, making the early years of the building block entities, the "WellCare group of companies," seem lethargic in comparison.

Soros Private Equity was led by financier George Soros, a Hungarian-born speculator with a net worth of roughly $9 billion. Soros and his fellow investors set their sights on the managed care business in the healthcare industry and formed WellCare Group, Inc., in May 2002. The company, the direct predecessor to WellCare Health Plans, was established for the express purpose of acquiring the WellCare group of companies, a purchase that would serve as a springboard for expansion. The investment group was intent on creating a new industry giant, an objective that became the mission of the executive hired by Soros Private Equity to lead WellCare Group, Todd S. Farha.

FARHA TAPPED TO LEAD THE NEW COMPANY

Named president and chief executive officer upon the inception of WellCare Group, Farha was 33 years old when he took the helm. A Harvard Business School graduate, Farha distinguished himself quickly in the healthcare industry, earning a reputation as an aggressive and skilled executive. Between 1990 and 1993, he held various positions at Physician Corporation of America, a Florida-based health plan serving Medicaid recipients, which led to a two-year stint as chief executive officer of a subsidiary owned by Oxford Health Plans. Next, Farha struck out on his own, founding Medical Technology Management LLC, a provider of shared medical equipment and services for physicians and hospitals. While serving as Medical Technology's chief executive officer, a title he held until joining WellCare Group, Farha also served in the same capacity for Best Doctors, Inc., a provider of information and referral services for patients suffering from critical illnesses.

The Soros-led investors looked to Farha to execute a major expansion of the WellCare group of companies and he fulfilled their wishes, spearheading an acquisition and marketing campaign that quickly turned the Florida, New York, and Connecticut operations into an industry leader. Under Farha's command, the businesses made their money the same way as they had before his arrival. An HMO profited by controlling medical costs, keeping its expenses lower than government reimbursements. The business model was the same, but Farha intended to provide managed care service on a much larger scale.

Before expansion began in earnest, Farha solidified the foundation upon which he would build. The company's New York operations were prohibited by the Centers of Medicare and Medicaid Services (CMS) from marketing Medicare plans in 1999. Under previous management, the business had failed to comply with the terms of its Medicare contract. Farha addressed the regulatory problem immediately, implementing a compliance program and hiring new senior management. In June 2003, the New York State Department of Health and CMS cleared the New York operations to market Medicare plans, enabling Farha to begin courting Medicare enrollees in New York.

PUBLIC DEBUT AND RAPID EXPANSION

Farha completed his first major acquisition one year after receiving the nod of approval from state and federal regulators for his New York operations. In June 2004, WellCare Group purchased Harmony Health Systems, which gave it 85,000 Medicaid members in Illinois and Indiana. The acquisition preceded a signal event that thrust the company into the public spotlight. In July 2004, the company completed its initial public offering (IPO) of stock, debuting at $17 per share, and changed its name to WellCare Health Plans, Inc., an event that spurred Farha's drive to expand.

When the IPO was completed, WellCare represented a formidable force as an insurer. The

KEY DATES

1985: WellCare Health Plans' earliest predecessor, Well Care HMO, is established by a group of physicians in Tampa, Florida.

1994: Well Care HMO begins offering managed care services for Medicaid recipients.

2000: HealthEase of Florida, Inc., is formed to acquire Tampa General Health Plan, Inc.

2002: Financially backed by Soros Private Equity Investors LP, WellCare Group, Inc., is formed to acquire Well Care HMO, HealthEase, and The WellCare Management Group, Inc., which provides managed care services in New York and Connecticut.

2004: WellCare Group completes its initial public offering (IPO) of stock and changes its name to WellCare Health Plans, Inc.

2007: State and federal agencies raid WellCare Health Plans' main offices, looking for evidence of Medicare and Medicaid fraud.

2008: Chairman, CEO, and President Todd S. Farha resigns.

company ranked as the largest managed care provider in Florida, serving nearly 500,000 individuals. In New York, the company served 56,000 individuals. In Connecticut, the company served 24,000 individuals. In Illinois and Indiana, the company served 85,000 individuals. To this base, Farha expanded WellCare's operations, adding new Medicaid and Medicare enrollees in the company's existing markets and steering the company into new markets. WellCare made its first geographic leap in September 2004, when it began offering managed care services in Louisiana. The company entered Georgia in 2005 and Missouri and Ohio in 2006, adding new markets and new members at a rapid pace. Meanwhile, the company launched a stand-alone Medicare prescription drug plan that would extend its operating territory, eventually giving the company a presence in all 50 states.

The financial growth recorded during the company's expansion was remarkable. Before Farha took control of the company, the Florida, New York, and Connecticut operations had generated $750 million in annual revenues. By the time the company completed its IPO, its annual sales volume had surpassed the $1 billion mark. By the end of 2006, the company's revenues had swelled to $3.72 billion, as its Medicare and Medicaid

membership swelled to 2.25 million, exponentially more than the approximately 615,000 members it served at the time of its IPO. WellCare's stock value responded to the tremendous growth achieved under Farha's watch, skyrocketing from its IPO price of $17 per share to more than $120 per share. Equally as impressive was the company's ability to convert its revenue growth into earnings growth, which had increased eightfold under Farha's leadership. WellCare recorded net earnings of $139 million in 2006, a profit margin that some analysts viewed with disbelief.

THE MAELSTROM OF 2007

WellCare's problems began when federal and state agencies began looking at its financial performance with the same puzzlement expressed by analysts. Concerns about inappropriate business practices by WellCare began to surface in 2007, casting a pall over the company that grew darker with each passing month. In the spring of 2007, it was revealed that some members of WellCare's Medicare plans in Georgia were dead when they were enrolled, a scandal blamed on independent sales agents. In May and June 2007, WellCare representatives sat alongside the representatives from six other insurers in a hearing held by the U.S. Congress, as lawmakers looked into over-aggressive Medicare marketing practices. WellCare and the six other companies promised to halt marketing one type of Medicare plan and said they would implement stringent consumer safeguards, but in August 2007 Medicare again cited WellCare for violating several provisions of its Medicare contract, including sales and practices. The unseemly events led up to WellCare's most calamitous moment, a day that sent the company reeling backward, leaving many industry observers to wonder if it would ever regain its footing.

On October 24, 2007, more than 200 state and federal agents raided WellCare's headquarters in Tampa. Employees were forced to exit the building as personnel from the Federal Bureau of Investigation, the U.S. Department of Health and Human Services, and Florida's Medicaid Fraud Control Unit began executing a search warrant, seizing computer hard drives and reams of documents. The federal and state agents, it was later revealed, were seeking evidence of "monetary overpayments" received from Medicare and Medicaid, as reported in the November 17, 2007 edition of the *Tampa Tribune*. One day after the raid, the U.S. Securities and Exchange Commission (SEC) announced it was joining the inquiry into WellCare. Before the day ended, class-action lawsuits were filed in the U.S. District Court for the Middle District of Florida on behalf of WellCare shareholders. The raid, conducted on a Wednesday, delivered a stunning blow to the company's reputation on Wall Street. By the end of the week, shares in WellCare had plummeted from $120 to $31.36, erasing more than $3.5 billion of the company's market value.

WellCare attempted to make the best out of a dire situation, saying it was cooperating with authorities and claiming no knowledge of any wrongdoing. In November 2007, the company announced Medicare contracts in three new markets, presenting a "business as usual" face to the public, but the debacle was difficult to ignore. In January 2008, Farha, who had been named chairman in 2006 in addition to his roles as president and chief executive officer, relinquished all titles and resigned from WellCare with two other senior executives, Paul Behrens, WellCare's chief financial officer, and Thaddeus Bereday, the company's general counsel. To replace Farha, the company's board of directors selected Heath Schiesser, a WellCare senior adviser who had been responsible for the launch of the company's nationwide prescription drug plan.

As WellCare moved forward, the federal and state investigation into its business practices continued. In August 2008, the company agreed to pay $35.2 million as part of an agreement with U.S. prosecutors, but, as the *St. Petersburg Times* reported on August 19, 2008, "the payment doesn't settle the case or limit the U.S. government and the state of Florida from making further claims in their continuing investigation." For WellCare, the road ahead was uncertain, made particularly murky by the turmoil in the credit markets in late 2008. In November 2008, the company announced it had defaulted on one loan, unable to secure access to cash to make its payment. News of the company's failure to meet its financial obligation sent its stock down 50 percent to $6.12 per share, far below the $120 heights during the halcyon days of the Farha era.

Jeffrey L. Covell

PRINCIPAL SUBSIDIARIES

WCG Health Management, Inc.; The WellCare Management Group, Inc.; WellCare of Florida, Inc.; HealthEase of Florida, Inc.; WellCare of New York, Inc.; WellCare of Connecticut, Inc.; Harmony Health Systems, Inc.; Harmony Health Plan of Illinois, Inc.; Harmony Health Management, Inc.; WellCare of Louisiana, Inc.; Harmony Behavioral Health, Inc.; Comprehensive Health Management, Inc.; Comprehensive Health Management of Florida, L.C.; Comprehensive Reinsurance, Ltd. (Cayman Islands); WellCare of Georgia, Inc.; WellCare Prescription Insurance, Inc.; WellCare of Ohio, Inc.; Comprehensive Logistics, LLC; WellCare Health Insurance of Arizona, Inc.; WellCare Health Insurance of Illinois, Inc.; WellCare Health Insurance of New York, Inc.

PRINCIPAL COMPETITORS

Centene Corporation; Humana, Inc.; WellPoint, Inc.; UnitedHealth Group Incorporated.

FURTHER READING

"Blue Chip News: Analysis of WellCare Health Plans, Inc.," *Europe Intelligence Wire,* March 29, 2007.

Boulton, Guy, "Investment Group to Profit from Success of WellCare Health Plans," *Tampa Tribune,* November 23, 2004.

Hundley, Kris, "FBI Raid Shutters Medicare Insurer," *St. Petersburg Times,* October 25, 2007, p. 1A.

———, "How WellCare Got So Rich," *St. Petersburg Times,* January 7, 2007, p. 1D.

———, "SEC Joins WellCare Inquiry," *St. Petersburg Times,* October 27, 2007, p. 1D.

———, "WellCare Run with Surgical Precision," *St. Petersburg Times,* January 22, 2008, p. 16A.

Mullins, Richard, "WellCare Raid Reaps CEO's Notes," *Tampa Tribune,* November 17, 2007, p. 1.

"Three Top Executives Resign from WellCare," *Tampa Tribune,* January 26, 2008, p. 1.

Watkins, Steve, "WellCare Health Plans," *Investor's Business Daily,* December 14, 2004, p. A9.

"WellCare Free Fall Goes On," *St. Petersburg Times,* November 14, 2008, p. 6B.

"WellCare to Offer Plans in 4 New Markets," *St. Petersburg Times,* November 10, 2007, p. 1D.

"WellCare to Pay $35.2M in Deal," *St. Petersburg Times,* August 19, 2008, p. 6B.

Wilh. Werhahn KG

Postfach 10 16 38
Neuss, D-41416
Germany
Telephone: (+49 02131) 916 0
Fax: (+49 02131) 9 16 418
Web site: http://www.werhahn.de

Private Company
Incorporated: 1871 as Offene Hg. Wilhelm Werhahn
Employees: 9,080
Sales: EUR 2.48 billion ($3.64 billion) (2007)
NAICS: 551112 Offices of Other Holding Companies

■ ■ ■

Wilh. Werhahn KG is one of Germany's oldest family-owned holding companies. With roots reaching back to the mid-19th century, the Neuss-based company directly controls an empire of more than 110 subsidiaries. Including associated and non-consolidated holdings, as well as minority shareholdings, the holdings extend to more than 350 companies. While Wilh. Werhahn provides the central strategic coordination for the group as well as overseeing the group's vast real estate holdings, the Werhahn subsidiaries themselves are run as independent enterprises grouped into five primary divisions. These include Aggregates, through Basalt AG, the German leader in natural stone products, as well as asphalt, concrete, and other construction materials. This division is also the company's largest, generating approximately half of its total EUR 2.5 billion ($3.6 billion) in 2007. The Baking Products division is another of the company's oldest areas of operation, and includes the Diamant and Goldpuder flour and baking mixtures brands. Companies leading this division include Georg Plange, Dresdener Mühlen, and Pfalzmühle Mannheim. The Slate division counts among the company's oldest, dating back to the family's acquisition of German slate leader Rathscheck Schiefer und Dach-Systeme in 1904. The Zwilling division represents Werhahn's control of knife-maker Zwilling J.A. Henckels Company, as well as related subsidiaries, including Jaguar, a maker of hairdressing and other scissors; Arcos, a leading cutlery producer in Spain; and Tweezerman, a U.S.-based specialist producer of tweezers and other beauty tools.

The final division is ABC Finance, a provider of leasing products to the corporate market. The Werhahn family also controls Bank Werhahn KG, and has long been one of Germany's most prominent banking families: at one time, the family's banking empire also included control of financial giant Kommerzbank. Many of the Werhahn group's companies also operate on an individual basis, although primarily in Western and Eastern Europe. Like many of the other top German business families, the Werhahn family has long remained extremely discreet about the full extent of its fortune. That fortune is nonetheless divided up among more than 300 family members, themselves grouped into three branches, each with its own class of shares. Anton Werhahn, representing the family's fifth generation, serves as the company's chief executive officer. His cousin Michael Werhahn, reportedly a bitter rival, serves as group chairman.

FOUNDING A NEUSS-BASED EMPIRE IN 1839

The Werhahn family business's emergence as one of 20th-century Germany's top family-owned fortunes began with a small general store opened by Peter Wilhelm Werhahn in Neuss in 1839. Born in 1802, Werhahn gradually expanded the business, taking advantage of the city of Neuss's status as a major German seaport to develop into a prominent trader. Werhahn focused particularly on the trade in timber and fertilizers.

The family's fortunes truly grew with the arrival of Werhahn's son, also named Peter, as the head of the family's operations. In 1871, Werhahn renamed the business Offene Hg. Wilhelm Werhahn.

Werhahn quickly began expanding the family's range of interests. One of Werhahn's first moves was to found a partnership, Werhahn & Nauen, which began business as an oil mill in 1871. That operation quickly led the company to expand into grain milling as well, and in 1873, the company acquired the Nix & Wex Krefelder mill in Neuss. That site later became the Werhahn group's headquarters. Flour milling and bakery products remained a major part of the Werhahn company's holdings.

By 1900, the Werhahn family had become one of Neuss's leading families. Their devout Catholicism earned them the nickname as the city's "Holy Family," and also provided them with connections with many of the region's most influential political and religious figures. Indeed, the extended family later included the archbishop of Cologne, whose brother became mayor of Neuss. Wilhelm Hermann Werhahn, great-grandson of the founder, later married Libeth Adenauer, daughter of Konrad Adenauer and de facto "first lady" of post–World War II Germany.

Marriage provided an important connection for the Werhahn family's interests when Wilhelm Peter Werhahn, the founder's grandson, married Adelgundis Cremer in 1907. The Cremer family owned a major detergent and soap company, founded in 1811, and also owned a number of grocery stores in Düsseldorf.

EARLY 20TH-CENTURY EXPANSION

Born in 1880, Wilhelm Peter Werhahn, more commonly known as Wilhelm Werhahn, became the true architect of the Werhahn family's business empire. Werhahn led the company through major diversification at the beginning of the 20th century, investing in a variety of areas, including lignite and coal mining as well as

banking. In 1904, the company entered the production of slate and other building materials, acquiring Rathscheck Schiefer. That company, founded in 1793, grew into Germany's leading supplier of slate roofing and siding products, as well as one of the largest in Europe. Werhahn later extended its construction materials operations to include aggregates, including shares in Basalt AG, a company founded in 1888, which became Germany's largest building materials producer.

When Adelgundis died ten years later, Werhahn married her younger sister; a decade after that, Werhahn took over control of the Cremer companies, extending its operations into the soap and detergents sector, as well as into the retail sector. Werhahn later emerged as one of Germany's leading supermarket groups, with chains including the Berlin-based Bolle chain, which also operated extensively in Hamburg; the Frankfurt-based Schade und Fullgrabe; and Mulheim-based Georg Schätzlein.

Flour milling remained a major focus for the family, however. In 1923, Werhahn paid the city of Neuss 64 million reichsmarks to acquire property near the city's newly built docks. Werhahn then built what became the largest flour mill in Europe. Operational in 1925, the Hansa mill had an initial capacity of 150,000 metric tons.

Throughout this period, the Werhahn family also built a wide-ranging portfolio of real estate properties in Neuss, Cologne, and elsewhere enabling the company to emerge relatively unscathed from Germany's long years of economic crisis, beginning with the hyperinflation years of the early 1920s through the Depression Era at the beginning of the next decade.

Negotiating a path during the Nazi-era presented the company with its own challenges, and opportunities. As devout Catholics, the Werhahns opposed the Nazi government, itself overtly hostile to the Catholic Church. When one member of the family chose to collaborate with the Nazi party, the family bought out his share of the company. As a result, Wilhelm Werhahn became the head of the Neuss chamber of commerce and even before the end of World War II had launched negotiations with the Allied forces for the rebuilding of the city. Werhahn's position enabled him to increase his financial and political influence in Neuss, earning him the new nickname "King of Neuss."

The Werhahn family fortune had also profited from the Nazi era. The so-called Aryanization policy of the Nazi government, which forced German Jews to sell their businesses and property to the Aryan population, often at prices far below the actual value, presented a number of growth opportunities for the Werhahns. In 1936, for example, Werhahn bought out the Jewish owners of Schade und Fullgrabe. While Werhahn reportedly paid less than that business was worth, the purchase nonetheless permitted the family to safely immigrate to the United States. Similarly, in that year Werhahn was able to expand its milling operations with the purchase of the Rheinischen Mühlenwerke in Duisberg; the owners of that company subsequently immigrated to South America.

POSTWAR GLORY YEARS

Neuss's strategic importance as a major German port led to the city's near destruction under the Allied bombing raids. Much of Werhahn's own businesses had been severely damaged as well. The postwar partition of Germany held further consequences for the company, as large portions of its operations fell within the Soviet-dominated East Germany.

Nonetheless, Werhahns' remaining holdings provided a strong foundation for the next phase in the family-owned company's growth. Under the leadership of Wilhelm Werhahn, the family fortune expanded significantly during Germany's postwar economic boom. By the beginning of the 1970s, the Werhahn family ranked among Germany's wealthiest.

Coal mining and trading played a central role in this growth, as the company added a number of new mining interests in the postwar period. Among these was a 15 percent stake in Heinrich Mining in Essen, making the family the largest shareholder in that company. Other holdings included Clarenberg AG, in Frechen, lignite producer Wachtberg, and the trading groups F.A. Meier in Berlin and Schunk & Dreschmann KG in Cologne. By the beginning of the 1960s, Werhahn had gained a major stake in Rheinbraun, which in turn gave the family a 10 percent stake in German power giant RWE. That position gave Wilhelm Werhahn (son of the preceding Wilhelm, who died in 1964) the presidency of RWE's board of directors.

Through this period, Werhahn had also established thriving banking and insurance operations as well. The company formed its own private bank, Bankhaus Wilh. Werhahn, in part to manage the family's own fortune. In the 1950s, the company founded WKV Warenkredit-Anstalt, providing installment loan products. Into the 1960s, Werhahn also gained a prominent shareholding in German financial giant Commerzbank AG. Werhahn's importance to that bank was underscored as Wilhelm Werhahn became Commerzbank's chairman of the board. The Werhahn family remained major shareholders in Commerzbank through the 1980s, with Werhahn's grandson, also Wilhelm, serving on the bank's supervisory board. In another foray into banking, the company launched AKB Privat- und Handelsbank AG, which became Germany's leading provider of car leasing and financing products. Werhahn sold that company in 2002, for EUR 1.1 billion, to Banco Santander Central Hispano, of Spain.

STREAMLINING FOR THE 21ST CENTURY

The second half of the 20th century, however, saw a major diversification of Werhahn's holdings. The group's original operations followed a certain logic. The entry into mining came, for example, as a result of that industry's strong demand for wood; similarly, the move into retail provided synergies with the group's oil and flour milling operations, as well as its soaps and detergents holdings.

Less clear, however, was the logic behind a number of the company's acquisitions in the 1970s and 1980s. In 1970, for example, Werhahn entered the production of knives and cutlery through its acquisition of the Zwilling knife group. Into the early 1980s, Werhahn moved into the beer brewing sector, acquiring control of Wuppertal-based Wickuler-Kupper Brauerei, then the third largest regional brewer in Germany. This acquisition nonetheless provided certain links with the group's other operations, notably because of its use of grains, as well as its sales through the retail sector. By then, Werhahn's various retail operations had grown strongly. Schade und Fullgrabe, for example, had grown to more than 100 stores by the 1980s. The company also invested in expanding its building materials operations, notably through the acquisition of full control of Basalt AG in 1978.

From the 1980s, however, Werhahn appeared to lose much of its entrepreneurial steam. While other family-controlled conglomerates, such as Heinkels and Haniels, achieved dramatic growth through the end of the century, Werhahn's own revenues remained more or less the same from year to year. Part of this was explained by the group's decision to exit a number of sectors. The company sold its retail operations, for example, including selling the Schade und Fullgrabe chain to Tengelmann in the early 1990s. The company attempted growth elsewhere, notably through the purchase of U.S.-based lubricants producer D.A. Stuart in 1995. However, by the latter part of that decade, Werhahn's fortunes had entered a sharp decline, as the company closed out the 1990s posting losses.

Part of the group's difficulties involved its shareholder base, consisting of more than 300 people, each claiming a share of the group's profits. The family by then had been essentially divided into three factions, each controlling its own class of shares. Rivalry among the different factions was increasing. Then, at the end of the 1990s, CEO Herbert Werhahn, considered the last of the family's truly entrepreneurial members, died in an accident.

In response, the family at last resolved to bring in an outsider to help lead the company, hiring Norbert Wiemers as chief executive. Wiemers brought in a new management team and began restructuring Werhahn's sprawling operations. In particular, Wiemers led the group on a major streamlining, trimming operations from 11 business areas to a core of just four or five.

Wiemers's tenure did not last long, however. In 2004, Wiemers attempted to merge the group's flour milling business with a larger French rival, in order to create a European leader. The family, fearful of losing control of one of its oldest components, opposed the move, however. Soon after, Anton Werhahn, son of Herbert and leader of the wealthiest family faction, took over as head of the family empire. Werhahn nonetheless continued the streamlining effort, culminating in the sale of several more business lines. This process appeared largely completed by the end of 2008, after the sale of the group's shopfittings division, Hansa Kontor Shopfitting, to Sweden's ITAB Shop Concept. Later that year, Werhahn sold the D.A. Stuart operation as well.

In the meantime, the company launched plans to expand its new core holdings. In 2006, the company acquired full control of Deutag, a major producer of asphalt and other building materials, previously operated as a joint venture with the Austro-German Stabag Group. The company also achieved a more modest expansion of its flour and bakery products division, acquiring a small U.K.-based trader in 2006. After seeing its total revenues dip below EUR 1.65 billion ($2 billion), Werhahn's turnover appeared once again on the rise, nearing EUR 2.5 billion at the end of 2007. As one of Germany's oldest family-owned conglomerates, Werhahn hoped to recapture part of its former glory in the new century.

M. L. Cohen

PRINCIPAL SUBSIDIARIES

"Jaguar" Stahlwarenfabrik GmbH & Co. KG; ABC Leasing GmbH; Bank Werhahn KG; Basalt-Actien-Gesellschaft; Deutag AG; Dresdener Mühlen GmbH; GB Plange Ltd. (UK); Georg Plange KG; Pfalzmühle Mannheim; Rathscheck Schiefer und Dach-Systeme KG; Tweezerman International LLC (USA); Werhahn Mühlen KG Hansastraße 6; Wilh. Werhahn KG ZN Haus & Grund; ZWILLING J.A. HENCKELS AG.

PRINCIPAL COMPETITORS

Allianz AG; HVB Group; Siemens AG; RWE AG; Wuestenrot and Wuerttembergische AG; Franz Haniel and Company GmbH; Celesio AG; Bertelsmann AG; The Linde Group; Vattenfall Europe AG.

FURTHER READING

"Expansion ins Ausland," *Die Welt,* June 24, 2004.

"New Werhahn Bid for Stuart Is Successful," *Globe & Mail,* January 13, 1995, p. B6.

"Rendite von Werhahn Schrumpft," *Handelsblatt,* June 26, 2006.

"Starke Marken aus Neuss," *Neuß-Grevenbroicher-Zeitung,* December 9, 2005.

"Strabag Trennt Sich Ganz von Deutag," *Borsen Zeitung,* May 13, 2006.

"Swedish Shop Interior Provider ITAB Shop Concept AB Expands, Acquires Hansa Kontor Shopfitting," *Nordic Business Report,* December 20, 2007.

"Werhahn: Messer, Mörtel, Mehl," *Die Welt,* June 29, 2004.

"Werhahn Seeks Profitable Investment Opportunities," *Handelsblatt,* July 23, 2003.

"Werhahn Starkt Auslandsgeschaft mit Akquisitionen," *Financial Times Deutschland,* June 23, 2004.

"Werhahn Sucht Neue Anlagfelder," *Handelsblatt,* July 23, 2003.

"Werhahns Prall Gefullte Kriegskasse," *Borsen Zeitung,* June 30, 2005.

Werres, Thomas, "Steinreich und Ideenarm," *Manager Magazin,* November 17, 2006, p. 96.

William Jackson & Son Ltd.

The Riverside Building, Livingstone Road
Hessle, HU13 0DZ
United Kingdom
Telephone: (+44 01482) 224 939
Fax: (+44 01482) 223 217
Web site: http://www.wjs.co.uk

Private Company
Incorporated: 1904 as William Jackson & Son Ltd.
Employees: 3,324
Sales: £119 million ($239.1 million) (2007)
NAICS: 311812 Commercial Bakeries; 311423 Dried
and Dehydrated Food Manufacturing

■ ■ ■

William Jackson & Son Ltd. is a holding company focused on the U.K. food manufacturing sector. Based in Hessle, Hull, the William Jackson Food Group (WJFG) operates through five primary subsidiaries: Aunt Bessie's, a leading producer of frozen Yorkshire pudding and other frozen traditional English meals; Jackson's Bakery, a major supplier of breads and baked goods to the industrial foods sector; Kwoks Foods, focused on the production of Asian foods; Hazeldene Foods, a producer of salads for the retail and catering sectors, acquired in 2005; and Parripak Foods, acquired in 2006, a grower and packager of onions, shallots, garlic, and other vegetables. Parripak also includes Solway Vegetable Peelers, based in Gretna and acquired in 2008 along with its sister company Ancient Recipes. In addition to its foods businesses, WJFG also owns a pub/

restaurant/inn complex, Ferguson Fawsitt Arms, in the town of Walkington. Founded in 1851, WJFG remains a family-owned company, led by Chairman Nicholas Oughtred, a direct descendant of the company's founder. Nonfamily member Norman Soutar serves as the group's managing director. In 2007 WJFG's total turnover reached approximately £119 million ($239 million).

HULL GROCER IN 1851

A farmer's son, William Jackson was 23 years old when he opened a grocer's shop in Hull in 1851. Jackson was joined by his wife Sarah; the couple's store opened for business on the afternoon of their wedding day. The Jacksons traded in groceries and tea, and soon gained a reputation for the exactitude of the measurements. This care earned Jackson the nickname "Mr. Split Currant."

The Jacksons' son George began working in his parents' shop as a youth; at the age of 25, the younger Jackson led the family's first expansion, with the opening of a second store in 1888. Two years later, the family expanded into food manufacturing, opening their first bakery in order to supply their shops. That facility produced bread, as well as other baked goods and confectionery.

Retail remained a family focus, however, and into the start of the 20th century, the family continued to add new shops. By that time under the leadership of George Jackson, the company incorporated as William Jackson & Son Limited in 1904. By the end of the first decade of the new century, the company counted 17 stores in the Yorkshire region. The retail operation was

COMPANY PERSPECTIVES

One of the guiding principles from our shareholders is that the company should not have "all its eggs in one basket." It is a policy that has served us well over the years and for that reason we have a portfolio of food businesses in attractive market areas which we are looking to grow and expand.

supported by a new, larger bakery, opened on Derringham Street in 1907, as well as the addition of a factory producing jam.

Although William Jackson remained active in the business until his death at the age of 84 in 1912, George Jackson launched the company on a new era of expansion. By 1916 William Jackson & Son had nearly doubled the number of shops in operation, to 32 stores. Into the next decade, George Jackson, who had changed his name to George Jackson Bentham and entered politics, was joined in the business by his daughters, Doris and Phyllis, who married brothers, Norman and Jack Oughtred.

Both of these brothers joined the company, then later took over the company's lead, with Jack Oughtred serving as the company's chairman, following their father-in-law's death in 1929. William Jackson & Son grew again soon after, acquiring Brown's Central Supply Stores Ltd. in 1931 and then rival grocer Francis Meyer Ltd. in 1932. Other investments soon followed. In 1934 the company added a modern oven to its Derringham Street factory, greatly boosting its output capacity. The higher output then led the company to invest in new automated slicing and packaging machinery soon after.

During this decade, the family-owned company took the unusual step of bringing in someone from outside the company to serve as its chairman. The family maintained ownership control of the company, while also following a policy of staffing the majority of its executive board with nonfamily members, into the 21st century. In the meantime, William Jackson & Son expanded strongly through the 1930s, motorizing its delivery fleet in order to serve its ever growing retail network. By the end of the 1930s, the company boasted 85 shops in Hull, as well as Bridlington, Doncaster, Goole, Leeds, and York. The company had also expanded its food production operations to include the preparation of meat-based products, such as sausages.

POSTWAR DIVERSIFICATION

The company suffered losses during World War II, seeing some of its facilities destroyed in the Nazi bombing raids. At the same time, the company's motorized fleet was requisitioned for the British war effort. The end of the war marked a new period of expansion for the family-owned company, however.

The company boosted its retail operations at the end of the 1940s, completing two acquisitions. The first came in 1947, with the takeover of Barkers (Grocers) Ltd. The second followed one year later, with the addition of John Cross Ltd. These acquisitions paved the way for an even greater growth phase in the early 1950s.

For this, the company restructured its operations, reincorporating as a privately owned holding company under the same name in 1952. The company then consisted of two areas of business, food manufacturing, including bakery operations, on the one hand, and retailing on the other. In 1954 the company launched an acquisition drive to expand both parts of its business. The group's purchases at the time included the retail company Harpers (Harrogate) Ltd.

William Jackson also added two bakeries, which included their own retail operations, in 1954, T. Swale Ltd. and Mitchell Ltd. By 1955 the company's operations included seven bakeries. The company then expanded its warehousing and distribution wing, buying T.A. Scott Ltd., which operated a distribution depot and retail store, in 1956. Meanwhile, the company had launched its first diversification beyond the food production and retail sectors, adding a Ford dealership under the name of Crystal Motors in 1953. Crystal Motors later added a number of other dealerships, becoming one of the largest in the Yorkshire region.

The next generation of the Jackson family, in the form of cousins Peter and Brian Oughtred, took over the business in 1958. The new generation also instituted a tradition of comanaging directorships, which was to remain a feature of the company's direction until the beginning of the next century.

SUPERMARKET GROWTH IN THE SIXTIES

William Jackson & Son continued to expand its range of businesses. By the beginning of the 1960s, the group's operations included two pubs, a restaurant, a catering business, and six off-license shops, three of which featured post office services.

Retail remained the major focus of the group's business, however. Into the early 1960s the company recognized the need to adapt its retail wing to the

KEY DATES

■

1851: William Jackson and wife Sarah open a grocer's shop in Hull, England, on their wedding day.

1888: Their son George opens a second store in Hull.

1890: Bakery operations are launched.

1904: The company incorporates as William Jackson & Son Ltd.

1916: William Jackson & Son operates 32 stores.

1953: The company begins to diversify, adding a car dealership.

1963: After converting a number of its grocer's shops to a supermarket format, the company acquires discount department store pioneer Grandways.

1975: The company begins producing frozen Yorkshire pudding, later placed under subsidiary Tryton Foods.

1991: As part of a restructuring, William Jackson begins sell-off of its Grandways operations.

1995: Tryton Foods relaunches its Yorkshire puddings under Aunt Bessie's name.

2000: William Jackson acquires Kwoks Foods, a leading Asian foods producer.

2004: William Jackson exits retail with the sale of Jackson's Stores to J. Sainsbury.

2006: The company enters the vegetable sector with purchase of Parripak Foods.

2008: William Jackson acquires Solway Vegetable Peelers and Ancient Recipes through Parripak.

emerging supermarket format, brought over to the United Kingdom from the United States in the previous decade. William Jackson began converting a number of its stores to the new self-service format, and by 1963 boasted 17 supermarkets among a total of 92 retail outlets. By the middle of the decade, nearly half of the group's grocery stores had been converted to the supermarket format.

By then, too, the group had made its first retailing foray beyond the grocery market, buying Grandways Stores Limited. Founded in 1961 as Associated & Independent Merchandisers Ltd., Grandways had pioneered the discount department store concept in the U.K. market, opening its first store in Leeds that year. The new store format played a major role in the ending of resale price maintenance legislation, which had al-

lowed manufacturers to control the minimum retail pricing of their goods.

William Jackson & Son went public in 1963. The access to capital helped fuel the group's continued expansion through the 1970s. The group expanded its slaughterhouse and meat-processing operations particularly, which in turn ultimately led to another successful branch of the company's business. In 1975 the company was approached by Butlins Holiday Camp to develop a frozen Yorkshire pudding product for its vacation camps. The success of this venture led William Jackson to establish a dedicated business for this production, which became known as Tryton Foods in 1985.

In another related extension of its operations, William Jackson & Son formed its own information systems division in 1976. The division was initially established to provide support services for the group's own business. By 1979, however, William Jackson had spun off the division into a dedicated systems and software subsidiary, Automatic Information Management Ltd. (AIM). AIM then began providing a range of information technology (IT) services to third parties, as well as continuing to support the operations of the William Jackson group.

RESTRUCTURING AND REFOCUSING IN THE NINETIES

William Jackson's highly diversified operations made the company vulnerable to new business trends in the 1980s. Consolidation within many of the group's areas of business had resulted in the emergence of a number of large-scale companies. The relatively small size of most of William Jackson's operations, however, left the company at a distinct competitive disadvantage in the new business era.

As a result, the company decided to restructure and refocus its operations on a smaller range of businesses. The company also went private again, as the Oughtred family regained control of nearly 90 percent of the group's shares. In the meantime, William Jackson had taken the first step in its restructuring process, selling its AIM computer and IT systems business to a management buyout backed by Melville Street Investments and the Bank of Scotland in 1987.

In the 1990s the company exited the restaurant, pub, and catering sectors, selling nearly all of its holdings, with the exception of a small pub, restaurant, and hotel complex, the Ferguson Fawsitt Arms. The company also began its exit of the discount retail sector, selling off part of the Grandways chain to Kwik Save Group Plc in 1991. The following year, the company completed the Grandways disposal, selling the remaining stores to Argyll Group PLC.

These disposals were followed by an exit from automobile dealerships, as the company sold part of the Crystal Motors of Hull dealership group to Sanderson Murray and Elder in 1993. The company completed its exit from this sector in 2000. At the same time, the company restructured part of its food production operations, selling its sausage-making facility, run by Tryton Foods, in 1994.

DEDICATED FOODS GROUP IN THE 21ST CENTURY

The restructuring of William Jackson's operations was not completed until the middle of the first decade of the 2000s, with the company's exit from the retail sector. This process had started during the 1980s, as the company adapted its chain of Jackson's Stores in the face of the growing competition from far-larger rivals such as Tesco, ASDA, and Sainsburys. In the 1990s the Jackson's Stores were converted from a supermarket to a convenience store format.

Competition in this retail area intensified in the late 1990s and into the first decade of the 2000s. William Jackson, by then under the leadership of Christopher Oughtred, great-grandson of the company's founder, decided to sell its retail business. In August 2004 the company reached an agreement to sell the Jackson's Stores chain to J. Sainsbury PLC. Terms of the sale included Sainsbury's guarantee that they would retain all of the retail network's employees, including Angus Oughtred, then serving as managing director of the Jackson's Stores. Sainsbury also agreed to maintain the Jackson name, renaming the store chain as Sainsbury's at Jacksons.

The sale marked the end of more than 150 years in retail for the company. Nonetheless, by then William Jackson had been reinventing itself as a major U.K. food manufacturer. The Jackson Bakery operations took a center role in the group's operations, emerging as a major supplier of bread to the industrial food sector, including the fast-growing sandwich production market.

The star of the company's operations, however, was its Aunt Bessie's brand. In 1995 the group's Tryton Foods subsidiary decided to reinvent itself. In that year, the company relaunched itself as Aunt Bessie's, a producer of frozen traditional English foods. The Aunt Bessie's brand, based on its flagship Yorkshire pudding, also permitted William Jackson to develop its own retail brand. By the dawn of the 21st century, Aunt Bessie's had become one of the best-selling Yorkshire pudding brands.

Fire nearly marred the Aunt Bessie's launch, when the company's production facility burned to the ground

three months later. Within a short time, however, the company had built a new factory, making the most of the situation by constructing a state-of-the-art facility. The modern equipment enabled the company to achieve operating efficiencies while also improving the quality of its product. By the middle of the first decade of the 2000s, the Aunt Bessie's operation was producing some 12 million Yorkshire "puddies" each week, and generating more than £110 million in sales.

With the Aunt Bessie's brand building strongly into the new decade, William Jackson took steps to expand its food production operations. The company entered the Asian foods market, buying a stake in Kwoks Foods in 2000; the company later gained majority control of that business.

Following the sale of Jackson's Stores, the William Jackson Food Group (WJFG), as the group became known, went in search of new growth prospects. This led the company to purchase majority control of Hazeldene, which produced salads for the retail and catering sectors, in 2005. Also in that year, the company hired Norman Soutar, formerly of Baxters Food Group, to become its managing director, ending its tradition of comanaging directorships.

WJFG bought Parripak Foods Ltd., a Shefford-based grower and packager of onions, shallots, garlic, and other vegetables, including organic vegetables, in 2006. By 2008 WJFG had strengthened its packaged vegetables business with the purchase of sister companies Solway Vegetable Peelers and Ancient Recipes, based in Gretna. With the next generation of the founding family becoming involved in the company's operations (in 2007 Nicholas Oughtred took over the role of chairman), William Jackson had successfully evolved from a single grocer's shop into a major U.K. foods producer.

M. L. Cohen

PRINCIPAL SUBSIDIARIES

Aunt Bessie's Ltd.; Hazeldene Foods Ltd.; Jackson's Bakery Ltd.; Kwoks Foods Ltd.; Parripak Foods Ltd.

PRINCIPAL COMPETITORS

Associated British Foods PLC; Wittington Investments Ltd.; United Biscuits Holdings PLC; Brake Brothers Ltd.; RHM PLC; Northern Foods PLC; Geest Ltd.; Greggs PLC; British Bakeries Ltd.; Warburtons Ltd.

FURTHER READING

"Firms Dig Deep in Dramatic Deals," *Europe Intelligence Wire*, January 29, 2007.

Hilpern, Kate, "'As English As Lasagne' … Try Telling That to the Roast Beef and Yorkshires Brigade," *Independent on Sunday,* September 5, 2004, p. 10.

"Jackson's Building New Specialist Bakehouse," *Bakeryandsnacks.com,* October 20, 2004.

"Major Changes at the Top for William Jackson," *Food Manufacture,* September 6, 2006.

"New Owner for Jacksons Stores," *Yorkshire Post,* August 17, 2004.

"New Role for Former Baxters Boss," *Aberdeen Press & Journal,* September 7, 2006.

Nicholson, Nigel, and Åsa Björnberg, "Case Reports: 2004 Family Business Honours," London Business School, JP-Morgan Private Bank, 2004.

"Soutar's Move," *Grocer,* September 16, 2006, p. 18.

"Tryton Foods: Aunt Bessie's Frozen Yorkshire Puddings," *Brand Strategy,* October 26, 1998.

Cumulative Index to Companies

A

A&E Television Networks, 32 3–7

A&P *see* The Great Atlantic & Pacific Tea Company, Inc.

A & W Brands, Inc., 25 3–5 *see also* Cadbury Schweppes PLC.

A-dec, Inc., 53 3–5

A-Mark Financial Corporation, 71 3–6

A.B. Chance Industries Co., Inc. *see* Hubbell Inc.

A.B.Dick Company, 28 6–8

A.B. Watley Group Inc., 45 3–5

A.C. Moore Arts & Crafts, Inc., 30 3–5

A.C. Nielsen Company, 13 3–5 *see also* ACNielsen Corp.

A. Duda & Sons, Inc., 88 1–4

A. F. Blakemore & Son Ltd., 90 1–4

A.G. Edwards, Inc., 8 3–5; **32** 17–21 (upd.)

A.H. Belo Corporation, 10 3–5; **30** 13–17 (upd.) *see also* Belo Corp.

A.L. Pharma Inc., 12 3–5 *see also* Alpharma Inc.

A.M. Castle & Co., 25 6–8

A. Moksel AG, 59 3–6

A. Nelson & Co. Ltd., 75 3–6

A. O. Smith Corporation, 11 3–6; **40** 3–8 (upd.); **93** 1–9 (upd.)

A.P. Møller - Maersk A/S, 57 3–6

A.S. Watson & Company Ltd., 84 1–4

A.S. Yakovlev Design Bureau, 15 3–6

A. Schulman, Inc., 8 6–8; **49** 3–7 (upd.)

A.T. Cross Company, 17 3–5; **49** 8–12 (upd.)

A.W. Faber-Castell Unternehmensverwaltung GmbH & Co., 51 3–6

AAF-McQuay Incorporated, 26 3–5

Aalborg Industries A/S, 90 5–8

AAON, Inc., 22 3–6

AAR Corp., 28 3–5

Aardman Animations Ltd., 61 3–5

Aarhus United A/S, 68 3–5

Aaron Brothers Holdings, Inc. *see* Michaels Stores, Inc.

Aaron Rents, Inc., 14 3–5; **35** 3–6 (upd.)

AARP, 27 3–5

Aavid Thermal Technologies, Inc., 29 3–6

Abar Corporation *see* Ipsen International Inc.

ABARTA, Inc., 100 1–4

Abaxis, Inc., 83 1-4

Abatix Corp., 57 7–9

ABB Ltd., II 1–4; **22** 7–12 (upd.); **65** 3–10 (upd.)

Abbey National plc, 10 6–8; **39** 3–6 (upd.)

Abbott Laboratories, I 619–21; **11** 7–9 (upd.); **40** 9–13 (upd.); **93** 10–18 (upd.)

ABC Appliance, Inc., 10 9–11

ABC Carpet & Home Co. Inc., 26 6–8

ABC Family Worldwide, Inc., 52 3–6

ABC, Inc. *see* Capital Cities/ABC Inc.

ABC Learning Centres Ltd., 93 19–22

ABC Rail Products Corporation, 18 3–5

ABC Stores *see* MNS, Ltd.

ABC Supply Co., Inc., 22 13–16

Abengoa S.A., 73 3–5

Abercrombie & Fitch Company, 15 7–9; **35** 7–10 (upd.); **75** 7–11 (upd.)

Abertis Infraestructuras, S.A., 65 11–13

ABF *see* Associated British Foods plc.

Abigail Adams National Bancorp, Inc., 23 3–5

Abiomed, Inc., 47 3–6

AbitibiBowater Inc., IV 245–47; **25** 9–13 (upd.); **99** 1–11 (upd.)

ABM Industries Incorporated, 25 14–16 (upd.)

ABN *see* Algemene Bank Nederland N.V.

ABN AMRO Holding, N.V., 50 3–7

Abrams Industries Inc., 23 6–8 *see also* Servidyne Inc.

Abraxas Petroleum Corporation, 89 1–5

Abril S.A., 95 1–4

Abt Associates Inc., 95 5–9

Abu Dhabi National Oil Company, IV 363–64; **45** 6–9 (upd.)

Academic Press *see* Reed Elsevier plc.

Academy of Television Arts & Sciences, Inc., 55 3–5

Academy Sports & Outdoors, 27 6–8

Agria Corporation, 101 9–13
Agrigenetics, Inc. *see* Mycogen Corp.
Agrium Inc., 73 21–23
AgustaWestland N.V., 75 18–20
Agway, Inc., 7 17–18; 21 17–19 (upd.)
see also Cargill Inc.
AHL Services, Inc., 27 20–23
Ahlstrom Corporation, 53 22–25
Ahmanson *see* H.F. Ahmanson & Co.
AHMSA *see* Altos Hornos de México, S.A. de C.V.
Ahold *see* Koninklijke Ahold NV.
AHP *see* American Home Products Corp.
AICPA *see* The American Institute of Certified Public Accountants.
AIG *see* American International Group, Inc.
AIMCO *see* Apartment Investment and Management Co.
Ainsworth Lumber Co. Ltd., 99 18–22
Air & Water Technologies Corporation, 6 441–42 *see also* Aqua Alliance Inc.
Air Berlin GmbH & Co. Luftverkehrs KG, 71 15–17
Air Canada, 6 60–62; 23 9–12 (upd.); 59 17–22 (upd.)
Air China, 46 9–11
Air Express International Corporation, 13 19–20
Air France *see* Societe Air France.
Air-India Limited, 6 63–64; 27 24–26 (upd.)
Air Jamaica Limited, 54 3–6
Air Liquide *see* L'Air Liquide SA.
Air Mauritius Ltd., 63 17–19
Air Methods Corporation, 53 26–29
Air Midwest, Inc. *see* Mesa Air Group, Inc.
Air New Zealand Limited, 14 10–12; 38 24–27 (upd.)
Air Pacific Ltd., 70 7–9
Air Partner PLC, 93 33–36
Air Products and Chemicals, Inc., I 297–99; 10 31–33 (upd.); 74 6–9 (upd.)
Air Sahara Limited, 65 14–16
Air T, Inc., 86 6–9
Air Wisconsin Airlines Corporation, 55 10–12
Air Zimbabwe (Private) Limited, 91 5–8
AirAsia Berhad, 93 37–40
Airborne Freight Corporation, 6 345–47; 34 15–18 (upd.) *see also* DHL Worldwide Network S.A./N.V.
Airborne Systems Group, 89 39–42
Airbus Industrie *see* G.I.E. Airbus Industrie.
Airgas, Inc., 54 7–10
Airguard Industries, Inc. *see* CLARCOR Inc.
Airlink Pty Ltd *see* Qantas Airways Ltd.
Airstream *see* Thor Industries, Inc.
AirTouch Communications, 11 10–12 *see also* Vodafone Group PLC.
Airtours Plc, 27 27–29, 90, 92
AirTran Holdings, Inc., 22 21–23
Aisin Seiki Co., Ltd., III 415–16; 48 3–5 (upd.)

Aitchison & Colegrave *see* Bradford & Bingley PLC.
Aiwa Co., Ltd., 30 18–20
Ajegroup S.A, 92 1–4
Ajinomoto Co., Inc., II 463–64; 28 9–11 (upd.)
AK Steel Holding Corporation, 19 8–9; 41 3–6 (upd.)
Akamai Technologies, Inc., 71 18–21
Akbank TAS, 79 18–21
Akerys S.A., 90 17–20
AKG Acoustics GmbH, 62 3–6
Akin, Gump, Strauss, Hauer & Feld, L.L.P., 33 23–25
Akorn, Inc., 32 22–24
Akro-Mills Inc. *see* Myers Industries, Inc.
Aktiebolaget SKF, III 622–25; 38 28–33 (upd.); 89 401–09 (upd.)
Akzo Nobel N.V., 13 21–23; 41 7–10 (upd.)
Al Habtoor Group L.L.C., 87 9–12
Al-Tawfeek Co. For Investment Funds Ltd. *see* Dallah Albaraka Group.
Alabama Farmers Cooperative, Inc., 63 20–22
Alabama National BanCorporation, 75 21–23
Aladdin Knowledge Systems Ltd., 101 14–17
Alain Afflelou SA, 53 30–32
Alain Manoukian *see* Groupe Alain Manoukian.
Alamo Group Inc., 32 25–28
Alamo Rent A Car, 6 348–50; 24 9–12 (upd.); 84 5–11 (upd.)
ALARIS Medical Systems, Inc., 65 17–20
Alascom, Inc. *see* AT&T Corp.
Alaska Air Group, Inc., 6 65–67; 29 11–14 (upd.)
Alaska Communications Systems Group, Inc., 89 43–46
Alaska Railroad Corporation, 60 6–9
Alba-Waldensian, Inc., 30 21–23 *see also* E.I. du Pont de Nemours and Co.
Albany International Corporation, 8 12–14; 51 11–14 (upd.)
Albany Molecular Research, Inc., 77 9–12
Albemarle Corporation, 59 23–25
Alberici Corporation, 76 12–14
The Albert Fisher Group plc, 41 11–13
Albert Heijn NV *see* Koninklijke Ahold N.V. (Royal Ahold).
Albert's Organics, Inc. *see* United Natural Foods, Inc.
Alberta Energy Company Ltd., 16 10–12; 43 3–6 (upd.)
Alberto-Culver Company, 8 15–17; 36 23–27 (upd.); 91 9–15 (upd.)
Albertson's, Inc., II 601–03; 7 19–22 (upd.); 30 24–28 (upd.); 65 21–26 (upd.)
Alcan Aluminium Limited, IV 9–13; 31 7–12 (upd.)
Alcatel S.A., 9 9–11; 36 28–31 (upd.)

Alco Health Services Corporation, III 9–10 *see also* AmeriSource Health Corp.
Alco Standard Corporation, I 412–13
Alcoa Inc., 56 7–11 (upd.)
Alderwoods Group, Inc., 68 11–15 (upd.)
Aldi Einkauf GmbH & Co. OHG, 13 24–26; 86 10–14 (upd.)
Aldila Inc., 46 12–14
Aldus Corporation, 10 34–36 *see also* Adobe Systems Inc.
Alès Groupe, 81 10–13
Alex Lee Inc., 18 6–9; 44 10–14 (upd.)
Alexander & Alexander Services Inc., 10 37–39 *see also* Aon Corp.
Alexander & Baldwin, Inc., 10 40–42; 40 14–19 (upd.)
Alexander's, Inc., 45 14–16
Alexandra plc, 88 5–8
Alexandria Real Estate Equities, Inc., 101 18–22
Alfa Corporation, 60 10–12
Alfa Group, 99 23–26
Alfa-Laval AB, III 417–21; 64 13–18 (upd.)
Alfa Romeo, 13 27–29; 36 32–35 (upd.)
Alfa, S.A. de C.V., 19 10–12
Alfesca hf, 82 1–4
Alfred A. Knopf, Inc. *see* Random House, Inc.
Alfred Dunhill Limited *see* Vendôme Luxury Group plc.
Alfred Kärcher GmbH & Co KG, 94 9–14
Alfred Ritter GmbH & Co. KG, 58 3–7
Alga *see* BRIO AB.
Algemene Bank Nederland N.V., II 183–84
Algerian Saudi Leasing Holding Co. *see* Dallah Albaraka Group.
Algo Group Inc., 24 13–15
Alico, Inc., 63 23–25
Alienware Corporation, 81 14–17
Align Technology, Inc., 94 15–18
Alimentation Couche-Tard Inc., 77 13–16
Alitalia–Linee Aeree Italiane, S.p.A., 6 68–69; 29 15–17 (upd.); 97 21–27 (upd.)
Aljazeera Satellite Channel, 79 22–25
All American Communications Inc., 20 3–7
The All England Lawn Tennis & Croquet Club, 54 11–13
All Nippon Airways Co., Ltd., 6 70–71; 38 34–37 (upd.); 91 16–20 (upd.)
Alldays plc, 49 16–19
Allders plc, 37 6–8
Alleanza Assicurazioni S.p.A., 65 27–29
Alleghany Corporation, 10 43–45; 60 13–16 (upd.)
Allegheny Energy, Inc., 38 38–41 (upd.)
Allegheny Ludlum Corporation, 8 18–20
Allegheny Power System, Inc., V 543–45 *see also* Allegheny Energy, Inc.

Allegheny Steel Distributors, Inc. *see* Reliance Steel & Aluminum Co.

Allegiance Life Insurance Company *see* Horace Mann Educators Corp.

Allegiant Travel Company, 97 28–31

Allegis Group, Inc., 95 24–27

Allen-Bradley Co. *see* Rockwell Automation.

Allen Brothers, Inc., 101 23–26

Allen Canning Company, 76 15–17

Allen-Edmonds Shoe Corporation, 61 20–23

Allen Foods, Inc., 60 17–19

Allen Organ Company, 33 26–29

Allen Systems Group, Inc., 59 26–28

Allerderm *see* Virbac Corp.

Allergan, Inc., 10 46–49; 30 29–33 (upd.); 77 17–24 (upd.)

Allgemeine Elektricitäts-Gesellschaft *see* AEG A.G.

Allgemeine Handelsgesellschaft der Verbraucher AG *see* AVA AG.

Allgemeiner Deutscher Automobil-Club e.V., 100 5–10

Alliance and Leicester plc, 88 9–12

Alliance Assurance Company *see* Royal & Sun Alliance Insurance Group plc.

Alliance Atlantis Communications Inc., 39 11–14

Alliance Boots plc, 83 20–28 (upd.)

Alliance Capital Management Holding L.P., 63 26–28

Alliance Entertainment Corp., 17 12–14 *see also* Source Interlink Companies, Inc.

Alliance Resource Partners, L.P., 81 18–21

Alliance UniChem Plc *see* Alliance Boots plc.

Alliant Techsystems Inc., 8 21–23; 30 34–37 (upd.); 77 25–31 (upd.)

Allianz AG, III 183–86; 15 10–14 (upd.); 57 18–24 (upd.)

Allied Corporation *see* AlliedSignal Inc.

The Allied Defense Group, Inc., 65 30–33

Allied Domecq PLC, 29 18–20

Allied Healthcare Products, Inc., 24 16–19

Allied Irish Banks, plc, 16 13–15; 43 7–10 (upd.); 94 19–24 (upd.)

Allied-Lyons plc, I 215–16 *see also* Carlsberg A/S.

Allied Plywood Corporation *see* Ply Gem Industries Inc.

Allied Products Corporation, 21 20–22

Allied-Signal Corp., I 414–16 *see also* AlliedSignal, Inc.

Allied Signal Engines, 9 12–15

Allied Waste Industries, Inc., 50 13–16

Allied Worldwide, Inc., 49 20–23

AlliedSignal Inc., 22 29–32 (upd.) *see also* Honeywell Inc.

Allison Gas Turbine Division, 9 16–19

Allmerica Financial Corporation, 63 29–31

Allou Health & Beauty Care, Inc., 28 12–14

Alloy, Inc., 55 13–15

The Allstate Corporation, 10 50–52; 27 30–33 (upd.)

ALLTEL Corporation, 6 299–301; 46 15–19 (upd.)

Alltrista Corporation, 30 38–41 *see also* Jarden Corp.

Allwaste, Inc., 18 10–13

Alma Media Corporation, 98 1–4

Almacenes Exito S.A., 89 47–50

Almaden Vineyards *see* Canandaigua Brands, Inc.

Almanij NV, 44 15–18 *see also* Algemeene Maatschappij voor Nijverheidskrediet.

Almay, Inc. *see* Revlon Inc.

Almost Family, Inc., 93 41–44

Aloha Airlines, Incorporated, 24 20–22

Alpargatas S.A.I.C., 87 13–17

Alpha Airports Group PLC, 77 32–35

Alpharma Inc., 35 22–26 (upd.)

Alpine Confections, Inc., 71 22–24

Alpine Electronics, Inc., 13 30–31

Alpine Lace Brands, Inc., 18 14–16 *see also* Land O'Lakes, Inc.

Alps Electric Co., Ltd., II 5–6; 44 19–21 (upd.)

Alrosa Company Ltd., 62 7–11

Alsco *see* Steiner Corp.

Alside Inc., 94 25–29

Altadis S.A., 72 6–13 (upd.)

ALTANA AG, 87 18–22

AltaVista Company, 43 11–13

Altera Corporation, 18 17–20; 43 14–18 (upd.)

Alternative Living Services *see* Alterra Healthcare Corp.

Alternative Tentacles Records, 66 3–6

Alternative Youth Services, Inc. *see* Res-Care, Inc.

Alterra Healthcare Corporation, 42 3–5

Alticor Inc., 71 25–30 (upd.)

Altiris, Inc., 65 34–36

Altos Hornos de México, S.A. de C.V., 42 6–8

Altran Technologies, 51 15–18

Altron Incorporated, 20 8–10

Aluar Aluminio Argentino S.A.I.C., 74 10–12

Alumalsa *see* Aluminoy y Aleaciones S.A.

Aluminum Company of America, IV 14–16; 20 11–14 (upd.) *see also* Alcoa Inc.

Alvin Ailey Dance Foundation, Inc., 52 14–17

Alvis Plc, 47 7–9

ALZA Corporation, 10 53–55; 36 36–39 (upd.)

Amalgamated Bank, 60 20–22

AMAX Inc., IV 17–19 *see also* Cyprus Amex.

Amazon.com, Inc., 25 17–19; 56 12–15 (upd.)

AMB Generali Holding AG, 51 19–23

AMB Property Corporation, 57 25–27

Ambac Financial Group, Inc., 65 37–39

Ambassadors International, Inc., 68 16–18 (upd.)

AmBev *see* Companhia de Bebidas das Américas.

Amblin Entertainment, 21 23–27

AMC Entertainment Inc., 12 12–14; 35 27–29 (upd.)

AMCC *see* Applied Micro Circuits Corp.

AMCOL International Corporation, 59 29–33 (upd.)

AMCON Distributing Company, 99 27–30

Amcor Ltd., IV 248–50; 19 13–16 (upd.); 78 1–6 (upd.)

AMCORE Financial Inc., 44 22–26

AMD *see* Advanced Micro Devices, Inc.

Amdahl Corporation, III 109–11; 14 13–16 (upd.); 40 20–25 (upd.) *see also* Fujitsu Ltd.

Amdocs Ltd., 47 10–12

Amec Spie S.A., 57 28–31

Amedysis, Inc., 53 33–36

Amer Group plc, 41 14–16

Amerada Hess Corporation, IV 365–67; 21 28–31 (upd.); 55 16–20 (upd.)

Amerchol Corporation *see* Union Carbide Corp.

AMERCO, 6 351–52; 67 11–14 (upd.)

Ameren Corporation, 60 23–27 (upd.)

Ameri-Kart Corp. *see* Myers Industries, Inc.

America Online, Inc., 10 56–58; 26 16–20 (upd.) *see also* CompuServe Interactive Services, Inc.; AOL Time Warner Inc.

America West Holdings Corporation, 6 72–74; 34 22–26 (upd.)

America's Car-Mart, Inc., 64 19–21

America's Favorite Chicken Company, Inc., 7 26–28 *see also* AFC Enterprises, Inc.

American & Efird, Inc., 82 5–9

American Airlines, I 89–91; 6 75–77 (upd.) *see also* AMR Corp.

American Apparel, Inc., 90 21–24

American Association of Retired Persons *see* AARP.

American Axle & Manufacturing Holdings, Inc., 67 15–17

American Banknote Corporation, 30 42–45

American Bar Association, 35 30–33

American Biltrite Inc., 16 16–18; 43 19–22 (upd.)

American Brands, Inc., V 395–97 *see also* Fortune Brands, Inc.

American Builders & Contractors Supply Co. *see* ABC Supply Co., Inc.

American Building Maintenance Industries, Inc., 6 17–19 *see also* ABM Industries Inc.

American Business Information, Inc., 18 21–25

American Business Interiors *see* American Furniture Company, Inc.

American Business Products, Inc., 20 15–17

American Campus Communities, Inc., 85 1–5

American Can Co. *see* Primerica Corp.

The American Cancer Society, 24 23–25
American Capital Strategies, Ltd., 91 21–24
American Cast Iron Pipe Company, 50 17–20
American Civil Liberties Union (ACLU), 60 28–31
American Classic Voyages Company, 27 34–37
American Coin Merchandising, Inc., 28 15–17; 74 13–16 (upd.)
American Colloid Co., 13 32–35 *see* AMCOL International Corp.
American Commercial Lines Inc., 99 31–34
American Cotton Growers Association *see* Plains Cotton Cooperative Association.
American Crystal Sugar Company, 11 13–15; 32 29–33 (upd.)
American Cyanamid, I 300–02; 8 24–26 (upd.)
American Eagle Outfitters, Inc., 24 26–28; 55 21–24 (upd.)
American Ecology Corporation, 77 36–39
American Electric Power Company, V 546–49; 45 17–21 (upd.)
American Express Company, II 395–99; 10 59–64 (upd.); 38 42–48 (upd.)
American Family Corporation, III 187–89 *see also* AFLAC Inc.
American Financial Group Inc., III 190–92; 48 6–10 (upd.)
American Foods Group, 43 23–27
American Furniture Company, Inc., 21 32–34
American General Corporation, III 193–94; 10 65–67 (upd.); 46 20–23 (upd.)
American General Finance Corp., 11 16–17
American Girl, Inc., 69 16–19 (upd)
American Golf Corporation, 45 22–24
American Gramaphone LLC, 52 18–20
American Greetings Corporation, 7 23–25; 22 33–36 (upd.); 59 34–39 (upd.)
American Healthways, Inc., 65 40–42
American Home Mortgage Holdings, Inc., 46 24–26
American Home Products, I 622–24; 10 68–70 (upd.) *see also* Wyeth.
American Homestar Corporation, 18 26–29; 41 17–20 (upd.)
American Institute of Certified Public Accountants (AICPA), 44 27–30
American International Group, Inc., III 195–98; 15 15–19 (upd.); 47 13–19 (upd.)
American Italian Pasta Company, 27 38–40; 76 18–21 (upd.)
American Kennel Club, Inc., 74 17–19
American Lawyer Media Holdings, Inc., 32 34–37
American Library Association, 86 15–19
American Licorice Company, 86 20–23
American Locker Group Incorporated, 34 19–21

American Lung Association, 48 11–14
American Machine and Metals *see* AMETEK, Inc.
American Maize-Products Co., 14 17–20
American Management Association, 76 22–25
American Management Systems, Inc., 11 18–20
American Media, Inc., 27 41–44; 82 10–15 (upd.)
American Medical Association, 39 15–18
American Medical International, Inc., III 73–75
American Medical Response, Inc., 39 19–22
American Metals Corporation *see* Reliance Steel & Aluminum Co.
American Modern Insurance Group *see* The Midland Co.
American Motors Corp., I 135–37 *see also* DaimlerChrysler AG.
América Móvil, S.A. de C.V., 80 5–8
American MSI Corporation *see* Moldflow Corp.
American National Insurance Company, 8 27–29; 27 45–48 (upd.)
American Olean Tile Company *see* Armstrong Holdings, Inc.
American Oriental Bioengineering Inc., 93 45–48
American Pad & Paper Company, 20 18–21
American Pfauter *see* Gleason Corp.
American Pharmaceutical Partners, Inc., 69 20–22
American Pop Corn Company, 59 40–43
American Power Conversion Corporation, 24 29–31; 67 18–20 (upd.)
American Premier Underwriters, Inc., 10 71–74
American President Companies Ltd., 6 353–55 *see also* APL Ltd.
American Printing House for the Blind, 26 13–15
American Re Corporation, 10 75–77; 35 34–37 (upd.)
American Red Cross, 40 26–29
American Reprographics Company, 75 24–26
American Residential Mortgage Corporation, 8 30–31
American Restaurant Partners, L.P., 93 49–52
American Retirement Corporation, 42 9–12 *see also* Brookdale Senior Living.
American Rice, Inc., 33 30–33
American Rug Craftsmen *see* Mohawk Industries, Inc.
American Safety Razor Company, 20 22–24
American Savings Bank *see* Hawaiian Electric Industries, Inc.
American Science & Engineering, Inc., 81 22–25

American Seating Company, 78 7–11
American Skiing Company, 28 18–21
American Society for the Prevention of Cruelty to Animals (ASPCA), 68 19–22
The American Society of Composers, Authors and Publishers (ASCAP), 29 21–24
American Software Inc., 22 214; 25 20–22
American Standard Companies Inc., III 663–65; 30 46–50 (upd.)
American States Water Company, 46 27–30
American Steamship Company *see* GATX.
American Stores Company, II 604–06; 22 37–40 (upd.) *see also* Albertson's, Inc.
American Superconductor Corporation, 97 32–36
American Technical Ceramics Corp., 67 21–23
American Telephone and Telegraph Company *see* AT&T.
American Tobacco Co. *see* B.A.T. Industries PLC.; Fortune Brands, Inc.
American Tourister, Inc., 16 19–21 *see also* Samsonite Corp.
American Tower Corporation, 33 34–38
American Vanguard Corporation, 47 20–22
American Water Works Company, Inc., 6 443–45; 38 49–52 (upd.)
American Woodmark Corporation, 31 13–16
American Yearbook Company *see* Jostens, Inc.
AmeriCares Foundation, Inc., 87 23–28
Amerigon Incorporated, 97 37–40
AMERIGROUP Corporation, 69 23–26
Amerihost Properties, Inc., 30 51–53
AmeriSource Health Corporation, 37 9–11 (upd.)
AmerisourceBergen Corporation, 64 22–28 (upd.)
Ameristar Casinos, Inc., 33 39–42; 69 27–31 (upd.)
Ameritech Corporation, V 265–68; 18 30–34 (upd.) *see also* AT&T Corp.
Ameritrade Holding Corporation, 34 27–30
Ameriwood Industries International Corp., 17 15–17 *see also* Dorel Industries Inc.
Amerock Corporation, 53 37–40
Ameron International Corporation, 67 24–26
Amersham PLC, 50 21–25
Ames Department Stores, Inc., 9 20–22; 30 54–57 (upd.)
AMETEK, Inc., 9 23–25
N.V. Amev, III 199–202 *see also* Fortis, Inc.
Amey Plc, 47 23–25
AMF Bowling, Inc., 40 30–33
Amfac/JMB Hawaii L.L.C., I 417–18; 24 32–35 (upd.)

Aviva PLC, 50 65–68 (upd.)
Avnet Inc., 9 55–57
Avocent Corporation, 65 56–58
Avon Products, Inc., III 15–16; 19 26–29 (upd.); 46 43–46 (upd.)
Avondale Industries, Inc., 7 39–41; 41 40–43 (upd.)
AVTOVAZ Joint Stock Company, 65 59–62
AVX Corporation, 67 41–43
AWA *see* America West Holdings Corp.
AWB Ltd., 56 25–27
Awrey Bakeries, Inc., 56 28–30
AXA Colonia Konzern AG, III 210–12; 49 41–45 (upd.)
Axcan Pharma Inc., 85 25–28
Axcelis Technologies, Inc., 95 36–39
Axel Johnson Group, I 553–55
Axel Springer Verlag AG, IV 589–91; 20 50–53 (upd.)
Axsys Technologies, Inc., 93 65–68
Aydin Corp., 19 30–32
Aynsley China Ltd. *see* Belleek Pottery Ltd.
Azcon Corporation, 23 34–36
Azelis Group, 100 44–47
Azerbaijan Airlines, 77 46–49
Azienda Generale Italiana Petroli *see* ENI S.p.A.
Aztar Corporation, 13 66–68; 71 41–45 (upd.)
AZZ Incorporated, 93 69–72

B

B&D *see* Barker & Dobson.
B&G Foods, Inc., 40 51–54
B&J Music Ltd. *see* Kaman Music Corp.
B&Q plc *see* Kingfisher plc.
B.A.T. Industries PLC, 22 70–73 (upd.) *see also* Brown and Williamson Tobacco Corporation
B. Dalton Bookseller Inc., 25 29–31 *see also* Barnes & Noble, Inc.
B/E Aerospace, Inc., 30 72–74
B.F. Goodrich Co. *see* The BFGoodrich Co.
B.J. Alan Co., Inc., 67 44–46
The B. Manischewitz Company, LLC, 31 43–46
B.R. Guest Inc., 87 43–46
B.W. Rogers Company, 94 49–52
BA *see* British Airways plc.
BAA plc, 10 121–23; 33 57–61 (upd.)
Baan Company, 25 32–34
Babbage's, Inc., 10 124–25 *see also* GameStop Corp.
The Babcock & Wilcox Company, 82 26–30
Babcock International Group PLC, 69 51–54
Babolat VS, S.A., 97 63–66
Baby Lock USA *see* Tacony Corp.
Baby Superstore, Inc., 15 32–34 *see also* Toys 'R Us, Inc.
Bacardi & Company Ltd., 18 39–42; 82 31–36 (upd.)
Baccarat, 24 61–63
Bachman's Inc., 22 58–60

Bachoco *see* Industrias Bachoco, S.A. de C.V.
Back Bay Restaurant Group, Inc., 20 54–56
Back Yard Burgers, Inc., 45 33–36
Backus y Johnston *see* Unión de Cervecerias Peruanas Backus y Johnston S.A.A.
Bad Boy Worldwide Entertainment Group, 58 14–17
Badger Meter, Inc., 22 61–65
Badger Paper Mills, Inc., 15 35–37
Badger State Ethanol, LLC, 83 33–37
BAE Systems Ship Repair, 73 46–48
Bahamas Air Holdings Ltd., 66 24–26
Bahlsen GmbH & Co. KG, 44 38–41
Baidu.com Inc., 95 40–43
Bailey Nurseries, Inc., 57 59–61
Bain & Company, 55 41–43
Baird & Warner Holding Company, 87 47–50
Bairnco Corporation, 28 42–45
Bajaj Auto Limited, 39 36–38
Baker *see* Michael Baker Corp.
Baker and Botts, L.L.P., 28 46–49
Baker & Daniels LLP, 88 17–20
Baker & Hostetler LLP, 40 55–58
Baker & McKenzie, 10 126–28; 42 17–20 (upd.)
Baker & Taylor Corporation, 16 45–47; 43 59–62 (upd.)
Baker Hughes Incorporated, III 428–29; 22 66–69 (upd.); 57 62–66 (upd.)
Bakkavör Group hf., 91 35–39
Balance Bar Company, 32 70–72
Balchem Corporation, 42 21–23
Baldor Electric Company, 21 42–44; 97 63–67 (upd.)
Baldwin & Lyons, Inc., 51 37–39
Baldwin Piano & Organ Company, 18 43–46 *see also* Gibson Guitar Corp.
Baldwin Richardson Foods Company, 100 48–52
Baldwin Technology Company, Inc., 25 35–39
Balfour Beatty Construction Ltd., 36 56–60 (upd.)
Ball Corporation, I 597–98; 10 129–31 (upd.); 78 25–29 (upd.)
Ball Horticultural Company, 78 30–33
Ballantine Books *see* Random House, Inc.
Ballantyne of Omaha, Inc., 27 56–58
Ballard Medical Products, 21 45–48 *see also* Kimberly-Clark Corp.
Ballard Power Systems Inc., 73 49–52
Ballistic Recovery Systems, Inc., 87 51–54
Bally Manufacturing Corporation, III 430–32
Bally Total Fitness Corporation, 25 40–42; 94 53–57 (upd.)
Balmac International, Inc., 94 58–61
Bâloise-Holding, 40 59–62
Baltek Corporation, 34 59–61
Baltika Brewery Joint Stock Company, 65 63–66
Baltimore & Ohio Railroad *see* CSX Corp.

Baltimore Aircoil Company, Inc., 66 27–29
Baltimore Gas and Electric Company, V 552–54; 25 43–46 (upd.)
Baltimore Orioles L.P., 66 30–33
Baltimore Technologies Plc, 42 24–26
The Bama Companies, Inc., 80 13–16
Banamex *see* Grupo Financiero Banamex S.A.
Banana Republic Inc., 25 47–49 *see also* Gap, Inc.
Banc One Corporation, 10 132–34 *see also* JPMorgan Chase & Co.
Banca Commerciale Italiana SpA, II 191–93
Banca Fideuram SpA, 63 52–54
Banca Intesa SpA, 65 67–70
Banca Monte dei Paschi di Siena SpA, 65 71–73
Banca Nazionale del Lavoro SpA, 72 19–21
Banca Serfin *see* Grupo Financiero Serfin, S.A.
Banco Bilbao Vizcaya Argentaria S.A., II 194–96; 48 47–51 (upd.)
Banco Bradesco S.A., 13 69–71
Banco Central, II 197–98; 56 65 *see also* Banco Santander Central Hispano S.A.
Banco Central del Paraguay, 100 53–56
Banco de Crédito del Perú, 9273–76
Banco de Crédito e Inversiones *see* Bci.
Banco Comercial Português, SA, 50 69–72
Banco de Chile, 69 55–57
Banco de Comercio, S.A. *see* Grupo Financiero BBVA Bancomer S.A.
Banco do Brasil S.A., II 199–200
Banco Espírito Santo e Comercial de Lisboa S.A., 15 38–40 *see also* Espírito Santo Financial Group S.A.
Banco Itaú S.A., 19 33–35
Banco Popular *see* Popular, Inc.
Banco Santander Central Hispano S.A., 36 61–64 (upd.)
Banco Serfin *see* Grupo Financiero Serfin, S.A.
Bancomer S.A. *see* Grupo Financiero BBVA Bancomer S.A.
Bandag, Inc., 19 36–38
Bandai Co., Ltd., 55 44–48
Banfi Products Corp., 36 65–67
Banfield, The Pet Hospital *see* Medical Management International, Inc.
Bang & Olufsen Holding A/S, 37 25–28; 86 24–29 (upd.)
Bank Austria AG, 23 37–39; 100 57–60 (upd.)
Bank Brussels Lambert, II 201–03
Bank Hapoalim B.M., II 204–06; 54 33–37 (upd.)
Bank Leumi le-Israel B.M., 60 48–51
Bank of America Corporation, 46 47–54 (upd.); 101 51–64 (upd.)
Bank of Boston Corporation, II 207–09 *see also* FleetBoston Financial Corp.
Bank of China, 63 55–57
Bank of Cyprus Group, 91 40–43
Bank of East Asia Ltd., 63 58–60

Bank of Granite Corporation, 89 87–91
Bank of Hawaii Corporation, 73 53–56
Bank of Ireland, 50 73–76
Bank of Mississippi, Inc., 14 40–41
Bank of Montreal, II 210–12; 46 55–58 (upd.)
Bank of New England Corporation, II 213–15
Bank of New York Company, Inc., II 216–19; 46 59–63 (upd.)
The Bank of Nova Scotia, II 220–23; 59 70–76 (upd.)
The Bank of Scotland *see* The Governor and Company of the Bank of Scotland.
Bank of the Ozarks, Inc., 91 44–47
Bank of the Philippine Islands, 58 18–20
Bank of Tokyo-Mitsubishi Ltd., II 224–25; 15 41–43 (upd.) *see also* Mitsubishi UFJ Financial Group, Inc.
Bank One Corporation, 36 68–75 (upd.) *see also* JPMorgan Chase & Co.
BankAmerica Corporation, II 226–28 *see also* Bank of America.
Bankers Trust New York Corporation, II 229–31
Banknorth Group, Inc., 55 49–53
Bankrate, Inc., 83 38–41
Banner Aerospace, Inc., 14 42–44; 37 29–32 (upd.)
Banorte *see* Grupo Financiero Banorte, S.A. de C.V.
Banque Nationale de Paris S.A., II 232–34 *see also* BNP Paribas Group.
Banta Corporation, 12 24–26; 32 73–77 (upd.); 79 50–56 (upd.)
Banyan Systems Inc., 25 50–52
Baptist Health Care Corporation, 82 37–40
Bar-S Foods Company, 76 39–41
Barbara's Bakery Inc., 88 21–24
Barclay Furniture Co. *see* LADD Furniture, Inc.
Barclays PLC, II 235–37; 20 57–60 (upd.); 64 46–50 (upd.)
BarclaysAmerican Mortgage Corporation, 11 29–30
Barco NV, 44 42–45
Barden Companies, Inc., 76 42–45
Bardwil Industries Inc., 98 15–18
Bare Escentuals, Inc., 91 48–52
Barilla G. e R. Fratelli S.p.A., 17 35–37; 50 77–80 (upd.)
Barings PLC, 14 45–47
Barlow Rand Ltd., I 422–24
Barmag AG, 39 39–42
Barnes & Noble, Inc., 10 135–37; 30 67–71 (upd.); 75 50–55 (upd.)
Barnes Group, Inc., 13 72–74; 69 58–62 (upd.)
Barnett Banks, Inc., 9 58–60 *see also* Bank of America Corp.
Barnett Inc., 28 50–52
Barney's, Inc., 28 53–55
Baron de Ley S.A., 74 27–29
Baron Philippe de Rothschild S.A., 39 43–46
Barr *see* AG Barr plc.

Barr Pharmaceuticals, Inc., 26 29–31; 68 46–49 (upd.)
Barratt Developments plc, I 556–57; 56 31–33 (upd.)
Barrett Business Services, Inc., 16 48–50
Barrett-Jackson Auction Company L.L.C., 88 25–28
Barrick Gold Corporation, 34 62–65
Barry Callebaut AG, 29 46–48; 71 46–49 (upd.)
Barry-Wehmiller Companies, Inc., 90 40–43
The Bartell Drug Company, 94 62–65
Barton Malow Company, 51 40–43
Barton Protective Services Inc., 53 56–58
The Baseball Club of Seattle, LP, 50 81–85
BASF Aktiengesellschaft, I 305–08; 18 47–51 (upd.); 50 86–92 (upd.)
Bashas' Inc., 33 62–64; 80 17–21 (upd.)
Basic Earth Science Systems, Inc., 101 65–68
The Basketball Club of Seattle, LLC, 50 93–97
Bass PLC, I 222–24; 15 44–47 (upd.); 38 74–78 (upd.)
Bass Pro Shops, Inc., 42 27–30
Bassett Furniture Industries, Inc., 18 52–55; 95 44–50 (upd.)
BAT Industries plc, I 425–27 *see also* British American Tobacco PLC.
Bata Ltd., 62 27–30
Bates Worldwide, Inc., 14 48–51; 33 65–69 (upd.)
Bath Iron Works Corporation, 12 27–29; 36 76–79 (upd.)
Battelle Memorial Institute, Inc., 10 138–40
Batten Barton Durstine & Osborn *see* Omnicom Group Inc.
Battle Mountain Gold Company, 23 40–42 *see also* Newmont Mining Corp.
Bauer Publishing Group, 7 42–43
Bauerly Companies, 61 31–33
Baugur Group hf, 81 45–49
Baumax AG, 75 56–58
Bausch & Lomb Inc., 7 44–47; 25 53–57 (upd.); 96 20–26 (upd.)
Bavaria S.A., 90 44–47
Baxi Group Ltd., 96 27–30
Baxter International Inc., I 627–29; 10 141–43 (upd.)
Baxters Food Group Ltd., 99 47–50
The Bay *see* The Hudson's Bay Co.
Bay State Gas Company, 38 79–82
Bayard SA, 49 46–49
BayBanks, Inc., 12 30–32
Bayer A.G., I 309–11; 13 75–77 (upd.); 41 44–48 (upd.)
Bayerische Hypotheken- und Wechsel-Bank AG, II 238–40 *see also* HVB Group.
Bayerische Motoren Werke A.G., I 138–40; 11 31–33 (upd.); 38 83–87 (upd.)

Bayerische Vereinsbank A.G., II 241–43 *see also* HVB Group.
Bayernwerk AG, V 555–58; 23 43–47 (upd.) *see also* E.On AG.
Bayou Steel Corporation, 31 47–49
BB&T Corporation, 79 57–61
BB Holdings Limited, 77 50–53
BBA *see* Bush Boake Allen Inc.
BBA Aviation plc, 90 48–52
BBAG Osterreichische Brau-Beteiligungs-AG, 38 88–90
BBC *see* British Broadcasting Corp.
BBDO Worldwide *see* Omnicom Group Inc.
BBGI *see* Beasley Broadcast Group, Inc.
BBN Corp., 19 39–42
BBVA *see* Banco Bilbao Vizcaya Argentaria S.A.
BCE, Inc., V 269–71; 44 46–50 (upd.)
Bci, 99 51–54
BDO Seidman LLP, 96 31–34
BE&K, Inc., 73 57–59
BEA *see* Bank of East Asia Ltd.
BEA Systems, Inc., 36 80–83
Beacon Roofing Supply, Inc., 75 59–61
Bear Creek Corporation, 38 91–94
Bear Stearns Companies, Inc., II 400–01; 10 144–45 (upd.); 52 41–44 (upd.)
Bearings, Inc., 13 78–80
Beasley Broadcast Group, Inc., 51 44–46
Beate Uhse AG, 96 35–39
Beatrice Company, II 467–69 *see also* TLC Beatrice International Holdings, Inc.
BeautiControl Cosmetics, Inc., 21 49–52
Beazer Homes USA, Inc., 17 38–41
bebe stores, inc., 31 50–52
Bechtel Corporation, I 558–59; 24 64–67 (upd.); 99 55–60 (upd.)
Beckett Papers, 23 48–50
Beckman Coulter, Inc., 22 74–77
Beckman Instruments, Inc., 14 52–54
Becton, Dickinson and Company, I 630–31; 11 34–36 (upd.); 36 84–89 (upd.); 101 69–77 (upd.)
Bed Bath & Beyond Inc., 13 81–83; 41 49–52 (upd.)
Beech Aircraft Corporation, 8 49–52 *see also* Raytheon Aircraft Holdings Inc.
Beech-Nut Nutrition Corporation, 21 53–56; 51 47–51 (upd.)
Beef O'Brady's *see* Family Sports Concepts, Inc.
Beer Nuts, Inc., 86 30–33
Beggars Group Ltd., 99 61–65
Behr GmbH & Co. KG, 72 22–25
Behring Diagnostics *see* Dade Behring Holdings Inc.
BEI Technologies, Inc., 65 74–76
Beiersdorf AG, 29 49–53
Bekaert S.A./N.V., 90 53–57
Bekins Company, 15 48–50
Bel *see* Fromageries Bel.
Bel Fuse, Inc., 53 59–62
Bel/Kaukauna USA, 76 46–48

Centocor Inc., 14 98–100
Central and South West Corporation, V 569–70
Central European Distribution Corporation, 75 90–92
Central European Media Enterprises Ltd., 61 56–59
Central Florida Investments, Inc., 93 137–40
Central Garden & Pet Company, 23 108–10; 58 57–60 (upd.)
Central Hudson Gas And Electricity Corporation, 6 458–60
Central Independent Television, 7 78–80; 23 111–14 (upd.)
Central Japan Railway Company, 43 103–06
Central Maine Power, 6 461–64
Central National-Gottesman Inc., 95 87–90
Central Newspapers, Inc., 10 207–09 *see also* Gannett Company, Inc.
Central Parking Corporation, 18 103–05
Central Soya Company, Inc., 7 81–83
Central Sprinkler Corporation, 29 97–99
Central Vermont Public Service Corporation, 54 53–56
Centrica plc, 29 100–05 (upd.)
Centuri Corporation, 54 57–59
Century Aluminum Company, 52 71–74
Century Business Services, Inc., 52 75–78
Century Casinos, Inc., 53 90–93
Century Communications Corp., 10 210–12
Century Telephone Enterprises, Inc., 9 105–07; 54 60–63 (upd.)
Century Theatres, Inc., 31 99–101
Cenveo Inc., 71 100–04 (upd.)
CEPCO *see* Chugoku Electric Power Company Inc.
Cephalon, Inc., 45 93–96
Cepheid, 77 93–96
Ceradyne, Inc., 65 100–02
Cerebos Gregg's Ltd., 100 96–99
Cerner Corporation, 16 92–94; 94 111–16 (upd.)
CertainTeed Corporation, 35 86–89
Certegy, Inc., 63 100–03
Cerveceria Polar, I 230–31 *see also* Empresas Polar SA.
Ceské aerolinie, a.s., 66 49–51
Cesky Telecom, a.s., 64 70–73
Cessna Aircraft Company, 8 90–93; 27 97–101 (upd.)
Cetelem S.A., 21 99–102
CeWe Color Holding AG, 76 85–88
ČEZ a. s., 97 112–15
CF Industries Holdings, Inc., 99 89–93
CG&E *see* Cincinnati Gas & Electric Co.
CGM *see* Compagnie Générale Maritime.
Chadbourne & Parke, 36 109–12
Chadwick's of Boston, Ltd., 29 106–08
Chalk's Ocean Airways *see* Flying Boat, Inc.

The Chalone Wine Group, Ltd., 36 113–16
Champion Enterprises, Inc., 17 81–84
Champion Industries, Inc., 28 74–76
Champion International Corporation, IV 263–65; 20 127–30 (upd.) *see also* International Paper Co.
Championship Auto Racing Teams, Inc., 37 73–75
Chancellor Beacon Academies, Inc., 53 94–97
Chancellor Media Corporation, 24 106–10
Chanel SA, 12 57–59; 49 83–86 (upd.)
Channel Four Television Corporation, 93 141–44
Chantiers Jeanneau S.A., 96 78–81
Chaoda Modern Agriculture (Holdings) Ltd., 87 96–99
Chaparral Steel Co., 13 142–44
Charal S.A., 90 117–20
Chargeurs International, 6 373–75; 21 103–06 (upd.)
Charisma Brands LLC, 74 75–78
The Charles Machine Works, Inc., 64 74–76
Charles River Laboratories International, Inc., 42 66–69
The Charles Schwab Corporation, 8 94–96; 26 64–67 (upd.); 81 62–68 (upd.)
The Charles Stark Draper Laboratory, Inc., 35 90–92
Charles Vögele Holding AG, 82 63-66
Charlotte Russe Holding, Inc., 35 93–96; 90 121–25 (upd.)
The Charmer Sunbelt Group, 95 91–94
Charming Shoppes, Inc., 8 97–98; 38 127–29 (upd.)
Charoen Pokphand Group, 62 60–63
Chart House Enterprises, Inc., 17 85–88; 96 82–86 (upd.)
Chart Industries, Inc., 21 107–09
Charter Communications, Inc., 33 91–94
ChartHouse International Learning Corporation, 49 87–89
Chas. Levy Company LLC, 60 83–85
Chase General Corporation, 91 102–05
The Chase Manhattan Corporation, II 247–49; 13 145–48 (upd.) *see also* JPMorgan Chase & Co.
Chateau Communities, Inc., 37 76–79
Chattanooga Bakery, Inc., 86 75–78
Chattem, Inc., 17 89–92; 88 47–52 (upd.)
Chautauqua Airlines, Inc., 38 130–32
CHC Helicopter Corporation, 67 101–03
Checker Motors Corp., 89 144–48
Checkers Drive-In Restaurants, Inc., 16 95–98; 74 79–83 (upd.)
CheckFree Corporation, 81 69–72
Checkpoint Systems, Inc., 39 77–80
Chedraui *see* Grupo Comercial Chedraui S.A. de C.V.
The Cheesecake Factory Inc., 17 93–96; 100 100–05 (upd.)

Chef Solutions, Inc., 89 149–52
Chello Zone Ltd., 93 145–48
Chelsea Milling Company, 29 109–11
Chelsea Piers Management Inc., 86 79–82
Chelsfield PLC, 67 104–06
Cheltenham & Gloucester PLC, 61 60–62
Chemcentral Corporation, 8 99–101
Chemed Corporation, 13 149–50
Chemfab Corporation, 35 97–101
Chemi-Trol Chemical Co., 16 99–101
Chemical Banking Corporation, II 250–52; 14 101–04 (upd.)
Chemical Waste Management, Inc., 9 108–10
Chemtura Corporation, 91 106–20 (upd.)
CHEP Pty. Ltd., 80 63–66
Cherokee Inc., 18 106–09
Cherry Lane Music Publishing Company, Inc., 62 64–67
Chesapeake Corporation, 8 102–04; 30 117–20 (upd.); 93 149–55 (upd.)
Chesapeake Utilities Corporation, 56 60–62
Cheshire Building Society, 74 84–87
Chesebrough-Pond's USA, Inc., 8 105–07
Cheung Kong (Holdings) Ltd., IV 693–95; 20 131–34 (upd.); 94 117–24 (upd.)
ChevronTexaco Corporation, IV 385–87;19 82–85 (upd.); 47 70–76 (upd.)
Cheyenne Software, Inc., 12 60–62
CHF Industries, Inc., 84 47–50
Chi-Chi's Inc., 13 151–53; 51 70–73 (upd.)
Chi Mei Optoelectronics Corporation, 75 93–95
Chiasso Inc., 53 98–100
Chiat/Day Inc. Advertising, 11 49–52 *see also* TBWA/Chiat/Day.
Chibu Electric Power Company, Incorporated, V 571–73
Chic by H.I.S., Inc., 20 135–37 *see also* VF Corp.
Chicago and North Western Holdings Corporation, 6 376–78 *see also* Union Pacific Corp.
Chicago Bears Football Club, Inc., 33 95–97
Chicago Blackhawk Hockey Team, Inc. *see* Wirtz Corp.
Chicago Board of Trade, 41 84–87
Chicago Bridge & Iron Company N.V., 82 67–73 (upd.)
Chicago Mercantile Exchange Holdings Inc., 75 96–99
Chicago National League Ball Club, Inc., 66 52–55
Chicago Pizza & Brewery, Inc., 44 85–88
Chicago Review Press Inc., 84 51–54
Chicago Tribune see Tribune Co.
Chick-fil-A Inc., 23 115–18; 90 126–31 (upd.)

Chicken of the Sea International, 24 114–16 (upd.)

Chico's FAS, Inc., 45 97–99

Children's Comprehensive Services, Inc., 42 70–72

Children's Healthcare of Atlanta Inc., 101 105–09

Children's Hospitals and Clinics, Inc., 54 64–67

The Children's Place Retail Stores, Inc., 37 80–82; 86 83–87 (upd.)

ChildrenFirst, Inc., 59 117–20

Childtime Learning Centers, Inc., 34 103–06 see also Learning Care Group, Inc.

Chiles Offshore Corporation, 9 111–13

China Airlines, 34 107–10

China Automotive Systems Inc., 87 100–103

China Construction Bank Corp., 79 101–04

China Eastern Airlines Co. Ltd., 31 102–04

China Life Insurance Company Limited, 65 103–05

China Merchants International Holdings Co., Ltd., 52 79–82

China National Cereals, Oils and Foodstuffs Import and Export Corporation (COFCO), 76 89–91

China National Petroleum Corporation, 46 86–89

China Nepstar Chain Drugstore Ltd., 97 116–19

China Netcom Group Corporation (Hong Kong) Limited, 73 80–83

China Shenhua Energy Company Limited, 83 68–71

China Southern Airlines Company Ltd., 33 98–100

China Telecom, 50 128–32

Chindex International, Inc., 101 110–13

Chinese Petroleum Corporation, IV 388–90; 31 105–08 (upd.)

Chipotle Mexican Grill, Inc., 67 107–10

CHIPS and Technologies, Inc., 9 114–17

Chiquita Brands International, Inc., 7 84–86; 21 110–13 (upd.); 83 72–79 (upd.)

Chiron Corporation, 10 213–14; 36 117–20 (upd.)

Chisholm-Mingo Group, Inc., 41 88–90

Chittenden & Eastman Company, 58 61–64

Chock Full o'Nuts Corp., 17 97–100

Chocoladefabriken Lindt & Sprüngli AG, 27 102–05

Choice Hotels International, Inc., 14 105–07; 83 80-83 (upd.)

ChoicePoint Inc., 65 106–08

Chorus Line Corporation, 30 121–23

Chr. Hansen Group A/S, 70 54–57

Chris-Craft Corporation, 9 118–19; 31 109–12 (upd.); 80 67–71 (upd.)

Christensen Boyles Corporation, 26 68–71

The Christian Broadcasting Network, Inc., 52 83–85

Christian Dalloz SA, 40 96–98

Christian Dior S.A., 19 86–88; 49 90–93 (upd.)

Christian Salvesen Plc, 45 100–03

The Christian Science Publishing Society, 55 99–102

Christie's International plc, 15 98–101; 39 81–85 (upd.)

Christofle SA, 40 99–102

Christopher & Banks Corporation, 42 73–75

Chromcraft Revington, Inc., 15 102–05

The Chronicle Publishing Company, Inc., 23 119–22

Chronimed Inc., 26 72–75

Chrysalis Group plc, 40 103–06

Chrysler Corporation, I 144–45; 11 53–55 (upd.) see also DaimlerChrysler AG

CHS Inc., 60 86–89

CH2M HILL Companies Ltd., 22 136–38; 96 72–77 (upd.)

Chubb Corporation, III 220–22; 14 108–10 (upd.); 37 83–87 (upd.)

Chubb, PLC, 50 133–36

Chubu Electric Power Company, Inc., V 571–73; 46 90–93 (upd.)

Chuck E. Cheese see CEC Entertainment, Inc.

Chugach Alaska Corporation, 60 90–93

Chugai Pharmaceutical Co., Ltd., 50 137–40

Chugoku Electric Power Company Inc., V 574–76; 53 101–04 (upd.)

Chunghwa Picture Tubes, Ltd., 75 100–02

Chunghwa Telecom Co., Ltd., 101 114–19 (upd.)

Chupa Chups S.A., 38 133–35

Church & Dwight Co., Inc., 29 112–15; 68 78–82 (upd.)

Church's Chicken, 66 56–59

Churchill Downs Incorporated, 29 116–19

Cia Hering, 72 66–68

Cianbro Corporation, 14 111–13

Ciba-Geigy Ltd., I 632–34; 8 108–11 (upd.) see also Novartis AG.

CIBC see Canadian Imperial Bank of Commerce.

Ciber, Inc., 18 110–12

CiCi Enterprises, L.P., 99 94–99

CIENA Corporation, 54 68–71

Cifra, S.A. de C.V., 12 63–65 see also Wal-Mart de Mexico, S.A. de C.V.

CIGNA Corporation, III 223–27; 22 139–44 (upd.); 45 104–10 (upd.)

Cimarex Energy Co., 81 73–76

Cimentos de Portugal SGPS S.A. (Cimpor), 76 92–94

Ciments Français, 40 107–10

Cimpor see Cimentos de Portugal SGPS S.A.

Cinar Corporation, 40 111–14

Cincinnati Bell, Inc., 6 316–18

Cincinnati Financial Corporation, 16 102–04; 44 89–92 (upd.)

Cincinnati Gas & Electric Company, 6 465–68 see also Duke Energy Corp.

Cincinnati Lamb Inc., 72 69–71

Cincinnati Milacron Inc., 12 66–69 see also Milacron, Inc.

Cincom Systems Inc., 15 106–08

Cinemark Holdings, Inc., 95 95–99

Cinemas de la República, S.A. de C.V., 83 84-86

Cinemeccanica S.p.A., 78 70–73

Cineplex Odeon Corporation, 6 161–63; 23 123–26 (upd.)

Cinnabon, Inc., 23 127–29; 90 132–36 (upd.)

Cinram International, Inc., 43 107–10

Cintas Corporation, 21 114–16; 51 74–77 (upd.)

CIPSA see Compañia Industrial de Parras, S.A. de C.V. (CIPSA).

CIPSCO Inc., 6 469–72 see also Ameren Corp.

The Circle K Company, II 619–20; 20 138–40 (upd.)

Circon Corporation, 21 117–20

Circuit City Stores, Inc., 9 120–22; 29 120–24 (upd.); 65 109–14 (upd.)

Circus Circus Enterprises, Inc., 6 203–05

Cirque du Soleil Inc., 29 125–28; 98 46–51 (upd.)

Cirrus Design Corporation, 44 93–95

Cirrus Logic, Inc., 11 56–57; 48 90–93 (upd.)

Cisco-Linksys LLC, 86 88–91

Cisco Systems, Inc., 11 58–60; 34 111–15 (upd.); 77 97–103 (upd.)

Cisneros Group of Companies, 54 72–75

CIT Group Inc., 76 95–98

Citadel Communications Corporation, 35 102–05

CitFed Bancorp, Inc., 16 105–07 see also Fifth Third Bancorp.

CITGO Petroleum Corporation, IV 391–93; 31 113–17 (upd.)

Citi Trends, Inc., 80 72–75

Citibank see Citigroup Inc

CITIC Pacific Ltd., 18 113–15

Citicorp, II 253–55; 9 123–26 (upd.) see also Citigroup Inc.

Citicorp Diners Club, Inc., 90 137–40

Citigroup Inc., 30 124–28 (upd.); 59 121–27 (upd.)

Citizen Watch Co., Ltd., III 454–56; 21 121–24 (upd.); 81 77–82 (upd.)

Citizens Communications Company, 79 105–08 (upd.)

Citizens Financial Group, Inc., 42 76–80; 87 104–112 (upd.)

Citizens Utilities Company, 7 87–89 see also Citizens Communications Company

Citrix Systems, Inc., 44 96–99

Citroën see PSA Peugeot Citroen S.A.

City Brewing Company LLC, 73 84–87

City Developments Limited, 89 153–56

City Public Service, 6 473–75

CJ Banks *see* Christopher & Banks Corp.

CJ Corporation, 62 68–70

CJSC Transmash Holding, 93 446–49

CKE Restaurants, Inc., 19 89–93; 46 94–99 (upd.)

Claire's Stores, Inc., 17 101–03; 94 125–29 (upd.)

CLARCOR Inc., 17 104–07; 61 63–67 (upd.)

Clare Rose Inc., 68 83–85

Clarion Company Ltd., 64 77–79

The Clark Construction Group, Inc., 8 112–13

Clark Equipment Company, 8 114–16

Classic Vacation Group, Inc., 46 100–03

Clayton Homes Incorporated, 13 154–55; 54 76–79 (upd.)

Clayton Williams Energy, Inc., 87 113–116

Clean Harbors, Inc., 73 88–91

Clear Channel Communications, Inc., 23 130–32 *see also* Live Nation, Inc.

Clearly Canadian Beverage Corporation, 48 94–97

Clearwire, Inc., 69 95–97

Cleary, Gottlieb, Steen & Hamilton, 35 106–09

Cleco Corporation, 37 88–91

The Clemens Family Corporation, 93 156–59

Clement Pappas & Company, Inc., 92 52–55

Cleveland-Cliffs Inc., 13 156–58; 62 71–75 (upd.)

Cleveland Indians Baseball Company, Inc., 37 92–94

Click Wine Group, 68 86–88

Clif Bar Inc., 50 141–43

Clifford Chance LLP, 38 136–39

Clinton Cards plc, 39 86–88

Cloetta Fazer AB, 70 58–60

Clopay Corporation, 100 106–10

The Clorox Company, III 20–22; 22 145–48 (upd.); 81 83–90 (upd.)

Close Brothers Group plc, 39 89–92

The Clothestime, Inc., 20 141–44

Clougherty Packing Company, 72 72–74

Club Méditerranée S.A., 6 206–08; 21 125–28 (upd.); 91 121–27 (upd.)

ClubCorp, Inc., 33 101–04

CMC *see* Commercial Metals Co.

CME *see* Campbell-Mithun-Esty, Inc.; Central European Media Enterprises Ltd.; Chicago Mercantile Exchange Inc.

CMG Worldwide, Inc., 89 157–60

CMGI, Inc., 76 99–101

CMIH *see* China Merchants International Holdings Co., Ltd.

CML Group, Inc., 10 215–18

CMO *see* Chi Mei Optoelectronics Corp.

CMP Media Inc., 26 76–80

CMS Energy Corporation, V 577–79; 14 114–16 (upd.); 100 111–16 (upd.)

CN *see* Canadian National Railway Co.

CNA Financial Corporation, III 228–32; 38 140–46 (upd.)

CNET Networks, Inc., 47 77–80

CNG *see* Consolidated Natural Gas Co.

CNH Global N.V., 38 147–56 (upd.); 99 100–112 (upd.)

CNP *see* Compagnie Nationale à Portefeuille.

CNPC *see* China National Petroleum Corp.

CNS, Inc., 20 145–47 *see also* GlaxoSmithKline plc.

Co-operative Group (CWS) Ltd., 51 86–89

Coach, Inc., 10 219–21; 45 111–15 (upd.); 99 113–120 (upd.)

Coach USA, Inc., 24 117–19; 55 103–06 (upd.)

Coachmen Industries, Inc., 77 104–07

Coal India Ltd., IV 48–50; 44 100–03 (upd.)

Coastal Corporation, IV 394–95; 31 118–21 (upd.)

Coats plc, V 356–58; 44 104–07 (upd.)

COBE Cardiovascular, Inc., 61 68–72

COBE Laboratories, Inc., 13 159–61

Coberco *see* Friesland Coberco Dairy Foods Holding N.V.

Cobham plc, 30 129–32

Coborn's, Inc., 30 133–35

Cobra Electronics Corporation, 14 117–19

Cobra Golf Inc., 16 108–10

Coca-Cola Bottling Co. Consolidated, 10 222–24

The Coca-Cola Company, I 232–35; 10 225–28 (upd.); 32 111–16 (upd.); 67 111–17 (upd.)

Coca-Cola Enterprises, Inc., 13 162–64

Cochlear Ltd., 77 108–11

Cockerill Sambre Group, IV 51–53; 26 81–84 (upd.) *see also* Arcelor Gent.

Codelco *see* Corporacion Nacional del Cobre de Chile.

Coeur d'Alene Mines Corporation, 20 148–51

COFCO *see* China National Cereals, Oils and Foodstuffs Import and Export Corp.

The Coffee Beanery, Ltd., 95 100–05

Coffee Holding Co., Inc., 95 106–09

Coflexip S.A., 25 103–05 *see also* Technip.

Cogent Communications Group, Inc., 55 107–10

Cogentrix Energy, Inc., 10 229–31

Cognex Corporation, 76 102–06

Cognizant Technology Solutions Corporation, 59 128–30

Cognos Inc., 44 108–11

Coherent, Inc., 31 122–25

Cohu, Inc., 32 117–19

Coinmach Laundry Corporation, 20 152–54

Coinstar, Inc., 44 112–14

Colas S.A., 31 126–29

Cold Spring Granite Company, 16 111–14; 67 118–22 (upd.)

Cold Stone Creamery, 69 98–100

Coldwater Creek Inc., 21 129–31; 74 88–91 (upd.)

Coldwell Banker Co. *see* CB Richard Ellis Group, Inc.

Cole National Corporation, 13 165–67; 76 107–10 (upd.)

Cole's Quality Foods, Inc., 68 92–94

The Coleman Company, Inc., 9 127–29; 30 136–39 (upd.)

Coleman Natural Products, Inc., 68 89–91

Coles Express Inc., 15 109–11

Coles Group Limited, V 33–35; 20 155–58 (upd.); 85 49–56 (upd.)

Colfax Corporation, 58 65–67

Colgate-Palmolive Company, III 23–26; 14 120–23 (upd.); 35 110–15 (upd.); 71 105–10 (upd.)

Collectors Universe, Inc., 48 98–100

Colliers International Property Consultants Inc., 92 56–59

Collins & Aikman Corporation, 13 168–70; 41 91–95 (upd.)

Collins Industries, Inc., 33 105–07

Colonial Properties Trust, 65 115–17

Colonial Williamsburg Foundation, 53 105–07

Color Kinetics Incorporated, 85 57–60

Colorado Baseball Management, Inc., 72 75–78

Colorado Boxed Beef Company, 100 117–20

Colorado MEDtech, Inc., 48 101–05

Colt Industries Inc., I 434–36

COLT Telecom Group plc, 41 96–99

Colt's Manufacturing Company, Inc., 12 70–72

Columbia Forest Products Inc., 78 74–77

The Columbia Gas System, Inc., V 580–82; 16 115–18 (upd.)

Columbia/HCA Healthcare Corporation, 15 112–14

Columbia House Company, 69 101–03

Columbia Sportswear Company, 19 94–96; 41 100–03 (upd.)

Columbia TriStar Motion Pictures Companies, II 135–37; 12 73–76 (upd.)

Columbus McKinnon Corporation, 37 95–98

Com Ed *see* Commonwealth Edison.

Comair Holdings Inc., 13 171–73; 34 116–20 (upd.)

Combe Inc., 72 79–82

Comcast Corporation, 7 90–92; 24 120–24 (upd.)

Comdial Corporation, 21 132–35

Comdisco, Inc., 9 130–32

Comerci *see* Controladora Comercial Mexicana, S.A. de C.V.

Comerica Incorporated, 40 115–17; 101 120–25 (upd.)

COMFORCE Corporation, 40 118–20

Comfort Systems USA, Inc., 101 126–29

Cominco Ltd., 37 99–102

Command Security Corporation, 57 71–73

Commerce Clearing House, Inc., 7 93–94 *see also* CCH Inc.

Commercial Credit Company, 8 117–19 *see also* Citigroup Inc.

Commercial Federal Corporation, 12 77–79; 62 76–80 (upd.)

Commercial Financial Services, Inc., 26 85–89

Commercial Metals Company, 15 115–17; 42 81–84(upd.)

Commercial Union plc, III 233–35 *see also* Aviva PLC.

Commercial Vehicle Group, Inc., 81 91–94

Commerzbank A.G., II 256–58; 47 81–84 (upd.)

Commodore International, Ltd., 7 95–97

Commonwealth Edison, V 583–85

Commonwealth Energy System, 14 124–26

Commonwealth Telephone Enterprises, Inc., 25 106–08

CommScope, Inc., 77 112–15

Community Coffee Co. L.L.C., 53 108–10

Community Health Systems, Inc., 71 111–13

Community Newspaper Holdings, Inc., 91 128–31

Community Psychiatric Centers, 15 118–20

Compagnia Italiana dei Jolly Hotels S.p.A., 71 114–16

Compagnie de Saint-Gobain, III 675–78; 16 119–23 (upd.); 64 80–84 (upd.)

Compagnie des Alpes, 48 106–08

Compagnie des Cristalleries de Baccarat *see* Baccarat.

Compagnie des Machines Bull S.A., III 122–23 *see also* Bull S.A.; Groupe Bull.

Compagnie Financière de Paribas, II 259–60 *see also* BNP Paribas Group.

Compagnie Financière Richemont AG, 50 144–47

Compagnie Financière Sucres et Denrées S.A., 60 94–96

Compagnie Générale d'Électricité, II 12–13

Compagnie Générale des Établissements Michelin, V 236–39; 42 85–89 (upd.)

Compagnie Générale Maritime et Financière, 6 379–81

Compagnie Maritime Belge S.A., 95 110–13

Compagnie Nationale à Portefeuille, 84 55–58

Companhia Brasileira de Distribuiçao, 76 111–13

Companhia de Bebidas das Américas, 57 74–77

Companhia de Tecidos Norte de Minas - Coteminas, 77 116–19

Companhia Energética de Minas Gerais S.A., 65 118–20

Companhia Siderúrgica Nacional, 76 114–17

Companhia Suzano de Papel e Celulose S.A., 94 130–33

Companhia Vale do Rio Doce, IV 54–57; 43 111–14 (upd.)

Compania Cervecerias Unidas S.A., 70 61–63

Compañia de Minas BuenaventuraS.A.A., 92160–63

Compañia Española de Petróleos S.A. (Cepsa), IV 396–98; 56 63–66 (upd.)

Compañia Industrial de Parras, S.A. de C.V. (CIPSA), 84 59–62

Compañia Sud Americana de Vapores S.A., 100 121–24

Compaq Computer Corporation, III 124–25; 6 221–23 (upd.); 26 90–93 (upd.) *see also* Hewlett-Packard Co.

Compass Bancshares, Inc., 73 92–94

Compass Group PLC, 34 121–24

Compass Minerals International, Inc., 79 109–12

CompDent Corporation, 22 149–51

CompHealth Inc., 25 109–12

Complete Business Solutions, Inc., 31 130–33

Comprehensive Care Corporation, 15 121–23

Comptoirs Modernes S.A., 19 97–99 *see also* Carrefour SA.

CompuAdd Computer Corporation, 11 61–63

CompuCom Systems, Inc., 10 232–34

CompuDyne Corporation, 51 78–81

CompUSA, Inc., 10 235–36; 35 116–18 (upd.)

CompuServe Interactive Services, Inc., 10 237–39; 27 106–08 (upd.) *see also* AOL Time Warner Inc.

Computer Associates International, Inc., 6 224–26; 49 94–97 (upd.)

Computer Data Systems, Inc., 14 127–29

Computer Learning Centers, Inc., 26 94–96

Computer Sciences Corporation, 6 227–29

ComputerLand Corp., 13 174–76

Computervision Corporation, 10 240–42

Compuware Corporation, 10 243–45; 30 140–43 (upd.); 66 60–64 (upd.)

Comsat Corporation, 23 133–36 *see also* Lockheed Martin Corp.

Comshare Inc., 23 137–39

Comstock Resources, Inc., 47 85–87

Comtech Telecommunications Corp., 75 103–05

Comverse Technology, Inc., 15 124–26; 43 115–18 (upd.)

Con Ed *see* Consolidated Edison, Inc.

Con-way Inc., 101 130–34

ConAgra Foods, Inc., II 493–95; 12 80–82 (upd.); 42 90–94 (upd.); 85 61–68 (upd.)

Conair Corporation, 17 108–10; 69 104–08 (upd.)

Conaprole *see* Cooperativa Nacional de Productores de Leche S.A. (Conaprole).

Concentra Inc., 71 117–19

Concepts Direct, Inc., 39 93–96

Concha y Toro *see* Viña Concha y Toro S.A.

Concord Camera Corporation, 41 104–07

Concord EFS, Inc., 52 86–88

Concord Fabrics, Inc., 16 124–26

Concurrent Computer Corporation, 75 106–08

Condé Nast Publications, Inc., 13 177–81; 59 131–34 (upd.)

Cone Mills LLC, 8 120–22; 67 123–27 (upd.)

Conexant Systems, Inc., 36 121–25

Confluence Holdings Corporation, 76 118–20

Congoleum Corporation, 18 116–19; 98 52–57 (upd.)

CONMED Corporation, 87 117–120

Conn-Selmer, Inc., 55 111–14

Conn's, Inc., 67 128–30

Connecticut Light and Power Co., 13 182–84

Connecticut Mutual Life Insurance Company, III 236–38

The Connell Company, 29 129–31

Conner Peripherals, Inc., 6 230–32

Connetics Corporation, 70 64–66

Connors Bros. Income Fund *see* George Weston Ltd.

ConocoPhillips, IV 399–402; 16 127–32 (upd.); 63 104–15 (upd.)

Conrad Industries, Inc., 58 68–70

Conseco Inc., 10 246–48; 33 108–12 (upd.)

Conso International Corporation, 29 132–34

CONSOL Energy Inc., 59 135–37

Consolidated Delivery & Logistics, Inc., 24 125–28 *see also* Velocity Express Corp.

Consolidated Edison, Inc., V 586–89; 45 116–20 (upd.)

Consolidated Freightways Corporation, V 432–34; 21 136–39 (upd.); 48 109–13 (upd.)

Consolidated Graphics, Inc., 70 67–69

Consolidated Natural Gas Company, V 590–91; 19 100–02 (upd.) *see also* Dominion Resources, Inc.

Consolidated Papers, Inc., 8 123–25; 36 126–30 (upd.)

Consolidated Products, Inc., 14 130–32

Consolidated Rail Corporation, V 435–37

Consorcio ARA, S.A. de C.V., 79 113–16

Consorcio Aviacsa, S.A. de C.V., 85 69–72

Consorcio G Grupo Dina, S.A. de C.V., 36 131–33

Constar International Inc., 64 85–88

Constellation Brands, Inc., 68 95–100 (upd.)

The Consumers Gas Company Ltd., 6 476–79; 43 154 *see also* Enbridge Inc.

Consumers Power Co., 14 133–36

Consumers Union, 26 97–99

Consumers Water Company, 14 137–39

The Container Store, 36 134–36

ContiGroup Companies, Inc., 43 119–22 (upd.)

Continental AG, V 240–43; 56 67–72 (upd.)

Continental Airlines, Inc., I 96–98; 21 140–43 (upd.); 52 89–94 (upd.)

Continental Bank Corporation, II 261–63 *see also* Bank of America.

Continental Cablevision, Inc., 7 98–100

Continental Can Co., Inc., 15 127–30

Continental Corporation, III 239–44

Continental General Tire Corp., 23 140–42

Continental Grain Company, 10 249–51; 13 185–87 (upd.) *see also* ContiGroup Companies, Inc.

Continental Group Co., I 599–600

Continental Medical Systems, Inc., 10 252–54

Continental Resources, Inc., 89 161–65

Continucare Corporation, 101 135–38

Continuum Health Partners, Inc., 60 97–99

Control Data Corporation, III 126–28 *see also* Seagate Technology, Inc.

Control Data Systems, Inc., 10 255–57

Controladora Comercial Mexicana, S.A. de C.V., 36 137–39

Controladora Mabe, S.A. de C.V., 82 74-77

Converse Inc., 9 133–36; 31 134–38 (upd.)

Conzzeta Holding, 80 76–79

Cooker Restaurant Corporation, 20 159–61; 51 82–85 (upd.)

Cookson Group plc, III 679–82; 44 115–20 (upd.)

CoolBrands International Inc., 35 119–22

CoolSavings, Inc., 77 120–24

Coop Schweiz Genossenschaftsverband, 48 114–16

Coopagri Bretagne, 88 53–56

Cooper Cameron Corporation, 20 162–66 (upd.); 58 71–75 (upd.)

The Cooper Companies, Inc., 39 97–100

Cooper Industries, Inc., II 14–17; 44 121–25 (upd.)

Cooper Tire & Rubber Company, 8 126–28; 23 143–46 (upd.)

Cooperativa Nacional de Productores de Leche S.A. (Conaprole),92 60–63

Coopers & Lybrand, 9 137–38 *see also* PricewaterhouseCoopers.

Coors Company *see* Adolph Coors Co.

Copa Holdings, S.A., 93 164–67

Copart Inc., 23 147–49

Copec *see* Empresas Copec S.A.

The Copley Press, Inc., 23 150–52

Coppel, S.A. de C.V., 82 78–81

The Copps Corporation, 32 120–22

Cora S.A./NV, 94 134–37

Corbis Corporation, 31 139–42

Corby Distilleries Limited, 14 140–42

The Corcoran Group, Inc., 58 76–78

Cordis Corporation, 19 103–05; 46 104–07 (upd.)

Cordon Bleu *see* Le Cordon Bleu S.A.

Corel Corporation, 15 131–33; 33 113–16 (upd.); 76 121–24 (upd.)

Corelio S.A./N.V., 96 87–90

CoreStates Financial Corp, 16 111–15 *see also* Wachovia Corp.

Corinthian Colleges, Inc., 39 101–04; 92 64–69 (upd.)

The Corky McMillin Companies, 98 58–62

Cornelsen Verlagsholding GmbH & Co., 90 141–46

Corning Inc., III 683–85; 44 126–30 (upd.); 90 147–53 (upd.)

Corporación Geo, S.A. de C.V., 81 95–98

Corporación Interamericana de Entretenimiento, S.A. de C.V., 83 87-90

Corporación Internacional de Aviación, S.A. de C.V. (Cintra), 20 167–69

Corporación José R. Lindley S.A., 92 70–73

Corporación Multi-Inversiones, 94 138–42

Corporacion Nacional del Cobre de Chile, 40 121–23

The Corporate Executive Board Company, 89 166–69

Corporate Express, Inc., 22 152–55; 47 88–92 (upd.)

Corporate Software Inc., 9 139–41

Corporation for Public Broadcasting, 14 143–45; 89 170–75 (upd.)

Correctional Services Corporation, 30 144–46

Corrections Corporation of America, 23 153–55

Correos y Telegrafos S.A., 80 80–83

Corrpro Companies, Inc., 20 170–73

CORT Business Services Corporation, 26 100–02

El Corte Inglés Group, 26 128–31 (upd.)

Cortefiel S.A., 64 89–91

Corticeira Amorim, Sociedade Gestora de Participaço es Sociais, S.A., 48 117–20

Corus Bankshares, Inc., 75 109–11

Corus Group plc, 49 98–105 (upd.)

Corvi *see* Grupo Corvi S.A. de C.V.

Cosi, Inc., 53 111–13

Cosmair Inc., 8 129–32 *see also* L'Oreal.

The Cosmetic Center, Inc., 22 156–58

Cosmo Oil Co., Ltd., IV 403–04; 53 114–16 (upd.)

Cosmolab Inc., 96 91–94

Cost Plus, Inc., 27 109–11

Cost-U-Less, Inc., 51 90–93

CoStar Group, Inc., 73 95–98

Costco Wholesale Corporation, 43 123–25 (upd.)

Coto Centro Integral de Comercializacion S.A., 66 65–67

Cott Corporation, 52 95–98

Cotter & Company, V 37–38 *see also* TruServ Corp.

Cotton Incorporated, 46 108–11

Coty, Inc., 36 140–42

Coudert Brothers, 30 147–50

Council on International Educational Exchange Inc., 81 99–102

Country Kitchen International, Inc., 76 125–27

Countrywide Financial, 16 133–36; 100 125–30 (upd.)

County Seat Stores Inc., 9 142–43

Courier Corporation, 41 108–12

Courtaulds plc, V 359–61; 17 116–19 (upd.) *see also* Akzo Nobel N.V.

Courts Plc, 45 121–24

Cousins Properties Incorporated, 65 121–23

Covance Inc., 30 151–53; 98 63–68 (upd.)

Covanta Energy Corporation, 64 92–95 (upd.)

Coventry Health Care, Inc., 59 138–40

Covidien Ltd., 91 132–35

Covington & Burling, 40 124–27

Cowen Group, Inc., 92 74–77

Cowles Media Company, 23 156–58 *see also* Primedia Inc.

Cox Enterprises, Inc., IV 595–97; 22 159–63 (upd.); 67 131–35 (upd.)

Cox Radio, Inc., 89 176–80

CP *see* Canadian Pacific Railway Ltd.

CPAC, Inc., 86 92–95

CPC International Inc., II 496–98 *see also* Bestfoods.

CPI Aerostructures, Inc., 75 112–14

CPI Corp., 38 157–60

CPL *see* Carolina Power & Light Co.

CPT *see* Chunghwa Picture Tubes, Ltd.

CR England, Inc., 63 116–18

CRA International, Inc., 93 168–71

CRA Limited, IV 58–61 *see also* Rio Tinto plc.

Cracker Barrel Old Country Store, Inc., 10 258–59 *see also* CBRL Group, Inc.

Craftmade International, Inc., 44 131–33

Craig Hospital, 99 121–126

craigslist, inc., 89 181–84

Crain Communications, Inc., 12 83–86; 35 123–27 (upd.)

Cram Company *see* The George F. Cram Company, Inc.

Cramer, Berkowitz & Co., 34 125–27

Crane & Co., Inc., 26 103–06; 30 42

Crane Co., 8 133–36; 30 154–58 (upd.); 101 139–47 (upd.)

Cranium, Inc., 69 109–11

Cranswick plc, 40 128–30

Crate and Barrel, 9 144–46 *see also* Euromarket Designs Inc.

Cravath, Swaine & Moore, 43 126–28

Crawford & Company, 87 121–126

Cray Inc., III 129–31; 16 137–40 (upd.); 75 115–21 (upd.)

Dennison Manufacturing Company *see* Avery Dennison Corp.

DENSO Corporation, 46 121–26 (upd.)

Dentsply International Inc., 10 270–72

Dentsu Inc., I 9–11; **16** 166–69 (upd.); **40** 140–44 (upd.)

Denver Nuggets, 51 94–97

DEP Corporation, 20 177–80

Department 56, Inc., 14 165–67; **34** 144–47 (upd.)

DEPFA BANK PLC, 69 115–17

Deposit Guaranty Corporation, 17 132–35

DePuy, Inc., 30 162–65; **37** 110–13 (upd.)

Derco Holding Ltd., 98 99–102

Desarrolladora Homex, S.A. de C.V., 87 127–130

Desc, S.A. de C.V., 23 170–72

Deschutes Brewery, Inc., 57 107–09

Deseret Management Corporation, 101 161–65

Designer Holdings Ltd., 20 181–84

Desnoes and Geddes Limited, 79 136–39

Destec Energy, Inc., 12 99–101

Detroit Diesel Corporation, 10 273–75; **74** 100–03 (upd.)

The Detroit Edison Company, V 592–95 *see also* DTE Energy Co.

The Detroit Lions, Inc., 55 119–21

The Detroit Pistons Basketball Company, 41 124–27

Detroit Red Wings, 74 104–06

Detroit Tigers Baseball Club, Inc., 46 127–30

Deutsch, Inc., 42 107–10

Deutsche Babcock AG, III 465–66

Deutsche Bahn AG, 46 131–35 (upd.)

Deutsche Bank AG, II 278–80; **40** 145–51 (upd.)

Deutsche Börse AG, 59 151–55

Deutsche BP Aktiengesellschaft, 7 140–43

Deutsche Bundepost Telekom, V 287–90 *see also* Deutsche Telekom AG

Deutsche Bundesbahn, V 444–47

Deutsche Fussball Bund e.V., 98 103–07

Deutsche Lufthansa AG, I 110–11; **26** 113–16 (upd.); **68** 105–09 (upd.)

Deutsche Post AG, 29 152–58

Deutsche Steinzeug Cremer & Breuer Aktiengesellschaft, 91 144–48

Deutsche Telekom AG, 48 130–35 (upd.)

Deutscher Sparkassen- und Giroverband (DSGV), 84 98–102

Deutz AG, 39 122–26

Deveaux S.A., 41 128–30

Developers Diversified Realty Corporation, 69 118–20

DeVito/Verdi, 85 85–88

Devon Energy Corporation, 61 73–75

Devoteam S.A., 94 151–54

Devro plc, 55 122–24

DeVry Inc., 29 159–61; **82** 86–90 (upd.)

Devtek Corporation *see* Héroux-Devtek Inc.

Dewberry, 78 83–86

Dewey Ballantine LLP, 48 136–39

Dex Media, Inc., 65 128–30

Dexia NV/SA, 42 111–13; **88** 66–69 (upd.)

The Dexter Corporation, I 320–22; **12** 102–04 (upd.) *see also* Invitrogen Corp.

DFS Group Ltd., 66 78–80

DH Technology, Inc., 18 138–40

DHB Industries Inc., 85 89–92

DHL Worldwide Network S.A./N.V., 6 385–87; **24** 133–36 (upd.); **69** 121–25 (upd.)

Di Giorgio Corp., 12 105–07

Diadora SpA, 86 121–24

Diageo plc, 24 137–41 (upd.); **79** 140–48 (upd.)

Diagnostic Products Corporation, 73 121–24

Diagnostic Ventures Inc. *see* DVI, Inc.

Dial-A-Mattress Operating Corporation, 46 136–39

The Dial Corporation, 8 144–46; **23** 173–75 (upd.)

Dialogic Corporation, 18 141–43

Diamond of California, 64 108–11 (upd.)

Diamond Shamrock Corporation , IV 408–11 *see also* Ultramar Diamond Shamrock Corp.

DiamondCluster International, Inc., 51 98–101

Diana Shipping Inc., 95 126–29

Diavik Diamond Mines Inc., 85 93–96

Dibrell Brothers, Incorporated, 12 108–10

dick clark productions, inc., 16 170–73

Dick Corporation, 64 112–14

Dick's Sporting Goods, Inc., 59 156–59

Dickten Masch Plastics LLC, 90 158–61

Dictaphone Healthcare Solutions, 78 87–92

Diebold, Incorporated, 7 144–46; **22** 183–87 (upd.)

Diedrich Coffee, Inc., 40 152–54

Diehl Stiftung & Co. KG, 79 149–53

Dierbergs Markets Inc., 63 127–29

Diesel SpA, 40 155–57

D'Ieteren S.A./NV, 98 75–78

Dietrich & Cie *see* De Dietrich & Cie.

Dietz and Watson, Inc., 92 88–92

Digex, Inc., 46 140–43

Digi International Inc., 9 170–72

Digital Equipment Corporation, III 132–35; **6** 233–36 (upd.) *see also* Compaq Computer Corp.

Digital River, Inc., 50 156–59

Digitas Inc., 81 107–10

Dillard Paper Company, 11 74–76 *see also* International Paper Co.

Dillard's Inc., V 45–47; **16** 174–77 (upd.); **68** 110–14 (upd.)

Dillingham Construction Corporation, 44 151–54 (upd.)

Dillingham Corp., I 565–66

Dillon Companies Inc., 12 111–13

Dime Savings Bank of New York, F.S.B., 9 173–74 *see also* Washington Mutual, Inc.

Dimension Data Holdings PLC, 69 126–28

DIMON Inc., 27 124–27

Dina *see* Consorcio G Grupo Dina, S.A. de C.V.

Diodes Incorporated, 81 111–14

Dionex Corporation, 46 144–46

Dior *see* Christian Dior S.A.

Dippin' Dots, Inc., 56 84–86

Direct Focus, Inc., 47 93–95

Direct Wines Ltd., 84 103–106

Directed Electronics, Inc., 87 131–135

Directorate General of Telecommunications, 7 147–49 *see also* Chunghwa Telecom Co., Ltd.

DIRECTV, Inc., 38 174–77; **75** 128–32 (upd.)

Dirk Rossmann GmbH, 94 155–59

Discount Auto Parts, Inc., 18 144–46

Discount Drug Mart, Inc., 14 172–73

Discount Tire Company Inc., 84 107–110

Discovery Communications, Inc., 42 114–17

Discovery Partners International, Inc., 58 93–95

Discreet Logic Inc., 20 185–87 *see also* Autodesk, Inc.

Disney *see* The Walt Disney Co.

Dispatch Printing Company, 100 140–44

Distillers Co. plc, I 239–41 *see also* Diageo PLC.

Distribución y Servicio D&S S.A., 71 123–26

Distrigaz S.A., 82 91-94

ditech.com, 93 181–84

The Dixie Group, Inc., 20 188–90; **80** 88–92 (upd.)

Dixon Industries, Inc., 26 117–19

Dixon Ticonderoga Company, 12 114–16; **69** 129–33 (upd.)

Dixons Group plc, V 48–50; **19** 121–24 (upd.); **49** 110–13 (upd.)

Djarum PT, 62 96–98

DKB *see* Dai-Ichi Kangyo Bank Ltd.

DKNY *see* Donna Karan International Inc.

DLJ *see* Donaldson, Lufkin & Jenrette.

DMB&B *see* D'Arcy Masius Benton & Bowles.

DMGT *see* Daily Mail and General Trust.

DMI Furniture, Inc., 46 147–50

Do it Best Corporation, 30 166–70

Dobrogea Grup S.A., 82 95-98

Dobson Communications Corporation, 63 130–32

Doctor's Associates Inc., 67 142–45 (upd.)

The Doctors' Company, 55 125–28

Doctors Without Borders *see* Médecins Sans Frontières.

Documentum, Inc., 46 151–53

Dofasco Inc., IV 73–74; **24** 142–44 (upd.)

Dogan Sirketler Grubu Holding A.S., 83 107-110

Dogi International Fabrics S.A., 52 99-102

Dolan Media Company, 94 160-63

Dolby Laboratories Inc., 20 191-93

Dolce & Gabbana SpA, 62 99-101

Dole Food Company, Inc., 9 175-76; 31 167-70 (upd.); 68 115-19 (upd.)

Dollar Thrifty Automotive Group, Inc., 25 142-45

Dollar Tree Stores, Inc., 23 176-78; 62 102-05 (upd.)

Dollywood Corporation *see* Herschend Family Entertainment Corp.

Doman Industries Limited, 59 160-62

Dominick & Dominick LLC, 92 93-96

Dominick's Finer Foods, Inc., 56 87-89

Dominion Homes, Inc., 19 125-27

Dominion Resources, Inc., V 596-99; 54 83-87 (upd.)

Dominion Textile Inc., 12 117-19

Domino Printing Sciences PLC, 87 136-139

Domino Sugar Corporation, 26 120-22

Domino's, Inc., 7 150-53; 21 177-81 (upd.); 63 133-39 (upd.)

Domtar Corporation, IV 271-73; 89 185-91 (upd.)

Don Massey Cadillac, Inc., 37 114-16

Donaldson Company, Inc., 16 178-81; 49 114-18 (upd.)

Donaldson, Lufkin & Jenrette, Inc., 22 188-91

Donatos Pizzeria Corporation, 58 96-98

Donna Karan International Inc., 15 145-47; 56 90-93 (upd.)

Donnelly Corporation, 12 120-22; 35 147-50 (upd.)

Donnkenny, Inc., 17 136-38

Donruss Playoff L.P., 66 81-84

Dooney & Bourke Inc., 84 111-114

Dorel Industries Inc., 59 163-65

Dorian Drake International Inc., 96 106-09

Dorling Kindersley Holdings plc, 20 194-96 *see also* Pearson plc.

Dorsey & Whitney LLP, 47 96-99

Doskocil Companies, Inc., 12 123-25 *see also* Foodbrands America, Inc.

Dot Foods, Inc., 69 134-37

Dot Hill Systems Corp., 93 185-88

Double-Cola Co.-USA, 70 74-76

DoubleClick Inc., 46 154-57

Doubletree Corporation, 21 182-85

Douglas & Lomason Company, 16 182-85

Doux S.A., 80 93-96

Dover Corporation, III 467-69; 28 101-05 (upd.); 90 162-67 (upd.)

Dover Downs Entertainment, Inc., 43 139-41

Dover Publications Inc., 34 148-50

The Dow Chemical Company, I 323-25; 8 147-50 (upd.); 50 160-64 (upd.)

Dow Jones & Company, Inc., IV 601-03; 19 128-31 (upd.); 47 100-04 (upd.)

Dow Jones Telerate, Inc., 10 276-78 *see also* Reuters Group PLC.

DP World, 81 115-18

DPL Inc., 6 480-82; 96 110-15 (upd.)

DXP Enterprises, Inc., 101 166-69

DQE, 6 483-85; 38 40

Dr. August Oetker KG, 51 102-06

Dr Pepper/Seven Up, Inc., 9 177-78; 32 154-57 (upd.)

Dr. Reddy's Laboratories Ltd., 59 166-69

Drackett Professional Products, 12 126-28 *see also* S.C. Johnson & Son, Inc.

Draftfcb, 94 164-68

Dragados y Construcciones *see* Grupo Dragados SA.

Drägerwerk AG, 83 111-114

Drake Beam Morin, Inc., 44 155-57

Draper and Kramer Inc., 96 116-19

Draper Fisher Jurvetson, 91 149-52

Dräxlmaier Group, 90 168-72

Dreams Inc., 97 133-3

DreamWorks SKG, 43 142-46

The Drees Company, Inc., 41 131-33

Dresdner Bank A.G., II 281-83; 57 110-14 (upd.)

Dresdner Kleinwort Wasserstein, 60 110-13 (upd.)

The Dress Barn, Inc., 24 145-46

Dresser Industries, Inc., III 470-73; 55 129-31 (upd.)

Drew Industries Inc., 28 106-08

Drexel Burnham Lambert Incorporated, II 407-09 *see also* New Street Capital Inc.

Drexel Heritage Furnishings Inc., 12 129-31

Dreyer's Grand Ice Cream, Inc., 17 139-41 *see also* Nestlé S.A.

The Dreyfus Corporation, 70 77-80

DRI *see* Dominion Resources, Inc.

Drie Mollen Holding B.V., 99 135-138

Dril-Quip, Inc., 81 119-21

Drinker, Biddle and Reath L.L.P., 92 97-101

DriveTime Automotive Group Inc., 68 120-24 (upd.)

Drs. Foster & Smith, Inc., 62 106-08

DRS Technologies, Inc., 58 99-101

Drug Emporium, Inc., 12 132-34 *see also* Big A Drug Stores Inc.

Drypers Corporation, 18 147-49

DryShips Inc., 95 130-33

DS Smith Plc, 61 76-79

DSC Communications Corporation, 12 135-37 *see also* Alcatel S.A.

DSGV *see* Deutscher Sparkassen- und Giroverband (DSGV).

DSM N.V., I 326-27; 56 94-96 (upd.)

DSW Inc., 73 125-27

DTAG *see* Dollar Thrifty Automotive Group, Inc.

DTE Energy Company, 20 197-201 (upd.); 94 169-76 (upd.)

DTS, Inc., 80 97-101

Du Pareil au Même, 43 147-49

Du Pont *see* E.I. du Pont de Nemours & Co.

Dualstar Entertainment Group LLC, 76 141-43

Duane Reade Holding Corp., 21 186-88

Ducati Motor Holding SpA, 30 171-73; 86 125-29 (upd.)

Duck Head Apparel Company, Inc., 42 118-21

Ducks Unlimited, Inc., 87 140-143

Duckwall-ALCO Stores, Inc., 24 147-49

Ducommun Incorporated, 30 174-76

Duferco Group, 94 177-80

Duke Energy Corporation, V 600-02; 27 128-31 (upd.)

Duke Realty Corporation, 57 115-17

The Dun & Bradstreet Corporation, IV 604-05; 19 132-34 (upd.); 61 80-84 (upd.)

Dun & Bradstreet Software Services Inc., 11 77-79

Dunavant Enterprises, Inc., 54 88-90

Duncan Aviation, Inc., 94 181-84

Duncan Toys Company, 55 132-35

Dunham's Athleisure Corporation, 98 108-11

Dunn-Edwards Corporation, 56 97-99

Dunn Industries, Inc. *see* JE Dunn Construction Group, Inc.

Dunnes Stores Ltd., 58 102-04

Duplex Products, Inc., 17 142-44

Dupont *see* E.I. du Pont de Nemours & Co.

Duracell International Inc., 9 179-81; 71 127-31 (upd.)

Durametallic, 21 189-91 *see also* Duriron Company Inc.

Duriron Company Inc., 17 145-47 *see also* Flowserve Corp.

Dürkopp Adler AG, 65 131-34

Duron Inc., 72 91-93 *see also* The Sherwin-Williams Co.

Dürr AG, 44 158-61

Duty Free International, Inc., 11 80-82 *see also* World Duty Free Americas, Inc.

DVI, Inc., 51 107-09

Duvernay Oil Corp., 83 115-118

Dyax Corp., 89 192-95

Dyckerhoff AG, 35 151-54

Dycom Industries, Inc., 57 118-20

Dyersburg Corporation, 21 192-95

Dylan's Candy Bar, LLC, 99 139-141

Dylex Limited, 29 162-65

Dynatec Corporation, 87 144-147

Dynaction S.A., 67 146-48

Dynamic Materials Corporation, 81 122-25

Dynatech Corporation, 13 194-96

Dynatronics Corporation, 99 142-146

DynCorp, 45 145-47

Dynea, 68 125-27

Dyneff S.A., 98 112-15

Dynegy Inc., 49 119-22 (upd.)

Dyson Group PLC, 71 132–34

E

E. & J. Gallo Winery, I 242–44; 7
154–56 (upd.); 28 109–11 (upd.)
E! Entertainment Television Inc., 17
148–50
E-Systems, Inc., 9 182–85
E*Trade Financial Corporation, 20
206–08; 60 114–17 (upd.)
E-Z Serve Corporation, 17 169–71
E-Z-EM Inc., 89 196–99
E H Booth & Company Ltd., 90
173–76
E.I. du Pont de Nemours and
Company, I 328–30; 8 151–54
(upd.); 26 123–27 (upd.); 73 128–33
(upd.)
E.On AG, 50 165–73 (upd.)
E.piphany, Inc., 49 123–25
E.W. Howell Co., Inc., 72 94–96 *see also*
Obayashi Corporation
The E.W. Scripps Company, IV 606–09;
7 157–59 (upd.); 28 122–26 (upd.);
66 85–89 (upd.)
EADS N.V. *see* European Aeronautic
Defence and Space Company EADS
N.V.
EADS SOCATA, 54 91–94
Eagle Hardware & Garden, Inc., 16
186–89 *see also* Lowe's Companies, Inc.
Eagle-Picher Industries, Inc., 8 155–58;
23 179–83 (upd.) *see also* PerkinElmer
Inc.
Eagle-Tribune Publishing Co., 91
153–57
Earl Scheib, Inc., 32 158–61
Earle M. Jorgensen Company, 82
99–102
The Earthgrains Company, 36 161–65
EarthLink, Inc., 36 166–68
East Japan Railway Company, V
448–50; 66 90–94 (upd.)
East Penn Manufacturing Co., Inc., 79
154–57
Easter Seals, Inc., 58 105–07
Eastern Airlines, I 101–03
The Eastern Company, 48 140–43
Eastern Enterprises, 6 486–88
EastGroup Properties, Inc., 67 149–51
Eastland Shoe Corporation, 82 103–106
Eastman Chemical Company, 14
174–75; 38 178–81 (upd.)
Eastman Kodak Company, III 474–77;
7 160–64 (upd.); 36 169–76 (upd.);
91 158–69 (upd.)
Easton Sports, Inc., 66 95–97
easyJet Airline Company Limited, 39
127–29; 52 330
Eateries, Inc., 33 138–40
Eaton Corporation, I 154–55; 10
279–80 (upd.); 67 152–56 (upd.)
Eaton Vance Corporation, 18 150–53
eBay Inc., 32 162–65; 67 157–61 (upd.)
Ebara Corporation, 83 119–122
EBSCO Industries, Inc., 17 151–53; 40
158–61 (upd.)

ECC Group plc, III 689–91 *see also*
English China Clays plc.
ECC International Corp., 42 122–24
Ecco Sko A/S, 62 109–11
Echlin Inc., I 156–57; 11 83–85 (upd.)
see also Dana Corp.
Echo Bay Mines Ltd., IV 75–77; 38
182–85 (upd.)
The Echo Design Group, Inc., 68
128–30
EchoStar Communications Corporation,
35 155–59
ECI Telecom Ltd., 18 154–56
Eckerd Corporation, 9 186–87 *see also*
J.C. Penney Company, Inc.
Eckes AG, 56 100–03
Eclipse Aviation Corporation, 87
148–151
Ecolab Inc., I 331–33; 13 197–200
(upd.); 34 151–56 (upd.); 85 97–105
(upd.)
eCollege.com, 85 106–09
Ecology and Environment, Inc., 39
130–33
The Economist Group Ltd., 67 162–65
Ecopetrol *see* Empresa Colombiana de
Petróleos.
ECS S.A., 12 138–40
Ed S.A.S., 88 70–73
Edasa *see* Embotelladoras del Atlántico,
S.A.
Eddie Bauer Holdings, Inc., 9 188–90;
36 177–81 (upd.); 87 152–159 (upd.)
Edeka Zentrale A.G., II 621–23; 47
105–07 (upd.)
edel music AG, 44 162–65
Edelbrock Corporation, 37 117–19
Edelman, 62 112–15
EDF *see* Electricité de France.
EDGAR Online, Inc., 91 170–73
Edgars Consolidated Stores Ltd., 66
98–100
Edge Petroleum Corporation, 67
166–68
Edipresse S.A., 82 107–110
Edison Brothers Stores, Inc., 9 191–93
Edison International, 56 104–07 (upd.)
Edison Schools Inc., 37 120–23
Éditions Gallimard, 72 97–101
Editis S.A., 78 93–97
Editora Abril S.A *see* Abril S.A.
Editorial Television, S.A. de C.V., 57
121–23
EdK *see* Edeka Zentrale A.G.
Edmark Corporation, 14 176–78; 41
134–37 (upd.)
EDO Corporation, 46 158–61
EDP Group *see* Electricidade de Portugal,
S.A.
The Edrington Group Ltd., 88 74–78
EDS *see* Electronic Data Systems Corp.
Educate Inc., 86 130–35 (upd.)
Education Management Corporation, 35
160–63
Educational Broadcasting Corporation,
48 144–47
Educational Testing Service, 12 141–43;
62 116–20 (upd.)

Edw. C. Levy Co., 42 125–27
Edward D. Jones & Company L.P., 30
177–79; 66 101–04 (upd.)
Edward Hines Lumber Company, 68
131–33
Edward J. DeBartolo Corporation, 8
159–62
Edwards and Kelcey, 70 81–83
Edwards Brothers, Inc., 92 102–06
Edwards Theatres Circuit, Inc., 31
171–73
EFJ, Inc., 81 126–29
EG&G Incorporated, 8 163–65; 29
166–69 (upd.)
Egan Companies, Inc., 94 185–88
EGAT *see* Electricity Generating Authority
of Thailand (EGAT).
Egghead.com, Inc., 9 194–95; 31
174–77 (upd.)
EGL, Inc., 59 170–73
Egmont Group, 93 189–93
EgyptAir, 6 84–86; 27 132–35 (upd.)
Egyptian General Petroleum
Corporation, IV 412–14; 51 110–14
(upd.)
eHarmony.com Inc., 71 135–38
Eiffage, 27 136–38
8x8, Inc., 94 189–92
800-JR Cigar, Inc., 27 139–41
84 Lumber Company, 9 196–97; 39
134–36 (upd.)
Eileen Fisher Inc., 61 85–87
Einstein/Noah Bagel Corporation, 29
170–73
eircom plc, 31 178–81 (upd.)
Eisai Co., Ltd., 101 170–73
Eka Chemicals AB, 92 107–10
Ekco Group, Inc., 16 190–93
El Al Israel Airlines Ltd., 23 184–87
El Camino Resources International,
Inc., 11 86–88
El Chico Restaurants, Inc., 19 135–38;
36 162–63
El Corte Inglés, S.A., V 51–53; 26
128–31 (upd.)
El Paso Corporation, 66 105–08 (upd.)
El Paso Electric Company, 21 196–98
El Paso Natural Gas Company, 12
144–46 *see also* El Paso Corp.
El Pollo Loco, Inc., 69 138–40
El Puerto de Liverpool, S.A.B. de C.V.,
97 137–40
Elamex, S.A. de C.V., 51 115–17
Elan Corporation PLC, 63 140–43
Elano Corporation, 14 179–81
The Elder-Beerman Stores Corp., 10
281–83; 63 144–48 (upd.)
Elders IXL Ltd., I 437–39
Electrabel N.V., 67 169–71
Electric Boat Corporation, 86 136–39
Electric Lightwave, Inc., 37 124–27
Electricidade de Portugal, S.A., 47
108–11
Electricité de France, V 603–05; 41
138–41 (upd.)
Electricity Generating Authority of
Thailand (EGAT), 56 108–10
Electro Rent Corporation, 58 108–10

Electrocomponents PLC, 50 174–77
Electrolux AB, 22 24–28 (upd.); 53 124–29 (upd.)
Electrolux Group, III 478–81
Electromagnetic Sciences Inc., 21 199–201
Electronic Arts Inc., 10 284–86; 85 110–15 (upd.)
Electronic Data Systems Corporation, III 136–38; 28 112–16 (upd.) *see also* Perot Systems Corp.
Electronics Boutique Holdings Corporation, 72 102–05
Electronics for Imaging, Inc., 15 148–50; 43 150–53 (upd.)
Elektra *see* Grupo Elektra, S.A. de C.V.
Elektra Entertainment Group, 64 115–18
Elektrowatt AG, 6 489–91 *see also* Siemens AG.
Element K Corporation, 94 193–96
Elementis plc, 40 162–68 (upd.)
Elephant Pharmacy, Inc., 83 123-126
Elf Aquitaine SA, 21 202–06 (upd.) *see also* Société Nationale Elf Aquitaine.
Eli Lilly and Company, I 645–47; 11 89–91 (upd.); 47 112–16 (upd.)
Elior SA, 49 126–28
Elite World S.A., 94 197–201
Elizabeth Arden, Inc., 8 166–68; 40 169–72 (upd.)
Eljer Industries, Inc., 24 150–52
Elkay Manufacturing Company, 73 134–36
ElkCorp, 52 103–05
Ellen Tracy, Inc., 55 136–38
Ellerbe Becket, 41 142–45
Ellett Brothers, Inc., 17 154–56
Elliott-Lewis Corporation, 100 145–48
Elma Electronic AG, 83 127-130
Elmer Candy Corporation, 88 79–82
Elmer's Restaurants, Inc., 42 128–30
Elpida Memory, Inc., 83 131-134
ElringKlinger AG, 100 149–55
Elscint Ltd., 20 202–05
Elsevier NV, IV 610–11 *see also* Reed Elsevier.
Elsinore Corporation, 48 148–51
Elvis Presley Enterprises, Inc., 61 88–90
EMAP plc, 35 164–66
EMBARQ Corporation, 83 135-138
Embers America Restaurants, 30 180–82
Embotelladora Andina S.A., 71 139–41
Embraer *see* Empresa Brasileira de Aeronáutica S.A.
Embrex, Inc., 72 106–08
EMC Corporation, 12 147–49; 46 162–66 (upd.)
EMCOR Group Inc., 60 118–21
EMCORE Corporation, 97 141–44
Emerson, 46 167–71 (upd.)
Emerson Electric Co., II 18–21
Emerson Radio Corp., 30 183–86
Emery Worldwide Airlines, Inc., 6 388–91; 25 146–50 (upd.)
Emge Packing Co., Inc., 11 92–93
EMI Group plc, 22 192–95 (upd.); 81 130–37 (upd.)

Emigrant Savings Bank, 59 174–76
The Emirates Group, 39 137–39; 81 138–42 (upd.)
Emmis Communications Corporation, 47 117–21
Empi, Inc., 27 132–35
Empire Blue Cross and Blue Shield, III 245–46 *see also* WellChoice, Inc.
The Empire District Electric Company, 77 138–41
Empire Resorts, Inc., 72 109–12
Empire Resources, Inc., 81 143–46
Employee Solutions, Inc., 18 157–60
Empresa Brasileira de Aeronáutica S.A. (Embraer), 36 182–84
Empresa Colombiana de Petróleos, IV 415–18
Empresas Almacenes Paris S.A., 71 142–44
Empresas CMPC S.A., 70 84–87
Empresas Copec S.A., 69 141–44
Empresas ICA Sociedad Controladora, S.A. de C.V., 41 146–49
Empresas Polar SA, 55 139–41 (upd.)
Empresas Públicas de Medellín S.A.E.S.P., 91 174–77
Enbridge Inc., 43 154–58
ENCAD, Incorporated, 25 151–53 *see also* Eastman Kodak Co.
Encompass Services Corporation, 33 141–44
Encore Acquisition Company, 73 137–39
Encore Computer Corporation, 13 201–02; 74 107–10 (upd.)
Encore Wire Corporation, 81 147–50
Encyclopedia Britannica, Inc., 7 165–68; 39 140–44 (upd.)
Endemol Entertainment Holding NV, 46 172–74; 53 154
ENDESA S.A., V 606–08; 46 175–79 (upd.)
Endo Pharmaceuticals Holdings Inc., 71 145–47
Endurance Specialty Holdings Ltd., 85 116–19
Energen Corporation, 21 207–09; 97 145–49 (upd.)
Energis plc, 44 363; 47 122–25
Energizer Holdings, Inc., 32 171–74
Energy Brands Inc., 88 83–86
Energy Conversion Devices, Inc., 75 133–36
Enersis S.A., 73 140–43
EnerSys Inc., 99 147–151
Enesco Corporation, 11 94–96
Engelhard Corporation, IV 78–80; 21 210–14 (upd.); 72 113–18 (upd.)
Engineered Support Systems, Inc., 59 177–80
Engle Homes, Inc., 46 180–82
English China Clays Ltd., 15 151–54 (upd.); 40 173–77 (upd.)
Engraph, Inc., 12 150–51 *see also* Sonoco Products Co.
ENI S.p.A., 69 145–50 (upd.)
ENMAX Corporation, 83 139-142

Ennis, Inc., 21 215–17; 97 150–54 (upd.)
Enodis plc, 68 134–37
EnPro Industries, Inc., 93 194–98
Enquirer/Star Group, Inc., 10 287–88 *see also* American Media, Inc.
Enrich International, Inc., 33 145–48
Enron Corporation, V 609–10; 19 139–41; 46 183–86 (upd.)
ENSCO International Incorporated, 57 124–26
Enserch Corp., V 611–13 *see also* Texas Utilities.
Enskilda S.A. *see* Skandinaviska Enskilda Banken AB.
Enso-Gutzeit Oy, IV 274–77 *see also* Stora Enso Oyj.
Ente Nazionale Idrocarburi, IV 419–22 *see also* ENI S.p.A.
Ente Nazionale per l'Energia Elettrica, V 614–17
Entercom Communications Corporation, 58 111–12
Entergy Corporation, V 618–20; 45 148–51 (upd.)
Enterprise Inns plc, 59 181–83
Enterprise Oil plc, 11 97–99; 50 178–82 (upd.)
Enterprise Rent-A-Car Company, 6 392–93; 69 151–54 (upd.)
Entertainment Distribution Company, 89 200–03
Entravision Communications Corporation, 41 150–52
Entreprise Nationale Sonatrach, IV 423–25 *see also* Sonatrach.
Envirodyne Industries, Inc., 17 157–60
Environmental Industries, Inc., 31 182–85
Environmental Power Corporation, 68 138–40
Environmental Systems Research Institute Inc. (ESRI), 62 121–24
Enzo Biochem, Inc., 41 153–55
Eon Labs, Inc., 67 172–74
EPAM Systems Inc., 96 120–23
EPCOR Utilities Inc., 81 151–54
Epic Systems Corporation, 62 125–28
EPIQ Systems, Inc., 56 111–13
Equant N.V., 52 106–08
Equifax, Inc., 6 23–25; 28 117–21 (upd.); 90 177–83 (upd.)
Equistar Chemicals, LP, 71 148–50
Equitable Life Assurance Society of the United States, III 247–49
Equitable Resources, Inc., 6 492–94; 54 95–98 (upd.)
Equity Marketing, Inc., 26 136–38
Equity Office Properties Trust, 54 99–102
Equity Residential, 49 129–32
Equus Computer Systems, Inc., 49 133–35
Eram SA, 51 118–20
Eramet, 73 144–47
Ercros S.A., 80 102–05
ERGO Versicherungsgruppe AG, 44 166–69

Ergon, Inc., 95 134–37
Erickson Retirement Communities, 57 127–30
Ericsson *see* Telefonaktiebolaget LM Ericsson.
Eridania Béghin-Say S.A., 36 185–88
Erie Indemnity Company, 35 167–69
ERLY Industries Inc., 17 161–62
Ermenegildo Zegna SpA, 63 149–52
Ernie Ball, Inc., 56 114–16
Ernst & Young, 9 198–200; **29** 174–77 (upd.)
Eroski *see* Grupo Eroski
Erste Bank der Osterreichischen Sparkassen AG, 69 155–57
ESCADA AG, 71 151–53
Escalade, Incorporated, 19 142–44
Eschelon Telecom, Inc., 72 119–22
ESCO Technologies Inc., 87 160–163
Eskimo Pie Corporation, 21 218–20
Espírito Santo Financial Group S.A., 79 158–63 (upd.)
ESPN, Inc., 56 117–22
Esporta plc, 35 170–72
Esprit de Corp., 8 169–72; **29** 178–82 (upd.)
ESS Technology, Inc., 22 196–98
Essar Group Ltd., 79 164–67
Essef Corporation, 18 161–63 *see also* Pentair, Inc.
Esselte, 64 119–21
Esselte Leitz GmbH & Co. KG, 48 152–55
Esselte Pendaflex Corporation, 11 100–01
Essence Communications, Inc., 24 153–55
Essex Corporation, 85 120–23
Essilor International, 21 221–23
The Estée Lauder Companies Inc., 9 201–04; **30** 187–91 (upd.); **92** 199–207 (upd.)
Esterline Technologies Corp., 15 155–57
Estes Express Lines, Inc., 86 140–43
Etablissements Economiques du Casino Guichard, Perrachon et ie, S.C.A., 12 152–54 *see also* Casino Guichard-Perrachon S.A.
Etablissements Franz Colruyt N.V., 68 141–43
Établissements Jacquot and Cie S.A.S., 92 111–14
Etam Developpement SA, 44 170–72
ETBD *see* Europe Through the Back Door.
Eternal Word Television Network, Inc., 57 131–34
Ethan Allen Interiors, Inc., 12 155–57; **39** 145–48 (upd.)
Ethicon, Inc., 23 188–90
Ethiopian Airlines, 81 155–58
Ethyl Corp., I 334–36; **10** 289–91 (upd.)
Etienne Aigner AG, 52 109–12
Etihad Airways PJSC, 89 204–07
EToys, Inc., 37 128–30
ETS *see* Educational Testing Service.

Euralis *see* Groupe Euralis.
Eurazeo, 80 106–09
The Eureka Company, 12 158–60 *see also* White Consolidated Industries Inc.
Euro Disney S.C.A., 20 209–12; **58** 113–16 (upd.)
Euro RSCG Worldwide S.A., 13 203–05
Eurocopter S.A., 80 110–13
Eurofins Scientific S.A., 70 88–90
Euromarket Designs Inc., 31 186–89 (upd.); **99** 152–157 (upd.)
Euronet Worldwide, Inc., 83 143–146
Euronext N.V., 37 131–33; **89** 208–11 (upd.)
Europe Through the Back Door Inc., 65 135–38
European Aeronautic Defence and Space Company EADS N.V., 52 113–16 (upd.)
European Investment Bank, 66 109–11
Eurotunnel Group, 13 206–08; **37** 134–38 (upd.)
EVA Airways Corporation, 51 121–23
Evans & Sutherland Computer Corporation, 19 145–49; **78** 98–103 (upd.)
Evans, Inc., 30 192–94
Everex Systems, Inc., 16 194–96
Evergreen Energy, Inc., 97 155–59
Evergreen International Aviation, Inc., 53 130–33
Evergreen Marine Corporation (Taiwan) Ltd., 13 209–11; **50** 183–89 (upd.)
Evergreen Solar, Inc., 101 174–78
Everlast Worldwide Inc., 47 126–29
Evialis S.A., 100 156–59
Evraz Group S.A., 97 160–63
EWTN *see* Eternal Word Television Network, Inc.
Exabyte Corporation, 12 161–63; **40** 178–81 (upd.)
Exactech, Inc., 101 179–82
Exar Corp., 14 182–84
EXCEL Communications Inc., 18 164–67
Excel Technology, Inc., 65 139–42
Executive Jet, Inc., 36 189–91 *see also* NetJets Inc.
Executone Information Systems, Inc., 13 212–14; **15** 195
Exel plc, 51 124–30 (upd.)
Exelon Corporation, 48 156–63 (upd.); **49** 65
Exide Electronics Group, Inc., 20 213–15
Exito *see* Almacenes Exito S.A.
Expand SA, 48 164–66
Expedia, Inc., 58 117–21
Expeditors International of Washington Inc., 17 163–65; **78** 104–08 (upd.)
Experian Information Solutions Inc., 45 152–55
Exponent, Inc., 95 138–41
Exportadora Bananera Noboa, S.A., 91 178–81
Express Scripts Inc., 17 166–68; **44** 173–76 (upd.)
Extended Stay America, Inc., 41 156–58

Extendicare Health Services, Inc., 6 181–83
Extreme Pizza *see* OOC Inc.
EXX Inc., 65 143–45
Exxon Mobil Corporation, IV 426–30; **7** 169–73 (upd.); **32** 175–82 (upd.); **67** 175–86 (upd.)
Eye Care Centers of America, Inc., 69 158–60
Ezaki Glico Company Ltd., 72 123–25
EZCORP Inc., 43 159–61

F

F&W Publications, Inc., 71 154–56
F.A.O. Schwarz *see* FAO Schwarz
The F. Dohmen Co., 77 142–45
F. Hoffmann-La Roche & Co. A.G., I 642–44; **50** 190–93 (upd.)
F. Korbel & Bros. Inc., 68 144–46
F.W. Webb Company, 95 142–45
Fab Industries, Inc., 27 142–44
Fabbrica D' Armi Pietro Beretta S.p.A., 39 149–51
Faber-Castell *see* A.W. Faber-Castell Unternehmensverwaltung GmbH & Co.
Fabri-Centers of America Inc., 16 197–99 *see also* Jo-Ann Stores, Inc.
Facebook, Inc., 90 184–87
Facom S.A., 32 183–85
FactSet Research Systems Inc., 73 148–50
Faegre & Benson LLP, 97 164–67
FAG—Kugelfischer Georg Schäfer AG, 62 129–32
Fair Grounds Corporation, 44 177–80
Fair, Isaac and Company, 18 168–71
Fairchild Dornier GmbH, 9 205–08; **48** 167–71 (upd.)
Fairclough Construction Group plc, I 567–68
Fairfax Financial Holdings Limited, 57 135–37
Fairfax Media Ltd., 94 202–08 (upd.)
Fairfield Communities, Inc., 36 192–95
Fairmont Hotels & Resorts Inc., 69 161–63
Faiveley S.A., 39 152–54
Falcon Products, Inc., 33 149–51
Falconbridge Limited, 49 136–39
Fallon Worldwide, 22 199–201; **71** 157–61 (upd.)
Family Christian Stores, Inc., 51 131–34
Family Dollar Stores, Inc., 13 215–17; **62** 133–36 (upd.)
Family Golf Centers, Inc., 29 183–85
Family Sports Concepts, Inc., 100 160–63
Famous Brands Ltd., 86 144–47
Famous Dave's of America, Inc., 40 182–84
Fannie Mae, 45 156–59 (upd.)
Fannie May Confections Brands, Inc., 80 114–18
Fansteel Inc., 19 150–52
Fanuc Ltd., III 482–83; **17** 172–74 (upd.); **75** 137–40 (upd.)

Foxboro Company, 13 233–35

FoxHollow Technologies, Inc., 85 132–35

FoxMeyer Health Corporation, 16 212–14 *see also* McKesson Corp.

Foxworth-Galbraith Lumber Company, 91 188–91

FPL Group, Inc., V 623–25; 49 143–46 (upd.)

Framatome SA, 19 164–67 aee also Alcatel S.A.; AREVA.

France Telecom S.A., V 291–93; 21 231–34 (upd.); 99 173–179 (upd.)

Francotyp-Postalia Holding AG, 92 123–27

Frank J. Zamboni & Co., Inc., 34 173–76

Frank Russell Company, 46 198–200

Frank's Nursery & Crafts, Inc., 12 178–79

Franke Holding AG, 76 157–59

Frankel & Co., 39 166–69

Frankfurter Allgemeine Zeitung GmbH, 66 121–24

Franklin Covey Company, 11 147–49; 37 149–52 (upd.)

Franklin Electric Company, Inc., 43 177–80

Franklin Electronic Publishers, Inc., 23 209–13

The Franklin Mint, 69 181–84

Franklin Resources, Inc., 9 239–40

Franz Inc., 80 122–25

Fraport AG Frankfurt Airport Services Worldwide, 90 197–202

Fraser & Neave Ltd., 54 116–18

Fred Alger Management, Inc., 97 168–72

Fred Meyer Stores, Inc., V 54–56; 20 222–25 (upd.); 64 135–39 (upd.)

Fred Usinger Inc., 54 119–21

The Fred W. Albrecht Grocery Co., 13 236–38

Fred Weber, Inc., 61 100–02

Fred's, Inc., 23 214–16; 62 144–47 (upd.)

Freddie Mac, 54 122–25

Frederick Atkins Inc., 16 215–17

Frederick's of Hollywood Inc., 16 218–20; 59 190–93 (upd.)

Freedom Communications, Inc., 36 222–25

Freeport-McMoRan Copper & Gold, Inc., IV 81–84; 7 185–89 (upd.); 57 145–50 (upd.)

Freescale Semiconductor, Inc., 83 151-154

Freeze.com LLC, 77 156–59

FreightCar America, Inc., 101 192–95

Freixenet S.A., 71 162–64

French Connection Group plc, 41 167–69

French Fragrances, Inc., 22 213–15 *see also* Elizabeth Arden, Inc.

Frequency Electronics, Inc., 61 103–05

Fresenius AG, 56 138–42

Fresh America Corporation, 20 226–28

Fresh Choice, Inc., 20 229–32

Fresh Enterprises, Inc., 66 125–27

Fresh Express Inc., 88 97–100

Fresh Foods, Inc., 29 201–03

FreshDirect, LLC, 84 130–133

Fretter, Inc., 10 304–06

Freudenberg & Co., 41 170–73

Fried, Frank, Harris, Shriver & Jacobson, 35 183–86

Fried. Krupp GmbH, IV 85–89 *see also* ThyssenKrupp AG.

Friedman, Billings, Ramsey Group, Inc., 53 134–37

Friedman's Inc., 29 204–06

Friedrich Grohe AG & Co. KG, 53 138–41

Friendly Ice Cream Corporation, 30 208–10; 72 141–44 (upd.)

Friesland Coberco Dairy Foods Holding N.V., 59 194–96

Frigidaire Home Products, 22 216–18

Frisch's Restaurants, Inc., 35 187–89; 92 128–32 (upd.)

Frito-Lay North America, 32 205–10; 73 151–58 (upd.)

Fritz Companies, Inc., 12 180–82

Fromageries Bel, 23 217–19; 25 83–84

Frontera Foods, Inc., 100 170–73

Frontier Airlines Holdings Inc., 22 219–21; 84 134–138 (upd.)

Frontier Corp., 16 221–23

Frontier Natural Products Co-Op, 82 121–24

Frontline Ltd., 45 163–65

Frost & Sullivan, Inc., 53 142–44

Frozen Food Express Industries, Inc., 20 233–35; 98 125–30 (upd.)

Frucor Beverages Group Ltd., 96 128–31

Fruehauf Corp., I 169–70

Fruit of the Loom, Inc., 8 200–02; 25 164–67 (upd.)

Fruth Pharmacy, Inc., 66 128–30

Fry's Electronics, Inc., 68 168–70

Frymaster Corporation, 27 159–62

FSI International, Inc., 17 192–94 *see also* FlightSafety International, Inc.

FTD Group, Inc., 99 180–185 (upd.)

FTI Consulting, Inc., 77 160–63

FTP Software, Inc., 20 236–38

Fubu, 29 207–09

Fuel Tech, Inc., 85 136–40

Fuel Systems Solutions, Inc., 97 173–77

FuelCell Energy, Inc., 75 150–53

Fugro N.V., 98 131–34

Fuji Bank, Ltd., II 291–93

Fuji Electric Co., Ltd., II 22–23; 48 180–82 (upd.)

Fuji Photo Film Co., Ltd., III 486–89; 18 183–87 (upd.); 79 177–84 (upd.)

Fuji Television Network Inc., 91 192–95

Fujisawa Pharmaceutical Company, Ltd., I 635–36; 58 132–34 (upd.) *see also* Astellas Pharma Inc.

Fujitsu-ICL Systems Inc., 11 150–51

Fujitsu Limited, III 139–41; 16 224–27 (upd.); 42 145–50 (upd.)

Fulbright & Jaworski L.L.P., 47 138–41

Fuller Smith & Turner P.L.C., 38 193–95

Funai Electric Company Ltd., 62 148–50

Funco, Inc., 20 239–41 *see also* GameStop Corp.

Fuqua Enterprises, Inc., 17 195–98

Fuqua Industries Inc., I 445–47

Furmanite Corporation, 92 133–36

Furniture Brands International, Inc., 39 170–75 (upd.)

Furon Company, 28 149–51 *see also* Compagnie de Saint-Gobain.

Furr's Restaurant Group, Inc., 53 145–48

Furr's Supermarkets, Inc., 28 152–54

Furukawa Electric Co., Ltd., III 490–92

Future Now, Inc., 12 183–85

Future Shop Ltd., 62 151–53

Fyffes Plc, 38 196–99

G

G&K Holding S.A., 95 159–62

G&K Services, Inc., 16 228–30

G A Pindar & Son Ltd., 88 101–04

G.D. Searle & Co., I 686–89; 12 186–89 (upd.); 34 177–82 (upd.)

G. Heileman Brewing Co., I 253–55 *see also* Stroh Brewery Co.

G.I.E. Airbus Industrie, I 41–43; 12 190–92 (upd.)

G.I. Joe's, Inc., 30 221–23 *see also* Joe's Sports & Outdoor.

G-III Apparel Group, Ltd., 22 222–24

G. Leblanc Corporation, 55 149–52

G.S. Blodgett Corporation, 15 183–85 *see also* Blodgett Holdings, Inc.

Gabelli Asset Management Inc., 30 211–14 *see also* Lynch Corp.

Gables Residential Trust, 49 147–49

Gadzooks, Inc., 18 188–90

GAF, I 337–40; 22 225–29 (upd.)

Gage Marketing Group, 26 147–49

Gaiam, Inc., 41 174–77

Gainsco, Inc., 22 230–32

Galardi Group, Inc., 72 145–47

Galaxy Investors, Inc., 97 178–81

Galaxy Nutritional Foods, Inc., 58 135–37

Gale International LLC, 93 221–24

Galenica AG, 84 139–142

Galeries Lafayette S.A., V 57–59; 23 220–23 (upd.)

Galey & Lord, Inc., 20 242–45; 66 131–34 (upd.)

Gallaher Group Plc, 49 150–54 (upd.)

Gallaher Limited, V 398–400; 19 168–71 (upd.)

Gallo Winery *see* E. & J. Gallo Winery.

The Gallup Organization, 37 153–56

Galoob Toys *see* Lewis Galoob Toys Inc.

Galp Energia SGPS S.A., 98 135–40

Galtronics Ltd., 100 174–77

Galyan's Trading Company, Inc., 47 142–44

The Gambrinus Company, 40 188–90

Gambro AB, 49 155–57

The GAME Group plc, 80 126–29

Gorton's, 13 243–44

Gosling Brothers Ltd., 82 146–49

Goss Holdings, Inc., 43 194–97

Gottschalks, Inc., 18 204–06; 91 211–15 (upd.)

Gould Electronics, Inc., 14 206–08

Gould Paper Corporation, 82 150–53

Goulds Pumps Inc., 24 188–91

The Governor and Company of the Bank of Scotland, 10 336–38

Goya Foods Inc., 22 245–47; 91 216–21 (upd.)

GP Strategies Corporation, 64 162–66 (upd.)

GPS Industries, Inc., 81 169–72

GPU *see* General Public Utilities Corp.

GPU, Inc., 27 182–85 (upd.)

Grace *see* W.R. Grace & Co.

GraceKennedy Ltd., 92 143–47

Graco Inc., 19 178–80; 67 191–95 (upd.)

Gradall Industries, Inc., 96 140–43

Graeter's Manufacturing Company, 86 165–68

Graham Corporation, 62 165–67

Graham Packaging Holdings Company, 87 192–196

Grampian Country Food Group, Ltd., 85 155–59

Grameen Bank, 31 219–22

Granada Group PLC, II 138–40; 24 192–95 (upd.)

Granaria Holdings B.V., 66 151–53

GranCare, Inc., 14 209–11

Grand Casinos, Inc., 20 268–70

Grand Hotel Krasnapolsky N.V., 23 227–29

Grand Metropolitan plc, I 247–49; 14 212–15 (upd.) *see also* Diageo plc.

Grand Piano & Furniture Company, 72 151–53

Grand Traverse Pie Company, 98 156–59

Grand Union Company, 7 202–04; 28 162–65 (upd.)

Grandoe Corporation, 98 160–63

Grands Vins Jean-Claude Boisset S.A., 98 164–67

GrandVision S.A., 43 198–200

Granite Broadcasting Corporation, 42 161–64

Granite City Food & Brewery Ltd., 94 214–17

Granite Construction Incorporated, 61 119–21

Granite Industries of Vermont, Inc., 73 169–72

Granite Rock Company, 26 175–78

Granite State Bankshares, Inc., 37 173–75

Grant Prideco, Inc., 57 162–64

Grant Thornton International, 57 165–67

Graphic Industries Inc., 25 182–84

Graphic Packaging Holding Company, 96 144–50 (upd.)

Gray Communications Systems, Inc., 24 196–200

Graybar Electric Company, Inc., 54 139–42

Great American Management and Investment, Inc., 8 228–31

The Great Atlantic & Pacific Tea Company, Inc., II 636–38; 16 247–50 (upd.); 55 164–69 (upd.)

Great Harvest Bread Company, 44 184–86

Great Lakes Bancorp, 8 232–33

Great Lakes Chemical Corp., I 341–42; 14 216–18 (upd.) *see also* Chemtura Corp.

Great Lakes Dredge & Dock Company, 69 194–97

Great Plains Energy Incorporated, 65 156–60 (upd.)

The Great Universal Stores plc, V 67–69; 19 181–84 (upd.) *see also* GUS plc.

Great-West Lifeco Inc., III 260–61 *see also* Power Corporation of Canada.

Great Western Financial Corporation, 10 339–41 *see also* Washington Mutual, Inc.

Great White Shark Enterprises, Inc., 89 242–45

Great Wolf Resorts, Inc., 91 222–26

Greatbatch Inc., 72 154–56

Grede Foundries, Inc., 38 214–17

Greek Organization of Football Prognostics S.A. (OPAP), 97 182–85

The Green Bay Packers, Inc., 32 223–26

Green Dot Public Schools, 99 186–189

Green Mountain Coffee, Inc., 31 227–30

Green Tree Financial Corporation, 11 162–63 *see also* Conseco, Inc.

The Greenalls Group PLC, 21 245–47

Greenberg Traurig, LLP, 65 161–63

The Greenbrier Companies, 19 185–87

Greencore Group plc, 98 168–71

Greene King plc, 31 223–26

Greene, Tweed & Company, 55 170–72

GreenMan Technologies Inc., 99 190–193

Greenpeace International, 74 128–30

GreenPoint Financial Corp., 28 166–68

Greenwood Mills, Inc., 14 219–21

Greg Manning Auctions, Inc., 60 145–46

Greggs PLC, 65 164–66

Greif Inc., 15 186–88; 66 154–56 (upd.)

Grévin & Compagnie SA, 56 143–45

Grey Global Group Inc., 6 26–28; 66 157–61 (upd.)

Grey Wolf, Inc., 43 201–03

Greyhound Lines, Inc., I 448–50; 32 227–31 (upd.)

Greyston Bakery, Inc., 101 220–23

Griffin Industries, Inc., 70 106–09

Griffin Land & Nurseries, Inc., 43 204–06

Griffith Laboratories Inc., 100 196–99

Griffon Corporation, 34 194–96

Grill Concepts, Inc., 74 131–33

Grinnell Corp., 13 245–47

Grist Mill Company, 15 189–91

Gristede's Foods Inc., 68 31 231–33; 180–83 (upd.)

Grohe *see* Friedrich Grohe AG & Co. KG.

Grolier Inc., 16 251–54; 43 207–11 (upd.)

Grolsch *see* Royal Grolsch NV.

Grossman's Inc., 13 248–50

Ground Round, Inc., 21 248–51

Group 4 Falck A/S, 42 165–68

Group Health Cooperative, 41 181–84

Group 1 Automotive, Inc., 52 144–46

Groupama S.A., 76 167–70

Groupe Air France, 6 92–94 *see also* Societe Air France.

Groupe Alain Manoukian, 55 173–75

Groupe André, 17 210–12 *see also* Vivarte SA.

Groupe Bolloré, 67 196–99

Groupe Bourbon S.A., 60 147–49

Groupe Bigard S.A., 96 151–54

Groupe Bull *see* Compagnie des Machines Bull.

Groupe Caisse d'Epargne, 100 200–04

Groupe Casino *see* Casino Guichard-Perrachon S.A.

Groupe Castorama-Dubois Investissements, 23 230–32 *see also* Kingfisher plc.

Groupe CECAB S.C.A., 88 131–34

Groupe Crit S.A., 74 134–36

Groupe Danone, 32 232–36 (upd.); 93 233–40 (upd.)

Groupe Dassault Aviation SA, 26 179–82 (upd.)

Groupe de la Cité, IV 614–16

Groupe DMC (Dollfus Mieg & Cie), 27 186–88

Groupe Euralis, 86 169–72

Groupe Flo S.A., 98 172–75

Groupe Fournier SA, 44 187–89

Groupe Genoyer, 96 155–58

Groupe Glon, 84 155–158

Groupe Go Sport S.A., 39 183–85

Groupe Guillin SA, 40 214–16

Groupe Henri Heuliez S.A., 100 205–09

Groupe Herstal S.A., 58 145–48

Groupe Jean-Claude Darmon, 44 190–92

Groupe Lactalis, 78 128–32 (upd.)

Groupe Lapeyre S.A., 33 175–77

Groupe LDC *see* L.D.C. S.A.

Groupe Le Duff S.A., 84 159–162

Groupe Léa Nature, 88 135–38

Groupe Legris Industries, 23 233–35

Groupe Les Echos, 25 283–85

Groupe Limagrain, 74 137–40

Groupe Louis Dreyfus S.A., 60 150–53

Groupe Monnoyeur, 72 157–59

Groupe Open, 74 141–43

Groupe Partouche SA, 48 196–99

Groupe Pinault-Printemps-Redoute *see* Pinault-Printemps-Redoute S.A.

Groupe Promodès S.A., 19 326–28

Groupe Rougier SA, 21 438–40

Groupe SEB, 35 201–03

Groupe Sidel S.A., 21 252–55

Groupe Soufflet SA, 55 176–78

Haemonetics Corporation, 20 277–79

Haftpflichtverband der Deutschen Industrie Versicherung auf Gegenseitigkeit V.a.G. *see* HDI (Haftpflichtverband der Deutschen Industrie Versicherung auf Gegenseitigkeit V.a.G.).

Hagemeyer N.V., 39 201–04

Haggar Corporation, 19 194–96; 78 137–41 (upd.)

Haggen Inc., 38 221–23

Hagoromo Foods Corporation, 84 175–178

Hahn Automotive Warehouse, Inc., 24 204–06

Haier Group Corporation, 65 167–70

Haights Cross Communications, Inc., 84 179–182

The Hain Celestial Group, Inc., 27 196–98; 43 217–20 (upd.)

Hair Club For Men Ltd., 90 222–25

Hakuhodo, Inc., 6 29–31; 42 172–75 (upd.)

HAL Inc., 9 271–73 *see also* Hawaiian Airlines, Inc.

Hal Leonard Corporation, 96 167–71

Hale-Halsell Company, 60 157–60

Half Price Books, Records, Magazines Inc., 37 179–82

Hall, Kinion & Associates, Inc., 52 150–52

Halliburton Company, III 497–500; 25 188–92 (upd.); 55 190–95 (upd.)

Hallmark Cards, Inc., IV 620–21; 16 255–57 (upd.); 40 228–32 (upd.); 87 205–212 (upd.)

Hamilton Beach/Proctor-Silex Inc., 17 213–15

Hammacher Schlemmer & Company Inc., 21 268–70; 72 160–62 (upd.)

Hammerson plc, IV 696–98; 40 233–35 (upd.)

Hammond Manufacturing Company Limited, 83 179-182

Hamon & Cie (International) S.A., 97 190–94

Hamot Health Foundation, 91 227–32

Hampton Affiliates, Inc., 77 175–79

Hampton Industries, Inc., 20 280–82

Hampshire Group Ltd., 82 170–73

Hancock Fabrics, Inc., 18 222–24

Hancock Holding Company, 15 207–09

Handleman Company, 15 210–12; 86 185–89 (upd.)

Handspring Inc., 49 183–86

Handy & Harman, 23 249–52

Hanesbrands Inc., 98 185–88

Hang Seng Bank Ltd., 60 161–63

Hanger Orthopedic Group, Inc., 41 192–95

Hanjin Shipping Co., Ltd., 50 217–21

Hankyu Corporation, V 454–56; 23 253–56 (upd.)

Hankyu Department Stores, Inc., V 70–71; 62 168–71 (upd.)

Hanmi Financial Corporation, 66 169–71

Hanna Andersson Corp., 49 187–90

Hanna-Barbera Cartoons Inc., 23 257–59, 387

Hannaford Bros. Co., 12 220–22

Hanover Compressor Company, 59 215–17

Hanover Direct, Inc., 36 262–65

Hanover Foods Corporation, 35 211–14

Hansen Natural Corporation, 31 242–45; 76 171–74 (upd.)

Hansgrohe AG, 56 149–52

Hanson Building Materials America Inc., 60 164–66

Hanson PLC, III 501–03; 7 207–10 (upd.); 30 228–32 (upd.)

Hanwha Group, 62 172–75

Hapag-Lloyd AG, 6 397–99; 97 195–203 (upd.)

Happy Kids Inc., 30 233–35

Harbert Corporation, 14 222–23

Harbison-Walker Refractories Company, 24 207–09

Harbour Group Industries, Inc., 90 226–29

Harcourt Brace and Co., 12 223–26

Harcourt Brace Jovanovich, Inc., IV 622–24

Harcourt General, Inc., 20 283–87 (upd.)

Hard Rock Cafe International, Inc., 12 227–29; 32 241–45 (upd.)

Harding Lawson Associates Group, Inc., 16 258–60

Hardinge Inc., 25 193–95

HARIBO GmbH & Co. KG, 44 216–19

Harkins Amusement Enterprises, Inc., 94 227–31

Harland and Wolff Holdings plc, 19 197–200

Harland Clarke Holdings Corporation, 94 232–35 (upd.)

Harlem Globetrotters International, Inc., 61 122–24

Harlequin Enterprises Limited, 52 153–56

Harley-Davidson, Inc., 7 211–14; 25 196–200 (upd.)

Harley Ellis Devereaux Corporation, 101 229–32

Harleysville Group Inc., 37 183–86

Harman International Industries, Incorporated, 15 213–15; 101 233–39 (upd.)

Harmon Industries, Inc., 25 201–04 *see also* General Electric Co.

Harmonic Inc., 43 221–23

Harmony Gold Mining Company Limited, 63 182–85

Harnischfeger Industries, Inc., 8 241–44; 38 224–28 (upd.)

Harold's Stores, Inc., 22 248–50

Harper Group Inc., 17 216–19

HarperCollins Publishers, 15 216–18

Harpo Inc., 28 173–75; 66 172–75 (upd.)

Harps Food Stores, Inc., 99 206–209

Harrah's Entertainment, Inc., 16 261–63; 43 224–28 (upd.)

Harris Corporation, II 37–39; 20 288–92 (upd.); 78 142–48 (upd.)

Harris Interactive Inc., 41 196–99; 92 148–53 (upd.)

Harris Publishing *see* Bernard C. Harris Publishing Company, Inc.

The Harris Soup Company (Harry's Fresh Foods),92 154–157

Harris Teeter Inc., 23 260–62; 72 163–66 (upd.)

Harrisons & Crosfield plc, III 696–700 *see also* Elementis plc.

Harrods Holdings, 47 171–74

Harry London Candies, Inc., 70 110–12

Harry N. Abrams, Inc., 58 152–55

Harry Winston Inc., 45 184–87

Harry's Farmers Market Inc., 23 263–66 *see also* Whole Foods Market, Inc.

Harry's Fresh Foods *see* The Harris Soup Company (Harry's Fresh Foods)

Harsco Corporation, 8 245–47 *see also* United Defense Industries, Inc.

Harte-Hanks Communications, Inc., 17 220–22; 63 186–89 (upd.)

Hartmann Inc., 96 172–76

Hartmarx Corporation, 8 248–50; 32 246–50 (upd.)

The Hartstone Group plc, 14 224–26

The Hartz Mountain Corporation, 12 230–32; 46 220–23 (upd.)

Harvey Norman Holdings Ltd., 56 153–55

Harveys Casino Resorts, 27 199–201 *see also* Harrah's Entertainment, Inc.

Harza Engineering Company, 14 227–28

Hasbro, Inc., III 504–06; 16 264–68 (upd.); 43 229–34 (upd.)

Haskel International, Inc., 59 218–20

Hastings Entertainment, Inc., 29 229–31

Hastings Manufacturing Company, 56 156–58

Hauser, Inc., 46 224–27

Havas, SA, 10 345–48; 33 178–82 (upd.) *see also* Vivendi Universal Publishing

Haverty Furniture Companies, Inc., 31 246–49

Hawaiian Airlines Inc., 22 251–53 (upd.) *see also* HAL Inc.

Hawaiian Electric Industries, Inc., 9 274–77

Hawaiian Holdings, Inc., 96 177–81 (upd.)

Hawk Corporation, 59 221–23

Hawker Siddeley Group Public Limited Company, III 507–10

Hawkeye Holdings LLC, 86 246–49

Hawkins Chemical, Inc., 16 269–72

Haworth Inc., 8 251–52; 39 205–08 (upd.)

Hay Group Holdings, Inc., 100 210–14

Hay House, Inc., 93 241–45

Hayel Saeed Anam Group of Cos., 92 158–61

Hayes Corporation, 24 210–14

Hayes Lemmerz International, Inc., 27 202–04

Haynes International, Inc., 88 163–66

Haynes Publishing Group P.L.C., 71 169–71

Hays plc, 27 205–07; 78 149–53 (upd.)

Hazelden Foundation, 28 176–79

Hazlewood Foods plc, 32 251–53

HBO *see* Home Box Office Inc.

HCA—The Healthcare Company, 35 215–18 (upd.)

HCI Direct, Inc., 55 196–98

HDI (Haftpflichtverband der Deutschen Industrie Versicherung auf Gegenseitigkeit V.a.G.), 53 159–63

HDOS Enterprises, 72 167–69

HDR Inc., 48 203–05

Head N.V., 55 199–201

Headlam Group plc, 95 170–73

Headwaters Incorporated, 56 159–62

Headway Corporate Resources, Inc., 40 236–38

Health Care & Retirement Corporation, 22 254–56

Health Communications, Inc., 72 170–73

Health Management Associates, Inc., 56 163–65

Health O Meter Products Inc., 14 229–31

Health Risk Management, Inc., 24 215–17

Health Systems International, Inc., 11 174–76

HealthExtras, Inc., 75 185–87

HealthMarkets, Inc., 88 167–72 (upd.)

HealthSouth Corporation, 14 232–34; 33 183–86 (upd.)

Healthtex, Inc., 17 223–25 *see also* VF Corp.

The Hearst Corporation, IV 625–27; 19 201–04 (upd.); 46 228–32 (upd.)

Heartland Express, Inc., 18 225–27

The Heat Group, 53 164–66

Hechinger Company, 12 233–36

Hecla Mining Company, 20 293–96

Heekin Can Inc., 13 254–56 *see also* Ball Corp.

Heelys, Inc., 87 213–216

Heery International, Inc., 58 156–59

HEICO Corporation, 30 236–38

Heidelberger Druckmaschinen AG, 40 239–41

Heidelberger Zement AG, 31 250–53

Heidrick & Struggles International, Inc., 28 180–82

Heijmans N.V., 66 176–78

Heileman Brewing Co *see* G. Heileman Brewing Co.

Heilig-Meyers Company, 14 235–37; 40 242–46 (upd.)

Heineken N.V., I 256–58; 13 257–59 (upd.); 34 200–04 (upd.); 90 230–36 (upd.)

Heinrich Deichmann-Schuhe GmbH & Co. KG, 88 173–77

Heinz Co *see* H.J. Heinz Co.

Helen of Troy Corporation, 18 228–30

Helene Curtis Industries, Inc., 8 253–54; 28 183–85 (upd.) *see also* Unilever PLC.

Helix Energy Solutions Group, Inc., 81 173–77

Hella KGaA Hueck & Co., 66 179–83

Hellenic Petroleum SA, 64 175–77

Heller, Ehrman, White & McAuliffe, 41 200–02

Helly Hansen ASA, 25 205–07

Helmerich & Payne, Inc., 18 231–33

Helmsley Enterprises, Inc., 9 278–80; 39 209–12 (upd.)

Helzberg Diamonds, 40 247–49

Hemisphere GPS Inc., 99 210–213

Hemlo Gold Mines Inc., 9 281–82 *see also* Newmont Mining Corp.

Henderson Land Development Company Ltd., 70 113–15

Hendrick Motorsports, Inc., 89 250–53

Henkel KGaA, III 31–34; 34 205–10 (upd.); 95 174–83 (upd.)

Henkel Manco Inc., 22 257–59

The Henley Group, Inc., III 511–12

Hennes & Mauritz AB, 29 232–34 *see also* H&M Hennes & Mauritz AB

Henry Boot plc, 76 175–77

Henry Crown and Company, 91 233–36

Henry Dreyfuss Associates LLC, 88 178–82

Henry Ford Health System, 84 183–187

Henry Modell & Company Inc., 32 263–65

Henry Schein, Inc., 31 254–56; 70 116–19 (upd.)

Hensel Phelps Construction Company, 72 174–77

Hensley & Company, 64 178–80

HEPCO *see* Hokkaido Electric Power Company Inc.

Her Majesty's Stationery Office, 7 215–18

Heraeus Holding GmbH, IV 98–100; 54 159–63 (upd.)

Herald Media, Inc., 91 237–41

Herbalife Ltd., 17 226–29; 41 203–06 (upd.); 92 162–67 (upd.)

Hercules Inc., I 343–45; 22 260–63 (upd.); 66 184–88 (upd.)

Hercules Technology Growth Capital, Inc., 87 217–220

Herley Industries, Inc., 33 187–89

Herman Goelitz, Inc., 28 186–88 *see also* Jelly Belly Candy Co.

Herman Goldner Company, Inc., 100 215–18

Herman Miller, Inc., 8 255–57; 77 180–86 (upd.)

Hermès International S.A., 14 238–40; 34 211–14 (upd.)

Hero Group, 100 219–24

Héroux-Devtek Inc., 69 205–07

Herr Foods Inc., 84 188–191

Herradura *see* Grupo Industrial Herradura, S.A. de C.V.

Herschend Family Entertainment Corporation, 73 173–76

Hershey Foods Corporation, II 510–12; 15 219–22 (upd.); 51 156–60 (upd.)

Herstal *see* Groupe Herstal S.A.

Hertie Waren- und Kaufhaus GmbH, V 72–74

The Hertz Corporation, 9 283–85; 33 190–93 (upd.); 101 240–45 (upd.)

Heska Corporation, 39 213–16

Heublein Inc., I 259–61

Heuer *see* TAG Heuer International SA.

Heuliez *see* Groupe Henri Heuliez S.A.

Hewitt Associates, Inc., 77 187–90

Hewlett-Packard Company, III 142–43; 6 237–39 (upd.); 28 189–92 (upd.); 50 222–30 (upd.)

Hexal AG, 69 208–10

Hexagon AB, 78 154–57

Hexcel Corporation, 28 193–95

hhgregg Inc., 98 189–92

HI *see* Houston Industries Inc.

Hibbett Sporting Goods, Inc., 26 189–91; 70 120–23 (upd.)

Hibernia Corporation, 37 187–90

Hickory Farms, Inc., 17 230–32

HickoryTech Corporation, 92 168–71

High Falls Brewing Company LLC, 74 144–47

High Tech Computer Corporation, 81 178–81

Highland Gold Mining Limited, 95 184–87

Highlights for Children, Inc., 95 188–91

Highmark Inc., 27 208–11

Highsmith Inc., 60 167–70

Highveld Steel and Vanadium Corporation Limited, 59 224–27

Hilmar Cheese Company, Inc., 98 193–96

Hilo Hattie *see* Pomare Ltd.

Hilb, Rogal & Hobbs Company, 77 191–94

Hildebrandt International, 29 235–38

Hill's Pet Nutrition, Inc., 27 212–14

Hillenbrand Industries, Inc., 10 349–51; 75 188–92 (upd.)

Hillerich & Bradsby Company, Inc., 51 161–64

The Hillhaven Corporation, 14 241–43 *see also* Vencor, Inc.

Hills Stores Company, 13 260–61

Hillsdown Holdings, PLC, II 513–14; 24 218–21 (upd.)

Hilti AG, 53 167–69

Hilton Group plc, III 91–93; 19 205–08 (upd.); 62 176–79 (upd.); 49 191–95 (upd.)

Hindustan Lever Limited, 79 198–201

Hines Horticulture, Inc., 49 196–98

Hino Motors, Ltd., 7 219–21; 21 271–74 (upd.)

HiPP GmbH & Co. Vertrieb KG, 88 183–88

Hiram Walker Resources Ltd., I 262–64

Hispanic Broadcasting Corporation, 35 219–22

HIT Entertainment PLC, 40 250–52

International Profit Associates, Inc., 87 248–251

International Rectifier Corporation, 31 263–66; 71 181–84 (upd.)

International Shipbreaking Ltd. L.L.C., 67 213–15

International Shipholding Corporation, Inc., 27 241–44

International Speedway Corporation, 19 221–23; 74 157–60 (upd.)

International Telephone & Telegraph Corporation, I 462–64; 11 196–99 (upd.)

International Total Services, Inc., 37 215–18

Interpool, Inc., 92 176–79

The Interpublic Group of Companies, Inc., I 16–18; 22 294–97 (upd.); 75 202–05 (upd.)

Interscope Music Group, 31 267–69

Intersil Corporation, 93 250–54

Interstate Bakeries Corporation, 12 274–76; 38 249–52 (upd.)

Interstate Hotels & Resorts Inc., 58 192–94

Intertek Group plc, 95 208–11

InterVideo, Inc., 85 179–82

Intevac, Inc., 92 180–83

Intimate Brands, Inc., 24 237–39

Intrado Inc., 63 202–04

Intrawest Corporation, 15 234–36; 84 192–196 (upd.)

Intres B.V., 82 178–81

Intuit Inc., 14 262–64; 33 208–11 (upd.); 73 188–92 (upd.)

Intuitive Surgical, Inc., 79 217–20

Invacare Corporation, 11 200–02; 47 193–98 (upd.)

Invensys PLC, 50 286–90 (upd.)

inVentiv Health, Inc., 81 205–08

The Inventure Group, Inc., 96 199–202 (upd.)

Inverness Medical Innovations, Inc., 63 205–07

Inversiones Nacional de Chocolates S.A., 88 199–202

Investcorp SA, 57 179–82

Investor AB, 63 208–11

Invitrogen Corporation, 52 182–84

Invivo Corporation, 52 185–87

Iogen Corporation, 81 209–13

Iomega Corporation, 21 294–97

IONA Technologies plc, 43 238–41

Ionatron, Inc., 85 183–86

Ionics, Incorporated, 52 188–90

Iowa Beef Processors see IBP, Inc.

Iowa Telecommunications Services, Inc., 85 187–90

Ipalco Enterprises, Inc., 6 508–09

IPC Magazines Limited, 7 244–47

Ipiranga S.A., 67 216–18

Ipsen International Inc., 72 192–95

Ipsos SA, 48 221–24

IranAir, 81 214–17

Irex Contracting Group, 90 245–48

IRIS International, Inc., 101 261–64

Irish Distillers Group, 96 203–07

Irish Life & Permanent Plc, 59 245–47

Irkut Corporation, 68 202–04

iRobot Corporation, 83 212-215

Iron Mountain, Inc., 33 212–14

IRSA Inversiones y Representaciones S.A., 63 212–15

Irvin Feld & Kenneth Feld Productions, Inc., 15 237–39 see also Feld Entertainment, Inc.

Irwin Financial Corporation, 77 213–16

Irwin Toy Limited, 14 265–67

Isbank see Turkiye Is Bankasi A.S.

Iscor Limited, 57 183–86

Isetan Company Limited, V 85–87; 36 289–93 (upd.)

Ishikawajima-Harima Heavy Industries Company, Ltd., III 532–33; 86 211–15 (upd.)

The Island ECN, Inc., 48 225–29

Isle of Capri Casinos, Inc., 41 217–19

Ispat Inland Inc., 30 252–54; 40 267–72 (upd.)

Israel Aircraft Industries Ltd., 69 215–17

Israel Chemicals Ltd., 55 226–29

ISS A/S, 49 221–23

Istituto per la Ricostruzione Industriale S.p.A., I 465–67; 11 203–06 (upd.)

Isuzu Motors, Ltd., 9 293–95; 23 288–91 (upd.); 57 187–91 (upd.)

Itaú see Banco Itaú S.A.

ITC Holdings Corp., 75 206–08

Itel Corporation, 9 296–99

Items International Airwalk Inc., 17 259–61

ITM Entreprises SA, 36 294–97

Ito En Ltd., 101 265–68

Ito-Yokado Co., Ltd., V 88–89; 42 189–92 (upd.)

ITOCHU Corporation, 32 283–87 (upd.)

Itoh see C. Itoh & Co.

Itoham Foods Inc., II 518–19; 61 138–40 (upd.)

Itron, Inc., 64 202–05

ITT Educational Services, Inc., 33 215–17; 76 200–03 (upd.)

ITT Sheraton Corporation, III 98–101 see also Starwood Hotels & Resorts Worldwide, Inc.

ITW see Illinois Tool Works Inc.

i2 Technologies, Inc., 87 252–257

Ivar's, Inc., 86 216–19

IVAX Corporation, 11 207–09; 55 230–33 (upd.)

IVC Industries, Inc., 45 208–11

iVillage Inc., 46 253–56

Iwerks Entertainment, Inc., 34 228–30

IXC Communications, Inc., 29 250–52

J

J & J Snack Foods Corporation, 24 240–42

J&R Electronics Inc., 26 224–26

J. & W. Seligman & Co. Inc., 61 141–43

J.A. Jones, Inc., 16 284–86

J. Alexander's Corporation, 65 177–79

J.B. Hunt Transport Services Inc., 12 277–79

J. Baker, Inc., 31 270–73

J C Bamford Excavators Ltd., 83 216-222

J. C. Penney Company, Inc., V 90–92; 18 269–73 (upd.); 43 245–50 (upd.); 91 263–72 (upd.)

J. Crew Group, Inc., 12 280–82; 34 231–34 (upd.); 88 203–08

J.D. Edwards & Company, 14 268–70 see also Oracle Corp.

J.D. Power and Associates, 32 297–301

J. D'Addario & Company, Inc., 48 230–33

J.F. Shea Co., Inc., 55 234–36

J.H. Findorff and Son, Inc., 60 175–78

J.I. Case Company, 10 377–81 see also CNH Global N.V.

J.J. Darboven GmbH & Co. KG, 96 208–12

J.J. Keller & Associates, Inc., 81 2180–21

The J. Jill Group, Inc., 35 239–41; 90 249–53 (upd.)

J.L. Hammett Company, 72 196–99

J Lauritzen A/S, 90 254–57

J. Lohr Winery Corporation, 99 229–232

The J. M. Smucker Company, 11 210–12; 87 258–265 (upd.)

J.M. Voith AG, 33 222–25

J.P. Morgan Chase & Co., II 329–32; 30 261–65 (upd.); 38 253–59 (upd.)

J.R. Simplot Company, 16 287–89; 60 179–82 (upd.)

J Sainsbury plc, II 657–59; 13 282–84 (upd.); 38 260–65 (upd.); 95 212–20 (upd.)

J. W. Pepper and Son Inc., 86 220–23

J. Walter Thompson Co. see JWT Group Inc.

Jabil Circuit, Inc., 36 298–301; 88 209–14

Jack Henry and Associates, Inc., 17 262–65; 94 258–63 (upd.)

Jack in the Box Inc., 89 265–71 (upd.)

Jack Morton Worldwide, 88 215–18

Jack Schwartz Shoes, Inc., 18 266–68

Jackpot Enterprises Inc., 21 298–300

Jackson Hewitt, Inc., 48 234–36

Jackson National Life Insurance Company, 8 276–77

Jacmar Companies, 87 266–269

Jaco Electronics, Inc., 30 255–57

Jacob Leinenkugel Brewing Company, 28 209–11

Jacobs Engineering Group Inc., 6 148–50; 26 220–23 (upd.)

Jacobs Suchard (AG), II 520–22 see also Kraft Jacobs Suchard AG.

Jacobson Stores Inc., 21 301–03

Jacor Communications, Inc., 23 292–95

Jacques Whitford, 92 184–87

Jacquot see Établissements Jacquot and Cie S.A.S.

Jacuzzi Brands Inc., 23 296–98; 76 204–07 (upd.)

JAFCO Co. Ltd., 79 221–24
Jaguar Cars, Ltd., 13 285–87
Jaiprakash Associates Limited, 101 269–72
JAKKS Pacific, Inc., 52 191–94
JAL *see* Japan Airlines Company, Ltd.
Jalate Inc., 25 245–47
Jamba Juice Company, 47 199–202
James Avery Craftsman, Inc., 76 208–10
James Beattie plc, 43 242–44
James Hardie Industries N.V., 56 174–76
James Original Coney Island Inc., 84 197–200
James Purdey & Sons Limited, 87 270–275
James River Corporation of Virginia, IV 289–91 *see also* Fort James Corp.
Jani-King International, Inc., 85 191–94
Janssen Pharmaceutica N.V., 80 164–67
JanSport, Inc., 70 134–36
Janus Capital Group Inc., 57 192–94
Japan Airlines Company, Ltd., I 104–06; 32 288–92 (upd.)
Japan Broadcasting Corporation, 7 248–50
Japan Leasing Corporation, 8 278–80
Japan Pulp and Paper Company Limited, IV 292–93
Japan Tobacco Inc., V 403–04; 46 257–60 (upd.)
Jarden Corporation, 93 255–61 (upd.)
Jardine Cycle & Carriage Ltd., 73 193–95
Jardine Matheson Holdings Limited, I 468–71; 20 309–14 (upd.); 93 262–71 (upd.)
Jarvis plc, 39 237–39
Jason Incorporated, 23 299–301
Jay Jacobs, Inc., 15 243–45
Jayco Inc., 13 288–90
Jaypee Group *see* Jaiprakash Associates Ltd.
Jays Foods, Inc., 90 258–61
Jazz Basketball Investors, Inc., 55 237–39
Jazzercise, Inc., 45 212–14
JB Oxford Holdings, Inc., 32 293–96
JBS S.A., 100 233–36
JCDecaux S.A., 76 211–13
JD Wetherspoon plc, 30 258–60
JDA Software Group, Inc., 101 273–76
JDS Uniphase Corporation, 34 235–37
JE Dunn Construction Group, Inc., 85 195–98
The Jean Coutu Group (PJC) Inc., 46 261–65
Jean-Georges Enterprises L.L.C., 75 209–11
Jeanneau *see* Chantiers Jeanneau S.A.
Jefferies Group, Inc., 25 248–51
Jefferson-Pilot Corporation, 11 213–15; 29 253–56 (upd.)
Jefferson Properties, Inc. *see* JPI.
Jefferson Smurfit Group plc, IV 294–96; 19 224–27 (upd.); 49 224–29 (upd.) *see also* Smurfit-Stone Container Corp.

Jel Sert Company, 90 262–65
Jeld-Wen, Inc., 45 215–17
Jelly Belly Candy Company, 76 214–16
Jenkens & Gilchrist, P.C., 65 180–82
Jennie-O Turkey Store, Inc., 76 217–19
Jennifer Convertibles, Inc., 31 274–76
Jenny Craig, Inc., 10 382–84; 29 257–60 (upd.); 92 188–93 (upd.)
Jenoptik AG, 33 218–21
Jeppesen Sanderson, Inc., 92 194–97
Jerónimo Martins SGPS S.A., 96 213–16
Jerry's Famous Deli Inc., 24 243–45
Jersey European Airways (UK) Ltd., 61 144–46
Jersey Mike's Franchise Systems, Inc., 83 223–226
Jervis B. Webb Company, 24 246–49
Jet Airways (India) Private Limited, 65 183–85
JetBlue Airways Corporation, 44 248–50
Jetro Cash & Carry Enterprises Inc., 38 266–68
Jewett-Cameron Trading Company, Ltd., 89 272–76
JFE Shoji Holdings Inc., 88 219–22
JG Industries, Inc., 15 240–42
Jillian's Entertainment Holdings, Inc., 40 273–75
Jim Beam Brands Worldwide, Inc., 14 271–73; 58 194–96 (upd.)
The Jim Henson Company, 23 302–04
The Jim Pattison Group, 37 219–22
Jimmy Carter Work Project *see* Habitat for Humanity International.
Jitney-Jungle Stores of America, Inc., 27 245–48
JJB Sports plc, 32 302–04
JLA Credit *see* Japan Leasing Corp.
JLG Industries, Inc., 52 195–97
JLL *see* Jones Lang LaSalle Inc.
JLM Couture, Inc., 64 206–08
JM Smith Corporation, 100 237–40
JMB Realty Corporation, IV 702–03 *see also* Amfac/JMB Hawaii L.L.C.
Jo-Ann Stores, Inc., 72 200–03 (upd.)
Joe's Sports & Outdoor, 98 218–22 (upd.)
Jockey International, Inc., 12 283–85; 34 238–42 (upd.); 77 217–23 (upd.)
The Joffrey Ballet of Chicago, 52 198–202
John B. Sanfilippo & Son, Inc., 14 274–76; 101 277–81 (upd.)
John Brown plc, I 572–74
The John D. and Catherine T. MacArthur Foundation, 34 243–46
John D. Brush Company Inc., 94 264–67
The John David Group plc, 90 266–69
John Deere *see* Deere & Co.
John Dewar & Sons, Ltd., 82 182–86
John Fairfax Holdings Limited, 7 251–54 *see also* Fairfax Media Ltd.
John Frieda Professional Hair Care Inc., 70 137–39
John H. Harland Company, 17 266–69

John Hancock Financial Services, Inc., III 265–68; 42 193–98 (upd.)
John Laing plc, I 575–76; 51 171–73 (upd.) *see also* Laing O'Rourke PLC.
John Lewis Partnership plc, V 93–95; 42 199–203 (upd.); 99 233–240 (upd.)
John Menzies plc, 39 240–43
The John Nuveen Company, 21 304–065
John Paul Mitchell Systems, 24 250–52
John Q. Hammons Hotels, Inc., 24 253–55
John W. Danforth Company, 48 237–39
John Wiley & Sons, Inc., 17 270–72; 65 186–90 (upd.)
Johnny Rockets Group, Inc., 31 277–81; 76 220–24 (upd.)
Johns Manville Corporation, 64 209–14 (upd.)
Johnson *see* Axel Johnson Group.
Johnson & Higgins, 14 277–80 *see also* Marsh & McLennan Companies, Inc.
Johnson & Johnson, III 35–37; 8 281–83 (upd.); 36 302–07 (upd.); 75 212–18 (upd.)
Johnson Controls, Inc., III 534–37; 26 227–32 (upd.); 59 248–54 (upd.)
Johnson Matthey PLC, IV 117–20; 16 290–94 (upd.); 49 230–35 (upd.)
Johnson Outdoors Inc., 84 201–205 (upd.)
Johnson Publishing Company, Inc., 28 212–14; 72 204–07 (upd.)
Johnson Wax *see* S.C. Johnson & Son, Inc.
Johnson Worldwide Associates, Inc., 28 215–17 *see also* Johnson Outdoors Inc.
Johnsonville Sausage L.L.C., 63 216–19
Johnston Industries, Inc., 15 246–48
Johnston Press plc, 35 242–44
Johnstown America Industries, Inc., 23 305–07
Jolly Hotels *see* Compagnia Italiana dei Jolly Hotels S.p.A.
Jones Apparel Group, Inc., 11 216–18; 39 244–47 (upd.)
Jones, Day, Reavis & Pogue, 33 226–29
Jones Intercable, Inc., 21 307–09
Jones Knowledge Group, Inc., 97 244–48
Jones Lang LaSalle Incorporated, 49 236–38
Jones Medical Industries, Inc., 24 256–58
Jones Soda Co., 69 218–21
Jongleurs Comedy Club *see* Regent Inns plc.
Jordache Enterprises, Inc., 23 308–10
The Jordan Company LP, 70 140–42
Jordan Industries, Inc., 36 308–10
Jordan-Kitt Music Inc., 86 224–27
Jos. A. Bank Clothiers, Inc., 31 282–85
José de Mello SGPS S.A., 96 217–20
Joseph T. Ryerson & Son, Inc., 15 249–51 *see also* Ryerson Tull, Inc.

Kerr Group Inc., 24 263–65
Kerr-McGee Corporation, IV 445–47; 22 301–04 (upd.); 68 217–21 (upd.)
Kerry Group plc, 27 258–60; 87 285–291 (upd.)
Kerry Properties Limited, 22 305–08
Kerzner International Limited, 69 222–24 (upd.)
Kesa Electricals plc, 91 285–90
Kesko Ltd (Kesko Oy), 8 293–94; 27 261–63 (upd.)
Ketchum Communications Inc., 6 38–40
Kettle Foods Inc., 48 240–42
Kewaunee Scientific Corporation, 25 259–62
Kewpie Kabushiki Kaisha, 57 202–05
Key Safety Systems, Inc., 63 224–26
Key Tronic Corporation, 14 284–86
KeyCorp, 8 295–97; 92 272–81 (upd.)
Keyes Fibre Company, 9 303–05
Keys Fitness Products, LP, 83 231-234
KeySpan Energy Co., 27 264–66
Keystone International, Inc., 11 225–27 *see also* Tyco International Ltd.
KFC Corporation, 7 265–68; 21 313–17 (upd.); 89 290–96 (upd.)
Kforce Inc., 71 188–90
KGHM Polska Miedz S.A., 98 223–26
KHD Konzern, III 541–44
KI, 57 206–09
Kia Motors Corporation, 12 293–95; 29 264–67 (upd.); 56 173
Kiabi Europe, 66 199–201
Kidde plc, I 475–76; 44 255–59 (upd.)
Kiehl's Since 1851, Inc., 52 209–12
Kikkoman Corporation, 14 287–89; 47 203–06 (upd.)
Kimball International, Inc., 12 296–98; 48 243–47 (upd.)
Kimberly-Clark Corporation, III 40–41; 16 302–05 (upd.); 43 256–60 (upd.)
Kimberly-Clark de México, S.A. de C.V., 54 185–87
Kimco Realty Corporation, 11 228–30
Kinder Morgan, Inc., 45 227–30
KinderCare Learning Centers, Inc., 13 298–300
Kinetic Concepts, Inc., 20 321–23
King & Spalding, 23 315–18
The King Arthur Flour Company, 31 292–95
King Kullen Grocery Co., Inc., 15 259–61
King Nut Company, 74 165–67
King Pharmaceuticals, Inc., 54 188–90
King Ranch, Inc., 14 290–92; 60 186–89 (upd.)
King World Productions, Inc., 9 306–08; 30 269–72 (upd.)
King's Hawaiian Bakery West, Inc., 101 282–85
Kingfisher plc, V 106–09; 24 266–71 (upd.); 83 235-242 (upd.)
Kingston Technology Corporation, 20 324–26
Kinki Nippon Railway Company Ltd., V 463–65

Kinko's Inc., 16 306–08; 43 261–64 (upd.)
Kinney Shoe Corp., 14 293–95
Kinray Inc., 85 209–12
Kinross Gold Corporation, 36 314–16
Kintera, Inc., 75 225–27
Kirby Corporation, 18 277–79; 66 202–04 (upd.)
Kirin Brewery Company, Limited, I 265–66; 21 318–21 (upd.); 63 227–31 (upd.)
Kirkland & Ellis LLP, 65 194–96
Kirlin's Inc., 98 227–30
Kirshenbaum Bond + Partners, Inc., 57 210–12
Kit Manufacturing Co., 18 280–82
Kitchell Corporation, 14 296–98
KitchenAid, 8 298–99
Kitty Hawk, Inc., 22 309–11
Kiva, 95 225–29
Kiwi International Airlines Inc., 20 327–29
KKR *see* Kohlberg Kravis Roberts & Co.
KLA-Tencor Corporation, 11 231–33; 45 231–34 (upd.)
Klabin S.A., 73 204–06
Klasky Csupo, Inc., 78 193–97
Klaus Steilmann GmbH & Co. KG, 53 192–95
Klein Tools, Inc., 95 230–34
Kleiner, Perkins, Caufield & Byers, 53 196–98
Kleinwort Benson Group PLC, II 421–23; 22 55 *see also* Dresdner Kleinwort Wasserstein.
Klement's Sausage Company, 61 147–49
KLM Royal Dutch Airlines *see* Koninklijke Luftvaart Maatschappij N.V.
Klöckner-Werke AG, IV 126–28; 58 201–05 (upd.)
Kluwer Publishers *see* Wolters Kluwer NV.
Kmart Corporation, V 110–12; 18 283–87 (upd.); 47 207–12 (upd.)
KMG Chemicals, Inc., 101 286–89
KN *see* Kühne & Nagel Group.
Knape & Vogt Manufacturing Company, 17 277–79
Knauf Gips KG, 100 245–50
K'Nex Industries, Inc., 52 206–08
Knight-Ridder, Inc., IV 628–30; 15 262–66 (upd.); 67 219–23 (upd.)
Knight Trading Group, Inc., 70 147–49
Knight Transportation, Inc., 64 218–21
Knoll, Inc., 14 299–301; 80 184–88 (upd.)
Knorr-Bremse AG, 84 226–231
Knorr Co. *see* C.H. Knorr Co.
The Knot, Inc., 74 168–71
Knott's Berry Farm, 18 288–90
Knowledge Learning Corporation, 51 197–99; 54 191
Knowledge Universe, Inc., 54 191–94
KnowledgeWare Inc., 9 309–11; 31 296–98 (upd.)
KOA *see* Kampgrounds of America, Inc.
Koala Corporation, 44 260–62

Kobe Steel, Ltd., IV 129–31; 19 238–41 (upd.)
Kobrand Corporation, 82 191–94
Koç Holding A.S., I 478–80; 54 195–98 (upd.)
Koch Enterprises, Inc., 29 215–17
Koch Industries, Inc., IV 448–49; 20 330–32 (upd.); 77 224–30 (upd.)
Kodak *see* Eastman Kodak Co.
Kodansha Ltd., IV 631–33; 38 273–76 (upd.)
Koenig & Bauer AG, 64 222–26
Kohl's Corporation, 9 312–13; 30 273–75 (upd.); 77 231–35 (upd.)
Kohlberg Kravis Roberts & Co., 24 272–74; 56 190–94 (upd.)
Kohler Company, 7 269–71; 32 308–12 (upd.)
Kohn Pedersen Fox Associates P.C., 57 213–16
Kolbenschmidt Pierburg AG, 97 249–53
The Koll Company, 8 300–02
Kollmorgen Corporation, 18 291–94
Kolmar Laboratories Group, 96 240–43
Komag, Inc., 11 234–35
Komatsu Ltd., III 545–46; 16 309–11 (upd.); 52 213–17 (upd.)
Konami Corporation, 96 244–47
KONE Corporation, 27 267–70; 76 225–28 (upd.)
Konica Corporation, III 547–50; 30 276–81 (upd.)
König Brauerei GmbH & Co. KG, 35 256–58 (upd.)
Koninklijke Ahold N.V., II 641–42; 16 312–14 (upd.)
Koninklijke Grolsch BV *see* Royal Grolsch NV.
Koninklijke Houthandel G Wijma & Zonen BV, 96 248–51
Koninklijke KPN N.V. *see* Royal KPN N.V.
Koninklijke Luchtvaart Maatschappij N.V., I 107–09; 28 224–27 (upd.)
Koninklijke Nederlandsche Hoogovens en Staalfabrieken NV, IV 132–34
N.V. Koninklijke Nederlandse Vliegtuigenfabriek Fokker, I 54–56; 28 327–30 (upd.)
Koninklijke Nedlloyd N.V., 6 403–05; 26 241–44 (upd.)
Koninklijke Numico N.V. *see* Royal Numico N.V.
Koninklijke Philips Electronics N.V., 50 297–302 (upd.)
Koninklijke PTT Nederland NV, V 299–301 *see also* Royal KPN NV.
Koninklijke Vendex KBB N.V. (Royal Vendex KBB N.V.), 62 206–09 (upd.)
Koninklijke Wessanen nv, II 527–29; 54 199–204 (upd.)
Koo Koo Roo, Inc., 25 263–65
Kookmin Bank, 58 206–08
Kooperativa Förbundet, 99 245–248
Koor Industries Ltd., II 47–49; 25 266–68 (upd.); 68 222–25 (upd.)
Kopin Corporation, 80 189–92

Koppers Industries, Inc., I 354–56; 26 245–48 (upd.)

Korbel Champagne Cellers *see* F. Korbel & Bros. Inc.

Körber AG, 60 190–94

Korea Electric Power Corporation (Kepco), 56 195–98

Korean Air Lines Co. Ltd., 6 98–99; 27 271–73 (upd.)

Koret of California, Inc., 62 210–13

Korn/Ferry International, 34 247–49

Kos Pharmaceuticals, Inc., 63 232–35

Koss Corporation, 38 277–79

Kotobukiya Co., Ltd., V 113–14; 56 199–202 (upd.)

KPMG International, 10 385–87; 33 234–38 (upd.)

KPN *see* Koninklijke PTT Nederland N.V.

Kraft Foods Inc., II 530–34; 7 272–77 (upd.); 45 235–44 (upd.); 91 291–306 (upd.)

Kraft Jacobs Suchard AG, 26 249–52 (upd.)

KraftMaid Cabinetry, Inc., 72 208–10

Kraus-Anderson Companies, Inc., 36 317–20; 83 243-248 (upd.)

Krause Publications, Inc., 35 259–61

Krause's Furniture, Inc., 27 274–77

Kredietbank N.V., II 304–056

Kreditanstalt für Wiederaufbau, 29 268–72

Kreisler Manufacturing Corporation, 97 254–57

Krispy Kreme Doughnut Corporation, 21 322–24; 61 150–54 (upd.)

The Kroger Company, II 643–45; 15 267–70 (upd.); 65 197–202 (upd.)

Kroll Inc., 57 217–20

Kronos, Inc., 18 295–97; 19 468; 100 251–55 (upd.)

Kruger Inc., 17 280–82

Krung Thai Bank Public Company Ltd., 69 225–27

Krupp AG *see* Fried. Krupp GmbH; ThyssenKrupp AG.

Kruse International, 88 227–30

The Krystal Company, 33 239–42

KSB AG, 62 214–18

KT&G Corporation, 62 219–21

KTM Power Sports AG, 100 256–59

K2 Inc., 16 295–98; 84 206–211 (upd.)

KU Energy Corporation, 11 236–38 *see also* LG&E Energy Corp.

Kubota Corporation, III 551–53

Kudelski Group SA, 44 263–66

Kuehne & Nagel International AG, V 466–69; 53 199–203 (upd.)

Kuhlman Corporation, 20 333–35

Kühne *see* Carl Kühne KG (GmbH & Co.).

Kühne & Nagel International AG, V 466–69

Kulicke and Soffa Industries, Inc., 33 246–48; 76 229–31 (upd.)

Kumagai Gumi Company, Ltd., I 579–80

Kumon Institute of Education Co., Ltd., 72 211–14

Kuoni Travel Holding Ltd., 40 284–86

Kurzweil Technologies, Inc., 51 200–04

The Kushner-Locke Company, 25 269–71

Kuwait Airways Corporation, 68 226–28

Kuwait Flour Mills & Bakeries Company, 84 232–234

Kuwait Petroleum Corporation, IV 450–52; 55 240–43 (upd.)

Kvaerner ASA, 36 321–23

Kwang Yang Motor Company Ltd., 80 193–96

Kwik-Fit Holdings plc, 54 205–07

Kwik Save Group plc, 11 239–41

Kymmene Corporation, IV 299–303 *see also* UPM-Kymmene Corp.

Kyocera Corporation, II 50–52; 21 329–32 (upd.); 79 231–36 (upd.)

Kyokuyo Company Ltd., 75 228–30

Kyowa Hakko Kogyo Co., Ltd., III 42–43; 48 248–50 (upd.)

Kyphon Inc., 87 292–295

Kyushu Electric Power Company Inc., V 649–51

L

L. and J.G. Stickley, Inc., 50 303–05

L-3 Communications Holdings, Inc., 48 251–53

L.A. Darling Company, 92 203–06

L.A. Gear, Inc., 8 303–06; 32 313–17 (upd.)

L.A. T Sportswear, Inc., 26 257–59

L.B. Foster Company, 33 255–58

L.D.C. SA, 61 155–57

L. Foppiano Wine Co., 101 290–93

L.L. Bean, Inc., 10 388–90; 38 280–83 (upd.); 91 307–13 (upd.)

The L.L. Knickerbocker Co., Inc., 25 272–75

L. Luria & Son, Inc., 19 242–44

L. M. Berry and Company, 80 197–200

L.S. Starrett Company, 13 301–03; 64 227–30 (upd.)

La Choy Food Products Inc., 25 276–78

La Doria SpA, 101 294–97

La Madeleine French Bakery & Café, 33 249–51

La Poste, V 270–72; 47 213–16 (upd.)

The La Quinta Companies, 11 242–44; 42 213–16 (upd.)

La Reina Inc., 96 252–55

La Seda de Barcelona S.A., 100 260–63

La Senza Corporation, 66 205–07

La Serenísima *see* Mastellone Hermanos S.A.

La-Z-Boy Incorporated, 14 302–04; 50 309–13 (upd.)

LAB *see* Lloyd Aéreo Boliviano S.A

LaBarge Inc., 41 224–26

Labatt Brewing Company Limited, I 267–68; 25 279–82 (upd.)

Labeyrie SAS, 80 201–04

LabOne, Inc., 48 254–57

Labor Ready, Inc., 29 273–75; 88 231–36 (upd.)

Laboratoires Arkopharma S.A., 75 231–34

Laboratoires de Biologie Végétale Yves Rocher, 35 262–65

Laboratoires Pierre Fabre S.A., 100 353–57

Laboratory Corporation of America Holdings, 42 217–20 (upd.)

LaBranche & Co. Inc., 37 223–25

LaCie Group S.A., 76 232–34

Lacks Enterprises Inc., 61 158–60

Laclede Steel Company, 15 271–73

LaCrosse Footwear, Inc., 18 298–301; 61 161–65 (upd.)

Ladbroke Group PLC, II 141–42; 21 333–36 (upd.) *see also* Hilton Group plc.

LADD Furniture, Inc., 12 299–301 *see also* La-Z-Boy Inc.

Ladish Co., Inc., 30 282–84

Lafarge Cement UK, 54 208–11 (upd.)

Lafarge Coppée S.A., III 703–05

Lafarge Corporation, 28 228–31

Lafuma S.A., 39 248–50

Laidlaw International, Inc., 80 205–08

Laing O'Rourke PLC, 93 282–85 (upd.)

L'Air Liquide SA, I 357–59; 47 217–20 (upd.)

Lakeland Industries, Inc., 45 245–48

Lakes Entertainment, Inc., 51 205–07

Lakeside Foods, Inc., 89 297–301

Lala *see* Grupo Industrial Lala, S.A. de C.V.

Lam Research Corporation, 11 245–47; 31 299–302 (upd.)

Lam Son Sugar Joint Stock Corporation (Lasuco), 60 195–97

Lamar Advertising Company, 27 278–80; 70 150–53 (upd.)

The Lamaur Corporation, 41 227–29

Lamb Weston, Inc., 23 319–21

Lamborghini *see* Automobili Lamborghini S.p.A.

Lamonts Apparel, Inc., 15 274–76

The Lamson & Sessions Co., 13 304–06; 61 166–70 (upd.)

Lan Chile S.A., 31 303–06

Lancair International, Inc., 67 224–26

Lancaster Colony Corporation, 8 307–09; 61 171–74 (upd.)

Lance, Inc., 14 305–07; 41 230–33 (upd.)

Lancer Corporation, 21 337–39

Land O'Lakes, Inc., II 535–37; 21 340–43 (upd.); 81 222–27 (upd.)

Land Securities PLC, IV 704–06; 49 246–50 (upd.)

LandAmerica Financial Group, Inc., 85 213–16

Landauer, Inc., 51 208–10

Landec Corporation, 95 235–38

Landmark Communications, Inc., 12 302–05; 55 244–49 (upd.)

Landmark Theatre Corporation, 70 154–56

Landor Associates, 81 228–31

Landry's Restaurants, Inc., 15 277–79; 65 203–07 (upd.)

Lands' End, Inc., 9 314–16; 29 276–79 (upd.); 82 195–200 (upd.)

Landsbanki Islands hf, 81 232–35

Landstar System, Inc., 63 236–38

Lane Bryant, Inc., 64 231–33

The Lane Co., Inc., 12 306–08

Lanier Worldwide, Inc., 75 235–38

Lanoga Corporation, 62 222–24 see also Pro-Build Holdings Inc.

Lapeyre S.A. see Groupe Lapeyre S.A.

Larry Flynt Publishing Inc., 31 307–10

Larry H. Miller Group, 29 280–83

Las Vegas Sands, Inc., 50 306–08

Laserscope, 67 227–29

LaSiDo Inc., 58 209–11

Lason, Inc., 31 311–13

Lassonde Industries Inc., 68 229–31

Lasuco see Lam Son Sugar Joint Stock Corp.

Latécoère S.A., 100 264–68

Latham & Watkins, 33 252–54

Latrobe Brewing Company, 54 212–14

Lattice Semiconductor Corp., 16 315–17

Lauda Air Luftfahrt AG, 48 258–60

Laura Ashley Holdings plc, 13 307–09; 37 226–29 (upd.)

The Laurel Pub Company Limited, 59 255–57

Laurent-Perrier SA, 42 221–23

Laurus N.V., 65 208–11

Lavoro Bank AG see Banca Nazionale del Lavoro SpA.

Lawson Software, 38 284–88

Lawter International Inc., 14 308–10 see also Eastman Chemical Co.

Layne Christensen Company, 19 245–47

Lazard LLC, 38 289–92

Lazare Kaplan International Inc., 21 344–47

Lazio see Società Sportiva Lazio SpA.

Lazy Days RV Center, Inc., 69 228–30

LCA-Vision, Inc, 85 217–20

LCC International, Inc., 84 235–238

LCI International, Inc., 16 318–20 see also Qwest Communications International, Inc.

LDB Corporation, 53 204–06

LDC, 68 232–34

LDC S.A.see L.D.C. S.A.

LDDS-Metro Communications, Inc., 8 310–12 see also MCI WorldCom, Inc.

LDI Ltd., LLC, 76 235–37

LDK Solar Co., Ltd., 101 298–302

Le Bon Marché see The Bon Marché.

Le Chateau Inc., 63 239–41

Le Cordon Bleu S.A., 67 230–32

Le Duff see Groupe Le Duff S.A.

Le Monde S.A., 33 308–10

Léa Nature see Groupe Léa Nature.

Leap Wireless International, Inc., 69 231–33

LeapFrog Enterprises, Inc., 54 215–18

Lear Corporation, 16 321–23; 71 191–95 (upd.)

Lear Siegler Inc., I 481–83

Learjet Inc., 8 313–16; 27 281–85 (upd.)

Learning Care Group, Inc., 76 238–41 (upd.)

The Learning Company Inc., 24 275–78

Learning Tree International Inc., 24 279–82

LeaRonal, Inc., 23 322–24 see also Rohm and Haas Co.

Leaseway Transportation Corp., 12 309–11

Leatherman Tool Group, Inc., 51 211–13

Lebhar-Friedman, Inc., 55 250–52

Leblanc Corporation see G. Leblanc Corp.

LeBoeuf, Lamb, Greene & MacRae, L.L.P., 29 284–86

LECG Corporation, 93 286–89

Leche Pascual see Grupo Leche Pascual S.A.

Lechmere Inc., 10 391–93

Lechters, Inc., 11 248–50; 39 251–54 (upd.)

Leclerc see Association des Centres Distributeurs E. Leclerc.

LeCroy Corporation, 41 234–37

Ledcor Industries Limited, 46 266–69

Ledesma Sociedad Anónima Agrícola Industrial, 62 225–27

Lee Apparel Company, Inc., 8 317–19

Lee Enterprises, Incorporated, 11 251–53; 64 234–37 (upd.)

Leeann Chin, Inc., 30 285–88

Lefrak Organization Inc., 26 260–62

Legal & General Group Plc, III 272–73; 24 283–85 (upd.); 101 303–08 (upd.)

The Legal Aid Society, 48 261–64

Legal Sea Foods Inc., 96 256–60

Legent Corporation, 10 394–96 see also Computer Associates International, Inc.

Legg Mason, Inc., 33 259–62

Leggett & Platt, Inc., 11 254–56; 48 265–68 (upd.)

Lego A/S, 13 310–13; 40 287–91 (upd.)

Legrand SA, 21 348–50

Lehigh Portland Cement Company, 23 325–27

Lehman Brothers Holdings Inc., 99 249–253 (upd.)

Leica Camera AG, 35 266–69

Leica Microsystems Holdings GmbH, 35 270–73

Leidy's, Inc., 93 290–92

Leinenkugel Brewing Company see Jacob Leinenkugel Brewing Co.

Leiner Health Products Inc., 34 250–52

Lend Lease Corporation Limited, IV 707–09; 17 283–86 (upd.); 52 218–23 (upd.)

LendingTree, LLC, 93 293–96

Lennar Corporation, 11 257–59

Lennox International Inc., 8 320–22; 28 232–36 (upd.)

Lenovo Group Ltd., 80 209–12

Lenox, Inc., 12 312–13

LensCrafters Inc., 23 328–30; 76 242–45 (upd.)

L'Entreprise Jean Lefebvre, 23 331–33 see also Vinci.

Leo Burnett Company, Inc., I 22–24; 20 336–39 (upd.)

The Leona Group LLC, 84 239–242

Leoni AG, 98 231–36

Leprino Foods Company, 28 237–39

Leroux S.A.S., 65 212–14

Leroy Merlin SA, 54 219–21

Les Boutiques San Francisco, Inc., 62 228–30

Les Echos see Groupe Les Echos.

Les Schwab Tire Centers, 50 314–16

Lesaffre see Societe Industrielle Lesaffre.

Lesco Inc., 19 248–50

The Leslie Fay Company, Inc., 8 323–25; 39 255–58 (upd.)

Leslie's Poolmart, Inc., 18 302–04

Leucadia National Corporation, 11 260–62; 71 196–200 (upd.)

Leupold & Stevens, Inc., 52 224–26

Level 3 Communications, Inc., 67 233–35

Levenger Company, 63 242–45

Lever Brothers Company, 9 317–19 see also Unilever.

Levi, Ray & Shoup, Inc., 96 261–64

Levi Strauss & Co., V 362–65; 16 324–28 (upd.)

Levitz Furniture Inc., 15 280–82

Levy Restaurants L.P., 26 263–65

Lewis Drug Inc., 94 272–76

Lewis Galoob Toys Inc., 16 329–31

LEXIS-NEXIS Group, 33 263–67

Lexmark International, Inc., 18 305–07; 79 237–42 (upd.)

LG&E Energy Corporation, 6 516–18; 51 214–17 (upd.)

LG Corporation, 94 277–83 (upd.)

Li & Fung Limited, 59 258–61

Libbey Inc., 49 251–54

The Liberty Corporation, 22 312–14

Liberty Livewire Corporation, 42 224–27

Liberty Media Corporation, 50 317–19

Liberty Mutual Holding Company, 59 262–64

Liberty Orchards Co., Inc., 89 302–05

Liberty Property Trust, 57 221–23

Liberty Travel, Inc., 56 203–06

Libyan National Oil Corporation, IV 453–55 see also National Oil Corp.

Liebherr-International AG, 64 238–42

Life Care Centers of America Inc., 76 246–48

Life is good, Inc., 80 213–16

Life Technologies, Inc., 17 287–89

Life Time Fitness, Inc., 66 208–10

LifeCell Corporation, 77 236–39

Lifeline Systems, Inc., 32 374; 53 207–09

LifeLock, Inc., 91 314–17

LifePoint Hospitals, Inc., 69 234–36

Lifetime Brands, Inc., 27 286–89; 73 207–11 (upd.)

Lifetime Entertainment Services, 51 218–22

Lifetouch Inc., 86 243–47

Lifeway Foods, Inc., 65 215–17
LifeWise Health Plan of Oregon, Inc., 90 276–79
Ligand Pharmaceuticals Incorporated, 10 48; 47 221–23
LILCO *see* Long Island Lighting Co.
Lillian Vernon Corporation, 12 314–15; 35 274–77 (upd.); 92 207–12 (upd.)
Lilly & Co *see* Eli Lilly & Co.
Lilly Endowment Inc., 70 157–59
Limagrain *see* Groupe Limagrain.
The Limited, Inc., V 115–16; 20 340–43 (upd.)
LIN Broadcasting Corp., 9 320–22
Linamar Corporation, 18 308–10
Lincare Holdings Inc., 43 265–67
Lincoln Center for the Performing Arts, Inc., 69 237–41
Lincoln Electric Co., 13 314–16
Lincoln National Corporation, III 274–77; 25 286–90 (upd.)
Lincoln Property Company, 8 326–28; 54 222–26 (upd.)
Lincoln Snacks Company, 24 286–88
Lincoln Telephone & Telegraph Company, 14 311–13
Lindal Cedar Homes, Inc., 29 287–89
Linde AG, I 581–83; 67 236–39 (upd.)
Lindley *see* Corporación José R. Lindley S.A.
Lindsay Manufacturing Co., 20 344–46
Lindt & Sprüngli *see* Chocoladefabriken Lindt & Sprüngli AG.
Linear Technology Corporation, 16 332–34; 99 254–258 (upd.)
Linens 'n Things, Inc., 24 289–92; 75 239–43 (upd.)
Lintas: Worldwide, 14 314–16
The Lion Brewery, Inc., 86 248–52
Lion Corporation, III 44–45; 51 223–26 (upd.)
Lion Nathan Limited, 54 227–30
Lionel L.L.C., 16 335–38; 99 259–265 (upd.)
Lions Gate Entertainment Corporation, 35 278–81
Lipman Electronic Engineering Ltd., 81 236–39
Lipton *see* Thomas J. Lipton Co.
Liqui-Box Corporation, 16 339–41
Liquidity Services, Inc., 101 309–13
Liquidnet, Inc., 79 243–46
LIRR *see* The Long Island Rail Road Co.
Litehouse Inc., 60 198–201
Lithia Motors, Inc., 41 238–40
Littelfuse, Inc., 26 266–69
Little Caesar Enterprises, Inc., 7 278–79; 24 293–96 (upd.) *see also* Ilitch Holdings Inc.
Little Switzerland, Inc., 60 202–04
Little Tikes Company, 13 317–19; 62 231–34 (upd.)
Littleton Coin Company Inc., 82 201–04
Littlewoods plc, V 117–19; 42 228–32 (upd.)

Litton Industries Inc., I 484–86; 11 263–65 (upd.) *see also* Avondale Industries; Northrop Grumman Corp.
LIVE Entertainment Inc., 20 347–49
Live Nation, Inc., 80 217–22 (upd.)
LivePerson, Inc., 91 318–21
Liz Claiborne, Inc., 8 329–31; 25 291–94 (upd.)
LKQ Corporation, 71 201–03
Lloyd Aéreo Boliviano S.A., 95 239–42
Lloyd's, III 278–81; 22 315–19 (upd.); 74 172–76 (upd.)
Lloyds TSB Group plc, II 306–09; 47 224–29 (upd.)
LM Ericsson *see* Telefonaktiebolaget LM Ericsson.
Loblaw Companies Limited, 43 268–72
Lockheed Martin Corporation, I 64–66; 11 266–69 (upd.); 15 283–86 (upd.); 89 306–11 (upd.)
Loctite Corporation, 8 332–34; 30 289–91 (upd.)
LodgeNet Entertainment Corporation, 28 240–42
Loehmann's Inc., 24 297–99
Loewe AG, 90 280–85
The Loewen Group, Inc., 16 342–44; 40 292–95 (upd.) *see also* Alderwoods Group Inc.
Loews Corporation, I 487–88; 12 316–18 (upd.); 36 324–28 (upd.); 93 297–304 (upd.)
Logan's Roadhouse, Inc., 29 290–92
Loganair Ltd., 68 235–37
Logica plc, 14 317–19; 37 230–33 (upd.)
Logicon Inc., 20 350–52 *see also* Northrop Grumman Corp.
Logitech International S.A., 28 243–45; 69 242–45 (upd.)
LoJack Corporation, 48 269–73
Lojas Americanas S.A., 77 240–43
Lojas Arapuã S.A., 22 320–22; 61 175–78 (upd.)
Loma Negra C.I.A.S.A., 95 243–46
London Drugs Ltd., 46 270–73
London Fog Industries, Inc., 29 293–96
London Regional Transport, 6 406–08
London Scottish Bank plc, 70 160–62
London Stock Exchange Limited, 34 253–56
Lone Star Steakhouse & Saloon, Inc., 51 227–29
Lonely Planet Publications Pty Ltd., 55 253–55
The Long & Foster Companies, Inc, 85 221–24
Long Island Bancorp, Inc., 16 345–47
Long Island Lighting Company, V 652–54
The Long Island Rail Road Company, 68 238–40
Long John Silver's, 13 320–22; 57 224–29 (upd.)
Long-Term Credit Bank of Japan, Ltd., II 310–11
The Longaberger Company, 12 319–21; 44 267–70 (upd.)

Longs Drug Stores Corporation, V 120; 25 295–97 (upd.); 83 249-253 (upd.)
Longview Fibre Company, 8 335–37; 37 234–37 (upd.)
Lonmin plc, 66 211–16 (upd.)
Lonrho Plc, 21 351–55 *see also* Lonmin plc.
Lonza Group Ltd., 73 212–14
Lookers plc, 71 204–06
Loos & Dilworth, Inc., 100 269–72
Loral Space & Communications Ltd., 8 338–40; 54 231–35 (upd.)
L'Oréal, III 46–49; 8 341–44 (upd.); 46 274–79 (upd.)
Los Angeles Lakers *see* California Sports, Inc.
Lost Arrow Inc., 22 323–25
LOT Polish Airlines (Polskie Linie Lotnicze S.A.), 33 268–71
LOT$OFF Corporation, 24 300–01
Lotte Confectionery Company Ltd., 76 249–51
Lotus Cars Ltd., 14 320–22
Lotus Development Corporation, 6 254–56; 25 298–302 (upd.)
LOUD Technologies, Inc., 95 247–50 (upd.)
Louis Dreyfus *see* Groupe Louis Dreyfus S.A.
Louis Vuitton, 10 397–99 *see also* LVMH Moët Hennessy Louis Vuitton SA.
The Louisiana Land and Exploration Company, 7 280–83
Louisiana-Pacific Corporation, IV 304–05; 31 314–17 (upd.)
Love's Travel Stops & Country Stores, Inc., 71 207–09
Lowe's Companies, Inc., V 122–23; 21 356–58 (upd.); 81 240–44 (upd.)
Löwenbräu AG, 80 223–27
Lowrance Electronics, Inc., 18 311–14
LPA Holding Corporation, 81 245–48
LSB Industries, Inc., 77 244–47
LSI *see* Lear Siegler Inc.
LSI Logic Corporation, 13 323–25; 64 243–47
LTU Group Holding GmbH, 37 238–41
The LTV Corporation, I 489–91; 24 302–06 (upd.)
The Lubrizol Corporation, I 360–62; 30 292–95 (upd.); 83 254-259 (upd.)
Luby's, Inc., 17 290–93; 42 233–38 (upd.); 99 266–273 (upd.)
Lucas Industries Plc, III 554–57
Lucasfilm Ltd., 12 322–24; 50 320–23 (upd.)
Lucent Technologies Inc., 34 257–60
Lucille Farms, Inc., 45 249–51
Lucky-Goldstar, II 53–54 *see also* LG Corp.
Lucky Stores Inc., 27 290–93
Ludendo S.A., 88 237–40
Lufkin Industries, Inc., 78 198–202
Lufthansa *see* Deutsche Lufthansa AG.
Luigino's, Inc., 64 248–50
Lukens Inc., 14 323–25 *see also* Bethlehem Steel Corp.
LUKOIL *see* OAO LUKOIL.

Maple Leaf Foods Inc., 41 249–53

Maple Leaf Sports & Entertainment Ltd., 61 188–90

Maples Industries, Inc., 83 260-263

Marble Slab Creamery, Inc., 87 304–307

March of Dimes, 31 322–25

Marchesi Antinori SRL, 42 245–48

Marchex, Inc., 72 222–24

marchFIRST, Inc., 34 261–64

Marco Business Products, Inc., 75 244–46

Marco's Franchising LLC, 86 264–67

Marcolin S.p.A., 61 191–94

Marconi plc, 33 286–90 (upd.)

Marcopolo S.A., 79 247–50

The Marcus Corporation, 21 359–63

Marelli see Magneti Marelli Holding SpA.

Marfin Popular Bank plc, 92 222–26

Margarete Steiff GmbH, 23 334–37

Marie Brizard et Roger International S.A.S., 22 342–44; 97 276–80 (upd.)

Marie Callender's Restaurant & Bakery, Inc., 28 257–59

Mariella Burani Fashion Group, 92 227–30

Marine Products Corporation, 75 247–49

MarineMax, Inc., 30 303–05

Mariner Energy, Inc., 101 326–29

Marion Laboratories Inc., I 648–49

Marion Merrell Dow, Inc., 9 328–29 (upd.)

Marionnaud Parfumeries SA, 51 233–35

Marisa Christina, Inc., 15 290–92

Maritz Inc., 38 302–05

Mark IV Industries, Inc., 7 296–98; 28 260–64 (upd.)

Mark T. Wendell Tea Company, 94 299–302

The Mark Travel Corporation, 80 232–35

Märklin Holding GmbH, 70 163–66

Marks and Spencer p.l.c., V 124–26; 24 313–17 (upd.); 85 239–47 (upd.)

Marks Brothers Jewelers, Inc., 24 318–20 see also Whitehall Jewellers, Inc.

Marlin Business Services Corp., 89 317–19

The Marmon Group, Inc., IV 135–38; 16 354–57 (upd.); 70 167–72 (upd.)

Marquette Electronics, Inc., 13 326–28

Marriott International, Inc., III 102–03; 21 364–67 (upd.); 83 264–270 (upd.)

Mars, Incorporated, 7 299–301; 40 302–05 (upd.)

Mars Petcare US Inc., 96 269–72

Marsh & McLennan Companies, Inc., III 282–84; 45 263–67 (upd.)

Marsh Supermarkets, Inc., 17 300–02; 76 255–58 (upd.)

Marshall & Ilsley Corporation, 56 217–20

Marshall Amplification plc, 62 239–42

Marshall Field's, 63 254–63 see also Target Corp.

Marshalls Incorporated, 13 329–31

Martek Biosciences Corporation, 65 218–20

Martell and Company S.A., 82 213–16

Marten Transport, Ltd., 84 243–246

Martha Stewart Living Omnimedia, Inc., 24 321–23; 73 219–22 (upd.)

Martignetti Companies, 84 247–250

Martin-Baker Aircraft Company Limited, 61 195–97

Martin Franchises, Inc., 80 236–39

Martin Guitar Company see C.F. Martin & Co., Inc.

Martin Industries, Inc., 44 274–77

Martin Marietta Corporation, I 67–69 see also Lockheed Martin Corp.

Martin's Super Markets, Inc., 101 330–33

MartinLogan, Ltd., 85 248–51

Martini & Rossi SpA, 63 264–66

Martz Group, 56 221–23

Marubeni Corporation, I 492–95; 24 324–27 (upd.)

Maruha Group Inc., 75 250–53 (upd.)

Marui Company Ltd., V 127; 62 243–45 (upd.)

Maruzen Co., Limited, 18 322–24

Marvel Entertainment, Inc., 10 400–02; 78 212–19 (upd.)

Marvin Lumber & Cedar Company, 22 345–47

Mary Kay Inc., 9 330–32; 30 306–09 (upd.); 84 251–256 (upd.)

Maryland & Virginia Milk Producers Cooperative Association, Inc., 80 240–43

Maryville Data Systems Inc., 96 273–76

Marzotto S.p.A., 20 356–58; 67 246–49 (upd.)

The Maschhoffs, Inc., 82 217–20

Masco Corporation, III 568–71; 20 359–63 (upd.); 39 263–68 (upd.)

Maserati see Officine Alfieri Maserati S.p.A.

Mashantucket Pequot Gaming Enterprise Inc., 35 282–85

Masland Corporation, 17 303–05 see also Lear Corp.

Masonite International Corporation, 63 267–69

Massachusetts Mutual Life Insurance Company, III 285–87; 53 210–13 (upd.)

Massey Energy Company, 57 236–38

MasTec, Inc., 55 259–63 (upd.)

Mastellone Hermanos S.A., 101 334–37

Master Lock Company, 45 268–71

MasterBrand Cabinets, Inc., 71 216–18

MasterCard Worldwide, 9 333–35; 96 277–81 (upd.)

MasterCraft Boat Company, Inc., 90 290–93

Matalan PLC, 49 258–60

Match.com, LP, 87 308–311

Material Sciences Corporation, 63 270–73

The MathWorks, Inc., 80 244–47

Matra-Hachette S.A., 15 293–97 (upd.) see also European Aeronautic Defence and Space Company EADS N.V.

Matria Healthcare, Inc., 17 306–09

Matrix Essentials Inc., 90 294–97

Matrix Service Company, 65 221–23

Matrixx Initiatives, Inc., 74 177–79

Matsushita Electric Industrial Co., Ltd., II 55–56; 64 255–58 (upd.)

Matsushita Electric Works, Ltd., III 710–11; 7 302–03 (upd.)

Matsuzakaya Company Ltd., V 129–31; 64 259–62 (upd.)

Matt Prentice Restaurant Group, 70 173–76

Mattel, Inc., 7 304–07; 25 311–15 (upd.); 61 198–203 (upd.)

Matth. Hohner AG, 53 214–17

Matthews International Corporation, 29 304–06; 77 248–52 (upd.)

Matussière et Forest SA, 58 220–22

Maui Land & Pineapple Company, Inc., 29 307–09; 100 273–77 (upd.)

Maui Wowi, Inc., 85 252–55

Mauna Loa Macadamia Nut Corporation, 64 263–65

Maurices Inc., 95 255–58

Maus Frères SA, 48 277–79

Maverick Ranch Association, Inc., 88 253–56

Maverick Tube Corporation, 59 280–83

Max & Erma's Restaurants Inc., 19 258–60; 100 278–82 (upd.)

Maxco Inc., 17 310–11

Maxicare Health Plans, Inc., III 84–86; 25 316–19 (upd.)

The Maxim Group, 25 320–22

Maxim Integrated Products, Inc., 16 358–60

MAXIMUS, Inc., 43 277–80

Maxtor Corporation, 10 403–05 see also Seagate Technology, Inc.

Maxus Energy Corporation, 7 308–10

Maxwell Communication Corporation plc, IV 641–43; 7 311–13 (upd.)

Maxwell Shoe Company, Inc., 30 310–12 see also Jones Apparel Group, Inc.

MAXXAM Inc., 8 348–50

Maxxim Medical Inc., 12 325–27

The May Department Stores Company, V 132–35; 19 261–64 (upd.); 46 284–88 (upd.)

May Gurney Integrated Services PLC, 95 259–62

May International see George S. May International Co.

Mayer, Brown, Rowe & Maw, 47 230–32

Mayfield Dairy Farms, Inc., 74 180–82

Mayflower Group Inc., 6 409–11

Mayo Foundation, 9 336–39; 34 265–69 (upd.)

Mayor's Jewelers, Inc., 41 254–57

Maytag Corporation, III 572–73; 22 348–51 (upd.); 82 221–25 (upd.)

Mazda Motor Corporation, 9 340–42; 23 338–41 (upd.); 63 274–79 (upd.)

Mazel Stores, Inc., 29 310–12
Mazzio's Corporation, 76 259–61
MBB *see* Messerschmitt-Bölkow-Blohm.
MBC Holding Company, 40 306–09
MBE *see* Mail Boxes Etc.
MBIA Inc., 73 223–26
MBK Industrie S.A., 94 303–06
MBNA Corporation, 12 328–30; 33
291–94 **(upd.)**
MC Sporting Goods *see* Michigan
Sporting Goods Distributors Inc.
MCA Inc., II 143–45 *see also* Universal
Studios.
McAfee Inc., 94 307–10
McAlister's Corporation, 66 217–19
McBride plc, 82 226–30
MCC *see* Morris Communications Corp.
McCain Foods Limited, 77 253–56
McCarthy Building Companies, Inc., 48
280–82
McCaw Cellular Communications, Inc.,
6 322–24 *see also* AT&T Wireless
Services, Inc.
McClain Industries, Inc., 51 236–38
The McClatchy Company, 23 342–44;
92 231–35 **(upd.)**
McCormick & Company, Incorporated,
7 314–16; 27 297–300 **(upd.)**
McCormick & Schmick's Seafood
Restaurants, Inc., 71 219–21
McCoy Corporation, 58 223–25
McDATA Corporation, 75 254–56
McDermott International, Inc., III
558–60; 37 242–46 **(upd.)**
McDonald's Corporation, II 646–48; 7
317–19 **(upd.);** 26 281–85 **(upd.);** 63
280–86 **(upd.)**
McDonnell Douglas Corporation, I
70–72; 11 277–80 **(upd.)** *see also*
Boeing Co.
McGrath RentCorp, 91 326–29
The McGraw-Hill Companies, Inc., IV
634–37; 18 325–30 **(upd.);** 51
239–44 **(upd.)**
MCI *see* Melamine Chemicals, Inc.
MCI WorldCom, Inc., V 302–04; 27
301–08 **(upd.)** *see also* Verizon
Communications Inc.
McIlhenny Company, 20 364–67
McJunkin Corporation, 63 287–89
McKechnie plc, 34 270–72
McKee Foods Corporation, 7 320–21;
27 309–11 **(upd.)**
McKesson Corporation, I 496–98; 12
331–33 **(upd.);** 47 233–37 **(upd.)**
McKinsey & Company, Inc., 9 343–45
McLane Company, Inc., 13 332–34
McLeodUSA Incorporated, 32 327–30
McMenamins Pubs and Breweries, 65
224–26
McMoRan *see* Freeport-McMoRan Copper
& Gold, Inc.
MCN Corporation, 6 519–22
McNaughton Apparel Group, Inc., 92
236–41 **(upd.)**
McPherson's Ltd., 66 220–22
McQuay International *see* AAF-McQuay
Inc.

MCSi, Inc., 41 258–60
McWane Corporation, 55 264–66
MDC Partners Inc., 63 290–92
MDU Resources Group, Inc., 7 322–25;
42 249–53 **(upd.)**
The Mead Corporation, IV 310–13; 19
265–69 **(upd.)** *see also* MeadWestvaco
Corp.
Mead Data Central, Inc., 10 406–08 *see
also* LEXIS-NEXIS Group.
Mead Johnson & Company, 84
257–262
Meade Instruments Corporation, 41
261–64
Meadowcraft, Inc., 29 313–15; 100
283–87 **(upd.)**
MeadWestvaco Corporation, 76 262–71
(upd.)
Measurement Specialties, Inc., 71
222–25
MEC *see* Mitsubishi Estate Company, Ltd.
Mecalux S.A., 74 183–85
Mechel OAO, 99 278–281
Mecklermedia Corporation, 24 328–30
see also Jupitermedia Corp.
Medarex, Inc., 85 256–59
Medco Containment Services Inc., 9
346–48 *see also* Merck & Co., Inc.
Médecins sans Frontières, 85 260–63
MEDecision, Inc., 95 263–67
Media Arts Group, Inc., 42 254–57
Media General, Inc., 7 326–28; 38
306–09 **(upd.)**
Mediacom Communications
Corporation, 69 250–52
MediaNews Group, Inc., 70 177–80
Mediaset SpA, 50 332–34
Medical Action Industries Inc., 101
338–41
Medical Information Technology Inc.,
64 266–69
Medical Management International,
Inc., 65 227–29
Medical Staffing Network Holdings,
Inc., 89 320–23
Medicis Pharmaceutical Corporation, 59
284–86
Medifast, Inc., 97 281–85
MedImmune, Inc., 35 286–89
Mediolanum S.p.A., 65 230–32
Medis Technologies Ltd., 77 257–60
Meditrust, 11 281–83
Medline Industries, Inc., 61 204–06
Medtronic, Inc., 8 351–54; 30 313–17
(upd.); 67 250–55 **(upd.)**
Medusa Corporation, 24 331–33
Mega Bloks, Inc., 61 207–09
Megafoods Stores Inc., 13 335–37
Meggitt PLC, 34 273–76
Meguiar's, Inc., 99 282–285
Meidensha Corporation, 92 242–46
Meier & Frank Co., 23 345–47 *see also*
Macy's, Inc.
Meijer, Inc., 7 329–31; 27 312–15
(upd.); 101 342–46 **(upd.)**
Meiji Dairies Corporation, II 538–39;
82 231–34 **(upd.)**

Meiji Mutual Life Insurance Company,
III 288–89
Meiji Seika Kaisha Ltd., II 540–41; 64
270–72 **(upd.)**
Mel Farr Automotive Group, 20 368–70
Melaleuca Inc., 31 326–28
Melamine Chemicals, Inc., 27 316–18
see also Mississippi Chemical Corp.
Melitta Unternehmensgruppe Bentz KG,
53 218–21
Mello Smello *see* The Miner Group
International.
Mellon Financial Corporation, II
315–17; 44 278–82 **(upd.)**
Mellon-Stuart Co., I 584–85 *see also*
Michael Baker Corp.
The Melting Pot Restaurants, Inc., 74
186–88
Melville Corporation, V 136–38 *see also*
CVS Corp.
Melvin Simon and Associates, Inc., 8
355–57 *see also* Simon Property Group,
Inc.
MEMC Electronic Materials, Inc., 81
249–52
Memorial Sloan-Kettering Cancer
Center, 57 239–41
Memry Corporation, 72 225–27
The Men's Wearhouse, Inc., 17 312–15;
48 283–87 **(upd.)**
Menasha Corporation, 8 358–61; 59
287–92 **(upd.)**
Mendocino Brewing Company, Inc., 60
205–07
The Mentholatum Company Inc., 32
331–33
Mentor Corporation, 26 286–88
Mentor Graphics Corporation, 11
284–86
MEPC plc, IV 710–12
Mercantile Bankshares Corp., 11
287–88
Mercantile Stores Company, Inc., V
139; 19 270–73 **(upd.)** *see also*
Dillard's Inc.
Mercer International Inc., 64 273–75
Mercian Corporation, 77 261–64
Merck & Co., Inc., I 650–52; 11
289–91 **(upd.);** 34 280–85 **(upd.);** 95
268–78 **(upd.)**
Mercury Air Group, Inc., 20 371–73
Mercury Communications, Ltd., 7
332–34 *see also* Cable and Wireless plc.
Mercury Drug Corporation, 70 181–83
Mercury General Corporation, 25
323–25
Mercury Interactive Corporation, 59
293–95
Mercury Marine Group, 68 247–51
Meredith Corporation, 11 292–94; 29
316–19 **(upd.);** 74 189–93 **(upd.)**
Merge Healthcare, 85 264–68
Meridian Bancorp, Inc., 11 295–97
Meridian Gold, Incorporated, 47
238–40
Merillat Industries, LLC, 13 338–39; 69
253–55 **(upd.)**
Merisant Worldwide, Inc., 70 184–86

Merisel, Inc., 12 334–36
Merit Medical Systems, Inc., 29 320–22
MeritCare Health System, 88 257–61
Meritage Corporation, 26 289–92
Merix Corporation, 36 329–31; 75
257–60 (upd.)
Merriam-Webster Inc., 70 187–91
Merrill Corporation, 18 331–34; 47
241–44 (upd.)
Merrill Lynch & Co., Inc., II 424–26;
13 340–43 (upd.); 40 310–15 (upd.)
Merry-Go-Round Enterprises, Inc., 8
362–64
The Mersey Docks and Harbour
Company, 30 318–20
Mervyn's California, 10 409–10; 39
269–71 (upd.) *see also* Target Corp.
Merz Group, 81 253–56
Mesa Air Group, Inc., 11 298–300; 32
334–37 (upd.); 77 265–70 (upd.)
Mesaba Holdings, Inc., 28 265–67
Messerschmitt-Bölkow-Blohm GmbH., I
73–75 *see also* European Aeronautic
Defence and Space Company EADS
N.V.
Mestek, Inc., 10 411–13
Metal Box plc, I 604–06 *see also* Novar
plc.
Metal Management, Inc., 92 247–50
Metaleurop S.A., 21 368–71
Metalico Inc., 97 286–89
Metallgesellschaft AG, IV 139–42; 16
361–66 (upd.)
Metalurgica Mexicana Penoles, S.A. *see*
Industrias Penoles, S.A. de C.V.
Metatec International, Inc., 47 245–48
Metavante Corporation, 100 288–92
Metcash Trading Ltd., 58 226–28
Meteor Industries Inc., 33 295–97
Methanex Corporation, 40 316–19
Methode Electronics, Inc., 13 344–46
MetLife *see* Metropolitan Life Insurance
Co.
Metris Companies Inc., 56 224–27
Metro AG, 50 335–39
Metro-Goldwyn-Mayer Inc., 25 326–30
(upd.); 84 263–270 (upd.)
Métro Inc., 77 271–75
Metro Information Services, Inc., 36
332–34
Metro International S.A., 93 309–12
Metrocall, Inc., 41 265–68
Metromedia Company, 7 335–37; 14
298–300 (upd.); 61 210–14 (upd.)
Métropole Télévision S.A., 76 272–74
(upd.)
Metropolitan Baseball Club Inc., 39
272–75
Metropolitan Financial Corporation, 13
347–49
Metropolitan Life Insurance Company,
III 290–94; 52 235–41 (upd.)
The Metropolitan Museum of Art, 55
267–70
Metropolitan Opera Association, Inc.,
40 320–23
Metropolitan Transportation Authority,
35 290–92

Metsä-Serla Oy, IV 314–16 *see also*
M-real Oyj.
Metso Corporation, 30 321–25 (upd.);
85 269–77 (upd.)
Mettler-Toledo International Inc., 30
326–28
Mexican Restaurants, Inc., 41 269–71
Mexichem, S.A.B. de C.V., 99 286–290
Meyer International Holdings, Ltd., 87
312–315
MFS Communications Company, Inc.,
11 301–03 *see also* MCI WorldCom,
Inc.
MG&E *see* Madison Gas and Electric.
MGA Entertainment, Inc., 95 279–82
MGIC Investment Corp., 52 242–44
MGM MIRAGE, 17 316–19; 98 237–42
(upd.)
MGM/UA Communications Company,
II 146–50 *see also*
Metro-Goldwyn-Mayer Inc.
MGN *see* Mirror Group Newspapers Ltd.
Miami Herald Media Company, 92
251–55
Michael Anthony Jewelers, Inc., 24
334–36
Michael Baker Corporation, 14 333–35;
51 245–48 (upd.)
Michael C. Fina Co., Inc., 52 245–47
Michael Foods, Inc., 25 331–34
Michael Page International plc, 45
272–74
Michaels Stores, Inc., 17 320–22; 71
226–30 (upd.)
Michelin *see* Compagnie Générale des
Établissements Michelin.
Michigan Bell Telephone Co., 14
336–38
Michigan National Corporation, 11
304–06 *see also* ABN AMRO Holding,
N.V.
Michigan Sporting Goods Distributors,
Inc., 72 228–30
Micrel, Incorporated, 77 276–79
Micro Warehouse, Inc., 16 371–73
MicroAge, Inc., 16 367–70
Microdot Inc., 8 365–68
Micron Technology, Inc., 11 307–09; 29
323–26 (upd.)
Micros Systems, Inc., 18 335–38
Microsemi Corporation, 94 311–14
Microsoft Corporation, 6 257–60; 27
319–23 (upd.); 63 293–97 (upd.)
MicroStrategy Incorporated, 87
316–320
Mid-America Apartment Communities,
Inc., 85 278–81
Mid-America Dairymen, Inc., 7 338–40
Midas Inc., 10 414–15; 56 228–31
(upd.)
Middle East Airlines - Air Liban S.A.L.,
79 251–54
The Middleby Corporation, 22 352–55
Middlesex Water Company, 45 275–78
The Middleton Doll Company, 53
222–25

Midland Bank plc, II 318–20; 17
323–26 (upd.) *see also* HSBC Holdings
plc.
The Midland Company, 65 233–35
Midway Airlines Corporation, 33
301–03
Midway Games, Inc., 25 335–38
Midwest Air Group, Inc., 35 293–95;
85 282–86 (upd.)
Midwest Grain Products, Inc., 49
261–63
Midwest Resources Inc., 6 523–25
Miele & Cie. KG, 56 232–35
MiG *see* Russian Aircraft Corporation
(MiG).
Migros-Genossenschafts-Bund, 68
252–55
MIH Limited, 31 329–32
Mikasa, Inc., 28 268–70
Mike-Sell's Inc., 15 298–300
Mikohn Gaming Corporation, 39
276–79
Milacron, Inc., 53 226–30 (upd.)
Milan AC S.p.A., 79 255–58
Milbank, Tweed, Hadley & McCloy, 27
324–27
Miles Laboratories, I 653–55 *see also*
Bayer A.G.
Millea Holdings Inc., 64 276–81 (upd.)
Millennium & Copthorne Hotels plc,
71 231–33
Millennium Pharmaceuticals, Inc., 47
249–52
Miller Brewing Company, I 269–70; 12
337–39 (upd.) *see also* SABMiller plc.
Miller Industries, Inc., 26 293–95
Miller Publishing Group, LLC, 57
242–44
Milliken & Co., V 366–68; 17 327–30
(upd.); 82 235–39 (upd.)
Milliman USA, 66 223–26
Millipore Corporation, 25 339–43; 84
271–276 (upd.)
The Mills Corporation, 77 280–83
Milnot Company, 46 289–91
Milton Bradley Company, 21 372–75
Milton CAT, Inc., 86 268–71
Milwaukee Brewers Baseball Club, 37
247–49
Mine Safety Appliances Company, 31
333–35
Minebea Co., Ltd., 90 298–302
The Miner Group International, 22
356–58
Minera Escondida Ltda., 100 293–96
Minerals & Metals Trading Corporation
of India Ltd., IV 143–44
Minerals Technologies Inc., 11 310–12;
52 248–51 (upd.)
Minnesota Mining & Manufacturing
Company, I 499–501; 8 369–71
(upd.); 26 296–99 (upd.) *see also* 3M
Co.
Minnesota Power, Inc., 11 313–16; 34
286–91 (upd.)
Minntech Corporation, 22 359–61
Minolta Co., Ltd., III 574–76; 18
339–42 (upd.); 43 281–85 (upd.)

The Minute Maid Company, 28 271–74

Minuteman International Inc., 46 292–95

Minyard Food Stores, Inc., 33 304–07; 86 272–77 (upd.)

Miquel y Costas Miquel S.A., 68 256–58

Mirage Resorts, Incorporated, 6 209–12; 28 275–79 (upd.) *see also* MGM MIRAGE.

Miramax Film Corporation, 64 282–85

Mirant Corporation, 98 243–47

Miroglio SpA, 86 278–81

Mirror Group Newspapers plc, 7 341–43; 23 348–51 (upd.)

Misonix, Inc., 80 248–51

Mississippi Chemical Corporation, 39 280–83

Misys PLC, 45 279–81; 46 296–99

Mitchell Energy and Development Corporation, 7 344–46 *see also* Devon Energy Corp.

Mitchells & Butlers PLC, 59 296–99

Mitel Corporation, 18 343–46

MITRE Corporation, 26 300–02

MITROPA AG, 37 250–53

Mitsubishi Bank, Ltd., II 321–22 *see also* Bank of Tokyo-Mitsubishi Ltd.

Mitsubishi Chemical Corporation, I 363–64; 56 236–38 (upd.)

Mitsubishi Corporation, I 502–04; 12 340–43 (upd.)

Mitsubishi Electric Corporation, II 57–59; 44 283–87 (upd.)

Mitsubishi Estate Company, Limited, IV 713–14; 61 215–18 (upd.)

Mitsubishi Heavy Industries, Ltd., III 577–79; 7 347–50 (upd.); 40 324–28 (upd.)

Mitsubishi Materials Corporation, III 712–13

Mitsubishi Motors Corporation, 9 349–51; 23 352–55 (upd.); 57 245–49 (upd.)

Mitsubishi Oil Co., Ltd., IV 460–62 *see also* Nippon Mitsubishi Oil Corp.

Mitsubishi Rayon Co. Ltd., V 369–71

Mitsubishi Trust & Banking Corporation, II 323–24

Mitsubishi UFJ Financial Group, Inc., 99 291–296 (upd.)

Mitsui & Co., Ltd., I 505–08; 28 280–85 (upd.)

Mitsui Bank, Ltd., II 325–27 *see also* Sumitomo Mitsui Banking Corp.

Mitsui Marine and Fire Insurance Company, Limited, III 295–96

Mitsui Mining & Smelting Co., Ltd., IV 145–46

Mitsui Mining Company, Limited, IV 147–49

Mitsui Mutual Life Insurance Company, III 297–98; 39 284–86 (upd.)

Mitsui O.S.K. Lines Ltd., V 473–76; 96 282–87 (upd.)

Mitsui Petrochemical Industries, Ltd., 9 352–54

Mitsui Real Estate Development Co., Ltd., IV 715–16

Mitsui Trust & Banking Company, Ltd., II 328

Mitsukoshi Ltd., V 142–44; 56 239–42 (upd.)

Mity Enterprises, Inc., 38 310–12

MIVA, Inc., 83 271–275

Mizuho Financial Group Inc., 25 344–46; 58 229–36 (upd.)

MNS, Ltd., 65 236–38

Mo och Domsjö AB, IV 317–19 *see also* Holmen AB

Mobil Corporation, IV 463–65; 7 351–54 (upd.); 21 376–80 (upd.) *see also* Exxon Mobil Corp.

Mobile Mini, Inc., 58 237–39

Mobile Telecommunications Technologies Corp., 18 347–49

Mobile TeleSystems OJSC, 59 300–03

Mocon, Inc., 76 275–77

Modell's Sporting Goods *see* Henry Modell & Company Inc.

Modern Times Group AB, 36 335–38

Modern Woodmen of America, 66 227–29

Modine Manufacturing Company, 8 372–75; 56 243–47 (upd.)

MoDo *see* Mo och Domsjö AB.

Modtech Holdings, Inc., 77 284–87

Moen Incorporated, 12 344–45

Moët-Hennessy, I 271–72 *see also* LVMH Moët Hennessy Louis Vuitton SA.

Mohawk Industries, Inc., 19 274–76; 63 298–301 (upd.)

Mohegan Tribal Gaming Authority, 37 254–57

Moksel *see* A. Moksel AG.

MOL *see* Mitsui O.S.K. Lines, Ltd.

MOL Rt, 70 192–95

Moldflow Corporation, 73 227–30

Molex Incorporated, 11 317–19; 14 27; 54 236–41 (upd.)

Moliflor Loisirs, 80 252–55

Molinos Río de la Plata S.A., 61 219–21

Molins plc, 51 249–51

The Molson Companies Limited, I 273–75; 26 303–07 (upd.)

Molson Coors Brewing Company, 77 288–300 (upd.)

Monaco Coach Corporation, 31 336–38

Monadnock Paper Mills, Inc., 21 381–84

Monarch Casino & Resort, Inc., 65 239–41

The Monarch Cement Company, 72 231–33

Mondadori *see* Arnoldo Mondadori Editore S.p.A.

Mondragón Corporación Cooperativa, 101 347–51

MoneyGram International, Inc., 94 315–18

Monfort, Inc., 13 350–52

Monnaie de Paris, 62 246–48

Monnoyeur Group *see* Groupe Monnoyeur.

Monoprix S.A., 86 282–85

Monro Muffler Brake, Inc., 24 337–40

Monrovia Nursery Company, 70 196–98

Monsanto Company, I 365–67; 9 355–57 (upd.); 29 327–31 (upd.); 77 301–07 (upd.)

Monsoon plc, 39 287–89

Monster Cable Products, Inc., 69 256–58

Monster Worldwide Inc., 74 194–97 (upd.)

Montana Coffee Traders, Inc., 60 208–10

The Montana Power Company, 11 320–22; 44 288–92 (upd.)

Montblanc International GmbH, 82 240–44

Montedison S.p.A., I 368–69; 24 341–44 (upd.)

Monterey Pasta Company, 58 240–43

Montgomery Ward & Co., Incorporated, V 145–48; 20 374–79 (upd.)

Montres Rolex S.A., 13 353–55; 34 292–95 (upd.)

Montupet S.A., 63 302–04

Moody's Corporation, 65 242–44

Moog Inc., 13 356–58

Moog Music, Inc., 75 261–64

Mooney Aerospace Group Ltd., 52 252–55

Moore Corporation Limited, IV 644–46 *see also* R.R. Donnelley & Sons Co.

Moore-Handley, Inc., 39 290–92

Moore Medical Corp., 17 331–33

Moran Towing Corporation, Inc., 15 301–03

The Morgan Crucible Company plc, 82 245–50

Morgan Grenfell Group PLC, II 427–29 *see also* Deutsche Bank AG.

The Morgan Group, Inc., 46 300–02

Morgan, Lewis & Bockius LLP, 29 332–34

Morgan Stanley Dean Witter & Company, II 430–32; 16 374–78 (upd.); 33 311–14 (upd.)

Morgan's Foods, Inc., 101 352 |B5–55

Morgans Hotel Group Company, 80 256–59

Morguard Corporation, 85 287–90

Morinaga & Co. Ltd., 61 222–25

Morinda Holdings, Inc., 82 251–54

Morningstar Inc., 68 259–62

Morris Communications Corporation, 36 339–42

Morris Travel Services L.L.C., 26 308–11

Morrison & Foerster LLP, 78 220–23

Morrison Knudsen Corporation, 7 355–58; 28 286–90 (upd.) *see also* The Washington Companies.

Morrison Restaurants Inc., 11 323–25

Morrow Equipment Co. L.L.C., 87 325–327

Morse Shoe Inc., 13 359–61

NIPSCO Industries, Inc., 6 532–33
Nissan Motor Company Ltd., I 183–84;
 11 350–52 (upd.); 34 303–07 (upd.);
 92 273–79 (upd.)
Nisshin Seifun Group Inc., II 554; 66
 246–48 (upd.)
Nisshin Steel Co., Ltd., IV 159–60
Nissho Iwai K.K., I 509–11
Nissin Food Products Company Ltd.,
 75 286–88
Nitches, Inc., 53 245–47
Nixdorf Computer AG, III 154–55 *see
 also* Wincor Nixdorf Holding GmbH.
NKK Corporation, IV 161–63; 28
 322–26 (upd.)
NL Industries, Inc., 10 434–36
Noah Education Holdings Ltd., 97
 303–06
Noah's New York Bagels *see*
 Einstein/Noah Bagel Corp.
Nobel Industries AB, 9 380–82 *see also*
 Akzo Nobel N.V.
Nobel Learning Communities, Inc., 37
 276–79; 76 281–85 (upd.)
Noble Affiliates, Inc., 11 353–55
Noble Roman's Inc., 14 351–53; 99
 297–302 (upd.)
Nobleza Piccardo SAICF, 64 291–93
Noboa *see also* Exportadora Bananera
 Noboa, S.A.
Nocibé SA, 54 265–68
NOF Corporation, 72 249–51
Nokia Corporation, II 69–71; 17
 352–54 (upd.); 38 328–31 (upd.); 77
 308–13 (upd.)
NOL Group *see* Neptune Orient Lines
 Ltd.
Noland Company, 35 311–14
Nolo.com, Inc., 49 288–91
Nomura Securities Company, Limited,
 II 438–41; 9 383–86 (upd.)
Noodle Kidoodle, 16 388–91
Noodles & Company, Inc., 55 277–79
Nooter Corporation, 61 251–53
Noranda Inc., IV 164–66; 7 397–99
 (upd.); 64 294–98 (upd.)
Norcal Waste Systems, Inc., 60 222–24
Norddeutsche Affinerie AG, 62 249–53
Nordea AB, 40 336–39
Nordex AG, 101 362–65
NordicTrack, 22 382–84 *see also* Icon
 Health & Fitness, Inc.
Nordisk Film A/S, 80 269–73
Nordson Corporation, 11 356–58; 48
 296–99 (upd.)
Nordstrom, Inc., V 156–58; 18 371–74
 (upd.); 67 277–81 (upd.)
Norelco Consumer Products Co., 26
 334–36
Norfolk Southern Corporation, V
 484–86; 29 358–61 (upd.); 75
 289–93 (upd.)
Norinchukin Bank, II 340–41
Norm Thompson Outfitters, Inc., 47
 275–77
Norrell Corporation, 25 356–59
Norsk Hydro ASA, 10 437–40; 35
 315–19 (upd.)

Norske Skogindustrier ASA, 63 314–16
Norstan, Inc., 16 392–94
Nortek, Inc., 34 308–12
Nortel Networks Corporation, 36
 349–54 (upd.)
North American Galvanizing &
 Coatings, Inc., 99 303–306
North Atlantic Trading Company Inc.,
 65 266–68
North Carolina National Bank
 Corporation *see* NCNB Corp.
The North Face, Inc., 18 375–77; 78
 258–61 (upd.)
North Fork Bancorporation, Inc., 46
 314–17
North Pacific Group, Inc., 61 254–57
North Star Steel Company, 18 378–81
The North West Company, Inc., 12
 361–63
North West Water Group plc, 11
 359–62 *see also* United Utilities PLC.
Northeast Utilities, V 668–69; 48
 303–06 (upd.)
Northern and Shell Network plc, 87
 341–344
Northern Foods plc, 10 441–43; 61
 258–62 (upd.)
Northern Rock plc, 33 318–21
Northern States Power Company, V
 670–72; 20 391–95 (upd.) *see also*
 Xcel Energy Inc.
Northern Telecom Limited, V 308–10
 see also Nortel Networks Corp.
Northern Trust Corporation, 9 387–89;
 101 366–72 (upd.)
Northland Cranberries, Inc., 38 332–34
Northrop Grumman Corporation, I
 76–77; 11 363–65 (upd.); 45 304–12
 (upd.)
Northwest Airlines Corporation, I
 112–14; 6 103–05 (upd.); 26 337–40
 (upd.); 74 204–08 (upd.)
Northwest Natural Gas Company, 45
 313–15
NorthWestern Corporation, 37 280–83
Northwestern Mutual Life Insurance
 Company, III 321–24; 45 316–21
 (upd.)
Norton Company, 8 395–97
Norton McNaughton, Inc., 27 346–49
 see also Jones Apparel Group, Inc.
Norwegian Cruise Lines *see* NCL
 Corporation
Norwich & Peterborough Building
 Society, 55 280–82
Norwood Promotional Products, Inc.,
 26 341–43
Nova Corporation of Alberta, V 673–75
NovaCare, Inc., 11 366–68
Novacor Chemicals Ltd., 12 364–66
Novar plc, 49 292–96 (upd.)
Novartis AG, 39 304–10 (upd.)
NovaStar Financial, Inc., 91 354–58
Novell, Inc., 6 269–71; 23 359–62
 (upd.)
Novellus Systems, Inc., 18 382–85
Noven Pharmaceuticals, Inc., 55 283–85

Novo Nordisk A/S, I 658–60; 61
 263–66 (upd.)
NOW *see* National Organization for
 Women, Inc.
NPC International, Inc., 40 340–42
The NPD Group, Inc., 68 275–77
NPM (Nationale Portefeuille
 Maatschappij) *see* Compagnie Nationale
 à Portefeuille.
NPR *see* National Public Radio, Inc.
NRG Energy, Inc., 79 290–93
NRT Incorporated, 61 267–69
NS *see* Norfolk Southern Corp.
NSF International, 72 252–55
NSK *see* Nippon Seiko K.K.
NSP *see* Northern States Power Co.
NSS Enterprises, Inc., 78 262–65
NTCL *see* Northern Telecom Ltd.
NTD Architecture, 101 373–76
NTL Inc., 65 269–72
NTN Buzztime, Inc., 86 308–11
NTN Corporation, III 595–96; 47
 278–81 (upd.)
NTTPC *see* Nippon Telegraph and
 Telephone Public Corp.
NU *see* Northeast Utilities.
Nu-kote Holding, Inc., 18 386–89
Nu Skin Enterprises, Inc., 27 350–53;
 31 386–89; 76 286–90 (upd.)
Nucor Corporation, 7 400–02; 21
 392–95 (upd.); 79 294–300 (upd.)
Nufarm Ltd., 87 345–348
Nuplex Industries Ltd., 92 280–83
Nutraceutical International
 Corporation, 37 284–86
NutraSweet Company, 8 398–400
Nutreco Holding N.V., 56 256–59
Nutrexpa S.A., 92 284–87
NutriSystem, Inc., 71 250–53
Nutrition for Life International Inc., 22
 385–88
Nutrition 21 Inc., 97 307–11
Nuveen *see* John Nuveen Co.
NVIDIA Corporation, 54 269–73
NVR Inc., 8 401–03; 70 206–09 (upd.)
NWA, Inc. *see* Northwest Airlines Corp.
NYK *see* Nippon Yusen Kabushiki Kaisha
 (NYK).
NYMAGIC, Inc., 41 284–86
NYNEX Corporation, V 311–13 *see also*
 Verizon Communications.
Nypro, Inc., 101 377–82
NYRG *see* New York Restaurant Group,
 Inc.
NYSE *see* New York Stock Exchange.
NYSEG *see* New York State Electric and
 Gas Corp.

O

O&Y *see* Olympia & York Developments
 Ltd.
O.C. Tanner Co., 69 279–81
Oak Harbor Freight Lines, Inc., 53
 248–51
Oak Industries Inc., 21 396–98 *see also*
 Corning Inc.
Oak Technology, Inc., 22 389–93 *see also*
 Zoran Corp.

Oakhurst Dairy, 60 225–28
Oakleaf Waste Management, LLC, 97 312–15
Oakley, Inc., 18 390–93; 49 297–302 (upd.)
Oaktree Capital Management, LLC, 71 254–56
Oakwood Homes Corporation, 13 155; 15 326–28
OAO AVTOVAZ *see* AVTOVAZ Joint Stock Co.
OAO Gazprom, 42 261–65
OAO LUKOIL, 40 343–46
OAO NK YUKOS, 47 282–85
OAO Severstal *see* Severstal Joint Stock Co.
OAO Siberian Oil Company (Sibneft), 49 303–06
OAO Tatneft, 45 322–26
Obayashi Corporation, 78 266–69 (upd.)
Oberto Sausage Company, Inc., 92 288–91
Obie Media Corporation, 56 260–62
Obrascon Huarte Lain S.A., 76 291–94
Observer AB, 55 286–89
Occidental Petroleum Corporation, IV 480–82; 25 360–63 (upd.); 71 257–61 (upd.)
Océ N.V., 24 360–63; 91 359–65 (upd.)
Ocean Beauty Seafoods, Inc., 74 209–11
Ocean Group plc, 6 415–17 *see also* Exel plc.
Ocean Spray Cranberries, Inc., 7 403–05; 25 364–67 (upd.); 83 284–290
Oceaneering International, Inc., 63 317–19
Ocesa *see* Corporación Interamericana de Entretenimiento, S.A. de C.V.
O'Charley's Inc., 19 286–88; 60 229–32 (upd.)
OCI *see* Orascom Construction Industries S.A.E.
OCLC Online Computer Library Center, Inc., 96 324–28
The O'Connell Companies Inc., 100 306–09
Octel Messaging, 14 354–56; 41 287–90 (upd.)
Ocular Sciences, Inc., 65 273–75
Odakyu Electric Railway Co., Ltd., V 487–89; 68 278–81 (upd.)
Odebrecht S.A., 73 242–44
Odetics Inc., 14 357–59
Odfjell SE, 101 383–87
ODL, Inc., 55 290–92
Odwalla, Inc., 31 349–51
Odyssey Marine Exploration, Inc., 91 366–70
OEC Medical Systems, Inc., 27 354–56
OENEO S.A., 74 212–15 (upd.)
Office Depot, Inc., 8 404–05; 23 363–65 (upd.); 65 276–80 (upd.)
OfficeMax Incorporated, 15 329–31; 43 291–95 (upd.); 101 388–94 (upd.)
OfficeTiger, LLC, 75 294–96

Officine Alfieri Maserati S.p.A., 13 376–78
Offshore Logistics, Inc., 37 287–89
Obagi Medical Products, Inc., 95 310–13
Ogden Corporation, I 512–14; 6 151–53 *see also* Covanta Energy Corp.
Ogilvy Group Inc., I 25–27 *see also* WPP Group.
Oglebay Norton Company, 17 355–58
Oglethorpe Power Corporation, 6 537–38
Ohbayashi Corporation, I 586–87
The Ohio Art Company, 14 360–62; 59 317–20 (upd.)
Ohio Bell Telephone Company, 14 363–65; *see also* Ameritech Corp.
Ohio Casualty Corp., 11 369–70
Ohio Edison Company, V 676–78
Oil and Natural Gas Commission, IV 483–84; 90 313–17 (upd.)
Oil-Dri Corporation of America, 20 396–99; 89 331–36 (upd.)
Oil States International, Inc., 77 314–17
Oil Transporting Joint Stock Company Transneft, 92 450–54
The Oilgear Company, 74 216–18
Oji Paper Co., Ltd., IV 320–22; 57 272–75 (upd.)
OJSC Novolipetsk Steel, 99 311–315
OJSC Wimm-Bill-Dann Foods, 48 436–39
Oki Electric Industry Company, Limited, II 72–74; 15 125; 21 390
Oklahoma Gas and Electric Company, 6 539–40
Okuma Holdings Inc., 74 219–21
Okura & Co., Ltd., IV 167–68
Olan Mills, Inc., 62 254–56
Old America Stores, Inc., 17 359–61
Old Dominion Freight Line, Inc., 57 276–79
Old Kent Financial Corp., 11 371–72 *see also* Fifth Third Bancorp.
Old Mutual PLC, IV 535; 61 270–72
Old National Bancorp, 15 332–34; 98 266–70 (upd.)
Old Navy, Inc., 70 210–12
Old Orchard Brands, LLC, 73 245–47
Old Republic International Corporation, 11 373–75; 58 258–61 (upd.)
Old Spaghetti Factory International Inc., 24 364–66
Old Town Canoe Company, 74 222–24
Olga's Kitchen, Inc., 80 274–76
Olin Corporation, I 379–81; 13 379–81 (upd.); 78 270–74 (upd.)
Olivetti S.p.A., 34 316–20 (upd.)
Olsten Corporation, 6 41–43; 29 362–65 (upd.) *see also* Adecco S.A.
Olympia & York Developments Ltd., IV 720–21; 9 390–92 (upd.)
OM Group, Inc., 17 362–64; 78 275–78 (upd.)
OMA *see* Grupo Aeroportuario del Centro Norte, S.A.B. de C.V.

Omaha Steaks International Inc., 62 257–59
Omega Protein Corporation, 99 316–318
O'Melveny & Myers, 37 290–93
Omni Hotels Corp., 12 367–69
Omnicare, Inc., 13 49 307–10
Omnicell, Inc., 89 337–40
Omnicom Group Inc., I 28–32; 22 394–99 (upd.); 77 318–25 (upd.)
Omnilife *see* Grupo Omnilife S.A. de C.V.
OmniSource Corporation, 14 366–67
OMNOVA Solutions Inc., 59 324–26
Omrix Biopharmaceuticals, Inc., 95 314–17
Omron Corporation, 28 331–35 (upd.); 53 46
Omron Tateisi Electronics Company, II 75–77
OMV AG, IV 485–87; 98 271–74 (upd.)
On Assignment, Inc., 20 400–02
1-800-FLOWERS, Inc., 26 344–46
1-800-GOT-JUNK? LLC, 74 225–27
180s, L.L.C., 64 299–301
One Price Clothing Stores, Inc., 20 403–05
O'Neal Steel, Inc., 95 306–09
Oneida Ltd., 7 406–08; 31 352–55 (upd.); 88 280–85 (upd.)
ONEOK Inc., 7 409–12
Onet S.A., 92 292–95
Onex Corporation, 16 395–97; 65 281–85 (upd.)
Onion, Inc., 69 282–84
Onoda Cement Co., Ltd., III 717–19 *see also* Taiheiyo Cement Corp.
Ontario Hydro Services Company, 6 541–42; 32 368–71 (upd.)
Ontario Teachers' Pension Plan, 61 273–75
Onyx Acceptance Corporation, 59 327–29
Onyx Software Corporation, 53 252–55
OOC Inc., 97 316–19
OPAP S.A. *see* Greek Organization of Football Prognostics S.A. (OPAP)
Opel AG *see* Adam Opel AG.
Open *see* Groupe Open.
Open Text Corporation, 79 301–05
Openwave Systems Inc., 95 318–22
Operadora Mexicana de Aeropuertos *see* Grupo Aeroportuario del Centro Norte, S.A.B. de C.V.
Operation Smile, Inc., 75 297–99
Opinion Research Corporation, 46 318–22
The Oppenheimer Group, 76 295–98
Oppenheimer Wolff & Donnelly LLP, 71 262–64
Opsware Inc., 49 311–14
OPTEK Technology Inc., 98 275–78
Option Care Inc., 48 307–10
Optische Werke G. Rodenstock, 44 319–23
Opus Corporation, 34 321–23; 101 395–99 (upd.)

Oracle Corporation, 6 272–74; 24 367–71 (upd.); 67 282–87 (upd.)
Orange Glo International, 53 256–59
Orange S.A., 84 286–289
Orascom Construction Industries S.A.E., 87 349–352
OraSure Technologies, Inc., 75 300–03
Orbital Sciences Corporation, 22 400–03
Orbitz, Inc., 61 276–78
Orbotech Ltd., 75 304–06
Orchard Supply Hardware Stores Corporation, 17 365–67
Ore-Ida Foods Inc., 13 382–83; 78 279–82 (upd.)
Oregon Chai, Inc., 49 315–17
Oregon Dental Service Health Plan, Inc., 51 276–78
Oregon Freeze Dry, Inc., 74 228–30
Oregon Metallurgical Corporation, 20 406–08
Oregon Steel Mills, Inc., 14 368–70
O'Reilly Automotive, Inc., 26 347–49; 78 283–87 (upd.)
O'Reilly Media, Inc., 99 307–310
Organic To Go Food Corporation, 99 319–322
Organic Valley (Coulee Region Organic Produce Pool), 53 260–62
Organización Soriana, S.A. de C.V., 35 320–22
Orgill, Inc., 99 323–326
ORI *see* Old Republic International Corp.
Orion Oyj, 72 256–59
Orion Pictures Corporation, 6 167–70 *see also* Metro-Goldwyn-Mayer Inc.
ORIX Corporation, II 442–43; 44 324–26 (upd.)
Orkla ASA, 18 394–98; 82 259–64 (upd.)
Orleans Homebuilders, Inc., 62 260–62
Ormat Technologies, Inc., 87 353–358
Ormet Corporation, 82 265–68
Orrick, Herrington and Sutcliffe LLP, 76 299–301
Orszagos Takarekpenztar es Kereskedelmi Bank Rt. (OTP Bank), 78 288–91
Orthodontic Centers of America, Inc., 35 323–26
Orthofix International NV, 72 260–62
The Orvis Company, Inc., 28 336–39
Oryx Energy Company, 7 413–15
Osaka Gas Company, Ltd., V 679–81; 60 233–36 (upd.)
Oscar Mayer Foods Corp., 12 370–72 *see also* Kraft Foods Inc.
Oshawa Group Limited, II 649–50
OshKosh B'Gosh, Inc., 9 393–95; 42 266–70 (upd.)
Oshkosh Corporation, 7 416–18; 98 279–84 (upd.)
Oshman's Sporting Goods, Inc., 17 368–70 *see also* Gart Sports Co.
OSI Restaurant Partners, Inc., 88 286–91 (upd.)
Osmonics, Inc., 18 399–401
Osram GmbH, 86 312–16

Österreichische Bundesbahnen GmbH, 6 418–20
Österreichische Elektrizitätswirtschafts-AG, 85 307–10
Österreichische Post- und Telegraphenverwaltung, V 314–17
O'Sullivan Industries Holdings, Inc., 34 313–15
Otari Inc., 89 341–44
Otis Elevator Company, Inc., 13 384–86; 39 311–15 (upd.)
Otis Spunkmeyer, Inc., 28 340–42
Otor S.A., 77 326–29
OTP Bank *see* Orszagos Takarekpenztar es Kereskedelmi Bank Rt.
OTR Express, Inc., 25 368–70
Ottakar's plc, 64 302–04
Ottaway Newspapers, Inc., 15 335–37
Otter Tail Power Company, 18 402–05
Otto Bremer Foundation *see* Bremer Financial Corp.
Otto Fuchs KG, 100 310–14
Otto Versand GmbH & Co., V 159–61; 15 338–40 (upd.); 34 324–28 (upd.)
Outback Steakhouse, Inc., 12 373–75; 34 329–32 (upd.) *see also* OSI Restaurant Partners, Inc.
Outboard Marine Corporation, III 597–600; 20 409–12 (upd.) *see also* Bombardier Inc.
Outdoor Research, Incorporated, 67 288–90
Outdoor Systems, Inc., 25 371–73 *see also* Infinity Broadcasting Corp.
Outlook Group Corporation, 37 294–96
Outokumpu Oyj, 38 335–37
Outrigger Enterprises, Inc., 67 291–93
Overhead Door Corporation, 70 213–16
Overhill Corporation, 51 279–81
Overland Storage Inc., 100 315–20
Overnite Corporation, 14 371–73; 58 262–65 (upd.)
Overseas Shipholding Group, Inc., 11 376–77
Overstock.com, Inc., 75 307–09
Owens & Minor, Inc., 16 398–401; 68 282–85 (upd.)
Owens Corning, III 720–23; 20 413–17 (upd.); 98 285–91 (upd.)
Owens-Illinois, Inc., I 609–11; 26 350–53 (upd.); 85 311–18 (upd.)
Owosso Corporation, 29 366–68
Oxfam GB, 87 359–362
Oxford Health Plans, Inc., 16 402–04
Oxford Industries, Inc., 8 406–08; 84 290–296 (upd.)

P

P&C Foods Inc., 8 409–11
P & F Industries, Inc., 45 327–29
P&G *see* Procter & Gamble Co.
P.C. Richard & Son Corp., 23 372–74
P.F. Chang's China Bistro, Inc., 37 297–99; 86 317–21 (upd.)

P.H. Glatfelter Company, 8 412–14; 30 349–52 (upd.); 83 291-297 (upd.)
P.W. Minor and Son, Inc., 100 321–24
PACCAR Inc., I 185–86; 26 354–56 (upd.)
Pacer International, Inc., 54 274–76
Pacer Technology, 40 347–49
Pacific Basin Shipping Ltd., 86 322–26
Pacific Clay Products Inc., 88 292–95
Pacific Coast Building Products, Inc., 94 338–41
Pacific Coast Feather Company, 67 294–96
Pacific Coast Restaurants, Inc., 90 318–21
Pacific Dunlop Limited, 10 444–46 *see also* Ansell Ltd.
Pacific Enterprises, V 682–84 *see also* Sempra Energy.
Pacific Ethanol, Inc., 81 269–72
Pacific Gas and Electric Company, V 685–87 *see also* PG&E Corp.
Pacific Internet Limited, 87 363–366
Pacific Mutual Holding Company, 98 292–96
Pacific Sunwear of California, Inc., 28 343–45; 47 425
Pacific Telecom, Inc., 6 325–28
Pacific Telesis Group, V 318–20 *see also* SBC Communications.
PacifiCare Health Systems, Inc., 11 378–80
PacifiCorp, Inc., V 688–90; 26 357–60 (upd.)
Packaging Corporation of America, 12 376–78; 51 282–85 (upd.)
Packard Bell Electronics, Inc., 13 387–89
Packeteer, Inc., 81 273–76
Paddock Publications, Inc., 53 263–65
Paddy Power plc, 98 297–300
PagesJaunes Groupe SA, 79 306–09
Paging Network Inc., 11 381–83
Pagnossin S.p.A., 73 248–50
PaineWebber Group Inc., II 444–46; 22 404–07 (upd.) *see also* UBS AG.
Pakistan International Airlines Corporation, 46 323–26
Pakistan State Oil Company Ltd., 81 277–80
PAL *see* Philippine Airlines, Inc.
Palace Sports & Entertainment, Inc., 97 320–25
Palfinger AG, 100 325–28
PALIC *see* Pan-American Life Insurance Co.
Pall Corporation, 9 396–98; 72 263–66 (upd.)
Palm Harbor Homes, Inc., 39 316–18
Palm, Inc., 36 355–57; 75 310–14 (upd.)
Palm Management Corporation, 71 265–68
Palmer & Cay, Inc., 69 285–87
Palmer Candy Company, 80 277–81
Palmer Co. *see* R. M. Palmer Co.
Paloma Industries Ltd., 71 269–71

Palomar Medical Technologies, Inc., 22 408–10

Pamida Holdings Corporation, 15 341–43

The Pampered Chef Ltd., 18 406–08; 78 292–96 (upd.)

Pamplin Corp. *see* R.B. Pamplin Corp.

Pan-American Life Insurance Company, 48 311–13

Pan American World Airways, Inc., I 115–16; 12 379–81 (upd.)

Panalpina World Transport (Holding) Ltd., 47 286–88

Panamerican Beverages, Inc., 47 289–91; 54 74

PanAmSat Corporation, 46 327–29

Panattoni Development Company, Inc., 99 327–330

Panavision Inc., 24 372–74

Pancho's Mexican Buffet, Inc., 46 330–32

Panda Restaurant Group, Inc., 35 327–29; 97 326–30 (upd.)

Panera Bread Company, 44 327–29

Panhandle Eastern Corporation, V 691–92 *see also* CMS Energy Corp.

Pantone Inc., 53 266–69

The Pantry, Inc., 36 358–60

Panzani, 84 297–300

Papa Gino's Holdings Corporation, Inc., 86 327–30

Papa John's International, Inc., 15 344–46; 71 272–76 (upd.)

Papa Murphy's International, Inc., 54 277–79

Papeteries de Lancey, 23 366–68

Papetti's Hygrade Egg Products, Inc., 39 319–21

Pappas Restaurants, Inc., 76 302–04

Par Pharmaceutical Companies, Inc., 65 286–88

The Paradies Shops, Inc., 88 296–99

Paradise Music & Entertainment, Inc., 42 271–74

Paradores de Turismo de Espana S.A., 73 251–53

Parallel Petroleum Corporation, 101 400–03

Parametric Technology Corp., 16 405–07

Paramount Pictures Corporation, II 154–56; 94 342–47 (upd.)

Paramount Resources Ltd., 87 367–370

PAREXEL International Corporation, 84 301–304

Parfums Givenchy S.A., 100 329–32

Paribas *see* BNP Paribas Group.

Paris Corporation, 22 411–13

Parisian, Inc., 14 374–76 *see also* Belk, Inc.

Park Corp., 22 414–16

Park-Ohio Holdings Corp., 17 371–73; 85 319–23 (upd.)

Parker Drilling Company, 28 346–48

Parker-Hannifin Corporation, III 601–03; 24 375–78 (upd.); 99 331–337 (upd.)

Parlex Corporation, 61 279–81

Parmalat Finanziaria SpA, 50 343–46

Parque Arauco S.A., 72 267–69

Parras *see* Compañia Industrial de Parras, S.A. de C.V. (CIPSA).

Parsons Brinckerhoff, Inc., 34 333–36

The Parsons Corporation, 8 415–17; 56 263–67 (upd.)

PartnerRe Ltd., 83 298-301

Partouche SA *see* Groupe Partouche SA.

Party City Corporation, 54 280–82

Pathé SA, 29 369–71 *see also* Chargeurs International.

Pathmark Stores, Inc., 23 369–71; 101 404–08 (upd.)

Patina Oil & Gas Corporation, 24 379–81

Patrick Industries, Inc., 30 342–45

Patriot Transportation Holding, Inc., 91 371–74

Patterson Dental Co., 19 289–91

Patterson-UTI Energy, Inc., 55 293–95

Patton Boggs LLP, 71 277–79

Paul Harris Stores, Inc., 18 409–12

Paul, Hastings, Janofsky & Walker LLP, 27 357–59

Paul Mueller Company, 65 289–91

Paul Reed Smith Guitar Company, 89 345–48

The Paul Revere Corporation, 12 382–83

Paul-Son Gaming Corporation, 66 249–51

Paul, Weiss, Rifkind, Wharton & Garrison, 47 292–94

Paulaner Brauerei GmbH & Co. KG, 35 330–33

Paxson Communications Corporation, 33 322–26

Pay 'N Pak Stores, Inc., 9 399–401

Paychex, Inc., 15 347–49; 46 333–36 (upd.)

Payless Cashways, Inc., 11 384–86; 44 330–33 (upd.)

Payless ShoeSource, Inc., 18 413–15; 69 288–92 (upd.)

PayPal Inc., 58 266–69

PBL *see* Publishing and Broadcasting Ltd.

PBS *see* Public Broadcasting Stations.

The PBSJ Corporation, 82 269–73

PC Connection, Inc., 37 300–04

PCA *see* Packaging Corporation of America.

PCA International, Inc., 62 263–65

PCC *see* Companhia Suzano de Papel e Celulose S.A.

PCC Natural Markets, 94 348–51

PCL Construction Group Inc., 50 347–49

PCM Uitgevers NV, 53 270–73

PCS *see* Potash Corp. of Saskatchewan Inc.

PDI, Inc., 52 272–75

PDL BioPharma, Inc., 90 322–25

PDO *see* Petroleum Development Oman.

PDQ Food Stores Inc., 79 310–13

PDS Gaming Corporation, 44 334–37

PDVSA *see* Petróleos de Venezuela S.A.

Peabody Energy Corporation, 10 447–49; 45 330–33 (upd.)

Peabody Holding Company, Inc., IV 169–72

Peace Arch Entertainment Group Inc., 51 286–88

The Peak Technologies Group, Inc., 14 377–80

Peapod, Inc., 30 346–48

Pearl Musical Instrument Company, 78 297–300

Pearle Vision, Inc., 13 390–92

Pearson plc, IV 657–59; 46 337–41 (upd.)

Peavey Electronics Corporation, 16 408–10; 94 352–56 (upd.)

Pechiney S.A., IV 173–75; 45 334–37 (upd.)

PECO Energy Company, 11 387–90 *see also* Exelon Corp.

Pediatric Services of America, Inc., 31 356–58

Pediatrix Medical Group, Inc., 61 282–85

Peebles Inc., 16 411–13; 43 296–99 (upd.)

Peek & Cloppenburg KG, 46 342–45

Peet's Coffee & Tea, Inc., 38 338–40; 100 333–37 (upd.)

Peg Perego SpA, 88 300–03

Pegasus Solutions, Inc., 75 315–18

Pei Cobb Freed & Partners Architects LLP, 57 280–82

Pelican Products, Inc., 86 331–34

Pelikan Holding AG, 92 296–300

Pella Corporation, 12 384–86; 39 322–25 (upd.); 89 349–53 (upd.)

Pemco Aviation Group Inc., 54 283–86

Pemex *see* Petróleos Mexicanos.

Penaflor S.A., 66 252–54

Penauille Polyservices SA, 49 318–21

Pendleton Grain Growers Inc., 64 305–08

Pendleton Woolen Mills, Inc., 42 275–78

Penford Corporation, 55 296–99

Pengrowth Energy Trust, 95 323–26

The Penguin Group, 100 338–42

The Peninsular and Oriental Steam Navigation Company, V 490–93; 38 341–46 (upd.)

Peninsular and Oriental Steam Navigation Company (Bovis Division), I 588–89 *see also* DP World.

Penn Engineering & Manufacturing Corp., 28 349–51

Penn National Gaming, Inc., 33 327–29

Penn Traffic Company, 13 393–95

Penn Virginia Corporation, 85 324–27

Penney's *see* J.C. Penney Company, Inc.

Pennington Seed Inc., 98 301–04

Pennon Group Plc, 45 338–41

Pennsylvania Blue Shield, III 325–27 *see also* Highmark Inc.

Pennsylvania Power & Light Company, V 693–94

Pennwalt Corporation, I 382–84

PennWell Corporation, 55 300–03
Pennzoil-Quaker State Company, IV
488–90; 20 418–22 (upd.); 50
350–55 (upd.)
Penske Corporation, V 494–95; 19
292–94 (upd.); 84 305–309 (upd.)
Pentair, Inc., 7 419–21; 26 361–64
(upd.); 81 281–87 (upd.)
Pentax Corporation, 78 301–05
Pentech International, Inc., 29 372–74
The Pentland Group plc, 20 423–25;
100 343–47 (upd.)
Penton Media, Inc., 27 360–62
Penzeys Spices, Inc., 79 314–16
People Express Airlines Inc., I 117–18
Peoples Energy Corporation, 6 543–44
PeopleSoft Inc., 14 381–83; 33 330–33
(upd.) *see also* Oracle Corp.
The Pep Boys—Manny, Moe & Jack, 11
391–93; 36 361–64 (upd.); 81
288–94 (upd.)
PEPCO *see* Potomac Electric Power Co.
Pepper *see* J. W. Pepper and Son Inc.
Pepper Hamilton LLP, 43 300–03
Pepperidge Farm, Incorporated, 81
295–300
The Pepsi Bottling Group, Inc., 40
350–53
PepsiAmericas, Inc., 67 297–300 (upd.)
PepsiCo, Inc., I 276–79; 10 450–54
(upd.); 38 347–54 (upd.); 93 333–44
(upd.)
Pequiven *see* Petroquímica de Venezuela
S.A.
Perdigao SA, 52 276–79
Perdue Farms Inc., 7 422–24; 23
375–78 (upd.)
Perfetti Van Melle S.p.A., 72 270–73
Performance Food Group, 31 359–62;
96 329–34 (upd.)
Perini Corporation, 8 418–21; 82
274–79 (upd.)
PerkinElmer, Inc., 7 425–27; 78 306–10
(upd.)
Perkins Coie LLP, 56 268–70
Perkins Family Restaurants, L.P., 22
417–19
Perkins Foods Holdings Ltd., 87
371–374
Perma-Fix Environmental Services, Inc.,
99 338–341
Pernod Ricard S.A., I 280–81; 21
399–401 (upd.); 72 274–77 (upd.)
Perot Systems Corporation, 29 375–78
Perrigo Company, 12 387–89; 59
330–34 (upd.)
Perry Ellis International, Inc., 41
291–94
Perry's Ice Cream Company Inc., 90
326–29
The Perseus Books Group, 91 375–78
Perstorp AB, I 385–87; 51 289–92
(upd.)
Pertamina, IV 491–93; 56 271–74
(upd.)
Perusahaan Otomobil Nasional Bhd., 62
266–68
Pescanova S.A., 81 301–04

Pet Incorporated, 7 428–31
Petco Animal Supplies, Inc., 29 379–81;
74 231–34 (upd.)
Pete's Brewing Company, 22 420–22
Peter Kiewit Sons' Inc., 8 422–24
Peter Piper, Inc., 70 217–19
Peterbilt Motors Company, 89 354–57
Petersen Publishing Company, 21
402–04
Peterson American Corporation, 55
304–06
Petit Bateau, 95 327–31
PetMed Express, Inc., 81 305–08
Petrie Stores Corporation, 8 425–27
Petro-Canada, IV 494–96; 99 342–349
(upd.)
Petrobrás *see* Petróleo Brasileiro S.A.
Petrobras Energia Participaciones S.A.,
72 278–81
Petroecuador *see* Petróleos del Ecuador.
Petrofac Ltd., 95 332–35
PetroFina S.A., IV 497–500; 26 365–69
(upd.)
Petrogal *see* Petróleos de Portugal.
Petrohawk Energy Corporation, 79
317–20
Petróleo Brasileiro S.A., IV 501–03
Petróleos de Portugal S.A., IV 504–06
Petróleos de Venezuela S.A., IV 507–09;
74 235–39 (upd.)
Petróleos del Ecuador, IV 510–11
Petróleos Mexicanos, IV 512–14; 19
295–98 (upd.)
Petroleum Development Oman LLC, IV
515–16; 98 305–09 (upd.)
Petroleum Helicopters, Inc., 35 334–36
Petroliam Nasional Bhd (Petronas), 56
275–79 (upd.)
Petrolite Corporation, 15 350–52 *see
also* Baker Hughes Inc.
Petromex *see* Petróleos de Mexico S.A.
Petron Corporation, 58 270–72
Petronas, IV 517–20 *see also* Petroliam
Nasional Bhd.
Petrossian Inc., 54 287–89
PETsMART, Inc., 14 384–86; 41
295–98 (upd.)
Peugeot S.A., I 187–88 *see also* PSA
Peugeot Citroen S.A.
The Pew Charitable Trusts, 35 337–40
Pez Candy, Inc., 38 355–57
The Pfaltzgraff Co. *see* Susquehanna
Pfaltzgraff Co.
Pfizer Inc., I 661–63; 9 402–05 (upd.);
38 358–67 (upd.); 79 321–33 (upd.)
PFSweb, Inc., 73 254–56
PG&E Corporation, 26 370–73 (upd.)
PGA *see* The Professional Golfers'
Association.
Phaidon Press Ltd., 98 310–14
Phantom Fireworks *see* B.J. Alan Co., Inc.
Phar-Mor Inc., 12 390–92
Pharmacia & Upjohn Inc., I 664–65; 25
374–78 (upd.) *see also* Pfizer Inc.
Pharmion Corporation, 91 379–82
Phat Fashions LLC, 49 322–24
Phelps Dodge Corporation, IV 176–79;
28 352–57 (upd.); 75 319–25 (upd.)

PHH Arval, V 496–97; 53 274–76
(upd.)
PHI, Inc., 80 282–86 (upd.)
Philadelphia Eagles, 37 305–08
Philadelphia Electric Company, V
695–97 *see also* Exelon Corp.
Philadelphia Gas Works Company, 92
301–05
Philadelphia Media Holdings LLC, 92
306–10
Philadelphia Suburban Corporation, 39
326–29
**Philharmonic-Symphony Society of New
York, Inc. (New York Philharmonic),**
69 293–97
Philip Environmental Inc., 16 414–16
Philip Morris Companies Inc., V
405–07; 18 416–19 (upd.); 44
338–43 (upd.) *see also* Kraft Foods Inc.
Philip Services Corp., 73 257–60
Philipp Holzmann AG, 17 374–77
Philippine Airlines, Inc., 6 106–08; 23
379–82 (upd.)
Philips Electronics N.V., 13 400–03
(upd.) *see also* Koninklijke Philips
Electronics N.V.
**Philips Electronics North America
Corp.,** 13 396–99
N.V. Philips Gloeilampenfabriken, II
78–80 *see also* Philips Electronics N.V.
Phillips, de Pury & Luxembourg, 49
325–27
Phillips Foods, Inc., 63 320–22; 90
330–33 (upd.)
Phillips International, Inc., 78 311–14
Phillips Petroleum Company, IV
521–23; 40 354–59 (upd.) *see also*
ConocoPhillips.
Phillips-Van Heusen Corporation, 24
382–85
Phoenix AG, 68 286–89
Phoenix Footwear Group, Inc., 70
220–22
Phoenix Mecano AG, 61 286–88
**The Phoenix Media/Communications
Group,** 91 383–87
Phones 4u Ltd., 85 328–31
Photo-Me International Plc, 83 302–306
PHP Healthcare Corporation, 22
423–25
PhyCor, Inc., 36 365–69
Physician Sales & Service, Inc., 14
387–89
Physio-Control International Corp., 18
420–23
Piaggio & C. S.p.A., 20 426–29; 100
348–52 (upd.)
PianoDisc *see* Burgett, Inc.
PIC International Group PLC, 24
386–88 (upd.)
Picanol N.V., 96 335–38
Picard Surgeles, 76 305–07
Piccadilly Cafeterias, Inc., 19 299–302
Pick 'n Pay Stores Ltd., 82 280–83
PictureTel Corp., 10 455–57; 27
363–66 (upd.)
Piedmont Natural Gas Company, Inc.,
27 367–69

PPB Group Berhad, 57 292–95
PPG Industries, Inc., III 731–33; 22 434–37 (upd.); 81 317–23 (upd.)
PPL Corporation, 41 314–17 (upd.)
PPR S.A., 74 244–48 (upd.)
PR Newswire, 35 354–56
PRS *see* Paul Reed Smith Guitar Co.
Prada Holding B.V., 45 342–45
Prairie Farms Dairy, Inc., 47 304–07
Pranda Jewelry plc, 70 233–35
Pratt & Whitney, 9 416–18
Praxair, Inc., 11 402–04; 48 321–24 (upd.)
Praxis Bookstore Group LLC, 90 339–42
Pre-Paid Legal Services, Inc., 20 434–37
Precision Castparts Corp., 15 365–67
Premark International, Inc., III 610–12 *see also* Illinois Tool Works Inc.
Premcor Inc., 37 309–11
Premier Industrial Corporation, 9 419–21
Premier Parks, Inc., 27 382–84 *see also* Six Flags, Inc.
Premium Standard Farms, Inc., 30 353–55
PremiumWear, Inc., 30 356–59
Preserver Group, Inc., 44 354–56
President Casinos, Inc., 22 438–40
Pressman Toy Corporation, 56 280–82
Presstek, Inc., 33 345–48
Preston Corporation, 6 421–23
Preussag AG, 17 378–82; 42 279–83 (upd.)
PreussenElektra Aktiengesellschaft, V 698–700 *see also* E.On AG.
PRG-Schultz International, Inc., 73 264–67
Price Communications Corporation, 42 284–86
The Price Company, V 162–64 *see also* Costco Wholesale Corp.
Price Pfister, Inc., 70 236–39
Price Waterhouse LLP, 9 422–24 *see also* PricewaterhouseCoopers
PriceCostco, Inc., 14 393–95 *see also* Costco Wholesale Corp.
Priceline.com Incorporated, 57 296–99
PriceSmart, Inc., 71 287–90
PricewaterhouseCoopers, 29 389–94 (upd.)
PRIDE Enterprises *see* Prison Rehabilitative Industries and Diversified Enterprises, Inc.
Pride International, Inc., 78 319–23
Primark Corp., 13 416–18 *see also* Thomson Corp.
Prime Hospitality Corporation, 52 280–83
Primedex Health Systems, Inc., 25 382–85
Primedia Inc., 22 441–43
Primerica Corporation, I 612–14
Prince Sports Group, Inc., 15 368–70
Princes Ltd., 76 312–14
Princess Cruise Lines, 22 444–46
The Princeton Review, Inc., 42 287–90

Principal Mutual Life Insurance Company, III 328–30
Printpack, Inc., 68 293–96
Printrak, A Motorola Company, 44 357–59
Printronix, Inc., 18 434–36
Prison Rehabilitative Industries and Diversified Enterprises, Inc. (PRIDE), 53 277–79
Pro-Build Holdings Inc., 95 344–48 (upd.)
The Procter & Gamble Company, III 50–53; 8 431–35 (upd.); 26 380–85 (upd.); 67 304–11 (upd.)
Prodigy Communications Corporation, 34 360–62
Proeza S.A. de C.V., 82 288–91
Professional Bull Riders Inc., 55 310–12
The Professional Golfers' Association of America, 41 318–21
Proffitt's, Inc., 19 323–25 *see also* Belk, Inc.
Programmer's Paradise, Inc., 81 324–27
Progress Energy, Inc., 74 249–52
Progress Software Corporation, 15 371–74
Progressive Corporation, 11 405–07; 29 395–98 (upd.)
Progressive Enterprises Ltd., 96 339–42
ProLogis, 57 300–02
Promus Companies, Inc., 9 425–27 *see also* Hilton Hotels Corp.
ProSiebenSat.1 Media AG, 54 295–98
Proskauer Rose LLP, 47 308–10
Protection One, Inc., 32 372–75
Provell Inc., 58 276–79 (upd.)
Providence Health System, 90 343–47
The Providence Journal Company, 28 367–69; 30 15
The Providence Service Corporation, 64 309–12
Provident Bankshares Corporation, 85 340–43
Provident Life and Accident Insurance Company of America, III 331–33 *see also* UnumProvident Corp.
Providian Financial Corporation, 52 284–90 (upd.)
Provigo Inc., II 651–53; 51 301–04 (upd.)
Provimi S.A., 80 292–95
Prudential Financial Inc., III 337–41; 30 360–64 (upd.); 82 292–98 (upd.)
Prudential plc, III 334–36; 48 325–29 (upd.)
PSA Peugeot Citroen S.A., 28 370–74 (upd.); 54 126
PSF *see* Premium Standard Farms, Inc.
PSI Resources, 6 555–57
Psion PLC, 45 346–49
Psychemedics Corporation, 89 358–61
Psychiatric Solutions, Inc., 68 297–300
PT Astra International Tbk, 56 283–86
PT Bank Buana Indonesia Tbk, 60 240–42
PT Indosat Tbk, 93 354–57
PTT Public Company Ltd., 56 287–90

Pubco Corporation, 17 383–85
Public Service Company of Colorado, 6 558–60
Public Service Company of New Hampshire, 21 408–12; 55 313–18 (upd.)
Public Service Company of New Mexico, 6 561–64 *see also* PNM Resources Inc.
Public Service Enterprise Group Inc., V 701–03; 44 360–63 (upd.)
Public Storage, Inc., 21 52 291–93
Publicis Groupe, 19 329–32; 77 346–50 (upd.)
Publishers Clearing House, 23 393–95; 64 313–16 (upd.)
Publishers Group, Inc., 35 357–59
Publishing and Broadcasting Limited, 54 299–302
Publix Super Markets Inc., 7 440–42; 31 371–74 (upd.)
Puck Lazaroff Inc. *see* The Wolfgang Puck Food Company, Inc.
Pueblo Xtra International, Inc., 47 311–13
Puerto Rico Electric Power Authority, 47 314–16
Puget Sound Energy Inc., 6 565–67; 50 365–68 (upd.)
Puig Beauty and Fashion Group S.L., 60 243–46
Pulaski Furniture Corporation, 33 349–52; 80 296–99 (upd.)
Pulitzer Inc., 15 375–77; 58 280–83 (upd.)
Pulsar Internacional S.A., 21 413–15
Pulte Homes, Inc., 8 436–38; 42 291–94 (upd.)
Puma AG Rudolf Dassler Sport, 35 360–63
Pumpkin Masters, Inc., 48 330–32
Punch International N.V., 66 258–60
Punch Taverns plc, 70 240–42
Puratos S.A./NV, 92 315–18
Pure World, Inc., 72 285–87
Purina Mills, Inc., 32 376–79
Puritan-Bennett Corporation, 13 419–21
Purolator Products Company, 21 416–18; 74 253–56 (upd.)
Putt-Putt Golf Courses of America, Inc., 23 396–98
PVC Container Corporation, 67 312–14
PW Eagle, Inc., 48 333–36
PWA Group, IV 323–25 *see also* Svenska Cellulosa.
Pyramid Breweries Inc., 33 353–55
Pyramid Companies, 54 303–05
PZ Cussons plc, 72 288–90

Q

Q.E.P. Co., Inc., 65 292–94
Qantas Airways Ltd., 6 109–13; 24 396–401 (upd.); 68 301–07 (upd.)
Qatar Airways Company Q.C.S.C., 87 404–407
Qatar National Bank SAQ, 87 408–411

Qatar Petroleum, IV 524–26; 98 324–28 (upd.)

Qatar Telecom QSA, 87 412–415

Qdoba Restaurant Corporation, 93 358–62

Qiagen N.V., 39 333–35

QLT Inc., 71 291–94

QRS Music Technologies, Inc., 95 349–53

QSC Audio Products, Inc., 56 291–93

QSS Group, Inc., 100 358–61

Quad/Graphics, Inc., 19 333–36

Quaker Chemical Corp., 91 388–91

Quaker Fabric Corp., 19 337–39

Quaker Foods North America, II 558–60; 12 409–12 (upd.); 34 363–67 (upd.); 73 268–73 (upd.)

Quaker State Corporation, 7 443–45; 21 419–22 (upd.) see also Pennzoil-Quaker State Co.

QUALCOMM Incorporated, 20 438–41; 47 317–21 (upd.)

Quality Chekd Dairies, Inc., 48 337–39

Quality Dining, Inc., 18 437–40

Quality Food Centers, Inc., 17 386–88 see also Kroger Co.

Quality Systems, Inc., 81 328–31

Quanex Corporation, 13 422–24; 62 286–89 (upd.)

Quanta Computer Inc., 47 322–24

Quanta Services, Inc., 79 338–41

Quantum Chemical Corporation, 8 439–41

Quantum Corporation, 10 458–59; 62 290–93 (upd.)

Quark, Inc., 36 375–79

Quebec Hydro-Electric Commission see Hydro-Quebec.

Quebecor Inc., 12 412–14; 47 325–28 (upd.)

Quelle Group, V 165–67 see also Karstadt Quelle AG.

Quest Diagnostics Inc., 26 390–92

Questar Corporation, 6 568–70; 26 386–89 (upd.)

The Quick & Reilly Group, Inc., 20 442–44

Quick Restaurants S.A., 94 357–60

Quicken Loans, Inc., 93 363–67

Quidel Corporation, 80 300–03

The Quigley Corporation, 62 294–97

Quiksilver, Inc., 18 441–43; 79 342–47 (upd.)

QuikTrip Corporation, 36 380–83

Quill Corporation, 28 375–77

Quilmes Industrial (QUINSA) S.A., 67 315–17

Quinn Emanuel Urquhart Oliver & Hedges, LLP, 99 350–353

Quintiles Transnational Corporation, 21 423–25; 68 308–12 (upd.)

Quixote Corporation, 15 378–80

The Quizno's Corporation, 42 295–98

Quovadx Inc., 70 243–46

QVC Inc., 9 428–29; 58 284–87 (upd.)

Qwest Communications International, Inc., 37 312–17

R

R&B, Inc., 51 305–07

R.B. Pamplin Corp., 45 350–52

R.C. Bigelow, Inc., 49 334–36

R.C. Willey Home Furnishings, 72 291–93

R.G. Barry Corp., 17 389–91; 44 364–67 (upd.)

R. Griggs Group Limited, 23 399–402; 31 413–14

R.H. Macy & Co., Inc., V 168–70; 8 442–45 (upd.); 30 379–83 (upd.) see also Macy's, Inc.

R.J. Reynolds Tobacco Holdings, Inc., 30 384–87 (upd.)

R. M. Palmer Co., 89 362–64

R.P. Scherer Corporation, I 678–80 see also Cardinal Health, Inc.

R.R. Bowker LLC, 100 362–66

R.R. Donnelley & Sons Company, IV 660–62; 38 368–71 (upd.)

Rabobank Group, 26 419; 33 356–58

RAC see Roy Anderson Corp.

Racal-Datacom Inc., 11 408–10

Racal Electronics PLC, II 83–84 see also Thales S.A.

Racing Champions Corporation, 37 318–20

Rack Room Shoes, Inc., 84 314–317

Radeberger Gruppe AG, 75 332–35

Radian Group Inc., 42 299–301 see also Onex Corp.

Radiation Therapy Services, Inc., 85 344–47

Radio Flyer Inc., 34 368–70

Radio One, Inc., 67 318–21

RadioShack Corporation, 36 384–88 (upd.); 101 416–23 (upd.)

Radius Inc., 16 417–19

RAE Systems Inc., 83 311-314

RAG AG, 35 364–67; 60 247–51 (upd.)

Rag Shops, Inc., 30 365–67

Ragdoll Productions Ltd., 51 308–11

Raiffeisen Zentralbank Österreich AG, 85 348–52

RailTex, Inc., 20 445–47

Railtrack Group PLC, 50 369–72

Rain Bird Corporation, 84 318–321

Rainforest Café, Inc., 25 386–88; 88 312–16 (upd.)

Rainier Brewing Company, 23 403–05

Raisio PLC, 99 354–357

Raleigh UK Ltd., 65 295–97

Raley's Inc., 14 396–98; 58 288–91 (upd.)

Rally's, 25 389–91; 68 313–16 (upd.)

Rallye SA, 54 306–09

Ralph Lauren see Polo/Ralph Lauren Corportion.

Ralphs Grocery Company, 35 368–70

Ralston Purina Company, II 561–63; 13 425–27 (upd.) see also Ralcorp Holdings, Inc.; Nestlé S.A.

Ramsay Youth Services, Inc., 41 322–24

Ramtron International Corporation, 89 365–68

Ranbaxy Laboratories Ltd., 70 247–49

Rand McNally & Company, 28 378–81; 53 122

Randall's Food Markets, Inc., 40 364–67 see also Safeway Inc.

Random House, Inc., 13 428–30; 31 375–80 (upd.)

Randon S.A. Implementos e Participações, 79 348–52

Randstad Holding n.v., 16 420–22; 43 307–10 (upd.)

Range Resources Corporation, 45 353–55

The Rank Group plc, II 157–59; 14 399–402 (upd.); 64 317–21 (upd.)

Ranks Hovis McDougall Limited, II 564–65; 28 382–85 (upd.)

RAO Unified Energy System of Russia, 45 356–60

Rapala-Normark Group, Ltd., 30 368–71

Rare Hospitality International Inc., 19 340–42

RAS see Riunione Adriatica di Sicurtà SpA.

Rascal House see Jerry's Famous Deli Inc.

Rasmussen Group see K.A. Rasmussen AS.

Rathbone Brothers plc, 70 250–53

RathGibson Inc., 90 348–51

ratiopharm Group, 84 322–326

Ratner Companies, 72 294–96

Raven Industries, Inc., 33 359–61

Ravensburger AG, 64 322–26

Raving Brands, Inc., 64 327–29

Rawlings Sporting Goods Co., Inc., 24 402–04

Raychem Corporation, 8 446–47

Raymond James Financial Inc., 69 308–10

Raymond Ltd., 77 351–54

Rayonier Inc., 24 405–07

Rayovac Corporation, 13 431–34; 39 336–40 (upd.)

Raytech Corporation, 61 306–09

Raytheon Aircraft Holdings Inc., 46 354–57

Raytheon Company, II 85–87; 11 411–14 (upd.); 38 372–77 (upd.)

Razorfish, Inc., 37 321–24

RCA Corporation, II 88–90

RCM Technologies, Inc., 34 371–74

RCN Corporation, 70 254–57

RCS MediaGroup S.p.A., 96 343–46

RDO Equipment Company, 33 362–65

RE/MAX International, Inc., 59 344–46

Read-Rite Corp., 10 463–64

The Reader's Digest Association, Inc., IV 663–64; 17 392–95 (upd.); 71 295–99 (upd.)

Reading International Inc., 70 258–60

The Real Good Food Company plc, 99 358–361

Real Madrid C.F., 73 274–76

Real Times, Inc., 66 261–65

Real Turismo, S.A. de C.V., 50 373–75

The Really Useful Group, 26 393–95

Rite Aid Corporation, V 174–76; 19 354–57 (upd.); 63 331–37 (upd.)

Ritter Sport *see* Alfred Ritter GmbH & Co. KG.

Ritter's Frozen Custard *see* RFC Franchising LLC.

Ritz Camera Centers, 34 375–77

The Ritz-Carlton Hotel Company, L.L.C., 9 455–57; 29 403–06 (upd.); 71 311–16 (upd.)

Ritz-Craft Corporation of Pennsylvania Inc., 94 365–68

Riunione Adriatica di Sicurtà SpA, III 345–48

Riva Fire *see* Gruppo Riva Fire SpA.

The Rival Company, 19 358–60

River Oaks Furniture, Inc., 43 314–16

River Ranch Fresh Foods LLC, 88 322–25

Riverbed Technology, Inc., 101 428–31

Riverwood International Corporation, 11 420–23; 48 340–44 (upd.) *see also* Graphic Packaging Holding Co.

Riviana Foods, 27 388–91

Riviera Holdings Corporation, 75 340–43

Riviera Tool Company, 89 373–76

RJR Nabisco Holdings Corp., V 408–10 *see also* R.J Reynolds Tobacco Holdings Inc., Nabisco Brands, Inc.; R.J. Reynolds Industries, Inc.

RM Auctions, Inc., 88 326–29

RMC Group p.l.c., III 737–40; 34 378–83 (upd.)

RMH Teleservices, Inc., 42 322–24

Roadhouse Grill, Inc., 22 464–66

Roadmaster Industries, Inc., 16 430–33

Roadway Express, Inc., V 502–03; 25 395–98 (upd.)

Roanoke Electric Steel Corporation, 45 368–70

Robbins & Myers Inc., 15 388–90

Roberds Inc., 19 361–63

Robert Bosch GmbH, I 392–93; 16 434–37 (upd.); 43 317–21 (upd.)

Robert Half International Inc., 18 461–63; 70 281–84 (upd.)

Robert Mondavi Corporation, 15 391–94; 50 386–90 (upd.)

Robert Talbott Inc., 88 330–33

Robert W. Baird & Co. Incorporated, 67 328–30

Robert Wood Johnson Foundation, 35 375–78

Robertet SA, 39 347–49

Roberts Pharmaceutical Corporation, 16 438–40

Robertson-Ceco Corporation, 19 364–66

Robins, Kaplan, Miller & Ciresi L.L.P., 89 377–81

Robinson Helicopter Company, 51 315–17

ROC *see* Royal Olympic Cruise Lines Inc.

Rocawear Apparel LLC, 77 355–58

Roche Biomedical Laboratories, Inc., 11 424–26 *see also* Laboratory Corporation of America Holdings.

Roche Bioscience, 14 403–06 (upd.)

Rochester Gas And Electric Corporation, 6 571–73

Rochester Telephone Corporation, 6 332–34

Röchling Gruppe, 94 369–74

Rock Bottom Restaurants, Inc., 25 399–401; 68 320–23 (upd.)

Rock-It Cargo USA, Inc., 86 339–42

Rock of Ages Corporation, 37 329–32

Rock-Tenn Company, 13 441–43; 59 347–51 (upd.)

The Rockefeller Foundation, 34 384–87

Rockefeller Group International Inc., 58 303–06

Rockford Corporation, 43 322–25

Rockford Products Corporation, 55 323–25

RockShox, Inc., 26 412–14

Rockwell Automation, 43 326–31 (upd.)

Rockwell International Corporation, I 78–80; 11 427–30 (upd.)

Rockwell Medical Technologies, Inc., 88 334–37

Rocky Mountain Chocolate Factory, Inc., 73 280–82

Rocky Shoes & Boots, Inc., 26 415–18

Rodale, Inc., 23 415–17; 47 336–39 (upd.)

Rodamco N.V., 26 419–21

Rodda Paint Company, 98 329–32

Rodriguez Group S.A., 90 357–60

ROFIN-SINAR Technologies Inc, 81 345–48

Rogers Communications Inc., 30 388–92 (upd.) *see also* Maclean Hunter Publishing Ltd.

Rogers Corporation, 61 310–13; 80 313–17 (upd.)

Rohde & Schwarz GmbH & Co. KG, 39 350–53

Röhm and Haas Company, I 391–93; 26 422–26 (upd.); 77 359–66 (upd.)

ROHN Industries, Inc., 22 467–69

Rohr Incorporated, 9 458–60 *see also* Goodrich Corp.

Roland Berger & Partner GmbH, 37 333–36

Roland Corporation, 38 389–91

Roland Murten A.G., 7 452–53

Rolex *see* Montres Rolex S.A.

Roll International Corporation, 37 337–39

Rollerblade, Inc., 15 395–98; 34 388–92 (upd.)

Rollins, Inc., 11 431–34

Rolls-Royce Allison, 29 407–09 (upd.)

Rolls-Royce Group PLC, 67 331–36 (upd.)

Rolls-Royce Motors Ltd., I 194–96

Rolls-Royce plc, I 81–83; 7 454–57 (upd.); 21 433–37 (upd.)

Rolta India Ltd., 90 361–64

Roly Poly Franchise Systems LLC, 83 326-328

Romacorp, Inc., 58 307–11

Roman Meal Company, 84 331–334

Ron Tonkin Chevrolet Company, 55 326–28

RONA, Inc., 73 283–86

Ronco Corporation, 15 399–401; 80 318–23 (upd.)

Ronson PLC, 49 337–39

Rooms To Go Inc., 28 389–92

Rooney Brothers Co., 25 402–04

Roosevelt Hospital *see* Continuum Health Partners, Inc.

Roots Canada Ltd., 42 325–27

Roper Industries, Inc., 15 402–04; 50 391–95 (upd.)

Ropes & Gray, 40 377–80

Rorer Group, I 666–68

Rosauers Supermarkets, Inc., 90 365–68

Rose Acre Farms, Inc., 60 255–57

Rose Art Industries, 58 312–14

Rose's Stores, Inc., 13 444–46

Roseburg Forest Products Company, 58 315–17

Rosemount Inc., 15 405–08 *see also* Emerson.

Rosenbluth International Inc., 14 407–09 *see also* American Express Co.

Rosetta Stone Inc., 93 375–79

Ross Stores, Inc., 17 408–10; 43 332–35 (upd.); 101 432–37 (upd.)

Rossignol Ski Company, Inc. *see* Skis Rossignol S.A.

Rossmann *see* Dirk Rossmann GmbH.

Rostelecom Joint Stock Co., 99 374–377

Rostvertol plc, 62 308–10

Rosy Blue N.V., 84 335–338

Rotary International, 31 395–97

Rothmans UK Holdings Limited, V 411–13; 19 367–70 (upd.)

Roto-Rooter, Inc., 15 409–11; 61 314–19 (upd.)

Rotork plc, 46 361–64

The Rottlund Company, Inc., 28 393–95

Rouge Steel Company, 8 448–50

Rougier *see* Groupe Rougier, SA.

Roularta Media Group NV, 48 345–47

Rounder Records Corporation, 79 357–61

Roundy's Inc., 14 410–12; 58 318–21 (upd.)

The Rouse Company, 15 412–15; 63 338–41 (upd.)

Roussel Uclaf, I 669–70; 8 451–53 (upd.)

Rover Group Ltd., 7 458–60; 21 441–44 (upd.)

Rowan Companies, Inc., 43 336–39

Rowntree Mackintosh PLC, II 568–70 *see also* Nestlé S.A.

The Rowohlt Verlag GmbH, 96 356–61

Roy Anderson Corporation, 75 344–46

Roy F. Weston, Inc., 33 369–72

Royal & Sun Alliance Insurance Group plc, 55 329–39 (upd.)

Royal Ahold N.V. *see* Koninklijke Ahold N.V.

Royal Appliance Manufacturing Company, 15 416–18

The Royal Bank of Canada, II 344–46; 21 445–48 (upd.); 81 349–55 (upd.)

The Royal Bank of Scotland Group plc, 12 421–23; 38 392–99 (upd.)

Royal Brunei Airlines Sdn Bhd, 99 378–381

Royal Canin S.A., 39 354–57

Royal Caribbean Cruises Ltd., 22 470–73; 74 277–81 (upd.)

Royal Crown Company, Inc., 23 418–20 *see also* Cott Corp.

Royal Doulton plc, 14 413–15; 38 400–04 (upd.)

Royal Dutch Petroleum Company, IV 530–32 *see also* Shell Transport and Trading Company p.l.c.

Royal Dutch/Shell Group, 49 340–44 (upd.)

Royal Grolsch NV, 54 315–18

Royal Group Technologies Limited, 73 287–89

Royal Insurance Holdings plc, III 349–51 *see also* Royal & Sun Alliance Insurance Group plc .

Royal KPN N.V., 30 393–95

Royal Nepal Airline Corporation, 41 335–38

Royal Numico N.V., 37 340–42

Royal Olympic Cruise Lines Inc., 52 297–99

Royal Packaging Industries Van Leer N.V., 30 396–98

Royal Ten Cate N.V., 68 324–26

Royal Vendex KBB N.V. *see* Koninklijke Vendex KBB N.V. (Royal Vendex KBB N.V.).

Royal Vopak NV, 41 339–41

RPC Group PLC, 81 356–59

RPC, Inc., 91 413–16

RPM International Inc., 8 454–57; 36 394–98 (upd.); 91 417–25 (upd.)

RSA Security Inc., 46 365–68

RSC *see* Rental Service Corp.

RSM McGladrey Business Services Inc., 98 333–36

RTI Biologics, Inc., 96 362–65

RTL Group SA, 44 374–78

RTM Restaurant Group, 58 322–24

RTZ Corporation PLC, IV 189–92 *see also* Rio Tinto plc.

Rubbermaid Incorporated, III 613–15; 20 454–57 (upd.) *see also* Newell Rubbermaid Inc.

Rubio's Restaurants, Inc., 35 379–81

Ruby Tuesday, Inc., 18 464–66; 71 317–20 (upd.)

Rudolph Technologies Inc., 94 375–78

The Rugby Group plc, 31 398–400

Ruger Corporation *see* Sturm, Ruger & Co., Inc.

Ruhrgas AG, V 704–06; 38 405–09 (upd.)

Ruhrkohle AG, IV 193–95 *see also* RAG AG.

Ruiz Food Products, Inc., 53 287–89

Rural Cellular Corporation, 43 340–42

Rural/Metro Corporation, 28 396–98

Rural Press Ltd., 74 282–85

Rush Communications, 33 373–75 *see also* Phat Fashions LLC.

Rush Enterprises, Inc., 64 336–38

Russ Berrie and Company, Inc., 12 424–26; 82 304–08 (upd.)

Russell Corporation, 8 458–59; 30 399–401 (upd.); 82 309–13 (upd.)

Russell Reynolds Associates Inc., 38 410–12

Russell Stover Candies Inc., 12 427–29; 91 426–32 (upd.)

Russian Aircraft Corporation (MiG), 86 343–46

Russian Railways Joint Stock Co., 93 380–83

Rust International Inc., 11 435–36

Rusty, Inc., 95 358–61

Ruth's Chris Steak House, 28 399–401; 88 338–42 (upd.)

RWD Technologies, Inc., 76 320–22

RWE Group, V 707–10; 50 396–400 (upd.)

Ryan Beck & Co., Inc., 66 273–75

Ryan Companies US, Inc., 99 382–385

Ryan's Restaurant Group, Inc., 15 419–21; 68 327–30 (upd.)

Ryanair Holdings plc, 35 382–85

Ryder System, Inc., V 504–06; 24 408–11 (upd.)

Ryerson Tull, Inc., 40 381–84 (upd.)

Ryko Corporation, 83 329-333

The Ryland Group, Inc., 8 460–61; 37 343–45 (upd.)

Ryoshoku Ltd., 72 300–02

RZB *see* Raiffeisen Zentralbank Österreich AG.

RZD *see* Russian Railways Joint Stock Co.

S

S&C Electric Company, 15 422–24

S&D Coffee, Inc., 84 339–341

S&K Famous Brands, Inc., 23 421–23

S&P *see* Standard & Poor's Corp.

S.A.C.I. Falabella, 69 311–13

S.A. Cockerill Sambre *see* Cockerill Sambre Group.

s.a. GB-Inno-BM *see* GIB Group.

S.C. Johnson & Son, Inc., III 58–59; 28 409–12 (upd.); 89 382–89 (upd.)

S-K-I Limited, 15 457–59

SAA (Pty) Ltd., 28 402–04

Saab Automobile AB, 32 386–89 (upd.); 83 334-339 (upd.)

Saab-Scania A.B., I 197–98; 11 437–39 (upd.)

Saarberg-Konzern, IV 196–99 *see also* RAG AG.

Saatchi & Saatchi plc, I 33–35; 33 328–31 (upd.)

SAB *see* South African Breweries Ltd.

Sabanci Holdings *see* Haci Omer Sabanci Holdings A.S.

Sabaté Diosos SA, 48 348–50 *see also* OENEO S.A.

Sabena S.A./N.V., 33 376–79

SABIC *see* Saudi Basic Industries Corp.

SABMiller plc, 59 352–58 (upd.)

Sabratek Corporation, 29 410–12

Sabre Holdings Corporation, 26 427–30; 74 286–90 (upd.)

Sadia S.A., 59 359–62

Safe Flight Instrument Corporation, 71 321–23

SAFECO Corporation, III 352–54

Safeguard Scientifics, Inc., 10 473–75

Safelite Glass Corp., 19 371–73

SafeNet Inc., 101 438–42

Safeskin Corporation, 18 467–70 *see also* Kimberly-Clark Corp.

Safety Components International, Inc., 63 342–44

Safety 1st, Inc., 24 412–15

Safety-Kleen Systems Inc., 8 462–65; 82 314–20 (upd.)

Safeway Inc., II 654–56; 24 416–19 (upd.); 85 362–69 (upd.)

Safeway PLC, 50 401–06 (upd.)

Saffery Champness, 80 324–27

Safilo SpA, 40 155–56; 54 319–21

Saga Communications, Inc., 27 392–94

The Sage Group, 43 343–46

SAGEM S.A., 37 346–48

Sagicor Life Inc., 98 337–40

Saia, Inc., 98 341–44

SAIC *see* Science Applications International Corp.

Sainsbury's *see* J Sainsbury PLC.

Saint-Gobain *see* Compagnie de Saint Gobain S.A.

St Ives plc, 34 393–95

St. James's Place Capital, plc, 71 324–26

The St. Joe Company, 31 422–25; 98 368–73 (upd.)

St. Joe Paper Company, 8 485–88

St. John Knits, Inc., 14 466–68

St. Jude Medical, Inc., 11 458–61; 43 347–52 (upd.); 97 350–58 (upd.)

St. Louis Music, Inc., 48 351–54

St. Luke's-Roosevelt Hospital Center *see* Continuum Health Partners, Inc.

St. Mary Land & Exploration Company, 63 345–47

St. Paul Bank for Cooperatives, 8 489–90

The St. Paul Travelers Companies, Inc., III 355–57; 22 492–95 (upd.); 79 362–69 (upd.)

Ste. Michelle Wine Estates Ltd., 96 408–11

Salem Communications Corporation, 97 359–63

salesforce.com, Inc., 79 370–73

Saks Inc., 24 420–23; 41 342–45 (upd.)

Salant Corporation, 12 430–32; 51 318–21 (upd.)

Salick Health Care, Inc., 53 290–92

Salix Pharmaceuticals, Ltd., 93 384–87

Sallie Mae *see* SLM Holding Corp.

Sally Beauty Company, Inc., 60 258–60

Salomon Inc., II 447–49; 13 447–50 (upd.) *see also* Citigroup Inc.

Salomon Worldwide, 20 458–60 *see also* adidas-Salomon AG.

Salt River Project, 19 374–76

Salton, Inc., 30 402–04; 88 343–48 (upd.)

The Salvation Army USA, 32 390–93

Salvatore Ferragamo Italia S.p.A., 62 311–13

Salzgitter AG, IV 200–01; 101 443–49 (upd.)

Sam Ash Music Corporation, 30 405–07

Sam Levin Inc., 80 328–31

Sam's Club, 40 385–87

Sam's Wine & Spirits, 96 366–69

Samick Musical Instruments Co., Ltd., 56 297–300

Samsonite Corporation, 13 451–53; 43 353–57 (upd.)

Samsung Electronics Co., Ltd., 14 416–18; 41 346–49 (upd.)

Samsung Group, I 515–17

Samuel Cabot Inc., 53 293–95

Samuels Jewelers Incorporated, 30 408–10

San Diego Gas & Electric Company, V 711–14 *see also* Sempra Energy.

San Diego Padres Baseball Club L.P., 78 324–27

San Francisco Baseball Associates, L.P., 55 340–43

San Miguel Corporation, 15 428–30; 57 303–08 (upd.)

Sanborn Hermanos, S.A., 20 461–63

Sanborn Map Company Inc., 82 321–24

SanCor Cooperativas Unidas Ltda., 101 450–53

The Sanctuary Group PLC, 69 314–17

Sandals Resorts International, 65 302–05

Sanders Morris Harris Group Inc., 70 285–87

Sanders\Wingo, 99 386–389

Sanderson Farms, Inc., 15 425–27

Sandia National Laboratories, 49 345–48

Sandoz Ltd., I 671–73 *see also* Novartis AG.

Sandvik AB, IV 202–04; 32 394–98 (upd.); 77 367–73 (upd.)

Sanford L.P., 82 325–29

Sanitec Corporation, 51 322–24

Sankyo Company, Ltd., I 674–75; 56 301–04 (upd.)

Sanlam Ltd., 68 331–34

SANLUIS Corporación, S.A.B. de C.V., 95 362–65

The Sanofi-Synthélabo Group, I 676–77; 49 349–51 (upd.)

SanomaWSOY Corporation, 51 325–28

Sanpaolo IMI S.p.A., 50 407–11

Sanrio Company, Ltd., 38 413–15

Santa Barbara Restaurant Group, Inc., 37 349–52

The Santa Cruz Operation, Inc., 38 416–21

Santa Fe Gaming Corporation, 19 377–79 *see also* Archon Corp.

Santa Fe International Corporation, 38 422–24

Santa Fe Pacific Corporation, V 507–09 *see also* Burlington Northern Santa Fe Corp.

Santa Margherita S.p.A. *see* Industrie Zignago Santa Margherita S.p.A.

Santos Ltd., 81 360–63

Sanwa Bank, Ltd., II 347–48; 15 431–33 (upd.)

SANYO Electric Co., Ltd., II 91–92; 36 399–403 (upd.); 95 366–73 (upd.)

Sanyo-Kokusaku Pulp Co., Ltd., IV 327–28

Sao Paulo Alpargatas S.A., 75 347–49

SAP AG, 16 441–44; 43 358–63 (upd.)

Sapa AB, 84 342–345

Sappi Limited, 49 352–55

Sapporo Holdings Limited, I 282–83; 13 454–56 (upd.); 36 404–07 (upd.); 97 364–69 (upd.)

Saputo Inc., 59 363–65

Sara Lee Corporation, II 571–73; 15 434–37 (upd.); 54 322–27 (upd.); 99 390–398 (upd.)

Sarnoff Corporation, 57 309–12

Sarris Candies Inc., 86 347–50

The SAS Group, 34 396–99 (upd.)

SAS Institute Inc., 10 476–78; 78 328–32 (upd.)

Sasol Limited, IV 533–35; 47 340–44 (upd.)

Saturn Corporation, 7 461–64; 21 449–53 (upd.); 80 332–38 (upd.)

Satyam Computer Services Ltd., 85 370–73

Saucony Inc., 35 386–89; 86 351–56 (upd.)

Sauder Woodworking Co., 12 433–34; 35 390–93 (upd.)

Saudi Arabian Airlines, 6 114–16; 27 395–98 (upd.)

Saudi Arabian Oil Company, IV 536–39; 17 411–15 (upd.); 50 412–17 (upd.)

Saudi Basic Industries Corporation (SABIC), 58 325–28

Sauer-Danfoss Inc., 61 320–22

Saul Ewing LLP, 74 291–94

Saur S.A.S., 92 327–30

Savannah Foods & Industries, Inc., 7 465–67 *see also* Imperial Sugar Co.

Savers, Inc., 99 399–403 (upd.)

Sawtek Inc., 43 364–66 (upd.)

Saxton Pierce Restaurant Corporation, 100 373–76

Sbarro, Inc., 16 445–47; 64 339–42 (upd.)

SBC Communications Inc., 32 399–403 (upd.)

SBC Warburg, 14 419–21 *see also* UBS AG.

Sberbank, 62 314–17

SBI *see* State Bank of India.

SBS Technologies, Inc., 25 405–07

SCA *see* Svenska Cellulosa AB.

SCANA Corporation, 6 574–76; 56 305–08 (upd.)

Scandinavian Airlines System, I 119–20 *see also* The SAS Group.

ScanSource, Inc., 29 413–15; 74 295–98 (upd.)

Scarborough Public Utilities Commission, 9 461–62

SCB Computer Technology, Inc., 29 416–18

SCEcorp, V 715–17 *see also* Edison International.

Schawk, Inc., 24 424–26

Scheels All Sports Inc., 63 348–50

Scheid Vineyards Inc., 66 276–78

Schell Brewing *see* August Schell Brewing Company Inc.

Schenck Business Solutions, 88 349–53

Schenker-Rhenus Ag, 6 424–26

Scherer *see* R.P. Scherer.

Scherer Brothers Lumber Company, 94 379–83

Schering A.G., I 681–82; 50 418–22 (upd.)

Schering-Plough Corporation, I 683–85; 14 422–25 (upd.); 49 356–62 (upd.); 99 404–414 (upd.)

Schibsted ASA, 31 401–05

Schieffelin & Somerset Co., 61 323–25

Schindler Holding AG, 29 419–22

Schlage Lock Company, 82 330–34

Schlotzsky's, Inc., 36 408–10

Schlumberger Limited, III 616–18; 17 416–19 (upd.); 59 366–71 (upd.)

Schmitt Music Company, 40 388–90

Schneider National, Inc., 36 411–13; 77 374–78 (upd.)

Schneider S.A., II 93–94; 18 471–74 (upd.)

Schneiderman's Furniture Inc., 28 405–08

Schneidersöhne Deutschland GmbH & Co. KG, 100 377–81

Schnitzer Steel Industries, Inc., 19 380–82

Scholastic Corporation, 10 479–81; 29 423–27 (upd.)

Scholle Corporation, 96 370–73

School Specialty, Inc., 68 335–37

School-Tech, Inc., 62 318–20

Schott Brothers, Inc., 67 337–39

Schott Corporation, 53 296–98

Schottenstein Stores Corp., 14 426–28 *see also* Retail Ventures, Inc.

Schouw & Company A/S, 94 384–87

Schreiber Foods, Inc., 72 303–06

Schroders plc, 42 332–35

Schuff Steel Company, 26 431–34

Schultz Sav-O Stores, Inc., 21 454–56; 31 406–08 (upd.)

Schurz Communications, Inc., 98 345–49

The Schwan Food Company, 7 468–70; 26 435–38 (upd.); 83 340–346 (upd.)

The Schwarz Group, 100 382–87

Schwebel Baking Company, 72 307–09

Schweitzer-Mauduit International, Inc., 52 300–02

Schweizerische Post-, Telefon- und Telegrafen-Betriebe, V 321–24

Schweppes Ltd. *see* Cadbury Schweppes PLC.

Shedd Aquarium Society, 73 297–99

Sheetz, Inc., 85 387–90

Shelby Williams Industries, Inc., 14 435–37

Sheldahl Inc., 23 432–35

Shell Oil Company, IV 540–41; 14 438–40 (upd.); 41 356–60 (upd.) *see also* Royal Dutch/Shell Group.

Shell Transport and Trading Company p.l.c., IV 530–32 *see also* Royal Dutch Petroleum Company; Royal Dutch/Shell.

Sheller-Globe Corporation, I 201–02 *see also* Lear Corp.

Shells Seafood Restaurants, Inc., 43 370–72

Shenandoah Telecommunications Company, 89 390–93

Shenhua Group *see* China Shenhua Energy Company Limited

Shepherd Neame Limited, 30 414–16

Sheplers, Inc., 96 387–90

The Sheridan Group, Inc., 86 357–60

Shermag, Inc., 93 392–97

The Sherwin-Williams Company, III 744–46; 13 469–71 (upd.); 89 394–400 (upd.)

Sherwood Brands, Inc., 53 302–04

Shikoku Electric Power Company, Inc., V 718–20; 60 269–72 (upd.)

Shimano Inc., 64 347–49

Shionogi & Co., Ltd., III 60–61; 17 435–37 (upd.); 98 350–54 (upd.)

Shiseido Company, Limited, III 62–64; 22 485–88 (upd.); 81 364–70 (upd.)

Shochiku Company Ltd., 74 302–04

Shoe Carnival Inc., 14 441–43; 72 326–29 (upd.)

Shoe Pavilion, Inc., 84 346–349

Shoney's, Inc., 7 474–76; 23 436–39 (upd.)

ShopKo Stores Inc., 21 457–59; 58 329–32 (upd.)

Shoppers Drug Mart Corporation, 49 367–70

Shoppers Food Warehouse Corporation, 66 290–92

Shorewood Packaging Corporation, 28 419–21

Showa Shell Sekiyu K.K., IV 542–43; 59 372–75 (upd.)

ShowBiz Pizza Time, Inc., 13 472–74 *see also* CEC Entertainment, Inc.

Showboat, Inc., 19 400–02 *see also* Harrah's Entertainment, Inc.

Showtime Networks, Inc., 78 343–47

Shred-It Canada Corporation, 56 319–21

Shriners Hospitals for Children, 69 318–20

Shubert Organization Inc., 24 437–39

Shuffle Master Inc., 51 337–40

Shure Inc., 60 273–76

Shurgard Storage Centers, Inc., 52 309–11

Shutterfly, Inc., 98 355–58

SHV Holdings N.V., 55 344–47

The Siam Cement Public Company Limited, 56 322–25

Sideco Americana S.A., 67 346–48

Sidel *see* Groupe Sidel S.A.

Siderar S.A.I.C., 66 293–95

Sidley Austin Brown & Wood, 40 400–03

Sidney Frank Importing Co., Inc., 69 321–23

Siebe plc *see* BTR Siebe plc.

Siebel Systems, Inc., 38 430–34

Siebert Financial Corp., 32 423–25

Siegel & Gale, 64 350–52

Siemens AG, II 97–100; 14 444–47 (upd.); 57 318–23 (upd.)

The Sierra Club, 28 422–24

Sierra Health Services, Inc., 15 451–53

Sierra Nevada Brewing Company, 70 291–93

Sierra On-Line, Inc., 15 454–56; 41 361–64 (upd.)

Sierra Pacific Industries, 22 489–91; 90 369–73 (upd.)

SIFCO Industries, Inc., 41

SIG plc, 71 334–36

Sigma-Aldrich Corporation, I 690–91; 36 429–32 (upd.); 93 398–404 (upd.)

Signet Banking Corporation, 11 446–48 *see also* Wachovia Corp.

Signet Group PLC, 61 326–28

Sikorsky Aircraft Corporation, 24 440–43

Silhouette Brands, Inc., 55 348–50

Silicon Graphics Inc., 9 471–73 *see also* SGI.

Siliconware Precision Industries Ltd., 73 300–02

Siltronic AG, 90 374–77

Silver Lake Cookie Company Inc., 95 378–81

Silver Wheaton Corp., 95 382–85

SilverPlatter Information Inc., 23 440–43

Silverstar Holdings, Ltd., 99 415–418

Silverstein Properties, Inc., 47 358–60

Simco S.A., 37 357–59

Sime Darby Berhad, 14 448–50; 36 433–36 (upd.)

Simmons Company, 47 361–64

Simon & Schuster Inc., IV 671–72; 19 403–05 (upd.); 100 393–97 (upd.)

Simon Property Group Inc., 27 399–402; 84 350–355 (upd.)

Simon Transportation Services Inc., 27 403–06

Simplex Technologies Inc., 21 460–63

Simplicity Manufacturing, Inc., 64 353–56

Simpson Investment Company, 17 438–41

Simpson Thacher & Bartlett, 39 365–68

Simula, Inc., 41 368–70

SINA Corporation, 69 324–27

Sinclair Broadcast Group, Inc., 25 417–19

Sine Qua Non, 99 419–422

Singapore Airlines Limited, 6 117–18; 27 407–09 (upd.); 83 355–359 (upd.)

Singapore Press Holdings Limited, 85 391–95

Singer & Friedlander Group plc, 41 371–73

The Singer Company N.V., 30 417–20 (upd.)

The Singing Machine Company, Inc., 60 277–80

Sir Speedy, Inc., 16 448–50

Sirius Satellite Radio, Inc., 69 328–31

Sirti S.p.A., 76 326–28

Siskin Steel & Supply Company, 70 294–96

Sistema JSFC, 73 303–05

Six Flags, Inc., 17 442–44; 54 333–40 (upd.)

Sixt AG, 39 369–72

SJW Corporation, 70 297–99

SK Group, 88 363–67

Skadden, Arps, Slate, Meagher & Flom, 18 486–88

Skalli Group, 67 349–51

Skandia Insurance Company, Ltd., 50 431–34

Skandinaviska Enskilda Banken AB, II 351–53; 56 326–29 (upd.)

Skanska AB, 38 435–38

Skechers U.S.A. Inc., 31 413–15; 88 368–72 (upd.)

Skeeter Products Inc., 96 391–94

SKF *see* Aktiebolaget SKF.

Skidmore, Owings & Merrill LLP, 13 475–76; 69 332–35 (upd.)

SkillSoft Public Limited Company, 81 371–74

skinnyCorp, LLC, 97 374–77

Skipton Building Society, 80 344–47

Skis Rossignol S.A., 15 460–62; 43 373–76 (upd.)

Skoda Auto a.s., 39 373–75

Skyline Chili, Inc., 62 325–28

Skyline Corporation, 30 421–23

SkyMall, Inc., 26 439–41

SkyWest, Inc., 25 420–24

Skyy Spirits LLC, 78 348–51

SL Green Realty Corporation, 44 383–85

SL Industries, Inc., 77 383–86

Sleeman Breweries Ltd., 74 305–08

Sleepy's Inc., 32 426–28

SLI, Inc., 48 358–61

Slim-Fast Foods Company, 18 489–91; 66 296–98 (upd.)

Slinky, Inc. *see* Poof-Slinky, Inc.

SLM Holding Corp., 25 425–28 (upd.)

Slough Estates PLC, IV 722–25; 50 435–40 (upd.)

Small Planet Foods, Inc., 89 410–14

Smart & Final LLC, 16 451–53; 94 392–96 (upd.)

Smart Balance, Inc., 100 398–401

SMART Modular Technologies, Inc., 86 361–64

SmartForce PLC, 43 377–80

Smarties *see* Ce De Candy Inc.

SMBC *see* Sumitomo Mitsui Banking Corp.

Smead Manufacturing Co., 17 445–48

571

SunOpta Inc., 79 406–10
SunPower Corporation, 91 467–70
The Sunrider Corporation, 26 470–74
Sunrise Greetings, 88 385–88
Sunrise Medical Inc., 11 486–88
Sunrise Senior Living, Inc., 81 380–83
Sunsweet Growers *see* Diamond of
California.
Suntech Power Holdings Company Ltd.,
89 432–35
Sunterra Corporation, 75 354–56
Suntory Ltd., 65 328–31
SunTrust Banks Inc., 23 455–58; 101
458–64 (upd.)
Super 8 Motels, Inc., 83 381-385
Super Food Services, Inc., 15 479–81
Supercuts Inc., 26 475–78
Superdrug Stores PLC, 95 390–93
Superior Energy Services, Inc., 65
332–34
Superior Essex Inc., 80 364–68
Superior Industries International, Inc.,
8 505–07
Superior Uniform Group, Inc., 30
455–57
Supermarkets General Holdings
Corporation, II 672–74 *see also*
Pathmark Stores, Inc.
SUPERVALU INC., II 668–71; 18
503–08 (upd.); 50 453–59 (upd.)
Suprema Specialties, Inc., 27 440–42
Supreme International Corporation, 27
443–46
Suramericana de Inversiones S.A., 88
389–92
OAO Surgutneftegaz, 48 375–78
Surrey Satellite Technology Limited, 83
386-390
The Susan G. Komen Breast
CancerFoundation, 78 373–76
Susquehanna Pfaltzgraff Company, 8
508–10
Sutherland Lumber Company, L.P., 99
431–434
Sutter Home Winery Inc., 16 476–78
Suzano *see* Companhia Suzano de Papel e
Celulose S.A.
Suzuki Motor Corporation, 9 487–89;
23 459–62 (upd.); 59 393–98 (upd.)
Sveaskog AB, 93 430–33
Svenska Cellulosa Aktiebolaget SCA, IV
338–40; 28 443–46 (upd.); 85
413–20 (upd.)
Svenska Handelsbanken AB, II 365–67;
50 460–63 (upd.)
Sverdrup Corporation, 14 475–78 *see
also* Jacobs Engineering Group Inc.
Sveriges Riksbank, 96 418–22
SWA *see* Southwest Airlines.
SWALEC *see* Scottish and Southern
Energy plc.
Swales & Associates, Inc., 69 336–38
Swank, Inc., 17 464–66; 84 380–384
(upd.)
Swarovski International Holding AG, 40
422–25
The Swatch Group SA, 26 479–81

Swedish Match AB, 12 462–64; 39
387–90 (upd.); 92 349–55 (upd.)
Swedish Telecom, V 331–33
SwedishAmerican Health System, 51
363–66
Sweet Candy Company, 60 295–97
Sweetheart Cup Company, Inc., 36
460–64
The Swett & Crawford Group Inc., 84
385–389
SWH Corporation, 70 307–09
Swift & Company, 55 364–67
Swift Energy Company, 63 364–66
Swift Transportation Co., Inc., 42
363–66
Swinerton Inc., 43 397–400
Swire Pacific Ltd., I 521–22; 16 479–81
(upd.); 57 348–53 (upd.)
Swisher International Group Inc., 23
463–65
Swiss Air Transport Company Ltd., I
121–22
Swiss Army Brands, Inc. *see* Victorinox
AG.
Swiss Bank Corporation, II 368–70 *see
also* UBS AG.
The Swiss Colony, Inc., 97 395–98
Swiss Federal Railways (Schweizerische
Bundesbahnen), V 519–22
Swiss International Air Lines Ltd., 48
379–81
Swiss Reinsurance Company
(Schweizerische
Rückversicherungs-Gesellschaft), III
375–78; 46 380–84 (upd.)
Swiss Valley Farms Company, 90
400–03
Swisscom AG, 58 336–39
Swissport International Ltd., 70 310–12
Sybase, Inc., 10 504–06; 27 447–50
(upd.)
Sybron International Corp., 14 479–81
Sycamore Networks, Inc., 45 388–91
Sykes Enterprises, Inc., 45 392–95
Sylvan, Inc., 22 496–99
Sylvan Learning Systems, Inc., 35
408–11 *see also* Educate Inc.
Symantec Corporation, 10 507–09; 82
372–77 (upd.)
Symbol Technologies, Inc., 15 482–84
see also Motorola, Inc.
Symrise GmbH and Company KG, 89
436–40
Syms Corporation, 29 456–58; 74
327–30 (upd.)
Symyx Technologies, Inc., 77 420–23
Synaptics Incorporated, 95 394–98
Synchronoss Technologies, Inc., 95
399–402
Syneron Medical Ltd., 91 471–74
Syngenta International AG, 83 391-394
Syniverse Holdings Inc., 97 399–402
SYNNEX Corporation, 73 328–30
Synopsys, Inc., 11 489–92; 69 339–43
(upd.)
SynOptics Communications, Inc., 10
510–12

Synovus Financial Corp., 12 465–67; 52
336–40 (upd.)
Syntel, Inc., 92 356–60
Syntex Corporation, I 701–03
Synthes, Inc., 93 434–37
Sypris Solutions, Inc., 85 421–25
SyQuest Technology, Inc., 18 509–12
Syratech Corp., 14 482–84
SYSCO Corporation, II 675–76; 24
470–72 (upd.); 75 357–60 (upd.)
System Software Associates, Inc., 10
513–14
Systemax, Inc., 52 341–44
Systems & Computer Technology Corp.,
19 437–39
Sytner Group plc, 45 396–98

T

T-Netix, Inc., 46 385–88
T-Online International AG, 61 349–51
T.J. Maxx *see* The TJX Companies, Inc.
T. Marzetti Company, 57 354–56
T. Rowe Price Associates, Inc., 11
493–96; 34 423–27 (upd.)
TA Triumph-Adler AG, 48 382–85
TAB Products Co., 17 467–69
Tabacalera, S.A., V 414–16; 17 470–73
(upd.) *see also* Altadis S.A.
TABCORP Holdings Limited, 44
407–10
TACA *see* Grupo TACA.
Taco Bell Corporation, 7 505–07; 21
485–88 (upd.); 74 331–34 (upd.)
Taco Cabana, Inc., 23 466–68; 72
344–47 (upd.)
Taco John's International Inc., 15
485–87; 63 367–70 (upd.)
Tacony Corporation, 70 313–15
TAG Heuer S.A., 25 459–61; 77 424–28
(upd.)
Tag-It Pacific, Inc., 85 426–29
Taiheiyo Cement Corporation, 60
298–301 (upd.)
Taittinger S.A., 43 401–05
Taiwan Semiconductor Manufacturing
Company Ltd., 47 383–87
Taiwan Tobacco & Liquor Corporation,
75 361–63
Taiyo Fishery Company, Limited, II
578–79 *see also* Maruha Group Inc.
Taiyo Kobe Bank, Ltd., II 371–72
Takara Holdings Inc., 62 345–47
Takashimaya Company, Limited, V
193–96; 47 388–92 (upd.)
Take-Two Interactive Software, Inc., 46
389–91
Takeda Chemical Industries, Ltd., I
704–06; 46 392–95 (upd.)
The Talbots, Inc., 11 497–99; 31
429–32 (upd.); 88 393–98 (upd.)
Talisman Energy Inc., 9 490–93; 47
393–98 (upd.)
Talk America Holdings, Inc., 70 316–19
Talley Industries, Inc., 16 482–85
TALX Corporation, 92 361–64
TAM Linhas Aéreas S.A., 68 363–65
Tambrands Inc., 8 511–13 *see also*
Procter & Gamble Co.

Trigen Energy Corporation, 42 386–89
Trilon Financial Corporation, II 456–57
TriMas Corp., 11 534–36
Trimble Navigation Limited, 40 441–43
Třinecké Železárny A.S., 92 384–87
Trinity Industries, Incorporated, 7 540–41
Trinity Mirror plc, 49 404–10 (upd.)
TRINOVA Corporation, III 640–42
TriPath Imaging, Inc., 77 446–49
Triple Five Group Ltd., 49 411–15
Triple P N.V., 26 496–99
Tripwire, Inc., 97 433–36
TriQuint Semiconductor, Inc., 63 396–99
Trisko Jewelry Sculptures, Ltd., 57 388–90
Triton Energy Corporation, 11 537–39
Triumph-Adler *see* TA Triumph-Adler AG.
Triumph Group, Inc., 31 446–48
Triumph Motorcycles Ltd., 53 334–37
Trizec Corporation Ltd., 10 529–32
The TriZetto Group, Inc., 83 416–419
TRM Copy Centers Corporation, 18 526–28
Tropicana Products, Inc., 28 473–77; 73 344–49 (upd.)
Troutman Sanders L.L.P., 79 427–30
True North Communications Inc., 23 478–80 *see also* Foote, Cone & Belding Worldwide.
True Religion Apparel, Inc., 79 431–34
True Temper Sports, Inc., 95 429–32
True Value Company, 74 353–57 (upd.)
Trump Organization, 23 481–84; 64 392–97 (upd.)
TRUMPF GmbH + Co. KG, 86 397–02
TruServ Corporation, 24 504–07 *see* True Value Co.
Trusthouse Forte PLC, III 104–06
TRW Automotive Holdings Corp., I 539–41; 11 540–42 (upd.); 14 510–13 (upd.); 75 376–82 (upd.)
TSA *see* Transaction Systems Architects, Inc.
Tsakos Energy Navigation Ltd., 91 483–86
TSB Group plc, 12 491–93
TSC *see* Tractor Supply Co.
Tsingtao Brewery Group, 49 416–20
TSMC *see* Taiwan Semiconductor Manufacturing Company Ltd.
TSYS *see* Total System Services, Inc.
TTL *see* Taiwan Tobacco & Liquor Corp.
TTX Company, 6 436–37; 66 328–30 (upd.)
Tubby's, Inc., 53 338–40
Tubos de Acero de Mexico, S.A. (TAMSA), 41 404–06
Tucows Inc., 78 411–14
Tucson Electric Power Company, 6 588–91
Tuesday Morning Corporation, 18 529–31; 70 331–33 (upd.)
TUF *see* Thai Union Frozen Products PCL.

TUI *see* Touristik Union International GmbH. and Company K.G.
TUI Group GmbH, 42 283; 44 432–35
Tulip Ltd., 89 454–57
Tullow Oil plc, 83 420-423
Tully's Coffee Corporation, 51 384–86
Tultex Corporation, 13 531–33
Tumaro's Gourmet Tortillas, 85 430–33
Tumbleweed, Inc., 33 412–14; 80 377–81 (upd.)
Tunisair *see* Société Tunisienne de l'Air-Tunisair.
Tupolev Aviation and Scientific Technical Complex, 24 58–60
Tupperware Brands Corporation, 28 478–81; 78 415–20 (upd.)
TurboChef Technologies, Inc., 83 424-427
Turkish Airlines Inc. (Türk Hava Yollari A.O.), 72 351–53
Turkiye Is Bankasi A.S., 61 377–80
Türkiye Petrolleri Anonim Ortakliği, IV 562–64
Turner Broadcasting System, Inc., II 166–68; 6 171–73 (upd.); 66 331–34 (upd.)
Turner Construction Company, 66 335–38
The Turner Corporation, 8 538–40; 23 485–88 (upd.)
Turtle Wax, Inc., 15 506–09; 93 465–70 (upd.)
Tuscarora Inc., 29 483–85
The Tussauds Group, 55 376–78
Tutogen Medical, Inc., 68 378–80
Tuttle Publishing, 86 403–06
TV Azteca, S.A. de C.V., 39 398–401
TV Guide, Inc., 43 431–34 (upd.)
TVA *see* Tennessee Valley Authority.
TVE *see* Television Española, S.A.
TVI, Inc., 15 510–12; 99 462–465 *see also* Savers, Inc.
TW Services, Inc., II 679–80
TWA *see* Trans World Airlines.
TWC *see* The Weather Channel Cos.
Tweeter Home Entertainment Group, Inc., 30 464–66
Twentieth Century Fox Film Corporation, II 169–71; 25 490–94 (upd.)
24 Hour Fitness Worldwide, Inc., 71 363–65
24/7 Real Media, Inc., 49 421–24
Twin Disc, Inc., 21 502–04
Twinlab Corporation, 34 458–61
II-VI Incorporated, 69 353–55
Ty Inc., 33 415–17; 86 407–11 (upd.)
Tyco International Ltd., III 643–46; 28 482–87 (upd.); 63 400–06 (upd.)
Tyco Toys, Inc., 12 494–97 *see also* Mattel, Inc.
Tyler Corporation, 23 489–91
Tyndale House Publishers, Inc., 57 391–94

Tyson Foods, Inc., II 584–85; 14 514–16 (upd.); 50 491–95 (upd.)

U

U.S. *see also* US.
U.S. Aggregates, Inc., 42 390–92
U.S. Army Corps of Engineers, 91 491–95
U.S. Bancorp, 14 527–29; 36 489–95 (upd.)
U.S. Borax, Inc., 42 393–96
U.S. Can Corporation, 30 474–76
U.S. Cellular Corporation, 31 449–52 (upd.); 88 408–13 (upd.)
U.S. Delivery Systems, Inc., 22 531–33 *see also* Velocity Express Corp.
U.S. Foodservice, 26 503–06
U.S. Healthcare, Inc., 6 194–96
U.S. Home Corporation, 8 541–43; 78 421–26 (upd.)
U.S. News & World Report Inc., 30 477–80; 89 458–63 (upd.)
U.S. Office Products Company, 25 500–02
U.S. Physical Therapy, Inc., 65 345–48
U.S. Premium Beef LLC, 91 487–90
U.S. Robotics Corporation, 9 514–15; 66 339–41 (upd.)
U.S. Satellite Broadcasting Company, Inc., 20 505–07 *see also* DIRECTV, Inc.
U.S. Steel Corp *see* United States Steel Corp.
U.S. Timberlands Company, L.P., 42 397–400
U.S. Trust Corp., 17 496–98
U.S. Vision, Inc., 66 342–45
U S West, Inc., V 341–43; 25 495–99 (upd.)
UAL Corporation, 34 462–65 (upd.)
UAP *see* Union des Assurances de Paris.
UAW (International Union, United Automobile, Aerospace and Agricultural Implement Workers of America), 72 354–57
Ube Industries, Ltd., III 759–61; 38 463–67 (upd.)
Ubi Soft Entertainment S.A., 41 407–09
UBS AG, 52 352–59 (upd.)
UCB Pharma SA, 98 409–12
UFA TV & Film Produktion GmbH, 80 382–87
UGI Corporation, 12 498–500
Ugine S.A., 20 498–500
Ugly Duckling Corporation, 22 524–27 *see also* DriveTime Automotive Group Inc.
UICI, 33 418–21 *see also* HealthMarkets, Inc.
Ukrop's Super Markets Inc., 39 402–04; 101 478–82 (upd.)
UL *see* Underwriters Laboratories, Inc.
Ulster Television PLC, 71 366–68
Ulta Salon, Cosmetics & Fragrance, Inc., 92471–73
Ultimate Electronics, Inc., 18 532–34; 69 356–59 (upd.)

University of Phoenix *see* Apollo Group, Inc.

Univision Communications Inc., 24 515–18; 83 434–439 (upd.)

UNM *see* United News & Media plc.

Uno Restaurant Holdings Corporation, 18 538–40; 70 334–37 (upd.)

Unocal Corporation, IV 569–71; 24 519–23 (upd.); 71 378–84 (upd.)

UNUM Corp., 13 538–40

UnumProvident Corporation, 52 376–83 (upd.)

Uny Co., Ltd., V 209–10; 49 425–28 (upd.)

UOB *see* United Overseas Bank Ltd.

UPC *see* United Pan-Europe Communications NV.

UPI *see* United Press International.

Upjohn Company, I 707–09; 8 547–49 (upd.) *see also* Pharmacia & Upjohn Inc.; Pfizer Inc.

UPM-Kymmene Corporation, 19 461–65; 50 505–11 (upd.)

UPS *see* United Parcel Service, Inc.

Uralita S.A., 96 438–41

Urban Outfitters, Inc., 14 524–26; 74 367–70 (upd.)

Urbi Desarrollos Urbanos, S.A. de C.V., 81 400–03

Urbium PLC, 75 389–91

URS Corporation, 45 420–23; 80 397–400 (upd.)

URSI *see* United Road Services, Inc.

US *see also* U.S.

US Airways Group, Inc., I 131–32; 6 131–32 (upd.); 28 506–09 (upd.); 52 384–88 (upd.)

US 1 Industries, Inc., 89 475–78

USA Interactive, Inc., 47 418–22 (upd.)

USA Mobility Inc., 97 437–40 (upd.)

USA Truck, Inc., 42 410–13

USAA, 10 541–43; 62 385–88 (upd.)

USANA, Inc., 29 491–93

USCC *see* United States Cellular Corp.

USF&G Corporation, III 395–98 *see also* The St. Paul Companies.

USG Corporation, III 762–64; 26 507–10 (upd.); 81 404–10 (upd.)

Ushio Inc., 91 496–99

Usinas Siderúrgicas de Minas Gerais S.A., 77 454–57

Usinger's Famous Sausage *see* Fred Usinger Inc.

Usinor SA, IV 226–28; 42 414–17 (upd.)

USO *see* United Service Organizations.

USPS *see* United States Postal Service.

USSC *see* United States Surgical Corp.

UST Inc., 9 533–35; 50 512–17 (upd.)

USX Corporation, IV 572–74; 7 549–52 (upd.) *see also* United States Steel Corp.

Utah Medical Products, Inc., 36 496–99

Utah Power and Light Company, 27 483–86 *see also* PacifiCorp.

UTG Inc., 100 430–33

Utilicorp United Inc., 6 592–94 *see also* Aquilla, Inc.

UTStarcom, Inc., 77 458–61

UTV *see* Ulster Television PLC.

Utz Quality Foods, Inc., 72 358–60

UUNET, 38 468–72

Uwajimaya, Inc., 60 312–14

Uzbekistan Airways National Air Company, 99 470–473

V

V&S Vin & Sprit AB, 91 504–11 (upd.)

VA TECH ELIN EBG GmbH, 49 429–31

Vail Resorts, Inc., 11 543–46; 43 435–39 (upd.)

Vaillant GmbH, 44 436–39

Valassis Communications, Inc., 8 550–51; 37 407–10 (upd.); 76 364–67 (upd.)

Valeo, 23 492–94; 66 350–53 (upd.)

Valero Energy Corporation, 7 553–55; 71 385–90 (upd.)

Valhi, Inc., 19 466–68; 94 431–35 (upd.)

Vallen Corporation, 45 424–26

Valley Media Inc., 35 430–33

Valley National Gases, Inc., 85 434–37

Valley Proteins, Inc., 91 500–03

ValleyCrest Companies, 81 411–14 (upd.)

Vallourec SA, 54 391–94

Valmet Oy, III 647–49 *see also* Metso Corp.

Valmont Industries, Inc., 19 469–72

Valora Holding AG, 98 425–28

Valorem S.A., 88 427–30

Valores Industriales S.A., 19 473–75

The Valspar Corporation, 8 552–54; 32 483–86 (upd.); 77 462–68 (upd.)

Value City Department Stores, Inc., 38 473–75 *see also* Retail Ventures, Inc.

Value Line, Inc., 16 506–08; 73 358–61 (upd.)

Value Merchants Inc., 13 541–43

ValueClick, Inc., 49 432–34

ValueVision International, Inc., 22 534–36

Valve Corporation, 101 483–86

Van Camp Seafood Company, Inc., 7 556–57 *see also* Chicken of the Sea International.

Van Hool S.A./NV, 96 442–45

Van Houtte Inc., 39 409–11

Van Lanschot NV, 79 456–59

Van Leer N.V. *see* Royal Packaging Industries Van Leer N.V.; Greif Inc.

Van's Aircraft, Inc., 65 349–51

Vance Publishing Corporation, 64 398–401

Vanderbilt University Medical Center, 99 474–477

The Vanguard Group, Inc., 14 530–32; 34 486–89 (upd.)

Vanguard Health Systems Inc., 70 338–40

Vans, Inc., 16 509–11; 47 423–26 (upd.)

Vapores *see* Compañia Sud Americana de Vapores S.A.

Varco International, Inc., 42 418–20

Vari-Lite International, Inc., 35 434–36

Varian Associates Inc., 12 504–06

Varian, Inc., 48 407–11 (upd.)

Variety Wholesalers, Inc., 73 362–64

Variflex, Inc., 51 391–93

VARIG S.A. (Viação Aérea Rio-Grandense), 6 133–35; 29 494–97 (upd.)

Varity Corporation, III 650–52 *see also* AGCO Corp.

Varlen Corporation, 16 512–14

Varsity Brands, Inc., 15 516–18; 94 436–40 (upd.)

Varta AG, 23 495–99

VASCO Data Security International, Inc., 79 460–63

Vastar Resources, Inc., 24 524–26

Vattenfall AB, 57 395–98

Vauxhall Motors Limited, 73 365–69

VBA - Bloemenveiling Aalsmeer, 88 431–34

VCA Antech, Inc., 58 353–55

Veba A.G., I 542–43; 15 519–21 (upd.) *see also* E.On AG.

Vebego International BV, 49 435–37

VECO International, Inc., 7 558–59 *see also* CH2M Hill Ltd.

Vector Aerospace Corporation, 97 441–44

Vector Group Ltd., 35 437–40 (upd.)

Vectren Corporation, 98 429–36 (upd.)

Vedior NV, 35 441–43

Veeco Instruments Inc., 32 487–90

Veidekke ASA, 98 437–40

Veit Companies, 43 440–42; 92 398–402 (upd.)

Velcro Industries N.V., 19 476–78; 72 361–64 (upd.)

Velocity Express Corporation, 49 438–41; 94 441–46 (upd.)

Velux A/S, 86 412–15

Venator Group Inc., 35 444–49 (upd.) *see also* Foot Locker Inc.

Vencor, Inc., 16 515–17

Vendex International N.V., 13 544–46 *see also* Koninklijke Vendex KBB N.V. (Royal Vendex KBB N.V.).

Vendôme Luxury Group plc, 27 487–89

Venetian Casino Resort, LLC, 47 427–29

Ventana Medical Systems, Inc., 75 392–94

Ventura Foods LLC, 90 420–23

Venture Stores Inc., 12 507–09

VeraSun Energy Corporation, 87 447–450

Verbatim Corporation, 14 533–35; 74 371–74 (upd.)

Vereinigte Elektrizitätswerke Westfalen AG, IV V 744–47

Veridian Corporation, 54 395–97

VeriFone, Inc., 18 541–44; 76 368–71 (upd.)

Verint Systems Inc., 73 370–72

VeriSign, Inc., 47 430–34

Veritas Software Corporation, 45 427–31

Verity Inc., 68 388–91

Verizon Communications Inc., 43 443–49 (upd.); 78 432–40 (upd.)

Verlagsgruppe Georg von Holtzbrinck GmbH, 35 450–53

Verlagsgruppe Weltbild GmbH, 98 441–46

Vermeer Manufacturing Company, 17 507–10

The Vermont Country Store, 93 478–82

Vermont Pure Holdings, Ltd., 51 394–96

The Vermont Teddy Bear Co., Inc., 36 500–02

Versace *see* Gianni Versace SpA.

Vertex Pharmaceuticals Incorporated, 83 440–443

Vertis Communications, 84 418–421

Vertrue Inc., 77 469–72

Vestas Wind Systems A/S, 73 373–75

Vestey Group Ltd., 95 433–37

Veuve Clicquot Ponsardin SCS, 98 447–51

VEW AG, 39 412–15

VF Corporation, V 390–92; 17 511–14 (upd.); 54 398–404 (upd.)

VHA Inc., 53 345–47

Viacom Inc., 7 560–62; 23 500–03 (upd.); 67 367–71 (upd.) *see also* Paramount Pictures Corp.

Viad Corp., 73 376–78

Viag AG, IV 229–32 *see also* E.On AG.

ViaSat, Inc., 54 405–08

Viasoft Inc., 27 490–93; 59 27

VIASYS Healthcare, Inc., 52 389–91

Viasystems Group, Inc., 67 372–74

Viatech Continental Can Company, Inc., 25 512–15 (upd.)

Vicat S.A., 70 341–43

Vickers plc, 27 494–97

Vicon Industries, Inc., 44 440–42

VICORP Restaurants, Inc., 12 510–12; 48 412–15 (upd.)

Victor Company of Japan, Limited, II 118–19; 26 511–13 (upd.); 83 444–449 (upd.)

Victoria Coach Station Ltd. *see* London Regional Transport.

Victoria Group, III 399–401; 44 443–46 (upd.)

Victorinox AG, 21 515–17; 74 375–78 (upd.)

Vicunha Têxtil S.A., 78 441–44

Victory Refrigeration, Inc., 82 403–06

Videojet Technologies, Inc., 90 424–27

Vidrala S.A., 67 375–77

Viel & Cie, 76 372–74

Vienna Sausage Manufacturing Co., 14 536–37

Viessmann Werke GmbH & Co., 37 411–14

Viewpoint International, Inc., 66 354–56

ViewSonic Corporation, 72 365–67

Viking Office Products, Inc., 10 544–46 *see also* Office Depot, Inc.

Viking Range Corporation, 66 357–59

Viking Yacht Company, 96 446–49

Village Roadshow Ltd., 58 356–59

Village Super Market, Inc., 7 563–64

Village Voice Media, Inc., 38 476–79

Villeroy & Boch AG, 37 415–18

Vilmorin Clause et Cie, 70 344–46

AO VimpelCom, 48 416–19

Vin & Spirit AB, 31 458–61 *see also* V&S Vin & Sprit AB.

Viña Concha y Toro S.A., 45 432–34

Vinci, 27 54; 43 450–52; 49 44

Vincor International Inc., 50 518–21

Vinmonopolet A/S, 100 434–37

Vinson & Elkins L.L.P., 30 481–83

Vintage Petroleum, Inc., 42 421–23

Vinton Studios, 63 420–22

Vion Food Group NV, 85 438–41

Virbac Corporation, 74 379–81

Virco Manufacturing Corporation, 17 515–17

Virgin Group Ltd., 12 513–15; 32 491–96 (upd.); 89 479–86 (upd.)

Virginia Dare Extract Company, Inc., 94 447–50

Viridian Group plc, 64 402–04

Visa International, 9 536–38; 26 514–17 (upd.)

Viscofan S.A., 70 347–49

Vishay Intertechnology, Inc., 21 518–21; 80 401–06 (upd.)

Vision Service Plan Inc., 77 473–76

Viskase Companies, Inc., 55 379–81

Vista Bakery, Inc., 56 365–68

Vista Chemical Company, I 402–03

Vistana, Inc., 22 537–39

VistaPrint Limited, 87 451–454

VISX, Incorporated, 30 484–86

Vita Food Products Inc., 99 478–481

Vita Plus Corporation, 60 315–17

Vital Images, Inc., 85 442–45

Vitalink Pharmacy Services, Inc., 15 522–24

Vitamin Shoppe Industries, Inc., 60 318–20

Vitasoy International Holdings Ltd., 94 451–54

Vitesse Semiconductor Corporation, 32 497–500

Vitro Corp., 10 547–48

Vitro Corporativo S.A. de C.V., 34 490–92

Vivarte SA, 54 409–12 (upd.)

Vivartia S.A., 82 407–10

Vivendi Universal S.A., 46 438–41 (upd.)

Vivra, Inc., 18 545–47 *see also* Gambro AB.

Vizio, Inc., 100 438–41

Vlasic Foods International Inc., 25 516–19

VLSI Technology, Inc., 16 518–20

VMware, Inc., 90 428–31

VNU N.V., 27 498–501

Vocento, 94 455–58

Vodafone Group Plc, 11 547–48; 36 503–06 (upd.); 75 395–99 (upd.)

voestalpine AG, IV 233–35; 57 399–403 (upd.)

Voith Sulzer Papiermaschinen GmbH *see* J.M. Voith AG.

Volcan Compañia Minera S.A.A., 92 403–06

Volcom, Inc., 77 477–80

Volga-Dnepr Group, 82 411–14

Volkert and Associates, Inc., 98 452–55

Volkswagen Aktiengesellschaft, I 206–08; 11 549–51 (upd.); 32 501–05 (upd.)

Volt Information Sciences Inc., 26 518–21

Volunteers of America, Inc., 66 360–62

AB Volvo, I 209–11; 7 565–68 (upd.); 26 9–12 (upd.); 67 378–83 (upd.)

Von Maur Inc., 64 405–08

Vonage Holdings Corp., 81 415–18

The Vons Companies, Incorporated, 7 569–71; 28 510–13 (upd.)

Vontobel Holding AG, 96 450–53

Vornado Realty Trust, 20 508–10

Vorwerk & Co., 27 502–04

Vosper Thornycroft Holding plc, 41 410–12

Vossloh AG, 53 348–52

Votorantim Participaçoes S.A., 76 375–78

Vought Aircraft Industries, Inc., 49 442–45

VSM *see* Village Super Market, Inc.

VTech Holdings Ltd., 77 481–84

Vueling Airlines S.A., 97 445–48

Vulcan Materials Company, 7 572–75; 52 392–96 (upd.)

W

W + K *see* Wieden + Kennedy.

W.A. Whitney Company, 53 353–56

W. Atlee Burpee & Co., 27 505–08

W.B Doner & Co., 56 369–72

W.B. Mason Company, 98 456–59

W.C. Bradley Co., 69 363–65

W.H. Brady Co., 16 518–21 *see also* Brady Corp.

W. H. Braum, Inc., 80 407–10

W H Smith Group PLC, V 211–13

W Jordan (Cereals) Ltd., 74 382–84

W.L. Gore & Associates, Inc., 14 538–40; 60 321–24 (upd.)

W.P. Carey & Co. LLC, 49 446–48

W.R. Berkley Corporation, 15 525–27; 74 385–88 (upd.)

W.R. Grace & Company, I 547–50; 50 522–29 (upd.)

W.W. Grainger, Inc., V 214–15; 26 537–39 (upd.); 68 392–95 (upd.)

W.W. Norton & Company, Inc., 28 518–20

Waban Inc., 13 547–49 *see also* HomeBase, Inc.

Wabash National Corp., 13 550–52

Wabtec Corporation, 40 451–54

Wachovia Bank of Georgia, N.A., 16 521–23

Wachovia Bank of South Carolina, N.A., 16 524–26

Wachovia Corporation, 12 516–20; 46 442–49 (upd.)

Wachtell, Lipton, Rosen & Katz, 47 435–38

The Wackenhut Corporation, 14 541–43; 63 423–26 (upd.)

Wacker-Chemie GmbH, 35 454–58

Wacker Construction Equipment AG, 95 438–41

Wacoal Corp., 25 520–24

Waddell & Reed, Inc., 22 540–43

Waffle House Inc., 14 544–45; 60 325–27 (upd.)

Wagers Inc. (Idaho Candy Company), 86 416–19

Waggener Edstrom, 42 424–26

Wagon plc, 92 407–10

Wah Chang, 82 415–18

Wahl Clipper Corporation, 86 420–23

Wahoo's Fish Taco, 96 454–57

Wakefern Food Corporation, 33 434–37

Wal-Mart de Mexico, S.A. de C.V., 35 459–61 (upd.)

Wal-Mart Stores, Inc., V 216–17; 8 555–57 (upd.); 26 522–26 (upd.); 63 427–32 (upd.)

Walbridge Aldinger Co., 38 480–82

Walbro Corporation, 13 553–55

Waldbaum, Inc., 19 479–81

Waldenbooks, 17 522–24; 86 424–28 (upd.)

Walgreen Co., V 218–20; 20 511–13 (upd.); 65 352–56 (upd.)

Walker Manufacturing Company, 19 482–84

Walkers Shortbread Ltd., 79 464–67

Walkers Snack Foods Ltd., 70 350–52

Wall Drug Store, Inc., 40 455–57

Wall Street Deli, Inc., 33 438–41

Wallace Computer Services, Inc., 36 507–10

Walsworth Publishing Company, Inc., 78 445–48

The Walt Disney Company, II 172–74; 6 174–77 (upd.); 30 487–91 (upd.); 63 433–38 (upd.)

Walter Industries, Inc., III 765–67; 22 544–47 (upd.); 72 368–73 (upd.)

Walton Monroe Mills, Inc., 8 558–60 see also Avondale Industries.

WaMu see Washington Mutual, Inc.

Wanadoo S.A., 75 400–02

Wang Laboratories, Inc., III 168–70; 6 284–87 (upd.) see also Getronics NV.

Warburtons Ltd., 89 487–90

WARF see Wisconsin Alumni Research Foundation.

The Warnaco Group Inc., 12 521–23; 46 450–54 (upd.) see also Authentic Fitness Corp.

Warner Chilcott Limited, 85 446–49

Warner Communications Inc., II 175–77 see also AOL Time Warner Inc.

Warner-Lambert Co., I 710–12; 10 549–52 (upd.) see also Pfizer Inc.

Warner Music Group Corporation, 90 432–37 (upd.)

Warners' Stellian Inc., 67 384–87

Warrantech Corporation, 53 357–59

Warrell Corporation, 68 396–98

Wärtsilä Corporation, 100 442–46

Warwick Valley Telephone Company, 55 382–84

Wascana Energy Inc., 13 556–58

The Washington Companies, 33 442–45

Washington Federal, Inc., 17 525–27

Washington Football, Inc., 35 462–65

Washington Gas Light Company, 19 485–88

Washington Mutual, Inc., 17 528–31; 93 483–89 (upd.)

Washington National Corporation, 12 524–26

Washington Natural Gas Company, 9 539–41 see also Puget Sound Energy Inc.

The Washington Post Company, IV 688–90; 20 515–18 (upd.)

Washington Scientific Industries, Inc., 17 532–34

Washington Water Power Company, 6 595–98 see also Avista Corp.

Wassall Plc, 18 548–50

Waste Connections, Inc., 46 455–57

Waste Holdings, Inc., 41 413–15

Waste Management, Inc., V 752–54

Water Pik Technologies, Inc., 34 498–501; 83 450–453 (upd.)

Waterford Wedgwood plc, 12 527–29; 34 493–97 (upd.)

Waterhouse Investor Services, Inc., 18 551–53

Waters Corporation, 43 453–57

Watkins-Johnson Company, 15 528–30

Watsco Inc., 52 397–400

Watson Pharmaceuticals Inc., 16 527–29; 56 373–76 (upd.)

Watson Wyatt Worldwide, 42 427–30

Wattie's Ltd., 7 576–78

Watts Industries, Inc., 19 489–91

Watts of Lydney Group Ltd., 71 391–93

Wausau-Mosinee Paper Corporation, 60 328–31 (upd.)

Waverly, Inc., 16 530–32

Wawa Inc., 17 535–37; 78 449–52 (upd.)

The Wawanesa Mutual Insurance Company, 68 399–401

WAXIE Sanitary Supply, 100 447–51

Waxman Industries, Inc., 9 542–44

WAZ Media Group, 82 419–24

WB see Warner Communications Inc.

WD-40 Company, 18 554–57; 87 455–460 (upd.)

We-No-Nah Canoe, Inc., 98 460–63

Weather Central Inc., 100 452–55

The Weather Channel Companies, 52 401–04 see also Landmark Communications, Inc.

Weatherford International, Inc., 39 416–18

Weaver Popcorn Company, Inc., 89 491–93

Webasto Roof Systems Inc., 97 449–52

Webber Oil Company, 61 384–86

Weber et Broutin France, 66 363–65

Weber-Stephen Products Co., 40 458–60

WebEx Communications, Inc., 81 419–23

WebMD Corporation, 65 357–60

Weeres Industries Corporation, 52 405–07

Weetabix Limited, 61 387–89

Weg S.A., 78 453–56

Wegener NV, 53 360–62

Wegmans Food Markets, Inc., 9 545–46; 41 416–18 (upd.)

Weider Nutrition International, Inc., 29 498–501

Weight Watchers International Inc., 12 530–32; 33 446–49 (upd.); 73 379–83 (upd.)

Weil, Gotshal & Manges LLP, 55 385–87

Weiner's Stores, Inc., 33 450–53

Wieden + Kennedy, 75 403–05

Wienerberger AG, 70 361–63

Weingarten Realty Investors, 95 442–45

The Weir Group PLC, 85 450–53

Weirton Steel Corporation, IV 236–38; 26 527–30 (upd.)

Weis Markets, Inc., 15 531–33; 84 422–426 (upd.)

The Weitz Company, Inc., 42 431–34

Welbilt Corp., 19 492–94; see also Enodis plc.

Welcome Wagon International Inc., 82 425–28

Weleda AG, 78 457–61

The Welk Group, Inc., 78 462–66

Wella AG, III 68–70; 48 420–23 (upd.)

WellCare Health Plans, Inc., 101 487–90

WellChoice, Inc., 67 388–91 (upd.)

Wellco Enterprises, Inc., 84 427–430

Wellcome Foundation Ltd., I 713–15 see also GlaxoSmithKline plc.

Wellman, Inc., 8 561–62; 52 408–11 (upd.)

WellPoint Health Networks Inc., 25 525–29

Wells Fargo & Company, II 380–84; 12 533–37 (upd.); 38 483–92 (upd.); 97 453–67

Wells-Gardner Electronics Corporation, 43 458–61

Wells Rich Greene BDDP, 6 50–52

Wells' Dairy, Inc., 36 511–13

Wendell see Mark T. Wendell Tea Co.

Wendy's International, Inc., 8 563–65; 23 504–07 (upd.); 47 439–44 (upd.)

Wenner Bread Products Inc., 80 411–15

Wenner Media, Inc., 32 506–09

Werhahn see Wilh. Werhahn KG.

Werner Enterprises, Inc., 26 531–33

Weru Aktiengesellschaft, 18 558–61

Wessanen see Koninklijke Wessanen nv.

West Bend Co., 14 546–48

West Coast Entertainment Corporation, 29 502–04

West Corporation, 42 435–37

West Fraser Timber Co. Ltd., 17 538–40; 91 512–18 (upd.)

West Group, 34 502–06 (upd.)

West Linn Paper Company, 91 519–22

Index to Industries

O.C. Tanner Co., 69
Oakleaf Waste Management, LLC, 97
Obie Media Corporation, 56
Observer AB, 55
OfficeTiger, LLC, 75
The Ogilvy Group, Inc., I
Olsten Corporation, 6; 29 (upd.)
Omnicom Group, I; 22 (upd.); 77 (upd.)
On Assignment, Inc., 20
1-800-FLOWERS, Inc., 26
Opinion Research Corporation, 46
Oracle Corporation, 67 (upd.)
Orbitz, Inc., 61
Outdoor Systems, Inc., 25
Paris Corporation, 22
Paychex, Inc., 15; 46 (upd.)
PDI, Inc., 52
Pegasus Solutions, Inc., 75
Pei Cobb Freed & Partners Architects
    LLP, 57
Penauille Polyservices SA, 49
PFSweb, Inc., 73
Philip Services Corp., 73
Phillips, de Pury & Luxembourg, 49
Pierce Leahy Corporation, 24
Pinkerton's Inc., 9
Plante & Moran, LLP, 71
PMT Services, Inc., 24
Posterscope Worldwide, 70
Priceline.com Incorporated, 57
Publicis Groupe, 19; 77 (upd.)
Publishers Clearing House, 23; 64 (upd.)
Quintiles Transnational Corporation, 68
    (upd.)
Quovadx Inc., 70
Randstad Holding n.v., 16; 43 (upd.)
RedPeg Marketing, 73
RedPrairie Corporation, 74
RemedyTemp, Inc., 20
Rental Service Corporation, 28
Rentokil Initial Plc, 47
Research Triangle Institute, 83
Resources Connection, Inc., 81
Rewards Network Inc., 70 (upd.)
The Richards Group, Inc., 58
Right Management Consultants, Inc., 42
Ritchie Bros. Auctioneers Inc., 41
Robert Half International Inc., 18
Roland Berger & Partner GmbH, 37
Ronco Corporation, 15; 80 (upd.)
Russell Reynolds Associates Inc., 38
Saatchi & Saatchi, I; 42 (upd.)
Sanders\Wingo, 99
Schenck Business Solutions, 88
Securitas AB, 42
ServiceMaster Limited Partnership, 6
Servpro Industries, Inc., 85
Shared Medical Systems Corporation, 14
Sir Speedy, Inc., 16
Skidmore, Owings & Merrill LLP, 13; 69
    (upd.)
SmartForce PLC, 43
SOS Staffing Services, 25
Sotheby's Holdings, Inc., 11; 29 (upd.);
    84 (upd.)
Source Interlink Companies, Inc., 75
Spencer Stuart and Associates, Inc., 14
Spherion Corporation, 52

Steiner Corporation (Alsco), 53
Strayer Education, Inc., 53
Superior Uniform Group, Inc., 30
Sykes Enterprises, Inc., 45
Sylvan Learning Systems, Inc., 35
Synchronoss Technologies, Inc., 95
TA Triumph-Adler AG, 48
Taylor Nelson Sofres plc, 34
TBA Global, LLC, 99
TBWA/Chiat/Day, 6; 43 (upd.)
Thomas Cook Travel Inc., 33 (upd.)
Ticketmaster, 76 (upd.)
Ticketmaster Group, Inc., 13; 37 (upd.)
TMP Worldwide Inc., 30
TNT Post Group N.V., 30
Towers Perrin, 32
Trader Classified Media N.V., 57
Traffix, Inc., 61
Transmedia Network Inc., 20
Treasure Chest Advertising Company, Inc.,
    32
TRM Copy Centers Corporation, 18
True North Communications Inc., 23
24/7 Real Media, Inc., 49
Tyler Corporation, 23
U.S. Office Products Company, 25
Unica Corporation, 77
UniFirst Corporation, 21
United Business Media plc, 52 (upd.)
United News & Media plc, 28 (upd.)
Unitog Co., 19
Valassis Communications, Inc., 37 (upd.);
    76 (upd.)
ValleyCrest Companies, 81 (upd.)
ValueClick, Inc., 49
Vebego International BV, 49
Vedior NV, 35
Vertis Communications, 84
Vertrue Inc., 77
Viad Corp., 73
W.B Doner & Co., 56
The Wackenhut Corporation, 14; 63
    (upd.)
Waggener Edstrom, 42
Warrantech Corporation, 53
WebEx Communications, Inc., 81
Welcome Wagon International Inc., 82
Wells Rich Greene BDDP, 6
Westaff Inc., 33
Whitman Education Group, Inc., 41
Wieden + Kennedy, 75
William Morris Agency, Inc., 23
Williams Scotsman, Inc., 65
Workflow Management, Inc., 65
WPP Group plc, 6; 48 (upd.)
Wunderman, 86
Xerox Corporation, III; 6 (upd.); 26
    (upd.); 69 (upd.)
Young & Rubicam, Inc., I; 22 (upd.); 66
    (upd.)
Zogby International, Inc., 99

Aerospace

A.S. Yakovlev Design Bureau, 15
Aerojet-General Corp., 63
Aeronca Inc., 46
Aerosonic Corporation, 69
The Aerospatiale Group, 7; 21 (upd.)

AeroVironment, Inc., 97
AgustaWestland N.V., 75
Airborne Systems Group, 89
Alliant Techsystems Inc., 30 (upd.)
Antonov Design Bureau, 53
Arianespace S.A., 89
Aviacionny Nauchno-Tehnicheskii
    Komplex im. A.N. Tupoleva, 24
Aviall, Inc., 73
Avions Marcel Dassault-Breguet Aviation,
    I
B/E Aerospace, Inc., 30
Ballistic Recovery Systems, Inc., 87
Banner Aerospace, Inc., 14
BBA Aviation plc, 90
Beech Aircraft Corporation, 8
Bell Helicopter Textron Inc., 46
The Boeing Company, I; 10 (upd.); 32
    (upd.)
Bombardier Inc., 42 (upd.); 87 (upd.)
British Aerospace plc, I; 24 (upd.)
CAE USA Inc., 48
Canadair, Inc., 16
Cessna Aircraft Company, 8
Cirrus Design Corporation, 44
Cobham plc, 30
CPI Aerostructures, Inc., 75
Daimler-Benz Aerospace AG, 16
DeCrane Aircraft Holdings Inc., 36
Derco Holding Ltd., 98
Diehl Stiftung & Co. KG, 79
Ducommun Incorporated, 30
Duncan Aviation, Inc., 94
EADS SOCATA, 54
Eclipse Aviation Corporation, 87
EGL, Inc., 59
Empresa Brasileira de Aeronáutica S.A.
    (Embraer), 36
European Aeronautic Defence and Space
    Company EADS N.V., 52 (upd.)
Fairchild Aircraft, Inc., 9
Fairchild Dornier GmbH, 48 (upd.)
Finmeccanica S.p.A., 84
First Aviation Services Inc., 49
G.I.E. Airbus Industrie, I; 12 (upd.)
General Dynamics Corporation, I; 10
    (upd.); 40 (upd.); 88 (upd.
GKN plc, III; 38 (upd.); 89 (upd.)
Goodrich Corporation, 46 (upd.)
Groupe Dassault Aviation SA, 26 (upd.)
Grumman Corporation, I; 11 (upd.)
Grupo Aeropuerto del Sureste, S.A. de
    C.V., 48
Gulfstream Aerospace Corporation, 7; 28
    (upd.)
HEICO Corporation, 30
International Lease Finance Corporation,
    48
Irkut Corporation, 68
Israel Aircraft Industries Ltd., 69
Kolbenschmidt Pierburg AG, 97
N.V. Koninklijke Nederlandse
    Vliegtuigenfabriek Fokker, I; 28 (upd.)
Kreisler Manufacturing Corporation, 97
Lancair International, Inc., 67
Learjet Inc., 8; 27 (upd.)
Lockheed Martin Corporation, I; 11
    (upd.); 15 (upd.); 89 (upd.)

Bio-Technology

Chemicals

Conglomerates

Construction

Post Properties, Inc., 26
Pulte Homes, Inc., 8; 42 (upd.)
Pyramid Companies, 54
Redrow Group plc, 31
Rinker Group Ltd., 65
RMC Group p.l.c., 34 (upd.)
Rooney Brothers Co., 25
The Rottlund Company, Inc., 28
Roy Anderson Corporation, 75
Ryan Companies US, Inc., 99
The Ryland Group, Inc., 8; 37 (upd.)
Sandvik AB, 32 (upd.)
Schuff Steel Company, 26
Seddon Group Ltd., 67
Servidyne Inc., 100 (upd.)
Shorewood Packaging Corporation, 28
Simon Property Group Inc., 27; 84 (upd.)
Skanska AB, 38
Skidmore, Owings & Merrill LLP, 69
  (upd.)
SNC-Lavalin Group Inc., 72
Speedy Hire plc, 84
Stabler Companies Inc. 78
Standard Pacific Corporation, 52
The Structure Tone Organization, 99
Stone & Webster, Inc., 64 (upd.)
Sundt Corp., 24
Swinerton Inc., 43
Tarmac Limited, III, 28 (upd.); 95 (upd.)
Taylor Woodrow plc, I; 38 (upd.)
Technical Olympic USA, Inc., 75
Terex Corporation, 7; 40 (upd.); 91
  (upd.)
ThyssenKrupp AG, IV; 28 (upd.); 87
  (upd.)
TIC Holdings Inc., 92
Toll Brothers Inc., 15; 70 (upd.)
Trammell Crow Company, 8
Tridel Enterprises Inc., 9
Turner Construction Company, 66
The Turner Corporation, 8; 23 (upd.)
U.S. Aggregates, Inc., 42
U.S. Home Corporation, 8; 78 (upd.)
Urbi Desarrollos Urbanos, S.A. de C.V.,
  81
VA TECH ELIN EBG GmbH, 49
Veidekke ASA, 98
Veit Companies, 43; 92 (upd.)
Wacker Construction Equipment AG, 95
Walbridge Aldinger Co., 38
Walter Industries, Inc., 22 (upd.)
The Weitz Company, Inc., 42
Whiting-Turner Contracting Company, 95
Willbros Group, Inc., 56
William Lyon Homes, 59
Wilson Bowden Plc, 45
Wood Hall Trust PLC, I
The Yates Companies, Inc., 62
Zachry Group, Inc., 95

Containers

Ball Corporation, I; 10 (upd.); 78 (upd.)
BWAY Corporation, 24
Chesapeake Corporation, 8; 30 (upd.); 93
  (upd.)
Clarcor Inc., 17
Continental Can Co., Inc., 15
Continental Group Company, I

Crown Cork & Seal Company, Inc., I; 13
  (upd.); 32 (upd.)
Crown Holdings, Inc., 83 (upd.)
Gaylord Container Corporation, 8
Golden Belt Manufacturing Co., 16
Graham Packaging Holdings Company,
  87
Greif Inc., 15; 66 (upd.)
Grupo Industrial Durango, S.A. de C.V.,
  37
Hanjin Shipping Co., Ltd., 50
Inland Container Corporation, 8
Interpool, Inc., 92
Kerr Group Inc., 24
Keyes Fibre Company, 9
Libbey Inc., 49
Liqui-Box Corporation, 16
The Longaberger Company, 12
Longview Fibre Company, 8
The Mead Corporation, 19 (upd.)
Metal Box PLC, I
Molins plc, 51
National Can Corporation, I
Owens-Illinois, Inc., I; 26 (upd.); 85
  (upd.)
Packaging Corporation of America, 51
  (upd.)
Primerica Corporation, I
PVC Container Corporation, 67
Rexam PLC, 32 (upd.); 85 (upd.)
Reynolds Metals Company, 19 (upd.)
Royal Packaging Industries Van Leer N.V.,
  30
RPC Group PLC, 81
Sealright Co., Inc., 17
Shurgard Storage Centers, Inc., 52
Smurfit-Stone Container Corporation, 26
  (upd.); 83 (upd.)
Sonoco Products Company, 8; 89 (upd.)
Thermos Company, 16
Toyo Seikan Kaisha, Ltd., I
U.S. Can Corporation, 30
Ultra Pac, Inc., 24
Viatech Continental Can Company, Inc.,
  25 (upd.)
Vidrala S.A., 67
Vitro Corporativo S.A. de C.V., 34

Drugs & Pharmaceuticals

A. Nelson & Co. Ltd., 75
A.L. Pharma Inc., 12
Abbott Laboratories, I; 11 (upd.); 40
  (upd.); 93 (upd.)
Actelion Ltd., 83
Adolor Corporation, 101
Akorn, Inc., 32
Albany Molecular Research, Inc., 77
Allergan, Inc., 77 (upd.)
Alpharma Inc., 35 (upd.)
ALZA Corporation, 10; 36 (upd.)
American Home Products, I; 10 (upd.)
American Oriental Bioengineering Inc., 93
American Pharmaceutical Partners, Inc.,
  69
AmerisourceBergen Corporation, 64
  (upd.)
Amersham PLC, 50
Amgen, Inc., 10; 89 (upd.)

Amylin Pharmaceuticals, Inc., 67
Andrx Corporation, 55
Angelini SpA, 100
Astellas Pharma Inc., 97 (upd.)
AstraZeneca PLC, I; 20 (upd.); 50 (upd.)
AtheroGenics Inc., 101
Axcan Pharma Inc., 85
Barr Pharmaceuticals, Inc., 26; 68 (upd.)
Bayer A.G., I; 13 (upd.)
Berlex Laboratories, Inc., 66
Biovail Corporation, 47
Block Drug Company, Inc., 8
Boiron S.A., 73
Bristol-Myers Squibb Company, III; 9
  (upd.); 37 (upd.)
BTG Plc, 87
C.H. Boehringer Sohn, 39
Caremark Rx, Inc., 10; 54 (upd.)
Carter-Wallace, Inc., 8; 38 (upd.)
Celgene Corporation, 67
Cephalon, Inc., 45
Chiron Corporation, 10
Chugai Pharmaceutical Co., Ltd., 50
Ciba-Geigy Ltd., I; 8 (upd.)
D&K Wholesale Drug, Inc., 14
Discovery Partners International, Inc., 58
Dr. Reddy's Laboratories Ltd., 59
Eisai Co., Ltd., 101
Elan Corporation PLC, 63
Eli Lilly and Company, I; 11 (upd.); 47
  (upd.)
Endo Pharmaceuticals Holdings Inc., 71
Eon Labs, Inc., 67
Express Scripts Inc., 44 (upd.)
F. Hoffmann-La Roche Ltd., I; 50 (upd.)
Fisons plc, 9; 23 (upd.)
Forest Laboratories, Inc., 52 (upd.)
FoxMeyer Health Corporation, 16
Fujisawa Pharmaceutical Company Ltd., I
G.D. Searle & Co., I; 12 (upd.); 34
  (upd.)
Galenica AG, 84
GEHE AG, 27
Genentech, Inc., I; 8 (upd.); 75 (upd.)
Genetics Institute, Inc., 8
Genzyme Corporation, 13, 77 (upd.)
Glaxo Holdings PLC, I; 9 (upd.)
GlaxoSmithKline plc, 46 (upd.)
Groupe Fournier SA, 44
Groupe Léa Nature, 88
H. Lundbeck A/S, 44
Hauser, Inc., 46
Heska Corporation, 39
Hexal AG, 69
Hospira, Inc., 71
Huntingdon Life Sciences Group plc, 42
ICN Pharmaceuticals, Inc., 52
Immucor, Inc., 81
Integrated BioPharma, Inc., 83
IVAX Corporation, 55 (upd.)
Janssen Pharmaceutica N.V., 80
Johnson & Johnson, III; 8 (upd.)
Jones Medical Industries, Inc., 24
The Judge Group, Inc., 51
King Pharmaceuticals, Inc., 54
Kinray Inc., 85
Kos Pharmaceuticals, Inc., 63
Kyowa Hakko Kogyo Co., Ltd., 48 (upd.)

Engineering & Management Services

Entertainment & Leisure

Financial Services: Banks

Seattle First National Bank Inc., 8
Security Capital Corporation, 17
Security Pacific Corporation, II
Shawmut National Corporation, 13
Signet Banking Corporation, 11
Singer & Friedlander Group plc, 41
Skandinaviska Enskilda Banken AB, II; 56 (upd.)
Société Générale, II; 42 (upd.)
Society Corporation, 9
Southern Financial Bancorp, Inc., 56
Southtrust Corporation, 11
Standard Chartered plc, II; 48 (upd.)
Standard Federal Bank, 9
Star Banc Corporation, 11
State Bank of India, 63
State Financial Services Corporation, 51
State Street Corporation, 8; 57 (upd.)
Staten Island Bancorp, Inc., 39
The Sumitomo Bank, Limited, II; 26 (upd.)
Sumitomo Mitsui Banking Corporation, 51 (upd.)
The Sumitomo Trust & Banking Company, Ltd., II; 53 (upd.)
The Summit Bancorporation, 14
Suncorp-Metway Ltd., 91
SunTrust Banks Inc., 23; 101 (upd.)
Svenska Handelsbanken AB, II; 50 (upd.)
Sveriges Riksbank, 96
Swiss Bank Corporation, II
Synovus Financial Corp., 12; 52 (upd.)
The Taiyo Kobe Bank, Ltd., II
TCF Financial Corporation, 47
The Tokai Bank, Limited, II; 15 (upd.)
The Toronto-Dominion Bank, II; 49 (upd.)
TSB Group plc, 12
Turkiye Is Bankasi A.S., 61
U.S. Bancorp, 14; 36 (upd.)
U.S. Trust Corp., 17
UBS AG, 52 (upd.)
Umpqua Holdings Corporation, 87
Unibanco Holdings S.A., 73
Union Bank of California, 16
Union Bank of Switzerland, II
Union Financière de France Banque SA, 52
Union Planters Corporation, 54
UnionBanCal Corporation, 50 (upd.)
United Community Banks, Inc., 98
United Overseas Bank Ltd., 56
USAA, 62 (upd.)
Van Lanschot NV, 79
Vontobel Holding AG, 96
Wachovia Bank of Georgia, N.A., 16
Wachovia Bank of South Carolina, N.A., 16
Washington Mutual, Inc., 17; 93 (upd.)
Wells Fargo & Company, II; 12 (upd.); 38 (upd.); 97 (upd.)
West One Bancorp, 11
Westamerica Bancorporation, 17
Westdeutsche Landesbank Girozentrale, II; 46 (upd.)
Westpac Banking Corporation, II; 48 (upd.)
Whitney Holding Corporation, 21

Wilmington Trust Corporation, 25
The Woolwich plc, 30
World Bank Group, 33
The Yasuda Trust and Banking Company, Ltd., II; 17 (upd.)
Zions Bancorporation, 12; 53 (upd.)

Financial Services: Excluding Banks

A.B. Watley Group Inc., 45
A.G. Edwards, Inc., 8; 32 (upd.)
ACCION International, 87
Accredited Home Lenders Holding Co., 91
ACE Cash Express, Inc., 33
Advanta Corporation, 8; 38 (upd.)
Ag Services of America, Inc., 59
Alliance Capital Management Holding L.P., 63
Allmerica Financial Corporation, 63
Ambac Financial Group, Inc., 65
America's Car-Mart, Inc., 64
American Capital Strategies, Ltd., 91
American Express Company, II; 10 (upd.); 38 (upd.)
American General Finance Corp., 11
American Home Mortgage Holdings, Inc., 46
Ameritrade Holding Corporation, 34
AMVESCAP PLC, 65
Apax Partners Worldwide LLP, 89
Arnhold and S. Bleichroeder Advisers, LLC, 97
Arthur Andersen & Company, Société Coopérative, 10
Avco Financial Services Inc., 13
Aviva PLC, 50 (upd.)
Bankrate, Inc., 83
Bear Stearns Companies, Inc., II; 10 (upd.); 52 (upd.)
Benchmark Capital, 49
Berwind Corporation, 100
Bill & Melinda Gates Foundation, 41; 100 (upd.
BlackRock, Inc., 79
Bolsa Mexicana de Valores, S.A. de C.V., 80
Bozzuto's, Inc., 13
Bradford & Bingley PLC, 65
Cantor Fitzgerald, L.P., 92
Capital One Financial Corporation, 52
Cardtronics, Inc., 93
Carnegie Corporation of New York, 35
Cash America International, Inc., 20; 61 (upd.)
Cash Systems, Inc., 93
Catholic Order of Foresters, 24; 97 (upd.)
Cattles plc, 58
Cendant Corporation, 44 (upd.)
Certegy, Inc., 63
Cetelem S.A., 21
The Charles Schwab Corporation, 8; 26 (upd.); 81 (upd.)
CheckFree Corporation, 81
Cheshire Building Society, 74
Chicago Mercantile Exchange Holdings Inc., 75
CIT Group Inc., 76

Citfed Bancorp, Inc., 16
Citicorp Diners Club, Inc., 90
Coinstar, Inc., 44
Comerica Incorporated, 40; 101 (upd.)
Commercial Financial Services, Inc., 26
Compagnie Nationale à Portefeuille, 84
Concord EFS, Inc., 52
Coopers & Lybrand, 9
Countrywide Financial, 16; 100 (upd.)
Cowen Group, Inc., 92
Cramer, Berkowitz & Co., 34
Credit Acceptance Corporation, 18
Cresud S.A.C.I.F. y A., 63
CS First Boston Inc., II
D. Carnegie & Co. AB, 98
Dain Rauscher Corporation, 35 (upd.)
Daiwa Securities Group Inc., II; 55 (upd.)
Datek Online Holdings Corp., 32
The David and Lucile Packard Foundation, 41
Dean Witter, Discover & Co., 12
Deutsche Börse AG, 59
ditech.com, 93
Dominick & Dominick LLC, 92
Dow Jones Telerate, Inc., 10
Draper Fisher Jurvetson, 91
Dresdner Kleinwort Wasserstein, 60 (upd.)
Drexel Burnham Lambert Incorporated, II
The Dreyfus Corporation, 70
DVI, Inc., 51
E*Trade Financial Corporation, 20; 60 (upd.)
Eaton Vance Corporation, 18
Edward D. Jones & Company L.P., 66 (upd.)
Edward Jones, 30
Eurazeo, 80
Euronet Worldwide, Inc., 83
Euronext N.V., 37; 89 (upd.)
Experian Information Solutions Inc., 45
Fair, Isaac and Company, 18
Fannie Mae, 45 (upd.)
Federal Agricultural Mortgage Corporation, 75
Federal Deposit Insurance Corporation, 93
Federal National Mortgage Association, II
Fidelity Investments Inc., II; 14 (upd.)
First Albany Companies Inc., 37
First Data Corporation, 30 (upd.)
The First Marblehead Corporation, 87
First USA, Inc., 11
FMR Corp., 8; 32 (upd.)
Forstmann Little & Co., 38
Fortis, Inc., 15
Frank Russell Company, 46
Franklin Resources, Inc., 9
Fred Alger Management, Inc., 97
Freddie Mac, 54
Friedman, Billings, Ramsey Group, Inc., 53
Gabelli Asset Management Inc., 30
Gilman & Ciocia, Inc., 72
Global Payments Inc., 91
The Goldman Sachs Group Inc., II; 20 (upd.); 51 (upd.)
Grede Foundries, Inc., 38
Green Tree Financial Corporation, 11

Food Products

Food Services & Retailers

CEC Entertainment, Inc., 31 (upd.)
Centerplate, Inc., 79
Chart House Enterprises, Inc., 17
Checkers Drive-In Restaurants, Inc., 16; 74 (upd.)
The Cheesecake Factory Inc., 17; 100 (upd.)
Chi-Chi's Inc., 13; 51 (upd.)
Chicago Pizza & Brewery, Inc., 44
Chick-fil-A Inc., 23; 90 (upd.)
Chipotle Mexican Grill, Inc., 67
Church's Chicken, 66
CiCi Enterprises, L.P., 99
Cinnabon Inc., 23; 90 (upd.)
The Circle K Corporation, II
CKE Restaurants, Inc., 19; 46 (upd.)
Coborn's, Inc., 30
The Coffee Beanery, Ltd., 95
Coffee Holding Co., Inc., 95
Cold Stone Creamery, 69
Coles Group Limited, V; 20 (upd.); 85 (upd.)
Compass Group PLC, 34
Comptoirs Modernes S.A., 19
Consolidated Products Inc., 14
Controladora Comercial Mexicana, S.A. de C.V., 36
Cooker Restaurant Corporation, 20; 51 (upd.)
The Copps Corporation, 32
Cosi, Inc., 53
Cost-U-Less, Inc., 51
Coto Centro Integral de Comercializacion S.A., 66
Country Kitchen International, Inc., 76
Cracker Barrel Old Country Store, Inc., 10
Cremonini S.p.A., 57
CulinArt, Inc., 92
Culver Franchising System, Inc., 58
D'Agostino Supermarkets Inc., 19
Dairy Mart Convenience Stores, Inc., 7; 25 (upd.)
Daniel Thwaites Plc, 95
Darden Restaurants, Inc., 16; 44 (upd.)
Dean & DeLuca, Inc., 36
Del Taco, Inc., 58
Delhaize "Le Lion" S.A., 44
DeMoulas / Market Basket Inc., 23
DenAmerica Corporation, 29
Denner AG, 88
Deschutes Brewery, Inc., 57
Diedrich Coffee, Inc., 40
Dierbergs Markets Inc., 63
Distribución y Servicio D&S S.A., 71
Doctor's Associates Inc., 67 (upd.)
Dominick's Finer Foods, Inc., 56
Domino's, Inc., 7; 21 (upd.); 63 (upd.)
Donatos Pizzeria Corporation, 58
E H Booth & Company Ltd., 90
Eateries, Inc., 33
Ed S.A.S., 88
Edeka Zentrale A.G., II; 47 (upd.)
Einstein/Noah Bagel Corporation, 29
El Chico Restaurants, Inc., 19
El Pollo Loco, Inc., 69
Elior SA, 49
Elmer's Restaurants, Inc., 42

Embers America Restaurants, 30
Etablissements Economiques du Casino Guichard, Perrachon et Cie, S.C.A., 12
Family Sports Concepts, Inc., 100
Famous Brands Ltd., 86
Famous Dave's of America, Inc., 40
Farmer Jack Supermarkets 78
Fatburger Corporation, 64
Fazoli's Management, Inc., 27; 76 (upd.)
Fiesta Mart, Inc., 101
Fili Enterprises, Inc., 70
Fired Up, Inc., 82
5 & Diner Franchise Corporation, 72
Five Guys Enterprises, LLC, 99
Flagstar Companies, Inc., 10
Flanigan's Enterprises, Inc., 60
Fleming Companies, Inc., II
Food Circus Super Markets, Inc., 88
The Food Emporium, 64
Food Lion LLC, II; 15 (upd.); 66 (upd.)
Foodarama Supermarkets, Inc., 28
Foodmaker, Inc., 14
Fox's Pizza Den, Inc., 98
The Fred W. Albrecht Grocery Co., 13
Fresh Choice, Inc., 20
Fresh Enterprises, Inc., 66
Fresh Foods, Inc., 29
Friendly Ice Cream Corporation, 30; 72 (upd.)
Frisch's Restaurants, Inc., 35; 92 (upd.)
Fuller Smith & Turner P.L.C., 38
Furr's Restaurant Group, Inc., 53
Furr's Supermarkets, Inc., 28
Galardi Group, Inc., 72
Galaxy Investors, Inc., 97
Garden Fresh Restaurant Corporation, 31
Gate Gourmet International AG, 70
The Gateway Corporation Ltd., II
Genuardi's Family Markets, Inc., 35
George Weston Ltd., II; 36 (upd.); 88 (upd.)
Ghirardelli Chocolate Company, 30
Giant Eagle, Inc., 86
Giant Food LLC, II; 22 (upd.); 83 (upd.)
Godfather's Pizza Incorporated, 25
Golden Corral Corporation, 10; 66 (upd.)
Golden Krust Caribbean Bakery, Inc., 68
Golden State Foods Corporation, 32
The Golub Corporation, 26; 96 (upd.)
Gordon Biersch Brewery Restaurant Group, Inc., 93
Gordon Food Service Inc., 8; 39 (upd.)
Grand Traverse Pie Company, 98
The Grand Union Company, 7; 28 (upd.)
The Great Atlantic & Pacific Tea Company, Inc., II; 16 (upd.); 55 (upd.)
Greggs PLC, 65
Grill Concepts, Inc., 74
Gristede's Foods Inc., 31; 68 (upd.)
Ground Round, Inc., 21
Groupe Flo S.A., 98
Groupe Le Duff S.A., 84
Groupe Promodès S.A., 19
Grupo Corvi S.A. de C.V., 86
Guyenne et Gascogne, 23
H.E. Butt Grocery Company, 13; 32 (upd.); 85 (upd.)
Haggen Inc., 38

Hannaford Bros. Co., 12
Hard Rock Cafe International, Inc., 12
Harps Food Stores, Inc., 99
Harris Teeter Inc., 23; 72 (upd.)
Harry's Farmers Market Inc., 23
HDOS Enterprises, 72
Hickory Farms, Inc., 17
Holberg Industries, Inc., 36
Holland Burgerville USA, 44
Hooters of America, Inc., 18; 69 (upd.)
Hops Restaurant Bar and Brewery, 46
Hoss's Steak and Sea House Inc., 68
Host America Corporation, 79
Hotel Properties Ltd., 71
Houchens Industries Inc., 51
Hughes Markets, Inc., 22
Hungry Howie's Pizza and Subs, Inc., 25
Hy-Vee, Inc., 36
ICA AB, II
Iceland Group plc, 33
IGA, Inc., 99
IHOP Corporation, 17; 58 (upd.)
Il Fornaio (America) Corporation, 27
In-N-Out Burger, 19
In-N-Out Burgers Inc., 74 (upd.)
Ingles Markets, Inc., 20
Inserra Supermarkets, 25
Inter Link Foods PLC, 61
International Dairy Queen, Inc., 10; 39 (upd.)
ITM Entreprises SA, 36
Ito-Yokado Co., Ltd., 42 (upd.)
Ivar's, Inc., 86
J Sainsbury plc, II; 13 (upd.); 38 (upd.); 95 (upd.)
J. Alexander's Corporation, 65
Jack in the Box Inc., 89 (upd.)
Jacmar Companies, 87
Jamba Juice Company, 47
James Original Coney Island Inc., 84
JD Wetherspoon plc, 30
Jean-Georges Enterprises L.L.C., 75
Jerónimo Martins SGPS S.A., 96
Jerry's Famous Deli Inc., 24
Jersey Mike's Franchise Systems, Inc., 83
Jitney-Jungle Stores of America, Inc., 27
John Lewis Partnership plc, V; 42 (upd.); 99 (upd.)
Johnny Rockets Group, Inc., 31; 76 (upd.)
KFC Corporation, 7; 21 (upd.); 89 (upd.)
King Kullen Grocery Co., Inc., 15
King's Hawaiian Bakery West, Inc., 101
Koninklijke Ahold N.V. (Royal Ahold), II; 16 (upd.)
Koo Koo Roo, Inc., 25
Kooperativa Förbundet, 99
The Kroger Co., II; 15 (upd.); 65 (upd.)
The Krystal Company, 33
Kwik Save Group plc, 11
La Madeleine French Bakery & Café, 33
Landry's Restaurants, Inc., 15; 65 (upd.)
The Laurel Pub Company Limited, 59
Laurus N.V., 65
LDB Corporation, 53
Leeann Chin, Inc., 30
Levy Restaurants L.P., 26

Thomas & Howard Company, Inc., 90
Timber Lodge Steakhouse, Inc., 73
Tops Markets LLC, 60
Total Entertainment Restaurant
    Corporation, 46
Toupargel-Agrigel S.A., 76
Trader Joe's Company, 13; 50 (upd.)
Travel Ports of America, Inc., 17
Tree of Life, Inc., 29
Triarc Companies, Inc., 34 (upd.)
Tubby's, Inc., 53
Tully's Coffee Corporation, 51
Tumbleweed, Inc., 33; 80 (upd.)
TW Services, Inc., II
Ukrop's Super Markets Inc., 39; 101
    (upd.)
Unified Grocers, Inc., 93
Unique Casual Restaurants, Inc., 27
United Dairy Farmers, Inc., 74
United Natural Foods, Inc., 32; 76 (upd.)
Uno Restaurant Holdings Corporation,
    18; 70 (upd.)
Uwajimaya, Inc., 60
Vail Resorts, Inc., 43 (upd.)
Valora Holding AG, 98
VICORP Restaurants, Inc., 12; 48 (upd.)
Victory Refrigeration, Inc., 82
Village Super Market, Inc., 7
The Vons Companies, Incorporated, 7; 28
    (upd.)
W. H. Braum, Inc., 80
Waffle House Inc., 14; 60 (upd.)
Wahoo's Fish Taco, 96
Wakefern Food Corporation, 33
Waldbaum, Inc., 19
Wall Street Deli, Inc., 33
Wawa Inc., 17; 78 (upd.)
Wegmans Food Markets, Inc., 9; 41
    (upd.)
Weis Markets, Inc., 15
Wendy's International, Inc., 8; 23 (upd.);
    47 (upd.)
The WesterN SizzliN Corporation, 60
Wetterau Incorporated, II
Whitbread PLC, I; 20 (upd.); 52 (upd.);
    97 (upd.)
White Castle Management Company, 12;
    36 (upd.); 85 (upd.)
White Rose, Inc., 24
Whittard of Chelsea Plc, 61
Whole Foods Market, Inc., 50 (upd.)
Wild Oats Markets, Inc., 19; 41 (upd.)
Willow Run Foods, Inc., 100
Winchell's Donut Houses Operating
    Company, L.P., 60
WinCo Foods Inc., 60
Winn-Dixie Stores, Inc., II; 21 (upd.); 59
    (upd.)
Wm. Morrison Supermarkets PLC, 38
Wolfgang Puck Worldwide, Inc., 26, 70
    (upd.)
Worldwide Restaurant Concepts, Inc., 47
Yoshinoya D & C Company Ltd., 88
Young & Co.'s Brewery, P.L.C., 38
Yucaipa Cos., 17
Yum! Brands Inc., 58

Zingerman's Community of Businesses,
    68

Health & Personal Care Products

Abaxis, Inc., 83
Abbott Laboratories, I; 11 (upd.); 40
    (upd.); 93 (upd.)
Accuray Incorporated, 95
Advanced Medical Optics, Inc., 79
Advanced Neuromodulation Systems, Inc.,
    73
Akorn, Inc., 32
ALARIS Medical Systems, Inc., 65
Alberto-Culver Company, 8; 36 (upd.); 91
    (upd.)
Alco Health Services Corporation, III
Alès Groupe, 81
Allergan, Inc., 10; 30 (upd.); 77 (upd.)
American Oriental Bioengineering Inc., 93
American Safety Razor Company, 20
American Stores Company, 22 (upd.)
Amway Corporation, III; 13 (upd.)
AngioDynamics, Inc., 81
ArthroCare Corporation, 73
Artsana SpA, 92
Ascendia Brands, Inc., 97
Atkins Nutritionals, Inc., 58
Aveda Corporation, 24
Avon Products, Inc., III; 19 (upd.); 46
    (upd.)
Bally Total Fitness Holding Corp., 25
Bare Escentuals, Inc., 91
Bausch & Lomb Inc., 7; 25 (upd.); 96
    (upd.)
Baxter International Inc., I; 10 (upd.)
BeautiControl Cosmetics, Inc., 21
Becton, Dickinson and Company, I; 11
    (upd.); 36 (upd.); 101 (upd.)
Beiersdorf AG, 29
Big B, Inc., 17
Bindley Western Industries, Inc., 9
Biolase Technology, Inc., 87
Biomet, Inc., 10; 93 (upd.)
BioScrip Inc., 98
Biosite Incorporated, 73
Block Drug Company, Inc., 8; 27 (upd.)
The Body Shop International plc, 53
    (upd.)
Boiron S.A., 73
Bolton Group B.V., 86
The Boots Company PLC, 24 (upd.)
Boston Scientific Corporation, 77 (upd.)
Bristol-Myers Squibb Company, III; 9
    (upd.)
Bronner Brothers Inc., 92
C.R. Bard Inc., 9
Candela Corporation, 48
Cantel Medical Corporation, 80
Cardinal Health, Inc., 18; 50 (upd.)
Carl Zeiss AG, III; 34 (upd.); 91 (upd.)
Carson, Inc., 31
Carter-Wallace, Inc., 8
Caswell-Massey Co. Ltd., 51
CCA Industries, Inc., 53
Chattem, Inc., 17; 88 (upd.)
Chesebrough-Pond's USA, Inc., 8
Chindex International, Inc., 101

Chronimed Inc., 26
Church & Dwight Co., Inc., 68 (upd.)
Cintas Corporation, 51 (upd.)
The Clorox Company, III; 22 (upd.); 81
    (upd.)
CNS, Inc., 20
Colgate-Palmolive Company, III; 14
    (upd.); 35 (upd.)
Combe Inc., 72
Conair Corp., 17
CONMED Corporation, 87
Connetics Corporation, 70
Cordis Corp., 19
Cosmair, Inc., 8
Cosmolab Inc., 96
Coty, Inc., 36
Covidien Ltd., 91
Cybex International, Inc., 49
Cytyc Corporation, 69
Dade Behring Holdings Inc., 71
Dalli-Werke GmbH & Co. KG, 86
Datascope Corporation, 39
Del Laboratories, Inc., 28
Deltec, Inc., 56
Dentsply International Inc., 10
DEP Corporation, 20
DePuy, Inc., 30
DHB Industries Inc., 85
Diagnostic Products Corporation, 73
The Dial Corp., 23 (upd.)
Direct Focus, Inc., 47
Drackett Professional Products, 12
Drägerwerk AG, 83
Dynatronics Corporation, 99
E-Z-EM Inc., 89
Elizabeth Arden, Inc., 8; 40 (upd.)
Empi, Inc., 26
Enrich International, Inc., 33
The Estée Lauder Companies Inc., 9; 30
    (upd.); 93 (upd.)
Ethicon, Inc., 23
Exactech, Inc., 101
Farouk Systems Inc. 78
Forest Laboratories, Inc., 11
Forever Living Products International Inc.,
    17
FoxHollow Technologies, Inc., 85
French Fragrances, Inc., 22
G&K Holding S.A., 95
Gambro AB, 49
General Nutrition Companies, Inc., 11;
    29 (upd.)
Genzyme Corporation, 13; 77 (upd.)
GF Health Products, Inc., 82
The Gillette Company, III; 20 (upd.)
Given Imaging Ltd., 83
GNC Corporation, 98 (upd.)
Golden Neo-Life Diamite International,
    Inc., 100
Groupe Yves Saint Laurent, 23
Grupo Omnilife S.A. de C.V., 88
Guerlain, 23
Guest Supply, Inc., 18
Guidant Corporation, 58
Guinot Paris S.A., 82
Hanger Orthopedic Group, Inc., 41
Helen of Troy Corporation, 18

Helene Curtis Industries, Inc., 8; 28 (upd.)
Henkel KGaA, III; 34 (upd.); 95 (upd.)
Henry Schein, Inc., 31; 70 (upd.)
Herbalife Ltd., 17; 41 (upd.); 92 (upd.)
Huntleigh Technology PLC, 77
Immucor, Inc., 81
Inamed Corporation, 79
Integra LifeSciences Holdings Corporation, 87
Integrated BioPharma, Inc., 83
Inter Parfums Inc., 35; 86 (upd.)
Intuitive Surgical, Inc., 79
Invacare Corporation, 11
IRIS International, Inc., 101
IVAX Corporation, 11
IVC Industries, Inc., 45
The Jean Coutu Group (PJC) Inc., 46
John Paul Mitchell Systems, 24
Johnson & Johnson, III; 8 (upd.); 36 (upd.); 75 (upd.)
Kanebo, Ltd., 53
Kao Corporation, III; 79 (upd.)
Kendall International, Inc., 11
Kensey Nash Corporation, 71
Keys Fitness Products, LP, 83
Kimberly-Clark Corporation, III; 16 (upd.); 43 (upd.)
Kolmar Laboratories Group, 96
Kyowa Hakko Kogyo Co., Ltd., III
Kyphon Inc., 87
L'Oréal SA, III; 8 (upd.); 46 (upd.)
Laboratoires de Biologie Végétale Yves Rocher, 35
The Lamaur Corporation, 41
Lever Brothers Company, 9
Lion Corporation, III; 51 (upd.)
Lush Ltd., 93
Luxottica SpA, 17; 52 (upd.)
Mandom Corporation, 82
Mannatech Inc., 33
Mary Kay Inc., 9; 30 (upd.); 84 (upd.)
Matrix Essentials Inc., 90
Maxxim Medical Inc., 12
Medco Containment Services Inc., 9
MEDecision, Inc., 95
Medical Action Industries Inc., 101
Medifast, Inc., 97
Medline Industries, Inc., 61
Medtronic, Inc., 8; 67 (upd.)
Melaleuca Inc., 31
The Mentholatum Company Inc., 32
Mentor Corporation, 26
Merck & Co., Inc., I; 11 (upd.); 34 (upd.); 95 (upd.)
Merit Medical Systems, Inc., 29
Merz Group, 81
Natura Cosméticos S.A., 75
Nature's Sunshine Products, Inc., 15
NBTY, Inc., 31
NeighborCare, Inc., 67 (upd.)
Neutrogena Corporation, 17
New Dana Perfumes Company, 37
Neways Inc. 78
Nikken Global Inc., 32
NutriSystem, Inc., 71
Nutrition for Life International Inc., 22
Nutrition 21 Inc., 97

Ocular Sciences, Inc., 65
OEC Medical Systems, Inc., 27
Obagi Medical Products, Inc., 95
OraSure Technologies, Inc., 75
Orion Oyj, 72
Parfums Givenchy S.A., 100
Patterson Dental Co., 19
Perrigo Company, 12
Pfizer Inc., 79 (upd.)
Physician Sales & Service, Inc., 14
Playtex Products, Inc., 15
PolyMedica Corporation, 77
The Procter & Gamble Company, III; 8 (upd.); 26 (upd.); 67 (upd.)
PZ Cussons plc, 72
Quidel Corporation, 80
Reckitt Benckiser plc, II; 42 (upd.); 91 (upd.)
Redken Laboratories Inc., 84
Reliv International, Inc., 58
Retractable Technologies, Inc., 99
Revlon Inc., III; 17 (upd.)
Roche Biomedical Laboratories, Inc., 11
S.C. Johnson & Son, Inc., III; 28 (upd.); 89 (upd.)
Safety 1st, Inc., 24
St. Jude Medical, Inc., 11; 43 (upd.); 97 (upd.)
Schering-Plough Corporation, I; 14 (upd.); 49 (upd.); 99 (upd.)
Sephora Holdings S.A., 82
Shaklee Corporation, 39 (upd.)
Shionogi & Co., Ltd., III; 17 (upd.); 98 (upd.)
Shiseido Company, Limited, III; 22 (upd.); 81 (upd.)
Slim-Fast Foods Company, 18; 66 (upd.)
Smith & Nephew plc, 17
SmithKline Beecham PLC, III
Soft Sheen Products, Inc., 31
Sola International Inc., 71
Spacelabs Medical, Inc., 71
STAAR Surgical Company, 57
Straumann Holding AG, 79
Stryker Corporation, 79 (upd.)
Sunrise Medical Inc., 11
Syneron Medical Ltd., 91
Synthes, Inc., 93
Tambrands Inc., 8
Terumo Corporation, 48
Thane International, Inc., 84
Tom's of Maine, Inc., 45
Transitions Optical, Inc., 83
The Tranzonic Companies, 37
Turtle Wax, Inc., 15; 93 (upd.)
Tutogen Medical, Inc., 68
Unicharm Corporation, 84
United States Surgical Corporation, 10; 34 (upd.)
USANA, Inc., 29
Utah Medical Products, Inc., 36
Ventana Medical Systems, Inc., 75
VHA Inc., 53
VIASYS Healthcare, Inc., 52
Vion Food Group NV, 85
VISX, Incorporated, 30
Vitamin Shoppe Industries, Inc., 60

Water Pik Technologies, Inc., 34; 83 (upd.)
Weider Nutrition International, Inc., 29
Weleda AG 78
Wella AG, III; 48 (upd.)
West Pharmaceutical Services, Inc., 42
Wright Medical Group, Inc., 61
Wyeth, 50 (upd.)
Zila, Inc., 46
Zimmer Holdings, Inc., 45

Health Care Services

Acadian Ambulance & Air Med Services, Inc., 39
Adventist Health, 53
Advocat Inc., 46
Almost Family, Inc., 93
Alterra Healthcare Corporation, 42
Amedysis, Inc., 53
The American Cancer Society, 24
American Healthways, Inc., 65
American Lung Association, 48
American Medical Association, 39
American Medical International, Inc., III
American Medical Response, Inc., 39
American Red Cross, 40
AMERIGROUP Corporation, 69
AmeriSource Health Corporation, 37 (upd.)
AmSurg Corporation, 48
The Andrews Institute, 99
Applied Bioscience International, Inc., 10
Assisted Living Concepts, Inc., 43
ATC Healthcare Inc., 64
Baptist Health Care Corporation, 82
Beverly Enterprises, Inc., III; 16 (upd.)
Bon Secours Health System, Inc., 24
Brookdale Senior Living, 91
C.R. Bard, Inc., 65 (upd.)
Cancer Treatment Centers of America, Inc., 85
Capital Senior Living Corporation, 75
Caremark Rx, Inc., 10; 54 (upd.)
Catholic Health Initiatives, 91
Children's Comprehensive Services, Inc., 42
Children's Healthcare of Atlanta Inc., 101
Children's Hospitals and Clinics, Inc., 54
Chindex International, Inc., 101
Chronimed Inc., 26
COBE Laboratories, Inc., 13
Columbia/HCA Healthcare Corporation, 15
Community Health Systems, Inc., 71
Community Psychiatric Centers, 15
CompDent Corporation, 22
CompHealth Inc., 25
Comprehensive Care Corporation, 15
Continental Medical Systems, Inc., 10
Continucare Corporation, 101
Continuum Health Partners, Inc., 60
Coventry Health Care, Inc., 59
Craig Hospital, 99
Cystic Fibrosis Foundation, 93
DaVita Inc., 73
Easter Seals, Inc., 58
Erickson Retirement Communities, 57
Express Scripts Incorporated, 17

Extendicare Health Services, Inc., 6
Eye Care Centers of America, Inc., 69
FHP International Corporation, 6
Fresenius AG, 56
Genesis Health Ventures, Inc., 18
Gentiva Health Services, Inc., 79
GranCare, Inc., 14
Group Health Cooperative, 41
Grupo Ángeles Servicios de Salud, S.A. de C.V., 84
Hamot Health Foundation, 91
Hazelden Foundation, 28
HCA - The Healthcare Company, 35 (upd.)
Health Care & Retirement Corporation, 22
Health Management Associates, Inc., 56
Health Risk Management, Inc., 24
Health Systems International, Inc., 11
HealthSouth Corporation, 14; 33 (upd.)
Henry Ford Health System, 84
Highmark Inc., 27
The Hillhaven Corporation, 14
Holiday Retirement Corp., 87
Hooper Holmes, Inc., 22
Hospital Central Services, Inc., 56
Hospital Corporation of America, III
Howard Hughes Medical Institute, 39
Humana Inc., III; 24 (upd.); 101 (upd.)
Intermountain Health Care, Inc., 27
Jenny Craig, Inc., 10; 29 (upd.); 92 (upd.)
Kinetic Concepts, Inc. (KCI), 20
LabOne, Inc., 48
Laboratory Corporation of America Holdings, 42 (upd.)
LCA-Vision, Inc., 85
Life Care Centers of America Inc., 76
Lifeline Systems, Inc., 53
LifePoint Hospitals, Inc., 69
Lincare Holdings Inc., 43
Manor Care, Inc., 6; 25 (upd.)
March of Dimes, 31
Marshfield Clinic Inc., 82
Matria Healthcare, Inc., 17
Maxicare Health Plans, Inc., III; 25 (upd.)
Mayo Foundation, 9; 34 (upd.)
McBride plc, 82
Médecins sans Frontières, 85
Medical Management International, Inc., 65
Medical Staffing Network Holdings, Inc., 89
Memorial Sloan-Kettering Cancer Center, 57
Merge Healthcare, 85
Merit Medical Systems, Inc., 29
MeritCare Health System, 88
Myriad Genetics, Inc., 95
National Health Laboratories Incorporated, 11
National Jewish Health, 101
National Medical Enterprises, Inc., III
National Research Corporation, 87
New York City Health and Hospitals Corporation, 60
New York Health Care, Inc., 72
NewYork-Presbyterian Hospital, 59

NovaCare, Inc., 11
NSF International, 72
Operation Smile, Inc., 75
Option Care Inc., 48
Orthodontic Centers of America, Inc., 35
Oxford Health Plans, Inc., 16
PacifiCare Health Systems, Inc., 11
Palomar Medical Technologies, Inc., 22
Pediatric Services of America, Inc., 31
Pediatrix Medical Group, Inc., 61
PHP Healthcare Corporation, 22
PhyCor, Inc., 36
PolyMedica Corporation, 77
Primedex Health Systems, Inc., 25
Providence Health System, 90
The Providence Service Corporation, 64
Psychemedics Corporation, 89
Psychiatric Solutions, Inc., 68
Quest Diagnostics Inc., 26
Radiation Therapy Services, Inc., 85
Ramsay Youth Services, Inc., 41
Renal Care Group, Inc., 72
Res-Care, Inc., 29
Response Oncology, Inc., 27
Rural/Metro Corporation, 28
Sabratek Corporation, 29
St. Jude Medical, Inc., 11; 43 (upd.); 97 (upd.)
Salick Health Care, Inc., 53
The Scripps Research Institute, 76
Select Medical Corporation, 65
Shriners Hospitals for Children, 69
Sierra Health Services, Inc., 15
Smith & Nephew plc, 41 (upd.)
Special Olympics, Inc., 93
The Sports Club Company, 25
SSL International plc, 49
Stericycle Inc., 33
Sun Healthcare Group Inc., 25
Sunrise Senior Living, Inc., 81
Susan G. Komen Breast Cancer Foundation 78
SwedishAmerican Health System, 51
Tenet Healthcare Corporation, 55 (upd.)
Twinlab Corporation, 34
U.S. Healthcare, Inc., 6
U.S. Physical Therapy, Inc., 65
Unison HealthCare Corporation, 25
United HealthCare Corporation, 9
United Nations International Children's Emergency Fund (UNICEF), 58
United Way of America, 36
Universal Health Services, Inc., 6
Vanderbilt University Medical Center, 99
Vanguard Health Systems Inc., 70
VCA Antech, Inc., 58
Vencor, Inc., 16
VISX, Incorporated, 30
Vivra, Inc., 18
Volunteers of America, Inc., 66
WellPoint Health Networks Inc., 25
World Vision International, Inc., 93
YWCA of the U.S.A., 45

Hotels

Accor S.A., 69 (upd.)
Amerihost Properties, Inc., 30
Ameristar Casinos, Inc., 69 (upd.)

Archon Corporation, 74 (upd.)
Arena Leisure Plc, 99
Aztar Corporation, 13; 71 (upd.)
Bass PLC, 38 (upd.)
Boca Resorts, Inc., 37
Boyd Gaming Corporation, 43
Boyne USA Resorts, 71
Bristol Hotel Company, 23
The Broadmoor Hotel, 30
Caesars World, Inc., 6
Candlewood Hotel Company, Inc., 41
Carlson Companies, Inc., 6; 22 (upd.); 87 (upd.)
Castle & Cooke, Inc., 20 (upd.)
Cedar Fair Entertainment Company, 22; 98 (upd.)
Cendant Corporation, 44 (upd.)
Choice Hotels International, Inc., 14; 83 (upd.)
Circus Circus Enterprises, Inc., 6
City Developments Limited, 89
Club Méditerranée S.A., 6; 21 (upd.); 91 (upd.)
Compagnia Italiana dei Jolly Hotels S.p.A., 71
Daniel Thwaites Plc, 95
Doubletree Corporation, 21
Extended Stay America, Inc., 41
Fairmont Hotels & Resorts Inc., 69
Fibreboard Corporation, 16
Four Seasons Hotels Inc., 9; 29 (upd.)
Fuller Smith & Turner P.L.C., 38
Gables Residential Trust, 49
Gaylord Entertainment Company, 11; 36 (upd.)
Global Hyatt Corporation, 75 (upd.)
Granada Group PLC, 24 (upd.)
Grand Casinos, Inc., 20
Grand Hotel Krasnapolsky N.V., 23
Great Wolf Resorts, Inc., 91
Grupo Posadas, S.A. de C.V., 57
Helmsley Enterprises, Inc., 9
Hilton Hotels Corporation, III; 19 (upd.); 49 (upd.); 62 (upd.)
Holiday Inns, Inc., III
Home Inns & Hotels Management Inc., 95
Hospitality Franchise Systems, Inc., 11
Hotel Properties Ltd., 71
Howard Johnson International, Inc., 17; 72 (upd.)
Hyatt Corporation, III; 16 (upd.)
ILX Resorts Incorporated, 65
Interstate Hotels & Resorts Inc., 58
ITT Sheraton Corporation, III
JD Wetherspoon plc, 30
John Q. Hammons Hotels, Inc., 24
Jumeirah Group, 83
Kerzner International Limited, 69 (upd.)
The La Quinta Companies, 11; 42 (upd.)
Ladbroke Group PLC, 21 (upd.)
Landry's Restaurants, Inc., 65 (upd.)
Las Vegas Sands, Inc., 50
Madden's on Gull Lake, 52
Mammoth Mountain Ski Area, 101
Mandalay Resort Group, 32 (upd.)
Manor Care, Inc., 25 (upd.)
The Marcus Corporation, 21

Marriott International, Inc., III; 21 (upd.); 83 (upd.)
McMenamins Pubs and Breweries, 65
MGM MIRAGE, 98 (upd.)
Millennium & Copthorne Hotels plc, 71
Mirage Resorts, Incorporated, 6; 28 (upd.)
Monarch Casino & Resort, Inc., 65
Morgans Hotel Group Company, 80
Motel 6, 13; 56 (upd.)
MTR Gaming Group, Inc., 75
MWH Preservation Limited Partnership, 65
NH Hoteles S.A., 79
Omni Hotels Corp., 12
Paradores de Turismo de Espana S.A., 73
Park Corp., 22
Players International, Inc., 22
Preussag AG, 42 (upd.)
Prime Hospitality Corporation, 52
Promus Companies, Inc., 9
Real Turismo, S.A. de C.V., 50
Red Roof Inns, Inc., 18
Regent Inns plc, 95
Resorts International, Inc., 12
The Ritz-Carlton Hotel Company, L.L.C., 9; 29 (upd.); 71 (upd.)
Riviera Holdings Corporation, 75
Sandals Resorts International, 65
Santa Fe Gaming Corporation, 19
The SAS Group, 34 (upd.)
SFI Group plc, 51
Shangri-La Asia Ltd., 71
Showboat, Inc., 19
Sol Meliá S.A., 71
Sonesta International Hotels Corporation, 44
Starwood Hotels & Resorts Worldwide, Inc., 54
Sun International Hotels Limited, 26
Sunburst Hospitality Corporation, 26
Super 8 Motels, Inc., 83
Thistle Hotels PLC, 54
Trusthouse Forte PLC, III
Vail Resorts, Inc., 43 (upd.)
WestCoast Hospitality Corporation, 59
Westin Hotels and Resorts Worldwide, 9; 29 (upd.)
Whitbread PLC, I; 20 (upd.); 52 (upd.); 97 (upd.)
Wyndham Worldwide Corporation (updates Cendant Corporation), 99 (upd.)
Young & Co.'s Brewery, P.L.C., 38

Information Technology

A.B. Watley Group Inc., 45
AccuWeather, Inc., 73
Acxiom Corporation, 35
Adaptec, Inc., 31
Adobe Systems Incorporated, 10; 33 (upd.)
Advanced Micro Devices, Inc., 6; 30 (upd.); 99 (upd.)
Agence France-Presse, 34
Agilent Technologies Inc., 38; 93 (upd.)
Akamai Technologies, Inc., 71
Aladdin Knowledge Systems Ltd., 101
Aldus Corporation, 10

Allen Systems Group, Inc., 59
AltaVista Company, 43
Altiris, Inc., 65
Amdahl Corporation, III; 14 (upd.); 40 (upd.)
Amdocs Ltd., 47
America Online, Inc., 10; 26 (upd.)
American Business Information, Inc., 18
American Management Systems, Inc., 11
American Software Inc., 25
AMICAS, Inc., 69
Amstrad PLC, III
Analex Corporation, 74
Analytic Sciences Corporation, 10
Analytical Surveys, Inc., 33
Anker BV, 53
Ansoft Corporation, 63
Anteon Corporation, 57
AOL Time Warner Inc., 57 (upd.)
Apollo Group, Inc., 24
Apple Computer, Inc., III; 6 (upd.); 77 (upd.)
aQuantive, Inc., 81
The Arbitron Company, 38
Ariba, Inc., 57
Asanté Technologies, Inc., 20
Ascential Software Corporation, 59
AsiaInfo Holdings, Inc., 43
ASK Group, Inc., 9
Ask Jeeves, Inc., 65
ASML Holding N.V., 50
The Associated Press, 73 (upd.)
AST Research Inc., 9
At Home Corporation, 43
AT&T Bell Laboratories, Inc., 13
AT&T Corporation, 29 (upd.)
AT&T Istel Ltd., 14
Atos Origin S.A., 69
Attachmate Corporation, 56
Autodesk, Inc., 10; 89 (upd.)
Autologic Information International, Inc., 20
Automatic Data Processing, Inc., III; 9 (upd.); 47 (upd.)
Autotote Corporation, 20
Avantium Technologies BV, 79
Avid Technology Inc., 38
Avocent Corporation, 65
Aydin Corp., 19
Baan Company, 25
Baidu.com Inc., 95
Baltimore Technologies Plc, 42
Bankrate, Inc., 83
Banyan Systems Inc., 25
Battelle Memorial Institute, Inc., 10
BBN Corp., 19
BEA Systems, Inc., 36
Bell and Howell Company, 9; 29 (upd.)
Bell Industries, Inc., 47
Billing Concepts, Inc., 26; 72 (upd.)
Blackbaud, Inc., 85
Blackboard Inc., 89
Blizzard Entertainment 78
Bloomberg L.P., 21
Blue Martini Software, Inc., 59
BMC Software, Inc., 55
Boole & Babbage, Inc., 25
Booz Allen Hamilton Inc., 10; 101 (upd.)

Borland International, Inc., 9
Bowne & Co., Inc., 23
Brite Voice Systems, Inc., 20
Broderbund Software, 13; 29 (upd.)
BTG, Inc., 45
Bull S.A., 43 (upd.)
Business Objects S.A., 25
C-Cube Microsystems, Inc., 37
CACI International Inc., 21; 72 (upd.)
Cadence Design Systems, Inc., 11
Caere Corporation, 20
Cahners Business Information, 43
CalComp Inc., 13
Cambridge Technology Partners, Inc., 36
Candle Corporation, 64
Canon Inc., III
Cap Gemini Ernst & Young, 37
Captaris, Inc., 89
CareerBuilder, Inc., 93
Caribiner International, Inc., 24
Cass Information Systems Inc., 100
Catalina Marketing Corporation, 18
CDC Corporation, 71
CDW Computer Centers, Inc., 16
Cerner Corporation, 16
CheckFree Corporation, 81
Cheyenne Software, Inc., 12
CHIPS and Technologies, Inc., 9
Ciber, Inc., 18
Cincom Systems Inc., 15
Cirrus Logic, Incorporated, 11
Cisco-Linksys LLC, 86
Cisco Systems, Inc., 11; 77 (upd.)
Citizen Watch Co., Ltd., III; 21 (upd.); 81 (upd.)
Citrix Systems, Inc., 44
CMGI, Inc., 76
CNET Networks, Inc., 47
Cogent Communications Group, Inc., 55
Cognizant Technology Solutions Corporation, 59
Cognos Inc., 44
Commodore International Ltd., 7
Compagnie des Machines Bull S.A., III
Compaq Computer Corporation, III; 6 (upd.); 26 (upd.)
Complete Business Solutions, Inc., 31
CompuAdd Computer Corporation, 11
CompuCom Systems, Inc., 10
CompUSA, Inc., 35 (upd.)
CompuServe Interactive Services, Inc., 10; 27 (upd.)
Computer Associates International, Inc., 6; 49 (upd.)
Computer Data Systems, Inc., 14
Computer Sciences Corporation, 6
Computervision Corporation, 10
Compuware Corporation, 10; 30 (upd.); 66 (upd.)
Comshare Inc., 23
Conner Peripherals, Inc., 6
Control Data Corporation, III
Control Data Systems, Inc., 10
Corbis Corporation, 31
Corel Corporation, 15; 33 (upd.); 76 (upd.)
Corporate Software Inc., 9
CoStar Group, Inc., 73

Netscape Communications Corporation, 15; 35 (upd.)
Network Appliance, Inc., 58
Network Associates, Inc., 25
Nextel Communications, Inc., 10
NFO Worldwide, Inc., 24
NICE Systems Ltd., 83
Nichols Research Corporation, 18
Nimbus CD International, Inc., 20
Nixdorf Computer AG, III
Noah Education Holdings Ltd., 97
Novell, Inc., 6; 23 (upd.)
NVIDIA Corporation, 54
Océ N.V., 24; 91 (upd.)
OCLC Online Computer Library Center, Inc., 96
Odetics Inc., 14
Onyx Software Corporation, 53
Open Text Corporation, 79
Openwave Systems Inc., 95
Opsware Inc., 49
Oracle Corporation, 6; 24 (upd.); 67 (upd.)
Orbitz, Inc., 61
Overland Storage Inc., 100
Packard Bell Electronics, Inc., 13
Packeteer, Inc., 81
Parametric Technology Corp., 16
PC Connection, Inc., 37
Pegasus Solutions, Inc., 75
PeopleSoft Inc., 14; 33 (upd.)
Perot Systems Corporation, 29
Phillips International Inc. 78
Pitney Bowes Inc., III
PLATINUM Technology, Inc., 14
Policy Management Systems Corporation, 11
Policy Studies, Inc., 62
Portal Software, Inc., 47
Primark Corp., 13
The Princeton Review, Inc., 42
Printrak, A Motorola Company, 44
Printronix, Inc., 18
Prodigy Communications Corporation, 34
Programmer's Paradise, Inc., 81
Progress Software Corporation, 15
Psion PLC, 45
QSS Group, Inc., 100
Quality Systems, Inc., 81
Quantum Corporation, 10; 62 (upd.)
Quark, Inc., 36
Quicken Loans, Inc., 93
Racal-Datacom Inc., 11
Razorfish, Inc., 37
RCM Technologies, Inc., 34
RealNetworks, Inc., 53
Red Hat, Inc., 45
Remedy Corporation, 58
Renaissance Learning, Inc., 39; 100 (upd.)
The Reynolds and Reynolds Company, 50
Ricoh Company, Ltd., III
Riverbed Technology, Inc., 101
Rocky Mountain Chocolate Factory, Inc., 73
Rolta India Ltd., 90
RSA Security Inc., 46
RWD Technologies, Inc., 76
SABRE Group Holdings, Inc., 26

SafeNet Inc., 101
The Sage Group, 43
salesforce.com, Inc., 79
The Santa Cruz Operation, Inc., 38
SAP AG, 16; 43 (upd.)
SAS Institute Inc., 10; 78 (upd.)
Satyam Computer Services Ltd., 85
SBS Technologies, Inc., 25
SCB Computer Technology, Inc., 29
Schawk, Inc., 24
Scientific Learning Corporation, 95
The SCO Group Inc., 78
SDL PLC, 67
Seagate Technology, Inc., 8
Siebel Systems, Inc., 38
Sierra On-Line, Inc., 15; 41 (upd.)
SilverPlatter Information Inc., 23
SINA Corporation, 69
SkillSoft Public Limited Company, 81
SmartForce PLC, 43
Softbank Corp., 13; 38 (upd.); 77 (upd.)
Sonic Solutions, Inc., 81
SonicWALL, Inc., 87
Spark Networks, Inc., 91
Specialist Computer Holdings Ltd., 80
SPSS Inc., 64
Square Enix Holdings Co., Ltd., 101
SRA International, Inc., 77
Standard Microsystems Corporation, 11
STC PLC, III
Steria SA, 49
Sterling Software, Inc., 11
Storage Technology Corporation, 6
Stratus Computer, Inc., 10
Sun Microsystems, Inc., 7; 30 (upd.); 91 (upd.)
SunGard Data Systems Inc., 11
Sybase, Inc., 10; 27 (upd.)
Sykes Enterprises, Inc., 45
Symantec Corporation, 10; 82 (upd.)
Symbol Technologies, Inc., 15
Synchronoss Technologies, Inc., 95
SYNNEX Corporation, 73
Synopsys, Inc., 11; 69 (upd.)
Syntel, Inc., 92
System Software Associates, Inc., 10
Systems & Computer Technology Corp., 19
T-Online International AG, 61
TALX Corporation, 92
Tandem Computers, Inc., 6
TechTarget, Inc., 99
TenFold Corporation, 35
Terra Lycos, Inc., 43
Terremark Worldwide, Inc., 99
The Thomson Corporation, 34 (upd.); 77 (upd.)
ThoughtWorks Inc., 90
3Com Corporation, 11; 34 (upd.)
The 3DO Company, 43
TIBCO Software Inc., 79
Timberline Software Corporation, 15
TomTom N.V., 81
TradeStation Group, Inc., 83
Traffix, Inc., 61
Transaction Systems Architects, Inc., 29; 82 (upd.)
Transiciel SA, 48

Trend Micro Inc., 97
Triple P N.V., 26
Tripwire, Inc., 97
The TriZetto Group, Inc., 83
Tucows Inc. 78
Ubi Soft Entertainment S.A., 41
Unica Corporation, 77
Unilog SA, 42
Unisys Corporation, III; 6 (upd.); 36 (upd.)
United Business Media plc, 52 (upd.)
United Internet AG, 99
United Online, Inc., 71 (upd.)
United Press International, Inc., 73 (upd.)
UUNET, 38
VASCO Data Security International, Inc., 79
Verbatim Corporation, 14
Veridian Corporation, 54
VeriFone Holdings, Inc., 18; 76 (upd.)
Verint Systems Inc., 73
VeriSign, Inc., 47
Veritas Software Corporation, 45
Verity Inc., 68
Viasoft Inc., 27
Vital Images, Inc., 85
VMware, Inc., 90
Volt Information Sciences Inc., 26
Wanadoo S.A., 75
Wang Laboratories, Inc., III; 6 (upd.)
Weather Central Inc., 100
WebMD Corporation, 65
WebEx Communications, Inc., 81
West Group, 34 (upd.)
Westcon Group, Inc., 67
Western Digital Corporation, 25; 92 (upd.)
Wikimedia Foundation, Inc., 91
Wind River Systems, Inc., 37
Wipro Limited, 43
Witness Systems, Inc., 87
Wolters Kluwer NV, 33 (upd.)
WordPerfect Corporation, 10
Wyse Technology, Inc., 15
Xerox Corporation, III; 6 (upd.); 26 (upd.); 69 (upd.)
Xilinx, Inc., 16; 82 (upd.)
Yahoo! Inc., 27; 70 (upd.)
YouTube, Inc., 90
Zanett, Inc., 92
Zapata Corporation, 25
Ziff Davis Media Inc., 36 (upd.)
Zilog, Inc., 15

Insurance

AEGON N.V., III; 50 (upd.)
Aetna Inc., III; 21 (upd.); 63 (upd.)
AFLAC Incorporated, 10 (upd.); 38 (upd.)
Alexander & Alexander Services Inc., 10
Alfa Corporation, 60
Alleanza Assicurazioni S.p.A., 65
Alleghany Corporation, 10
Allianz AG, III; 15 (upd.); 57 (upd.)
Allmerica Financial Corporation, 63
The Allstate Corporation, 10; 27 (upd.)
AMB Generali Holding AG, 51
American Family Corporation, III

The Standard Life Assurance Company, III
State Auto Financial Corporation, 77
State Farm Mutual Automobile Insurance Company, III; 51 (upd.)
State Financial Services Corporation, 51
Stewart Information Services Corporation 78
Sumitomo Life Insurance Company, III; 60 (upd.)
The Sumitomo Marine and Fire Insurance Company, Limited, III
Sun Alliance Group PLC, III
Sun Life Financial Inc., 85
SunAmerica Inc., 11
Suncorp-Metway Ltd., 91
Suramericana de Inversiones S.A., 88
Svenska Handelsbanken AB, 50 (upd.)
The Swett & Crawford Group Inc., 84
Swiss Reinsurance Company (Schweizerische Rückversicherungs-Gesellschaft), III; 46 (upd.)
Teachers Insurance and Annuity Association-College Retirement Equities Fund, III; 45 (upd.)
Texas Industries, Inc., 8
TIG Holdings, Inc., 26
The Tokio Marine and Fire Insurance Co., Ltd., III
Torchmark Corporation, 9; 33 (upd.)
Transatlantic Holdings, Inc., 11
The Travelers Corporation, III
UICI, 33
Union des Assurances de Pans, III
United National Group, Ltd., 63
Unitrin Inc., 16; 78 (upd.)
UNUM Corp., 13
UnumProvident Corporation, 52 (upd.)
USAA, 10
USF&G Corporation, III
UTG Inc., 100
Victoria Group, 44 (upd.)
VICTORIA Holding AG, III
Vision Service Plan Inc., 77
W.R. Berkley Corporation, 15; 74 (upd.)
Washington National Corporation, 12
The Wawanesa Mutual Insurance Company, 68
WellCare Health Plans, Inc., 101
WellChoice, Inc., 67 (upd.)
Westfield Group, 69
White Mountains Insurance Group, Ltd., 48
Willis Group Holdings Ltd., 25; 100 (upd.)
Winterthur Group, III; 68 (upd.)
The Yasuda Fire and Marine Insurance Company, Limited, III
The Yasuda Mutual Life Insurance Company, III; 39 (upd.)
Zurich Financial Services, 42 (upd.); 93 (upd.)
Zürich Versicherungs-Gesellschaft, III

Legal Services

Akin, Gump, Strauss, Hauer & Feld, L.L.P., 33

American Bar Association, 35
American Lawyer Media Holdings, Inc., 32
Amnesty International, 50
Andrews Kurth, LLP, 71
Arnold & Porter, 35
Baker & Daniels LLP, 88
Baker & Hostetler LLP, 40
Baker & McKenzie, 10; 42 (upd.)
Baker and Botts, L.L.P., 28
Bingham Dana LLP, 43
Brobeck, Phleger & Harrison, LLP, 31
Cadwalader, Wickersham & Taft, 32
Chadbourne & Parke, 36
Cleary, Gottlieb, Steen & Hamilton, 35
Clifford Chance LLP, 38
Coudert Brothers, 30
Covington & Burling, 40
CRA International, Inc., 93
Cravath, Swaine & Moore, 43
Davis Polk & Wardwell, 36
Debevoise & Plimpton, 39
Dechert, 43
Dewey Ballantine LLP, 48
Dorsey & Whitney LLP, 47
Drinker, Biddle and Reath L.L.P., 92
Faegre & Benson LLP, 97
Fenwick & West LLP, 34
Fish & Neave, 54
Foley & Lardner, 28
Fried, Frank, Harris, Shriver & Jacobson, 35
Fulbright & Jaworski L.L.P., 47
Gibson, Dunn & Crutcher LLP, 36
Greenberg Traurig, LLP, 65
Heller, Ehrman, White & McAuliffe, 41
Hildebrandt International, 29
Hogan & Hartson L.L.P., 44
Holland & Knight LLP, 60
Holme Roberts & Owen LLP, 28
Hughes Hubbard & Reed LLP, 44
Hunton & Williams, 35
Jenkens & Gilchrist, P.C., 65
Jones, Day, Reavis & Pogue, 33
Kelley Drye & Warren LLP, 40
King & Spalding, 23
Kirkland & Ellis LLP, 65
Latham & Watkins, 33
LeBoeuf, Lamb, Greene & MacRae, L.L.P., 29
LECG Corporation, 93
The Legal Aid Society, 48
Mayer, Brown, Rowe & Maw, 47
Milbank, Tweed, Hadley & McCloy, 27
Morgan, Lewis & Bockius LLP, 29
Morrison & Foerster LLP 78
O'Melveny & Myers, 37
Oppenheimer Wolff & Donnelly LLP, 71
Orrick, Herrington and Sutcliffe LLP, 76
Patton Boggs LLP, 71
Paul, Hastings, Janofsky & Walker LLP, 27
Paul, Weiss, Rifkind, Wharton & Garrison, 47
Pepper Hamilton LLP, 43
Perkins Coie LLP, 56
Pillsbury Madison & Sutro LLP, 29
Pre-Paid Legal Services, Inc., 20

Proskauer Rose LLP, 47
Quinn Emanuel Urquhart Oliver & Hedges, LLP, 99
Robins, Kaplan, Miller & Ciresi L.L.P., 89
Ropes & Gray, 40
Saul Ewing LLP, 74
Seyfarth Shaw LLP, 93
Shearman & Sterling, 32
Sidley Austin Brown & Wood, 40
Simpson Thacher & Bartlett, 39
Skadden, Arps, Slate, Meagher & Flom, 18
Snell & Wilmer L.L.P., 28
Southern Poverty Law Center, Inc., 74
Stroock & Stroock & Lavan LLP, 40
Sullivan & Cromwell, 26
Troutman Sanders L.L.P., 79
Vinson & Elkins L.L.P., 30
Wachtell, Lipton, Rosen & Katz, 47
Weil, Gotshal & Manges LLP, 55
White & Case LLP, 35
Williams & Connolly LLP, 47
Willkie Farr & Gallagher LLP, 95
Wilson Sonsini Goodrich & Rosati, 34
Winston & Strawn, 35
Womble Carlyle Sandridge & Rice, PLLC, 52

Manufacturing

A-dec, Inc., 53
A. Schulman, Inc., 49 (upd.)
A.B.Dick Company, 28
A.O. Smith Corporation, 11; 40 (upd.); 93 (upd.)
A.T. Cross Company, 17; 49 (upd.)
A.W. Faber-Castell Unternehmensverwaltung GmbH & Co., 51
AAF-McQuay Incorporated, 26
Aalborg Industries A/S, 90
AAON, Inc., 22
AAR Corp., 28
Aarhus United A/S, 68
ABB Ltd., 65 (upd.)
ABC Rail Products Corporation, 18
Abiomed, Inc., 47
ACCO World Corporation, 7; 51 (upd.)
Accubuilt, Inc., 74
Acindar Industria Argentina de Aceros S.A., 87
Acme United Corporation, 70
Acme-Cleveland Corp., 13
Acorn Products, Inc., 55
Acuity Brands, Inc., 90
Acushnet Company, 64
Acuson Corporation, 36 (upd.)
Adams Golf, Inc., 37
Adolf Würth GmbH & Co. KG, 49
Advanced Circuits Inc., 67
Advanced Neuromodulation Systems, Inc., 73
AEP Industries, Inc., 36
AeroGrow International, Inc., 95
Aftermarket Technology Corp., 83
Ag-Chem Equipment Company, Inc., 17
Aga Foodservice Group PLC, 73
AGCO Corporation, 13; 67 (upd.)
Agfa Gevaert Group N.V., 59

INTERNATIONAL DIRECTORY OF COMPANY HISTORIES, VOLUME 101

Materials

Manville Corporation, III; 7 (upd.)
Material Sciences Corporation, 63
Matsushita Electric Works, Ltd., III; 7
  (upd.)
McJunkin Corporation, 63
Medusa Corporation, 24
Mitsubishi Materials Corporation, III
Nevamar Company, 82
Nippon Sheet Glass Company, Limited,
  III
North Pacific Group, Inc., 61
Nuplex Industries Ltd., 92
OmniSource Corporation, 14
Onoda Cement Co., Ltd., III
Otor S.A., 77
Owens-Corning Fiberglass Corporation,
  III
Pacific Clay Products Inc., 88
Pilkington Group Limited, III; 34 (upd.);
  87 (upd.)
Pioneer International Limited, III
PolyOne Corporation, 87 (upd.)
PPG Industries, Inc., III; 22 (upd.); 81
  (upd.)
Redland plc, III
Rinker Group Ltd., 65
RMC Group p.l.c., III
Rock of Ages Corporation, 37
Rogers Corporation, 80 (upd.)
Royal Group Technologies Limited, 73
The Rugby Group plc, 31
Scholle Corporation, 96
Schuff Steel Company, 26
Sekisui Chemical Co., Ltd., III; 72 (upd.)
Severstal Joint Stock Company, 65
Shaw Industries, 9
The Sherwin-Williams Company, III; 13
  (upd.); 89 (upd.)
The Siam Cement Public Company
  Limited, 56
SIG plc, 71
Simplex Technologies Inc., 21
Siskin Steel & Supply Company, 70
Solutia Inc., 52
Sommer-Allibert S.A., 19
Southdown, Inc., 14
Spartech Corporation, 19; 76 (upd.)
Ssangyong Cement Industrial Co., Ltd.,
  III; 61 (upd.)
Steel Technologies Inc., 63
Sun Distributors L.P., 12
Symyx Technologies, Inc., 77
Tarmac Limited, III, 28 (upd.); 95 (upd.)
Tilcon-Connecticut Inc., 80
TOTO LTD., III; 28 (upd.)
Toyo Sash Co., Ltd., III
Tuscarora Inc., 29
U.S. Aggregates, Inc., 42
Ube Industries, Ltd., III
United States Steel Corporation, 50 (upd.)
USG Corporation, III; 26 (upd.); 81
  (upd.)
Usinas Siderúrgicas de Minas Gerais S.A.,
  77
Vicat S.A., 70
voestalpine AG, 57 (upd.)
Vulcan Materials Company, 7; 52 (upd.)
Wacker-Chemie GmbH, 35

Walter Industries, Inc., III
Waxman Industries, Inc., 9
Weber et Broutin France, 66
Wienerberger AG, 70
Wolseley plc, 64
ZERO Corporation, 17; 88 (upd.)
Zoltek Companies, Inc., 37

Mining & Metals

A.M. Castle & Co., 25
Acindar Industria Argentina de Aceros
  S.A., 87
African Rainbow Minerals Ltd., 97
Aggregate Industries plc, 36
Agnico-Eagle Mines Limited, 71
Aktiebolaget SKF, III; 38 (upd.); 89
  (upd.)
Alcan Aluminium Limited, IV; 31 (upd.)
Alcoa Inc., 56 (upd.)
Alleghany Corporation, 10
Allegheny Ludlum Corporation, 8
Alliance Resource Partners, L.P., 81
Alrosa Company Ltd., 62
Altos Hornos de México, S.A. de C.V., 42
Aluminum Company of America, IV; 20
  (upd.)
AMAX Inc., IV
AMCOL International Corporation, 59
  (upd.)
Amsted Industries Incorporated, 7
Anglo American Corporation of South
  Africa Limited, IV; 16 (upd.)
Anglo American PLC, 50 (upd.)
Aquarius Platinum Ltd., 63
ARBED S.A., IV, 22 (upd.)
Arcelor Gent, 80
Arch Coal Inc., 98
Arch Mineral Corporation, 7
Armco Inc., IV
ASARCO Incorporated, IV
Ashanti Goldfields Company Limited, 43
Atchison Casting Corporation, 39
Barrick Gold Corporation, 34
Battle Mountain Gold Company, 23
Benguet Corporation, 58
Bethlehem Steel Corporation, IV; 7
  (upd.); 27 (upd.)
BHP Billiton, 67 (upd.)
Birmingham Steel Corporation, 13; 40
  (upd.)
Boart Longyear Company, 26
Bodycote International PLC, 63
Boliden AB, 80
Boral Limited, 43 (upd.)
British Coal Corporation, IV
British Steel plc, IV; 19 (upd.)
Broken Hill Proprietary Company Ltd.,
  IV, 22 (upd.)
Brush Engineered Materials Inc., 67
Brush Wellman Inc., 14
Buderus AG, 37
Cameco Corporation, 77
Caparo Group Ltd., 90
Carpenter Technology Corporation, 13;
  95 (upd.)
Chaparral Steel Co., 13
China Shenhua Energy Company
  Limited, 83

Christensen Boyles Corporation, 26
Cleveland-Cliffs Inc., 13; 62 (upd.)
Coal India Ltd., IV; 44 (upd.)
Cockerill Sambre Group, IV; 26 (upd.)
Coeur d'Alene Mines Corporation, 20
Cold Spring Granite Company Inc., 16;
  67 (upd.)
Cominco Ltd., 37
Commercial Metals Company, 15; 42
  (upd.)
Companhia Siderúrgica Nacional, 76
Companhia Vale do Rio Doce, IV; 43
  (upd.)
Compañia de Minas Buenaventura S.A.A.,
  93
CONSOL Energy Inc., 59
Corporacion Nacional del Cobre de Chile,
  40
Corus Group plc, 49 (upd.)
CRA Limited, IV
Cyprus Amax Minerals Company, 21
Cyprus Minerals Company, 7
Daido Steel Co., Ltd., IV
De Beers Consolidated Mines Limited/De
  Beers Centenary AG, IV; 7 (upd.); 28
  (upd.)
Degussa Group, IV
Diavik Diamond Mines Inc., 85
Dofasco Inc., IV; 24 (upd.)
Dynatec Corporation, 87
Earle M. Jorgensen Company, 82
Echo Bay Mines Ltd., IV; 38 (upd.)
Engelhard Corporation, IV
Eramet, 73
Evergreen Energy, Inc., 97
Evraz Group S.A., 97
Falconbridge Limited, 49
Fansteel Inc., 19
Fluor Corporation, 34 (upd.)
Freeport-McMoRan Copper & Gold, Inc.,
  IV; 7 (upd.); 57 (upd.)
Fried. Krupp GmbH, IV
Gencor Ltd., IV, 22 (upd.)
Geneva Steel, 7
Gerdau S.A., 59
Glamis Gold, Ltd., 54
Gold Fields Ltd., IV; 62 (upd.)
Goldcorp Inc., 87
Grupo Mexico, S.A. de C.V., 40
Gruppo Riva Fire SpA, 88
Handy & Harman, 23
Hanson Building Materials America Inc.,
  60
Hanson PLC, 30 (upd.)
Harmony Gold Mining Company
  Limited, 63
Haynes International, Inc., 88
Hecla Mining Company, 20
Hemlo Gold Mines Inc., 9
Heraeus Holding GmbH, IV
Highland Gold Mining Limited, 95
Highveld Steel and Vanadium
  Corporation Limited, 59
Hitachi Metals, Ltd., IV
Hoesch AG, IV
Homestake Mining Company, 12; 38
  (upd.)
Horsehead Industries, Inc., 51

Paper & Forestry

Personal Services

Petroleum

Publishing & Printing

Andrews McMeel Universal, 40
The Antioch Company, 40
AOL Time Warner Inc., 57 (upd.)
Arandell Corporation, 37
Archie Comics Publications, Inc., 63
Arnoldo Mondadori Editore S.p.A., IV;
  19 (upd.); 54 (upd.)
The Associated Press, 31 (upd.); 73 (upd.)
The Atlantic Group, 23
Audible Inc., 79
Axel Springer Verlag AG, IV; 20 (upd.)
Banta Corporation, 12; 32 (upd.); 79
  (upd.)
Bauer Publishing Group, 7
Bayard SA, 49
Berlitz International, Inc., 13
Bernard C. Harris Publishing Company,
  Inc., 39
Bertelsmann A.G., IV; 15 (upd.); 43
  (upd.); 91 (upd.)
Bibliographisches Institut & F.A.
  Brockhaus AG, 74
Big Flower Press Holdings, Inc., 21
Blackwell Publishing Ltd. 78
Blue Mountain Arts, Inc., 29
Bobit Publishing Company, 55
Bonnier AB, 52
Book-of-the-Month Club, Inc., 13
Bowne & Co., Inc., 23; 79 (upd.)
Broderbund Software, 13; 29 (upd.)
Brown Printing Company, 26
Burda Holding GmbH. & Co., 23
The Bureau of National Affairs, Inc., 23
Butterick Co., Inc., 23
Cadmus Communications Corporation,
  23
Cahners Business Information, 43
Carl Allers Etablissement A/S, 72
Carus Publishing Company, 93
CCH Inc., 14
Central Newspapers, Inc., 10
Champion Industries, Inc., 28
Cherry Lane Music Publishing Company,
  Inc., 62
Chicago Review Press Inc., 84
ChoicePoint Inc., 65
The Christian Science Publishing Society,
  55
The Chronicle Publishing Company, Inc.,
  23
Chrysalis Group plc, 40
CMP Media Inc., 26
Commerce Clearing House, Inc., 7
Community Newspaper Holdings, Inc.,
  91
Concepts Direct, Inc., 39
Condé Nast Publications, Inc., 13; 59
  (upd.)
Consolidated Graphics, Inc., 70
Consumers Union, 26
The Copley Press, Inc., 23
Corelio S.A./N.V., 96
Cornelsen Verlagsholding GmbH & Co.,
  90
Courier Corporation, 41
Cowles Media Company, 23
Cox Enterprises, Inc., IV; 22 (upd.)

Crain Communications, Inc., 12; 35
  (upd.)
Current, Inc., 37
Cygnus Business Media, Inc., 56
Dai Nippon Printing Co., Ltd., IV; 57
  (upd.)
Daily Journal Corporation, 101
Daily Mail and General Trust plc, 19
Dawson Holdings PLC, 43
Day Runner, Inc., 14
DC Comics Inc., 25; 98 (upd.)
De La Rue plc, 10; 34 (upd.)
DeLorme Publishing Company, Inc., 53
Deluxe Corporation, 7; 22 (upd.); 73
  (upd.)
Dennis Publishing Ltd., 62
Dex Media, Inc., 65
Dispatch Printing Company, 100
Donruss Playoff L.P., 66
Dorling Kindersley Holdings plc, 20
Dover Publications Inc., 34
Dow Jones & Company, Inc., IV; 19
  (upd.); 47 (upd.)
The Dun & Bradstreet Corporation, IV;
  19 (upd.)
Duplex Products Inc., 17
The E.W. Scripps Company, IV; 7 (upd.);
  28 (upd.); 66 (upd.)
Eagle-Tribune Publishing Co., 91
The Economist Group Ltd., 67
Edipresse S.A., 82
Éditions Gallimard, 72
Editis S.A. 78
Edmark Corporation, 14
Edwards Brothers, Inc., 92
Egmont Group, 93
Electronics for Imaging, Inc., 43 (upd.)
Elsevier N.V., IV
EMAP plc, 35
EMI Group plc, 22 (upd.); 81 (upd.)
Encyclopaedia Britannica, Inc., 7; 39
  (upd.)
Engraph, Inc., 12
Enquirer/Star Group, Inc., 10
Entravision Communications Corporation,
  41
Essence Communications, Inc., 24
F&W Publications, Inc., 71
Farm Journal Corporation, 42
Farrar, Straus and Giroux Inc., 15
Flint Ink Corporation, 13
Follett Corporation, 12; 39 (upd.)
Forbes Inc., 30; 82 (upd.)
Frankfurter Allgemeine Zeitung GmbH,
  66
Franklin Electronic Publishers, Inc., 23
Freedom Communications, Inc., 36
G A Pindar & Son Ltd., 88
Gannett Company, Inc., IV; 7 (upd.); 30
  (upd.); 66 (upd.)
GateHouse Media, Inc., 91
Geiger Bros., 60
Gibson Greetings, Inc., 12
Giesecke & Devrient GmbH, 83
Golden Books Family Entertainment, Inc.,
  28
Goss Holdings, Inc., 43
Graphic Industries Inc., 25

Gray Communications Systems, Inc., 24
Grolier Incorporated, 16; 43 (upd.)
Groupe de la Cite, IV
Groupe Les Echos, 25
Grupo Clarín S.A., 67
Grupo Televisa, S.A., 54 (upd.)
Guardian Media Group plc, 53
The H.W. Wilson Company, 66
Hachette, IV
Hachette Filipacchi Medias S.A., 21
Haights Cross Communications, Inc., 84
Hal Leonard Corporation, 96
Hallmark Cards, Inc., IV; 16 (upd.); 40
  (upd.); 87 (upd.)
Harcourt Brace and Co., 12
Harcourt Brace Jovanovich, Inc., IV
Harcourt General, Inc., 20 (upd.)
Harlequin Enterprises Limited, 52
HarperCollins Publishers, 15
Harris Interactive Inc., 41; 92 (upd.)
Harry N. Abrams, Inc., 58
Harte-Hanks Communications, Inc., 17
Havas SA, 10; 33 (upd.)
Hay House, Inc., 93
Haynes Publishing Group P.L.C., 71
Hazelden Foundation, 28
Health Communications, Inc., 72
The Hearst Corporation, IV; 19 (upd.);
  46 (upd.)
Her Majesty's Stationery Office, 7
Herald Media, Inc., 91
Highlights for Children, Inc., 95
N.V. Holdingmaatschappij De Telegraaf,
  23
Hollinger International Inc., 24; 62 (upd.)
HOP, LLC, 80
Houghton Mifflin Company, 10; 36
  (upd.)
IDG Books Worldwide, Inc., 27
IHS Inc. 78
Independent News & Media PLC, 61
Informa Group plc, 58
Information Holdings Inc., 47
International Data Group, Inc., 7; 25
  (upd.)
IPC Magazines Limited, 7
J.J. Keller & Associates, Inc., 81
Jeppesen Sanderson, Inc., 92
John Fairfax Holdings Limited, 7
John H. Harland Company, 17
John Wiley & Sons, Inc., 17; 65 (upd.)
Johnson Publishing Company, Inc., 28;
  72 (upd.)
Johnston Press plc, 35
Jostens, Inc., 25 (upd.); 73 (upd.)
Journal Communications, Inc., 86
Journal Register Company, 29
Jupitermedia Corporation, 75
Kaplan, Inc., 42
Kelley Blue Book Company, Inc., 84
Kensington Publishing Corporation, 84
Kinko's, Inc., 43 (upd.)
Knight Ridder, Inc., 67 (upd.)
Knight-Ridder, Inc., IV; 15 (upd.)
The Knot, Inc., 74
Kodansha Ltd., IV; 38 (upd.)
Krause Publications, Inc., 35

Retail & Wholesale

INTERNATIONAL DIRECTORY OF COMPANY HISTORIES, VOLUME 101

INDEX TO INDUSTRIES

Celebrate Express, Inc., 70
Celebrity, Inc., 22
CellStar Corporation, 83
Cencosud S.A., 69
Central European Distribution
  Corporation, 75
Central Garden & Pet Company, 23
Cenveo Inc., 71 (upd.)
Chadwick's of Boston, Ltd., 29
Charlotte Russe Holding, Inc., 35; 90
  (upd.)
Charming Shoppes, Inc., 38
Chas. Levy Company LLC, 60
ChevronTexaco Corporation, 47 (upd.)
Chiasso Inc., 53
The Children's Place Retail Stores, Inc.,
  37; 86 (upd.)
China Nepstar Chain Drugstore Ltd., 97
Christian Dior S.A., 49 (upd.)
Christopher & Banks Corporation, 42
Cifra, S.A. de C.V., 12
The Circle K Company, 20 (upd.)
Circuit City Stores, Inc., 9; 29 (upd.); 65
  (upd.)
Clare Rose Inc., 68
Clinton Cards plc, 39
The Clothestime, Inc., 20
CML Group, Inc., 10
Co-operative Group (CWS) Ltd., 51
Coach, Inc., 45 (upd.); 99 (upd.)
Coborn's, Inc., 30
Coinmach Laundry Corporation, 20
Coldwater Creek Inc., 21; 74 (upd.)
Cole National Corporation, 13; 76 (upd.)
Cole's Quality Foods, Inc., 68
Coles Group Limited, V; 20 (upd.); 85
  (upd.)
Collectors Universe, Inc., 48
Columbia House Company, 69
Comdisco, Inc., 9
Compagnie Financière Sucres et Denrées
  S.A., 60
Companhia Brasileira de Distribuiçao, 76
CompUSA, Inc., 10
Computerland Corp., 13
Concepts Direct, Inc., 39
Conn's, Inc., 67
The Container Store, 36
Controladora Comercial Mexicana, S.A.
  de C.V., 36
CoolSavings, Inc., 77
Coop Schweiz Genossenschaftsverband, 48
Coppel, S.A. de C.V., 82
Corby Distilleries Limited, 14
Corporate Express, Inc., 22; 47 (upd.)
Cortefiel S.A., 64
The Cosmetic Center, Inc., 22
Cost Plus, Inc., 27
Costco Wholesale Corporation, V; 43
  (upd.)
Cotter & Company, V
County Seat Stores Inc., 9
Courts Plc, 45
CPI Corp., 38
Crate and Barrel, 9
Croscill, Inc., 42
CROSSMARK, 79
Crowley, Milner & Company, 19

Crown Books Corporation, 21
Cumberland Farms, Inc., 17; 84 (upd.)
CVS Corporation, 45 (upd.)
D&H Distributing Co., 95
Daffy's Inc., 26
The Daiei, Inc., V; 17 (upd.); 41 (upd.)
The Daimaru, Inc., V; 42 (upd.)
Dairy Farm International Holdings Ltd.,
  97
Dairy Mart Convenience Stores, Inc., 25
  (upd.)
Daisytek International Corporation, 18
Damark International, Inc., 18
Dart Group Corporation, 16
Darty S.A., 27
David Jones Ltd., 60
David's Bridal, Inc., 33
Dayton Hudson Corporation, V; 18
  (upd.)
Deb Shops, Inc., 16; 76 (upd.)
Debenhams Plc, 28; 101 (upd.)
Deli Universal NV, 66
dELiA*s Inc., 29
Department 56, Inc., 34 (upd.)
Designer Holdings Ltd., 20
Deveaux S.A., 41
DFS Group Ltd., 66
Dick's Sporting Goods, Inc., 59
Diesel SpA, 40
Digital River, Inc., 50
Dillard Department Stores, Inc., V; 16
  (upd.)
Dillard's Inc., 68 (upd.)
Dillon Companies Inc., 12
Discount Auto Parts, Inc., 18
Discount Drug Mart, Inc., 14
Dixons Group plc, V; 19 (upd.); 49
  (upd.)
Do it Best Corporation, 30
Dollar Tree Stores, Inc., 23; 62 (upd.)
Donna Karan International Inc., 56 (upd.)
Dorian Drake International Inc., 96
Dreams Inc., 97
The Dress Barn, Inc., 24; 55 (upd.)
Drs. Foster & Smith, Inc., 62
Drug Emporium, Inc., 12
DSW Inc., 73
Du Pareil au Même, 43
Duane Reade Holding Corp., 21
Duckwall-ALCO Stores, Inc., 24
Dunham's Athleisure Corporation, 98
Dunnes Stores Ltd., 58
Duron Inc., 72
Duty Free International, Inc., 11
Dylan's Candy Bar, LLC, 99
Dylex Limited, 29
E-Z Serve Corporation, 17
Eagle Hardware & Garden, Inc., 16
Eastman Kodak Company, III; 7 (upd.);
  36 (upd.); 91 (upd.)
eBay Inc., 32
Eckerd Corporation, 9; 32 (upd.)
Eddie Bauer Holdings, Inc., 9; 36 (upd.);
  87 (upd.)
Edgars Consolidated Stores Ltd., 66
Edward Hines Lumber Company, 68
Egghead.com, Inc., 31 (upd.)
Eileen Fisher Inc., 61

El Corte Inglés Group, V
El Puerto de Liverpool, S.A.B. de C.V., 97
The Elder-Beerman Stores Corp., 10; 63
  (upd.)
Electrocomponents PLC, 50
Electronics Boutique Holdings
  Corporation, 72
Elephant Pharmacy, Inc., 83
Ellett Brothers, Inc., 17
EMI Group plc, 22 (upd.); 81 (upd.)
Empresas Almacenes Paris S.A., 71
Ermenegildo Zegna SpA, 63
ESCADA AG, 71
The Estée Lauder Companies Inc., 9; 30
  (upd.); 93 (upd.)
Etablissements Franz Colruyt N.V., 68
Ethan Allen Interiors, Inc., 39 (upd.)
EToys, Inc., 37
Euromarket Designs Inc., 31 (upd.); 99
  (upd.)
Evans, Inc., 30
Eye Care Centers of America, Inc., 69
EZCORP Inc., 43
F.W. Webb Company, 95
The F. Dohmen Co., 77
Family Christian Stores, Inc., 51
Family Dollar Stores, Inc., 13; 62 (upd.)
Fannie May Confections Brands, Inc., 80
Farmacias Ahumada S.A., 72
Fastenal Company, 14; 42 (upd.); 99
  (upd.)
Faultless Starch/Bon Ami Company, 55
Fay's Inc., 17
Federated Department Stores, Inc., 9; 31
  (upd.)
Fenaco, 86
Fielmann AG, 31
Fila Holding S.p.A., 20; 52 (upd.)
Finarte Casa d'Aste S.p.A., 93
Findel plc, 60
Fingerhut Companies, Inc., 9; 36 (upd.)
The Finish Line, Inc., 29; 68 (upd.)
Finlay Enterprises, Inc., 16; 76 (upd.)
Finning International Inc., 69
First Cash Financial Services, Inc., 57
Fleming Companies, Inc., 17 (upd.)
Florsheim Shoe Group Inc., 9; 31 (upd.)
FNAC, 21
Follett Corporation, 12
Foot Locker, Inc., 68 (upd.)
Footstar, Incorporated, 24
Forever 21, Inc., 84
Fortunoff Fine Jewelry and Silverware
  Inc., 26
The Forzani Group Ltd., 79
Foxworth-Galbraith Lumber Company, 91
Frank's Nursery & Crafts, Inc., 12
Fred Meyer Stores, Inc., V; 20 (upd.); 64
  (upd.)
Fred's, Inc., 23; 62 (upd.)
Frederick Atkins Inc., 16
Frederick's of Hollywood, Inc., 59 (upd.)
Freeze.com LLC, 77
Fretter, Inc., 10
Friedman's Inc., 29
Fruth Pharmacy, Inc., 66
Fry's Electronics, Inc., 68
FTD Group, Inc., 99 (upd.)

PETsMART, Inc., 14; 41 (upd.)
PFSweb, Inc., 73
Phar-Mor Inc., 12
Phones 4u Ltd., 85
Photo-Me International Plc, 83
Pick 'n Pay Stores Ltd., 82
Pier 1 Imports, Inc., 12; 34 (upd.); 95 (upd.)
Piercing Pagoda, Inc., 29
Pilot Corporation, 49
Pinault-Printemps Redoute S.A., 19 (upd.)
Pitman Company, 58
Polartec LLC, 98 (upd.)
Pomeroy Computer Resources, Inc., 33
Powell's Books, Inc., 40
PPR S.A., 74 (upd.)
Praxis Bookstore Group LLC, 90
The Price Company, V
PriceCostco, Inc., 14
PriceSmart, Inc., 71
Pro-Build Holdings Inc., 95 (upd.)
Proffitt's, Inc., 19
Provell Inc., 58 (upd.)
Provigo Inc., 51 (upd.)
Publishers Clearing House, 64 (upd.)
Puig Beauty and Fashion Group S.L., 60
Purina Mills, Inc., 32
Quelle Group, V
QuikTrip Corporation, 36
Quiksilver, Inc., 79 (upd.)
Quill Corporation, 28
QVC Inc., 58 (upd.)
R.C. Willey Home Furnishings, 72
R.H. Macy & Co., Inc., V; 8 (upd.); 30 (upd.)
RadioShack Corporation, 36 (upd.); 101 (upd.)
Rag Shops, Inc., 30
Raley's Inc., 14; 58 (upd.)
Rallye SA, 54
Rapala-Normark Group, Ltd., 30
Ratner Companies, 72
RDO Equipment Company, 33
Reckitt Benckiser plc, II; 42 (upd.); 91 (upd.)
Recoton Corp., 15
Recreational Equipment, Inc., 18; 71 (upd.)
Red McCombs Automotive Group, 91
Red Wing Shoe Company, Inc., 9; 30 (upd.); 83 (upd.)
Redlon & Johnson, Inc., 97
Reeds Jewelers, Inc., 22
Rejuvenation, Inc., 91
Reliance Steel & Aluminum Company, 70 (upd.)
Rent-A-Center, Inc., 45
Rent-Way, Inc., 33; 75 (upd.)
Restoration Hardware, Inc., 30; 96 (upd.)
Retail Ventures, Inc., 82 (upd.)
Revco D.S., Inc., V
REX Stores Corp., 10
Rhodes Inc., 23
Richton International Corporation, 39
Riklis Family Corp., 9
Rinascente S.p.A., 71
Rite Aid Corporation, V; 19 (upd.); 63 (upd.)

Ritz Camera Centers, 34
RM Auctions, Inc., 88
Roberds Inc., 19
Rocky Shoes & Boots, Inc., 26
Rogers Communications Inc., 30 (upd.)
RONA, Inc., 73
Ronco Corporation, 15; 80 (upd.)
Rooms To Go Inc., 28
Roots Canada Ltd., 42
Rose's Stores, Inc., 13
Ross Stores, Inc., 17; 43 (upd.); 101 (upd.)
Rosy Blue N.V., 84
Roundy's Inc., 14
Rush Enterprises, Inc., 64
Ryoshoku Ltd., 72
S&K Famous Brands, Inc., 23
S.A.C.I. Falabella, 69
Saks Inc., 24; 41 (upd.)
Sally Beauty Company, Inc., 60
Sam Ash Music Corporation, 30
Sam Levin Inc., 80
Sam's Club, 40
Samuels Jewelers Incorporated, 30
Sanborn Hermanos, S.A., 20
SanomaWSOY Corporation, 51
Savers, Inc., 99 (upd.)
Scheels All Sports Inc., 63
Schmitt Music Company, 40
Schneiderman's Furniture Inc., 28
School Specialty, Inc., 68
Schottenstein Stores Corp., 14
Schultz Sav-O Stores, Inc., 31
The Score Board, Inc., 19
Scotty's, Inc., 22
The Scoular Company, 77
SCP Pool Corporation, 39
Seaman Furniture Company, Inc., 32
Sean John Clothing, Inc., 70
Sears plc, V
Sears Roebuck de México, S.A. de C.V., 20
Sears, Roebuck and Co., V; 18 (upd.); 56 (upd.)
SED International Holdings, Inc., 43
Seibu Department Stores, Ltd., V; 42 (upd.)
Seigle's Home and Building Centers, Inc., 41
The Seiyu, Ltd., V; 36 (upd.)
Selfridges Plc, 34
Service Merchandise Company, Inc., V; 19 (upd.)
7-Eleven, Inc., 32 (upd.)
Seventh Generation, Inc., 73
Shaklee Corporation, 12
The Sharper Image Corporation, 10; 62 (upd.)
Sheetz, Inc., 85
Sheplers, Inc., 96
The Sherwin-Williams Company, 89 (upd.)
Shoe Carnival Inc., 14; 72 (upd.)
ShopKo Stores Inc., 21; 58 (upd.)
Shoppers Drug Mart Corporation, 49
Shoppers Food Warehouse Corporation, 66
SIG plc, 71

Signet Group PLC, 61
skinnyCorp, LLC, 97
SkyMall, Inc., 26
Sleepy's Inc., 32
Smith & Hawken, Ltd., 68
Snapfish, 83
Solo Serve Corporation, 28
Sophus Berendsen A/S, 49
Sound Advice, Inc., 41
Source Interlink Companies, Inc., 75
Southern States Cooperative Incorporated, 36
Spartan Stores Inc., 66 (upd.)
Spec's Music, Inc., 19
Spector Photo Group N.V., 82
Spiegel, Inc., 10; 27 (upd.)
Sport Chalet, Inc., 16
Sport Supply Group, Inc., 23
Sportmart, Inc., 15
Sports & Recreation, Inc., 17
The Sports Authority, Inc., 16; 43 (upd.)
The Sportsman's Guide, Inc., 36
Stage Stores, Inc., 24; 82 (upd.)
Stanhome Inc., 15
Staple Cotton Cooperative Association (Staplcotn), 86
Staples, Inc., 10; 55 (upd.)
Starbucks Corporation, 13; 34 (upd.); 77 (upd.)
Starcraft Corporation, 30
Stefanel SpA, 63
Stein Mart Inc., 19; 72 (upd.)
Steve & Barry's LLC, 88
Stewart's Shops Corporation, 80
Stinnes AG, 8
The Stop & Shop Companies, Inc., 24 (upd.)
Storehouse PLC, 16
Strauss Discount Auto, 56
Stride Rite Corporation, 8
The Strober Organization, Inc., 82
Strouds, Inc., 33
Stuller Settings, Inc., 35
Successories, Inc., 30
Sun Television & Appliances Inc., 10
Sunglass Hut International, Inc., 21; 74 (upd.)
Superdrug Stores PLC, 95
Supreme International Corporation, 27
Sutherland Lumber Company, L.P., 99
Swarovski International Holding AG, 40
The Swiss Colony, Inc., 97
Syms Corporation, 29; 74 (upd.)
Systemax, Inc., 52
Takashimaya Company, Limited, V; 47 (upd.)
The Talbots, Inc., 11; 31 (upd.); 88 (upd.)
Target Corporation, 61 (upd.)
Target Stores, 10; 27 (upd.)
Tati SA, 25
Tattered Cover Book Store, 43
Tech Data Corporation, 10; 74 (upd.)
Tengelmann Group, 27
Tesco plc, 24 (upd.); 68 (upd.)
Things Remembered, Inc., 84
Thomsen Greenhouses and Garden Center, Incorporated, 65

Textiles & Apparel

Pluma, Inc., 27
Polo/Ralph Lauren Corporation, 12; 62 (upd.)
Pomare Ltd., 88
Prada Holding B.V., 45
PremiumWear, Inc., 30
Puma AG Rudolf Dassler Sport, 35
Quaker Fabric Corp., 19
Quiksilver, Inc., 18; 79 (upd.)
R.G. Barry Corporation, 17; 44 (upd.)
Rack Room Shoes, Inc., 84
Raymond Ltd., 77
Recreational Equipment, Inc., 18
Red Wing Shoe Company, Inc., 9; 30 (upd.); 83 (upd.)
Reebok International Ltd., V; 9 (upd.); 26 (upd.)
Reliance Industries Ltd., 81
Renfro Corporation, 99
Rieter Holding AG, 42
Robert Talbott Inc., 88
Rocawear Apparel LLC, 77
Rollerblade, Inc., 15
Royal Ten Cate N.V., 68
Russell Corporation, 8; 30 (upd.); 82 (upd.)
Rusty, Inc., 95
St. John Knits, Inc., 14
Salant Corporation, 51 (upd.)
Salvatore Ferragamo Italia S.p.A., 62
Sao Paulo Alpargatas S.A., 75
Saucony Inc., 35; 86 (upd.)
Schott Brothers, Inc., 67
Seattle Pacific Industries, Inc., 92
Shaw Industries, Inc., 40 (upd.)
Shelby Williams Industries, Inc., 14
Shoe Pavilion, Inc., 84
Skechers U.S.A. Inc., 31; 88 (upd.)
skinnyCorp, LLC, 97
Sole Technology Inc., 93
Sophus Berendsen A/S, 49
Spanx, Inc., 89
Springs Global US, Inc., V; 19 (upd.); 90 (upd.)
Starter Corp., 12
Stefanel SpA, 63
Steiner Corporation (Alsco), 53
Steven Madden, Ltd., 37
Stirling Group plc, 62
Stoddard International plc, 72
Stone Manufacturing Company, 14; 43 (upd.)
Stride Rite Corporation, 8; 37 (upd.); 86 (upd.)
Stussy, Inc., 55
Sun Sportswear, Inc., 17
Superior Uniform Group, Inc., 30
Tag-It Pacific, Inc., 85
The Talbots, Inc., 11; 31 (upd.); 88 (upd.)
Tamfelt Oyj Abp, 62
Tarrant Apparel Group, 62
Ted Baker plc, 86
Teijin Limited, V
Thanulux Public Company Limited, 86
Thomaston Mills, Inc., 27
Tilley Endurables, Inc., 67
The Timberland Company, 13; 54 (upd.)

Tommy Hilfiger Corporation, 20; 53 (upd.)
Too, Inc., 61
Toray Industries, Inc., V
True Religion Apparel, Inc., 79
Tultex Corporation, 13
Under Armour Performance Apparel, 61
Unifi, Inc., 12; 62 (upd.)
United Merchants & Manufacturers, Inc., 13
United Retail Group Inc., 33
Unitika Ltd., V
Umbro plc, 88
Vans, Inc., 16; 47 (upd.)
Varsity Spirit Corp., 15
VF Corporation, V; 17 (upd.); 54 (upd.)
Vicunha Têxtil S.A. 78
Volcom, Inc., 77
Walton Monroe Mills, Inc., 8
The Warnaco Group Inc., 12; 46 (upd.)
Wellco Enterprises, Inc., 84
Wellman, Inc., 8; 52 (upd.)
West Point-Pepperell, Inc., 8
WestPoint Stevens Inc., 16
Weyco Group, Incorporated, 32
Williamson-Dickie Manufacturing Company, 14
Wolverine World Wide, Inc., 16; 59 (upd.)
Woolrich Inc., 62
Zara International, Inc., 83

Tobacco

Altadis S.A., 72 (upd.)
American Brands, Inc., V
B.A.T. Industries PLC, 22 (upd.)
British American Tobacco PLC, 50 (upd.)
Brooke Group Ltd., 15
Brown & Williamson Tobacco Corporation, 14; 33 (upd.)
Culbro Corporation, 15
Dibrell Brothers, Incorporated, 12
DIMON Inc., 27
800-JR Cigar, Inc., 27
Gallaher Group Plc, V; 19 (upd.); 49 (upd.)
General Cigar Holdings, Inc., 66 (upd.)
Holt's Cigar Holdings, Inc., 42
House of Prince A/S, 80
Imasco Limited, V
Imperial Tobacco Group PLC, 50
Japan Tobacco Incorporated, V
KT&G Corporation, 62
Nobleza Piccardo SAICF, 64
North Atlantic Trading Company Inc., 65
Philip Morris Companies Inc., V; 18 (upd.)
R.J. Reynolds Tobacco Holdings, Inc., 30 (upd.)
RJR Nabisco Holdings Corp., V
Rothmans UK Holdings Limited, V; 19 (upd.)
Seita, 23
Souza Cruz S.A., 65
Standard Commercial Corporation, 13; 62 (upd.)
Swedish Match AB, 12; 39 (upd.); 92 (upd.)

Swisher International Group Inc., 23
Tabacalera, S.A., V; 17 (upd.)
Taiwan Tobacco & Liquor Corporation, 75
Universal Corporation, V; 48 (upd.)
UST Inc., 9; 50 (upd.)
Vector Group Ltd., 35 (upd.)

Transport Services

Abertis Infraestructuras, S.A., 65
The Adams Express Company, 86
Aegean Marine Petroleum Network Inc., 89
Aéroports de Paris, 33
Air Express International Corporation, 13
Air Partner PLC, 93
Air T, Inc., 86
Airborne Freight Corporation, 6; 34 (upd.)
Alamo Rent A Car, Inc., 6; 24 (upd.); 84 (upd.)
Alaska Railroad Corporation, 60
Alexander & Baldwin, Inc., 10, 40 (upd.)
Allied Worldwide, Inc., 49
AMCOL International Corporation, 59 (upd.)
Amerco, 6
AMERCO, 67 (upd.)
American Classic Voyages Company, 27
American Commercial Lines Inc., 99
American President Companies Ltd., 6
Anderson Trucking Service, Inc., 75
Anschutz Corp., 12
APL Limited, 61 (upd.)
Aqua Alliance Inc., 32 (upd.)
Arlington Tankers Ltd., 101
Arriva PLC, 69
Atlas Van Lines, Inc., 14
Attica Enterprises S.A., 64
Avis Group Holdings, Inc., 75 (upd.)
Avis Rent A Car, Inc., 6; 22 (upd.)
BAA plc, 10
Bekins Company, 15
Berliner Verkehrsbetriebe (BVG), 58
Bollinger Shipyards, Inc., 61
Boyd Bros. Transportation Inc., 39
Brambles Industries Limited, 42
The Brink's Company, 58 (upd.)
British Railways Board, V
Broken Hill Proprietary Company Ltd., 22 (upd.)
Buckeye Partners, L.P., 70
Budget Group, Inc., 25
Budget Rent a Car Corporation, 9
Burlington Northern Santa Fe Corporation, V; 27 (upd.)
C.H. Robinson Worldwide, Inc., 40 (upd.)
Canadian National Railway Company, 71 (upd.)
Canadian National Railway System, 6
Canadian Pacific Railway Limited, V; 45 (upd.); 95 (upd.)
Cannon Express, Inc., 53
Carey International, Inc., 26
Carlson Companies, Inc., 6; 22 (upd.); 87 (upd.)
Carolina Freight Corporation, 6

Smithway Motor Xpress Corporation, 39
Société Nationale des Chemins de Fer
  Français, V; 57 (upd.)
Société Norbert Dentressangle S.A., 67
Southern Pacific Transportation Company,
  V
Spee-Dee Delivery Service, Inc., 93
Stagecoach Holdings plc, 30
Stelmar Shipping Ltd., 52
Stevedoring Services of America Inc., 28
Stinnes AG, 8; 59 (upd.)
Stolt-Nielsen S.A., 42
Sunoco, Inc., 28 (upd.); 83 (upd.)
Swift Transportation Co., Inc., 42
The Swiss Federal Railways
  (Schweizerische Bundesbahnen), V
Swissport International Ltd., 70
Teekay Shipping Corporation, 25; 82
  (upd.)
Tibbett & Britten Group plc, 32
Tidewater Inc., 11; 37 (upd.)
TNT Freightways Corporation, 14
TNT Post Group N.V., V; 27 (upd.); 30
  (upd.)
Tobu Railway Company Ltd., 6; 98
  (upd.)
Tokyu Corporation, V
Totem Resources Corporation, 9
TPG N.V., 64 (upd.)
Trailer Bridge, Inc., 41
Transnet Ltd., 6
Transport Corporation of America, Inc.,
  49
Trico Marine Services, Inc., 89
Tsakos Energy Navigation Ltd., 91
TTX Company, 6; 66 (upd.)
U.S. Delivery Systems, Inc., 22
Union Pacific Corporation, V; 28 (upd.);
  79 (upd.)
United Parcel Service of America Inc., V;
  17 (upd.)
United Parcel Service, Inc., 63
United Road Services, Inc., 69
United States Postal Service, 14; 34 (upd.)
US 1 Industries, Inc., 89
USA Truck, Inc., 42
Velocity Express Corporation, 49
Werner Enterprises, Inc., 26
Wheels Inc., 96
Wincanton plc, 52
Wisconsin Central Transportation
  Corporation, 24
Wright Express Corporation, 80
Yamato Transport Co. Ltd., V; 49 (upd.)
Yellow Corporation, 14; 45 (upd.)
Yellow Freight System, Inc. of Delaware,
  V
YRC Worldwide Inc., 90 (upd.)

Utilities

AES Corporation, 10; 13 (upd.); 53
  (upd.)
Aggreko Plc, 45
Air & Water Technologies Corporation, 6
Alberta Energy Company Ltd., 16; 43
  (upd.)
Allegheny Energy, Inc., V; 38 (upd.)
Ameren Corporation, 60 (upd.)

American Electric Power Company, Inc.,
  V; 45 (upd.)
American States Water Company, 46
American Water Works Company, Inc., 6;
  38 (upd.)
Aquarion Company, 84
Aquila, Inc., 50 (upd.)
Arkla, Inc., V
Associated Natural Gas Corporation, 11
Atlanta Gas Light Company, 6; 23 (upd.)
Atlantic Energy, Inc., 6
Atmos Energy Corporation, 43
Avista Corporation, 69 (upd.)
Baltimore Gas and Electric Company, V;
  25 (upd.)
Bay State Gas Company, 38
Bayernwerk AG, V; 23 (upd.)
Berlinwasser Holding AG, 90
Bewag AG, 39
Big Rivers Electric Corporation, 11
Black Hills Corporation, 20
Bonneville Power Administration, 50
Boston Edison Company, 12
Bouygues S.A., I; 24 (upd.); 97 (upd.)
British Energy Plc, 49
British Gas plc, V
British Nuclear Fuels plc, 6
Brooklyn Union Gas, 6
California Water Service Group, 79
Calpine Corporation, 36
Canadian Utilities Limited, 13; 56 (upd.)
Cap Rock Energy Corporation, 46
Carolina Power & Light Company, V; 23
  (upd.)
Cascade Natural Gas Corporation, 9
Centerior Energy Corporation, V
Central and South West Corporation, V
Central Hudson Gas and Electricity
  Corporation, 6
Central Maine Power, 6
Central Vermont Public Service
  Corporation, 54
Centrica plc, 29 (upd.)
ČEZ a. s., 97
Chesapeake Utilities Corporation, 56
China Shenhua Energy Company
  Limited, 83
Chubu Electric Power Company, Inc., V;
  46 (upd.)
Chugoku Electric Power Company Inc.,
  V; 53 (upd.)
Cincinnati Gas & Electric Company, 6
CIPSCO Inc., 6
Citizens Utilities Company, 7
City Public Service, 6
Cleco Corporation, 37
CMS Energy Corporation, V, 14 (upd.);
  100 (upd.)
The Coastal Corporation, 31 (upd.)
Cogentrix Energy, Inc., 10
The Coleman Company, Inc., 9
The Columbia Gas System, Inc., V; 16
  (upd.)
Commonwealth Edison Company, V
Commonwealth Energy System, 14
Companhia Energética de Minas Gerais
  S.A. CEMIG, 65

Compañia de Minas Buenaventura S.A.A.,
  93
Connecticut Light and Power Co., 13
Consolidated Edison, Inc., V; 45 (upd.)
Consolidated Natural Gas Company, V;
  19 (upd.)
Consumers Power Co., 14
Consumers Water Company, 14
Consumers' Gas Company Ltd., 6
Covanta Energy Corporation, 64 (upd.)
Dalkia Holding, 66
Destec Energy, Inc., 12
The Detroit Edison Company, V
Dominion Resources, Inc., V; 54 (upd.)
DPL Inc., 6; 96 (upd.)
DQE, Inc., 6
DTE Energy Company, 20 (upd.)
Duke Energy Corporation, V; 27 (upd.)
E.On AG, 50 (upd.)
Eastern Enterprises, 6
Edison International, 56 (upd.)
El Paso Electric Company, 21
El Paso Natural Gas Company, 12
Electrabel N.V., 67
Electricidade de Portugal, S.A., 47
Electricité de France, V; 41 (upd.)
Electricity Generating Authority of
  Thailand (EGAT), 56
Elektrowatt AG, 6
The Empire District Electric Company,
  77
Empresas Públicas de Medellín S.A.E.S.P.,
  91
Enbridge Inc., 43
ENDESA S.A., V; 46 (upd.)
Enersis S.A., 73
ENMAX Corporation, 83
Enron Corporation, V; 46 (upd.)
Enserch Corporation, V
Ente Nazionale per L'Energia Elettrica, V
Entergy Corporation, V; 45 (upd.)
Environmental Power Corporation, 68
EPCOR Utilities Inc., 81
Equitable Resources, Inc., 6; 54 (upd.)
Exelon Corporation, 48 (upd.)
Florida Progress Corporation, V; 23 (upd.)
Florida Public Utilities Company, 69
Fortis, Inc., 15; 47 (upd.)
Fortum Corporation, 30 (upd.)
FPL Group, Inc., V; 49 (upd.)
Gas Natural SDG S.A., 69
Gaz de France, V; 40 (upd.)
General Public Utilities Corporation, V
Générale des Eaux Group, V
GPU, Inc., 27 (upd.)
Great Plains Energy Incorporated, 65
  (upd.)
Gulf States Utilities Company, 6
Hawaiian Electric Industries, Inc., 9
Hokkaido Electric Power Company Inc.
  (HEPCO), V; 58 (upd.)
Hokuriku Electric Power Company, V
Hong Kong and China Gas Company
  Ltd., 73
Hongkong Electric Holdings Ltd., 6; 23
  (upd.)
Houston Industries Incorporated, V
Hyder plc, 34

Waste Services

Geographic Index

GEOGRAPHIC INDEX

Technip 78
Télévision Française 1, 23
Terrena L'Union CANA CAVAL, 70
Thales S.A., 42
THOMSON multimedia S.A., II; 42
(upd.)
Total Fina Elf S.A., IV; 24 (upd.); 50
(upd.)
Toupargel-Agrigel S.A., 76
Touton S.A., 92
Transiciel SA, 48
Ubi Soft Entertainment S.A., 41
Ugine S.A., 20
Unibail SA, 40
Unilog SA, 42
Union des Assurances de Pans, III
Union Financière de France Banque SA,
52
Usinor SA, IV; 42 (upd.)
Valeo, 23; 66 (upd.)
Vallourec SA, 54
Veuve Clicquot Ponsardin SCS, 98
Vicat S.A., 70
Viel & Cie, 76
Vilmorin Clause et Cie, 70
Vinci, 43
Vivarte SA, 54 (upd.)
Vivendi Universal S.A., 46 (upd.)
Wanadoo S.A., 75
Weber et Broutin France, 66
Worms et Cie, 27
Zodiac S.A., 36

Germany

A. Moksel AG, 59
A.W. Faber-Castell
Unternehmensverwaltung GmbH &
Co., 51
Adam Opel AG, 7; 21 (upd.); 61 (upd.)
adidas Group AG, 14; 33 (upd.); 75
(upd.)
Adolf Würth GmbH & Co. KG, 49
AEG A.G., I
Air Berlin GmbH & Co. Luftverkehrs
KG, 71
Aldi Einkauf GmbH & Co. OHG 13; 86
(upd.)
Alfred Kärcher GmbH & Co KG, 94
Alfred Ritter GmbH & Co. KG, 58
Allgemeiner Deutscher Automobil-Club
e.V., 100
Allianz AG, III; 15 (upd.); 57 (upd.)
ALTANA AG, 87
AMB Generali Holding AG, 51
Andreas Stihl AG & Co. KG, 16; 59
(upd.)
AOK-Bundesverband (Federation of the
AOK) 78
Aral AG, 62
ARD, 41
August Storck KG, 66
AVA AG (Allgemeine Handelsgesellschaft
der Verbraucher AG), 33
AXA Colonia Konzern AG, 27; 49 (upd.)
Axel Springer Verlag AG, IV; 20 (upd.)
Bahlsen GmbH & Co. KG, 44
Barmag AG, 39

BASF Aktiengesellschaft, I; 18 (upd.); 50
(upd.)
Bauer Publishing Group, 7
Bayer A.G., I; 13 (upd.); 41 (upd.)
Bayerische Hypotheken- und
Wechsel-Bank AG, II
Bayerische Motoren Werke AG, I; 11
(upd.); 38 (upd.)
Bayerische Vereinsbank A.G., II
Bayernwerk AG, V; 23 (upd.)
Beate Uhse AG, 96
Behr GmbH & Co. KG, 72
Beiersdorf AG, 29
Berliner Stadtreinigungsbetriebe, 58
Berliner Verkehrsbetriebe (BVG), 58
Berlinwasser Holding AG, 90
Bertelsmann A.G., IV; 15 (upd.); 43
(upd.); 91 (upd.)
Bewag AG, 39
Bibliographisches Institut & F.A.
Brockhaus AG, 74
Bilfinger & Berger AG, I; 55 (upd.)
Brauerei Beck & Co., 9; 33 (upd.)
Braun GmbH, 51
Brenntag Holding GmbH & Co. KG, 8;
23 (upd.); 101 (upd.)
Brose Fahrzeugteile GmbH & Company
KG, 84
BSH Bosch und Siemens Hausgeräte
GmbH, 67
Buderus AG, 37
Burda Holding GmbH. & Co., 23
C&A Brenninkmeyer KG, V
C. Bechstein Pianofortefabrik AG, 96
C.H. Boehringer Sohn, 39
Carl Kühne KG (GmbH & Co.), 94
Carl Zeiss AG, III; 34 (upd.); 91 (upd.)
CeWe Color Holding AG, 76
Commerzbank A.G., II; 47 (upd.)
Continental AG, V; 56 (upd.)
Cornelsen Verlagsholding GmbH & Co.,
90
Dachser GmbH & Co. KG, 88
Daimler-Benz Aerospace AG, 16
DaimlerChrysler AG, I; 15 (upd.); 34
(upd.); 64 (upd.)
Dalli-Werke GmbH & Co. KG, 86
dba Luftfahrtgesellschaft mbH, 76
Debeka Krankenversicherungsverein auf
Gegenseitigkeit, 72
Degussa Group, IV
Degussa-Huls AG, 32 (upd.)
Deutsche Babcock A.G., III
Deutsche Bahn AG, 46 (upd.)
Deutsche Bank AG, II; 14 (upd.); 40
(upd.)
Deutsche BP Aktiengesellschaft, 7
Deutsche Bundesbahn, V
Deutsche Bundespost TELEKOM, V
Deutsche Börse AG, 59
Deutsche Fussball Bund e.V., 98
Deutsche Lufthansa AG, I; 26 (upd.); 68
(upd.)
Deutsche Post AG, 29
Deutsche Steinzeug Cremer & Breuer
Aktiengesellschaft, 91
Deutsche Telekom AG, 48 (upd.)

Deutscher Sparkassen- und Giroverband
(DSGV), 84
Deutz AG, 39
Diehl Stiftung & Co. KG 79
Dirk Rossmann GmbH, 94
Dr. August Oetker KG, 51
Drägerwerk AG, 83
Dräxlmaier Group, 90
Dresdner Bank A.G., II; 57 (upd.)
Dürkopp Adler AG, 65
Dürr AG, 44
Dyckerhoff AG, 35
E.On AG, 50 (upd.)
Eckes AG, 56
Edeka Zentrale A.G., II; 47 (upd.)
edel music AG, 44
ElringKlinger AG, 100
ERGO Versicherungsgruppe AG, 44
ESCADA AG, 71
Esselte Leitz GmbH & Co. KG, 48
Etienne Aigner AG, 52
FAG—Kugelfischer Georg Schäfer AG, 62
Fairchild Dornier GmbH, 48 (upd.)
Feldmuhle Nobel A.G., III
Fielmann AG, 31
Francotyp-Postalia Holding AG, 92
Frankfurter Allgemeine Zeitung GmbH,
66
Fraport AG Frankfurt Airport Services
Worldwide, 90
Fresenius AG, 56
Freudenberg & Co., 41
Fried. Krupp GmbH, IV
Friedrich Grohe AG & Co. KG, 53
GEA AG, 27
GEHE AG, 27
Gelita AG, 74
GEMA (Gesellschaft für musikalische
Aufführungs- und mechanische
Vervielfältigungsrechte), 70
geobra Brandstätter GmbH & Co. KG,
48
Gerhard D. Wempe KG, 88
Gerling-Konzern Versicherungs-
Beteiligungs-Aktiengesellschaft, 51
Gerresheimer Glas AG, 43
Gerry Weber International AG, 63
Getrag Corporate Group, 92
GfK Aktiengesellschaft, 49
Giesecke & Devrient GmbH, 83
Gildemeister AG 79
Groz-Beckert Group, 68
Grundig AG, 27
Hansgrohe AG, 56
Hapag-Lloyd AG, 6; 97 (upd.)
HARIBO GmbH & Co. KG, 44
HDI (Haftpflichtverband der Deutschen
Industrie Versicherung auf
Gegenseitigkeit V.a.G.), 53
Heidelberger Druckmaschinen AG, 40
Heidelberger Zement AG, 31
Heinrich Deichmann-Schuhe GmbH &
Co. KG, 88
Hella KGaA Hueck & Co., 66
Henkel KGaA, III; 34 (upd.); 95 (upd.)
Heraeus Holding GmbH, IV; 54 (upd.)
Hertie Waren- und Kaufhaus GmbH, V
Hexal AG, 69

Ghana

Greece

Guatemala

Hong Kong

China Merchants International Holdings Co., Ltd., 52
CITIC Pacific Ltd., 18
Dairy Farm International Holdings Ltd., 97
First Pacific Company Limited, 18
The Garden Company Ltd., 82
GOME Electrical Appliances Holding Ltd., 87
Guangzhou R&F Properties Co., Ltd., 95
Hang Seng Bank Ltd., 60
Henderson Land Development Company Ltd., 70
Hong Kong and China Gas Company Ltd., 73
Hong Kong Dragon Airlines Ltd., 66
Hong Kong Telecommunications Ltd., 6
The Hongkong and Shanghai Banking Corporation Limited, II
Hongkong Electric Holdings Ltd., 6; 23 (upd.)
Hongkong Land Holdings Limited, IV; 47 (upd.)
Hopson Development Holdings Ltd., 87
Hutchison Whampoa Limited, 18; 49 (upd.)
Kerry Properties Limited, 22
Meyer International Holdings, Ltd., 87
Nam Tai Electronics, Inc., 61
New World Development Company Limited, IV; 38 (upd.)
Next Media Ltd., 61
Pacific Basin Shipping Ltd., 86
Playmates Toys, 23
Shangri-La Asia Ltd., 71
The Singer Company N.V., 30 (upd.)
Swire Pacific Limited, I; 16 (upd.); 57 (upd.)
Techtronic Industries Company Ltd., 73
Tommy Hilfiger Corporation, 20; 53 (upd.)
Vitasoy International Holdings Ltd., 94
VTech Holdings Ltd., 77

Hungary
Magyar Telekom Rt. 78
Malév Plc, 24
MOL Rt, 70
Orszagos Takarekpenztar es Kereskedelmi Bank Rt. (OTP Bank) 78

Iceland
Alfesca hf, 82
Bakkavör Group hf., 91
Baugur Group hf, 81
Icelandair, 52
Icelandic Group hf, 81
Landsbanki Islands hf, 81

India
Adani Enterprises Ltd., 97
Aditya Birla Group 79
Air Sahara Limited, 65
Air-India Limited, 6; 27 (upd.)
Bajaj Auto Limited, 39
Bharti Tele-Ventures Limited, 75
Coal India Limited, IV; 44 (upd.)
Dr. Reddy's Laboratories Ltd., 59

Essar Group Ltd. 79
Hindustan Lever Limited 79
Indian Airlines Ltd., 46
Indian Oil Corporation Ltd., IV; 48 (upd.)
Infosys Technologies Ltd., 38
Jaiprakash Associates Limited, 101
Jet Airways (India) Private Limited, 65
Minerals and Metals Trading Corporation of India Ltd., IV
MTR Foods Ltd., 55
Neyveli Lignite Corporation Ltd., 65
Oil and Natural Gas Corporation Ltd., IV; 90 (upd.)
Ranbaxy Laboratories Ltd., 70
Raymond Ltd., 77
Reliance Industries Ltd., 81
Rolta India Ltd., 90
Satyam Computer Services Ltd., 85
State Bank of India, 63
Steel Authority of India Ltd., IV; 66 (upd.)
Sun Pharmaceutical Industries Ltd., 57
Tata Iron & Steel Co. Ltd., IV; 44 (upd.)
Tata Tea Ltd., 76
Wipro Limited, 43

Indonesia
Djarum PT, 62
Garuda Indonesia, 6; 58 (upd.)
PERTAMINA, IV
Pertamina, 56 (upd.)
PT Astra International Tbk, 56
PT Bank Buana Indonesia Tbk, 60
PT Indosat Tbk, 93

Iran
IranAir, 81
National Iranian Oil Company, IV; 61 (upd.)

Ireland
Aer Lingus Group plc, 34; 89 (upd.)
Allied Irish Banks, plc, 16; 43 (upd.); 94 (upd.)
Baltimore Technologies Plc, 42
Bank of Ireland, 50
CRH plc, 64
DEPFA BANK PLC, 69
Dunnes Stores Ltd., 58
eircom plc, 31 (upd.)
Elan Corporation PLC, 63
Fyffes Plc, 38
Glanbia plc, 59
Glen Dimplex 78
Greencore Group plc, 98
Harland and Wolff Holdings plc, 19
IAWS Group plc, 49
Independent News & Media PLC, 61
IONA Technologies plc, 43
Irish Distillers Group, 96
Irish Life & Permanent Plc, 59
Jefferson Smurfit Group plc, IV; 19 (upd.); 49 (upd.)
Jurys Doyle Hotel Group plc, 64
Kerry Group plc, 27; 87 (upd.)
Musgrave Group Plc, 57

Paddy Power plc, 98
Ryanair Holdings plc, 35
Shannon Aerospace Ltd., 36
SkillSoft Public Limited Company, 81
Telecom Eireann, 7
Thomas Crosbie Holdings Limited, 81
Waterford Wedgwood plc, 34 (upd.)

Israel
Aladdin Knowledge Systems Ltd., 101
Amdocs Ltd., 47
Bank Hapoalim B.M., II; 54 (upd.)
Bank Leumi le-Israel B.M., 60
Blue Square Israel Ltd., 41
BVR Systems (1998) Ltd., 93
Castro Model Ltd., 86
ECI Telecom Ltd., 18
El Al Israel Airlines Ltd., 23
Elscint Ltd., 20
Galtronics Ltd., 100
Given Imaging Ltd., 83
IDB Holding Corporation Ltd., 97
Israel Aircraft Industries Ltd., 69
Israel Chemicals Ltd., 55
Koor Industries Ltd., II; 25 (upd.); 68 (upd.)
Lipman Electronic Engineering Ltd., 81
Makhteshim-Agan Industries Ltd., 85
NICE Systems Ltd., 83
Orbotech Ltd., 75
Scitex Corporation Ltd., 24
Strauss-Elite Group, 68
Syneron Medical Ltd., 91
Taro Pharmaceutical Industries Ltd., 65
Teva Pharmaceutical Industries Ltd., 22; 54 (upd.)

Italy
AgustaWestland N.V., 75
Alfa Romeo, 13; 36 (upd.)
Alitalia—Linee Aeree Italiana, S.p.A., 6; 29 (upd.); 97 (upd.)
Alleanza Assicurazioni S.p.A., 65
Angelini SpA, 100
Aprilia SpA, 17
Arnoldo Mondadori Editore S.p.A., IV; 19 (upd.); 54 (upd.)
Artsana SpA, 92
Assicurazioni Generali SpA, III; 15 (upd.)
Autogrill SpA, 49
Automobili Lamborghini Holding S.p.A., 13; 34 (upd.); 91 (upd.)
Autostrada Torino-Milano S.p.A., 101
Azelis Group, 100
Banca Commerciale Italiana SpA, II
Banca Fideuram SpA, 63
Banca Intesa SpA, 65
Banca Monte dei Paschi di Siena SpA, 65
Banca Nazionale del Lavoro SpA, 72
Barilla G. e R. Fratelli S.p.A., 17; 50 (upd.)
Benetton Group S.p.A., 10; 67 (upd.)
Brioni Roman Style S.p.A., 67
Bulgari S.p.A., 20
Cantine Giorgio Lungarotti S.R.L., 67
Capitalia S.p.A., 65
Cinemeccanica SpA 78

Compagnia Italiana dei Jolly Hotels S.p.A., 71
Credito Italiano, II
Cremonini S.p.A., 57
Davide Campari-Milano S.p.A., 57
De'Longhi S.p.A., 66
Diadora SpA, 86
Diesel SpA, 40
Dolce & Gabbana SpA, 62
Ducati Motor Holding SpA, 30; 86 (upd.)
ENI S.p.A., 69 (upd.)
Ente Nazionale Idrocarburi, IV
Ente Nazionale per L'Energia Elettrica, V
Ermenegildo Zegna SpA, 63
Fabbrica D' Armi Pietro Beretta S.p.A., 39
FASTWEB S.p.A., 83
Ferrari S.p.A., 13; 36 (upd.)
Ferrero SpA, 54
Ferretti Group SpA, 90
Fiat SpA, I; 11 (upd.); 50 (upd.)
Fila Holding S.p.A., 20; 52 (upd.)
Finarte Casa d'Aste S.p.A., 93
Finmeccanica S.p.A., 84
Gianni Versace SpA, 22
Giorgio Armani S.p.A., 45
Gruppo Coin S.p.A., 41
Gruppo Riva Fire SpA, 88
Guccio Gucci, S.p.A., 15
illycaffè SpA, 50
Industrie Natuzzi S.p.A., 18
Industrie Zignago Santa Margherita S.p.A., 67
Ing. C. Olivetti & C., S.p.a., III
Istituto per la Ricostruzione Industriale S.p.A., I; 11
Juventus F.C. S.p.A, 53
La Doria SpA, 101
Luxottica SpA, 17; 52 (upd.)
Magneti Marelli Holding SpA, 90
Marchesi Antinori SRL, 42
Marcolin S.p.A., 61
Mariella Burani Fashion Group, 92
Martini & Rossi SpA, 63
Marzotto S.p.A., 20; 67 (upd.)
Mediaset SpA, 50
Mediolanum S.p.A., 65
Milan AC, S.p.A. 79
Miroglio SpA, 86
Montedison SpA, I; 24 (upd.)
Officine Alfieri Maserati S.p.A., 13
Olivetti S.p.A., 34 (upd.)
Pagnossin S.p.A., 73
Parmalat Finanziaria SpA, 50
Peg Perego SpA, 88
Perfetti Van Melle S.p.A., 72
Piaggio & C. S.p.A., 20; 100 (upd.)
Pirelli & C. S.p.A., 75 (upd.)
Pirelli S.p.A., V; 15 (upd.)
RCS MediaGroup S.p.A., 96
Reno de Medici S.p.A., 41
Rinascente S.p.A., 71
Riunione Adriatica di Sicurtè SpA, III
Safilo SpA, 54
Salvatore Ferragamo Italia S.p.A., 62
Sanpaolo IMI S.p.A., 50
Seat Pagine Gialle S.p.A., 47
Sirti S.p.A., 76

Società Finanziaria Telefonica per Azioni, V
Società Sportiva Lazio SpA, 44
Stefanel SpA, 63
Targetti Sankey SpA, 86
Telecom Italia Mobile S.p.A., 63
Telecom Italia S.p.A., 43
Tiscali SpA, 48

Jamaica
Air Jamaica Limited, 54
Desnoes and Geddes Limited 79
GraceKennedy Ltd., 92
Wray & Nephew Group Ltd., 98

Japan
AEON Co., Ltd., 68 (upd.)
Aisin Seiki Co., Ltd., III; 48 (upd.)
Aiwa Co., Ltd., 30
Ajinomoto Co., Inc., II; 28 (upd.)
All Nippon Airways Co., Ltd., 6; 38 (upd.); 91 (upd.)
Alpine Electronics, Inc., 13
Alps Electric Co., Ltd., II; 44 (upd.)
Anritsu Corporation, 68
Asahi Breweries, Ltd., I; 20 (upd.); 52 (upd.)
Asahi Denka Kogyo KK, 64
Asahi Glass Company, Ltd., III; 48 (upd.)
Asahi National Broadcasting Company, Ltd., 9
Asatsu-DK Inc., 82
ASICS Corporation, 57
Astellas Pharma Inc., 97 (upd.)
Autobacs Seven Company Ltd., 76
Bandai Co., Ltd., 55
Bank of Tokyo-Mitsubishi Ltd., II; 15 (upd.)
Benesse Corporation, 76
Bourbon Corporation, 82
Bridgestone Corporation, V; 21 (upd.); 59 (upd.)
Brother Industries, Ltd., 14
C. Itoh & Company Ltd., I
Canon Inc., III; 18 (upd.); 79 (upd.)
Capcom Company Ltd., 83
CASIO Computer Co., Ltd., III; 16 (upd.); 40 (upd.)
Central Japan Railway Company, 43
Chubu Electric Power Company, Inc., V; 46 (upd.)
Chugai Pharmaceutical Co., Ltd., 50
Chugoku Electric Power Company Inc., V; 53 (upd.)
Citizen Watch Co., Ltd., III; 21 (upd.); 81 (upd.)
Clarion Company Ltd., 64
Cosmo Oil Co., Ltd., IV; 53 (upd.)
Dai Nippon Printing Co., Ltd., IV; 57 (upd.)
The Dai-Ichi Kangyo Bank Ltd., II
Daido Steel Co., Ltd., IV
The Daiei, Inc., V; 17 (upd.); 41 (upd.)
Daihatsu Motor Company, Ltd., 7; 21 (upd.)
Daiichikosho Company Ltd., 86
Daikin Industries, Ltd., III

Daiko Advertising Inc. 79
The Daimaru, Inc., V; 42 (upd.)
Daio Paper Corporation, IV, 84 (upd.)
Daishowa Paper Manufacturing Co., Ltd., IV; 57 (upd.)
The Daiwa Bank, Ltd., II; 39 (upd.)
Daiwa Securities Group Inc., II; 55 (upd.)
DDI Corporation, 7
DENSO Corporation, 46 (upd.)
Dentsu Inc., I; 16 (upd.); 40 (upd.)
East Japan Railway Company, V; 66 (upd.)
Ebara Corporation, 83
Eisai Co., Ltd., 101
Elpida Memory, Inc., 83
Ezaki Glico Company Ltd., 72
Fanuc Ltd., III; 17 (upd.); 75 (upd.)
The Fuji Bank, Ltd., II
Fuji Electric Co., Ltd., II; 48 (upd.)
Fuji Photo Film Co., Ltd., III; 18 (upd.); 79 (upd.)
Fuji Television Network Inc., 91
Fujisawa Pharmaceutical Company, Ltd., I; 58 (upd.)
Fujitsu Limited, III; 16 (upd.); 42 (upd.)
Funai Electric Company Ltd., 62
The Furukawa Electric Co., Ltd., III
General Sekiyu K.K., IV
Hakuhodo, Inc., 6; 42 (upd.)
Hankyu Department Stores, Inc., V; 23 (upd.); 62 (upd.)
Hagoromo Foods Corporation, 84
Hino Motors, Ltd., 7; 21 (upd.)
Hitachi, Ltd., I; 12 (upd.); 40 (upd.)
Hitachi Metals, Ltd., IV
Hitachi Zosen Corporation, III; 53 (upd.)
Hokkaido Electric Power Company Inc. (HEPCO), V; 58 (upd.)
Hokuriku Electric Power Company, V
Honda Motor Company Ltd., I; 10 (upd.); 29 (upd.); 96 (upd.)
Honshu Paper Co., Ltd., IV
Hoshino Gakki Co. Ltd., 55
Idemitsu Kosan Co., Ltd., IV; 49 (upd.)
The Industrial Bank of Japan, Ltd., II
INPEX Holdings Inc., 97
Isetan Company Limited, V; 36 (upd.)
Ishikawajima-Harima Heavy Industries Company, Ltd., III; 86 (upd.)
Isuzu Motors, Ltd., 9; 23 (upd.); 57 (upd.)
Ito En Ltd., 101
Ito-Yokado Co., Ltd., V; 42 (upd.)
ITOCHU Corporation, 32 (upd.)
Itoham Foods Inc., II; 61 (upd.)
Japan Airlines Company, Ltd., I; 32 (upd.)
JAFCO Co. Ltd. 79
Japan Broadcasting Corporation, 7
Japan Leasing Corporation, 8
Japan Pulp and Paper Company Limited, IV
Japan Tobacco Inc., V; 46 (upd.)
JFE Shoji Holdings Inc., 88
JSP Corporation, 74
Jujo Paper Co., Ltd., IV
JUSCO Co., Ltd., V
Kajima Corporation, I; 51 (upd.)

Kanebo, Ltd., 53
Kanematsu Corporation, IV; 24 (upd.)
The Kansai Electric Power Company, Inc.,
    V; 62 (upd.)
Kansai Paint Company Ltd., 80
Kao Corporation, III; 20 (upd.); 79
    (upd.)
Katokichi Company Ltd., 82
Kawai Musical Instruments Mfg Co. Ltd.
    78
Kawasaki Heavy Industries, Ltd., III; 63
    (upd.)
Kawasaki Kisen Kaisha, Ltd., V; 56 (upd.)
Kawasaki Steel Corporation, IV
Keio Corporation, V; 96 (upd.)
Kenwood Corporation, 31
Kewpie Kabushiki Kaisha, 57
Kikkoman Corporation, 14; 47 (upd.)
Kinki Nippon Railway Company Ltd., V
Kirin Brewery Company, Limited, I; 21
    (upd.); 63 (upd.)
Kobe Steel, Ltd., IV; 19 (upd.)
Kodansha Ltd., IV; 38 (upd.)
Komatsu Ltd., III; 16 (upd.); 52 (upd.)
Konami Corporation, 96
Konica Corporation, III; 30 (upd.)
Kotobukiya Co., Ltd., V; 56 (upd.)
Kubota Corporation, III; 26 (upd.)
Kumagai Gumi Company, Ltd., I
Kumon Institute of Education Co., Ltd.,
    72
Kyocera Corporation, II; 21 (upd.); 79
    (upd.)
Kyokuyo Company Ltd., 75
Kyowa Hakko Kogyo Co., Ltd., III; 48
    (upd.)
Kyushu Electric Power Company Inc., V
Lion Corporation, III; 51 (upd.)
Long-Term Credit Bank of Japan, Ltd., II
Mabuchi Motor Co. Ltd., 68
Makita Corporation, 22; 59 (upd.)
Mandom Corporation, 82
Marubeni Corporation, I; 24 (upd.)
Maruha Group Inc., 75 (upd.)
Marui Company Ltd., V; 62 (upd.)
Maruzen Co., Limited, 18
Matsushita Electric Industrial Co., Ltd.,
    II; 64 (upd.)
Matsushita Electric Works, Ltd., III; 7
    (upd.)
Matsuzakaya Company Ltd., V; 64 (upd.)
Mazda Motor Corporation, 9; 23 (upd.);
    63 (upd.)
Meidensha Corporation, 92
Meiji Dairies Corporation, II; 82 (upd.)
The Meiji Mutual Life Insurance
    Company, III
Meiji Seika Kaisha Ltd., II; 64 (upd.)
Mercian Corporation, 77
Millea Holdings Inc., 64 (upd.)
Minebea Co., Ltd., 90
Minolta Co., Ltd., III; 18 (upd.); 43
    (upd.)
The Mitsubishi Bank, Ltd., II
Mitsubishi Chemical Corporation, I; 56
    (upd.)
Mitsubishi Corporation, I; 12 (upd.)

Mitsubishi Electric Corporation, II; 44
    (upd.)
Mitsubishi Estate Company, Limited, IV;
    61 (upd.)
Mitsubishi Heavy Industries, Ltd., III; 7
    (upd.); 40 (upd.)
Mitsubishi Materials Corporation, III
Mitsubishi Motors Corporation, 9; 23
    (upd.); 57 (upd.)
Mitsubishi Oil Co., Ltd., IV
Mitsubishi Rayon Co., Ltd., V
The Mitsubishi Trust & Banking
    Corporation, II
Mitsubishi UFJ Financial Group, Inc., 99
    (upd.)
Mitsui & Co., Ltd., 28 (upd.)
The Mitsui Bank, Ltd., II
Mitsui Bussan K.K., I
Mitsui Marine and Fire Insurance
    Company, Limited, II
Mitsui Mining & Smelting Co., Ltd., IV
Mitsui Mining Company, Limited, IV
Mitsui Mutual Life Insurance Company,
    III; 39 (upd.)
Mitsui O.S.K. Lines, Ltd., V; 96 (upd.)
Mitsui Petrochemical Industries, Ltd., 9
Mitsui Real Estate Development Co.,
    Ltd., IV
The Mitsui Trust & Banking Company,
    Ltd., II
Mitsukoshi Ltd., V; 56 (upd.)
Mizuho Financial Group Inc., 58 (upd.)
Mizuno Corporation, 25
Morinaga & Co. Ltd., 61
Nagasakiya Co., Ltd., V; 69 (upd.)
Nagase & Co., Ltd., 8; 61 (upd.)
NEC Corporation, II; 21 (upd.); 57
    (upd.)
NGK Insulators Ltd., 67
NHK Spring Co., Ltd., III
Nichii Co., Ltd., V
Nichimen Corporation, IV; 24 (upd.)
Nichirei Corporation, 70
Nichiro Corporation, 86
Nidec Corporation, 59
Nihon Keizai Shimbun, Inc., IV
The Nikko Securities Company Limited,
    II; 9 (upd.)
Nikon Corporation, III; 48 (upd.)
Nintendo Co., Ltd., III; 7 (upd.); 28
    (upd.); 67 (upd.)
Nippon Credit Bank, II
Nippon Electric Glass Co. Ltd., 95
Nippon Express Company, Ltd., V; 64
    (upd.)
Nippon Life Insurance Company, III; 60
    (upd.)
Nippon Light Metal Company, Ltd., IV
Nippon Meat Packers Inc., II, 78 (upd.)
Nippon Oil Corporation, IV; 63 (upd.)
Nippon Seiko K.K., III
Nippon Sheet Glass Company, Limited,
    III
Nippon Shinpan Co., Ltd., II; 61 (upd.)
Nippon Soda Co., Ltd., 85
Nippon Steel Corporation, IV; 17 (upd.);
    96 (upd.)
Nippon Suisan Kaisha, Ltd., II; 92 (upd.)

Nippon Telegraph and Telephone
    Corporation, V; 51 (upd.)
Nippon Yusen Kabushiki Kaisha (NYK),
    V; 72 (upd.)
Nippondenso Co., Ltd., III
Nissan Motor Company Ltd., I; 11
    (upd.); 34 (upd.); 92 (upd.)
Nisshin Seifun Group Inc., II; 66 (upd.)
Nisshin Steel Co., Ltd., IV
Nissho Iwai K.K., I
Nissin Food Products Company Ltd., 75
NKK Corporation, IV; 28 (upd.)
NOF Corporation, 72
Nomura Securities Company, Limited, II;
    9 (upd.)
Norinchukin Bank, II
NTN Corporation, III; 47 (upd.)
Obayashi Corporation 78
Odakyu Electric Railway Co., Ltd., V; 68
    (upd.)
Ohbayashi Corporation, I
Oji Paper Co., Ltd., IV; 57 (upd.)
Oki Electric Industry Company, Limited,
    II
Okuma Holdings Inc., 74
Okura & Co., Ltd., IV
Omron Corporation, II; 28 (upd.)
Onoda Cement Co., Ltd., III
ORIX Corporation, II; 44 (upd.)
Osaka Gas Company, Ltd., V; 60 (upd.)
Otari Inc., 89
Paloma Industries Ltd., 71
Pearl Corporation 78
Pentax Corporation 78
Pioneer Electronic Corporation, III; 28
    (upd.)
Rengo Co., Ltd., IV
Ricoh Company, Ltd., III; 36 (upd.)
Roland Corporation, 38
Ryoshoku Ltd., 72
Sankyo Company, Ltd., I; 56 (upd.)
Sanrio Company, Ltd., 38
The Sanwa Bank, Ltd., II; 15 (upd.)
SANYO Electric Co., Ltd., II; 36 (upd.);
    95 (upd.)
Sanyo-Kokusaku Pulp Co., Ltd., IV
Sapporo Holdings Limited, I; 13 (upd.);
    36 (upd.); 97 (upd.)
SEGA Corporation, 73
Seibu Department Stores, Ltd., V; 42
    (upd.)
Seibu Railway Company Ltd., V; 74
    (upd.)
Seiko Corporation, III; 17 (upd.); 72
    (upd.)
Seino Transportation Company, Ltd., 6
The Seiyu, Ltd., V; 36 (upd.)
Sekisui Chemical Co., Ltd., III; 72 (upd.)
Sharp Corporation, II; 12 (upd.); 40
    (upd.)
Shikoku Electric Power Company, Inc., V;
    60 (upd.)
Shimano Inc., 64
Shionogi & Co., Ltd., III; 17 (upd.); 98
    (upd.)
Shiseido Company, Limited, III; 22
    (upd.), 81 (upd.)
Shochiku Company Ltd., 74

Sompo Japan Insurance, Inc., 98 (upd.)
Showa Shell Sekiyu K.K., IV; 59 (upd.)
Snow Brand Milk Products Company, Ltd., II; 48 (upd.)
Softbank Corp., 13; 38 (upd.)
Sojitz Corporation, 96 (upd.)
Sony Corporation, II; 12 (upd.); 40 (upd.)
Square Enix Holdings Co., Ltd., 101
The Sumitomo Bank, Limited, II; 26 (upd.)
Sumitomo Chemical Company Ltd., I; 98 (upd.)
Sumitomo Corporation, I; 11 (upd.)
Sumitomo Electric Industries, Ltd., II
Sumitomo Heavy Industries, Ltd., III; 42 (upd.)
Sumitomo Life Insurance Company, III; 60 (upd.)
The Sumitomo Marine and Fire Insurance Company, Limited, III
Sumitomo Metal Industries Ltd., IV; 82 (upd.)
Sumitomo Metal Mining Co., Ltd., IV
Sumitomo Mitsui Banking Corporation, 51 (upd.)
Sumitomo Realty & Development Co., Ltd., IV
Sumitomo Rubber Industries, Ltd., V
The Sumitomo Trust & Banking Company, Ltd., II; 53 (upd.)
Suntory Ltd., 65
Suzuki Motor Corporation, 9; 23 (upd.); 59 (upd.)
Taiheiyo Cement Corporation, 60 (upd.)
Taiyo Fishery Company, Limited, II
The Taiyo Kobe Bank, Ltd., II
Takara Holdings Inc., 62
Takashimaya Company, Limited, V; 47 (upd.)
Takeda Chemical Industries, Ltd., I; 46 (upd.)
Tamron Company Ltd., 82
TDK Corporation, II; 17 (upd.); 49 (upd.)
TEAC Corporation 78
Teijin Limited, V; 61 (upd.)
Terumo Corporation, 48
Tobu Railway Company Ltd., 6; 98 (upd.)
Tohan Corporation, 84
Toho Co., Ltd., 28
Tohoku Electric Power Company, Inc., V
The Tokai Bank, Limited, II; 15 (upd.)
The Tokio Marine and Fire Insurance Co., Ltd., III
The Tokyo Electric Power Company, 74 (upd.)
The Tokyo Electric Power Company, Incorporated, V
Tokyo Gas Co., Ltd., V; 55 (upd.)
Tokyu Corporation, V; 47 (upd.)
Tokyu Department Store Co., Ltd., V; 32 (upd.)
Tokyu Land Corporation, IV
Tomen Corporation, IV; 24 (upd.)
Tomy Company Ltd., 65

TonenGeneral Sekiyu K.K., IV; 16 (upd.); 54 (upd.)
Topcon Corporation, 84
Toppan Printing Co., Ltd., IV; 58 (upd.)
Toray Industries, Inc., V; 51 (upd.)
Toshiba Corporation, I; 12 (upd.); 40 (upd.); 99 (upd.)
Tosoh Corporation, 70
TOTO LTD., III; 28 (upd.)
Toyo Sash Co., Ltd., III
Toyo Seikan Kaisha, Ltd., I
Toyoda Automatic Loom Works, Ltd., III
Toyota Motor Corporation, I; 11 (upd.); 38 (upd.); 100 (upd.)
Trend Micro Inc., 97
Ube Industries, Ltd., III; 38 (upd.)
ULVAC, Inc., 80
Unicharm Corporation, 84
Uniden Corporation, 98
Unitika Ltd., V; 53 (upd.)
Uny Co., Ltd., V; 49 (upd.)
Ushio Inc., 91
Victor Company of Japan, Limited, II; 26 (upd.); 83 (upd.)
Wacoal Corp., 25
Yamada Denki Co., Ltd., 85
Yamaha Corporation, III; 16 (upd.); 40 (upd.); 99 (upd.)
Yamaichi Securities Company, Limited, II
Yamato Transport Co. Ltd., V; 49 (upd.)
Yamazaki Baking Co., Ltd., 58
The Yasuda Fire and Marine Insurance Company, Limited, III
The Yasuda Mutual Life Insurance Company, III; 39 (upd.)
The Yasuda Trust and Banking Company, Ltd., II; 17 (upd.)
The Yokohama Rubber Company, Limited, V; 19 (upd.); 91 (upd.)
Yoshinoya D & C Company Ltd., 88

Jordan
Arab Potash Company, 85

Kenya
Kenya Airways Limited, 89

Kuwait
Kuwait Airways Corporation, 68
Kuwait Flour Mills & Bakeries Company, 84
Kuwait Petroleum Corporation, IV; 55 (upd.)

Latvia
A/S Air Baltic Corporation, 71

Lebanon
Middle East Airlines - Air Liban S.A.L. 79

Libya
National Oil Corporation, IV; 66 (upd.)

Liechtenstein
Hilti AG, 53

Luxembourg
ARBED S.A., IV; 22 (upd.)
Cactus S.A., 90

Cargolux Airlines International S.A., 49
Elite World S.A., 94
Espèrito Santo Financial Group S.A. 79 (upd.)
Gemplus International S.A., 64
Metro International S.A., 93
RTL Group SA, 44
Société Luxembourgeoise de Navigation Aérienne S.A., 64
Tenaris SA, 63

Malaysia
AirAsia Berhad, 93
Berjaya Group Bhd., 67
Gano Excel Enterprise Sdn. Bhd., 89
Genting Bhd., 65
Malayan Banking Berhad, 72
Malaysian Airlines System Berhad, 6; 29 (upd.); 97 (upd.)
Perusahaan Otomobil Nasional Bhd., 62
Petroliam Nasional Bhd (Petronas), IV; 56 (upd.)
PPB Group Berhad, 57
Sime Darby Berhad, 14; 36 (upd.)
Telekom Malaysia Bhd, 76
Yeo Hiap Seng Malaysia Bhd., 75

Mauritius
Air Mauritius Ltd., 63

Mexico
Alfa, S.A. de C.V., 19
Altos Hornos de México, S.A. de C.V., 42
América Móvil, S.A. de C.V., 80
Apasco S.A. de C.V., 51
Bolsa Mexicana de Valores, S.A. de C.V., 80
Bufete Industrial, S.A. de C.V., 34
Casa Cuervo, S.A. de C.V., 31
Celanese Mexicana, S.A. de C.V., 54
CEMEX S.A. de C.V., 20; 59 (upd.)
Cifra, S.A. de C.V., 12
Cinemas de la República, S.A. de C.V., 83
Compañia Industrial de Parras, S.A. de C.V. (CIPSA), 84
Consorcio ARA, S.A. de C.V. 79
Consorcio Aviacsa, S.A. de C.V., 85
Consorcio G Grupo Dina, S.A. de C.V., 36
Controladora Comercial Mexicana, S.A. de C.V., 36
Controladora Mabe, S.A. de C.V., 82
Coppel, S.A. de C.V., 82
Corporación Geo, S.A. de C.V., 81
Corporación Interamericana de Entretenimiento, S.A. de C.V., 83
Corporación Internacional de Aviación, S.A. de C.V. (Cintra), 20
Desarrolladora Homex, S.A. de C.V., 87
Desc, S.A. de C.V., 23
Editorial Television, S.A. de C.V., 57
Empresas ICA Sociedad Controladora, S.A. de C.V., 41
El Puerto de Liverpool, S.A.B. de C.V., 97
Ford Motor Company, S.A. de C.V., 20
Gruma, S.A. de C.V., 31
Grupo Aeroportuario del Centro Norte, S.A.B. de C.V., 97

Grupo Aeroportuario del Pacífico, S.A. de C.V., 85
Grupo Aeropuerto del Sureste, S.A. de C.V., 48
Grupo Ángeles Servicios de Salud, S.A. de C.V., 84
Grupo Carso, S.A. de C.V., 21
Grupo Casa Saba, S.A. de C.V., 39
Grupo Comercial Chedraui S.A. de C.V., 86
Grupo Corvi S.A. de C.V., 86
Grupo Cydsa, S.A. de C.V., 39
Grupo Elektra, S.A. de C.V., 39
Grupo Financiero Banamex S.A., 54
Grupo Financiero Banorte, S.A. de C.V., 51
Grupo Financiero BBVA Bancomer S.A., 54
Grupo Financiero Serfín, S.A., 19
Grupo Gigante, S.A. de C.V., 34
Grupo Herdez, S.A. de C.V., 35
Grupo IMSA, S.A. de C.V., 44
Grupo Industrial Bimbo, 19
Grupo Industrial Durango, S.A. de C.V., 37
Grupo Industrial Herradura, S.A. de C.V., 83
Grupo Industrial Lala, S.A. de C.V., 82
Grupo Industrial Saltillo, S.A. de C.V., 54
Grupo Mexico, S.A. de C.V., 40
Grupo Modelo, S.A. de C.V., 29
Grupo Omnilife S.A. de C.V., 88
Grupo Posadas, S.A. de C.V., 57
Grupo Televisa, S.A., 18; 54 (upd.)
Grupo TMM, S.A. de C.V., 50
Grupo Transportación Ferroviaria Mexicana, S.A. de C.V., 47
Grupo Viz, S.A. de C.V., 84
Hylsamex, S.A. de C.V., 39
Industrias Bachoco, S.A. de C.V., 39
Industrias Penoles, S.A. de C.V., 22
Internacional de Ceramica, S.A. de C.V., 53
Jugos del Valle, S.A. de C.V., 85
Kimberly-Clark de México, S.A. de C.V., 54
Mexichem, S.A.B. de C.V., 99
Nadro S.A. de C.V., 86
Organización Soriana, S.A. de C.V., 35
Petróleos Mexicanos, IV; 19 (upd.)
Proeza S.A. de C.V., 82
Pulsar Internacional S.A., 21
Real Turismo, S.A. de C.V., 50
Sanborn Hermanos, S.A., 20
SANLUIS Corporación, S.A.B. de C.V., 95
Sears Roebuck de México, S.A. de C.V., 20
Telefonos de Mexico S.A. de C.V., 14; 63 (upd.)
Tubos de Acero de Mexico, S.A. (TAMSA), 41
TV Azteca, S.A. de C.V., 39
Urbi Desarrollos Urbanos, S.A. de C.V., 81
Valores Industriales S.A., 19
Vitro Corporativo S.A. de C.V., 34

Wal-Mart de Mexico, S.A. de C.V., 35 (upd.)

Nepal
Royal Nepal Airline Corporation, 41

Netherlands
ABN AMRO Holding, N.V., 50
AEGON N.V., III; 50 (upd.)
Akzo Nobel N.V., 13; 41 (upd.)
Algemene Bank Nederland N.V., II
Amsterdam-Rotterdam Bank N.V., II
Arcadis NV, 26
ASML Holding N.V., 50
Avantium Technologies BV 79
Baan Company, 25
Blokker Holding B.V., 84
Bols Distilleries NV, 74
Bolton Group B.V., 86
Buhrmann NV, 41
The Campina Group, The 78
Chicago Bridge & Iron Company N.V., 82 (upd.)
CNH Global N.V., 38 (upd.); 99 (upd.)
CSM N.V., 65
Deli Universal NV, 66
Drie Mollen Holding B.V., 99
DSM N.V., I; 56 (upd.)
Elsevier N.V., IV
Endemol Entertainment Holding NV, 46
Equant N.V., 52
Euronext N.V., 89 (upd.)
European Aeronautic Defence and Space Company EADS N.V., 52 (upd.)
Friesland Coberco Dairy Foods Holding N.V., 59
Fugro N.V., 98
Getronics NV, 39
Granaria Holdings B.V., 66
Grand Hotel Krasnapolsky N.V., 23
Greenpeace International, 74
Gucci Group N.V., 50
Hagemeyer N.V., 39
Head N.V., 55
Heijmans N.V., 66
Heineken N.V., I; 13 (upd.); 34 (upd.); 90 (upd.)
IHC Caland N.V., 71
IKEA Group, 94 (upd.)
Indigo NV, 26
Intres B.V., 82
Ispat International N.V., 30
Koninklijke Ahold N.V. (Royal Ahold), II; 16 (upd.)
Koninklijke Houthandel G Wijma & Zonen BV, 96
Koninklijke Luchtvaart Maatschappij, N.V. (KLM Royal Dutch Airlines), I; 28 (upd.)
Koninklijke Nederlandsche Hoogovens en Staalfabrieken NV, IV
Koninklijke Nedlloyd N.V., 6; 26 (upd.)
Koninklijke Philips Electronics N.V., 50 (upd.)
Koninklijke PTT Nederland NV, V
Koninklijke Vendex KBB N.V. (Royal Vendex KBB N.V.), 62 (upd.)

Koninklijke Wessanen nv, II; 54 (upd.)
KPMG International, 10; 33 (upd.)
Laurus N.V., 65
Mammoet Transport B.V., 26
MIH Limited, 31
N.V. AMEV, III
N.V. Holdingmaatschappij De Telegraaf, 23
N.V. Koninklijke Nederlandse Vliegtuigenfabriek Fokker, I; 28 (upd.)
N.V. Nederlandse Gasunie, V
Nationale-Nederlanden N.V., III
New Holland N.V., 22
Nutreco Holding N.V., 56
Océ N.V., 24; 91 (upd.)
PCM Uitgevers NV, 53
Philips Electronics N.V., II; 13 (upd.)
PolyGram N.V., 23
Prada Holding B.V., 45
Qiagen N.V., 39
Rabobank Group, 33
Randstad Holding n.v., 16; 43 (upd.)
Rodamco N.V., 26
Royal Dutch/Shell Group, IV; 49 (upd.)
Royal Grolsch NV, 54
Royal KPN N.V., 30
Royal Numico N.V., 37
Royal Packaging Industries Van Leer N.V., 30
Royal Ten Cate N.V., 68
Royal Vopak NV, 41
SHV Holdings N.V., 55
Telegraaf Media Groep N.V., 98 (upd.)
Tennet BV 78
TNT Post Group N.V., V, 27 (upd.); 30 (upd.)
Toolex International N.V., 26
TomTom N.V., 81
TPG N.V., 64 (upd.)
Trader Classified Media N.V., 57
Triple P N.V., 26
Unilever N.V., II; 7 (upd.); 32 (upd.)
United Pan-Europe Communications NV, 47
Van Lanschot NV 79
VBA - Bloemenveiling Aalsmeer, 88
Vebego International BV, 49
Vedior NV, 35
Velcro Industries N.V., 19
Vendex International N.V., 13
Vion Food Group NV, 85
VNU N.V., 27
Wegener NV, 53
Wolters Kluwer NV, 14; 33 (upd.)
Zentiva N.V./Zentiva, a.s., 99

Netherlands Antilles
Orthofix International NV, 72
Velcro Industries N.V., 72

New Zealand
Air New Zealand Limited, 14; 38 (upd.)
Carter Holt Harvey Ltd., 70
Cerebos Gregg's Ltd., 100
Fletcher Challenge Ltd., IV; 19 (upd.)
Fonterra Co-Operative Group Ltd., 58
Frucor Beverages Group Ltd., 96
Nuplex Industries Ltd., 92

Progressive Enterprises Ltd., 96
Telecom Corporation of New Zealand
  Limited, 54
Wattie's Ltd., 7

Nigeria
Nigerian National Petroleum Corporation,
  IV; 72 (upd.)

Norway
Braathens ASA, 47
Den Norse Stats Oljeselskap AS, IV
Helly Hansen ASA, 25
Jotun A/S, 80
K.A. Rasmussen AS, 99
Kvaerner ASA, 36
Norsk Hydro ASA, 10; 35 (upd.)
Norske Skogindustrier ASA, 63
Odfjell SE, 101
Orkla ASA, 18; 82 (upd.)
Schibsted ASA, 31
Statoil ASA, 61 (upd.)
Stolt Sea Farm Holdings PLC, 54
Telenor ASA, 69
Veidekke ASA, 98
Vinmonopolet A/S, 100
Wilh. Wilhelmsen ASA, 94
Yara International ASA, 94

Oman
Petroleum Development Oman LLC, IV;
  98 (upd.)
The Zubair Corporation L.L.C., 96

Pakistan
Pakistan International Airlines
  Corporation, 46
Pakistan State Oil Company Ltd., 81

Panama
Autoridad del Canal de Panamá, 94
Copa Holdings, S.A., 93
Panamerican Beverages, Inc., 47
Willbros Group, Inc., 56

Papua New Guinea
Steamships Trading Company Ltd., 82

Paraguay
Banco Central del Paraguay, 100

Peru
Ajegroup S.A., 92
Banco de Crédito del Perú, 93
Compañia de Minas Buenaventura S.A.A.,
  93
Corporación José R. Lindley S.A., 92
Grupo Brescia, 99
Southern Peru Copper Corporation, 40
Unión de Cervecerias Peruanas Backus y
  Johnston S.A.A., 92
Volcan Compañia Minera S.A.A., 92

Philippines
Bank of the Philippine Islands, 58
Benguet Corporation, 58

Manila Electric Company (Meralco), 56
Mercury Drug Corporation, 70
Petron Corporation, 58
Philippine Airlines, Inc., 6; 23 (upd.)
San Miguel Corporation, 15; 57 (upd.)

Poland
Agora S.A. Group, 77
LOT Polish Airlines (Polskie Linie
  Lotnicze S.A.), 33
KGHM Polska Miedz S.A., 98
Narodowy Bank Polski, 100
Polski Koncern Naftowy ORLEN S.A., 77
Telekomunikacja Polska SA, 50
Zakłady Azotowe Puławy S.A., 100

Portugal
Banco Comercial Português, SA, 50
Banco Espírito Santo e Comercial de
  Lisboa S.A., 15
BRISA Auto-estradas de Portugal S.A., 64
Cimentos de Portugal SGPS S.A.
  (Cimpor), 76
Corticeira Amorim, Sociedade Gestora de
  Participaço es Sociais, S.A., 48
Electricidade de Portugal, S.A., 47
Galp Energia SGPS S.A., 98
Grupo Portucel Soporcel, 60
Jerónimo Martins SGPS S.A., 96
José de Mello SGPS S.A., 96
Madeira Wine Company, S.A., 49
Mota-Engil, SGPS, S.A., 97
Petróleos de Portugal S.A., IV
Portugal Telecom SGPS S.A., 69
Sonae SGPS, S.A., 97
TAP—Air Portugal Transportes Aéreos
  Portugueses S.A., 46
Transportes Aereos Portugueses, S.A., 6

Puerto Rico
Puerto Rico Electric Power Authority, 47

Qatar
Aljazeera Satellite Channel 79
Qatar Airways Company Q.C.S.C., 87
Qatar General Petroleum Corporation, IV
Qatar National Bank SAQ, 87
Qatar Petroleum, 98
Qatar Telecom QSA, 87

Republic of Yemen
Hayel Saeed Anam Group of Cos., 92

Romania
Dobrogea Grup S.A., 82
TAROM S.A., 64

Russia
A.S. Yakovlev Design Bureau, 15
Aeroflot - Russian Airlines JSC, 6; 29
  (upd.); 89 (upd.)
Alfa Group, 99
Alrosa Company Ltd., 62
AO VimpelCom, 48
Aviacionny Nauchno-Tehnicheskii
  Komplex im. A.N. Tupoleva, 24

AVTOVAZ Joint Stock Company, 65
Baltika Brewery Joint Stock Company, 65
Evraz Group S.A., 97
Golden Telecom, Inc., 59
Interfax News Agency, 86
Irkut Corporation, 68
JSC MMC Norilsk Nickel, 48
Mechel OAO, 99
Mobile TeleSystems OJSC, 59
OAO Gazprom, 42
OAO LUKOIL, 40
OAO NK YUKOS, 47
OAO Siberian Oil Company (Sibneft), 49
OAO Surgutneftegaz, 48
OAO Tatneft, 45
OJSC Novolipetsk Steel, 99
OJSC Wimm-Bill-Dann Foods, 48
RAO Unified Energy System of Russia, 45
Rostelecom Joint Stock Co., 99
Rostvertol plc, 62
Russian Aircraft Corporation (MiG), 86
Russian Railways Joint Stock Co., 93
Sberbank, 62
Severstal Joint Stock Company, 65
Sistema JSFC, 73
Sukhoi Design Bureau Aviation
  Scientific-Industrial Complex, 24
CJSC Transmash Holding, 93
Oil Transporting Joint Stock Company
  Transneft, 93
Volga-Dnepr Group, 82

Saudi Arabia
Dallah Albaraka Group, 72
Saudi Arabian Airlines, 6; 27 (upd.)
Saudi Arabian Oil Company, IV; 17
  (upd.); 50 (upd.)
Saudi Basic Industries Corporation
  (SABIC), 58

Scotland
Arnold Clark Automobiles Ltd., 60
Distillers Company PLC, I
General Accident PLC, III
The Governor and Company of the Bank
  of Scotland, 10
The Royal Bank of Scotland Group plc,
  12
Scottish & Newcastle plc, 15
Scottish Hydro-Electric PLC, 13
Scottish Media Group plc, 32
ScottishPower plc, 19
Stagecoach Holdings plc, 30
The Standard Life Assurance Company,
  III

Singapore
Asia Pacific Breweries Limited, 59
City Developments Limited, 89
Creative Technology Ltd., 57
Flextronics International Ltd., 38
Fraser & Neave Ltd., 54
Hotel Properties Ltd., 71
Jardine Cycle & Carriage Ltd., 73
Keppel Corporation Ltd., 73
Neptune Orient Lines Limited, 47
Pacific Internet Limited, 87
Singapore Airlines Limited, 6; 27 (upd.);
  83 (upd.)

Singapore Press Holdings Limited, 85
StarHub Ltd., 77
United Overseas Bank Ltd., 56

South Africa

African Rainbow Minerals Ltd., 97
Anglo American Corporation of South
   Africa Limited, IV; 16 (upd.)
Barlow Rand Ltd., I
De Beers Consolidated Mines Limited/De
   Beers Centenary AG, IV; 7 (upd.); 28
   (upd.)
Dimension Data Holdings PLC, 69
Edgars Consolidated Stores Ltd., 66
Famous Brands Ltd., 86
Gencor Ltd., IV; 22 (upd.)
Gold Fields Ltd., IV; 62 (upd.)
Harmony Gold Mining Company
   Limited, 63
Highveld Steel and Vanadium
   Corporation Limited, 59
Iscor Limited, 57
Naspers Ltd., 66
New Clicks Holdings Ltd., 86
Pick 'n Pay Stores Ltd., 82
SAA (Pty) Ltd., 28
Sanlam Ltd., 68
Sappi Limited, 49
Sasol Limited, IV; 47 (upd.)
The South African Breweries Limited, I;
   24 (upd.)
Transnet Ltd., 6

South Korea

Anam Group, 23
Asiana Airlines, Inc., 46
CJ Corporation, 62
Daesang Corporation, 84
Daewoo Group, III; 18 (upd.); 57 (upd.)
Electronics Co., Ltd., 14
Goldstar Co., Ltd., 12
Hanjin Shipping Co., Ltd., 50
Hanwha Group, 62
Hite Brewery Company Ltd., 97
Hyundai Group, III; 7 (upd.); 56 (upd.)
Kia Motors Corporation, 12; 29 (upd.)
Kookmin Bank, 58
Korea Electric Power Corporation
   (Kepco), 56
Korean Air Lines Co., Ltd., 6; 27 (upd.)
KT&G Corporation, 62
LG Corporation, 94 (upd.)
Lotte Confectionery Company Ltd., 76
Lucky-Goldstar, II
Pohang Iron and Steel Company Ltd., IV
POSCO, 57 (upd.)
Samick Musical Instruments Co., Ltd., 56
Samsung Electronics Co., Ltd., I; 41
   (upd.)
SK Group, 88
Ssangyong Cement Industrial Co., Ltd.,
   III; 61 (upd.)
Tong Yang Cement Corporation, 62

Spain

Abengoa S.A., 73
Abertis Infraestructuras, S.A., 65
Acciona S.A., 81

Adolfo Dominguez S.A., 72
Altadis S.A., 72 (upd.)
Banco Bilbao Vizcaya Argentaria S.A., II;
   48 (upd.)
Banco Central, II
Banco do Brasil S.A., II
Banco Santander Central Hispano S.A.,
   36 (upd.)
Baron de Ley S.A., 74
Campofrío Alimentación S.A, 59
Chupa Chups S.A., 38
Compañia Española de Petróleos S.A.
   (Cepsa), IV; 56 (upd.)
Cortefiel S.A., 64
Correos y Telegrafos S.A., 80
Dogi International Fabrics S.A., 52
El Corte Inglés Group, V; 26 (upd.)
ENDESA S.A., V; 46 (upd.)
Ercros S.A., 80
Federico Paternina S.A., 69
Freixenet S.A., 71
Gas Natural SDG S.A., 69
Grupo Dragados SA, 55
Grupo Eroski, 64
Grupo Ferrovial, S.A., 40
Grupo Ficosa International, 90
Grupo Leche Pascual S.A., 59
Grupo Lladró S.A., 52
Grupo Planeta, 94
Iberdrola, S.A., 49
Iberia Líneas Aéreas de España S.A., 6; 36
   (upd.); 91 (upd.)
Industria de Diseño Textil S.A., 64
Instituto Nacional de Industria, I
La Seda de Barcelona S.A., 100
Mecalux S.A., 74
Miquel y Costas Miquel S.A., 68
Mondragón Corporación Cooperativa,
   101
NH Hoteles S.A. 79
Nutrexpa S.A., 92
Obrascon Huarte Lain S.A., 76
Paradores de Turismo de Espana S.A., 73
Pescanova S.A., 81
Puig Beauty and Fashion Group S.L., 60
Real Madrid C.F., 73
Repsol-YPF S.A., IV; 16 (upd.); 40 (upd.)
Sol Meliá S.A., 71
Tabacalera, S.A., V; 17 (upd.)
Telefónica S.A., V; 46 (upd.)
TelePizza S.A., 33
Television Española, S.A., 7
Terra Lycos, Inc., 43
Unión Fenosa, S.A., 51
Uralita S.A., 96
Vidrala S.A., 67
Viscofan S.A., 70
Vocento, 94
Vueling Airlines S.A., 97
Zara International, Inc., 83
Zed Group, 93

Sweden

A. Johnson & Company H.B., I
AB Volvo, I; 7 (upd.); 26 (upd.); 67
   (upd.)
Aktiebolaget Electrolux, 22 (upd.)

Aktiebolaget SKF, III; 38 (upd.); 89
   (upd.)
Alfa Laval AB, III; 64 (upd.)
Astra AB, I; 20 (upd.)
Atlas Copco AB, III; 28 (upd.); 85 (upd.)
Autoliv, Inc., 65
Billerud AB, 100
Boliden AB, 80
Bonnier AB, 52
BRIO AB, 24
Cardo AB, 53
Cloetta Fazer AB, 70
D. Carnegie & Co. AB, 98
Electrolux AB, III; 53 (upd.)
Eka Chemicals AB, 92
FöreningsSparbanken AB, 69
Gambro AB, 49
Gunnebo AB, 53
H&M Hennes & Mauritz AB, 98 (upd.)
Hennes & Mauritz AB, 29
Hexagon AB 78
Holmen AB, 52 (upd.)
ICA AB, II
Investor AB, 63
Kooperativa Förbundet, 99
Mo och Domsjö AB, IV
Modern Times Group AB, 36
NetCom Systems AB, 26
Nobel Industries AB, 9
Nordea AB, 40
Observer AB, 55
Perstorp AB, I; 51 (upd.)
Saab Automobile AB, I; 11 (upd.); 32
   (upd.); 83 (upd.)
Sandvik AB, IV; 32 (upd.); 77 (upd.)
Sapa AB, 84
The SAS Group, 34 (upd.)
Scandinavian Airlines System, I
Securitas AB, 42
Skandia Insurance Company, Ltd., 50
Skandinaviska Enskilda Banken AB, II; 56
   (upd.)
Skanska AB, 38
SSAB Svenskt Stål AB, 89
Stora Kopparbergs Bergslags AB, IV
Sveaskog AB, 93
Svenska Cellulosa Aktiebolaget SCA, IV;
   28 (upd.); 85 (upd.)
Svenska Handelsbanken AB, II; 50 (upd.)
Sveriges Riksbank, 96
Swedish Match AB, 12; 39 (upd.); 92
   (upd.)
Swedish Telecom, V
Telefonaktiebolaget LM Ericsson, V; 46
   (upd.)
TeliaSonera AB, 57 (upd.)
Trelleborg AB, 93
Vattenfall AB, 57
V&S Vin & Sprit AB, 91 (upd.)
Vin & Spirit AB, 31

Switzerland

ABB ASEA Brown Boveri Ltd., II; 22
   (upd.)
ABB Ltd., 65 (upd.)
Actelion Ltd., 83
Adecco S.A., 36 (upd.)
Adia S.A., 6

Arthur Andersen & Company, Société
  Coopérative, 10
Ascom AG, 9
Bâloise-Holding, 40
Barry Callebaut AG, 29; 71 (upd.)
Bernina Holding AG, 47
Bodum Design Group AG, 47
Bon Appetit Holding AG, 48
Charles Vögele Holding AG, 82
Chocoladefabriken Lindt & Sprüngli AG,
  27
Ciba-Geigy Ltd., I; 8 (upd.)
Compagnie Financiere Richemont AG, 50
Conzzeta Holding, 80
Coop Schweiz Genossenschaftsverband, 48
Credit Suisse Group, II; 21 (upd.); 59
  (upd.)
Danzas Group, V; 40 (upd.)
De Beers Consolidated Mines Limited/De
  Beers Centenary AG, IV; 7 (upd.); 28
  (upd.)
Denner AG, 88
Duferco Group, 94
Edipresse S.A., 82
Elektrowatt AG, 6
Elma Electronic AG, 83
F. Hoffmann-La Roche Ltd., I; 50 (upd.)
Fédération Internationale de Football
  Association, 27
Fenaco, 86
Firmenich International S.A., 60
Franke Holding AG, 76
Galenica AG, 84
Gate Gourmet International AG, 70
Geberit AG, 49
Georg Fischer AG Schaffhausen, 61
Givaudan SA, 43
Hero Group, 100
Holderbank Financière Glaris Ltd., III
International Olympic Committee, 44
Jacobs Suchard A.G., II
Julius Baer Holding AG, 52
Keramik Holding AG Laufen, 51
Kraft Jacobs Suchard AG, 26 (upd.)
Kudelski Group SA, 44
Kuehne & Nagel International AG, V; 53
  (upd.)
Kuoni Travel Holding Ltd., 40
Liebherr-International AG, 64
Logitech International S.A., 28; 69 (upd.)
Lonza Group Ltd., 73
Maus Frères SA, 48
Médecins sans Frontières, 85
Mettler-Toledo International Inc., 30
Migros-Genossenschafts-Bund, 68
Montres Rolex S.A., 13; 34 (upd.)
Nestlé S.A., II; 7 (upd.); 28 (upd.); 71
  (upd.)
Novartis AG, 39 (upd.)
Panalpina World Transport (Holding)
  Ltd., 47
Pelikan Holding AG, 92
Phoenix Mecano AG, 61
Ricola Ltd., 62
Rieter Holding AG, 42
Roland Murten A.G., 7
Sandoz Ltd., I
Schindler Holding AG, 29

Schweizerische Post-, Telefon- und
  Telegrafen-Betriebe, V
Selecta AG, 97
Serono S.A., 47
STMicroelectronics NV, 52
Straumann Holding AG 79
Sulzer Ltd., III; 68 (upd.)
Swarovski International Holding AG, 40
The Swatch Group SA, 26
Swedish Match S.A., 12
Swiss Air Transport Company, Ltd., I
Swiss Bank Corporation, II
The Swiss Federal Railways
  (Schweizerische Bundesbahnen), V
Swiss International Air Lines Ltd., 48
Swiss Reinsurance Company
  (Schweizerische
  Rückversicherungs-Gesellschaft), III; 46
  (upd.)
Swisscom AG, 58
Swissport International Ltd., 70
Syngenta International AG, 83
Synthes, Inc., 93
TAG Heuer International SA, 25; 77
  (upd.)
Tamedia AG, 53
Tetra Pak International SA, 53
UBS AG, 52 (upd.)
Underberg AG, 92
Union Bank of Switzerland, II
Valora Holding AG, 98
Victorinox AG, 21; 74 (upd.)
Vontobel Holding AG, 96
Weleda AG 78
Winterthur Group, III; 68 (upd.)
Xstrata PLC, 73
Zurich Financial Services, 42 (upd.); 93
  (upd.)
Zürich Versicherungs-Gesellschaft, III

Taiwan
Acer Incorporated, 16; 73 (upd.)
AU Optronics Corporation, 67
BenQ Corporation, 67
Chi Mei Optoelectronics Corporation, 75
China Airlines, 34
Chunghwa Picture Tubes, Ltd., 75
Chunghwa Telecom Co., Ltd., 101 (upd.)
D-Link Corporation, 83
Directorate General of
  Telecommunications, 7
EVA Airways Corporation, 51
Evergreen Marine Corporation (Taiwan)
  Ltd., 13; 50 (upd.)
First International Computer, Inc., 56
Formosa Plastics Corporation, 14; 58
  (upd.)
Giant Manufacturing Company, Ltd., 85
High Tech Computer Corporation, 81
Hon Hai Precision Industry Co., Ltd., 59
Kwang Yang Motor Company Ltd., 80
Pou Chen Corporation, 81
Quanta Computer Inc., 47
Siliconware Precision Industries Ltd., 73
Taiwan Semiconductor Manufacturing
  Company Ltd., 47
Taiwan Tobacco & Liquor Corporation,
  75

Tatung Co., 23
United Microelectronics Corporation, 98
Winbond Electronics Corporation, 74
Yageo Corporation, 16; 98 (upd.)

Thailand
Charoen Pokphand Group, 62
Electricity Generating Authority of
  Thailand (EGAT), 56
Krung Thai Bank Public Company Ltd.,
  69
Pranda Jewelry plc, 70
PTT Public Company Ltd., 56
The Siam Cement Public Company
  Limited, 56
Thai Airways International Public
  Company Limited, 6; 27 (upd.)
Thai Union Frozen Products PCL, 75
Thanulux Public Company Limited, 86
The Topaz Group, Inc., 62

Tunisia
Société Tunisienne de l'Air-Tunisair, 49

Turkey
Akbank TAS 79
Anadolu Efes Biracilik ve Malt Sanayii
  A.S., 95
Dogan Sirketler Grubu Holding A.S., 83
Haci Omer Sabanci Holdings A.S., 55
Koç Holding A.S., I; 54 (upd.)
Turkish Airlines Inc. (Türk Hava Yollari
  A.O.), 72
Turkiye Is Bankasi A.S., 61
Türkiye Petrolleri Anonim Ortakliği, IV

Ukraine
Antonov Design Bureau, 53

United Arab Emirates
Abu Dhabi National Oil Company, IV;
  45 (upd.)
Al Habtoor Group L.L.C., 87
DP World, 81
The Emirates Group, 39; 81 (upd.)
Etihad Airways PJSC, 89
Gulf Agency Company Ltd. 78
Jumeirah Group, 83

United Kingdom
A. F. Blakemore & Son Ltd., 90
A. Nelson & Co. Ltd., 75
Aardman Animations Ltd., 61
Abbey National plc, 10; 39 (upd.)
Acergy SA, 97
Adams Childrenswear Ltd., 95
Aegis Group plc, 6
AG Barr plc, 64
Aga Foodservice Group PLC, 73
Aggregate Industries plc, 36
Aggreko Plc, 45
AgustaWestland N.V., 75
Air Partner PLC, 93
Airtours Plc, 27
The Albert Fisher Group plc, 41
Alexandra plc, 88

Phaidon Press Ltd., 98
Phones 4u Ltd., 85
Photo-Me International Plc, 83
PIC International Group PLC, 24 (upd.)
Pilkington Group Limited, III; 34 (upd.); 87 (upd.)
PKF International 78
The Plessey Company, PLC, II
The Porcelain and Fine China Companies Ltd., 69
Portmeirion Group plc, 88
Post Office Group, V
Posterscope Worldwide, 70
Powell Duffryn plc, 31
Powergen PLC, 11; 50 (upd.)
Princes Ltd., 76
Prudential plc, 48 (upd.)
Psion PLC, 45
Punch Taverns plc, 70
PZ Cussons plc, 72
R. Griggs Group Limited, 23
Racal Electronics PLC, II
Ragdoll Productions Ltd., 51
Railtrack Group PLC, 50
Raleigh UK Ltd., 65
The Rank Group plc, II; 14 (upd.); 64 (upd.)
Ranks Hovis McDougall Limited, II; 28 (upd.)
Rathbone Brothers plc, 70
The Real Good Food Company plc, 99
The Really Useful Group, 26
Reckitt Benckiser plc, II; 42 (upd.); 91 (upd.)
Redland plc, III
Redrow Group plc, 31
Reed Elsevier plc, IV; 17 (upd.); 31 (upd.)
Regent Inns plc, 95
Renishaw plc, 46
Rentokil Initial Plc, 47
Reuters Group PLC, IV; 22 (upd.); 63 (upd.)
Rexam PLC, 32 (upd.); 85 (upd.)
Ricardo plc, 90
Rio Tinto PLC, 19 (upd.); 50 (upd.)
RMC Group p.l.c., III; 34 (upd.)
Rolls-Royce Group PLC, 67 (upd.)
Rolls-Royce plc, I; 7 (upd.); 21 (upd.)
Ronson PLC, 49
Rothmans UK Holdings Limited, V; 19 (upd.)
Rotork plc, 46
Rover Group Ltd., 7; 21 (upd.)
Rowntree Mackintosh, II
Royal & Sun Alliance Insurance Group plc, 55 (upd.)
The Royal Bank of Scotland Group plc, 38 (upd.)
Royal Doulton plc, 14; 38 (upd.)
Royal Dutch Petroleum Company/ The Shell Transport and Trading Company p.l.c., IV
Royal Insurance Holdings PLC, III
RPC Group PLC, 81
The RTZ Corporation PLC, IV
The Rugby Group plc, 31
Saatchi & Saatchi PLC, I
SABMiller plc, 59 (upd.)

Safeway PLC, 50 (upd.)
Saffery Champness, 80
The Sage Group, 43
St. James's Place Capital, plc, 71
The Sanctuary Group PLC, 69
SBC Warburg, 14
Schroders plc, 42
Scottish & Newcastle plc, 35 (upd.)
Scottish and Southern Energy plc, 66 (upd.)
Scottish Power plc, 49 (upd.)
Scottish Radio Holding plc, 41
SDL PLC, 67
Sea Containers Ltd., 29
Sears plc, V
Securicor Plc, 45
Seddon Group Ltd., 67
Selfridges Plc, 34
Serco Group plc, 47
Severn Trent PLC, 12; 38 (upd.)
SFI Group plc, 51
Shanks Group plc, 45
Shepherd Neame Limited, 30
SIG plc, 71
Signet Group PLC, 61
Singer & Friedlander Group plc, 41
Skipton Building Society, 80
Slough Estates PLC, IV; 50 (upd.)
Smith & Nephew plc, 17;41 (upd.)
SmithKline Beecham plc, III; 32 (upd.)
Smiths Industries PLC, 25
Somerfield plc, 47 (upd.)
Southern Electric PLC, 13
Specialist Computer Holdings Ltd., 80
Speedy Hire plc, 84
Spirax-Sarco Engineering plc, 59
SSL International plc, 49
St Ives plc, 34
Standard Chartered plc, II; 48 (upd.)
Stanley Leisure plc, 66
STC PLC, III
Stirling Group plc, 62
Stoddard International plc, 72
Stoll-Moss Theatres Ltd., 34
Stolt-Nielsen S.A., 42
Storehouse PLC, 16
Strix Ltd., 51
Superdrug Stores PLC, 95
Surrey Satellite Technology Limited, 83
Sun Alliance Group PLC, III
Sytner Group plc, 45
Tarmac Limited, III; 28 (upd.); 95 (upd.)
Tate & Lyle PLC, II; 42 (upd.); 101 (upd.)
Taylor & Francis Group plc, 44
Taylor Nelson Sofres plc, 34
Taylor Woodrow plc, I; 38 (upd.)
Ted Baker plc, 86
Tesco plc, II; 24 (upd.); 68 (upd.)
Thames Water plc, 11; 90 (upd.)
Thistle Hotels PLC, 54
Thorn Emi PLC, I
Thorn plc, 24
Thorntons plc, 46
3i Group PLC, 73
365 Media Group plc, 89
TI Group plc, 17
Tibbett & Britten Group plc, 32

Tiger Aspect Productions Ltd., 72
Time Out Group Ltd., 68
Tomkins plc, 11; 44 (upd.)
Tottenham Hotspur PLC, 81
Travis Perkins plc, 34
Trinity Mirror plc, 49 (upd.)
Triumph Motorcycles Ltd., 53
Trusthouse Forte PLC, III
TSB Group plc, 12
Tulip Ltd., 89
Tullow Oil plc, 83
The Tussauds Group, 55
Ulster Television PLC, 71
Ultimate Leisure Group PLC, 75
Ultramar PLC, IV
Umbro plc, 88
Unigate PLC, II; 28 (upd.)
Unilever, II; 7 (upd.); 32 (upd.); 89 (upd.)
Uniq plc, 83 (upd.)
United Biscuits (Holdings) plc, II; 42 (upd.)
United Business Media plc, 52 (upd.)
United News & Media plc, IV; 28 (upd.)
United Utilities PLC, 52 (upd.)
Urbium PLC, 75
Vauxhall Motors Limited, 73
Vendôme Luxury Group plc, 27
Vestey Group Ltd., 95
Vickers plc, 27
Virgin Group Ltd., 12; 32 (upd.); 89 (upd.)
Viridian Group plc, 64
Vodafone Group Plc, 11; 36 (upd.); 75 (upd.)
Vosper Thornycroft Holding plc, 41
W Jordan (Cereals) Ltd., 74
Wagon plc, 92
Walkers Shortbread Ltd. 79
Walkers Snack Foods Ltd., 70
Warburtons Ltd., 89
Wassall Plc, 18
Waterford Wedgwood Holdings PLC, 12
Watson Wyatt Worldwide, 42
Watts of Lydney Group Ltd., 71
Weetabix Limited, 61
The Weir Group PLC, 85
The Wellcome Foundation Ltd., I
WH Smith PLC, V, 42 (upd.)
Whatman plc, 46
Whitbread PLC, I; 20 (upd.); 52 (upd.); 97 (upd.)
Whittard of Chelsea Plc, 61
Wilkinson Hardware Stores Ltd., 80
Wilkinson Sword Ltd., 60
William Grant & Sons Ltd., 60
William Hill Organization Limited, 49
William Jackson & Son Ltd., 101
William Reed Publishing Ltd. 78
Willis Group Holdings Ltd., 25; 100 (upd.)
Wilson Bowden Plc, 45
Wincanton plc, 52
Wm. Morrison Supermarkets PLC, 38
Wolseley plc, 64
The Wolverhampton & Dudley Breweries, PLC, 57
Wood Hall Trust PLC, I

The Woolwich plc, 30
Woolworths Group plc, 83
WPP Group plc, 6; 48 (upd.)
WS Atkins Plc, 45
Xstrata PLC, 73
Yell Group PLC 79
Young & Co.'s Brewery, P.L.C., 38
Young's Bluecrest Seafood Holdings Ltd., 81
Yule Catto & Company plc, 54
Zeneca Group PLC, 21
Zomba Records Ltd., 52

United States

A & E Television Networks, 32
A & W Brands, Inc., 25
A-dec, Inc., 53
A-Mark Financial Corporation, 71
A. Schulman, Inc., 8; 49 (upd.)
A.B. Watley Group Inc., 45
A.B.Dick Company, 28
A.C. Moore Arts & Crafts, Inc., 30
A. Duda & Sons, Inc., 88
A.G. Edwards, Inc., 8; 32
A.H. Belo Corporation, 10; 30 (upd.)
A.L. Pharma Inc., 12
A.M. Castle & Co., 25
A.O. Smith Corporation, 11; 40 (upd.); 93 (upd.)
A.T. Cross Company, 17; 49 (upd.)
AAF-McQuay Incorporated, 26
AAON, Inc., 22
AAR Corp., 28
Aaron Rents, Inc., 14; 35 (upd.)
AARP, 27
Aavid Thermal Technologies, Inc., 29
ABARTA, Inc., 100
Abatix Corp., 57
Abaxis, Inc., 83
Abbott Laboratories, I; 11 (upd.); 40 (upd.); 93 (upd.)
ABC Appliance, Inc., 10
ABC Carpet & Home Co. Inc., 26
ABC Family Worldwide, Inc., 52
ABC Rail Products Corporation, 18
ABC Supply Co., Inc., 22
Abercrombie & Fitch Company, 15; 35 (upd.); 75 (upd.)
Abigail Adams National Bancorp, Inc., 23
Abiomed, Inc., 47
ABM Industries Incorporated, 25 (upd.)
Abrams Industries Inc., 23
Abraxas Petroleum Corporation, 89
Abt Associates Inc., 95
Academy of Television Arts & Sciences, Inc., 55
Academy Sports & Outdoors, 27
Acadian Ambulance & Air Med Services, Inc., 39
ACCION International, 87
Acclaim Entertainment Inc., 24
ACCO World Corporation, 7; 51 (upd.)
Accredited Home Lenders Holding Co., 91
Accubuilt, Inc., 74
Accuray Incorporated, 95
AccuWeather, Inc., 73
ACE Cash Express, Inc., 33

Ace Hardware Corporation, 12; 35 (upd.)
Aceto Corp., 38
AchieveGlobal Inc., 90
Ackerley Communications, Inc., 9
Acme United Corporation, 70
Acme-Cleveland Corp., 13
ACNielsen Corporation, 13; 38 (upd.)
Acorn Products, Inc., 55
Acosta Sales and Marketing Company, Inc., 77
Acsys, Inc., 44
Action Performance Companies, Inc., 27
Activision, Inc., 32; 89 (upd.)
Actuant Corporation, 94 (upd.)
Acuity Brands, Inc., 90
Acushnet Company, 64
Acuson Corporation, 10; 36 (upd.)
Acxiom Corporation, 35
The Adams Express Company, 86
Adams Golf, Inc., 37
Adaptec, Inc., 31
ADC Telecommunications, Inc., 10; 30 (upd.); 89 (upd.)
Adelphia Communications Corporation, 17; 52 (upd.)
ADESA, Inc., 71
Administaff, Inc., 52
Adobe Systems Inc., 10; 33 (upd.)
Adolor Corporation, 101
Adolph Coors Company, I; 13 (upd.); 36 (upd.)
ADT Security Services, Inc., 12; 44 (upd.)
Adtran Inc., 22
Advance Auto Parts, Inc., 57
Advance Publications Inc., IV; 19 (upd.); 96 (upd.)
Advanced Circuits Inc., 67
Advanced Fibre Communications, Inc., 63
Advanced Marketing Services, Inc., 34
Advanced Medical Optics, Inc. 79
Advanced Micro Devices, Inc., 6; 30 (upd.); 99 (upd.)
Advanced Neuromodulation Systems, Inc., 73
Advanced Technology Laboratories, Inc., 9
Advanstar Communications, Inc., 57
Advanta Corporation, 8; 38 (upd.)
Advantica Restaurant Group, Inc., 27 (upd.)
Adventist Health, 53
The Advertising Council, Inc., 76
The Advisory Board Company, 80
Advo, Inc., 6; 53 (upd.)
Advocat Inc., 46
AECOM Technology Corporation 79
AEI Music Network Inc., 35
AEP Industries, Inc., 36
AeroGrow International, Inc., 95
Aerojet-General Corp., 63
Aeronca Inc., 46
Aéropostale, Inc., 89
Aeroquip Corporation, 16
Aerosonic Corporation, 69
AeroVironment, Inc., 97
The AES Corporation, 10; 13 (upd.); 53 (upd.)
Aetna Inc., III; 21 (upd.); 63 (upd.)
AFC Enterprises, Inc., 32; 83 (upd.)

Affiliated Computer Services, Inc., 61
Affiliated Foods Inc., 53
Affiliated Managers Group, Inc. 79
Affiliated Publications, Inc., 7
Affinity Group Holding Inc., 56
AFLAC Incorporated, 10 (upd.); 38 (upd.)
Africare, 59
After Hours Formalwear Inc., 60
Aftermarket Technology Corp., 83
Ag Services of America, Inc., 59
Ag-Chem Equipment Company, Inc., 17
AGCO Corporation, 13; 67 (upd.)
Agere Systems Inc., 61
Agilent Technologies Inc., 38; 93 (upd.)
Agilysys Inc., 76 (upd.)
Agri Beef Company, 81
Agway, Inc., 7; 21 (upd.)
AHL Services, Inc., 27
Air & Water Technologies Corporation, 6
Air Express International Corporation, 13
Air Methods Corporation, 53
Air Products and Chemicals, Inc., I; 10 (upd.); 74 (upd.)
Air T, Inc., 86
Air Wisconsin Airlines Corporation, 55
Airborne Freight Corporation, 6; 34 (upd.)
Airborne Systems Group, 89
Airgas, Inc., 54
AirTouch Communications, 11
AirTran Holdings, Inc., 22
AK Steel Holding Corporation, 19; 41 (upd.)
Akamai Technologies, Inc., 71
Akin, Gump, Strauss, Hauer & Feld, L.L.P., 33
Akorn, Inc., 32
Alabama Farmers Cooperative, Inc., 63
Alabama National BanCorporation, 75
Alamo Group Inc., 32
Alamo Rent A Car, 6; 24 (upd.); 84 (upd.)
ALARIS Medical Systems, Inc., 65
Alaska Air Group, Inc., 6; 29 (upd.)
Alaska Communications Systems Group, Inc., 89
Alaska Railroad Corporation, 60
Alba-Waldensian, Inc., 30
Albany International Corporation, 8; 51 (upd.)
Albany Molecular Research, Inc., 77
Albemarle Corporation, 59
Alberici Corporation, 76
Alberto-Culver Company, 8; 36 (upd.); 91 (upd.)
Albertson's, Inc., II; 7 (upd.); 30 (upd.); 65 (upd.)
Alco Health Services Corporation, III
Alco Standard Corporation, I
Alcoa Inc., 56 (upd.)
Aldila Inc., 46
Aldus Corporation, 10
Alex Lee Inc., 18; 44 (upd.)
Alexander & Alexander Services Inc., 10
Alexander & Baldwin, Inc., 10; 40 (upd.)
Alexander's, Inc., 45
Alexandria Real Estate Equities, Inc., 101

AmeriSource Health Corporation, 37 (upd.)
AmerisourceBergen Corporation, 64 (upd.)
Ameristar Casinos, Inc., 33; 69 (upd.)
Ameritech Corporation, V; 18 (upd.)
Ameritrade Holding Corporation, 34
Ameriwood Industries International Corp., 17
Amerock Corporation, 53
Ameron International Corporation, 67
Ames Department Stores, Inc., 9; 30 (upd.)
AMETEK, Inc., 9
AMF Bowling, Inc., 40
Amfac/JMB Hawaii L.L.C., I; 24 (upd.)
Amgen, Inc., 10; 30 (upd.); 89 (upd.)
AMICAS, Inc., 69
Amkor Technology, Inc., 69
Amoco Corporation, IV; 14 (upd.)
Amoskeag Company, 8
AMP Incorporated, II; 14 (upd.)
Ampacet Corporation, 67
Ampco-Pittsburgh Corporation 79
Ampex Corporation, 17
Amphenol Corporation, 40
AMR Corporation, 28 (upd.); 52 (upd.)
AMREP Corporation, 21
Amscan Holdings, Inc., 61
AmSouth Bancorporation, 12; 48 (upd.)
Amsted Industries Incorporated, 7
AmSurg Corporation, 48
Amtran, Inc., 34
Amway Corporation, III; 13 (upd.); 30 (upd.)
Amy's Kitchen Inc., 76
Amylin Pharmaceuticals, Inc., 67
Anacomp, Inc., 94
Anadarko Petroleum Corporation, 10; 52 (upd.)
Anaheim Angels Baseball Club, Inc., 53
Analex Corporation, 74
Analog Devices, Inc., 10
Analogic Corporation, 23
Analysts International Corporation, 36
Analytic Sciences Corporation, 10
Analytical Surveys, Inc., 33
Anaren Microwave, Inc., 33
Anchor Bancorp, Inc., 10
Anchor BanCorp Wisconsin, Inc., 101
Anchor Brewing Company, 47
Anchor Gaming, 24
Anchor Hocking Glassware, 13
Andersen, 10; 29 (upd.); 68 (upd.)
Anderson Trucking Service, Inc., 75
The Anderson-DuBose Company, 60
The Andersons, Inc., 31
Andin International, Inc., 100
Andis Company, Inc., 85
Andrew Corporation, 10; 32 (upd.)
The Andrews Institute, 99
Andrews Kurth, LLP, 71
Andrews McMeel Universal, 40
Andronico's Market, 70
Andrx Corporation, 55
Angelica Corporation, 15; 43 (upd.)
AngioDynamics, Inc., 81

Anheuser-Busch InBev, I; 10 (upd.); 34 (upd.); 100 (upd.)
Anixter International Inc., 88
Annie's Homegrown, Inc., 59
Annin & Co., 100
AnnTaylor Stores Corporation, 13; 37 (upd.); 67 (upd.)
ANR Pipeline Co., 17
The Anschutz Company, 12; 36 (upd.); 73 (upd.)
Ansoft Corporation, 63
Anteon Corporation, 57
Anthem Electronics, Inc., 13
Anthony & Sylvan Pools Corporation, 56
The Antioch Company, 40
AOL Time Warner Inc., 57 (upd.)
Aon Corporation, III; 45 (upd.)
Apache Corporation, 10; 32 (upd.); 89 (upd.)
Apartment Investment and Management Company, 49
Apex Digital, Inc., 63
APi Group, Inc., 64
APL Limited, 61 (upd.)
Apogee Enterprises, Inc., 8
Apollo Group, Inc., 24
Applause Inc., 24
Apple & Eve L.L.C., 92
Apple Bank for Savings, 59
Apple Computer, Inc., III; 6 (upd.); 36 (upd.); 77 (upd.)
Applebee's International Inc., 14; 35 (upd.)
Appliance Recycling Centers of America, Inc., 42
Applica Incorporated, 43 (upd.)
Applied Bioscience International, Inc., 10
Applied Films Corporation, 48
Applied Materials, Inc., 10; 46 (upd.)
Applied Micro Circuits Corporation, 38
Applied Power, Inc., 9; 32 (upd.)
Applied Signal Technology, Inc., 87
AptarGroup, Inc., 69
Aqua Alliance Inc., 32 (upd.)
aQuantive, Inc., 81
Aquarion Company, 84
Aquent, 96
Aquila, Inc., 50 (upd.)
AR Accessories Group, Inc., 23
ARA Services, II
ARAMARK Corporation, 13; 41 (upd.)
Arandell Corporation, 37
The Arbitron Company, 38
Arbor Drugs Inc., 12
Arby's Inc., 14
Arch Chemicals Inc. 78
Arch Coal Inc., 98
Arch Mineral Corporation, 7
Arch Wireless, Inc., 39
Archer Daniels Midland Company, I; 11 (upd.); 32 (upd.); 75 (upd.)
Archie Comics Publications, Inc., 63
Archon Corporation, 74 (upd.)
Archstone-Smith Trust, 49
Archway Cookies, Inc., 29
ARCO Chemical Company, 10
Arctco, Inc., 16
Arctic Cat Inc., 40 (upd.); 96 (upd.)

Arctic Slope Regional Corporation, 38
Arden Group, Inc., 29
Arena Resources, Inc., 97
Argon ST, Inc., 81
Argosy Gaming Company, 21
Ariba, Inc., 57
Ariens Company, 48
ARINC Inc., 98
Aris Industries, Inc., 16
The Aristotle Corporation, 62
Ark Restaurants Corp., 20
Arkansas Best Corporation, 16; 94 (upd.)
Arkla, Inc., V
Armco Inc., IV
Armor All Products Corp., 16
Armor Holdings, Inc., 27
Armstrong Holdings, Inc., III; 22 (upd.); 81 (upd.)
Army and Air Force Exchange Service, 39
Arnhold and S. Bleichroeder Advisers, LLC, 97
Arnold & Porter, 35
Arotech Corporation, 93
ArQule, Inc., 68
ARRIS Group, Inc., 89
Arrow Air Holdings Corporation, 55
Arrow Electronics, Inc., 10; 50 (upd.)
The Art Institute of Chicago, 29
Art Van Furniture, Inc., 28
Art's Way Manufacturing Co., Inc., 101
Artesyn Technologies Inc., 46 (upd.)
ArthroCare Corporation, 73
The Arthur C. Clarke Foundation, 92
Arthur D. Little, Inc., 35
Arthur J. Gallagher & Co., 73
Arthur Murray International, Inc., 32
Artisan Entertainment Inc., 32 (upd.)
ArvinMeritor, Inc., 8; 54 (upd.)
Asanté Technologies, Inc., 20
ASARCO Incorporated, IV
Asbury Automotive Group Inc., 60
Asbury Carbons, Inc., 68
ASC, Inc., 55
Ascend Communications, Inc., 24
Ascendia Brands, Inc., 97
Ascential Software Corporation, 59
Ash Grove Cement Company, 94
Ashland Inc., 19; 50 (upd.)
Ashland Oil, Inc., IV
Ashley Furniture Industries, Inc., 35
Ashworth, Inc., 26
ASK Group, Inc., 9
Ask Jeeves, Inc., 65
Aspect Telecommunications Corporation, 22
Aspen Skiing Company, 15
Asplundh Tree Expert Co., 20; 59 (upd.)
Assisted Living Concepts, Inc., 43
Associated Estates Realty Corporation, 25
Associated Grocers, Incorporated, 9; 31 (upd.)
Associated Milk Producers, Inc., 11; 48 (upd.)
Associated Natural Gas Corporation, 11
The Associated Press, 13; 31 (upd.); 73 (upd.)
Association of Junior Leagues International Inc., 60

GEOGRAPHIC INDEX

AST Research Inc., 9
Astec Industries, Inc. 79
AstenJohnson Inc., 90
Astoria Financial Corporation, 44
Astronics Corporation, 35
Asurion Corporation, 83
ASV, Inc., 34; 66 (upd.)
At Home Corporation, 43
AT&T Bell Laboratories, Inc., 13
AT&T Corporation, V; 29 (upd.); 68 (upd.)
AT&T Wireless Services, Inc., 54 (upd.)
ATA Holdings Corporation, 82
Atari Corporation, 9; 23 (upd.); 66 (upd.)
ATC Healthcare Inc., 64
Atchison Casting Corporation, 39
AtheroGenics Inc., 101
The Athlete's Foot Brands LLC, 84
The Athletics Investment Group, 62
Atkins Nutritionals, Inc., 58
Atkinson Candy Company, 87
Atlanta Bread Company International, Inc., 70
Atlanta Gas Light Company, 6; 23 (upd.)
Atlanta National League Baseball Club, Inc., 43
Atlantic American Corporation, 44
Atlantic Coast Airlines Holdings, Inc., 55
Atlantic Energy, Inc., 6
The Atlantic Group, 23
Atlantic Premium Brands, Ltd., 57
Atlantic Richfield Company, IV; 31 (upd.)
Atlantic Southeast Airlines, Inc., 47
Atlantis Plastics, Inc., 85
Atlas Air, Inc., 39
Atlas Van Lines, Inc., 14
Atmel Corporation, 17
ATMI, Inc., 93
Atmos Energy Corporation, 43
Attachmate Corporation, 56
Atwood Mobil Products, 53
Atwood Oceanics, Inc., 100
Au Bon Pain Co., Inc., 18
The Auchter Company, The 78
Audible Inc. 79
Audio King Corporation, 24
Audiovox Corporation, 34; 90 (upd.)
August Schell Brewing Company Inc., 59
Ault Incorporated, 34
Auntie Anne's, Inc., 35
Aurora Casket Company, Inc., 56
Aurora Foods Inc., 32
The Austin Company, 8; 72 (upd.)
Austin Powder Company, 76
Authentic Fitness Corporation, 20; 51 (upd.)
Auto Value Associates, Inc., 25
Autobytel Inc., 47
Autocam Corporation, 51
Autodesk, Inc., 10; 89 (upd.)
Autologic Information International, Inc., 20
Automatic Data Processing, Inc., III; 9 (upd.); 47 (upd.)
AutoNation, Inc., 50
Autotote Corporation, 20
AutoTrader.com, L.L.C., 91
AutoZone, Inc., 9; 31 (upd.)

Auvil Fruit Company, Inc., 95
Avado Brands, Inc., 31
Avalon Correctional Services, Inc., 75
AvalonBay Communities, Inc., 58
Avco Financial Services Inc., 13
Aveda Corporation, 24
Avedis Zildjian Co., 38
Aventine Renewable Energy Holdings, Inc., 89
Avery Dennison Corporation, IV; 17 (upd.); 49 (upd.)
Aviall, Inc., 73
Aviation Sales Company, 41
Avid Technology Inc., 38
Avis Group Holdings, Inc., 75 (upd.)
Avis Rent A Car, Inc., 6; 22 (upd.)
Avista Corporation, 69 (upd.)
Avnet Inc., 9
Avocent Corporation, 65
Avon Products, Inc., III; 19 (upd.); 46 (upd.)
Avondale Industries, 7; 41 (upd.)
AVX Corporation, 67
Awrey Bakeries, Inc., 56
Axcelis Technologies, Inc., 95
Axsys Technologies, Inc., 93
Aydin Corp., 19
Azcon Corporation, 23
Aztar Corporation, 13; 71 (upd.)
AZZ Incorporated, 93
B&G Foods, Inc., 40
B. Dalton Bookseller Inc., 25
The B. Manischewitz Company, LLC, 31
B/E Aerospace, Inc., 30
B.J. Alan Co., Inc., 67
B.R. Guest Inc., 87
B.W. Rogers Company, 94
Babbage's, Inc., 10
The Babcock & Wilcox Company, 82
Baby Superstore, Inc., 15
Bachman's Inc., 22
Back Bay Restaurant Group, Inc., 20
Back Yard Burgers, Inc., 45
Bad Boy Worldwide Entertainment Group, 58
Badger Meter, Inc., 22
Badger Paper Mills, Inc., 15
Badger State Ethanol, LLC, 83
BAE Systems Ship Repair, 73
Bailey Nurseries, Inc., 57
Bain & Company, 55
Baird & Warner Holding Company, 87
Bairnco Corporation, 28
Baker & Daniels LLP, 88
Baker & Hostetler LLP, 40
Baker & McKenzie, 10; 42 (upd.)
Baker & Taylor Corporation, 16; 43 (upd.)
Baker and Botts, L.L.P., 28
Baker Hughes Incorporated, III; 22 (upd.); 57 (upd.)
Balance Bar Company, 32
Balchem Corporation, 42
Baldor Electric Company, 21; 97 (upd.)
Baldwin & Lyons, Inc., 51
Baldwin Piano & Organ Company, 18
Baldwin Richardson Foods Company, 100
Baldwin Technology Company, Inc., 25

Ball Corporation, I; 10; 78 (upd.)
Ball Horticultural Company 78
Ballantyne of Omaha, Inc., 27
Ballard Medical Products, 21
Ballistic Recovery Systems, Inc., 87
Bally Manufacturing Corporation, III
Bally Total Fitness Corporation, 25; 94 (upd.)
Balmac International, Inc., 94
Baltek Corporation, 34
Baltimore Aircoil Company, Inc., 66
Baltimore Gas and Electric Company, V; 25 (upd.)
Baltimore Orioles L.P., 66
The Bama Companies, Inc., 80
Banana Republic Inc., 25
Bandag, Inc., 19
Banfi Products Corp., 36
Bank of America Corporation, 46 (upd.); 101 (upd.)
Bank of Boston Corporation, II
Bank of Granite Corporation, 89
Bank of Hawaii Corporation, 73
Bank of Mississippi, Inc., 14
Bank of New England Corporation, II
The Bank of New York Company, Inc., II; 46 (upd.)
Bank of the Ozarks, Inc., 91
Bank One Corporation, 10; 36 (upd.)
BankAmerica Corporation, II; 8 (upd.)
Bankers Trust New York Corporation, II
Banknorth Group, Inc., 55
Bankrate, Inc., 83
Banner Aerospace, Inc., 14; 37 (upd.)
Banta Corporation, 12; 32 (upd.); 79 (upd.)
Banyan Systems Inc., 25
Baptist Health Care Corporation, 82
Bar-S Foods Company, 76
BarclaysAmerican Mortgage Corporation, 11
Barbara's Bakery Inc., 88
Barden Companies, Inc., 76
Bardwil Industries Inc., 98
Bare Escentuals, Inc., 91
Barnes & Noble, Inc., 10; 30 (upd.); 75 (upd.)
Barnes Group Inc., 13; 69 (upd.)
Barnett Banks, Inc., 9
Barnett Inc., 28
Barney's, Inc., 28
Barr Pharmaceuticals, Inc., 26; 68 (upd.)
Barrett Business Services, Inc., 16
Barrett-Jackson Auction Company L.L.C., 88
Barry-Wehmiller Companies, Inc., 90
The Bartell Drug Company, 94
Barton Malow Company, 51
Barton Protective Services Inc., 53
The Baseball Club of Seattle, LP, 50
Bashas' Inc., 33; 80 (upd.)
Basic Earth Science Systems, Inc., 101
The Basketball Club of Seattle, LLC, 50
Bass Pro Shops, Inc., 42
Bassett Furniture Industries, Inc., 18; 95 (upd.)
Bates Worldwide, Inc., 14; 33 (upd.)
Bath Iron Works, 12; 36 (upd.)

buy.com, Inc., 46
BWAY Corporation, 24
C&K Market, Inc., 81
C & S Wholesale Grocers, Inc., 55
C-COR.net Corp., 38
C-Cube Microsystems, Inc., 37
C.F. Martin & Co., Inc., 42
The C.F. Sauer Company, 90
C.H. Guenther & Son, Inc., 84
C.H. Heist Corporation, 24
C.H. Robinson Worldwide, Inc., 11; 40 (upd.)
C.R. Bard, Inc., 9; 65 (upd.)
C.R. Meyer and Sons Company, 74
C-Tech Industries Inc., 90
Cabela's Inc., 26; 68 (upd.)
Cabletron Systems, Inc., 10
Cablevision Electronic Instruments, Inc., 32
Cablevision Systems Corporation, 7; 30 (upd.)
Cabot Corporation, 8; 29 (upd.); 91 (upd.)
Cache Incorporated, 30
CACI International Inc., 21; 72 (upd.)
Cactus Feeders, Inc., 91
Cadence Design Systems, Inc., 11; 48 (upd.)
Cadmus Communications Corporation, 23
Cadwalader, Wickersham & Taft, 32
CAE USA Inc., 48
Caere Corporation, 20
Caesars World, Inc., 6
Cagle's, Inc., 20
Cahners Business Information, 43
Cal-Maine Foods, Inc., 69
CalAmp Corp., 87
Calavo Growers, Inc., 47
CalComp Inc., 13
Calcot Ltd., 33
Caldor Inc., 12
Calgon Carbon Corporation, 73
California Cedar Products Company, 58
California Pizza Kitchen Inc., 15; 74 (upd.)
California Sports, Inc., 56
California Steel Industries, Inc., 67
California Water Service Group 79
Caliper Life Sciences, Inc., 70
Callanan Industries, Inc., 60
Callard and Bowser-Suchard Inc., 84
Callaway Golf Company, 15; 45 (upd.)
Callon Petroleum Company, 47
Calloway's Nursery, Inc., 51
CalMat Co., 19
Calpine Corporation, 36
Caltex Petroleum Corporation, 19
Calvin Klein, Inc., 22; 55 (upd.)
Cambrex Corporation, 16; 44 (upd.)
Cambridge SoundWorks, Inc., 48
Cambridge Technology Partners, Inc., 36
Camden Property Trust, 77
Camelot Music, Inc., 26
Cameron & Barkley Company, 28
Campagna-Turano Bakery, Inc., 99
Campbell-Ewald Advertising, 86
Campbell-Mithun-Esty, Inc., 16

Campbell Scientific, Inc., 51
Campbell Soup Company, II; 7 (upd.); 26 (upd.); 71 (upd.)
Campo Electronics, Appliances & Computers, Inc., 16
Canandaigua Brands, Inc., 13; 34 (upd.)
Cancer Treatment Centers of America, Inc., 85
Candela Corporation, 48
Candie's, Inc., 31
Candle Corporation, 64
Candlewood Hotel Company, Inc., 41
Cannon Design, 63
Cannon Express, Inc., 53
Cannondale Corporation, 21
Cano Petroleum Inc., 97
Cantel Medical Corporation, 80
Canterbury Park Holding Corporation, 42
Cantor Fitzgerald, L.P., 92
Cap Rock Energy Corporation, 46
Cape Cod Potato Chip Company, 90
Capel Incorporated, 45
Capezio/Ballet Makers Inc., 62
Capital Cities/ABC Inc., II
Capital Holding Corporation, III
Capital One Financial Corporation, 52
Capitol Records, Inc., 90
Capital Senior Living Corporation, 75
CapStar Hotel Company, 21
Capstone Turbine Corporation, 75
Captain D's, LLC, 59
Captaris, Inc., 89
Car Toys, Inc., 67
Caraustar Industries, Inc., 19; 44 (upd.)
The Carbide/Graphite Group, Inc., 40
Carborundum Company, 15
Cardinal Health, Inc., 18; 50 (upd.)
Cardone Industries Inc., 92
Cardtronics, Inc., 93
Career Education Corporation, 45
CareerBuilder, Inc., 93
Caremark Rx, Inc., 10; 54 (upd.)
Carey International, Inc., 26
Cargill, Incorporated, II; 13 (upd.); 40 (upd.); 89 (upd.)
Carhartt, Inc., 30; 77 (upd.)
Caribiner International, Inc., 24
Caribou Coffee Company, Inc., 28; 97 (upd.)
Carlisle Companies Inc., 8; 82 (upd.)
Carlson Companies, Inc., 6; 22 (upd.); 87 (upd.)
Carlson Restaurants Worldwide, 69
Carlson Wagonlit Travel, 55
Carma Laboratories, Inc., 60
CarMax, Inc., 55
Carmichael Lynch Inc., 28
Carmike Cinemas, Inc., 14; 37 (upd.); 74 (upd.)
Carnation Company, II
Carnegie Corporation of New York, 35
The Carnegie Hall Corporation, 101
Carnival Corporation, 6; 27 (upd.); 78 (upd.)
Carolina First Corporation, 31
Carolina Freight Corporation, 6
Carolina Power & Light Company, V; 23 (upd.)

Carolina Telephone and Telegraph Company, 10
Carpenter Technology Corporation, 13; 95 (upd.)
CARQUEST Corporation, 29
Carr-Gottstein Foods Co., 17
CarrAmerica Realty Corporation, 56
The Carriage House Companies, Inc., 55
Carriage Services, Inc., 37
Carrier Access Corporation, 44
Carrier Corporation, 7; 69 (upd.)
Carrizo Oil & Gas, Inc., 97
Carroll's Foods, Inc., 46
Carrols Restaurant Group, Inc., 92
The Carsey-Werner Company, L.L.C., 37
Carson Pirie Scott & Company, 15
Carson, Inc., 31
Carter Hawley Hale Stores, Inc., V
Carter Lumber Company, 45
Carter-Wallace, Inc., 8; 38 (upd.)
Carus Publishing Company, 93
Carvel Corporation, 35
Carver Bancorp, Inc., 94
Carver Boat Corporation LLC, 88
Carvin Corp., 89
Cascade Corporation, 65
Cascade General, Inc., 65
Cascade Natural Gas Corporation, 9
Casco Northern Bank, 14
Casey's General Stores, Inc., 19; 83 (upd.)
Cash America International, Inc., 20; 61 (upd.)
Cash Systems, Inc., 93
Cass Information Systems Inc., 100
Castle & Cooke, Inc., II; 20 (upd.)
Casual Corner Group, Inc., 43
Casual Male Retail Group, Inc., 52
Caswell-Massey Co. Ltd., 51
Catalina Lighting, Inc., 43 (upd.)
Catalina Marketing Corporation, 18
Catalytica Energy Systems, Inc., 44
Catellus Development Corporation, 24
Caterpillar Inc., III; 15 (upd.); 63 (upd.)
Catherines Stores Corporation, 15
Catholic Charities USA, 76
Catholic Health Initiatives, 91
Catholic Order of Foresters, 24; 97 (upd.)
Cato Corporation, 14
Cattleman's, Inc., 20
Cavco Industries, Inc., 65
CB Commercial Real Estate Services Group, Inc., 21
CB Richard Ellis Group, Inc., 70 (upd.)
CBI Industries, Inc., 7
CBRL Group, Inc., 35 (upd.); 86 (upd.)
CBS Corporation, II; 6 (upd.); 28 (upd.)
CBS Television Network, 66 (upd.)
CCA Industries, Inc., 53
CCC Information Services Group Inc., 74
CCH Inc., 14
CDI Corporation, 6; 54 (upd.)
CDW Computer Centers, Inc., 16; 52 (upd.)
Ce De Candy Inc., 100
CEC Entertainment, Inc., 31 (upd.)
Cedar Fair Entertainment Company, 22; 98 (upd.)
Celadon Group Inc., 30

Celanese Corporation, I
Celebrate Express, Inc., 70
Celebrity, Inc., 22
Celera Genomics, 74
Celestial Seasonings, Inc., 16
Celgene Corporation, 67
CellStar Corporation, 83
Cendant Corporation, 44 (upd.)
Centel Corporation, 6
Centennial Communications Corporation, 39
Centerior Energy Corporation, V
Centerplate, Inc. 79
Centex Corporation, 8; 29 (upd.)
Centocor Inc., 14
Central and South West Corporation, V
Central European Distribution Corporation, 75
Central Florida Investments, Inc., 93
Central Garden & Pet Company, 23; 58 (upd.)
Central Hudson Gas and Electricity Corporation, 6
Central Maine Power, 6
Central National-Gottesman Inc., 95
Central Newspapers, Inc., 10
Central Parking Corporation, 18
Central Soya Company, Inc., 7
Central Sprinkler Corporation, 29
Central Vermont Public Service Corporation, 54
Centuri Corporation, 54
Century Aluminum Company, 52
Century Business Services, Inc., 52
Century Casinos, Inc., 53
Century Communications Corp., 10
Century Telephone Enterprises, Inc., 9; 54 (upd.)
Century Theatres, Inc., 31
Cenveo Inc., 71 (upd.)
Cephalon, Inc., 45
Cepheid, 77
Ceradyne, Inc., 65
Cerner Corporation, 16; 94 (upd.)
CertainTeed Corporation, 35
Certegy, Inc., 63
Cessna Aircraft Company, 8; 27 (upd.)
CF Industries Holdings, Inc., 99
Chadbourne & Parke, 36
Chadwick's of Boston, Ltd., 29
The Chalone Wine Group, Ltd., 36
Champion Enterprises, Inc., 17
Champion Industries, Inc., 28
Champion International Corporation, IV; 20 (upd.)
Championship Auto Racing Teams, Inc., 37
Chancellor Beacon Academies, Inc., 53
Chancellor Media Corporation, 24
Chaparral Steel Co., 13
Charisma Brands LLC, 74
The Charles Machine Works, Inc., 64
Charles River Laboratories International, Inc., 42
The Charles Schwab Corporation, 8; 26 (upd.); 81 (upd.)
The Charles Stark Draper Laboratory, Inc., 35

Charlotte Russe Holding, Inc., 35; 90 (upd.)
The Charmer Sunbelt Group, 95
Charming Shoppes, Inc., 8; 38
Chart House Enterprises, Inc., 17
Chart Industries, Inc., 21; 96 (upd.)
Charter Communications, Inc., 33
ChartHouse International Learning Corporation, 49
Chas. Levy Company LLC, 60
Chase General Corporation, 91
The Chase Manhattan Corporation, II; 13 (upd.)
Chateau Communities, Inc., 37
Chattanooga Bakery, Inc., 86
Chattem, Inc., 17; 88 (upd.)
Chautauqua Airlines, Inc., 38
Checker Motors Corp., 89
Checkers Drive-In Restaurants, Inc., 16; 74 (upd.)
CheckFree Corporation, 81
Checkpoint Systems, Inc., 39
The Cheesecake Factory Inc., 17; 100 (upd.)
Chef Solutions, Inc., 89
Chelsea Milling Company, 29
Chelsea Piers Management Inc., 86
Chemcentral Corporation, 8
Chemed Corporation, 13
Chemfab Corporation, 35
Chemi-Trol Chemical Co., 16
Chemical Banking Corporation, II; 14 (upd.)
Chemical Waste Management, Inc., 9
Chemtura Corporation, 91 (upd.)
CHEP Pty. Ltd., 80
Cherokee Inc., 18
Cherry Lane Music Publishing Company, Inc., 62
Chesapeake Corporation, 8; 30 (upd.); 93 (upd.)
Chesapeake Utilities Corporation, 56
Chesebrough-Pond's USA, Inc., 8
ChevronTexaco Corporation, IV; 19 (upd.); 47 (upd.)
Cheyenne Software, Inc., 12
CHF Industries, Inc., 84
Chi-Chi's Inc., 13; 51 (upd.)
Chiasso Inc., 53
Chiat/Day Inc. Advertising, 11
Chic by H.I.S, Inc., 20
Chicago and North Western Holdings Corporation, 6
Chicago Bears Football Club, Inc., 33
Chicago Board of Trade, 41
Chicago Mercantile Exchange Holdings Inc., 75
Chicago National League Ball Club, Inc., 66
Chicago Review Press Inc., 84
Chick-fil-A Inc., 23; 90 (upd.)
Chicken of the Sea International, 24 (upd.)
Chico's FAS, Inc., 45
Children's Comprehensive Services, Inc., 42
Children's Healthcare of Atlanta Inc., 101
Children's Hospitals and Clinics, Inc., 54

The Children's Place Retail Stores, Inc., 37; 86 (upd.)
ChildrenFirst, Inc., 59
Childtime Learning Centers, Inc., 34
Chiles Offshore Corporation, 9
Chindex International, Inc., 101
Chipotle Mexican Grill, Inc., 67
CHIPS and Technologies, Inc., 9
Chiquita Brands International, Inc., 7; 21 (upd.); 83 (upd.)
Chiron Corporation, 10; 36 (upd.)
Chisholm-Mingo Group, Inc., 41
Chittenden & Eastman Company, 58
Chock Full o' Nuts Corp., 17
Choice Hotels International Inc., 14; 83 (upd.)
ChoicePoint Inc., 65
Chorus Line Corporation, 30
Chris-Craft Corporation, 9; 31 (upd.); 80 (upd.)
Christensen Boyles Corporation, 26
The Christian Broadcasting Network, Inc., 52
The Christian Science Publishing Society, 55
Christopher & Banks Corporation, 42
Chromcraft Revington, Inc., 15
The Chronicle Publishing Company, Inc., 23
Chronimed Inc., 26
Chrysler Corporation, I; 11 (upd.)
CHS Inc., 60
CH2M HILL Companies Ltd., 22; 96 (upd.)
The Chubb Corporation, III; 14 (upd.); 37 (upd.)
Chugach Alaska Corporation, 60
Church & Dwight Co., Inc., 29; 68 (upd.)
Church's Chicken, 66
Churchill Downs Incorporated, 29
Cianbro Corporation, 14
Ciber, Inc., 18
CiCi Enterprises, L.P., 99
CIENA Corporation, 54
CIGNA Corporation, III; 22 (upd.); 45 (upd.)
Cimarex Energy Co., 81
Cincinnati Bell, Inc., 6
Cincinnati Financial Corporation, 16; 44 (upd.)
Cincinnati Gas & Electric Company, 6
Cincinnati Lamb Inc., 72
Cincinnati Milacron Inc., 12
Cincom Systems Inc., 15
Cinemark Holdings, Inc., 95
Cinnabon, Inc., 23; 90 (upd.)
Cintas Corporation, 21; 51 (upd.)
CIPSCO Inc., 6
The Circle K Company, II; 20 (upd.)
Circon Corporation, 21
Circuit City Stores, Inc., 9; 29 (upd.); 65 (upd.)
Circus Circus Enterprises, Inc., 6
Cirrus Design Corporation, 44
Cirrus Logic, Inc., 11; 48 (upd.)
Cisco-Linksys LLC, 86

Fastenal Company, 14; 42 (upd.); 99 (upd.)
Fatburger Corporation, 64
Faultless Starch/Bon Ami Company, 55
Fay's Inc., 17
Faygo Beverages Inc., 55
Fazoli's Management, Inc., 76 (upd.)
Fazoli's Systems, Inc., 27
Featherlite Inc., 28
Fedders Corporation, 18; 43 (upd.)
Federal Agricultural Mortgage Corporation, 75
Federal Deposit Insurance Corporation, 93
Federal Express Corporation, V
Federal National Mortgage Association, II
Federal Paper Board Company, Inc., 8
Federal Prison Industries, Inc., 34
Federal Signal Corp., 10
Federal-Mogul Corporation, I; 10 (upd.); 26 (upd.)
Federated Department Stores Inc., 9; 31 (upd.)
FedEx Corporation, 18 (upd.); 42 (upd.)
Feed The Children, Inc., 68
FEI Company 79
Feld Entertainment, Inc., 32 (upd.)
Fellowes Manufacturing Company, 28
Fender Musical Instruments Company, 16; 43 (upd.)
Fenwick & West LLP, 34
Ferolito, Vultaggio & Sons, 27; 100 (upd.)
Ferrara Fire Apparatus, Inc., 84
Ferrara Pan Candy Company, 90
Ferrellgas Partners, L.P., 35
Ferro Corporation, 8; 56 (upd.)
F5 Networks, Inc., 72
FHP International Corporation, 6
FiberMark, Inc., 37
Fibreboard Corporation, 16
Fidelity Investments Inc., II; 14 (upd.)
Fidelity National Financial Inc., 54
Fidelity Southern Corporation, 85
Fieldale Farms Corporation, 23
Fieldcrest Cannon, Inc., 9; 31 (upd.)
Fiesta Mart, Inc., 101
Fifth Third Bancorp, 13; 31 (upd.)
Figgie International Inc., 7
Fiji Water LLC, 74
FileNet Corporation, 62
Fili Enterprises, Inc., 70
Film Roman, Inc., 58
FINA, Inc., 7
Fingerhut Companies, Inc., 9; 36 (upd.)
Finisar Corporation, 92
The Finish Line, Inc., 29; 68 (upd.)
FinishMaster, Inc., 24
Finlay Enterprises, Inc., 16; 76 (upd.)
Firearms Training Systems, Inc., 27
Fired Up, Inc., 82
Fireman's Fund Insurance Company, III
First Albany Companies Inc., 37
First Alert, Inc., 28
The First American Corporation, The 52
First Aviation Services Inc., 49
First Bank System Inc., 12
First Brands Corporation, 8

First Cash Financial Services, Inc., 57
First Chicago Corporation, II
First Colony Coffee & Tea Company, 84
First Commerce Bancshares, Inc., 15
First Commerce Corporation, 11
First Data Corporation, 30 (upd.)
First Empire State Corporation, 11
First Executive Corporation, III
First Fidelity Bank, N.A., New Jersey, 9
First Financial Management Corporation, 11
First Hawaiian, Inc., 11
First Industrial Realty Trust, Inc., 65
First Interstate Bancorp, II
The First Marblehead Corporation, 87
First Mississippi Corporation, 8
First Nationwide Bank, 14
First of America Bank Corporation, 8
First Security Corporation, 11
First Solar, Inc., 95
First Team Sports, Inc., 22
First Tennessee National Corporation, 11; 48 (upd.)
First Union Corporation, 10
First USA, Inc., 11
First Virginia Banks, Inc., 11
The First Years Inc., 46
Firstar Corporation, 11; 33 (upd.)
Fiserv Inc., 11; 33 (upd.)
Fish & Neave, 54
Fisher Communications, Inc., 99
Fisher Companies, Inc., 15
Fisher Controls International, LLC, 13; 61 (upd.)
Fisher Scientific International Inc., 24
Fisher-Price Inc., 12; 32 (upd.)
Fisk Corporation, 72
5 & Diner Franchise Corporation, 72
Five Guys Enterprises, LLC, 99
Flagstar Companies, Inc., 10
Flanders Corporation, 65
Flanigan's Enterprises, Inc., 60
Flatiron Construction Corporation, 92
Fleer Corporation, 15
FleetBoston Financial Corporation, 9; 36 (upd.)
Fleetwood Enterprises, Inc., III; 22 (upd.); 81 (upd.)
Fleming Companies, Inc., II; 17 (upd.)
Flexsteel Industries Inc., 15; 41 (upd.)
Flight Options, LLC, 75
FlightSafety International, Inc., 9; 29 (upd.)
Flint Ink Corporation, 13; 41 (upd.)
FLIR Systems, Inc., 69
Florida Crystals Inc., 35
Florida East Coast Industries, Inc., 59
Florida Gaming Corporation, 47
Florida Progress Corporation, V; 23 (upd.)
Florida Public Utilities Company, 69
Florida Rock Industries, Inc., 46
Florida's Natural Growers, 45
Florists' Transworld Delivery, Inc., 28
Florsheim Shoe Group Inc., 9; 31 (upd.)
Flotek Industries Inc., 93
Flour City International, Inc., 44
Flow International Corporation, 56
Flowers Industries, Inc., 12; 35 (upd.)

Flowserve Corporation, 33; 77 (upd.)
Fluke Corporation, 15
Fluor Corporation, I; 8 (upd.); 34 (upd.)
Flying Boat, Inc. (Chalk's Ocean Airways), 56
Flying J Inc., 19
FMC Corporation, I; 11 (upd.); 89 (upd.)
FMR Corp., 8; 32 (upd.)
Foamex International Inc., 17
Focus Features 78
Foley & Lardner, 28
Follett Corporation, 12; 39 (upd.)
Food Circus Super Markets, Inc., 88
The Food Emporium, 64
Food For The Poor, Inc., 77
Food Lion LLC, II; 15 (upd.); 66 (upd.)
Foodarama Supermarkets, Inc., 28
FoodBrands America, Inc., 23
Foodmaker, Inc., 14
Foot Locker, Inc., 68 (upd.)
Foot Petals L.L.C., 95
Foote, Cone & Belding Worldwide, I; 66 (upd.)
Footstar, Incorporated, 24
Forbes Inc., 30; 82 (upd.)
Force Protection Inc., 95
The Ford Foundation, 34
Ford Motor Company, I; 11 (upd.); 36 (upd.); 64 (upd.)
FORE Systems, Inc., 25
Foremost Farms USA Cooperative, 98
Forest City Enterprises, Inc., 16; 52 (upd.)
Forest Laboratories, Inc., 11; 52 (upd.)
Forest Oil Corporation, 19; 91 (upd.)
Forever Living Products International Inc., 17
Forever 21, Inc., 84
FormFactor, Inc., 85
Formica Corporation, 13
Forrester Research, Inc., 54
Forstmann Little & Co., 38
Fort Howard Corporation, 8
Fort James Corporation, 22 (upd.)
Fortune Brands, Inc., 29 (upd.); 68 (upd.)
Fortunoff Fine Jewelry and Silverware Inc., 26
Forward Air Corporation, 75
Forward Industries, Inc., 86
Fossil, Inc., 17
Foster Poultry Farms, 32
Foster Wheeler Corporation, 6; 23 (upd.)
Foster Wheeler Ltd., 76 (upd.)
FosterGrant, Inc., 60
Foundation Health Corporation, 12
Fountain Powerboats Industries, Inc., 28
Four Winns Boats LLC, 96
4Kids Entertainment Inc., 59
Fourth Financial Corporation, 11
Fox Entertainment Group, Inc., 43
Fox Family Worldwide, Inc., 24
Fox's Pizza Den, Inc., 98
Foxboro Company, 13
FoxHollow Technologies, Inc., 85
FoxMeyer Health Corporation, 16
Foxworth-Galbraith Lumber Company, 91
FPL Group, Inc., V; 49 (upd.)
Frank J. Zamboni & Co., Inc., 34

Frank Russell Company, 46
Frank's Nursery & Crafts, Inc., 12
Frankel & Co., 39
Franklin Covey Company, 11; 37 (upd.)
Franklin Electric Company, Inc., 43
Franklin Electronic Publishers, Inc., 23
The Franklin Mint, 69
Franklin Resources, Inc., 9
Franz Inc., 80
Fred Alger Management, Inc., 97
Fred Meyer Stores, Inc., V; 20 (upd.); 64
  (upd.)
Fred Usinger Inc., 54
The Fred W. Albrecht Grocery Co., 13
Fred Weber, Inc., 61
Fred's, Inc., 23; 62 (upd.)
Freddie Mac, 54
Frederick Atkins Inc., 16
Frederick's of Hollywood, Inc., 16; 59
  (upd.)
Freedom Communications, Inc., 36
Freeport-McMoRan Copper & Gold, Inc.,
  IV; 7 (upd.); 57 (upd.)
Freescale Semiconductor, Inc., 83
Freeze.com LLC, 77
FreightCar America, Inc., 101
French Fragrances, Inc., 22
Frequency Electronics, Inc., 61
Fresh America Corporation, 20
Fresh Choice, Inc., 20
Fresh Enterprises, Inc., 66
Fresh Express Inc., 88
Fresh Foods, Inc., 29
FreshDirect, LLC, 84
Fretter, Inc., 10
Fried, Frank, Harris, Shriver & Jacobson,
  35
Friedman's Inc., 29
Friedman, Billings, Ramsey Group, Inc.,
  53
Friendly Ice Cream Corporation, 30; 72
  (upd.)
Frigidaire Home Products, 22
Frisch's Restaurants, Inc., 35; 92 (upd.)
Frito-Lay North America, 32; 73 (upd.)
Fritz Companies, Inc., 12
Frontera Foods, Inc., 100
Frontier Airlines Holdings Inc., 22; 84
  (upd.)
Frontier Corp., 16
Frontier Natural Products Co-Op, 82
Frost & Sullivan, Inc., 53
Frozen Food Express Industries, Inc., 20;
  98 (upd.)
Fruehauf Corporation, I
Fruit of the Loom, Inc., 8; 25 (upd.)
Fruth Pharmacy, Inc., 66
Fry's Electronics, Inc., 68
Frymaster Corporation, 27
FSI International, Inc., 17
FTD Group, Inc., 99 (upd.)
FTI Consulting, Inc., 77
FTP Software, Inc., 20
Fubu, 29
Fuel Systems Solutions, Inc., 97
Fuel Tech, Inc., 85
FuelCell Energy, Inc., 75
Fujitsu-ICL Systems Inc., 11

Fulbright & Jaworski L.L.P., 47
Funco, Inc., 20
Fuqua Enterprises, Inc., 17
Fuqua Industries, Inc., I
Furmanite Corporation, 92
Furniture Brands International, Inc., 39
  (upd.)
Furon Company, 28
Furr's Restaurant Group, Inc., 53
Furr's Supermarkets, Inc., 28
Future Now, Inc., 12
G&K Services, Inc., 16
G-III Apparel Group, Ltd., 22
G. Heileman Brewing Company Inc., I
G. Leblanc Corporation, 55
G.A.F., I
G.D. Searle & Company, I; 12 (upd.); 34
  (upd.)
G.I. Joe's, Inc., 30
G.S. Blodgett Corporation, 15
Gabelli Asset Management Inc., 30
Gables Residential Trust, 49
Gadzooks, Inc., 18
GAF Corporation, 22 (upd.)
Gage Marketing Group, 26
Gaiam, Inc., 41
Gainsco, Inc., 22
Galardi Group, Inc., 72
Galaxy Investors, Inc., 97
Galaxy Nutritional Foods, Inc., 58
Gale International Llc, 93
Galey & Lord, Inc., 20; 66 (upd.)
The Gallup Organization, 37
Galyan's Trading Company, Inc., 47
The Gambrinus Company, 40
GameStop Corp., 69 (upd.)
Gaming Partners International
  Corporation, 93
Gander Mountain Company, 20; 90
  (upd.)
Gannett Company, Inc., IV; 7 (upd.); 30
  (upd.); 66 (upd.)
Gantos, Inc., 17
The Gap, Inc., V; 18 (upd.); 55 (upd.)
Garan, Inc., 16; 64 (upd.)
Garden Fresh Restaurant Corporation, 31
Garden Ridge Corporation, 27
Gardenburger, Inc., 33; 76 (upd.)
Gardner Denver, Inc., 49
Gart Sports Company, 24
Gartner, Inc., 21; 94 (upd.)
Garst Seed Company, Inc., 86
GateHouse Media, Inc., 91
The Gates Corporation, 9
Gateway, Inc., 10; 27 (upd.); 63 (upd.)
The Gatorade Company, 82
GATX Corporation, 6; 25 (upd.)
Gaylord Bros., Inc., 100
Gaylord Container Corporation, 8
Gaylord Entertainment Company, 11; 36
  (upd.)
GC Companies, Inc., 25
GE Aircraft Engines, 9
GE Capital Aviation Services, 36
Geerlings & Wade, Inc., 45
Geffen Records Inc., 26
Gehl Company, 19
GEICO Corporation, 10; 40 (upd.)

Geiger Bros., 60
Gemini Sound Products Corporation, 58
Gen-Probe Incorporated 79
GenCorp Inc., 8; 9
Genentech, Inc., I; 8 (upd.); 32 (upd.);
  75 (upd.)
General Atomics, 57
General Bearing Corporation, 45
General Binding Corporation, 10; 73
  (upd.)
General Cable Corporation, 40
The General Chemical Group Inc., 37
General Cigar Holdings, Inc., 66 (upd.)
General Cinema Corporation, I
General DataComm Industries, Inc., 14
General Dynamics Corporation, I; 10
  (upd.); 40 (upd.); 88 (upd.)
General Electric Company, II; 12 (upd.);
  34 (upd.); 63 (upd.)
General Employment Enterprises, Inc., 87
General Growth Properties, Inc., 57
General Host Corporation, 12
General Housewares Corporation, 16
General Instrument Corporation, 10
General Maritime Corporation, 59
General Mills, Inc., II; 10 (upd.); 36
  (upd.); 85 (upd.)
General Motors Corporation, I; 10 (upd.);
  36 (upd.); 64 (upd.)
General Nutrition Companies, Inc., 11;
  29 (upd.)
General Public Utilities Corporation, V
General Re Corporation, III; 24 (upd.)
General Signal Corporation, 9
General Tire, Inc., 8
Genesco Inc., 17; 84 (upd.)
Genesee & Wyoming Inc., 27
Genesis Health Ventures, Inc., 18
Genesis Microchip Inc., 82
Genetics Institute, Inc., 8
Geneva Steel, 7
Genmar Holdings, Inc., 45
Genovese Drug Stores, Inc., 18
GenRad, Inc., 24
Gentex Corporation, 26
Gentiva Health Services, Inc. 79
Genuardi's Family Markets, Inc., 35
Genuine Parts Company, 9; 45 (upd.)
Genzyme Corporation, 13; 38 (upd.); 77
  (upd.)
The Geon Company, 11
GeoResources, Inc., 101
George A. Hormel and Company, II
The George F. Cram Company, Inc., 55
George P. Johnson Company, 60
George S. May International Company,
  55
George W. Park Seed Company, Inc., 98
Georgia Gulf Corporation, 9; 61 (upd.)
Georgia-Pacific LLC, IV; 9 (upd.); 47
  (upd.); 101 (upd.)
Geotek Communications Inc., 21
Gerald Stevens, Inc., 37
Gerber Products Company, 7; 21 (upd.)
Gerber Scientific, Inc., 12; 84 (upd.)
German American Bancorp, 41
Getty Images, Inc., 31
Gevity HR, Inc., 63

INTERNATIONAL DIRECTORY OF COMPANY HISTORIES, VOLUME 101

Monrovia Nursery Company, 70
The Mosaic Company, 91
Monsanto Company, I; 9 (upd.); 29 (upd.); 77 (upd.)
Monster Cable Products, Inc., 69
Monster Worldwide Inc., 74 (upd.)
Montana Coffee Traders, Inc., 60
The Montana Power Company, 11; 44 (upd.)
Monterey Pasta Company, 58
Montgomery Ward & Co., Incorporated, V; 20 (upd.)
Moody's Corporation, 65
Moog Inc., 13
Moog Music, Inc., 75
Mooney Aerospace Group Ltd., 52
Moore Medical Corp., 17
Moore-Handley, Inc., 39
Moran Towing Corporation, Inc., 15
The Morgan Group, Inc., 46
Morgan, Lewis & Bockius LLP, 29
Morgan Stanley Dean Witter & Company, II; 16 (upd.); 33 (upd.)
Morgan's Foods, Inc., 101
Morgans Hotel Group Company, 80
Morinda Holdings, Inc., 82
Morningstar Inc., 68
Morris Communications Corporation, 36
Morris Travel Services L.L.C., 26
Morrison & Foerster LLP 78
Morrison Knudsen Corporation, 7; 28 (upd.)
Morrison Restaurants Inc., 11
Morrow Equipment Co. L.L.C., 87
Morse Shoe Inc., 13
Morton International Inc., I; 9 (upd.); 80 (upd.)
Morton Thiokol, Inc., I
Morton's Restaurant Group, Inc., 30; 88 (upd.)
Mosinee Paper Corporation, 15
Mossimo, 27; 96 (upd.)
Motel 6, 13; 56 (upd.)
Mothers Against Drunk Driving (MADD), 51
Mothers Work, Inc., 18
The Motley Fool, Inc., 40
Moto Photo, Inc., 45
Motor Cargo Industries, Inc., 35
Motorcar Parts & Accessories, Inc., 47
Motorola, Inc., II; 11 (upd.); 34 (upd.); 93 (upd.)
Motown Records Company L.P., 26
Mott's Inc., 57
Mountain States Mortgage Centers, Inc., 29
Movado Group, Inc., 28
Movie Gallery, Inc., 31
Movie Star Inc., 17
MPS Group, Inc., 49
MPW Industrial Services Group, Inc., 53
Mr. Coffee, Inc., 15
Mr. Gasket Inc., 15
Mr. Gatti's, LP, 87
Mrs. Baird's Bakeries, 29
Mrs. Fields' Original Cookies, Inc., 27
Mrs. Grossman's Paper Company Inc., 84
MSC Industrial Direct Co., Inc., 71

Mt. Olive Pickle Company, Inc., 44
MTR Gaming Group, Inc., 75
MTS Inc., 37
Mueller Industries, Inc., 7; 52 (upd.)
Mullen Advertising Inc., 51
Multi-Color Corporation, 53
Multimedia Games, Inc., 41
Multimedia, Inc., 11
Murdock Madaus Schwabe, 26
Murphy Family Farms Inc., 22
Murphy Oil Corporation, 7; 32 (upd.); 95 (upd.)
The Musco Family Olive Co., 91
Musco Lighting, 83
Musicland Stores Corporation, 9; 38 (upd.)
The Mutual Benefit Life Insurance Company, III
The Mutual Life Insurance Company of New York, III
The Mutual of Omaha Companies, 98
Muzak, Inc., 18
MWH Preservation Limited Partnership, 65
MWI Veterinary Supply, Inc., 80
Mycogen Corporation, 21
Myers Industries, Inc., 19; 96 (upd.
Mylan Laboratories Inc., I; 20 (upd.); 59 (upd.)
Myriad Restaurant Group, Inc., 87
Myriad Genetics, Inc., 95
N.F. Smith & Associates LP, 70
Nabisco Foods Group, II; 7 (upd.)
Nabors Industries, Inc., 9
NACCO Industries Inc., 7; 78 (upd.)
Nalco Holding Company, I; 12 (upd.); 89 (upd.)
Nantucket Allserve, Inc., 22
Napster, Inc., 69
NASD, 54 (upd.)
The NASDAQ Stock Market, Inc., 92
Nash Finch Company, 8; 23 (upd.); 65 (upd.)
Nashua Corporation, 8
Nastech Pharmaceutical Company Inc. 79
Nathan's Famous, Inc., 29
National Amusements Inc., 28
National Aquarium in Baltimore, Inc., 74
National Association for Stock Car Auto Racing, 32
National Association of Securities Dealers, Inc., 10
National Audubon Society, 26
National Auto Credit, Inc., 16
The National Bank of South Carolina, 76
National Beverage Corporation, 26; 88 (upd.)
National Broadcasting Company, Inc., II; 6 (upd.); 28 (upd.)
National Can Corporation, I
National Car Rental System, Inc., 10
National City Corporation, 15; 97 (upd.)
National Collegiate Athletic Association, 96
National Convenience Stores Incorporated, 7
National Discount Brokers Group, Inc., 28

National Distillers and Chemical Corporation, I
National Educational Music Co. Ltd., 47
National Envelope Corporation, 32
National Equipment Services, Inc., 57
National Financial Partners Corp., 65
National Football League, 29
National Frozen Foods Corporation, 94
National Fuel Gas Company, 6; 95 (upd.)
National Geographic Society, 9; 30 (upd.); 79 (upd.)
National Grape Cooperative Association, Inc., 20
National Grid USA, 51 (upd.)
National Gypsum Company, 10
National Health Laboratories Incorporated, 11
National Heritage Academies, Inc., 60
National Hockey League, 35
National Home Centers, Inc., 44
National Instruments Corporation, 22
National Intergroup, Inc., V
National Jewish Health, 101
National Journal Group Inc., 67
National Media Corporation, 27
National Medical Enterprises, Inc., III
National Medical Health Card Systems, Inc. 79
National Oilwell, Inc., 54
National Organization for Women, Inc., 55
National Patent Development Corporation, 13
National Picture & Frame Company, 24
National Presto Industries, Inc., 16; 43 (upd.)
National Public Radio, Inc., 19; 47 (upd.)
National R.V. Holdings, Inc., 32
National Railroad Passenger Corporation (Amtrak), 22; 66 (upd.)
National Record Mart, Inc., 29
National Research Corporation, 87
National Rifle Association of America, 37
National Sanitary Supply Co., 16
National Semiconductor Corporation, II; VI, 26 (upd.); 69 (upd.)
National Service Industries, Inc., 11; 54 (upd.)
National Standard Co., 13
National Starch and Chemical Company, 49
National Steel Corporation, 12
National TechTeam, Inc., 41
National Thoroughbred Racing Association, 58
National Weather Service, 91
National Wine & Spirits, Inc., 49
NationsBank Corporation, 10
Natrol, Inc., 49
Natural Alternatives International, Inc., 49
Natural Ovens Bakery, Inc., 72
Natural Selection Foods, 54
Natural Wonders Inc., 14
Naturally Fresh, Inc., 88
The Nature Conservancy, 28
Nature's Sunshine Products, Inc., 15
Naumes, Inc., 81
Nautica Enterprises, Inc., 18; 44 (upd.)

Navarre Corporation, 24
Navigant Consulting, Inc., 93
Navigant International, Inc., 47
The Navigators Group, Inc., 92
Navistar International Corporation, I; 10
    (upd.)
NAVTEQ Corporation, 69
Navy Exchange Service Command, 31
Navy Federal Credit Union, 33
NBD Bancorp, Inc., 11
NBGS International, Inc., 73
NBTY, Inc., 31
NCH Corporation, 8
NCI Building Systems, Inc., 88
NCL Corporation 79
NCNB Corporation, II
NCO Group, Inc., 42
NCR Corporation, III; 6 (upd.); 30
    (upd.); 90 (upd.)
Nebraska Book Company, Inc., 65
Nebraska Furniture Mart, Inc., 94
Nebraska Public Power District, 29
Neenah Foundry Company, 68
Neff Corp., 32
NeighborCare, Inc., 67 (upd.)
The Neiman Marcus Group, Inc., 12; 49
    (upd.)
Nektar Therapeutics, 91
Neogen Corporation, 94
NERCO, Inc., 7
NetCracker Technology Corporation, 98
Netezza Corporation, 69
Netflix, Inc., 58
NETGEAR, Inc., 81
NetIQ Corporation 79
NetJets Inc., 96 (upd.)
Netscape Communications Corporation,
    15; 35 (upd.)
Network Appliance, Inc., 58
Network Associates, Inc., 25
Network Equipment Technologies Inc., 92
Neuberger Berman Inc., 57
NeuStar, Inc., 81
Neutrogena Corporation, 17
Nevada Bell Telephone Company, 14
Nevada Power Company, 11
Nevamar Company, 82
New Balance Athletic Shoe, Inc., 25; 68
    (upd.)
New Belgium Brewing Company, Inc., 68
New Brunswick Scientific Co., Inc., 45
New Chapter Inc., 96
New Dana Perfumes Company, 37
New England Business Service Inc., 18;
    78 (upd.)
New England Confectionery Co., 15
New England Electric System, V
New England Mutual Life Insurance
    Company, III
New Jersey Devils, 84
New Jersey Manufacturers Insurance
    Company, 96
New Jersey Resources Corporation, 54
New Line Cinema, Inc., 47
New Orleans Saints LP, 58
The New Piper Aircraft, Inc., 44
New Plan Realty Trust, 11
New Seasons Market, 75

New Street Capital Inc., 8
New Times, Inc., 45
New Valley Corporation, 17
New World Pasta Company, 53
New World Restaurant Group, Inc., 44
New York City Health and Hospitals
    Corporation, 60
New York City Off-Track Betting
    Corporation, 51
New York Community Bancorp Inc. 78
New York Daily News, 32
New York Health Care, Inc., 72
New York Life Insurance Company, III;
    45 (upd.)
New York Restaurant Group, Inc., 32
New York Shakespeare Festival
    Management, 93
New York State Electric and Gas, 6
New York Stock Exchange, Inc., 9; 39
    (upd.)
The New York Times Company, IV; 19
    (upd.); 61 (upd.)
Neways Inc. 78
Newcor, Inc., 40
Newell Rubbermaid Inc., 9; 52 (upd.)
Newfield Exploration Company, 65
Newhall Land and Farming Company, 14
Newly Weds Foods, Inc., 74
Newman's Own, Inc., 37
Newmont Mining Corporation, 7; 94
    (upd.)
Newpark Resources, Inc., 63
Newport Corporation, 71
Newport News Shipbuilding Inc., 13; 38
    (upd.)
News America Publishing Inc., 12
NewYork-Presbyterian Hospital, 59
Nexstar Broadcasting Group, Inc., 73
Nextel Communications, Inc., 10; 27
    (upd.)
NFL Films, 75
NFO Worldwide, Inc., 24
NGC Corporation, 18
Niagara Corporation, 28
Niagara Mohawk Holdings Inc., V; 45
    (upd.)
Nichols Research Corporation, 18
Nicklaus Companies, 45
Nicole Miller, 98
Nicor Inc., 6; 86 (upd.)
Nielsen Business Media, Inc., 98
NIKE, Inc., V; 8 (upd.); 36 (upd.); 75
    (upd.)
Nikken Global Inc., 32
Niman Ranch, Inc., 67
Nimbus CD International, Inc., 20
Nine West Group, Inc., 11; 39 (upd.)
99¢ Only Stores, 25; 100 (upd.)
NIPSCO Industries, Inc., 6
Nitches, Inc., 53
NL Industries, Inc., 10
Nobel Learning Communities, Inc., 37;
    76 (upd.)
Noble Affiliates, Inc., 11
Noble Roman's Inc., 14; 99 (upd.)
Noland Company, 35
Nolo.com, Inc., 49
Noodle Kidoodle, 16

Noodles & Company, Inc., 55
Nooter Corporation, 61
Norcal Waste Systems, Inc., 60
NordicTrack, 22
Nordson Corporation, 11; 48 (upd.)
Nordstrom, Inc., V; 18 (upd.); 67 (upd.)
Norelco Consumer Products Co., 26
Norfolk Southern Corporation, V; 29
    (upd.); 75 (upd.)
Norm Thompson Outfitters, Inc., 47
Norrell Corporation, 25
Norstan, Inc., 16
Nortek, Inc., 34
North American Galvanizing & Coatings,
    Inc., 99
North Atlantic Trading Company Inc., 65
The North Face, Inc., 18; 78 (upd.)
North Fork Bancorporation, Inc., 46
North Pacific Group, Inc., 61
North Star Steel Company, 18
Northeast Utilities, V; 48 (upd.)
Northern States Power Company, V; 20
    (upd.)
Northern Trust Corporation, 9; 101
    (upd.)
Northland Cranberries, Inc., 38
Northrop Grumman Corporation, I; 11
    (upd.); 45 (upd.)
Northwest Airlines, I; 6
    (upd.); 26 (upd.); 74 (upd.)
Northwest Natural Gas Company, 45
NorthWestern Corporation, 37
Northwestern Mutual Life Insurance
    Company, III; 45 (upd.)
Norton Company, 8
Norton McNaughton, Inc., 27
Norwood Promotional Products, Inc., 26
NovaCare, Inc., 11
NovaStar Financial, Inc., 91
Novell, Inc., 6; 23 (upd.)
Novellus Systems, Inc., 18
Noven Pharmaceuticals, Inc., 55
NPC International, Inc., 40
The NPD Group, Inc., 68
NRG Energy, Inc. 79
NRT Incorporated, 61
NSF International, 72
NSS Enterprises Inc. 78
NTD Architecture, 101
NTN Buzztime, Inc., 86
Nu Skin Enterprises, Inc., 27; 76 (upd.)
Nu-kote Holding, Inc., 18
Nucor Corporation, 7; 21 (upd.); 79
    (upd.)
Nutraceutical International Corporation,
    37
NutraSweet Company, 8
Nutrition 21 Inc., 97
NutriSystem, Inc., 71
Nutrition for Life International Inc., 22
NVIDIA Corporation, 54
NVR Inc., 8; 70 (upd.)
NYMAGIC, Inc., 41
NYNEX Corporation, V
Nypro, Inc., 101
O.C. Tanner Co., 69
Oak Harbor Freight Lines, Inc., 53
Oak Industries Inc., 21

Panavision Inc., 24
Pancho's Mexican Buffet, Inc., 46
Panda Restaurant Group, Inc., 35; 97 (upd.)
Panera Bread Company, 44
Panhandle Eastern Corporation, V
Pantone Inc., 53
The Pantry, Inc., 36
Papa Gino's Holdings Corporation, Inc., 86
Papa John's International, Inc., 15; 71 (upd.)
Papa Murphy's International, Inc., 54
Papetti's Hygrade Egg Products, Inc., 39
Pappas Restaurants, Inc., 76
Par Pharmaceutical Companies, Inc., 65
The Paradies Shops, Inc., 88
Paradise Music & Entertainment, Inc., 42
Parallel Petroleum Corporation, 101
Parametric Technology Corp., 16
Paramount Pictures Corporation, II; 94 (upd.)
PAREXEL International Corporation, 84
Paris Corporation, 22
Parisian, Inc., 14
Park Corp., 22
Park-Ohio Industries Inc., 17; 85 (upd.)
Parker Drilling Company, 28
Parker-Hannifin Corporation, III; 24 (upd.); 99 (upd.)
Parlex Corporation, 61
Parsons Brinckerhoff, Inc., 34
The Parsons Corporation, 8; 56 (upd.)
Party City Corporation, 54
Pathmark Stores, Inc., 23; 101 (upd.)
Patina Oil & Gas Corporation, 24
Patrick Industries, Inc., 30
Patriot Transportation Holding, Inc., 91
Patterson Dental Co., 19
Patterson-UTI Energy, Inc., 55
Patton Boggs LLP, 71
Paul Harris Stores, Inc., 18
Paul, Hastings, Janofsky & Walker LLP, 27
Paul Mueller Company, 65
Paul Reed Smith Guitar Company, 89
The Paul Revere Corporation, 12
Paul, Weiss, Rifkind, Wharton & Garrison, 47
Paul-Son Gaming Corporation, 66
Paxson Communications Corporation, 33
Pay 'N Pak Stores, Inc., 9
Paychex, Inc., 15; 46 (upd.)
Payless Cashways, Inc., 11; 44 (upd.)
Payless ShoeSource, Inc., 18; 69 (upd.)
PayPal Inc., 58
The PBSJ Corporation, 82
PC Connection, Inc., 37
PCA International, Inc., 62
PCC Natural Markets, 94
PDI, Inc., 52
PDL BioPharma, Inc., 90
PDQ Food Stores, Inc. 79
PDS Gaming Corporation, 44
Peabody Coal Company, 10
Peabody Energy Corporation, 45 (upd.)
Peabody Holding Company, Inc., IV
The Peak Technologies Group, Inc., 14

Peapod, Inc., 30
Pearle Vision, Inc., 13
Peavey Electronics Corporation, 16; 94 (upd.)
PECO Energy Company, 11
Pediatric Services of America, Inc., 31
Pediatrix Medical Group, Inc., 61
Peebles Inc., 16; 43 (upd.)
Peet's Coffee & Tea, Inc., 38; 100 (upd.)
Pegasus Solutions, Inc., 75
Pei Cobb Freed & Partners Architects LLP, 57
Pelican Products, Inc., 86
Pella Corporation, 12; 39 (upd.); 89 (upd.)
Pemco Aviation Group Inc., 54
Pendleton Grain Growers Inc., 64
Pendleton Woolen Mills, Inc., 42
Penford Corporation, 55
Penn Engineering & Manufacturing Corp., 28
Penn National Gaming, Inc., 33
Penn Traffic Company, 13
Penn Virginia Corporation, 85
Pennington Seed Inc., 98
Pennsylvania Blue Shield, III
Pennsylvania Power & Light Company, V
Pennwalt Corporation, I
PennWell Corporation, 55
Pennzoil-Quaker State Company, IV; 20 (upd.); 50 (upd.)
Penske Corporation, V; 19 (upd.); 84 (upd.)
Pentair, Inc., 7; 26 (upd.); 81 (upd.)
Pentech International, Inc., 29
Penton Media, Inc., 27
Penzeys Spices, Inc. 79
People Express Airlines, Inc., I
Peoples Energy Corporation, 6
PeopleSoft Inc., 14; 33 (upd.)
The Pep Boys—Manny, Moe & Jack, 11; 36 (upd.); 81 (upd.)
Pepper Hamilton LLP, 43
Pepperidge Farm, Incorporated, 81
The Pepsi Bottling Group, Inc., 40
PepsiAmericas, Inc., 67 (upd.)
PepsiCo, Inc., I; 10 (upd.); 38 (upd.); 93 (upd.)
Perma-Fix Environmental Services, Inc., 99
Perdue Farms Inc., 7; 23 (upd.)
Performance Food Group, 31; 96 (upd.)
Perini Corporation, 8; 82 (upd.)
PerkinElmer Inc. 7; 78 (upd.)
Perkins Coie LLP, 56
Perkins Family Restaurants, L.P., 22
Perot Systems Corporation, 29
Perrigo Company, 12; 59 (upd.)
Perry Ellis International, Inc., 41
Perry's Ice Cream Company Inc., 90
The Perseus Books Group, 91
Pet Incorporated, 7
Petco Animal Supplies, Inc., 29; 74 (upd.)
Pete's Brewing Company, 22
Peter Kiewit Sons' Inc., 8
Peter Piper, Inc., 70
Peterbilt Motors Company, 89
Petersen Publishing Company, 21

Peterson American Corporation, 55
PetMed Express, Inc., 81
Petrie Stores Corporation, 8
Petrohawk Energy Corporation 79
Petroleum Helicopters, Inc., 35
Petrolite Corporation, 15
Petrossian Inc., 54
PETsMART, Inc., 14; 41 (upd.)
The Pew Charitable Trusts, 35
Pez Candy, Inc., 38
Pfizer Inc., I; 9 (upd.); 38 (upd.); 79 (upd.)
PFSweb, Inc., 73
PG&E Corporation, 26 (upd.)
Phar-Mor Inc., 12
Pharmacia & Upjohn Inc., I; 25 (upd.)
Pharmion Corporation, 91
Phat Fashions LLC, 49
Phelps Dodge Corporation, IV; 28 (upd.); 75 (upd.)
PHH Arval, V; 53 (upd.)
PHI, Inc., 80 (upd.)
Philadelphia Eagles, 37
Philadelphia Electric Company, V
Philadelphia Gas Works Company, 92
Philadelphia Media Holdings LLC, 92
Philadelphia Suburban Corporation, 39
Philharmonic-Symphony Society of New York, Inc. (New York Philharmonic), 69
Philip Morris Companies Inc., V; 18 (upd.); 44 (upd.)
Philip Services Corp., 73
Philips Electronics North America Corp., 13
Phillips, de Pury & Luxembourg, 49
Phillips Foods, Inc., 63; 90 (upd.)
Phillips International Inc. 78
Phillips Petroleum Company, IV; 40 (upd.)
Phillips-Van Heusen Corporation, 24
Phoenix Footwear Group, Inc., 70
The Phoenix Media/Communications Group, 91
PHP Healthcare Corporation, 22
PhyCor, Inc., 36
Physician Sales & Service, Inc., 14
Physio-Control International Corp., 18
Piccadilly Cafeterias, Inc., 19
PictureTel Corp., 10; 27 (upd.)
Piedmont Natural Gas Company, Inc., 27
Pier 1 Imports, Inc., 12; 34 (upd.); 95 (upd.)
Pierce Leahy Corporation, 24
Piercing Pagoda, Inc., 29
Piggly Wiggly Southern, Inc., 13
Pilgrim's Pride Corporation, 7; 23 (upd.); 90 (upd.
Pillowtex Corporation, 19; 41 (upd.)
The Pillsbury Company, II; 13 (upd.); 62 (upd.)
Pillsbury Madison & Sutro LLP, 29
Pilot Air Freight Corp., 67
Pilot Corporation, 49
Pilot Pen Corporation of America, 82
Pinkerton's Inc., 9
Pinnacle Airlines Corp., 73

Riklis Family Corp., 9
Rimage Corp., 89
Ripley Entertainment, Inc., 74
Riser Foods, Inc., 9
Rite Aid Corporation, V; 19 (upd.); 63 (upd.)
Ritz Camera Centers, 34
The Ritz-Carlton Hotel Company, L.L.C., 9; 29 (upd.); 71 (upd.)
Ritz-Craft Corporation of Pennsylvania Inc., 94
The Rival Company, 19
River Oaks Furniture, Inc., 43
River Ranch Fresh Foods LLC, 88
Riverbed Technology, Inc., 101
Riverwood International Corporation, 11; 48 (upd.)
Riviana Foods Inc., 27
Riviera Holdings Corporation, 75
Riviera Tool Company, 89
RJR Nabisco Holdings Corp., V
RMH Teleservices, Inc., 42
Roadhouse Grill, Inc., 22
Roadmaster Industries, Inc., 16
Roadway Express, Inc., V; 25 (upd.)
Roanoke Electric Steel Corporation, 45
Robbins & Myers Inc., 15
Robins, Kaplan, Miller & Ciresi L.L.P., 89
Roberds Inc., 19
Robert Half International Inc., 18; 70 (upd.)
Robert Mondavi Corporation, 15; 50 (upd.)
Robert Talbott Inc., 88
Robert W. Baird & Co. Incorporated, 67
Robert Wood Johnson Foundation, 35
Roberts Pharmaceutical Corporation, 16
Robertson-Ceco Corporation, 19
Robinson Helicopter Company, 51
Rocawear Apparel LLC, 77
Roche Bioscience, 11; 14 (upd.)
Rochester Gas and Electric Corporation, 6
Rochester Telephone Corporation, 6
Rock Bottom Restaurants, Inc., 25; 68 (upd.)
Rock-It Cargo USA, Inc., 86
Rock of Ages Corporation, 37
Rock-Tenn Company, 13; 59 (upd.)
The Rockefeller Foundation, 34
Rockefeller Group International Inc., 58
Rockford Corporation, 43
Rockford Products Corporation, 55
RockShox, Inc., 26
Rockwell Automation, 43 (upd.)
Rockwell International Corporation, I; 11 (upd.)
Rockwell Medical Technologies, Inc., 88
Rocky Mountain Chocolate Factory, Inc., 73
Rocky Shoes & Boots, Inc., 26
Rodale, Inc., 23; 47 (upd.)
Rodda Paint Company, 98
ROFIN-SINAR Technologies Inc., 81
Rogers Corporation, 61; 80 (upd.)
Rohm and Haas Company, I; 26 (upd.); 77 (upd.)
ROHN Industries, Inc., 22
Rohr Incorporated, 9

Roll International Corporation, 37
Rollerblade, Inc., 15; 34 (upd.)
Rollins, Inc., 11
Rolls-Royce Allison, 29 (upd.)
Roly Poly Franchise Systems LLC, 83
Romacorp, Inc., 58
Roman Meal Company, 84
Ron Tonkin Chevrolet Company, 55
Ronco Corporation, 15; 80 (upd.)
Rooms To Go Inc., 28
Rooney Brothers Co., 25
Roper Industries, Inc., 15; 50 (upd.)
Ropes & Gray, 40
Rorer Group, I
Rosauers Supermarkets, Inc., 90
Rose Acre Farms, Inc., 60
Rose Art Industries, 58
Rose's Stores, Inc., 13
Roseburg Forest Products Company, 58
Rosemount Inc., 15
Rosenbluth International Inc., 14
Rosetta Stone Inc., 93
Ross Stores, Inc., 17; 43 (upd.); 101 (upd.)
Rotary International, 31
Roto-Rooter, Inc., 15; 61 (upd.)
The Rottlund Company, Inc., 28
Rouge Steel Company, 8
Rounder Records Corporation 79
Roundy's Inc., 14; 58 (upd.)
The Rouse Company, 15; 63 (upd.)
Rowan Companies, Inc., 43
Roy Anderson Corporation, 75
Roy F. Weston, Inc., 33
Royal Appliance Manufacturing Company, 15
Royal Caribbean Cruises Ltd., 22; 74 (upd.)
Royal Crown Company, Inc., 23
RPC, Inc., 91
RPM International Inc., 8; 36 (upd.); 91 (upd.)
RSA Security Inc., 46
RSM McGladrey Business Services Inc., 98
RTI Biologics, Inc., 96
RTM Restaurant Group, 58
Rubbermaid Incorporated, III; 20 (upd.)
Rubio's Restaurants, Inc., 35
Ruby Tuesday, Inc., 18; 71 (upd.)
Rudolph Technologies Inc., 94
Ruiz Food Products, Inc., 53
Rural Cellular Corporation, 43
Rural/Metro Corporation, 28
Rush Communications, 33
Rush Enterprises, Inc., 64
Russ Berrie and Company, Inc., 12; 82 (upd.)
Russell Corporation, 8; 30 (upd.); 82 (upd.)
Russell Reynolds Associates Inc., 38
Russell Stover Candies Inc., 12; 91 (upd.)
Rust International Inc., 11
Rusty, Inc., 95
Ruth's Chris Steak House, 28; 88 (upd.)
RWD Technologies, Inc., 76
Ryan Beck & Co., Inc., 66
Ryan Companies US, Inc., 99

Ryan's Restaurant Group, Inc., 15; 68 (upd.)
Ryder System, Inc., V; 24 (upd.)
Ryerson Tull, Inc., 40 (upd.)
Ryko Corporation, 83
The Ryland Group, Inc., 8; 37 (upd.)
S&C Electric Company, 15
S&D Coffee, Inc., 84
S&K Famous Brands, Inc., 23
S-K-I Limited, 15
S.C. Johnson & Son, Inc., III; 28 (upd.); 89 (upd.)
Saatchi & Saatchi, 42 (upd.)
Sabratek Corporation, 29
SABRE Group Holdings, Inc., 26
Sabre Holdings Corporation, 74 (upd.)
Safe Flight Instrument Corporation, 71
SAFECO Corporaton, III
Safeguard Scientifics, Inc., 10
Safelite Glass Corp., 19
SafeNet Inc., 101
Safeskin Corporation, 18
Safety Components International, Inc., 63
Safety 1st, Inc., 24
Safety-Kleen Systems Inc., 8; 82 (upd.)
Safeway Inc., II; 24 (upd.); 85 (upd.)
Saga Communications, Inc., 27
Saia, Inc., 98
The St. Joe Company, 31; 98 (upd.)
St. Joe Paper Company, 8
St. John Knits, Inc., 14
St. Jude Medical, Inc., 11; 43 (upd.); 97 (upd.)
St. Louis Music, Inc., 48
St. Mary Land & Exploration Company, 63
St. Paul Bank for Cooperatives, 8
The St. Paul Travelers Companies, Inc. III; 22 (upd.); 79 (upd.)
Ste. Michelle Wine Estates Ltd., 96
Saks Inc., 24; 41 (upd.)
Salant Corporation, 12; 51 (upd.)
Salem Communications Corporation, 97
salesforce.com, Inc. 79
Salick Health Care, Inc., 53
Salix Pharmaceuticals, Ltd., 93
Sally Beauty Company, Inc., 60
Salomon Inc., II; 13 (upd.)
Salt River Project, 19
Salton, Inc., 30; 88 (upd.)
The Salvation Army USA, 32
Sam Ash Music Corporation, 30
Sam Levin Inc., 80
Sam's Club, 40
Sam's Wine & Spirits, 96
Samsonite Corporation, 13; 43 (upd.)
Samuel Cabot Inc., 53
Samuels Jewelers Incorporated, 30
San Diego Gas & Electric Company, V
San Diego Padres Baseball Club LP 78
Sanborn Map Company Inc., 82
Sandals Resorts International, 65
Sanders Morris Harris Group Inc., 70
Sanders\Wingo, 99
Sanderson Farms, Inc., 15
Sandia National Laboratories, 49
Sanford L.P., 82
Santa Barbara Restaurant Group, Inc., 37

Sierra Nevada Brewing Company, 70
Sierra On-Line, Inc., 15; 41 (upd.)
Sierra Pacific Industries, 22; 90 (upd.)
SIFCO Industries, Inc., 41
Sigma-Aldrich Corporation, I; 36 (upd.); 93 (upd.)
Signet Banking Corporation, 11
Sikorsky Aircraft Corporation, 24
Silhouette Brands, Inc., 55
Silicon Graphics Incorporated, 9
Silver Lake Cookie Company Inc., 95
SilverPlatter Information Inc., 23
Silverstar Holdings, Ltd., 99
Silverstein Properties, Inc., 47
Simmons Company, 47
Simon & Schuster Inc., IV; 19 (upd.); 100 (upd.)
Simon Property Group Inc., 27; 84 (upd.)
Simon Transportation Services Inc., 27
Simplex Technologies Inc., 21
Simplicity Manufacturing, Inc., 64
Simpson Investment Company, 17
Simpson Thacher & Bartlett, 39
Simula, Inc., 41
Sinclair Broadcast Group, Inc., 25
Sine Qua Non, 99
The Singing Machine Company, Inc., 60
Sir Speedy, Inc., 16
Sirius Satellite Radio, Inc., 69
Siskin Steel & Supply Company, 70
Six Flags, Inc., 17; 54 (upd.)
SJW Corporation, 70
Skadden, Arps, Slate, Meagher & Flom, 18
Skechers U.S.A. Inc., 31; 88 (upd.)
Skeeter Products Inc., 96
Skidmore, Owings & Merrill LLP, 13; 69 (upd.)
skinnyCorp, LLC, 97
Skyline Chili, Inc., 62
Skyline Corporation, 30
SkyMall, Inc., 26
SkyWest, Inc., 25
Skyy Spirits LLC 78
SL Green Realty Corporation, 44
SL Industries, Inc., 77
Sleepy's Inc., 32
SLI, Inc., 48
Slim-Fast Foods Company, 18; 66 (upd.)
SLM Holding Corp., 25 (upd.)
Small Planet Foods, Inc., 89
Smart & Final LLC, 16; 94 (upd.)
Smart Balance, Inc., 100
SMART Modular Technologies, Inc., 86
SmartForce PLC, 43
Smead Manufacturing Co., 17
Smith & Hawken, Ltd., 68
Smith & Wesson Corp., 30; 73 (upd.)
Smith Barney Inc., 15
Smith Corona Corp., 13
Smith International, Inc., 15; 59 (upd.)
Smith's Food & Drug Centers, Inc., 8; 57 (upd.)
Smith-Midland Corporation, 56
Smithfield Foods, Inc., 7; 43 (upd.)
SmithKline Beckman Corporation, I
Smithsonian Institution, 27
Smithway Motor Xpress Corporation, 39

Smurfit-Stone Container Corporation, 26 (upd.); 83 (upd.)
Snap-On, Incorporated, 7; 27 (upd.)
Snapfish, 83
Snapple Beverage Corporation, 11
Snell & Wilmer L.L.P., 28
Society Corporation, 9
Soft Sheen Products, Inc., 31
Softbank Corporation, 77 (upd.)
Sola International Inc., 71
Solar Turbines Inc., 100
Sole Technology Inc., 93
Solectron Corporation, 12; 48 (upd.)
Solo Serve Corporation, 28
Solutia Inc., 52
Sonat, Inc., 6
Sonesta International Hotels Corporation, 44
Sonic Automotive, Inc., 77
Sonic Corp., 14; 37 (upd.)
Sonic Innovations Inc., 56
Sonic Solutions, Inc., 81
SonicWALL, Inc., 87
Sonoco Products Company, 8; 89 (upd.)
SonoSite, Inc., 56
Sorbee International Ltd., 74
Soros Fund Management LLC, 28
Sorrento, Inc., 24
SOS Staffing Services, 25
Sotheby's Holdings, Inc., 11; 29 (upd.); 84 (upd.)
Sound Advice, Inc., 41
Souper Salad, Inc., 98
The Source Enterprises, Inc., 65
Source Interlink Companies, Inc., 75
South Beach Beverage Company, Inc., 73
South Dakota Wheat Growers Association, 94
South Jersey Industries, Inc., 42
Southdown, Inc., 14
Southeast Frozen Foods Company, L.P., 99
The Southern Company, V; 38 (upd.)
Southern Connecticut Gas Company, 84
Southern Financial Bancorp, Inc., 56
Southern Indiana Gas and Electric Company, 13
Southern New England Telecommunications Corporation, 6
Southern Pacific Transportation Company, V
Southern Poverty Law Center, Inc., 74
Southern States Cooperative Incorporated, 36
Southern Union Company, 27
Southern Wine and Spirits of America, Inc., 84
The Southland Corporation, II; 7 (upd.)
Southtrust Corporation, 11
Southwest Airlines Co., 6; 24 (upd.); 71 (upd.)
Southwest Gas Corporation, 19
Southwest Water Company, 47
Southwestern Bell Corporation, V
Southwestern Electric Power Co., 21
Southwestern Public Service Company, 6
Southwire Company, Inc., 8; 23 (upd.)
Sovran Self Storage, Inc., 66

Spacehab, Inc., 37
Spacelabs Medical, Inc., 71
Spaghetti Warehouse, Inc., 25
Spangler Candy Company, 44
Spanish Broadcasting System, Inc., 41
Spansion Inc., 80
Spanx, Inc., 89
Spark Networks, Inc., 91
Spartan Motors Inc., 14
Spartan Stores Inc., 8; 66 (upd.)
Spartech Corporation, 19; 76 (upd.)
Sparton Corporation, 18
Spear & Jackson, Inc., 73
Spear, Leeds & Kellogg, 66
Spec's Music, Inc., 19
Special Olympics, Inc., 93
Specialized Bicycle Components Inc., 50
Specialty Coatings Inc., 8
Specialty Equipment Companies, Inc., 25
Specialty Products & Insulation Co., 59
Spectrum Control, Inc., 67
Spectrum Organic Products, Inc., 68
Spee-Dee Delivery Service, Inc., 93
SpeeDee Oil Change and Tune-Up, 25
Speedway Motorsports, Inc., 32
Speidel Inc., 96
Speizman Industries, Inc., 44
Spelling Entertainment, 14; 35 (upd.)
Spencer Stuart and Associates, Inc., 14
Spherion Corporation, 52
Spiegel, Inc., 10; 27 (upd.)
Spinnaker Exploration Company, 72
Spirit Airlines, Inc., 31
Sport Chalet, Inc., 16; 94 (upd.)
Sport Supply Group, Inc., 23
Sportmart, Inc., 15
Sports & Recreation, Inc., 17
The Sports Authority, Inc., 16; 43 (upd.)
The Sports Club Company, 25
The Sportsman's Guide, Inc., 36
Springs Global US, Inc., V; 19 (upd.); 90 (upd.)
Sprint Corporation, 9; 46 (upd.)
SPS Technologies, Inc., 30
SPSS Inc., 64
SPX Corporation, 10; 47 (upd.)
Spyglass Entertainment Group, LLC, 91
Square D, 90
Squibb Corporation, I
SRA International, Inc., 77
SRAM Corporation, 65
SRC Holdings Corporation, 67
SRI International, Inc., 57
SSOE Inc., 76
STAAR Surgical Company, 57
Stabler Companies Inc. 78
Stage Stores, Inc., 24; 82 (upd.)
Stanadyne Automotive Corporation, 37
StanCorp Financial Group, Inc., 56
Standard Candy Company Inc., 86
Standard Commercial Corporation, 13; 62 (upd.)
Standard Federal Bank, 9
Standard Microsystems Corporation, 11
Standard Motor Products, Inc., 40
Standard Pacific Corporation, 52
The Standard Register Company, 15, 93 (upd.)

INTERNATIONAL DIRECTORY OF COMPANY HISTORIES, VOLUME 101

Vitro Corp., 10
Vivra, Inc., 18
Vizio, Inc., 100
Vlasic Foods International Inc., 25
VLSI Technology, Inc., 16
VMware, Inc., 90
Volcom, Inc., 77
Volkert and Associates, Inc., 98
Volt Information Sciences Inc., 26
Volunteers of America, Inc., 66
Von Maur Inc., 64
Vonage Holdings Corp., 81
The Vons Companies, Incorporated, 7; 28 (upd.)
Vornado Realty Trust, 20
Vought Aircraft Industries, Inc., 49
Vulcan Materials Company, 7; 52 (upd.)
W. Atlee Burpee & Co., 27
W.A. Whitney Company, 53
W.B Doner & Co., 56
W.B. Mason Company, 98
W.C. Bradley Co., 69
W. H. Braum, Inc., 80
W.H. Brady Co., 17
W.L. Gore & Associates, Inc., 14; 60 (upd.)
W.P. Carey & Co. LLC, 49
W.R. Berkley Corporation, 15; 74 (upd.)
W.R. Grace & Company, I; 50 (upd.)
W.W. Grainger, Inc., V; 26 (upd.); 68 (upd.)
W.W. Norton & Company, Inc., 28
Waban Inc., 13
Wabash National Corp., 13
Wabtec Corporation, 40
Wachovia Bank of Georgia, N.A., 16
Wachovia Bank of South Carolina, N.A., 16
Wachovia Corporation, 12; 46 (upd.)
Wachtell, Lipton, Rosen & Katz, 47
The Wackenhut Corporation, 14; 63 (upd.)
Waddell & Reed, Inc., 22
Waffle House Inc., 14; 60 (upd.)
Wagers Inc. (Idaho Candy Company), 86
Waggener Edstrom, 42
Wah Chang, 82
Wahl Clipper Corporation, 86
Wahoo's Fish Taco, 96
Wakefern Food Corporation, 33
Wal-Mart Stores, Inc., V; 8 (upd.); 26 (upd.); 63 (upd.)
Walbridge Aldinger Co., 38
Walbro Corporation, 13
Waldbaum, Inc., 19
Waldenbooks, 17; 86 (upd.)
Walgreen Co., V; 20 (upd.); 65 (upd.)
Walker Manufacturing Company, 19
Wall Drug Store, Inc., 40
Wall Street Deli, Inc., 33
Wallace Computer Services, Inc., 36
Walsworth Publishing Co. 78
The Walt Disney Company, II; 6 (upd.); 30 (upd.); 63 (upd.)
Walter Industries, Inc., II; 22 (upd.); 72 (upd.)
Walton Monroe Mills, Inc., 8
Wang Laboratories, Inc., III; 6 (upd.)

The Warnaco Group Inc., 12; 46 (upd.)
Warner Communications Inc., II
Warner Music Group Corporation, 90 (upd.)
Warner-Lambert Co., I; 10 (upd.)
Warners' Stellian Inc., 67
Warrantech Corporation, 53
Warrell Corporation, 68
Warwick Valley Telephone Company, 55
The Washington Companies, 33
Washington Federal, Inc., 17
Washington Football, Inc., 35
Washington Gas Light Company, 19
Washington Mutual, Inc., 17; 93 (upd.)
Washington National Corporation, 12
Washington Natural Gas Company, 9
The Washington Post Company, IV; 20 (upd.)
Washington Scientific Industries, Inc., 17
Washington Water Power Company, 6
Waste Connections, Inc., 46
Waste Holdings, Inc., 41
Waste Management, Inc., V
Water Pik Technologies, Inc., 34; 83 (upd.)
Waterhouse Investor Services, Inc., 18
Waters Corporation, 43
Watkins-Johnson Company, 15
Watsco Inc., 52
Watson Pharmaceuticals Inc., 16; 56 (upd.)
Watson Wyatt Worldwide, 42
Watts Industries, Inc., 19
Wausau-Mosinee Paper Corporation, 60 (upd.)
Waverly, Inc., 16
Wawa Inc., 17; 78 (upd.)
WAXIE Sanitary Supply, 100
Waxman Industries, Inc., 9
WD-40 Company, 18; 87 (upd.)
We-No-Nah Canoe, Inc., 98
Weather Central Inc., 100
The Weather Channel Companies, The 52
Weatherford International, Inc., 39
Weaver Popcorn Company, Inc., 89
Webasto Roof Systems Inc., 97
Webber Oil Company, 61
Weber-Stephen Products Co., 40
WebEx Communications, Inc., 81
WebMD Corporation, 65
Weeres Industries Corporation, 52
Wegmans Food Markets, Inc., 9; 41 (upd.)
Weider Nutrition International, Inc., 29
Weight Watchers International Inc., 12; 33 (upd.); 73 (upd.)
Weil, Gotshal & Manges LLP, 55
Weiner's Stores, Inc., 33
Weingarten Realty Investors, 95
Weirton Steel Corporation, IV; 26 (upd.)
Weis Markets, Inc., 15; 84 (upd.)
The Weitz Company, Inc., 42
Welbilt Corp., 19
Welcome Wagon International Inc., 82
The Welk Group Inc. 78
WellCare Health Plans, Inc., 101
WellChoice, Inc., 67 (upd.)
Wellco Enterprises, Inc., 84

Wellman, Inc., 8; 52 (upd.)
WellPoint Health Networks Inc., 25
Wells Fargo & Company, II; 12 (upd.); 38 (upd.); 97 (upd.)
Wells Rich Greene BDDP, 6
Wells' Dairy, Inc., 36
Wells-Gardner Electronics Corporation, 43
Wendy's International, Inc., 8; 23 (upd.); 47 (upd.)
Wenner Bread Products Inc., 80
Wenner Media, Inc., 32
Werner Enterprises, Inc., 26
West Bend Co., 14
West Coast Entertainment Corporation, 29
West Corporation, 42
West Group, 34 (upd.)
West Linn Paper Company, 91
West Marine, Inc., 17; 90 (upd.)
West One Bancorp, 11
West Pharmaceutical Services, Inc., 42
West Point-Pepperell, Inc., 8
West Publishing Co., 7
Westaff Inc., 33
Westamerica Bancorporation, 17
Westar Energy, Inc., 57 (upd.)
WestCoast Hospitality Corporation, 59
Westcon Group, Inc., 67
Westell Technologies, Inc., 57
Westerbeke Corporation, 60
Western Atlas Inc., 12
Western Beef, Inc., 22
Western Company of North America, 15
Western Digital Corporation, 25; 92 (upd.)
Western Gas Resources, Inc., 45
Western Publishing Group, Inc., 13
Western Resources, Inc., 12
The WesterN SizzliN Corporation, 60
Western Union Financial Services, Inc., 54
Western Wireless Corporation, 36
Westfield Group, 69
Westin Hotels and Resorts Worldwide, 9; 29 (upd.)
Westinghouse Electric Corporation, II; 12 (upd.)
Westmoreland Coal Company, 7
WestPoint Stevens Inc., 16
Westport Resources Corporation, 63
Westvaco Corporation, IV; 19 (upd.)
Westwood One, Inc., 23
The Wet Seal, Inc., 18; 70 (upd.)
Wetterau Incorporated, II
Weyco Group, Incorporated, 32
Weyerhaeuser Company, IV; 9 (upd.); 28 (upd.); 83 (upd.)
WFS Financial Inc., 70
WGBH Educational Foundation, 66
Wham-O, Inc., 61
Wheaton Industries, 8
Wheaton Science Products, 60 (upd.)
Wheelabrator Technologies, Inc., 6; 60 (upd.)
Wheeling-Pittsburgh Corporation, 7; 58 (upd.)
Wheels Inc., 96